Teacher's Wraparound Edition

GLENCOE

Writer's Choice

Grammar and Composition
Grade 10

 Glencoe McGraw-Hill

New York, New York   Columbus, Ohio   Woodland Hills, California   Peoria, Illinois

ACKNOWLEDGMENTS

Grateful acknowledgment is given authors, publishers, photographers, museums, and agents for permission to reprint the following copyrighted material. Every effort has been made to determine copyright owners. In case of any omissions, the Publisher will be pleased to make suitable acknowledgments in future editions.

Acknowledgments continued on page 965.

The Standardized Test Practice pages in this book were written by The Princeton Review, the nation's leader in test preparation. Through its association with McGraw-Hill, The Princeton Review offers the best way to help students excel on standardized assessments.

The Princeton Review is not affiliated with Princeton University or Educational Testing Service.

The **Facing the Blank Page** feature in this book was prepared in collaboration with the writers and editors of *Time* magazine.

Glencoe/McGraw-Hill

A Division of the **McGraw-Hill** *Companies*

Copyright © 2001 by The McGraw-Hill Companies, Inc. All rights reserved. Except as permitted under the United States Copyright Act of 1976, no part of this publication may be reproduced or distributed in any form or means, or stored in a database or retrieval system, without the prior written permission of the publisher.

PRINTED IN THE UNITED STATES OF AMERICA

Send all inquiries to:
GLENCOE/MCGRAW-HILL
8787 Orion Place
Columbus, OH 43240-4027

ISBN 0-02-818149-2
(Student Edition)
ISBN 0-07-822659-7
(Teacher's Wraparound Edition)

2 3 4 5 6 7 8 9 10 027/043 05 04 03 02 01 00

CONTENTS

Teacher's Wraparound Edition

Organization of Teacher's Wraparound Edition **T4**

Professional Articles

The program editors have italicized key phrases in the professional articles and have noted in the margins the specific *Writer's Choice* features that address each professional concern.

Confidence and Competence in Writing by William Strong **T6**

Integrating the Language Arts by Denny Wolfe **T8**

Cultural Diversity by Arnold Webb **T10**

Teaching Students with Different Abilities
                 by Bonnie S. Sunstein and Dan-Ling Fu **T12**

Journal Writing by Sharyn Lowenstein **T14**

Portfolios by Bonnie S. Sunstein **T16**

Writing Across the Curriculum by Denny Wolfe **T18**

Thinking and Writing by Carol Booth Olson **T20**

Cooperative Learning by Judith Summerfield **T22**

Sentence Combining and the Writing Process by William Strong **T24**

Assessment by Charles R. Duke **T26**

Visual Learning **T28**

Technology by Barbara King-Shaver **T30**

The Teacher's Wraparound Edition provides an effective resource for presenting the lessons in *Writer's Choice.* Each lesson plan has four parts: Focus, Teach, Assess, and Close. The margins offer additional information and strategies to meet a wide range of teaching situations.

Teach provides varied strategies for customizing the lesson and addressing the needs of basic-to-average and advanced learners.

Strategies and background information support critical thinking, cultural diversity, English language learners, cross-curricular connections, fine art, and civic literacy.

Focus clearly sets the objectives with writing, thinking, and listening and speaking skills as well as motivating activities for the lesson.

Resource Manager lists ancillaries that extend and support the lesson.

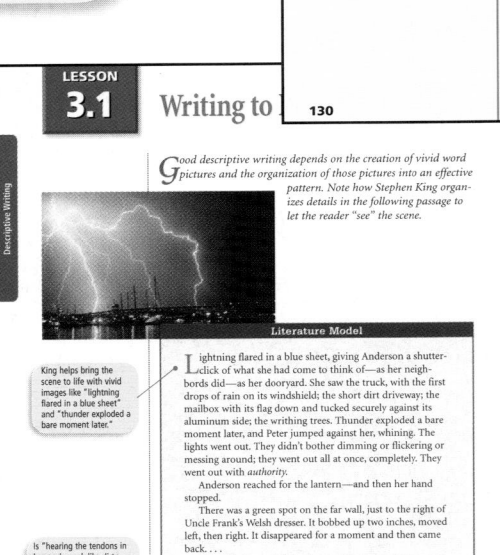

3.1

Teach

Guided Practice

Teaching Tip
To help students understand that one place can evoke different images depending on a writer's use of detail, bring in a photo of a unique place. Suggest that groups of students meet and think of an event that might occur there, such as a party or an accident. Ask students to determine the effect the setting might have on this event and write a descriptive topic sentence giving that impression. Groups can list the details in the picture that support their topic sentence. When the class reconvenes, ask groups to share topic sentences to illustrate the variety of images that can come from one source. **L2**

Using the Model
In discussing the model, help students see that transition words such as "overhead" and "on either side" indicate that Lonn is using spatial order. As he moves near to far, he describes such details as the "sheer cliff walls" and the "wind-twisted pine trees." **L1**

Additional Resources

Writing Process Transparencies, 9, 13–17
Writing Across the Curriculum
Cooperative Learning Activities

For further stimuli for descriptive writing, see *Fine Art Transparencies*, 13–18.
Thinking and Study Skills, pp. 10, 15
Sentence Combining Practice, pp. 28–29
Speaking and Listening Activities, pp. 1, 2, 19, 21
Composition Practice, p. 19

The topic sentence states the main idea: to describe Picture Canyon and explain why it has a special effect on people.

In what order does Rider arrange his details in describing Picture Canyon? What details does he use?

Transition words such as "overhead," "on either side," and "looking ahead" help the reader follow the organization.

Revising Tip
When you revise your writing, add transition words to help the reader follow the organization of your descriptive details. For help refer to Lesson 2.7, page 72.

Put It All Together

After you've created your images and organized them around sentence, you should have an effective description. Notice how Lonn Rider used specific and vivid details to create a clear im favorite place.

Student Model

Picture Canyon, though not the most beautiful of pl has a special, enigmatic effect on people. As you ente canyon, the soft golden sandstone walls begin to build a loom overhead until they meet the electric-blue skyline Native American drawings etched inside the canyon co sheer cliff walls on either side, illustrating a past long si forgotten. The rugged floor of the canyon is scattered w multitudes of small, algae-covered ponds with a few we beaten, sandstone roadways. Looking ahead, there are sr wind-twisted pine trees with a multitude of squirrels fe on the pea-sized piñon nuts. Each playfully eats his fill stores the excess in bulging cheeks. As the sun sets over horizon, the jagged, golden rock formations on the skyl seem to radiate an eerie, golden energy known only to a infrequent visitors and to the Native Americans who liv the canyon centuries ago.

Lonn Rider, Centennial High School, Pueblo, Co

Like Rider, you can enhance your descriptions by carefully your ideas and supporting details. Follow these guidelines wl write your own descriptive paragraphs.

Guidelines for Descriptive Writing

1. Gather vivid details that will help you re-create a scene or an experien your readers.
2. Decide which kind of organization will be more appropriate for your s spatial order or order of importance.
3. Write a topic sentence, and decide whether it will be more effective p at the beginning or the end of the paragraph.
4. Use appropriate transitions to make the organization and relationship ideas clear.

130 Unit 3 Descriptive Writing

130

Critical Thinking

Identifying Relationships
Descriptive details may be related in many ways, such as spatially, by importance or distinctiveness, and chronologically. The writer's task is to identify which relationship suits the purpose of the description. Spatial organization conveys a vivid picture to the reader; organization by

importance helps the reader form opinions ab or place; chronological order emphasizes chan of students to list ideas for descriptive paragr decide which kind of organization they would for each.

3.1

Focus

Lesson Overview

Objective
• To write a descriptive paragraph using an organization plan for concrete and sensory details

Skills
• examining characteristics of descriptive writing; organizing details; writing a topic sentence; using prepositional phrases in descriptions

Critical Thinking
• comparing; visualizing; analyzing

Listening and Speaking
• discussing; evaluating; explaining a process

Bellringer
Daily Language Activity
When students enter the classroom, have this assignment on the board: *Write five sentences that accurately and completely describe the front of this classroom.*

Grammar Link to the Bellringer
Tell students to underline the prepositional phrases used in their descriptions.

See also *Daily Language Practice*

Motivating Activity
At the start of the movie *The Wizard of Oz*, the main character, Dorothy, wishes she could be "somewhere over the rainbow." Ask students to describe some details about a favorite place to another classmate without naming where they would like to be. Have students see how quickly their partners can guess the places described.

LESSON
3.1

Writing to

Good descriptive writing depends on the creation of vivid word pictures and the organization of those pictures into an effective pattern. Note how Stephen King organizes details in the following passage to let the reader "see" the scene.

King helps bring the scene to life with vivid images like "lightning flared in a blue sheet" and "thunder exploded a bare moment later."

Is "hearing the tendons in her neck creak like dirty doorhinges" an effective image? Why?

Literature Model

Lightning flared in a blue sheet, giving Anderson a shutter-click of what she had come to think of—as her neighbords did—as her dooryard. She saw the truck, with the first drops of rain on its windshield; the short dirt driveway; the mailbox with its flag down and tucked securely against its aluminum side; the writhing trees. Thunder exploded a bare moment later, and Peter jumped against her, whining. The lights went out. They didn't bother dimming or flickering or messing around; they went out all at once, completely. They went out with *authority.*

Anderson reached for the lantern—and then her hand stopped.

There was a green spot on the far wall, just to the right of Uncle Frank's Welsh dresser. It bobbed up two inches, moved left, then right. It disappeared for a moment and then came back. . . .

She turned toward Peter, hearing the tendons in her neck creak like dirty doorhinges, knowing what she was going to see. The light was coming from Peter's eye. His left eye. It glared with the witchy green light of St. Elmo's fire drifting over a swamp after a still, muggy day.

Stephen King, *The Tommyknockers*

126 Unit 3 Descriptive Writing

way of organizing descriptive writing is to arrange details in spatial order—that is, left to right, front to back, near to far, clockwise, or counterclockwise. How did Iowa writer Sharon Oard Warner organize the details of her description?

Literature Model

The pediatric waiting room is divided into two unequal sections by a length of Plexiglas that juts out into the middle of the room. A table at one end keeps people from walking into the flat edge. Orange and brown upholstered chairs line both sides of this transparent wall, back to back, as though some enormous game of musical chairs is about to begin. The smaller section of the room is reserved for well patients, and a prominent sign directs the rest of us to the other side.

When I carried Jancey in this morning, I stopped in the entrance, momentarily confused. Some redecorating had gone on since our last visit. A large oval braided rug covered an expanse of institutional carpet in the unwell section, and a baby not much older than Jancey was seated in the middle of it. While I watched, he crawled to the edge and then back again, as though the rug were an island and he was marooned.

Sharon Oard Warner, "A Simple Matter of Hunger"

Journal Writing
Experiment with spatial organization of details by writing a brief description of a special place or secret hideaway where you go to get away from it all.

Resource Manager

Planning Resources
• *Lesson Plans*

Transparencies
• *Bellringer*
• *Daily Language Practice*
• *Fine Art* 13–18
• *Two-Minute Skill Drill*
• *Writing Process* 9, 13–17

Other Print Resources
• *Composition Enrichment* p. 19
• *Composition Practice*, p. 19
• *Composition Reteaching* p. 19
• *Cooperative Learning Activities*, pp. 13–16
• *Listening and Speaking Activities*, pp. 1, 2, 19, 21

• *Sentence-Combining Practice*, pp. 28–29
• *Thinking and Study Skills*, pp. 10, 15
• *Writing Across the Curriculum*
• *Writing Assessment and Evaluation Rubrics*

126

3.1 Writing Activities

Write a Descriptive Paragraph

Write a description of the painting below that is so specific that someone who has never seen it would immediately recognize it. Use the guidelines on page 130 to help you.

PURPOSE To describe a painting
AUDIENCE Someone who has never seen it
LENGTH 1 paragraph

WRITING RUBRICS To write an effective descriptive paragraph, you should
- use specific details
- order details spatially or by order of importance
- write a clear topic sentence

Listening and Speaking

COOPERATIVE LEARNING Write a paragraph about a possession you had in your early childhood. Describe the object's most unusual features, without naming the object. Read your paragraph aloud with those of a group, identify the objects, and discuss which specific details helped identify the objects.

Blackbear Bosin, *Prairie Fire*, 1953

Grammar Link

Use prepositional phrases to show spatial relationships.

The literature models in this lesson used prepositional phrases, such as "in the middle of the floor," to establish spatial relationships.

Clarify position or location by adding at least one prepositional phrase to each sentence below.

1. A bookcase stood.
2. An overstuffed blue chair squatted.
3. A patchwork quilt of primary colors covered the bed.
4. Clothes were strewn in heaps.
5. A matching chair and desk of oak faced the window.

See Lesson 12.1, pages 523–524.

Cross-Curricular Activity

SCIENCE Work with a partner to research information about the role of fire in maintaining the prairie environment. Write a few paragraphs and present your facts to the class.

3.1 Writing to Describe **131**

Assess

Evaluation Rubrics

Write a Descriptive Paragraph
Each paragraph should include
- a number of specific details from the painting
- an organization pattern, such as left to right or cause and effect

See also the Teacher's Guide to Writing Assessment.

Listening and Speaking
When students read their descriptions within their groups, have classmates ask the following questions.
- What mood or impression did you perceive?
- What details could be added, or made more vivid and specific?
- Are details arranged in a logical order?

Cross-Curricular Activity
Students' paragraphs should
- be based on accurate information from reliable sources.
- use clear, non-technical language.

Reteaching
Composition Reteaching, p. 19

Enrichment
Composition Enrichment, p. 19

Fine Art Transparencies Use *Fine Art Transparencies*, 13–18, for enrichment activities also.

Close

Ask students to name different purposes for which they might use descriptive writing. Ask students to look for examples of descriptive writing in a variety of publications.

Assess presents Writing Activities Evaluation Rubrics to help you critique and assess student writing.

Close gives tips for reviewing, applying, and extending the lesson.

Grammar units contain an abundance of practical suggestions for helping students master grammar and improve their writing.

Grammar Link

Answers
(Answers will vary.)
1. next to the wall
2. near the fireplace
3. in the guest room down the hall
4. around the room
5. near the door

Viewing the Art

Blackbear Bosin, *Prairie Fire*, 1953
Native-American artist Blackbear Bosin filled his watercolor *Prairie Fire* (23 by 33 1/4 inches, Philbrook Art Center, Tulsa) with details provoking the senses. The viewer smells and feels the searing heat of the fire and hears its roar and the pounding of hooves.

131

Teach

Guided Practice

Using the Model
You might suggest that students close their eyes and visualize the waiting room as you read its description aloud. Afterward, ask whether any of the details were difficult to imagine. In discussing the model, point out that Warner has chosen to organize her description around the most prominent object in the room, the Plexiglas divider. She discusses other objects in relation to the divider: the table at one end and the back-to-back arrangement of the chairs against it. **L2**

Two-Minute Skill Drill

Write the following sentences on the board and have students insert prepositional phrases.

1. Mary ran _____.
2. Bees flew _____.

See also *Two-Minute Skill Drill Transparency 3.1*

Journal Writing Tip

Identifying Spatial Relationships
Before students complete the journal activity, suggest they list all the spatial details that come to mind about their special places. If some students have difficulty, you might suggest they sketch their secret hideaways to help them identify the location and placement of significant details.

127

Bellringer

Daily Language Activity
When students enter the classroom, have this assignment on the board: *List some common abbreviations you use every day.*

See also *Daily Language Practice*

Teach

Capitalization of Abbreviations

☑ **Teaching Tip**
Certain expressions used in formal writing may sometimes be written as abbreviations with periods. For example, *i.e.* is an abbreviation of *id est; e.g.,* of *exempli gratia; viz.,* of *videlicet; ca.* or *c.,* of *circa; cf.,* of *confer;* and *etc.,* of *et cetera.*

☑ **Vocabulary Link**
The term *abbreviation* comes from a Latin verb meaning "to shorten." It is related to the English word *brief.*

Abbreviations

...tions are shortened forms of words. They are used to save space ...d to avoid wordiness. For example, it is more concise and easier ...b.c. than to write *800 years before the birth of Christ.* Periods follow ...breviations. For guidance on how to write a particular abbrevia...dictionary.

...eviation occurs at the end of a sentence that would ordinarily ...riod, do not add an additional closing period

...ing to Washington, **D.C.**

...eviation occurs at the end of a sentence that ends with a question mark or an exclamation point, use the period for the abbreviation *and* the second mark of punctuation.

Have you been to Washington, **D.C.?**
I can't wait to go to Washington, **D.C.!**

Capitalization of Abbreviations

■ Capitalize abbreviations of proper nouns.

Dwight **D.** Eisenhower
135 Claremont **Ave.**
U.S. Department of Labor

The names of many organizations and agencies, whether pronounced letter by letter or as words, are abbreviated by using the initial letters of the complete name without periods.

NAACP   YMCA   CIA   FCC   UN   NATO

Capitalize these abbreviations related to historical dates:

A.D. (*anno Domini*), "in the year of the Lord" (since the birth of Christ); place before the date: **A.D.** 66

B.C. (before Christ); place after the date: 336 **B.C.**

B.C.E. (before the common era; equivalent to **B.C.**); place after the date: 1000 **B.C.E.**

C.E. (common era; equivalent to **A.D.**); place after the date: 60 **C.E.**

A.M. (*ante meridiem*), "before noon"; place after exact times: 2:45 **A.M.**

P.M. (*post meridiem*), "after noon"; place after exact times: 10:30 **P.M.**

766 Unit 21 Punctuation, Abbreviations, and Numbers

State Abbreviations

In ordinary prose, spell out state names. When addressing mail, however, use the abbreviations of state names that appear in the list below. (*Note:* No comma appears between the state postal abbreviation and the number in a zip code.)

State	Abbr.	State	Abbr.
Alabama	AL	Montana	MT
Alaska	AK	Nebraska	NE
Arizona	AZ	Nevada	NV
Arkansas	AR	New Hampshire	NH
California	CA	New Jersey	NJ
Colorado	CO	New Mexico	NM
Connecticut	CT	New York	NY
Delaware	DE	North Carolina	NC
Florida	FL	North Dakota	ND
Georgia	GA	Ohio	OH
Hawaii	HI	Oklahoma	OK
Idaho	ID	Oregon	OR
Illinois	IL	Pennsylvania	PA
Indiana	IN	Rhode Island	RI
Iowa	IA	South Carolina	SC
Kansas	KS	South Dakota	SD
Kentucky	KY	Tennessee	TN
Louisiana	LA	Texas	TX
Maine	ME	Utah	UT
Maryland	MD	Vermont	VT
Massachusetts	MA	Virginia	VA
Michigan	MI	Washington	WA
Minnesota	MN	West Virginia	WV
Mississippi	MS	Wisconsin	WI
Missouri	MO	Wyoming	WY

The zip code form for the District of Columbia, for use on envelopes only, is **DC.**

Exercise 23   Using Abbreviations

On your paper, write the abbreviations for the italicized words or phrases in the following sentences. If an abbreviation should not be used, write *correct.*

1. The *Young Men's Christian Association* has been promoting family and recreational activities since *anno Domini* 1881.
2. The *United States* Capitol is located in Washington, D.C.
3. One zip code for Fargo, *North Dakota,* is 58103.
4. The *Federal Aviation Administration* establishes regulations for airline companies.
5. Many Americans begin work at 9:00 *ante meridiem* and end at 5:00 *post meridiem.*

21.13 Abbreviations **767**

Teach

State Abbre...

☑ **Grammar Tip**
Periods have traditionally... abbreviations in the Engl... trend today, however, is a... of periods in abbreviation... scientific writing. Abbrev... the metric system, which... scientific writing, are rare... periods.

☑ **Teaching Tip**
Point out that in a perso... appropriate to use a stat... the address. In other for... as expository writing, stu... out the name of a state... paper on the tourist trade... dents should always spe... name.

Practice... and Ass...

Answers: Exercise...
1. YMCA; A.D.
2. U.S. *or* correct
3. correct
4. FAA *or* correct
5. A.M.; P.M.

Resource Manager

Planning Resources
- *Lesson Plans*

Transparencies
- *Bellringer*
- *Daily Language Practice*

Other Print Resources
- *Grammar and Composition Handbook*
- *Grammar Practice,* p. 52
- *Grammar Workbook,* Lesson 91

766

English Language Learners

Listing Common Abbreviations
Because many of the abbreviated words used in this lesson may be unfamiliar to students new to English, provide students with a list of words that are commonly abbreviated. Encourage students to copy the list into their journals. Suggest that they highlight the periods in the abbreviations so that they remember to include them.

Confidence and Competence in Writing

by William Strong

Professor of Secondary Education at Utah State University, Director of the Utah Writing Project, and a member of the National Writing Project Advisory Board

The blank page awaits our words. For many of our students—and perhaps even for us, occasionally—the blank page inspires a queasy sensation, a primitive *fear.* Do we have anything to say? Will words really come? Will we sound stupid?

Doubts like these remind us that writing is hard work as well as an audaciously public act, one that not only exposes our thoughts to the world but gives them independent being. Our words stand by themselves, naked to the scrutiny of others. No wonder we are tentative!

A state-of-the-art composition program helps students overcome such basic fears. Our aim as secondary teachers, after all, is to graduate young people who are both *confident* and *competent* in dealing with the many challenges of the blank page, whether in college, in the workplace, or in their personal lives.

How Do We Improve Writing Confidence?

Thanks to the efforts of the National Writing Project, many of us now see fluency as a prerequisite skill for composing. To help students achieve increased ease with the task itself, we ask for *frequent writing*—for example, in journals or learning logs. While such work may be checked for completion, it is generally not "graded."

Helping students *manage the complexity of writing tasks* also reduces apprehension. By taking students through prewriting strategies, for example, we generate both ideas and energy. By inviting students to "talk through" their ideas with others, we make the transition to writing less intimidating. By encouraging students to choose angles and topics of genuine interest, we promote a sense of ownership.

Not surprisingly, students develop confidence in classrooms where there is clear, sure direction from their teachers and where, in addition, their peers

---

Writer's Choice provides invitations and instruction for frequent writing:
- Every four-page composition lesson includes a journal activity.
- Every four-page composition lesson ends with a full page of activities.
- Remarkable variety of writing opportunities includes writing based on Media Connections, on literature, and on content areas.

Writer's Choice helps students manage the complexity of writing tasks:
- Complete instruction in the writing process
- Writing Process Tips throughout composition lessons for help with writing process
- Writing Assignments—realistic writing prompts with real-world contexts
- **Troubleshooter** to help solve common grammar, usage, and mechanics errors

give helpful response to drafts. According to Sarah Freedman, in NCTE Research Report No. 23 (1987), "allowing students time and support while they work to communicate their ideas" (160) is a distinguishing characteristic of successful teachers.

How *we* respond to writing is also important. For example, one of Donald Murray's favorite responses to student writing begins with five words—"I like the way you"—which he encourages teachers to finish in any way they choose. In reviewing the effects of criticism and the importance of "learning to praise," Donald Daiker notes that he allows himself only positive comments as he first reads a student essay.

How Do We Improve Writing Competence?

Most students acquire increasing *confidence* as their *competence* improves. We improve writing competence by showing students how to do what we expect them to do, then *structuring the environment for problem solving and success.*

According to George Hillocks in *Research on Written Composition* (NCTE/ERIC, 1986), the most effective teaching emphasizes "structured problem-solving activities, with clear objectives, planned to enable students to deal with similar problems in composing" (247). In such contexts, three teaching practices have proven to be highly effective: (1) inquiry teaching (e.g., focusing on a concrete data set and involving students in one or two strategies); (2) the use of grading scales, explicit criteria, and specific questions to guide individual or group work; and (3) sentence combining practice.

Beyond these research-based recommendations, the hard-won savvy of expert teachers charts our direction. We can improve students' writing competence by sharing drafts-in-progress, by modeling response strategies, and by *teaching skills in context* rather than in isolation. Such approaches redefine our relationship with students.

Moreover, by encouraging students to explore their own writing processes and to evaluate their own products in portfolios, we put the responsibility for learning where it should be—with students themselves. As students see what they can do with words, they come to regard writing as an important act of self-definition and knowledge construction. What is clearly at stake in this new kind of teaching is each student's sense of pride and personal authority.

Students become hooked when text itself becomes their teacher—infinitely flexible, patient, and recursive. Then the blank page seems not so much a threat as *an engaging array of options,* each waiting to be enacted. Ah, so many *choices!* So little time!

Writer's Choice is a structured environment for problem solving and success:
- Manageable lessons address specific writing situations with workable strategies.
- Writing assignments and Writing Process in Action provide substantial contexts and criteria for self-evaluation.
- Complete unit on sentence combining demonstrates multiple strategies.

Writer's Choice presents skills in context:
- Composition lessons use annotated models to show specific skills in action.
- Writing Process Tips integrate composition with grammar and vocabulary skills.
- Grammar Reviews integrate grammar, usage, and mechanics with literature.

Writer's Choice gives students and teachers an engaging array of options:
- Composition lessons in a unit may be used in order, or a choice of lessons may be linked to particular writing needs.
- Writing Activity pages offer a variety of workable assignments and degrees of guidance.
- Grammar instruction is delivered through discrete units with a wealth of exercises, literature-based Grammar Reviews, the **Troubleshooter,** and Grammar Links.

Integrating the Language Arts

Writer's Choice encourages total language growth through reading, responding, writing, and reflecting:
- Manageable lessons with Journal Writing activities
- Writing Activities with a variety of contexts, curriculum areas, and degrees of guidance
- Literature selections
- Short literature models
- Writing process instruction that demonstrates how thinking and writing go hand in hand

Writer's Choice encourages the exchange of perceptions:
- Student Models by real student writers
- Readers Respond—real student responses to literature
- Peer Editing built into writing assignments
- Cooperative Learning activities
- Listening and Speaking activities

Writer's Choice embodies the interdependence of all language processes:
- Literature integrated into composition—through literature selections and models
- Grammar integrated into composition—through the **Troubleshooter** and Grammar Links
- Composition integrated into grammar—through Writing Applications
- Literature integrated into grammar—through selections in Grammar Reviews

by Denny Wolfe

Professor of English Education at Old Dominion University in Norfolk, Virginia; Director of the Tidewater Virginia Writing Project

Why Integrate the Language Arts?

As English teachers, we have a unique responsibility: to assist students in their growth toward language maturity. Specifically, our challenge is to help students read, write, speak, and listen capably and effectively. To the extent we are successful in meeting this challenge, students learn to *think* critically and imaginatively.

Reading, writing, speaking, and listening are complementary processes. That is, growth in any one enhances growth in the others. We want students to achieve both *oracy* (speaking and listening competence) and *literacy* (reading and writing competence), and each feeds the other. Our curriculum, therefore, should function to give students *opportunities for total language growth.* By talking and by listening to others, students often are stimulated to read or write; during and after reading or writing, the *exchange of perceptions* through further oral and written activities both broadens and deepens students' understanding.

We must lead students toward a recognition of the *interdependence of all language processes.* Students can then become truly competent readers, writers, speakers, and listeners. The process works much like learning to drive a car. The competent driver must accomplish many tasks simultaneously—managing the steering wheel, operating the gas pedal, using the brake, looking ahead at the road, glancing behind through the rear-view mirror, paying attention to road signs. All of these are necessary to making the car work for us. Similarly, for language to work for us, we must use all the processes together, capitalizing on each to make the others meaningful.

How Can We Integrate the Language Arts?

One conception of the English curriculum is that it is about literature—in both print and nonprint forms—and that it is about experience. *The world of literature* and the world of students' experience must be drawn together if the English classroom is to be an exciting, dynamic place. When we as teachers attempt to draw these two worlds together, we create conditions for integrating the language arts.

For example, a poet may write about a sunset. Before asking students to read the poem (or hear it read), we can invite them to talk or to write about a sunset—a memorable experience, a place or a person they associate with a sunset, or a generic description of one. We might relate an experience or two of our own. Afterwards, when students approach the poem, they have established a mindset for reading it, and they are potentially able to relate to it in special ways. Upon finishing the poem, they might talk in groups about how the poem is different from or similar to their own experiences. Or, they may be invited to make journal entries. Such discussions or personal reflections in journals may lead to a full, even formal, piece of writing on some interesting aspect of the poem, perhaps drafted several times and finally released to the teacher. In these ways, students practice reading, writing, speaking, and listening to clarify and to enhance their thoughts and feelings about a literary experience.

How Do Students Benefit from Integrating the Language Arts?

When students engage in experiences that invite reading, writing, speaking, and listening to be used in concert, they gain a sense of the wholeness of English. They cease to think of these language processes as discrete—reading as one thing, writing another, and speaking and listening something else. They develop *a sense of community* as they talk together, share perceptions from their reading, and respond to each other's written drafts. Most importantly, they grow *toward full language maturity*, recognizing that each language process contributes to the development of all others. Finally, they become better thinkers, a major goal of all instruction.

Writer's Choice is literature-rich:
- Literature selections from the finest contemporary writers
- Annotated Literature Models to take the mystery out of writing well
- Writing About Literature lessons with practical instruction for specific writing situations
- Literature-based Grammar Reviews

Writer's Choice helps students develop a sense of community through the use of language in their own lives, in the classroom, and in the world at large:
- Media Connections—writing in the real world
- Journal Writing—for response and reflection
- Peer Editing—for shared responses
- Cooperative Learning—reading, writing, speaking, listening, and thinking toward common goals
- Readers Respond—students talking to students

Writer's Choice provides a framework for each student's growth toward full language maturity:
- Choice among writing assignments empowers students to draw on their own experiences.
- Writing Process in Action includes criteria for students' self-evaluations.

Cultural Diversity

by Arnold Webb

Senior Research Associate, Research for Better Schools, Philadelphia, Pennsylvania

What Is Cultural Diversity?

Cultural diversity is one of those terms to which we educators nod knowingly when we hear it. We nod, secure in righteous affirmation of a concept that is second only to motherhood, and with which no one would dare disagree. We also believe that we are all using essentially the same definitional parameters and, therefore, can communicate with each other on this issue from a common (and enlightened) conceptual base.

As comforting as the above notion may be, it is not entirely accurate. Perceptions concerning what constitutes meaningful cultural diversity in our classrooms range from fostering and stressing a common culture to celebrating and supporting different cultures. Hard-core adherents to each of these views believe strongly that their approach is the only viable way to *channel the dynamic cultural and ethnic mix in our classrooms* into areas that support and strengthen our democratic society.

I agree with Asa Hilliard who said,

> I do not believe that it is necessary to choose between (cultural) commonality and uniqueness. This is a false dichotomy. Human minds and systems are powerful and flexible enough to handle both.

The truth is that both are essential. We must provide an environment in which children can understand the world around them and their place (and responsibility) in that society as citizens and as contributors to the perpetuation of democratic precepts and ideals. We cannot do this, however, without empowering every child to recognize and value his/her individual worth. That empowerment for many children can only occur when they are in an educational environment that provides opportunities for them to understand and appreciate the unique historic and ongoing contributions of their ethnic and cultural heritage to their land of origin and to the American dream.

Writer's Choice helps you channel the cultural mix in your classroom:

- Student Advisory Board ensured student involvement in creation of the series.
- Student Models reflect diverse population.
- Literature, grammar exercises, and fine art present cultural variety.

How Do We Strike the Right Balance?

How does a teacher strike a balance between providing youngsters with a positive sense of self-worth through pride in their cultural heritage and still engender appreciation of our unique shared culture as Americans? It is a daunting task, but it must be accomplished. Perhaps one might begin by taking a self-administered test and responding candidly to the following questions:

- What do I believe about the children I teach? What are the bases of my expectations of them?
- What do I know about the history, mores, and culture of my students?
- How is this knowledge utilized in my planning and teaching?
- Does the curriculum I teach reflect *the truths of a pluralistic society?* In what ways?
- What opportunities are provided in my classroom for children to know, understand, and *relate to classmates from other backgrounds and cultures?*
- What skills are my students learning that enable them to *contribute positively to an evolving, diverse, and demanding democracy?*

Your answers to the questions posed above should provide some private insights for you into the impact of cultural diversity in your own classroom. Do not believe for a moment, however, that you are alone in the struggle to celebrate diversity and to make it a viable aspect of our educational systems.

In the final analysis, we teachers (all of us) must be responsive to the needs and exigencies of our changing society. For example, the 1990 Census revealed that one of every four Americans is a person of color. This demographic and economic imperative must be dealt with realistically in America's classrooms. Cultural and ethnic diversity is endemic, and we can shy away from its impact to our detriment, or we can build upon its strengths and benefit us all. What happens in our classrooms as we address this issue will markedly affect the rest of the nation's response. It's up to us!

Writer's Choice reflects the truths of a pluralistic society:
- Contemporary photographs
- Fine art
- Cultural Diversity annotations in Teacher's Wraparound Edition

Writer's Choice helps students relate to people of other backgrounds:
- Cultural diversity in Media Connections and in assignment and exercise topics
- Cultural diversity in models and literature

Writer's Choice empowers students to learn the skills of civic literacy:
- Civic Literacy annotations in Teacher's Wraparound Edition pinpoint skills and concepts.
- Media Connections exemplify variety of social roles and contributions.

Teaching Students with Different Abilities

by Bonnie S. Sunstein

Associate Professor of English and Director of the Master of Arts in Teaching Program at Rivier College, Nashua, New Hampshire

and Dan-Ling Fu

Assistant Professor of English at Nanjing University in the People's Republic of China and doctoral candidate at the University of New Hampshire

How Can We Teach Writing to Students with Different Abilities?

In the early 1970s, when Public Law 94-142 offered assistance to millions of students and teachers throughout the United States by providing special education programs and allowing for individualized educational plans, many students who had not been previously included joined regular classes. But with the help came uncomfortable labels: "language deficient," "minimally dysfunctional," "linguistically disadvantaged," "educationally impaired." Our immigrant students, too, were considered "at risk" because they had learned a first language other than English.

These labels (and the tests that created them) suggested a deficit model: that the students were missing certain parts of the mental apparatus that would allow them a complete education. Educational plans followed the defects that the tests revealed; curriculum was designed for repair. In short, for many of our students, curriculum became based on what they *couldn't* do rather than what they could, on how they were *different* from other students rather than how they were the *same.*

Trends are beginning to change again. Much has been written recently about creating curriculum that begins with students' abilities rather than their disabilities. A *coherent writing plan based on personal choice* can offer students a place to connect what they already know, to work with what language skill they already have, and then learn to shape it.

Writer's Choice offers a coherent writing plan based on personal choice:
- Short, manageable lessons to meet specific writing needs and goals
- Wide variety of writing prompts with different degrees of guidance
- Journal writing and portfolio keeping
- Alternative strategies for Basic and Advanced students and for English Language Learners (Teacher's Wraparound Edition)

How Can We Teach Writing to Students Who Have Difficulty with Language?

1. *Start with the students, not the curriculum.* Let them put their ideas to paper: in pictures, in broken English, in invented spelling, even in body language or words dictated to someone more able to write. Once a student has something to say and a reason to say it, there is reason to connect meaning to her sentence. Once she has a meaningful sentence, there is reason to learn to construct it with standard conventions for someone else to read.

2. *Students need to talk first, then write.* Composition theorists and researchers have taught us that meaningful speech must come before the written word (James Moffett, James Britton, Gordon Wells). Speaking is a rehearsal for writing. If students don't have a chance to speak the language or listen to others using it, they won't be able to write it. Our students who have difficulty with language need more opportunities to use it, not a silent classroom with the soft sound of pencil marks on worksheets. They need to tell their stories and listen to others' stories for inspiration: the teachers, the other students, the aides in the class. In a *language-rich classroom,* no opportunity for talk is a waste.

3. *To have control of language, students need to choose what they say.* If students are responsible for creating their own content, the ideas are there and there is a reason to find the language to match their intended meaning. The work of Eleanor Duckworth and Donald Graves has taught us that when students gather their own ideas, they have reason to work toward reshaping those ideas for others.

4. *When students write, we need to highlight the conventions they know how to use, not offer them empty structures in which to fit their writing.* Intuitively, students use many of the narrative and analytical conventions we teach, such as topic sentences, conclusions, characterization, use of specific detail, cause and effect, comparison and contrast. We must look for these structures and help students name them, record them, and document those conventions they already know.

5. *Students need a supportive, literate community.* Students with language difficulties need to spend time in school with people who want to read and write. In Mike Rose's words, they must "enter the conversation." When we assume that they are *members of a literate community* (Nancie Atwell, Mike Rose), they begin to function as one.

Writer's Choice starts with students:
- Personal writing beginning each book
- Journal writing for reflection and self-expression
- Writing prompts with a variety of student-friendly contexts
- Student models by real students
- Literature responses by real students

Writer's Choice helps students and teacher together create a language-rich classroom through the sheer variety of language experiences:
- Media Connections
- Literature discussion
- Student Models
- Writing conferences
- Journal Writing
- Writing Across the Curriculum
- Listening and Speaking opportunities
- Peer responses
- Cooperative Learning Activities

Writer's Choice includes *all* students as members of a literate community:
- Choices among lessons and array of contexts for assignments enable all students to feel involved.
- Media Connections, Student Models, and Readers Respond encourage participation by example.
- *Practice, Reteaching,* and *Enrichment* blackline masters meet individual needs.

Journal Writing

by Sharyn Lowenstein

Associate Professor and Director of the Academic Support Center, Lesley College, Cambridge, Massachusetts

What Can Students Learn from Journal Writing?

Because journal writing is very close to inner speech—what we're actually thinking without having to translate it to others—students using journals can really grow aware of *what's on their minds.* They can plainly see the other "voices" interfering in their work, the way in which they (yes, even in the journal!) have come to censor their work, the many audiences they're trying to please. The journal gives them a chance to complain, to get frustrated, to change their minds, and often, once they take this opportunity, they are able to return with deeper concentration to other academic tasks.

Journal writing often promotes free association, gives students "permission" to wander; often, in that wandering they recapture memories, which in turn can be mined. Through memory work students may realize their personal and familial *connections to topics they are studying* in history, science, and mathematics, etc., topics they may have previously thought were unimportant or too abstract or unrelated to their lives. Journals store moments much like scrapbooks store pictures. Thus, when students go back to reread their entries, they are able to retrieve and ultimately relive the incidents and processes described in the journal. Students report this re-experiencing of incidents as often very pleasurable.

When students keep journals focusing on project-related work, they learn how to describe sometimes very subtle aspects of their problem-solving behaviors. By reviewing their journals they can keep track of the various approaches they tried; they can identify their challenges, and they can better appreciate their successes. Ultimately because the journal can help students see the picture of how they accomplished a task or completed a project, the journal helps students evaluate their own learning: they can see where they became stuck and how they became "unstuck." They come to recognize that learning takes time, that one must try numerous approaches. They eventually can come to see themselves as learners in a dynamic process: often, they report becoming more patient with themselves and more clear about the questions they need to ask as they attempt to learn.

Writer's Choice provides consistent invitations for students to express themselves in journals:
- Personal Writing Unit, including lessons on Writing as Self-Discovery, Keeping a Writer's Journal, and Keeping a Commonplace Book
- Journal Writing—a brief prompt halfway through each composition lesson
- Writing Process in Action with suggestions for journal writing as a means for students to reflect on their writing experiences

Writer's Choice encourages journal writing as a tool for unifying students' educational experiences:
- Lessons on Writing to Learn, Keeping a Reader-Response Journal, and Using a Learning Log help students become more aware of themselves as learners.
- Cross-curricular writing prompts help students practice and transfer composition skills to writing done in other classes and in the world of work.

Why Do Both Students and Teachers Enjoy Journal Writing?

Journal keeping promotes the writing of papers because it helps to incubate ideas, without having to evaluate them. The journal can be a safe place to "play" with ideas, topics, and approaches. By encouraging students to write from several perspectives on the same topic, teachers help students develop their arguments, and ultimately their papers will become more convincing.

Many teachers assign journal work outside of class, which helps individualize the lessons and, in effect, extend instruction. When teachers respond to students' entries, especially when they reveal anything even slightly personal about themselves or their own learning, students have the opportunity to develop or deepen their relationship to their teachers.

Toby Fulwiler and others have written extensively about journal use in the class. Journals can be used to provide time to start the class with a journal question, *to summarize class discussion, to articulate confusions, to anticipate new information, to synthesize or evaluate material.* When teachers sense that class discussion or their presentation of information is unclear or they don't know how to interpret students' reactions, journal writing in class (and subsequent sharing) helps the teacher identify student concerns and helps the students assess their knowledge about the subject. Journal writing in class also helps the more quiet students or the students who require more time to process information. Journal keeping is a kind of equalizer in which every student can access his or her thoughts, and then better contribute to class discussion.

When all students keep journals (and especially if the teacher keeps one too), the class is taking writing risks together, and this shared experience contributes to community building. Many classes have even experimented with class journals, which further promote collaborative learning and empower students as active participants in their classrooms.

Writer's Choice invites students to experiment, summarize, articulate, anticipate, synthesize, and evaluate:
- Journal Writing activities suggest a variety of relevant stimuli for helping students start out and set frameworks for problem solving, pose questions for follow-through, and engage higher-order thinking skills.

Portfolios

by **Bonnie S. Sunstein**

Associate Professor of English and Director of the Master of Arts in Teaching Program at Rivier College, Nashua, New Hampshire

How Do People Use Portfolios?

Artists, musicians, heads of state, and financiers use portfolios at intervals during their careers, gathering samples to represent depth and breadth in their work. They select different artifacts at different times, depending on who will be looking at their portfolios, and for what purposes. Over the last two centuries there is evidence that portfolios have appeared in tooled leather cases, carved wooden boxes, ornate display stands, and makeshift cloth carrying cases. The word *portfolio* derives from the Latin *portare* ("to carry") and *fogli* ("leaves or sheets of paper").

In the last decade, we've seen similarly colorful and energetic varieties of portfolios in schools and colleges. They appear on our classroom shelves in plastic boxes, shoe boxes, loose-leaf scrapbooks, neon-colored trapper-keepers, and metal drawers full of sedate manila folders. With homage to their heritage, all portfolios "carry" representative "leaves" of paper for the display of their owner's work. With portfolios, students can document their own histories as learners. They can *become their own authorities* rather than relying on external authorities to judge what's good or bad about their work. The use of portfolios to represent students' accomplishments is in its infancy, and the possibilities for learning from portfolios are open and exciting.

How Can Portfolios Help Students and Teachers?

As students, teachers, classes, and whole school systems experiment with portfolios, we are shifting our thinking about the terms *assessment* and *evaluation*. For students, a collection of writing over time can offer insights as they *write reflectively about their own learning*. For teachers, portfolios enable us to include our students in our evaluation process. When we keep our own portfolios along with our students, our own written reflections point out the time we devote to our students and to our own personal literacy.

Writer's Choice empowers students to become their own authorities:
- Portfolio and Reflecting ideas at the end of every composition unit
- Writing Portfolios for collecting student work

Writer's Choice encourages students to write reflectively about their own learning:
- Student models of writing to learn
- Journal Writing
- Reflecting and Portfolio Activities

Because evaluation is inextricably tied to instruction, portfolios teach us more about our teaching. For whole classes, teachers and students can view progress over time and make more informed decisions about curriculum coverage. For school systems, large-scale use of portfolios can offer new kinds of information and raise questions we've never been able to ask before. In other words, portfolios can help us to evaluate where we've been, assess where we are, and project where we want to go next. When we collect our reading and writing for display and analysis, we connect our present to our past and our future.

What Goes into a Portfolio—and Why?

As this is being written, there are as many kinds of portfolios as there are people working with them, and that's a healthy sign. Some are distilled folders, holding samples of students' "best" work. Deciding what's "best" becomes a negotiation between a teacher and a student in which they decide what is important in writing. The decisions may offer surprises as we discover what issues we most value in our evaluations. Portfolios offer us a multidimensional look at ourselves.

Portfolios complete with students' reflections—commentaries about why the paper is included—offer *opportunities for metacognition*—to think about their own thinking and document it. A "best" paper might be the one with the least errors or one that follows the teacher's assignment perfectly. But a "best" paper might be the one in which the student took a risk, worked out a nagging question, researched and synthesized a new idea, reached beyond the teacher's assignment. This paper might not have followed the assignment exactly, but it might represent a new moment in a student's thinking.

Portfolios are not writing folders redone; they are documented collections of literary decisions made at certain times among certain people. They reflect our philosophies of reflection, evaluation, and learning. Portfolio keeping is decision making, and making decisions involves asking tough questions—of ourselves and our students—about what we value in writing and reading.

Writer's Choice offers opportunities for metacognition:
- Writing activities point the way at each stage of the writing process.
- Rubrics for self-evaluation accompany every Writing Process in Action.
- The Unit Review helps students ask the right questions about their work.

Writing Across the Curriculum

Writer's Choice provides numerous opportunities for students to tell what they've learned:

- Writing assignments cover art, biology, geography, history, home economics, journalism, mathematics, music, science, and, of course, literature.
- TIME Facing the Blank Page and Media Connections explore and model how today's professionals write in the world of work.
- Research Paper unit in each book focuses on a topic in social studies, science, or art.
- *Writing Across the Curriculum* blackline masters provide practical help for writing in content areas.
- *Research Paper and Report Writing* blackline masters offer cross-curricular support.

Writer's Choice encourages students to write to learn:

- Individual lessons cover such topics as Keeping a Learning Log, Writing to Learn, and Keeping a Reader-Response Journal.
- Annotations in the Teacher's Wraparound Edition identify points of intersection between English and other curriculum areas.

by Denny Wolfe

Professor of English Education at Old Dominion University in Norfolk, Virginia; Director of the Tidewater Virginia Writing Project

Why Teach Students to Write to Learn?

Heuristic is an English adjective derived from a Greek verb meaning "to find out." In composition theory it is often used to describe how we go about learning. Writing—historically used in schools as a means of testing what students already know—can become a powerful *heuristic* strategy for students—i.e., a way of inventing, investigating, and discovering.

Traditionally, only half the power of writing has been exploited in our schools. Typically, we ask students to write for the purpose of *telling us what they've learned*—about literature, social studies, science, mathematics, and so on; or we ask them to write to show us what they've learned about writing itself—how to structure sentences, organize their ideas, make their thoughts cohere, punctuate, and spell. This remains, as it should, an important function of writing in school.

But the other half of writing's power is quite different. It is the writing we do primarily for ourselves, not others. It is the writing we do to *find out what we know and do not know.* This is ungraded writing, writing not meant to be judged by an audience beyond the writer. As adults, and sometimes as students, many of us have discovered for ourselves just how useful this kind of writing can be. We make lists to organize our days; we set goals for ourselves; we keep diaries and journals; we write pros and cons to aid in important decision-making; and we simply "brainstorm" on paper. Admitting this kind of writing into our classrooms can work to improve students' learning. Why should they have to wait—to learn by accident the power of this second half of writing?

How Can We Help Students Write to Learn?

Some students believe that the only writing worth doing is the writing that teachers grade. Somehow we must break this myth. If we wish students to improve as writers, they must write far more than we can possibly grade. An analogy might be helpful. If the only time a professional golfer played golf were in a tournament, he or she would never win a prize. The golfer must practice, practice, practice—often when no one is watching—to develop his or her game. Of course, the same is true with writing. One must write *a lot* to hone the craft of writing. Response to writing is necessary, but not to *all* writing.

Short, in-class invitations to write can be a start. Asking students to come into class, go to their places, and write for two or three minutes about where the class ended yesterday can focus their attention upon what is coming up today. Or, asking them to write something they have learned at the end of class today can pay instructional dividends tomorrow. Writing to summarize reading can help students monitor their own comprehension. Pausing in a lecture to ask students to write a question can lead to rich discussion. Of course, journal keeping can become a major source of learning for students, as well. It can help them determine what they know and do not know, as well as record and pursue ideas for the future writing of formal papers.

The point is that writing briefly to inquire, clarify, interpret, define, decide, explore—even play—can be a fertile tool for teaching and learning.

How Do Students Benefit from Writing to Learn?

When students write just for themselves, they often get to cob-webbed crevices in their heads they have never before visited. They invent and discover knowledge, questions, gaps in their understanding, and even attitudes that surprise them. The quality of surprise that comes from this kind of writing can be instructional, enlightening, and exciting. Further, writing just for the sake of inventing, investigating, and discovering makes one reflective, introspective, and curious—qualities that go a long way toward defining good learners. Finally, students become more comfortable and able as language users, and the writing we *do* grade often becomes better, more sparkling, and pleasurable to read.

Writer's Choice is a program of invitation and instruction:
- Journal Writing activities occur in every composition lesson.
- Annotated models invite student response.
- Media Connections and literature selections invite student response.
- Writing and cross-curricular assignments invite the kinds of choices that generate student engagement.
- Writing Process in Action gives even more extended modeling and guidance.

Thinking and Writing

by Carol Booth Olson

Director of the UCI Writing Project and a faculty member in the Department of Education at the University of California, Irvine

What Are the Fundamental Premises About Thinking That Can Inform the Teaching of Writing?

Writing is a mode of thinking. In order to produce a composition, writers must generate ideas, plan for both the process of writing and for the written product itself, translate thought into print, revise what they have articulated, and evaluate the effectiveness of their efforts. In short, in moving from conception to completion, writers tap all of the levels of Bloom's taxonomy of the cognitive domain.

If thinking and writing are so inextricably connected, then a number of fundamental premises about thinking can and should inform the teaching of writing:

- *Thinking is developmental.* It is an evolving process that grows with maturity and experience. A developmental writing curriculum should *start from where the kids are* in terms of interests and maturity levels, tap a range of different intellectual strengths or what Howard Gardner would call "areas of potential" (linguistic, musical, logical-mathematical, kinesthetic, etc.), and build bridges from the student's personal experience to the world of school. Instruction should be challenging enough to stimulate students to stretch intellectually and yet be accessible enough to be attainable with guidance from the teacher.

- *Thinking is progressive.* As Piaget observed, the mind is better able to make cognitive leaps when learning moves from the concrete to the abstract. Individual thinking/writing tasks should begin by focusing on something tangible and/or concrete. For example, students can observe a seashell and be encouraged to think analogically by creating similes about what the seashell is like. An overall writing curriculum

Writer's Choice is built on the belief that writing is a mode of thinking:
- Clear, manageable lessons help students think through specific writing situations.
- Journal Writing activities support each composition lesson.
- Writing Objectives, as well as critical thinking and listening and speaking skills, are identified in the Teacher's Wraparound Edition for every composition lesson.

Writer's Choice starts from where students are in interest and maturity level:
- Student-friendly text and visuals
- Student Models by real students
- Literature that engages contemporary readers
- Readers Respond pages that foster critical thinking
- Choices of assignments that enable students to draw on their own personal experiences and cross-curricular interests

should also move progressively. This might take the form of sequencing the domains of writing from descriptive to narrative to expository, or it might involve moving from known to unknown audiences.

- *Thinking is cumulative and recursive.* All thinking experiences build upon one another. However, the pathway to more complex thought is not a linear one. Researchers have noted that *writing, in particular, is a recursive process.* Writers often go back in their thinking in order to move forward with their writing. Therefore, teachers who use a stage process model of composition which moves from prewriting to writing to revising, editing, and so forth should invite students to continually revisit what they have written and to think about their thinking and their writing. So, too, a writing curriculum should be scaffolded in such a way that students must go back to prior learning in order to move forward to the next assignment.

- *Thinking is not taught but fostered.* Thinking is an innate capacity which can be enhanced through the act of writing. Hilda Taba concludes that "how people think may depend largely on the kinds of 'thinking experience' they have had." The teacher, then, plays a crucial role by providing students with thinking experiences that facilitate cognitive growth. Writing is one of the most complex and challenging thinking experiences the teacher can provide.

What Can a Composition Teacher Do to Encourage the Development of Independent Thinking and Writing?

The key to *independent thinking and writing* is *practice.* Teachers need to provide students with enough guided practice in a range of thinking and writing tasks to enable them to develop and internalize a repertoire of problem-solving strategies that they can apply with confidence as autonomous learners to future thinking/writing challenges.

Writer's Choice recognizes that writing is a recursive process:
- Writing Process Tips recur throughout composition lessons.
- Writing Process in Action reinforces "revisiting" of previous thinking and writing.
- Media Connections exemplify recursive writing process in the real world.

TIME Facing the Blank Page takes students inside the writing process to explore other writers' approaches.

Writer's Choice fosters independent thinking and writing:
- Writing Process in Action includes criteria for self-evaluation.
- Reflecting and Adding to Your Portfolio in Unit Reviews focus students' thoughts about their writing.
- **Troubleshooter** helps students help themselves.
- *Thinking and Study Skills* blackline masters provide additional practice and activities.

Cooperative Learning

by Judith Summerfield

Associate Professor of English, Queens College,
City University of New York

Writer's Choice incorporates practical cooperative learning activities:
- Writing Activities often include a choice of a Cooperative Learning activity.
- Additional optional cooperative activities appear in Teacher's Wraparound Edition.
- Peer response and peer editing are encouraged.

Writer's Choice includes cooperative learning activities that fit a variety of purposes:
- Choices include brainstorming for prewriting, peer response for revision, responding to literature, responding to fine art, group problem solving, and research for group writing.

Why Are Twenty Heads Better Than One?

Cooperative learning—or collaborative learning—is a new name for the old adage: Two heads are better than one. And nowhere is cooperative learning better than in the writing classroom, where one of the gifts we can give to our students is to allow time for them to write—right in the classroom—and to read their own writing to their peers and listen to the writing of others.

But "How?" you ask—particularly when twenty in the English classroom might, in actuality, be forty. How, when there is so much else to do? How, when there is so much that I, the teacher, have to teach, given the pressures to cover material, to get students ready for state exams or for the SAT's? And how, when the seats are bolted to the floor—when I don't have the mobility of the classroom itself?

Perhaps it might be useful to think about cooperative learning in two ways: (1) *whole class activity* and (2) *small group work.*

How Can a Whole Class Activity Be Cooperative?

The whole class reads around, quickly, without comment, a short piece of their own writing, a journal entry, a brainstorming idea, a response to something they have read. Within a few minutes, the entire class is given voice.

Here's how it might work:

1. Write William Carlos Williams's "The Red Wheelbarrow" on the board and ask students to imitate the poem, beginning with "So much depends upon" followed by two separate images. Ten minutes. (You write, too.)
2. Now have the entire class read very quickly around the room. (In a class of twenty, this will take about ten minutes.)
3. See what happens.

Being willing to "see what happens," to allow for surprise, the unexpected, the unpredictable, the happy accidents that arise when writers write, begins to turn your class into a writing class. I used the Williams exercise recently in a literature class when students, having read the Williams poem, protested loudly. One student said, "Well, it's fine for *him* to have the leisure to spend his time looking at wheelbarrows and chickens. But we don't have that kind of time." Another student said, "Right, and you can be sure he's not a she! She'd be in the kitchen cooking the chicken." Another complained, "I hate farm poetry." And another asked, "What's the point?"

Rather than allow their energy to dissipate, or to evaporate in classroom chat, I *used* it: I asked them to take out their writers' notebooks and imitate Williams's poem, using the same form: "so much depends upon" + two separate images. Then they all read their reactions aloud. I believe that what they realized through their own writing was an appreciation for what can be said in such a short, tight, confined space; how a poem "does" rather than "explains"; how many more words they would have needed to translate the impulses or feelings of the "so much depends upon" into an essay or into a short story; how these city kids had their own wheelbarrows, which they could use and respect in their own writing; and how thirty heads produced thirty little ventures, of great richness and variety. The class cooperative turned us all into poets.

How Is Small-Group Work Cooperative?

Students gather in pairs, trios, quartets, quintets, depending upon the task. Giving up your own center in the classroom can be a bit disconcerting, but the benefits are uncountable. Here, too, the tasks must be very *carefully planned and defined.* Students can use each other, as writers do, to plan or brainstorm, to throw ideas around, to read each others' drafts, or to edit or proofread. Writers' groups can be stable—for a month or a semester. Or you can develop specialized groups. In a basic writing course I recently taught, several students became "punctuation experts," and they were the ones designated to help in proofreading and editing, particularly when we were working together on a class book of students' writings (which they entitled *Roll Over, Hemingway!*).

Students realize that they, too, can make things happen on the page, which, added up, can be turned into a portfolio of their own writing—their own book; or a collection of the class writings, which is the ultimate cooperative venture.

Writer's Choice offers cooperative learning activities that are carefully planned and defined:
- Students are given clear, step-by-step guidance for cooperative activities.
- Teacher's Wraparound Edition provides detailed, concrete suggestions for additional cooperative activities, including round-robin, pairs check, think-pair-share, roundtable, and partners.

Sentence Combining and the Writing Process

by **William Strong**

Professor of Secondary Education at Utah State University, Director of the Utah Writing Project, and a member of the National Writing Project Advisory Board

What Is the Role of Sentence Combining in Writing Instruction?

Because teachers *know* what works, interest in sentence combining (SC) has paralleled the rise of writing process since the early 1970s. Our focus on what students *do* as they compose has led many of us to welcome SC into our classes.

Happily, research has confirmed our intuitions. For example, George Hillocks concluded in *Research on Written Composition* (NCTE/ERIC, 1986) that "research shows sentence combining, on the average, to be more than twice as effective as freewriting as a means of enhancing the quality of student writing" (249).

Practice in SC apparently enables students to say more in fewer words and to write more *varied* sentences than they would otherwise manage. Moreover, the gains in sentence fluency (or maturity) seem to be linked with qualitative gains (better writing) in a number of studies.

To explain these associations, Hillocks suggests that "perhaps sentence combining practice provides writers with systematic knowledge of syntactic possibilities, the access to which allows them to sort through alternatives in their heads as well as on paper and to choose those which are most apt" (150).

One approach to SC involves *whole-discourse models* of descriptive, narrative, expository, and persuasive text. As students combine sentences and consider options, they make decisions *in context*, just as they do in their own writing. An important bonus is that paragraph-length exercises help students internalize methods of development—such as spatial ordering or comparison/contrast—in different modes of writing.

Writer's Choice includes whole-discourse sentence combining:
- Sentence Combining unit in each book includes instruction and exercises for descriptive, narrative, expository, and persuasive writing.

Moreover, the paragraphs that students construct from whole-discourse SC can serve as motivating *springboards*, particularly for work in journals. In this way, SC not only promotes sentence fluency and decision making but also stimulates prewriting and drafting.

A second approach to SC instruction involves "*cued*," or "*signaled*," exercises. Whereas whole-discourse exercises have many right answers and help us teach revision, cued exercises serve a different purpose: to help students acquire the know-how to make specific transformations with ease. Such exercises provide support for English language learners or for others needing direct, structured approaches in sentence construction.

Because SC is essentially a revising activity, students should understand its basic aim: to help them make *good* sentences, not merely long ones. We should explain how SC practice simulates and stimulates sentence-level revision, then encourage similar "moves" in our writing workshops. By teaching for transfer, we help students see the connection between SC practice and the work in their portfolios.

How Does Experience with Sentence Combining Improve Students' Writing Style?

Sorting and choosing are familiar strategies to us as writing teachers. We encourage rhetorical and stylistic options. Often, however, we teach students who "play it safe" because they fear mistakes.

SC provides a no-risk context in which students can not only explore stylistic options but also make mistakes and *learn* from them. Doing exercises orally, either with the whole class or in small groups, is a particularly effective activity. Because SC is collaborative—and because students see many right answers, not just one—they often begin to take risks in their own writing.

Of course, good instruction can support such efforts to find a personal style. Inviting students to compare sentences and make decisions about those they prefer builds skill and self-confidence. Publicly praising various stylistic moves—such as parallelism, sentence variety, or interruption for effect—encourages more risk-taking. Challenging students to *compare their style with that of a professional writer* leads to insights and surprises.

When the oral emphasis of SC workshops is coupled with a focus on stylistic decision-making, we have a potent combination for helping students develop and improve their writing style. And by marking "SC" in the margin of choppy drafts, we help students *apply* what they have learned.

Writer's Choice includes "cued," or "signaled," exercises:
- *Sentence Combining Practice* blackline masters provide signaled as well as unsignaled exercises.

Writer's Choice offers opportunities for students to compare their styles with professional writers':
- Literature-based sentence combining activities invite insight and surprise.

Assessment

by **Charles R. Duke**

Dean of the College of Education and Human Services, Clarion University, Clarion, Pennsylvania

What Is Assessment?

Assessment can mean responding much as we might if we were present as a potter worked with clay or as a painter worked on canvas. At this stage in the creative process, response, usually called "formative evaluation," takes the form of questions and comments about the process, all designed to assist the creator in achieving his or her purpose. In another sense, assessment can mean the response made at the completion of a task. This "summative evaluation" measures the product against established standards and usually, but not always, results in the recording of some form of judgment such as a letter grade, percentile, or published critique.

What Is the Role of Formative Evaluation?

For teachers to use assessment effectively in conjunction with the writing process, both formative and summative evaluation are necessary, but the most important, when working with young writers, is the formative. Central to formative evaluation is diagnosis, seeing where the writer is at any given stage of the writing process and providing feedback designed to assist the writer to move to the next stage. To achieve this, teachers must pay close attention to the *signals in students' composing processes* and avoid passing summative judgments early in the process on what is being produced. Instead, teachers play the role of collaborator, responding to drafts as readers, not judges, and providing responses which help the writers clarify meaning and purpose.

But teachers need not do this all by themselves. *Peer response* groups can not only provide useful formative responses but also enlarge the writer's audience. Once established in the classroom, response groups often free the teacher, particularly in the early stages of the writing process, from providing extensive written feedback because peers perform the same function more immediately. This frees teachers from having to read so many early

---

Writer's Choice pays close attention to the signals in students' composing processes:
- Evaluation Rubrics in the Teacher's Wraparound Edition provide specific suggestions for giving students feedback.
- *Teacher's Guide to Writing Assessment* offers additional models and guidelines for assessment.

Writer's Choice encourages peer response and discussion:
- Writing Process in Action suggests peer response and peer editing.
- Students are instructed in effective methods of peer response.

drafts and allows them instead to offer concise focused feedback in more one-to-one brief conferences with students at significant moments in their composing process.

Throughout all assessment, teachers need to be alert to the developmental aspects of their students' writing. Not all writers develop at the same pace, nor are they all necessarily able to handle the same writing tasks at the same time and level. *Establishing writing options* based upon diagnosis of students' abilities, needs, and interests and developing clear criteria for their completion will not only individualize the writing process but also assist both student and teacher in understanding what must be done to complete a particular task successfully.

How Can I Best Prepare for Summative Evaluation?

Finally, of course, teachers are expected to report the results of student writing achievement, a summative evaluation of where students are at a given point in their writing development. A useful way of preparing for such assessment is the establishment of *writing portfolios*. Such portfolios may range in complexity from single folders with representative samples of student work to more complex ones kept by students themselves; these can include student commentary on their progress, self-evaluation of their achievement, and self-selection of pieces for thorough evaluation based upon criteria clearly established at the beginning of a marking period, school year, etc.

If teachers establish first a classroom within which formative evaluation is an on-going activity, *summative evaluation* emerges easily and clearly as a final report on that formative activity, and represents a collaboration between student and teacher that will enhance student writing achievement.

Writer's Choice is based upon establishing a range of writing opportunities:
- Short, manageable lessons address specific writing situations.
- Variety of assignments and strategies address students of varying interests, abilities, and stages of development.

Writer's Choice helps students establish and maintain portfolios with
- Writing Rubrics for self-evaluation on Writing Activity pages and in Writing Process in Action
- Reflecting and Portfolio help

Writer's Choice provides instruments for summative evaluation:
- Both objective and holistic forms
- Composition tests with criteria for the student's self-evaluation
- Pretests and Mastery Tests for Grammar, Usage, Mechanics, and Resources
- Tests in print form and in *Testmaker* software (IBM, Apple, Macintosh)

Visual Learning

Writer's Choice encourages visual literacy:
- Viewing and Representing unit with instruction in deconstructing and interpreting visual images and media presentations
- Viewing and Representing activities in many composition lessons
- Viewing the Art discussion prompts in Teacher's Wraparound Edition

Writer's Choice enhances instruction by effectively combining visual and verbal elements:
- Sparkling visuals that grab and hold students' attention
- Computer graphics that clearly illustrate concepts and processes
- Visual Thinking annotations in the Teacher's Wraparound Edition with strategies for improving students' thinking and writing

Why Are Visual Learning Strategies Important?

To be truly literate in a modern technological culture, we need to comprehend and use both verbal and visual literacies." This claim made by Richard Sinatra and Josephine Stahl-Gemake in *Using the Right Brain in the Language Arts* has important ramifications for the English classroom. Clearly, English teachers consider the development of verbal literacy as central to their mission, but what do we mean by visual literacy? Loosely defined, visual literacy encompasses a set of skills that enable an individual to decode and interpret images and visual representations of concepts, to use images and visual representations to communicate effectively, and to understand and enjoy the creative works of visual artists.

In a culture permeated by television, the Internet, computer games, and other electronic media, students come to school with a rich experience in receiving and interpreting messages that are at once both visual and verbal. Rather than presenting a cause for alarm, this experience offers an opportunity for effective instructional materials and strategies to meet the learning needs of all students.

We can begin to use visual strategies to enhance instruction by first acknowledging that *presentations which effectively combine visual and verbal elements* are more compelling than text alone, particularly for students who have grown up in a video culture. We know from brain research that visual messages are processed largely in the brain's right hemisphere, while the processing of verbal messages takes place mainly in the left hemisphere. In essence then, the compelling nature of video derives in large measure from its dual message that simultaneously stimulates two discrete regions of the brain. In the classroom, visuals that relate instructionally to the text can engage students' attention and serve as a gateway to a concept or skill to be explored verbally. This function of engagement and connection to personal experience is a necessary first step in the learning process.

An integrated combination of visual and verbal presentations can also provide greater access to concepts and skills for students of varied learning styles. For example, graphic organizers are a particularly powerful means of representing processes and relationships. Not just visual learners but all students can benefit from using a flow chart to represent the steps in a process or a Venn diagram to highlight similarities and differences.

In addition, *a memorable graphic representation of a key concept or relationship* provides a useful mnemonic tool for all learners. Again brain research indicates that visual memories are formed and retrieved very differently from verbal memories. Thus the association of an image with a particular concept can enhance students' ability to recall and apply that concept.

How Can Visuals Promote the Development of Student Writing?

Photographs and fine art can provide *points of entry to writing through visual exploration.* At the most basic level, students can write a personal response to a visual just as they would to a piece of literature. Similarly, they can describe what they see, narrate the story depicted, or write persuasively about their aesthetic judgment of the painting or photo.

At a more significant level, however, students can explore analogies between the writing process and the creative processes of photography and painting. Opportunities to explore the process of composing a photograph or other visual message can help students discover principles that they can apply to their written compositions. Like a writer, a photographer must select a subject, a focus, and a point of view. Similarly, both photographers and writers create a mood—one through the choice of lighting and camera angles, the other through the choice of words and sentence structure.

The ultimate payoff from these visual-verbal approaches to instruction lies in helping students become more effective communicators and more discerning recipients of communication. As they come to recognize the parallels between written and visual communication, they become better equipped to apply critical thinking skills both in their reading and writing and in their viewing.

Writer's Choice provides memorable graphic representations of key concepts and relationships:
- State-of-the-art graphics to help students see the connections between observing, thinking, and writing
- Visuals that offer an alternate mode of information delivery that is especially helpful for today's visually oriented students

Writer's Choice provides points of entry to writing through visual exploration:
- Fine art and contemporary photography for stimulating thinking and writing
- Fine Art Overhead Transparencies for additional writing prompts
- Writing Process Overhead Transparencies for easy-to-use graphic organizers and revision models

Technology

by Barbara King-Shaver

Supervisor of English, South Brunswick High School, Monmouth Junction, New Jersey

Does Using Computers Make a Difference in Students' Writing?

When most students write using a computer, they are more enthusiastic about writing, they tend to write more, and they produce better finished products. Because the computer is very forgiving, allowing writers to make changes easily, *students are less intimidated* by the writing process and more willing to experiment with their writing. Writing using a computer *supports the writing process* approach to writing. The computer can be a successful tool for helping students of all abilities prewrite, draft, revise, and edit.

As a prewriting tool, the computer helps students overcome writer's block by offering them an inviting surface on which to write. Students have reported that staring at a blank, white lined journal page is more inhibiting than staring at a computer screen with a cursor blinking its invitation to write. During prewriting, students feel free to play with ideas and experiment with language. In addition, when students freewrite on the computer, they have less tendency to stop and edit what they have written, thus supporting the goal of prewriting: to generate ideas and develop fluency.

The computer is also a great tool for composing, drafting a text. The ease with which words can be typed on a computer keyboard takes the drudgery out of handwriting a paper. Many students are reluctant writers because of the physical strain of writing or because they have terrible handwriting and cannot reread what they have written. Drafting on the computer eliminates these problems. As with prewriting, drafting on the computer helps focus the writer on the act of drafting, getting ideas down in an organized way: the tendency to interrupt drafting to edit what has been written is lessened.

Perhaps the most successful use of the computer in writing can be seen during the revising process. When students who write papers by hand are asked to revise their papers, many resist because of the physical work required in rewriting. Therefore, students who revise by hand usually make

Writer's Choice takes every opportunity to develop computer-proficient writers:
- Using Computers ideas in composition lessons suggest ways to use a computer to solve particular writing problems.
- Technology Tips in the Teacher's Wraparound Editions provide useful on-the-spot ideas for helping students write with computers.
- Electronic Resources unit provides instruction and practice for using a variety of technological resources for research, for communicating, and for word processing.
- *Word Processing* ancillary provides additional *instruction* to familiarize students with word processing and *practice* in using technology to write.

Writer's Choice offers the student advice for using computers at each stage of the writing process:
- Using Computers features pinpoint strategies for prewriting, drafting, revising, editing, and presenting.
- *Word Processing* ancillary provides practice for all stages of the writing process.

only limited changes in their papers, while students who have composed their first drafts on the computer are willing to make more changes in their texts. On the computer, it is a simple task to add or delete ideas and rearrange sentences or paragraphs by using the cut and paste functions. Students who use the computer for writing sometimes report that they never really understood the revising process before they used computers.

Once students have revised their papers, the computer can aid in editing drafts by providing clean copy that can be easily read. In order to edit carefully for errors in mechanics and usage, students must be able to reread a paper carefully. In addition, students may use editing software programs that help them search their papers for specific errors. The students must then decide how to correct the errors.

Where Do Teacher and Peers Come into the Writing Process When Students Use a Computer?

The use of a computer for writing does not mean that students sit in front of a screen all alone prewriting, drafting, revising, and editing without any feedback. One of the advantages of writing using a computer is that the writer can print out a hard copy at any time, even during the first draft, and then has a legible copy for anyone to read. Conferencing with peers or the teacher is a key component of the writing process. Conferencing can take place at any stage of the writing process just as it does when students compose by hand. The teacher can build conferencing time into the computer writing process by giving students deadlines by which a draft must be completed and printed out for peer-group feedback.

An added advantage of writing using the computer is the unofficial conferencing that goes on all the time during the writing process. Because of the public nature of the computer screen, students often read each other's work as it appears on the computer screen and make informal comments. Collaboration happens informally all the time in a computer writing lab. Therefore, *the communal nature of writing* is supported as an important part of the whole writing process.

Writer's Choice Web site at writerschoice.glencoe.com provides writing prompts and other online support for student writers.

Writer's Choice encourages the community of writers through feedback, conferencing, and collaborating:
- Using Computers reminds students of practical collaborative techniques.

GLENCOE

Writer's Choice

Grammar and Composition
Grade 10

 Glencoe McGraw-Hill

New York, New York   Columbus, Ohio   Woodland Hills, California   Peoria, Illinois

ACKNOWLEDGMENTS

Grateful acknowledgment is given authors, publishers, photographers, museums, and agents for permission to reprint the following copyrighted material. Every effort has been made to determine copyright owners. In case of any omissions, the Publisher will be pleased to make suitable acknowledgments in future editions.

Acknowledgments continued on page 965.

The Standardized Test Practice pages in this book were written by The Princeton Review, the nation's leader in test preparation. Through its association with McGraw-Hill, The Princeton Review offers the best way to help students excel on standardized assessments.

The Princeton Review is not affiliated with Princeton University or Educational Testing Service.

The **Facing the Blank Page** feature in this book was prepared in collaboration with the writers and editors of *TIME* magazine.

Glencoe/McGraw-Hill

A Division of the **McGraw-Hill** *Companies*

PRINTED IN THE UNITED STATES OF AMERICA

Send all inquiries to:
GLENCOE/MCGRAW-HILL
8787 Orion Place
Columbus, OH 43240-4027

ISBN 0-02-818149-2
(Student Edition)
ISBN 0-07-822659-7
(Teacher's Wraparound Edition)

2 3 4 5 6 7 8 9 10 027/043 05 04 03 02 01 00

ii

PROGRAM CONSULTANTS

Mark Lester is Professor of English at Eastern Washington University. He formerly served as Chair of the Department of English as a Second Language, University of Hawaii. He is the author of *Grammar in the Classroom* (Macmillan, 1990) and of numerous other professional books and articles.

Sharon O'Neal is Assistant Professor at the College of Education, Southwest Texas State University, where she teaches courses in reading instruction. She formerly served as Director of Reading and Language Arts of the Texas Education Agency and has authored, and contributed to, numerous articles and books on reading instruction and teacher education.

Jacqueline Jones Royster is Associate Professor of English at The Ohio State University. She is also on the faculty at the Bread Loaf School of English at Middlebury College in Middlebury, Vermont. In addition to the teaching of writing, Dr. Royster's professional interests include the rhetorical history of African American women and the social and cultural implications of literate practices.

William Strong is Professor of Secondary Education at Utah State University, Director of the Utah Writing Project, and a member of the National Writing Project Advisory Board. A nationally known authority on the teaching of composition, he is the author of many volumes, including *Writing Incisively: Do-It-Yourself Prose Surgery* (McGraw-Hill, 1991).

Jeffrey Wilhelm, a former English and reading teacher, is currently an assistant professor at the University of Maine, where he teaches courses in middle and secondary level literacy. Author of several books and articles on the teaching of reading and the use of technology, he also works with local schools as part of the Adolescent Literacy Project.

Denny Wolfe, a former high school English teacher and department chair, is Professor of English Education, Director of the Tidewater Virginia Writing Project, and Director of the Center for Urban Education at Old Dominion University in Norfolk, Virginia. Author of more than seventy-five articles and books on teaching English, Dr. Wolfe is a frequent consultant to schools and colleges on the teaching of English language arts.

Advisors

Michael Angelotti
Head of Division of Teacher
 Education
College of Education
University of Oklahoma

Larry Beason
Assistant Professor
 of English
Eastern Washington
 University

Charles Duke
Dean of the College
 of Education and
 Human Services
Clarion University

Carol Booth Olson
Director
University of California,
 Irvine, Writing Project

Willis L. Pitkin
Professor of English
Utah State University

Judith Summerfield
Associate Professor
 of English
Queens College,
City University of New York

Bonnie S. Sunstein
Associate Professor of
 English and Director,
 Master of Arts in
 Teaching Program
Rivier College

Educational Reviewers

Lenore Croudy
Flint Community School
Flint, Michigan

John A. Grant
St. Louis Public Schools
St. Louis, Missouri

Vicki Haker
Mead Junior High School
Mead, Washington

Frederick G. Johnson
Georgia Department of
 Education
Atlanta, Georgia

Sterling C. Jones Jr.
Detroit Public Schools
Detroit, Michigan

Barry Kincaid
Raytown School District
Kansas City, Missouri

Evelyn G. Lewis
Newark Public Schools
Newark, New Jersey

M. DeAnn Morris
Crescenta Valley High School
La Crescenta, California

Anita Moss
University of North Carolina
Charlotte, North Carolina

Ann S. O'Toole
Chesterfield County Schools
Richmond, Virginia

Suzanne Owens
Glendale High School
Glendale, California

Sally P. Pfeifer
Lewis and Clark High School
Spokane, Washington

Marie Rogers
Independence High School
Charlotte, North Carolina

Barbara Schubert
Santa Clara County Office
 of Education
San Jose, California

Ronnie Spilton
Chattahoochee High School
Alpharetta, Georgia

Robert Stolte
Huntington Beach High
 School
Huntington Beach, California

Student Advisory Board

The Student Advisory Board was formed in an effort to ensure student involvement in the development of
Writer's Choice. The editors wish to thank members of the board for their enthusiasm and dedication to the
project. The editors also wish to thank the many student writers whose models appear in this book.

BOOK OVERVIEW

Part 1 Composition

Unit 1   Personal Writing 2
Unit 2   The Writing Process 40
TIME Facing the Blank Page 109
Unit 3   Descriptive Writing 120
Unit 4   Narrative Writing 164
Unit 5   Expository Writing 214

Unit 6   Persuasive Writing 276
Unit 7   Research Paper Writing 320
Unit 8   Sentence Combining 358
Unit 9   Troubleshooter 386
Business and Technical Writing 412

Part 2 Grammar, Usage, and Mechanics

Unit 10 Parts of Speech 438
Unit 11 Parts of the Sentence 496
Unit 12 Phrases 522
Unit 13 Clauses and Sentence Structure 542
Unit 14 Diagraming Sentences 574
Unit 15 Verb Tenses and Voice 584
Unit 16 Subject-Verb Agreement 612

Unit 17 Using Pronouns Correctly 636
Unit 18 Using Modifiers Correctly 662
Unit 19 Usage Glossary 690
Unit 20 Capitalization 712
Unit 21 Punctuation, Abbreviations,
             and Numbers 732

Part 3 Resources and Skills

Unit 22 History and Development
             of English 782
Unit 23 Library Resources 798
Unit 24 Using Dictionaries 811
Unit 25 Vocabulary 818
Unit 26 Spelling 827

Unit 27 Study Skills 835
Unit 28 Taking Tests 846
Unit 29 Listening and Speaking 882
Unit 30 Viewing and Representing 894
Unit 31 Electronic Resources 908

Writing and Language Glossary 928
Spanish Glossary 938

Index 950
Acknowledgments 965

CONTENTS

Part 1 | Composition

UNIT 1 Personal Writing 2

Writing in the Real World 4

The Personal Journals of Denise Chavez
Journal Writing by Denise Chavez

Instruction and Practice

1.1 Writing to Discover Your World 8
Write a Journal Entry; Listening and Speaking;
Cooperative Learning; **Grammar Link**

1.2 Using a Learning Log 12
Write a Learning Log; Using Computers; Viewing and
Representing; **Grammar Link**

1.3 Keeping a Commonplace Book 16
Write Commonplace Book Annotations; Viewing and
Representing; Spelling; **Grammar Link**

Writing About Literature

1.4 Using a Reader-Response Journal 20
Write a Reader-Response Journal Entry; Cross-Curricular
Activity; Listening and Speaking; **Grammar Link**

Writing About Literature

1.5 Responding to a Short Story 24
Write a Reader-Response Journal Entry; Viewing and
Representing; Using Computers; **Grammar Link**

Writing Process in Action

Personal Writing Project 28
Write a personal narrative about an event or a situation that
caused you to change.
• Prewriting • Drafting • Revising
• Editing/Proofreading • Publishing/Presenting

Literature Model

from *Blue Highways: A Journey into America* 32
by William Least Heat-Moon

Linking Writing and Literature

Exploring William Least Heat-Moon's personal writing 38

UNIT 1 Review   Reflecting on the Unit

🗂 Adding to Your Portfolio

Writing Across the Curriculum **39**

UNIT 2

The Writing Process **40**

🎩 *Writing in the Real World* **42**

Trahant Investigates Nuclear Transport
Newspaper Article by Mark N. Trahant

Instruction and Practice

2.1 Stages of the Writing Process **46**
Write a Personal Response; Listening and Speaking;
Cross-Curricular Activity; Grammar Link

2.2 Prewriting: Finding a Writing Topic **50**
Write to Find a Topic; Viewing and Representing;
Cross-Curricular Activity; Grammar Link

2.3 Prewriting: Identifying Purpose and Audience . . **56**
Identify Purpose and Audience; Listening and Speaking;
Using Computers; Grammar Link

2.4 Prewriting: Exploring a Topic **60**
Make a Plan for Writing; Cross-Curricular Activity;
Viewing and Representing; Grammar Link

2.5 Prewriting: Interviewing **64**
Interview to Gather Information; Using Computers;
Listening and Speaking; Grammar Link

2.6 Drafting: Writing a Paragraph **68**
Write a Draft; Cross-Curricular Activity; Viewing and
Representing; Grammar Link

2.7 Drafting: Organizing a Paragraph **72**
Plan Ordered Paragraphs; Cross-Curricular Activity;
Viewing and Representing; Grammar Link

2.8 Revising: Checking Unity and Coherence **76**
Revise for Effective Paragraphs; Listening and Speaking;
Using Computers; Grammar Link

2.9 Editing/Proofreading: Toward a Final Version . . . **82**
Edit Your Draft; Using Computers; Listening and Speaking;
Grammar Link

2.10 Publishing/Presenting: Sharing Your Writing . . 86
Present Your Writing; Viewing and Representing;
Using Computers; Grammar Link

Writing About Literature
2.11 Analyzing Point of View. 90
Write from a Particular Point of View; Cross-Curricular
Activity; Listening and Speaking; Grammar Link

Writing Process in Action
The Writing Process Project. 94
Write about your personal history or heritage
• Prewriting • Drafting • Revising
• Editing/Proofreading • Publishing/Presenting

Literature Model
from ***My Furthest-Back Person—The African*** 98
by Alex Haley

Linking Writing and Literature
Examining Alex Haley's writing techniques 107

UNIT 2 Review
Reflecting on the Unit
Adding to Your Portfolio
Writing Across the Curriculum 108

Facing the Blank Page 109

Writing for *TIME* • Prewriting • Drafting • Revising
• Editing/Proofreading • Publishing/Presenting

UNIT 3
Descriptive Writing 120

Writing in the Real World 122

from ***Equator*** Travel Writing by Thurston Clarke

Instruction and Practice
3.1 Writing to Describe. 126
Write a Descriptive Paragraph; Listening and Speaking;
Cross-Curricular Activity; Grammar Link

3.2 Observing and Taking Notes 132
Write About a Painting; Listening and Speaking;
Using Computers; Grammar Link

3.3 Using Energetic Verbs **136**
Write with Energetic Verbs; Listening and Speaking;
Using Computers; **Grammar Link**

3.4 Describing from Vantage Points **140**
Write from a Moving Vantage Point; Listening and Speaking;
Cross-Curricular Activity; **Grammar Link**

Writing About Literature

3.5 Responding to Imagery in Poetry **144**
Write a Response Poem; Using Computers;
Listening and Speaking; **Grammar Link**

3.6 Analyzing Setting in a Short Story **148**
Write a Setting Analysis; Listening and Speaking;
Cross-Curricular Activity; **Grammar Link**

Writing Process in Action
Descriptive Writing Project **152**
Write a description of a place that you know well.
• Prewriting • Drafting • Revising
• Editing/Proofreading • Publishing/Presenting

Literature Model
from ***The Solace of Open Spaces*** by Gretel Ehrlich **156**

Linking Writing and Literature
Analyzing Gretel Ehrlich's descriptive techniques **162**

UNIT 3 Review
Reflecting on the Unit
Adding to Your Portfolio
Writing Across the Curriculum **163**

UNIT 4 Narrative Writing **164**

Writing in the Real World **166**
from **"Perseus and the Gorgon"** **Storytelling** by Bobby Norfolk

Instruction and Practice
4.1 Narrating a Personal Experience **170**
Write a Personal Narrative; Cross-Curricular Activity;
Viewing and Representing; **Grammar Link**

4.2 Developing a Fictional Narrative **174**
Write the Solution for a Story Problem; Listening
and Speaking; Cross-Curricular Activity; **Grammar Link**

4.3 Organizing a Fictional Narrative **180**
Write a Story Opening; Using Computers;
Listening and Speaking; **Grammar Link**

4.4 Writing Dialogue. 184
Write a Dialogue; Listening and Speaking; Viewing
and Representing; **Grammar Link**

4.5 Theme and Anecdote. 188
Write an Anecdote; Using Computers; Listening
and Speaking; **Grammar Link**

4.6 The Plot Summary 192
Write a Plot Summary; Cross-Curricular Activity; Viewing
and Representing; **Grammar Link**

4.7 Analyzing Conflict. 196
Write a Conflict Analysis; Listening and Speaking;
Using Computers; **Grammar Link**

Writing About Literature

Writing Process in Action

Narrative Writing Project. 200
Plan a short story and write the beginning of it.
● Prewriting ● Drafting ● Revising
● Editing/Proofreading ● Publishing/Presenting

Literature Model

from ***Tortuga*** by Rudolfo A. Anaya 204

Linking Writing and Literature

Exploring Rudolfo A. Anaya's narrative. 212

UNIT 4 Review

Reflecting on the Unit
Adding to Your Portfolio
Writing Across the Curriculum 213

UNIT 5 Expository Writing 214

Writing in the Real World 216
from **"Drowsy America"**
Magazine Article by Anastasia Toufexis

Instruction and Practice

5.1 Writing to Inform and Explain. 220
Write an Explanation of an Event; Using Computers;
Cross-Curricular Activity; **Grammar Link**

5.2 Knowing Your Audience. 224
Write an Explanation of a Painting; Cross-Curricular
Activity; Viewing and Representing; **Grammar Link**

Writing About Literature

Writing Process in Action

Literature Model

Linking Writing and Literature

UNIT 5 Review

5.3 **Writing About a Process**. 228
Write a "How-to" Article; Viewing and Representing;
Using Computers; **Grammar Link**

5.4 **Writing About Cause and Effect** 232
Write a Cause-and-Effect Paragraph; Viewing and
Representing; Using Computers; **Grammar Link**

5.5 **Comparing and Contrasting** 236
Write a Comparison-Contrast Article; Cross-Curricular
Activity; Listening and Speaking; **Grammar Link**

5.6 **Writing Effective Definitions** 240
Write a Definition; Listening and Speaking;
Using Computers; **Grammar Link**

5.7 **Using Graphs in Exposition** 244
Write to Compare Information; Using Computers;
Viewing and Representing; **Grammar Link**

5.8 **Writing a News Article**. 248
Write a News Article; Listening and Speaking;
Using Computers; **Grammar Link**

5.9 **Taking an Essay Test** 252
Write an Essay Answer; Cross-Curricular Activity;
Listening and Speaking; **Grammar Link**

5.10 **Comparing and Contrasting Literature** 258
Write a Comparison-Contrast Essay; Viewing and
Representing; Using Computers; **Grammar Link**

Expository Writing Project. 262
Write an explanation of a process.
● Prewriting ● Drafting ● Revising
● Editing/Proofreading ● Publishing/Presenting

from *A Book of Bees . . . and How to Keep Them* 266
by Sue Hubbell

Examining Sue Hubbell's expository techniques. 274

Reflecting on the Unit
Adding to Your Portfolio
Writing Across the Curriculum 275

UNIT 6 Persuasive Writing 276

 Writing in the Real World 278

Membership at the MCA: What Will It Do To You?
Advertisements by an advertising agency

Instruction and Practice

6.1 **Understanding Persuasive Writing** 282
Write an Opinion; Viewing and Representing; Listening
and Speaking; **Grammar Link**

6.2 **Evidence in Persuasive Writing** 286
Write an Editorial; Cross-Curricular Activity; Listening
and Speaking; **Grammar Link**

6.3 **Presenting an Opinion** 290
Write a Letter; Cross-Curricular Activity; Using Computers;
Grammar Link

6.4 **Writing a Product Evaluation** 294
Write an Evaluation of a Place; Viewing and Representing;
Cross-Curricular Activity; **Grammar Link**

6.5 **Creating an Ad** 298
Write an Ad; Cross-Curricular Activity; Using Computers;
Grammar Link

6.6 **Writing a Letter of Complaint** 302
Write a Complaint Letter; Using Computers; Listening
and Speaking; **Grammar Link**

Writing About Literature

6.7 **Reviewing a Nonfiction Book** 306
Write a Book Review; Cross-Curricular Activity; Viewing
and Representing; **Grammar Link**

Writing Process in Action

Persuasive Writing Project 310
Write a letter persuading someone in authority to change a rule in a
favorite game or sport.
● Prewriting ● Drafting ● Revising
● Editing/Proofreading ● Publishing/Presenting

Literature Model

"A Plague on Tennis" by Mark Mathabane 314

Linking Writing and Literature

Analyzing Mark Mathabane's persuasive writing 318

UNIT 6 Review   Reflecting on the Unit

📁 Adding to Your Portfolio

Writing Across the Curriculum 319

UNIT 7

Research Paper Writing 320

Instruction and Practice

7.1 Prewriting: Planning and Researching 322
Types of Research Papers; Draw Up a Schedule; Select
a Topic; Examine a Topic; Locate Information; Develop
a Working Bibliography; Take Notes; Examine Sources
Critically; Avoid Plagiarism

7.2 Prewriting: Outlining 328
Develop an Outline; Develop a Thesis Statement

7.3 Drafting 332
Use Your Outline and Notes; Write an Introduction
and a Conclusion

7.4 Citing Sources 336
Document Appropriately; Format Citations Properly;
Format Your List of Works Cited

7.5 Revising 342
Improve Your Paper; Revise Your Paper

7.6 Editing and Presenting: A Model Paper 346
Prepare the Final Copy; Present Your Paper

Student Model   **The *Titanic*: Was It the End of an Era?** 349

UNIT 7 Review   Reflecting on the Unit

📁 Adding to Your Portfolio

Writing Across the Curriculum 357

UNIT 8

Sentence Combining 358

Instruction and Practice

Style Through Sentence Combining 360
Varying Sentence Length and Structure; Using Parallelism,
Interrupting Phrases, and Unusual Patterns for Emphasis

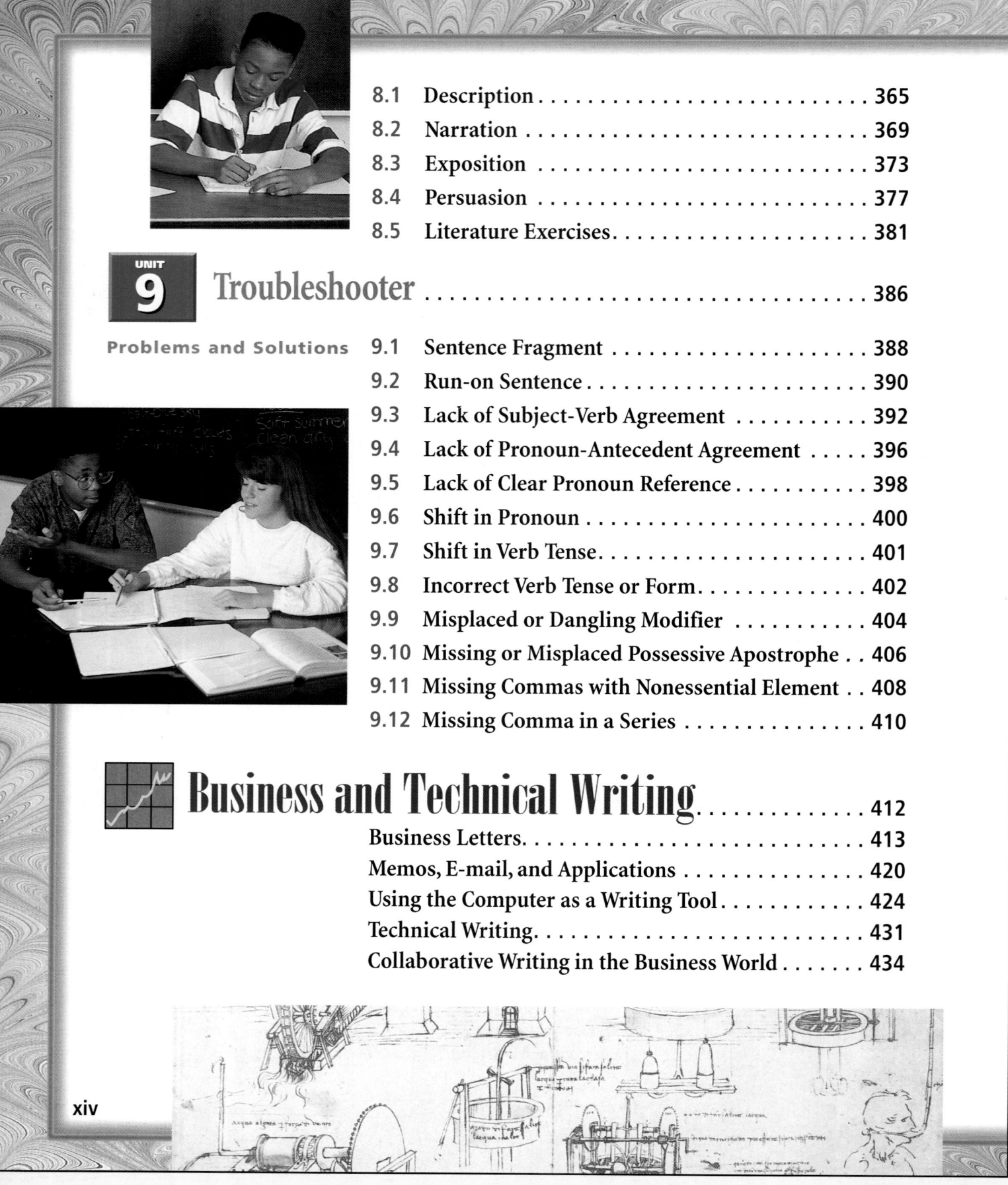

8.1 Description 365

8.2 Narration 369

8.3 Exposition 373

8.4 Persuasion 377

8.5 Literature Exercises. 381

UNIT 9

Troubleshooter

Troubleshooter 386

Problems and Solutions

9.1 Sentence Fragment 388

9.2 Run-on Sentence 390

9.3 Lack of Subject-Verb Agreement 392

9.4 Lack of Pronoun-Antecedent Agreement 396

9.5 Lack of Clear Pronoun Reference 398

9.6 Shift in Pronoun 400

9.7 Shift in Verb Tense. 401

9.8 Incorrect Verb Tense or Form. 402

9.9 Misplaced or Dangling Modifier 404

9.10 Missing or Misplaced Possessive Apostrophe . . 406

9.11 Missing Commas with Nonessential Element . . 408

9.12 Missing Comma in a Series 410

Business and Technical Writing

Business and Technical Writing 412

Business Letters. 413

Memos, E-mail, and Applications 420

Using the Computer as a Writing Tool 424

Technical Writing. 431

Collaborative Writing in the Business World 434

Part 2 Grammar, Usage, and Mechanics

UNIT 10 Parts of Speech 438

Instruction and Practice

    10.1 **Nouns** 439

    10.2 **Pronouns** 445

    10.3 **Verbs** 453

    10.4 **Adjectives** 460

    10.5 **Adverbs**. 466

    10.6 **Prepositions** 473

    10.7 **Conjunctions**. 476

    10.8 **Interjections** 482

Grammar Review   **Parts of Speech** 484

Literature Model   from **The Sound of Waves** by Yukio Mishima 484

Writing Application   Adverbs in Writing; Techniques with Adverbs; Practice. 495

UNIT 11 Parts of the Sentence 496

Instruction and Practice

11.1 Simple Subjects and Simple Predicates...... 497

11.2 Complete Subjects and Complete Predicates.. 498

11.3 Compound Subjects and
Compound Predicates 500

11.4 Order of Subject and Predicate........... 503

11.5 Complements 506

Grammar Review   Parts of the Sentence....................... 512

Literature Model   from *Palace Walk* by Naguib Mahfouz 512

Writing Application   Sentence Patterns in Writing; Techniques with
Sentence Patterns; Practice 521

UNIT 12 Phrases 522

Instruction and Practice

12.1 Prepositional Phrases 523

12.2 Appositives and Appositive Phrases 525

12.3 Verbals and Verbal Phrases 527

Grammar Review   Phrases................................. 532

Literature Model   from *The Stuff of Heroes* by Miguel Delibes 532

Writing Application   Phrases in Writing; Techniques with Phrases; Practice 541

xvi

UNIT 13 Clauses and Sentence Structure 542

Instruction and Practice

13.1 Main Clauses 543

13.2 Subordinate Clauses 544

13.3 Simple and Compound Sentences 545

13.4 Complex and Compound-Complex Sentences 547

13.5 Adjective Clauses 549

13.6 Adverb Clauses 551

13.7 Noun Clauses 553

13.8 Four Kinds of Sentences 556

13.9 Sentence Fragments 557

13.10 Run-on Sentences 559

Grammar Review Clauses and Sentence Structure 562

Literature Model from *Death Comes for the Archbishop* by Willa Cather . . . 562

Writing Application Sentence Structure in Writing; Techniques with Sentence Structure; Practice 573

UNIT 14 Diagraming Sentences 574

Instruction and Practice

14.1 Diagraming Simple Sentences 575

14.2 Diagraming Simple Sentences with Phrases 578

14.3 Diagraming Sentences with Clauses 581

UNIT 15 Verb Tenses and Voice 584

Instruction and Practice

15.1 Principal Parts of Verbs 585

15.2 Regular and Irregular Verbs 586

15.3 Tense of Verbs 589

15.4 Perfect Tenses 593

15.5 Progressive and Emphatic Forms 596

15.6 Compatibility of Tenses 598

15.7 Voice of Verbs 600

Grammar Review   Verb Tenses and Voice 602

Literature Model   from *The Fellowship of the Ring* by J. R. R. Tolkien 602

Writing Application   Verbs in Writing; Techniques with Verbs; Practice 611

UNIT 16 Subject-Verb Agreement 612

Instruction and Practice   16.1 Intervening Prepositional Phrases 613

16.2 Agreement with Linking Verbs 615

16.3 Agreement in Inverted Sentences 616

16.4 Agreement with Special Subjects 618

16.5 Agreement with Compound Subjects 620

16.6 Intervening Expressions 621

16.7 Indefinite Pronouns as Subjects 623

Grammar Review   Subject-Verb Agreement 626

Literature Model   from *Elsewhere, Perhaps* by Amos Oz 626

Writing Application   Subject-Verb Agreement in Writing; Techniques
with Subject-Verb Agreement; Practice 635

UNIT 17 Using Pronouns Correctly 636

Instruction and Practice   17.1 Case of Personal Pronouns 637

17.2 Pronouns with and as Appositives 639

17.3 Pronouns After *Than* and *As* 641

17.4 *Who* and *Whom* in Questions and
Subordinate Clauses 642

17.5 **Pronoun-Antecedent Agreement** 644

17.6 **Clear Pronoun Reference** 649

Grammar Review   **Using Pronouns Correctly** 652

Literature Model   from *The African* by William Conton. 652

Writing Application   Personal Pronouns in Writing; Techniques
with Personal Pronouns; Practice 661

UNIT 18 Using Modifiers Correctly 662

Instruction and Practice   18.1 **The Three Degrees of Comparison** 663

18.2 **Irregular Comparisons** 666

18.3 **Double Comparisons** 668

18.4 **Incomplete Comparisons** 670

18.5 *Good* or *Well; Bad* or *Badly*. 671

18.6 **Double Negatives**. 673

18.7 **Misplaced and Dangling Modifiers**. 674

Grammar Review   **Using Modifiers Correctly** 680

Literature Model   from *A Soldier of the Great War* by Mark Helprin 680

Writing Application   Modifiers in Writing; Techniques with Modifiers; Practice 689

UNIT 19 Usage Glossary 690

Instruction and Practice   19.0 **Usage Glossary** 691

Grammar Review   Usage Glossary 704

Literature Model   **Quotations About Nature** 704

Writing Application   Word Usage in Writing; Techniques with Nouns; Practice 711

UNIT 20 Capitalization 712

Instruction and Practice

20.1 **Capitalization of Sentences** 713

20.2 **Capitalization of Proper Nouns** 715

20.3 **Capitalization of Proper Adjectives**....... 722

Grammar Review   **Capitalization** 726

Literature Model   from ***In Patagonia*** by Bruce Chatwin 726

Writing Application   Capitalization in Writing;
Capitalization Techniques; Practice.................... 731

UNIT 21 Punctuation, Abbreviations, and Numbers....... 732

Instruction and Practice

21.1 **The Period**........................... 733

21.2 **The Exclamation Point**................. 734

21.3 **The Question Mark** 735

21.4 **The Colon** 737

21.5 **The Semicolon**...................... 740

21.6 **The Comma**......................... 743

21.7 **The Dash**.......................... 752

21.8 **Parentheses**........................ 753

21.9 **Quotation Marks** 755

21.10 **Italics (Underlining)** 758

21.11 **The Apostrophe**..................... 760

21.12 **The Hyphen**........................ 763

21.13 **Abbreviations** 766

21.14 **Numbers and Numerals**.............. 769

Grammar Review   **Punctuation** 772

Literature Model   from ***One Writer's Beginnings*** by Eudora Welty 772

Writing Application   Colons and Commas in Writing; Techniques with Colons
and Commas; Practice........................... 779

Part 3 | Resources and Skills

UNIT 22 History and Development of English 782

Instruction and Practice

22.1 How Language Began 783

    Wordworks ACRONYMS 785

22.2 From Speaking to Writing 786

    Wordworks MALAPROPISMS 788

22.3 Indo-European Language Family 789

    Wordworks IDIOMS 791

22.4 Old and Middle English 792

    Wordworks WEASEL WORDS 794

22.5 Modern English. 795

    Wordworks JARGON 797

UNIT 23 Library Resources 798

Instruction and Practice

23.1 Arrangement of a Library 799

23.2 Locating Books and Other Library Materials 801

23.3 Searching for Periodicals 806

23.4 Using Reference Sources 808

xxi

UNIT 24 Using Dictionaries. 811

Instruction and Practice   24.1 General Dictionaries 812

24.2 Using a Thesaurus 816

UNIT 25 Vocabulary 818

Instruction and Practice   25.1 Building Vocabulary 819

25.2 Word Parts 822

UNIT 26 Spelling. 827

Instruction and Practice   26.1 Improving Your Spelling 828

26.2 Spelling Difficult Words. 833

UNIT 27 Study Skills. 835

Instruction and Practice   27.1 Studying Effectively. 836

27.2 Reading Graphs and Diagrams. 842

UNIT 28 Taking Tests 846

Instruction and Practice

28.1 **Preparing for Classroom Tests** 847

THE PRINCETON REVIEW

28.2 **Preparing for Standardized Tests** 851

28.3 **Standardized Test Practice** 857

UNIT 29 Listening and Speaking 882

Instruction and Practice

29.1 **Listening Effectively** 883

29.2 **Speaking Effectively** 887

29.3 **Working in Groups** 891

29.4 **Conducting an Interview** 892

xxiii

UNIT 30 Viewing and Representing 894

Instruction and Practice

30.1 Understanding Visual Messages 895

30.2 Examining Media Messages 902

30.3 Making Your Own Media Messages 905

UNIT 31 Electronic Resources 908

Instruction and Practice

31.1 Electronic Resources and the Writing Process   909

31.2 Research and Resources 913

31.3 Communicating Visually 917

31.4 Visual Analysis 921

31.5 Producing in Multimedia 924

Writing and Language Glossary 928

Spanish Glossary 938

Index 950

Acknowledgments 965

LITERATURE MODELS

Composition Models

Each literature selection is an extended example of the mode of writing taught in the unit.

William Least Heat-Moon, from *Blue Highways: A Journey into America*   32

Alex Haley, from "My Furthest-Back Person—The African"   98

Gretel Ehrlich, from *The Solace of Open Spaces*   156

Rudolfo A. Anaya, from *Tortuga*   204

Sue Hubbell, from *A Book of Bees . . . and How to Keep Them*   266

Mark Mathabane, "A Plague on Tennis"   314

Skill Models

Excerpts from outstanding works of fiction and nonfiction exemplify specific writing skills.

Sylvia Plath, from *The Journals of Sylvia Plath*   8

John Updike, from *Picked-Up Pieces*   24

J. D. Salinger, from "For Esmé—with Love and Squalor"   24

Wayne Swanson, from "Exploring Proud Past of Indians"   50

Lewis Mumford, from *Technics and Civilization*   57

Roy Blount Jr., from *About Three Bricks Shy of a Load*   57

William M. Mathers, from "*Nuestra Señora de la Concepción*"   68

Bette Bao Lord, from *Legacies: A Chinese Mosaic*   70

Robert D. Ballard, from "The *Bismarck* Found"   74

Stephen King, from *The Tommyknockers*   126

Sharon Oard Warner, from "A Simple Matter of Hunger"   127

Eugenia Collier, from "Marigolds"   128

Alice Munro, from "Boys and Girls"   129

Ameena Meer, from "The Only Living Boy in New York"   132

Virginia Woolf, from *To the Lighthouse*   137

McCandlish Phillips, from *City Notebook*   137

Edward Abbey, from "The Most Beautiful Place on Earth"   141, 142

A. R. Ammons, from "Corsons Inlet"   144

Amber Coverdale Sumrall, from "Home Stretch"   170

James Thurber, from *My Life and Hard Times*   173

Max Brand, from "Wine on the Desert"   174

T. Ernesto Bethancourt, from "User Friendly"   182

Mary Lavin, from "The Story of the Widow's Son"   184–185

Will Steger, from "Six Across Antarctica," *National Geographic*   188

Mary Crow Dog and Richard Erdoes, from *Lakota Woman*   220

LITERATURE MODELS

Skill Models *continued*

Betsy Armstrong and Knox Williams, from
The Avalanche Book   222

Gretel Ehrlich, from *The Solace of Open
Spaces*   224

David Lamb, from *The Africans*   226

James Wagenvoord, from *Hangin' Out: City Kids,
City Games*   228

Frank Trippett, from "The Great American
Cooling Machine"   232

Phil Sudo, from *Scholastic Update*   236

Wendell Berry, from "A Defense of the Family
Farm"   240

Gina Lubrano, from "2 Condors to Fly Free
Late in '91"   248

Rachel Carson, from *Silent Spring*   258

Newton Minow, from Address to the Broadcasting
Industry   282

Tom Shales, from "MTV Has Shallow Look
of Success"   286

George Varga, from "Is It MTV or Is It
'Empty-V'?"   287

Jewelbox Advocates and Manufacturers, from
"A Strong Case for a Strong Case"   288

Consumer Reports, from "In-Line Skates: They
Aren't Just for Kids"   288

Betty Berry, from *NEA Today*   290

Jennifer March, from *NEA Today*   290

David Fricke, from "Sam Phillips and the Birth
of Rock & Roll,"*Rolling Stone*   302

Language Models

*Each Grammar Review uses excerpts to link
grammar, usage, or mechanics to literature.*

Yukio Mishima, from *The Sound of Waves,*
translated from the Japanese by Meredith
Weatherby   484

Naguib Mahfouz, from *Palace Walk,* translated
from the Arabic by William Maynard
Hutchins and Olive E. Kenny   512

Miguel Delibes, from *The Stuff of Heroes,*
translated from the Spanish by Frances M.
López-Morillas   532

Willa Cather, from *Death Comes for the
Archbishop*   562

J. R. R. Tolkien, from *The Fellowship of the
Ring*   602

Amos Oz, from *Elsewhere, Perhaps,* translated from
the Hebrew by Nicholas de Lange   626

William Conton, from *The African*   652

Mark Helprin, from *A Soldier of the
Great War*   680

William Blake, from "Auguries of
Innocence"   704

Heinerich Heine, from *The Romantic
School*   704

George Sand, from *Nouvelles Lettres d'un
Voyageur*   704

Willa Cather, from *O Pioneers!*   704

Robert Frost, from "Mending Wall"   704

Bruce Chatwin, from *In Patagonia*   726

Eudora Welty, from *One Writer's Beginnings*   772

FINE ART

Fine art—paintings, drawings, photos, and sculpture—is used to teach and stimulate ideas for writing.

Albert Bierstadt, Study for The Last of the Buffalo   xxviii

Carmen Lomas Garza, *Cumpleaños de Lala y Tudi*   11

Henri Rousseau, *The Sleeping Gypsy*   27

Maynard Dixon, *Earth Knower*   33

Jaune Quick-To-See Smith, *Osage Orange*   35

Pawnee, Ceremonial drum, nineteenth century   37

Edna Jackson, *Kaaswoot*   55

Vincent van Gogh, *The Potato Eaters*   63

David Hockney, *Paul Explaining Pictures to Mie Kakigahara*   72

Sofonisba Anguissola, *Three of the Artist's Sisters Playing Chess*   93

Howardena Pindell, *Autobiography: Water/Ancestors, Middle Passage/Family Ghosts*   101

Beverly Buchanan, *Barnesville*   128

Blackbear Bosin, *Prairie Fire*   131

Childe Hassam, *Fifth Avenue*   135

Arthur Dove, *Sunrise*   145

Sonia Terk Delaunay, *Electric Prisms*   146

Frederic Remington, *The Fall of the Cowboy*   157

Ann Taylor, *Red Riding*   159

José Gamarra, *Five Centuries Later*   179

Richard Bosman, *Flight*   183

Gilberto Ruiz, *The Good News Call*   187

Edvard Munch, *The Scream*   196

Melissa Miller, *Salmon Run*   199

Rufino Tamayo, *Interior with Alarm Clock*   209

Zinaida Serebriakova, *Castle of Cards*   223

Jacob Lawrence, *Strike*   227

M. C. Escher, *Day and Night*   231

Alma Thomas, *Iris, Tulips, Jonquils and Crocuses*   239

Ben Schonzeit, *Parrot Tulip*   243

Vincent van Gogh, *View of Arles*   268

Vincent van Gogh, *View of Arles with Irises*   271

Ernest Lawson, *Garden Landscape*   272

Jonathan Franklin, *Mad Hatters*   285

Mandy Martin, *Powerhouse*   289

Claude Monet, *Les Coquelicots (Wild Poppies)*   301

Charles March Gere, *The Tennis Party*   314

Andō Hiroshige, *Imagiri Promontory from Maizaka*   493

Henri Matisse, *The Casbah Gate*   519

Henri Cartier-Bresson, *Seville*   539

Georgia O'Keeffe, *Gate of Adobe Church*   571

Samuel Palmer, *Early Morning*   609

Elias Newman, *Wadi Musserara*   633

Clementine Hunter, patchwork quilt   659

Albert Bierstadt, *Sunrise on the Matterhorn*   687

Louis Comfort Tiffany, *Autumn Landscape*   709

Unknown artist, *Butch Cassidy and the Gang*   729

Winslow Homer, *Girl on a Garden Seat*   777

Unknown artist, *Portrait of a Woman*   780

PART 1
Composition

Objectives

- to compose in a variety of forms
- to write for a variety of purposes and audiences
- to compose using a recursive writing process
- to draw on technology in the process of writing
- to write clearly, legibly, and effectively using the conventions and mechanics of English
- to use writing as a tool for research and inquiry and to compile and represent information using available technology
- to analyze the writing strategies of others
- to work collaboratively to analyze and evaluate their own writing and that of their peers

Viewing the Art

Albert Bierstadt's painting reflects the artist's admiration for the natural beauty of the American West. Born near Düsseldorf, Germany in 1830, Bierstadt moved with his family to Massachusetts two years later. Though he later returned to Germany for formal training as an artist, he spent the greater part of his professional life attempting to capture the grandeur of the skies and mountain ranges he encountered on six extended trips through the West. He died in 1902.

Interpret and Analyze Use the following questions for discussion:

- What elements of Bierstadt's painting suggest its unfinished state?
- How does Bierstadt's *Study. . .* reflect his feelings about the natural world of the American West?

"*The white mares of the moon rush along the sky*
Beating their golden hoofs upon the glass heavens . . ."

—Amy Lowell

Resource Manager

Use the following resources to customize your teaching of the units in Part 1.

Planning Resources
- Lesson Plans
- Block Scheduling

 Transparencies
- *Bellringer*
- *Daily Language Practice*
- *Fine Art*

- *Two-Minute Skill Drill*
- *Writing Process*

📂 **Other Print Resources**
- *Business and Technical Writing Activities*
- *Composition Enrichment*
- *Composition Practice*
- *Composition Reteaching*
- *Cooperative Learning Activities*
- *Glencoe Literature Library*

- *Grammar and Composition Handbook*
- *Grammar Workbook*
- *Guide to Using the Internet and Other Electronic Resources*
- *Listening and Speaking Activities*
- *Research Paper and Report Writing*
- *Sentence-Combining Practice*
- *Spelling Power*
- *Style and Documentation Sourcebook for Writers*

Albert Bierstadt,
*Study for the Last of
the Buffalo*, 1888

P A R T 1

Composition

Unit 1   **Personal Writing**   *2*

Unit 2   **The Writing Process**   *40*

TIME   **Facing the Blank Page**   *109*

Unit 3   **Descriptive Writing**   *120*

Unit 4   **Narrative Writing**   *164*

Unit 5   **Expository Writing**   *214*

Unit 6   **Persuasive Writing**   *276*

Unit 7   **Research Paper Writing**   *320*

Unit 8   **Sentence Combining**   *358*

Unit 9   **Troubleshooter**   *386*

Business and Technical Writing   *412*

1

Discussing the Quotation

Direct students to Amy Lowell's "Night Clouds" on page 677 of *Glencoe Literature,* Course 5. Discuss with them the tenets of Imagism which Lowell practiced—a belief in the power of vivid, concrete language to convey meaning. Have students discuss any similarities or differences that they see between Lowell's words and Bierstadt's painting.

Writing Prompt Ask students to freewrite brief, impressionistic responses to Lowell's and Bierstadt's works, expressing what they think the images reveal about the artists' feelings and intentions.

- *Taking Standardized Tests*
- *Tests with Answer Key and Rubrics*
- *Thinking and Study Skills*
- *Vocabulary Power*
- *Writing Across the Curriculum*
- *Writing Assessment and Evaluation Rubrics*
- *Writing in the Real World*
- *English II End of Course Preparation and Practice Workbook*

Video
- *Facing the Blank Page*
- *MindJogger Videoquizzes*

Software
- *Interactive Grammar and Language Workbook*
- *Presentation Plus!*
- *Revising with Style*
- *Testmaker*

- *Vocabulary Power Puzzlemaker*
- *Writer's Assistant*
- *Writer's Choice Puzzlemaker*

Web Sites
- *writerschoice.glencoe.com*
- *lit.glencoe.com*

Personal Writing

Viewing the Art

The rustic garden in the photograph indicates a quiet or private place, the sort of setting to which a person might go to reflect or to read. While the bench and baskets suggest a kind of rational order, the uneven stones and leafy abundance convey a certain disorder. In the same way, personal writing might be orderly and organized, yet in need of editing to trim and shape it.

Interpret and Analyze Use the following questions for discussion:

• How would you describe the tone or atmosphere of the setting shown in the photograph?

• What details in the setting contribute to that tone or atmosphere? How?

Discussing the Quotation

The quotation comes from "How I Changed the War and Won the Game," by Mary Helen Ponce (b. 1938). Ask students to speculate about who the "I" in the quote might be, and what is suggested by the news of war delivered in an apparently peaceful setting. Point out that the use of the first person will be stressed in this unit, and that the kind of anecdote suggested here is often the basis for the best personal writing. To help students establish a context for the quotation, direct them to the full selection, in *Glencoe Literature,* Course 5, page 1055.

Writing Prompt Not everyone has a quiet garden to retreat to when they want privacy and peace. In a paragraph, describe a place that you find private and peaceful, being specific about what, exactly, makes the place appealing to you.

> "There, among the geraniums and pots of yerbubuena I would bring to them the news of the war."
>
> —Mary Helen Ponce, "How I Changed the War and Won the Game"

Resource Manager

Planning Resources
• *Lesson Plans*
• *Block Scheduling*

Transparencies
• *Bellringer*
• *Daily Language Practice*
• *Fine Art*

• *Two-Minute Skill Drill*
• *Writing Process*

Other Print Resources
• *Composition Enrichment*
• *Composition Practice*
• *Composition Reteaching*
• *Cooperative Learning Activities*

• *Glencoe Literature Library*
• *Grammar and Composition Handbook*
• *Grammar Workbook*
• *Listening and Speaking Activities*
• *Tests with Answer Key and Rubrics*
• *Thinking and Study Skills*
• *Writing Across the Curriculum*

UNIT 1
Personal Writing

Writing in the Real World: *Denise Chavez* 4

Lesson **1.1** **Writing to Discover Your World** 8

Lesson **1.2** **Using a Learning Log** 12

Lesson **1.3** **Keeping a Commonplace Book** 16

Lesson **1.4** **Writing About Literature: Using a
Reader-Response Journal** 20

Lesson **1.5** **Writing About Literature:
Responding to a Short Story** 24

Writing Process in Action 28

**Literature Model: from *Blue Highways*,
by William Least Heat-Moon** 32

Unit 1 Review 39

Objectives

- To develop an understanding of varieties of written expression
- To explore self-development through personal writing in commonplace books and journals
- To learn to respond in writing to a literary work

✔ ASSESSMENT OPTIONS

Tests with Answer Key & Rubrics
Unit 1 Choice A Test, p. 1
Unit 1 Choice B Test, p. 2
Unit 1 Composition Objective
Test, pp. 3–4

Testmaker
Unit 1 Choice A Test
Unit 1 Choice B Test
Unit 1 Composition Objective Test

You may wish to administer either the Unit 1 Choice A Test or the Unit 1 Choice B Test as a pretest.

Key to Ability Levels

L1 Level 1 activities are within the basic ability range of students.

L2 Level 2 activities are within the ability range of average students.

L3 Level 3 activities are more challenging activities.

- *Writing Assessment and Evaluation Rubrics*
- *Writing in the Real World*

Video
- *MindJogger Videoquizzes*

Software
- *Presentation Plus!*
- *Revising with Style*
- *Testmaker*
- *Writer's Assistant*
- *Writer's Choice Puzzlemaker*

Web Sites
- *writerschoice.glencoe.com*
- *lit.glencoe.com*

Focus

Lesson Overview

Objectives

- To analyze and deconstruct media
- To analyze one writer's process and strategies
- To explore the elements of personal writing

Skills

- freewriting; establishing a daily writing habit; using descriptive words

Critical Thinking

- evaluating; analyzing; synthesizing

Listening and Speaking

- discussing; presenting personal observations

Bellringer
Daily Language Activity

When students enter the classroom, have this assignment on the board: *Freewrite about a favorite memory of a person, place, or event.*

Grammar Link to the Bellringer

Encourage students to use adjective clauses to expand their writing.

See also *Daily Language Practice*

Motivating Activity

Discuss students' responses to the Bellringer assignment. Ask them if they regularly record their thoughts and daily experiences in a diary or a journal. Lead them to see that these records are important because they help people understand who they are, where they've been, and where they might be going. Explain that many well-known writers, such as Denise Chavez, have developed a habit of daily journal writing and that students will have an opportunity to try this technique for themselves.

Personal Writing

Writing in the Real World

MEDIA Connection
Journal Writing

Journal writers, unlike other writers, usually compose just for themselves. Keeping a journal helps these writers to explore the world around them and to examine their own lives. It can also serve as a source of ideas for other types of writing. The following is a journal entry by Denise Chavez, an award-winning playwright, poet, and fiction writer.

The Personal Journals of Denise Chavez

By Denise Chavez

August 28
Beginning
9:00 a m Wednesday in my new notebook—the paper seems harsh, perhaps too crisp, but I am happy to be writing in this new Journal—it indicates to me a time of Beginning—it is the Birth of many new things in my life, although at the same time (ironically, comically.) it signifies perhaps too, the Death of many things . . . this time of year . . .

When Chavez forgets her journal and an idea hits her, she'll write on whatever is handy—whether a check stub or a restaurant napkin.

Author Denise Chavez

Resource Manager

Planning Resources
- *Lesson Plans*

Transparencies
- *Bellringer*
- *Daily Language Practice*
- *Writing Process* 1

Other Print Resources
- *Cooperative Learning Activities,* pp. 5–8
- *Thinking and Study Skills,* pp. 2, 3, 29–30
- *Writing Assessment and Evaluation Rubrics*
- *Writing in the Real World,* pp. 1–4

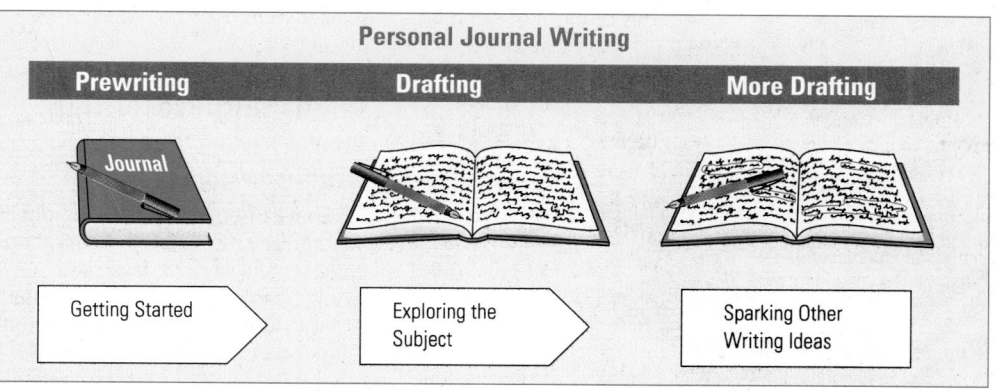

Personal Journal Writing

Prewriting	Drafting	More Drafting
Getting Started	Exploring the Subject	Sparking Other Writing Ideas

A Writer's Process

Prewriting:
Getting Started

Denise Chavez completes two or three personal journals each year, which she stores on a shelf in her back room. "I've kept a journal for almost as long as I can remember," she says; "I feel healthier and happier when I'm recording." Chavez's journals help her both to look within herself and to explore the world around her. "Writing a journal helps me keep abreast of what's going on in my life," explains Chavez. "Looking back over my journal, I can see patterns of my own behavior and personality. I've learned a lot by what I've loved and by what I've chosen. Keeping a journal is something I do for mental health."

Before beginning a new journal, Chavez gives it a title. She explains, "I may call it 'On the Road' or 'Becoming.' Each journal represents a chunk of time in which I'll be working on some personal goal, and the title gives me a point of focus. It's with great joy that I greet these new journals."

Drafting/Revising:
Exploring the Subject

Chavez usually writes in her journal just before going to bed, but she also carries her journal with her, in case she is inspired to jot something down. Chavez doesn't have to look far to find things to write about. She says, "I write more when I travel, but I don't have to go beyond my own house to find things to write about. We got a cat whom we named Pascualita.

A personal journal can be a record of your thoughts and memories. Whatever you choose to record, it's a place where you can try out your writing ideas in private.

Teach

Building Background

Warm-up
Ask students to list some of the topics they might write about in a daily journal. Topics might include
- family or school events
- favorite movies and books
- places they have visited
- personal reflections
- sports or games they enjoy

Personal Writing and Speaking
Tell students that they can use a journal to record quotations or any fragments of dialogue they hear or utter in their own conversations. Point out that these recorded speeches can be included in a learning log, used to develop a character in a narrative, or used to trigger writing ideas. Ask students to think of other ways they can use speech in a personal journal.

Journal Keeping and Writing
Discuss any published journals or diaries that students have read or heard about. Ask students whether they have read the diaries or journals of people such as Anne Frank, Sylvia Plath, or Leonardo da Vinci. Then pose the following questions:
- Why do people enjoy reading these private journals?
- What do these journals tell the reader about the writer's life and times?

Reading Media
Have students read the title and focus of the Media Connection. Ask students to discuss the value of keeping a personal journal. Then have them read the journal entries.

Cultural Connections

Exploring Journal Keeping
You might encourage students to explore generational and other cultural differences in the kinds of records people keep. Encourage them to ask their parents, grandparents, and other older relatives whether they ever kept a diary or journal or a collection of personal letters—and if so, why. This discussion might yield some surprises.

Writing in the Real World

Personal Writing

Teach

Discussion Prompts

- What subjects would you like to explore in your journal? (Students should note that they can address any subject in a journal.)
- What techniques could you use to overcome writer's block? (Possibilities include freewriting, timed writing, and using writing prompts.)
- How often should you write in your journal? (Point out that writing in a journal every day is ideal, but that students should adapt their writing to their schedules and their whims.)
- Why shouldn't you worry about grammar, spelling, and punctuation when you write in a journal? (Students should feel free to concentrate on getting their thoughts down.)

Discussion

Stimulate a discussion of the Media Connection. You may also want to invite students to talk about

- how they can use journal entries as a source for stories, essays, letters, and other types of writing
- how the writing process stages for personal writing differ from the stages they have used for other modes of writing
- whether they were surprised to read about the many possible uses of a journal
L2

Additional Resources

Writing Process Transparencies, 1
Writing in the Real World, pp. 1–4
Cooperative Learning Activities
Thinking and Study Skills, pp. 2, 3, 29–30

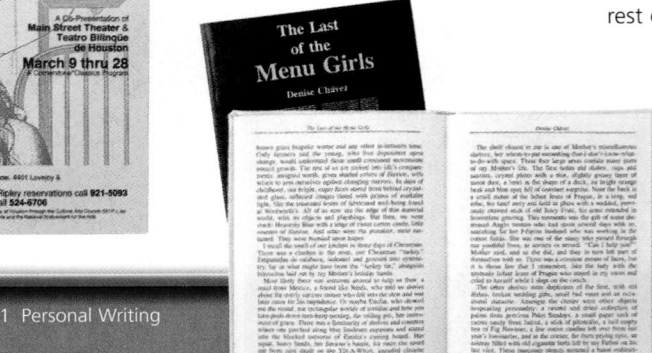

Years of journal keeping can result in a personal library of journals.

This brought to mind an aunt of my mother's and I found myself writing about Aunt Pascualita for several days."

Chavez writes her journal entries in longhand. She says, "I like the physical feeling of moving the pen across the paper. I've always liked paper, the feel of it. I use artists' sketch pads, because I never write with lines. I think lines are very restrictive and don't allow for the organic, natural process. If I want to draw a picture or put in a newspaper clipping, I have room."

"Sometimes," she continues, "I write all the way around the page. That's when the writing is coming so fast, I can't stop. There's no time to flip the page. At other times, I may allow myself to put just one word on a page."

As she writes, Chavez pays little attention to grammar or spelling, since for her the ideas are more important than the syntax or

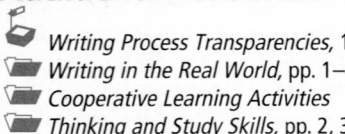

spelling. She does not edit or revise her entries.

Publishing/Presenting:
Journal Writing Leads to Published Works

Chavez frequently uses her journal entries to stimulate other writing projects. She says, "I have seen whole plays come out of my journal. Or I may use the journal to work out problems in my plays, such as biographical data about the characters or the setting."

Chavez began working on her short story "Evening in Paris" in her journal. She says, "I had a deadline to get this story in to a magazine. I just started writing about Christmas and putting together some of the smells. I remembered that we always had a chicken for Christmas because we couldn't afford a turkey. I kept writing down things and I worked on it every day. Finally, I had pages of notes in my journal. When I began to write the story, I already had my guide, my road map, in the journal, so I was pretty sure of the road I'd be driving on as I wrote the story."

Chavez's journal writing exploration seems unlimited. She notes, "I never run out of things to write about. In fact, I'm booked for the rest of my life."

Denise Chavez's novel The Last of the Menu Girls *was also produced as a play.*

6   Unit 1   Personal Writing

Enrichment and Extension

Exploring Personal History

You might suggest that students bring to class items they have chosen to save over the years—ticket stubs, autographed baseballs, matchbooks, and other souvenirs. Ask students to show these to a partner and explain their significance. Recall Chavez's statement, "I've learned a lot by

what I've loved and by what I've chosen." Invite students to discuss with their partner what they have discovered about themselves from the things they have loved and chosen.

Examining Writing in the Real World

Analyzing the Media Connection

Discuss these questions about the journal entry on page 4.

1. How does Chavez begin her journal entry? Do you think this is a typical way for journal writers to begin? Why or why not?
2. Why do you think Chavez uses dashes in her entry instead of periods?
3. What subjects does Chavez explore in her entry?
4. How would you characterize the style of writing Chavez uses in her entry?
5. How might Chavez use this journal entry as a springboard for her professional writing?

Analyzing a Writer's Process

Discuss these questions about Denise Chavez's writing process.

1. What are some reasons that Chavez gives for keeping a journal?
2. When does Chavez write in her journal?

3. Describe Chavez's technique for drafting her journal entries.
4. Where does Chavez get ideas for her journal writing?
5. What role do Chavez's journal entries play in her professional writing?

Grammar Link

Use adjective clauses to create variety in sentence structure.

An *adjective clause* is a subordinate clause that modifies a noun or a pronoun. For example, Denise Chavez writes the following:

> We got a cat **whom we named Pascualita.**

An adjective clause that is not needed to make the meaning of a sentence clear is set off by commas.

Add an adjective clause to each sentence below, using correct punctuation.

1. My brother James keeps a journal.
2. He writes a lot about sports and about our dog.
3. Sometimes he also writes for the school paper.
4. James wrote a great story about the basketball team.
5. The coach wants him to do a feature story about sports injuries.

See Lesson 13.5, pages 549–550.

Grammar Link

Answers

(Answers will vary; suggestions follow.)

1. My brother James, who wants to be a screen-writer, keeps a journal.
2. He writes a lot about sports and about our dog, who provides some funny material.
3. Sometimes he also writes for the school paper, which is published daily.
4. James wrote a great story about the basketball team that won the state championship.
5. The coach wants him to do a feature story about sports injuries which can be prevented easily.

Assess

Analyzing the Media Connection

Answers will vary; samples shown below:

1. Chavez begins with the day and the time. Most journal entries begin with the date.
2. Chavez may use dashes to allow for a freer flow of ideas.
3. Chavez describes her thoughts and feelings as she begins a new journal.
4. Students may say Chavez's style is informal and natural.
5. Students might respond that Chavez could use the entry to write a work exploring the themes of birth and death.

Analyzing a Writer's Process

Answers will vary, but might resemble the following:

1. Chavez keeps a journal to examine her growth as a human being and to foster good mental health.
2. Chavez usually writes at night.
3. Chavez writes in longhand, sometimes at length, sometimes writing only one word. She pays little attention to spelling or grammar.
4. Chavez gets ideas from real life.
5. Chavez's journals serve as a source of ideas and as a place where she can work out problems in a literary piece.

Reteaching

Have students think of something in their house—a pet, a piece of furniture, a painting—and write in their journals about what it means to them.

Enrichment

Challenge students to pose questions in their journals about their futures and to freewrite about the answers.

Close

Have students freewrite about a friend or family member and then discuss how they could use the character sketch in another piece of writing.

Focus

Lesson Overview

Objective

- To begin a personal journal for collecting personal experiences, and to record them as journal entries

Skills

- starting a journal; experimenting with new writing ideas

Critical Thinking

- analyzing; recalling

Listening and Speaking

- discussing

Bellringer
Daily Language Activity

When students enter the classroom, have this assignment on the board: *Write three sentences about subjects you might like to record in a personal journal.*

Grammar Link to the Bellringer

Have students analyze the pronouns they used in their list. Is it clear to whom or to what these pronouns refer?

See also *Daily Language Practice*

Motivating Activity

Ask whether the students have ever kept a diary or journal and, if so, why. Elicit that the writer of a diary or journal is also its audience, but that some famous journals and diaries, such as Leonardo da Vinci's and Sylvia Plath's, were eventually published in book form and read by many others. Ask why readers are interested in other people's diaries. What might readers learn there and nowhere else? Whose diary would the students like to read, and why?

LESSON 1.1

Writing to Discover Your World

Recording ideas and feelings in a personal journal is a risk-free way to learn about yourself and your world.

> Da Vinci, Renaissance artist, filled his notebooks with detailed drawings and diagrams dealing with art, engineering, architecture, and other topics.

> Plath, a modern American poet, wrote this entry when she was eighteen. What does this passage reveal about her reasons for keeping a journal?

Literature Model

Some things are hard to write about. After something happens to you, you go to write it down, and either you over-dramatize it or underplay it, exaggerate the wrong parts or ignore the important ones. At any rate, you never write it quite the way you want to. I've just got to put down what happened to me this afternoon. I can't tell Mother; not yet, anyway. She was in my room when I came home, fussing with clothes, and she didn't even sense that something had happened. She just kept scolding and chattering on and on. So I couldn't stop and tell her. No matter how it comes out, I have to write it.

Sylvia Plath, *The Journals of Sylvia Plath*

Resource Manager

Planning Resources
- *Lesson Plans*

 Transparencies
- *Bellringer*
- *Daily Language Practice*
- *Fine Art* 1–6
- *Writing Process* 1

 Other Print Resources
- *Composition Enrichment,* p. 1
- *Composition Practice,* p. 1
- *Composition Reteaching,* p. 1
- *Cooperative Learning Activities,* pp. 5–8
- *Listening and Speaking Activities,* pp. 9, 19, 20

- *Thinking and Study Skills,* pp. 5, 23, 29–30
- *Writing Across the Curriculum*
- *Writing Assessment and Evaluation Rubrics*

Start Your Own Personal Journal

A personal journal is a place where you can try out your writing ideas without risk. You can follow your thoughts wherever they lead, explore new ideas, and sort out feelings. Here are some tips for getting started with your own personal journal.

Tips for Journal Writing
1. Write whatever comes to mind. Write about thoughts and memories that have special significance for you.
2. Write on a regular basis, either every day or every other day.
3. Date each journal entry for future reference.

Try Out New Writing Ideas

A journal is the ideal place for exploring personal thoughts, and it is perfect for other kinds of writing, too. Some people experiment with poetry. Others try out ideas for stories and plays. You don't have to limit yourself to writing. You can include original cartoons, comic strips, even doodles. The following chart shows other kinds of items you can include in your journal.

Personal Journal Entries			
Unsent Letters	Dear Gabby Letters	Tongue in Cheek Ads	Words and Music
to parents or friends dealing with problems that you would like to discuss face to face— but can't	about problems that bug you (you might want to play Gabby and write the replies, too)	about diet and exercise, mixing sound advice about nutrition and health with good-natured humor	for original songs —pop, country, or rock-and-roll (the choice is up to you)

Journal Writing

People choose a variety of formats for their personal journals— spiral notebooks, loose-leaf notebooks, even computer disks. Decide which format will work best for you, and start your own personal journal. In your first entry, write what you hope journal writing will do for you.

Teach

Using the Model

After students read the model on the opposite student page, ask them to recall a time when something happened that needed telling right away. Ask what they did about it. Did they tell a family member or a friend? Maybe they told no one even though they felt the need. Plath's reasons for making this entry were twofold: she had to "put down what happened," and she couldn't tell her mother. Ask whether students see any advantages in writing the experience down before telling someone about it. **L2**

Two-Minute Skill Drill

Have students rewrite the following sentence to clarify the vague pronoun reference:

Monday, Jim went to see a play that Mark was in which made him very happy.

See also *Two-Minute Skill Drill Transparency 1.1*

Journal Writing Tip

Decision Making Before students write their first journal entry, have them make decisions about what format they wish to use: spiral notebook, looseleaf notebook, or word processor. Chances are they will continue to use the same format throughout the year; however, they should be encouraged to experiment with other formats, too.

Teach

Trying Freewriting

Freewriting can be considered a form of doodling in words. Some students who have difficulty dealing with abstract concepts may prefer putting their thoughts down in quick sketches—doodles—rather than words. Illustrated experience maps such as the one on this student page may be as useful as written entries for reminding students of earlier experiences, feelings, or impressions that they could incorporate into their writing. **L1**

Keeping a Journal

While taking care to ensure privacy and security for students' journals, encourage students to use their journals to work out personal problems by writing about them. It might become a useful lifetime habit. **L2**

Additional Resources

For further stimuli for journal writing, see *Fine Art Transparencies*, 1–6.

Writing Process Transparencies, 1
Writing Across the Curriculum
Cooperative Learning Activities
Thinking and Study Skills, pp. 5, 23, 29–30
Listening and Speaking Activities, pp. 9, 19, 20
Composition Practice, p. 1

Personal Writing

Don't Be Afraid to Experiment

You will want to experiment with different ways of recording information in your journal. Da Vinci, for example, filled his notebooks with drawings and diagrams, and he wrote backward. The following examples demonstrate different ways of exploring the same early childhood experiences.

Methods of Recording Information

Freewriting

I was born in the Texas Hill Country, and I remember spending most of my free time scrambling up and down the canyons that crisscross the landscape, chasing armadillos through the underbrush and flushing roadrunners out into the open. Rattlesnakes, too. I'll never forget the day I was edging down a cliff and found myself nose to nose with a diamondback! My happiest memory, though, is of fishing in the streams on my grandfather's ranch. There were always plenty of catfish and sunfish, but the bass were the best!

My family moved to Illinois when I was nine, and I didn't like it at first. The land was flat, so different from the wild canyons in Texas, but the fishing was just as good. Ice fishing in the wintertime—that was new to me, and I really enjoyed it.

> **One way of exploring early childhood memories is to write freely about each experience as it comes to mind.**

> **Another way is to create an experience map, with captions highlighting significant events.**

Mapping

I loved living in Texas (although I must admit I didn't really like those rattlesnakes).

My father took me ice fishing the first winter after we moved to Illinois, and I soon became an expert.

MEETING INDIVIDUAL NEEDS

English Language Learners

Writing Entries

Students who have difficulty writing in English usually are relieved to learn that their journal entries will not be graded for spelling and grammar. In fact, most teachers will not read journal entries unless invited to do so by a student. Make clear that the journal is a place to record private thoughts in words—or, as da Vinci did, in words and drawings—without fear of ridicule or criticism. Encourage students to use English in their journal whenever possible.

Write a Journal Entry

The painting below shows an extended family at a birthday celebration. Examine the scene carefully. Then write your personal reactions in your journal.

PURPOSE Self-discovery
AUDIENCE Yourself
LENGTH 2–3 paragraphs

WRITING RUBRICS To write an effective journal entry, you should

- explore feelings and memories similar to those shown in the painting
- experiment with different ways of recording ideas
- be sure your writing is legible and that it is meaningful to you

Cooperative Learning

In a small group, assign each member a family role. Role-play for five minutes a family conversation—perhaps about an after-school activity.

Carmen Lomas Garza, *Cumpleaños de Lala y Tudi*, 1989

Grammar Link

Avoid vague pronoun references.

Even your private writing should make sense when you reread it.

Revise each sentence below to make the pronoun reference clear.

1. Frank got maps for the Saturday hike to Nelson Park, which was a great idea.
2. That day they took along a picnic lunch, but it was cold.
3. Some folks climbed the firetower, which was a spectacular view.
4. The rangers had closed off one park trail, and that changes their plans.
5. The group wants to go on some longer hikes, and it will probably be during spring vacation.

See Lesson 17.6, pages 649–651.

Each group member should write a journal entry about the conversation from the point of view of the role he or she played. Share journal entries and compare reactions.

Listening and Speaking

Imagine you are one of the characters in the painting on this page. Write a journal entry for that character. What might the person be thinking or feeling at the celebration? Read your journal entry aloud to the class. Remember to speak clearly and to read at an appropriate speed.

Personal Writing

Assess

Evaluation Rubrics

Write a Journal Entry

Use these criteria when evaluating your students' writing. The entries should

- describe the student's feelings and memories of family holidays
- reflect a variety of journal writing modes

See also *Writing Assessment and Evaluation Rubrics.*

Cooperative Learning

Journal entries should
- reflect the viewpoint appropriate to the family member whose role was assumed
- reflect insights and self-discoveries from the role-play

To encourage students' self-evaluation discuss this question: Do you see any benefit in doing this at home after an argument?

Listening and Speaking

Journal entries should reflect thoughts and feelings appropriate to the chosen character.

Reteaching

Composition Reteaching, p. 1

Enrichment

Composition Enrichment, p. 1

Use *Fine Art Transparencies* 1–6 for enrichment activities also.

Close

Have students work in small groups to discuss the types of things they might record in their journals.

Grammar Link

Answers

(Answers will vary. The first three sentences in the exercise are provided as examples.)

1. That Frank brought maps for the Saturday hike to Nelson Park was a great idea.
2. That day they took along a picnic lunch, which became cold.
3. Some folks climbed the firetower and got a spectacular view from there.

Viewing the Art

Carmen Lomas Garza, *Cumpleaños de Lala y Tudi*, 1989

Carmen Lomas Garza uses her art to express her cultural identity: "I wanted to depict in fine art form all the things of our culture that are important or beautiful or very moving." *Cumpleaños de Lala y Tudi*, a 36–by–40–inch gouache (opaque watercolor) on paper, is in the collection of the artist.

Focus

Lesson Overview

Objective
- To initiate the habits of keeping a learning log
- To restructure and formulate questions for better understanding

Skills
- writing on a daily basis; writing to learn; writing a learning log

Critical Thinking
- synthesizing; defining and clarifying

Listening and Speaking
- note taking

Bellringer
Daily Language Activity
When students enter the classroom, have this assignment on the board: *In paragraph form, write an explanation of the material you learned in a recent class.*

Grammar Link to the Bellringer
Have students check to see if they used commas to separate any points in a series in the paragraph.

See also *Daily Language Practice*

Motivating Activity
To begin establishing the value of a learning log, initiate a discussion about how the students keep track of their assignments. Do students write down assignments and, if so, where? What other notes do students take for their classes? Explain that a learning log can help students with all their subjects, especially the hard ones. A learning log can help make sense out of hard-to-understand material, answer questions about it, and even improve grades.

Using a Learning Log

A learning log is a special kind of journal that can help you clarify your ideas about concepts covered in various classes. The example below shows a page from a learning log for biology, written after a class discussion of nutrition.

> **The log entry begins with the date and a brief summary of the discussion in class.**

> **The entry includes a notation. It could also have indicated a point for further exploration. What other kinds of notations might you make?**

> **The entry ends with the class assignment.**

Biology   September 15, 1993

Finally began the study of nutrition. Boy, was that an eye-opener! I like burgers and fries—at least I get enough protein. But according to the U.S.D.A. food pyramid, I'm not eating nearly enough fruit and vegetables. Four pieces of fruit a day! I never knew that! I still don't understand how nutritionists decide which foods are best. Why do they recommend so much fish and poultry? And why so few eggs? I'll have to remember to ask about that tomorrow.

Homework Assignment: Read Chapter 3, pp. 45–65 which discusses how regular exercise relates to overall health.

Resource Manager

Planning Resources
- *Lesson Plans*

Transparencies
- *Bellringer*
- *Daily Lanuage Practice*
- *Fine Art 1–6*
- *Two-Minute Skill Drill*
- *Writing Process 1*

Other Print Resources
- *Composition Enrichment*, p. 2
- *Composition Practice*, p. 2
- *Composition Reteaching*, p. 2
- *Cooperative Learning Activities*, pp. 5–8
- *Listening and Speaking Activities*, pp. 9, 19, 20

- *Thinking and Study Skills*, pp. 4, 14, 23, 26
- *Writing Across the Curriculum*
- *Writing Assessment and Evaluation Rubrics*

Write on a Daily Basis

Learning logs work best when you use them on a day-to-day basis, with a separate section for each class. Here are a few tips for using a learning log to keep your studies on track.

Keeping a Learning Log			
Characterize	**Identify**	**Discuss**	**Evaluate**
the main ideas discussed in class. Did you learn anything new?	difficult concepts you want to examine further. Where can you go for help?	a controversial idea that came up in class. Where do you stand on this issue?	your progress on a weekly basis. How are you doing in this class?

Write to Learn

Writing can help you make sense out of new information in any subject area. You never fully know something until you can state it in your own words. The following chart shows some writing-to-learn techniques that you can use to clarify ideas and concepts. Remember that your goal is to make the information make sense to *you*.

A Variety of Writing Ideas	
Idea	**Example**
1. Try to summarize the significance of what you are studying in a single clear sentence.	1. "The study of nutrition teaches us how to select the best diet for better health and longer life."
2. Begin with a particular topic, start freewriting, and see where it leads.	2. "Diet and exercise, exercise and diet, that's all you hear about these days. . . . "
3. As you write, continue to ask why until you exhaust all questions.	3. "Why do we need so much fruit in our diet? For the vitamins, I know, but why are vitamins important?"
4. Set down your point of view, and then deliberately argue against it.	4. "I am dead set against junk food, but . . . "

Journal Writing

In your journal write at least two questions about today's class work in one of your school subjects. Note what you might do to answer your questions.

Teach

Summarizing Learning Logs

Have students summarize what they've learned about the value of learning logs thus far. Suggest they do this in one clear sentence. **L2**

Using a Learning Log

Students who perform well in their schoolwork can benefit from using a learning log. Encourage these students to use a learning log to "talk back" to textbooks on issues that they disagree on and might avoid in class. **L3**

Two-Minute Skill Drill

Add appropriate commas in the following sentences:

I will take out the trash mow the lawn and clean the garage after I ride my bike.

Josie boarded the plane closed her eyes and dreamed of Europe.

Yesterday you should have read seventy pages outlined five chapters and completed one hundred math problems!

See also *Two-Minute Skill Drill Transparency 1.2*

Journal Writing Tip

Identifying Learning Log Benefits
To identify the many possible beneficial effects of a learning log, students may approach the issue from several angles—first thinking of general benefits and then zeroing in on benefits in specific subjects. Another angle would be to consider what academic problems they have and how a learning log could help them solve each problem.

Teach

Analyzing Diagrams

You might take a few minutes to help students analyze Jenny's diagram carefully to see how it clarifies the cause-effect relationships. Point out that each arrow shows a cause leading to an effect. Then ask questions like this: *Why do arrows lead both to and from greater muscle mass?* (It is both an effect, of exercise, and a cause, of greater muscle strength.) **L2**

Writing a Learning Log

Students may need help in seeing how Jenny's diagram clarifies the meaning of the text passage. Bring out that the passage moves from an effect (muscle strength) to a cause (exercise). The diagram shows the relationships clearly by starting with exercise, the main cause, at the top. Elicit that Jenny's paragraph reflects the same cause-effect relationships as her diagram. Then have students write their own learning log based on the passage and diagram. **L1**

Additional Resources

 For further stimuli for journal writing, see *Fine Art Transparencies*, 1–6.

 Writing Process Transparencies, 1
 Writing Across the Curriculum
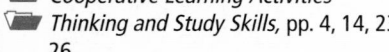 *Cooperative Learning Activities*
Thinking and Study Skills, pp. 4, 14, 23, 26
Listening and Speaking Activities, pp. 9, 19, 20
Composition Practice, p. 2

Personal Writing

Make a Learning Log Work for You

Jenny King found the following passage in her biology textbook difficult to understand, so she used her learning log to help clarify the ideas. She began by creating a diagram to show how ideas in the passage relate. Then she rewrote the passage in her own words.

Muscle strength does not depend on the number of fibers, but rather on their thickness and on how many of them contract at one time. Thicker fibers are stronger and contribute to muscle mass. Exercise stresses muscles slightly; as a result, the fibers increase in size.

Regular exercise can result in overall body fitness and endurance that can affect muscle strength. Body fitness is related to the condition of the heart and the number of capillaries in body tissue. One component of physical fitness is the efficiency of the heart in pumping blood to the tissues. Increased physical fitness results in a greater number of capillaries in the muscle tissue. Endurance is a measure of how long you can continue to exercise and depends on how much fuel your muscles can store. A muscle that is continually exercised is stronger and can store more fuel.

King made a diagram like this to show how the main ideas in the passage relate.

Student Model

What evidence can you find that King used her diagram to rewrite the passage?

Muscle strength depends on the thickness of muscle fibers, how many of the fibers contract at one time, and the amount of fuel stored within the muscle tissue. Exercise relates to all three categories. Exercising the muscles causes slight stress. This stress causes the muscle fibers to increase in thickness and controls the fiber contractions. Exercise also improves the condition of the heart and increases the number of capillaries in body tissue, including muscle tissue. These increased capillaries increase the amount of energy stored within the muscle; therefore, muscle endurance is increased.

Jenny King, Henry Clay High School, Lexington, Kentucky

MEETING INDIVIDUAL NEEDS

English Language Learners

Making Sense of Unfamiliar Words

Students who have difficulty reading and writing English will often hear unfamiliar words and phrases used in their content courses. Suggest that they use their learning logs to write down such words and phrases at the time, leaving space after each one. Later they can look up the word or phrase or ask for help, writing down the explanation.

Write a Learning Log

Start using your learning log today in your English, history, or math class, and keep it going for a week. Then reread your log entries. Think about how they have helped you understand your class. Then write a log entry evaluating your experience.

PURPOSE To clarify concepts discussed in class
AUDIENCE Yourself
LENGTH 2–4 paragraphs
WRITING RUBRICS To write an effective learning log, you should

- write for at least three to five minutes for each class session
- begin each entry with a brief summary of the class discussion
- make notes for concepts you do not understand
- be sure your learning log is legible and that it is clear to you

Viewing and Representing

PEER REVIEW Share completed learning logs with your classmates. Discuss the various graphic organizers that you and others used. What makes these particular graphics effective? Discuss your responses in small groups.

Using Computers

If you have access to a personal computer, you may want to keep your learning log electronically. Set up separate files for different classes. As you experiment with writing-to-learn techniques, save and date entries.

Grammar Link

Use commas to separate three or more words, phrases, or clauses in a series.

Muscle strength depends on the thickness of muscle fibers, how many of the fibers contract at one time, and the amount of fuel stored within the muscle tissue.

Add any needed comma or commas to each sentence below.

1. Our subway ride to the museum yesterday was long hot and crowded.
2. Over the weekend I had homework assignments for my science math history and English classes.
3. I can't decide whether to join the drama club the school debating team or a new after-school jazz club.
4. The jazz club will meet at our school at a neighboring school and at a professional jazz club downtown.
5. My music and German classes meet on Monday Wednesday and Friday.
6. We got to the museum at one stood in line for an hour and finally toured the exhibit with 35 fourth graders.
7. By Monday I have to memorize a poem finish a history paper plan my science project and make a poster.
8. I'm not sure whether the poem paper project or poster is the place to start.
9. My older brother says I am disorganized forgetful and hopeless.
10. Of course, he can't remember anyone's birthday our parents' anniversary or his own weekend plans.

See Lesson 21.6, page 743.

Assess

Evaluation Rubrics

Write a Learning Log
Use these criteria when evaluating your students' logs. Students should
- make daily entries
- summarize class discussion
- identify a puzzling concept
- explain the next assignment

See also *Writing Assessment and Evaluation Rubrics.*

Using Computers
To further clarify ideas, encourage students to use software that creates diagrams, time lines, and charts.

Viewing and Representing
Students' responses to the graphic organizers should
- identity their purposes.
- evaluate their effectiveness.

Reteaching
📁 *Composition Reteaching,* p. 2

Enrichment
📁 *Composition Enrichment,* p. 2

Close

Discuss with students the advantages of keeping a separate learning log for home, school, and extra-curricular activities. Challenge them to write in their learning logs after each practice or event for one week.

Grammar Link

Answers
1. . . . long, hot, and crowded.
2. . . . science, math, history, and English classes.
3. . . . drama club, the school debating team, or a new after-school jazz club.
4. . . . club will meet at our school, at a neighboring school, and . . .
5. . . . on Monday, Wednesday, and Friday.
6. . . . one, stood in line for an hour, and . . .
7. . . . poem, finish a history paper, plan my science project, and . . .
8. . . . poem, paper, project, or . . .
9. . . . disorganized, forgetful, and hopeless.
10. . . . birthday, our parents' anniversary, or . . .

Focus

Lesson Overview

Objective
- To start keeping a commonplace book with personal items as a source of writing ideas

Skills
- keeping a commonplace book; exploring ideas for writing

Critical Thinking
- evaluating; relating

Listening and Speaking
- note taking

 Bellringer
Daily Language Activity

When students enter the classroom, have this assignment on the board: *Write down a favorite quote or saying and briefly explain in writing how it might give you an idea for a story.*

Grammar Link to the Bellringer

Have students analyze the subjects and verbs in their Bellringer. Do they all agree?

See also *Daily Language Practice*

Motivating Activity

The term *commonplace book* may be new to your students, but the motivation for keeping one may find other outlets. Ask if students have ever had a bulletin board at home. If so, what purpose did it serve? Have they ever kept a scrapbook or a photo album? What did they put into it, and why? Explain that a commonplace book is something like each of these, but it serves another important purpose. Students can use it as a source of ideas when they can't think of anything to write about.

Personal Writing

Keeping a Commonplace Book

A commonplace book is a collection of items that have some special significance for you personally and that may eventually become a source of writing ideas that you can use for other writing. The model shows entries from a commonplace book assembled by poet Sheila P. Donohue.

> Donohue collected several quotations that help her clarify her view of the world.

> What do Donohue's notes reveal about her reasons for keeping the quotations for future reference?

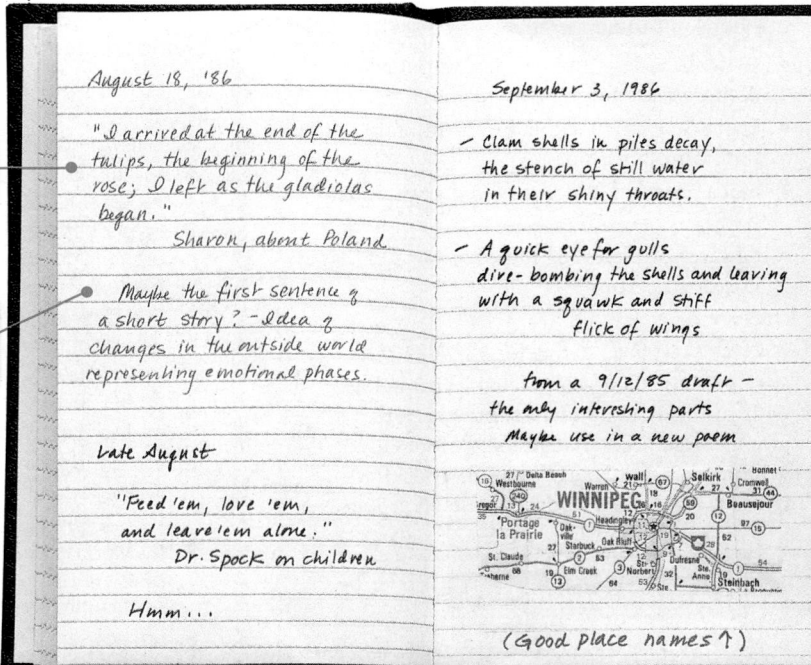

16 Unit 1 Personal Writing

 Resource Manager

Planning Resources
- *Lesson Plans*

Transparencies
- *Bellringer*
- *Daily Lanuage Practice*
- *Fine Art* 1–6
- *Two-Minute Skill Drill*
- *Writing Process* 1

Other Print Resources
- *Composition Enrichment,* p. 3
- *Composition Practice,* p. 3
- *Composition Reteaching,* p. 3
- *Cooperative Learning Activities* pp. 5–8
- *Listening and Speaking Activities,* pp. 9, 19, 20

- *Thinking and Study Skills,* pp. 3, 5, 11
- *Writing Across the Curriculum*
- *Writing Assessment and Evaluation Rubrics*

Start Your Own Commonplace Book

You can collect whatever you want in your commonplace book—quotations, song lyrics, jokes, menus—anything that you find interesting or thought-provoking. The following display shows other kinds of items you might keep in your book.

TIME

For more about the writing process, see **TIME Facing the Blank Page,** pp. 109–119.

Journal Writing

Do some freewriting in your journal, assessing different kinds of items you might want to keep in you own commonplace book.

Teach

Using the Model

Students will understand the uses of a commonplace book better if they observe this one in detail, answering questions such as these: Why did Sheila date her entries? What shows that she is a poet? Does she write anything besides poetry? How might the map fragment prove useful to her later? Point out Sheila's comment "maybe use in a new poem" to show that she kept interesting items even if she didn't know how she would use them. **L2**

Listening and Speaking

To stress the value of a commonplace book, you might ask each student to bring to class a brief but meaningful passage (a verse from a poem or song, or a quotation from a speech, article or book) to read aloud. After each reading, allow a minute or two for students to write notes in their commonplace book, including their personal responses and the source of the passage, if they wish to find it later. **L3**

Two-Minute Skill Drill

Have students complete the following sentence:

Movies (is, are) his only form of entertainment.

 See also *Two-Minute Skill Drill Transparency 1.3*

Journal Writing Tip

Classifying Before students begin their freewriting, have them draw several circles and label them with aspects of their lives. Have them write in each circle some items they might collect. Those items that have the greatest personal significance should be put into their commonplace books.

Teach

Using the Model

In discussing Nina's story, have students compare sentences like "Still, there was nothing she could do" with her earlier annotations, such as "Take charge." Help students see that when Nina wrote her story, she decided to approach the same theme from the opposite direction, showing the unhappy results of Sophie's failure to take responsibility. **L2**

Finding Good Ideas

Students might enjoy explaining to their classmates where some of their best writing ideas have originated. For example, a letter written by a long-deceased great-grandfather might have sparked an idea for a piece about immigration. The whimsical names a restaurant gave its menu items might have inspired a "found poem" (a poem created by using words and phases that unintentionally read like poetry). The range of items that can go into a commonplace book is limitless. **L3**

Additional Resources

For further stimuli for personal writing, see *Fine Art Transparencies*, 1–6.

Writing Process Transparencies, 1
Writing Across the Curriculum
Cooperative Learning Activities
Thinking and Study Skills, pp. 3, 6, 11
Listening and Speaking Activities, pp. 9, 19, 20
Composition Practice, p. 3

Personal Writing

Explore Ideas for Writing

In her reading Nina Molumby ran across a quotation about responsibility. She wrote a note explaining why she thought the quotation worth saving, and she put the item in her commonplace book. Months later, Nina came across the item again, and it started her thinking. She decided to write a story about responsibility, but with a twist. She would show what could happen to a person who refused to take responsibility for her life.

> Character—the willingness to accept responsibility for one's own life—is the source from which self-respect springs.
>
> Joan Didion
>
> *Responsibility—that's a word you hear more and more these days:*
> *"Take charge."*
> *"Accept responsibility."*
> *"Just say no."*

Student Model

Sophie sat at her desk in her room, thinking about her life. Last year her mother had left, leaving Sophie alone with her father. Their family problems had intensified over the years with her father's drinking, her mother's irrational behavior, and Sophie's poor performance in school. Eventually, Sophie stopped seeing her friends, replacing busy afternoons of swimming practice and telephone calls with solitude. The only thing that seemed to matter any more was her orchids. She poured into them all her love, since she was unable to share it with anyone else. They served as a barrier, protecting Sophie from her family problems, her teachers' questions, and her own fear of being vulnerable.

Sophie broke out of her daze and drifted back into the present. A feeling of frustration swept over her. Was she another crack-up like her parents? How did other people resolve their problems? All that her family had tried usually failed. Still, there was nothing she could do. Her parents were the ones with the problem. They caused all the agony, leaving her only one place to hide—in her room with her orchids. How could she accept responsibility for a life that was already ruined by others? As for self-respect, the only pride she had was in her plants.

Nina Molumby, Evanston Township High School,
Evanston, Illinois

> Molumby's story revolves around a character named Sophie, whose life is on hold because of family troubles.

> What echoes of Molumby's journal entry do you hear in these sentences?

As you look through your commonplace book for a writing idea, don't feel constrained by an annotation you wrote long before. It's just a starting point. Open your mind. Follow your ideas wherever they lead. If one leads nowhere, choose another.

18 Unit 1 Personal Writing

Exploring Language

Sharing Ideas

Have students work with partners. To demonstrate the usefulness of an item in a commonplace book, write on the board an interesting quote that could spark a writing idea. For example, write the statement, "You cannot be a hero without being a coward" (George Bernard Shaw). Have the partners discuss what this quote reminds them of. Ask students to make a list of their ideas and to then discuss how these ideas might be turned into a story.

Write Commonplace Book Annotations

Set up your own commonplace book, and start collecting items that interest you. Look for things related to the themes of self-discovery and self-improvement. You can include such things as a cartoon, a photo, or lines from a song.

PURPOSE Self-discovery
AUDIENCE Yourself
LENGTH 4 or more annotations

WRITING RUBRICS To write an effective commonplace book, you should

- choose items that are important to you
- write a brief note explaining each item
- make notes for concepts you do not understand
- be sure your annotations are clear and legible

Spelling

LEARNING NEW WORDS As you gather information for your commonplace book, you will probably come across words that are new to you. When you first hear a new word, you can make a note of it, attempting to spell it correctly. Later, to be sure of the correct spelling, use a dictionary or spelling-checker software. Usually, you will be able to spell enough of a word to find it in a dictionary or with a spelling-checker. If you don't find the word at first, try other possible spellings. (Spelling-checker software will suggest possible spellings if you've spelled the word incorrectly.)

Grammar Link

A verb must agree with its subject, not with the predicate nominative that follows it.

In the student model, Nina Molumby correctly writes, *The only thing that seemed to matter . . . was her orchids.*

Complete each sentence to make the subject and verb agree.

1. In northern states, snowmobiles (is, are) a common form of winter transportation.
2. The puppies (is, are) an added expense for the family.
3. The first item on the agenda (was, were) the needs of the new tenants.
4. Baseball cards (is, are) his only topic of conversation.
5. The favorite dessert (was, were) strawberries with ice cream.

See Lesson 16.2, page 615.

Viewing and Representing

With a small group of classmates, create a "commonplace bulletin board" for the classroom. Choose a general theme for your collection. Have each group member contribute things he or she makes. Decide how to assemble the items for display.

Personal Writing

Assess

Evaluation Rubrics

Write Commonplace Book Annotations

In their commonplace books, students should include
- explanations of items' importance
- description of items

In evaluating annotations, look for
- details about who, what, when, where, why, how
- ideas for writing

See also *Writing Assessment and Evaluation Rubrics.*

Viewing and Representing

Students' bulletin boards should
- be related to the designated general theme.
- include contributions from each member of the group.

Reteaching

📁 *Composition Reteaching*, p. 3

Enrichment

📁 *Composition Enrichment*, p. 3

✍ Use *Fine Art Transparencies* 1–6 for enrichment activities also.

Close

Have students list three items they would include in their commonplace books and explain why they might be useful later as story ideas.

Grammar Link

Answers
1. are
2. are
3. was
4. are
5. was

Focus

Lesson Overview

Objective
- To record personal responses to literature in a reader-response journal

Skills
- responding to literature; interpreting impressions

Critical Thinking
- analyzing; evaluating; recalling

Listening and Speaking
- evaluating

 Bellringer

Daily Language Activity

When students enter the classroom, have this assignment on the board: *List the creative ways you respond to what you read.*

Grammar Link to the Bellringer

Suggest that students proofread their responses to make sure they contain no sentence fragments.

See also *Daily Language Practice*

Motivating Activity

Ask students if they've ever read a poem, story, or novel to which they had an especially strong reaction: that is, they either really liked it or really disliked it. For example, they were dissatisfied with the ending, or they agreed strongly with the author's message. Explain that in a reader-response journal they have a chance to "talk back" and express their feelings about a work, sometimes making discoveries about themselves in the process.

Personal Writing

LESSON

1.4

Using a Reader-Response Journal

You can use a reader-response journal to record personal reactions to whatever you read. Notice how one student's reaction to the poem "The Eagle" changed when she read it a second time.

The Eagle

He clasps the crag with crooked hands;
Close to the sun in lonely lands,
Ringed with the azure world he stands.

The wrinkled sea beneath him crawls;
He watches from his mountain walls,
And like a thunderbolt he falls.

Alfred, Lord Tennyson

> **How does Clare's response draw on particular lines from the poem?**

Student Model

When I first read, "The Eagle," I wasn't too impressed, but reading it a second time made me change my mind. The poem is short and compact, but oh so powerful! There's just so much beauty and majestic feeling. Here we have an eagle, high above lonely lands, soaring through a sun-filled sky. Then, without warning, it drops from the sky and attacks! The image this poem conveys is so breathtaking it lingers in the mind like a fond memory.

Avilonia Clare, Kelvyn Park High School, Chicago, Illinois

Resource Manager

Planning Resources
- *Lesson Plans*

 Transparencies
- *Bellringer*
- *Daily Lanuage Practice*
- *Fine Art* 1–6
- *Two-Minute Skill Drill*
- *Writing Process* 1

 Other Print Resources
- *Composition Enrichment*, p. 4
- *Composition Practice*, p. 4
- *Composition Reteaching*, p. 4
- *Cooperative Learning Activities*, pp. 5–8
- *Listening and Speaking Activities*, pp. 9, 19, 20

- *Thinking and Study Skills*, pp. 5, 21, 31–32
- *Writing Across the Curriculum*
- *Writing Assessment and Evaluation Rubrics*

Set Up the Journal

A reader-response journal gives you the opportunity to discover what you really think about the things that you read. You can set up a reader-response journal in a separate notebook or in a special section of your personal journal or learning log.

Once you set up your reader-response journal, start writing. Here are a number of creative ways of responding to works of fiction and nonfiction. What others can you think of?

Think of a story or novel that has a character you find appealing. Explain why you identify with the character.

Write a brief review of the book. Note its strengths and weaknesses as well as any suggestions you might have for making the book better.

Create a magazine ad that you think would help sell the book.

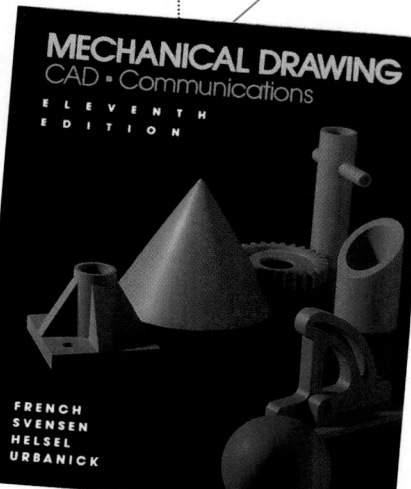

Rewrite an important scene from a different point of view.

Create a dust jacket with a new cover design and information about the author on the inside flap.

List questions you have about how the book is organized.

Journal Writing

Use the first page in your reader-response journal to begin exploring your reactions to what you read. Jot down an annotated list of some things you have read recently—perhaps the funniest, the saddest, or something with which you strongly disagree.

Teach

Using the Model

Before students open their books, ask them to listen as you give a dramatic reading of "The Eagle." Afterward, have them compare their reactions to Avilonia's. Help them see how her words—"lonely lands," "sun-filled sky," "Then, without warning, it drops from the sky and attacks"—echo ideas and images from the poem. **L2**

Using Audio Aids

Students who have reading recall problems might benefit from using a tape recorder. While they are reading, either at home or at school, they can have their recorder nearby, ready to use each time they have a specific response to record. Then, when they finish reading, they can play the tape back, stopping whenever they come to something they'd like to put into their reader-response journal. **L1**

 Two-Minute Skill Drill

Write the following words on the board. Have students list their initial impressions of each genre.

poetry	*short story*
novel	*nonfiction*

See also *Two-Minute Skill Drill Transparency 1.4*

Journal Writing Tip

Recalling Suggest that students look through their current class anthology or their bookshelves at home to help them remember earlier reading experiences.

Teach

Using the Model

Have students closely examine the student model. Ask students what Dan contrasts in his journal entry (the pessimism of many modern writers and intellectuals with the optimism he sees in novelist John Steinbeck). Discuss how Dan responds to his reading of Steinbeck's novel by praising the author's positive message about the triumph of the human spirit. **L2**

Discussing Personal Responses

Before students write their personal responses to a specific piece, they might benefit from discussing them with partners. Suggest that they bring their ideas into focus by answering the questions in the chart at the bottom of page 22. Students often need help in developing their ideas. Explaining their responses to a classmate, especially one who is unfamiliar with the piece, will direct their thinking and encourage the flow of creativity. **L3**

Additional Resources

For further stimuli for personal writing, see *Fine Art Transparencies*, 1–6.

Writing Process Transparencies, 1
Writing Across the Curriculum
Cooperative Learning Activities
Thinking and Study Skills, pp. 5, 21, 31–32
Listening and Speaking Activities, pp. 9, 19, 20
Composition Practice, p. 4

Personal Writing

Unleash Your Imagination

Reading is a process of discovery, helping us gain insight into the world around us, the people we know, and ourselves. When student Dan Felten read John Steinbeck's novel *The Grapes of Wrath*, he was particularly struck by the courage with which ordinary people face adversity. He explored his reaction in his reader-response journal.

Student Model

> **Felten begins by discussing the undue pessimism he finds in some modern writers and intellectuals.**

I think that far too often writers and so-called intellectuals consider the human race to be basically hopeless. The problem with this kind of thinking is that it is usually based on personal assumptions about the human race as a whole. It rarely takes into account the personal hopes and triumphs of individuals.

> **He then explains why he likes the boundless optimism he always finds in the works of Steinbeck.**

John Steinbeck's novel *The Grapes of Wrath* does not neglect these hopes and triumphs. When I finished the book, I was left with the feeling that perhaps people aren't quite as hopeless as they sometimes seem. As always, Steinbeck is blunt in discussing various evils that people inflict upon one another, but he also helps us see how they strive to overcome these evils. This is Steinbeck's main point in *The Grapes of Wrath,* a point that I feel is often overlooked. Officials can be evil and do evil things, but they cannot stamp out the hopes and dreams of ordinary people. At the end of the novel, Steinbeck helps us understand that the hope that flames within the Joads will never be quenched.

Dan Felten, Evanston Township High School,
Evanston, Illinois

Here is a list of questions to consider before you record your personal response to a piece of writing.

Questions to Consider

1. How did you feel when you finished reading? Happy? Sad? Inspired? Confused? Puzzled? Angry?
2. What did you like best about the piece? Is there anything you would change? What?
3. Did you agree with everything you read? Would you like to argue with the author? What would you say?
4. Did you learn anything that you didn't know before? What?

Enabling Strategies

Recording Impressions

To help students who find writing difficult, suggest that when writing in their reader-response journals they pretend they are talking to someone about the literature. Emphasize the exploratory, free-flowing nature of personal journal writing. Tell students that they should not worry about grammar, spelling, or punctuation conventions at first, but concentrate on recording their immediate impressions.

Write a Reader-Response Journal Entry

Write a journal entry about a piece of literature that you have recently read and enjoyed. Use the following list to help you explore your feelings and reactions.

PURPOSE To explore your response to literature
AUDIENCE Yourself
LENGTH 4–6 paragraphs

WRITING RUBRICS To write an effective reader-response journal entry, you should

- explain clearly what you like or dislike about the literature
- describe any self-discoveries you made or insights into others you had
- explain how you felt when you finished reading
- be sure your entry is clear and legible

Cross-Curricular Activity

JOURNALISM The school paper has asked you to write a two-page review of a short story or book you have read recently. Look through your reader-response journal, and base your review on an entry you have made.

Outline your review carefully before writing. Use your journal entry to remind yourself of what you liked or didn't like. Write about what the literature might say—or not say—to your classmates and peers. Conclude by giving your fellow students your recommendation as to whether they should or should not read the literature.

Grammar Link

In general, avoid sentence fragments in your writing.

A *sentence fragment* is an error that occurs when an incomplete sentence is punctuated as if it were complete.

Revise the paragraph below to eliminate all sentence fragments.

¹I really liked the book I just finished reading. ²Because it was both funny and exciting. ³I'd like to read more by that author. ⁴One of his plays, maybe. ⁵Although I think it's more difficult to read a play than a story. ⁶Someday I would like to try writing a one-act play. ⁷With a nice juicy part for myself. ⁸We could try it out in English class. ⁹If I ever have the nerve to let anybody else read it! ¹⁰That is.

See Lesson 13.9, pages 557–558.

Listening and Speaking

Deliver your literature review as an oral presentation to the class. Consider the most effective method to persuade the class of your recommendation concerning that short story or book. What techniques can you use to persuade listeners to read (or not read) the literature?

Personal Writing

Assess

Evaluation Rubrics

Write a Reader-Response Journal Entry

Use these criteria when evaluating your students' writing:
- Did the entry show strong emotion?
- Did the entry show evidence of self-discovery?
- Did the student use references to specific elements of the literature?

See also *Writing Assessment and Evaluation Rubrics.*

Cross-Curricular Activity

Evaluate the review on the following:
- whether the reactions were based on a journal entry
- the work's relevance to classmates
- whether the review would encourage or discourage peer reading

Listening and Speaking

Students' oral reviews should
- use arguments supported by evidence in the texts.
- employ effective verbal and nonverbal strategies.

Reteaching

📁 *Composition Reteaching,* p. 4

Enrichment

📁 *Composition Enrichment,* p. 4

Close

Suggest that students write to an author of a favorite book, mailing their letter in care of the publisher. Students may prefer to review the book for the school newspaper.

Grammar Link

Answers

Revised paragraph should read:

I really liked the book I just finished reading because it was both funny and exciting. I'd like to read more by that author—one of his plays, maybe—although I think it's more difficult to read a play than a story. Someday I would like to try writing a one-act play, with a nice juicy part for myself. We could try it out in English class—if I ever have the nerve to let anybody else read it, that is!

Focus

Lesson Overview

Objectives
- To write a personal response to a short story
- To make a critical assessment of a story's elements

Skills
- responding to literature; interpreting impressions; using story elements

Critical Thinking
- analyzing; evaluating; recalling

Listening and Speaking
- evaluating

Bellringer
Daily Language Activity

When students enter the classroom, have this assignment on the board: *List the titles of the short stories you've read most recently. Then state your reactions to the stories.*

Grammar Link to the Bellringer

The Bellringer provides an opportunity to teach capitalization in titles.

See also *Daily Language Practice*

Motivating Activity

Ask students what kind of stories they like best. Do they have favorite stories, and if so, what are they? What about those stories appeals to students? Do they try to find other stories by the same authors? Most students will have reading preferences, including some rather strong ones, but they may not have given much thought to their reasons. Encourage responses that include the students' experiences, interests, and aspirations.

Personal Writing

LESSON 1.5

WRITING ABOUT LITERATURE
Responding to a Short Story

Novelist John Updike as a young man

*R*esponding to a story in your reader-response journal can teach you something about yourself. Plot, theme, setting, and characters may evoke interesting opinions and connections. Notice how novelist John Updike responded to J. D. Salinger's stories.

How does Updike signal in the first sentence the effect that J. D. Salinger's stories had on him?

Updike found Salinger's stories especially meaningful because they contain characters with whom he could identify.

Literature Models

*I*t's in Salinger that I first heard, as a college student in the early Fifties, the tone that spoke to my condition. I had a writing teacher . . . who read aloud to us some of Salinger's stories as they appeared in *The New Yorker*. They seemed to me to say something about the energies of people and the ways they encounter each other that I did not find in the short stories of Hemingway or John O'Hara or Dorothy Parker or any of that "wised-up" style of short-story writing. Salinger's stories were not wised up. They were very open to tender invasions.

John Updike, *Picked-Up Pieces*

"*I* looked down at Charles, who was now resting the side of his face on his chair seat. When he saw that I was looking at him, he closed his eyes, sleepily, angelically, then stuck out his tongue—an appendage of startling length—and gave out what in *my* country would have been a glorious tribute to a myopic baseball umpire."

J. D. Salinger, "For Esmé—with Love and Squalor"

24 Unit 1 Personal Writing

Resource Manager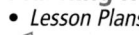

Planning Resources
- *Lesson Plans*

 Transparencies
- *Bellringer*
- *Daily Language Practice*
- *Fine Art* 1–6
- *Two-Minute Skill Drill*
- *Writing Process* 1

📁 **Other Print Resources**
- *Composition Enrichment*, p. 5
- *Composition Practice*, p. 5
- *Composition Reteaching*, p. 5
- *Cooperative Learning Activities*, pp. 5–8
- *Listening and Speaking Activities*, pp. 9, 19, 20

- *Thinking and Study Skills*, pp. 13, 21, 25
- *Writing Across the Curriculum*
- *Writing Assessment and Evaluation Rubrics*

Get into the Spirit

The best way to find out how you really feel about a piece of literature is to write a personal response in your reader-response journal. As you explore your feelings about and reactions to a piece, you may even discover that you have an opinion different from the one you originally had. The following graphic lists a variety of ways you can respond to a short story.

Ways of Responding to a Short Story	
Characters The individuals in a story	• Pick one character you like and write a dialogue between the two of you. • Write a letter to a character in the story, making connections with your life.
Setting The time and place of the action	• Tell why the setting of the story has a special appeal for you. • Create a drawing or painting depicting the setting of a major event.
Plot The sequence of events	• Tell what you like or don't like about the ending of the story. • Get a new perspective on the story by writing a different ending.
Theme The underlying meaning	• Compare the story with another story that has the same general theme. • Write about an experience of your own that had a similar meaning for you.

Journal Writing

What is the last story you read? Did you like it? Why or why not? Which story element influenced your reaction the most? Spend a few minutes freewriting about your reaction in your reader-response journal.

Personal Writing

Teach

Creating a Chart

Some students may find it easier to respond to a particular story if they begin by creating a chart like the one on this student page. First, they can list the characters, setting, events, and theme of their story on the left side of their chart. On the right side, they can take notes on their responses, using suggestions on this page as a guide, either as they read or afterward. Finally, students can decide on their overall personal response. **L1**

 Two-Minute Skill Drill

Write the following words on the board. Have students give an example of each story element from a story they have recently read.

character   *setting*
plot   *theme*

 See also *Two-Minute Skill Drill Transparency 1.8*

Journal Writing Tip

Personal Preferences Encourage students to think about their literary likes and dislikes before considering a specific story in their freewriting. Some might state their overall reaction to the story and then mention details that explain it. Some might do the opposite, starting with the details and ending with their reactions.

Teach

Giving a Dramatic Reading

Grade school students aren't the only ones who enjoy hearing stories read aloud. High school students derive the same pleasure and benefit in similar ways. You might give a dramatic reading of a story like Doris Lessing's "A Sunrise on the Veld." (Explain that a veld is a flat *grassland,* usually in southern Africa, that contains a sprinkling of bushy areas and a few trees.) **L2**

Thematic Similarities

You might call attention to the fact that although Lessing's story reflects a culture different from Robin's, the student relates to the main character's feeling of helplessness in the face of death, a universal experience that transcends cultural differences. Emphasize the point that cultural and language differences need not separate readers from the literature of other times and places, since great themes such as love, hope, fear, and betrayal are common to the experience of all humans. **L3**

Additional Resources

For further stimuli for journal writing, see *Fine Art Transparencies,* 1–6.

Writing Process Transparencies, 1
Writing Across the Curriculum
Cooperative Learning Activities
Thinking and Study Skills, pp. 13, 21, 25
Listening and Speaking Activities, pp. 9, 19, 20
Composition Practice, p. 5

Respond in Your Own Way

Most people like stories that have a character with whom they can identify, so they usually begin their personal response there. Don't overlook other elements of a short story. Speculating about setting, plot, and theme can be just as fruitful in discovering why a story has special appeal for you.

The following model shows how student Robin Borland responded to the short story "A Sunrise on the Veld" by Doris Lessing. The story tells how a fifteen-year-old boy in southern Africa, rejoicing in his own good health, suddenly comes face to face with the unpredicability of death. This theme touched Borland deeply because it reminded her of a time when she herself had come face to face with mortality.

Borland begins by providing a brief summary of the story theme.

She then connects the story theme with something that happened in her own life.

Notice how she uses her own experience to give her a deeper understanding of the story.

Student Model

To feel helpless is just about the worst emotion a person can experience, especially to feel helpless for the first time. At the beginning of "A Sunrise on the Veld," the boy is brimming with enthusiasm for life. He is completely unprepared for the reality of death—in himself or in any other living creature. Then he stumbles upon a buck covered with ants, and he watches, powerless, as the shadows of death swarm over the dying animal. Had he not been there, the same thing would have happened, yet now he is left scarred with an image of mortality—an image he had no inkling of up until this time.

I came face to face with this reality when a close friend of mine passed away this year. He was seventeen and had been fighting kidney disease for over three years. I continued to visit him during that time, holding fast to an inner belief that everything would be fine. I believed that life is great, that everything is eternal, that nothing goes wrong in this great place. There was no way that my friend was going to die. But then he died.

I know now that there was nothing I could have done. My visits weren't enough; the doctors weren't enough. I know how the boy in "Sunrise on the Veld" felt as he watched the ants swarm over the prey. The ants took away the boy's innocence. Death is unpredictable and unmerciful; it is not something that you can prepare for. It is the ultimate shock of feeling completely helpless.

Robin Borland, Evanston Township High School, Evanston, Illinois

---

Listening and Speaking

Listening to Stories

Some students will benefit from listening to stories and responding to them in class. Play recorded stories or read them aloud. Encourage students to vary their responses by acting out dialogues between characters and themselves or sketching major plot events in their reader-response journals.

Write a Reader-Response Journal Entry

Reread a favorite short story. Then write a creative response in your journal.

PURPOSE To respond creatively to a short story
AUDIENCE Yourself
LENGTH 4–6 paragraphs
WRITING RUBRICS To write an effective reader-response journal entry, you should

- respond specifically to the characters and the setting of the story
- consider the story's plot and theme in your entry
- explain how you felt when you finished reading
- be sure your entry is clear and legible

Viewing and Representing

In your journal, write your response to the painting below. Is the scene realistic? What do you imagine is happening, and what might happen next? Respond in prose or poetry.

Using Computers

Work with a partner to research various readers' responses on the Internet. Choose a novel that you and your partner have read. Find out what other readers have to say about that novel on the Internet. You might start your search by visiting online bookstore sites. Are readers' reviews based on careful analysis of characters, setting, plot, and theme? Are the reviews based on subjective feelings? Do you agree with other readers' responses?

Grammar Link

Avoid double negatives in writing.

Notice that Robin Borland uses only one negative word in a sentence.

There was no way that my friend was going to die.

Revise the sentences below to eliminate double negatives.

1. When the fire began, the Robinson family didn't notice no smoke.
2. When they saw the flames, they did not have no time to save their belongings.
3. There wasn't no room for the fire trucks to get through the street.
4. The Robinsons didn't have nowhere to sleep that night.
5. The place was a mess, but they felt lucky because they hadn't lost nothing that was really important to them.

See Lesson 18.6, page 673.

Henri Rousseau, *The Sleeping Gypsy,* 1897

1.5 Responding to a Short Story **27**

Personal Writing

Assess

Evaluation Rubrics

Write a Reader-Response Journal Entry

Use these criteria when evaluating your students' writing:

- Does the entry elaborate on the story's character, setting, plot, or theme?
- Does the entry reveal new insights?
- Does the entry respond in creative ways?

See also *Writing Assessment and Evaluation Rubrics.*

Viewing and Representing

Evaluate the responses on the following:
- how imaginatively the student interprets the story in the painting
- if the entry shows strong emotion
- if the student relates the painting to his or her life or to literature

Using Computers

Students' search efforts should include
- an appraisal of the credibility of the sources they find.
- discussion with their partners of any differing opinions they find.

Reteaching

📁 *Composition Reteaching,* p. 5

Enrichment

📁 *Composition Enrichment,* p. 5

✏️ Use *Fine Art Transparencies* 1–6 for enrichment activities also.

Close

Ask students to list several short stories they have responded to or intend to respond to in their reader-response journals.

Grammar Link

Answers

(Answers will vary; suggestions follow.)
1. . . . didn't notice smoke.
2. . . . they did not have time . . .
3. There wasn't room . . .
4. . . . didn't have anywhere . . .
5. . . . they hadn't lost anything . . .

Viewing the Art

Henri Rousseau, *The Sleeping Gypsy,* 1897
Henri Rousseau described his painting: "A wandering woman, playing her mandolin, with her jar beside her sleeps deeply, worn out by fatigue. A lion wanders by, detects her and doesn't devour her." This 51-by-79-inch oil painting is in the Museum of Modern Art in New York City.

Focus

Lesson Overview

Objective
• To apply the writing process to the task of writing a personal narrative about an incident involving personal change

Skills
• using the five stages of the writing process: prewriting, drafting, revising, editing, presenting

Critical Thinking
• synthesizing; relating; summarizing

Listening and Speaking
• evaluating

Bellringer
Daily Language Activity

When students enter the classroom, have this assignment on the board: *Write three sentences about an experience that changed your life.*

Grammar Link to the Bellringer
Students should check responses for fragments and double negatives.

See also *Daily Language Practice*

Motivating Activity

You can set an example by sharing your own story about an experience that changed you, and any lessons you learned from the incident.

Personal Writing

Writing Process in Action

Personal Writing

In preceding lessons you've learned about—and had the chance to practice—using personal writing to keep journals, learning logs, commonplace books, and reader-response journals. Now it's time to put together what you've learned. In this lesson you're invited to write a personal narrative about how you were changed as a result of something that happened to you—a turning point in your life.

WRITING Online
Visit the Writer's Choice Web site at **writerschoice. glencoe.com** for additional writing prompts.

Assignment

Context
Your new class journal, *Start Me Up,* is to serve as a source of models and inspiration for student writing. The class has chosen the issue of change and growth as the first topic for writing. Submission of articles for publication will be voluntary.

Purpose
To write a brief account of an incident or experience that caused you to change.

Audience
Yourself and maybe some of your peers

Length
1–2 pages

The following pages can help you plan and write your narrative. Read through them, and then refer to them when necessary, but don't feel limited by them. You are in charge of your own writing process.

Resource Manager

Planning Resources
• *Lesson Plans*

 Transparencies
• *Bellringer*
• *Daily Language Practice*
• *Writing Process* 1

Other Print Resources
• *Composition Enrichment,* p. 6
• *Composition Practice,* p. 6
• *Composition Reteaching,* p. 6
• *Grammar Workbook,* Lessons 31, 36
• *Thinking and Study Skills,* pp. 5, 13, 23, 24
• *Writing Assessment and Evaluation Rubrics*

Software
• *Writer's Assistant*

Web Sites
• *writerschoice.glencoe.com*
• *lit.glencoe.com*

Writing Process in Action

Prewriting

First you need to select the right incident to write about—one that is clearly an experience that caused a change in you. If one does not immediately pop into your mind, you might get an idea by looking through your journal or commonplace book. Still stuck?

- Write the heads "People" and "Places," and list memories that come to mind in each category.
- Think back to earlier school years.
- Look at old photographs, or reminisce with your family or a close friend.

When you have selected one incident for your narrative, try to recall what happened as fully as possible. Make a list of specific details about the incident. The questions to the right may help you.

Drafting

To begin drafting your narrative, simply tell what happened, step by step. Don't worry about how it sounds or the flow of the writing. Your goal in drafting is to set down your ideas without worrying about polishing them. A straight chronological retelling—writing in the order events took place—is often best, but you may want to experiment with other arrangements. You may want to take a humorous approach or use dialogue to make your narrative lively. Remember to tell why the event was important to you.

Since this is a personal narrative, it should include details that give readers a sense of who you are. Your narrative should sound like you, even if you are writing about something that happened to you a long time ago. You will also want to give the details that bring this particular incident to life. In the passage that follows, notice how William Least Heat-Moon provides specific information and sensory details that tell how he is feeling and allow the reader to picture the scene clearly.

Prewriting Questions

- Who was involved in this incident?
- What happened, and where?
- How did I feel while it was going on?
- What did I learn from this experience?
- What might others learn from my telling about it?

Personal Writing

Drafting Tip

For more information about starting to get your ideas down on paper, see Lesson 1.1, page 8.

Writing Process in Action **29**

Teach

Prewriting

Developing Ideas for Personal Writing

Some students find it difficult to recognize how their own experiences have caused them to change. These students will benefit from class time spent brainstorming about the kinds of experiences that are most likely to influence a young person, such as moving to a new place; starting a new sport or hobby that becomes very important; experiencing an unexpected success, failure, injury, or illness; or having a change in one's family situation caused by death, divorce, or a new family member. **L1**

Drafting

Cooperative Learning

Students often find it beneficial to have several responses to their early drafts. Divide the class into groups of four, and use a Roundtable strategy. Each student passes his or her draft to the student on the right, who reads it and writes brief comments and suggestions directly on the draft.

Stress that the most helpful comments are specific: "You said you learned a lesson. What was it?" or "Why did you react so strongly at the time?" or "How exactly were you different after this incident?"

After each draft has been passed to all group members, students can evaluate the comments and then revise and edit their own narrative accordingly, incorporating only the suggestions they think will improve it. Encourage them to share their final products with their groups and, if they wish, with the rest of the class. **L2**

Teach

Prewriting

Peer Editing

Students can work in writing conferences with peer editors before they revise their writing. You may want to duplicate the Peer Response forms in *Writing Assessment and Evaluation Rubrics.* Suggest that peer editors respond to the following:

- Does the writing convey specific examples of change?
- Does the personal writing illustrate feelings as well as actions?
- Does the reader get a sense that a lesson was learned? **L2**

Editing

Peer Editing

After students have edited their own work, have them edit another student's writing. Remind them to refer to the Editing Checklist on student page 31. **L2**

Presenting

If students wish to publish their papers, emphasize the importance of the final draft.

Additional Resources

 Writing Process Transparencies, 1
 Thinking and Study Skills, pp. 5, 13, 23, 24
Composition Practice, p. 6

 Grammar Workbook, Lessons 31, 36

Journal Writing Tip

Asking Questions Students can do a mini freewrite, listing questions about the journal topics.

Personal Writing

Literature Model

I turned up the heater to blast level, went to the back, and wrapped a blanket around the sleeping bag. I undressed fast and got into a sweatsuit, two pairs of socks, my old Navy-issue watch cap, a pair of gloves. When I cut the engine, snow already had covered the windshield. Only a quarter tank of gas. While the warmth lasted, I hurried into the bag and pulled back the curtain to watch the fulminous [related to thunder and lightning] clouds blast the mountain. That sky was bent on having a storm, and I was in for a drubbing.

William Least Heat-Moon, *Blue Highways*

Revising

To begin revising, read over your draft to make sure that what you've written fits your purpose and audience. Then have a **writing conference.** Read your draft to a partner or small group. Use your audience's reactions and the Revising Checklist below to help you evaluate your work.

Revising Tip

To give your peer reviewers some ideas about questions they might consider when responding to your personal narrative, see Lesson 1.4, page 22.

Revising Checklist

- Does my personal narrative tell my story clearly?
- Does it deal with my personal change or growth?
- Does it show why the incident was important to me?
- Does a sense of "me" come through?

Enrichment and Extension

Follow-up Ideas

- Set aside a time for students to celebrate the conclusion of their writing projects.
- Consider class publication. All of students' writing in response to this assignment can be collected, illustrated, bound, and placed in the school library.

Extending Personal Writing

- Explore opportunities for personal writing beyond the classroom, such as writing letters to friends and relatives, writing an advice column for the school newspaper, and keeping a personal journal.

Editing/Proofreading

Once you are satisfied with the content and style of your narrative, **proofread** it carefully for errors in grammar, usage, mechanics, and spelling. Use the questions at the right as a guide.

In addition to proofreading, use the self-evaluation list below to make sure your narrative does all the things you want it to do. When you're satisfied, make a clean copy of your narrative and proofread it once more.

Self-Evaluation

Make sure your personal narrative—

✔ focuses on a situation that caused you to change

✔ orients readers with a clear narration of what happened

✔ uses personal frames of reference to personalize the incident

✔ explains why the experience was important to you

✔ follows standard grammar, usage, mechanics, and spelling

Publishing/Presenting

You may wish to offer your narrative for inclusion in the class journal along with those of your classmates. If you feel your sketch is too personal to share with such a wide audience, keep it with your personal journal.

Editing Checklist

- Have I avoided sentence fragments?
- Have I used commas correctly in a series?
- Have I avoided double negatives?
- Are my pronoun references clear?
- Have I checked spellings of any words I'm unsure of?

Personal Writing

Proofreading

For proofreading symbols, see page 84.

Journal Writing

Reflect on your writing process experience. Answer these questions in your journal: What do you like best about your personal narrative? What was the hardest part of writing it? What did you learn in your writing conference? What new things have you learned as a writer?

Assess

Evaluation Rubrics

Use the following questions to evaluate the student's finished writing:

- Is there a clear account of the details of the incident?
- Is there an indication of the changes that resulted from the incident?
- Is there a description of the writer's feelings?
- Do you get a sense of the writer as a person, including a personal tone?
- Do details about the characters and setting make the incident clear and orient readers?
- Does the writing clearly indicate what the writer learned and what others might learn?

See also *Writing Assessment and Evaluation Rubrics.*

Reteaching

📁 *Composition Reteaching,* p. 6

Enrichment

📁 *Composition Enrichment,* p. 6

Close

Discuss with students that change is one of the themes most often explored in personal narratives. Students might think of other common themes, such as the end or beginning of a relationship, the solution to a problem, or a personal discovery to record in their journals as separate page headings. Later, they can record on these pages experiences that fit these themes. These entries could become the basis for other personal narratives.

Cultural Connections

Looking at Change

Change has positive as well as negative connotations, and cultures vary somewhat in their ideas about change. Progress and opportunity are typically American values, while other cultures place greater value on honoring tradition and family history. Ask whether students have heard comments from older relatives or other sources that indicate values about change in their particular cultural heritages.

Literature Model

About the Author

William Least Heat-Moon turned personal and professional crises into opportunity. Having just lost his job, 38-year-old Heat-Moon began the 13,000-mile journey that became the book Blue Highways. During the journey, Heat-Moon found ways to tap his greatest resource—himself. Students may also have important personal resources to discover.

Focus

Lesson Overview

Objective
• To travel vicariously on a writer's journey of self-discovery

Skills
• reading comprehension

Critical Thinking
• analyzing; making inferences

Listening and Speaking
• questioning; discussing

Bellringer
Daily Language Activity

When students enter the classroom, have this assignment on the board: *Write four or five sentences explaining an experience you've had out in nature.*

See also *Daily Language Practice*

Motivating Activity

Ask students to share any human-against-nature experiences they've had. Maybe they tried unsuccessfully to beat a storm home and suffered the consequences. As students share, ask what the experience told them about themselves.

Personal Writing

Literature Model

FROM

A Journey into America
Blue Highways

by William Least Heat-Moon

William Least Heat-Moon is the pen name of writer William Trogdon, a Native American of Sioux ancestry. In 1978 Trogdon packed his small truck and began a journey across rural America—to discover both his country and himself. As you read this excerpt from his book Blue Highways: A Journey into America, *note what you think the author discovered about himself during his travels. Then complete the activities in Linking Writing and Literature on page 38.*

Somewhere out there was the Colorado River perfectly hidden in the openness. The river wasn't more than a mile away, but I couldn't make out the slightest indication of it in the desert stretching level and unbroken for twenty or thirty miles west, although I was only fifty miles above where it enters Grand Canyon. This side of the Colorado gorge[1] was once an important

---

1 gorge a steep narrow pass between great heights

Resource Manager

Planning Resources
• *Lesson Plans*

 Transparencies
• *Bellringer*
• *Daily Language Practice*
• *Fine Art* 1–6

📁 Other Print Resources
• *Listening and Speaking Activities,* pp. 9, 19, 20
• *Thinking and Study Skills,* pp. 5, 17
• *Writing Assessment and Evaluation Rubrics*

🖥 Web Sites

• *writerschoice.glencoe.com*
• *lit.glencoe.com*

Literature Model

Maynard Dixon, *Earth Knower,* C. 1932

Teach

Guided Reading

- What is the setting of this narrative? Be as precise as you can.
- What contrast is brought out here by the narrator? **L2**

Hopi[2] trail south, and, some say, the route Hopi guides took when they first led white men to the canyon. While the arid[3] path followed the river cleft,[4] water was an inaccessible four hundred feet down. Typically, the flexible Hopi solved the desert: women buried gourds of water at strategic points on the outward journey for use on the return.

The highway made an unexpected jog toward Navajo Bridge, a melding of silvery girders and rock cliffs. Suddenly, there it was, far below in the deep and scary canyon of sides so sheer they might have been cut with a stone saw, the naturally silted[5] water turned an unnatural green (*colorado* means "reddish") by the big settling basin a few miles upriver called Glen Canyon Dam. Navajo Bridge, built in 1929 when paved roads began opening the area, is the only crossing over the Colorado between Glen Canyon and Hoover Dam several hundred river miles downstream.

---

2 **Hopi** (ho′pē) a Native American group from northeastern Arizona
3 **arid** (ar′ id) dry and barren
4 **cleft** An opening or crevice
5 **silted** filled or clogged with fine-grained sediment

Literature Model **33**

Viewing the Art

Maynard Dixon, *Earth Knower,* c. 1932
A self-taught artist born in California, Maynard Dixon (1875–1946) produced, in his long career, hundreds of paintings, drawings, and murals of the American West. With their bold, angular forms and vivid sky and earth tones, Dixon's paintings convey a sense of the western desert. *Earth Knower* is a 50-by-40–inch oil painting from the collection of the Oakland (California) Museum.

Teach

Guided Reading

- Reread the paragraph beginning "In 1776 . . ." What is the tone of the paragraph? List four phrases that contribute to that tone.
- What sentence on this page foreshadows an event in the narrative? **L2**

Personal Writing

West of the gorge lay verdant[6] rangeland, much of it given to a buffalo herd maintained by the Arizona Game Commission; the great beasts lifted their heads to watch me pass, their dark, wet eyes catching the late sun. To the north rose the thousand-foot butt end of the Vermillion Cliffs; the cliffs weren't truly vermillion,[7] but contrasting with the green valley in the orange afternoon light, they seemed so.

In 1776, a few months after white-stockinged men in Philadelphia had declared independence, a Spanish expedition led by missionaries Francisco Silvestre Velez de Escalante and Francisco Atanasio Dominguez, returning from an unsuccessful search for a good northern route to the California missions, wandered dispiritedly along the Vermillion Cliffs as they tried to find in the maze of the Colorado a point to cross the river chasm.[8] They looked for ten days and were forced to eat boiled cactus and two of their horses before finding a place to ford; even then, they had to chop out steps to get down and back up the four-hundred-foot perpendicular walls. My crossing, accomplished sitting down, took twenty seconds. What I saw as a remarkable sight, the Spaniards saw as a terror that nearly did them in.

Escalante's struggles gave perspective to the easy passage I'd enjoyed across six thousand miles of America. Other than weather, some bad road, and a few zealous police, my difficulties had been only those of mind. In light of what was about to happen, my guilt over easy transit proved ironic.

I went up an enormous geologic upheaval called the Kaibab Plateau; with startling swiftness, the small desert bushes changed to immense conifers as the Kaibab forest deepened: ponderosa, fir, spruce. At six thousand feet, the temperature was sixty: a drop of thirty degrees in ten miles. On the north edge of the forest, the highway made a long gliding descent off the plateau into Utah. Here lay Kane and Garfield counties, a place of multicolored rock and baroque[9] stone columns and, under it all, the largest unexploited coalfield in the country. A land certain one day to be fought over.

At dusk I considered going into the Coral Sand Dunes for the night, but I'd had enough warmth and desert for a while, so I pushed north toward Cedar Breaks in the severe and beautiful Markagunt Plateau. The cool would refresh me. Sporadic splats of rain, not enough to pay attention to, hit the windshield. I turned onto Utah 14, the cross-mountain road to Cedar City. In the dim light of a mountainous sky, I could just make out a large sign:

ELEVATION 10,000 FEET
ROAD MAY BE IMPASSIBLE
DURING WINTER MONTHS.

So? It was nearly May. The rain popped, then stopped, popped and stopped. The incline became steeper and light rain fell steadily, rolling red desert dust off the roof; I hadn't hit showers since east Texas. It was good. The pleasant cool turned to cold, and I switched on the heater. The

---

6 **verdant** (verd′ ənt) green
7 **vermillion** (vər mil′ yən) a bright red or scarlet
8 **chasm** (kaz′ m) a deep crack in the earth's surface
9 **baroque** (bə rok′) irregular in shape

34   Unit 1 Personal Writing

Writing in the Real World

Genre and Style

To place *Blue Highways* in a context, read this quote by Norbert Blei (in the *Chicago Sun-Times*): "Steinbeck's *Travels with Charley* is one of the best [on-the-road books], and William Least Heat-Moon is even better." Explain (or have a volunteer explain) that *Travels with Charley* is also a book about an author's trip across America, accompanied by his dog Charley. Both writers explore what Robert Penn Warren calls "the unsung side of America."

Literature Model

Jaune Quick-To-See Smith, *Osage Orange*, 1985

headlights glared off snowbanks edging closer to the highway as it climbed, and the rain became sleet. That's when I began thinking I might have made a little miscalculation. I looked for a place to turn around, but there was only narrow, twisted road. The sleet got heavier, and the headlights were cutting only thirty feet into it. Maybe I could drive above and out of the storm. At eight thousand feet, the wind came up—a rough, nasty wind that bullied me about the slick road. Lear,[10] daring the storm to "strike flat the thick rotundity[11] of the world," cries, "Blow, winds, and crack your cheeks! Rage! Blow!" And that's just what they did.

A loud, sulphurous blast of thunder rattled the little truck, then another, and one more. Never had I seen lightning or heard thunder in a snowstorm. Although there were no signs, the map showed a campground near the summit. It would be suicide to stop, and maybe the same to go on. The wind pushed on Ghost Dancing[12] so, I was afraid of getting blown over the

---

10 Lear a legendary British king and the central character of a tragedy by William Shakespeare
11 rotundity (rō tun′ di tē) roundness or fullness
12 Ghost Dancing the name that the author uses for his 1975 Econoline van

Literature Model **35**

Teach

Guided Reading

- What does the narrator mean when he writes, "That's when I began thinking I might have made a little miscalculation"? This kind of statement is called irony, since the miscalculation was a very big one. Write an example of irony that you might use.
- Explain what the driver's choices are at this point. **L2**

Viewing the Art

Jaune Quick-To-See Smith, *Osage Orange*, 1985

Artist Jaune Quick-To-See Smith, a member of the Flathead/Shoshone tribe in Montana, has combined her study of petroglyphs (rock carvings), Native-American geometrical forms, and colors drawn from southwestern nature to create *Osage Orange*. This narrative landscape conveys the power of nature, with "the landscape in motion." Its title refers to a small bush used by Osage Indians to make bows. The 48-by-72-inch oil painting is in the Bernice Steinbaum Gallery in New York.

Teach

Guided Reading

- Point out three or four examples of descriptive writing. What effect does the writer achieve by using description?
- Relate this part of the selection to the title of Heat-Moon's book.
- What is the root word for *calamitously?* What does the word mean? Why is this a good word to describe the narrator's feelings at this point?
- If you had been in the van, how would you have answered the question at the bottom of this student page? **L2**

Personal Writing

invisible edge. Had not the falling snow taken away my vision, I might have needed a blindfold like the ones medieval travelers wore to blunt their terror of crossing the Alps. A rule of the blue road: Be careful going in search of adventure—it's ridiculously easy to find.

Then I was on the top, ten thousand feet up. UP. The wind was horrendous. Utah 14 now cut through snowbanks higher than the truck. At the junction with route 143, a sign pointed north toward Cedar Breaks campground. I relaxed. I was going to live. I puffed up at having beaten the mountain.

Two hundred yards up 143, I couldn't believe what I saw. I got out and walked to it as the raving wind whipped my pantlegs and pulled my hair on end. I couldn't believe it. There it was, the striped centerline, glowing through the sleet, disappearing under a seven-foot snowbank. Blocked.

Back to the truck. My heart dropped like a stone through new snow. There had to be a mistake. I mean, this wasn't 1776. The days of Escalante were gone. But the only mistake was my judgment. I was stopped on state 143, and 143 lay under winter ice.

I turned up the heater to blast level, went to the back, and wrapped a blanket around the sleeping bag. I undressed fast and got into a sweatsuit, two pairs of socks, my old Navy-issue watch cap, a pair of gloves. When I cut the engine, snow already had covered the windshield. Only a quarter tank of gas. While the warmth lasted, I hurried into the bag and pulled back the curtain to watch the fulminous[13] clouds blast the mountain. That sky was bent on having a storm, and I was in for a drubbing.

At any particular moment in a man's life, he can say that everything he has done and not done, that has been done and not been done to him, has brought him to that moment. If he's being installed as Chieftain or receiving a Nobel Prize, that's a fulfilling notion. But if he's in a sleeping bag at ten thousand feet in a snowstorm, parked in the middle of a highway and waiting to freeze to death, the idea can make him feel calamitously stupid.

A loud racketing of hail fell on the steel box, and the wind seemed to have hands, it shook the Ghost so relentlessly. Lightning tried to outdo thunder in scaring me. So did those things scare me? No. Not *those* things. It was something else. I was certain of a bear attack. That's what scared me.

Lightning strikes the earth about eight million times each day and kills a hundred and fifty Americans every year. I don't know how many die from exposure[14] and hypothermia,[15] but it must be at least a comparable number. As for bears eating people who sleep inside steel trucks, I haven't been able to find that figure. It made no sense to fear a bear coming out of hibernation in such weather to attack a truck. Yet I lay a long time, waiting for the beast, shaggy and immense, to claw through the metal, its hot breath on my head, to devour me like a gumdrop and roll the van over the edge.

---

13 fulminous (fool′ mə nəs) of or related to thunder and lightning
14 exposure (ik spō′ zhər) being overly exposed to extreme weather conditions
15 hypothermia (hi′ pə ther′ mēə) an extremely low body temperature

Writing in the Real World

Appreciating Humor

To help students appreciate Heat-Moon's tongue-in-cheek-humor, discuss his "rule of the blue road": "Be careful going in search of adventure—it's ridiculously easy to find." Ask what this means and why Heat-Moon calls it a rule. (Here the word rule doesn't mean "a regulation," but "something that usually happens." Those looking for adventure often find more of it than they want.)

Pawnee, Ceremonial drum, nineteenth century

Perhaps fatigue or strain prevented me from worrying about the real fear; perhaps some mechanism of mind hid the true and inescapable threat. Whatever it was, it finally came to me that I was crazy. Maybe I was already freezing to death. Maybe this was the way it happened. Black Elk prays for the Grandfather Spirit to help him face the winds and walk the good road to the day of quiet. Whitman too:

> O to be self-balanced for contingencies,
> To confront night, storms, hunger, ridicule,
> accidents, rebuffs, as the trees and animals do.

I wondered how long I might have to stay in the Breaks before I could drive down. The cold didn't worry me much: I had insulated the rig myself and slept in it once when the windchill was thirty-six below. I figured to survive if I didn't have to stay on top too long. Why hadn't I listened to friends who advised carrying a CB?[16] The headline showed darkly: FROZEN MAN FOUND IN AVALANCHE. The whole night I slept and woke, slept and woke, while the hail fell like iron shot, and thunder slammed around, and lightning seared the ice.

---

16 **CB** a citizens' band radio, sometimes used for communication among cars and trucks on highways

Literature Model **37**

Personal Writing

Teach

Guided Reading
- What does Heat-Moon mean by the phrase ". . . perhaps some mechanism of mind hid the true and inescapable threat"?
- How does the narrator combine ancient beliefs, education, and modern technology as he waits through the night? What does this tell the reader about William Least Heat-Moon? **L2**

Additional Resources

Fine Art Transparencies, 1–6
Listening and Speaking Activities, pp. 9, 19–20
Thinking and Study Skills, pp. 5, 17

Viewing the Art

Pawnee, *Ceremonial drum*, nineteenth century
Drums have long been used in Native American wars and rituals. This Pawnee ceremonial drum, on display at Chicago's Field Museum of Natural History, depicts the mythical source of violent plains storms.

Real World Connection

Geography
Ask students to trace part of the author's journey on a road map. This excerpt began in northern Arizona near the Colorado River and ended in Utah on Highway 143 en route to the Cedar Breaks campground. Lead students in pinpointing such landmarks as the Grand Canyon and Coral Sand Dunes.

Linking Writing and Literature

Assess

Evaluation Rubrics

As your students discuss the selection, either in small groups or as a class, encourage them to begin with a personal response. The student responses on this page might be used as a starting point.

Look for evidence that students
- have read the selection
- can state some of the writer's ideas in their own words
- understand the writer's point of view
- have connected the content to their own knowledge and experiences
- understand the ideas and implications of the selection

Some possible responses to the discussion questions on this page:
1. The writer expresses guilt about his easy journey, fear of a bear, and relief at being safe.
2. He constantly refers to the Native Americans, Spanish explorers, and various writers.
3. It gives the reader a clear description, making it almost seem a place he or she has been.
4. He knows that he is in the company of many others who have had similar experiences.

Close

Have small groups of students create a character web that displays traits that define the author. Ask groups to share with one another, supporting their choices with details from the story, to create a class character web.

Personal Writing

Linking Writing and Literature

Readers Respond to the Model

What makes William Least Heat-Moon's account of his journey both personal and memorable?

Explore William Least Heat-Moon's personal writing by answering these questions. Then read what other students liked about Heat-Moon's autobiographical account.

1. What are some of the most vivid personal details that the author includes in this personal account?
2. How does the author interweave information about past travelers with the story of his own journey? What impact does this have on the reader?
3. What is the effect of the author's precise description of the landscape through which he travels?
4. What do you think the author discovers about himself during this experience? Explain.

What Students Say

❝This selection was about a man caught in a severe snowstorm while on a dangerous mountain road. The part I remember most clearly was when the man had to stop his truck during the storm. The cliff-hanging description of how he lived through the night kept my attention. It created a feeling of waiting and suspense.

The narrator's point of view was first person. I believe Mr. Heat-Moon chose it to make the story very personal and believable. It helped bring the reality of his situation to life.❞

Rachel Hansen

❝In this selection from *Blue Highways,* William Least Heat-Moon created a suspenseful mood by detailing the possible danger that was awaiting him. This suspense kept me interested in the story; I wanted to read on and find out what happened next.❞

Claire Monty

Cooperative Learning

Sharing Books

To relate reading to self-discovery, remind students that the narrator took along several books that he valued. Ask them to think of a book they might take along on a journey of self-discovery, and to choose a favorite passage from the book to read aloud to classmates. On the day of the reading, have the students form groups. After reading aloud, students should explain what their chosen book and passage mean to them.

UNIT 1 Review

Reflecting on the Unit

Summarize what you learned in this unit by answering the following questions.

1 What are the important functions of a personal journal in your development as an individual and as a writer?

2 How can a learning log help you become actively involved in your school work?

3 What is a commonplace book and what uses does it serve?

4 How can a reader-response journal help in both your reading and your writing?

Adding to Your Portfolio

CHOOSE A SELECTION FOR YOUR PORTFOLIO Look over the personal writing you have done in this unit. Select a completed piece of writing to put into your portfolio. The piece you choose should show one or both of the following:

- reactions to something you have seen, experienced, read, or studied
- your own personal thoughts and feelings

REFLECTING ON YOUR CHOICE Attach a note to the piece you chose, explaining briefly why you chose it and what you learned from writing it.

SET GOALS FOR YOUR WRITING How can you improve your writing? What skill will you focus on the next time you write?

Writing Across the Curriculum

MAKE A SCIENCE CONNECTION Choose a science concept that interests you, and write a learning log entry about it. Summarize what you already know about the subject. Identify aspects of the concept that you want to examine further. Discuss any controversial ideas that relate to the concept. Make a list of questions you have that relate to the concept. Use pictures, charts, or diagrams as part of your entry.

Review **39**

Review

Reflecting on the Unit

You may have students respond to Reflecting on the Unit in writing or through discussion.

Writing Across the Curriculum

Discuss learning logs in terms of how students have used them. Encourage students to work with partners to select a science concept for a learning log entry and to work together to consider ideas and plan visual images. Each student can then write his or her own log entry.

Adding to Your Portfolio

Suggest students work with a partner and evaluate each other's work, using the criteria on this page. Partners can discuss reasons for their choices before making their final selections.

Portfolio Evaluation

If you grade the portfolio selections, you might want to award two marks—one each for content and form. Explain your assessment criteria before students make their selections.

Commend

- experimentation with creative prewriting techniques
- clear, concise writing in which the main idea, audience, and purpose are evident
- successful revisions
- work that shows a flair for language

The objects in this photograph seem to reflect a human presence even though no one is actually present. The open bookcases and cluttered windowsills help create a sense of someone studying or doing research in the room.

Interpret and Analyze Use the following questions for discussion:

- Describe the objects and furniture in the room? What do they add to the picture and what information do they convey to the viewer?
- Notice how the daylight is coming through the window and shining on the objects in the room. Describe the effect of the light. What mood does it help establish?

"He was sitting behind a brown table upon which stood piles of dust and cobweb-covered books and papers."

—Mark Mathabane, *Kaffir Boy*

40

Discussing the Quotation

Discuss this quotation from *Kaffir Boy,* an autobiography by Mark Mathabane (born 1960), with the class. What do the table, dust piles, and books tell about the person sitting behind them? Who might be observing this person? To find out more information about the author and the story from which this quotation was taken, see *Glencoe Literature,* Course 5, p. 444.

Writing Prompt Have students use the quotation as the opening of a short narrative. Ask students to use the photograph to help them focus on details and description in their writing.

Resource Manager

Planning Resources
- *Lesson Plans*
- *Block Scheduling*

 Transparencies
- *Bellringer*
- *Daily Language Practice*
- *Fine Art*

- *Two-Minute Skill Drill*
- *Writing Process*

 Other Print Resources
- *Composition Enrichment*
- *Composition Practice*
- *Composition Reteaching*
- *Cooperative Learning Activities*

- *Glencoe Literature Library*
- *Grammar and Composition Handbook*
- *Grammar Workbook*
- *Listening and Speaking Activities*
- *Spelling Power*
- *Tests with Answer Key and Rubrics*

UNIT 2

The Writing Process

Writing in the Real World: *Mark Trahant*   42

Lesson 2.1   **Stages of the Writing Process**   46

Lesson 2.2   **Prewriting: Finding a Writing Topic**   50

Lesson 2.3   **Prewriting: Identifying Purpose and Audience**   56

Lesson 2.4   **Prewriting: Exploring a Topic**   60

Lesson 2.5   **Prewriting: Interviewing**   64

Lesson 2.6   **Drafting: Writing a Paragraph**   68

Lesson 2.7   **Drafting: Organizing a Paragraph**   72

Lesson 2.8   **Revising: Checking Unity and Coherence**   76

Lesson 2.9   **Editing/Proofreading: Toward a Final Version**   82

Lesson 2.10   **Publishing/Presenting: Sharing Your Writing**   86

Lesson 2.11   **Writing About Literature: Analyzing Point of View**   90

Writing Process in Action   94

Literature Model: from "My Furthest-Back Person—The African" by Alex Haley   98

Unit 2 Review   108

Objectives

- To develop an understanding of the five stages of the writing process
- To employ the five stages of the writing process to write an analysis of point of view in a literary work

✔ ASSESSMENT OPTIONS

 Tests With Answer Key & Rubrics
Unit 2 Choice A Test, p. 5
Unit 2 Choice B Test, p. 6
Unit 2 Composition Objective Test, pp. 7-8

💾 *Testmaker*
Unit 2 Choice A Test
Unit 2 Choice B Test
Unit 2 Composition Objective Test

You may wish to administer either the Unit 2 Choice A Test or the Unit 2 Choice B Test as a pretest.

- *Thinking and Study Skills*
- *Writing Across the Curriculum*
- *Writing Assessment and Evaluation Rubrics*
- *Writing in the Real World*

📺 Video
- *MindJogger Videoquizzes*

💾 Software
- *Presentation Plus!*
- *Revising with Style*
- *Testmaker*

- *Writer's Assistant*
- *Writer's Choice Puzzlemaker*

 Web Sites
- *writerschoice.glencoe.com*
- *lit.glencoe.com*

Focus

Lesson Overview

Objectives
- To analyze and deconstruct media
- To analyze one writer's process and strategies
- To explore the stages of the writing process

Skills
- evaluating facts; using main ideas

Critical Thinking
- analysis; making inferences; building background

Listening and Speaking
- interviewing; note taking; questioning

Bellringer
Daily Language Activity

When students come into the classroom, have this assignment on the board: *List some ways in which a reporter is like a detective.*

Grammar Link to the Bellringer

Have students underline the subjects they used in their responses and circle the corresponding verbs.

See also *Daily Language Practice*

Motivating Activity

Ask students to share their list of the ways in which a reporter is like a detective. (Both conduct investigations. A detective investigates the facts behind a crime; a reporter investigates the facts behind a story.) Then ask students where they think reporters get their facts. (The sources vary widely: books, magazines, the Yellow Pages, phone and face-to-face interviews, radio and TV shows.) A reporter must do a great deal of investigating before writing.

The Writing Process

Writing in the Real World

MEDIA Connection
Newspaper

Skilled investigative reporters, like detectives, spend countless hours searching for the truth behind a story. Then they must be sure to use fair and accurate writing to present their findings. The following is an excerpt from an investigative newspaper story reporter Mark Trahant wrote for the *Arizona Republic.*

Trahant Investigates Nuclear Transport

by Mark Trahant

Investigative Reporter Mark Trahant

It's about an hour shy of dusk as the white 18-wheeler races toward the setting sun at speeds occasionally topping 70 mph.

The truck and its trailer are inconspicuous. There are no markings of any kind. But you can see its U.S. government license plates, an odd crop of antennas fenced in on the truck's roof and an escort of four sinister-appearing Chevy Suburbans that lead and follow the rig.

This is no ordinary truck. It's a "safe secure trailer" [SST] from the U.S. Department of Energy and probably is carrying a cargo of missile components, weapons-grade plutonium or hydrogen bombs. Behind the dark windows of the escort Suburbans are enough guns to launch a small war—including turret-mounted machine guns in some vehicles.

It's life in the nuclear lane on Interstate 40.

Tractor-trailers ferrying nuclear materials travel most of America's interstates as well as many main highways. The rig in the next lane could be carrying plutonium, uranium or a host of other products of fission.

The potential for accidents grows with each additional truck on the road. On . . . Interstate 85 in China Grove, N.C., a car crashed head-on into a tractor-trailer carrying low-level radioactive material.

One person was killed and more than 225 were evacuated for about five hours while officials surveyed the area for radioactive leaks. . . .

Federal investigators have found that many trucks on the highways—including

---

Resource Manager

Planning Resources
- *Lesson Plans*

Transparencies
- *Bellringer*
- *Daily Language Practice*
- *Writing Process 2–8*

Other Print Resources
- *Cooperative Learning Activities,* pp. 9–12
- *Thinking and Study Skills* pp. 3, 13, 23
- *Writing Assessment and Evaluation Rubrics*
- *Writing in the Real World,* pp. 5–8

those that carry nuclear freight—have serious mechanical problems. At the same time, the Department of | Energy is considering a number of plans that would increase the amount of nuclear freight on public | highways, especially in the Southwest, in the next two decades. . . .

A Writer's Process

Prewriting:
Investigating the Transports

Mark Trahant's interest in the transport of radioactive materials evolved from research he did on a New Mexico nuclear waste project—a plan to bury millions of cubic feet of plutonium waste in the desert near Carlsbad. While researching this topic, he met townspeople who said they saw nuclear transport trucks all the time. Soon after, he discovered that almost 3 million loads of nuclear freight crisscross U.S. highways each year.

Once his editor gave him the go-ahead for a story, Trahant dug up every bit of information he could on these nuclear transport trucks. "Successful investigative reporters are, above all, very good reporters," Trahant said. "They are curious. They want to see how a story affects people—the population of a city or county, as well as one person." They also have to doggedly seek out every side of the story. "Investigative reporters can't be seen as advocates of any side," Trahant stressed.

For four weeks, ten to eighteen hours a day, Trahant traveled, talked, listened, and read. He scoured four years' worth of transportation records and safety complaints in Denver, El Paso, and Phoenix federal courts. He conducted more than fifty interviews with people on all sides of the issue—the Department of Energy, experts on nuclear transport safety, scientists, peace activists, terrorism experts, and people who live on the main routes. He even tried, unsuccessfully, to talk to people in Texas at a major weapons manufacturing plant.

After a month of research, Trahant had four notebooks full of

Sleuthing for evidence—it's not a glamouous adventrue but a demanding search for the facts.

Teach

Building Background

Warm-up
Have students list as many ways as they can in which an investigative report can be presented.

The Writing Process in Speaking
Have students think of situations in which everyday conversation might become part of the writing process.

The Writing Process in Writing
Discuss any investigative reports students have read. Use prompts such as the following:
- Have you ever read a newspaper article in which a scandal or criminal activity was revealed? How was the article organized?
- What kinds of evidence do investigative reporters use?

Preview the Media Connection
Have students preview the title and focus of the Media Connection. Explain that Mark Trahant is an award-winning investigative reporter who wrote an article about how nuclear materials are transported. Then have students read the newspaper article.

Writing in the Real World

Writers and Writing
Mark Trahant, who lives in Arizona, is an award-winning investigative reporter. Students might be interested to know that reporters may belong to the staff of a particular publication as Trahant did when he conducted the investigation of nuclear transport described here. Or they may work independently as Trahant does now, submitting proposals and articles to various publications.

The Writing Process

Discussion Prompts

- Do you think Trahant's statement "Journalism is literature in a hurry" is an accurate description? Why or why not?
- How did Trahant organize the information in the report?
- What did Trahant mean when he said he checked his story for "good rhythm"?
- What kind of research did Trahant conduct for his report?
- Why do you think it is important for investigative reporters to remain impartial?
- Trahant says that investigative reporters are good, curious reporters. Can you think of other qualities that might benefit investigative reporters?

Discussion

Stimulate a discussion of the Media Connection. You may also want to invite students to talk about
- why three editors reviewed Trahant's story
- what kinds of changes an editor might make and what an editor might want to check with the writer

Additional Resources

Writing Process Transparencies, 2–8
Writing in the Real World, pp. 5–8
Cooperative Learning Activities
Thinking and Study Skills, pp. 3, 13, 23

notes and several file drawers of photocopied documents. At that point, he met with his editor, explained where the story was going, and asked for a full page in the newspaper.

Drafting/Revising:
Recording and Supporting Key Ideas

Trahant approached the job of drafting the story with a reporter's strategy—write it fast the first time; then rewrite. "Journalism is literature in a hurry," he said.

To open the piece, Trahant described the truck he clocked at 72 miles an hour, an anecdote he had marked "lead" in his notebook. Then he drafted the body of the story, keeping in mind three or four key ideas that presented all sides of the story and the need to interest readers. "Good writing is surprising [to the reader]," Trahant said. "It tells the reader something unusual, not expected. It's also concrete. It puts the reader there with examples of color, how something looked or sounded."

Trahant closed with an attention-grabbing quotation, despite knowing that editors often cut stories from the end. "Most editors realize that a good story has a beginning, a middle, and an end," he said. After finishing a draft, Trahant went back and inserted supporting details and quotations. Then he read the story aloud, checking to be sure the language flowed smoothly.

Reporter Mark Trahant defines journalism as "literature in a hurry."

Revising/Editing:
Making Necessary Changes

Three editors reviewed Trahant's article to ensure complete and fair coverage and to check for correct style and grammar. Then Trahant made his final revisions. Most newspapers ask an attorney to review very touchy stories before publication to be sure the paper won't be sued, but Trahant's piece went to press without legal review. "There was no real bad guy in this story," explained Trahant. His research pointed out two areas of public concern: the large percentage (20 percent) of all SSTs in poor mechanical condition and the growing potential for accidents as the number of trucks on the roads increases.

Publishing/Presenting:
Getting the Story Out

What did Trahant hope to accomplish by publishing this article? "I always hope my work will result in improvements, but I know one story won't change much," he said. "My job is to dig up the information and present it in an interesting way. I leave change to the public."

By the time a story reaches the morning breakfast table, an investigative reporter is following fresh leads for the next story and beginning the writing process again.

Real World Connection

Using Investigative Techniques

Many workers use an investigative reporter's techniques (researching, interviewing, writing) every day. Police officers and private detectives are obvious examples. Ask students to name others (fire inspectors, lawyers, medical examiners, salespeople).

Examining Writing in the Real World

Analyzing the Media Connection

Discuss these questions about the article on page 42.

1. In your opinion, does the lead, or opening, of Trahant's article capture the reader's interest? Why or why not?

2. What details create a sense of drama and urgency in the story?

3. What tragedy does Trahant mention? For what reasons does he mention this tragedy?

4. In your opinion, does Trahant do a good job of persuading the reader that change is necessary? Why or why not?

5. Describe the style of writing Trahant uses in his article. How is it similar to or different from your own style of writing?

Analyzing a Writer's Process

Discuss these questions about Mark Trahant's writing process.

1. What prompted Mark Trahant to write an article about the transport of nuclear materials?

2. How did Trahant research his topic? What kinds of evidence did he gather?

3. What basic strategy did Trahant take in drafting his story?

4. Describe the steps Trahant followed in drafting his story? Why do you think he followed that order?

5. What did Trahant's editors look for in his story? How did Trahant view the outcome of his work?

Grammar Link

Make verbs agree with nouns of amount.

The verb that follows a noun of amount is plural if the noun refers to individual units: *Almost 3 million* **loads** *of nuclear freight* **crisscross** *U.S. highways.* The verb is singular if the noun refers to a single unit: *Three million* **loads** *is a lot.*

Complete each sentence with the correct form of the verb in parentheses.

1. Three-fourths of Trahant's article (focuses, focus) on nuclear transports.

2. One-and-a-half file drawers (was, were) full of photocopied documents.

3. Four weeks (is, are) a long time to spend gathering evidence.

4. The 100 inches of copy space (was, were) more than most articles get.

5. Twenty percent of all SSTs (was, were) in poor mechanical condition.

See Lesson 16.4, pages 618–619.

Grammar Link

Answers

1. focuses
2. were
3. is
4. was
5. was

Close

Invite students to conduct mini-investigations of topics that arouse their curiosity. Suggest that they do some preliminary research before they record their findings in a notebook.

Analyzing the Media Connection

Responses will vary.

1. Students may respond that the high speed and the vivid language captured their attention.

2. Students may note the U.S. government plates, the possible contents of the truck, and the arsenal of weapons in the Suburbans.

3. Trahant mentions a car-truck collision, perhaps to underscore the danger posed by the transport of nuclear weapons.

4. Students may respond that Trahant's arresting lead, clear thesis, and compelling evidence are persuasive.

5. Students may note that Trahant is precise, objective, and careful about word choices.

Analyzing a Writer's Process

Discussion responses will vary; some possibilities follow:

1. Trahant's earlier work on a nuclear waste project prompted this article.

2. Trahant traveled, talked, listened, read, and did research and interviews with various sources.

3. He drafted his story quickly.

4. Trahant drafted the lead, then the body, then the conclusion, perhaps to be certain he had a clear direction.

5. The editors wanted completeness, fairness, and clear, grammatical language. Trahant appeared satisfied with his work.

See also *Writing Assessment & Evaluation Rubrics.*

Reteaching

Have students watch an investigative report on television and then write a review of the report. Student reviews should include the purpose of the report and the types of evidence and documentation the reporter(s) used. Students should evaluate the report's conclusions on the basis of its objectivity and fairness.

Enrichment

Invite students to find another media coverage of the same event they watched in the televised investigative report. Suggest that students look in newspapers, magazines, or on the Internet. Have them write a comparison/contrast essay in which they critique each media's representation of the event.

Focus

Lesson Overview

Objective
- To employ a recursive process that includes five stages—prewriting, drafting, revising, editing/proofreading, and publishing/presenting

Skills
- identifying writing process stages; moving among stages

Critical Thinking
- identifying main ideas; classifying

Listening and Speaking
- discussing

Bellringer
Daily Language Activity

When students enter the classroom, have this assignment on the board: *Write a few sentences about something you have investigated lately.*

Grammar Link to the Bellringer

Have students correct any run-on sentences they might have written in their Bellringer assignments.

See also *Daily Language Practice*

Motivating Activity

To underscore the unit theme, announce that you're conducting an investigation and you want the students to join you in it. Ask when students have conducted an investigation (such as researching a science project or exploring a new vacation spot). Explain that this lesson deals with a kind of investigation they may not have thought of—writing and the writing process.

The Writing Process

Stages of the Writing Process

*T*he five stages of the writing process allow you to explore, investigate, and write about any topic. In the following pages you will follow the investigation and writing process of a high school student, Shella Calamba.

The Five Writing Process Stages

Writing is a process with different stages. Professional and student writers all follow processes made up of combinations of the stages shown below.

The Writing Process

Prewriting → Drafting → Revising → Editing/Proofreading → Publishing/Presenting

PREWRITING The first stage, called prewriting, is the idea stage. By probing your thoughts, you can discover a topic and a purpose for writing about it. This is the stage in which information or details are gathered and the paper is planned. Shella Calamba began investigating her family's history by using a prewriting technique called freewriting.

During the freewriting stage, Calamba's ideas are random and free flowing, but they lead to a writing topic.

Exploring my family's history. Chinese and Spanish ancestors. Great-grandparents half Chinese. Great-grandfather Filipino. Great-grandmother very religious according to my mother. My mother was named after my great-grandmother, Josefa Parcarey. My great-grandfather was the mayor of the town. Both my grandparents were farmers. I could write about my mother's genealogy.

Resource Manager

Planning Resources
- *Lesson Plans*

Transparencies
- *Bellringer*
- *Daily Language Practice*
- *Fine Art 7–12*

- *Two-Minute Skill Drill*
- *Writing Process 2–8*

Other Print Resources
- *Composition Enrichment*, p. 7
- *Composition Practice*, p. 7
- *Composition Reteaching*, p. 7
- *Cooperative Learning Activities*

- *Listening and Speaking Activities* pp. 6–8
- *Thinking and Study Skills*, pp. 5, 13, 26
- *Writing Across the Curriculum*
- *Writing Assessment and Evaluation Rubrics*

DRAFTING Drafting is writing your ideas down in related sentences and paragraphs. The goal during drafting is to let your writing flow without worrying about grammar or mechanics. Notice how Calamba has combined related ideas in a paragraph.

> It is far from a coincidence that my mother was named after my great-grandmother, Josefa. My mother spent her early childhood years under my great-grandmother's watchful, firm eye. Later, she spent her teenage years in Manila, where she studied in high school and college.

How does Calamba give structure to her ideas in the drafting stage?

REVISING Revision means reading your draft closely, reminding yourself of your purpose, and reworking and clarifying your ideas, as Calamba did here.

> My great-grandfather was the mayor of a Philippine province. My great-grandmother, Josefa, a religious woman, taught my mother Latin prayers. They ~~would~~ used to pray together, every afternoon at precisely five.
>
> My grandparents raised eight children. Two aunts ~~were~~ became teachers, and one ~~has~~ owns a store. (My mother is a pharmacist in Chicago.) One uncle is ~~in business~~ a restaurant owner, and one is a nurse in Australia.

In revising this passage, what details has Calamba added? What effect do they have? What other changes did Calamba make?

Journal Writing

In your journal analyze your own writing process. Which of these first three stages do you find easy? What are your stumbling blocks? Do you always move straight forward, or do you sometimes return to a previous stage?

Teach

Using the Model

Ask students to mention specific ways that each stage of Calamba's writing is different from the prior stage. (In drafting, Calamba expressed her ideas in full sentences, adding a paragraph about her mother's early years, arranged in time order. In revising, Calamba added details like "every afternoon at precisely five" and "a restaurant owner" to provide a clearer picture of her family and background. She also moved a sentence to add emphasis and changed certain words to express her meaning more exactly.) **L2**

Freewriting

Ask what students notice about Calamba's freewriting. (She wrote mainly in words and phrases.) Explain that correct grammar and spelling do not matter in freewriting. The idea is to capture thoughts on paper. **L1**

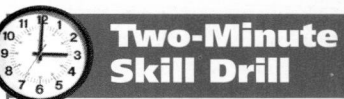 **Two-Minute Skill Drill**

Have students write three ways to correct run-on sentences.

📖 **See also** *Two-Minute Skill Drill Transparency 2.1*

Journal Writing Tip

Recalling Before students begin this activity, you might have them each examine a few pieces of their best earlier writing. Ask them to recall where they got their ideas—from daydreams, friends, or their own experiences, for example—and what process students engaged in to get the finished pieces of writing. Encourage them to record discoveries they make about how they write.

47

Teach

Using the Model

Examining editing changes in Calamba's paragraph, students wonder why Calamba decided to spell out "U.S." Explain that names of countries are usually spelled out when used as nouns. Stress that even such small details should be corrected in editing so that the final version makes a good impression when presented to an audience. **L2**

Additional Resources

 For further stimuli for writing, see *Fine Art Transparencies*, 7–12.
 Writing Across the Curriculum
Cooperative Learning Activities

 Writing Process Transparencies, 2–8
 Thinking and Study Skills, pp. 5, 13, 26
Listening and Speaking Activities, pp. 6–8
Composition Practice, p. 7

The Writing Process

EDITING/PROOFREADING In this stage look closely at each paragraph, each sentence, and each word. Do your sentences flow smoothly? Are they grammatically correct? Are your spelling and punctuation correct? Notice how Calamba edited the paragraph below.

> My mother came here to the ~~U.S.~~ *United States* and became a pharmacist. All seven of her sisters and brothers have raised ~~familys~~ *families* of their own. For this reason, I have many cousins; I've never had to live in the ~~isalated~~ *isolated* world of the proverbial only child.

In editing and proofreading this paragraph, Calamba corrected spelling and punctuation.

PUBLISHING/PRESENTING Sometimes sharing your writing with a reader simply means handing it in to your teacher. At other times you want your thoughts and ideas to go far beyond the teacher's desk. For example, Calamba might decide to submit her essay to her high school's prose and poetry magazine.

Move Among the Stages

Good writers move back and forth among stages in the writing process. For example, you might reach the revising stage and notice that one section needs more explanation. You could return to a prewriting task, such as freewriting, to explore those ideas in greater detail.

When you write, your mind is in a state of motion. This perpetual motion is absolutely necessary; after all, you are involved in an investigation to discover your thoughts.

48 Unit 2 The Writing Process

Listening and Speaking

Prewriting

To help students who find writing difficult, suggest that during prewriting and drafting they pretend they are talking to someone about their topic. Emphasize the exploratory, free-flowing nature of the early writing stages—prewriting and drafting. Tell students that they needn't worry about grammar, spelling, or punctuation conventions until a later stage.

Write a Personal Response

Follow the five stages of the writing process as you write a response to a painting in this book. What does the subject or mood of the painting remind you of?

PURPOSE To use the stages of the writing process
AUDIENCE Your classmates
LENGTH 1-2 paragraphs

WRITING RUBRICS To write a personal response, you should

- freewrite to explore your associations
- focus on one aspect of your response at a time as you draft
- revise to clarify your ideas
- check spelling, grammar, and punctuation as you edit

Cross-Curricular Activity

MUSIC Use the writing process to draft a paragraph about a song or a music video. Begin by listening to the music or viewing the video. Notice the artistic qualities of the performers' presentations. Then identify your topic and your purpose for writing about it. Progress through the steps of the writing process to create your paragraph.

Grammar Link

When you edit, correct run-on sentences.

Imagine that you are in the editing stage of the writing process. Rewrite the run-on sentences below.

1. Writing is a journey that is seldom smooth often it is an exploration of your thoughts and ideas.
2. There are five stages in the writing process prewriting is the first.
3. During the freewriting stage ideas are random but they can lead to a writing topic.
4. A good writer moves back and forth among stages for example while revising, a writer may choose to add details.
5. Presenting is the final stage you share your writing with a reader.

See Lesson 13.10, pages 559-561.

Listening and Speaking

SPELLING Exchange your personal response from the writing activity with a partner. Work together to correct any spelling errors in your papers. Keep a list of words that have given you difficulty. Use your list as a resource and check against it as you proofread your work.

Assess

Evaluation Rubrics

Write a Personal Response

Use these criteria when evaluating your students' writing. Students should

- freewrite to explore associations
- focus on a single subject
- revise to clarify
- check grammar, spelling, and punctuation

See also *Writing Assessment & Evaluation Rubrics.*

Cross-Curricular Activity

Student copy should include these elements:
- clear topic
- statement of purpose

Reteaching

📁 *Composition Reteaching,* p. 7

Enrichment

📁 *Composition Enrichment,* p. 7

🖱 Use *Fine Art Transparencies* 7–12 for enrichment activities also.

Close

Have students list the five stages of the writing process and write a one-sentence definition of each.

Grammar Link

Answers
1. smooth; often
2. process. Prewriting
3. random, but
4. stages. For example,
5. stage; you share

Focus

Lesson Overview

Objective
- To develop a list of writing topics by freewriting, brainstorming, and/or clustering

Skills
- discovering ideas; freewriting; brainstorming; clustering; narrowing the focus

Critical Thinking
- identifying; generating new information

Listening and Speaking
- discussing; brainstorming

Bellringer
Daily Language Activity

When students enter the classroom, have this assignment on the board: *Write three sentences about the places you sometimes daydream about visiting.*

Grammar Link to the Bellringer

Have students identify what the capitalized words in their sentences have in common (they are proper nouns or they begin sentences).

See also *Daily Language Practice*

Motivating Activity

Initiate a discussion of daydreaming as one source of writing ideas, inviting students to share some of the subjects of their daydreams. First, name some examples: becoming a rock star, winning a basketball championship, traveling to a tropical island. Comment that freewriting allows students to daydream on paper, putting down ideas as quickly as possible before they are lost. Stress that students' freewriting needn't be spelled correctly or even make sense to an outsider. Freewriting is for the writer only.

The Writing Process

LESSON 2.2

Prewriting: Finding a Writing Topic

W riters may use various techniques to zero in on a topic. When asked to write a feature story on Native Americans in southern California, journalist Wayne Swanson began by jotting down some ideas. Compare his freewriting with the first part of his article to see how he used his notes.

> Through his freewriting, Swanson focused on a topic—glimpses of a lost Native American heritage.

Sad truth, little left of Native American culture—time, conquest, conversion, development have buried. But long history, and if know where to look, possible to catch a glimpse of world before white people came.

So. I could focus on glimpses of their lost heritage, baskets and cemetery plots at missions, but also evidence of power that eradicated most of their history. Perhaps draw a picture of life along San Luis Rey valley. Where were their settlements? What did they do?

> How did the comments in the prewriting notes about drawing a picture lead to this introduction?

Literature Model

Imagine a time when the San Luis Rey River ran freely, even in dry years. Imagine irrigated fields of corn and grain thriving in its valleys. Imagine small, self-sufficient villages up along the valley slopes, scattered all the way from the ocean to Mt. Palomar and beyond.

In other words, imagine San Diego County before European adventurers claimed it for their own. As development moves relentlessly up the valley, the evidence of this earlier era becomes ever harder to find. Nevertheless, glimpses remain. They remain in the landscape and in the efforts of Native Americans and others to hold on to what is left.

Wayne Swanson, "Exploring Proud Past of Indians"
Los Angeles Times

Resource Manager

Planning Resources
- *Lesson Plans*

Transparencies
- *Bellringer*
- *Daily Language Practice*
- *Fine Art 7–12*
- *Two-Minute Skill Drill*
- *Writing Process 2–8*

Other Print Resources
- *Composition Enrichment,* p. 8
- *Composition Practice,* p. 8
- *Composition Reteaching,* p. 8
- *Cooperative Learning Activities*

- *Listening and Speaking Activities* pp. 6–8
- *Thinking and Study Skills,* pp. 17, 24–25
- *Writing Across the Curriculum*
- *Writing Assessment and Evaluation Rubrics*

Discover Ideas

Like Wayne Swanson, you have countless ideas hidden in your mind, waiting to be uncovered. How can you get at them? There are several techniques you can use.

FREEWRITING Freewriting consists of writing nonstop for a set time, usually only five or ten minutes. The idea is to keep pace with your thoughts, getting them on paper before they vanish. Freewriting can start anywhere and go anywhere. Sometimes it begins with an assignment. Sometimes it grows out of a class discussion—for example, a biology class discussion on using animals in medical research. Read Shella Calamba's freewriting to see what ideas she uncovered as she thought about this topic.

TIME

For more about the writing process, see TIME Facing the Blank Page, pp. 109–119.

Student Model

The role of animals in medical research is an interesting topic. But what aspect? Which animals are used and why? Maybe pick one species and describe an experiment done on it. I can include safety precautions involved in using animals. I could write about rights and laws that protect animals. Controversy surrounding animals and research. I could investigate this. I could give my own opinions on the vital role of animals in research.

Shella Calamba, Lincoln Park High School, Chicago, Illinois

Freewriting Tips

1. Let your thoughts flow—ideas, memories, anything that comes to mind.
2. Don't edit or judge your thoughts; just write them down. You can evaluate them later.
3. Don't worry about spelling, punctuation, grammar, or even sense; just keep writing.
4. If you stop, rewrite your last sentence, or write "I'm stuck" until a new idea pops up.

Journal Writing

In your journal, spend five minutes freewriting about whatever comes to mind. Then make a list of the different ideas you came up with.

Teach

Using the Model

Point out that Swanson's freewriting note about drawing a picture resulted in the vivid opening description he later put in his article. Ask students to find other prewriting ideas he used (the toll that development has taken on Native American culture and the glimpses that remain of an earlier era). **L2**

Freewriting Dialogue

You might challenge students who demonstrate a command of the language to try freewriting dialogue as a way to investigate story ideas. Suggest students select speakers and situations, both real and imaginary—parents and their teenager discussing curfew, or two television characters discussing a social cause, for example. Encourage students to use their journals and let the conversations flow freely. **L3**

Two-Minute Skill Drill

List two of the four freewriting tips.

See also *Two-Minute Skill Drill Transparency 2.2*

Journal Writing Tip

Identifying Main Ideas After students have completed the journal activity, suggest they read their freewriting. They can identify main ideas for potential writing projects by circling words or phrases that seem interesting or spark other ideas.

Teach

Learning Cooperatively

You might lead students in an activity to develop a list of writing topics related to what leaders can accomplish. Form groups of four. Each group member should pick a leader and write the following heading at the top of a sheet of paper: *If I were (school principal, president, football coach, mayor, etc.), I would . . . .* Students should pass each paper around their group, and each member should write an ending for the sentence, indicating the changes or accomplishments the student would try to achieve in that leadership role. When all four papers have circled the group, the last member to get each paper should read the ideas aloud. Members should record in their journals those ideas that sound interesting as writing topics. **L2**

Cross-reference: Listening and Speaking

For more information on ways to facilitate brainstorming and other group activities, refer students to Lesson 29.3, page 891.

BRAINSTORMING You freewrite on your own, but like the students shown below, you can brainstorm ideas with others. The student at the right is tossing out a question, and the others will answer it. These ideas will lead to new ideas as each student's comment starts the others thinking. The result of this interplay of ideas is a list like the one below. You should allow a set amount of time, ten to fifteen minutes, for each brainstorming session.

Brainstorming Tips
1. Choose someone to list ideas as they are called out.
2. Start with a topic (such as inventions) or a question.
3. Encourage everyone to join in freely.
4. Accept all ideas; do not evaluate them now.
5. Follow each idea as far as it goes.

OK, what's the most important invention of all time?

Inventions

- Most important inventions: wheel, internal-combustion engine, movable type, electricity, penicillin, telephone
- Unsuccessful inventions
- How inventions happen
- Inventions still needed

Viewing and Representing

Creating an Idea Map

Students may have difficulty brainstorming alone. If time permits, demonstrate on the chalkboard just how easy and effective it is to create a giant idea map. Start with a topic of interest to students—rock music, grades, school rules, fads, part-time jobs. Then have students make idea maps of their own on a topic that interests them. **L1**

CLUSTERING Brainstorming is often a group activity, but you can also brainstorm by yourself. One way to focus your brainstorming is by clustering. Start by circling a word or phrase. Surround it with related ideas, and connect each of those ideas with others, creating groups, or clusters, of ideas. The following cluster started with one word, *inventions*.

Clustering Tips

1. Start with a key word or phrase circled in the center of your paper.
2. Brainstorm to discover related ideas; circle each one, and connect it to the central idea.
3. Branch out with new ideas that refine existing ideas by adding details.
4. Review your chart, looking for ideas or clusters of ideas that interest you.

Journal Writing

Some writers prefer to work alone, while others like working in groups. Write in your journal about the pros and cons of group activities like brainstorming and individual efforts like freewriting and clustering. Which approach do you think works better for you? Why?

Teach

Using Brainstorming

Emphasize to students the practical applications of brainstorming. You might point out that brainstorming is often used in business. Creative teams meet to bounce around ideas for products, improving service, handling problems, and so forth. Business leaders agree that the time is well spent. **L1**

Journal Writing Tip

Drawing Conclusions If this activity follows immediately after the students have practiced freewriting, brainstorming, and clustering, they will be able to draw conclusions about the different activities more accurately—and eagerly.

Cultural Connections

Clustering

If your students represent a variety of national and ethnic backgrounds, suggest using the country of the student's or a parent's origin as a starting point for a clustering activity. Initial clusters might include topics such as land, people, customs, economy, government, holidays, and history. The details in the clusters will be as diverse as the students' backgrounds.

Teach

Getting Started

If students have difficulty getting started, suggest they begin by writing a sentence, a phrase, even a word, over and over again until the ideas begin to flow. Students needing a topic for looping or clustering should scout their journals for ideas. Point out that this page is about finding a topic by narrowing your focus. A general idea like "sports" is too broad for a writing topic. You might demonstrate how students can use looping or clustering to get to a more specific topic. **L2**

Exploring an Issue

Students may use one or more of the freewriting techniques in this lesson to explore a current issue of great interest or concern, such as the destruction of tropical rain forests or homelessness. Afterward, instruct students to go through the writing process to write a focused essay on one aspect of the issue. Encourage students to present their finished essays as letters to the editor of a publication that has covered the issue. **L3**

Additional Resources

For further stimuli for freewriting, see *Fine Art Transparencies*, 7–12.
Writing Across the Curriculum
Cooperative Learning Activities

Writing Process Transparencies, 2–8
Thinking and Study Skills, pp. 17, 24–25
Listening and Speaking Activities, pp. 6–8
Composition Practice, p. 8

Narrow Your Focus

Prewriting techniques—freewriting, brainstorming, clustering—help you discover your thoughts and ideas, but they have another value, too. They can help you narrow a topic so that you can use it for a short piece of writing, even a single paragraph.

RETURN TO FREEWRITING Looping is one way to narrow your topic. Start by reading some of your freewriting, and choose one idea you touched upon that interests you. Freewrite about that idea for another five minutes. Review that freewriting, choose an idea from it, and try to focus it further in another freewriting session. Repeat the process two or three times. As shown below, your idea will be narrower and more focused with each "loop" until you discover a topic for writing.

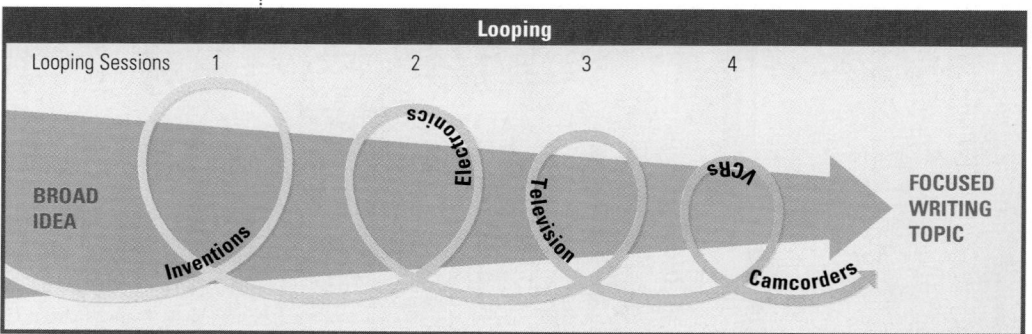

RETURN TO CLUSTERING Writing additional clusters is another way to narrow your topic. Look at the clustering you did to search for ideas, and choose an idea that seems promising—for example, "How inventions happen" from the cluster on page 53. Write it at the center of a new page, and start clustering again.

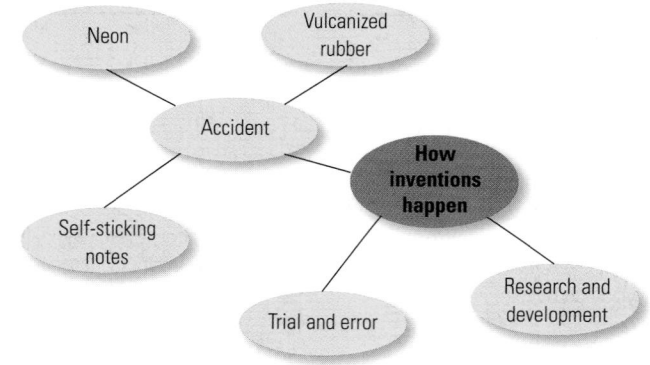

Viewing and Representing

Writing Invisibly

Students with access to a computer might experiment with "invisible writing." They can follow the same procedure suggested in the looping activity with one exception. They freewrite at the computer with the monitor turned off, freeing them from concern over spelling and other errors. Afterward, they can boldface the words or ideas they will use in their next "invisible writing" session.

Write to Find a Topic

As you study this unit, you will be writing an investigative report. Use the prewriting methods discussed in this lesson to choose two or three possible topics for your report.

PURPOSE To select writing topics
AUDIENCE Yourself
LENGTH 1-2 pages

WRITING RUBRICS To find a topic, you should

- freewrite and use different sources to collect ideas
- brainstorm to generate related ideas
- use looping and clustering to narrow your focus

Edna Jackson, *Kaaswoot,* 1983

Viewing and Representing

COOPERATIVE LEARNING In a small group, study the self-portrait on this page. The artist is of Native American and European descent. How does the portrait reflect the artist's dual heritage? Use your group's ideas to write a paragraph each about the painting.

Grammar Link

Capitalize proper nouns.

Rewrite the following sentences, adding or dropping capital letters as necessary.

1. The aztec built majestic Temples and Palaces in Central Mexico.
2. They built the City of Tenochtitlán on a swampy Island in lake Texcoco.
3. By the Fifteenth Century, this city was one of the largest in the World.

See Lesson 20.2, pages 715–721.

Cross-Curricular Activity

ART Visit the Web site for the National Portrait Gallery. Write a paragraph comparing and contrasting two portraits. How is each figure shown (standing, seated, a head-and-shoulders view)? Does the figure hold anything? What do you learn about the subject by looking at the portrait?

Assess

Evaluation Rubrics

Write to Find a Topic

Have each student evaluate his or her process as follows:

- How did freewriting help to collect ideas?
- How did clustering or brainstorming help generate ideas?
- How did looping and clustering help to narrow the focus?

See also *Writing Assessment & Evaluation Rubrics.*

Viewing and Representing

Commend paragraphs about narrowed topics such as

- a comparison of Jackson's dual heritage with the student's own
- a description of the mask
- a "mask" the student wears

Cross-Curricular Activity

Responses to the portraits should

- describe the portrait specifically
- explain how physical details imply other characteristics

Reteaching

📁 *Composition Reteaching,* p. 8

Enrichment

📁 *Composition Enrichment,* p. 8

🔧 Use *Fine Art Transparencies* 7–12 for enrichment activities also.

Close

Have a discussion with students about narrowing a topic in which you compare the process to some other activity. For example, you might compare narrowing a topic in writing with zeroing in on an object with a microscope. Scientists adjust their lens to get a close-up view of a small object, just as writers focus on details to narrow their topics.

Grammar Link

Answers

Only the following words should be capitalized:

1. The, Aztec, Mexico
2. They, Tenochtitlán, Lake Texcoco
3. By

Viewing the Art

Edna Jackson, *Kaaswoot,* 1983.
Edna Jackson created *Kaaswoot* with handmade cedar paper, prismacolor pencil on black silk, and a beaded box. The sculpture, 14 1/2 by 8 1/2 by 2 inches, belongs to the artist's personal collection.

Focus

Lesson Overview

Objective

- To formulate a main idea statement suitable for a particular topic, purpose, and audience

Skills

- clarifying purpose; identifying audience; using main idea

Critical Thinking

- analyzing; evaluating

Listening and Speaking

- discussing; evaluating

Bellringer
Daily Language Activity

When students enter the classroom, have this assignment on the board: *Write a brief cereal commercial aimed at young children.*

Grammar Link to the Bellringer

Have students check whether they used simple sentences and easy-to-understand vocabulary in writing for a young audience.

See also *Daily Language Practice*

Motivating Activity

Ask students to pretend they are advertisers and tell what they might say in a cereal commercial aimed at preschool children. Then ask how students would change the commercial to target teenagers or fitness buffs. How would a commercial for a brand-new cereal need to be different from one for a well-known product? Point out that the nature of their commercial would depend on both their target audience and their purpose. Stress that the same is true of any piece of writing.

2.3
Prewriting: Identifying Purpose and Audience

Knowing your purpose and audience will help determine your main idea, or what you want a piece of writing to say. Mike had different purposes and audiences in mind as he wrote the postcards below.

Decide on Your Purpose

Deciding on a purpose will help you determine what to include in your writing. To clarify your purpose, answer these questions:

1. Why do I want to write about this topic?
2. Is my purpose to describe? Inform? Narrate? Amuse? Persuade?
3. Will I have more than one purpose in this piece of writing?

> Purpose: to persuade
> *What is Mike's purpose in writing to his parents? How do his details reflect his purpose and audience?*

> Purpose: to inform

> Purpose: to describe
> *How does Mike select details that relate to his friend's experience as he describes the Hall of Fame?*

Pro Football Hall of Fame
CANTON, OHIO

Dear Mom and Dad,
My visit with the Andersons is going well. Yesterday we visited the Football Hall of Fame. Today we're going to an art museum. I think it would be worthwhile for me to stay all summer! Let me know if it's ok. Send money! Mike

Dear Grandfather,
Ever since you told me about the Pro Football Hall of Fame, I've wanted to see it, and today I got my chance. I'll tell you all about it when I get home.
Michael

Dear Todd,
The Hall of Fame was just as great as we thought. There are all sorts of displays, recordings, and videos. One display shows the old leather headgear the players used to wear. We'd die if we had to wear those things.
Mike

Post Card
Todd Lyons
211 Dixon Drive
Brownsville, TX 78520

Post Card
Mrs. George Ruiz
2008 Finley Street
Houston, TX 77001

Resource Manager

Planning Resources
- *Lesson Plans*

Transparencies
- *Bellringer*
- *Daily Language Practice*
- *Fine Art 7–12*
- *Two-Minute Skill Drill*
- *Writing Process 2–8*

Other Print Resources
- *Composition Enrichment, p. 9*
- *Composition Practice, p. 9*
- *Composition Reteaching, p. 9*
- *Cooperative Learning Activities*

- *Listening and Speaking Activities pp. 6–8*
- *Thinking and Study Skills, pp. 13, 17, 23*
- *Writing Across the Curriculum*
- *Writing Assessment and Evaluation Rubrics*

Identify Your Reader

Your audience is anyone who will be reading your writing. Sometimes you write just for yourself. More often, however, you write to share information with others. The audience may include a few friends or family members, your classmates, or the population at large.

The writers of both excerpts below wrote with a similar purpose, to inform. Note that each had a different audience in mind.

The Writing Process

Literature Model

[The sports hero] exhibits that complete skill to which the amateur vainly aspires. Instead of being looked upon as a servile and ignoble being, because of the very perfection of his physical efforts, as the Athenians in Socrates' time looked upon the professional athletes and dancers, this new hero represents the summit of the amateur's effort.

Lewis Mumford, *Technics and Civilization*

> What words and details does Mumford use to appeal to his scholarly, academic audience?

Literature Model

Pro football players are adults who fly through the air in plastic hats and smash each other for a living. I now know a bunch of them, and I think they are good folks.

Roy Blount Jr., *About Three Bricks Shy of a Load*

> The writer's informal tone and choice of details appeal to a general-interest audience.

As you write, consider these questions about your audience:

1. Who will my audience be: What do I want to say to them?
2. What do my readers already know about my topic?
3. What types of information will interest my audience?

Journal Writing

Reread one sample of your recent writing and jot down your thoughts about these questions: How could I use the same ideas to write for a different purpose? How could I make this appeal to a different audience?

Teach

Writing a Main Idea Statement

Some students may have difficulty in using abstract reasoning. Display a familiar object—an athletic shoe, for example. Suggest an audience, such as a shoe-store customer, an athlete, a parent, or a young child. Lead students in brainstorming purposes for writing about the object for each audience. Students can then choose an audience and purpose and write a main idea statement they could use in writing about the object.
L1

Two-Minute Skill Drill

List these types of writing on the board and have students suggest an appropriate audience for each.

doctoral thesis

court opinion

eulogy

acceptance speech

See also *Two-Minute Skill Drill Transparency 2.3*

Journal Writing Tip

Restructuring Suggest students discuss their writing pieces with partners to decide what they want to say, to whom, and why.

Teach

Writing Main Idea Statements

Discuss with students the elements that make up a strong main idea statement as described on student page 58. Students who struggle with the main-idea concept might benefit from taking a look at magazine ads, which typically focus on one big idea that is recognizable because of large, bold type. The purpose and audience for such ads are easy to identify. Afterward, ask volunteers to choose an item and develop a main idea statement for an ad. Their purpose would be to sell the product, and they can specify an audience. **L2**

Additional Resources

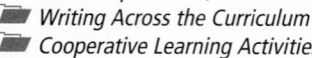 For further stimuli for writing, see *Fine Art Transparencies*, 7–12.

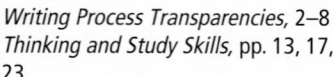 *Writing Across the Curriculum*
Cooperative Learning Activities

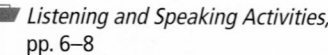 *Writing Process Transparencies*, 2–8
Thinking and Study Skills, pp. 13, 17, 23
Listening and Speaking Activities, pp. 6–8
Composition Practice, p. 9

The Writing Process

Write Your Main Idea Statement

With a topic, a purpose, and an audience in mind, you're almost ready to write. In the next step ask yourself, What's the most important idea? Answer the question in one sentence. That sentence will be your main idea statement.

No matter how big or small your writing project is—a single paragraph or a twenty-page research paper—you should write a main idea statement. It will tell what you want your entire piece to say and will help you choose appropriate details for your topic. Later, as you draft your piece, it will keep your writing on track. As the chart below indicates, the main idea statement is central to any writing; all other ideas depend on it.

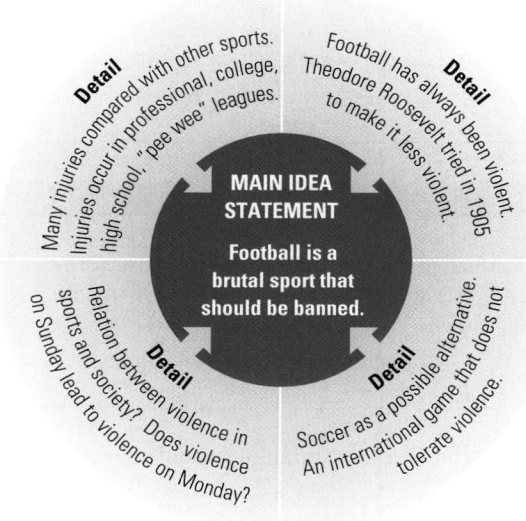

Now consider a different main idea statement about football: *Football is a game built on teamwork, discipline, and strategy.* To what audience might this topic appeal? What kinds of details could you use to develop the main idea?

Ask yourself the following questions as you develop your main idea statement for any piece of writing:

1. What point do I want to make?
2. Will my audience be interested in the idea?
3. Do I need to narrow my topic further?

MEETING INDIVIDUAL NEEDS — English Language Learners

Developing a Main Idea

Encourage students who have trouble writing in English to continue to work on their writing. However, to have a free flow of ideas when they use prewriting techniques such as listing, questioning, or writing a main idea-statement, students may occasionally want to use words and phrases from their first language. You or a peer editor can help students translate these ideas into English.

Identify Purpose and Audience

Before you make the final choice of topic for your investigative report, decide on your audience and your purpose.

PURPOSE To identify audience and purpose; to select a topic

AUDIENCE Yourself

LENGTH 1-2 pages

WRITING RUBRICS To focus your topic ideas, you should

- identify your purpose. Is it to point out a problem? encourage people to take some action? provide background information?
- identify your audience. Is it your classmates? your family? a club? readers of the school newspaper?

Listening and Speaking

COOPERATIVE LEARNING In a small group, brainstorm ideas for changes or improvements in your community. Then choose one idea about which you could write. Discuss how your writing might vary for different audiences. For example, how would you approach a good friend versus the CEO of a major corporation? Possible audiences to consider in your discussion include the following: the principal, your parents, the mayor, a restaurant owner, a friend, or the president of the United States. As a group, prepare a few samples that show how your writing would vary depending on the audience. Present the samples to the class.

Grammar Link

Tailor your writing style to your audience.

When you write for a young audience, try using simple sentences and easy-to-understand vocabulary.

Rewrite the following sentences into simple sentences. Change wording as necessary.

1. Despite the fact that writing can be complex and time-consuming, it is frequently quite enjoyable.
2. Acquaintances who no longer live in the area savor receiving letters from me.
3. Now and again I take advantage of e-mail, which is extraordinarily fast, to communicate with my friends.
4. My older sibling has created a screenplay that is being filmed in San Antonio, Texas.

See Lesson 13.3, pages 545–546.

Using Computers

On the Internet locate speeches by past leaders, such as Franklin D. Roosevelt and Martin Luther King Jr. Determine the intended audience and the purpose of the speech. With a partner, discuss how the speaker used language to reach the intended audience.

The Writing Process

Assess

Evaluation Rubrics

Identify Purpose and Audience

Use these criteria when evaluating your students' responses. Writing should have

- a specific audience—classmates, family, newspaper—identified
- a specific statement of purpose formulated

See also *Writing Assessment & Evaluation Rubrics.*

Listening and Speaking

Evaluate the samples on the following:
- Are the recommendations reasonable?
- Are the main ideas clear?
- Are the recommendations clear?
- Are the recommendations persuasive?
- Is the tone of the recommendations respectful?

Reteaching

📂 *Composition Reteaching*, p. 9

Enrichment

📂 *Composition Enrichment*, p. 9

Close

Students might examine editorials from the school or local newspaper and identify the editorials' messages by writing main idea statements.

Grammar Link

Answers

(Answers will vary; suggestions follow.)

1. Writing is difficult and takes a lot of time. Writing is also fun.
2. Sometimes friends move away. I write letters to them. My friends like letters.
3. Sometimes I use e-mail to communicate with my friends. It speeds up communication a lot.
4. My older brother has written a screenplay. It is being filmed in San Antonio, Texas.

Focus

Lesson Overview

Objective
• To explore a topic by listing factual, creative, and personal questions about it

Skills
• observing closely; listing details; asking questions; using outside sources; analyzing the topic

Critical Thinking
• discussing; analyzing; classifying; evaluating

Listening and Speaking
• evaluating; questioning; note taking; discussing

Bellringer
Daily Language Activity

When students enter the classroom, have this assignment on the board: *Write a few sentences about topics you would like to investigate and write about.*

Grammar Link to the Bellringer

Have students rewrite their sentences so they have compound subjects joined by *and*.

See also *Daily Language Practice*

Motivating Activity

Ask students to share the topics they want to investigate. They may need to learn about something for a class, or they may have a personal interest in a topic, such as what summer job to apply for. Allow students five minutes to list details, and then another five minutes to list questions about their topics. Explain that students have just used two valuable techniques for exploring a writing topic.

The Writing Process

LESSON 2.4

Prewriting: Exploring a Topic

After you've identified a writing topic, explore it further by listing and organizing details, asking questions, and doing research.

Observe Closely

One good starting point for exploring a topic is simply to observe closely and list the details you see. What do you observe in this photo of 1960s students that reflects the social unrest of the time? List the details that you observe.

The next step is to arrange the items on your list into categories. For example, the details you listed about the photograph might fit into broad categories such as clothes, hairstyles, body language, and attitudes. The categories you choose depend on the details you observe and your writing goal. If you were going to describe a place—say, the campus where these students attended school—you might arrange your details according to the five senses, what you smell, hear, see, taste, and touch.

Resource Manager

Planning Resources
• *Lesson Plans*

 Transparencies
• *Bellringer*
• *Daily Language Practice*
• *Fine Art 7–12*
• *Two-Minute Skill Drill*
• *Writing Process 2–8*

 Other Print Resources
• *Composition Enrichment,* p. 10
• *Composition Practice,* p. 10
• *Composition Reteaching,* p. 10
• *Cooperative Learning Activities*

• *Listening and Speaking Activities* pp. 6–8
• *Thinking and Study Skills,* pp. 3–5, 11, 15, 17, 23
• *Writing Across the Curriculum*
• *Writing Assessment and Evaluation Rubrics*

Ask Questions

Asking questions is another way of exploring a topic and is central to any investigation. Questions help you get at the facts of the matter. They also help you see your topic in new ways and probe its meaning. Jot down questions about your topic in a notebook or journal. Notice the three kinds of questions listed below.

Questions for Exploring a Topic

Factual	Creative	Personal

Factual

1. What did 1960s young people wear? Did they all dress alike?
2. What music did they listen to? What books and magazines did they read?
3. What events and causes were important to them, and why?
4. How are they similar to kids today? How are they different?

Creative

1. How do today's styles in clothing and music reflect the 1960s?
2. Would I feel at home in the 1960s? Why or why not?
3. What if one of the kids in the photo were my parent?
4. What kind of conversation might I have with a student from the 1960s? What would we ask each other?

Personal

1. Why do I want to know about 1960s students?
2. What can I learn from them? What could they learn from me?
3. What causes did 1960s kids support? Were their causes similar to mine?
4. What about their dreams?

Journal Writing

Observe something in the room around you and record details about it. Use one or more of the techniques explained in this lesson to find out as much as possible about the essential qualities of your subject.

Teach

Using Photographs

Point out that photographs and art can provide writing ideas as well as details to support those ideas. Ask students to look at the photo on student page 60 and to discuss the details in the photo.

- long hair and beards
- casual, unconventional clothing
- flowers, worn or carried by both males and females
- guitar (folk music and protest songs were popular) **L2**

Identifying Question Types

Discuss the uses of each type of question identified on student page 61 by asking students for additional examples. Some students might benefit from creating an easy-to-use chart that lists tags or starter phrases that distinguish each type of question. For example: "How do I feel about . . .?" (personal); "What if . . .?" (creative); "Who/What/ When/Where/How . . .?" (factual). **L2**

Two-Minute Skill Drill

Have students list the three kinds of questions for exploring a topic and give one example of each.

See also *Two-Minute Skill Drill Transparency 2.3*

Journal Writing Tip

Observing and Restructuring
Suggest that students structure their lists into five separate lists, one for each of the senses.

Teach

Organizing Information

Students who grasp both concrete and abstract concepts easily will see that the idea tree is a kind of pictorial outline. Explain that the parts of an idea tree can be arranged to form a traditional outline. Discuss other types of diagrams, such as comparison charts (p. 237), pie charts (p. 246), and flow charts (p. 46) that students might find helpful as tools for organizing information. **L3**

 Cross-reference: Library Resources

For more information on finding and gathering information, refer students to Unit 23, pp. 799–810.

Additional Resources

Writing Process Transparencies, 2–8
Writing Across the Curriculum
Cooperative Learning Activities

For further stimuli for writing, see *Fine Art Transparencies, 7–12.*
Thinking and Study Skills, pp. 3–5, 11, 15, 17, 23
Listening and Speaking Activities, pp. 6–8
Composition Practice, p. 10

The Writing Process

Search Out Information

Outside sources of reliable information are important when you explore a topic. These sources include encyclopedias, books, articles, and a wide range of formal and informal sources. Are there Web sites, photographs, filmstrips, records, videos, TV programs, interviews, field trips, or other resources that would give you information about your topic? The more creative you are in searching out information, the more likely you are to find full and satisfactory answers to the questions about your topic.

Create an Idea Tree

As you gather your information, you may begin to wonder how it all fits together. Creating an idea tree can help you analyze your topic. An idea tree like the one below can often make the relationships among the parts of your topic stand out and may even show you a plan for organizing your writing.

MEETING INDIVIDUAL NEEDS — English Language Learners

Making Lists and Questioning

Assure students who have difficulty writing in English that their exploratory lists and questions are part of their prewriting; students will not be graded for spelling or grammar. Help students understand that listing and questioning are techniques intended to help them find out what they might say about their topic, how to make their topic personal, and what it is about the topic that intrigues them.

Make a Plan for Writing

Look at the topic you chose for your investigative report, and begin to plan your writing.

PURPOSE To plan your writing
AUDIENCE Yourself
LENGTH 1-2 pages

WRITING RUBRICS To develop an effective writing plan, you should
- identify your main idea
- list your main points, questions, details, or incidents
- arrange your ideas legibly and in an order to suit your purpose

Cross-Curricular Activity

ART Study the painting on this page. What can you tell about the people pictured? How do you think the artist felt about these people? Write a list of questions you would like to answer by consulting an outside source for information about the artist, the place in which he lived, or the time period of the painting.

Vincent van Gogh, *The Potato Eaters*, 1885

Grammar Link

Make verb agree with compound subjects.

A compound subject that is joined by *and* is plural unless its parts are thought of as one unit, such as "ham and eggs."

Complete each sentence below by choosing the correct verb.

1. How (does, do) today's music and movies reflect the culture of the 1990s?
2. Both Tom Hanks and Brad Pitt (is, are) actors who are popular with teenagers.
3. Salsa and chips (is, are) a favorite snack.
4. The balanced budget amendment and health care reform (is, are) controversial issues.
5. By the mid-1990s, the House of Representatives and the Senate (was, were) controlled by the Republicans.

See Lesson 16.5, page 620.

Viewing and Representing

ELEMENTS OF DESIGN Find out more about van Gogh's paintings, including *The Potato Eaters.* How does he use light, color, and texture, and how does this change in his later work? View his works. Research his techniques and the topics he chose. Record notes and write a research summary.

Assess

Evaluation Rubrics

Make a Plan for Writing

Use these criteria when evaluating your students' writing. Does the student
- identify the main idea?
- list main points, questions, details, or incidents?
- arrange them in an order that fits the purpose?

See also *Writing Assessment & Evaluation Rubrics.*

Cross-Curricular Activity

Students' questions should reflect observation of details in the painting and should center on the artist, the place he lived, or the time period of the painting.

Viewing and Representing

Students' summaries should show evidence of having carefully observed van Gogh's techniques and topics.

Reteaching

📁 *Composition Reteaching,* p. 10

Enrichment

📁 Composition Enrichment, p. 10

📋 Use *Fine Art Transparencies,* 7–12, for enrichment activities also.

Close

Suggest that students discuss the consequences of not investigating important issues. Ask students to brainstorm examples of problems that result from missing or incomplete information—such as the unhappy discovery that you helped to elect an incompetent person for a government office.

Grammar Link

Answers
1. do
2. are
3. is
4. are
5. were

Viewing the Art

Vincent van Gogh, *The Potato Eaters,* 1885
Dutch painter Vincent van Gogh (1853–1890) portrayed people as he saw them—poverty-stricken and miserable, living drab, relentlessly routine lives. Nowhere is this more evident than in *The Potato Eaters.*

Focus

Lesson Overview

Objective
- To record information from interviews in a form accessible for a composition project

Skills
- planning an interview; writing and asking questions; taking notes

Critical Thinking
- analyzing; generating new information; categorizing; evaluating; synthesizing

Listening and Speaking
- discussing; interviewing; note taking; evaluating answers

Bellringer
Daily Language Activity

When students enter the classroom, have this assignment on the board: *Write two questions you would like to ask your favorite actor or actress, as well as the answers you think he or she might give.*

Grammar Link to the Bellringer

Have students set off the answers they just wrote with quotation marks.

See also *Daily Language Practice*

Motivating Activity

Play a taped interview by a popular TV talk-show host. Then ask students what they learned about the guest and how the interviewer obtained that information. Point out that even though the interview may have seemed impromptu, the interviewer had most likely planned the questions to draw out the desired information.

The Writing Process

Prewriting: Interviewing

Interviewing someone is often the best way to get information on a topic. Successful interviews begin with carefully thought-out and organized questions.

Go Straight to the Source

An interview is a focused, structured encounter for which the interviewer has a topic and purpose firmly in mind. Interviewing is a vital part of prewriting for many writing projects, and the firsthand information you collect will add liveliness to your writing.

Journalist Wayne Swanson researched the Native American heritage of southern California for a newspaper feature story. His investigation took him to an archaeologist who is an expert on the subject. Here are some of the questions Swanson asked, along with their answers.

Q. How did you get involved in studying the Native Americans of southern California?

A. When I was in college, I went on an archaeological dig outside San Diego. When we discovered some artifacts, I felt an immediate link with the people. I wanted to learn more about them.

> This question shows that Swanson has already done some research on his topic. But he wants to know more.

Q. Why has so little been written about them?

A. They did not fit the popular image of warriors on horseback. They had few confrontations with white people. Instead, they had a stable, self-sufficient culture.

Q. What is notable about these early Native Americans?

A. They are renowned for basketry and pottery making. They also had a remarkable knowledge of plants and pharmacology.

Resource Manager

Planning Resources
- *Lesson Plans*

Transparencies
- *Bellringer*
- *Daily Language Practice*
- *Fine Art 7–12*
- *Two-Minute Skill Drill*
- *Writing Process 2–8*

Other Print Resources
- *Composition Enrichment*, p. 11
- *Composition Practice*, p. 11
- *Composition Reteaching*, p. 11
- *Cooperative Learning Activities*

- *Listening and Speaking Activities* pp. 6–8
- *Thinking and Study Skills*, pp. 4, 11, 13, 23, 25
- *Writing Assessment and Evaluation Rubrics*

Ask Questions and Take Notes

As Swanson's interview shows, the success of an interview depends on asking good questions. Keep these points in mind when you prepare your interview questions:

1. Ask questions that require more than *yes* or *no* answers.
2. Ask questions that are clearly worded and easily understood.
3. Ask questions that relate directly to your topic and purpose.

DO BACKGROUND RESEARCH Before an interview you should do preliminary research about the person and the topic. Informed questions will get you informative answers. What do the questions below tell you about the interviewer's preparation?

> Q: Why do we have so little evidence today of early Native American settlements?
>
> A: They built few permanent structures and had few material possessions. In this warm climate they had no need for elaborate housing or warm clothing.

> Q: How did the arrival of the Spanish affect the Native American people?
>
> A: The Spanish impact was devastating. It drastically reduced the population. The Native Americans lacked immunity to common European diseases, and many died of smallpox, measles, and influenza.

Notes

Warm climate
didn't need sturdy
    houses, warm clothes

"The Spanish impact
    was devastating."
Many died of European
    diseases.

DON'T WRITE EVERY WORD You want to capture your subject's ideas, but you don't have to become a human tape recorder. Listen carefully, and write down words and phrases that summarize the ideas. When the person makes a point in a way that stands out, write the exact words and enclose them in quotation marks. Even if you use a tape recorder, note taking can help you organize and summarize the information.

Journal Writing

Think about an interview you've read in a newspaper or magazine or watched on television. What questions helped to make the interview effective? List them.

Teach

Using the Model

Ask students to compare the archaeologist's answers with Swanson's notes. Why did Swanson write the exact words "The Spanish impact was devastating"? (It is likely he wanted to quote this dramatic statement later in the article.) Discuss the kinds of statements an interviewer likes to record as direct quotes (strong or controversial opinions, summarizing statements, emotional or humorous comments). **L2**

Planning Topics and Interviews

Ask students to work with partners to think of possible interview topics and candidates. Encourage them to investigate their own cultural heritages by each interviewing someone who is knowledgeable about it. Both professional and amateur experts are easy to find. Good sources are local colleges and universities, and newspaper articles about people, shops, or activities that relate to the culture. **L3**

Two-Minute Skill Drill

Have students list the three points to keep in mind when they prepare interview questions.

See also *Two-Minute Skill Drill Transparency 2.5*

Journal Writing Tip

Evaluating Before directing students to complete the journal activity, suggest that they look for questions that probe deeply into an issue and questions that take advantage of on-the-spot opportunities to explore the why's and wherefore's.

Teach

Ordering Questions

Point out to students that interviewers need to consider categories of questions and the order in which to ask them. Ask students to think of categories they could use to order questions for a personal interview, such as early life, education, career, or future plans. Ask students to think of alternative methods of arrangement, including time order, order of importance, and cause and effect. **L2**

Preparing Questions

Have students observe and participate in an interview and analyze and evaluate it later. Invite a guest to visit your classroom to be interviewed by one or several students. The guest could be a school employee or someone with an interesting career or position in the community. Have the panel members prepare for the interview by doing background research on the person or the type of work he or she does and formulating their questions in advance. **L3**

Additional Resources

 Writing Process Transparencies, 2–8
Cooperative Learning Activities

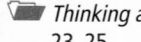 For further stimuli for interviewing, see *Fine Art Transparencies,* 7–12.
Thinking and Study Skills, pp. 4, 11, 13, 23, 25
Listening and Speaking Activities, pp. 6–8
Composition Practice, p. 11

The Writing Process *(vertical sidebar)*

ASK ON-THE-SPOT QUESTIONS Some of the best questions can't be planned in advance. Listen closely to the subject's answers and be aware of opportunities to ask follow-up questions. Notice in the graphic below the insight that is lost when the interviewer plows ahead with a prepared question instead of considering a follow-up question.

Prepared question: What is the state of the Native American heritage today?

A. Some aspects of Native American language and customs are lost with each generation. But the culture is resilient.

 Not This

Next prepared question: How many Native Americans live in southern California

A. Many. About ten thousand in San Diego County alone.

 But This

 ?

Follow-up question: What do you mean by "resilient"?

A. The Native American culture never dies. It just reinvents itself.

? Another follow-up question

FOLLOW THESE STEPS The following chart can help you plan and carry out an effective interview.

Set It Up	Listen More, Say Less	Get It All Down
• Request an interview, explain your purpose, and make an appointment. • Do background research about the person and the topic. • Write a list of focused questions. • Ask permission to tape the interview.	• Be polite, friendly, and businesslike. • Listen well, and try not to interrupt. Let the person explain fully. • Ask appropriate follow-up questions. • In taking notes, summarize the main ideas, and quote well-stated remarks.	• Listen to your tape. Review your notes. Then freewrite about your topic. • If some information is unclear, check back with the person for clarification. • Send the person a copy of your finished writing.

Listening and Speaking

Practicing Interviewing

Have students work with partners and take turns playing interviewer and interviewee. Have them choose topics they know about, such as an after-school job or sport. Tell students to record their practice interviews on audio tape. Afterward, discuss which questions led to the most interesting or informative answers, allowing students to draw conclusions about valuable interviewing techniques. Have students listen to their recorded interviews and decide which words, phrases, or questions they need to improve.

Interview to Gather Information

Plan and conduct an interview to gather information about the topic of your investigative report. After the interview, summarize your findings.

PURPOSE To plan and carry out an interview
AUDIENCE Yourself
LENGTH 1-2 pages

WRITING RUBRICS To conduct an interview, you should

- set up the interview and explain your purpose to the person you will interview (your subject)
- research to learn about the subject and the topic
- accurately record main points and quotations during the interview

Using Computers

You might want to write up your interview as a script. You could also prepare a dialogue for a mock interview to perform in front of the class. Use a word processing program to put your questions and answers in a script format—indent the text after the name of the person speaking. Make one person's dialogue italic, and the other's bold. Such visual distinctions make it easier to keep your place on the page.

Grammar Link

Enclose direct quotations in quotation marks.

When you take notes during an interview, enclose the subject's own exact words in quotation marks.

Rewrite any incorrect sentences below, adding quotation marks when they are needed.

1. In a recent interview, a telecommunications executive made this statement: The bottom line is that the information superhighway is changing the way we live.
2. She added that the information superhighway will dramatically affect the way we work and play.
3. The executive then went on to enumerate how the superhighway would transform the workplace.
4. What do you think will be the most significant change in the next five years? asked the interviewer.

See Lesson 21.9, pages 755–757.

Listening and Speaking

COOPERATIVE LEARNING Before conducting an interview for your investigative report, conduct a practice interview with a partner. Critique each other's questions and techniques to sharpen your performances.

The Writing Process

Assess

Evaluation Rubrics

Interview to Gather Information

Use these criteria when evaluating your students' writing. The summary and notes should reveal

- a clearly stated, specific purpose
- research about the interview subject and the topic
- clear thoughtful questions
- an accurate record of the main points and quotations

See also *Writing Assessment & Evaluation Rubrics.*

Using Computers

Look for consistency in styling of the dialogue.

Listening and Speaking

Students' critiques should offer constructive advice on questioning techniques and on methods of recording main points and quotations.

Reteaching

📁 *Composition Reteaching,* p. 11

Enrichment

📁 *Composition Enrichment,* p. 11

Close

Discuss with students specific uses for interviews and why information learned during an interview may not always be reliable.

Grammar Link

Answers

1. "The bottom line is that the information superhighway is going to change the way we live."
2. (no quotation marks)
3. (no quotation marks)
4. "What do you think will be the most significant change in the next five years?"

Focus

Lesson Overview

Objective
- To draft a piece of writing with a main idea and several supporting details

Skills
- writing a topic sentence; including supporting details

Critical Thinking
- main idea; categorizing; generalizing

Listening and Speaking
- discussing

Bellringer
Daily Language Activity

When students enter the classroom, have this assignment on the board: *Write a sentence in which you state your opinion of the most beautiful scenery you have ever seen. Then write several sentences that include details to support your opinion.*

Grammar Link to the Bellringer

Have students review their paragraphs and add commas after any introductory phrases or clauses they might have used.

See also *Daily Language Practice*

Motivating Activity

Ask students to look over the paragraph each has written and use it to define what a paragraph is (typical explanation: a group of related sentences that develop one topic, indicated by starting a new line with the first word indented). Have students find examples of paragraphs in their textbooks to see if their definition fits.

The Writing Process

Drafting: Writing a Paragraph

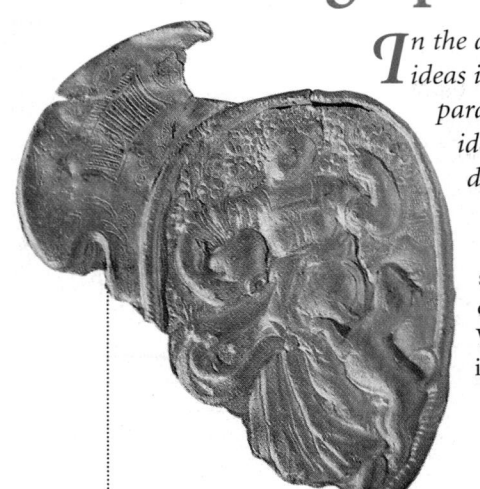

In the drafting stage, you write down your ideas in sentences and paragraphs. Each paragraph should have a topic or main idea sentence that is supported by details.

A paragraph is a group of related sentences that work together to develop one main idea. Notice how William Mathers states the main idea in each paragraph in the model below.

> The first sentence introduces the main idea: the author finds a small metal object. The supporting sentences describe the object in detail.

> The first sentence makes an observation about the nature of some items that were found. How do the following sentences support the first?

Literature Model

And then I catch a glimpse of metal—a small, luminous object poking from the sand. Probing carefully, I uncover a three-inch-wide fragment of hand-tooled gold plate. I am captivated by the image on the fragment: A woman in a swirling gown cradles a vase of flowers. Her left hand holds a cluster of roses. A small dog springs up at her feet. Floral designs embellish the fragment's border. . . .

Some items were touchingly personal. Along the edges of a small gold comb I made out "AÑOS 1618" inscribed in appliquéd gold dots. An abbreviated name, "DOÑA CATAL D GUSMA" (short for Doña Catalina de Guzmán) was also visible. Later research revealed that she was a widow residing in Manila in 1634. Had she been aboard the stricken vessel? What was her ultimate fate? No one knows.

William M. Mathers, *"Nuestra Señora de la Concepción"*

Resource Manager

Planning Resources
- *Lesson Plans*

Transparencies
- *Bellringer*
- *Daily Language Practice*
- *Fine Art 7–12*
- *Two-Minute Skill Drill*
- *Writing Process 2–8*

Other Print Resources
- *Composition Enrichment*, p. 12
- *Composition Practice*, p. 12
- *Composition Reteaching*, p. 12
- *Cooperative Learning Activities*

- *Listening and Speaking Activities* pp. 6–8
- *Thinking and Study Skills*, pp. 17, 22–23
- *Writing Across the Curriculum*
- *Writing Assessment and Evaluation Rubrics*

The Topic Sentence

In many paragraphs the main idea is stated in a topic sentence, and then all the details in the paragraph develop that idea. The wheel illustrates the vital role of a topic sentence in controlling the paragraph. All the details must not only be on the same topic, but must also help support the idea in the topic sentence.

In the literature model on the opposite page, the topic sentence comes at the beginning of each paragraph. Sometimes, though, the topic sentence comes at the end or in the middle. Wherever it is, it should tell two things: what your topic is and what your paragraph will say about it. Notice how Shella Calamba used a topic sentence to keep this paragraph on track.

Supporting detail

Supporting detail

Supporting detail

Topic Sentence

Supporting detail

Supporting detail

Supporting detail

Supporting detail

The Writing Process

Student Model

In investigating my mother's family history, I think I've discovered the origin of many of my own traits. My grandfather, who enjoyed listening to music as loud as any teenager today, willed me his love of music. My grandmother taught me to be responsible and open-minded. Because two of my aunts were teachers, I learned to value education. I inherited my dark, sarcastic sense of humor from one of my uncles. He would play bizarre practical jokes, and of many I was the victim. My interest in history and politics came from my great-grandfather, once the mayor of a small Philippine province. Finally, I credit my mother with teaching me to be independent, strong-minded, and determined in going after whatever goals I set.

Shella Calamba, Lincoln Park High School, Chicago, Illinois

> The topic sentence states the main idea, which Calamba has supported with details—in this case, specific examples.

Journal Writing

Examine some of your topic sentences in a piece of your recent writing. Experiment with ways you could make your topic sentences better.

Teach

Using the Model

After students read the model, ask them to identify Calamba's topic sentence (the first one) and point out details she used to develop her main idea. (She describes each relative's specific trait that she inherited.) **L2**

Applying and Extending

Help students see that what they are learning about writing can help them become more effective readers, too. Suggest they choose a passage from the text for a course such as biology or world history. Ask them to skim through it, looking for topic sentences, which usually begin or end a paragraph. Explain that starting a textbook reading assignment by skimming for topic sentences can increase comprehension later when students read the passage slowly and carefully. **L2**

Two-Minute Skill Drill

Have students list the two things that a topic sentence should tell.

See also *Two-Minute Skill Drill Transparency 2.6*

Journal Writing Tip

Identifying Main Ideas Before students complete the journal activity, suggest that they reread their paragraphs and identify main ideas by underlining the topic sentences. Have students check to see that each of the other sentences is a specific detail that relates to the broader topic in the topic sentence.

Teach

Sorting Sentences

Have students work in groups of two or three to write topic sentences about something related to school. Have them use graphics like the one on student page 69 and write their topic sentences in the center. As they think of supporting details, remind them that their details must prove, clarify, or expand on the main topic. After completing their graphics, they should check that their details are relevant and then rewrite them as paragraphs. **L1**

Generalizing

Students at home with abstract ideas might think of topic and supporting sentences in terms of general and specific ideas. They can discuss the topic sentence as a generalization about something, and the detail sentences as specific details supporting (or relating to, or proving) the generalization. Point out that in the model on student page 69, Calamba's topic sentence is a generalization. **L3**

Additional Resources

 For further stimuli for writing, see *Fine Art Transparencies*, 7–12.

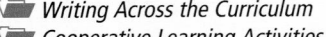 *Writing Process Transparencies*, 2–8
📁 *Writing Across the Curriculum*
📁 *Cooperative Learning Activities*
📁 *Thinking and Study Skills*, p. 17, 22–23
📁 *Listening and Speaking Activities*, pp. 6–8
📁 *Composition Practice*, p. 12

The Writing Process

Include Supporting Details

The details you include in your supporting sentences should prove, clarify, or expand on your main idea. The types of details that you decide to use will vary, but they will generally fall into the categories shown in the following chart.

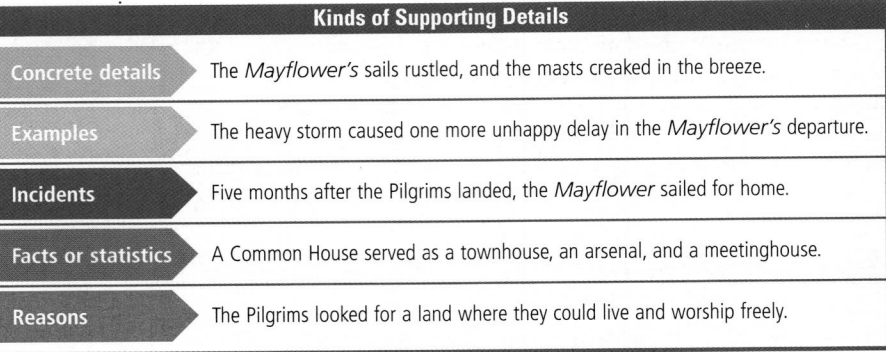

Kinds of Supporting Details	
Concrete details	The *Mayflower's* sails rustled, and the masts creaked in the breeze.
Examples	The heavy storm caused one more unhappy delay in the *Mayflower's* departure.
Incidents	Five months after the Pilgrims landed, the *Mayflower* sailed for home.
Facts or statistics	A Common House served as a townhouse, an arsenal, and a meetinghouse.
Reasons	The Pilgrims looked for a land where they could live and worship freely.

In some paragraphs all the supporting details are the same type, as in the student model on page 69. More frequently, a paragraph will contain two or more types of details, all working to support the main idea. In a family memoir, Bette Bao Lord used concrete details and reasons to develop a paragraph about her grandfather's grave site in China. How do the two kinds of details work together to create a sense of the president and the forever, rather than a sense of the past and time?

Literature Model

Concrete details describe the grave site.

What kind of details explain why the grave site is important to the family?

Grandfather sleeps in the earth near Suzhou. He has mountains to shelter him from the wind, green farm lands to gaze upon, the shade of a bamboo grove, the vast tranquillity of Tai Hu Lake, and the singing mists just over the horizon. And he has a name. It is carved in stone. This man was born and lived and died. The stone will not be plowed under or smashed or abandoned or carted away. It will stand. It will endure. For my grandfather. For us. For my Chinese roots. So when one day the children of my children and their children, who won't speak Chinese, look Chinese or know China, visit this lone ancestor they will feel Chinese, as I did that afternoon at his grave.

Bette Bao Lord, *Legacies: A Chinese Mosaic*

70 Unit 2 The Writing Process

Writing in the Real World

Deconstructing Media

Analyzing Magazines Ask your students to bring in their favorite magazines. Invite students to browse through them and choose a short article to read. Afterward, have each student examine a few paragraphs in his or her article and identify topic and supporting sentences. (Explain that some paragraphs don't include topic sentences—the main ideas are implied, not stated.) Help students see how supporting sentences build a paragraph, and paragraphs build an article.

Write a Draft

You have planned for your investigative report. Now it is time to begin your draft. Just begin writing. Skip every other line to leave room for changes. Don't worry about correctness. At this stage, you are still exploring what you want to say.

PURPOSE To create a draft
AUDIENCE Yourself
LENGTH 1-2 pages

WRITING RUBRICS To write an effective draft, you should

- use your prewriting notes for ideas
- get your ideas down on paper
- add ideas that support or relate to your topic sentences

Cross-Curricular Activity

SOCIAL STUDIES Locate a photograph of a person in the newspaper. Read the accompanying article about why the person is pictured. Imagine that you are going to interview the subject as part of an investigative report. What would you ask, and how would you use the information? Then make a list of questions for the interview.

Viewing and Representing

COOPERATIVE LEARNING With a partner, select a painting from this book. Where are the figures placed, and how are they presented? Notice the title. What main idea does the painting express? Take notes on your reactions to the painting. Together, compose a topic sentence based on your responses and write a paragraph using the details you discussed.

Grammar Link

Use commas after introductory phrases and clauses.

Shella Calambra said: *Because two of my aunts were teachers, I learned to value education.*

Rewrite the sentences below, adding commas where they are needed.

1. Working with the latest underwater equipment the salvage team explored the ocean bottom.

2. Because they were seeking whatever remained of the Spanish ship's cargo they spent over two years in the islands.

3. During the long search for the treasure many of the divers almost gave up hope.

4. By the time the project was completed the team had recovered almost 2,000 pieces of treasure.

5. Of the many items found a gold comb appliquéd with gold dots was the most interesting.

See Lesson 21.6, pages 743–751.

2.6 Drafting: Writing a Paragraph **71**

Assess

Evaluation Rubrics

Write a Draft

Use these criteria when evaluating your students' writing. The draft should show

- use of prewriting notes
- ideas put down on paper without too much attention to correctness

See also *Writing Assessment & Evaluation Rubrics.*

Cross-Curricular Activity

Students' list of questions should

- reflect an accurate reading and understanding of the article.
- stem from main issues or ideas mentioned in the article.

Viewing and Representing

Students with contrasting views of the painting's main idea or message could present their paragraphs as a mini-debate. Each debater could cite details in the painting to support his or her view.

Reteaching

📁 *Composition Reteaching*, p. 12

Enrichment

📁 *Composition Enrichment*, p. 12

✍ *Use Fine Art Transparencies* 7–12 for enrichment activities also.

Close

Have students discuss the different kinds of supporting details. Have students suggest which might work best with different kinds of writing.

Grammar Link

Answers
Add commas after the following words:
1. equipment
2. cargo
3. treasure
4. completed
5. found

Focus

Lesson Overview

Objective
- To draft unified, coherent paragraphs and to organize paragraph details in a meaningful whole

Skills
- ordering details; linking details

Critical Thinking
- identifying main idea; classifying

Listening and Speaking
- discussing; listening; reading aloud

Bellringer
Daily Language Activity

When students enter the classroom, have this assignment on the board: *Write a short paragraph describing possible subjects of jigsaw puzzles—geographical forms, portraits, works of art, and so forth.*

Grammar Link to the Bellringer

In the paragraphs they have written, have students use a semicolon to replace a comma and a coordinating conjunction that join two main clauses in a sentence, or have them rewrite the sentence as two sentences.

See also *Daily Language Practice*

Motivating Activity

Spread the pieces of a jigsaw puzzle on a large table. Allow time for students to try to put some of the pieces together. Afterward, ask how students went about it (grouping like colors, comparing shapes, trial and error). Then ask them to explain how writing is something like putting together the pieces of a jigsaw puzzle (grouping like or related ideas or aspects of a topic, often in one paragraph).

The Writing Process

Drafting: Organizing a Paragraph

Writers, like artists, put together pieces to create meaning. Just as the artist connected pieces of small snapshots to give his collage a meaning, a writer arranges and links details to express a main idea.

David Hockney, *Paul Explainir Pictures to Mie Kakigahara, 198*

Order the Details

As you prepare to write, you accumulate many unconnected ideas and pieces of information. Before you begin to write, your task is to sort out and organize your main ideas and the details that support them.

When you arrange details to express a main idea in writing, you can use one of several kinds of order.

SPATIAL ORDER One student, Mark Center, explored a department store on a busy day. Later, he described the store in spatial order, arranging the details according to their closeness to each other.

72 Unit 2 The Writing Process

Resource Manager

Planning Resources
- *Lesson Plans*

Transparencies
- *Bellringer*
- *Daily Language Practice*
- *Fine Art 7–12*
- *Two-Minute Skill Drill*
- *Writing Process 2–8*

📁 Other Print Resources
- *Composition Enrichment,* p. 13
- *Composition Practice,* p. 13
- *Composition Reteaching,* p. 13
- *Cooperative Learning Activities*

- *Listening and Speaking Activities* pp. 6–8
- *Thinking and Study Skills,* pp. 11, 13, 15, 17, 23
- *Writing Across the Curriculum*
- *Writing Assessment and Evaluation Rubrics*

Student Model

In the store's display window, two mannequins pose stiffly, showing off the season's newest styles. Inside, next to the window, an extravagant tropical tree reaches to the ceiling, its limbs spreading over racks of pastel plaid shorts and matching shirts. Behind the service counter, a salesman rings up a purchase for a distressed mother looking around for her child. The little girl is peering into a glass case filled with glittering jewelry. A few steps beyond, a thin, glamorous model tries to shower passing customers with perfume. A frantic father drags his two small boys onto an escalator, while they fuss and cry. The store's rear entrance is jammed with exhausted shoppers leaving and enthusiastic shoppers entering.

Mark Center, Jefferson Davis High School,
Montgomery, Alabama

> **Center begins with the display window in the front of the store and ends with the rear entrance.**

> **What words does Center use to help his readers locate objects in this scene?**

OTHER KINDS OF ORDER Spatial order works well for descriptive writing, but when your primary purpose is to narrate, you will usually choose chronological order. Be aware of other types of order as well.

Four Kinds of Order

Chronological	Importance	Cause and Effect	Compare and Contrast
To explain how a medical researcher went about her work, arrange the steps in time order.	To persuade people to donate money for cancer research, end with your strongest argument.	To convince someone that a certain drug is harmful, explain what happened to some of its users.	To explain a new and unfamiliar medical procedure, compare it with a familiar one.

Journal Writing

List possible topics that would be best described by each of the five kinds of order presented in this lesson.

Teach

Using the Model

Invite students to recall a busy department store shopping scene and to compare their mental pictures to the description in the model as you read it aloud. Help students spot words and phrases used to indicate location, such as "inside" and "behind the service counter." **L2**

Presenting a Demonstration

Provide students an opportunity to demonstrate something they do well—French-braid, for example. Ask them to demonstrate their skill for a partner, who can jot down the steps in order. Then partners can work together to complete the list of steps, making sure all necessary details are correctly described and sequenced. Partners can take turns teaching and learning new skills, first to each other and then, if they wish, to the class. **L1**

 Two-Minute Skill Drill

Have students list the five different kinds of order mentioned on this page.

See also *Two-Minute Skill Drill Transparency 2.7*

Journal Writing Tip

Using Different Kinds of Order If ideas are slow in coming, you might have students look at the examples on the student page and try to give similar examples.

Teach

Using the Model

Before students examine the model, ask them to listen as you read it aloud. Challenge them to identify the order Ballard used to organize the details about the *Bismarck* (chronological). What transitions and other verbal clues indicate this? (Students should notice time references such as "this time," "soon," "when," and "then at last.") **L2**

Making Smooth Transitions

To underscore the importance of smooth transitions, ask students to bring in newspaper or magazine articles and then circle all the transition words and phrases. To stress the importance of transitions, suggest students read their articles again, this time omitting all circled transition words. **L1**

Additional Resources

Writing Process Transparencies, 2–9
Writing Across the Curriculum
Cooperative Learning Activities

For further stimuli for paragraph writing, see *Fine Art Transparencies,* 7–12.
Thinking and Study Skills, pp. 11, 13, 15, 17, 23
Listening and Speaking Activities, pp. 6–8
Composition Practice, p. 13

The Writing Process

Link the Details

Mark Center arranged his details about the department store in a logical order, but he also connected his ideas smoothly to each other and to the main idea. Mark used transition words and phrases as signposts to point his reader in the right direction. Notice how transitions help you follow the ideas in the paragraph below. It describes the discovery of a German battleship, the *Bismarck,* that sank in the North Atlantic in 1941.

> Transition words and phrases—"soon," "then," "at last"—clarify the order of the events and add coherence. The words "this" and "these" add coherence by referring to something mentioned earlier.

Literature Model

We had been fooled by the debris from the clipper ship, but this time it would prove to be *Bismarck.* Following the trail northwestward, we soon encountered one of the battleship's four massive gun turrets. These had been held in place by the force of gravity, and they had fallen free when *Bismarck* capsized on her way to the bottom. Then at last on June 8 [1988] we came upon *Bismarck* herself, a great phantom shape resting in her grave three miles beneath the surface.

Robert D. Ballard, "The *Bismarck* Found"

The transition words and phrases you choose will depend on your topic and purpose. The chart below shows some transitions you can use to connect ideas that are related in different ways. Not every sentence, however, needs a transition word or phrase. Too many transitions will make your writing sound awkward and artificial.

Transition Words and Phrases	
Time	first, when, until, next, before, later, finally, afterward, that night, meanwhile, then
Location	above, below, here, underneath, inside, next to, around the corner, in the distance
Importance	first, mainly, primarily, last, most important, secondly, next
Cause and Effect	as a result, because, consequently, for that reason, therefore, then
Compare	similarly, like, just as, also, in the same way
Contrast	but, even so, however, in contrast, on the other hand, unlike, on the contrary

---

MEETING INDIVIDUAL NEEDS English Language Learners

Listing Words

A list of transition words and phrases might be useful for students learning English. Suggest that students make a chart like the one on this page and color code the category heads. Students can keep the list in their journal for quick reference. Encourage them to add to their chart as they discover other useful transitions.

Plan Ordered Paragraphs

Review the draft of your investigative report. Pick out two of the main ideas and plan an ordered paragraph for each.

PURPOSE To plan the structure of paragraphs
AUDIENCE Yourself
LENGTH 2 paragraphs

WRITING RUBRICS To develop an effective plan for your paragraphs, you should

- consider the order that best suits the content and purpose of the paragraphs
- arrange the supporting details in a suitable order
- use transitions to link details

Cross-Curricular Activity

HISTORY Look through the table of contents and the historical atlas of your U.S. history textbook. Locate information and maps showing the territorial growth of the country. Use the information and maps to write a report describing the expansion of the United States from 1783 to 1853. You can tell about the events in chronological order; in spatial order, tracing expansion from east to west or north to south; or in order of importance.

Viewing and Representing

VISUALS Present to the class the main points of your report from the Cross-Curricular Activity, along with a visual in the form of a map, a chart, or a time line. Make sure that your visual is clear and legible and that it clarifies information in your report.

Grammar Link

Use a semicolon to separate main clauses joined by a conjunctive adverb (such as *however, therefore*) or by an expression (such as *for example* or *in fact*).

In such sentences the expression or adverb is also set off by a comma:

Divers finally located the sunken ship; however, it took more than 40 years.

This type of sentence structure is often useful when you write using transitions.

Rewrite the following sentences, using correct punctuation.

1. Each supporting detail in a paragraph is like a piece of a jigsaw puzzle in fact it may have little meaning by itself.
2. Spatial order works well for descriptive writing however it seldom works for narrative writing.
3. The relationship between sentences needs to be made clear for that reason transition words are often used to tie ideas together.
4. Transition words clarify the order of supporting details therefore they add coherence to your writing.
5. Not every sentence needs a transition furthermore too many transitions may make your writing awkward.

See Lesson 21.5, page 740, and Lesson 21.6, pages 746–748.

2.7 Drafting: Organizing a Paragraph **75**

The Writing Process

Assess

Evaluation Rubrics

Plan Ordered Paragraphs

Use these criteria when evaluating your students' writing. Paragraphs should show

- suitable order for the purpose of the paragraph
- suitable order of supporting details
- use of transitions

See also *Writing Assessment & Evaluation Rubrics.*

Cross-Curricular Activity

Check reports for the following:
- a clear main idea
- clear organization
- appropriate supporting details
- appropriate transition words and phrases

Viewing and Representing

Students' visuals should
- be clear and legible
- be relevant to the main points in the students' reports
- clarify information in the reports

Reteaching

 Composition Reteaching, p. 13.

Enrichment

Composition Enrichment, p. 13

Close

Students might enjoy writing a review in which they compare and contrast a movie with its sequel. Each student should write a main idea statement supported by specific details from both films to complete his or her review.

Grammar Link

Answers
1. puzzle; in fact,
2. writing; however,
3. clear; for that reason,
4. details; therefore,
5. transition; furthermore,

Focus

Lesson Overview

Objective
- To revise a piece of writing, strengthening it for unity and coherence

Skills
- evaluating a draft; using peer reviewer comments; revising for unity and coherence

Critical Thinking
- evaluating; defining and clarifying

Listening and Speaking
- discussing; evaluating; reading aloud; listening

 Bellringer
Daily Language Activity

When students enter the classroom, have this assignment on the board: *Write a paragraph describing the clothes you would wear to a big party at your school.*

Grammar Link to the Bellringer

Have students look through the paragraph they have written for any misplaced or dangling modifiers.

See also *Daily Language Practice*

Motivating Activity

Ask whether students have ever dressed for a big occasion but then changed clothes because they weren't satisfied with their outfit. They tried a different shirt or sweater. Point out that they were revising their outfit—changing a shirt here or adding a jacket there until they were satisfied. That revision is like the revision that writers do, except that writers change words, not clothes.

The Writing Process

LESSON 2.8

Revising: Checking Unity and Coherence

*W*hen you revise your writing, work with a peer reviewer. Check unity; all sentences and details should help support the main idea. Also check for coherence, adding transitions to connect ideas.

All writers, even famous ones, keep trying to improve their writing. Here's how author E. B. White revised the conclusion of an essay about the day American astronauts first set foot on the moon.

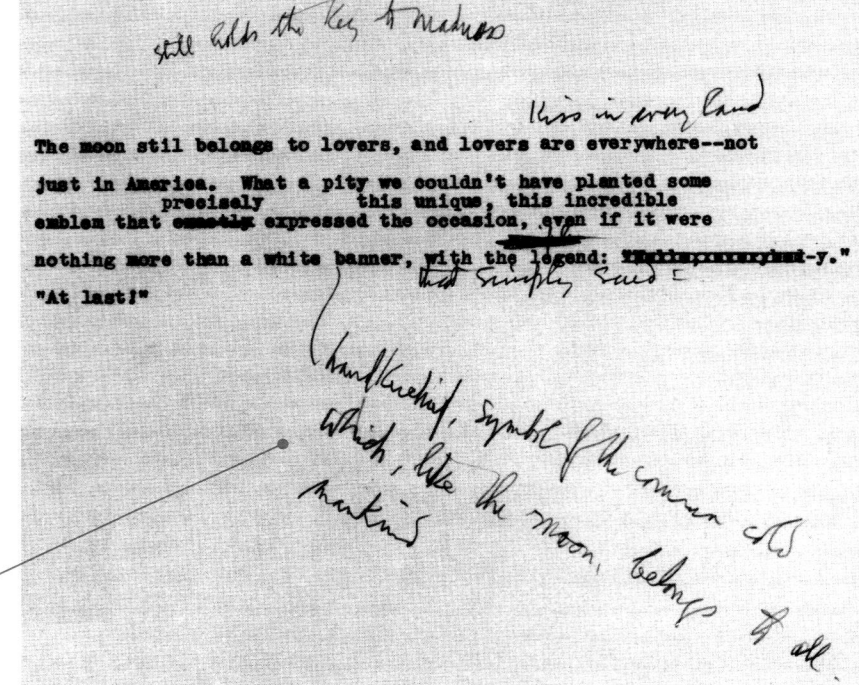

This humorous ending adds unity by supporting the idea that the moon belongs to everyone, not just Americans.

76 Unit 2 The Writing Process

Resource Manager

Planning Resources
- *Lesson Plans*

 Transparencies
- *Bellringer*
- *Daily Language Practice*
- *Fine Art 7–12*
- *Two-Minute Skill Drill*
- *Writing Process 2–8*

📁 Other Print Resources
- *Composition Enrichment,* p. 14
- *Composition Practice,* p. 14
- *Composition Reteaching,* p. 14
- *Cooperative Learning Activities*

- *Listening and Speaking Activities* pp. 6–8
- *Thinking and Study Skills,* pp. 23, 25, 27–28
- *Writing Assessment and Evaluation Rubrics*

Evaluate Your First Draft

Writers need to evaluate their first drafts objectively, at times ruthlessly. Often it helps to put your draft aside, returning to it a few days later. Then you can look at it objectively, asking yourself questions like the ones in the chart.

Your fellow writers are facing the same challenges, and you can help one another. A classmate can serve as a peer reviewer, who points out what works well in your draft and what does not. Here are three ways to work with a peer reviewer.

Questions to Consider
1. Is my writing interesting?
2. Is it easy to follow?
3. What do I like best about it?
4. How can I make it better?

Working with a Peer Reviewer

1. Read your first draft aloud; then discuss it with a peer reviewer.

2. Let your peer reviewer read your first draft silently, making comments right on the page.

3. Give your peer reviewer an evaluation form to fill out.

Journal Writing

How successful are you at evaluating your own work? List ways in which a peer reviewer can help you. What other strategies might help you revise more successfully?

Teach

Editing by Peers

To guide peer editor discussions, remind editors to read the piece carefully and take time to think about how it affects them. Is it interesting? Is the writing clear? Does the piece make sense? Do the parts hang together? Do the words put them "on the scene"? Encourage editors to begin with a positive statement before mentioning problems. Emphasize that it's all right to indicate where they see problems, with or without suggestions about how to correct them. **L2**

Tape-recording a Draft

Students who have difficulty with reading comprehension and analysis might benefit from tape-recording their draft before they revise it. Suggest that they replay the tape, draft in hand, listening and marking words or parts they want to change. After revising, they might want to retape a reading of their work and then play it for discussion with a peer editor. **L1**

Two-Minute Skill Drill

List the three steps in working with a peer reviewer.

See also *Two-Minute Skill Drill Transparency 2.8*

Journal Writing Tip

Assessing Take time to discuss students' prior experiences with self-editing and peer editing. If peer editing hasn't helped them improve their writing before, encourage them to give it another try, following the techniques suggested in this lesson. Bring out the writer's responsibility to recognize problems and to work hard to correct them.

Teach

Using the Model

As students examine the model, point out that the boxed questions are those of the peer reviewer; the changes and revisions in the article itself were made by the writer after reading the peer reviewer's comments. To illustrate, you might read each boxed item aloud and then ask a volunteer to find and read the corresponding revision. Help students see that in the second paragraph, moving the next-to-last sentence near the beginning of the paragraph helped correct a unity problem since both sentences are about the New York *World*. **L2**

Peer Editing Strategies

Sometimes teachers prefer to provide peer editors with evaluation forms that incorporate both checklist and short-answer items. A form might include questions such as "Did you feel a sense of satisfaction at the end?" and "What questions still need answers?" Allow space for the editor to add editorial comments. **L2**

The Writing Process

Use a Peer Reviewer's Comments

A peer reviewer can spot problems you may not be able to see. Notice how a peer reviewer's comments, shown in the margin, helped one writer.

> I'd like to know when Bly was born.

> I really like your introduction, but this detail about the name of the town doesn't seem to belong here.

> How did the editor come up with that name?

Nellie Bly, who was born *in 1867* in Cochran Mills, Pennsylvania, became the first celebrated woman investigative reporter in the United States. "Nellie Bly" was actually just her pen name. Her real name was Elizabeth Cochran. ~~I guess her family must have owned the town they lived in, because it had the same name.~~ Her pen name was suggested by the managing editor at The Pittsburgh Dispatch, where she was a reporter. *He took the name from a song by Stephen Foster.*

The paragraph below needed more extensive changes. Again, read the peer reviewer's suggestions in the margin. Which change corrected a problem in unity?

> I don't think this sentence belongs here.

> Shouldn't this sentence come after the first one?

> What were the conditions like?

In 1887, Nellie had joined the New York World. ~~At the Dispatch, she had written about slum life and divorce.~~ *Nellie* ~~She~~ pretended to be insane so that she could be admitted to Blackwell's Island, an insane asylum near New York. The World specialized in "muckraking," journalism that exposed corruption and scandal. She saw ~~the conditions~~ *the horrifying and inhumane treatment of the helpless inmates.* firsthand. Her story brought about reforms at Blackwell's Island.

MEETING INDIVIDUAL NEEDS — English Language Learners

Focusing

Students who have difficulty writing in English will be more successful if they have only one type of problem to look for as they edit a peer's writing. You might put the editing focus on the chalkboard in the form of a question and ask them to write their comments and suggestions on the writer's draft. Examples of questions are as follows: Is the writing organized in a way that is easy to follow? Which details support the main idea, and which do not?

Revise for Unity

In a unified paragraph, all sentences work together to support the main idea. When you revise, look at each paragraph to see whether every sentence relates to your main idea. Any sentences that introduce irrelevant ideas should be eliminated. The questions below will help you revise your paragraphs for unity.

Checking for Unity
1. Does my topic sentence accurately state what I want to say about my topic? Can it be more tightly focused?
2. Have I fully supported my topic sentence? Do I need to add details?
3. Do all supporting statements relate to the topic sentence? Should any be eliminated?

Examine the changes this writer made in response to her peer reviewer's comments. Which changes add unity to her writing? Which changes add detail to support her topic sentence?

Bly's ~~biggest~~ *greatest* triumph was her attempt to beat the record for traveling around the world set by Phileas Fogg in Jules Verne's novel <u>Around the World in Eighty Days</u>. ~~This popular book was made into an equally popular movie.~~ Bly sailed *from New York* on November 14, 1889. She rode ~~on many forms of~~ *ships, trains, sampans, horses, and burros* ~~transportation~~ as she circled the globe. She returned to New York 72 days, 6 hours, 11 minutes, and 14 seconds later. *She had beaten the record and given her readers a thrilling adventure to share.*

> This is an interesting fact, but I don't think it relates to your topic sentence.

> I think your readers would like to know what kinds of transportation.

Journal Writing

Look at a recent piece of writing and examine it for unity. In your journal experiment with ways you can change specific paragraphs to add unity to your writing.

Teach

Peer Editing Strategies

If the peer editor will be commenting directly on the page, suggest that students double-space their early drafts. Caution peer editors to resist making wording changes. Their job is to comment on the current draft and suggest changes that the writer will then consider making. Editors should make their comments in red, green, or other colored pencil or pen that is easily spotted. **L2**

Using Technology

Students who regularly use word processors will want to take advantage of the many options available for revision. One of these allows users to delete and move text at the press of a button. Students are likely to discover that they will do more and better revision as they become increasingly proficient at using their word-processing program. Invite student volunteers to explain to the class basic word-processing functions that can help to expedite revision. **L2**

Journal Writing Tip

Restructuring Some students may get sidetracked correcting errors in spelling and punctuation. Remind them that their focus in the revising stage is unity: they should make sure that the writing has one clear main idea and that the details clearly support the main idea. Suggest that they use the questions on this page as a guide.

The Writing Process

Cooperative Learning

Gathering Responses

Some students benefit from the responses of more than one peer editor, so you may wish to use a Roundrobin technique from time to time. Here's how it works. In small groups, students take turns reading their drafts aloud.

Group members comment on the drafts as writers take notes. Afterward, on their own, writers weigh the comments and make their revisions. Stress that a writer has the final choice about whether to accept the suggestions.

Teach

Learning Together

After students have revised their paragraphs, they might like to work in small groups to discuss the decisions they have made about peer review comments. Have each student explain why they chose to use or ignore suggestions. If reviewers suggested different possible revisions for the same problem, ask students why they chose one revision over another. **L3**

Additional Resources

Writing Process Transparencies, 2–8
Cooperative Learning Activities

For further stimuli for paragraph writing, see *Fine Art Transparencies*, 7–12.
Thinking and Study Skills, pp. 23, 25, 27–28
Listening and Speaking Activities, pp. 6–8
Composition Practice, p. 14

Revise for Coherence

In a coherent paragraph, sentences are clearly and logically connected to each other. Look over your writing to see whether your paragraphs flow smoothly from one idea to the next. These questions can help you revise your paragraphs for coherence.

Checking for Coherence
1. Does each sentence follow in a logical order?
2. Would another means of organizing my ideas work better?
3. Do transition words and phrases clarify the relationships between ideas?

Notice how changes in the following paragraph reflect the peer reviewer's comments shown in the margin. How do the changes add coherence to the writing?

> I think you're getting the story out of sequence here.

> This belongs near the sentence where you mention the contest.

While Bly circled the globe, the editors at the World made her journey a national story. In fact, when she returned to San Francisco, a special train waited to carry her to New York. In addition to daily stories about Bly's exploits, the World, aiming to increase its circulation, held a contest. Whoever came closest to guessing the time of her journey would win a prize. The contest worked. The World received almost one million contest entries from readers who were following Bly's race around the world. Steaming across the country, the train was met at every stop by large crowds, brass bands, and fireworks. What's more, the contest winner would get a trip to Europe. Bly's triumph sparked the nation's imagination.

Enrichment and Extension

Reviewing Across the Curriculum

Suggest that students bring to class something they are presently writing or working on for a specific purpose or audience—such as a book report, a history paper, a speech, or a poem. Allow them to work with a peer reviewer, in an editing group, or by themselves to revise their writing. As they work, circulate among them, listening and offering help when asked.

Revise for Effective Paragraphs

Take another look at the draft of your investigative report. Work with a peer reviewer. Then revise your paragraphs incorporating useful peer reviewer suggestions.

PURPOSE To revise for paragraph unity
AUDIENCE Yourself
LENGTH Changes on the draft

WRITING RUBRICS To revise for unity in each paragraph, you should

- make sure that all the sentences are about one main idea
- check to see whether the paragraph needs a topic sentence
- see whether transition words are needed

Using Computers

To check your use of transitions, convert all your transition words and phrases into boldface type. Check for awkward transitions, and see where transitions may be needed. When you have finished revising, convert the entire file back to regular text.

Grammar Link

When revising for clarity, look for misplaced or dangling modifiers.

In your sentences, place modifiers as close as possible to the words they modify so that your meaning is clear. For example, in the model on page 80 the writer states:

Steaming across the country, the train was met at every stop by large crowds, brass bands, and fireworks.

The reader understands that the modifier describes the train.

Rewrite the sentences below, correcting the misplaced or dangling modifier in each.

1. The main character in Jules Verne's novel *Around the World in Eighty Days,* reporter Nellie Bly wanted to break the travel record of Phileas Fogg.
2. She rode on horses and camels traveling around the world.
3. Beating Fogg's record, newspaper readers shared Bly's thrilling experience.
4. While circling the globe, the editors at the *World* made Bly's journey a front-page story.

See Lesson 18.7, pages 674–679.

Listening and Speaking

COOPERATIVE LEARNING To review paragraphs with a partner, try reading aloud first to evaluate content. After arranging your paragraphs as they will appear in the finished product, read the paragraphs aloud again and check for unity and coherence.

2.8 Revising: Checking Unity and Coherence **81**

Assess

Evaluation Rubrics

Revise for Effective Paragraphs

Use these criteria when evaluating your students' writing. Commend revisions that
- produce strong, focused topic sentences
- provide appropriate details
- achieve coherence with appropriate transitions

See also *Writing Assessment & Evaluation Rubrics.*

Using Computers

Students might need individual instruction in how to accomplish this activity. Student volunteers might show other students how to convert transition words and phrases into boldface type and back again to plain text.

Listening and Speaking

Students working in pairs should evaluate each other's paragraphs by listening carefully for a clear presentation of topic and checking for unity and coherence.

Reteaching

Composition Reteaching, p. 14

Enrichment

Composition Enrichment, p. 14

Close

Discuss with students the purpose of revising their writing and some of the techniques of revision. Help students see that revising their writing will make it more unified and coherent.

Grammar Link

Answers

(Answers will vary. The first five sentences in the exercise are provided as examples.)
1. The reporter Nellie Bly wanted to break the travel record of Phineas Fogg, the main character. . . .
2. Traveling around the world, she rode on horses and camels.
3. Newspaper readers shared Bly's thrilling experience of beating . . .
4. While Bly circled the globe, the editors at the *World* made . . .

Focus

Lesson Overview

Objective
- To identify and correct errors in a piece of writing

Skills
- editing to correct errors; proofreading for spelling and mechanics

Critical Thinking
- identifying; evaluating

Listening and Speaking
- discussing

 Bellringer
Daily Language Activity

When students enter the classroom, have this assignment on the board: *Imagine that you are looking into your closet. Which items could you throw away? Which items should you fix or repair? Write a short paragraph in which you describe your closet.*

Grammar Link to the Bellringer

Have students review the paragraphs they have written for subject-verb agreement.

See also *Daily Language Practice*

Motivating Activity

You might begin by displaying a pair of shoes—one clean and polished, the other dusty and dirty. Ask students to tell which shoe presents a more favorable image and why. Point out that editing one's writing is much like polishing shoes: writers polish their writing to make it more presentable to an audience.

LESSON
2.9

Editing/Proofreading: Toward a Final Version

The fourth stage in the writing process is editing/proofreading. Like the framers of the United States Constitution, shown below, you correct your errors so that they do not distract the reader from your ideas.

"So, then . . . Would that be 'us the people' or 'we the people'?"

 Resource Manager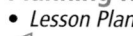

Planning Resources
- *Lesson Plans*

Transparencies
- *Bellringer*
- *Daily Language Practice*
- *Fine Art 7–12*
- *Two-Minute Skill Drill*
- *Writing Process 2–8*

Other Print Resources
- *Composition Enrichment,* p. 15
- *Composition Practice,* p. 15
- *Composition Reteaching,* p. 15
- *Cooperative Learning Activities*
- *Listening and Speaking Activities* pp. 6–8

- *Thinking and Study Skills,* pp. 13, 20, 25
- *Writing Across the Curriculum*
- *Writing Assessment and Evaluation Rubrics*

Edit to Correct Sentence Errors

Begin the editing stage by taking a careful look at your sentences. Make sure that each sentence expresses a complete thought in a way that is grammatically correct. Compare the edited draft below with the checklist. Which sentence-editing guidelines did the writer apply?

Sentence-Editing Checklist	
1. Have I avoided sentence fragments?	4. Are all verbs used correctly?
2. Have I avoided run-on sentences?	5. Have I avoided double negatives?
3. Are all pronouns used correctly?	6. Have I avoided wordiness?

Scientists ~~who are~~ searching for clues about what ~~it was that~~ caused the extinction of the dinosaurs ~~has~~ *have* debated various theories. One theory suggests that dinosaurs became extinct suddenly. ∧After a gigantic comet or meteor collided with the earth. The impact spewed debris into the atmosphere. The sunlight was blocked for months. Temperatures dropped, *and*∧many species of plants and animals

Journal Writing

Perhaps you have found yourself in this situation: a teacher likes the content of your paper but has given you a lower mark because of errors. "But you know what I meant," you complain. "Why does it matter how I said it?" Write a response from your teacher's point of view.

Teach

Starting Out Slowly

Students who have trouble editing their writing independently might be helped by starting out slowly. With their drafts before them, students read item 1 of the sentence-editing checklist about sentence fragments. Then they check their own drafts with just that one item in mind. Answer questions about fragments before moving on to item 2. Encourage students to put copies of the checklist inside their journals for easy reference. **L1**

Finding Cartoons

Magazines and newspapers often include cartoons like the one on student page 82, dealing with aspects of language such as vocabulary, grammar, and spelling. Encourage students to be on the lookout for these and contribute them to a class bulletin board displaying language-related cartoons. **L3**

Two-Minute Skill Drill

Have students list the six sentence-editing guidelines in the checklist.

 See also *Two-Minute Skill Drill Transparency 2.8*

Journal Writing Tip

Predicting Before students complete the journal activity, you might ask partners to take turns role-playing the student and the teacher. Suggest that students use their actual work as props. To help them see things from the teacher's point of view, they can ask questions such as "Do misspellings make the paper hard to read?"

Teach

Using Proofreading Symbols

To give students practice in using proofreading symbols, duplicate a typed, double-spaced paragraph from a magazine or newspaper, omitting some punctuation and capital letters, and an occasional word. Challenge students to proofread the paragraph, correcting all sentence and punctuation errors. Then distribute copies of the original for students to check and compare. **L2**

Using a Roundtable Technique

You might have groups of three students assume author, editor, and proofreader roles, using a Simultaneous Roundtable technique. All three students bring a draft they have written and hand it to the group member on their right, who serves as their editor and suggests revisions. They take their draft back, revise it, and pass it to the student on their left, their proofreader. After each proofreader marks corrections, each author prepares a final copy. **L3**

Additional Resources

Writing Process Transparencies, 2–8
Writing Across the Curriculum
Cooperative Learning Activities

For further stimuli for writing, see *Fine Art Transparencies*, 7–12.
Thinking and Study Skills, pp. 13, 20, 25
Listening and Speaking Activities, pp. 6–8
Composition Practice, p. 15

The Writing Process

Proofread for Spelling and Mechanics

Proofreading is the part of editing that focuses on spelling and on mechanics—capital letters and punctuation marks. Use the checklist below to identify errors. Use the proofreading symbols as a kind of shorthand to mark needed changes.

Proofreading

Checklist

1. Does each sentence have the right end punctuation?
2. Are commas and semicolons used as needed?
3. Are other punctuation marks used as needed?
4. Are all words spelled correctly?
5. Are possessives and contractions written correctly?
6. Are capital letters used as needed?

Symbols

Symbol	Meaning
∧	Insert
ℒ	Remove
⁀	Exchange
¶	New paragraph
⊙	Add period
∧	Add comma
≡	Uppercase
/	Lowercase
⌣	Close space

> What change does each proofreading symbol indicate?

¶Until recently, many scientists theorized that the extinction of the dinosaur was a gradual process. One theory held that poisons slowly built up in earth's vegetation over the years, slowly killing the dinosaurs. Another theory was that mamals ate the dinosaur eggs still another theory was that dinosaurs could not adapt to gradual changes in earth's climate and plant life. Today, however most scientists think that a sudden and catastrophic event--perhaps caused by a crashing Meteor or colliding planet--caused the extinction of dinosaurs.

Proofreading is the last part of the editing process. Your investigation of your subject, which may have started with just a glimpse of an idea, has resulted in a fully developed piece of writing. Now is the time to prepare your final version and present your writing to its audience.

84 Unit 2 The Writing Process

Enrichment and Extension

Exploring Language

Using Spell Check Students might profit from using the Spell Check feature on the word processor as a final editing tool. Caution them that while the program can check the spelling of words like *hear* and *here,* it cannot tell whether the writer has chosen the correct word.

Edit Your Draft

When you are satisfied that your investigative report says what you want it to say, it is time to edit your writing.

PURPOSE To edit and proofread
AUDIENCE Yourself
LENGTH Changes on the draft

WRITING RUBRICS To edit and proofread your draft, you should

- use the editing and proofreading checklists from this lesson
- proofread for one kind of error at a time
- use proofreading symbols

Using Computers

Sharpen your keyboard skills as well as your proofreading skills by having a paragraph from this textbook read aloud to you while you sit at your computer. As you listen to the passage, type it as a document in your word processing program. Later check for typographical errors you may have made, as well as errors in punctuation, spelling, and capitalization.

Listening and Speaking

COOPERATIVE LEARNING Work with a partner to read aloud various stages of your edited investigative reports. Listening to a report can help make grammatical errors and errors in usage more obvious.

Grammar Link

Make sure subjects and verbs agree in person and number.

Check subject-verb agreement as you edit your work. Be especially careful with sentences in which phrases intervene between the subject and the verb. For example, look at the first sentence of the model on page 83. The subject, *scientists,* is plural. The writer changed the verb to its plural form to agree with the subject.

Rewrite the sentences below to make subjects and verbs agree.

1. Scientists from all over the world is studying the effects of climate changes.
2. This scientist, in addition to many of his colleagues, believe that severe climate changes caused the extinction of dinosaurs.
3. An ice age thousands of years ago probably were responsible for migrations of early people.
4. Perhaps the poisons slowly building up in the earth's vegetation was the cause of dinosaurs disappearing.
5. A definitive answer to this question, as well to the reason for migrations, continue to elude scientists.

See Lessons 16.1, page 614; and Lesson 16.6, pages 621–622.

Assess

Evaluation Rubrics

Edit Your Draft

Use these criteria when evaluating your students' drafts. You should see
- sentence errors that have been corrected
- spelling errors that have been corrected
- mechanical errors that have been corrected
- use of proofreading symbols

See also *Writing Assessment & Evaluation Rubrics.*

Using Computers

You may wish to point out egregious errors in punctuation to students, but since this is an auditory activity in which they type what they hear, there will be some variation in punctuation.

Listening and Speaking

Students should speak slowly and clearly when reading their reports to each other. As students notice errors in their reports, they should jot down corrections on their hard copy before making changes in the computer.

Reteaching

📁 *Composition Reteaching,* p. 15

Enrichment

📁 *Composition Enrichment,* p. 15

Close

Encourage students to read newspapers and magazines with an editor's eye, looking for errors in spelling, usage, and punctuation.

Grammar Link

Answers

1. Scientists . . . are
2. This scientist . . . believes
3. An ice age . . . was
4. poisons . . . were
5. A definitive answer . . . continues

The Writing Process

Focus

Lesson Overview

Objective

• To create and publish a class magazine

Skills

• targeting an audience; publishing a magazine

Critical Thinking

• analyzing; evaluating; establishing and evaluating criteria

Listening and Speaking

• evaluating; questioning

Bellringer
Daily Language Activity

When students enter the classroom, have this assignment on the board: *Draft a short letter to a magazine editor asking to have your work published.*

Grammar Link to the Bellringer

Ask students to write a correct return address (theirs) with date and an inside address (imaginary) for their letters. Ask them to correctly capitalize and punctuate.

See also *Daily Language Practice*

Motivating Activity

Invite students to tell why they endure football or basketball practice day after day, why they train so hard for swimming or running, why they spend hours practicing the piano or guitar. In other words, what's the payoff for trying to improve performance? (Rewards include doing one's best in a big game, a marathon, a recital, or a performance.) Emphasize that writers revise, edit, and proofread their work for the same reason: so that what they present to an audience will be their very best work.

LESSON 2.10

Publishing/Presenting: Sharing Your Writing

P resenting your work—sharing it with others—is the final stage in the writing process. You may think your job is done when you hand your work in to your teacher; but other avenues are available to help you get the word out.

Shown below are just a few possible places where you could present your work. When you've spent the time and effort to put your thoughts on paper, you owe it to yourself—and your potential readers—to share your ideas.

Resource Manager

Planning Resources
• *Lesson Plans*

Transparencies
• *Bellringer*
• *Daily Language Practice*
• *Fine Art* 7–12
• *Two-Minute Skill Drill*
• *Writing Process* 2–8

Other Print Resources
• *Composition Enrichment*, p. 16
• *Composition Practice*, p. 16
• *Composition Reteaching*, p. 16
• *Cooperative Learning Activities*
• *Listening and Speaking Activities*, pp. 6–8

• *Thinking and Study Skills*, pp. 2, 24–25
• *Writing Assessment and Evaluation Rubrics*

Prewriting: "None of my friends are cooks. How can I interest them in salsa recipes?"

Drafting: "A description of a rock concert will grab my readers' attention."

Revising: "My cousin doesn't use a computer. I'd better explain how to use a mouse."

Editing/Proofreading: "Is it *o-s-m-o-s-e-s?* Mr. Dorn teaches science, so I'd better spell it right."

Publishing/Presenting: "Hey, I think I've got it now. Got a minute to listen to this?"

Reach Your Audience

Whenever you write, you're writing for an audience. As the photos suggest, your audience should affect every stage of your writing process. Your audience can be yourself when you write in your journal or a friend when you scribble a note. It can be the large and far-flung audience you reach by publishing your work. Who might learn from your writing, be entertained or persuaded by it, or be interested in some other way by your work? Here are some ways to present what you write.

Places to Publish	
Publication	**Audience**
School publications: literary magazine, newspaper, yearbook	Your fellow students
General-interest newspapers and magazines	The general student and adult population
Special interest newsletters and magazines	People interested in a particular subject: hobby, sport, cause, career
Computer networks: on-line bulletin boards, special-interest networks	Computer users linked by common interests

Journal Writing

Choose a piece of writing from your journal. Write about the audience you'd like to present it to and how you'd prepare it.

The Writing Process

Teach

Entering Writing Contests

After discussing writing audiences and places to publish, some students might consider entering their work in one of the many writing contests sponsored by various literary magazines and professional organizations, including the National Council of Teachers of English. It is a good idea to meet with students before they submit their work. Review contest rules, especially those specifying topic and length. **L3**

Two-Minute Skill Drill

Have students write the stages of the writing process and circle the ones that are hardest for them.

✎ **See also** *Two-Minute Skill Drill Transparency 2.10*

Journal Writing Tip

Identifying Audience Suggest that students browse through copies of school newspapers, literary magazines, and special-interest publications such as *PC World, Road & Track,* and *Guitar Player.* Encourage students to notice and describe the style and tone of each publication, as well as the content of the articles. These observations can help them assess where they ought to send their work and what changes they would need to make if they did.

Teach

Exploring Publishing

Have students discuss the types of publications described on student page 88 and the many people that contribute to the process. Emphasize how important it is to understand the purpose, audience, and message of the written work in order to design the appropriate presentation. Some students may enjoy exploring careers that focus on the presentation stage of the writing process. These include layout editors, book designers, and graphic designers. **L2**

Cutting for Space

Often an article has to be shortened to fit the available space in a publication. If this should happen, suggest to students that a member of the editorial committee go back to the writer to discuss any cuts or changes. Point out that professional publishers often follow this procedure. **L2**

Additional Resources

Writing Process Transparencies, 2–8
Cooperative Learning Activities

For further stimuli for writing, see *Fine Art Transparencies*, 7–12.
Thinking and Study Skills, pp. 2, 24–25
Listening and Speaking Activities, pp. 6–8
Composition Practice, p. 16

The Writing Process

Publish Together

Today it's easier than ever for writers to see their work in print. Desktop publishing allows anyone with access to a computer and a printer to produce high-quality graphic art and professional-looking layouts. Even without a computer, you can create interesting and effective publications—with just a typewriter and a copy machine.

What type of publication could your class produce? Would you like to produce a literary magazine that will be a forum for stories, poetry, and reviews? Or a general magazine covering topics of interest to your class? Or perhaps a series of special reports, each covering one topic or issue in depth? Look at the examples below for ideas your class might use to create its own publication.

A Do-It-Yourself Class Publication

1. Decide what kind of publication you want to produce.
☐ Literary Magazine
☑ General Magazine
☐ Special Reports

2. Decide what everyone will contribute.
• poetry
• short stories
• articles
• editorials

3. Make a schedule.

Monthly Planner
1	2	3	4	5
6	7	8	9	10	11	12
13	14	15	16	17	18	19
20	21	22	23	24	25	26
27	28	29	30	31

Format the writing on a computer or a typewriter. Shown on this computer is a grid used to format writing for publication.

4. Follow the five-stage writing process to create the writing for your publication.

Prewriting ▸ Drafting ▸ Revising ▸ Editing/Proofreading ▸ Publishing/Presenting

Prepare art and photos. Don't forget to add captions and credit lines.

Proofread the writing one more time just before you print the publication.

88 Unit 2 The Writing Process

MEETING INDIVIDUAL NEEDS — English Language Learners

Translating into English

For their class publication some students can submit poems or other pieces written in a language other than English. For example, a student whose first language is Spanish might submit a poem in Spanish with an accompanying English translation.

Present Your Writing

You have taken your report through prewriting, drafting, revising, and editing/proofreading. Now it's time for sharing your writing!

PURPOSE To present your finished work
AUDIENCE The audience you chose when you began to write
LENGTH Whatever is appropriate for your purpose

WRITING RUBRICS To prepare your writing for final presentation, you should

- use a format that is appropriate for your audience and purpose
- include illustrations or other images if desired
- make your paper neat and legible

Using Computers

You might present your final investigative report in the form of a Web page on the Internet. (First check your school's policy.) Investigate Web page–building software, and choose the one most appropriate for your purpose and audience. Before publishing, check your report once more for accuracy in content, spelling, and grammar.

Viewing and Representing

COOPERATIVE LEARNING In a small group, brainstorm to create a list of magazines and other publishing vehicles, including electronic ones, in which you and your classmates might publish your writings. Begin by considering the audiences that might be interested in individual and class writing samples. Present your list to the class. Visit your library and check out publications that feature student writing to display in the classroom.

Grammar Link

Use correct punctuation for each part of a business letter.

When you submit a piece of your writing to the editor of a publication, you should write a cover letter to go with it. Be sure to use the correct form and punctuation for your letter.

Use commas to separate city from state, day from year, the addressee's name from his or her title, and after the closing. Use a colon after the greeting. Use correct punctuation with abbreviations.

Write the parts of the business letter below using correct punctuation.

1. 120 N Merrill Street
   Park Ridge IL 60068
   March 6 1997
2. Mr. Paul Oscar Feature Editor
   The Shore Weekly
   1 Sunrise Lane
3. Westport CT 06880
4. Dear Mr. Oscar
5. Sincerely yours

See Lesson 21.4, page 739; Lesson 21.6, pages 749–750; and Lesson 21.13, pages 766–768.

Assess

Evaluation Rubrics

Present Your Writing

Use these criteria when evaluating your students' writing:

- Is the report presented in the most effective way?
- Is the report neat and attractive?
- Did the student use illustrations?

See also *Writing Assessment & Evaluation Rubrics.*

Viewing and Representing

Advise students to look in the reference section of their school or public library for books that classify magazines by type, subject matter, age, kinds of articles, and so on. These reference books also give the publishing criteria for specific magazines and tell students how to submit their own writing. Students could also search online for sites for writers. Have students explain how they selected magazines or online sites to which they might like to submit their writing.

Reteaching

📁 *Composition Reteaching,* p. 16

Enrichment

📁 *Composition Enrichment,* p. 16

Close

Work with students to create a large bulletin-board display that highlights the stages of the writing process. Post separate pieces of writing taken from each stage. Try to involve everyone in the decision-making process concerning what contributions to display.

Grammar Link

Answers

1. 120 N. Merrill Street
   Park Ridge, IL 60068
   March 6, 1997
2. Mr. Paul Oscar, Feature Editor
   The Shore Weekly
   1 Sunrise Lane
3. Westport, CT 06880
4. Dear Mr. Oscar:
5. Sincerely yours,

Focus

Lesson Overview

Objective
- To discuss the point of view in a novel or a short story

Skills
- identifying point of view; drafting an analysis

Critical Thinking
- analyzing; identifying

Listening and Speaking
- discussing

Bellringer
Daily Language Activity

When students enter the classroom, have this assignment on the board: *Use the following as the first sentence of the opening paragraph of a story in either the first person or the third person:*

Strange tracks led away from the path and into the undergrowth.

Grammar Link to the Bellringer

Have students review the paragraphs they have written to make sure that the use of pronouns is consistent with the point of view.

See also *Daily Language Practice*

Motivating Activity

Bring in photos showing people, animals, or objects seen from unusual angles. Display the photos, and ask students where they think the camera was positioned for each one. Point out that what we see depends on the angle from which the photographer takes the picture. Similarly, what we know as we read a story depends on the writer's angle of vision or point of view.

The Writing Process

LESSON 2.11

WRITING ABOUT LITERATURE
Analyzing Point of View

*P*oint of view is the angle from which you see people, objects, or events. In the cartoon you see what is outside the window from the point of view of Gladys Murphy. In other words, you see only what she sees. In a short story or novel, point of view controls what the reader knows.

"Hello, Emily. This is Gladys Murphy up the street. Fine, thanks . . . Say, could you go to your window and describe what's in my front yard?"

Identify Point of View

The paragraphs that follow tell the same story from different points of view. Read them to discover the three main points of view that story writers use: first-person, third-person limited, and third-person omniscient (all-knowing). The paragraph is part of a mystery story involving a police investigation. The characters are the detective, Sergeant Rivera, and the suspect, Carson. For each version ask these questions: Who is the narrator, or the teller of the story? How much is known to the narrator, and therefore to the reader?

The writer has Rivera tell the story from his own point of view, using the first-person pronouns *I* and *me*. This point of view allows readers to know the character better and gives a "you-are-there" feeling.

First Person

We walked to the swimming pool. I leaned against the diving board, wondering if now were the moment to spring my trap, to ask Carson just how his emerald stickpin had wound up on the floor of Jasmine Tsing's abandoned car. Carson sank into the *chaise longue,* clearly puzzled by my silence. I knew he thought he'd left no clues, no evidence along that secluded stretch of Evergeen Road. Time and time again, he told me that he'd never even met Jasmine Tsing. Carson had no idea that a small chunk of fiery green crystal was about to call him a liar.

90   Unit 2 The Writing Process

Resource Manager

Planning Resources
- *Lesson Plans*

Transparencies
- *Bellringer*
- *Daily Language Practice*
- *Fine Art* 7–12
- *Two-Minute Skill Drill*
- *Writing Process* 2–8

Other Print Resources
- *Composition Enrichment,* p. 17
- *Composition Practice,* p. 17
- *Composition Reteaching,* p. 17
- *Cooperative Learning Activities*
- *Listening and Speaking Activities,* pp. 6–8

- *Thinking and Study Skills,* pp. 5, 19, 24
- *Writing Across the Curriculum*
- *Writing Assessment and Evaluation Rubrics*

Third-Person Limited

They walked to the swimming pool. As Rivera leaned against the diving board, Carson sank into the *chaise longue*. Why, he wondered, was Rivera so silent? Carson was certain he had left no clues, no evidence along that solitary stretch of Evergeen Road where Jasmine Tsing's abandoned car had been discovered. No, he told himself, Rivera couldn't possibly suspect him. Hadn't he told the police more than once that he'd never met Jasmine Tsing?

> A third-person limited narrator tells the story from one character's point of view—in this case, Carson's. What does the reader learn about other characters' thoughts and feelings? What clues are given?

Third-Person Omniscient

They walked to the swimming pool. Rivera leaned against the diving board, wondering if now were the moment to spring the trap, to ask how Carson's emerald stickpin had wound up on the floor of Jasmine Tsing's abandoned car. Carson sank into the *chaise longue*. He was puzzled by Rivera's silence but certain he'd left no clues, no evidence along that secluded stretch of Evergreen Road. Hadn't he told the police more than once that he'd never even met Jasmine Tsing?

> A third-person omniscient narrator knows everything about the characters. How does this affect the way the reader views the characters?

When you are planning an analysis of point of view in a story, your prewriting begins with reading the work closely. Then you are ready to use the following questionnaire.

Questionnaire on Point of View

1. What point of view is used—first-person, third-person limited, or third-person omniscient?
2. How does the point of view affect your attitude toward the characters and the events?
3. How does the point of view affect your overall understanding of the story?
4. How would the story be different if the author had told it from another point of view?
5. What point of view would you use if you were writing this story? Why?

Journal Writing

Use the questionnaire to analyze point of view in a favorite short story. Do you view the story differently now? Explain your answer.

2.11 Analyzing Point of View **91**

The Writing Process

Teach

Using the Models

Point out that the third-person limited model tells the reader nothing about Rivera's thoughts or feelings—only Carson's. (Note that Rivera's silence suggests his suspicion of Carson.) In the third-person omniscient model both points of view are presented in a neutral, objective way. Suggest students compare these points of view and vote on which they would use if they were writing the story. **L2**

Using the Questionnaire

Help students paraphrase each of the five questionnaire items to check their understanding of these key concepts: point of view and person. As a group exercise, refer to a short story that was previously analyzed and discussed in class. After reviewing its main elements—setting, characters, plot—help students examine the point of view orally, using the questionnaire. **L1**

Two-Minute Skill Drill

Have students list the three main points of view that story writers use.

👆 **See also** *Two-Minute Skill Drill Transparency 2.11*

Journal Writing Tip

Inferring Before students complete the journal activity, you might provide practice with point of view. Ask them to find and reread the introductory paragraphs and other excerpts from a literary selection they've read in this text. Ask them to write a paragraph with a topic sentence in which they infer the author's point of view and explain what details enabled them to do so.

Teach

Applying and Extending

To understand a writer's process of choosing a point of view, students might work in small groups to create a realistic story for which various points of view are possible: for example, an auto accident as seen by a driver, a victim, and a police officer. Each group brainstorms for details of action and for dialogue. Members choose a point of view and write independently. Afterward, have students compare stories, analyzing differences resulting from point of view. **L2**

Using the Model

Some students may have read Willa Cather's *My Ántonia*. If so, invite them to share and compare their responses. In discussing Katherine Jane Wise's analysis, point out that although she says Cather "tells the story through Jim Burden's eyes," she goes on to comment that his eyes "become her eyes, too." Ask students to discuss the effect of that point of view on Wise. (It made the book seem like a biography, not a novel.) **L3**

Additional Resources

 For further stimuli for writing, see *Fine Art Transparencies*, 7–12.

 Writing Process Transparencies, 2–8
 Writing Across the Curriculum
Cooperative Learning Activities
Thinking and Study Skills, pp. 5, 19, 24
Listening and Speaking Activities, pp. 6–8
Composition Practice, p. 17

The Writing Process

Draft Your Analysis

Once you've completed the questionnaire, you are ready to draft your analysis of the point of view in a story or novel. You've seen that first-person point of view uses the pronoun *I*. Third-person point of view, limited or omniscient, uses *he*, *she*, and *it*. But as you will see in Katherine Wise's analysis of Willa Cather's *My Ántonia*, point of view goes far beyond grammar.

Student Model

> Wise provides background by referring to Cather's introduction.

> According to Wise, the story is told through whose eyes? What effect does this create?

> This paragraph describes the student's strong personal response to a powerful story.

Willa Cather and Jim Burden were crossing Iowa on the same train. They began talking about the small Nebraska town where they had grown up together. In her introduction to the novel *My Ántonia*, Cather says that the conversation kept centering around a Bohemian girl who, better than anyone else, seemed to epitomize their prairie childhood. Over the years Burden had written down the things he remembered about her, and he showed his manuscript to Cather. He had entitled it *Ántonia* but after a little thought changed it to *My Ántonia*. From there came what is considered Willa Cather's greatest work.

Cather tells the story through Jim Burden's eyes. But they become her eyes, too. The book is so real that you keep flipping back to the introduction to see that yes, this was written by Cather, and that no, this is not a biography—it is a novel.

Cather is able to maintain this feeling of reality because as the narrator she remains completely objective. She describes everything through Jim's eyes, but she never states what his feelings or emotions are. This seems strange at times, but it would not have been as sincere if Cather had tried to apply her own feelings to Jim, or if she had tried to imagine what his feelings might be. Instead her objectivity emphasizes the fact that the book is not about Jim, but about Ántonia.

Burden and Cather had "agreed that no one who had not grown up in a little prairie town could know anything about it." But they proved themselves wrong. Cather took me there—to Black Hawk, Nebraska—swept away on the prairie winds of her words. Her writing is as plain, simple, and harsh as the land it is about, and just as beautiful.

Katherine Jane Wise, Perrysburg High School,
Perrysburg, Ohio

Cooperative Learning

Analyzing Literature

Choose four or five short stories that your students are currently studying or know well. As a group exercise, divide the class into small groups, and have each group choose one story to use for the following activity. Each group member answers one of the questions on the questionnaire on student page 91. After members discuss their answers, each group presents its analysis to the class as a panel discussion.

Write from a Particular Point of View

Look at the painting and its title below. Write a short description of what might be happening in the scene from one of these points of view: the first-person point of view of one of the people pictured, third-person limited, or third-person omniscient.

PURPOSE To explore point of view
AUDIENCE Your classmates
LENGTH 2 paragraphs

WRITING RUBRICS To present point of view correctly, you should

• make the point of view clear
• keep the point of view consistent
• use pronouns correctly

Cross-Curricular Activity

MUSIC In a small group, listen to the lyrics of a ballad. Discuss the point of view used in the song and why that point of view may have been chosen by the lyricist.

Sofonisba Anguissola,
Three of the Artist's Sisters Playing Chess, 1555

Listening and Speaking

NARRATIVE Consider the viewpoint of different characters in a story. Discuss which viewpoints offer the most interesting perspectives on story events. Then take turns telling parts of the story as first-person narration by different characters.

Grammar Link

Be consistent in presenting point of view when writing.

When you write in the first person, use the pronouns *I* and *we*. In the third person, refer to characters as *he, she, one,* and *they*. In the second person, use *you*. The writer of the first-person narration in the model on page 90 used pronouns consistently:

*I leaned against the diving board, wondering if now was the moment to spring **my** trap. . . .*

Revise each sentence below to eliminate the incorrect shifts in pronouns.

1. When you analyze first-person point of view, we decide how much we can learn from the first-person narrator.
2. If they are writing from a third-person point of view, you can narrate the actions and words of all the characters.
3. If a story captures one's curiosity, your interest usually follows.
4. When one is interested in a story, I keep on reading.
5. She and I like reading the same kinds of books in their spare time.

See Lesson 17.5, page 644.

The Writing Process

Assess

Evaluation Rubrics

Write from a Particular Point of View

Use these criteria when evaluating your students' writing. Commend paragraphs that
• clearly illustrate one of the three points of view
• reflect careful observation

See also *Writing Assessment & Evaluation Rubrics.*

Cross-Curricular Activity

Students' discussions should
• demonstrate that students have listened attentively to the lyrics
• demonstrate a clear understanding of point of view
• include ideas as to why the lyricist chose that point of view

Listening and Speaking

Commend
• consistent use of one character's perspective
• details showing how first-person narration affects understanding of personality and attitudes

Reteaching

📁 *Composition Reteaching*, p. 17

Enrichment

📁 *Composition Enrichment*, p. 17

📦 Use *Fine Art Transparencies*, 7–12, for enrichment activities also.

Close

Read aloud a cogent critical comment on a work previously discussed in class and have students analyze the comment.

Grammar Link

Answers
1. *we* analyze, we decide, we can learn.
2. *you* are writing, you can narrate.
3. one's curiosity, *one's* interest.
4. *I am* interested, I keep on reading.
5. She and I; *our* spare time.

Viewing the Art

Sofonisba Anguissola, *Three of the Artist's Sisters Playing Chess*, 1555
The oldest of a family of six girls and one boy, the artist created this painting when she was 20, a remarkable accomplishment in Renaissance Italy when women did not usually attend school.

Focus

Lesson Overview

Objective
• To describe the results of an investigation into personal history or heritage

Skills
• using the five stages of the writing process: prewriting, drafting, revising, editing/proofreading, publishing/presenting; using descriptive language to describe an aspect of a life; organizing information; using supporting details; using standard grammar, usage, and mechanics

Critical Thinking
• recalling; relating

Listening and Speaking
• discussing; presenting orally

Bellringer
Daily Language Activity

When students enter the classroom, have this assignment on the board: *Write a list of three interesting facts about your family history.*

Grammar Link to the Bellringer

Have students review their lists, checking for capitalized proper nouns.

See also *Daily Language Practice*

Motivating Activity

Ask students if they've ever tried to construct a family tree or a project requiring an investigation into family history. What information did they uncover? Suggest that they begin an investigation by scouting around for old letters, diaries, family Bibles, and photo albums to get ideas and information about their roots.

UNIT 2
Writing Process in Action

The Writing Process

In preceding lessons you learned about the five stages of the writing process—prewriting, drafting, revising, editing/proofreading, and publishing/presenting. You also had an opportunity to practice each of these stages. Now you will use the writing process to put together a piece of writing about your personal history or heritage.

WRITING Online

Visit the Writer's Choice Web site at **writerschoice. glencoe.com** for additional writing prompts.

Assignment

Context

As part of a world history assignment, class members have been asked to write about some aspect of their personal history or heritage. Suggested topics include family histories, descriptions of family or relatives, and autobiographical accounts. The goal of the assignment is to show how you are part of history and of the history-making process.

Purpose

To briefly describe a particular aspect of your personal history or heritage

Audience

Your teacher and peers, and perhaps your family members

Length

1-2 pages

For advice on how to approach this assignment, you will find the next few pages helpful. You can come back to these pages as you write, getting help where and when you need it. Don't feel limited by the suggestions here. You're in charge of your own writing process.

Resource Manager

Planning Resources
• *Lesson Plans*

Transparencies
• *Bellringer*
• *Daily Language Practice*
• *Writing Process 2–8*

 Other Print Resources
• *Composition Enrichment,* p. 18
• *Composition Practice,* p. 18
• *Composition Reteaching,* p. 18
• *Grammar Workbook,* Lesson 71
• *Thinking and Study Skills,* pp. 5–7, 11
• *Writing Assessment and Evaluation Rubrics*

 Software
• *Writer's Assistant*

 Web Sites
• *writerschoice.glencoe.com*
• *lit.glencoe.com*

Prewriting

Do you remember listening spellbound to a tale about your past or your family's past? Maybe you have your own stories—memories that hold their shape and color despite the passage of time. Search your memory for a story you'd like to explore. If you're looking for an idea, try the prewriting suggestions.

Next, review the assignment. Your main purpose is to inform your readers about an aspect of your personal history or heritage. Is there anything else you want to accomplish? For example, do you want to persuade your readers to be proud of their own roots? Also keep in mind the needs of your audience. Be sure to provide enough background information so that family relationships and other details that you take for granted will make sense to your teacher and classmates.

Then, work on a main idea statement to help you choose details and keep your writing on track. To find details, start with family photo albums or videos. Interview family members and family friends to get firsthand information. Make notes on what you learn to help you as you draft.

Drafting

Now it's time to start getting your story down on paper. Review your prewriting notes and main idea statement. Then find a place to jump in—either at the beginning, or at the part that is clearest in your mind, even if that's somewhere in the middle. The goal of drafting is to get your ideas down, even if they're not exactly in the right order or in a polished form.

How will you organize your draft? If you're telling a story about your past, chronological order may be your best choice. If you are describing a special place, you may want to use spatial order.

As you write, look for ways you can use details to intrigue your readers. In his autobiography, Alex Haley, the author of *Roots*, introduces his readers to the strange sounding words that were clues to his African heritage. Read the following passage and notice Haley's effective use of details.

Prewriting Options

- Read your journal. Look for autobiographical entries.
- Prewrite about yourself. Try to answer the question, Who am I?
- Brainstorm with family members.
- Create an idea tree. Start by circling the word <u>family</u>.

Prewriting Tip

For tips on interviewing, see Lesson 2.5, pages 64–67.

Drafting Tip

For examples of different types of supporting details, see Lesson 2.6, page 70.

Teach

Prewriting

Visualizing Flashbacks

Some students might benefit from using their mind's eye to see "flashbacks" of past events they have experienced or heard about repeatedly, such as an ocean voyage, leaving the "old country," a holiday memory, a family trip, or a special time with a relative. Students can jot down each event in their journals, along with key words or phrases to jog their memories and to flesh out the event with details. **L2**

Exploring Topics

Suggest that students create an idea map. Have them start by writing and circling the word *family* on a sheet of paper. Tell them to make as many associations to this word as they can. Have them write each association around the word *family*. Clustering in this way will help students probe their memories for specific details and find ideas about which to write. **L1**

Drafting

Using the Model

Have students take a close look at the Literature Model on page 96. Point out that Haley had heard the story of his family and "Kin-tay" so often that, even as a child, he began picturing the events in his mind. Point out that often-repeated stories become so vivid that they beg to be recorded and shared. Some students might try writing a brief summary of a vivid childhood memory similar to Haley's example in the model. **L2**

Teach

Revising

Peer Editing

Students can work in writing conferences with peer editors before they revise their writing. Suggest that peer editors respond to the following questions:
- Is the story clearly organized?
- Where might additional details strengthen the story?

You may want to duplicate the Peer Response forms in *Writing Assessment & Evaluation Rubrics.* **L2**

Editing

Peer Editing

After students have edited their own work, have them edit another student's writing. Have them refer to the Editing Checklist on the student page. **L2**

Presenting

Before students present their personal histories, discuss ways for them to publish their papers.

Additional Resources

Writing Process Transparencies, 2–8

Thinking and Study Skills, pp. 5–7, 11

Composition Practice, p. 18

Grammar Workbook, Lesson 71

The Writing Process

Literature Model

Anyway, all of this is how I was growing up in Henning at Grandma's, listening from behind her rocking chair as she and the other visiting old women talked of that African . . . who said his name was "*Kintay,*" and said "*ko*" for banjo, "*Kamby Bolong*" for river, and a jumble of other "*k*"-beginning sounds that Grandma privately muttered. . . .

Alex Haley, "My Furthest-Back Person—The African"

Once you've got everything down, take a break from your writing, even if you're not particularly satisfied with your draft. You'll be able to evaluate your draft more objectively after a few hours or a day away from it.

Revising Tip

For advice on how to work with a peer reviewer, see Lesson 2.8, page 77.

Revising

To begin revising, read over your draft to make sure that what you've written fits your purpose and audience. Then have a **writing conference.** Read your draft to a partner or small group. Use your audience's reactions and the Revising Checklist below to help you evaluate your work.

Revising Checklist

- Does my writing reveal something interesting about my personal history?
- Have I narrowed my topic to get a tight focus?
- Is each paragraph coherent and unified?
- Will my writing appeal to my audience—my teacher and peers?

Enrichment and Extension

Follow-up Ideas
- Set aside time for students to celebrate the conclusion of their writing projects.
- Consider class publication. All of students' writing in response to this assignment can be collected, illustrated, bound, and placed in the school library.

Extending the Writing Process
- Explore opportunities for extending the writing process beyond the classroom, such as creating a community history for new families who move into the community.

The Writing Process

Editing/Proofreading

When you have revised your writing for basic content and organization, **proofread** it carefully for grammar, usage, and mechanics errors that can distract readers. Use the questions at the right as a guide.

Now use the Self-Evaluation list below to judge your overall work. When you're satisfied with your personal history, make a clean copy of it and proofread one more time.

Editing/Proofreading Checklist

- Have I capitalized proper nouns, especially names of places and people?
- Have I made sure that all pronouns are correct?
- Have I added commas and semicolons where they are needed?
- Have I set off direct quotes with quotations marks?
- Have I checked carefully for possible misspellings?

Reflection

Make sure that your personal history —

✔ describes an aspect of your life or heritage
✔ uses an appropriate method of organization
✔ includes supporting details, humor, or suspense to maintain audience interest
✔ reveals something interesting about your background
✔ follows correct grammar, usage, mechanics, and spelling

Publishing/Presenting

If you choose to do so, share your writing with the class. You also may want to publish your writing in a local history journal or in a magazine that publishes students' writing.

Proofreading

For proofreading symbols, see page 84.

Journal Writing

Reflect on your writing process experience. Answer these questions in your journal: What do you like best about your personal history? What was the hardest part of writing it? What did you learn in your writing conference? What new things have you learned as a writer?

Assess

Evaluation Rubrics

Use the following criteria to evaluate the students' finished writing. The writing should

- describe an aspect of personal history or heritage
- contain factual information indicating thorough and careful investigation of the topic
- follow a clear, logical plan of organization
- reflect careful editing for errors in grammar and mechanics

See also *Writing Assessment & Evaluation Rubrics.*

Reteaching

📁 *Composition Reteaching,* p. 18

Enrichment

📁 *Composition Enrichment,* p. 18

Journal Writing Tip

Reflecting on the Writing Process
Remind students that writing about the writing process in their journals can help them gain insight into the creative process.

Close

Suggest that students rewrite their stories as poems and share them with the class.

Listening and Speaking

Making Oral Presentations

Many of these stories will lend themselves to entertaining oral presentations. Consider holding a Personal History Day for students to read their work to their classmates, to another class, or even to a wider audience. Encourage readers to tape-record their readings beforehand and play them back, noting where they want to slow down, speed up, or change volume or pitch. Remind them to include pauses for dramatic effect, laughter, and, of course, applause. Have the class listen to, respond to, and appropriately evaluate each presentation.

About the Author

Although his parents were both teachers and Alex Haley (1921–1992) himself attended two colleges, he considered the sea his alma mater; it was there he taught himself to write. Haley spent twelve years researching and writing *Roots.*

Focus

Lesson Overview

Objective
- To trace a prewriting investigation that led to a book idea and provided details used in the book

Skills
- reading comprehension

Critical Thinking
- analyzing; evaluating; visualizing

Listening and Speaking
- questioning; discussing

Bellringer
Daily Language Activity

When students enter the classroom, have this assignment on the board: *Have you ever been completely absorbed with a single goal or activity? If so, what was it?*

See also *Daily Language Practice*

Motivating Activity

Students familiar with *Roots,* the book or the TV miniseries, might give the class an informal review. Explain that students will read a piece in which the author tells how he got the idea for *Roots.*

✔ ASSESSMENT OPTIONS

📂 *Writing Assessment & Evaluation Rubrics*

The Writing Process

My Furthest-Back Person

THE AFRICAN
by Alex Haley

Alex Haley wrote the tremendously popular Roots, *an account of seven generations of his own African American family. In the following autobiographical selection, Haley provides a glimpse of his own writing process as he shows how he got the original idea for* Roots. *As you read, note how he began researching the full story. Then try the activities in Linking Writing and Literature on page 107.*

My Grandma Cynthia Murray Palmer lived in Henning, Tenn. (pop. 500), about 50 miles north of Memphis. Each summer as I grew up there, we would be visited by several women relatives who were mostly around Grandma's age, such as my Great Aunt Liz Murray who taught in Oklahoma, and Great Aunt Till Merriwether from Jackson, Tenn., or their considerably younger niece, Cousin Georgia Anderson from Kansas City, Kan., and some others. Always after the supper dishes had been washed, they would go out to take seats and talk in the rocking chairs on the front porch, and I would scrunch down, listening, behind Grandma's squeaky chair, with the dusk deepening into night and the lightning bugs flicking on and off above the now shadowy honeysuckles. Most often they talked about our family—the story had been passed down for generations—until the whistling blur of lights of the southbound Panama Limited train whooshing through Henning at 9:05 p.m. signaled our bedtime.

So much of their talking of people, places and events I didn't understand: For instance, what was an "Ol' Massa," an "Ol' Missus" or a "plantation"? But early I gathered that white folks had done lots of bad things to our folks, though I couldn't figure out why. I guessed that all that they talked

---

Literature Model

about had happened a long time ago, as now or then Grandma or another, speaking of someone in the past, would excitedly thrust a finger toward me, exclaiming, "Wasn't big as *this* young 'un!" And it would astound me that anyone as old and grey-haired as they could relate to my age. But in time my head began both a recording and picturing of the more graphic scenes they would describe, just as I also visualized David killing Goliath with his slingshot, Old Pharaoh's army drowning, Noah and his ark, Jesus feeding that big multitude with nothing but five loaves and two fishes, and other wonders that I heard in my Sunday school lessons at our New Hope Methodist Church.

The furthest-back person Grandma and the others talked of—always in tones of awe, I noticed—they would call "The African." They said that some ship brought him to a place that they pronounced "'Naplis." They said that then some "Mas' John Waller" bought him for his plantation in "Spotsylvania County, Va." This African kept on escaping, the fourth time trying to kill the "hateful po' cracker" slave-catcher, who gave him the punishment choice of castration or of losing one foot. This African took a foot being chopped off with an ax against a tree stump, they said, and he was about to die. But his life was saved by "mas' John's" brother—"Mas' William Waller," a doctor, who was so furious about what had happened that he bought the African for himself and gave him the name "Toby."

Crippling about, working in "Mas' William's" house and yard, the African in time met and mated with "the big house

cook named Bell," and there was born a girl named Kizzy. As she grew up her African daddy often showed her different kinds of things, telling her what they were in his native tongue. Pointing at a banjo, for example, the African uttered, "*ko*"; or pointing at a river near the plantation, he would say, "*Kamby Bolong.*" Many of his strange words started with a "k" sound, and the little, growing Kizzy learned gradually that they identified different things.

When addressed by other slaves as "Toby," the master's name for him, the African said angrily that his name was "*Kintay.*" And as he gradually learned English, he told young Kizzy some things about himself—for instance, that he was not far from his village, chopping wood to make himself a drum, when four men had surprised, overwhelmed, and kidnaped him.

So Kizzy's head held much about her African daddy when at age 16 she was sold away onto a much smaller plantation in North Carolina. Her new "Mas' Tom Lea" fathered her first child, a boy she named George. And Kizzy told her boy all about his African grandfather. George grew up to be such a gamecock[1] fighter that he was called "Chicken George," and people would come from all over and "bet big money" on his cockfights. He mated with Matilda, another of Lea's slaves; they had seven children, and he told them the stories and strange sounds of their African great-grandfather. And one of those children,

---

1 **gamecock** (gām' käk') a rooster bred and trained to fight other roosters in events called cockfights

Teach

Guided Reading

- How would you describe the genre of this passage?
- Who is the main character in this passage?
- Describe how Haley reveals his relatives' feelings about the African. **L2**

Teach

Guided Reading

- What does Haley mean when he says that the African's sounds and stories had become the "family's prideful treasure"?
- Beginning with the tenth paragraph ("To compress my next . . ."), Haley shifts the focus of the piece. What did he accomplish in the beginning nine paragraphs? **L2**

The Writing Process

Literature Model

Tom, became a blacksmith who was bought away by a "Mas' Murray" for his tobacco plantation in Alamance County, N.C.

Tom mated there with Irene, a weaver on the plantation. She also bore seven children, and Tom now told them all about their African great-great-grandfather, the faithfully passed-down knowledge of his sounds and stories having become by now the family's prideful treasure.

The youngest of that second set of seven children was a girl, Cynthia, who became my maternal Grandma (which today I can only see as fated). Anyway, all of this is how I was growing up in Henning at Grandma's, listening from behind her rocking chair as she and the other visiting old women talked of that African (never then comprehended as *my* great-great-great-great-grandfather) who said his name was "*Kin-tay*," and said "*ko*" for banjo, "*Kamby Bolong*" for river, and a jumble of other "k"-beginning sounds that Grandma privately muttered, most often while making beds or cooking, and who also said that near his village he was kidnaped while chopping wood to make himself a drum.

The story had become nearly as fixed in my head as in Grandma's by the time Dad and Mama moved me and my two younger brothers, George and Julius, away from Henning to be with them at the small black agricultural and mechanical college in Normal, Ala., where Dad taught.

To compress my next 25 years: When I was 17 Dad let me enlist as a mess boy in the U.S. Coast Guard. I became a ship's cook out in the South Pacific during World War II, and at night down by my bunk I began trying to write sea adventure stories,

mailing them off to magazines and collecting rejection slips for eight years before some editors began purchasing and publishing occasional stories. By 1949 the Coast Guard had made me its first "journalist"; finally with 20 years' service, I retired at the age of 37, determined to make a full time career of writing. I wrote mostly magazine articles; my first book was "The Autobiography of Malcom X."

Then one Saturday in 1965 I happened to be walking past the National Archives building in Washington. Across the interim years I had thought of Grandma's old stories—otherwise I can't think what diverted me up the Archives' steps. And when a main reading room desk attendant asked if he could help me, I wouldn't have dreamed of admitting to him some curiosity hanging on from boyhood about my slave forebears. I kind of bumbled that I was interested in census records of Alamance County, North Carolina, just after the Civil War.

The microfilm rolls were delivered, and I turned them through the machine with a building sense of intrigue, viewing in different census takers' penmanship an endless parade of names. After about a dozen microfilmed rolls, I was beginning to tire, when in utter astonishment I looked upon the names of Grandma's parents: Tom Murray, Irene Murray . . . older sisters of Grandma's as well—every one of them a name that I'd heard countless times on her front porch.

It wasn't that I hadn't believed Grandma. You just *didn't* not believe my Grandma. It was simply so uncanny actually seeing those names in print and in official U.S. Government records.

Writing in the Real World

Genre and Style

Inventing a Genre Haley wrote both fiction and nonfiction books and articles, but *Roots,* by the nature of its content, had to be something different, its own genre. Haley called his book "faction." Invite students to infer the meaning of the word. (*Roots* is a mixture of fact and fiction.) "My Furthest-Back Person—The African," like *Roots,* describes intense moments of self-discovery when Haley realizes who he is, where he came from, and what his discovery represents for all African Americans.

Howardena Pindell, *Autobiography: Water/Ancestors, Middle Passage/Family Ghosts*, 1988.

The Writing Process

Library. (Whenever black attendants understood the idea of my search, documents I requested reached me with miraculous speed.) In one source or another during 1966 I was able to document at least the highlights of the cherished family story. I would have given anything to have told Grandma, but sadly, in 1949 she had gone. So I went and told the only survivor of those Henning front-porch storytellers: Cousin Georgia Anderson now in her 80's in Kansas City, Kan. Wrinkled, bent, not well herself, she was so overjoyed, repeating to me the old stories and sounds; they were like Henning echoes: "Yeah, boy, that African say his name was '*Kin-tay*'; he say the banjo was 'ko,' an' the river 'Kamby-Bolong,' an' he was off choppin' some wood to make his drum when they grabbed 'im!" Cousin Georgia grew so excited we had to stop her, calm her down, "You go' head, boy! Your grandma an' all of 'em—they up there watching what you do!"

That week I flew to London on a magazine assignment. Since by now I was steeped in the old, in the past, scarcely a tour guide missed me—I was awed at so many historical places and treasures I'd heard of and

During the next several months I was back in Washington whenever possible, in the Archives, the Library of Congress, the Daughters of the American Revolution

Literature Model **101**

Teach

Guided Reading
- How did Haley begin his family history research?
- What made Haley enter the National Archives building?
- Why does Haley call the discovery of his great-grandparents' names "uncanny"? **L2**

Viewing the Art

Howardena Pindell, *Autobiography: Water/Ancestors, Middle Passage/Family Ghosts*, 1988

This collage by artist Howardena Pindell is from a series called *Autobiography.* The piece measures 118 by 71 inches and is made with acrylic, tempera, and mixed media on sewn canvas. The collage centers around a template of the artist's body, with her whitened self-portrait. The white shape of a slave ship reflects the artist's African ancestors. References to twins indicate the frequency of twins in her family and may also suggest the merging of two cultures.

Teach

Guided Reading

- Why were a few bits of strange-sounding *k* words so important?
- Can you think of other clues Haley could have researched? **L2**

The Writing Process

Literature Model

read of. I came upon the Rosetta stone[2] in the British Museum, marveling anew at how Jean Champollion, the French archaeologist, had miraculously deciphered its ancient demotic and hieroglyphic[3] texts. . . .

The thrill of that just kept hanging around in my head. I was on a jet returning to New York when a thought hit me. Those strange, unknown-tongue sounds, always part of our family's old story . . . they were obviously bits of our original African "Kin-tay's" native tongue. What specific tongue? Could I somehow find out?

Back in New York, I began making visits to the United Nations Headquarters lobby; it wasn't hard to spot Africans. I'd stop any I could, asking if my bits of phonetic sounds held any meaning for them. A couple of dozen Africans quickly looked at me, listened, and took off— understandably dubious about some Tennessean's accent alleging "African" sounds.

> *I was awed at so many historical places and treasures I'd heard of and read of.*

My research assistant, George Sims (we grew up together in Henning), brought me some names of ranking scholars of African linguistics. One was particularly intriguing: a Belgian- and English-educated Dr. Jan Vansina; he had spent his early career living in West African villages, studying and tape-recording countless oral histories that were narrated by certain very old African men; he had written a standard textbook, "The Oral Tradition."

So I flew to the University of Wisconsin to see Dr. Vansina. In his living room I told him every bit of the family story in the fullest detail that I could remember

it. Then, intensely, he queried me about the story's relay across the generations, about the gibberish of "k" sounds Grandma had fiercely muttered to herself while doing her housework, with my brothers and me giggling beyond her hearing at what we had dubbed "Grandma's noises."

Dr. Vansina, his manner very serious, finally said, "These sounds your family has kept sound very probably of the tongue called 'Mandinka.'"

I'd never heard of any "Mandinka." Grandma just told of the African saying "*ko*" for banjo, or "*Kamby Bolong*" for a Virginia river.

Among Mandinka stringed instruments, Dr. Vansina said, one of the oldest was the "*kora.*"

"*Bolong,*" he said, was clearly Mandinka for "river." Preceded by "Kamby," it very likely meant "Gambia River."

Dr. Vasina telephoned an eminent Africanist colleague, Dr. Philip Curtin. He said that the phonetic "*Kin-tay*" was correctly spelled "Kinte," a very old clan that had originated in Old Mali. The Kinte men traditionally were blacksmiths, and the women were potters and weavers.

---

2 **Rosetta** (rō zet′ ə) **stone** an ancient tablet found in Egypt with inscriptions in both Greek and Egyptian, thus giving researchers a key to understanding ancient Egyptian writings
3 **demotic** (di mot′ik), **hieroglyphic** (hī′ ər ə glif′ik) two ancient Egyptian systems of writing

Cultural Connections

History

Explain that the Rosetta stone, which was discovered in 1799 by a French officer in Napoleon's army, held the key to much of our current knowledge of ancient Egypt's history and culture. Point out that the writing on the stone is in two languages, Egyptian and Greek, and three writing systems, hieroglyphics, demotic script (a simplified form of Egyptian writing), and the Greek alphabet. Until the Rosetta stone was found and deciphered, no one knew how to read hieroglyphics. Ask volunteers to read about the Rosetta stone in an encyclopedia.

Literature Model

I knew I must get to the Gambia River.

The first native Gambian I could locate in the U.S. was named Ebou Manga, then a junior attending Hamilton College in upstate Clinton, N.Y. He and I flew to Dakar, Senegal, then took a smaller plane to Yundum Airport, and rode in a van to Gambia's capital, Bathurst. Ebou and his father assembled eight Gambia government officials. I told them Grandma's stories, every detail I could remember, as they listened intently, then reacted. "'*Kamby Bolong*' of course is Gambia River!" I heard. "But more clue is your forefather's saying his name was '*Kinte*.'" Then they told me something I would never even have fantasized—that in places in the back country lived very old men, commonly called *griots,* who could tell centuries of the histories of certain very old family clans. As for *Kintes,* they pointed out to me on a map some family villages, Kinte-Kundah, and Kinte-Kundah Janneh-Ya, for instance.

The Gambian officials said they would try to help me. I returned to New York dazed. It is embarrassing to me now, but despite Grandma's stories, I'd never been concerned much with Africa, and I had the routine images of African people living mostly in exotic jungles. But a compulsion[4] now laid hold of me to learn all I could, and I began devouring books about Africa, especially about the slave trade. Then one Thursday's mail contained a letter from one of the Gambian officials, inviting me to return there.

Monday I was back in Bathurst. It galvanized[5] me when the officials said that a griot had been located who told the *Kinte* clan history—his name was Kebba Kanga

Fofana. To reach him, I discovered, required a modified safari: renting a launch to get upriver, two land vehicles to carry supplies by a roundabout land route, and employing finally 14 people, including three interpreters and four musicians, since a *griot* would not speak the reversed clan histories without background music.

The boat Baddibu vibrated upriver, with me acutely tense: Were these Africans maybe viewing me as but another of the pith-helmets?[6] After about two hours, we put in at James Island, for me to see the ruins of the once British-operated James Fort. Here two centuries of slave ships had loaded thousands of cargoes of Gambian tribespeople. The crumbling stones, the deeply oxidized[7] swivel cannon, even some remnant links of chain seemed all but impossible to believe. Then we continued upriver to the left-bank village of Albreda, and there put ashore to continue on foot to Juffure, village of the *griot.* Once more we stopped, for me to see *toubob kolong,* "the white man's well," now almost filled in, in a swampy area with abundant, tall, saw-toothed grass. It was dug two centuries ago to "17 men's height deep" to insure survival drinking water for long-driven, famishing coffles[8] of slaves.

---

4 compulsion (kəm pul' shən) a driving force
5 galvanized (gal' və nīzd') excited, as if by an electric shock
6 pith-helmets (pith' hel' mət) a reference to earlier European explorers of Africa, who wore such helmets
7 oxidized (ok'sə dīzd') rusted
8 coffles (kô' fəlz) groups of slaves fastened or driven together

Literature Model **103**

The Writing Process

Teach

Guided Reading

- How were Haley's research techniques similar to investigative reporter Mark Trahant's, as described in the Media Connection?
- What effect does Haley achieve by listing all the people and equipment needed to reach the isolated village where the *griot* lived? **L2**

Critical Thinking

Identifying Temporal Relationships

To help students appreciate the time and energy Haley put into his investigation, you might suggest that as they read, they list important events such as the oft-told stories of Haley's grandmother and Cousin Georgia, his first trip to the National Archives where he discovered his great-grandparents' names, his discovery of the language connection, and his meeting with Dr. Jan Vansina. Stress that Haley's work illustrates what it takes to make the breakthrough discoveries that move an investigation forward.

Teach

Guided Reading

- How do the vivid verbs that Haley uses affect this passage?
- How does Haley reveal the *griot's* status among his fellow villagers?
- How did Haley regard the *griot?* **L2**

Literature Model

Walking on, I kept wishing that Grandma could hear how her stories had led me to the "*Kamby Bolong.*" (Our surviving story-teller Cousin Georgia died in a Kansas City hospital during this same morning, I would learn later.) Finally, Juffure village's playing children, sighting us, flashed an alert. The 70-odd people came rushing from their cir-cular, thatch-roofed, mud-walled huts, with goats bounding up and about, and parrots squawking from up in the palms. I sensed him in advance somehow, the small man amid them, wearing a pillbox cap and an off-white robe—the *griot.* Then the inter-preters went to him, as the villagers thronged around me.

And it hit me like a gale wind: every one of them, the whole crowd, was *jet black.* An enormous sense of guilt swept me—a sense of being some kind of hybrid[9] . . . a sense of being impure among the pure. It was an awful sensation.

The old *griot* stepped away from my interpreters and the crowd quickly swarmed around him—all of them buzzing. An interpreter named A. B. C. Salla came to me; he whispered: "Why they stare at you so, they have never seen here a black American." And that hit me: I was symbol-izing for them twenty-five millions of us they had never seen. What did they think of me—of us?

Then abruptly the old *griot* was briskly walking toward me. His eyes boring into mine, he spoke in Mandinka, as if instinc-tively I should understand—and A. B. C. Salla translated:

It was as if some ancient scroll were printed indelibly within the griot's *brain.*

"Yes . . . we have been told by the forefa-thers . . . that many of us from this place are in exile . . . in that place called America . . . and in other places."

I suppose I physically wavered, and they thought it was the heat; rustling whispers went through the crowd, and a man brought me a low stool. Now the whisper-ing hushed—the musicians had softly begun playing *kora* and *balafon,* and a can-vas sling lawn seat was taken by the *griot,* Kebba Kanga Fofana, aged 73 "rains" (one rainy season each year). He seemed to gather himself into a physical rigidity, and he begin speaking the *Kinte* clan's ancestral oral history; it came rolling from his mouth across the next hours . . . 17th- and 18th-century *Kinte* lineage details, pre-dominantly what men took wives; the children they "begot," in the order of their births; those children's mates and children.

Events frequently were dated by some proximate singular physical occurrence. It was as if some ancient scroll were printed indelibly within the *griot's* brain. Each few sentences or so, he would pause for an interpreter's translation to me. I distill here the essence:

The *Kinte* clan began in Old Mali, the men generally blacksmiths ". . . who con-quered fire," and the women potters and weavers. One large branch of the clan

---

9 **hybrid** (hī′ brid) the offspring of individuals of unlike genetic background, such as of peo-ple of different races

MEETING INDIVIDUAL NEEDS English Language Learners

Performing a Dramatic Reading

These next three pages present Haley's encounter with the *griot,* the cli-mactic event in the quest for his roots. For new speakers of English, you might want to read these pages aloud, starting with the first full paragraph on this student page. Or enlist some of your better readers to prepare a dramatic reading. Such a reading can highlight the emotional impact of the events on Haley, including his recognition that what he would later write was not his story alone, but that of all African Americans.

The Writing Process

moved to Mauretania from where one son of the clan, Kairaba Kunta Kinte, a Moslem Marabout holy man, entered Gambia. He lived first in the village of Pakali N'Ding; he moved next to Jiffarong village; ". . . and then he came here, into our own village of Juffure."

In Juffure, Kairaba Kunta Kinte took his first wife, ". . . a Mandinka maiden, whose name was Sireng. By her, he begot two sons, whose names were Janneh and Saloum. Then he got a second wife, Yaisa. By her, he begot a son, Omoro."

The three sons became men in Juffure. Janneh and Saloum went off and found a new village, Kinte-Kundah Janneh-Ya. "And then Omoro, the youngest son, when he had 30 rains, took as a wife a maiden, Binta Kebba.

"And by her, he begot four sons—Kunta, Lamin, Suwadu, and Madi . . ."

Sometimes, a "begotten," after his naming, would be accompanied by some later occurring detail, perhaps as ". . . in time of big water (flood), he slew a water buffalo." Having named those four sons, now the *griot* stated such a detail.

"About the time the king's soldiers came, the eldest of these four sons, Kunta, when he had about 16 rains, went away from this village, to chop wood to make a drum . . . and he was never seen again . . ."

Goose-pimples the size of lemons seemed to pop all over me. In my knapsack were my cumulative notebooks, the first of them including how in my boyhood, my Grandma, Cousin Georgia and the others told of the African "*Kin-tay*" who always said he was kidnaped near his village—while chopping wood to make a drum . . .

I showed the interpreter, he showed and told the *griot,* who excitedly told the people; they grew very agitated. Abruptly then they formed a human ring, encircling me, dancing and chanting. Perhaps a dozen of the women carrying their infant babies rushed in toward me, thrusting the infants into my arms—conveying, I would later learn, "the laying on of hands . . . through this flesh which is us, we are you, and you are us." The men hurried me into their mosque[10], their Arabic praying later being translated outside: "Thanks be to Allah for returning the long lost from among us." Direct descendants of Kunta Kinte's blood brothers were hastened, some of them from nearby villages, for a family portrait to be taken with me, surrounded by actual ancestral sixth cousins. More symbolic acts filled the remaining day.

When they would let me leave, for some reason I wanted to go away over the African land. Dazed, silent in the bumping Land Rover, I heard the cutting staccato[11] of talking drums. Then when we sighted the next village, its people came thronging to meet us. They were all—little naked ones to wizened[12] elders—waving, beaming, amid a cacophony[13] of crying out; and then my ears identified their words: "*Meester Kinte! Meester Kinte!*"

Let me tell you something: I am a man. But I remember the sob surging up from

---

10 **mosque** (mäsk) a Muslim place of worship
11 **staccato** (stə kät′ ō) a pattern of rapid, abrupt sounds with quick, distinct breaks
12 **wizened** (wiz′ ənd) withered, wrinkled
13 **cacophony** (kə kof′ ə nē) jarring, dissonant sounds

Literature Model **105**

Teach

Guided Reading

- How does Haley capture the emotional power in this scene?
- What effect does Haley's repeating the *griot's* words have? **L2**

 Cultural Connections

Literature

You might mention another oral tradition that passed on stories about real events. During the Middle Ages, the bards of Scotland, Ireland, and Wales were singer-poets. The stories they sang, often satirical, told about the deeds of national heroes. They accompanied themselves on harps and other stringed instruments. Today the word *bard* is used for certain folksingers and poets, including Shakespeare in the expression *the bard of Avon.*

Teach

Guided Reading

- Why did the villagers become agitated when the *griot* told them about Haley's notebook?
- How effective is Haley in describing his emotions? Why? **L2**

Additional Resources

  Fine Art Transparencies, 7–12
  Listening and Speaking Activities,
    pp. 6–8
  Thinking and Study Skills, p. 14

The Writing Process

Literature Model

my feet, flinging up my hands before my face and bawling as I had not done since I was a baby . . . the jet-black Africans were jostling, staring . . . I didn't care, with the feelings surging. If you really knew the odyssey of us millions of black Americans, if you really knew how we came in the seeds of our forefathers, captured, driven, beaten, inspected, bought, branded, chained in foul ships, if you really knew, you needed weeping . . .

Writing in the Real World

Writers and Writing

Changing Direction Haley relates an experience common to all writers—a change in direction during the writing process. He meant to write the story of his family. After his African experience, he knew he had to do more: "I knew that what I must write, really, was our black saga, where any individual's past is the essence of the millions."

Literature Model

Linking Writing and Literature

Readers Respond to the Model

How did Alex Haley's purpose and point of view affect his writing process?

Explore Alex Haley's techniques by answering these questions. Then read what other students liked about Haley's writing.

1. How did Alex Haley come up with the idea to write a book tracing his roots back to his "furthest-back person"?
2. What sources did Haley consult to research his African heritage?

3. How did Haley order and present the information he collected? In what other ways could he have structured and told his story?
4. To which part of Alex Haley's story did you personally relate? Why?

What Students Say

"This piece was about Alex Haley becoming more interested in his roots and how he traced them all the way back to a specific Gambian family. The part I remember most clearly was when Haley met his family in Gambia. It was an emotional, climactic scene."

Chris Fickes

"This selection was about a person trying to find out about his heritage. Haley wrote in first person because he was talking about his own experience. The mood was one of curiosity. Haley was curious, and as a reader I was, too. I found what the author was looking for as he found it. The writer created this mood by telling his story in chronological order. I enjoyed this selection and would recommend it to people who are interested in their heritage."

Yahna Awazu

Literature Model **107**

The Writing Process

Linking Writing and Literature

Assess

Evaluation Rubrics

As your students discuss the selection, either in small groups or as a class, encourage them to begin with a personal response. The student responses on this page might be used as a starting point.

Look for evidence that students
- have read the selection
- can state some of the writer's ideas in their own words
- understand the writer's point of view
- have connected the content to their own knowledge and experiences
- understand the ideas and implications of the selection

Some possible responses to the discussion questions on this page include the following:
1. Haley had been thinking about his Grandma's stories.
2. He read old census records; he talked to leading scholars of African linguistics. Haley also read everything he could find on Africa and the slave trade. He went to Gambia once he knew that his ancestor was from there.
3. He organized his information in chronological order, from his early childhood memories to meeting the *griot* in Africa. He could have started with his visit to Africa and then moved on to flashbacks of his childhood and book research.
4. I identified with his description of how his relatives would sit around on the porch telling stories.

Close

Have students write a paragraph or two detailing research they might do to find out their own family history.

107

Review

Reflecting on the Unit

You may have students respond to Reflecting on the Unit in writing or through discussion.

Writing Across the Curriculum

As students work on this assignment, have them think of themselves as candidates running for political office. Clear, concise language is essential in helping an audience to understand complex issues and their opinions.

☛ Adding to Your Portfolio

Suggest that students select pieces for which they have a good "how-I-wrote-this" story to share with those who review their portfolio.

Portfolio Evaluation

If you grade the portfolio selections, you may want to award two marks—one each for content and form. Explain your assessment criteria before students make their selections.

Commend
- experimentation with creative prewriting techniques
- clear, concise writing in which the main idea, audience, and purpose are evident
- successful revisions
- work that shows a flair for language

✓ ASSESSMENT OPTIONS

 Tests With Answer Key & Rubrics
Unit 2 Choice A Test, p. 5
Unit 2 Choice B Test, p. 6
Unit 2 Composition Objective Test, pp. 7-8

 Testmaker
Unit 2 Choice A Test
Unit 2 Choice B Test
Unit 2 Composition Objective Test

You may wish to administer one of these tests as a mastery test.

💾 MindJogger Videoquizzes

Reflecting on the Unit

Summarize what you learned in this unit by answering the following questions.

❶ What are the five stages of the writing process?
❷ What are the important elements of each stage?
❸ What techniques, tools, or procedures can help you successfully complete each stage of the process?
❹ What are some of the main things to consider when you analyze point of view in literature?

Adding to Your Portfolio

CHOOSE A SELECTION FOR YOUR PORTFOLIO Look over the writing you have done during this unit. Select a completed piece of writing to put in your portfolio. The piece you choose should show some or all of the following:

- a specific audience and writing purpose
- a clear topic sentence or sentences supported by appropriate details
- a logical ordering of ideas
- unity and coherence
- careful editing and proofreading

Reflect on Your Choice

Attach a note to the piece you chose, explaining briefly why you chose it and what you learned from writing it.
SET GOALS How can you improve your writing? What skill will you focus on the next time you write?

Writing Across the Curriculum

MAKE A SOCIAL STUDIES CONNECTION Scan your government textbook or a magazine or newspaper for topics relating to local, state, or national politics. Choose a subject that interests you. Write two related topic sentences and list details that will help support each. Try to include each type of supporting detail: a concrete detail, an example, a fact or statistic, and a reason. Then follow the other stages of the writing process. Use your topic sentences and supporting details to draft, revise, and edit two unified paragraphs that describe a political issue. Write legibly and be sure to check for errors in spelling and grammar. You may wish to present your finished writing to an audience of other students.

TIME
Facing the Blank Page

Inside the writing process with TIME writers and editors

Focus

Lesson Overview

Objectives

- To apply the strategies of professional writers to all stages of the writing process
- To develop visual aids to enhance written and oral presentations
- To use print and electronic resources to research writing topics
- To generate ideas for writing by using prewriting strategies
- To develop ideas through the use of the drafting process
- To revise writing based on peer and self-directed evaluation
- To edit writing for specific purposes and for clarity and conciseness
- To use available technology to support aspects of creating, revising, editing, and publishing texts

🔔 Bellringer
Daily Language Activity

When students come into the classroom, have this assignment on the board: *You have been asked to write an article for a new magazine for high school students. What steps will you need to take to complete the assignment?*

See also 📖 *Daily Language Practice*

Motivating Activity

As students answer the bellringer question, list their responses on the board, in the order in which students give them. Do not sequence or edit the steps. Have students form small groups, and direct groups to develop and organize the steps on the board into a coherent process. (Define *process* as a sequence of interconnected steps that lead to a desired goal.) Tell groups that they may reword, add, combine, or omit steps from the list.

Resource Manager

Planning Resources
- *Lesson Plans*

📖 **Transparencies**
- *Writing Process*

📂 **Other Print Resources**
- *Composition Enrichment*
- *Composition Practice*
- *Composition Reteaching*

- *Grammar and Composition Handbook*
- *Guide to Using the Internet and Other Electronic Resources*
- *Writing Assessment and Evaluation Rubrics*

📼 **Video**
- *Facing the Blank Page*

💾 **Software**
- *Presentation Plus!*
- *Revising with Style*

🖥 **Web Sites**
- *writerschoice.glencoe.com*
- *lit.glencoe.com*

Teach

Discussion Prompt

The professionals at TIME say that collaboration helps them learn from one another. What did you learn by collaborating in groups? Did working together make it easier to think of all the steps that might be involved in writing an article? To identify omissions or ineffective repetition? To express ideas and organize them?

Think about the writing process— prewriting, drafting, revising, editing and proofreading, publishing and presenting. Which steps in the writing process lend themselves to collaboration? (Most of the steps can benefit from collaboration, such as brainstorming or peer editing.) How might collaboration be helpful when writing? (Answers might include the following: Collaboration can help a writer generate ideas, refine thoughts, or catch errors.)

Viewing the Chart

Have students read the chart and summarize what each member of the TIME writing team contributes to the process. (*Writer:* helps come up with a story idea; reads, selects, and organizes information; drafts story; revises story. *Correspondent:* helps come up with a story idea, investigates and interviews, reviews writer's draft and makes suggestions. *Researcher:* gathers material from reliable sources, compiles and submits research files, checks accuracy of draft. *Editor:* helps come up with a story idea; reviews draft; suggests revisions; reviews revisions; "greens"; chooses to print, hold, or "kill" story. *Copyeditor:* checks style, grammar, mechanics, and spelling.) Ask students to compare and contrast their writing processes with the process that the professionals at TIME follow. What steps, if any, would students like add to their processes? Why?

Writing for TIME

The stories published each week in TIME are the work of experienced professionals. The writing is strong; the facts are accurate; the grammar, spelling, and punctuation are error-free (or close!). Behind the scenes, however, there is another story to be told. As these pages reveal, TIME staffers struggle with many of the same challenges that students face in the messy, trial-and-error process that is writing: selecting among topics; finding information; getting organized; starting to draft; and then revising, revising, and revising some more.

Is there a secret to the quality of writing in TIME? Beyond experience and hard work, the key lies in collaboration. As the chart on these pages illustrates, writers are assisted at each stage of the process by other members of the staff in a kind of "group journalism" that has become the magazine's hallmark. The writers and editors teach and learn from one another every week; student writers can do the same. Try out and adapt the writing and collaboration strategies presented in "Facing the Blank Page" to discover what works for you.

PREWRITING

Senior Editor in New York   **Staff Writer** in New York   **Correspondent** in the field

Story idea is proposed and assigned

Writer takes assignment, refines topic, sends "query" to correspondents and researchers

Research begins

Correspondents investigate, conduct interviews   **Researchers** gather material from reliable sources: "clips" from articles, studies, statistics

DRAFTING

Correspondents send their reporting or "files" to writer   **Researchers** compile and submit research files

Writer reads and organizes information, drafts the story

Viewing and Representing

Visual Aids

As a class, discuss the advantages to writers of presenting information in chart form. (Charting can help writers organize information logically and express ideas concisely.) How do charts benefit readers? (Charts present information in a brief, organized, easy-to-follow format.) Ask students to review recent pieces of their own writing to see which might be enhanced by visual aids. Encourage students to create and add the visuals.

REVISING

Editor reads draft, asks for revisions

Correspondents
check interpretation,
make suggestions

Writer revises, resubmits for comments

Researchers
check accuracy,
details

Writer and editor revise again, "green" (edit for length)

EDITING AND PROOFREADING

Checks for conformity to TIME
style and conventions

Copy Desk

Checks and corrects grammar,
mechanics, spelling

PUBLISHING AND PRESENTING

Managing Editor chooses to print, hold, or "kill" (omit) story

Circulation of TIME
rises or falls

Readers respond to published story

E-mail and letters
to the editor

111

Teach

Discussing the Steps

Point out that the capitalized headings of the TIME chart describe stages in the writing process, while the brief descriptions below the headings describe steps. Ask students to discuss the difference between stages and steps. (Stages are general phases of a process; steps are specific tasks performed during each stage.) As a class, generate a list of steps one must follow to complete a simple process, such as changing a tire. Then challenge students to group the steps into stages and to label each stage. (The tire-changing process might include these stages: gathering tools, taking safety pre-cautions, removing the damaged tire, attaching and securing the spare tire, replacing tools.)

Charting a Process

Ask students to jot down the steps in a process that they have studied in another class, such as geometry, chemistry, psychol-ogy, or physical education. Have students group the steps in their processes and write headings that describe the stages in the process. Then ask students to create charts based on their notes.

Listening and Speaking

Reporting on the Charts

Have students use the process-analysis charts they created as the basis for brief oral reports. To help students build skills in using visual aids, encourage students to prepare and organize their reports while consider-ing the information in their visuals. Then have presenters display and refer to their charts during their reports. Allow time for class members to ask clear questions and to have presenters respond appropriately.

Teach

Prewriting Strategies

Encourage students to discuss their experiences with freewriting. Point out that there is no single "right" prewriting strategy. Individual preferences often dictate which strategy one uses. But also note that students should continue to try different approaches. Young writers may find that an approach they usually avoid is helpful for a particular writing project.

Assess

Evaluation Rubrics

Try It Out

Students should
- select an appropriate subject.
- write a statement or question about the subject.
- freewrite continuously for fifteen minutes.
- identify the main idea or ideas in their freewriting.

Prewriting

Getting Started: Freewriting

In the early stages of writing an essay or article for TIME, Contributor Lance Morrow uses freewriting to help him discover what the focus of his piece should be.

Lance Morrow:

Lance Morrow: Test your assumptions.

"A great help to me in writing is making notes. I record information or snippets of quotations from books or sources and then I think, 'Hey, what about that? Well, that's interesting, but where does it lead?' I follow that road, and then that idea leads down another road. So I go down the next road a bit. And then I put it all into notes. By writing, you are forming your own thinking. You are assembling the materials, but you are also defining the questions that you want to address. What's important here? What is the essence?

What you want to do is honestly accompany the idea. Don't pre-cook the ideas in a piece of writing—test yourself. Test your assumptions. Don't think that you've got it when you start out on the journey, because, to me, the whole point is that you learn in the process of writing."

WRITING TIP

Facing the Essay
"There is a feeling that the essay is an imposing form. Don't be intimidated by it. An essay is simply a somewhat organized exercise in discussing, having a conversation about a particular subject. Approach the essay the way you would approach discussing this subject with an intelligent, reasonably well-informed friend."
—**Lance Morrow**

LEARNING FROM THE WRITER

TRY IT OUT
Try Morrow's freewriting technique. At the top of a blank piece of paper, name an issue in school, local or national news, or an important topic you have discussed in any one of your classes. On the next line, write a statement or a question about this topic. Then continue to write freely, allowing one idea or argument to lead to another. Write without stopping for 15 minutes. Now stop, reread your writing, and circle the word, phrase or sentence that answers Morrow's question: What's important here? What is the essence?

HOW I WRITE
1. Is freewriting a technique that works for you? Have you ever tried it before? What other strategies have you used to find the focus for a piece of writing?
2. Review the work in your writing folder and journal. Identify a piece of writing in which you tested yourself and challenged your assumptions. Specifically, what did you learn in the process of writing?

Enrichment and Extension

Using Quotations

Morrow points out that quotations can be a source of inspiration for generating topics. Ask students to use print or electronic resources to find interesting quotations. Skim the index to a collection of quotations, and assign each student a different subject to research. Have students bring their favorite quotations to class. Then ask for volunteers to compile a master list of the quotations and create a class Web quotation site.

Thinking and writing freely can also help you organize ideas before drafting. Here is a technique that works for television critic James Poniewozik.

James Poniewozik:

❝ I don't use outlines, but what I often do is just free-associate on a page. I will freely write down the dozen topics or points that should be mentioned at some point in the piece, and then maybe I'll write numbers by them—either to show their relative importance or to put them in what seems to make for a smooth flow of the article.

And an order emerges: I say, 'I should start with this, and then I'll jump to this, and this segues to this,' and so on. Then I can start to write. ❞

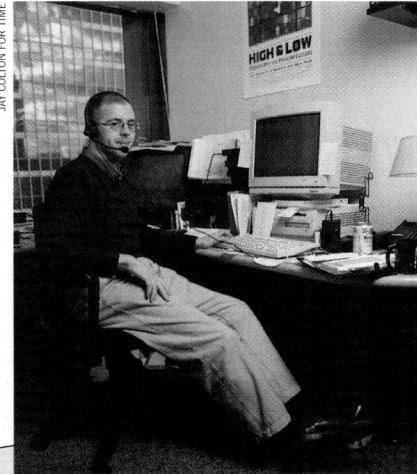

James Poniewozik: Writing freely to find a structure.

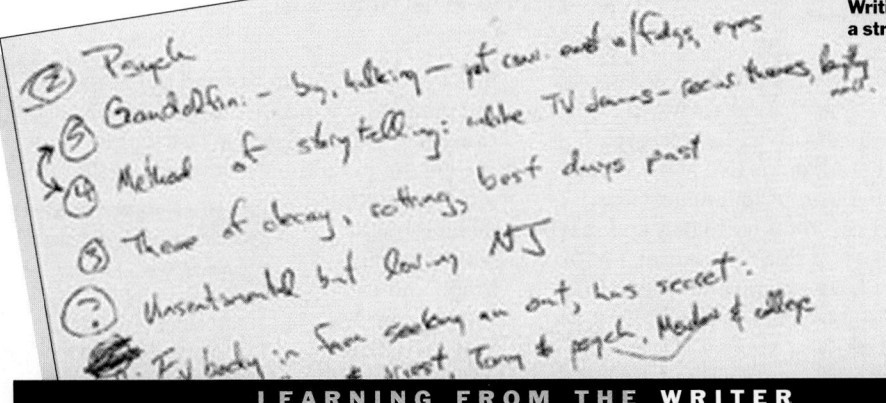

LEARNING FROM THE WRITER

TRY IT OUT
1. Review by the numbers. Poniewozik's reviews of television shows appear frequently in TIME. The notes above are for a piece he wrote naming *The Sopranos* the best television program of 1999. Use his writing strategy to prepare your own review. Think of a program you have seen recently. Now "free-associate" on a sheet of paper: describe characters and plot, offer analysis and comparisons, tell about your personal response to the show. Get down on paper every point you might wish to make about this program. Then look back over your writing and number items as Poniewozik did. Does an order for a review emerge? Write the review!
2. Compare Poniewozik's technique to the suggestions for finding and focusing a topic presented in Lesson 2.2. Which strategy works best for you?

Writing in the Real World

Reviewing Books

Major Web bookstores include e-mail message boxes where readers can write reviews of books that they have read. Encourage students to write reviews of favorite novels or other books and publish their reviews on-line. Or, have students write a review of a favorite movie. Student reviews should demonstrate that the students recognize how visual and sound techniques, including special effects, editing, camera angles, reaction shots, sequencing, and music, convey messages in the movie.

Teach

Technology Tip

Drafting Encourage students to word-process first drafts. Copy, paste, and delete functions make it easy for writers to experiment with different patterns of organization when they write. Encourage students to use the shading function of their program to highlight problem sentences while drafting. Highlighting can help students avoid "getting stuck" and breaking their train of thought. Remind students that they should revise shaded portions after first getting their ideas down on paper.

Learning about Leads

Discuss and Evaluate Ask students to paraphrase the TIME definition for *lead*. (Students should see that the *lead* is the introduction.) As a class, discuss the functions that a lead or an introduction should fulfill. Write students' reponses in key words on the board; then have students recast the responses into a list of questions that they can use to evaluate their own introductory paragraphs. (*Sample list:* Does the introduction include an effective attention-getting device? Motivate readers to continue reading? State or imply the main idea of the piece?) Encourage students to select recent pieces of writing from their portfolios and use the questions to evaluate and revise the introductions to the pieces.

Drafting
The Flow of Ideas: Leads and Transitions

Jesse Birnbaum: Each sentence calls forth the next.

MARIANNE BARCELLONA

When a TIME staff writer is ready to begin drafting, he or she faces a desk piled high with material supplied by the research department, along with "files" or reports written by TIME correspondents around the country and around the world. From here, no two writers proceed in exactly the same way.

Recalls writer Jesse Birnbaum, "The late Paul O'Neill, a famous writer at TIME, would take all the folders on his desk, read them twice, and then put them all away. He would sit down and write the cover story without ever once looking back at the material. His idea was that the things you remembered were the things that were worth saying, and that the details you didn't remember were not worth telling the reader about."

Birnbaum's own method is different, and easier to test as a model:

❝I will try to absorb all the research that has been gathered and arrive at an idea for the story. I might underline material as I read, so that I can refer to it later, and maybe make some notes. I don't do a formal outline. For me, there is an organization I can find without working too mechanically. That is: get your lead written, know what you want to say, and let every sentence call forth the next idea.❞

When each sentence and paragraph leads to the next, the result is a coherent, organized draft. A story or review by Jesse Birnbaum is held together by logical and elegant transitions between paragraphs and ideas.

Birnbaum on transitions:

❝Transitions move the reader on to another subject from the end of the preceding paragraph. One way to find good transitions is to look back at the last sentence, or maybe the penultimate sentence of the previous paragraph. Get a thought from that paragraph and evoke the idea, or even a key word, from what came before. Pause and look back to help you find a transition into your next subject, the next scene.

Finally, as you go toward the end, it helps organize a story to evoke (in your last paragraph or last sentence) a thought that was made in your lead.❞

> **TIME LEXICON**
>
> **Lead:** The opening paragraph or paragraphs of a piece, designed to draw in the reader and show the reader what the story will be about. "The lead," says Birnbaum, "is a road map for the rest of the story."

Cooperative Learning

Researching and Writing

Identify a subject of general interest to your students, and ask them to freewrite about it. Have students review their freewriting to identify subtopics that they would like to research. Organize the class into research groups, and challenge each group to find and present to the class at least one current print or electronic article by an expert on the subtopic that the group is investigating. The members of each group should take turns as speakers, using effective verbal and nonverbal strategies, and should speak clearly and effectively in presenting the article to the class. When each group presents its article to the class, other groups should take notes on major points. After all groups have presented their articles, assign students to use their notes to write a feature story about the subject.

Read this excerpt from one of Jesse Birnbaum's book reviews in TIME:

Roads Not Taken:
What If Some of Our History Had Happened a Little Differently?

Military history is a gallimaufry of choices and chance, of opportunities taken, of roads forsaken.

It is this truism that drives *What If?*, a collection of essays by 34 military historians, journalists and novelists, all indulging in "counterfactual" conjecture.

In 334 B.C., for example, the 22-year-old Macedonian King Alexander charged with his cavalry into the ranks of Persian forces at the Granicus River in what is now Turkey. A Persian soldier clubbed Alexander with an ax, but before he could deal a second and fatal blow, the King's bodyguard killed him.

What if Alexander had died at Granicus? Goodbye to all the conquests of Alexander the Great, says Princeton historian Josiah Ober. The Persian Empire would have overtaken the known world. The great promise of Hellenism would have lost its way; the growing Roman Empire would have atrophied; Judea would have remained a backwater, Jesus merely "a local religious figure," and Christianity and Judaism insignificant provincial oddities. There would have been no need for a Martin Luther, no Reformation, no Renaissance, no Enlightenment, no Western culture.

In 1944 General Dwight Eisenhower was prepared to invade Normandy on June 5, but when his weather officer predicted storms over the English Channel, Ike postponed D-day for 24 hours. What if the Channel weather had not abated on June 6? World War II chronicler Stephen Ambrose argues that without air cover and paratrooper support, the first waves of Allied troops would have been incapable of fighting. Hitler could have held his positions, and Operation Overlord, the master plan for reconquering Europe, would have disintegrated.

—**Jesse Birnbaum**

DISCUSSION

1. How does Birnbaum's lead work as a "road map" for the reader and the writer?

2. Study his transitions. How does the first sentence of each paragraph harken back to a word or an idea in the preceding paragraph?

3. Look at one paragraph closely and evaluate Birnbaum's writing. Does each sentence "call forth the next idea"? Cite an example or counter-example.

TRY IT OUT

1. Select a piece of writing from your portfolio and evaluate it as you did Jesse Birnbaum's writing. Do the paragraphs follow a logical organization? Are there transitions to lead the reader smoothly from one paragraph to the next? Identify one paragraph that would benefit from a clearer transition and revise it.

2. Recall and describe how you organized the writing of this piece. How does your writing strategy compare to Jesse Birnbaum's? Could his approach work for you? Why or why not?

Listening and Speaking

Point out that many of the guidelines offered by the TIME staff for writing articles and essays also apply to speech writing. Challenge each student to prepare, organize, and present a two- or three-minute speech based on a recent piece of persuasive writing. Then have students use this feedback to evaluate their own effectiveness and to make a list of goals for future presentations.

- compare the structure of their piece to the structure of Birnbaum's.
- decide whether to adopt Birnbaum's approach.

Teach

Comparing Leads

Have students read the lead to the article on page 115. Then have students locate news articles on the Internet and read the leads to these articles. Have students also watch a televised nightly news report and a television documentary, paying close attention to how the announcers use leads. Have students record their findings from all sources. Then have students analyze their findings by comparing and contrasting how a newsmagazine, Internet news articles, the nightly news, and a documentary use leads in their presentations. Students should also point out the unique properties of each genre.

Assess

Evaluation Rubrics

Discussion

1. Jesse Birnbaum's lead works as a "road map" by stating the main idea, or thesis, of the book that he is reviewing. Follow up by discussing how the general statement logically leads to the specific examples that follow and support it.

2. Students should identify the following transitional devices: *paragraph two*—transitional phrase ("for example"); *paragraph three*—rhetorical question that restates the subject of paragraph two; *paragraph four*—repetition created through the use of similar examples.

3. Through analysis of paragraph structure, students should see that each sentence calls forth the next idea. Note, for example, how the chronologically sequenced chain of events described in the third paragraph answers the rhetorical question presented in the topic sentence.

Try It Out

1. Students should
- select a piece of writing from their portfolio.
- review the organization of each paragraph and the piece as a whole.
- evaluate the effectiveness of the transitional devices.
- identify a weak transition and revise it.

2. Students should
- identify and describe the organizational pattern of their piece of writing.

Teach

Discussion Prompt

What are your thoughts about giving criticism? Receiving it? Together, discuss effective ways to offer constructive criticism. (You might use the following guidelines: adopt a positive or neutral tone, criticize the writing rather than the writer, be specific, and explain how revising will improve the writing.)

Assess

Evaluation Rubrics

Discussion

1. Through discussion, students should see that the TIME editor acts as a thoughtful reader who evaluates the clarity, development, and coherence of stories. Encourage students to discuss how feedback might help them improve their writing.

2. Students should identify similarities and difference between classroom writing conferences and the writing conferences that TIME writers and editors hold.

Try It Out

1. Students should
- collaborate on a list of questions to use during writing conferences.
- apply the questions during a writing conference.
- use feedback to revise a piece of writing.

2. Students should
- recall times that they experimented with new writing strategies.
- evaluate what they learned through experimentation.
- describe specific ways that they might encourage one another to experiment.

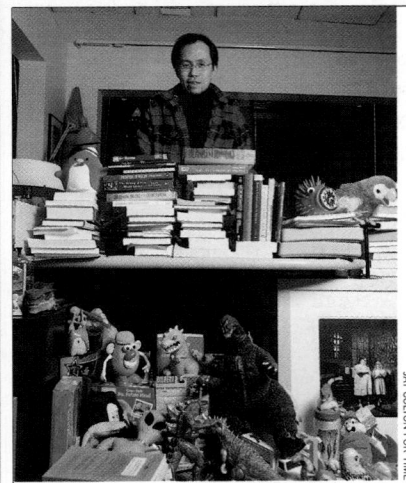

Howard Chua-Eoan: Even the best writers need an editor.

JAY COLTON FOR TIME

Revising
The Editor's Role

TIME magazine works in much the same way that many writing classes do: through collaboration, conferences, and peer review. TIME's writers revise with the help of their editors and fellow writers.

Senior Editor Howard Chua-Eoan:

❝Someone has to read your copy to make sure the point you're trying to get across gets put across. You might think you've made your point clearly, but then when someone else reads it—which is always the test—and it's not clear, then you've got to go back and do it over again—all of it, or perhaps just a sentence or two.

Even the best writers need an editor, because sometimes you think you've figured everything out, but you've slid over an essential step in reasoning a story. An editor can say, 'I know what you're trying to do, and I agree with it, but you're missing how you get from this point to that point.'

Students should focus on whether or not the message gets across. Next, see if the message is delivered coherently. Then ask: Is there a structure embedded in the story that holds it together? The structure is very important; how you begin the story, the paragraph where you say what the story is all about, what it means. Details, quotes, style should be left to the writer's discretion.❞

WRITING TIP

"When you write, it's important to have structural elements firmly in place, but then you should experiment. If you can just do a story, you're not special. But if you can do special things within the existing structure—that's what's great."
—**Howard Chua-Eoan**

LEARNING FROM THE EDITOR

DISCUSSION
1. What is the role of an editor at TIME? Have you ever had a good editor?
2. How is a classroom writing conference similar to or different from the writer/editor relationship at TIME?

TRY IT OUT
1. Questions for revision. Based on Howard Chua-Eoan's advice, make a list of questions to help you and your listeners in a writing conference. Use them to help revise a piece of writing in progress.

2. Recall a time when you freely experimented with your writing. What did you try to do? Was it successful? How can you, your teacher, and your classmates encourage each other to experiment with your writing this year?

116 TIME Facing the Blank Page

Cooperative Learning

Pair students and ask them to exchange pieces of their writing. Encourage students to assume the role of editor, evaluate each other's papers, and offer specific suggestions for revising. After students respond to their peers' feedback, have them revise their own papers. Then have students take turns presenting their papers orally to the class. Students should speak clearly and effectively, using appropriate pitch and tone of voice, posture, and eye contact.

Sentence Variety: Making It Move

Time Correspondent James Willwerth was asked to give one essential tip for writers. Jim grabbed a marker and explained:

66 This is my advice. Here is 'straight-line writing': 'Bill went to the store to get some bread.' That's a fine, declarative sentence. But in the next sentence, instead of using another straight declarative, vary it and write: 'Because he had to get some bread, Bill went to the store.' That variety is the wavy line. If you front-load some sentences with clauses, back-load others, and use the straight declarative, too, then your narrative moves. Your narrative has some rhythm to it. 99

Don't write like this | Write like this

LEARNING FROM THE **WRITER**

Side by Side in Santa Paula: One School's Success

Math teacher Zbigniew Zielina was puzzled by the silence. It was early in the school year, he was about to begin his algebra class, and the Santa Paula High School instructor detected none of the loud talk and scraping chairs that usually marked his students' entrance. He turned to investigate. "I see 30 kids quietly copying the questions," he recalls. "They were ready to

work. In all my years, I have never seen this."

Until last September, no one in Santa Paula, Calif., had. That's when the tiny (population: 27,000) farm community, about 65 miles northwest of Los Angeles, decided to integrate its college-prep and "general" education students so that slow, average and accelerated learners would sit side by side. It is a bold experiment. Segregating students

by ability—a vintage classroom organizational tool known as "tracking" or "ability grouping"—is practiced in at least 80% of U.S. high schools, according to the National Center for Education Statistics. But in Santa Paula, anger at the grouping system had smoldered for decades. "This is a small town that's been run the same way forever," says special-programs teacher Lisa Salas.   **—James Willwerth**

TRY IT OUT
1. Does Jim Willwerth follow his own advice? Look closely at the lead paragraphs from Willwerth's story, "Side by Side," above. Does Willwerth vary the length and structure of his sentences? Find an example. Identify the longest and shortest sentences in the paragraph. Transform the longest into two or three short, declarative sentences.

Combine his shortest with the sentence that comes before or after it. Read the sets of sentences together. Why do you think Willwerth made the choices he did?
2. Analyze a sample of your writing. Take a paragraph you have written, from either a work-in-progress or a completed piece in your portfolio. Would James Willwerth call your paragraph "straight-line

writing" or "wavy-line writing"? Why?

Now rewrite the paragraph by adding more variety to the length and structure of the sentences. Your goal is to find the right balance for your own writing. Read the paragraphs aloud to a partner, but don't specify which is the original. Which version does your partner feel has more movement and rhythm?

TIME Facing the Blank Page **117**

TIME
Facing the Blank Page

Teach

Technology Tip

Revising Most word-processing programs have a revising function that allows editors to mark revisions without deleting the original first draft. Encourage students to practice using this revising function and to make use of any other online editing functions.

Assess

Evaluation Rubrics

Try It Out

1. Students should see that James Willwerth varies the length and structure of his sentences. The longest sentence—sentence two—is followed by the shortest.

Students should
- revise Willwerth's sentence patterning.
- compare their revisions with Willwerth's draft.
- explain why Willwerth might have made his choices.

2. Students should
- select a paragraph that they have written.
- evaluate the sentence variety.
- revise the sentence structure of the paragraph.
- elicit peer feedback about the original and revised drafts.

Exploring Language

Levels of Usage
Many young writers rely on slang and colloquialisms to express their ideas. Have students review the diction of recent pieces of one another's writing and underline overly informal or unclear language. Give students time to discuss and revise.

117

Teach

 Technology Tip

Editing and Proofreading Most word-processing programs have a spell-check function that can be customized to include words a writer frequently misspells. Remind students to use the function during the editing and proofreading stage of the writing process, but warn them that even the best spell-checkers are incapable of finding all spelling errors. Students must still proofread carefully.

Assess

Evaluation Rubrics

Discussion

1. Through discussion, students should see that the objective case *whom* is needed because the pronoun functions as a direct object.
2. *Sample revision:* When the PAC Man Calls
3. *Common misuse of whom:* "Whom shall I say is calling?"
4. *Sample answer:* People are more likely to notice a written grammatical error because they can reread and ponder written statements, and because people generally expect written statements to be polished.
5. Students should voice their opinions about the editors' decision and support their opinions with persuasive reasons.

Try It Out

Students should be able to
- identify and correct common errors in usage.
- differentiate between conscious and unconscious breeches in usage.

 # Editing and Proofreading

Following the Rules— and Breaking Them!

It is the job of TIME's copy editors to ensure that every article, caption, and headline appearing in the magazine is correct. The Copy Desk catches and changes misspellings and errors in grammar and usage.

Imagine that you are a copy editor at TIME. On Saturday, the cover of Monday morning's magazine lands on your desk. The cover text—"Who's This Man Calling?"—contains an error. Can you find it?

Deputy Copy Chief Judy Paul spotted it right away:

"We told the editors that the first word should be *whom*. But changing it to *whom* made the line awkward. We suggested to the editors that they rewrite the cover line to work around the problem, but they said, 'No. We're going to go with it.' A Managing Editor always gets what he wants, so we left it alone. We received a slew of letters on that one. *Who's This Man Calling?* was technically incorrect. We were incorrect on the cover! But that was a conscious decision, not a mistake.

At TIME, if there is a good reason for breaking a usage rule, we will sometimes go ahead and break the rules. But if you just do it because you like it, that's a problem. **"**

LEARNING FROM THE EDITOR

DISCUSSION
1. Explain why the cover line was incorrect. For help, refer to Lesson 17.4.
2. Look closely at the cover photo, title, and subtitle. Write an alternative that works around the *who/whom* usage problem.
3. In your daily speech, do you use *who* and *whom* correctly? Give an example of a common misuse of *who* or *whom* in spoken English.

4. On paper, do you use the two pronouns correctly? Why is there more emphasis on correct usage of pronouns in written English than in spoken English?
5. Why do you think TIME's editors chose to run this cover as originally written? Would you have made the same choice? Do magazines and newspapers have a special responsibility to follow standard usage rules at all times?

TRY IT OUT
Hunt for usage errors. Go on a search for usage errors in print. Begin at a newspaper and magazine rack, scanning cover titles and subtitles, headlines, and advertising copy. Pay attention to signage in stores and on the street. For every error you identify, write a corrected version. Which errors do you think are the result of a conscious decision to break standard usage rules?

Viewing and Representing

Charting Errors

Encourage each student to create a "Frequently Made Errors" chart and to update it every time you return a graded piece of writing. Remind students to refer to their charts whenever they proofread and edit their writing.

Publishing and Presenting

Rewards and Challenges

"Writing," admits Senior Editor Janice Simpson, "is very, very hard work." Does getting published make it all worthwhile?

Janice Simpson reflects:

❝ It isn't necessarily being published that I find rewarding. What drew me to journalism was the fact that I'd actually get paid to be a dilettante! I like going into other people's worlds. I like finding out about those worlds. Then I tell other people about them. Journalism still excites me because it allows me to do that.

Yes, writing is hard work, but there's also an element of fun about what we do, and the best writing reflects that joy. That joy is

Janice Simpson: Going into other people's worlds.

JAY COLTON FOR TIME

transmitted in writing, in finding the right word. I think we've all had the experience of reading something and thinking, 'Aha! Let me write that down. That's just the way I feel about it.' When that happens, the writer has transmitted some of the joy he or she is feeling, some of the emotion, to you, the reader. And that's very much what writing and storytelling and journalism are about. ❞

Janice Simpson's first "official" published piece of writing appeared when she was 15. Simpson was the *Portland Press-Herald* correspondent for her high school in Portland, Maine.

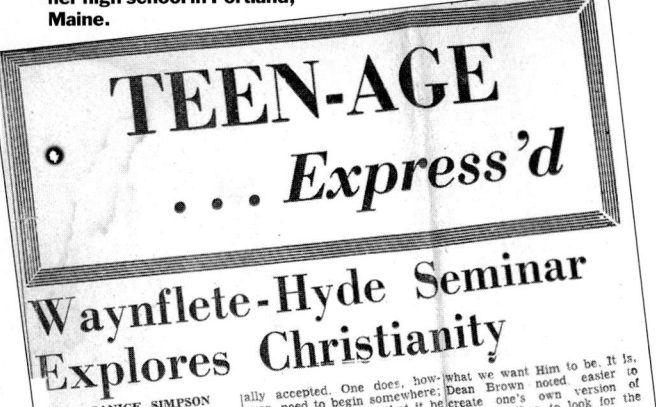

TEEN-AGE ... Express'd

Waynflete-Hyde Seminar Explores Christianity

By JANICE SIMPSON

Who was Jesus? Master, teacher, heretic, son of man, or forerunner of the Hippie movement? All of these titles, except the last, have been attributed to Jesus in the Gospels. But who or what was he?

ally accepted. One does, however, need to begin somewhere; Dean Brown suggests that it be with the search for the historical Jesus.

Everyone has his own concept of Jesus. Dean Brown likens this to the test in which a person looks at an ink blot and

what we want Him to be. It is, Dean Brown noted, easier to create one's own version of something than to look for the correct one.

Dean Brown conceded that the search wouldn't be an easy one, for the Gospels, our earliest record of Jesus, never come out and tell us who He was. And of Calcedon which

Teach

Using Feedback

Although publishing and presenting are the final stage of the writing process for professional writers, they need not be the final stage for students. Discuss how to use the feedback that you provide on final drafts. Encourage students to revise errors and weaknesses in graded writing assignments. Remind students that revision will help them remember difficulties that they have had so that they can avoid repeating mistakes.

Close

Team writing Divide the class into writing teams of five or more students. Assign each student the role of editor, writer, correspondent, researcher, or copyeditor. Have members of each team work together to develop a story idea that would appeal to students their age. Then guide students through the process of researching and organizing, drafting and revising, editing and proofreading their stories. Refer them to the advice that the professionals at TIME offer. Finally, act as managing editor and publish the stories in a classroom newspaper. As a follow-up to this activity, have students discuss what they learned from this process, including what difficulties they faced and how they solved the difficulties.

JOURNAL WRITING

REFLECT ON WRITING AND READING

1. Describe a time you found satisfaction in learning about other people's worlds as either a writer or a reader.

2. Recall a time when you had an "Aha!" experience as a reader. What was the genre: comic strip, novel, article? Write about your response.

3. Do you agree that writing is "very, very hard work"? When has hard work paid off for you as a writer? Are some forms of writing easier than others? Why?

TIME Facing the Blank Page **119**

Writing in the Real World

Internet Connection

The Internet has several online magazines for teenaged writers. Encourage students to submit their writing to online magazines and other sites for young writers. Some sites that accept young writers' work are: Global Wave (http://www.cs.bilkent.edu.tr/~david/derya/gw/gw12-1.htm), Young People's Press Online (http://www.ypp.net/), The Young Writer's Club (http://www.cs.bilkent.edu.tr/~david/derya/ywc.html), and Writer's Gallery (http://www.onestep.com:80/writers/). You should review these sites to be sure the content is appropriate for your class.

"*The jungle was wide and full of twitterings, rustlings, murmurs, and sighs. Suddenly it all ceased, as if someone had shut a door.*"

—Ray Bradbury, "A Sound of Thunder"

Viewing the Art

This photograph, which shows several leaves from a single type of plant in close-up, captures some of the themes and variations that are visible in nature. One might notice, for example, the gradations of the color green or the nuanced repetitions of heart shapes and vein patterns. The photographer, Douglas Peebles, finds the material for many of his pictures in his travels to Pacific islands.

Interpret and Analyze Use the following questions for discussion:
- What specific elements of design, such as color and texture, do you see repeated in the photograph? How are they varied?
- What is the center of interest in the photograph? How do elements of design and the camera angle draw the viewer to this point of interest?

Discussing the Quotation

The quotation is from "A Sound of Thunder," a short story by Ray Bradbury (born 1920) in which a single misstep of a traveler back in time has subtle but grave consequences for his present. Have students discuss what senses the quotation evokes, what mood it creates, and how it evokes that mood. To find out more information about the author and the story from which this quotation was taken, see *Glencoe Literature,* Course 5, p. 315.

Writing Prompt Write a brief paragraph comparing and contrasting the ways in which the photograph and quotation portray nature.

120

Resource Manager

Planning Resources
- *Lesson Plans*
- *Block Scheduling*

Transparencies
- *Bellringer*
- *Daily Language Practice*
- *Fine Art*
- *Two-Minute Skill Drill*
- *Writing Process*

Other Print Resources
- *Composition Enrichment*
- *Composition Practice*
- *Composition Reteaching*
- *Cooperative Learning Activities*
- *Glencoe Literature Library*
- *Grammar and Composition Handbook*
- *Grammar Workbook*
- *Listening and Speaking Activities*

- *Sentence-Combining Practice*
- *Tests with Answer Key and Rubrics*
- *Thinking and Study Skills*
- *Writing Across the Curriculum*
- *Writing Assessment and Evaluation Rubrics*
- *Writing in the Real World*

UNIT 3 Descriptive Writing

Writing in the Real World: *Thurston Clarke*   *122*

Lesson 3.1   **Writing to Describe**   *126*

Lesson 3.2   **Observing and Taking Notes**   *132*

Lesson 3.3   **Using Energetic Verbs**   *136*

Lesson 3.4   **Describing from Vantage Points**   *140*

Lesson 3.5   **Writing About Literature: Responding to Imagery in Poetry**   *144*

Lesson 3.6   **Writing About Literature: Analyzing Setting in a Short Story**   *148*

Writing Process in Action: Descriptive Writing   *152*

Literature Model: from *The Solace of Open Spaces* by Gretel Ehrlich   *156*

Linking Writing and Literature   *162*

Unit 3 Review   *163*

121

Objectives

- To develop an understanding of effective techniques for descriptive writing
- To demonstrate control over techniques of descriptive writing by using them to write responses to literature

 ASSESSMENT OPTIONS

📁 *Tests with Answer Key & Rubrics*
Unit 3 Choice A Test, p. 9
Unit 3 Choice B Test, p. 10
Unit 3 Composition Objective Test, pp. 11–12

💾 *Testmaker*
Unit 3 Choice A Test
Unit 3 Choice B Test
Unit 3 Composition Objective Test

You may wish to administer either the Unit 3 Choice A Test or the Unit 3 Choice B Test as a pretest.

Key to Ability Levels

L1 Level 1 activities are within the basic ability range of students.

L2 Level 2 activities are within the ability range of average students.

L3 Level 3 activities are more challenging activities.

 Video
- *MindJogger Videoquizzes*

💾 **Software**
- *Presentation Plus!*
- *Revising with Style*
- *Testmaker*
- *Writer's Assistant*
- *Writer's Choice Puzzlemaker*

🖥 **Web Sites**
- *writerschoice.glencoe.com*
- *lit.glencoe.com*

Focus

Lesson Overview

Objective

- To examine how a professional travel writer brings a place to life using colorful details, background facts, and strong impressions

Skills

- using description; taking notes; researching; writing descriptive details

Critical Thinking

- recalling; generating new information; synthesizing

Listening and Speaking

- discussing; oral reports

Bellringer
Daily Language Activity

When students enter the classroom, have this assignment on the board: *Describe the most exciting vacation you have ever taken. What made it so exciting?*

Grammar Link to the Bellringer

Have students reread their vacation descriptions, looking for verbs that could be replaced with stronger verbs.

See also *Daily Language Practice*

Motivating Activity

Have students talk about their favorite places to visit. Ask students to describe the physical appearance of the place or relate experiences that reveal its unique character. Encourage students to include colorful details that will help the rest of the class visualize the place. Tell students that travel writers also use descriptive details to convey a sense of a particular place and bring it to life.

Descriptive Writing

Writing in the Real World

MEDIA
Travel Writing
Connection

To create a vivid picture of a place, travel writers use descriptive writing. Good descriptive writing includes details that appeal to one or more of the senses. The following is an excerpt from a travel book about countries located near the equator. It was written by Thurston Clarke.

from *Equator*

by Thurston Clarke

*Travel Writer
Thurston Clarke*

MY CLOTHES ARE EXHAUSTED, thin as silk from being slapped on rocks and scorched by irons heated over charcoal. I slip them on and smell, I think, the equator: sweat, charcoal, and low tide.

Souvenirs litter my rooms. There is a paper clip from Albert Schweitzer's desk, a box with a pop-out snake, and a chunk of propeller from a plane crashed on a Pacific atoll by Amelia Earhart, or so I was told. I have a T-shirt saying Happy Trails, in Indonesian. I won it racing Baptist missionaries up a Borneo hill. I keep pencils in a soapstone box from Somalia, as white and square as the houses of Muqdisho. I weight papers with a gold-flecked rock from a Sumatran mine. My wife says it is fool's gold.

I have become a connoisseur of heat. There is the heat that reflects off coral and scorches and softens the face like a tomato held over a fire. There is the greasy heat of a tropical city, a milky heat that steams a jungle river like a pan of nearly boiled water, a blinding heat that explodes off tin roofs like *paparazzi's* flashbulbs, . . .

. . . Before a journey a map is an impersonal menu; afterwards, it is intimate as a diary. Before, I had stared at my maps and wondered if there was still a Jardin Botanique in the middle of Zaïre. Did passenger ships sail between Sumatra and Borneo? . . . And what should I make of the black dots signaling a "difficult or dangerous" road? Now I know, and these maps have become as comfortable as my canvas boots. I enjoy touching them, imagining I can feel, as if printed in Braille, the mountains, rivers, roads, and railways, all the familiar contours of the longest circular route on earth.

Why do maps attract the finger? . . . What child has not traveled by spinning a globe? I owned an illuminated one. I switched it on and darkened

122   Unit 3 Descriptive Writing

Resource Manager

Planning Resources
- *Lesson Plans*

Transparencies
- *Bellringer*
- *Daily Language Practice*
- *Writing Process* 9, 13–17

Other Print Resources
- *Cooperative Learning Activities*
- *Thinking and Study Skills,* pp. 1, 3, 6–8, 22
- *Writing Assessment and Evaluation Rubrics*
- *Writing in the Real World,* pp. 9–12

the room and it became the glowing, revolving planet that introduced travelogues and newsreels. Then I closed my eyes, stabbed at it with a finger, and imagined going wherever I landed.

My journey began this way on a snowy February evening in New York when I grabbed a globe off a friend's bookshelf and spun it into a whirling bouquet of continents and oceans.

A Writer's Process

Prewriting:
Researching and Traveling

Clarke spent several months organizing his expedition to South American, African, and Asian countries located on the equator. Research took up a major portion of his time. "I spent two or three months in libraries, reading about each country, especially newspaper articles," he said.

As he read the articles, Clarke jotted down the names of missionaries, politicians, Peace Corps workers, and other individuals. "It's important to have a couple of people to call who live in a place," he said. "They can give you a briefing about the country, tell you where to go, and what to avoid, describe the political situation, and introduce you to other people." Clarke's research also helped him develop a loose itinerary for a series of trips that lasted about eight months.

Clarke decided to travel west to east beginning in the small city of Macapá, Brazil. In Macapá, he found the Park of the Equator—a place with a long wall faced in blue tiles and a garden. Clarke would return

to this park two years later "to complete the circle."

Wherever he went, Clarke jotted down his first impressions. "First impressions are very important for any writer," he said. "I schedule nothing the first day. I take long walks and notice everything new, scary, wonderful. I jot down a few words about something that strikes me. If I hear a conversation I want, I write a summary. In the evening I expand my notes into a paragraph or two about what impressed me."

Drafting/Revising:
Putting the Trip into Words

When Clarke revisited Macapá, the Park of the Equator had been replaced by an "eight-story concrete slab." Clarke decided the time had come for him to return home and start writing.

By the time Clarke sat down to write, much of the book had already taken shape in his mind. "The trip itself defines the book, so as I experienced and did things they determined the book," he

Teach

Building Background

Warm-up
Have students list instances where descriptions are helpful.

Description in Speaking
Discuss how and when descriptions are used. For example, people use descriptions when giving directions, when talking about an object during a telephone conversation, when telling a story, and so on.
- Name ways descriptions enliven speech and help a person visualize the subject.

Description in Writing
Discuss any descriptions that students may have read.
- How vivid were the descriptions?
- What impression did the descriptions make on you?

Previewing the Media Connection

Have students read the title and the focus at the beginning of the Media Connection. Ask students to make predictions as to how descriptions aid travel writers. Then have students read the Media Connection.

Discussion Prompts
- What part did research play in helping Clarke be descriptive in his writing?
- What impressions did you gain about descriptive writing, based on Clarke's writing process?
- How does note taking help a writer such as Clarke?
- What places have you seen that created as strong an impression on you as the equator did on Clarke?
- What types of visual aids should a writer use to help his or her readers understand the logistics of an area?

Cultural Connections

Broadening One's Horizons
Travel writers like Thurston Clarke bring the world to readers who may never leave their homes. Travel writers invite their audience to appreciate different lands and cultures. As the world becomes smaller and more homogeneous, a travel writer may also serve as a kind of historian, recording a way of life before it changes. For example, at the beginning of his travels, Clarke recorded his impressions of the Park of the Equator in Macapá. Only two years later the park had been replaced by a modern building.

Teach

Discussion Prompts

Stimulate a discussion of the media connection. You may also want to invite students to talk about
- what part revision plays in the writing process
- why Clarke preferred using active verbs to adjectives
- the decision that a piece is considered finished or ready for submission
- Clarke's reliance upon his editor to help him cut the book **L2**

Additional Resources

Writing Process Transparencies, 9, 13–17

 Writing in the Real World, pp. 9–12

 Cooperative Learning Activities

Thinking and Study Skills, pp. 1, 3, 6–8, 22

Cross-reference: Writing

For instruction and practice in deciding what details and experiences to include in a piece of writing, refer students to Lesson 2.3, pp. 56–59.

---

reflected. Still, Clarke had to choose material from a dozen notebooks and the newspaper clips he collected along the way. "Travel books depend on variety," he said. "So I used my best, most interesting stuff." With this rule in mind, Clarke began to write. "I always write a first draft fast, just to get something down. Often the sentences run on, there's a lot of repetition, and the transitions aren't very good. I just keep moving to get a first draft," he said.

Revising/Editing:
Adding the Finishing Touches

Once he finished a draft, Clarke started revising. "I really think of writing as editing," Clarke explained. "I edit so many times that the writing happens for me when I edit. That's when I put in the transitions and play with the copy. I enjoy editing a lot."

During this phase, Clarke took care to create powerful descrip-

tions, using active verbs—not adjectives. "If you're describing a landscape or a city, there are always things going on; there's always motions and movement," he said. For example, Clarke wrote: "My first sunset . . . was a classic equatorial one, with the sun hesitating an instant as if taking a deep breath, before jumping into the sea. The wind dropped, clouds froze, and the sails of a native canoe sagged. The sun fell and the lagoon turned silver."

Clarke revised manuscript six or seven times, a process that took almost a year. The manuscript Clarke sent to the publisher was about 650 well-crafted pages. "I never submit a book until it's absolutely ready." said Clarke. Clarke's editor asked him to make no major changes to his manuscript —except to cut it down. With his editor's help, Clarke trimmed 20,000 words from *Equator.*

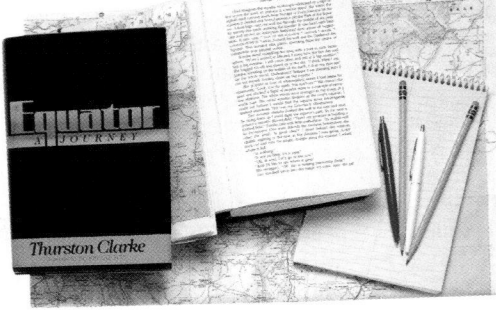

The task of writing does not end with a polished manuscript. Often substantial changes are required before a book can be published.

Enrichment and Extension

Describing Places

Point out to students that they can find interesting places to write about in their own community—a shopping mall, a dentist's office, or their own kitchen can provide plenty of rich material. Suggest that students select an everyday place in their community and try to make it come alive in a piece of descriptive writing. Encourage students to write about their own past experiences to convey a sense of the place. Collect the finished pieces in a book for the whole class to read.

Descriptive Writing

Analyzing the Media Connection

Discuss these questions about the book excerpt on page 122.

1. What sensory details does Clarke use in the opening paragraph? To what senses do they appeal?

2. What purpose does the list of souvenirs serve?

3. What figure of speech does Clarke use in describing heat? How does its use add to the description?

4. List some active verbs that enrich Clarke's writing. How do they contribute to the overall effect of the piece?

5. Clarke describes a spinning globe as "a whirling bouquet of continents and oceans." What does this description suggest about his feelings about globes?

Analyzing a Writer's Process

Discuss these questions about Thurston Clarke's writing process.

1. How did Clarke prepare for his trip?

2. Why was it important for Clarke to jot down his first impressions?

3. What approach did Clarke take in writing a first draft?

4. How does Clarke define writing? Do you agree with his definition? Why or why not?

5. Why does Clarke consider active verbs important in travel writing?

Grammar Link

Use strong verbs.

Strong verbs, not adjectives, create powerful descriptions such as this one:

> The wind **dropped,** clouds **froze,** and the sails of a native canoe **sagged.**

Rewrite these sentences, replacing weak verbs with stronger ones to paint a vivid picture, making other changes too.

1. As the wind blew, the trees moved.

2. A convertible that looked as if it were held together with bandages and tape came in our direction.

3. Its driver had on an orange jumpsuit and matching cap that caught the eye of everyone on the street.

4. When the car got closer to us, the driver motioned.

5. We couldn't hear what he said over the racket his car was making.

See Lesson 10.3, page 453.

A river meanders through the grasslands around Kampala, Uganda.

Grammar Link

Answers

(Answers will vary.)

1. As the wind blustered and shrieked, the trees flailed.

2. A convertible that appeared to be held together with bandages and tape roared in our direction.

3. Its driver wore an orange jumpsuit and matching cap that assaulted the eye of everyone on the street.

4. When the car neared, the driver gestured wildly.

5. We couldn't hear him over the din his car created.

Assess

Annalyzing the Media Connection

1. The sensory details include elements like *silk, slapped, scorched, heated* (touch); *sweat* and *charcoal* (smell); *low tide* (sight, sound, and smell).

2. Among other things, the souvenirs established Clarke's credentials as an experienced traveler.

3. Clarke uses similes. Students may respond that his similes make the descriptions more vivid and sensual.

4. Students may list such verbs as *slapped, scorched, smell, crashed, explodes, spinning switched,* and *grabbed.* The active verbs contribute to the pace and vividness of the piece.

5. The description suggests that Clarke has a romantic attachment to globes.

Analyzing a Writer's Process

1. Clarke read extensively and compiled a list of possible contact people in each country.

2. Clarke feels his first impressions help him identify what is "new, scary, and wonderful" about a place.

3. At first, Clarke wrote quickly, to get his ideas and impressions down on paper.

4. Clarke thinks of writing as editing. Students' opinions will vary.

5. Clarke feels that active verbs help readers picture the motions and movements of a place and its people.

Reteaching

Remind students to record their first impressions about a place in brief notes that can be expanded later.

Enrichment

Challenge students to use vivid action verbs when they describe a location.

Close

Ask students to read a travel article and discuss the details the writer used to convey a sense of the place.

Focus

Lesson Overview

Objective
- To write a descriptive paragraph using an organization plan for concrete and sensory details

Skills
- examining characteristics of descriptive writing; organizing details; writing a topic sentence; using prepositional phrases in descriptions

Critical Thinking
- comparing; visualizing; analyzing

Listening and Speaking
- discussing; evaluating; explaining a process

Bellringer
Daily Language Activity

When students enter the classroom, have this assignment on the board: *Write five sentences that accurately and completely describe the front of this classroom.*

Grammar Link to the Bellringer

Tell students to underline the prepositional phrases used in their descriptions.

See also *Daily Language Practice*

Motivating Activity

At the start of the movie *The Wizard of Oz*, the main character, Dorothy, wishes she could be "somewhere over the rainbow." Ask students to describe some details about a favorite place to another classmate without naming where they would like to be. Have students see how quickly their partners can guess the places described.

Descriptive Writing

LESSON
3.1

Writing to Describe

Good descriptive writing depends on the creation of vivid word pictures and the organization of those pictures into an effective pattern. Note how Stephen King organizes details in the following passage to let the reader "see" the scene.

King helps bring the scene to life with vivid images like "lightning flared in a blue sheet" and "thunder exploded a bare moment later."

Is "hearing the tendons in her neck creak like dirty doorhinges" an effective image? Why?

Literature Model

Lightning flared in a blue sheet, giving Anderson a shutter-click of what she had come to think of—as her neighbords did—as her dooryard. She saw the truck, with the first drops of rain on its windshield; the short dirt driveway; the mailbox with its flag down and tucked securely against its aluminum side; the writhing trees. Thunder exploded a bare moment later, and Peter jumped against her, whining. The lights went out. They didn't bother dimming or flickering or messing around; they went out all at once, completely. They went out with *authority*.

Anderson reached for the lantern—and then her hand stopped.

There was a green spot on the far wall, just to the right of Uncle Frank's Welsh dresser. It bobbed up two inches, moved left, then right. It disappeared for a moment and then came back. . . .

She turned toward Peter, hearing the tendons in her neck creak like dirty doorhinges, knowing what she was going to see. The light was coming from Peter's eye. His left eye. It glared with the witchy green light of St. Elmo's fire drifting over a swamp after a still, muggy day.

Stephen King, *The Tommyknockers*

126   Unit 3 Descriptive Writing

Resource Manager

Planning Resources
- *Lesson Plans*

 Transparencies
- *Bellringer*
- *Daily Language Practice*
- *Fine Art* 13–18
- *Two-Minute Skill Drill*
- *Writing Process* 9, 13–17

📂 Other Print Resources
- *Composition Enrichment,* p. 19
- *Composition Practice,* p. 19
- *Composition Reteaching,* p. 19
- *Cooperative Learning Activities*
- *Listening and Speaking Activities,* pp. 1, 2, 19, 21
- *Sentence-Combining Practice,* pp. 28–29

- *Thinking and Study Skills,* pp. 10, 15
- *Writing Across the Curriculum*
- *Writing Assessment and Evaluation Rubrics*

Organize Details in Spatial Order

Good descriptive writing depends on the effective use of details, and the organization of those details into meaningful patterns. One natural way of organizing descriptive writing is to arrange details in spatial order—that is, left to right, front to back, near to far, clockwise, or counterclockwise. How did Iowa writer Sharon Oard Warner organize the details of her description?

Grammar Tip

When you write descriptions, you can use prepositional phrases, as Warner does, to establish spatial relationships between objects. For more information about prepositional phrases, see Lesson 12.1, page 523.

Descriptive Writing

Literature Model

The pediatric waiting room is divided into two unequal sections by a length of Plexiglas that juts out into the middle of the room. A table at one end keeps people from walking into the flat edge. Orange and brown upholstered chairs line both sides of this transparent wall, back to back, as though some enormous game of musical chairs is about to begin. The smaller section of the room is reserved for well patients, and a prominent sign directs the rest of us to the other side.

When I carried Jancey in this morning, I stopped in the entrance, momentarily confused. Some redecorating had gone on since our last visit. A large oval braided rug covered an expanse of institutional carpet in the unwell section, and a baby not much older than Jancey was seated in the middle of it. While I watched, he crawled to the edge and then back again, as though the rug were an island and he was marooned.

Sharon Oard Warner, "A Simple Matter of Hunger"

"Island" and "marooned" reinforce the sense of rigidly divided space.

Journal Writing

Experiment with spatial organization of details by writing a brief description of a special place or secret hideaway where you go to get away from it all.

Teach

Using the Model

You might suggest that students close their eyes and visualize the waiting room as you read its description aloud. Afterward, ask whether any of the details were difficult to imagine. In discussing the model, point out that Warner has chosen to organize her description around the most prominent object in the room, the Plexiglas divider. She discusses other objects in relation to the divider: the table at one end and the back-to-back arrangement of the chairs against it. **L2**

Two-Minute Skill Drill

Write the following sentences on the board and have students insert prepositional phrases.

1. Mary ran _____.
2. Bees flew _____.

See also *Two-Minute Skill Drill Transparency 3.1*

Journal Writing Tip

Identifying Spatial Relationships
Before students complete the journal activity, suggest they list all the spatial details that come to mind about their special places. If some students have difficulty, you might suggest they sketch their secret hideaways to help them identify the location and placement of significant details.

Teach

Teaching from the Art

You may wish to initiate a discussion about organizing descriptive details, using Beverly Buchanan's oil pastel *Barnesville,* which hangs in the Bernice Steinbaum Gallery, New York. Ask students to examine the picture and tell what is unusual about the size and placement of the barns. (The barns in front would normally appear larger, but in the painting they are much smaller than the barns in the background.) Point out that an artist or writer is free to deviate from a realistic organization to achieve a desired mood or impression. **L2**

Organizing Details

Challenge students to consider the reasons behind the varied ways writers choose to organize details. First, suggest that students examine passages describing different settings, such as in Sherwood Anderson's "Sophistication" or Juan A. A. Sedillo's "Gentleman of Rio en Medio." Does the writer want to build suspense or create some other mood or feeling? Where does the author place the best or strongest image? Point out that a writer's purpose usually determines the order he or she uses in a specific piece of writing. **L3**

Descriptive Writing

Organize Details According to Importance

Writers sometimes arrange details in order of importance, from the least important detail to the most important. This lets the description build to a climax, leaving the strongest image for the end. In the passage below, African American writer Eugenia Collier recalls several details about childhood summers that made a lasting impression on her.

Beverly Buchanan, *Barnesville,* 1989

In this case, order of importance means moving from the general and pervasive—"dust"—to the specific and sharply focused—"a brilliant splash of sunny yellow."

Literature Model

When I think of the home town of my youth, all that I seem to remember is dust—the brown, crumbly dust of late summer—arid, sterile dust that gets into the eyes and makes them water, gets into the throat and between the toes of bare brown feet. I don't know why I should remember only the dust. Surely there must have been lush green lawns and paved streets under leafy shade trees somewhere in town; but memory is an abstract painting—it does not present things as they are, but rather as they *feel.* And so, when I think of that time and that place, I remember only the dry September of the dirt roads and grassless yards of the shanty-town where I lived. And one other thing I remember, another incongruency of memory—a brilliant splash of sunny yellow against the dust—Miss Lottie's marigolds.

Eugenia Collier, "Marigolds"

Special Needs

Understanding Spatial Order

Students who have difficulty expressing themselves in writing might benefit from first experimenting with spatial order in a more artistic fashion. Suggest they draw or paint a dramatic scene, such as the scene of a heroic act, crime, or accident. They should include details in strategic places that show the sequence of dramatic events. Invite students to trade pictures and use spatial organization to describe the scene as if reporting it for a news broadcast.

Focus on the Topic Sentence

Topic sentences are as important in writing descriptions as in any other form of writing. Where you place your topic sentence—at the beginning of the paragraph or at the end—depends upon the effect you want to achieve. The model below begins with a topic sentence, setting the stage for a scary night for two children.

Literature Model

We were afraid at night in the winter. . . . The upstairs of our house was not finished. A brick chimney went up one wall. In the middle of the floor was a square hole, with a wooden railing around it; that was where the stairs came up. On the other side of the stairwell were the things that nobody had any use for anymore. . . . I had told Laird, as soon as he was old enough to understand such things, that bats and skeletons lived over there; whenever a man escaped from the county jail, twenty miles away, I imagined that he had somehow let himself in the window and was hiding behind the linoleum.

Alice Munro, "Boys and Girls"

The topic sentence states the main idea—the children were afraid at night—and the rest of the paragraph describes why they were afraid.

The next paragraph takes a different approach, beginning leisurely and developing a vivid picture one detail at a time. Everything builds toward the topic sentence at the end.

Model

Tall bookshelves stood at attention along the right wall; the books toed a straight line. Two uncomfortable chairs were deployed strategically across the room. Matching brass trays holding paper clips and pens were set up across the front of the desk. Rosa's office clearly revealed her personality.

What can you infer from the description about Rosa's personality?

Journal Writing

Find a paragraph that begins with a topic sentence. Rewrite the paragraph with the topic sentence at the end. Compare the two versions. Explain which you like better.

Teach

Writing Topic Sentences

Encourage students to keep travel journals when they go on trips or outings to particularly scenic or picturesque places. They have a chance to practice what they learn in this lesson if they each write a topic sentence for a postcard or letter describing a favorite scene. They can organize specific details to suit their purpose—whether to create a mood or leave a strong final impression. **L2**

Using the Models

As students discuss the models, help them see how the details in each paragraph support the topic sentence. For example, the straight rows of books on Rosa's shelves suggest that she is a disciplined, orderly, and no-nonsense kind of person. **L2**

Journal Writing Tip

Comparing Topic Sentence Placement Suggest that partners work together to assess both original paragraphs and rewrites. Using the second model on this page as an example, one might ask if the impact would be lessened by *telling* about Rosa before *showing* her office.

Cooperative Learning

Moving the Topic Sentence

Involve students in a Partners activity to identify the topic sentences in descriptive paragraphs and evaluate their placement for effect. Suggest that partners select a descriptive paragraph from a literature selection. After reading the paragraph, partners should write down the topic sentence and note how its placement at the beginning, middle, or end contributes to the paragraph's total effect. Next, have each pair meet with another pair to compare their findings. Ask students how moving the topic sentence would alter the intended effect.

Teach

Teaching Tip

To help students understand that one place can evoke different images depending on a writer's use of detail, bring in a photo of a unique place. Suggest that groups of students meet and think of an event that might occur there, such as a party or an accident. Ask students to determine the effect the setting might have on this event and write a descriptive topic sentence giving that impression. Groups can list the details in the picture that support their topic sentence. When the class reconvenes, ask groups to share topic sentences to illustrate the variety of images that can come from one source. **L2**

Using the Model

In discussing the model, help students see that transition words such as "overhead" and "on either side" indicate that Lonn is using spatial order. As he moves near to far, he describes such details as the "sheer cliff walls" and the "wind-twisted pine trees." **L1**

Additional Resources

Writing Process Transparencies, 9, 13–17

Writing Across the Curriculum

Cooperative Learning Activities

For further stimuli for descriptive writing, see *Fine Art Transparencies,* 13–18.

Thinking and Study Skills, pp. 10, 15

Sentence-Combining Practice, pp. 28–29

Listening and Speaking Activities, pp. 1, 2, 19, 21

Composition Practice, p. 19

130

Descriptive Writing

Put It All Together

After you've created your images and organized them around a topic sentence, you should have an effective description. Notice how student Lonn Rider used specific and vivid details to create a clear image of a favorite place.

> The topic sentence states the main idea: to describe Picture Canyon and explain why it has a special effect on people.

> In what order does Rider arrange his details in describing Picture Canyon? What details does he use?

> Transition words such as "overhead," "on either side," and "looking ahead" help the reader follow the organization.

Student Model

Picture Canyon, though not the most beautiful of places, has a special, enigmatic effect on people. As you enter the canyon, the soft golden sandstone walls begin to build and loom overhead until they meet the electric-blue skyline. Native American drawings etched inside the canyon cover sheer cliff walls on either side, illustrating a past long since forgotten. The rugged floor of the canyon is scattered with multitudes of small, algae-covered ponds with a few weather-beaten, sandstone roadways. Looking ahead, there are small, wind-twisted pine trees with a multitude of squirrels feeding on the pea-sized piñon nuts. Each playfully eats his fill and stores the excess in bulging cheeks. As the sun sets over the horizon, the jagged, golden rock formations on the skyline seem to radiate an eerie, golden energy known only to a few infrequent visitors and to the Native Americans who lived in the canyon centuries ago.

Lonn Rider, Centennial High School, Pueblo, Colorado

Like Rider, you can enhance your descriptions by carefully organizing your ideas and supporting details. Follow these guidelines when you write your own descriptive paragraphs.

Revising Tip

When you revise your writing, add transition words to help the reader follow the organization of your descriptive details. For help refer to Lesson 2.7, page 72.

Guidelines for Descriptive Writing

1. Gather vivid details that will help you re-create a scene or an experience for your readers.
2. Decide which kind of organization will be more appropriate for your subject—spatial order or order of importance.
3. Write a topic sentence, and decide whether it will be more effective positioned at the beginning or the end of the paragraph.
4. Use appropriate transitions to make the organization and relationships among ideas clear.

Critical Thinking

Identifying Relationships

Descriptive details may be related in many ways, such as spatially, by importance or distinctiveness, and chronologically. The writer's task is to identify which relationship suits the purpose of the description. Spatial organization conveys a vivid picture to the reader; organization by importance helps the reader form opinions about a person or place; chronological order emphasizes change. Ask pairs of students to list ideas for descriptive paragraphs and decide which kind of organization they would recommend for each.

Write a Descriptive Paragraph

Write a description of the painting below that is so specific that someone who has never seen it would immediately recognize it. Use the guidelines on page 130 to help you.

PURPOSE To describe a painting
AUDIENCE Someone who has never seen it
LENGTH 1 paragraph

WRITING RUBRICS To write an effective descriptive paragraph, you should

- use specific details
- order details spatially or by order of importance
- write a clear topic sentence

Listening and Speaking

COOPERATIVE LEARNING Write a paragraph about a possession you had in your early childhood. Describe the object's most unusual features, without naming the object. Read your paragraph aloud with those of a group, identify the objects, and discuss which specific details helped identify the objects.

Blackbear Bosin, *Prairie Fire*, 1953

Grammar Link

Use prepositional phrases to show spatial relationships.

The literature models in this lesson used prepositional phrases, such as "in the middle of the floor," to establish spatial relationships.

Clarify position or location by adding at least one prepositional phrase to each sentence below.

1. A bookcase stood.
2. An overstuffed blue chair squatted.
3. A patchwork quilt of primary colors covered the bed.
4. Clothes were strewn in heaps.
5. A matching chair and desk of oak faced the window.

See Lesson 12.1, pages 523–524.

Cross-Curricular Activity

SCIENCE Work with a partner to research information about the role of fire in maintaining the prairie environment. Write a few paragraphs and present your facts to the class.

Assess

Evaluation Rubrics

Write a Descriptive Paragraph

Each paragraph should include
- a number of specific details from the painting
- an organization pattern, such as left to right or cause and effect

See also *Writing Assessment & Evaluation Rubrics.*

Listening and Speaking

When students read their descriptions within their groups, have classmates ask the following questions.
- What mood or impression did you perceive?
- What details could be added, or made more vivid and specific?
- Are details arranged in a logical order?

Cross-Curricular Activity

Students' paragraphs should
- be based on accurate information from reliable sources.
- use clear, non-technical language.

Reteaching

📁 *Composition Reteaching,* p. 19

Enrichment

📁 *Composition Enrichment,* p. 19

🔖 **Fine Art Transparencies** Use *Fine Art Transparencies,* 13–18, for enrichment activities also.

Close

Ask students to name different purposes for which they might use descriptive writing. Ask students to look for examples of descriptive writing in a variety of publications.

Grammar Link

Answers

(Answers will vary.)
1. next to the wall
2. near the fireplace
3. in the guest room down the hall
4. around the room
5. near the door

Viewing the Art

Blackbear Bosin, *Prairie Fire*, 1953
Native American artist Blackbear Bosin filled his watercolor *Prairie Fire* (23 by 33 1/4 inches, Philbrook Art Center, Tulsa) with details provoking the senses. The viewer smells and feels the searing heat of the fire and hears its roar and the pounding of hooves.

Focus

Lesson Overview

Objective
• To draft a description using vibrant and incisive details

Skills
• observing and recording details; writing from notes

Critical Thinking
• note taking; evaluating; recalling

Listening and Speaking
• discussing; evaluating

Bellringer
Daily Language Activity

When students enter the classroom, have this assignment on the board: *Test your observational skills. Take a good look at your classmates for about a minute. Then close your eyes and count to thirty. When you open your eyes, make a list of details about what your classmates are wearing without looking at anyone again.*

Grammar Link to the Bellringer

Have students check their use of possessive pronouns. Did they use the correct form for each possessive pronoun?

See also *Daily Language Practice*

Motivating Activity

Invite students to share experiences they may have had taking photographs or making videotapes. Ask what students try to capture on film or tape and how they attempt to do it. Comment that writers use words as their film to capture an experience or feeling by focusing on specific details.

Descriptive Writing

LESSON
3.2

Observing and Taking Notes

Striking, image-creating details bring a place to life. The most effective way to "capture" such details is through direct observation and note taking. What direct observations were used to enliven this description of an Indian restaurant in Queens, New York?

Specific visual images like "red plastic tables," "yellow turmeric stains," and "styrofoam bowls" evoke a strong sense of place.

What do words like "wheaty," "bitter," and "sting" add to the description of the scene:

1 **turmeric** (turʹmer ik) an orange-colored spice
2 **dal** (däl) lentil sauce
3 **chapati** (chə pätʹē) bread
4 **masala** (mə sälʹa) spice mixture

Literature Model

Adam is in an Indian restaurant in Queens, little red plastic tables with yellow turmeric[1] stains on them, styrofoam bowls of dal[2] and chicken curry, slippery with orange oil.

Adam's fingers tear a chapati[3] and dip it into the dal. He gulps it down, the smoothness of the dal mixing with the wheaty taste of the chapati. He eats some chicken, carefully licking all the masala[4] from his fingers, almost tasting each spice alone, the sweet cinnamon and cardamom, the bitter cumin and coriander, the sting of the chilies. The smell makes him so homesick his eyes start watering. He thinks of his grandmother's chicken curry.

"Food all right, sir? Not too spicy?"

Adam swallows. The chicken is so sweet. He looks up at the waiter. "It's perfect," he says.

The waiter looks worried. "You want some yogurt, sir? To make it less spicy. Some raita. That is yogurt with cucumber in it. You know, cucumber."

"No, thank you," says Adam, smiling. "I know what raita is."

"Oh yes, a lot of Europeans eat Indian food now. It's very popular in England as well. Yes, I can see you know how to eat like an Indian," leaning on the table now, he hangs the wet cloth over the back of the chair. "Me, I like American food. I never eat here. I eat at McDonald's or Kentucky Chicken. It's so funny, isn't it? Indians like American food and Americans like Indian food."

Ameena Meer, "The Only Living Boy in New York."

132　Unit 3　Descriptive Writing

Resource Manager

Planning Resources
• *Lesson Plans*

Transparencies
• *Bellringer*
• *Daily Language Practice*
• *Fine Art* 13–18
• *Two-Minute Skill Drill*
• *Writing Process* 9, 13–17

📂 **Other Print Resources**
• *Composition Enrichment*, p. 20
• *Composition Practice*, p. 20
• *Composition Reteaching*, p. 20
• *Cooperative Learning Activities*
• *Listening and Speaking Activities*, pp. 1, 2, 19, 21
• *Sentence-Combining Practice*, pp. 28–29

• *Thinking and Study Skills*, pp. 6–7
• *Writing Across the Curriculum*
• *Writing Assessment and Evaluation Rubrics*

Use Direct Observation

Revisiting a scene through memory is one kind of observation, but you can get a better sense of a place if you revisit the location in person. In both cases you will want to consider the same questions as you think about re-creating the scene in words: What is the most striking thing about the scene? What colors do you see? What sounds do you hear? What scents do you smell? What will you have to include in the description so that your readers will see what you saw, feel as you felt?

Take Notes

If you don't have a photographic memory, draw a sketch, make a video, or take notes in your personal journal. Do whatever you think will help you re-create the scene later when you sit down to write. Here is a set of notes that student Michelle Kalski took in preparation for writing a description of her favorite getaway spot.

Prewriting Tip
You may want to record your observations in a notebook. Keep a list there of your first impressions.

<u>Sight</u>
green grass, sunlight and shadows, sun-kissed water, rippling waves, white sails, cobalt-blue sky, cotton-fluffy clouds, snow-white gulls

<u>Sound</u>	<u>Smell</u>	<u>Touch</u>
chirping birds,	fresh greenery,	soft summer breeze,
whispering trees	fragrant pines	clean dry grass

Journal Writing

Look carefully around you right now. Think about the questions above under "Use Direct Observation." Make notes answering these questions.

Teach

Observing Through Touch

To help students understand that observation is not limited to vision, you might try the following tactile exercise. Select several ordinary objects, such as a rubber stamp, a pen, or a hole punch, and put them in a bag. Have students take turns reaching inside the bag and identifying the object they touch. Students should record their observations in their journals. Afterward suggest that students combine their observations to describe the objects in the bag. **L2**

Thinking Visually

Point out to students that as they collect information and take notes, they might find it helpful to create a chart categorizing their images by sense, as Kalski did on the student page. The chart will remind students to use details from senses such as smell and taste. **L1**

Two-Minute Skill Drill

Write possessive pronouns for each parenthetical description.

1. *The family on the right is _____ (the family belonging to them).*
2. *The clock on the mantel is _____ (the clock belonging to us).*

See also *Two-Minute Skill Drill Transparency 3.2*

Journal Writing Tip

Observing Suggest that students develop the habit of recording sensory images in their journals for later use in their writing. Since sight tends to dominate the other senses, students may grow more aware of the other senses by closing their eyes.

Teach

Using the Model

Ask students to listen as you read the model aloud. Afterward ask what impression Kalski gives of her place (peaceful, pleasant, friendly). Point out that Kalski's description is effective because she includes details that the reader doesn't expect—like "tie-dye configurations" and "trees discussing old times." Her notes helped her recall these perceptions. **L3**

Listing Details

If students have trouble focusing on subtle smells or sounds, they might benefit from a more hands-on approach to observation and recording. Bring in several objects that would produce strong sensory impressions, such as a kaleidoscope, bells, or cinnamon sticks. Instruct students to examine the objects and then list or tape-record at least three sensory details they could use in a descriptive paragraph about each object. Encourage students to include words and images that appeal to as many of the senses as are appropriate. **L1**

Additional Resources

 Writing Process Transparencies, 9, 13–17
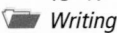 *Writing Across the Curriculum*
Cooperative Learning Activities

 For further stimuli for descriptive writing, *see Fine Art Transparencies,* 13–18.
 Thinking and Study Skills, pp. 6–7
Listening and Speaking Activities, pp. 1, 2, 19, 21
 Sentence-Combining Practice, pp. 28–29
Composition Practice, p. 20

Descriptive Writing

Publishing Tip

You might want to get together with others to create a poster display of your descriptive writing.

Write from Notes

The student model below shows how Kalski used her notes to write a descriptive paragraph. She began with a topic sentence stating the main idea. She then organized the supporting details in order of importance, saving strong, mood-capturing details for the end.

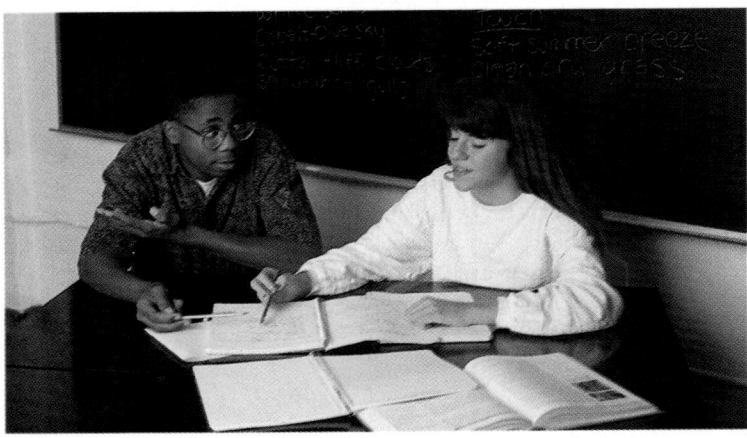

Kalski relied on her notes for specific sensory details like "green dry grass," "warm breeze," and "glistening lake."

How do original and unusual details make this passage more effective?

Student Model

School is out in gorgeous weather, and there isn't much to worry about except sleeping too late into the afternoon. I head out to my favorite spot, a small patch of space to separate me from the busy lives of all the bustling people. As I lie there, the green dry grass plays hide and seek with my fingers and toes. Sun and shade spot me like tie-dye configurations, while a warm breeze keeps me company. The trees overhead say "Hello," as if they were old friends; they shade and protect me just in case the sky might fall. I feel a warm sun penetrating through the trees, making conversation with the breeze as if they'd known each other for a thousand years. I'm surrounded and encompassed by nature. I look over the glistening lake and see ripples kissing the water's surface. Scattered cotton clouds on blue wait to absorb everything around in just one season. The only things heard are birds chirping and the breeze and trees discussing old times. Peace is all around until sunset and later on.

Michelle Kalski, Evanston Township High School, Evanston, Illinois

134 Unit 3 Descriptive Writing

MEETING INDIVIDUAL NEEDS — English Language Learners

Using Prewriting Techniques

Students who lack proficiency in English may feel more comfortable if they make their prewriting notes in their primary language and then translate them into English words, phrases, and sentences. To gain fluency, they may also want to talk through their descriptions with a tape recorder before writing them in English.

Write About a Painting

The painting on this page portrays an interesting impression of Fifth Avenue in New York. Take notes on the style, colors used, and effect of the painting. Then write a descriptive paragraph about the painting.

PURPOSE To observe and describe paintings
AUDIENCE Your teacher
LENGTH 1 paragraph

WRITING RUBRICS To write an effective descriptive paragraph, you should

- compose a topic sentence for your paragraph
- use observation and list details
- include details that appeal to different senses

Listening and Speaking

COOPERATIVE LEARNING In a small group, explore an outdoor location. Ask each group member to take detailed notes about the plant and animal life in one section. Write the combined notes into a group description.

Using Computers

SPELLING To refine your spelling skills, work with a partner to check each other's spelling on printouts of your paragraphs. Then verify any suggested spelling corrections using the spell-check feature on the computer.

Grammar Link

Form possessive pronouns correctly.

Possessive pronouns do not use apostrophes. Do not confuse the possessive pronoun *its* with the contraction *it's* (it is):

> "It's perfect," he [Adam] says.

Choose the right words to complete each sentence below.

1. (Her's, Hers) is the backpack that's bigger than (your's, yours).
2. This canvas backpack is (he's, his).
3. The backpacks left on the bus must be (their's, theirs).
4. (Our's, Ours) were not on the bus.
5. Ted's backpack is torn; (it's, its) time for him to find (it's, its) replacement.

See Lesson 17.1, pages 637–638.

Childe Hassam, *Fifth Avenue*, 1919

3.2 Observing and Taking Notes **135**

Assess

Evaluation Rubrics

Write About Paintings

Each student's descriptive paragraph should
- have a clear topic sentence
- use spatial order or order of importance

See also *Writing Assessment & Evaluation Rubrics.*

Listening and Speaking

Look for the following in each group's paragraph:
- mention of physical features, plants, and animals at the location
- input from all members' notes

Using Computers

Remind students that most spell-check features will not detect homonyms such as *boar* and *bore* or *pair* and *pear*. Encourage them to pay special attention to such words as they check their own and their partners' paragraphs.

Reteaching

📂 *Composition Reteaching,* p. 20

Enrichment

📂 *Composition Enrichment,* p. 20

✎ Use *Fine Art Transparencies* 13–18 for enrichment activities also.

Close

Suggest that students take the time to observe a piece of architecture, a piece of art, or a place. Have them take notes and report on their observations in class.

Grammar Link

Answers

1. Hers/yours
2. his
3. theirs
4. Ours
5. it's/its

Forming Possessive Nouns Correctly

For information on correct pronoun forms, refer students to Lesson 17.1, pages 637–638.

Viewing the Art

Childe Hassam, *Fifth Avenue*, 1919
Hassam's impressionist oil painting (24 1/8 by 20 1/4 inches) is in the Cleveland Museum of Art.

LESSON
3.3

Focus

Lesson Overview

Objective
- To compare energetic, lively verbs with dull, overused ones
- To use the more colorful verbs to enliven a piece of descriptive writing

Skills
- choosing exact verbs; revising with exact verbs; writing with energetic verbs

Critical Thinking
- comparing; evaluating

Listening and Speaking
- informal speaking; discussing

 Bellringer
Daily Language Activity

When students enter the classroom, have this assignment on the board: *List four verbs that show vivid action.*

Grammar Link to the Bellringer
Have students change the verbs to their past forms.

See also *Daily Language Practice*

Motivating Activity

Building upon this lesson's opening example, you might ask students to mention their favorite comic-book heroes or heroines, and discuss why comic books are popular. (They are exciting and have a lot of action.) Ask students to examine the exciting words on this page and think of other examples of words cartoonists use to convey action—*chase* and *punch,* for instance. Stress the excitement created by such action-filled word choices.

Descriptive Writing

LESSON
3.3

Using Energetic Verbs

Cartoonists highlight words like BAM, POW, and BWHOOOOOSH. You can bring the same kind of energy to your own writing by using specific, action-packed words.

Choose Exact Verbs

Exact verbs create mood and strong mental images in descriptive writing. Notice how the writers of the following models have used energetic verbs.

 Resource Manager

Planning Resources
- *Lesson Plans*

Transparencies
- *Bellringer*
- *Daily Language Practice*
- *Fine Art* 13–18
- *Two-Minute Skill Drill*
- *Writing Process* 9, 13–17

Other Print Resources
- *Composition Enrichment,* p. 21
- *Composition Practice,* p. 21
- *Composition Reteaching,* p. 21
- *Cooperative Learning Activities*
- *Listening and Speaking Activities,* pp. 1, 2, 19, 21
- *Sentence-Combining Practice,* pp. 28–29

- *Thinking and Study Skills,* pp. 10–11
- *Writing Across the Curriculum*
- *Writing Assessment and Evaluation Rubrics*

Literature Model

The nights now are full of wind and destruction; the trees plunge and bend and their leaves fly helter skelter until the lawn is plastered with them and they lie packed in gutters and choke rain pipes and scatter damp paths.

Virginia Woolf, *To the Lighthouse*

Literature Model

The crowds are thick on the sidewalks and street vendors work on nearly every block. The litter baskets—they look like volcanoes of trash that have just erupted—are overloaded from a Sunday's use. Debris is strewn over the pavement and in the gutters. A wind stirs up scraps and creates a funnel of newspaper that swirls up in a mad ballet.

McCandlish Phillips, *City Notebook*

> What verbs in these passages create strong mental pictures? What pictures do they create?

Descriptive Writing

To choose just the right verb to use in a particular situation, do what many professional writers do—use a thesaurus, which is a collection of synonyms. Just keep in mind that synonyms are not necessarily interchangeable. For example, you wouldn't write "The horse *jogs*" when you mean "The horse *gallops*," even though *jog* and *gallop* are both synonyms for *run*.

Sometimes you may not be certain of the precise meanings of synonyms. See the thesaurus entry at the right, for example: you might have to consult a dictionary to find the exact meanings of *aggrandize* and *augment*.

Vocabulary Tip

During the revising stage, replace verb-adverb pairs with a single verb. For instance, change "Pablo smiled happily" to "Pablo beamed."

INCREASE—V.
Increase, enhance, aggrandize, augment; intensify, step up, raise, boost.
  grow, surge, swell, fill out, inflate; skyrocket; overgrow, spread.

Journal Writing

Choose a recent entry in your journal. Underline all the verbs. Replace them with more vivid ones. How does this change your entry?

Teach

Judging Verbs

Some students may find it difficult to judge which words are lively and which are dull and may need a rule-of-thumb to guide them. Mention that it is often effective to substitute a strong verb that can carry more meaning by itself than a weaker verb-adverb combination. For example, instead of writing that someone "spoke quickly," the writer can substitute "jabbered." Encourage students to examine paragraphs they have written for verb-adverb pairs that may be replaced with single verbs. **L2**

⇄ Cross-reference: Thesaurus

For more information on determining the appropriateness of synonyms, see Lesson 24.2, pages 816–817.

Two-Minute Skill Drill

Have students choose the correct verb for each of the following sentences:

1. *Yesterday I (squelched, squelch) the urge to scream.*
2. *My dog (lays, lies) in his own corner of the kitchen floor.*

See also *Two-Minute Skill Drill Transparency 3.3*

Journal Writing Tip

Evaluating Students will need to establish criteria for deciding whether or not to replace a verb. Dull verbs give little information about how or why an action occurred; often such verbs require an adverb while a more specific verb does not. Repetition or overuse of a verb should also prompt a writer to replace it with an appropriate synonym.

Teach

Using a Thesaurus

To provide an example of how to use a thesaurus, write the following sentence on the board: "We *conversed* on the phone for hours." Point out that the thesaurus lists *conversed* as a synonym for *talked*, but *conversed* sounds stilted. Ask students to use the thesaurus to find words that would be more appropriate for an informal discussion. Stress that the main reason to use a thesaurus is to avoid overusing a word like *talked*, but that students should choose replacements carefully. **L2**

Sporting Verbs

Students interested in sports may be surprised at the variety of energetic verbs used to describe one team's victory over another. Suggest that students collect examples from sports magazines to add to their personal journals and word banks. Also, radio and TV broadcasters use a seemingly infinite variety of lively verbs. **L1**

Additional Resources

For further stimuli for descriptive writing, see *Fine Art Transparencies*, 13–18.

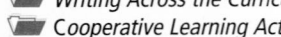

Writing Process Transparencies, 9, 13–17

Writing Across the Curriculum

Cooperative Learning Activities

Thinking and Study Skills, pp. 10–11

Sentence-Combining Practice, pp. 28–29

Listening and Speaking Activities, pp. 1, 2, 19, 21

Composition Practice, p. 21

Descriptive Writing

Revise with Exact Verbs

The best time to check the effectiveness of your verbs is in the revising stage, after you've gotten all your ideas down. Notice how much the replacement verbs in the following model strengthen the images the writer is trying to create. The guidelines below the model provide a plan for systematically checking and improving verbs.

Model

It stopped raining at noon, but clouds continued to ~~flow~~ *sweep* down the craggy mountain into the valley below. Despite the weather, we were determined to hike up at least one mountain in Switzerland. We ~~climbed~~ *trudged* up the steep slope behind the Klausen Pass Hotel, picking our way through fields of sharp rock and over spongelike clumps of wet lichen. After an hour of heavy climbing, we ~~sat~~ *plopped* down on a chilly slab to revive ourselves with water and chocolate. Suddenly, the clouds that had been moving down the mountain spread over our slope, enveloping us in mist. Like it or not, we knew we had to turn back. Disappointed, we ~~walked~~ *stumbled* blindly downward until we came to the road to our hotel.

- Sweep gives a better feeling of relentless motion than "flow."
- How is "trudged" better than "climbed"?
- What does "plopped" tell you?
- "Stumbled" calls up a more vivid mental image than "walked." How does "stumbled" build on the impression created by "plopped" and "trudged"?

Grammar Tip

When you get to the editing stage, pay particular attention to consistency of tenses. See Lessons 15.3–15.6, pages 589–597.

Guidelines for Revision

1. Read your first draft carefully, highlighting each verb with a yellow marker.
2. Scrutinize each verb. Does it call up a vivid mental picture? If not, try to substitute one that does.
3. Consult a thesaurus for help in finding specific, interesting verbs.

138 Unit 3 Descriptive Writing

MEETING INDIVIDUAL NEEDS — English Language Learners

Learning Nuances

Students who are just learning English may not understand the nuances and differences between verbs. As students reexamine their writing, you might suggest they work with a peer editor. Have them take turns reading their descriptions aloud and making suggestions regarding more energetic and precise verbs.

Descriptive Writing

Write with Energetic Verbs

Use one of the following verbs to help you visualize an activity in a location with which you are familiar: *slide, kick, skip, lunge, swoop, shriek, whirl, toss.*

Picture both the location and the action. Write a description of what you visualized. First, make a list of striking details you want to include in the description. Then, write a first draft, using your details to create a vivid word picture. Revise your paragraph, replacing simple verbs with action-packed verbs where appropriate. Consult a thesaurus if you need help finding synonyms.

PURPOSE To use action verbs to describe
AUDIENCE Yourself and your teacher
LENGTH 1 paragraph

WRITING RUBRICS To use action verbs to describe, you should

- choose exact verbs
- use verbs that are descriptive and energetic
- replace overused, uninteresting verbs

Using Computers

If your computer has an electronic thesaurus, use it to help you choose energetic verbs. The electronic thesaurus will quickly give you options for synonyms of verbs, or any other words, that you highlight. The thesaurus may even replace the original word automatically with the new word you have chosen.

Grammar Link

Use verbs correctly.

Even vivid verbs will not be effective if you do not use them correctly. Remember to use the past form without a helping verb (I *went*) and the past participle form with a helping verb (I *have gone*). Remember also to use the correct verb in confusing pairs such as *lie* and *lay.*

Rewrite each sentence below, inserting the correct form of the verb in parentheses.

1. I have (grew, grown) up reading English writer Virginia Woolf.
2. She (wrote, written) several excellent novels, including *To the Lighthouse.*
3. I have (read, readed) most of Virginia Woolf's books.
4. I have sometimes (thunk, thought) that they are among my favorites.
5. Occasionally, Woolf's characters have (drove, driven) me crazy.

See Lessons 15.1 and 15.2, pages 585– 588.

Listening and Speaking

COOPERATIVE LEARNING Working in a small group, take turns reading your descriptive paragraphs aloud without identifying the place in your description. Have your listeners guess the place or type of place you have written about.

Grammar Link

Answers
1. grown
2. wrote
3. read
4. thought
5. driven

Assess

Evaluation Rubrics

Write with Energetic Verbs
The descriptions should
- include energetic verbs
- focus on one or two prominent features of a geographical site
- convey an overall impression of the place
- evoke imaginative, lively images

See also *Writing Assessment & Evaluation Rubrics.*

Using Computers
Demonstrate to students how to use the electronic thesaurus on the computer. Also show them how to select and replace a word with a new word suggested by the thesaurus.

Listening and Speaking
Encourage listeners to sketch the images that emerge from the readings. Have them share the sketches with the readers to illustrate which details and actions made the strongest impressions.

Reteaching
📂 *Composition Reteaching,* p. 21

Enrichment
📂 *Composition Enrichment,* p. 21

Close

Like comic books, political cartoons combine words and pictures in action-packed, often humorous ways. Political cartoons have long been used to satirize current events and issues. Ask students to bring in political cartoons and discuss how the artist exaggerates details for dramatic or humorous effect. Point out that writers also emphasize certain details in descriptions to make a point.

Focus

Lesson Overview

Objective
- To produce descriptions reflecting a consistent vantage point

Skills
- making verbs and subjects agree in inverted sentences; using chronology in a description

Critical Thinking
- classifying; visualizing; identifying

Listening and Speaking
- discussing; listening to a reading

 Bellringer
Daily Language Activity

When students enter the classroom, have this assignment on the board: *Write a paragraph describing the movement of a planet with two moons around an imaginary sun.*

Grammar Link to the Bellringer
Have students read their work to a partner and check for grammatical accuracy, especially in subject-verb agreement.

See also *Daily Language Practice*

Motivating Activity

Place a chair on top of a desk and ask students to describe what they see. How would the chair look if they were looking down from the ceiling? How would a baby crawling on the floor see it? Point out that the vantage point a writer chooses has a direct effect on descriptive writing.

Descriptive Writing

Describing from Vantage Points

*T*he term vantage point *refers to the location from which a writer observes a scene. A writer can describe a scene from a stationary vantage point or, if the scene continually changes, from a moving vantage point. Which vantage point would be used to describe the cockpit below? the scene outside it?*

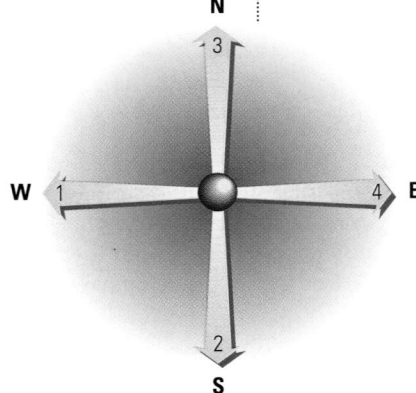

Stationary Vantage Points

A stationary vantage point is a fixed position from which to view a scene. In the following model, American writer Edward Abbey describes a scene from such a vantage point. He views a mountain landscape from a central focus, describing the view to each compass point in turn, first west, then south and north, and finally east. The graphic at the right diagrams this spatial organization.

Resource Manager

Planning Resources
- *Lesson Plans*

Transparencies
- *Bellringer*
- *Daily Language Practice*
- *Fine Art* 13–18
- *Two-Minute Skill Drill*
- *Writing Process* 9, 13–17

Other Print Resources
- *Composition Enrichment*, p. 22
- *Composition Practice*, p. 22
- *Composition Reteaching*, p. 22
- *Cooperative Learning Activities*
- *Listening and Speaking Activities*, pp. 1, 2, 19, 21
- *Sentence-Combining Practice*, pp. 28–29

- *Thinking and Study Skills*, pp. 2, 11, 12, 29–30
- *Writing Across the Curriculum*
- *Writing Assessment and Evaluation Rubrics*

Literature Model

The view is open and perfect in all directions except to the west where the ground rises and the skyline is only a few hundred yards away. Looking toward the mountains I can see the dark gorge of the Colorado River five or six miles away, carved through the sandstone mesa, though nothing of the river itself down inside the gorge. Southward, on the far side of the river, lies the Moab valley between thousand-foot walls of rock, with the town of Moab somewhere on the valley floor, too small to be seen from here. Beyond the Moab valley is more canyon and tableland stretching away to the Blue Mountains fifty miles south. On the north and northwest I see the Roan Cliffs and the Book Cliffs, the two-level face of the Uinta Plateau. . . . To the east, under the spreading sun-rise, are more mesas, more canyons, league on league of red cliff and arid tablelands, extending through purple haze over the bulging curve of the planet to the ranges of Colorado— a sea of desert.

Edward Abbey, "The Most Beautiful Place on Earth"

> **What words give you a sense of direction in this passage?**

Descriptive Writing

Prewriting Tip

Creating a diagram before you begin drafting a description can help you focus your writing. Use arrows and numbers to show the ordering of specific details.

Journal Writing

Think about your daily trip to school. List details you would use to describe that trip. In your journal write a few sentences about your trip. Experiment with creating a graphic for organizing a description of your trip from a stationary vantage point.

Teach

Using the Model

Ask students to pretend they are in the center of the graphic as you read the model aloud. Point out that the phrase "to the west" defines the first vantage point and that Abbey's description of the mountains and mesa gives the reader a sense of what the writer can see in that direction. Ask students to mention other direction words and details that help them orient themselves in the scene. **L2**

Using Vantage Points

Some students may have trouble visualizing from different vantage points. Point out a classroom object, such as an aquarium or overhead projector. Divide students into two groups. Invite the first group to look at the object from above and note their impressions. Have the second group observe the object only from the side and note their impressions. Discuss how a vantage point determines what the viewer sees. **L1**

Two-Minute Skill Drill

Ask students to choose the correct verb for this sentence:

My two cousins (live, lives) down the street.

Then have students rewrite the sentence so that the subject follows the verb.

 See also *Two-Minute Skill Drill Transparency 3.4*

Journal Writing Tip

Representing Suggest that graphic representation will be easier if students consider what their line of sight would be in varied physical situations.

Teach

Using the Model

Read the passage aloud slowly and have students follow the diagram at the top of the page, moving a finger from one dot to the next when they hear the appropriate transitional phrase. Ask for reasons the author might have chosen to switch from spatial order (used in the preceding model) to chronological order. Ask what transitions indicate the shift. (Transitions like "farther on" and "through the beams of my lights" indicate that Abbey is driving his pickup truck. He is no longer stationary and neither is his description.) **L3**

Additional Resources

Writing Process Transparencies, 9, 13–17

Writing Across the Curriculum

Cooperative Learning Activities

For further stimuli for descriptive writing, see *Fine Art Transparencies,* 13–18.

Thinking and Study Skills, pp. 2, 11, 12, 29–30

Listening and Speaking Activities, pp. 1, 2, 19, 21

Composition Practice, p. 22

Sentence-Combining Practice, pp. 28–29

Descriptive Writing

Moving the Vantage Points

A moving vantage point occurs when the position of the viewer continually changes. Usually a writer switches to chronological, or time, order when describing a scene from a moving vantage point. The diagram graphically shows the model's chronological organization.

Moving along points on a path, you describe each scene as you come upon it.

You can get a better feel for the chronological nature of Abbey's organization by comparing the description with the diagram.

Vocabulary Tip

When you revise descriptions written from a moving vantage point, you can make chronological order clearer by using transitions that suggest the passage of time: *until, later, then, after.*

Literature Model

I drove twelve miles farther north on the highway until I came to a dirt road on the right, where a small wooden sign pointed the way: ARCHES NATIONAL MONUMENT EIGHT MILES. I left the pavement, turned east into the howling wilderness. Wind roaring out of the northwest, black clouds across the stars—all I could see were clumps of brush and scattered junipers along the roadside. Then another modest signboard:

WARNING: QUICKSAND
DO NOT CROSS WASH WHEN WATER IS RUNNING

The wash looked perfectly dry in my headlights. I drove down, across, up the other side and on into the night. Glimpses of weird humps of pale rock on either side, like petrified elephants, dinosaurs, stone-age hobgoblins. Now and then something alive scurried across the road: kangaroo mice, a jackrabbit, an animal that looked like a cross between a raccoon and a squirrel—the ringtail cat. Farther on a pair of mule deer started from the brush and bounded obliquely through the beams of my lights, raising puffs of dust which the wind, moving faster than my pickup truck, caught and carried ahead of me out of sight into the dark. The road, narrow and rocky, twisted sharply left and right, dipped in and out of tight ravines, climbing by degrees toward a summit which I would see only in the light of the coming day.

Edward Abbey, "The Most Beautiful Place on Earth"

142   Unit 3 Descriptive Writing

English Language Learners

Choosing Words

If students are unfamiliar with some of the transition words in the model, it may be helpful for them to make a list of phrases such as "farther north," "turned east," "out of the northwest," and so forth. Ask each student to select one of these phrases and use it in a sentence, and then identify the opposite direction and use it in another sentence. This may help students understand how to visualize a vantage point.

Write from a Moving Vantage Point

Write a description of a place from a moving vantage point, such as a landscape viewed from a train window or a canyon as you climb down into it.

PURPOSE To describe a scene from a moving vantage point

AUDIENCE Your classmates

LENGTH 2–3 paragraphs

WRITING RUBRICS To describe a scene from a moving vantage point, you should

- select an interesting scene to describe
- use chronological order to describe the moving scene
- use transitions when your vantage point changes

Cross-Curricular Activity

GEOGRAPHY Think of a city that you have studied recently or one with which you are familiar. Choose one stationary vantage point from which to describe a view of the city. Write a paragraph telling what you see from that vantage point. Then select an area of the city that you might like to walk through, and write a paragraph describing sites from that moving vantage point. Decide which description communicates a better sense of the city.

Grammar Link

Make subjects agree with verbs in inverted sentences.

A subject must agree with a verb even when it follows that verb.

*To the east, under the spreading sunrise, **are** more **mesas**. . . .*

Rewrite any faulty sentence below so that the verb agrees with the subject. Do not confuse subjects with objects of prepositions that precede the verb.

1. Behind the emerald hills, in the distance, loom the hazy shapes of a snow-capped mountain range.
2. There is adventures to be found in those mountains.
3. Here comes two backpackers.
4. There go another two backpackers in the distance.
5. On the mountain lives deer and bears.
6. Near my house is two national parks.

See Lesson 16.3, pages 616–617.

Listening and Speaking

SPELLING Work with a partner and use a dictionary or the spell-checking feature on your computer to make sure that your descriptions are spelled correctly. Correct your misspellings and discuss what your most common spelling errors have in common. How might you avoid these errors in your future writing?

Descriptive Writing

Assess

Evaluation Rubrics

Write from a Moving Vantage Point

Use these criteria when evaluating your students' writing.

- Is there a clearly defined, consistent moving vantage point?
- Are details ordered chronologically with appropriate transitions?
- Do the descriptions evoke a vivid impression for the reader?

See also *Writing Assessment & Evaluation Rubrics.*

Cross-Curricular Activity

Use these criteria when evaluating your students' writing.

- Are the two vantage points distinct?
- Does each give readers a good description of what can be viewed from that vantage point?
- Does the student give logical details to support his or her choice of the more effective vantage point?

Reteaching

📁 *Composition Reteaching*, p. 22

Enrichment

📁 *Composition Enrichment*, p. 22

Close

Students can work with partners to write descriptions. Have them select a view both can describe. One student should write from a stationary vantage point, the other from a moving vantage point. They might then review one another's drafts, write a revised paragraph, and share with other pairs or with the class.

Grammar Link

Answers

1. (no error)
2. There are adventures to be found . . .
3. Here come two backpackers.
4. (no error)
5. On the mountain live deer and bears.
6. Near my house are two national parks.

Descriptive Writing

Focus

Lesson Overview

Objective
• To record personal responses to a poem

Skills
• using precise descriptive words

Critical Thinking
• analyzing; visualizing; making inferences

Listening and Speaking
• listening to poetry; discussing

Bellringer
Daily Language Activity

When students enter the classroom, have this assignment on the board: *Write one sentence describing the use of color on a book or CD cover.*

Grammar Link to the Bellringer

Have volunteers read their sentences aloud. Discuss students' use of precise adjectives when describing any object.

See also *Daily Language Practice*

Motivating Activity

To dispel some students' uneasiness with poetry, you might comment that if music is a part of their lives, then poetry is, too. To explore this connection, bring in the recording of a popular song that would be appropriate to evaluate as poetry. Play the recording and analyze and discuss its artistic elements of rhyme, rhythm, form, imagery, and use of language.

LESSON
3.5

WRITING ABOUT LITERATURE
Responding to Imagery in Poetry

The images a poet uses enable readers to share the poet's unique experience of the world. How would you respond to the images in the following poem? by writing your own poem? by painting a picture such as the one on page 145?

TIME

For more about the writing process, see **TIME Facing the Blank Page,** pp. 109–119.

Literature Model

Corsons Inlet

I went for a walk over the dunes again this morning
to the sea,
then turned right along
   the surf
        rounded a naked headland
        and returned

   along the inlet shore:

it was muggy sunny, the wind from the sea steady and high,
crisp in the running sand,
   some breakthroughs of sun
 but after a bit

continuous overcast:

the walk liberating, I was released from forms,
from the perpendiculars,
     straight lines, blocks, boxes, binds
of thought
into the hues, shadings, rises, flowing bends and blends
     of sight . . .

               A. R. Ammons

Resource Manager

Planning Resources
• *Lesson Plans*

 Transparencies
• *Bellringer*
• *Daily Language Practice*
• *Fine Art* 13–18
• *Two-Minute Skill Drill*
• *Writing Process* 9, 13–17

📁 Other Print Resources
• *Composition Enrichment,* p. 23
• *Composition Practice,* p. 23
• *Composition Reteaching,* p. 23
• *Cooperative Learning Activities*
• *Listening and Speaking Activities,* pp. 1, 2, 19, 21
• *Sentence-Combining Practice,* pp. 28–29

• *Thinking and Study Skills,* pp. 16, 21, 24
• *Writing Across the Curriculum*
• *Writing Assessment and Evaluation Rubrics*

Respond Creatively

Sometimes people are so affected by a poem that they feel a need to respond in a creative way. For example, some people turn poetic images into pictures—pencil sketches, watercolors, even quilts. Others pick an image and respond by choreographing a dance. The following chart shows four other creative ways of responding to imagery in a poem.

Creative Responses to Poetic Images
1. Create a collage that expresses the image's meaning to you.
2. Use your journal to explore the feelings the image arouses in you.
3. Write a poem based on an image that inspires you.
4. Read the poem aloud for a friend or group of classmates.

Descriptive Writing

Arthur Dove, *Sunrise*, 1924

Prewriting Tip

You may want to discuss your idea for responding to a poem with a classmate before working it out on your own. Such interaction will help you clarify and focus your own ideas.

Grammar Tip

When you revise poems you have written as responses, add vivid adjectives to bring images to life. For more information about adjectives, see Lesson 10.4, pages 460–465.

Journal Writing

Think about different ways of responding to a favorite poem. In your journal, discuss which of the responses listed above would work best for you.

Teach

Using the Model

Read or have a student read aloud the poem on the opposite student page. Then ask students to study the painting *Sunrise*. Discuss the sensory language in the poem—some might be auditory or kinesthetic rather than visual. **L2**

Creating a Response

Challenge students to find a poem and respond to it creatively. An image can arouse a feeling or trigger a memory that can be the focus of a response. Responses might include composing music, creating a visual image, performing a dance, or writing in any literary genre. **L3**

Two-Minute Skill Drill

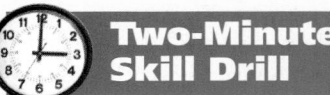

List the following general adjectives on the board and have students write a more specific adjective for each.

happy   *colorful*

interesting   *sad*

See also *Two-Minute Skill Drill Transparency 3.5*

Journal Writing Tip

Drawing Conclusions As students consider the best response for their poem's image, suggest they ask themselves questions such as, "How do I express myself best—on paper, on canvas, on the guitar?" and "Does my response match the mood (place, event, picture) conveyed by the poem?" Students can elaborate on their answers in their journals.

Teach

Teaching from the Art

You might ask students to reexamine the paintings on this and the previous page. Can students see any similarities between the paintings and Ammons's images in "Corsons Inlet" (p. 144)? The painting *Sunrise* (p. 145; oil on plywood, 18 1/4 by 20 7/8 inches, Milwaukee Art Museum) may suggest the "bends and blends of sight." *Electric Prisms* (oil on canvas, 93 3/4 by 98 3/4 inches, Musée National d'Art Moderne in Paris) may remind students of "blocks, boxes, binds of thought." **L2**

Using the Model

Help students contrast the two stanzas. Point out that the first has images of soft, changing shapes of nature, and that the second describes hard, straight lines of artificial things that obstruct vision and cloud thought. Show them that the diner counter serves as a bridge between the two halves of the poem. **L1**

Additional Resources

 For further stimuli for descriptive writing, see *Fine Art Transparencies*, 13–18.

 Writing Process Transparencies 9, 13–17

 Cooperative Learning Activities
Thinking and Study Skills, pp. 16, 21, 24
Sentence-Combining Practice, pp. 28–29
Listening and Speaking Activities, pp. 1, 2, 19, 21
Composition Practice, p. 23

Descriptive Writing

Respond to Poetry

Sometimes it isn't easy to respond to a poem. New York poet Kenneth Koch found a way to help his students—children as young as 8 and adults as old as 98. Koch taught reading poetry and writing poetry as one subject. The two were brought together by "poetry ideas," suggestions for writing that echo the theme of a poem being studied.

Sonia Terk Delaunay, *Electric Prisms*, 1914

To see how to apply Koch's idea, look back at the selection "Corsons Inlet" on page 144. Notice how Ammons contrasts the changing shapes and movement of nature—the dunes, the sea, the wind, and the sun—with the rigid perpendiculars, straight lines, and binds of his own thinking. One writer took that as his "poetry idea": how thinking often gets in the way of really seeing.

Model

The writer uses Ammons's images of nature as a springboard for the new poem.

Why does the poet suddenly include the image of a diner counter? What does it point to?

In the second stanza the writer details how thinking gets in the way of seeing.

I wish the hard part
would be forms. Catching the trees right,
getting the sea to cooperate
Or the sun, coaxing the sun out
when everything is right
and you want it shining.
But all this is easy, soothing, and natural.
As bright and spotless as a diner counter.

The real difficulty is eyeing the flat,
plain, and level. Scaffolding,
the high wires, the firefighter's ladders,
disarrange the subject. Then
an ocean has thoughts; the wind
calls collect, a whispering relative. Your signature
is on everything
saying names and hiding shapes.

146 Unit 3 Descriptive Writing

MEETING INDIVIDUAL NEEDS — English Language Learners

Responding to Poetry

Students who have difficulty reading in English would benefit from reading and responding to poetry in their first language. Ask them to explain to others in the class the images, the comparisons or contrasts, and the beauty of their chosen poems. Ask how they themselves would respond to the poem.

Write a Response Poem

Write a poem in response to one of the images in the poem at the beginning of this lesson or to an image in another poem of your own choosing. First, find a "poetry idea" in the original poem. Then, freewrite to build on this idea.

PURPOSE To respond to a poetic image
AUDIENCE Yourself and your teacher
LENGTH 1 page

WRITING RUBRICS To write an effective poem, you should

- choose a subject that lends itself to descriptive words and images
- list impressions as you visualize your subject
- use your list of impressions to help you write
- use vivid adjectives to create your images

Using Computers

As you are writing your poem, you might experiment with how the words look on the page. Try breaking your lines at different places. Try a different typeface or size. The shape and size of the letters can affect the "feel" of your poem. Print out different versions of your poem and compare them. If you want to achieve a special effect, change the typeface of only one line or word. Use tabs or alignment commands to scatter your text across the page. See which changes bring the most meaning to your poem.

Grammar Link

Use clear, precise adjectives to improve your descriptions.

Adjectives such as *muggy, flowing,* and *soothing* from the models in this lesson help create precise word pictures. Look at this example by A. R. Ammons:

> it was **muggy sunny**, the wind from the sea **steady** and **high**,
> **crisp** in the **running** sand . . .

Revise the following sentences by adding at least one vivid adjective to each.

1. I walked over the dunes.
2. The sea grass grew.
3. The sea beckoned me.
4. The waves lapped the shore.
5. A boat bobbed, straining at its anchor.
6. The sun barely penetrated the mist.
7. The air tickled my nose.
8. I laughed.

See Lesson 10.4, pages 460–465.

Listening and Speaking

COOPERATIVE LEARNING After drafting your poem, work with a partner to review each other's work. Read each other's poems and make suggestions for improvement. How might you make images more "real"? What other words might you use to make a description more vivid? Incorporate some of your partner's suggestions into your final draft. Then read your completed poems aloud.

Descriptive Writing

Assess

Evaluation Rubrics

Write a Poem

Use these criteria when evaluating your students' writing.
- a single, unifying image based on another poem
- a consistent poetic style or voice, either patterned after the other poet or original to the student
- use of vivid adjectives that create images

See also *Writing Assessment & Evaluation Rubrics.*

Using Computers

When evaluating students' use of computer programs, look for a use of fonts, text arrangement, and graphics or illustrations that support the poem.

Listening and Speaking

Encourage students to use at least one image of their own in their responses to the imagery in another poem.

Reteaching

📁 *Composition Reteaching,* p. 23

Enrichment

📁 *Composition Enrichment,* p. 23

Close

Have volunteers plan an exhibit of materials students have prepared as responses to poetry. When their work has been displayed, discuss the variety of ways readers can relate to the same poem. Expand the discussion by encouraging students to describe the elements of poetry that elicit a personal response from them.

Grammar Link

Answers

(Answers will vary, but suggestions are given for the first seven sentences.)
1. I walked over the breezy dunes.
2. The lazy blue sea grass grew.
3. The weary sea beckoned me.
4. The waves lapped the tired shore.
5. A wee boat bobbed, straining at its nagging anchor.
6. The mournful sun barely penetrated the liquid mist.
7. The sticky air tickled my nose.

Focus

Lesson Overview

Objective
• To describe the significance of a story's setting

Skills
• analyzing setting; describing the setting of a short story

Critical Thinking
• analyzing; relating setting to story elements

Listening and Speaking
• discussing

Bellringer
Daily Language Activity

When students enter the classroom, have this assignment on the board: *Choose one of the characters below, and write three sentences giving details of a setting where your character might be found:*
a doctor, a teacher, a construction worker.

Grammar Link to the Bellringer

Ask several students to read their descriptions. Then have other students identify the adjectives and adverbs in the descriptions.

See also *Daily Language Practice*

Motivating Activity

To establish the importance of setting, discuss students' preferences regarding the setting for various activities. For example, ask students where they would rather picnic—on a beach or at a park; where they would rather camp—in the woods or on a mountainside; and where they would rather go to a concert—at a stadium or in a small theater. Ask students how each place would influence their enjoyment of the experience.

LESSON
3.6

WRITING ABOUT LITERATURE
Analyzing Setting in a Short Story

*S*etting is the environment—the time and place—in which the action of a story takes place. When you analyze setting, you describe the setting and then look at how it relates to other important elements of the story.

The graphic below illustrates some important uses of setting. Consider these uses when you analyze the setting of any story.

Uses of Setting		
Use	**Example**	**Explanation**
To create mood	During the whole of a dull, dark, and soundless day in the autumn of the year, when the clouds hung oppressively low in the heavens, I had been passing alone, on horseback, through a singularly dreary tract of country, and at length found myself, as the shades of evening drew on, within view of the melancholy House of Usher. Edgar Allan Poe, "The Fall of the House of Usher"	The setting creates a mood of depression and impending doom.
To affect action	The house was very still about me and yet alive, as if it breathed softly. . . . I shivered and crept to the wide-open window. The faint dawn light, scarcely less than darkness, showed only the silhouette of the birch trees. The moon was down. The garden was totally indistinct. Iris Murdoch, "The Italian Girl"	The setting is crucial as a backdrop for the action.
To develop character	"It's pretty over there," she said. . . . "I go there all the time. Ride over. Especially the graveyard. Down where Spring Creek runs into the Clear Fork. Daddy says it's dangerous because of the copperheads but I go there anyway." A. C. Greene, "The Girl at Cabe Ranch"	The setting conveys information about the main character.

Resource Manager

Planning Resources
• *Lesson Plans*

Transparencies
• *Bellringer*
• *Daily Language Practice*
• *Fine Art* 13–18
• *Two-Minute Skill Drill*
• *Writing Process* 9, 13–17

Other Print Resources
• *Composition Enrichment,* p. 24
• *Composition Practice,* p. 24
• *Composition Reteaching,* p. 24
• *Cooperative Learning Activities*
• *Listening and Speaking Activities,* pp. 1, 2, 19, 21
• *Sentence-Combining Practice,* pp. 28–29

• *Thinking and Study Skills,* pp. 3, 13–14
• *Writing Across the Curriculum*
• *Writing Assessment and Evaluation Rubrics*

Look for Connections

Relating the setting of a story to other elements such as mood, plot, and character, you may find that the setting tells about the other elements. For example, setting may foreshadow disaster or create an atmosphere of terror. The contrast between two settings in a story—a farmhouse and a city apartment, for instance—may reveal a character's feelings. The details of setting—color of walls, neatness of a desk, contents of a drawer—may provide important information about a character.

Setting may also be used as an active participant in a story—for example, a mountain that must be scaled. In this case the setting is something that a character must struggle against. Below is a questionnaire that you can use to help you analyze a story setting.

Grammar Tip

As you analyze story setting, notice the author's use of adverbs to present a more vivid picture of place. For more information about adverbs, see Lesson 10.5, pages 466–472.

Analyzing a Story Setting

General	**1.** What is the name of the story? **2.** Where does most of the story action take place? When does it take place? Is there historical significance to the setting?
Setting and Mood	**3.** What is the general mood of the story? cheerful or gloomy? comforting or threatening? hopeful or despairing? **4.** How does the story setting contribute to the mood?
Setting and Plot	**5.** What is the plot in the story? **6.** Is the setting crucial to the plot? Would it matter much if the story had a different setting? Does the description of the setting change as the story progresses?
Setting and Character	**7.** Who is the main character in the story? What is this person like? **8.** How do we learn about the main character? Does the author convey any important information about the main character through setting?

Journal Writing

Use the questionnaire to begin analyzing setting in a favorite short story. Answer the questions as thoroughly as possible.

Teach

Identifying Components

Discuss how the setting is used in each example on the opposite student page. To see how the setting functions, students can try two approaches: (1) identifying specific details during reading (such as Poe's "dull, dark, and soundless day") and analyzing them to determine what the overall effect is (a mood of depression); or (2) identifying the overall effect after a first reading (an adventurous character in Green's passage) and then going back to identify specific details that contribute to that effect (such as "Daddy says it's dangerous . . . but I go there anyway"). **L3**

Two-Minute Skill Drill

List the following general adverbs on the board and have students write a more vivid adverb for each:

slowly	*happily*
loudly	*quietly*
rapidly	*timidly*

☞ **See also** *Two-Minute Skill Drill Transparency 3.6*

Journal Writing Tip

Identifying Correlations The questionnaire will help students organize their investigation of how the setting of the story correlates with all other elements. Whenever students need to do this kind of analysis, they will find it helpful to create a similar list of questions or issues to be sure of covering the most important correlations.

Teach

Using the Model

As students examine the model, emphasize that the writer did not simply write the answers to the questionnaire; he used them as a tool to help develop the analysis. In discussing the quotations from the story, show how the writer uses them to support the connection between setting and Chee's character as one "who always tries to live in harmony with nature," and to back up the statement that "the plot and setting are intertwined." **L2**

Answering a Questionnaire

Select a story in which the setting plays an important part (such as the literature selection from this unit). Assign each of four groups a section of the questionnaire on page 149. Suggest that each group member read the story and individually answer the questions from their group's section of the questionnaire. Next, have members regroup and discuss their answers. When the class reconvenes, a member from each group should share the group's answers. **L2**

Additional Resources

 For further stimuli for descriptive writing, see *Fine Art Transparencies,* 13–18.

 Writing Process Transparencies, 9, 13–17

 Cooperative Learning Activities
 Writing Across the Curriculum
Thinking and Study Skills, pp. 3, 13–14
Sentence-Combining Practice, pp., 28–29
Listening and Speaking Activities, pp. 1, 2, 19, 21
Composition Practice, p. 24

Descriptive Writing

The introductory paragraph points out that setting plays a major role in the story.

How does the writer use direct quotations from the story?

How does the writer use evidence from the story to support the arguments of the analysis?

Create Your Analysis

After you identify the connections between setting and the other story elements, plan an effective analysis. Use the questionnaire on page 149 as a guide while developing your main points and the support for your arguments. Notice how the questionnaire relates to the following model. Below the model is a set of guidelines you can use to write your own essay about setting in a short story.

Model

In some stories setting isn't very important. It's only background to the main action. In other stories, however, setting plays a major role, creating a unifying thread that touches everyone and everything. Such is the case with the setting in "Chee's Daughter."

Chee is a Navajo who always tries to live in harmony with nature. He has a "feeling of wholeness and of oneness with the sun and earth and growing things." As the story begins, we learn that Chee's wife has died, leaving a three-year-old daughter who, according to Navajo custom, now lives with the mother's relatives.

The story revolves around Chee's efforts to get his daughter back, and the plot and the setting are intertwined every step of the way. For example, the story begins in the cold of winter, so when Chee first asks the grandparents if the daughter can stay with him, we know what the answer will be: a frigid no. We soon learn, however, that "spring-time transformed the mesas," and we realize immediately that it will transform Chee, too. He has a new plan—to place his trust in the land, grow a bountiful harvest, and exchange the food for the child. In the end, Chee's faith is vindicated, and he gets his daughter back.

Guidelines for Writing About Setting

1. Read the story carefully, completing the questionnaire as you go.
2. Write an introductory paragraph that states the main idea of your essay.
3. Use information from the questionnaire in developing your major points.
4. Cite specific evidence from the story to support your argument.
5. End with a brief paragraph summarizing your conclusions.

MEETING INDIVIDUAL NEEDS Less Proficient Readers

Analyzing Setting

Students who have trouble reading may have a hard time analyzing setting as well. Encourage such students to start by looking at just one aspect of setting, such as weather. Select a story in which weather plays an important part, such as Ray Bradbury's "All Summer in a Day."

As students read the story, suggest that they work together and take notes on a "weather chart." On it they can record the weather conditions in the story and the resulting events. Afterward, read the story aloud to students and help them draw conclusions.

Write a Setting Analysis

Select a painting from this book. Think of a general plot for a story that could accompany the painting. Then write an explanation of how the painting's setting affects the story.

PURPOSE To analyze setting
AUDIENCE Your teacher
LENGTH 2-3 paragraphs

WRITING RUBRICS To write an effective analysis of setting, you should

- describe the mood created by the setting
- explain how the setting might affect the actions or feelings of the characters
- cite details from the artwork to support your views

Cross-Curricular Activity

HISTORY Read a short story that takes place in a specific historical period. Write an analysis of how the story's setting, including the historical context, affects the story's mood, action, and character development.

Grammar Link

Use strong adverbs to make descriptions more precise.

Notice how Edgar Allan Poe uses the adverbs *oppressively, alone,* and *singularly* in the model on page 148.

Revise the following sentences by adding at least one vivid adverb to each. (You may make other changes, too, if you wish.)

1. The thunder faded into the distance.
2. Gray clouds raced overhead.
3. The countryside lay sodden and silent.
4. The weary plop of a horse's hooves reached my ears.
5. A solitary rider approached.

See Lesson 10.5, page 466.

Listening and Speaking

ILLUSTRATING Imagine moving the figures from the painting you used for your setting analysis to a different setting. It might be the beach or an amusement park. Orally describe the scene you imagine. Be sure to provide vivid details. What mood describes your setting? How does the setting affect the characters?

Descriptive Writing

Assess

Evaluation Rubrics

Write a Setting Analysis

Use these criteria when evaluating your students' writing.

- Did the writer create a mood with the setting?
- Is the effect of the setting on character clear?
- Is the relationship of plot to setting clear?

See also *Writing Assessment & Evaluation Rubrics.*

Cross-Curricular Activity

Students' writing must analyze the effect of the period on character, mood, and action.

Listening and Speaking

Students' oral descriptions should

- employ vivid details to establish the nature of the new setting.
- reflect an understanding of how setting may affect other story elements.

Reteaching

 Composition Reteaching, p. 24

Enrichment

Composition Enrichment, p. 24

Fine Art Transparencies
Use *Fine Art Transparencies,* 13–18, for enrichment activities also.

Close

Have students discuss whether setting is always important in a short story. Have students give examples to support their ideas.

Grammar Link

Answers
(Answers will vary, but some suggestions are given below.)
1. . . . faded grudgingly . . .
2. . . . raced far and fast overhead.
3. . . . understandably silent.
4. . . . barely reached my ears.
5. . . . approached slowly.

Focus

Objective

- To use facts, statistics, vivid images, and engaging anecdotes in a description

Skills

- using the five stages of the writing process: prewriting, drafting, revising, editing/proofreading, and publishing/presenting; writing a description using a strong lead; elaborating on details using strong verbs and good transitions

Critical Thinking

- recalling; analyzing; generating new information

Listening and Speaking

- interviewing; role-playing; discussing

 Bellringer
Daily Language Activity

When students come into the classroom, have this assignment on the board: *Write a paragraph describing one incident on your first day of high school or on your first day at a new school.*

Grammar Link to the Bellringer

Have students check the verbs they used in their descriptions and evaluate how strong an impression the verbs help create.

See also *Daily Language Practice*

Motivating Activity

Invite students to recall their first few days at their present school. What do they wish someone had told them about the school? Encourage students to discuss the answers to their questions in descriptive detail.

Descriptive Writing

WRITING *Online*

Visit the Writer's Choice Web site at **writerschoice. glencoe.com** for additional writing prompts.

Descriptive Writing

In preceding lessons, you've learned how to describe a place by choosing a vantage point, observing and organizing details carefully, and using energetic verbs. You've also had a chance to write a poem and an essay about story setting. In this lesson you'll put together what you've learned by describing a place that you know well.

Assignment

Context

A student from another state is moving to your school. Your principal has sent the student a variety of orientation materials—class schedules, copies of the school newspaper, last year's yearbook. The student writes back, politely explaining that what she or he really wants is a description of the new school that will allow her or him to "see" the place and the people in it. You've been asked to respond to this request.

Purpose

To write a description of your school that will convey what it's like from a student's point of view

Audience

A student moving to your school from another state

Length

1 to 2 pages

You will find the next few pages helpful as you plan and write your description. Read through the pages, and refer to them as you need to, but remember that they are only guidelines. After all, you're in charge of your own writing process.

Resource Manager

Planning Resources
- *Lesson Plans*

 Transparencies
- *Bellringer*
- *Daily Language Practice*
- *Writing Process* 9, 13–17

Other Print Resources
- *Composition Enrichment,* p. 25
- *Composition Practice,* p. 25
- *Composition Reteaching,* p. 25
- *Grammar Workbook,* Lesson 5
- *Sentence-Combining Practice,* pp. 28–29
- *Thinking and Study Skills,* pp. 3, 14, 21

- *Writing Assessment and Evaluation Rubrics*

 Software
- *Writer's Assistant*

 Web Sites
- *writerschoice.glencoe.com*
- *lit.glencoe.com*

Writing Process in Action

Prewriting

How will you describe your school? What details will you use to present a picture of the building? What details will bring the people in the school to life for your future schoolmate? The questions on the right may help you choose details and a method of organizing the details that will help you write a vivid description.

Jot down notes of details as they occur to you. If you decide to describe the school from a moving vantage point, walk through the building, noting any striking images to include in your description. If necessary, research facts by checking with the school administration.

Once you've collected your details, decide which ones you want to use, and organize your notes. Does a fact or an image stand out? If so, use that for your lead—the first sentence or two that will grab your reader's attention. Look at the lead that Gretel Ehrlich uses in this description of her subject, Wyoming. Note how this passage presents a general picture of Wyoming and uses a quotation to sharpen the picture.

Prewriting Questions

- What images—verbal snapshots—will allow my reader to see the school as I see it?
- What personal anecdotes or quotations can I include?
- What facts and statistics will provide useful information?
- What vantage point would give life to my description?

Literature Model

To live and work in this kind of open country, with its hundred-mile views, is to lose the distinction between background and foreground. When I asked an older ranch hand to describe Wyoming's openness, he said, "It's all a bunch of nothing—wind and rattlesnakes—and so much of it you can't tell where you're going or where you've been and it don't make much difference."

Gretel Ehrlich, *The Solace of Open Spaces*

Teach

Prewriting

Developing Ideas for Descriptive Writing

Encourage students to use an anecdote—either humorous or thought-provoking—in their lead paragraphs. The anecdote should reveal some aspect of school life that the student wants to highlight in the description. Suggest that students first determine a point they want to make about the school and then freewrite to come up with an anecdote that illustrates that point. **L2**

Drafting

Drafting Tips

Before beginning their drafts, encourage students to think through or talk through their descriptions, trying different kinds of organization. Discuss the advantages and disadvantages of using chronological order, order of importance, cause and effect, or compare and contrast. As students write their drafts, they might want to share their organizational preferences. **L2**

Teach

Revising

Peer Editing

Students can work in writing conferences with peer editors before they revise their writing. Suggest that peer editors respond to the following questions:

- Did the description engage your interest immediately? Why or why not?
- Can you suggest other details the student can use to support an idea?
- Can you identify irrelevant details that could be deleted?

You may want to duplicate the Peer Response forms in *Writing Assessment & Evaluation Rubrics.* **L2**

Editing

Peer Editing

After students have edited their own work, have them edit another student's writing. Remind them to refer to the Editing Checklist on student page 155.

Presenting

Before students present their descriptive writing, discuss how to prepare their papers for publication. Emphasize the importance of the final draft and that it must be neatly done.

Additional Resources

Writing Process Transparencies, 9, 13–17
Thinking and Study Skills, pp. 3, 14, 21
Sentence-Combining Practice, p. 28–29

Composition Practice, p. 25

Grammar Workbook, Lesson 5

Descriptive Writing

Drafting Tip

To review how to organize details, see Lesson 2.7, pages 72–75, and Lesson 3.1, pages 126–131.

Revising Tip

If you are having trouble with word choice, consult the Guidelines for Revision chart, Lesson 3.3, page 138.

Drafting

To begin drafting, imagine where you are—the place you'll begin your tour or where you will stand to describe all that you see around you—or look at your lead. Then just start writing.

As you write, be aware of details unique to your school that might need special explanation. Try to look at your school with a "fresh" eye so you can make the description clear for the new student.

Visualize what you are describing. Use your notes to help you remember details, but don't stop writing at this stage to find the perfect verb or image. If you get stuck, take a break, talk about your description with a friend, or start over.

Revising

To begin revising, read over your draft to make sure that what you've written fits your purpose and audience. Then have a **writing conference.** Read your draft to a partner or small group. Use your audience's reactions and the Revising Checklist below to help you evaluate your work.

Revising Checklist

- Did I use a lead that grabbed the reader?
- Did I select good details and organize them logically around topic sentences?
- Were the images I used clear and striking?
- Did I use exact, energetic verbs to enliven my description?
- Did I write from a vantage point that made sense?

Enrichment and Extension

Follow-up Ideas

- Set aside time for students to celebrate the conclusion of their writing projects.
- Consider class publication. All of the students' writing for this assignment can be collected, illustrated, bound, and placed in the school library.

Extending Description

- Explore opportunities for extending descriptive writing beyond the classroom. Students might create a community resources description for senior citizens or write family descriptions and interests to update distant relatives.

Editing/Proofreading

When you are satisfied with your description, **proofread** it carefully for errors in grammar, usage, mechanics, and spelling. Use the quotations at the right as a guide.

In addition to proofreading, use the Self-Evaluation guidelines to make sure your writing describes the school well. When you feel that it does, make a clean copy of your description and proofread it one more time.

Self-Evaluation

Make sure your description—

✔ uses a strong lead
✔ uses different kinds of vivid supporting details
✔ uses strong verbs and good transitions
✔ follows correct grammar, usage, mechanics, and spelling

Editing, like revising, is best accomplished in a series of passes through your work. It's easier to watch for one type of error than to be on the lookout for ten kinds. The guidelines for editing presented in Lesson 2.9, pages 82–85 can also help. Don't let the fact that you know your work lull you into missing obvious errors.

Publishing/Presenting

You might want to have someone from another state read your description. Your reader might be a friend who has moved away, a relative, or a pen pal. Feedback from such a reading would tell you how well your description works.

Editing/Proofreading Checklist

- Have I used verbs correctly?
- Have I formed possessive pronouns correctly?
- Do my subjects and verbs agree?
- Have I used precise, vivid word choices?
- Have I checked spellings of any words of which I'm unsure?

Proofreading

For proofreading symbols, see page 84. Use the spell-check and grammar-check features on the computer to examine your work.

Journal Writing

Reflect on your writing-process experience. Answer these questions in your journal: What do you like best about your description? What was the hardest part of writing it? What did you learn in your writing conference? What new things have you learned as a writer?

Assess

Evaluation Rubrics

Use the following questions to evaluate the students' finished writing:

- Does the prewriting focus on facts, images, and anecdotes that provide revealing glimpses of school life?
- Does the draft begin with an attention-grabbing lead?
- Does the draft develop the prewriting ideas into vivid details and images?
- Do the ideas in the revision flow from sentence to sentence and from paragraph to paragraph?
- Do transitions connect ideas in the revised description?
- Are ideas in the revision organized logically?
- Has the student replaced passive, boring verbs with more vivid ones in the revised description?
- Is the edited version free of grammar, usage, and mechanical errors?

See also *Writing Assessment & Evaluation Rubrics.*

Reteaching

📁 *Composition Reteaching,* p. 25

Enrichment

📁 *Composition Enrichment,* p. 25

Journal Writing Tip

Evaluating the Writing Process
Remind students to follow the Self-Evaluation list to evaluate their work.

Cultural Connections

Investigating Differences

Suggest that students compile interesting facts and statistics about the various cultural groups represented at their school. How are the groups alike? How are they different? Students might want to describe holidays celebrated at their school or in family gatherings. Encourage students to describe how the cultural diversity of the school has enriched their learning experience.

Close

Have students discuss how writing this description has helped them look more closely at their school. What did they find was the most difficult part of writing this description?

UNIT 3
Literature Model

About the Author

Gretel Ehrlich feels bound to Wyoming where she ranches and which she has come to know at least partially through sensory knowledge. Ehrlich believes that people should come to know a place by seeking equality with the place, not dominance over it: "If we go out in order to find, not to impose, the landscape touches us and we it. Only then is a sense of place born."

Focus

Lesson Overview

Objective
• To examine a professional writer's use of descriptive writing

Skills
• reading comprehension; identifying supporting details

Critical Thinking
• analyzing

Listening and Speaking
• discussing; reporting

Bellringer
Daily Language Activity

When students enter the classroom, have this activity on the board: *Describe briefly the most enjoyable place you have been.*

See also *Daily Language Practice*

Motivating Activity

Ask students if they like the peace of rural areas, or if they feel more at home in small towns or in the fast-paced energy of the big city. Encourage students to use descriptive details and anecdotes to explain why they prefer that environment.

✔ ASSESSMENT OPTIONS

🗁 *Writing Assessment & Evaluation Rubrics*

Descriptive Writing

FROM

The Solace of Open Spaces

by Gretel Ehrlich

In this excerpt from her book The Solace of Open Spaces, *Gretel Ehrlich, who lives on a ranch in Wyoming, uses descriptive writing to portray her adopted home state, its land, and its people. Pay particular attention to the images, the facts, and the anecdotes Ehrlich uses to engage the reader in her description. Then try the activities in Linking Writing and Literature on page 162.*

To live and work in this kind of open country, with its hundred-mile views, is to lose the distinction between background and foreground. When I asked an older ranch hand to describe Wyoming's openness, he said, "It's all a bunch of nothing—wind and rattlesnakes—and so much of it you can't tell where you're going or where you've been and it don't make much difference." John, a sheepman I know, is tall and handsome and has an explosive temperament. He has a perfect intuition about people and sheep. They call him "Highpockets," because he's so long-legged; his graceful stride matches the distances he has to cover. He says, "Open space hasn't affected me at all. It's all the people moving in on

---

Resource Manager

Planning Resources
• *Lesson Plans*

🗁 **Transparencies**
• *Bellringer*
• *Daily Language Practice*
• *Fine Art 13–18*

🗁 **Other Print Resources**
• *Listening and Speaking Activities,* pp. 1, 2, 19, 21

• *Thinking and Study Skills,* pp. 3, 14, 19
• *Writing Assessment and Evaluation Rubrics*

🖥 **Web Sites**
• *writerschoice.glencoe.com*
• *lit.glencoe.com*

Literature Model

Frederic Remington, *The Fall of the Cowboy*, 1895

it." The huge ranch he was born on takes up much of one county and spreads into another state; to put 100,000 miles on his pickup in three years and never leave home is not unusual. A friend of mine has an aunt who ranched on Powder River and didn't go off her place for eleven years. When her husband died, she quickly moved to town, bought a car, and drove around the States to see what she'd been missing.

Most people tell me they've simply driven through Wyoming, as if there were nothing to stop for. Or else they've skied in Jackson Hole, a place Wyomingites acknowledge uncomfortably because its green beauty and chic affluence[1] are mis-

matched with the rest of the state. Most of Wyoming has a "lean-to" look. Instead of big, roomy barns and Victorian houses, there are dugouts, low sheds, log cabins, sheep camps, and fence lines that look like driftwood blown haphazardly into place. People here still feel pride because they live in such a harsh place, part of the glamorous cowboy past, and they are determined not to be the victims of a mining-dominated future.

---

1 **chic affluence** (shēk′ af′ loo əns) stylish wealth

Literature Model **157**

Descriptive Writing

Teach

Guided Reading

- Of what kind of creative work does the opening sentence (on student page 156) remind you? How does Ehrlich carry out that same idea in the first two paragraphs?
- How does Ehrlich use comparison and contrast in these opening paragraphs? **L2**

Viewing the Art

Frederic Remington, *The Fall of the Cowboy*, 1895
American artist Frederic Remington (1861–1909) is known for paintings and sculptures depicting the Old West. The 25 by 35 1/8-inch oil painting is in the Amon Carter Museum in Fort Worth, Texas.

Teach

Guided Reading

- Ehrlich writes that she came to Wyoming to "lose myself"—to find "numbness." Did she achieve her goal? Explain why or why not.
- While writing of the people, Ehrlich continues to emphasize the space and shape of Wyoming. Give several examples. **L2**

Descriptive Writing

Most characteristic of the state's landscape is what a developer euphemistically[2] describes as "indigenous growth right up to your front door"—a reference to waterless stands of salt sage, snakes, jack rabbits, deerflies, red dust, a brief respite of wildflowers, dry washes, and no trees. In the Great Plains the vistas look like music, like Kyries[3] of grass, but Wyoming seems to be the doing of a mad architect—tumbled and twisted, ribboned with faded, deathbed colors, thrust up and pulled down as if the place had been startled out of a deep sleep and thrown into a pure light.

I came here four years ago. I had not planned to stay, but I couldn't make myself leave. John, the sheepman, put me to work immediately. It was spring, and shearing time. For fourteen days of fourteen hours each, we moved thousands of sheep through sorting corrals to be sheared, branded, and deloused.[4] I suspect that my original motive for coming here was to "lose myself" in new and unpopulated territory. Instead of producing the numbness I thought I wanted, life on the sheep ranch woke me up. The vitality of the people I was working with flushed out what had become a hallucinatory[5] rawness inside me. I threw away my clothes and bought new ones; I cut my hair. The arid country was a clean slate. Its absolute indifference steadied me.

Sagebrush covers 58,000 square miles of Wyoming. The biggest city has a population of fifty thousand, and there are only five settlements that could be called cities in the whole state. The rest are towns, scattered across the expanse with as much as sixty miles between them, their populations two thousand, fifty, or ten. They are fugitive-looking, perched on a barren, windblown bench, or tagged onto a river or a railroad, or laid out straight in a farming valley with implement stores and a block-long Mormon church. In the eastern part of the state, which slides down into the Great Plains, the new mining settlements are boomtowns, trailer cities, metal knots on flat land.

Despite the desolate look, there's a coziness to living in this state. There are so few people (only 470,000) that ranchers who buy and sell cattle know one another statewide; the kids who choose to go to college usually go to the state's one university, in Laramie; hired hands work their way around Wyoming in a lifetime of hirings and firings. And despite the physical separation, people stay in touch, often driving two or three hours to another ranch for dinner.

Seventy-five years ago, when travel was by buckboard or horseback, cowboys who were temporarily out of work rode the grub line—drifting from ranch to ranch, mending fences or milking cows, and receiving in exchange a bed and meals. Gossip and messages traveled this slow

---

2 **euphemistically** (yōō fə mis' tik lē) using a word or phrase in place of another that is distasteful or offensive
3 **Kyries** (kir' ē āz) parts of Church liturgy, often set to music
4 **deloused** (dē lousd') rid of lice
5 **hallucinatory** (ha lōōs' sə nə tor' ē) characterized by, or producing, sights or sounds that are not really present

Listening and Speaking

Genre and Style

Ehrlich uses descriptive writing to create vivid images of Wyoming and its people in *The Solace of Open Spaces*. Written from the first-person point of view, the selection invites the reader to discover Wyoming through the eyes of the writer. Ehrlich combines facts with anecdotes to paint a picture of a place and its people who seem made of the same windswept rocks and earth.

Ask student volunteers to read sections of the excerpt aloud. Have the rest of the class listen, respond, and appropriately evaluate the presentation. In a discussion, students should identify and analyze the effect of the excerpt's literary elements including description, setting, character development, imagery, and language.

Literature Model

Ann Taylor, *Red Riding*, 1982

Teach

Guided Reading

- Make an idea web around the word space. Include only the details on pages 159–160. Remember to use concepts from *Red Riding* in your web.
- What do you think Ehrlich means by this sentence about westerners: "These detached looks of quiet amusement are sometimes cynical, but they can also come from a dry-eyed humility. . . ."? **L2**

circuit with them, creating an intimacy between ranchers who were three and four weeks' ride apart. One old-time couple I know, whose turn-of-the-century homestead was used by an outlaw gang as a relay station for stolen horses, recalls that if you were traveling, desperado or not, any lighted ranch house was a welcome sign. Even now, for someone who lives in a remote spot, arriving at a ranch or coming to town for supplies is cause for celebration. To emerge from isolation can be disorienting.[6] Everything looks bright, new, vivid. After I had been herding sheep for only three days, the sound of the camp tender's pickup flustered me. Longing for human company, I felt a foolish grin take over my face; yet I had to resist an urgent temptation to run and hide.

Things happen suddenly in Wyoming, the change of seasons and weather; for people, the violent swings in and out of isolation. But good-naturedness is

---

6 disorienting (dis ôr′ ē ent′ iŋ) causing one to lose one's bearings

Viewing the Art

Ann Taylor, *Red Riding,* 1982

Ann Taylor, a self-taught artist, was born in New York in 1941 but has lived in Arizona. Her simple, spare landscapes reveal her love of wide-open, largely uninhabited places. One critic claimed that Taylor had painted "the very air" in her "reach for solitude." The oil painting measures 84 by 52 inches and is contained in a private collection in New York City.

Teach

Guided Reading

- What very appropriate metaphor does Ehrlich use to describe the speech of westerners?
- Find sentences in the two paragraphs beginning with "Sentence structure . . ." in which Ehrlich contrasts what may seem true with what is really true about Wyoming people. **L2**

Additional Resources

Fine Art Transparencies, 13–18
Listening and Speaking Activities, pp. 1, 2, 19, 21
Thinking and Study Skills, pp. 3, 14, 19

Literature Model

Descriptive Writing

concomitant with severity.[7] Friendliness is a tradition. Strangers passing on the road wave hello. A common sight is two pickups stopped side by side far out on a range, on a dirt track winding through the sage. The drivers will share a cigarette, uncap their thermos bottles, and pass a battered cup, steaming with coffee, between windows. These meetings summon up the details of several generations, because, in Wyoming, private histories are largely public knowledge.

Because ranch work is a physical and, these days, economic strain, being "at home on the range" is a matter of vigor, self-reliance, and common sense. A person's life is not a series of dramatic events for which he or she is applauded or exiled but a slow accumulation of days, seasons, years, fleshed out by the generational weight of one's family and anchored by a land-bound sense of place.

In most parts of Wyoming, the human population is visibly outnumbered by the animal. Not far from my town of fifty, I rode into a narrow valley and startled a herd of two hundred elk. Eagles look like small people as they eat car-killed deer by the road. Antelope, moving in small, graceful bands, travel at sixty miles an hour, their mouths open as if drinking in the space.

The solitude in which westerners live makes them quiet. They telegraph thoughts and feelings by the way they tilt their heads and listen; pulling their Stetsons into a steep dive over their eyes, or pigeon-toeing one boot over the other, they lean against a fence with a fat wedge of Copenhagen beneath their lower lips and take in the whole scene. These detached looks of quiet

amusement are sometimes cynical, but they can also come from a dry-eyed humility as lucid as the air is clear.

Conversation goes on in what sounds like a private code; a few phrases imply a complex of meanings. Asking directions, you get a curious list of details. While trailing sheep I was told to "ride up to that kinda upturned rock, follow the pink wash, turn left at the dump, and then you'll see the water hole." One friend told his wife on roundup to "turn at the salt lick and the dead cow," which turned out to be a scattering of bones and no salt lick at all.

Sentence structure is shortened to the skin and bones of a thought. Descriptive words are dropped, even verbs; a cowboy looking over a corral full of horses will say to a wrangler, "Which one needs rode?" People hold back their thoughts in what seems to be a dumbfounded silence, then erupt with an excoriating[8] perceptive remark. Language, so compressed, becomes metaphorical. A rancher ended a relationship with one remark: "You're a bad check," meaning bouncing in and out was intolerable, and even coming back would be no good.

What's behind this laconic[9] style is shyness. There is no vocabulary for the subject of feelings. It's not a hangdog[10] shyness, or anything coy—always there's a robust spirit in evidence behind the

---

7 **is concomitant with severity** (kən käm' ə tənt) (se ver' ə tē) is related to harshness
8 **excoriating** (ik skôr' ē āt'ŋ) harsh; abrasive
9 **laconic** (lə kän' ik) brief or succinct in speech
10 **hangdog** ashamed; cringing

Writing in the Real World

Writers and Writing

Ehrlich claims that Wyoming changed her life. The "hallucinatory rawness" of an urban environment was flushed out, and the writer felt as if she could begin all over again in Wyoming. "The arid country was a clean slate." Ask students if any place has had a similarly strong impact on their lives.

Literature Model

restraint, as if the earth-dredging wind that pulls across Wyoming had carried its people's voices away but everything else in them had shouldered confidently into the breeze.

I've spent hours riding to sheep camp at down in a pickup when nothing was said; eaten meals in the cookhouse when the only words spoken were a mumbled "Thank you, ma'am" at the end of dinner. The silence is profound. Instead of talking, we seem to share one eye. Keenly observed, the world is transformed. The landscape is engorged with detail, every movement on it chillingly sharp. The air between people is charged. Days unfold, bathed in their own music. Nights become hallucinatory; dreams, prescient.[11]

---

11 **prescient** (prē′ shē ənt) able to know of things before they occur

Teach

Guided Reading

- Summarize the ways in which Ehrlich characterizes the speech of the people of Wyoming.
- According to Ehrlich, what are some of the factors which affect the speech of her Wyoming neighbors?

Literature Model **161**

Linking Writing and Literature

Assess

Evaluation Rubrics

As your students discuss the selection, either in small groups or as a class, encourage them to begin with a personal response. The student responses on this page might be used as a starting point.

Look for evidence that students
- have read the selection
- can state some of the writer's ideas in their own words
- understand the writer's point of view
- have connected the content to their own knowledge and experiences
- understand the ideas and implications of the selection

The following are possible responses to the discussion questions on this page:
1. Ehrlich added layers of descriptive details to engulf the reader in a sense of Wyoming. She included details of the land, work, animals, and people.
2. Students' writing should list specific details to support their choices.
3. The moods vary: a sense of openness, a feeling of respect or admiration.
4. The people are described as silent, competent, wry—quite different from something created by a "mad architect."

Close

In her description of Wyoming, Ehrlich shows her love for the land. Have students write brief descriptions of a place, real or imaginary, in which the narrator expresses dislike of the environment and a desire to leave it. Discuss details and anecdotes appropriate to this type of description. Have students share their writing by reading their descriptions aloud.

Descriptive Writing

Literature Model

Linking Writing and Literature

Readers Respond to the Model

What makes Gretel Ehrlich's description effective?

Explore Gretel Ehrlich's description by answering these questions. Then read how other students reacted to Ehrlich's narrative.

1. How did Ehrlich convey a "sense of place"?
2. Choose one descriptive paragraph. What specific details or images made it work?
3. What mood does Ehrlich's description evoke? How?
4. Explain how the following description of the geography contrasts with Ehrlich's of the people: "Wyoming seems to be the doing of a mad architect—tumbled and twisted, ribboned with faded, deathbed colors, thrust up and pulled down as if the place had been startled out of a deep sleep . . . ."

What Students Say

"I truly admire Gretel Ehrlich's passion for Wyoming's desolate country and her ability to make such a seemingly barren land come to life. Her description was phenomenal; it made me see the whole state. Ehrlich's first-person point of view made the selection very lyrical and personal, without being clichéd. Her writing had a real human quality. I believe the author wrote as she did because she is akin to the land and its people.

The part I remember best was when Ehrlich talked about how the people rarely spoke, about their having a silent language. It seemed both straightforward and cryptic; it made me feel somehow included in the private, secretive lives of the ranchers. I would recommend this selection to a friend because it is so personal and truthful. It made me understand how someone can have so much love for a place."

Rachel Hansen

"Although Ehrlich's descriptions were good, this selection did not interest me very much—perhaps because of the quiet and peaceful nature of the place. The writer simply failed to keep my attention."

Claire Monty

Writing in the Real World

Writers and Writing

Point out to students that Ehrlich paints a picture of the people of Wyoming in a few descriptive sentences. The reader can see them leaning against a fence, gazing into the distance. Suggest that students try writing a similar word picture of someone they know. The description should capture the person's characteristic mannerisms and physical attributes, and convey a sense of his or her personality.

UNIT **3** Review

Reflecting on the Unit

Summarize what you learned in this unit by answering the following questions.

1 How can you gather details for descriptive writing?

2 What are some effective ways to organize descriptive details to create effective images?

3 How can choice of verbs affect the vitality of your writing?

4 How does vantage point relate to description of a place?

5 What are some important elements in analyzing the setting of a story?

 ## Adding to Your Portfolio

CHOOSE A SELECTION FOR YOUR PORTFOLIO Look over the descriptive writing you have done during this unit. Select a completed piece of writing to put into your portfolio. The piece you choose should show some or all of the following:

- descriptive details arranged in an effective order
- a basis in observation and note taking
- precise, vivid verbs
- the use of a clear vantage point

REFLECT ON YOUR CHOICE Attach a note to the piece you chose, explaining briefly why you chose it and what you learned from writing it.

SET GOALS How can you improve your writing? What skill will you focus on the next time you write?

Writing Across the Curriculum

MAKE A GEOGRAPHY CONNECTION Think about the description of your school that you wrote and about Gretel Ehrlich's description of Wyoming. What images spring to mind when you think about your town or county? Take notes and organize your descriptive details. Create a lead using colorful images, quotations, anecdotes, or background facts. Then write a two- or three-paragraph description of your town or county. Use topic sentences to focus the details in your paragraphs and action-packed verbs to make your vision come to life for the reader. Write legibly and check spelling for your final copy.

Review

Reflecting on the Unit

You may have students respond to Reflecting on the Unit in writing or through discussion.

Writing Across the Curriculum

Suggest that students brainstorm with partners or small groups to focus on an overall tone for their descriptions. Students might want to emphasize colors, chaos, or openness, for example.

Adding to Your Portfolio

Suggest that students begin the selection process by choosing five writing samples that use colorful details, sensory language, and strong verbs to create vivid mental images. They may then exchange their work with their classmates and use peer responses as an additional guide.

Portfolio Evaluation

If you grade the portfolio selections, you may want to award two marks—one each for content and form. Explain your assessment criteria before students make their selections.

Commend
- experimentation with creative prewriting techniques
- clear, concise writing in which the main idea, audience, and purpose are evident
- successful revisions
- work that shows a flair for language

✔ ASSESSMENT OPTIONS

📁 *Tests With Answer Key and Rubrics*
Unit 3 Choice A Test, p. 9
Unit 3 Choice B Test, p. 10
Unit 3 Composition Objective Test, pp. 11–12

💾 *Testmaker*
Unit 3 Choice A Test
Unit 3 Choice B Test
Unit 3 Composition Objective Test

You may wish to administer one of these tests as a mastery test.

📺 *MindJogger Videoquizzes*

Narrative Writing

Viewing the Art

The photographer presents a view of the canyon of Big Bend National Park in south-western Texas from the top of the canyon's south rim. The image is notable for its dramatic contrasts of light and shadow as well as for its juxtaposition of the spiky cacti in the foreground and the sharp peaks of the hills in the background. The photographer uses details to help tell a story in much the same way that narrative writers use details to relate a sequence of events.

Interpret and Analyze Use the following questions for discussion:

- What adjectives would you use to describe the canyon and the other details in the photograph? What effect do these details have on the viewer?

- Compare the foreground (the plants) with the background (the hills). How are they similar? How are they different? What do they tell the viewer about the climate and character of the canyon?

Discussing the Quotation

Discuss this quotation from "Lullaby," a short story by Leslie Marmon Silko (born 1948), with the class, and ask students what sense of place it conveys. How would they further describe this place? How might it be similar to or different from the location depicted in the photograph? To find out more information about the author and the story from which this quotation was taken, see *Glencoe Literature,* Course 5, p. 329.

Writing Prompt Have students write a short narrative that is set in a place similar to the one described in Silko's words or in the photograph.

"She stayed up in the hills for the rest of the day, sitting on a black lava boulder in the sunshine where she could see for miles all around her."

—Leslie Marmon Silko, "Lullaby"

164

Resource Manager

Planning Resources
- *Lesson Plans*
- *Block Scheduling*

Transparencies
- *Bellringer*
- *Daily Language Practice*
- *Fine Art*
- *Two-Minute Skill Drill*
- *Writing Process*

Other Print Resources
- *Composition Enrichment*
- *Composition Practice*
- *Composition Reteaching*
- *Cooperative Learning Activities*
- *Glencoe Literature Library*
- *Grammar and Composition Handbook*
- *Grammar Workbook*

- *Listening and Speaking Activities*
- *Research Paper and Report Writing*
- *Sentence-Combining Practice*
- *Tests with Answer Key and Rubrics*
- *Thinking and Study Skills*
- *Writing Across the Curriculum*
- *Writing Assessment and Evaluation Rubrics*
- *Writing in the Real World*

UNIT 4 Narrative Writing

Writing in the Real World: *Bobby Norfolk*   *166*

   Lesson **4.1**   **Narrating a Personal Experience**   *170*

   Lesson **4.2**   **Developing a Fictional Narrative**   *174*

   Lesson **4.3**   **Organizing a Fictional Narrative**   *180*

   Lesson **4.4**   **Writing Dialogue**   *184*

   Lesson **4.5**   **Theme and Anecdote**   *188*

   Lesson **4.6**   **Writing About Literature: The Plot Summary**   *192*

   Lesson **4.7**   **Writing About Literature: Analyzing Conflict**   *196*

Writing Process in Action: Narrative Writing   *200*

Literature Model: from *Tortuga* by Rudolfo A. Anaya   *204*

Unit 4 Review   *213*

Objectives

- To become familiar with narratives through reading and discussion
- To identify and understand the characteristics of various kinds of narratives
- To demonstrate control over narrative techniques by writing effective narratives with developed elements of plot, character, setting, conflict, and resolution

ASSESSMENT OPTIONS

Tests with Answer Key & Rubrics
Unit 4 Choice A Test, p. 13
Unit 4 Choice B Test, p. 14
Unit 4 Composition Objective Test, pp. 15–16

Testmaker
Unit 4 Choice A Test
Unit 4 Choice B Test
Unit 4 Composition Objective Test

You may wish to administer either the Unit 4 Choice A Test or the Unit 4 Choice B Test as a pretest.

Key to Ability Levels

L1   Level 1 activities are within the basic ability range of students.

L2   Level 2 activities are within the ability range of average students.

L3   Level 3 activities are more challenging activities.

165

Video
- *MindJogger Videoquizzes*

 Software
- *Presentation Plus!*
- *Revising with Style*
- *Testmaker*
- *Writer's Assistant*
- *Writer's Choice Puzzlemaker*

 Web Sites
- *writerschoice.glencoe.com*
- *lit.glencoe.com*

Focus

Lesson Overview

Objective
- To explore how narrative writing and the writing process are used in a real-life application

Skills
- analyzing; discussing; creating or adapting a narrative; telling a story

Critical Thinking
- evaluating; visualizing; generating new information

Listening and Speaking
- informal speaking; narrating and performing a story

Bellringer
Daily Language Activity

When students enter the classroom, have this assignment on the board: *Write a paragraph about a fictional character. Describe how you would make that character come to life if you were an actor.*

Grammar Link to the Bellringer

Encourage students to edit their descriptions, using participles to add lively details to their writing.

See also *Daily Language Practice*

Motivating Activity

Ask students to recall their own experiences listening to stories. Some may remember an adult who told them stories or read to them. Then ask them what makes someone a good storyteller. (Ruth Tooze, a children's literature specialist, values imagination, perception, insight, enthusiasm, spontaneity, the desire to share experiences, and sensitivity to the needs and moods of listeners.)

Narrative Writing

Writing in the Real World

MEDIA Connection
Storytelling

Like a story written for a book, a story created for the stage has characters, a plot, and a setting. In the case of a told story, however, character and plot are usually emphasized more than setting is. The following excerpt is from a work written for the stage by storyteller Bobby Norfolk. It is based on classical scholar Edith Hamilton's written version of the myth of Perseus.

From "Perseus and the Gorgon"

by Bobby Norfolk

Perseus stood up in the king's court and shouted: "I will go off and bring back the head of Medusa!" Everyone gasped. "The boy must be mad!" someone said. No man in his right mind would try to kill Medusa. Medusa was one of the Gorgons. She stood about eight feet tall and had scales of green hue. Her fingernails were long and sharp, and she had canine teeth that hung from her mouth—used for tearing flesh from bone. Her hair was a mass of living snakes, hissing and twirling about constantly. Medusa had a long serpentlike tail that [dragged] behind her for six feet. That was not the most hideous thing about Medusa however. She had blood-red eyes that lit up when any person looked upon her. That person would immediately turn into stone. . . .

. . . Perseus was guided by Hermes, over ocean and sea to the Terrible Sisters Island. As fate would have it, the Terrible Sisters were all asleep when Perseus found them. In the mirror, he could see them clearly, hideous creatures with scales, and hair, a mass of twisting snakes. Perseus hovered low enough to be within striking distance of Medusa. The two messengers were with him, and gave Perseus explicit instructions on which monster was Medusa. Two of the Gorgons were immortal, [hence] only Medusa could be killed. Perseus carefully aimed his sword by way of the mirror at the Gorgon's neck, and hovering above the trio, [launched] his surprise attack.

With one fell swoop, . . . Perseus cut the head of Medusa off and it landed on the floor of the cave. He then flew down low enough to grab the head up and place it in [his] pouch. The other Gorgons were enraged upon finding their

---

Resource Manager

Planning Resources
- *Lesson Plans*

Transparencies
- *Bellringer*
- *Daily Language Practice*
- *Writing Process* 10, 18–22

Other Print Resources
- *Cooperative Learning Activities,* pp. 17–20
- *Thinking and Study Skills,* pp. 21–22
- *Writing Assessment and Evaluation Rubrics*
- *Writing in the Real World,* pp. 13–16

A Writer's Process

Prewriting
Finding the Story

Some storytellers write their own stories. Others retell narratives that they have heard or read. Storyteller Bobby Norfolk, for example, finds most of his stories in books. "I live in libraries and bookstores," he says.

After rereading Edith Hamilton's *Mythology*, Norfolk chose to retell the tale of Perseus, one of the heroes of Greek mythology, "because it was the most visual of all the myths. This one gets as close as you can to classic horror," he explains, "so I knew kids would relish it."

As told by Edith Hamilton, the story of Perseus unfolds like a fairy tale. Perseus's extraordinary adventures begin with his boast that he will slay Medusa, a monster with "snaky hair," who turns people who look at her into stone. Naturally, Perseus needs help to accomplish this task, which comes from three witches and several Greek gods. Norfolk says, "As I read the story, I visualized the three witches who had to share one eye, and Perseus's meeting with the Greek gods. I knew I could convey these vivid images to my listeners."

Drafting/Revising
Adapting the Story

To adapt Hamilton's tale for the stage, Norfolk expanded the dialogue. He also supplied details to emphasize the scene that he considered the climax of the story—when the king and his court are turned into stone all at once. In Norfolk's adaptation, a series of pantomimes show five or six courtiers becoming petrified in turn. This technique extends the action and underlines the climactic moment.

In addition to adding dialogue and highlighting plot elements, Norfolk also enlarged upon the descriptions of several characters. Hamilton describes Medusa's locks as "snaky hair, most horrible to mortals." Norfolk's version supplies many other vivid details his listeners can visualize as he speaks.

Revising/Editing
Fine-Tuning the Story

No matter how often storytellers practice and revise a story, storytelling is an improvisational art. As they perform, storytellers make many

The foundation of world literature lies in the stories of ancient mythology.

Edith Hamilton's book Mythology *inspired Norfolk to create his version of the Perseus tale.*

Teach

Building Background

Warm-up
Have students list as many occasions as they can think of where narration is used.

Narration in Speaking
Remind students that they use narration every day when they are speaking, such as relating a movie's plot to a friend or telling their parents what happened on the way home from school.

Invite students to discuss other times when they have really wanted to capture their audience's attention with a good story.

Narration in Writing
Discuss any narratives students have read. Use prompts such as these:

- Have you ever read a newspaper account of events leading up to a crime? How does the writer of the article grab your attention?
- What details do writers use to enliven the retelling of a historical event?

Reading Media
Have students preview the title and focus of the Media Connection. Discuss with students how Bobby Norfolk adapts stories and makes them his own through his performance. Then have students read the story.

Viewing and Representing

Performing Art
Like dance, theater, and music, storytelling is a performing art. Storytellers' voices and bodies are the media through which they share their art. As with all performing arts, variables such as the audience's response or the storyteller's mood make each performance unique. Encourage student groups to adapt a story and perform it before the class. Ask a volunteer to videotape the performances and/or the audience's responses to play back later and use in evaluating each group's storytelling skills.

Teach

Discussion Prompts

- Why does Norfolk add dialogue and highlight plot elements in his storytelling performances?
- What details help you visualize the Gorgon Medusa? How do these details appeal to the senses?

Additional Resources

 Writing Process Transparencies, 10, 18–22

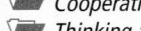 Writing in the Real World, pp. 13–16

Cooperative Learning Activities

Thinking and Study Skills, pp. 21–22

Narrative Writing

Portraying various moods and gestures, Norfolk performs the tale of Perseus.

adjustments. "As I tell my story," notes Norfolk, "I look around the audience and gauge their response. Sometimes I insert a modern reference, as in describing Perseus. I say he's built like Hulk Hogan, and then I growl and flex my muscles. The first time I told this story, I made clicking noises as the three witches in turn plucked the eye out of their forehead. The kids all said 'oooh,' so I knew that part had to stay. They also loved the part where I act out Medusa. I made my ten fingers the snakes wriggling on my head. I hissed like a snake, and then I did hand movements like silhouettes on the wall, rising through the air."

Storytellers, like other kinds of writers, revise their stories numerous times. In their case, however, the audience serves as editor. "If I don't get a satisfactory reaction," states Norfolk, "I know I have to rework my story. I usually get an audience's rapt attention. If people are glancing off, I know they have mentally strayed. But if the story is hot, if the audience is very upbeat, then I know I've done the right thing. That's how I critique myself."

Publishing/Presenting

Performing the Story

The style a storyteller uses to perform a story is comparable to the style an author uses to write. Some authors write using spare prose, just as some storytellers tell their tales with little fanfare. Not Bobby Norfolk. Norfolk's dramatic storytelling style incorporates his skills in acrobatics and sound effects so that

Norfolk pantomimes Medusa's snaky hair.

his audience can "see, hear, taste, touch, and smell the story."

While many storytellers publish or produce tapes of their stories, they may still continue to change them with each telling. Norfolk has written down his version of "Perseus and the Gorgon," but the storyteller says, "I've revised the story since I originally performed it. If you saw it, you would probably notice some parts that are different from my written version."

Norfolk performs at Miller Plaza in Chattanooga to celebrate the county library's summer reading program.

168 Unit 4 Narrative Writing

 ## Cultural Connections

Appreciating Other Cultures' Stories

By revealing the interests, values, and ideals of a people, storytelling can generate appreciation for other cultures. Students may recall the African *griot* in the literature selection for Unit 2 on page 103. *Griots* tell both the history and the stories of their people, and both of these help us know the culture better. Point out that since certain experiences happen everywhere, many folktales are universal, often passing from one culture to another.

Examining Writing in the Real World

Analyzing the Media Connection

Discuss these questions about the excerpt on pages 166–167.

1. How does Norfolk use concrete details to create terrifying images of Medusa's fingernails and teeth?

2. What verbs does Norfolk use to describe the movements of Medusa's hair? Why might he have chosen these particular verbs?

3. What, according to Norfolk, was most hideous about Medusa?

4. What does this excerpt reveal about Perseus as a character?

5. Norfolk calls the Perseus myth "the most visual of all the [Greek] myths." Why?

Analyzing a Writer's Process

Discuss these questions about Bobby Norfolk's writing process.

1. Where does Bobby Norfolk find most of his stories?

2. What changes did Norfolk make to Hamilton's version of the myth in adapting it for storytelling?

3. Why did Norfolk make changes to Hamilton's version?

4. For what reasons does Norfolk revise his story as he tells it?

5. Describe Norfolk's style of story-telling? Why might his approach to storytelling engage an audience?

Narrative Writing

Use participles, correctly punctuated, to add lively details to a story.

A *participle* is a verb form used as an adjective. Introductory participles and participial phrases and those that are not essential to the meaning of a sentence are set off by commas.

> *Her hair was a mass of **living** snakes, **hissing** and **twirling** about constantly.*

Use each present participle below in a sentence. Insert commas where necessary.

1. screeching
2. whining
3. snaking
4. clutching
5. hammering
6. honking
7. snarling
8. glistening
9. sprinting
10. rumbling

See Lesson 12.3, pages 527–531, and Lesson 21.6, pages 743–751.

Assess

Analyzing the Media Connection

1. He says her nails are "long and sharp" and that her "canine teeth" are "used for tearing flesh from bone."
2. He says her hair was "hissing and twirling," to evoke a snake-like image.
3. He says her "blood-red eyes" were her most hideous trait.
4. The excerpt reveals Perseus' courage, strength, and resourcefulness.
5. Medusa's extraordinary appearance makes this a most visual myth.

Analyzing a Writer's Process

1. Norfolk finds his stories in libraries and bookstores.
2. He expanded the dialogue and added details for emphasis.
3. He made the changes to make the story more vivid.
4. He revises his story to engage his audience more fully.
5. His style is energetic and animated, which would appeal especially to young audiences.

Reteaching

Have students listen to recordings and watch videotapes of storytellers in action. Discuss the variety of ways in which the storytellers achieved their effects.

Close

Challenge students to deliver a short speech to the class in the persona of a well-known character. Have the class guess who each character is.

Answers

(Answers will vary. The first seven sentences in the exercise are provided as examples.)

1. The screeching tires stopped inches before his feet.
2. Whining loudly, the child ran home.
3. The snaking road led nowhere.
4. Clutching the mail, she burst into the room.
5. We watched him hammering nails.
6. Honking his horn, the driver tried to chase the dog off the street.
7. The snarling tiger leapt at her prey.

Civic Literacy

Storytelling in Society

Storytellers contribute much to society and can reach a wide audience. Also, as a shared experience, storytelling draws people together. It teaches children how to listen, expands their vocabulary and appreciation of language, and helps them develop empathy for others. The governments of some African nations, newly independent in the last century, have even made use of storytellers to help their people develop a spirit of unity and national identity.

Focus

Lesson Overview

Objective
- To relate the meaning of an experience in a personal narrative

Skills
- finding ideas for a personal narrative; writing a personal narrative

Critical Thinking
- recalling; relating

Listening and Speaking
- brainstorming; discussing

Bellringer
Daily Language Activity

When students enter the classroom, have this assignment on the board: *Jot down a list of important events that have happened to you.*

Grammar Link to the Bellringer

Have students identify the first-person pronouns they have used in their list of important events.

See also *Daily Language Practice*

Motivating Activity

To help students reflect on their own experiences, direct their attention to the teddy bear pictured on this student page. Ask volunteers to tell about a teddy bear (or other toy) that was special to them when they were small. Volunteers might share such details as how they got the toy, where they played with it, and how they used it in creating imaginary worlds.

Narrative Writing

Narrating a Personal Experience

A personal narrative allows you to focus on important events of your life and their significance. Notice how Amber Sumrall uses first person and chronological order in relating an event from early childhood.

Literature Model

After setting the scene, Sumrall narrates the event vividly and dramatically.

> When I was five we went to Yosemite for our first vacation. As my mother and father sat outside our cabin in Tuolomne Meadows reading the newspaper I played near the river with Bear, dipping his furry feet into the icy water. He was my best friend; I took him everywhere, could not fall asleep at night without him. Suddenly the current swept him out of my hands. I ran screaming and crying to my father, "Daddy, hurry, Bear's gone down the river." In a matter of seconds he'd tossed his newspaper aside and followed me to the place where I last saw Bear. Leaping from boulder to boulder he seemed to be flying down the creek, his red flannel shirt billowing like a flag, finally disappearing from view. When he returned an hour later, drenched and disheveled, he had Bear in his hands. Until that moment I had never been conscious of loving my father. I wonder if he realized then just how thoroughly Bear had taken his place. And if he knew what a disaster it would be for both of us if he'd returned empty-handed.

What meaning did the event have for the writer? Why does she remember it so vividly? Explain in your own words.

> Amber Coverdale Sumrall, "Home Stretch"

Resource Manager

Planning Resources
- *Lesson Plans*

Transparencies
- *Bellringer*
- *Daily Language Practice*
- *Fine Art* 19–24
- *Two-Minute Skill Drill*
- *Writing Process* 10, 18–22

Other Print Resources
- *Composition Enrichment*, p. 26
- *Composition Practice*, p. 26
- *Composition Reteaching*, p. 26
- *Cooperative Learning Activities*, pp. 17–20
- *Listening and Speaking Activities*, pp. 13, 18, 20, 21

- *Sentence-Combining Practice*, pp. 30–31
- *Thinking and Study Skills*, pp. 5, 12, 19, 23
- *Writing Across the Curriculum*
- *Writing Assessment and Evaluation Rubrics*

Find Ideas for Your Personal Narrative

A personal narrative, such as the one you just read, comes directly from the writer's experience; it tells a real-life story. It also takes readers beyond the events to the meaning of those events. Two strategies—charting and mapping—can help you find ideas for personal narratives.

Charting involves making a chart of events grouped in categories. It includes such categories as important firsts, like the first day of school or a first date; turning points, like moving or joining a team; worst times, such as a disastrous summer job or an unfriendly sleepover.

Mapping involves making a map of your life. Draw a winding path showing high and low points, turning points, roads not taken. How would your personal map compare with the one below?

Map of Important Events in My Life

Important life event — Little sister born
Got lost in park
First day of kindergarten
Grandmother died
Started swimming lessons
Moved to another state — **Important life event**
Joined a swim team
Broke my arm
Major crush on D. B.
Important life event
First "A" on English paper
Got lead in school play
Quit swim team to pursue drama
Taught swimming to handicapped children
Road not taken

Journal Writing

Explore ideas for a personal narrative by charting and mapping. In your journal try out each strategy for about ten minutes. Compare the results. Write a few sentences about which strategy uncovered more of your memories and why.

Teach

Mapping Your Experience

Have each student create a map of his or her life, showing the high and low points. An experience map can help students see their lives as a whole, with each experience as a part of that whole rather than an isolated event. The events on their personal paths should be arranged in time order, but the ups and downs, the twists and turns that they draw, needn't have any meaning, unless students choose to give them meaning. Students do not need to draw footsteps—a line is enough. Some may wish to illustrate their map, but they don't have to. Stress that the map is not the goal; it's a tool, like the chart, to help them uncover their memories. **L2**

Two-Minute Skill Drill

Have students identify the first-person pronouns in the following sentences:

1. *I saw the light.*
2. *The movie made me sad.*
3. *Jim and I went to the game.*
4. *Please give me a cookie.*

See also *Two-Minute Skill Drill Transparency 4.1*

Journal Writing Tip

Comparing Results Students might tell which activity, mapping or charting, would work better for different types of personal narratives.

Teach

Using Specific Details

Help students see the value of including specific facts and details by pointing out how Van Ngo enlivens her narrative. Her family's flight from Vietnam happened six years before Van wrote her story, but she tells where they landed and what church sponsored them. Specific names of people and places are among the details that bring narrative writing to life. **L2**

Preparing for Publication

Encourage students to prepare one of their personal narratives for publication. Explain that Van Ngo's story first appeared in *Merlyn's Pen,* a national magazine of student writing. If possible, show the class a copy. You can obtain a free sample for your classroom by calling 1-800-247-2027. If your school or local library subscribes to this magazine, some students might wish to read the rest of Van Ngo's story, which appeared in the October/November 1989 issue. **L3**

Additional Resources

 For further stimuli for journal writing, see *Fine Art Transparencies,* 19–24.

 Writing Process Transparencies, 10, 18–22

 Writing Across the Curriculum

 Cooperative Learning Activities

Thinking and Study Skills, pp. 5, 12, 19, 23

Listening and Speaking Activities, pp. 13, 18, 20, 21

Composition Practice, p. 26

Narrative Writing

Grammar Tip

When you revise your personal narrative, check for correct use of first-person pronouns. For help, see Lesson 17.1, pages 637–638.

Write Your Personal Narrative

After you find a personal experience to write about, use a prewriting strategy such as brainstorming to recall as many details as possible. Complete your prewriting by deciding what meaning your experience had for you. Then follow these guidelines to write your narrative.

Guidelines for Writing a Personal Narrative

1. In prewriting, list the events chronologically—the order in which they happened.

2. Maintain a first-person point of view, using the pronoun *I*.

3. Enliven your narrative with specific facts and details.

4. Use language—concrete nouns, vivid verbs, precise adjectives—to help readers share your excitement, sorrow, or anger.

5. Build a conclusion that expresses your thoughts and feelings about your experience and tell what it means to you.

Van Ngo followed this last guideline in her personal narrative. She related an experience that happened six years earlier, when she and her family fled from Vietnam. Their voyage in her uncle's small boat meant many hardships, even a death—but finally a new home. Following is her conclusion, in which the writer gives meaning to her experience.

Student Model

"Mimi, wake up. You're going to be late for school," my mom's voice cut through my dream.

I got slowly out of bed, dazed and disoriented. For a few moments, I didn't even know where I was. Then I remembered, and my dreams and memories came flooding back. I remembered that long journey and the day after my cousin's death when we finally found land. We'd landed on a Malaysian island and stayed for sixteen months before being sponsored by St. Mary's Church in Ohio. The Lord had answered all our prayers!

Six years have passed, but I still occasionally have dreams about my long journey to America. I feel so lucky and grateful that we found land and a new life in America. I learned that life should be appreciated and loved. Above all, I learned never to give up hope.

Van Ngo, Thomas Jefferson High School, Alexandria, Virginia
First appeared in *Merlyn's Pen: The National Magazine of Student Writing*

Here Van provides information she had intentionally omitted earlier in order to focus on the sea voyage.

The experience has more than one meaning for Van. What does she say is the most important lesson she learned?

MEETING INDIVIDUAL NEEDS English Language Learners

Reviewing First-Person Pronouns

Students who have difficulty with English may need extra assistance in using first-person pronouns correctly. Review these pronouns with students, emphasizing the use of *I* for subjects and *me* for objects. Read aloud and repeat illustrative sentences to reinforce the patterns.

Write a Personal Narrative

Charles Dickens began his famous novel *A Tale of Two Cities* with these words: "It was the best of times, it was the worst of times." Write a narrative about your own personal best time or worst time. Use mapping or charting to choose an event.

PURPOSE To write a personal narrative
AUDIENCE English class
LENGTH 3–4 paragraphs

WRITING RUBRICS To write an effective personal narrative, you should

- present events chronologically
- maintain a first-person point of view
- build to a conclusion that explains what the experience meant to you
- use *I* and *me* correctly

Cross-Curricular Activity

SCIENCE Read James Thurber's account of his continuing failure in biology class. Then write a short narrative about an experience you've had in a science class. Read your narrative aloud to a small group.

I never once saw a cell through a microscope. This used to enrage my instructor. He would wander around the laboratory pleased with the progress all the students were making in drawing the involved and, so I am told, interesting structure of flower cells, until he came to me. I would just be standing there. "I can't see anything," I would say. He would begin patiently enough, explaining how anybody can see through a microscope, but he would always end up in a fury, claiming that I could too see through a microscope but just pretended that I couldn't.

James Thurber, *My Life and Hard Times*

Grammar Link

Use *I* and *me* correctly.

Personal writing involves much use of first-person pronouns. In compound constructions be particularly careful to use *I* for subjects and *me* for objects.

> . . . *followed **me** to the place where **I** last saw Bear.*

Complete each sentence below by adding *I* or *me*.

1. Chin and _____ have bicycled together before.
2. Yet this was a major trip for both him and _____.
3. Vanessa's description of a family bike trip had so impressed Chin and _____ that we decided to follow the same route.
4. My parents made my friend and _____ sandwiches for two days' lunches.
5. Since we had arranged to stay with Chin's uncle overnight, Chin and _____ planned to eat dinner and the next day's breakfast with his uncle's family.

See Lesson 17.1, pages 637–638.

Viewing and Representing

COOPERATIVE LEARNING After everyone has read an account of a humorous experience in science class, work together to create a graph or chart that shows the types of humorous events that have taken place in science classes.

Assess

Evaluation Rubrics

Write a Personal Narrative
Use these criteria when evaluating your students' narratives.
- Events are presented chronologically.
- The narrative maintains first-person point of view.
- The narrative builds to a conclusion that explains what the experience means to the student.

See also *Writing Assessment and Evaluation Rubrics.*

Cross-Curricular Activity
The narrative should include vivid details that bring the story to life.

Viewing and Representing
The graph or chart should
- employ a sensible principle of organization.
- allow for some whimsical representations.
- permit inclusion of all students' experiences.

Reteaching
📁 *Composition Reteaching,* p. 26

Enrichment
📁 *Composition Enrichment,* p. 26

Close

Have students work in small groups to find personal narratives in magazines, books, and newspapers. You might have students share their findings with the class.

Grammar Link

Answers
1. I; **2.** me; **3.** me; **4.** me; **5.** I

Using *I* and *Me*
Have students complete the following sentences by using *I* or *me.*
1. _____ said that Yosemite could be more spectacular than Yellowstone.
2. He and _____ argued on that point for hours.
3. Aunt Flora forced Father and _____ to take several ridiculous photos of the park rangers.

Focus

Lesson Overview

Objective
- To create a list of problems and solutions that will lead to interesting stories

Skills
- using story elements; finding and evaluating a story idea; developing a story

Critical Thinking
- identifying; analyzing; defining; clarifying

Listening and Speaking
- discussing; evaluating

Bellringer
Daily Language Activity

When students enter the classroom, have this assignment on the board: *List some of your favorite characters from books and movies.*

Grammar Link to the Bellringer

Some students may have listed compound subjects for their favorite characters, such as Batman and Robin. Have students identify compound subjects.

See also *Daily Language Practice*

Motivating Activity

Ask students to imagine themselves sitting around a campfire as you relate this story starter:

Marty and Annie toiled through the dense undergrowth, searching for a way out. The night noises—and the feeling they were being followed—kept them moving.

Ask each student to add a sentence or two. A typical story starter introduces characters, a problem, and a setting.

Narrative Writing

LESSON 4.2

Developing a Fictional Narrative

Like any other narrative, a fictional narrative tells a story. A short story is a tightly constructed narrative built around a complication. Note the characters, the setting, the events that form the plot, and the point of view from which the story below is told.

> Someone fleeing from someone else has formed the basic action in countless fictional narratives, both short stories and novels.

> Durante, ruthless and single-minded, confronts kind, trusting Tony. Through the ages, writers have told stories about the struggle between good and evil.

Literature Model

They went out from the house. The sun turned the sweat of Durante to hot water and then dried his skin so that his clothes felt transparent. "Tony, I gotta be mean," said Durante. "Stand right there where I can see you. Don't try to get close. Now listen. The sheriff's gunna be along this trail sometime today, looking for me. He'll load up himself and all his gang with water out of your tanks. Then he'll follow my sign across the desert. Get me? He'll follow if he finds water on the place. But he's not gunna find water."

"What you done, poor Dick?" said Tony. "Now look, I could hide you in the old wine cellar where nobody—"

"The sheriff's not gunna find water," said Durante. "It's gunna be like this."

He put the rifle to his shoulder, aimed, fired. The shot struck the base of the nearest tank, ranging down through the bottom. A semicircle of darkness began to stain the soil near the edge of the iron wall.

Tony fell on his knees. "No, no, Dick! Good Dick!" he said. "Look! All the vineyard. It will die. It will turn into old, dead wood, Dick. . . ."

"Shut your face," said Durante. "Now I've started, I kinda like the job."

Max Brand, "Wine on the Desert"

174 Unit 4 Narrative Writing

Resource Manager

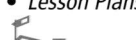

Planning Resources
- *Lesson Plans*

Transparencies
- *Bellringer*
- *Daily Language Practice*
- *Fine Art* 19–24
- *Two-Minute Skill Drill*
- *Writing Process* 10, 18–22

Other Print Resources
- *Composition Enrichment*, p. 27
- *Composition Practice*, p. 27
- *Composition Reteaching*, p. 27
- *Cooperative Learning Activities*, pp. 17–20
- *Listening and Speaking Activities*, pp. 13, 18, 20, 21

- *Sentence-Combining Practice*, pp. 30–31
- *Thinking and Study Skills*, pp. 13, 19, 25, 27–28
- *Writing Across the Curriculum*
- *Writing Assessment and Evaluation Rubrics*

The Elements of a Short Story

This lesson will focus on the short story, one kind of fictional narrative. It is created in the writer's imagination and tells about some made-up event or occurrence. In a short story, an event or series of events forms the **plot.** The events happen to **characters,** usually people. They happen in a time and place—**the setting**—and are told from a certain angle, or **point of view.** In the chart below, examine the elements that make up the short story "Wine on the Desert."

Elements of a Narrative

Element	Explanation	Example
Plot	The plot is the story's action and events. Most plots focus on a problem faced by the main character.	Durante is being pursued by the sheriff. He destroys Tony's water tanks to solve this problem.
Character	The characters of a story are the people or animals involved in the plot.	Tony and Durante are the characters. The sheriff is pursuing Durante, but doesn't appear in the story.
Setting	The setting is the time and place in which the events of a story happen. Setting can create mood or atmosphere.	The desert setting of "Wine on the Desert" creates an atmosphere of starkness and danger.
Point of View	Point of view is the particular vantage point from which the story is told.	"Wine on the Desert" is told from Durante's point of view.

Prewriting Tip

A story's point of view is usually chosen during prewriting. For more about point of view, see Lesson 2.11, on pages 90–93.

Narrative Writing

Journal Writing

Think of a short story you've read recently. In your journal summarize the plot, characters, setting, and point of view. Explain how any one of these elements contributes to the short story.

Teach

Identifying Story Elements

To help students understand the chart, ask them to identify the four elements in stories they have read on their own or as a class. Volunteers should pattern their description of each element after the examples on the chart. Encourage them to comment on the part each element plays in advancing the narrative. **L2**

Using the Model

Ask students what elements in the model characterize it as a story. (It is fictional; it has characters, action, conflict, suspense, and a setting.) Invite speculation about what will happen to Durante. Then encourage volunteers to find the story in the library, read it, and report the actual ending to the class. **L3**

Two-Minute Skill Drill

Have students list the elements of a narrative or short story.

See also *Two-Minute Skill Drill Transparency 4.2*

Journal Writing Tip

Inferring Tell students that if they can recall one element above others, they can infer that it was prominent in the story. It might even have been the writer's starting point—the element that gave the writer an idea. Encourage students to speculate about what element the author may have thought of first.

Teach

Noting Cultural Diversity

Point out that many narratives—personal narratives, novels, and short stories—deal with situations that arise when different cultures meet and sometimes clash. For example, the main character may struggle to fit in with the culture that predominates in a country. N. Scott Momaday writes about his experience as a Native American, Maya Angelou as an African American, and Richard Rodriguez as a Mexican American. Have students find other examples of such narratives. **L2**

Promoting Discussion

Ask students to identify complications and resolutions in stories they've read or those they've seen in movies or on television. To help students determine whether these elements actually form the basis of each story's plot, suggest this test: If someone asked, "What is the story about?" would the answer include this complication and resolution? If so, it is probably the central conflict. **L2**

Narrative Writing

Add Other Story Elements

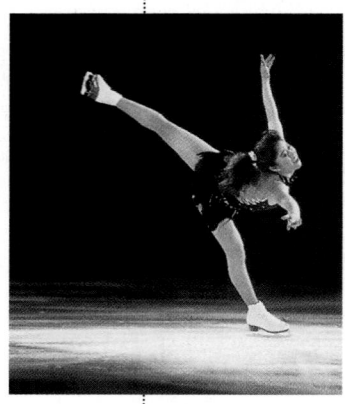

Plot, character, setting, and point of view provide the basic language for talking about a story. But there are other, equally important, story elements. Jon Franklin, Pulitzer-Prize-winning feature story writer, says that a story "consists of a sequence of actions that occur when a sympathetic character encounters a complicating situation that he [or she] confronts and solves." In other words, a story centers around a problem, or **complication,** and its solution, or **resolution.**

THE COMPLICATION The most attention-grabbing element of a story is the complication. The complication may be external: Leo struggles to keep his boat afloat in a storm. Or it may be internal: Lisa is torn between loyalty and honesty when her friend shoplifts. Above all, the problem must be basic to human experience, and the central character must care deeply about it.

THE RESOLUTION A story's plot moves forward in a series of actions resulting from the complication and moving toward the resolution, which is the solution to the character's problem. The resolution must grow out of the story; a character's problem can't be solved by having the roof cave in on the villain. Often, the resolution teaches the character—and the reader—a lesson about coping with the world.

News photos that present actual events can spark ideas for fictional narratives. A photo of a farm blighted by drought illustrates a problem. A photo of a daring rescue from a burning building illustrates both a problem and a solution. To a writer, the photo of a skating competition on this page could suggest a story complication; the photo of the winner could suggest a resolution.

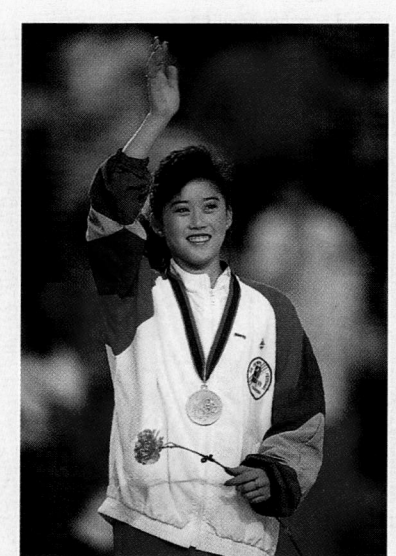

Kristi Yamaguchi

176 Unit 4 Narrative Writing

MEETING INDIVIDUAL NEEDS Less Proficient Readers

Understanding Solutions

Students who have difficulty understanding abstract English words such as *complication* and *resolution* might be helped by thinking of these as *problem* and *solution.* Point out that in some stories the complication is not a bad problem or crisis but a situation that calls for effort, such as competing in an athletic contest. In such a case, the resolution is what happens to the character in the contest.

Find a Story Idea

For many short-story writers, thinking of a good idea is the hardest part about writing. However, good ideas are everywhere, in other people's lives and in your own life. Behind almost every action in real life lies an attempt to solve a problem or conflict. The chart below shows some strategies for using real-life problems and solutions to find and evaluate story ideas.

Using Complications To . . .	
Find Story Ideas	**Evaluate Story Ideas**
• Look for external problems: Kelly's father was ill.	• Does the complication concern basic human experiences such as love, hate, loyalty, faith, sorrow, pain, survival, death?
• Look for internal problems: Ana had to make a moral decision.	
• Look for action: What action did Otis take to solve a problem?	• Does the complication matter deeply to the character?
• Look for motivations: Why did Anita quit her job?	• Does the complication create an opportunity for the character to learn something?

Using Resolutions To . . .	
Find Story Ideas	**Evaluate Story Ideas**
• Look for newspaper stories about achievement.	• Does the resolution grow directly out of the complication?
• Look for changes in a person, condition, or situation.	• Is the resolution the result of a character's own efforts?
• Work backward from a resolution to a complication—if someone received an award, ask how.	• Does the resolution teach readers a lesson about how to deal with life?
	• Does the character change or grow by resolving the complication?

> ## Journal Writing
>
> List four or five problems that would make interesting stories. Then list possible solutions for each problem. Ideas might come from your own experience, from photos, or from other sources.

TIME

For more about the writing process, see **TIME Facing the Blank Page,** pp. 109–119.

Teach

Browsing and Brainstorming

Ask students to bring in local newspapers to use for story ideas. After allowing a few minutes for browsing, begin a brainstorming session about the photos and articles students find that suggest complications and resolutions. Encourage students to evaluate their ideas against the questions on the chart. **L2**

Two-Minute Skill Drill

Have students define *complication* and *resolution*.

📖 **See also** *Two-Minute Skill Drill Transparency 4.2*

> ## Journal Writing Tip
>
> **Solving Problems** Franklin warns beginning writers that although most of life's problems don't have solutions, a complication without a resolution makes a poor story. Encourage students to think of solutions for their main character's problem.

Critical Thinking

Establishing Evaluation Criteria

Point out that students should evaluate story ideas objectively rather than subjectively. Students' evaluations need to go beyond "I like it" or "It's interesting." (Someone might suggest this complication: a student wonders whether to eat lunch with a friend who is not part of the "in" crowd. Students might say, "The complication involves loyalty, a basic human quality, and the character will learn about the relationship of loyalty to friendship.")

Teach

Using the Model

Ask students to identify hints that Jeanine Skendzel has given about the nature of her story's complication. (In the last three sentences of the first paragraph, Ben is painfully reminded of his brother Drew's absence.) Point out that these sentences also serve as a transition between the present, when Ben is on his way to his family's lake cottage, and the past, when something happened to his brother at the lake. Note how in the flashback Jeanine tells not only events but how characters felt about the events. ("I grin back, pleased that I have finally outwitted him at something.") Have students find examples of how she also tells how characters related to each other. ("He holds an unfair advantage, but I never complain." "We glare at each other, flashing our ugliest poses. Finally, we break down laughing. . .") **L2**

Additional Resources

 For further stimuli for narrative writing, see *Fine Art Transparencies*, 19–24.

 Writing Process Transparencies, 10, 18–22

 Writing Across the Curriculum

Cooperative Learning Activities

Thinking and Study Skills, pp. 13, 19, 25, 27–28

Listening and Speaking Activities, pp. 13, 18, 20, 21

Composition Practice, p. 27

Sentence Combining Practice, pp. 30–31

Drafting Tip

In drafting your story, you usually relate the events in chronological order—but not always. "Summer's End," for example, tells the central event through a flashback that "looks back" at an earlier event.

How does Skendzel prepare you in this paragraph for the problem that is the basis of her story's plot?

What details demonstrate that Skendzel is interested not only in the actions and events but also in how actions and events affect her characters?

Develop Your Story

A short story can start with a problem or solution. You decide who the characters are, what problems they confront, how they solve them, and what they learn. Refer to the chart and the excerpt from Jeanine Skendzel's "Summer's End" for development ideas.

How to Write a Story

• Create a character.	• Show the character reacting to the situation.
• Confront the character with a problem.	• Allow the character to resolve the problem.

Student Model

We're heading to our cottage on Scenic Lake. A dull ache pounds in my head, and my stomach churns in rhythm with the motor. I stretch out comfortably halfway across the seat until I accidentally hit my sleeping sister, Tracy. Just a few months ago we could hardly fit in this back seat: that's when my brother, Drew, was here. He would take up half the seat alone. The pain stabs me and the memories quickly flood back.

We're diving for Drew's waterproof wristwatch as we do every year. Drew or I throw the watch as far as possible and the other person dives to find it. Since Drew is seventeen and I'm only fourteen, he holds an unfair advantage, but I never complain. This time it's my turn to throw it. He has already beaten me three times today by thirty seconds each, so this particular time I secretly throw the watch behind me. Drew bobs up and down the dock, searching for a glint of silver in the hot summer sun.

"Come on, Ben! What'd ya do with it?" he frustratedly whines. I foolishly grin back, pleased that I have finally outwitted him at something. Grabbing my arm, he strongly twists it into a horrible snake bite.

"Tell me, Ben, or you know what's coming," he whispers, checking for our parents. We glare at each other, flashing our ugliest poses. Finally, we break down laughing and I point happily toward the watch.

"You little . . . " is all I hear before he sprints off the dock and pulls into a flawless dive.

Jeanine Skendzel, Traverse City Senior High School, Traverse City, Michigan. First appeared in *Merlyn's Pen: The National Magazine of Student Writing*

Cooperative Learning

Developing Plot

To create a story idea-bank using Franklin's formula, ask students to break into small groups. Each student invents a character and describes the person briefly on the top of a sheet of paper. After five minutes, students pass their papers to the right, and the student who gets the paper confronts the character on it with a problem. The next student tells how the character reacts, and the fourth student resolves the problem.

4.2 Writing Activities

Write the Solution for a Story Problem

In his short story "The Lady, or the Tiger?" Frank Stockton presents the following unresolved complication:

A young man dared to love a princess. He was brought to an arena, where he must open one of two identical doors. Behind one, a fierce, hungry tiger was waiting; behind the other, a beautiful lady—not the princess—was waiting to marry him.

Write an ending to the story.

PURPOSE To create a story resolution
AUDIENCE Your English class
LENGTH 1 paragraph

WRITING RUBRICS To write a dramatic solution for a story problem, you should

- clearly identify and describe the characters and their actions
- resolve the conflict
- use correct spelling and grammar

José Gamarra, *Five Centuries Later*, 1986

Cross-Curricular Activity

FINE ART Freewrite about the scene in the painting. Consider the plants, people, water, and lighting. Jot down story ideas that the painting suggests. Choose one idea, and plan a short story about it.

Listening and Speaking

COOPERATIVE LEARNING Work together with a partner to create a dramatic telling of the story you invented about the painting. Make sure that your story contains a problem and a possible solution that would be appropriate for your audience.

Make verbs agree with compound subjects.

When you have a compound subject joined by *or* or *nor* or *either . . . or* or *neither . . . nor,* the verb always agrees with the subject nearer the verb.

*Drew or I **throw** the watch . . . .*

Choose the correct form of the verb for each sentence below.

1. Fur or feathers (covers/cover) many living creatures.
2. Neither people nor a bird (is/are) cold-blooded.
3. Either feathers or hair (keeps/keep) the body warm.
4. However, neither a fur coat nor feathers nor warm blood alone (identifies/identify) a mammal.

See Lesson 16.5, page 620.

4.2 Developing a Fictional Narrative **179**

Grammar Link

Answers
1. cover
2. is
3. keeps
4. identifies

Viewing the Art

José Gamarra, *Five Centuries Later,* 1986
This landscape depicts an unspoiled paradise. Its serenity is marred by people whose clothing is of the period of European conquest. The title implies that Latin America is still being spoiled by outsiders.

Narrative Writing

Assess

Evaluation Rubrics

Write the Solution for a Story Problem

Use these criteria when evaluating your students' endings.
- Look for an idea that resolves the complication by telling the young man's choice.
- Look for an idea that explains why he made the choice.
- Look for an idea that explains the results.

See also *Writing Assessment and Evaluation Rubrics.*

Cross-Curricular Activity

You might have students share the ideas they have generated.

Listening and Speaking

The dramatic renderings of the stories should
- include the use of appropriate verbal effects.
- express a problem and solution clearly enough for an audience to follow.

Reteaching

Composition Reteaching, p. 27

Enrichment

Composition Enrichment, p. 27

 Use *Fine Art Transparencies* 19–24 for enrichment activities also.

Close

Ask students to find a news story that provides a resolution but no complication. Then invite students to turn their news story into a fictional narrative by supplying the missing complication, developing a story idea, and evaluating their idea by using the chart on student page 177.

Focus

Lesson Overview

Objective
- To create a story opening that incorporates a given main character, setting, and complication

Skills
- creating a story outline; drafting a story opening

Critical Thinking
- categorizing; analyzing; ordering

Listening and Speaking
- discussing

Bellringer
Daily Language Activity

When students enter the classroom, have this assignment on the board: *Write a brief outline of a story you recently told a friend.*

Grammar Link to the Bellringer

If students have listed three or more events in a series, make sure they have used commas to separate the items.

See also *Daily Language Practice*

Motivating Activity

Lead a discussion about how story writers work. Is it likely that they sit down at the typewriter or computer and await inspiration? (That would be unlikely if they use the prewriting techniques students have been learning.) Do writers spend years collecting details? (Some do; historical novels, for example, require extensive research.) Do writers scrupulously plan each event, or does the story take them by surprise? (Writers work in a wide variety of ways.)

180

Narrative Writing

Organizing a Fictional Narrative

After you've identified your story idea, a main character, and a problem, you're ready to plan your story. Creating a story outline or diagram can help you organize the events for your plot.

Plan Your Story

Look at the outline for a story called "Same Difference," written by student Yannie ten Broeke. Note how it orders the events of the plot.

Outline for a Story	
1. Introduce a main character.	Mrs. Kreager, a poor, elderly woman
2. Introduce a problem (complication, conflict).	Mrs. Kreager, who lives alone in a city apartment, walks to the park on her birthday to feed the pigeons.
3. List the actions and events (in chronological order, the order in which they happen).	1. Mrs. Kreager gathers bread crumbs in a small bag. 2. She goes to the park to feed the pigeons. 3. She tries to feed Henry, her pet pigeon.
4. Tell the climax (the point of highest tension in the story).	When Sam, a younger pigeon, keeps Henry from eating, Mrs. Kreager accidentally hits Henry. Henry will never recover.
5. Suggest the resolution (how the problem is solved or not solved).	Mrs. Kreager leaves the park, never to return.

Resource Manager

Planning Resources
- *Lesson Plans*

Transparencies
- *Bellringer*
- *Daily Language Practice*
- *Fine Art* 19–24
- *Two-Minute Skill Drill*
- *Writing Process* 10, 18–22

Other Print Resources
- *Composition Enrichment*, p. 28
- *Composition Practice*, p. 28
- *Composition Reteaching*, p. 28
- *Cooperative Learning Activities*, pp. 17–20
- *Listening and Speaking Activities*, pp. 13, 18, 20, 21

- *Sentence-Combining Practice*, pp. 30–31
- *Thinking and Study Skills*, pp. 9, 12–13
- *Writing Across the Curriculum*
- *Writing Assessment and Evaluation Rubrics*

With the elements shown in the outline, Yannie ten Broeke has forged a moving story that focuses on cheerful, plucky Mrs. Kreager, whose one pleasure is feeding pigeons in the park. Read from her story's ending.

Student Model

Henry fell over on his side, stunned, and made no attempt to get to his feet. Mrs. Kreager's eyes opened wide with horror, and her hands covered her mouth. She lurched with such quickness that all the pigeons scattered, leaving an immobile Henry. She put him in her hands, and although he was not dead, it seemed he had given up life. . . .

She stood up, still clutching the warm little body, and began to walk home, leaving the bag on the bench to be thrown away by the Park Service and the stick to be found by some child in search of an imaginary Excalibur. She knew she would not be back.

Yannie ten Broeke, Rutgers Preparatory School, Somerset, New Jersey. First appeared in *Merlyn's Pen: The National Magazine of Student Writing*

> Do you think the resolution solves the problem? Why or why not?

A plot diagram like the one below can be a handy tool to help you visualize the structure of the story you will write. Notice how the diagram reflects the basic structure of a story.

OPENING → ACTION 1 → ACTION 2 → ACTION 3 → CLIMAX → RESOLUTION

Journal Writing

Use the diagram above to examine a short story you've read. List the main character, the complication, the main events, the climax, and the resolution.

Teach

Aiding Memory

For students with a verbal learning disability, visual symbols like the sign shapes in the plot diagram can serve as memory aids. Go over these symbols with students. The story opening, indicated by a circle, gets the action going by introducing the main character, setting, and conflict. Rectangular signs are informational. In this plot diagram, rectangles enclose the actions or events that build to a climax. The diamond shape of a warning sign indicates the climax, or turning point; readers learn which side wins or how the conflict is resolved. Some stories stop there; others, like Yannie's, include an outcome that tells more about what happens to the characters. For the outcome, the eight-sided shape of a stop sign is appropriate. Ask students to come up with other symbols that might work in diagraming a plot. **L1**

Two-Minute Skill Drill

Have students define the following story terms:

opening	climax
actions	resolution
outcome	

See also *Two-Minute Skill Drill Transparency 4.3*

Journal Writing Tip

Examining the Elements Students might examine the story on page 174, "Wine on the Desert," by Max Brand, or another story of their own choice.

Teach

Using the Model

Ask students to identify the main character (Kevin, a 13-year-old computer buff), the complication (Kevin's computer asking him an unprogrammed question), and the setting (Kevin's bedroom). Initiate a discussion about how the story opening pulls the reader in and invite students to give examples. (The complication—a thinking, feeling computer—is interesting in itself, but the writer makes it more so by surprising the reader. Kevin's automatic actions and commonplace morning rituals lull readers into thinking it's an average day—and then the unexpected happens.) **L2**

Additional Resources

 For further stimuli for narrative writing, see *Fine Art Transparencies*, 19–24.

 Writing Process Transparencies, 10, 18–22

 Writing Across the Curriculum

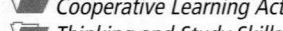 *Cooperative Learning Activities*

Thinking and Study Skills, pp. 9, 12–13

Listening and Speaking Activities, pp. 13, 18, 20, 21

Composition Practice, p. 28

Sentence Combining Practice, pp. 30–31

Narrative Writing

Draft Your Opening

Once you have a story outline, your next step is to draft your opening. Does the story opening below snag your interest? If so, how?

> **What main character does the writer introduce in his opening?**

> **Notice how the opening also establishes a setting—both time and place. What details show that the day begins as an average one for Kevin?**

> **What problem or complication does the writer introduce?**

Grammar Tip

"User Friendly" is told from a first-person point of view, with Kevin the *I* of the story. When drafting, be careful to maintain your point of view and not to shift pronouns. See Lesson 17.5, pages 644–648.

Literature Model

I reached over and shut off the insistent buzzing of my bedside alarm clock. I sat up, swung my feet over the edge of the bed, and felt for my slippers on the floor. Yawning, I walked toward the bathroom. As I walked by the corner of my room, where my computer table was set up, I pressed the on button, slid a diskette into the floppy drive, then went to brush my teeth. By the time I got back, the computer's screen was glowing greenly, displaying the message: *Good Morning, Kevin.*

I sat down before the computer table, addressed the keyboard and typed: *Good Morning, Louis.* The computer immediately began to whirr and promptly displayed a list of items on its green screen.

Today is Monday, April 22, the 113th day of the year. There are 254 days remaining. Your 14th birthday is five days from this date.

Math test today, 4th Period.

Your history project is due today. Do you wish printout: Y/N?

I punched the letter *Y* on the keyboard and flipped on the switch to the computer's printer. At once the printer sprang to life and began *eeek*ing out page one. I went downstairs to breakfast. . . .

When I returned to my room to shower and dress for the day, my history project was already printed out. I had almost walked by Louis, when I noticed there was a message on the screen. It wasn't the usual:

Printout completed. Do you wish to continue: Y/N?

Underneath the printout question were two lines:

When are you going to get me my voice module, Kevin?

I blinked. It couldn't be. There was nothing in Louis's basic programming that would allow for a question like this.

T. Ernesto Bethancourt, "User Friendly"

MEETING INDIVIDUAL NEEDS — Less Proficient Readers

Reading Openings

Students who have limited experience with fiction might have trouble creating strong story openings. Ask volunteers to describe a short story with an interest-grabbing opening or, if possible, read the opening with a partner. Discuss each opening using the following questions: What story elements does it introduce? How does it pull readers into the story? Is the opening primarily narration, dialogue, description, or action?

Write a Story Opening

Plan an original short story for your school's literary magazine based on the painting shown here. Write a plot diagram and the opening for the story you will submit.

PURPOSE To write a story opening that introduces character, setting, and complication
AUDIENCE Readers of the school literary magazine
LENGTH 3–4 paragraphs

Richard Bosman, *Flight*, 1981–82

WRITING RUBRICS To write an effective plot diagram and story opening, you should

- chart the conflict, action, climax, and resolution of the plot
- draft your opening, making sure to establish character, setting, point of view, and conflict
- use correct spelling and grammar

Using Computers

Use your computer's drawing software to create the plot diagram for your story. Make sure to include the conflict, action, climax, and resolution.

Listening and Speaking

COOPERATIVE LEARNING In a small group, find a short story in your literature book or another source. After reading the story, discuss the resolution and possible alternative resolutions. Which resolution seems most satisfying? Why?

Grammar Link

Use commas to separate three or more items in a series.

Note how Bethancourt uses commas to separate parts of a series in this sentence from "User Friendly."

I sat up, swung my feet over the edge of the bed, and felt for my slippers on the floor.

Rewrite the following sentences, inserting commas as necessary.

1. My little brother scowled stamped his right foot stuck out his lower lip and announced that he was mad.
2. His face was pale wrinkled and angry.
3. He cast furious glances at me at our mother and toward the cat.
4. I bristled my mother looked puzzled and the cat stalked away.
5. "I want milk bread jelly and peanut butter right now," announced the little tyrant.

See Lesson 21.6, pages 743–751.

Narrative Writing

Assess

Evaluation Rubrics

Write a Story Opening

Use these criteria when evaluating your students' writing:

- The opening should introduce the main character, setting, and complication.
- The opening should elaborate on the above elements, filling in the details.
- The opening should pull readers in, making them wonder what happens next.

See also *Writing Assessment and Evaluation Rubrics.*

Listening and Speaking

Ask each group to read the story to the whole class.

Reteaching

📁 *Composition Reteaching,* p. 28

Enrichment

📁 *Composition Enrichment,* p. 28

✏ Use *Fine Art Transparencies* 19–24 for enrichment activities also.

Close

Have students find opening paragraphs in stories that they think are especially effective. Invite volunteers to read paragraphs they have chosen to the class.

Grammar Link

Answers

Commas should be placed after the following words in each sentence:
1. scowled, foot, lip,
2. pale, wrinkled,
3. me, mother,
4. bristled, puzzled,
5. milk, bread, jelly,

Viewing the Art

Richard Bosman, *Flight,* 1981–1982
Richard Bosman's paintings are narrative in content, often suggesting impending disaster and depicting characters engaged in struggle and violence. *Flight,* a 72-by-42-inch oil painting, is in the Des Moines Art Center in Iowa.

Focus

Lesson Overview

Objective
- To identify ways in which dialogue enhances a story and to use personal conversation as the basis for a piece of fictional dialogue

Skills
- using dialogue to advance a story; writing dialogue

Critical Thinking
- recalling; contrasting

Listening and Speaking
- listening to speech

Bellringer
Daily Language Activity
When students enter the classroom, have this assignment on the board: *Write down—word-for-word, if you can—two to three lines from a recent conversation you had.*

Grammar Link to the Bellringer
Have students look at the conversation they wrote and add quotation marks and other punctuation.

See also *Daily Language Practice*

Motivating Activity
Show students a brief videotaped excerpt of dialogue from a movie or television program. Ask students to imagine what the dialogue would look like if it were written as a story. Help them realize that some of what they saw and heard on the videotape might be missing, including pauses, tone of voice, gestures, and facial expressions. Brainstorm words and phrases they could use to capture these elements.

Narrative Writing

LESSON 4.4 Writing Dialogue

It's about time they let us speak for ourselves! If I hear myself described one more time as a puffed-up, blustering fool, I'll . . .

At least they gave you a personality. I'm portrayed so vaguely that if I ever get to open my mouth, I won't know what to say, much less how to say it.

A dialogue is a conversation between two or more persons. Note how Mary Lavin uses dialogue in the model below to bring characters and events to life.

Literature Model

How does the dialogue create a vivid sense of time and place?

A neighbor passed.
"Waiting for Packy?" said the neighbor, pleasantly, and he stood for a minute to take off his hat and wipe the sweat of the day from his face. He was an old man.
"It's a hot day!" he said. "It will be a hard push for Packy on that battered old bike of his. I wouldn't like to have to face into four miles on a day like this!"

The dialogue shows the widow's deep pride in Packy.

"Packy would travel three times that distance if there was a book at the other end of the road!" said the widow, with the pride of those who cannot read more than a line or two without wearying.
The minutes went by slowly. The widow kept looking up at the sun.

The dialogue contains a subtle foreshadowing, or hint of possible trouble to come. What is it?

"I suppose the heat is better than the rain!" she said, at last. "The heat can do a lot of harm too, though," said the neighbor, absent-mindedly, as he pulled a long blade of grass from between the stones of the wall and began to chew the end of it. "You could get sunstroke on a day like this!" He looked up at the sun. "The sun is a terror," he said. "It could

Where does the dialogue contain another hint of possible danger?

cause you to drop down dead like a stone!"
The widow strained out further over the gate. She looked up the hill in the direction of the town.

184 Unit 4 Narrative Writing

Resource Manager

Planning Resources
- *Lesson Plans*

Transparencies
- *Bellringer*
- *Daily Language Practice*
- *Fine Art* 19–24
- *Two-Minute Skill Drill*
- *Writing Process* 10, 18–22

Other Print Resources
- *Composition Enrichment,* p. 29
- *Composition Practice,* p. 29
- *Composition Reteaching,* p. 29
- *Cooperative Learning Activities,* pp. 17–20
- *Listening and Speaking Activities,* pp. 13, 18, 20, 21

- *Sentence-Combining Practice,* pp. 30–31
- *Thinking and Study Skills,* pp. 13, 19
- *Writing Across the Curriculum*
- *Writing Assessment and Evaluation Rubrics*

"He will have a good cool breeze on his face coming down the hill, at any rate," she said.

The man looked up the hill. "That's true. On the hottest day of the year you would get a cool breeze coming down that hill on a bicycle. You would feel the air streaming past your cheeks like silk. And in the winter it's like two knives flashing to either side of you, and peeling off your skin like you'd peel the bark off a sally-rod [willow twig]." He chewed the grass meditatively. "That must be one of the steepest hills in Ireland," he said. "That hill is a hill worthy of the name of a hill." He took the grass out of his mouth. "It's my belief," he said, earnestly looking at the widow—"it's my belief that that hill is to be found marked with a name in the Ordnance Survey map!"

"If that's the case," said the widow, "Packy will be able to tell you all about it. When it isn't a book he has in his hand it's a map."

"Is that so?" said the man. "That's interesting. A map is a great thing. A map is not an ordinary thing. It isn't everyone can make out a map."

The widow wasn't listening.

"I think I see Packy!" she said, and she opened the gate and stepped out into the roadway.

Mary Lavin, "The Story of the Widow's Son"

The dialogue adds liveliness and realism. Even this unnamed old man has a personality— warm, friendly, interested in people and places.

How does this part of the dialogue advance the plot?

Use Dialogue to Advance Your Story

Good dialogue can serve many purposes in a narrative. Mary Lavin uses it to create a sense of time and place, tell about character, foreshadow possible trouble, and move the plot along. When you write a story, you can use dialogue for all these purposes—and more.

Revising Tip

In revising, read your dialogue aloud to test whether it sounds like real conversation. Keep revising and rereading until your characters' words sound right.

Journal Writing

Find and examine some dialogue in a novel or short story. Explore the purposes of the dialogue by writing what it reveals about the setting, the characters, or the plot.

Teach

Writing What You Hear

Ask students to tape-record a short conversation. Then play the tape, pausing after each sentence so that students can write the words down. Afterward, allow time for students to rewrite the dialogue as it might appear in a narrative, adding the tag lines, paragraphing, punctuation, and capitalization. (Point out that while standard usage requires new paragraphs for each new speaker, Lavin doesn't always observe this rule.) Replay the tape so students can add information about pauses and tone of voice. **L2**

Two-Minute Skill Drill

Have students rewrite the following sentences as lively, descriptive dialogue, adding punctuation marks and capital letters as necessary.

1. *Latisha said the house was on fire.*
2. *Jason said he received an A on his story.*

See also *Two-Minute Skill Drill Transparency 4.4*

Journal Writing Tip

Analyzing Have students start by looking at a single page in a story or novel. Ask them to list anything they find out about the setting, the characters, or the plot on that page. Then have them go back and highlight any of this information that was revealed through dialogue.

Teach

Listening for Characters

Read students a dialogue in which the characters have widely divergent ways of speaking. Choose an example from a short story or novel, focusing on vocabulary, tone of voice, dialect, and other features used to reveal and distinguish between characters. Ask about specific information that a character's speech can reveal (such as age, cultural and educational background, location, personality). **L2**

Writing Dialect

Have students collect and study examples of dialogue in which the writer attempts to capture a regional dialect. (Examples can be found in Mark Twain's *The Adventures of Huckleberry Finn*, John Steinbeck's *The Grapes of Wrath*, and Harper Lee's *To Kill a Mockingbird*.) Challenge students to write a brief dialogue in a dialect they've read or heard in real life. Caution students that dialect is difficult to write well. **L3**

Additional Resources

 For further stimuli for narrative writing see *Fine Art Transparencies*, 19–24.

 Writing Process Transparencies, 10, 18–22

 Writing Across the Curriculum
 Cooperative Learning Activities
Thinking and Study Skills, pp. 13, 19
Listening and Speaking Activities, pp. 13, 18, 20, 21
Sentence Combining Practice, pp. 30–31
Composition Practice, p. 29

Narrative Writing

Grammar Tip

If you need to review the mechanics of writing dialogue, see Lesson 21.9, pages 755–757.

Write Dialogue

Essentially, a dialogue is a series of direct quotations. A direct quotation is a character's own words enclosed in quotation marks. An indirect quotation is a report of what someone said. Compare the following quotations.

Direct quotation: "I think I see Packy!" she said.
Indirect quotation: The widow said that she thought she saw Packy.

In a dialogue, the words that identify the speaker, such as "said the widow," are called tag lines. Without tag lines, readers might have trouble figuring out who is saying what. Too few tag lines can make a dialogue confusing; too many tag lines can make it choppy.

Mary Lavin uses the verb *said* eleven times in the passage you read. You might think that the story would be more interesting if she had substituted synonyms such as *replied* and *remarked*. However, Lavin chose her verbs carefully. Later, to emphasize the difference in the widow's tone of voice, she used vivid verbs in her tag lines:

"He's only in a weakness!" *screamed* the widow. . . . "Get a doctor!" she *cried*.

In addition to tag lines, your dialogue can include descriptions of characters' facial expressions, tone of voice, gestures, and mannerisms. Here is an example:

"The heat can do a lot of harm too, though," said the neighbor, absent-mindedly, as he pulled a long blade of grass from between the stones of the wall and began to chew the end of it.

The following guidelines will help you write effective dialogue in your fictional narratives.

Guidelines for Writing Dialogue

1. Make sure your dialogue has a purpose: to reveal character, to highlight the relationships between characters, to intensify the action, to add suspense, or a combination.

2. Write dialogue in words and phrases appropriate to each character. Consider the character's age, personality, and educational background. Consider the character's emotional state.

3. Use dialogue to reveal character and personality. What are this character's beliefs? Desires? Fears? Is the character shy? Honest? Nervous? Ignorant? Boastful?

4. Make your dialogue sound like real conversation by using interruptions and pauses.

5. Make your dialogue easy to follow by using clear tag lines and correct paragraphing and punctuation.

MEETING INDIVIDUAL NEEDS English Language Learners

Writing in Pairs

Students for whom English is a second language may have difficulty creating English dialogue that sounds natural. Pair them up with an English-proficient peer editor. Have the peer editor write the conversation down as his or her partner dictates it. Have them work together to revise the dialogue to make it sound natural.

Narrative Writing

Write a Dialogue

Recall an interesting conversation you heard or took part in. Then write a fictional dialogue based on what you remember.

PURPOSE To create a dialogue
AUDIENCE Your teacher and classmates
LENGTH 1-2 pages

WRITING RUBRICS To write realistic dialogue, you should

- reveal something about your speakers
- use appropriate words and phrases for each speaker
- use clear tag lines and correct paragraphing, punctuation, and capitalization

Listening and Speaking

With a partner, write a short dramatic scene based on this painting. Rehearse your dialogue and then present it to your class.

Gilberto Ruiz, *The Good News Call*, 1986

Viewing and Representing

COOPERATIVE LEARNING In a group of four, make a video of one of the dialogues you wrote for the activities on this page. One person should direct the production, one person should operate the camera, and the other two should act out the dialogue. Share your completed video with the class.

Grammar Link

Capitalize and punctuate direct and indirect quotations correctly.

Reread Mary Lavin's dialogue and page 186. Then rewrite the following sentences correctly. Write *correct* for any sentence that needs no changes.

1. Abraham Lincoln gave a speech in which he said the ballot is stronger than the bullet.

2. In a later speech, Lincoln said that nobody had ever expected him to be President.

3. I feel somewhat like the boy in Kentucky who stubbed his toe while running to see his sweetheart Lincoln replied in answer to a question in 1862. The boy said he was too big to cry, and far too badly hurt to laugh.

4. These words of Lincoln are in John Bartlett's *Familiar Quotations* my teacher said. do you know what that book is?

5. I've heard of it I admitted but I don't know whether I've ever seen it.

See Lesson 20.1, pages 713–714 and 21.9, pages 755–757.

4.4 Writing Dialogue **187**

Assess

Evaluation Rubrics

Write a Dialogue

Use these criteria when evaluating your students' writing.

- The dialogue should use appropriate language for each character.
- The dialogue should help reveal each character's personality and beliefs.
- The writing should be lively and realistic.
- The writer should use tag lines, paragraphs, and correct punctuation and capitalization.

See also *Writing Assessment and Evaluation Rubrics.*

Listening and Speaking

The dramatic scenes should reflect reasonable interpretations of the painting.

Viewing and Representing

Suggest that students create a dialogue for four characters. The dialogue should sound lively and realistic.

Reteaching

📁 *Composition Reteaching,* p. 29

Enrichment

📁 *Composition Enrichment,* p. 29

✎ Use *Fine Art Transparencies,* 19–24, for enrichment activities also.

Close

Have students create a list of things to consider when they write dialogue. (They should shape their dialogues carefully. They should strive for realism by using sentence fragments and slang. They should also make sure every speech has a purpose.)

Grammar Link

Answers

1. correct   2. correct
3. "I feel . . . sweetheart," Lincoln replied . . . in 1862. "The boy said he . . . laugh."
4. "These words . . . *Familiar Quotations,*" my teacher said. "Do . . . is?"
5. "I've heard of it," I admitted, "but I . . . it."

Viewing the Art

Gilberto Ruiz, *The Good News Call,* 1986
Gilberto Ruiz, born in Cuba, calls his narrative paintings pictograms. In each he offers a dramatic view of an event but no explanation, thus creating a sense of mystery. *The Good News Call* is a 55-by-35-inch oil painting.

Focus

Lesson Overview

Objective
- To create an anecdote that illustrates a theme

Skills
- using anecdotes to support a theme; writing anecdotes

Critical Thinking
- recalling; relating

Listening and Speaking
- informal speaking

Bellringer
Daily Language Activity

When students enter the classroom, have this assignment on the board: *Write two or three sentences summarizing a memorable story a parent, teacher, or friend told you.*

Grammar Link to the Bellringer

Have students add an appositive or appositive phrase to one of the descriptions in their sentences.

See also *Daily Language Practice*

Motivating Activity

Ask students to share some memorable, meaningful stories told to them by coaches, neighbors, or relatives. Usually the point of a meaningful story is a truth about life that the adult hopes to pass on, such as the value of careful study to achieve academic success or the value of rigorous daily practice to achieve athletic success. Point out that the very fact that students remember these anecdotes illustrates their value.

Narrative Writing

LESSON 4.5
Theme and Anecdote

An anecdote is a brief story that makes a point. The theme of a work is its main idea or underlying message. Look for the point that Will Steger makes with this anecdote.

> How is this anecdote a story within a story? Why do you think Steger decided to use it as his introduction?

> Why does Steger use a direct quotation in his anecdote? Why not just say "I called Keizo by name"?

Literature Model

Tears of frustration and despair blinded me more than the stinging wind or snow. For 24 hours a storm had pinned us in our camp only 16 miles from our goal—the far edge of Antarctica. We had come too far, endured too much suffering, to lose a man now, I thought bitterly. We had to find him.

We clung to a long rope as we searched; the end was tied to a sled to keep us from straying, as he had, into the raging whiteout. "Keizo!" I yelled into the blizzard. "Keizo! . . . Keizo!"

Faintly I heard the others shouting his name as they too groped in a tethered arc around the tents and sleds. Our Japanese teammate, Keizo Funatsu—gentle, compassionate Keizo—had crawled out of his tent at 4:30 the afternoon before to check on his dogs. By six we knew he was lost. We searched into the night, calling and listening, flashlight beams futile against the swirling snow.

Now in the first faint wash of daylight we were searching again.

It was unthinkable that one of us could be gone after what we had come through together for nearly seven months: Trudging, antlike, across 3,700 miles of brutal terrain, from sea level to lonely elevations above 11,000 feet . . . battered for weeks by continuous storms . . . winds that howled at 90 miles an hour.

We had challenged a foreign place, a place not meant for warm-blooded animals. Antarctica's terrible interior tries to turn men into its own image—frozen. Yet this endurance test had forged a deep and permanent bond among us: six dissimilar men from six nations, attempting to complete the first crossing of the continent by dogsled.

188 Unit 4 Narrative Writing

Resource Manager

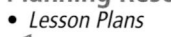

Planning Resources
- *Lesson Plans*

Transparencies
- *Bellringer*
- *Daily Language Practice*
- *Fine Art* 19–24
- *Two-Minute Skill Drill*
- *Writing Process* 10, 18–22

Other Print Resources
- *Composition Enrichment*, p. 30
- *Composition Practice*, p. 30
- *Composition Reteaching*, p. 30
- *Cooperative Learning Activities*, pp. 17–20
- *Listening and Speaking Activities*, pp. 13, 18, 20, 21

- *Sentence-Combining Practice*, pp. 30–31
- *Thinking and Study Skills*, pp. 13–14, 22
- *Writing Across the Curriculum*
- *Writing Assessment and Evaluation Rubrics*

I envisioned the worst—carrying Keizo these last few miles wrapped in the flag of his homeland—and my stomach knotted in anguish. "Keizo!" I bellowed, over and over again.

I couldn't believe it when I glimpsed him—a wraith emerging from the driving curtain of snow. "I am alive," he said. In seconds we were clutching each other. Both of us were crying.

Keizo is a skilled survivor. Once lost, he scraped a shallow trench with pliers, the only tool he had, and curled up in it like a shed dog, allowing the blizzard to bury him. And there, with Zen-like calm, he waited for 13 hours, until he heard our calls.

It was then—but only then—that I was certain our expedition was a success.

> How does this last sentence suggest the point of the anecdote?

Will Steger, "Six Across Antarctica," *National Geographic*

Understand the Theme

Steger's anecdote forcefully introduces his article. It also illustrates his theme, or main idea: Six men from dissimilar cultural backgrounds could work together under some of the cruelest conditions on the planet.

The chart below explains some of the characteristics of a theme. Notice that it discusses themes in fiction as well as nonfiction.

The Characteristics of a Theme	
A Theme is . . .	**A Theme is Not . . .**
• A theme is a general insight about life or human nature.	• A theme is not the topic or subject of the work.
• In nonfiction, a theme is often stated, as in Steger's article.	• A theme is not a summary of a plot or story line.
• In fiction, a theme is usually implied, as in a story in which the events show how love overcomes prejudice.	• A theme is not a moral or lesson about life, though it may suggest one.

Journal Writing

Find a theme in something you have written. In your journal express the theme as a general statement about life or human nature.

Teach

Comparing Themes

Have students work together to discover the theme of a short story familiar to the whole class. First, each student should write a statement of the story's theme. Then, they should join with a partner to share and discuss the two statements and agree on one. Afterward, one student from each pair should read the pair's statement to the class. In class discussion of the statements, bring out that although there is no one correct way to state a theme, some statements may seem more appropriate or relevant than others. **L2**

Prewriting Help

Help students find and articulate a theme for their anecdote. Talk with them about the details—their story's characters and actions, their problem and solution—and then help students formulate and write the general idea their anecdote will illustrate. **L1**

 Two-Minute Skill Drill

Have students add an appositive or appositive phrase to each of the following descriptions:

> *a furry dog   a yellow shirt*
> *a cold day   a homemade raft*

See also *Two-Minute Skill Drill Transparency 4.5*

Journal Writing Tip

Summarizing Challenge students to express their themes as general statements, without referring to specific people or events in their stories.

Teach

Matching Themes

List a variety of familiar fairy tales on the board. Then ask pairs of students to write a statement about each story's theme on a sheet of paper. Collect the theme statements. Randomly read theme statements and see if students can match the theme with its fairy tale. **L2**

Collecting Anecdotes

Have students interview people in the community and write down their most interesting anecdotes. Then have students compile the anecdotes. Students may want to group the anecdotes by theme. Share the collected anecdotes with the rest of the class. **L3**

Additional Resources

 For further stimuli for narrative writing, see *Fine Art Transparencies,* 19–24.

 Writing Process Transparencies, 10, 18–22

Writing Across the Curriculum

Cooperative Learning Activities

Thinking and Study Skills, pp. 13–14, 22

Sentence Combining Practice, pp. 30–31

Listening and Speaking Activities, pp. 13, 18, 20, 21

Composition Practice, p. 30

Narrative Writing

Use Anecdotes to Support the Theme

An anecdote in fiction is a story within a story. Claire Edwards has included the following anecdote in "Kay," a fictional story about the death of the narrator's best friend, an event that happened when both girls were teenagers. Underlying Edwards's story is a theme about a strong friendship that the narrator believes will endure forever. Notice how this anecdote supports the theme.

This anecdote has all the elements of any narrative. Can you identify the characters, the setting, the complication, and the resolution?

This last sentence expresses the point of the anecdote. How does the anecdote support the theme of the whole story?

Student Model

Kay and I met on the first day of third grade. Fate brought us together—literally! We collided on the front steps of our school building, and I ended up dropping all my new books. A freckled face peered into mine and gasped, "Oh, I'm sorry! Would you believe this is the second time today I've bumped into someone? I'm not always this clumsy, but I woke up late, and my mom made me eat all my breakfast, bite by bite. It took such a long time, and I don't think I'm quite fully awake yet. By the way, my name's Katherine Montgomery, but all my friends call me Kay." It was only a matter of weeks before Kay and I were inseparable.

Claire Edwards, New Trier East Township High School, Winnetka, Illinois. First appeared in *Merlyn's Pen: The National Magazine of Student Writing*

Revising Tip

In revising, make your anecdote short and lively. Cut out unnecessary details, but keep those that make your writing interesting. A peer reviewer can help you make cuts.

When writing either nonfiction or fiction, think of anecdotes you might use to support your theme. For example, a nonfiction article about the importance of animals to children could include an anecdote about the writer's own pet. A fiction story about a teenager who works in a restaurant could include a humorous anecdote showing how his job teaches him valuable lessons about people. Once you have an idea for an anecdote, answer the following questions to plan it.

Prewriting Your Anecdote

- What is the setting?
- Who are the characters?
- What problem, challenge, or conflict do they face?
- How is the problem solved?
- What's the point?

 ## Cultural Connections

Appreciating Ethnic Anecdotes

Different cultures may have different anecdotes that are used to get across common themes. Have students share anecdotes or stories they were told to emphasize the importance of themes such as never telling a lie, getting enough sleep, or the importance of eating breakfast.

Write an Anecdote

Adults often tell young children stories about lessons learned through experience. These stories are anecdotes. Write an anecdote for young children based on your own experience.

PURPOSE To write an anecdote
AUDIENCE Young children
LENGTH 4-6 paragraphs

WRITING RUBRICS To write a meaningful anecdote, you should

- illustrate a theme or lesson
- reveal the setting, characters, conflict, and resolution
- make the point of your anecdote clear
- ensure that your word choice is appropriate for a young audience

Using Computers

Anecdotes, like jokes, benefit in special ways from revision, since they succeed best when they are brief and lively, saying much in little space. Use the copy feature of your word-processing program to help you revise your anecdotes. Make several copies of the original, and revise each one, creating different versions. Compare them, and select the best version. If you're unsure which is really your best, print out two you like, and ask a peer reviewer to read and respond to them.

Listening and Speaking

After you have written your anecdote, practice reading it aloud before presenting it to the class. Decide how you will tell the story. Use storytelling techniques to make your anecdote more interesting. After all the presentations, the class should create a questionnaire to elicit students' views on the characteristics of successful presentations.

Grammar Link

Use and punctuate appositives and appositive phrases correctly.

An *appositive* is a noun or pronoun placed next to another noun or pronoun to provide additional information. An *appositive phrase* is an appositive plus any words that modify it.

Add at least one appositive or appositive phrase to each sentence below. Use commas as needed.

1. In 1832, Charles Darwin sailed from England on the HMS *Beagle*.
2. Darwin collected 68 different species of small beetles in a forest outside Rio de Janeiro.
3. During the next three years, the *Beagle* sailed south to round Cape Horn and north again up the coast of Chile.
4. The expedition eventually came to the Galápagos Islands where Darwin made more studies of wildlife.
5. There Darwin found cormorants, iguanas, and tortoises that were very different from those on the mainland.

See Lesson 12.2, pages 525–526.

Assess

Evaluation Rubrics

Write an Anecdote

Use these criteria when evaluating your students' writing.

- The anecdote should be appropriate for children in content, style, and word choice.
- The anecdote should include these narrative elements: characters, setting, problem or conflict, and solution.
- The anecdote should make a valid point about life.
- The anecdote should be short and interest-grabbing.

See also *Writing Assessment and Evaluation Rubrics.*

Using Computers

If necessary, demonstrate to the class how to copy one of their anecdotes and edit it in several different ways.

Listening and Speaking

Students' presentations should employ appropriate techniques to enliven the anecdotes.

Reteaching

📁 *Composition Reteaching*, p. 30

Enrichment

📁 *Composition Enrichment*, p. 30

Close

Ask students to suggest some real-world purposes for anecdotes. (Anecdotes are used by politicians to make speeches more compelling, by lecturers to illustrate complex ideas, by coaches to inspire players, and by advertisers to affirm the benefits of their products.)

Grammar Link

Answers
(Answers will vary.)
1. . . . scientist Charles Darwin . . .
2. . . . outside Rio de Janeiro, a seaport in southeast Brazil.
3. . . . Cape Horn, the most southerly part of South America, and . . .
4. . . . Galápagos Islands, a group of islands on the equator, where . . .
5. There Darwin, the naturalist, found cormorants . . .

Focus

Lesson Overview

Objective
- To write a summary of a short story's plot, following a three-paragraph structure

Skills
- identifying a story's main idea and conflict; writing a plot summary

Critical Thinking
- summarizing

Listening and Speaking
- listening for information

Bellringer
Daily Language Activity

When students enter the classroom, have this assignment on the board: *Write a paragraph summarizing a story you have read or heard.*

Grammar Link to the Bellringer

Have students change all the verbs in their paragraph to present tense.

See also *Daily Language Practice*

Motivating Activity

Ask students how useful they find the plot summaries on the back of video boxes, on the inner flaps of book jackets, and in television listings. What other plot summaries do they read? (Students might mention those within book or movie reviews and at the end of history lessons.) Then discuss the uses of plot summaries.

Narrative Writing

LESSON
4.6

WRITING ABOUT LITERATURE
The Plot Summary

A plot summary is a shortened version of a story built around the main character's problem. Like a traveler's passport, it shows important stopping points but does not tell whether the trip was enjoyable. As you read the plot summary of "The Most Dangerous Game," note how it summarizes the narrative elements of the story.

Literature Model

The short story "The Most Dangerous Game," by Richard Connell, pits two great hunters against each other. Rainsford, the main character, falls from a yacht and swims to an island owned by General Zaroff. We as readers see the events through Rainsford's eyes. Zaroff, bored with hunting animals, hunts men instead. Rainsford's horror grows as he finds himself the unwilling quarry in Zaroff's deadly game.

According to the rules of that game, Rainsford must elude his foe for three days or be killed. He begins his flight in panic, then gathers his wits and draws on his vast knowledge of hunting. Rainsford knows terror when Zaroff tracks his intricate trail but deliberately saves him for another day's sport. The next day, Rainsford escapes death and wins his

> What elements of the plot does the summary introduce in the first paragraph?

Resource Manager

Planning Resources
- *Lesson Plans*

Transparencies
- *Bellringer*
- *Daily Language Practice*
- *Fine Art* 19–24
- *Two-Minute Skill Drill*
- *Writing Process* 10, 18–22

Other Print Resources
- *Composition Enrichment*, p. 31
- *Composition Practice*, p. 31
- *Composition Reteaching*, p. 31
- *Cooperative Learning Activities*, pp. 17–20
- *Listening and Speaking Activities*, pp. 13, 18, 20, 21

- *Sentence-Combining Practice*, pp. 30–31
- *Thinking and Study Skills*, pp. 1, 10, 17, 22
- *Writing Across the Curriculum*
- *Writing Assessment and Evaluation Rubrics*

foe's respect by building ingenious traps that wound Zaroff and kill one of his dogs. The third day, Zaroff pursues him with a pack of ferocious dogs led by his savage servant, Ivan. Rainsford's last trap misses its intended victim but kills the servant. Finally, knowing he cannot outrun the dogs, Rainsford leaps into the sea.

The climax comes later that night. Retiring to his bedroom, Zaroff finds himself face to face with Rainsford, who swam across the cove to the chateau. Surprised, the general congratulates Rainsford for winning the game. Rainsford lets his enemy know the game isn't over, and both men realize that the loser will be fed to the dogs. We know who that is in the last sentence, when Rainsford decides that he "never slept in a better bed."

> Notice that the second paragraph sums up the main events that build suspense.

> What is the writer's purpose in this third paragraph?

Why Write a Plot Summary?

A plot summary is intended to sum up the main events in a story—specifically, the main character's problem and how it is resolved. It does not include personal opinion or evaluation.

Plot summaries can be valuable in a number of ways. Read the chart for ideas of how to use summaries.

Uses of a Plot Summary

- Preparing a plot summary will help you recognize the story line and other narrative elements.
- Writing the summary will help you clarify your understanding of action, complication, resolution, and theme.
- Reading the plot summary later will help you review for a test.

Journal Writing

Think of a movie or TV program you saw recently. How would you summarize it in two or three sentences for a friend? Write your summary in your journal.

Narrative Writing

Teach

Identifying Main Events

Some students may need help isolating main events from incidental ones. Have students list the events as they read a story, beginning with the introduction of the complication and ending with the outcome. Help them decide which events belong in a summary by weighing the events' importance to the solution of the problem. Explain that if the outcome makes sense without a particular event, students should leave that event out of the summary. **L2**

Summarizing Novels

Challenge students to tackle writing a plot summary of a novel. Point out that they may need to write a longer summary than this lesson's models; several paragraphs should describe the novel's main events. Remind students that a plot summary is not a review. The goal here is simply to summarize, not evaluate. **L3**

 ### Two-Minute Skill Drill

Have students change the following verbs to present tense:

1. *galloped*
2. *has gone*
3. *will fly*
4. *screamed*
5. *was climbing*

See also *Two-Minute Skill Drill Transparency 4.6*

Journal Writing Tip

Listing Encourage students to start by randomly listing anything they can remember about the movie or program. Then have them use this information to write their plot summary.

Teach

Plotting Visually

Show students a short cartoon or film clip. Then work with students to outline the plot summary in a three-box diagram like the one on student page 194. The diagram reinforces the summary's focus on the main character's problem. The information in the first box introduces the problem; the information in the second box tells the steps taken to resolve the problem; and the information in the third box solves the problem. **L1**

Plotting History

Much of what students read about history is written in summary form, focusing on the key participants and the main events. Have students write a plot summary of a major event in history. **L3**

Additional Resources

 For further stimuli for narrative writing, see *Fine Art Transparencies,* 19–24.

 Writing Process Transparencies, 10, 18–22

Writing Across the Curriculum
Cooperative Learning Activities
Thinking and Study Skills, pp. 1, 10, 17, 22
Listening and Speaking Activities, pp. 13, 18, 20, 21
Composition Practice, p. 31
Sentence Combining Practice, pp. 30–31

Narrative Writing

Write a Plot Summary

As with most writing you do, prewriting is crucial to preparing a plot summary. The first step is to read the work carefully. As you read, take notes regarding the elements listed in the chart below. Most plot summaries, including both of the models in this lesson, are organized as shown. Notice the focus on the main character's problem.

Paragraph 1	**Paragraph 2**	**Paragraph 3**
List the title, author, main character(s), setting, and point of view. Then describe the main character's problem.	Explain the main events in chronological order (the order in which they happen).	Describe the climax or turning point, when readers know how the problem will be solved and how the story ends.

Literary terms, such as *complication* and *climax,* can help you summarize the story line, but their use isn't necessary. In her plot summary below, Laurie Valle used very literary terms.

Revising Tip

In revising your plot summary, be sure to verify your facts and organization against the original work.

Although the plot summary is written in Valle's own words, it includes this brief quotation. Why did Valle choose to use these words from the story?

How does Mrs. Mallard's story illustrate irony, a contrast between what appears to be true and what really is true?

Student Model

"The Story of an Hour" by Kate Chopin begins with a delicate situation. Louise Mallard, who has a serious heart condition, must be told that her husband is dead. Her sister Josephine and her husband's friend Richards have come to her home, where they gently break the news of the tragic railroad accident.

Louise retires to her bedroom, overcome with weeping. Alone, she thinks about the accident and the effect it will have on her life. The reader learns that she did not love her husband. She feels no grief at his death but rather, exultation. Now she is free, able to run her own life.

Then Brently Mallard walks through the door unscathed. He was not on the train at all and was, in fact, very far from the accident. The irony of the situation is in the way Louise Mallard dies. The doctor says her sudden death is from "heart disease—joy that kills." But the reader knows it isn't joy that kills Louise Mallard. Instead, seeing her husband alive has destroyed her new sense of freedom, killing her joy and causing her death.

Laurie Valle, Edison High School, Edison, New Jersey

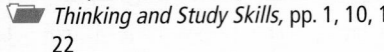 ## Less Proficient Readers

MEETING INDIVIDUAL NEEDS

Expanding a Summary

Have students start with the television listing for a program they have seen or a book jacket from a book they have read. (The program listing or book jacket does not have to be in English.) Have them try to expand or edit the plot summary to fit the three-paragraph structure.

Write a Plot Summary

Summarize the plot of a short story you read or a movie you saw recently.

PURPOSE To summarize a short story or movie
AUDIENCE Your classmates
LENGTH 3 paragraphs

WRITING RUBRICS To write an effective plot summary, you should

- describe setting, point of view, and the main character's conflict
- explain the important events up through the climax and resolution
- exclude personal opinions
- use verbs in the present tense

Cross-Curricular Activity

WORLD HISTORY History is usually told as a narrative, with the events related in chronological order. Summarizing requires careful reading, so a useful technique for studying history is to summarize the story line of a chapter or unit in your history text. Try it. Write a one- to two-page summary of the material that will be covered on your next history test.

Viewing and Representing

CREATING AN AD Use one of the plot summaries you wrote to create a print ad for the work. Make sure that your ad is visually appealing. Illustrate your print ad and display it in the classroom.

Grammar Link

Avoid unnecessary shifts in verb tenses.

When summarizing or analyzing literature, use verbs in the present tense. Note how Laurie Valle uses the present tense when speaking of Louise Mallard.

> Louise Mallard . . . **has** a serious heart condition.

Then note the verbs in the rest of Valle's plot summary.

Revise the plot summary below, correcting shifts from the present tense.

1. In "The Most Dangerous Game," General Zaroff played a deadly game in which he hunts people, not animals.
2. Rainsford, the main character, tried to escape from Zaroff, who hunted him.
3. Although Zaroff finds Rainsford on the first day, Rainsford is not killed because Zaroff wanted to track him for one more day.
4. On the second day Rainsford fought back and made a clever trap, which kills one of Zaroff's tracking dogs.
5. On the final day of the hunt, Rainsford escaped from the dogs and jumps into the sea.
6. He will be the victor, though, because he will become the hunter and confront Zaroff when he least expected it.

See Lesson 15.6, pages 598–599.

Assess

Evaluation Rubrics

Write a Plot Summary

Use these criteria when evaluating your students' writing.

- The summary should include three paragraphs that correspond to those in the chart on student page 194.
- The summary should focus on the main character's problem.
- The summary should include main events.
- The summary should accurately relate the significance of events.
- The summary should not include minor points or personal opinions.

See also *Writing Assessment and Evaluation Rubrics.*

Cross-Curricular Activity

You might have students from the same history class form small groups. Encourage students to compare their summaries, revising to add important information and delete minor events.

Viewing and Representing

The ads should reveal students' creativity while accurately reflecting the tone and substance of the book.

Reteaching

📁 *Composition Reteaching*, p. 31

Enrichment

📁 *Composition Enrichment*, p. 31

Close

Read a short story aloud in class, and then ask students to summarize it. Remind them to include the story's main events.

Grammar Link

Answers
(Answers list only the verbs.)
1. plays; hunts
2. tries; hunts
3. finds; is not killed; wants
4. fights; makes; kills
5. escapes; jumps
6. is; becomes; confronts; expects

Focus

Lesson Overview

Objective
- To recognize the conflict in fiction and determine how the conflict interacts with other story elements

Skills
- recognizing conflict; writing a conflict analysis

Critical Thinking
- identifying; classifying; analyzing

Listening and Speaking
- discussing

Bellringer
Daily Language Activity

When students enter the classroom, have this assignment on the board: *List three examples of conflict you have read about or witnessed.*

Grammar Link to the Bellringer

Have students underline each noun in their list and then write its possessive form.

See also *Daily Language Practice*

Motivating Activity

Ask students what makes them want to see a movie or read a story. (One explanation is that people are interested in conflicts and how they are resolved.) Spend time brainstorming with students about different kinds of conflicts (such as a disciplinary dispute with a teacher or a fight with a sibling over a game). List suggestions on the chalkboard under headings such as the following: at school, at home, with friends, with self.

Narrative Writing

LESSON 4.7

WRITING ABOUT LITERATURE
Analyzing Conflict

One way to understand a story is to examine its conflict, or the struggle between opposing forces. Read the analysis below of W.W. Jacobs's "The Monkey's Paw." Who or what are the opposing forces in the conflict?

Edvard Munch, *The Scream*, 1893

Literature Model

The analysis begins with this thesis sentence, which is a statement about the nature of the conflict.

1 **fakir:** (fə kir') a Hindu or Muslim holy man

According to the analysis, readers can predict which side of this conflict will win. What causes the suspense that makes readers want to read on?

In the short story "The Monkey's Paw," members of an ordinary family come into conflict with fate. The family suffers because they try to change their lives by using the magic in the monkey's paw.

Mr. White is intrigued with magic and the unknown, so he rescues the paw when his guest, Morris, throws it into the fire. Later, Mr. White's first wish is granted. When the Whites hear of their son's death, they realize the awful truth of the fakir's[1] words: "that fate ruled people's lives, and that those who interfered with it did so to their sorrow."

As readers, we know that the monkey's paw always brings tragedy. Before the action of the story, the paw had caused one death and left Morris with terrible memories. Still, much of our interest in this story is created by its suspense. We don't know what the tragedy will be, or how it will happen, and we care about this family. We identify with Mrs. White in her desire to get her son back, but we know the monkey's paw can bring nothing good, even if he returns. In the end, the Whites have learned a great deal about fate, but with their knowledge has come the sorrow that the fakir had promised.

196 Unit 4 Narrative Writing

Resource Manager

Planning Resources
- *Lesson Plans*

Transparencies
- *Bellringer*
- *Daily Language Practice*
- *Fine Art* 19–24
- *Two-Minute Skill Drill*
- *Writing Process* 10, 18–22

Other Print Resources
- *Composition Enrichment*, p. 32
- *Composition Practice*, p. 32
- *Composition Reteaching*, p. 32
- *Cooperative Learning Activities*, pp. 17–20
- *Listening and Speaking Activities*, pp. 13, 18, 20, 21

- *Research Paper and Report Writing*, p. 49
- *Sentence-Combining Practice*, pp. 30–31
- *Thinking and Study Skills*, p. 13, 21, 24
- *Writing Across the Curriculum*
- *Writing Assessment and Evaluation Rubrics*

Recognize Conflict

Most stories focus on a complication, a problem in the main characters' lives. Usually, the complication is a conflict, a struggle between opposing forces. The conflict can be important (two soldiers fight to the death) or petty (a sister and brother argue over their inheritance). The conflict can be external (a family fight to save their house from a flood) or internal (a girl is torn between love for her mother and desire for independence). Conflict engages readers by creating suspense, a desire to find out what happens. The suspense ends when the conflict is resolved and readers know which opposing force will prevail.

Near the story's beginning, the conflict motivates the characters, leading them to act. By the story's end, the characters have usually learned something significant. The chart below gives examples of conflicts found in fiction.

Revising Tip

In prewriting a conflict analysis, you may find it helpful to discuss the story with another person who has read it.

Conflicts in Fiction		
Kind	**Example**	**Plot**
Person vs. Person	"The Most Dangerous Game" by Richard Connell	Rainsford, who has become General Zaroff's unwilling prey, must elude his hunter for three days or be killed.
Person vs. Nature	"To Build a Fire" by Jack London	A man struggles to keep from freezing to death in the extreme cold of winter in the Klondike region of western Canada.
Person vs. Society	"The Lottery" by Shirley Jackson	A woman is selected by lot for death by stoning in a ritual mandated and carried out by the community.
Person vs. Self	"Through the Tunnel" by Doris Lessing	A boy struggles to overcome his fear of drowning in order to satisfy his desire to swim through an underwater tunnel.
Person vs. Machine	"Trucks" by Stephen King	People who are being held hostage by trucks must decide whether to meet the trucks' demands.
Person vs. the Supernatural	*The Odyssey* by Homer	Odysseus is delayed in his return to Ithaca by various characters, including the sea god Poseidon.

Journal Writing

Why do you think conflict is an element of most good fiction? Is it because readers can identify with conflicts they have experienced? Is it because the resolution of conflict gives meaning to events? Explore these questions in your journal.

Teach

Identifying Conflict

Challenge students to think of other familiar works—novels, short stories, and movies—that illustrate the conflicts listed in the chart. If students think of narratives with more than one major conflict, point out that one is usually primary. For example, a story might tell about a character pitted against an opponent in a bitter election campaign (person against person) who must also overcome a sense of personal inadequacy (person against self). **L2**

Two-Minute Skill Drill

Have students write the possessive form of the following nouns:

congresswomen

mother-in-law

Mr. Jones

classes

See also *Two-Minute Skill Drill Transparency 4.7*

Journal Writing Tip

Drawing Conclusions Urge students to use examples from their reading as they draw conclusions about the value of conflict in fiction. What stories or books have they found interesting? Why? Did they identify with the main character's conflict? Did they learn anything from its resolution?

Teach

Working Together to Analyze Conflict

Form small groups, assigning a familiar story to each. Have each group member answer one or two of the chart's questions about the group's story. One member serves as a recorder, and another presents the group's analysis to the class. Discuss any questions class members have about another group's analysis. **L1**

Analyzing Real-Life Conflicts

Challenge students to analyze real-life conflicts using the techniques they've learned for analyzing fictional conflicts. Real conflicts—personal, school, political, environmental—have the elements that are summed up in the chart on student page 197. Students can identify the opposing forces and some possible resolutions. **L3**

Additional Resources

 For further stimuli for narrative writing, see *Fine Art Transparencies*, 19–24.

 Writing Process Transparencies, 10, 18–22

 Writing Across the Curriculum
Cooperative Learning Activities
 Thinking and Study Skills, pp. 13, 21, 24
Listening and Speaking Activities, pp. 13, 18, 20, 21
Composition Practice, p. 32
Sentence Combining Practice, pp. 30–31

Narrative Writing

Grammar Tip

When you revise your analysis, you might discover places to use direct quotations to support your ideas. For information about punctuating direct quotations, see Lesson 21.9, pages 755–757.

What is the thesis statement in Chaffee's analysis, and what is its purpose?

Why do you think the writer chose to quote from the story? What do the direct quotations add to her analysis?

Write About Conflict

As you prepare to write a conflict analysis, first pinpoint the conflict. Use the questions in the chart below to help you plan your analysis.

Questions About Conflict
1. What are the opposing forces in the conflict?
2. Is the conflict external, internal, or both?
3. How does the writer create and maintain interest in the conflict?
4. How is the conflict resolved?
5. What new understanding do the characters reach as a result of the conflict and its resolution? What new understanding do readers discover?
6. How does the conflict help the author develop the story's theme?

A conflict analysis is not a plot summary. Refer to the plot only as it relates to the conflict, as Cary Chaffee does in the analysis below.

Student Model

In the short story "Eveline," from James Joyce's *Dubliners*, the conflict is internal; it is Eveline versus herself. Eveline's dilemma—whether to stay in an unhappy home or seize an opportunity to escape to another place and a better life—is with herself alone. It is a conflict that many readers will recognize. Like many people, Eveline must choose between security and happiness.

Eveline lives a terrible life. On her job she is unappreciated, and in her home she is little more than a household drudge. Her father, a drunkard, has recently begun to threaten her with the same kind of violence he once used on her brothers. Now she has a chance to escape. "Why should she be unhappy? She had a right to happiness."

Eveline realizes, though, that no matter how bad things are, she is secure at home with her father. "It was hard work—a hard life—but now that she was about to leave it she did not find it a wholly undesirable life." Eveline's inner struggle makes readers want to urge her to marry her lover and be happy. Her uncertainty creates to marry her lover and be happy. Her uncertainty creates suspense. In her decision to stay, readers can discover a theme: you can become happy only by taking risks.

Cary Chaffee, Quartz Hill High School, Quartz Hill, California

MEETING INDIVIDUAL NEEDS — Less Proficient Readers

Defining Suspense

Make sure students understand what suspense is. (Suspense is the uncertainty readers feel when they don't know how a story will turn out.) Demonstrate suspense by reading an exciting passage from a story and stopping just before the action is resolved. Point out that suspense makes readers want to read on; it makes viewers want to see the end of the movie. Suspense creates feelings of excitement and pleasure. People want to find out which side wins. Suggest that one way to identify the conflict in a story is to ask what creates the suspense.

Write a Conflict Analysis

Write an analysis of the conflict in one of the following short stories: "The Use of Force" by William Carlos Williams; "Barn Burning" by William Faulkner; or "Through the Tunnel" by Doris Lessing.

PURPOSE To analyze conflict in a short story
AUDIENCE Your teacher and classmates
LENGTH 3-4 paragraphs

WRITING RUBRICS To write an effective analysis, you should

- identify the conflict and the forces involved in it
- explain the development of the conflict and its resolution
- tell what new understandings the characters and the reader reach

Listening and Speaking

COOPERATIVE LEARNING In a small group discuss the elements of conflict in the painting *Salmon Run*. Brainstorm to list examples of conflict in nature: animal vs. environment; one animal species vs. another; conflict among animals of the same species. What resolutions are possible in these conflicts?

Using Computers

Conduct research on the Internet or various newsmagazines to find out more about a conflict between two groups over an environmental issue. Create a poster presentation, using printouts from your research, additional photographs, and text that shows how this conflict might be resolved.

Grammar Link

Form possessive nouns correctly.

The writer of the conflict analysis of "The Monkey's Paw" used a number of singular possessive nouns. To refer to the paws of more than one monkey, you would write "*monkeys' paws.*"

Complete each sentence below with the correct possessive form.

1. The teacher collected one (class's, classes') papers.
2. She announced that all (student's, students') writing had improved.
3. Each (paper's, papers') subject was conflict.
4. Many (paper's, papers') thesis statements related to the nature of the conflict analyzed.
5. Mrs. (Harris's, Harris') comments were generally favorable.

See Lesson 21.11, pages 760–762.

Melissa Miller, *Salmon Run*, 1984

4.7 Analyzing Conflict **199**

Assess

Evaluation Rubrics

Write a Conflict Analysis

Use these criteria when evaluating your students' writing. The analysis should

- identify the conflict in a clear thesis statement
- specify whether the forces in the conflict are internal or external
- explain the development and resolution of the conflict

See also *Writing Assessment and Evaluation Rubrics.*

Listening and Speaking

Analyses should identify two forces that oppose the salmon and discuss how instinct relates to the struggle. Students' analyses should refer to details from the painting.

Viewing and Representing

The graph or chart should
- use a sensible principle of organization.
- allow for some whimsical representations.
- permit inclusion of all students' experiences.

Reteaching

Composition Reteaching, p. 32

Enrichment

Composition Enrichment, p. 32

Use *Fine Art Transparencies* 19–24 for enrichment activities also.

Close

Have students look at the conflicts that they listed at the beginning of the lesson. With a partner, have them discuss whether any of these conflicts have helped them understand their own problems.

Viewing the Art

Melissa Miller, *Salmon Run,* 1984
In boldly colored scenes from nature, Melissa Miller focuses on a conflict—the upstream struggle of salmon facing strong currents and hungry bears. Although the struggles are instinctive, the painting invites viewers to draw parallels with human struggles.

Grammar Link

Answers

1. class's
2. students'
3. paper's
4. papers'
5. Harris's

Focus

Lesson Overview

Objective
- To write a narrative that could serve as an introduction to a longer work of fiction

Skills
- using the five stages of the writing process: prewriting, drafting, revising, editing, presenting; focusing on an interesting complication; establishing setting, characters, and conflict; using dialogue and/or anecdotes effectively

Critical Thinking
- recalling; generating new information

Listening and Speaking
- informal speaking

Bellringer
Daily Language Activity

When students enter the room, have this assignment on the board: *Think about the most exciting opening to a narrative that you have ever read and briefly describe it.*

Grammar Link to the Bellringer

Have students make sure they have correctly used commas with items in a series.

See also *Daily Language Practice*

Motivating Activity

Ask students to recall the openings of specific television dramas, miniseries, or movies. Discuss what kinds of information are introduced in the first few minutes. What keeps viewers waiting through a commercial break?

Writing Process in Action

Narrative Writing

Narrative Writing

In preceding lessons you've learned about the basics of narrative writing—character, setting, plot, point of view, conflict, and resolution. You've also had a chance to practice writing parts of narratives, as well as plot summaries and conflict analyses. Now it's time to put together everything you've learned. In this lesson, you're invited to plan a short story of your own and to write the beginning of it.

WRITING Online

Visit the Writer's Choice Web site at **writerschoice. glencoe.com** for additional writing prompts.

Assignment

Content

You are a faithful reader of *To Be Continued . . .* , a magazine that publishes serialized student fiction in short monthly installments. You plan to submit a story to the magazine. In the first installment of your story, you will introduce the characters, setting, plot, and the complication you plan to develop in the succeeding installments.

Purpose

To write a narrative that could serve as an introduction to a longer work of fiction

Audience

Editors and teenage readers of *To Be Continued . . .*

Length

1-2 pages

You will find the next few pages helpful for planning your story and writing its first installment. Begin by reading through the pages, but don't feel you have to remember everything on them. You can refer back to the pages as you need to. After all, you're in charge of your own writing process.

Resource Manager

Planning Resources
- *Lesson Plans*

 Transparencies
- *Bellringer*
- *Daily Language Practice*
- *Writing Process* 10, 18–22

 Other Print Resources
- *Composition Enrichment,* p. 33

- *Composition Practice,* p. 33
- *Composition Reteaching,* p. 33
- *Grammar Workbook,* Lesson 77
- *Sentence-Combining Practice,* pp. 30–31
- *Thinking and Study Skills,* pp. 5, 23, 31–32
- *Writing Assessment and Evaluation Rubrics*

 Software
- *Writer's Assistant*

 Web Sites
- *writerschoice.glencoe.com*
- *lit.glencoe.com*

Writing Process in Action

Prewriting

If you have trouble coming up with an idea, the prewriting options shown here may help.

After choosing your idea, do the following:

- Make notes to identify characters, setting, point of view, and the basic events of your plot.
- Freewrite about your story's plot.
- Outline or diagram the basic events of your story.
- Decide whether you will use a first-person, third-person limited, or third-person omniscient narrator, and, if limited, from which character's point of view you will tell the story.

Prewriting Options

- Skim your journal for ideas.
- Brainstorm with family members or friends.
- Browse through newspapers and magazines to find references to interesting characters or real-life problems and solutions.
- Select a theme, conflict, or character type that interests you.

Drafting

Sometimes writers don't tell a story from its beginning. Look at what Rudolfo A. Anaya does in these opening paragraphs of his novel *Tortuga*.

Prewriting Tip

If you want to review creating a story outline or plot diagram, see Lesson 4.3, pages 180–183.

Literature Model

I awoke from a restless sleep. For a moment I couldn't remember where I was, then I heard Filomón and Clepo talking up front and I felt the wind sway the old ambulance. I tried to turn my body, but it was impossible. Upon waking it was always the same; I tried to move but the paralysis held me firmly in its grip.

I could turn my head and look out the small window. The cold winter rain was still falling. It had been only a gray drizzle when we left the hospital, but the farther south we went into the desert the sheets of icy rain became more intense. For a great part of the trip we had been surrounded by darkness. Only the flashes of lightning which tore through the sky illuminated the desolate landscape.

Rudolfo A. Anaya, *Tortuga*

Teach

Prewriting

Dictating Ideas

Students may dictate their ideas into a tape recorder, a practice that allows ideas to flow freely. Most people talk faster—and more easily—than they write. **L2**

Using Franklin's Plan

Students who have difficulty synthesizing information they've learned about narrative writing might respond to the simplicity of Jon Franklin's plan on student page 176. You might work with students individually or allow them to work with partners to complete the first steps: thinking of a character and giving the character a problem. Students can then complete their stories by showing their characters reacting to the situations and resolving the problems. **L1**

Drafting

Fleshing Out the Story

After students have decided on a story idea for *To Be Continued,* encourage them to work with a partner. Have partners read each other's story plan and respond with specific questions to help the writer fill in the missing pieces. Partners can also discuss different ways of opening their stories. **L2**

Opening Powerfully

Challenge students to create a powerful mood in their opening—as Rudolfo Anaya did. Some might do this through their description of the setting. Others might start with dialogue, using it to establish the opening situation as well as the mood. **L3**

Teach

Revising

Peer Editing

Students can work in writing conferences with peer editors before they revise their writing. Have peer editors respond to the following questions:

- Will the story create suspense?
- What will make readers want to read another installment?

You may want to duplicate the Peer Response form in the *Teacher's Guide to Writing Assessment* for use in writing conferences. **L2**

Editing

Peer Editing

After students have edited their own work, have them edit another student's writing. **L2**

Presenting

Before students present their narrative writing, discuss how to prepare their papers for publication. Emphasize the importance of a neat final draft.

Additional Resources

 Writing Process Transparencies, 10, 18–22

 Thinking and Study Skills, pp. 5, 23, 31–32

Sentence Combining Practice, pp. 30–31

 Composition Practice, p. 33

 Grammar Workbook Lesson 77

Narrative Writing

Drafting Tip

For help in structuring your introduction as an anecdote, see Lesson 4.5, pages 188–191.

Revising Tip

If your peer reviewers suggest that more or better dialogue would improve your story introduction, see Lesson 4.4, pages 184–187.

Anaya introduces the main elements of his narrative—the character and complication—in the first paragraphs of his book. Later he will have to go back in time to explain the origin of the complication—how the boy came to be paralyzed—and move forward in time to resolve the complication.

However you start your story, you need to construct a beginning that grabs your reader, moves the story along, lets readers get to know your characters, and gives them some idea of what lies ahead. Since you are writing the first installment of a continuing narrative, you can't really wrap up your story at the end. You can and should, however, leave your readers eager to find out more. Think about raising a compelling question, introducing a mysterious character, or even creating a suspenseful cliff-hanger.

Revising

To begin revising, read over your draft to make sure that what you've written fits your purpose and audience. Then have a **writing conference.** Read your draft to a partner or small group. Use your audience's reactions and the Revising Checklist below to help you evaluate your work.

Revising Checklist

- Did I introduce characters, setting, plot, and complication?
- Was the complication or conflict introduced potentially interesting to my audience?
- Did I end in a way that made my audience want to continue reading?
- Did I present a clear and consistent point of view?

Enrichment and Extension

Follow-up Ideas

- Set aside a time for students to celebrate the conclusion of their writing projects. Encourage them to share their finished pieces with the class.
- If students are sending their work out of the classroom, make sure that photocopies are retained.

Extending Narration

- Brainstorm with students for ways they can use their expertise in narrative writing in other subject areas, such as making a scientific discovery come to life or making a historical event more realistic.

Editing

When you are satisfied with your story introduction, proofread it carefully for errors in grammar, usage, mechanics, and spelling. Use the questions at the right as a guide.

In addition to proofreading, use the self-evaluation list below to make sure your story introduction does all the things you want it to do. When you feel that it does, make a clean copy of your story and proofread it one more time.

Reflection

Make sure your narrative introduction—

✔ focuses on an interesting complication
✔ establishes setting, characters, and conflict
✔ has a compelling beginning and ending
✔ ends in a way that keeps the reader guessing
✔ uses dialogue and/or anecdotes effectively
✔ is written from a consistent point of view
✔ follows correct grammar, usage, mechanics, and spelling

Presenting

Many magazines publish student writing. Check such references as *Writer's Market* to identify publications and determine their policy for submissions. If you decide to send your chapter to a real magazine, attach a brief letter informing the editors that you are submitting your story for publication. Be sure to include your address and phone number so that they can respond to your work.

Editing Checklist

- Have I punctuated appositives, participles, and their phrases correctly?
- Have I punctuated direct quotations correctly?
- Have I formed possessive nouns correctly?
- Have I used commas to separate items in a series?
- Have I checked spellings of any words of which I'm unsure?

Proofreading

For proofreading symbols, see page 84.

Journal Writing

Reflect on your writing process experience. Answer these questions in your journal: What do you like best about your narrative introduction? What was the hardest part of writing it? What did you learn in your writing conference? What new things have you learned as a writer?

Assess

Evaluation Rubrics

Use the following questions to evaluate students' finished writing:

- Did the student introduce characters, a setting, and a plot suitable for a longer fictional narrative?
- Is the point of view consistent?
- Did the student use mood, foreshadowing, or dialogue to move the story along?
- Is the writing vivid and expressive?
- Is the writing grammatically correct?
- As a reader, would you like to read further installments?

See also *Writing Assessment and Evaluation Rubrics.*

Reteaching

📁 *Composition Reteaching,* p. 33

Enrichment

📁 *Composition Enrichment,* p. 33

Journal Writing Tip

Freewrite Encourage students to freewrite to discover the answer to each question. They might want to use a key word in each question as a prompt.

Close

Ask students to discuss what this process has taught them about narrative writing. What writing techniques did they try that they had never tried before? What do they consider their strengths and weaknesses in narrative writing? What kinds of narrative writing do they prefer, and why?

About the Author

Rudolfo Alfonso Anaya grew up in a Spanish-speaking community in New Mexico. He has taught in the Albuquerque public schools and is now a professor of English at the University of New Mexico. He has published articles, reviews, plays, short stories, a mock-heroic epic poem, and a television screenplay. He's best known for his novels and has said, "Writing novels seems to be the medium which allows me to bring together all the questions I ask about life, the characters I have met, the haunting beauty of the people and the land."

Focus

Lesson Overview

Objective

- To read a literature passage and identify the narrative elements a professional writer uses to develop and embellish a story

Skills

- reading comprehension

Critical Thinking

- analyzing; evaluating; visualizing

Listening and Speaking

- discussing; formal reading

 Bellringer

Daily Language Activity

When students enter the classroom, have this assignment on the board: *List four of your favorite characters from books and movies.*

Literature Model

Narrative Writing

Tortuga

by Rudolfo A. Anaya

Mexican American writer Rudolfo A. Anaya, who was born in New Mexico, says he learned "from the old storytellers" in his native state "how to re-create the narrative and pass it on." In this beginning to the third novel of his trilogy about growing up a Mexican American in the Southwest, notice how the author creates mood while introducing characters and plot. Then complete the activities in Linking Writing and Literature on page 212.

Resource Manager

Planning Resources
- *Lesson Plans*

📋 **Transparencies**
- *Bellringer*
- *Daily Language Practice*
- *Fine Art 19–24*

📁 **Other Print Resources**
- *Listening and Speaking Activities,* pp. 13, 18, 20, 21
- *Thinking and Study Skills,* pp. 10, 13
- *Writing Assessment and Evaluation Rubrics*

 Web Sites
- *writerschoice.glencoe.com*
- *lit.glencoe.com*

Literature Model

I awoke from a restless sleep. For a moment I couldn't remember where I was, then I heard Filomón and Clepo talking up front and I felt the wind sway the old ambulance. I tried to turn my body, but it was impossible. Upon waking it was always the same; I tried to move but the paralysis held me firmly in its grip.

I could turn my head and look out the small window. The cold winter rain was still falling. It had been only a gray drizzle when we left the hospital, but the farther south we went into the desert the sheets of icy rain became more intense. For a great part of the trip we had been surrounded by darkness. Only the flashes of lightning which tore through the sky illuminated the desolate land-scape.

I had slept most of the way; the rain drumming against the ambulance and the rumble of the distant thunder lulled me to sleep. Now I blinked my eyes and remembered that we had left at daybreak, and Filomón had said that it would be mid-afternoon before we arrived at the new hospital.

Your new home, he had said.

Home. Up north, at home, it would be snowing, but here it was only the dark, dismal rain which swept across the wide desert and covered us with its darkness. I tried to turn again, but the paralysis compounded by the bone-chilling cold held me. I cursed silently.

"It's never been this dark before," I heard Clepo whisper.

For a great part of the trip we had been surrounded by darkness. Only the flashes of lightning which tore through the sky illuminated the desolate landscape.

"Don't worry," Filomón answered, "it'll get better before it gets worse. You have to know the desert to know rain don't last. It can be raining one minute and blowing dust devils[1] the next. But the clouds are beginning to break, see, to the west."

I turned my head and looked out the window. In the distance I could see the bare outline of a mountain range. Around us the desert was alkaline[2] and white. Only the most tenacious shrubs and brittle grasses seemed to grow, clinging to the harsh land like tufts of mouldy hair. Overhead, the sun struggled to break through the clouds. To the east, a diffused, distorted rainbow stretched across the vast, gray sky.

I remembered the rainbows of my childhood, beautifully sculptured arches reaching from north to south, shafts of light so pure their harmony seemed to wed the sky and earth. My mother had taught me to look at rainbows, the mantle[3] of the Blessed Virgin Mary she called them. When a summer thunderstorm passed she would take me out and we would stand in the thin drops which followed the storm. We would turn our faces up to the sky, and the large, glistening drops of rain would pelt our faces. She would open her mouth and hold out her tongue to receive the large, golden drops. She would stir the muddy ponds and pick up the little

---

1 **dust devils** small whirlwinds of dust
2 **alkaline** (al' kə līn) containing mineral salts
3 **mantle** a cloak or cape

Literature Model **205**

Motivating Activity

Ask students to recall stories and novels they've enjoyed because they were able to identify with the main character. Were the stories written from the first-person point of view, with the main character the "I" of the story? Discuss student selections using this point of view, along with familiar examples, such as *The Adventures of Huckleberry Finn*. How does a first-person point of view affect readers? (Readers empathize with the main character because they are able to see and feel and think along with that person.)

Teach

Guided Reading

- Why can't the narrator turn to look out the ambulance window? How does his paralysis affect the description of the story? Why does the character's paralysis limit the reader's view of the setting as well?

- What image triggers the narrator's flash-back? How does the rainbow he sees from the ambulance compare with those he recalls from his childhood? How might the rainbow symbolize the narrator's past and present? **L2**

Teach

Guided Reading

- How do the narrator's memories of his mother help advance the plot? What point does the anecdote about the narrator's mother make?
- What seems to be the story's central conflict? Encourage students to make predictions about its outcome. **L2**

Narrative Writing

Literature Model

frogs which came with the rain. "They are like you," she told me, "blessed by the rain, children of the water." When I was hurt she would take me in her arms and sing . . . .

> Sana, sana
>   colita de rana
> Si no sanas hoy
>   sanarás mañana . . . [4]

And her touch could drive away the worst of pains. But then the paralysis had come, and suddenly her prayers and her touch were not enough. Her face grew pale and thin, her eyes grew dark. "It is God's will," she had said.

"It's clearing now," Filomón said, "see, the sun is beginning to break through!"

"Yes, the sun!" Clepo shouted. He was Filomón's assistant, a small impish man with hunched shoulders. I noticed he limped when they loaded me on the ambulance.

"I think I see the top of the mountain!" Filomón cried cheerfully.

I was fully awake. The last images of the dreams faded as the darkness of the rain moved over us and eastward. Only occasional peals of thunder rumbled across the sky. Beneath us the ambulance rocked like a ship. Memories of my life moved in and out of my troubled consciousness. My mother's face appeared again and again. She had cried when they loaded me on the ambulance, but she knew it was necessary. The doctors there had helped as much as they

My mother's face appeared again and again. She had cried when they loaded me on the ambulance. . . .

could. Now, they insisted, they had to move me to this new hospital in the south where they specialized in taking care of crippled children. If there was any hope of regaining the use of my stiff limbs, it was there. So early in the morning they wheeled me on a gurney[5] to the outpatient area, loaded me onto Filomón's ambulance and the journey began.

"There!" Filomón shouted again, "There's the mountain!"

I tried to turn my head to see, but I couldn't. "What mountain?" I asked.

"Tortuga Mountain," he said and looked back, "it's right by the hospital. Don't worry, I'll stop so you can see it." He sounded happy, revived, after the long, monotonous drive across the desert. I felt a sense of urgency as he pulled the ambulance onto the shoulder of the road. We bounced along until he found the right spot, then he stopped the ambulance and turned off the motor. He climbed over the seat to where I lay strapped on the small cot.

---

4 Sana, sana / colita de rana / Si no sanas hoy / sanarás mañana . . . Spanish for "Get well, get well / little frogtail / If you don't get well today / you will tomorrow . . . ."
5 gurney (gurʹnē) a wheeled stretcher or cot used to move hospital patients

---

Cultural Connections

Being Bilingual

New Mexico has a large Mexican-American population, and many people speak both English and Spanish. Ask students to name some advantages of being bilingual—speaking two languages equally well. (A bilingual person is at home in two cultures.) Rudolfo Anaya, who grew up in a Spanish-speaking family and community, had to overcome language barriers to achieve success as a writer. In his desire to help other Spanish-speaking Americans, he has edited and translated several anthologies of their work.

Literature Model

"Ah, Filo," Clepo grumbled, "you've stopped here every time we bring a new kid. Don't you ever get tired of showing them that . . . mountain?"

"It's always a new kid," Filomón smiled as he loosened the straps that held me, "and each kid deserves to see the mountain from here. I want the boy to see it."

Filomón was an old man with a deep wrinkled face and rough, calloused hands, but he moved like a younger man as he lifted me tenderly so I could look out the window and see the mountain.

"There it is," he nodded, "that's Tortuga." His eyes sparkled as he looked at the volcanic mountain that loomed over the otherwise empty desert. It rose so magically into the gray sky that it seemed to hold the heavens and the earth together. It lay just east of the river valley, and the afternoon sun shining on it after the rain covered it with a sheen of silver.

"It's a magic mountain," Filomón whispered, and I felt his heart beating against me as he held me. "See!" he whispered, "See!" I tried to see beyond the volcanic slabs and granite boulders which formed the outline of a turtle, I tried to sense the steady rhythm of his pulse which seemed to be draining into the giant mountain, but I couldn't. I was too tired, and my faith in magic had drained out the night the paralysis came and in the ensuing nights and days

His eyes sparkled as he looked at the volcanic mountain that loomed over the otherwise empty desert.

which I spent without movement on the hospital bed.

I shook my head.

"That's okay," he smiled, "it comes slowly sometimes. But now at least you know it's there—" He seemed very tired. It had been a long trip for him too. He had had to keep the ambulance on course through one of the worst storms I could remember. But now we were almost there.

"Where's the hospital?" I asked.

"It's on this side of the river, you can't see it from here. See the smoke rising in the valley? That's Agua Bendita.[6] It's a small town, but people come from all over to bathe in the mineral waters from the springs which drain from the mountain—"

"It's a town full of old arthritics," Clepo giggled, "old people who think they can escape the pains of old age by dipping themselves in the mountain's water, but they can't run fast enough from death!" He slapped his thigh and laughed.

Filomón didn't answer. He sat beside the cot and looked out the window into the desert. "Even as terrible as the storm was for us, it will be good for the plants in the spring. After a good, wet winter the desert blooms like a garden," he nodded and rolled a cigarette. There was something about the

---

6 **Agua Bendita** (ä′ gwə ben dē′ tə) Spanish for "holy water"

Literature Model **207**

Teach

Guided Reading

- What does their dialogue reveal about Filomón's and Clepo's characters?
- How might Filomón's comments about the mountain foreshadow future events? **L2**

Viewing and Representing

Painting the Scene

Invite students to imagine they are artists whose job is to illustrate *Tortuga* by painting the scene described on this page. Ask what words and phrases would help them paint the scene, especially the mountain ("loomed . . . empty . . . gray . . . shining . . . sheen of silver . . . volcanic slabs . . . granite boulders . . . outline of a turtle"). Discuss what colors they'd use in their paintings, and why. Volunteers might like to paint or draw the scene.

Teach

Guided Reading

- How does Filomón describe the desert and the river valley? What does his description tell the reader about his beliefs? Why is it fitting that Filomón converted a hearse into an ambulance?

- How does the reader discover more information about the narrator's physical condition? Why is it more effective to show this information through dialogue than to tell it in a lengthy description? **L2**

Narrative Writing

way he spoke, the strength of his face, that reminded me of someone I had known—my grandfather perhaps, but I hadn't thought of him in years.

"These old villages cling to the river like the beads of a rosary,"[7] he continued, thinking aloud.

"Whoever crosses this desert has a lot of praying to do," Clepo agreed, "it's a journey of death."

"No, a journey of life. Our forefathers have wandered up and down this river valley for a long, long time. First the Indians roamed up and down this river, then others came, but they all stopped here at this same place: the springs of Tortuga, the place of the healing water—"

He talked and smoked. The dull sun shone through the window and played on the swirling smoke. I was fully awake now, but I felt feverish, and I couldn't help wondering what a strange day it had been to ride all this way with the old man and his assistant. I shivered, but not from the cold. The inside of the ambulance was now stifling. It glowed with white smoke and golden light which poured through the window. Filomón's eyes shone.

"How long have you been bringing kids to the hospital?" I asked.

"As long as I can remember," Filomón answered. "I bought this old hearse[8] in a

> *"Whoever crosses this desert has a lot of praying to do," Clepo agreed, "it's a journey of death."*

junk yard and I fixed it up like an ambulance. I've been transporting kids ever since."

"We get thirty dollars a kid, dead or alive," Clepo laughed. "And we get to hear a lot of interesting stories. We've taken every kind of diseased body there is to the hospital. Why, Filo and I could become doctors if we wanted to, couldn't we Filo? But we don't know anything about you. You slept most of the way." He leaned over the seat and peered at me.

"He's tired," Filomón said.

"Yeah, but he's awake now," Clepo grinned.

"So how did he get crippled? I know it ain't polio, I know polio. And how come his left hand is bandaged, huh? There's quite a story there, but he hasn't said a word!"

He seemed put out that I had slept most of the way and had not told the story of my past. But since the paralysis the past didn't matter. It was as if everything had died, except the dreams and the memories which kept haunting me. And even those were useless against the terrible weight which had fallen over me and which I cursed until I could curse no more.

---

7 rosary (rō′ zər ē) a string of beads used in prayer to keep count
8 hearse an automobile used to carry the corpse during a funeral

Writing in the Real World

Discussing Writing Processes

Rudolfo Anaya says he tries to write every day when he's working on a novel. "I tell my students that writing is not learned by formula, it is learned by writing a lot. There is no shortcut for work in writing." About revising, he says, "Writing is never quite learned. I have to rewrite and rewrite each manuscript before I'm satisfied." Ask students to compare their own writing process with Anaya's.

Literature Model

Teach

Guided Reading

- How would you describe the relationship between Filomón and Clepo? What new insights does their exchange on this page provide? Why do you think the cynical Clepo stays with the optimistic Filomón?
- How does Filomón's description of the river and the desert in spring appeal to the senses? What images does the description bring to mind? **L2**

Rufino Tamayo, *Interior with Alarm Clock*, 1928

Literature Model **209**

Viewing the Art

Rufino Tamayo, *Interior with Alarm Clock*, 1928

Rufino Tamayo was born in Oaxaca, Mexico, in 1899. As an artist, he often depicted strange, enigmatic situations, and *Interior with Alarm Clock* is an example. Here, the viewer's eye moves through the heavy-lined interior to the mountains beyond, which seem liberated by comparison. The clock's missing numbers give a sense of fractured time, of waiting.

Teach

Guided Reading

- Do you accept, wonder about, or reject the "magic" Filomón refers to—his faith in the mystical powers of Tortuga and its healing waters? Do you think the narrator will come to share Filomón's faith? **L2**

Narrative Writing

"Do you take the kids back?" I asked.

"No, we don't!" Clepo said, "That's against the rules!"

"I picked you up," Filomón reminded him.

"I was hitch-hiking," Clepo said smartly, "somebody would have picked me up."

"You were lost. I found you in the middle of a sandstorm, crying. Lucky for you I came along."

"I wasn't crying, I had sand in my eyes," Clepo insisted.

Filomón smiled. "It doesn't matter, you've been a good assistant." That seemed to satisfy Clepo, he grunted and sat back down. Filomón drew close and looked at me. "We can't take anybody back, that's not our job. But when you get better you can make the trip back home by yourself. Just wait till spring, and you'll be better. I know it looks bad now, but in the spring the river comes alive and the desert dresses like a young bride. The lizards come out to play in the warm sun, and even the mountain moves—" He touched my forehead with his fingers, then he leaned close to me and I felt his forehead touch mine, perhaps he was just leaning to retrieve one of the straps to tie me up again, but I felt his forehead brush mine, and I felt a relief from the paralysis which I hadn't felt since it came. Then he tied the strap and climbed back into the driver's seat.

> *. . . I couldn't move. I could only turn my head and watch the mountain across the valley.*

"Filomón says you gotta keep your eyes on the mountain," Clepo said to fill in the silence.

"Well, it's helped us," Filomón answered, "it's been our faith in this wasteland . . . and it's helped a lot of kids. There's a strong power there."

He started the ambulance and let it coast down the long slope of the hill into the valley. I knew he was still looking at the mountain, still feeling the strange power that resided there for him.

"The water from the mountain springs is holy," he mused aloud, "long ago the place was used as a winter ceremonial ground by the Indians. They came to purify themselves by bathing in the warm waters . . . the water of the turtle . . . Later, when the Spaniards came, they called the springs Los Ojos de la Tortuga,[9] and when they discovered the waters could cure many illnesses they called the village Agua Bendita . . ."

"Who lives here?" I asked. We had entered the edge of the small town. Through the window I could see the tops of rundown gas stations, motels and cafes. There was a dilapidated movie house, a brownstone hotel, and many signs which

---

9 **Los Ojos de la Tortuga** (lōs ō' hōs dā lä tôr tōō' gə) Spanish for "the eyes of the turtle"

Cultural Connections

History

Native Americans have probably lived in the region that is now New Mexico for more than 20,000 years. The Spanish arrived in the early 1500s, and Spain ruled the region for about two centuries. Later Mexico ruled until the United States took possession in 1848, after the Mexican War. Thus, New Mexico's history helps explain today's large Mexican-American and Native-American populations.

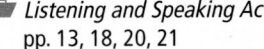
creaked in the wind as they advertised the hot mineral baths.

"Mostly old people who come for the baths, people who work at the hospital, and a few of the old people who try to make a living from the small farms along the river—"

Filomón turned the ambulance and I caught a glimpse of a weathered sign that read *Crippled Children and Orphans Hospital.* The arrow pointed up the hill, so from the highway which ran through the small town we had to turn up the hill again towards the washed-out buildings which

huddled together at the top. I struggled to turn to see more, instinctively, as I had so many times before, but it was useless, I couldn't move. I could only turn my head and watch the mountain across the valley. An air of hopelessness brooded over the dull mountain as the remaining winter clouds huddled at its peak. It seemed lost and out of place in the immense desert which surrounded it, and I wondered what secret rested in its core. Whatever it was, it was something that made Filomón's voice ring with hope and made his eyes sparkle even after the fatigue of the long journey.

Teach

Guided Practice

- What is the mood at the end of the passage? What details help create this mood?

Additional Resources

 Fine Art Transparencies, 19–24

Listening and Speaking Activities, pp. 13, 18, 20, 21

Thinking and Study Skills, pp. 10, 13

Linking Writing and Literature

Assess

Evaluation Rubrics

As your students discuss the selection, either in small groups or as a class, encourage them to begin with a personal response. The student responses on this page might be used as a starting point.

Look for evidence that students
- have read the selection
- can state some of the writer's ideas in their own words
- understand the writer's point of view
- have connected the content to their own knowledge and experiences
- understand the ideas and implications of the selection

Some possible responses to the discussion questions on this page:
1. Filomón, because of his good nature, his hope, his optimism, and his faith; Clepo, because of his cynicism and realistic outlook on life; or the narrator, because of his lively mind and curiosity
2. The narrator's illness and his trip to the hospital; the narrator's memories of his mother
3. The mood was sad and depressing, and the gray skies, gray mountain, and dimly lit desert added to that feeling.
4. The reader might not identify as strongly with the narrator.

Close

Encourage students to write personal narratives or short stories in which, like Anaya, they explore the meaning of a personal experience.

Narrative Writing

Literature Model

Linking Writing and Literature

Readers Respond to the Model

How does Rudolfo A. Anaya use character and complication to create mood in his narrative?

Explore Rudolfo A. Anaya's narrative by answering these questions. Then read what other students liked about Anaya's narrative.

1. Choose a character that you particularly liked. Explain how Anaya's description of this character contributes to the narrative.
2. What is the basic conflict in the narrative? What background information does the author provide to set up this conflict and make it appear realistic?
3. How did the author use setting to create mood?
4. How would the story have changed if the author had told it in the third person rather than the first?

What Students Say

❝The boy was my favorite character because, although he had a handicap, he still believed he would be healed someday. These details made the boy's character very realistic. The vivid description of Clepo, from his little limp to his facial expressions, also made that character seem real. I liked Filomón's story about the first inhabitants of the land and about the significance of Tortuga Mountain because it showed the importance of knowing your background. I would recommend this selection to a friend because it gives you an idea of how other cultures tell stories about healing and myths. ❞

Torré Triplett

❝The dominant mood of the selection was uneasiness. The author set up that mood from the beginning by showing the boy thinking about how different and unfamiliar the weather was in the desert than at his home. Just as the setting was unfamiliar, the hospital where the boy was being taken was also unfamiliar. The boy had no idea what awaited him. ❞

Lucino Vences

UNIT 4 Review

Reflecting on the Unit

Summarize what you learned in this unit by answering the following questions.

❶ What are the characteristics of personal narrative writing, and what strategies can help you find ideas for your personal narratives?

❷ What are the basic elements of a work of fiction, and what characterizes plot?

❸ How does dialogue serve narrative writing?

❹ What is an anecdote? How can anecdotes serve theme in fiction and nonfiction?

❺ What are the important aspects of plot summary and conflict analysis and the uses of each?

Adding to Your Portfolio

CHOOSE A SELECTION FOR YOUR PORTFOLIO Look over the narrative writing you have done during this unit. Select a completed piece of writing to put into your portfolio. The piece you choose should show some or all of the following:

- the basic narrative elements—characters, setting, plot, and point of view
- a character in a conflict or complication that leads to a climax and a resolution
- dialogue that advances plot or reveals character
- an anecdote that reinforces the theme of the story

Reflecting on Your Choice

Attach a note to the piece you chose, explaining briefly why you chose it and what you learned from writing it.

SET GOALS How can you improve your writing? What skill will you focus on the next time you write?

Writing Across the Curriculum

MAKE A LITERATURE CONNECTION Select a work of literature you read in class this year—a story, novel, or personal narrative. Then write a one- or two-page story introduction that would get someone interested in reading the story. Include setting, characters, complication, and resolution.

Review **213**

Review

Reflecting on the Unit

You may have students respond to Reflecting on the Unit in writing or through discussion.

Writing Across the Curriculum

As they do this assignment, have students think of themselves as book editors. Their introductions will be printed on the book jackets. An effective introduction could put their books or stories on the best-seller list.

Adding to Your Portfolio

If students are having difficulty making their selections, have them work with one or two peer editors. Encourage them to work together to select the best pieces of work.

Portfolio Evaluation

If you grade the portfolio selections, you might want to award two marks—one each for content and form. Explain your assessment criteria before students make their selections. Commend

- experimentation with creative prewriting techniques
- clear, concise writing in which the main idea, audience, and purpose are evident
- successful revisions
- work that shows a flair for language

✔ ASSESSMENT OPTIONS

📁 *Tests With Answer Key and Rubrics*
Unit 4 Choice A Test, p. 13
Unit 4 Choice B Test, p. 14
Unit 4 Composition Objective Test, pp. 15-16

💾 *Testmaker*
Unit 4 Choice A Test
Unit 4 Choice B Test
Unit 4 Composition Objective Test

You may wish to administer one of these tests as a mastery test.

📼 *MindJogger Videoquizzes*

213

Expository Writing

Viewing the Art

This photograph of ice floes south of the Antarctic Circle off Adelaide Island illustrates various aspects of nature. The large blocks of ice floating in the cold sea and the snow-covered hills in the distance call to mind a brutally cold climate. Yet the sunlight reflected on the water and shining through the ice conveys a sense of oncoming warmer weather. The breakup of ice signals a change in weather and hints that further melting will take place.

Interpret and Analyze Use the following questions for discussion:
- What is the mood of the photograph? What details convey that mood?
- What features of nature does the photograph highlight?
- How does this photograph suggest an environment in flux?

Discussing the Quotation

This quotation is from "Exploring Antarctic Ice," a magazine article by Jane Ellen Stevens (born 1948). Encourage students to discuss their responses to the quotation. Ask students to tell why they agree or disagree with the point the author makes. Ask students why, in their opinion, Stevens uses the words *presumably* and *perhaps* and what effect these words have on the quotation's meaning. To find out more information about the author and the article from which this quotation is taken, see *Glencoe Literature,* Course 5, p. 531.

Writing Prompt Have students write a paragraph explaining how the photograph might illustrate the concerns raised in the quotation.

"What disruptions would occur if a warming or cooling trend were to shrink or expand the winter sea ice? Presumably ocean currents would shift, perhaps causing drastic shifts in climate."

—Jane Ellen Stevens, "Exploring Antarctic Ice"

214

Resource Manager

Planning Resources
- *Lesson Plans*
- *Block Scheduling*

Transparencies
- *Bellringer*
- *Daily Language Practice*
- *Fine Art*
- *Two-Minute Skill Drill*
- *Writing Process*

Other Print Resources
- *Composition Enrichment*
- *Composition Practice*
- *Composition Reteaching*
- *Cooperative Learning Activities*
- *Glencoe Literature Library*
- *Grammar and Composition Handbook*
- *Grammar Workbook*

- *Listening and Speaking Activities*
- *Research Paper and Report Writing*
- *Sentence-Combining Practice*
- *Tests with Answer Key and Rubrics*
- *Thinking and Study Skills*
- *Writing Across the Curriculum*
- *Writing Assessment and Evaluation Rubrics*
- *Writing in the Real World*

UNIT 5

Expository Writing

Writing in the Real World: *Anastasia Toufexis*   216

Lesson 5.1   **Writing to Inform and Explain**   220

Lesson 5.2   **Knowing Your Audience**   224

Lesson 5.3   **Writing About a Process**   228

Lesson 5.4   **Writing About Cause and Effect**   232

Lesson 5.5   **Comparing and Contrasting**   236

Lesson 5.6   **Writing Effective Definitions**   240

Lesson 5.7   **Using Graphs in Exposition**   244

Lesson 5.8   **Writing a News Article**   248

Lesson 5.9   **Taking an Essay Test**   252

Lesson 5.10   **Writing About Literature: Comparing and Contrasting Literature**   258

Writing Process in Action   262

Literature Model: from *A Book of Bees . . . and How to Keep Them* by Sue Hubbell   266

Unit 5 Review   275

Objectives

- To develop, through example and instruction, an understanding of expository writing
- To learn written and graphic techniques that will help an expository writer explain processes, causes and effects, categories, and similarities and differences
- To apply the techniques learned to writing an informative article

✔ ASSESSMENT OPTIONS

 Tests with Answer Key & Rubrics
Unit 5 Choice A Test, p. 17
Unit 5 Choice B Test, p. 18
Unit 5 Composition Objective Test, pp. 19–20

💾 *Testmaker*
Unit 5 Choice A Test
Unit 5 Choice B Test
Unit 5 Composition Objective Test

You may wish to administer either the Unit 5 Choice A Test or the Unit 5 Choice B Test as a pretest.

Key to Ability Levels

L1 Level 1 activities are within the ability range of students.

L2 Level 2 activities are within the ability range of average students.

L3 Level 3 activities are more challenging activities.

215

 Video
- *MindJogger Videoquizzes*

 Software
- *Presentation Plus!*
- *Revising with Style*
- *Testmaker*
- *Writer's Assistant*
- *Writer's Choice Puzzlemaker*

🖥 **Web Sites**
- *writerschoice.glencoe.com*
- *lit.glencoe.com*

Focus

Lesson Overview

Objective

- To explore the process behind writing a science feature for a national magazine

Skills

- varying sentence structure; writing a review of a science feature article; evaluating components of expository writing

Critical Thinking

- generating new information; analyzing

Listening and Speaking

- discussing; formulating questions

 Bellringer
Daily Language Activity

When students enter the classroom, have this assignment on the board: *How many hours of sleep do you get each night, on average? Write a paragraph describing the amount of sleep you need in order to function normally. Explain why you need that amount.*

Grammar Link to the Bellringer

Have students identify each type of sentence they used in their paragraphs (simple, compound, complex).

See also *Daily Language Practice*

Motivating Activity

Take a class poll to figure out the average number of hours students sleep per night. How many hours does the whole class average? Tell students that by exploring their answers to questions like these, they can draw their own conclusions about the importance of sleep.

Writing in the Real World

Expository Writing

L ike other kinds of exposition written for a general audience, science writing uses plain talk and concrete examples to bring a subject to life. The following is an expository article by Anastasia Toufexis, health and behavior editor at *Time* magazine.

from "Drowsy America"

by Anastasia Toufexis

A t 7 a.m. or 6 or maybe even 5, the blare of the alarm breaks the night, and another workday dawns. As an arm gropes to stop the noise and the whole body rebels against the harsh call of morning, the thought is almost always the same: *I have to get more sleep.* That night, after 17 or 18 hours of fighting traffic, facing deadlines and racing the clock,

the weary soul collapses into bed once again for an all-too-brief respite. And just before the slide into slumber, the nagging thought returns: *I have to get more sleep.*

Millions of Americans make this complaint, but how many do anything about it? Sleep is a biological imperative, but do people consider it as vital as food or drink? Not in today's rock-around-the-clock world. Not in a society in which mothers work, stores don't close, assembly lines never stop. . . .

To some night owls, the very idea of spending more than 20 years of one's life in idle snoozing is appalling. Listen to Harvey Bass. Between a job as a computer-systems manager in New York City and free-lance

consulting, he gets no more than five hours of sleep a night and sometimes only two. He admits that the schedule occasionally leaves him with a "tingling around my head." Even so, he says, "if I live a normal life span, I will have lived 20% more than the average person because I'm awake."

That may sound like an attractive exchange, but scientists are increasingly making the case that forgoing rest is a foolish and often perilous bargain. In fact, evidence is mounting that sleep deprivation has become one of the most pervasive health problems facing the U.S. . . . [S]tudies show that mental alertness and performance can suffer badly. "Sleepiness is one of the least recognized

216 Unit 5 Expository Writing

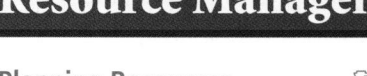

Resource Manager

Planning Resources

- *Lesson Plans*

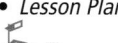 **Transparencies**

- *Bellringer*
- *Daily Language Practice*
- *Writing Process* 11, 23–27

Other Print Resources

- *Cooperative Learning Activities,* pp. 21–24
- *Thinking and Study Skills,* pp. 3, 4, 13
- *Writing Assessment and Evaluation Rubrics*
- *Writing in the Real World,* pp. 17–20

sources of disability in our society," declares Dr. Charles Pollak, head of the sleep-disorder center at Cornell University's New York Hospital. . . . "[P]eople who don't get enough sleep can't think, they can't make appropriate judgments, they can't maintain long attention spans."

Such mental fatigue can be as threatening as a heart attack. Recent evidence indicates that drowsiness is a leading cause of traffic fatalities and industrial mishaps.

A Writer's Process

Prewriting
Getting the Facts

In preparing her story on sleep, Toufexis enlisted the help of correspondents in six *Time* bureaus around the country. She sent each one a query explaining the gist of the story, a list of questions to research, and the names of a few information sources.

Toufexis worked with a team in order to gather information from all around the country. "There would be no way to get national coverage unless we had an enormous amount of time [for me to] travel around the country, stopping in each and every place to get experts' views and analyses of their research plus finding people locally," she explained.

Local people—pilots, students, stockbrokers, truck drivers, working moms—were critical to the story. "We didn't want a dry academic treatise on the lack of sleep," Toufexis said. "We wanted to humanize the problem, make it alive."

Toufexis did considerable reading herself, in books, in *Time*'s clip folder of articles on sleep, in professional journals, and in her bulging file of reports on sleep research. She also interviewed several experts in the field.

After a month of detective work, Toufexis and her team had a stack of research material standing a foot and a half high that revealed a national health problem. The problem ranged from scary tales of sleepy airplane pilots to statistics showing that up to 200,000 truck accidents a year may be related to fatigue.

Drafting/Revising
Selecting and Condensing Facts

Before trying to turn the mountain of data into a lively article, Toufexis laid some important groundwork. She organized her notes into topics. Then she typed the most important facts, studies, and quotes into her computer. The result: three or four pages of information for each topic. Next, Toufexis noted

Press conferences, such as the one on "America's Sleep Debt," sometimes offer a forum for individuals to present their research on a topic.

Teach

Discussion Prompts

- What part did research play in helping Toufexis write her article?
- How important do you think it is for an article like this one to relate science to everyday life? Explain.
- Describe Toufexis's drafting process. Why, do you think, did she spend so much time writing the lead paragraph?
- How does Toufexis try to keep her readers' attention?
- How do you develop ideas for science-related articles?
- How does Toufexis's position as health and behavior editor at *Time* magazine provide her with the opportunity to reach a diverse group of readers?
- How do you choose a topic that will educate as well as interest your readers?

Additional Resources

Writing Process Transparencies, 11, 23–27

Writing in the Real World, pp. 17–20

Cooperative Learning Activities

Thinking and Study Skills, pp. 3–4, 13

Assess

Analyzing the Media Connection

1. Toufexis reels her readers in by describing a scenario they themselves have experienced.
2. Toufexis begins two sentences with the phrase "Not in." Answers will vary. Students may respond that the parallelism functions to create rhythm and to underscore the idea that people are too busy to worry about getting enough sleep.
3. The anecdote serves to illustrate the idea presented in the previous paragraph that people don't consider sleep to be of great importance.

Expository Writing (sidebar)

the length her story should be— 4,000 to 5,000 words.

Toufexis's first challenge was to write a gripping lead. "Within the first two or three paragraphs, I have to be clear about why I'm doing the story so I can get people interested," she said. "Then I try to hit them with the billboard: Why is this important? How does it affect you?" For this article, Toufexis chose to begin with the common experience of struggling awake to an alarm clock.

With her lead resolved, Toufexis began writing. She presented her main idea and selected key research to support it. She explained the research clearly and then illustrated it with examples from her interviews. For instance, she cited one study that found that adolescents need at least nine and a half hours of sleep a night. Do they get it? Toufexis answered this question with two examples. One example came from a fifteen-year-old from California who was horrified at the notion of sleeping nearly ten hours a night. The second example came from teachers who were interviewed and described "sleepy youngsters arriving late to class. . . . "

All over the country, the correspondents found that school, part-time work, and social demands keep teens from getting necessary sleep.

After selecting and condensing material, Toufexis had a complete draft. It was still "way too long, portions were unbalanced, but the draft was finished," Toufexis said. She let the draft sit for a couple of days before starting to revise.

Revising/Editing
Checking Accuracy and Sense

After a week of revising her story, Toufexis released it to the senior editor, who edited it for interest and sense. The magazine's managing editor and other high-level editors also reviewed the story, as did the correspondents, who were asked to respond to a list of fact-checking questions.

The week before Toufexis's story ran, she and a researcher worked long hours improving the story by responding to questions of grammar, punctuation, sense, and style raised by *Time*'s copyeditors. As the deadline neared, Toufexis and her researcher fit the story to the layout, wrote captions, and held a final review with the science editor. Finally, "Drowsy America" was ready for publication.

Publishing/Presenting
Making People Aware

Was all the effort worth it? "I hope my work has an impact," Toufexis said, "but for the most part, I work to get a piece of information across. If I make people aware that a subject is something they should think of, I've done my job."

Through collaborative effort, a large group of people made this cover story possible.

Cultural Connections

Understanding Differences

Toufexis states that the fast pace of American life makes people sleep deprived. Many workers labor long hours in high-pressure, stressful jobs. You might ask students to name other factors in modern society that prevent people from getting the sleep they need. Tell students that, in some countries with very warm climates, people observe a period of rest during the afternoon hours. Most offices, stores, and museums close during this time. As a result, the pace of life there is much more relaxed than it is in American society. Ask students if they would prefer living in a more relaxed culture.

Examining Writing in the Real World

Analyzing the Media Connection

Discuss these questions about the article on page 216.

1. How does Toufexis capture the reader's interest with her opening paragraph?

2. What example of parallelism does Toufexis use in the second paragraph? How does it contribute to the impact of the article?

3. Why do you think Toufexis includes the anecdote about Harvey Bass?

4. How do the quotations from a sleep-disorder expert advance the story?

5. Why do you think Toufexis choose the title "Drowsy America" for her article? How appropriate is this title?

Analyzing a Writer's Process

Discuss these questions about Anastasia Toufexis's writing process.

1. For what reason did Toufexis enlist the help of other *Time* correspondents?

2. How did Toufexis and her team gather information on sleep deprivation?

3. How did Toufexis organize the data she and her team collected?

4. Describe Toufexis's writing process. Do you think it is effective? Why or why not?

5. What was the role of each editor who reviewed Toufexis's article?

Vary sentence structure to create interest.

Reread the media connection. Note how the sentences vary in structure and in length. In addition to simple sentences, there are compound sentences: *It was "way too long, portions were unbalanced, but it was finished,"* . . . There are also complex sentences: *As the deadline neared, Toufexis and her researcher fit the story to the layout.* . . .

Follow these directions to create different types of sentences.

1. Write a simple sentence or choose one in the media connection.

2. Rework it, making it a compound sentence.

3. Rework the simple sentence again to make it part of a complex sentence.

4. Rework your compound sentence into a compound-complex sentence.

5. Write a fifth related sentence, and tell what type of sentence it is.

See Lesson 13.3, pages 545–546; and Lesson 13.4, pages 547–548.

4. The quotations drive home the idea that sleep deprivation is a serious problem.

5. Toufexis chose the title to evoke the image of a country whose citizens are in a state of constant drowsiness. Most students will respond that the title suits the contents of the article.

Analyzing a Writer's Process

1. Toufexis enlisted the help of other *Time* correspondents in order to gather information from around the country.

2. Toufexis and her team interviewed experts in the field of sleep deprivation, as well as ordinary citizens. Toufexis also read articles and reports on the subject.

3. She organized the data into topics and under each topic typed relevant facts, studies, and quotes.

4. Toufexis began by writing the lead and then wrote the body of the article. In the body, she explained the key research and then illustrated it with specific examples. Answers will vary.

5. The senior editor edited Toufexis's story for interest and sense. The managing editor and other high-level editors also reviewed the story. The copy editors edited the story for grammar, punctuation, sense, and style.

Reteaching

Remind students that a science feature should explain a topic's importance—how it could affect the reader.

Enrichment

Invite students to find a science feature in a specialized magazine and rewrite it for a general audience.

Close

Invite students to study professional examples of science writing. Journals such as *Scientific American* and *Discover* are good sources of science articles written for the general public.

Grammar Link

Answers

(*Answers will vary. The first three sentences in the exercise are provided as examples.*)

1. The ruby-throated hummingbird is one of the smallest birds in the country.

2. The ruby-throated hummingbird is one of the smallest birds in the country, and the eagle is one of the largest birds.

3. The ruby-throated hummingbird, which is one of the smallest birds in the country, grows to a length of four inches.

219

Focus

Lesson Overview

Objective
- To become familiar with six forms of expository writing and to practice using them

Skills
- writing an expository essay

Critical Thinking
- analyzing; classifying; synthesizing; comparing

Listening and Speaking
- discussing

Bellringer
Daily Language Activity

When students enter the classroom, have this assignment on the board: *List three things you understand or know how to do and could explain in writing.*

Grammar Link to the Bellringer

Have students write an inverted sentence about one of the three things they listed in the Bellringer.

See also *Daily Language Practice*

Motivating Activity

Have students decide what forms of expository writing would help them explain the topics they listed in the Bellringer activity—for example, game instructions, a how-to article, or a recipe.

Expository Writing

LESSON 5.1

Writing to Inform and Explain

Expository writing is what you use to give directions, explain a new term or idea, compare one thing to another, or explain how to do something. In the model below, Mary Crow Dog and Richard Erdoes explain the importance of the tiyospaye[1] *in Lakota Sioux society.*

Literature Model

> At the center of the old Sioux society was the *tiyospaye*, the extended family group, the basic hunting band, which included grandparents, uncles, aunts, in-laws, and cousins. The tiyospaye was like a warm womb cradling all within it. Kids were never alone, always fussed over by not one but several mothers, watched and taught by several fathers. The real father, as a matter of fact, selected a second father, some well-thought-of-relative with special skills as a hunter or medicine man, to help him bring up a boy, and such a person was called "Father" too. And the same was true for the girls. Grandparents in our tribe always held a special place in caring for the little ones, because they had more time to devote to them, when the father was out hunting, taking the mother with him to help with the skinning and butchering.
>
> Mary Crow Dog and Richard Erdoes,
> *Lakota Woman*

The topic sentence defines "tiyospaye."

Supporting sentences use comparison and several examples to explain the specific qualities of a tiyospaye.

1 tiyospaye tē′ yō shpä′ yā

Resource Manager

Planning Resources
- *Lesson Plans*

Transparencies
- *Bellringer*
- *Daily Language Practice*
- *Fine Art 25–28*
- *Two-Minute Skill Drill*
- *Writing Process 11, 23–27*

Other Print Resources
- *Composition Enrichment, p. 34*
- *Composition Practice, p. 34*
- *Composition Reteaching, p. 34*
- *Cooperative Learning Activities, pp. 21–24*
- *Listening and Speaking Activities, pp. 15–16*
- *Research Paper and Report Writing, pp. 43–48*

- *Sentence-Combining Practice, pp. 32–33*
- *Thinking and Study Skills, pp. 11, 13*
- *Writing Across the Curriculum*
- *Writing Assessment and Evaluation Rubrics*

Choose a Kind of Expository Writing

An essay is the most general form of expository writing. The introduction of an essay includes a thesis statement, a one-sentence summary of purpose. The body is made up of one or more paragraphs of details that support the thesis. The conclusion states the implications of the thesis. Within the general essay format, the specific kind of exposition you write depends on your goal, as the chart shows.

Six Kinds of Expository Writing		
Kind	**Attribute**	**Examples**
Process Explanation	Uses step-by-step organization to explain how something happens, works, or is done	How do you run a computer program? How are homes built? How does the human body process food?
Cause and Effect	Identifies the causes and/or effects of something and examines the relationship between causes and effects	What causes freckles? What causes sunspots? What are the effects of poverty on children?
Comparison and Contrast	Examines similarities and differences to find relationships and draw conclusions	Compare jazz and rap, or blues and country music. Compare and contrast basketball and ballet.
Definition	Explains a term or concept by listing and examining its qualities or characteristics	What is hypothermia? What is "grandstanding"? What was the Harlem Renaissance?
Classification	Organizes subjects into categories and examines qualities or characteristics of those categories	What organisms are considered fungi? How would you characterize the writing of Stephen King?
Problem and Solution	Examines aspects of a complex problem and explores or proposes possible solutions	How can your community increase literacy? What can be done to protect wilderness areas?

Grammar Tip

In the editing stage, check that words used to represent themselves have been italicized or underlined. For more information about italics, see Lesson 21.10, pages 758–759.

Journal Writing

If you were asked to write about any aspect of school life for your school's newspaper, what would you write about? Choose a topic and tell which kind of expository writing would help you meet your goal.

Teach

Using the Model

After students read the Literature Model on student page 220, have them give a synopsis of what they learned about the Lakota Sioux family hierarchy. How does the model define the term *tiyospaye?* Ask students to compare the Lakota Sioux family hierarchy with their own families. How are they alike? different? **L2**

Finding Examples

Write the six kinds of expository writing from student page 221 on the board and have students suggest examples of each. Students might include a cookbook recipe for process explanation or a field guide for classification. **L2**

Two-Minute Skill Drill

Have students complete these inverted sentences, making the verb and subject agree.

Sitting beside me (was, were)
Included on the list (was, were)
In the dark cave (live, lives)
Over the hill (come, comes)

See also *Two-Minute Skill Drill Transparancy 5.1*

Journal Writing Tip

Identifying Purpose If students have difficulty deciding what kind of expository writing is best for their newspaper article, ask them to state the article's purpose.

Teach

Using the Model

After students identify the kinds of expository writing in the Literature Model on student page 222, have them suggest other questions the authors might answer about the topic, using other kinds of expository writing. **L2**

Additional Resourses

 Writing Process Transparencies, 11, 23–27

 For further stimuli for expository writing, see *Fine Art Transparencies*, 25–28

 Writing Across the Curriculum

Cooperative Learning Activities

Thinking and Study Skills, pp. 11, 13

Sentence-Combining Practice, pp. 32–33

Listening and Speaking Activities, pp. 15–16

Composition Practice, p. 34

Expository Writing

Revising Tip

Whenever you revise expository writing, ask yourself whether using a different kind of exposition would help you develop your topic more clearly or completely.

What is the cause-and-effect relationship between human settlement and an increase in avalanches?

How do the writers explain reforestation in Ursental, Switzerland, as the solution to a problem?

Combine Various Kinds of Exposition

To fully explore the qualities and characteristics of a topic, you will most often need to use a combination of expository types. In the following passage, authors Betsy Armstrong and Knox Williams write about an avalanche-prone area in Switzerland. The authors begin by explaining how forests tend to inhibit avalanches. Then they discuss what happens when areas are deforested for building or heating purposes. Finally, the authors describe how reforestation can prevent avalanches. As you read, try to pick out the specific kinds of expository writing the authors use.

Literature Model

In many cases, the villagers made the avalanche problem worse. Before settlement, dense forests covered many of the steep slopes above the valleys. The forests inhibited large avalanches, since catastrophic avalanches do not originate in a heavy forest, and avalanches traveling into such a forest will often slow as the snow encounters the trees. [A forest] tends to diminish the speed of the snow and break up the avalanche. However, villagers often cut down the forests for building and heating purposes. In many areas the trees never grew back, leaving the slopes bare and smooth—a perfect track for the run of a snow avalanche. A prime example of deforestation is in the valley of Ursental in central Switzerland. Above the town of Andermatt, there remains just a wedge of trees, while the remainder of the steep slope is bare. Up valley, near the Furka Pass, is the town of Hospental, which also maintains its own protective wedge of trees. As the story is told, the inhabitants of the valley systematically cut down the forests that covered the steep slopes on both sides. Almost too late they realized their mistake: they saw that on the bare, treeless slopes, huge avalanches began descending to the valley floor, making travel between towns extremely dangerous. All tree-cutting stopped and the wedges of trees above the towns were preserved. Reforestation, the systematic planting of trees, continues today in the Ursental, to thicken the wedges that are periodically thinned by avalanches.

Betsy Armstrong and Knox Williams, *The Avalanche Book*

MEETING INDIVIDUAL NEEDS English Language Learners

Summarizing

Students who are less familiar with the English language might have difficulty understanding the Literature Model on page 222. Have them work with a partner to summarize the main ideas before they try to identify the kinds of expository strategies used in the model.

Write an Explanation of an Event

Examine the painting *Castle of Cards*. Who do you think the four people are, and how might they be related? What's going on? Write an essay explaining the event you see in the painting.

PURPOSE To explain an event portrayed in a piece of art
AUDIENCE Your teacher and classmates
LENGTH 2–3 paragraphs

WRITING RUBRICS To write an effective explanation of an event, you should

- combine the kinds of exposition you use
- include an introduction, a body, and a conclusion

Using Computers

SPELLING Check your explanation for correct spelling. List any consistent spelling errors you make and store them in the spell-check section labeled "Options" on your computer so that these words will be automatically checked and corrected in the future.

Zinaida Serebriakova, *Castle of Cards*, 1918

Grammar Link

Make subjects and verbs agree in inverted sentences.

Subjects and verbs must agree in inverted sentences—sentences in which the subject follows the verb. The selection from *Lakota Woman* begins with this inverted sentence:

> *At the center of the old Sioux society was the tiospaye. . . .*

Rewrite each sentence below, adding the verb that agrees with the subject.

1. There (is, are) usually many people in an extended family group.
2. Included in the extended family (is, are) in-laws and grandparents.
3. Hovering behind the children in that photograph (stands, stand) several mothers.
4. Under the huge tree (sits, sit) that young boy's second "father."
5. Here (comes, come) the cousins now.

See Lesson 16.3, pages 616–617.

Cross-Curricular Activity

SCIENCE In a small group, select a natural phenomenon: a hurricane, earthquake, glacier, iceberg, sunspots, or any other you'd like to explore. Work together to compile a list of questions based on the six kinds of exposition. Divide the questions among group members. Do some basic research using your science textbook, and write a paragraph answering your question. Then combine the paragraphs into a fact sheet on your subject to share with the class.

Expository Writing

Assess

Evaluation Rubrics

Write an Explanation of an Event

When evaluating students' explanations, look for

- a well-developed introduction, body, and conclusion
- several types of exposition explaining the event in the painting

See also *Writing Assessment & Evaluation Rubrics*.

Cross-Curricular Activity

Each fact sheet should

- use six types of exposition.
- include facts about the subject that are accurate and clearly expressed.

Reteaching

📁 *Composition Reteaching,* p. 34

Enrichment

📁 *Composition Enrichment,* p. 34

Use *Fine Art Transparencies* 25–28 for enrichment activities also.

Close

Have students give examples of expository writing they might find at home and identify which of the six categories of exposition each example belongs to.

Grammar Link

Answers
1. are
2. are
3. stand
4. sits
5. come

Viewing the Art

Zinaida Serebriakova, *Castle of Cards*, 1918
Serebriakova's delicate use of line and color matches the delicate way the children are playing the game in *Castle of Cards*. The painting is in the Russian Museum in St. Petersburg.

Focus

Lesson Overview

Objective
• To learn how to write engagingly and informatively for specific audiences

Skills
• writing for a specific audience; identifying an audience; understanding an audience

Critical Thinking
• analyzing; defining and clarifying; comparing; contrasting; identifying

Listening and Speaking
• discussing

Bellringer
Daily Language Activity

When students enter the classroom, have this assignment on the board: *Write three sentences telling about a party you have attended.*

Grammar Link to the Bellringer

Have students check to see that they answered the Bellringer in complete sentences and not in sentence fragments.

See also *Daily Language Practice*

Motivating Activity

Ask students whether they would describe the same party differently to a close friend, a parent, and an acquaintance from another culture. Ask them to write brief notes explaining how each version might differ from the others and then to discuss their notes in class. What factors would they consider when deciding what to tell and what to omit?

LESSON 5.2
Knowing Your Audience

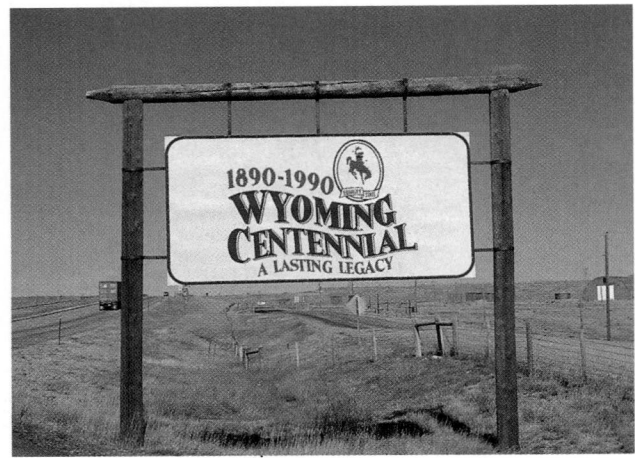

Identifying your audience will help you focus your writing and choose details. In the model below, one-time California filmmaker Gretel Ehrlich explains her attraction to a place that her audience, most of them city dwellers, regard as isolated and desolate.

> Ehrlich provides two examples to show what she means when she says the people are "tenderhearted about quirky behavior."

> This quotation brings a sense of immediacy to the writing. How might Cliff's comment help Ehrlich's readers to understand her words "strong on scruples"?

Literature Model

In all this open space, values crystallize quickly. People are strong on scruples but tenderhearted about quirky behavior. . . . A friend, Cliff, who runs a trapline in the winter, cut off half his foot while chopping a hole in the ice. Alone, he dragged himself to his pickup and headed for town, stopping to open the ranch gate as he left, and getting out to close it again, thus losing, in his observance of rules, precious time and blood. Later, he commented, "How would it look, them having to come to the hospital to tell me their cows had gotten out?"

Accustomed to emergencies, my friends doctor each other from the vet's bag with relish. When one old-timer suffered a heart attack in hunting camp, his partner quickly stirred up a brew of red horse liniment and hot water and made the half-conscious victim drink it, then tied him onto a horse and led him twenty miles to town. He regained consciousness and lived.

Gretel Ehrlich, *The Solace of Open Spaces*

224 Unit 5 Expository Writing

 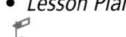

Resource Manager

Planning Resources
• *Lesson Plans*

Transparencies
• *Bellringer*
• *Daily Language Practice*
• *Fine Art 25–28*
• *Two-Minute Skill Drill*
• *Writing Process 11, 23–27*

Other Print Resources
• *Composition Enrichment*, p. 35
• *Composition Practice*, p. 35
• *Composition Reteaching*, p. 35
• *Cooperative Learning Activities*, pp. 21–24
• *Listening and Speaking Activities*, pp. 15–16
• *Research Paper and Report Writing*, pp. 43–48

• *Sentence-Combining Practice*, pp. 32–33
• *Thinking and Study Skills*, pp. 13, 20
• *Writing Across the Curriculum*
• *Writing Assessment and Evaluation Rubrics*

Write to Someone

Thinking about your particular audience for each piece of expository writing will help you zero in on what your readers need to know. Even if your main readers are your teachers, you should remember every teacher is different. Think about what each teacher is looking for as you complete your assignments.

Besides teachers, classmates and other peers will often read and critique your writing. In addition, when you write personal notes, letters to friends, job or college applications, or news stories for the school paper, you must consider various readers. The following questions can help you develop a feel for your audience.

Understanding Your Audience

Interest	• Does this audience care about my topic already, or must I convince them of its importance? • Will I need to find ways to overcome apathy or dislike of my topic? • If this audience has a strong interest in my topic, how can I move forward swiftly to maintain their interest?
Background	• How much does this audience already know about my topic? • Do I need to define basic terms and concepts? • Do I need to probe deeply for new insights in order to tell this audience something it doesn't already know, or should I concentrate on clarifying the main points?
Vocabulary	• Should I use formal or informal language to reach this audience? • Should I present my points in nontechnical language? • Will my audience be able to follow complex explanations, or should I keep sentences short and simple?

Journal Writing

Using the chart above, analyze a piece of writing you have already completed. Would you change anything now? Record your reactions in your journal.

5.2 Knowing Your Audience   **225**

Revising Tip

A peer editor can give you valuable feedback on how well you have responded to the needs of your audience.

Expository Writing

Teach

Using the Model

Ask students to consider why Gretel Ehrlich states her main idea at the beginning of the model. (Ehrlich wants to grab the reader's attention right from the start and use entertaining examples to prove her point and maintain interest.) Ask students how the comment made by Ehrlich's friend Cliff demonstrates that he is "strong on scruples." (Cliff's comment shows that he considered others, even in the face of a personal emergency. His words also suggest his belief that other people would have expected no less of him.) **L2**

Using the Chart

You might suggest that students use the questions in the chart on student page 225 to analyze a model of expository writing in this unit and to determine its intended audience. Stress that they should back up their conclusions with examples from the piece. For example, if they infer that the writer assumed apathy on the part of the audience, they should briefly explain how the writer tried to overcome this apathy. **L3**

Journal Writing Tip

Identifying Audience Before students analyze their expository writing, suggest they clearly identify its intended audience. Then ask them to underline the details in their writing that address the interest level, background, and vocabulary of this audience.

Teach

Using the Model

Have students point out the strategies David Lamb used to appeal to his audience's level of knowledge and interest. Ask which supporting details appeal most to their own level of knowledge about the subject. (Students may mention the comparison between the Sahara and the size of the United States.) Ask why this detail is so effective. (Most readers in the United States will understand the comparison.) **L2**

Two-Minute Skill Drill

Have students identify and correct these sentence fragments.

My sister's two pets, a dog and a cat.
A big party at John's house.

📖 **See also** *Two-Minute Skill Drill Transparancy 5.2*

Additional Resources

📖 *Writing Process Transparencies*, 11, 25–28

📖 For further stimuli for expository writing, see *Fine Art Transparencies*, 25–28.

📁 *Writing Across the Curriculum*
📁 *Cooperative Learning Activities*
📁 *Thinking and Study Skills*, pp. 13, 20
📁 *Sentence-Combining Practice*, pp. 32–33
📁 *Research Paper and Report Writing*, pp. 43–48
📁 *Listening and Speaking Activities*, pp. 15–16
📁 *Composition Practice*, p. 35

Expository Writing

Grammar Tip

When editing expository writing, check that all proper nouns and proper adjectives are capitalized, as in the literature model. To review capitalization rules, see Lessons 20.2 and 20.3, pages 715 and 721.

Use Details to Appeal to Your Audience

Identifying your audience is just the first step. Here are some strategies you can use to support your main ideas and make connections clear to your audience.

Supporting Details and Good Connections

Examples	Support main ideas with vivid, interesting examples to help readers grasp unfamiliar information or relate information to their own experiences.
Facts and Statistics	Use facts and statistics to help readers understand the magnitude of an issue, set the time frame, provide historical background, or support technical points.
Comparisons	Use analogies, metaphors, similes, and other forms of comparison to help readers understand unfamiliar concepts by relating them to something readers *do* understand.
Quotations	Use engaging quotations from experts on your topic to clarify meanings or lend authority to your writing. Or use a relevant quotation at the beginning of your writing to set the tone.

Literature Model

Statistics help give readers a sense of the vastness of the continent.

Africa occupies 20 percent of the earth's land surface, or 11.7 million square miles. Only Asia is larger. Africa is 5,000 miles long, reaching from the God-forsaken deserts of the north to the lush wine country in the south, and 4,600 miles wide. Its coastline measures 18,950 miles—shorter than Europe's because of the absence of inlets and bays—and the equator cuts Africa just about in half. Africa's climate varies wildly, from temperate in the high plateaus, to tropical along the coastal plains to just plain intolerable in the sizzling deserts.

Lamb compares the size of the Sahara and the United States. What does this comparison tell you that statistics alone cannot?

The coastal strip around Africa is narrow, and the interior plateaus are characterized by wide belts of tropical rain forest, wooded savanna and grassland plains. In the far north is the Sahara, the world's largest desert. It covers one quarter of the continent, an area as large as the United States mainland. In the far south is the Kalahari Desert, the world's seventh largest. The highest point in Africa is Mount Kilimanjaro in Tanzania, 19,340 feet tall and snow-capped the year round. . . .

David Lamb, *The Africans*

226 Unit 5 Expository Writing

MEETING INDIVIDUAL NEEDS Less Proficient Readers

Reading the Models

Students who lack proficiency in English may not understand the jargon and geographical terms in the Literature Models in this lesson. Pair these students with more proficient readers to read and discuss the models.

Write an Explanation of a Painting

Look carefully at the painting on this page and read the title. Write a short explanation of what is happening in the picture. Your audience is a foreign exchange student unfamiliar with the game of baseball. Think about what your audience needs to know.

PURPOSE To explain baseball to someone unfamiliar with the game

AUDIENCE A foreign exchange student

LENGTH 2–3 paragraphs

WRITING RUBRICS To write an effective explanation of a painting, you should

- use language that your audience will understand
- use details to support your main idea
- make good, clear connections

Cross-Curricular Activity

SCIENCE In a small group, choose a complex biological term, such as *ecosystem, biodiversity,* or *molecular*. Each of you should choose a different audience—for example, a younger child, a parent, or a biology teacher—and write a paragraph defining the term. Compare definitions to identify techniques each writer used to reach a particular audience.

Viewing and Representing

COOPERATIVE LEARNING After you have defined your term, work as a group to illustrate your term for your audience. Use appropriate materials to represent your expository paragraphs visually.

Grammar Link

Avoid sentence fragments.

A *sentence fragment* is an incomplete sentence punctuated as if it were a complete sentence.

Rewrite the following items, correcting all sentence fragments.

1. Expository writing can be dry and boring. Often lacks feeling.
2. Your readers have different levels of knowledge. And varying degrees of interest in your topic.
3. What kind of language should you use to reach a younger audience? Probably informal.
4. Regardless of their background. Make sure that your audience understands technical terms you introduce.
5. Support your main ideas with comparisons. For example, analogies, metaphors, and similes.

See Lesson 13.9, pages 557–558.

Jacob Lawrence, *Strike,* 1949

5.2 Knowing Your Audience **227**

Expository Writing

Assess

Evaluation Rubrics

Write an Explanation of a Painting

When evaluating students' explanations, look for

- details about baseball that students might take for granted
- details from the painting that help readers grasp the information

See also *Writing Assessment & Evaluation Rubrics.*

Cross-Curricular Activity

Students should use

- vocabulary appropriate for their audiences
- comparisons that appeal to the audiences' levels of knowledge

Reteaching

📁 *Composition Reteaching,* p. 35

Enrichment

📁 *Composition Enrichment,* p. 35

🖨 Use *Fine Art Transparencies* 25–28 for enrichment activities also.

Close

Have students give three possible audiences for an article on the human brain and tell how the three versions of the article might differ.

Grammar Link

Answers

(*Answers will vary. The first two sentences in the exercise are provided as examples.*)

1. Expository writing that lacks feeling can be dry and boring.
2. Your readers have different levels of knowledge and varying degrees of interest in your topic.

Viewing the Art

Jacob Lawrence, *Strike,* 1949

Jacob Lawrence painted scenes depicting the African American urban experience. *Strike* (1949), on display at Howard University in Washington, D. C., was painted a year after Satchel Paige became the first African American pitcher in the American League.

Focus

Lesson Overview

Objective
- To learn strategies for explaining a process clearly in writing

Skills
- writing about a process; ordering steps; defining terms; taking notes

Critical Thinking
- analyzing; evaluating; visualizing

Listening and Speaking
- discussing; questioning

Bellringer
Daily Language Activity

When students enter the classroom, have this assignment on the board: *Explain step by step one simple process that you went through to get ready for school.*

Grammar Link to the Bellringer

Ask students to use strong, exact verbs in their explanations.

See also *Daily Language Practice*

Motivating Activity

Have students read aloud the explanations they wrote for the Bellringer activity while a partner mimes the process exactly as it is read. Students can note where they omitted important steps (for example, uncapping a toothpaste tube before squeezing) or where steps are unclear.

Expository Writing

LESSON
5.3

Writing About a Process

When you explain a process, you describe the steps involved in completing it. Notice the details James Wagenvoord uses in his explanation.

Literature Model

Stickball's a little closer to the big game than stoopball. Instead of playing the width of a street, it stretches down the block as far as a hollow Spaldeen can be powered with a cut-off broom handle. It's often an impressive distance. There are neighborhood variations upon variations. If there's a basic version it's the street game—the hitter flipping the ball into the air, fixedly eyeing its bounce in front of him, and then, as it rises to its apex, stepping into the ball to slash at it with the bat. When the ball is smashed into the playing area, the standard baseball rules take over—again with variations. A ball landing and staying on the rooftop—fair or foul—is an automatic out. But a fair ball skimming off fire escapes, window frames, and dribbling down building faces is in play. There's a version of the game called slow pitch which, with a pitcher, becomes baseball except for the size of the ball and the narrow bat. And there's "off the wall," a tailoring of the classic to interior courtyards, a reversed mirror-image form. The pitcher stands behind the batter, outfielders ranging behind them and all facing the same wall, as the batter waits for his crack until a pitch has been flung at the wall and rebounds to him. His hit is in play the moment that, on the fly, it again strikes the wall. Then stoopball bounce rules take over. One bounce before being caught is a single, and a home run is four bounces or a smash hopelessly beyond reach of the defenders.

James Wagenvoord, *Hangin' Out: City Kids, City Games*

> Wagenvoord discusses several different variations of stickball, beginning with the basic version.

> What kind of details does Wagenvoord use to characterize stickball?

228 Unit 5 Expository Writing

Resource Manager

Planning Resources
- *Lesson Plans*

Transparencies
- *Bellringer*
- *Daily Language Practice*
- *Fine Art* 25–28
- *Two-Minute Skill Drill*
- *Writing Process* 11, 23–27

Other Print Resources
- *Composition Enrichment*, p. 36
- *Composition Practice*, p. 36
- *Composition Reteaching*, p. 36
- *Cooperative Learning Activities*
- *Listening and Speaking Activities*, pp. 15–16
- *Research Paper and Report Writing*, pp. 43–48

- *Sentence-Combining Practice*, pp. 32–34
- *Thinking and Study Skills*, pp. 13, 17, 23
- *Writing Across the Curriculum*
- *Writing Assessment and Evaluation Rubrics*

Explain One Step at a Time

When you write about a process, you must take care to remember all the little details. Unless you can describe the process completely and accurately, your readers will be left in the dark. You must also take into consideration the level of knowledge of your readers. If they know little about the process, you may need to define basic terms and concepts. If your readers are familiar with the process, you don't want to bore them with general information they already know. The following steps can help you write about a process.

Explaining a Process	
1. Investigate	Watch someone perform the process, do it yourself, ask questions about it, or read about it. Take notes as you go.
2. Observe	Identify the main parts of the process and the specific steps needed to carry it out.
3. Arrange	Put the steps in chronological order. You may wish to "walk through" the process mentally to make sure nothing is missing.
4. Elaborate	Decide what background information and examples you need to include so that your audience will understand your explanation. Be sure to define any unfamiliar terms.
5. Polish	Use transitions such as *first, next, meanwhile, then, finally,* and *last* to point the way as you write.
6. Review	Check to make sure your explanation is complete, clear, and accurate.

Journal Writing

What steps do you take to get ready for a party or a school dance? Try listing the steps in your journal. Be careful not to leave anything out or take anything for granted. You may be surprised at how complex such a routine process turns out to be.

Teach

Using the Model

Ask students to discuss the kinds of details James Wagenvoord uses to describe stickball. (The writer describes stickball largely in terms of baseball.) What do these descriptions suggest about his intended audience? (They suggest that Wagenvoord wrote for an audience with a basic knowledge of baseball.) What details in the model support this deduction? (Undefined baseball terms such as *single* support the deduction.) Ask students how they would revise the model if it were intended for someone who had absolutely no knowledge of baseball. (The writer would have to explain baseball clearly enough to enable the reader to see the similarities with stickball.) **L2**

Two-Minute Skill Drill

List these verbs on the board and have students write a more colorful, exact one for each.

walk	go	give
get	move	

See also *Two-Minute Skill Drill Transparancy 5.3*

Journal Writing Tip

Ordering Steps Students who have difficulty including and ordering all the steps may find the following questions useful:

- Does each step flow logically from the preceding step?
- Can a step be broken down into smaller ones?

Encourage students to try to see themselves performing the process as they list the steps.

229

Teach

Explaining a Process

Encourage students to revise their drafts so that each step of a process is clearly explained in a separate paragraph. Point out that the topic sentences should serve as a sort of outline that students can use to check the clarity, completeness, and accuracy of their drafts. Remind students to use transitions to connect the paragraphs. You might also suggest that students underline any key terms or concepts in their drafts and ask themselves if any of the words or phrases need to be defined or expanded upon. **L1**

Additional Resources

For further stimuli for expository writing, see *Fine Art Transparencies,* 25–28.

Writing Process Transparencies, 11, 23–27

Writing Across the Curriculum
Cooperative Learning Activities
Thinking and Study Skills, pp. 1, 5, 13–14, 21
Sentence-Combining Practice, pp. 32–33
Research Paper and Report Writing, pp. 43–48
Listening and Speaking Activities, pp. 15–16
Composition Practice, p. 36

Expository Writing

Prewriting Tip

Explaining a process to a peer editor before writing can help you identify steps or essential background information you may have overlooked.

Grammar Tip

When describing a process, be sure to use the same verb tense throughout the explanation. For help, see Lesson 15.6, pages 598–599.

How does the topic sentence in each paragraph make the steps of the process clearer?

The writer also defines terms that she knows might be unfamiliar.

Revise Your Explanation

When you revise an explanation, your main goals are clarity, completeness, and accuracy. Make sure that the information you present and the way you present it are appropriate for your audience.

The first draft below is taken from an essay that explains the stages of building a house. It is intended for a general audience with no specific background in home building. What changes would you make in order to improve the passage's clarity and appropriateness for that audience?

Model

Next, workers bolt wooden sills to the top of the foundation. Floor joists are placed across the foundation on the sills, and the floorboards are nailed to the top of the joists, forming the bottom layer of the floor. Each wall frame is lifted into place along the sill and braced temporarily. When all the outside walls have been set in place, they are nailed together and braced permanently.

When the writer reviewed the draft, she made some vocabulary changes. She realized her readers might not know some basic terms, such as *sills* and *joists.* Also, they might understand the process more easily if she drew attention to the distinct stages of the process. Notice the changes she made.

Model

The next step is to build the frame. Workers start by bolting wooden sills, called base plates, to the top of the foundation. These sills support the outside walls. Next, floor joists, or support beams, are placed across the foundation on the sills, and the floor boards are nailed to the top of the joists, forming the bottom layer of the floor.

At this point the structure is solid enough to hold the wall frames. Carpenters assemble each wall frame separately. Then each one is lifted into place along the sill and braced temporarily. When all the outside walls have been set in place, they are nailed together and braced permanently.

MEETING INDIVIDUAL NEEDS **English Language Learners**

Explaining the Steps

Students whose first language is not English may feel they lack the knowledge or the vocabulary to explain a process in English. Pair these students with students whose first language is English to help them list the steps in a process. Ask the students to explain a game or some other process from their native country to their partners. Encourage the partners to take notes and ask questions to fill in gaps in the information.

Write a "How-to" Article

Write a 2- to 3-paragraph explanation of a process you are very familiar with, such as how to care for tropical fish or how to train for a 10K race. Assume that your audience is fellow students who are unfamiliar with the process.

PURPOSE To explain a familiar process to somebody unfamiliar with it
AUDIENCE Other students
LENGTH 2–3 paragraphs

WRITING RUBRICS To write an effective "How-to" article, you should

- arrange the steps in chronological order
- explain one step at a time
- tailor your explanation to your audience
- proofread your article

Viewing and Representing

COOPERATIVE LEARNING In a small group, discuss processes in M. C. Escher's *Day and Night* shown on this page. Refer to a process that is portrayed in the picture, a process used by the artist to achieve his effects, or both. Then each member should write a paragraph about the picture. Share and compare responses.

Using Computers

With a partner, search the Internet for other works by M. C. Escher and critical responses to his art. In three or four paragraphs, summarize how you found the information and what you learned about Escher's art and reputation. Share your findings and processes with the class.

Grammar Link

Use exact action verbs.

James Wagenvoord uses forms of strong, exact action verbs—*powered, flipping, eyeing, slash, smashed, flung.*

Rewrite the explanation below, using exact verbs. (You may make other changes, too.)

1. In football, two teams try to get possession of the ball and move it across their opponent's goal line for a touchdown.
2. The offensive team, led by a quarterback, must go ten yards in four downs to keep the ball.
3. The defending team runs after the ball carrier to keep him from advancing.
4. When a player gets a touchdown, his team has six points.
5. The team gets another point if its kicker sends the ball over the goal posts.

See Lesson 3.3, pages 136–139, and Lesson 10.3, pages 453–459.

M. C. Escher, *Day and Night,* 1938

Assess

Evaluation Rubrics

Write a "How-to" Article
When evaluating students' articles, look for
- a step-by-step explanation of an activity
- chronological ordering of steps
- background information appropriate to the reader's level of knowledge
- transitions that clarify the explanation

See also *Writing Assessment and Evaluation Rubrics.*

Viewing and Representing
Students' paragraphs may
- describe how the squares in the field gradually turn into birds
- discuss the relation between the black birds and the white birds

Reteaching
Composition Reteaching, p. 36

Enrichment
Composition Enrichment, p. 36

Use *Fine Art Transparencies* 25–28 for enrichment activities also.

Close

Have students explain the process they selected in the Bellringer to a partner again, using what they learned in this lesson.

Grammar Link

Answers
(*Answers will vary. The first two sentences in the exercise are provided as examples.*)
1. . . . teams battle for possession of the ball and run it . . .
2. . . . team, spearheaded by a quarterback, must advance ten yards . . . to retain the ball.

Viewing the Art

Maurits Cornelis Escher, *Day and Night,* 1938
Dutch artist M. C. Escher was inspired by the interlocking Moorish mosaics of Spain and often employed geometric figures and orderly progressions in his work. The above woodcut is on view at the Cincinnati Art Museum.

Focus

Lesson Overview

Objective
- To learn how to determine cause-and-effect relationships and explain them in writing

Skills
- identifying cause-and-effect relationships; writing about cause and effect; gathering and organizing information

Critical Thinking
- identifying; analyzing; evaluating; clarifying

Listening and Speaking
- discussing

Bellringer
Daily Language Activity

When students enter the classroom, have this assignment on the board: *Write three simple cause-and-effect relationships.*

Grammar Link to the Bellringer

Have students circle the indefinite pronouns in their cause-and-effect relationships.

See also *Daily Language Practice*

Motivating Activity

Encourage students to think of a whole chain of causes and effects stemming from the examples they wrote for the Bellringer activity (cause: student forgot to set his alarm clock; effect: student woke up late; cause: student woke up late; effect: student was late for school).

Expository Writing

Writing About Cause and Effect

*C*ause-and-effect writing explains relationships between events or facts—specifically, that one event or fact caused another. In the model below, reporter Frank Trippett describes several revolutionary effects of air conditioning.

Trippett begins by identifying the cause and then explains the effects.

Trippett gives details about a series of effects of air conditioning.

Literature Model

In fact, air conditioning has substantially altered the country's character and folkways. . . . Many of its byproducts are so conspicuous that they are scarcely noticed. To begin with, air conditioning transformed the face of urban America by making possible those glassy, boxy, sealed-in skyscrapers on which the once humane geometries of places like San Francisco, Boston and Manhattan have been impaled. It has been indispensable, no less, to the functioning of sensitive advanced computers, whose high operating temperatures require that they be constantly cooled. Thus, in a very real way, air conditioning has made possible the ascendancy of computerized civilization. . . . It has also reshaped the national economy and redistributed political power simply by encouraging the burgeoning of the sultry southerly swatch of the country, profoundly influencing major migration trends of people and industry. Sunbelt cities like Phoenix, Atlanta, Dallas and Houston (where shivering indoor frigidity became a mark of status) could never have mushroomed so prosperously without air conditioning; some communities—Las Vegas in the Nevada desert and Lake Havasu City on the Arizona-California border—would shrivel and die overnight if it were turned off.

Frank Trippett, "The Great American Cooling Machine"

Resource Manager

Planning Resources
- *Lesson Plans*

Transparencies
- *Bellringer*
- *Daily Language Practice*
- *Fine Art 25–28*
- *Two-Minute Skill Drill*
- *Writing Process 11, 23–27*

Other Print Resources
- *Composition Enrichment,* p. 37
- *Composition Practice,* p. 37
- *Composition Reteaching,* p. 37
- *Cooperative Learning Activities,* pp. 21–24
- *Listening and Speaking Activities,* pp. 15–16
- *Research Paper and Report Writing,* pp. 43–48

- *Sentence-Combining Practice,* pp. 32–33
- *Thinking and Study Skills,* pp. 11, 14, 21
- *Writing Across the Curriculum*
- *Writing Assessment and Evaluation Rubrics*

Identify the Relationship

In a simple chronological relationship, one event simply follows another in time. In a cause-and-effect relationship, however, one event *causes* another—for example, according to Frank Trippett, the birth of skyscrapers occurred because of air conditioning. You can test for a cause-and-effect relationship by asking the following: If the "cause" hadn't happened, would the "effect" have happened?

Cause-and-effect relationships are not always simple and straight-forward. One cause can have several effects; one effect can result from several causes. Individual causes and effects can also form a chain of events, each one leading to the next. The graphic below will help you to visualize these relationships.

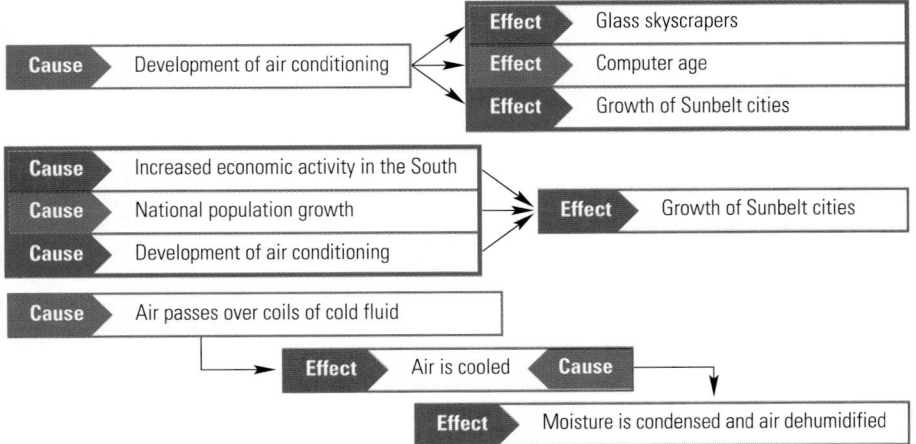

When you write about cause-and-effect relationships, you generally use one of two patterns of organization. With the cause-and-effect pattern, you start by explaining the cause (or causes) and then proceed to the effects. In the effect-to-cause pattern, you examine the effect (or effects) first and then explain what caused them.

Journal Writing

In your journal brainstorm a list of positive and negative effects of the computer. Then write a short paragraph exploring this question. On the whole, have the effects of the computer on modern society been beneficial or harmful?

Teach

Using the Model

Invite students to imagine what life would be like if air conditioning had not been invented. (Computers would probably not be used extensively, if at all; cities would not be filled with skyscrapers; the sunbelt cities would not have become major industrial centers.) Ask students how these differences would affect them. **L2**

Asking Why

As students use an effect-to-cause pattern of organization, call on volunteers to explain what caused a particular effect. Invite the other students to ask themselves the same questions about all cause-and-effect patterns. **L3**

Two-Minute Skill Drill

List the following indefinite pronouns on the board and have students write the present-tense form of *to be* that agrees with each.

all   *none*   *somebody*

everybody   *many*

See also *Two-Minute Skill Drill Transparancy 5.4*

Journal Writing Tip

Classifying Suggest students use separate brainstorming lists to classify the positive and negative effects of the computer. Encourage students to form their opinions after they have prepared the lists. When they write their paragraphs, they should use transitions such as *although* and *on the other hand* to connect the details supporting their opinions.

Teach

Generating Causes and Effects

Divide the class into two groups. Provide students with a focus, such as the introduction of shoes. Then ask the groups to generate details explaining the event in terms of cause and effect. Ask one group to generate causes by answering the following question: *Why were shoes introduced?* Ask the other group to generate effects by answering this question: *What happened as a result of the introduction of shoes?* Give each group a piece of paper and a pencil to pass around so that each member can write down one answer. When both groups have finished, invite all of the students to discuss what they have written. **L2**

Using the Model

Some students may have difficulty keeping track of the causes and effects explained in the model. Suggest students organize causes and effects in a chart. You could point out that the phrase *As a result* signals an effect. **L1**

Additional Resources

For further stimuli for expository writing, see *Fine Art Transparencies,* 25–28.

Writing Process Transparencies, 11, 23–27

Writing Across the Curriculum

Cooperative Learning Activities

Thinking and Study Skills, pp. 11, 14, 21

Sentence-Combining Practice, pp. 32–33

Listening and Speaking Activities, pp. 15–16

Research Paper and Report Writing, pp. 43–48

Composition Practice, p. 37

Expository Writing

Vocabulary Tip

Transitions such as *accordingly, as a result, consequently, therefore,* and *thus* can help you show connections between causes and effects.

Explore Relationships

Examining causes and effects is a skill frequently used in the natural and social sciences and in journalistic writing. The following guidelines can help you explore cause-and-effect relationships.

Guidelines for Writing a Cause-and-Effect Essay

1. Test the cause-and-effect relationship. Does one action actually *cause* another to happen, or does one merely follow the other?
2. Explore the cause-and-effect relationship. How are causes and effects related? What are the most significant aspects of the relationship?
3. Choose a focus. Do you want to emphasize causes, effects, or both?
4. Gather details. Find examples, facts and statistics, and other details to explain the cause-and-effect relationship. Keep in mind the interest level and prior knowledge of your audience.
5. Organize your writing. Should you use cause-to-effect order or effect-to-cause order? Or should you explain a chain of causes and effects in chronological order?
6. Clarify relationships. Use paragraphing and transitions to draw distinctions between causes and effects.

This cause-and-effect paragraph is from an essay about the benefits and drawbacks of air conditioning. What is the cause? What are the effects? What transitions show these relationships?

Model

Which phrases help to show the relationship between causes and effects?

This specific example elaborates on one effect.

Despite its benefits, air conditioning has caused its share of problems as well. Air conditioners require tremendous amounts of power. Consequently, as more homes and businesses installed air conditioning, power utilities were forced to increase their capacities. Some coal-burning utilities began burning far more fuel to meet the demand. As a result, pollution increased. Other utilities began ambitious nuclear power projects. Some citizens, concerned about the safety of nuclear power, protested. As a result, many of these projects were halted or forced to exceed their budgets to meet new safety requirements. In many large cities, even increased utility capacity could not keep up with the demand. Summer became a time of frequent "brownouts," when certain parts of a city would experience brief periods of reduced power. In some cases, power would be lost completely.

MEETING INDIVIDUAL NEEDS English Language Learners

Illustrating Causes and Effects

Students who are acquiring English might have difficulty with the vocabulary in the model. Have them work with partners to illustrate causes and effects in a diagram with pictures and simple phrases.

5.4 | Writing Activities

Write a Cause-and-Effect Paragraph

The following poems, both by Robert Frost, contain causes and effects. Choose one of the poems and write a paragraph explaining its meaning in terms of cause and effect.

PURPOSE   To explain a cause-and-effect relationship in poetry

AUDIENCE   Your English teacher

LENGTH   1 paragraph

WRITING RUBRICS   To write an effective cause-and-effect paragraph, you should

- identify the cause-and-effect relationship
- use a pattern of organization from the chart on page 233
- clarify relationships with clear transitions

Fire and Ice
Some say the world will end in fire,
Some say in ice.
From what I've tasted of desire
I hold with those who favor fire.
But if it had to perish twice,
I think I know enough of hate
To say that for destruction ice
Is also great
And would suffice.

Dust of Snow
The way a crow
Shook down on me
The dust of snow
From a hemlock tree

Has given my heart
A change of mood
And saved some part
Of a day I'd rued.

Viewing and Representing

COOPERATIVE LEARNING   With a small group,

Grammar Link

Make verbs agree with indefinite pronoun subjects.

Some indefinite pronouns are singular and require singular verbs; others are plural and take plural verbs. Note how the indefinite pronoun subject *many* is used in this sentence from the model on page 232. "*Many* of its byproducts *are* . . . scarcely noticed." There are also indefinite pronouns whose number depends on the nouns to which they refer.

Write sentences using each of the ten indefinite pronouns below as the subject. Make each subject agree with a present-tense verb.

1. nothing
2. some
3. several
4. one
5. each
6. few
7. both
8. everyone
9. most
10. either

See Lesson 16.7, pages 623–625.

create visuals of the poems, depicting important causes and effects. Share your work.

Using Computers

Many word-processing programs include an outlining feature that enables you to create an outline and a skeleton "draft" at the same time.

Assess

Evaluation Rubrics

Write a Cause-and-Effect Paragraph

Use these criteria when evaluating your students' writing. Each paragraph should

- accurately explain the poem's meaning in terms of cause-and-effect relationships
- be clearly organized
- use transitions to clarify cause-and-effect relationships

See also *Writing Assessment & Evaluation Rubrics.*

Reteaching

📂 *Composition Reteaching,* p. 37

Enrichment

📂 *Composition Enrichment,* p. 37

Close

Have groups of students try to think of a long chain of causes and effects. Students should explain causes and effects in complete sentences and should use a variety of transitional phrases.

Grammar Link

Answers

The verbs students choose will vary, but they should all be in the present tense.

1. singular
2. singular or plural
3. plural
4. singular
5. singular
6. plural
7. plural
8. singular
9. singular or plural
10. singular

Focus

Lesson Overview

Objective
- To compare and contrast elements, using graphic representations and logical organization

Skills
- creating graphic organizers; organizing a comparison

Critical Thinking
- comparing; contrasting

Listening and Speaking
- discussing

Bellringer
Daily Language Activity

When students enter the classroom, have this assignment on the board: *Write three sentences that compare high school with junior high or middle school.*

Grammar Link to the Bellringer

Have students reread their sentences to make sure they have not made any double comparisons.

See also *Daily Language Practice*

Motivating Activity

Ask students if they agree with Naohiko Hirata's perception of life in a U.S. high school. Do they study a maximum of two hours a day? Do they have after-school jobs? Does socializing detract from their studies? Maybe some students have more in common with Naohiko's experience in a Japanese school. Have they had no choice in selecting their classes and teachers? Encourage students to compare and contrast their own high school experiences with those of Naohiko in both the United States and Japan.

Expository Writing

LESSON 5.5

Comparing and Contrasting

When you compare two or more subjects, you explain how they are similar. When you contrast them, you explain how they are different. Note how writer Phil Sudo uses comparison and contrast to discuss the likes and dislikes of a Japanese exchange student studying in the United States.

高等学校

> The first sentence introduces the main ideas—"the radical differences" between Japanese and U.S. schools.

> Sudo compares features of Japanese and U.S. schools: study habits, teacher-student relationships, social life.

Student Model

Life in America has exposed Naohiko to the radical differences between Japanese and U.S. schools. [In the United States] students rarely study more than two hours a night. In part, that's because so many have part-time jobs. "In my high school in Japan, they said we couldn't get jobs. 'If you get a job, you can't study,' they said." But also, he says, some students [in the United States] take advantage of the free environment. "I don't understand why it's so easy to skip class," says Naohiko. . . .

On the positive side, . . . is the open curriculum. "Here we can choose our classes and choose our teachers. In Japan, I didn't like teachers and they didn't like students. In America, a teacher is like a friend."

He also likes the social aspects of school. He has an American girlfriend, and goes to school dances. "In Japan, school is for studying. There's not many good experiences. In America, we get a lot of good experiences. It makes a lot of nice memories."

Phil Sudo, *Scholastic Update*

When comparing and contrasting, you do more than list similarities and differences. You investigate relationships and draw conclusions.

236   Unit 5 Expository Writing

Resource Manager

Planning Resources
- *Lesson Plans*

Transparencies
- *Bellringer*
- *Daily Language Practice*
- *Fine Art 25–28*
- *Two-Minute Skill Drill*
- *Writing Process* 11, 23–27

Other Print Resources
- *Composition Enrichment,* p. 38
- *Composition Practice,* p. 38
- *Composition Reteaching,* p. 38
- *Cooperative Learning Activities,* pp. 21–24
- *Listening and Speaking Activities,* pp. 15–16
- *Research Paper and Report Writing,* pp. 43–48

- *Sentence-Combining Practice,* pp. 32–33
- *Thinking and Study Skills,* pp. 10,12
- *Writing Across the Curriculum*
- *Writing Assessment and Evaluation Rubrics*

Create Graphic Organizers

In preparing to write a comparison-contrast essay, you may find two kinds of graphic organizers particularly useful.

VENN DIAGRAMS A Venn diagram can help you explore similarities and differences in your subjects. Here's how to create a Venn diagram:

1. Draw two intersecting circles.

2. In the left-hand circle, list features unique to Subject A. In the right-hand circle, list features unique to Subject B.

3. Where the circles overlap, list the important features that both subjects share.

Japanese Schools
- More than two hours of homework; no jobs
- No choice of classes or teachers
- School for studying; no socializing

Similarities
- Standardized tests
- Competitive environment

U.S. Schools
- Limited homework because of part-time jobs and extracurricular activities
- Some required courses, some electives; some choice of teachers
- Social life a big part of school

COMPARISON FRAMES If you know the categories you want to compare and contrast, use a comparison frame. Follow these steps:

Write the two subjects being compared as headings.

List the categories you will compare and contrast.

Fill in the boxes.

Subjects		
Categories	**U.S. Schools**	**Japanese Schools**
Study Habits	Limited homework because of activities and jobs	Often more than two hours of homework; no jobs
Student Choice	Some required courses and some electives	Courses prescribed by government
Social Life	Social life an important aspect of school	School for studying, not socializing

Grammar Tip

When comparing two items, use the comparative form of a modifier. For help, see Lesson 18.1, pages 663–665.

Journal Writing

How would you compare and contrast two things, such as rugby and football, or two movies? In your journal, create a Venn diagram or comparison frame.

Teach

Thinking Visually

Suggest that students use a Venn diagram or a comparison frame to compare Japanese and U.S. schools. For example, students could use a Venn diagram to list general similarities and differences between Japanese and U.S. schools or students. In a comparison frame, students could compare and contrast such categories as homework, social life, part-time jobs, curriculum, and so on. **L2**

Making Decisions

Point out that being able to organize thoughts, observations, and findings into a comparison-and-contrast framework could help students make life decisions. **L1**

Two-Minute Skill Drill

Have students eliminate the double comparison in the following sentence:

Students in the U.S. are more likelier to have long summer vacations than Japanese students are.

See also *Two-Minute Skill Drill Transparency 5.5*

Journal Writing Tip

Making and Using Graphic Organizers If students use a Venn diagram to compare and contrast the items, suggest they use the areas where the circles overlap to list similarities. If students use a comparison frame, suggest they first write freely about the items to determine the categories they will compare and contrast.

Teach

Using the Model

Discuss the questions in the marginal boxes. Students should note that the first two sentences prepare the reader for a contrast between the writer's expectations and her actual observations of killer whales. The last sentence summarizes the contrast between the writer's positive expectations and her negative observations. **L2**

Using Both Methods

Challenge students to write two different comparison and contrast pieces on the some topic, such as the life of the tiger in captivity compared to that of a tiger in the jungle. In one piece, students should compare and contrast the two subjects feature by feature (in the example, features might include diet and longevity). In the other piece, students should describe features of one subject and then describe features of the second subject. **L3**

Additional Resources

For further stimuli for expository writing, see *Fine Art Transparencies*, 25–28.

Writing Process Transparencies, 11, 23–24

Writing Across the Curriculum

Cooperative Learning Activities

Thinking and Study Skills, pp. 10, 12, 14, 21

Sentence-Combining Practice, pp. 32–33

Listening and Speaking Activities, pp. 15–16

Research Paper and Report Writing, pp. 43–48

Composition Practice, p. 38

Expository Writing

Organize Your Comparison

Sudo's essay comparing Japanese and U.S. high schools uses the compare-and-contrast method of organization. Another method, shown in this model, discusses feature by feature all aspects first of one subject, then of the other. The chart below clarifies each method.

> **How do the first two sentences set the stage for a contrast?**

> **The writer compares by presenting subjects separately. The first subject is her expectations. The second subject is her actual observations.**

> **What is the purpose of the last sentence?**

Model

The only reason I cared about going to Florida on vacation with my family was to see the killer whales at Sea World. But what I saw was not what I had expected. I pictured the killer whales I had seen on television: huge creatures—twenty to thirty feet long—with shiny backs and white bellies. I recalled them swimming freely through ocean waters at speeds as fast as twenty-five miles an hour in groups as large as twenty or more, stopping occasionally for a joyful roll through the water or a leap above the surface.

The killer whales I saw at Sea World certainly looked as I had expected, but everything else about them surprised and disappointed me. They lived in tanks—gigantic to you and me, but puny compared to the vast ocean. They traveled at rates that never even approached their top ocean speeds and were alone or in pairs rather than in large groups. Their flips and leaps were commanded by the trainer and didn't seem quite so joyful and free. After a short time, all I felt was sadness for these captives of an environment not their own.

Grammar Tip

Eliminate any double comparisons—that is, comparisons that add both the ending -er or -est and the word *more* or *most* to the modifier. See Lesson 18.3, pages 668–669.

How to Organize a Comparison-Contrast Essay

Feature by Feature	Subject by Subject

1. Study Habits
   A. Japan
   B. United States
2. Student Choice
   A. Japan
   B. United States
3. Social Life
   A. Japan
   B. United States
	1. What I expected
	   A. Swimming in ocean
	   B. Groups of twenty or more
	   C. Free, joyful actions
	2. What I observed
	   A. Confined to tanks
	   B. Alone or in pairs
	   C. Actions on command

MEETING INDIVIDUAL NEEDS   English Language Learners

Comparing Objects

Students whose first language is not English may have difficulty finding the right words for their observations. Suggest that students discuss their observations with an English-proficient partner who can help transcribe the findings.

Write a Comparison-Contrast Article

Write an article comparing and contrasting the abstract painting below with the realistic floral painting on page 243 in regard to color, composition, and total effect on the viewer. First, explore similarities and differences in a Venn diagram. Then, list your categories and information in a comparison frame.

PURPOSE To compare and contrast two paintings
AUDIENCE Your classmates and teacher
LENGTH 2–3 paragraphs

WRITING RUBRICS To write an effective comparison-contrast article, you should

- use an appropriate method of organization
- draw clear conclusions
- check your spelling and sentence structure

Cross-Curricular Activity

SCIENCE Write an article comparing and contrasting the optimist's view of the future of the planet with that of the pessimist. The optimist thinks that the environment will be saved by people who are committed to recycling and

Alma Thomas, *Iris, Tulips, Jonquils and Crocuses*, 1969

Grammar Link

Avoid double comparisons.

The comparative form of an adjective or adverb is formed with *-er* or *more/less*. Using both together creates an incorrect double comparison.

Rewrite each sentence below to eliminate the double comparison.

1. U.S. schools are more easier than Russian schools.
2. Russian students have homework more frequenter than American students.
3. Russian teachers are less friendlier than American teachers.
4. Russian schools offer more fewer electives than U.S. schools.
5. American students attend social events more oftener than do Russian students.

See Lesson 18.3, pages 668–669.

ending pollution. The pessimist thinks that the environment is in decline and that people have neither the capacity nor the commitment to adequately care for the planet.

Listening and Speaking

MAKING A SPEECH Deliver your article on the future of the environment as a speech to a specific audience, such as retired NASA scientists, a group of kindergartners, or a U.S. Senate committee. Ask your classmates if they can identify the audience you are aiming at and how effectively you adapted your article to this audience.

5.5 Comparing and Contrasting **239**

Assess

Evaluation Rubrics

Write a Comparison-Contrast Article

Use these criteria when evaluating your students' writing. Articles may

- state that Thomas's painting recalls colorful flowers on a sunny day
- compare the warmth of Thomas's work with the cold realism of Schonzeit's

See also *Writing Assessment & Evaluation Rubrics.*

Cross-Curricular Activity

Students should

- use a single method of organization
- draw their own conclusions about the subject

Reteaching

📁 *Composition Reteaching,* p. 38

Enrichment

📁 *Composition Enrichment,* p. 38

🖨 Use *Fine Art Transparencies* 25–28 for enrichment activities also.

Close

Have students work in small groups to compare and contrast two of their favorite stories, books, or games. Encourage them to record the results of their discussion in a Venn diagram or comparison frame.

Grammar Link

Answers
1. U.S. schools are easier . . .
2. . . . have homework more frequently . . .
3. . . . are less friendly than . . .
4. . . . offer fewer electives than . . .
5. . . . attend social events more often than . . .

Viewing the Art

Alma Thomas, *Iris, Tulips, Jonquils and Crocuses*, 1969
African American artist Alma Thomas used dabs of paint to suggest a garden of colorful flowers on a breezy day. The acrylic-on-canvas painting is in the National Museum of Women in the Arts in Washington, D.C.

Focus

Lesson Overview

Objective
• To see the differences between a formal definition and a personal definition and incorporate them in writing

Skills
• word mapping; listing details

Critical Thinking
• defining and clarifying; inferring; classifying

Listening and Speaking
• listening critically

 Bellringer
Daily Language Activity

When students enter the classroom, have this assignment on the board: *Write a short definition of your favorite kind of exercise.*

Grammar Link to the Bellringer

Have students circle the specific nouns in their definitions.

See also *Daily Language Practice*

Motivating Activity

Invite students to volunteer their definitions of slang terms for talking, relaxing, or exercising. Encourage students to define a word formally by placing it in a general category and comparing it to a similar object or idea. Then ask students to explain what the word means to them personally. Discuss which definition provided the most information. Explain that either a formal or a personal approach—or a combination of both—may be used to write an effective definition.

Expository Writing

LESSON 5.6

Writing Effective Definitions

Basic definitions of words can be found in dictionaries. To present more elaborate concepts of words, however, lengthier writing is often needed. Notice how Wendell Berry gives both a formal and a personal definition of "family farm" in this excerpt from an essay.

What is Berry's definition of a family farm?

> ### Literature Model
>
> What I shall mean by the term "family farm" is a farm small enough to be farmed by a family and one that *is* farmed by a family, perhaps with a small amount of hired help. I shall *not* mean a farm that is owned by a family and worked by other people. The family farm is both the home and the workplace of the family that owns it. . . .
>
> Furthermore, the term "family farm" implies longevity in the connection between family and farm. A family farm is not a farm that a family has bought on speculation and is only occupying and using until it can be profitably sold.
>
> Wendell Berry, "A Defense of the Family Farm"

What two types of farm does Berry exclude from his definition?

Write a Formal Definition

A formal definition places a word or subject in a general category and examines how it differs from other words in its category. One way to get started in writing a formal definition is to create a word map.

240 Unit 5 Expository Writing

 ## Resource Manager

Planning Resources
• *Lesson Plans*

 Transparencies
• *Bellringer*
• *Daily Language Practice*
• *Fine Art* 25–28
• *Two-Minute Skill Drill*
• *Writing Process* 11, 23–27

📁 Other Print Resources
• *Composition Enrichment*, p. 39
• *Composition Practice*, p. 39
• *Composition Reteaching*, p. 39
• *Cooperative Learning Activities*
• *Listening and Speaking Activities*, pp. 15–16
• *Research Paper and Report Writing*, pp. 43–48

• *Sentence-Combining Practice*, pp. 32–33
• *Thinking and Study Skills*, pp. 10–13, 19
• *Writing Across the Curriculum*
• *Writing Assessment and Evaluation Rubrics*

Word Map

```
What is it?          ┌──────────────┐
                     │ An aquatic   │
                     │ environment  │
                     └──────┬───────┘
                            │          ┌──────────┐
Word to be        ┌─────────┴──┐       │  Ocean   │   What is
defined           │  Estuary   │───────│  meets   │   it like?
                  └─┬────┬────┬─┘       │  river   │
                    │    │    │         └──────────┘
       ┌────────┐   │    │    │    ┌──────────────┐    What are
       │ Puget  │───┘    │    └────│ San Francisco│    some
       │ Sound  │   ┌────┴─────┐   │     Bay      │    examples?
       └────────┘   │Chesapeake│   └──────────────┘
                    │   Bay    │
                    └──────────┘
```

Naming your word's general category (What is it?) helps identify its broadest, most basic meaning. Naming other words in the same category (What is it like?) helps pinpoint the meanings that are unique to your word. Citing examples helps clarify the specific qualities included in the meaning of your word.

The word map above was helpful in writing this definition of *estuary*. As you read the definition, refer to the word map.

Model

Puget Sound, San Francisco Bay, and Chesapeake Bay may seem to be just busy waterways in the middle of large urban areas; but they have something else in common as well. They are all estuaries, aquatic environments with unique combinations of physical surroundings and life forms.

Estuaries are located where rivers and oceans meet, and the mixing of salt water from the ocean and fresh water from the river produces a unique environment. In addition, the action of ocean tides creates currents that deposit sediments and organic debris, making estuaries rich in minerals and nutrients. These conditions also make estuaries productive breeding grounds for shellfish.

> Familiar examples help readers picture the meaning of the term being defined.

> The explanation about oceans and rivers shows how estuaries are related to these other aquatic environments.

Journal Writing

Experiment with writing formal definitions. Create a word map for one or more of the following words: *horror movie, personal computer, frog, medicine*.

Teach

Using the Models

After students read the Literature Model on page 240, point out that Wendell Berry assumes the reader is already familiar with the dictionary definition of *farm*. Ask students to name the characteristics of a family farm according to Berry. Then have students read the model on page 241. What clues are given to help the reader understand the term described? **L2**

Making a Word Map

Encourage students to use a dictionary, a thesaurus, and an encyclopedia when they create word maps for formal definitions. The dictionary will help students identify the words' most basic meanings. The thesaurus can provide synonyms that may increase students' understanding of the words. The encyclopedia may offer familiar examples to help students understand the words' meanings. **L1**

 Two-Minute Skill Drill

List these words on the board and have students provide a synonym for each.

relief	*help*	*strong*
transport	*decay*	

See also *Two-Minute Skill Drill Transparancy 5.6*

Journal Writing Tip

Representing Words Remind students that a word map is a prewriting tool they can use to represent the word or term they want to define. Encourage students to modify the questions in the sample word map to suit the word or term they choose.

Expository Writing

Teach

Using the Model

Point out that the writer clarifies his or her personal definition of an environmentalist by providing two points of comparison: the dictionary definition and a personal opinion of extremists. Have students identify the feelings and experiences the writer uses to elaborate on his or her personal definition of an environmentalist. Ask students what evidence demonstrates that the writer's own definition of the term lies between a dictionary definition and that of an extremist? **L2**

Cooperative Learning

Divide the class into groups. Provide each group with a different word and ask students to write a brief personal definition of it. Encourage students to use the guidelines on this page to help them. After students have finished, they should read and discuss their definitions. **L2**

Additional Resources

- For further stimuli for expository writing, see *Fine Art Transparencies*, 25–28.
- *Writing Process Transparencies*, 11, 23–27
- *Writing Across the Curriculum*
- *Cooperative Learning Activities*
- *Thinking and Study Skills*, pp. 10–13, 19
- *Sentence-Combining Practice*, pp. 32–33
- *Research Paper and Report Writing*, pp. 43–48
- *Listening and Speaking and Activities*, pp. 15–16
- *Composition Practice*, p. 39

Vocabulary Tip

You may find that you need to combine the techniques of writing formal and personal definitions to fully explore the meaning of some words.

Write a Personal Definition

Formal definitions of words like *love* only scratch the surface. An informal definition—involving your language, your style, your meaning—can often do a better job. Look at the guidelines below.

Guidelines for Writing Personal Definitions

1. Examine what the word means to you personally. How does the word affect you? What feelings or experiences does the word bring to mind?
2. Examine other viewpoints. What is the dictionary definition? What other personal definitions can you find? How is your definition different from others?
3. Find details to support your definition.

Notice the techniques this writer used to develop a personal definition of the term *environmentalist*.

> **A dictionary definition "anchors" the personal definition and provides a basis for comparison.**

> **Examples elaborate on the personal definition.**

Model

I consider myself an environmentalist. According to the dictionary, an *environmentalist* is interested in preserving and improving the environment, and I certainly fit that description. To me, however, being an environmentalist requires a greater commitment than just being "interested."

For me, every day is Earth Day. I try to buy only those products that are packaged in biodegradable materials. I recycle paper, aluminum, and plastics. I persuaded my brother and sister-in-law to stop buying disposable diapers for my nephew Mark. My biggest accomplishment, however, was getting my parents to stop using weed killers on our lawn. No more pesticides for us. If we see a few weeds, that's OK. We can live with weeds.

Some environmental activists are more extreme. They chain themselves to trees in the forest to keep them from being cut down. They lie down in front of bulldozers. They ride out in boats to interfere with commercial fishing and nuclear testing. I support their goals, but not their tactics. I believe we've done enough violence to the environment without doing more harm to one another. I just want future generations to live in a world that is a little cleaner and a little less threatening than the one I am growing up in.

242 Unit 5 Expository Writing

MEETING INDIVIDUAL NEEDS · English Language Learners

Word Mapping

Help students acquiring English try to explain a word or term from their native language. First ask students to think of a word they would like to define. Then pair each student with an English-proficient partner. The partner should ask questions to help identify the word's most basic meaning and to pinpoint situations in which the word or term may be used. Based on answers to these questions, the pair can make a word map for the definition.

Write a Definition

The style of the painting shown on this page is sometimes called *photorealism*. Look at the painting closely, and use it to write your own definition of photorealism. Before you write your definition, prepare a word map.

PURPOSE To define *photorealism*, using a painting as an example

AUDIENCE Your teacher and classmates

LENGTH 1–2 paragraphs

WRITING RUBRICS To write an effective definition, you should

- identify feelings and experiences the word or painting brings to mind
- use details to support your definition
- make sure your writing is legible and clear

Listening and Speaking

COOPERATIVE LEARNING In a small group, prepare a presentation on current slang. Brainstorm to generate a list of terms, starting with words for *good* and *bad*. Assign each student to compose several creative definitions and examples. Share your definitions within the group. Then present them as an oral reading to the class.

Ben Schonzeit, *Parrot Tulip*, 1976

Grammar Link

Use precise nouns to clarify meaning.

When you write definitions, use specific nouns to make clear what you mean. Note how precise nouns are used as supporting details in the model definitions.

Rewrite the definitions for the italicized words below, replacing the general nouns with nouns that are more exact.

1. A *community* is a collection of things.
2. A *habitat* is a place where things live and grow.
3. *Ecologists* are people who study science.
4. *Air* is the item all things breathe.
5. *Water* is another thing all things need to live.

See Lesson 10.1, pages 439–444.

Using Computers

Investigate similarities and differences in definitions among various Internet sites and software such as Encyclopaedia Britannica, Encarta, and Webster's Dictionary. Choose six words to look up using each research tool and note the respellings, origins, and definitions provided for each word. Write a summary of your findings.

5.6 Writing Effective Definitions **243**

Assess

Evaluation Rubrics

Write a Definition

Use these criteria when evaluating your students' writing. The writing should

- contain a dictionary definition of the term *photorealism*
- point out details in the painting that would also be captured in a photo
- contrast the reality represented in a painting with that in a photo

See also *Writing Assessment & Evaluation Rubrics.*

Listening and Speaking

Evaluate student work based on the following:

- Does the student describe the personal feelings and experiences the words bring to mind?
- Has the student included the viewpoint of others in the definitions?

Reteaching

📂 *Composition Reteaching,* p. 39

Enrichment

📂 *Composition Enrichment,* p. 39

🖌 Use *Fine Art Transparencies* 25–28 for enrichment activities also.

Close

Discuss with students the degree to which definitions (other than dictionary definitions) depend on the personal experiences and feelings of the definer. What implications do students think this would have for writers in a business or political environment?

Grammar Link

Answers

(*Answers will vary. The first two sentences are provided as samples.*)

1. A community is a group of people.
2. A habitat is a home where animals or plants live and grow.

Viewing the Art

Ben Schonzeit, *Parrot Tulip*, 1976
The sharpness of detail in Ben Schonzeit's painting is so perfect that the flower appears real. The 60-by-72–inch acrylic painting is in the Chase Manhattan Collection in New York City.

Focus

Lesson Overview

Objective

• To communicate numerical data in a graph and to utilize the graph in an expository paper

Skills

• graphing numerical data

Critical Thinking

• relating data to writing; visualizing

Listening and Speaking

• discussing; questioning

Bellringer
Daily Language Activity

When students enter the classroom, have this assignment on the board: *Write what percentage of your day is spent in school. List the subjects you are studying now.*

Grammar Link to the Bellringer

Have students check that their class subjects are capitalized appropriately.

See also *Daily Language Practice*

Motivating Activity

Initiate a discussion about the amount of time students spend on their various activities each day. What percentage of time do they spend in school? at part-time jobs? doing homework? socializing? Make a pie chart representing the amount of time one student allocates to each activity per day. Be sure to label each section of the graph and indicate percentages. Explain that the pie chart presents the information in a format that is easy to read and understand

244

Expository Writing

LESSON
5.7

Using Graphs in Exposition

Expository writers often use graphs to present information that may be too difficult or boring to present in words. Notice how the graph below shows that the population of Phoenix more than doubled from 1960 to 1990.

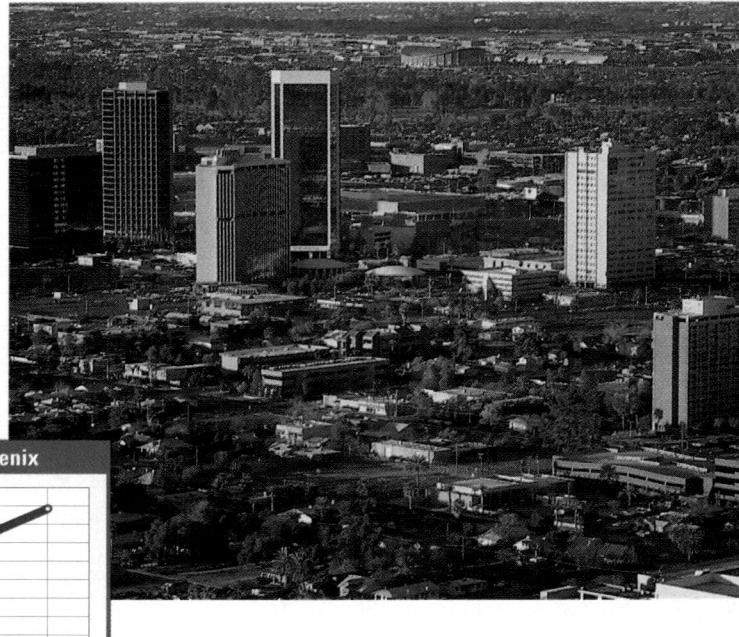

Population Growth in Phoenix

Use Graphs for Clarification

Writing filled with statistics can be deadly, with numbers cluttering up the sentences, making them hard to read and understand. Study the two examples on the next page carefully. Which model does a better job of presenting the information about the 10 largest cities in the United States—the one with the graph or the one without?

244 Unit 5 Expository Writing

Resource Manager

Planning Resources
• *Lesson Plans*

Transparencies
• *Bellringer*
• *Daily Language Practice*
• *Fine Art 25–28*
• *Two-Minute Skill Drill*
• *Writing Process* 11, 23–27

Other Print Resources
• *Composition Enrichment,* p. 40
• *Composition Practice,* p. 40
• *Composition Reteaching,* p. 40
• *Cooperative Learning Activities*
• *Listening and Speaking Activities,* pp. 15–16
• *Research Paper and Report Writing,* pp. 43–48

• *Sentence-Combining Practice,* pp. 32–33
• *Thinking and Study Skills,* pp. 12, 24
• *Writing Across the Curriculum*
• *Writing Assessment and Evaluation Rubrics*

Model: Text Only

The census figures show that New York is still the nation's largest city, with 7.3 million people, even though the city's population shrank by almost a half million between 1960 and 1990. Los Angeles became the second largest city, growing by one million people to 3.5 million, and Chicago dropped to third. Houston edged past Philadelphia—now in the fifth position—to become the fourth largest city, and San Diego jumped to sixth place, ahead of Detroit, Dallas, Phoenix, and San Antonio. Phoenix, number 29 on the list in 1960, rose to ninth.

> Burying statistics in a paragraph makes the data hard to find and hard to follow.

Model: Text and Graph

The latest census figures reveal a reshuffling of the order of the nation's largest cities. As the graph below shows, New York remains by far the nation's most populous city, and Los Angeles has moved past Chicago into second place. Other cities to make the top ten were Houston, Phoenix, and San Diego. Baltimore, which was sixth in 1960, failed to make the top ten this time around.

> Presenting the statistics in a graph enables the reader to take in the information at a glance.

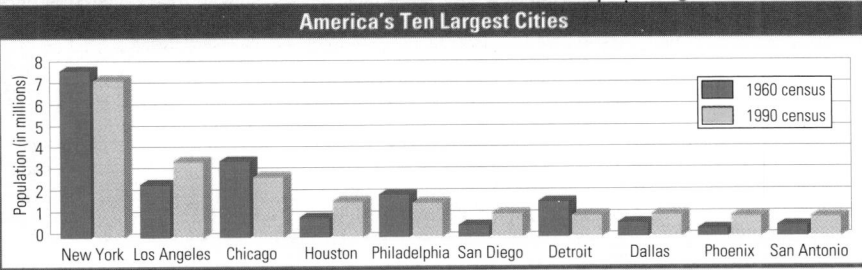

America's Ten Largest Cities

The bar graphs helps readers visualize the information. It allows readers to see which cities are larger and also how much larger.

Journal Writing

List some kinds of data that can be graphed, such as height, weight, test scores, and so on. What is the advantage to presenting this kind of information in a graph?

Teach

Using the Models

Ask students what information the model with the accompanying graph provides that the other model does not. (The model with the graph provides population figures for all ten cities from both the 1960 and the 1990 censuses. The graph also allows the reader to compare the relative size of the cities and note the rate of an individual city's growth.) **L2**

Using Graphs in Writing

When students write papers, remind them to avoid restating in words information their graphs show visually. Point out that the writer of the model summarizes the general results of the census without actually repeating information given in the graph. **L1**

Two-Minute Skill Drill

Rewrite the following sentence, capitalizing where necessary.

on our trip to chicago, my aunt amelia promised us we would see the lincoln park zoo, the planetarium, and the field museum of natural history.

See also *Two-Minute Skill Drill Transparancy 5.7*

Journal Writing Tip

Drawing Conclusions Suggest that students study graphs in newspapers, magazines, and textbooks. The conclusions they draw from these graphs can help them understand the advantages of various types of graphs in conveying information.

Teach

Analyzing Patterns

Suggest students use a graph to show the grades they received in each class a year ago and those for the most recent marking period. They may use a bar graph or a line graph (by plotting two sets of points). Show students how graphing the two sets of grades can show improvement trends and areas of study that need work. **L2**

Creating Graphs

Suggest that students try to show the same statistics on both a line graph and a bar graph. For example, suppose students were writing an expository essay about baseball. How would they represent a player's year-to-year batting average on the graphs? (Students should plot the years the athlete played on the horizontal axis and numbers 100, 200, 300, 400, and 500 on the vertical axis.) Supply students with the statistics, and, as they work, check that they can use the information to prepare the two graphs. **L3**

Additional Resources

- For further stimuli for expository writing, see *Fine Art Transparencies,* 25–28.

- *Writing Process Transparencies,* 11, 23–27
- *Cooperative Learning Activities,* pp. 21–24
- *Thinking and Study Skills,* pp. 12, 24
- *Listening and Speaking Activities,* pp. 15–16
- *Sentence-Combining Practice,* pp. 32–33
- *Research Paper and Report Writing,* pp. 43–48
- *Composition Practice,* p. 40

246

Expository Writing

Presenting Tip

Include a graph, diagram, map, or other graphic with your final draft to enhance a reader's understanding of your exposition.

Revising Tip

Make sure that readers recognize how the graph relates to the text. If necessary, add a specific reference or caption to make the connection clear.

Choose the Right Graph

You can choose specific types of graphs to clarify different relationships among statistics. Examine the models below. Then use the guidelines below the models to determine when and how to include graphs in your expository writing.

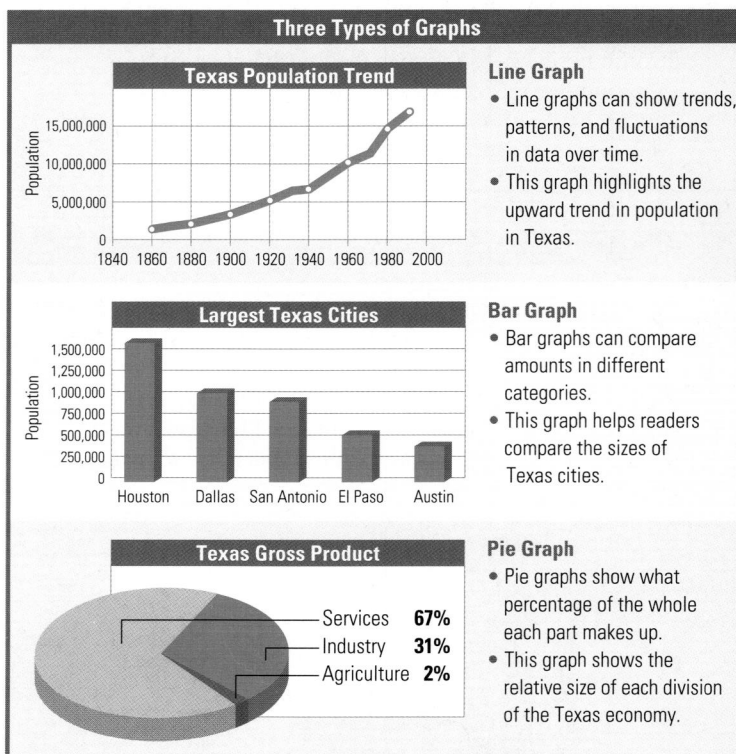

Three Types of Graphs

Texas Population Trend

Line Graph
- Line graphs can show trends, patterns, and fluctuations in data over time.
- This graph highlights the upward trend in population in Texas.

Largest Texas Cities

Bar Graph
- Bar graphs can compare amounts in different categories.
- This graph helps readers compare the sizes of Texas cities.

Texas Gross Product

Services **67%**
Industry **31%**
Agriculture **2%**

Pie Graph
- Pie graphs show what percentage of the whole each part makes up.
- This graph shows the relative size of each division of the Texas economy.

Guidelines for Making Graphs

1. Examine your data to determine whether or not a graph will help. Can you present the data more clearly in a graph than in sentences alone?
2. Decide whether you want to emphasize trends, comparisons, or parts of a whole. Choose the type of graph that meets your needs.
3. Add titles and labels that explain the information you are presenting.

246 Unit 5 Expository Writing

MEETING INDIVIDUAL NEEDS — English Language Learners

Understanding Graphs

Students who are less proficient in English may need help understanding how graphs track statistical information. First, make sure students understand the difference between a pie graph, bar graph, and line graph. The pictured graphs and their accompanying definitions will make understanding the differences easy to discern. Explain that a pie graph, also called a pie chart, gets its name from its pie shape. Then help students track the information analyzed in each graph.

Write to Compare Information

Write a paragraph in which you compare and contrast the average high and low temperatures in Flagstaff and Phoenix and their implications for travelers. Use the graph for information.

PURPOSE To compare and contrast high and low temperatures using a graph to present information
AUDIENCE Travelers
LENGTH 1 paragraph

WRITING RUBRICS To write an effective comparison, you should

- include facts from the graph
- organize your information in a coherent manner

Viewing and Representing

COOPERATIVE LEARNING Work together with a partner to construct one of the graphs discussed in this lesson: line graph, bar graph, or pie graph. Choose a meaningful subject and decide which graph would be most appropriate. Make your graph clear and legible.

Using Computers

Your electronic spell-checker can help you proofread, but you have to be careful. For example, if you've used the wrong homonym, such as *here* when you meant *hear,* your spell-checker will not catch the error. Be sure to check manually the proper nouns not in the spell-checker.

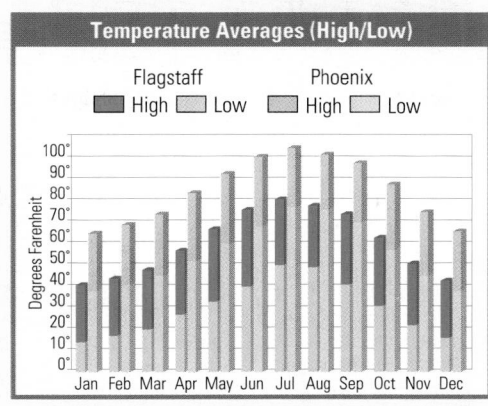

Temperature Averages (High/Low)

Flagstaff: High, Low Phoenix: High, Low

Degrees Farenheit (100° 90° 80° 70° 60° 50° 40° 30° 20° 10° 0°) — Jan Feb Mar Apr May Jun Jul Aug Sep Oct Nov Dec

Expository Writing

Grammar Link

Capitalize names and titles in a graphic correctly.

Capitalize all proper nouns in a graphic, including the beginning and key words in its title.

Rewrite the following sentences, adding capital letters as necessary.

1. The time line shows the establishment of the massachusetts bay colony, virginia, maryland, and other english colonies.
2. The title of the diagram is how a bill becomes a law.
3. The map shows bull run, gettysburg, vicksburg, and other battle sites of the civil war.
4. The line graph compares the population growth rate of hispanics, african americans, asians, and other ethnic groups.

See Lesson 20.2, pages 715–721 and Lesson 20.3, pages 722–725.

5.7 Using Graphs in Exposition **247**

Assess

Evaluation Rubrics

Write to Compare Information

Use these criteria when evaluating your students' writing.

- Does the student base recommendations for travel on a comparison of the temperatures given in the graph?
- Does the student refer to the information in the graph without repeating all of the information in sentences?

See also *Writing Assessment & Evaluation Rubrics.*

Using Computers

Invite students to demonstrate the use of the spell-checker. You might also ask them to talk about any problems they have had using a spell-checker.

Reteaching

Composition Reteaching, p. 40

Enrichment

Composition Enrichment, p. 40

Close

Invite students to look again at the graph of average temperatures in Flagstaff and Phoenix that appears on page 247. Do students feel that the information could have been displayed using another type of graph, perhaps a line graph or a pictorial graph? Have students discuss the advantages and disadvantages of graphing this information in another way.

Grammar Link

Answers

1. The time line shows the establishment of the Massachusetts Bay Colony, Virginia, Maryland, and other English colonies.
2. The title of the diagram is "How a Bill Becomes a Law."
3. The map shows Bull Run, Gettysburg, Vicksburg, and other battle sites of the Civil War.
4. The line graph compares the population growth rate of Hispanics, African Americans, Asians, and other ethnic groups.

Focus

Lesson Overview

Objective
- To compose a news article that answers the six basic questions: *who, what, when, where, why, how*

Skills
- planning; gathering and ordering details; outlining; drafting; proofreading

Critical Thinking
- establishing and evaluating criteria; generating new information; summarizing

Listening and Speaking
- interviewing; discussing

Bellringer
Daily Language Activity

When students enter the classroom, have this assignment on the board: *List the subjects and the titles of recent news stories you have read. Include any quotations you remember.*

Grammar Link to the Bellringer

Have students evaluate whether the correct punctuation was used with the quotations they wrote for the Bellringer activity.

See also *Daily Language Practice*

Motivating Activity

Initiate a discussion about news stories that students have recently read or heard about on television. Why did these particular stories catch their interest? Then ask students to consider how they would write a news article about something that happened to them. Invite students to think of a lead sentence that summarizes the story and captures the reader's attention.

Expository Writing

LESSON
5.8

Writing a News Article

The primary purpose of a news story is to inform; thus, it presents its most important information first. Note the organization of the following article.

> The first paragraph— the lead—captures attention and summarizes the main points of the story.

> In what order are paragraphs arranged in this article?

TIME
For more about the writing process, see TIME Facing the Blank Page, pp. 109–119

2 Condors to Fly Free Late in '91
Release plans follow unexpected success of captive breeding

By Gina Lubrano
Staff Writer

LOS ANGELES — Two California condors will be reintroduced into the wilds of Ventura County late this year in a gamble that the once nearly extinct birds can live free, officials said yesterday.

"The time is now for the condors' return," said Marvin Plenert, Pacific regional director of the U.S. Fish and Wildlife Service.

"We have the birds. We have the site. We have the expertise, and we have the dedication."

Chocuyens, hatched at the San Diego Wild Animal Park on May 29, and Hoi-Ne-Wut, hatched at the Los Angeles Zoo three weeks earlier, are the million-dollar babies selected for release.

"Frankly, we will be taking a gamble," Plenert said. "The chance of losing a young condor faced with the uncertainties of life in the wild is extremely high."

Marc Weitzel, manager of the Hopper Mountain National Wildlife Refuge in Ventura County, tells where two endangered California condors will be released into the wild.

248   Unit 5 Expository Writing

Resource Manager

Planning Resources
- *Lesson Plans*

Transparencies
- *Bellringer*
- *Daily Language Practice*
- *Fine Art* 25–28
- *Two-Minute Skill Drill*
- *Writing Process* 11, 23–27

Other Print Resources
- *Composition Enrichment*, p. 41
- *Composition Practice*, p. 41
- *Composition Reteaching*, p. 41
- *Cooperative Learning Activities*, pp. 21–24
- *Listening and Speaking Activities*, pp. 15–16

- *Sentence-Combining Practice*, pp. 32–33
- *Thinking and Study Skills*, pp. 3–4, 8, 15
- *Writing Assessment and Evaluation Rubrics*

Get the Facts

Most of the details in a news story are facts—statements, events, and observations that can be proved or disproved. The readers of news articles—a broad, general-interest audience—want to know what happened, not what the writer's opinions are. The goal of a news article is to answer six basic questions, the five *W*s and an *H*.

5 *W*s and *H*	
Who?	Who did it? Who caused the action? Who else is affected?
What?	What happened? What was the action? What were the reactions?
When?	When did it take place? When will related actions occur?
Where?	Where did it happen? What was the scene like?
Why?	Why did it happen? Why is it significant?
How?	How did it happen? How does it work? How will it affect people?

Start with a Lead

An effective lead, or opening paragraph, attracts attention and provides a capsule summary of the article—all in the space of a sentence or two. The lead presents the essential facts, answering some or all of the six basic questions. Notice which questions are answered in this lead.

> Two California condors will be reintroduced into the wilds of Ventura County late this year in a gamble that the once nearly extinct birds can live free, officials said yesterday.

WHO?
WHAT?
WHERE?
WHEN?
WHY?

Journal Writing

As you go about your daily activities, try to see things through the eyes of a reporter. What news do you see in your classes, in the cafeteria, and on your way to and from school? In your journal practice writing leads about two or more scenes, trying to answer as many of the six basic questions as possible.

Teach

Learning Cooperatively

Divide the class into groups of six. Ask each group to write a lead for a possible news article about something that interests all group members: a recent field trip, a school sports event, and so on. Each student in a group should answer one of the six basic questions while one student takes notes. Invite the groups to share their material. **L2**

Using 5*W*s and *H*

Some students may have difficulty remembering what elements they must include in a news article. Suggest that students write out their answers to the six basic questions before they try to write a lead for a news article. Encourage them to label each answer with its appropriate question word. Students can use the list of answers to write the lead. **L1**

Two-Minute Skill Drill

Ask students to punctuate the following quote correctly.

I just don't know where my energy goes sighed Sarah. It's always the same. When lunch is over I'm ready to go home.

See also *Two-Minute Skill Drill Transparancy 5.8*

Journal Writing Tip

Formulating Questions To help students see things from a reporter's point of view, suggest that they study the style and content of several news article leads. Encourage students to try to formulate the six basic questions answered in the lead.

Teach

Using the Model

Ask students how the lead draws the reader into the story. (The lead creates a sense of curiosity and excitement about the team by mentioning two new and unknown factors.) Which of the six basic questions does Michael answer in the lead? (who—the Cookeville Cavaliers; what—prepare for a game; where—at Warren County; when—tonight; and how—with a new football coach and a new enthusiasm) **L2**

Taping Responses

Encourage students to tape-record the responses of people they want to quote in their articles. Then when they begin to organize the details, they can select the recorded material that supports their lead and quote it accurately. Students who don't have access to a tape recorder should carefully transcribe the quotations in a notebook. Make sure students choose portions of the response to quote, rather than incorporating their interviewee's entire response. **L3**

Additional Resources

For further stimuli for expository writing, see *Fine Art Transparencies*, 25–28.

Writing Process Transparencies, 11, 23–27

Cooperative Learning Activities

Thinking and Study Skills, pp. 3–4, 8, 15

Listening and Speaking Activities, pp. 15–16

Sentence-Combining Practice, pp. 32–33

Composition Practice, p. 41

Expository Writing

Present the Details

The events in a fictional story usually build up to a climax or turning point, often the most important event in the story. Reporters turn this pattern upside down. They start with a lead that sums up the most important event and relate other events in decreasing order of importance. This organization makes it easier for editors to make last-minute cuts in the story. Read Michael Han's story to see how it follows this pattern. Then review guidelines for writing a news article.

> How does Michael's lead draw readers into the story? Which of the five *W*s does he answer in the lead?

> After presenting the most important part of the story at the beginning, Michael adds less important material.

Grammar Tip

As you gather information for a news article, listen for direct quotations, which will add authority and interest to your writing. Set off direct quotes with quotation marks. For information on using quotation marks, see Lesson 21.9, pages 755–757.

Student Model

The Cookeville Cavaliers head into their game at Warren County tonight with a new football coach and a new enthusiasm.

"I'm looking forward to the season," said senior Jerald Bryant. "I think it's going to be a great one."

Jake Libbey begins his second stint as the head football coach of the Cavaliers with what could best be described as a "rebuilding" year. The team has only 32 players, 17 of them seniors.

The season began last Friday here in Cookeville with a win against Hillsboro. The Cavaliers are staring at a demanding schedule with five away games, including Oakland and McGavock. The Homecoming game will be against Riverdale on October 5.

"We are just going to have to take this schedule one game at a time," said Coach Libbey. "We can't look before us or behind us. We're really going to have to rise to the occasion with courage and desire."

Michael Han, Cookeville High School, Cookeville, Tennessee

Guidelines for Writing a News Article

1. Gather information that will add authority and interest to your writing.
2. Write a strong lead. Grab the reader's attention and summarize your main points.
3. Present information in order of importance. Start with the most important points.
4. Be fair. Cover all sides of the story, and keep your own opinions out of your article.
5. Make sure your facts are accurate and that proper names are spelled correctly.

250 Unit 5 Expository Writing

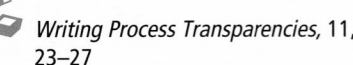 **Less Proficient Readers**

Organizing Ideas

Pair students who are less proficient in English with students whose first language is English and have them work together to brainstorm ideas for the articles. Then encourage students to make lists of information to support their ideas in their native languages and number them in order of importance to the articles, with the most important idea first. Students can then read the lists to their partners, who can help them organize the ideas. Students can use the lists as outlines.

Write a News Article

Imagine that you were a reporter who was present on the historic day when the Berlin Wall was opened. Write a news article using these facts:

- Wall is opened November 9, 1989.
- At an all-night celebration, people dance on the wall itself.
- People travel freely between East and West Berlin for the first time since 1961.
- At exactly midnight, people begin crossing.
- The wall is twenty-six miles long.
- Tens of thousands of East and West Berliners swarm across the wall.
- Some chisel off pieces for souvenirs.
- One elderly East Berliner who crosses over the wall is overheard saying, "I can't believe I'm here. We have dreamed of this."

PURPOSE To write a news story about a major historical event
AUDIENCE Readers of your local newspaper, all ages
LENGTH 2–3 paragraphs

WRITING RUBRICS To write an effective news article, you should

- write a strong lead
- present details in decreasing order of importance
- avoid personal opinions

Using Computers

In revising, if you discover a misspelled word that you use again and again, save time by using the Search and Replace feature of your word-processing program.

Punctuate direct quotations correctly.

Note how the writer punctuated this direct quote in her news article about condors:

> *"Frankly, we will be taking a gamble,"*
> *Plenert said. "The chance of losing a*
> *young condor . . . is extremely high."*

Rewrite the following sentences, adding or correcting punctuation as necessary.

1. For years, the Japanese assumed that their cities were earthquake resistant, a news reporter commented.
2. "Twenty seconds of terror shattered that belief" said one reporter, "when a 7.2 earthquake hit Kobe, Japan, in 1995"
3. A government official admitted, I never felt so powerless in my life.
4. A second official confessed, "The government's initial response was pure panic and confusion."
5. "Revamping disaster-relief plans and revising building codes are the only way to avoid future disasters" seismologists warn.

See Lesson 21.9, pages 755–757.

Listening and Speaking

BROADCAST NEWS Rewrite your news article or a news article on another event as a TV report for the nightly news. Deliver your report in the style of a network news anchor. Discuss with the class the major difference between a written news article and a TV news report.

5.8 Writing a News Article **251**

Expository Writing

Assess

Evaluation Rubrics

Write a News Article

Use these criteria when evaluating your students' writing.

- Does the lead sum up the story's main points?
- Has the student organized the article's details according to their decreasing order of importance?
- Is the article strictly factual, unclouded by the student's personal opinions?
- Has the student spelled proper nouns correctly in the article?
- Has the student answered the six basic questions in the article?

See also *Writing Assessment & Evaluation Rubrics.*

Using Computers

Invite volunteers to demonstrate the Search and Replace feature to the class and to explain its use.

Reteaching

📁 *Composition Reteaching,* p. 41

Enrichment

📁 *Composition Enrichment,* p. 41

Close

Encourage students to find and bring to class both especially good and very bad examples of articles from newspapers and magazines. Challenge them to become critical readers of news articles and to spot incomplete leads or misleading details.

Grammar Link

Answers

1. "For years, . . . resistant," a news reporter commented.
2. "Twenty . . . belief," said one reporter, "when . . . 1995."
3. . . . admitted, "I . . . life."
4. . . . confessed, "The . . . confusion."
5. "Revamping . . . disasters," seismologists warn.

Focus

Lesson Overview

Objective
- To learn to budget time during an essay test, to identify key words in essay questions, and to reword a question in the thesis statement of the answer

Skills
- scanning; estimating; outlining

Critical Thinking
- clarifying; goal setting; making decisions

Listening and Speaking
- listening to directions

Bellringer
Daily Language Activity

When students enter the classroom, have this assignment on the board: *Quickly jot down what ideas ran through your mind just before you took your last essay test.*

Grammar Link to the Bellringer
Have students check whether they used complete sentences to express their thoughts. Have them rewrite their ideas if necessary.

See also *Daily Language Practice*

Motivating Activity

Encourage students to talk about their fears and frustrations about taking essay tests. Do they feel ill-prepared and panic-stricken? Do they feel they aren't given enough time to finish tests? Do they spend too much time on one answer? Do they have trouble writing coherent paragraphs under the pressure of a time limit? Invite students who have overcome these problems to share their strategies.

Expository Writing

LESSON
5.9

Taking an Essay Test

Do you react like the character in the cartoon when you have to take an essay test? In this lesson you will learn some ways to examine test questions and compose illuminating answers.

Look at the sample test below. How would you go about answering the following questions?

> Answer all the questions below. You will have one hour to complete this test.
> 1. Define the term <u>biome</u>. (20 points)
> 2. Discuss the characteristics of desert biomes. (20 points)
> 3. Compare the qualities of tropical savannas to those of temperate grasslands. (20 points)
> 4. Analyze the factors that affect the distribution of biomes. (40 points)
> 5. Describe the vegetation found in the tropical rain forest.
> 6. Summarize the problems facing tropical rain forests today.

252   Unit 5 Expository Writing

Resource Manager

Planning Resources
- *Lesson Plans*

 Transparencies
- *Bellringer*
- *Daily Language Practice*
- *Fine Art* 25–28
- *Two-Minute Skill Drill*
- *Writing Process* 11, 23–27

☞ Other Print Resources
- *Composition Enrichment*, p. 42
- *Composition Practice*, p. 42
- *Composition Reteaching*, p. 42
- *Cooperative Learning Activities*, pp. 21–24
- *Listening and Speaking Activities*, pp. 15–16
- *Research Paper and Report Writing*, pp. 43–48

- *Sentence-Combining Practice*, pp. 32–33
- *Thinking and Study Skills*, pp. 1–2, 15, 17, 26
- *Writing Across the Curriculum*
- *Writing Assessment and Evaluation Rubrics*

Develop a Plan of Attack

When you sit down to take a test like the one on the previous page, don't jump right in and start writing answers. Instead, take a moment to look over the individual questions and the test as a whole. That way you can make plans that will help you answer all the questions in the time available. Keep the following steps in mind.

Read the directions. Are you expected to answer *all* the questions, or do you have a choice? How much time do you have to complete the test?

▶

Read each question. Which ones will be easier or will take less time to answer? Are you unprepared to answer any of the questions?

▶

Note the point value for each question. Are some questions worth more than others? Does the test include any extra credit questions?

To avoid the problem of time being up while you are still writing answers, estimate how much time you will need for each question. Consider both how much you know about the subject and how many points the question is worth. The greater the point value, the more time you should plan to devote to the question, especially if it's one about which you know a great deal. The graphic below shows one way to divide your time among four unequally weighted questions. How might your time allotment vary if you knew little about question 2?

Time allotted for test:
1 hour

Question Value:
#1: **20 points**
#2: **20 points**
#3: **20 points**
#4: **40 points**

| 9:00 A.M. Start 1 | 9:12 A.M. Start 2 | 9:24 A.M. Start 3 | 9:36 A.M. Start 4 | 10:00 A.M. Finish |

Journal Writing

In your journal, reflect on your test-taking experiences. Write about some ways that previewing tests and budgeting your time could help you improve your performance.

Teach

Staying with the Plan

Tell students that once they determine how much time to allot for a question, they should stick to that limit—even when they don't complete the answer. Encourage them to move on to the next question. Explain that one or two of the remaining questions will probably require less time than they have estimated. After they have answered the remaining questions, they can go back and finish answering earlier questions. **L2**

Two-Minute Skill Drill

How should you divide your time in a half-hour essay test with three questions: a 60-point question and two 20-point questions?

See also *Two-Minute Skill Drill Transparency 5.9*

Journal Writing Tip

Analyzing Tests Suggest that students analyze tests they have taken recently to help them identify past mistakes. Did they do poorly because they didn't follow directions? Were points taken off because an answer was incomplete? Did they take too much time answering one question? A critical analysis of students' test-taking experiences may help improve their performance on future essay tests.

Teach

Practicing Essay Questions

Have students work in pairs to practice answering essay questions on material recently covered in this text or in the text for another course in which both partners are enrolled. Encourage students to ask each other questions about the material, making sure the student partner understands how to respond. As the students answer the questions with the help of his or her partner, both partners should take notes, outlining the main points made. Students can use these notes for further study. **L1**

Understand the Questions

Make sure you understand each question before you start to respond. Focus on key words that tell exactly what you have to do. Below are some questions that include common key words and some strategies for answering the questions.

Key Words in Essay Questions		
Question	**Key Word**	**Strategy for Answering**
Define the term *biome*. **Define**		Tell what the term means, and explain what distinguishes it from other similar terms.
Discuss the characteristics of desert biomes.	**Discuss**	Look at your subject from several viewpoints, and provide facts and other details to explain its characteristics or qualities.
Compare the qualities of tropical savannas with those of temperate grasslands.	**Compare**	Tell how two or more subjects are alike and how they are different. Support your ideas with details and examples.
Analyze the factors that affect the distribution of biomes.	**Analyze**	Identify the important parts of your subject, examine each part, and explain how each part relates to the others.
Describe the vegetation found in tropical rain forests.	**Describe**	Create and organize concrete sensory images that vividly illustrate the qualities of your subject.
Summarize the problems facing tropical rain forests today.	**Summarize**	Present the main points or concepts of your subject, and give a brief explanation for each.

English Language Learners

Identifying Key Words

Non-native English speakers may have difficulty understanding what kind of answer each key word requires. Help these students understand the key words in essay questions by supplying them with concrete examples of answers to actual questions. While these students take notes, ask students who are native English speakers to answer the questions in the chart or to respond to essay questions of your own (perhaps gleaned from old tests).

Write a Thesis Statement

An effective thesis statement, a sentence that communicates the main idea you intend to develop in an answer, can point you in the right direction as you begin writing. Such a statement also tells the reader how you will respond to the key word in the question and helps you determine what types of details you must include to develop your essay. Often you can rephrase the question as a statement and indicate how you will respond to it, as in the example below.

> 2. Discuss the characteristics of desert biomes. (20 points)
>
> *Desert biomes are characterized by a variety of harsh conditions, chief of which is a lack of water.*

Create a Plan

Since you probably will not have much time to revise your answer, it pays to plan what you intend to say before you start writing. Your plan should be simple, logically organized, and easy to follow. Create an outline, a cluster diagram, or a comparison-contrast chart to identify and organize your main points. Notice how brief your organizing plan can be.

> 2. Discuss the characteristics of desert biomes. (20 points)
>
> *A. Amount of precipitation*
> *B. Range of temperatures*
> *C. Types of plants*
> *D. Types of animals*

Journal Writing

Look at the questions in the chart on the previous page. In your journal, write thesis statements for several by rewording the questions and anticipating how you might respond to them.

Drafting Tip

As you write, keep looking back at your thesis statement to remind yourself of your focus.

5.9

Teach

Trying Thesis Statements

Students may waste precious time trying to frame the first sentence of their essays. As an exercise in jump-starting essay responses, post some comic questions on the chalkboard for your students to respond to. Students need not be entirely serious in their answers but should draft their statements to respond to the questions. Make sure each question contains a key word or phrase for students to use as a starting point. **L2**

Evaluating Answers

Encourage students to look over their old essay tests and evaluate their answers using the following questions. Does each answer begin with a thesis statement that introduces the main idea? Do supporting details develop the main idea? Does each paragraph address a topic that supports the main idea? Are the sentences in each answer linked by transitions? Does each answer conclude by restating the main idea? Invite students to rewrite the answers that do not adhere to this format. **L3**

Journal Writing Tip

Identifying Main Idea Suggest that students try to identify the main idea they want to develop in an essay before they begin writing thesis statements for the questions. The thesis statement should introduce the main idea in general terms; subsequent sentences should develop and support the main idea.

Cultural Connections

Preparing for Essay Tests

High school students in many western European countries must take a series of essay tests in order to graduate and qualify for university study. The essay questions cover a broad range of subjects and require students to apply everything they have learned in the course of their high school careers. Some students cannot withstand the pressures and fail the tests as a result. Ask students how they would prepare for a similar series of essay tests.

Teach

Evaluating Answers

Ask students if the answer addresses every main point in the rough outline on page 255. (All points are covered. The items identified as "types of plants" and "types of animals" are introduced by a general statement in the first sentence of the second paragraph.) Ask students to identify some of the specific details used to support this generalization. (The writer's discussion of how the saguaro cactus, the desert dandelion, and nocturnal animals have adapted to desert life supports the generalization.) **L2**

Additional Resources

For further stimuli for expository writing, see *Fine Art Transparencies*, 25–28.

Writing Process Transparencies, 11, 23–27

Cooperative Learning Activities
Writing Across the Curriculum
Thinking and Study Skills, pp. 1–2, 15, 17, 26
Sentence-Combining Practice, pp. 32–33
Listening and Speaking Activities, pp. 15–16
Research Paper and Report Writing, pp. 43–48
Composition Practice, p. 42

Draft Your Answer

Because your time is limited, you need to use a simple, straightforward format for writing your answer. Your thesis statement, which introduces your main idea, can serve as your first sentence. Then you can let your outline or graphic aid guide you as you compose your answer, adding solid facts and other supporting details that elaborate on your thesis. Remember to use appropriate transition words and phrases to connect ideas. Finally, end your answer with a brief conclusion that restates your main ideas.

The answer begins with the thesis statement. Each paragraph addresses a topic that supports the thesis. The conclusion restates the main point.

What specific details are used to support generalizations?

2. Discuss the characteristics of desert biomes. (20 points)

Desert biomes are characterized by harsh conditions, including a lack of water. Deserts get little rain, so plants are few and widely scattered. The soil is often mainly sand. The lack of ground cover affects temperatures. The land heats up rapidly during the day and cools off rapidly at night, so temperature ranges are extreme.

Plants and animals have adapted to the desert in various ways. Some plants, such as the saguaro cactus, store water in their tissues during rains and use it later in dry periods. Others, such as the desert dandelion, grow only when there is enough moisture. Many desert animals are nocturnal, sleeping in the shade during the day.

In the harsh conditions of desert biomes, only hardy plants and animals survive.

Editing Tip

Even though time is limited, be sure to proofread your work. Pay special attention to the spelling and usage of those key terms and concepts on which you are being tested.

There's no getting away from essay tests; you will face them throughout your school years. By following the steps summarized below, you can probably improve your performance.

Guidelines for Taking an Essay Test

1. Preview the test by reading all directions and questions.
2. Budget your time, using the point value of each question as a guide.
3. Prepare a thesis statement and brief outline or graphic aid before you begin drafting your essay.
4. Start your essay with your thesis statement, follow your outline, and support each point with specific facts and details. Conclude by restating your thesis.

Real World Connection

Using What You Learn

Tell students that they probably won't have to take essay tests once they have completed their formal education. However, you might point out that adults are often required to write essay answers when they fill out job applications or college applications, apply for loans, or complete surveys.

5.9 | Writing Activities

Write an Essay Answer

Read the following excerpt from *Sand County Almanac,* and take the essay test that follows it. Allow yourself thirty minutes. Read the whole test before you begin.

PURPOSE To take an essay test on literature
AUDIENCE Your English teacher
LENGTH 3–6 paragraphs

When I was a boy, there was an old German merchant who lived in a little cottage in our town. On Sundays he used to go out and knock chips off the limestone ledges along the Mississippi, and he had a great tonnage of these chips, all labeled and catalogued. The chips contained little fossil stems of some defunct water creatures called crinoids. The townspeople regarded this gentle old fellow as just a little bit abnormal, but harmless. One day the newspaper reported the arrival of certain titled strangers. It was whispered that these visitors were great scientists. Some of them were from foreign lands, and some among the world's leading paleontologists. They came to visit the harmless old man and to hear his pronouncements on crinoids, and they accepted these pronouncements as law. When the old German died, the town awoke to the fact that he was a world authority on his subject, a creator of knowledge, a maker of scientific history. He was a great man — a man beside whom the local captains of industry were mere bushwhackers. His collection went to a national museum, and his name is known in all the nations of the earth.

Aldo Leopold, *Sand County Almanac*

Essay Test

• Compare and contrast what the German merchant was like with what people in the town thought he was like. (60 points)
• Summarize Leopold's main point in telling this story. (40 points)

WRITING RUBRICS To write an effective answer to an essay question, you should

• budget your time and plan your answers
• study the key words in each question
• write a clear thesis statement

Grammar Link

Use commas in compound sentences to avoid run-ons.

Commas and coordinating conjunctions are needed between the clauses in a compound sentence.

Rewrite the following compound sentences, adding commas as necessary.

1. Energy cannot be created or destroyed yet it can change form.
2. Energy is needed to maintain all aspects of life for you use it even when you sleep.
3. All living things get their energy from the sun but plants get it directly.
4. Energy conversions always involve a loss nor is any conversion 100-percent efficient.

See Lesson 21.6, page 743–751.

Cross-Curricular Activity

PROOFREADING In a small group, exchange essay answers and check for misspelled words and illegible writing. Discuss common strengths and weaknesses.

Listening and Speaking

COOPERATIVE LEARNING In a small group, brainstorm for essay questions on a science topic you are studying. Discuss various ways of responding to the questions.

Assess

Evaluation Rubrics

Write an Essay Answer

Use these criteria when evaluating your students' writing:

• Was an outline or graphic used to organize ideas?
• Did each answer begin with a thesis statement?
• Did specific examples from the passage support ideas?
• Are all the main points in the outline or graphic addressed in the answer?

See also *Writing Assessment & Evaluation Rubrics.*

Listening and Speaking

Evaluate each student's work using these criteria.

• Does the key word in each question indicate exactly what kind of answer is required?
• Did the student use the key word to frame the thesis statement and select details for the answer?
• Does the thesis statement provide a focus for the entire essay?

Reteaching

📁 *Composition Reteaching,* p. 42

Enrichment

📁 *Composition Enrichment,* p. 42

Close

Have students answer a final essay question:

Summarize what you have learned in this lesson about taking an essay test.

Grammar Link

Answers

1. Energy cannot be created or destroyed, yet it can change form.
2. Energy is needed to maintain all aspects of life, for you use it even when you sleep.
3. All living things get their energy from the sun, but plants get it directly.
4. Energy conversions always involve a loss, nor is any conversion 100-percent efficient.

Focus

Lesson Overview

Objective
- To develop a comparison of two or more literary works

Skills
- rereading; taking notes; prewriting

Critical Thinking
- recalling; analyzing

Listening and Speaking
- discussing

Bellringer
Daily Language Activity
When students enter the classroom, have this assignment on the board: *Briefly compare two or three authors whose work you admire.*

Grammar Link to the Bellringer
Have students check that the comparisons of their authors are clear.

See also *Daily Language Practice*

Motivating Activity
Ask students what literary genre, such as mystery, science fiction, or poetry, they prefer to read. Invite students to compare and discuss two of their favorite authors within the genre. Does one author create more believable characters or plots than the other? How do the authors treat a similar theme, such as death or love? Does one author write seriously about serious subjects, while the other takes a more light-hearted approach? Tell students that they can write effective literary criticism by comparing character, plot, theme, tone, or other elements of literature.

258

Expository Writing

LESSON 5.10

WRITING ABOUT LITERATURE
Comparing and Contrasting Literature

There are many approaches you can take in comparing and contrasting works of literature. For example, you might compare this modern fable with a traditional fable.

> The first sentence introduces a style and tone similar to those of traditional fables.

Literature Model

There was once a town in the heart of America where all life seemed to live in harmony with its surroundings. The town lay in the midst of a checkerboard of prosperous farms, with fields of grain and hillsides of orchards where, in spring, white clouds of bloom drifted above the green fields. In autumn, oak and maple and birch set up a blaze of color that flamed and flickered across a backdrop of pines. Then foxes barked in the hills and deer silently crossed the fields, half hidden in the mists of the fall mornings.

Along the roads, laurel, viburnum and alder, great ferns and wildflowers delighted the traveler's eye through much of the year. Even in winter the roadsides were places of beauty, where countless birds came to feed on the berries and on the seed heads of the dried weeds rising above the snow. The countryside was, in fact, famous for the abundance and variety of its bird life, and when the flood of migrants was pouring through in spring and fall, people traveled from great distances to observe them. Others came to fish the streams, which flowed clear and cold out of the hills and contained shady pools where trout lay. So it had been from the days many years ago when the first settlers raised their houses, sank their wells, and built their barns.

Then a strange blight crept over the area and everything began to change. Some evil spell had settled on the community: mysterious maladies swept the flocks of chickens; the cattle and sheep sickened and died. Everywhere was a shadow of death. The farmers spoke of much illness among their families. In the town the doctors had become more and more puzzled by new kinds of sickness appearing among their

---

Resource Manager

Planning Resources
- *Lesson Plans*

Transparencies
- *Bellringer*
- *Daily Language Practice*
- *Fine Art* 25–28
- *Two-Minute Skill Drill*
- *Writing Process* 11, 23–27

Other Print Resources
- *Composition Enrichment*, p. 43
- *Composition Practice*, p. 43
- *Composition Reteaching*, p. 43
- *Cooperative Learning Activities*, pp. 21–24
- *Listening and Speaking Activities*, pp. 15–16
- *Research Paper and Report Writing*, pp. 43–48

- *Sentence-Combining Practice*, pp. 32–33
- *Thinking and Study Skills*, pp. 3, 5, 10
- *Writing Across the Curriculum*
- *Writing Assessment and Evaluation Rubrics*

patients. There had been several sudden and unexplained deaths, not only among adults but even among children, who would be stricken suddenly while at play and die within a few hours.

There was a strange stillness. The birds, for example— where had they gone? Many people spoke of them, puzzled and disturbed. The feeding stations in the back yards were deserted. The few birds seen anywhere were moribund; they trembled violently and could not fly. It was a spring without voices. On the mornings that had once throbbed with the dawn chorus of robins, catbirds, doves, jays, wrens, and scores of other bird voices there was now no sound; only silence lay over the fields and woods and marsh. . . .

No witchcraft, no enemy action had silenced the rebirth of new life in this stricken world. The people had done it themselves.

Rachel Carson, *Silent Spring*

> Most traditional fables end with a moral. Carson's fable ends with an accusation. How does her accusation serve as a kind of moral?

Expository Writing

Teach

Using the Model

Read the model aloud to the class. Ask students to discuss how the selection's setting compares with that of a traditional fable. (The town in the model is not anchored in a specified time or place.) How does Rachel Carson's accusation serve as a kind of moral for the reader? (The accusation warns the reader that destruction can happen anywhere if people do not protect the environment.) **L2**

Organizing Comparisons

Suggest that students organize the similarities and differences between literary works in a Venn diagram or a comparison frame (see p. 237). A Venn diagram can help students explore as many similarities and differences as they can identify in the works. Students should use a comparison frame once they have determined which literary elements they want to compare and contrast. **L1**

Two-Minute Skill Drill

Have students write a short paragraph in which they compare the characteristics of any two of the following: fables, plays, poems, short stories, or novels.

✏ **See also** *Two-Minute Skill Drill Transparency 5.10*

Evaluate Literary Elements

Depending on what your precise topic is, your literary analysis will examine some or all of the elements listed below.

Analyzing Basic Elements of Literature	
Element	**Question to Ask**
Theme, or central focus	Does the work address a universal problem or teach a moral?
Style	Is the language formal or informal, figurative or objective?
Tone	Is it serious? Sad? Humorous?
Setting	What is the role of time and place?
Plot	What is the main conflict?
Characters	How do we know what the characters are like?

Prewriting Tip

It is often helpful to write down your initial impressions about a piece of literature as you read.

Journal Writing

Reread a short literary piece you've read recently. In your journal, note what you see now that you hadn't seen before.

Journal Writing Tip

Recalling Major Elements Before students reread, suggest that they try to recall the major elements in the work. After students reread the work, they can observe whether their earlier impressions changed.

Teach

Using the Model

Ask students how the writer uses the quotation from Carson to compare the form of her fable with that of traditional fables. (The quotation provides an example of the fable's simple, direct style. It also introduces the contrast between the fable's style and its serious message.) What does the writer contrast at the end? (The simple truths of traditional fables are contrasted with Carson's weightier warning.) **L2**

Additional Resources

For further stimuli for expository writing, see *Fine Art Transparencies*, 25–28.

Writing Process Transparencies, 11, 23–27

Writing Across the Curriculum

Cooperative Learning Activities

Thinking and Study Skills, pp. 3, 5, 10

Listening and Speaking Activities, pp. 15–16

Sentence-Combining Practice, pp. 32–33

Research Paper and Report Writing, p. 41

Composition Practice, p. 43

Expository Writing *(vertical tab)*

Grammar Tip

When comparing literary pieces, use quotation marks to set off the titles of short works, such as short stories and poems. Italicize, or underline, the titles of longer works, such as novels. See Lesson 21.9, page 755, and 21.10, page 758.

Make Your Point

After you've identified the elements on which you will focus, examine similarities and differences about each element. Look also for direct quotations you can use to help you make your points. Use these guidelines to help you.

Guidelines for Writing a Literary Comparison and Contrast

1. Write an introductory paragraph stating your main idea.
2. Use information from your reading to shape your writing.
3. Include quotations, when appropriate, to support your points.
4. Write an effective conclusion, summing up your main idea in a sentence or two.

The following model compares and contrasts Rachel Carson's fable with the traditional form of the fable. Note how it uses the guidelines.

Model

For thousands of years, people have told fables to teach a lesson or to pass on wisdom. Fables were part of the oral tradition of many early cultures, and the well-known Aesop's fables date to the sixth century B.C. Yet, the form of the fable still has value today, as Rachel Carson demonstrates in "A Fable for Tomorrow."

Carson uses a simple, direct style common to fables. In fact, her style and tone are seemingly directed at children. "There was once a town in the heart of America where all life seemed to live in harmony with its surroundings," her fable begins, borrowing some familiar words from many age-old fables. Behind the simple style, however, is a serious message intended for everyone.

In contrast to traditional fables, Carson's story ends with an accusation instead of a moral. She warns of the environmental dangers facing society, and she teaches that people must take responsibility for saving their environment.

The themes of traditional fables often deal with simple truths about everyday life. In contrast, Carson's theme is a more weighty warning about environmental destruction. Nevertheless, Carson proves that a simple literary form that has been passed down through the ages can still be used today to draw attention to important truths.

The form of Carson's fable is compared to that of traditional fables.

How does this quotation contribute to the overall passage?

What does the writer contrast at the end? How does the writer achieve this effect?

MEETING INDIVIDUAL NEEDS — Less Proficient Readers

Making Comparisons

Some students may feel that their command of English is not sufficient to compare and contrast literary works written in that language. You might suggest that these students analyze works they have read (and which were originally written) in their first language. Explain that students should write their analyses in English, translating any quotations from the works that they want to include to support their points.

Write a Comparison-Contrast Essay

The two poems on this page were both written by William Carlos Williams. Write a comparison-contrast essay about the two poems.

PURPOSE To compare and contrast works of a poet
AUDIENCE Your English teacher and classmates
LENGTH 2 paragraphs

WRITING RUBRICS To write an effective comparison-contrast essay, you should

- identify key elements in each poem
- explore similarities and differences for each element
- identify quotations to support your points
- check your spelling

This Is Just to Say
I have eaten
the plums
that were in
the icebox

and which
you were probably
saving for breakfast

Forgive me
they were delicious
so sweet
and so cold

The Red Wheelbarrow
so much depends
upon

a red wheel
barrow

glazed with rain
water

beside the white
chickens

Using Computers

To write effective literary criticism, you must find the right words to express your meaning. If your word-processing program has an electronic thesaurus, be sure to use it, especially in revising.

Grammar Link

Make clear and complete comparisons.

In the model, note how the student clearly states one difference between Rachel Carson's fable and more traditional fables:

In contrast to traditional fables, Carson's story ends with an accusation instead of a moral.

Rewrite each sentence below to correct the unclear comparison.

1. Rachel Carson, a marine biologist, wrote more books on the environment than any scientist.

2. She has had more influence on environmental beliefs than anyone.

3. Carson portrayed people's role in silencing the rebirth of new life as greater than witchcraft or enemy action.

4. Traditional fables deal with simpler truths than Carson.

5. Still, in their own way yesterday's fables are as valuable as today.

See Lesson 18.4, page 670.

Viewing and Representing

COOPERATIVE LEARNING Work with a partner to create a visual image to represent the poems. Discuss the following questions with your partner before you start. How will you depict the ideas in each poem? What materials will you use to create your images? Display your work along with the text of each poem.

Expository Writing

Assess

Evaluation Rubrics

Write a Comparison-Contrast Essay

Use these criteria when evaluating your students' writing.

- Have students examined the basic literary elements—especially style and tone—that play a major role in both poems?
- Did students examine how the works are similar or different on a number of points?
- Were quotations used where appropriate to support a point?

See also *Writing Assessment & Evaluation Rubrics.*

Using Computers

Invite volunteers to demonstrate the use of the electronic thesaurus. Give students a list of words for which they can find synonyms.

Reteaching

📁 *Composition Reteaching,* p. 43

Enrichment

📁 *Composition Enrichment,* p. 43

Close

Discuss with students the purpose of comparing and contrasting literary works. Ask whether students feel that writing their essays helped them understand more about the characteristics of the literary works they chose to write about.

Grammar Link

Answers

(*Answers will vary.*)
1. . . . than any other scientist.
2. . . . than anyone else.
3. Carson suggested that people's role in silencing the rebirth of new life was greater than the role of witchcraft or enemy action.
4. . . . than Carson's fable does.
5. . . . are as valuable as today's.

Focus

Lesson Overview

Objective
- To produce a piece of expository writing that explains a process for a general audience

Skills
- using the five stages of the writing process: prewriting, drafting, revising, editing, and presenting; explaining a process; organizing steps in a clear, logical order; using appropriate vocabulary; following standards of grammar, usage, and mechanics

Critical Thinking
- analyzing; generating new information; organizing

Listening and Speaking
- evaluating; discussing; informal speaking; formal speaking; questioning

Bellringer
Daily Language Activity

When students enter the classroom, have this assignment on the board: *Write a brief paragraph describing an experience you've had using written directions, such as assembly instructions for toys or equipment.*

Grammar Link to the Bellringer

Have students review their answers for subjects and verbs that do not agree.

See also *Daily Language Practice*

Motivating Activity

Invite students to discuss a favorite pastime such as fixing a car or doing tricks with a yo-yo. Ask them to explain how they carry out the process.

Writing Process in Action

Expository Writing

WRITING *Online*

Visit the Writer's Choice Web site at **writerschoice.glencoe.com** for additional writing prompts.

Expository Writing

In preceding lessons you learned about the different kinds of expository writing, the purpose of each, and ways to make exposition informative and engaging. You've had a chance to write comparison-contrasts, definitions, and news articles. Now you are invited to write a practical or whimsical explanation of a process that is familiar and enjoyable for you.

Assignment

Context

You are a member of a team of writers selected to write a book entitled *How to Do Just About Anything.* You have been asked to write an entry explaining a process with which you are familiar and that you enjoy. The subject you select can be practical or whimsical, and your writing style should be light and engaging.

Purpose

To write a practical or whimsical explanation of a familiar process

Audience

Teenagers and adults who read general-interest books

Length

1–2 pages

The guidelines on the following pages can help you plan and write your book entry. Read through the guidelines, and then refer back to them as you complete this assignment. However, don't feel tied down by them. Remember, you're in charge of your own writing process.

Resource Manager

Planning Resources
- *Lesson Plans*

 Transparencies
- *Bellringer*
- *Daily Language Practice*
- *Writing Process* 11, 23–27

 Other Print Resources
- *Composition Enrichment*, p. 44
- *Composition Practice*, p. 44
- *Composition Reteaching*, p. 44
- *Grammar Workbook*, Lessons 44–51
- *Sentence-Combining Practice*, pp. 32–33
- *Thinking and Study Skills*, pp. 13, 25

- *Writing Assessment and Evaluation Rubrics*

 Software
- *Writer's Assistant*

 Web Sites
- *writerschoice.glencoe.com*
- *lit.glencoe.com*

Writing Process in Action

Prewriting

A good way to find a topic is to think about your talents and your interests. Let your mind wander for a few minutes. Additional ways to probe your thoughts are listed to the right.

Once you've found a topic, think about what you want to accomplish with this piece. You might want to clear up misconceptions about something, persuade readers to look at your process in a new light, or just entertain your readers. Try freewriting to explore how you really feel about your topic; develop a main idea statement.

Next, think about your audience. The fact that you will be writing for a general readership means you can't assume readers will have any prior knowledge of your process. It also means they probably won't have enough interest to wade through piles of dry facts.

Drafting

The challenge in explaining a process is to make your writing more than just a monotonous list of steps. The key is finding a way to make your writing flow. Start by figuring out how to break down your subject. What are the major terms and concepts you need to explain? What are the processes related to these concepts?

Next, think about how you can weave the concepts and processes into an engaging expository essay. Don't let yourself get bogged down in technicalities. Keep your audience in mind, and consider what details will grab their attention and maintain their interest. Note how naturalist writer Sue Hubbell mixes factual data with first-person observations in the model that follows.

Prewriting Options

- Freewrite about your areas of expertise. Explore jobs, hobbies, sports, and school subjects.
- List "how to" topics.
- Hold a brainstorming session with your classmates.

Prewriting Tip

To gain better understanding of your audience, ask yourself the questions listed in Lesson 5.2, page 224.

Teach

Developing Ideas for Expository Writing

To help students develop ideas for their entries, ask them to write "I'm good at" at the top of a piece of paper and then complete the statement, listing four or five areas of personal expertise. Then divide the class into pairs for a Partners Activity. Ask partners to exchange their lists and challenge each other to briefly explain one of the processes on the lists. If a student has trouble explaining one process, the partner should select another from the student's list. Encourage the partners to ask questions about the process. Once both students in a pair have found a process they are comfortable discussing, they should discuss these processes with another team. **L2**

Drafting

Developing Paragraphs

Students who have trouble developing topics into expository articles may be able to choose processes and think of several parts of the processes but be unable to order the parts. Suggest that they use each part as a topic sentence for a paragraph and then develop it and support it with more information. If necessary, help students write each paragraph on a separate note card or sheet of paper and then tie the paragraphs together at the end. **L1**

Enrichment and Extension

Extending Exposition

- Brainstorm for ways to use expository writing in other subjects.
- Explore opportunities for extending expository writing beyond the classroom, such as an article about how to improve a local recycling program.

Teach

Revising

Peer Editing

Students can work with peer editors before they revise their writing. You might duplicate the Peer Response forms in *Writing Assessment & Evaluation Rubrics.* Suggest that peer editors respond to these questions:

• Are the steps easy to follow?
• Does the writing flow smoothly?
• Would more background information be helpful? **L2**

Editing

Peer Editing

After students have edited their work, have them edit another student's writing. Remind them to refer to the Editing Checklist on student page 265. **L2**

Presenting

Before students present their expository writing, discuss how to prepare their papers for publication. Emphasize the importance of neatness.

Additional Resources

 Writing Process Transparencies, 11, 23–27

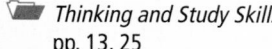 *Thinking and Study Skills,* pp. 13, 25

Sentence-Combining Practice, pp. 32–33

Composition Practice, p. 44

 Grammar Workbook, Lessons 44–51

Expository Writing

Drafting Tip

For tips on writing about a process, see Lesson 5.3, pages 228–231.

Revising Tip

For additional tips on revising expository writing, see Lesson 5.3, page 230.

Literature Model

I n early springtime, the bees' need for pollen may be greater than what is available, and then they will compulsively gather up almost any fine granular material—sawdust, bits of plastic packing materials, ashes—whether it is useful to them or not. I often see them at the bird feeder, picking through the wild bird feed. At that time of year, I often get a telephone call from a dairy farmer who lives near one of my beeyards.

"Hey, Sue," he says. "How about coming over and feeding your bees? They're in the calf feed again."

Sue Hubbell, *A Book of Bees . . . and How to Keep Them*

Revising

To begin revising, read over your draft to make sure that what you have written fits your purpose and your audience. Then have a **writing conference.** Read your draft to a partner or small group. Use your audience's reactions to help you evaluate your work so far. The questions in the Revising Checklist can help you and your listeners.

An easy way to check your explanation for completeness is to visualize yourself actually doing the process. Walk through each step of the process mentally, checking your work as you go. Sharing your draft with a peer reader is another way to identify holes in your explanation. Ask for feedback about steps that are unclear, terms that are unfamiliar, background information that would be helpful.

Next, look closely at how your explanation flows. Make sure you use strong topic sentences to tell readers where you are headed with each paragraph. Within paragraphs, use transitions to move readers along the steps of the process.

Revising Checklist

• Is my explanation complete, clear, and accurate?
• Are the steps of the process easy to follow?
• Have I used a writing style that a general audience will enjoy?
• Have I defined any unfamiliar terms and concepts?

Journal Writing Tip

Expository Writing If students found one part of the writing process particularly frustrating, it might be a good topic for this journal entry.

Enrichment and Extension

Follow-up Ideas

• Set aside time for students to celebrate completing their projects.
• If students are sending their work out of the classroom for publication or sharing, make sure that photocopies are retained.

Editing

Once you have revised your article for basic content and organization, **proofread** it carefully for errors in grammar, usage, mechanics, and spelling. Use the questions at the right as a guide.

In addition to proofreading, use the list below to make sure your explanation does all the things you want it to do. When you're satisfied, make a clean copy of your explanation and proofread it one more time.

Editing Checklist

- Have I avoided sentence fragments and run-on sentences?
- Do my subjects and verbs agree?
- Have I used correct capitalization?
- Have I made any comparisons clear and logical?
- Have I checked carefully for possible misspellings?

Reflection

Make sure your exposition—

- ✔ focuses on explaining a process
- ✔ presents steps in a clear, easy-to-follow order
- ✔ uses terms and concepts related to the process in an appropriate way
- ✔ uses a light, engaging style of writing
- ✔ follows correct grammar, usage, mechanics, and spelling

Proofreading

For proofreading symbols, see page 84.

Presenting

With your classmates, compile a class "how to" book. Create a cover, table of contents, and an introduction for the volume. Have interested classmates either draw or find illustrations to include in the book.

Journal Writing

Reflect on your writing process experience. Answer these questions in your journal: What do you like best about your process explanation? What was the hardest part of writing it? What did you learn in your writing conference? What new things have you learned as a writer?

Assess

Evaluation Rubrics

Use the following questions to evaluate the students' finished writing:

- Does the prewriting focus on a process that is appropriate for this article?
- Does the article present the steps in a logical order?
- Does the lead contain attention-grabbing details to hook the reader?
- Has the student used a light, engaging writing style?
- Do the topic sentences in the revised article prepare the reader for the information contained in each paragraph?
- Has the student used transitions in the revised article to move readers through the steps of the process?
- Has the edited article been checked for errors in grammar, usage, and mechanics?
- Have unfamiliar terms and concepts been defined or explained in the edited article?

See also *Writing Assessment & Evaluation Rubrics*.

Reteaching

📂 *Composition Reteaching*, p. 44

Enrichment

📂 *Composition Enrichment*, p. 44

Close

Ask students to discuss whether it is easier to explain a complex process orally or in writing. Invite students to give examples and perhaps experiment by explaining a process orally and then in writing, inviting feedback from the audience.

MEETING INDIVIDUAL NEEDS — English Language Learners

Choosing Details

Students who are not proficient in the use of English may have trouble listing the steps in a process and coming up with attention-grabbing details. Pair these students with students whose first language is English. Ask the student whose primary language is English to perform the process as the other student reads his or her draft aloud. (The student who is not proficient in English should provide any materials necessary.) Students should work together to identify missing or confusing steps and to suggest humorous or descriptive details that would enliven the draft.

Literature Model

About the Author

Sue Hubbell divides her time between a home in Washington, D.C., and her ninety-acre farm in the Ozark Mountains of southern Missouri. Hubbell believes that living part of the year in the city and part in the country helps her appreciate both environments.

Focus

Lesson Overview

Objective

- To appreciate how a professional writer uses different types of exposition to share her knowledge of bees and her observations of nature

Skills

- reading comprehension

Critical Thinking

- synthesizing; classifying; visualizing

Listening and Speaking

- explaining process

Bellringer
Daily Language Activity

When students enter the classroom, have this assignment on the board: *List three things you know or have heard about bees.*

Motivating Activity

Tell students that in this passage Sue Hubbell shares her knowledge of bees and her experiences as a beekeeper. Ask students whether they have ever taken care of an animal. Then tell them that they could turn their experiences with animals into expository essays.

Literature Model

Expository Writing

A Book of Bees . . . and How to Keep Them

by Sue Hubbell

Sue Hubbell, a self-taught naturalist, spends much of the year on her Missouri farm, taking care of her 300 beehives and approximately 12 million bees. As you read the selection below from A Book of Bees . . . and How to Keep Them, *note how Hubbell reaches out to her readers as she guides them through the beekeeper's year. Then try the activities in Linking Writing and Literature on page 274.*

266 Unit 5 Expository Writing

Resource Manager

Planning Resources
- *Lesson Plans*

Transparencies
- *Bellringer*
- *Daily Language Practice*
- *Fine Art* 25–28

Other Print Resources
- *Listening and Speaking Activities,* pp. 15–16

- *Thinking and Study Skills,* pp. 3, 8, 11
- *Writing Assessment and Evaluation Rubrics*

Web Sites
- *writerschoice.glencoe.com*
- *lit.glencoe.com*

Literature Model

Spring for bees, and so for beekeepers as well, has nothing to do with the calendar. In protected hollows even in the Missouri winter, bees can find a bit of springtime in flowers with enough pollen to feed the first young bees growing from the eggs the queen has begun to lay.

Various species of maples, all members of the genus *Acer,* with their delicate blossoms ranging from yellow-green to red, are one of the earliest to bloom. Maples are tall trees, and their blossoms are borne high in the crowns, where they often are not seen by humans. The bees, of course, have no trouble in finding them. The American hazel, *Corylus americana,* is a smaller tree—hardly more than a shrub—that is another early source of pollen, and easier for us to see. It grows wild throughout most of temperate North America and produces the nuts we call filberts. In late winter and early spring when most other plants are at rest, hazel generously produces pollen on long, dangling catkins.[1] In the winter, I like to stop on my walk down to the mailbox and draw one of the yellowish brown catkins between my thumb and forefinger and watch the powdery golden pollen collect in my palm. On days warm enough, bees, having declared it springtime, will be on the catkins collecting pollen.

Skunk cabbage, *Symplocarpus foetidus,* with its coarsely sheathed flower and supposedly vile odor, makes spring for bees in February in northern parts of the country. If a walker in the wet woods or swamps takes the time to look inside the skunk-cabbage spathe[2] on a mild day, he will usually find a honeybee there, packing pollen into the carrying baskets on her back legs.

Mature adult bees are carbohydrate feeders. They live on nectar and honey, which are almost exclusively carbohydrate in composition except for a few traces of minerals, vitamins and other materials. But young and developing bees need protein to grow muscles, glands and other tissues, and it is pollen—variously rich in protein, depending on its source—that provides it.

It takes about three weeks for a bee to grow from egg to adult. Three days after the queen bee has laid an egg, it hatches out into a nearly white larva that, throughout its instars, or developmental stages, has a ferocious need for food high in protein. Bee larvae don't move around looking for food as some insects do in their early stages; they are not wriggly caterpillars as are those of moths or butterflies. They merely lie passively in their cells, growing, changing. They are small animals, with disproportionately large stomachs waiting to be filled by nurse bees—young adults just emerged from pupation.[3] These nurse bees feed on the gathered pollen and produce secretions from their hypopharyngeal[4] glands (glands under the pharynx), which they will use as food for the developing larvae.

---

1 **catkins** (kat′ kinz) drooping, scaly spikes that hang down from trees such as poplars and birches
2 **spathe** (spāth) a leaflike part of a plant that encloses a fleshy spike or tiny flower
3 **pupation** (pyoo pā′ shən) the developmental stage between larva and adult insect
4 **hypopharyngeal** (hī′ pō fə rin′ jē ə l) [for pronunciation only; see above for definition]

Teach

Guided Reading

- From what point of view is the essay written? How does Hubbell use this perspective to engage the reader? How would the description of the catkins differ if it were told from the third-person point of view?
- What type of expository writing does Hubbell use when she explains how a bee grows from egg to adult? What strategy does she use to describe how bee larvae differ from the larvae of other insects? **L2**

Teach

Guided Reading

- Why do you think Hubbell uses an anecdote to begin her discussion of pollen? What effect does the anecdote have on the reader?
- How can you use context clues to understand the meaning of the word *empiricist?* **L2**

Expository Writing

Literature Model

Vincent van Gogh, *View of Arles*

In recent years, vendors of nostrums[5] to the health-food industry have been delighted by Ronald Reagan's public consumption of pollen, and pollen has become a hot item in health-food stores. Claims are made that humans who eat pollen are stronger, sexier, livelier and more cheerful, but there is no good medical evidence to back up these claims so far. And as a matter of fact, some people have experienced severe allergic reactions after eating it.

---

5 nostrums (näs' trəmz) medicines, sometimes sold with exaggerated claims of what they can do

Viewing the Art

Vincent van Gogh, *View of Arles*, 1889

Much of the work of Dutch-born painter Vincent van Gogh (1853–1890) was done in the last three years of his life. Most of that period he lived in Arles in southern France. In *View of Arles,* he used richly textured brushstrokes to convey the creative energy of nature.

Writing in the Real World

Examining Essays

A Book of Bees . . . and How to Keep Them is a series of expository essays examining the development and activities of bees throughout the seasons. Written in the first person, the book is a personal record of Hubbell's observations and reflections on the world she shares with bees.

Literature Model

Pollen from a hay-fever sufferer's local area is also said to cure him of his allergy. I have an open mind. I am an empiricist.[6] I have hay fever. And, after all, bee venom[7] does help my arthritis. So one summer, when my eyes were running and I was sneezing exquisitely from ragweed, I gathered and ate pollen from my bees. Pollen has a bitter taste. It is no fun to eat, but in the interests of testing the efficacy[8] of the stuff I dutifully continued to eat it—and to sneeze. It is possible pollen may cure someone else's hay fever, but it doesn't cure mine.

I am always eager to start working with the bees in the spring. I miss them in the winter and want to be back with them again. But I sternly remind myself I can do more harm than good if I open their hives before the daffodils bloom, so when the crocuses flower around my cabin I have to content myself with crouching down beside those purple, white and yellow blossoms to watch the field bees gathering pollen.

Each worker bee is covered with stiff hairs. These catch the granules when the bee brushes against the flower's pollen-bearing anthers.[9] She is soon covered and stops to use her two front pairs of legs to comb the sticky pollen from her body and pack it into the baskets on her rear pair of legs. When her legs are heavy with their wads of pollen she returns to her hive to unload. House bees arrange the pollen granules in the honeycomb cells around the developing bee larvae, where it is conveniently available to the nurse bees.

In the springtime, a typical frame of brood—as beekeepers call developing bees—contains a large central semicircle of cells containing eggs and larvae in various stages. The eggs and larvae are there to see, but the oldest brood, stomachs full, have spun themselves cocoons in which to pupate, and are hidden from human eyes, sealed in their cells by a tough, velvety brown covering, from beneath which they will emerge as adults. The entire semicircle of brood is bordered by a ring of pollen-filled cells, which in turn is surrounded by honey, or, as the season progresses, nectar.

In this part of the country most of the early pollen collected is yellow and makes a bright ring around the fuzzy brown sealed brood area. But as the season advances and the days lengthen, more pollen sources are available. Serviceberry, *Amelanchier arborea,* frosts the slopes of the hills near the rivers with white blossoms. Redbud, *Cercis canadensis,* flourishes in the wood's understory, with dramatic purplish red clusters of blossom. Henbit, *Lamium amplexicaule,* which everyone except beekeepers think of as an unwelcome weed, covers the ground with a low-growing thatch of purple-blue flowers. The wild fruit trees—plum, cherry and peach—bloom extravagantly. These flowers all have different-colored pollens, and the pollen cells ringing the bees' brood are as various: scarlet, pale green, yellow, and orange—as beautiful as a stained-glass window.

---

6 **empiricist** (em pir′ ə sist) one willing to learn through experiment and observation
7 **venom** (ven′ əm) a secreted poison
8 **efficacy** (ef′ i kə sē) effectiveness
9 **anthers** (an′ thərz) pollen sacs

Literature Model **269**

Expository Writing

Teach

Guided Reading

- What vivid verbs and descriptive language does Hubbell use to discuss the bees' activities?
- How does the writer's description of the flowers and the different-colored pollens enrich her essay? **L2**

Real World Connection

Comparing Urban and Rural Life

Hubbell says that spring for bees and beekeepers "has nothing to do with the calendar." In the country the writer lives in harmony with nature and marks the seasons by observing her bees. By contrast, most city dwellers recognize the animal life around them only as pets. Encourage students to compare the concerns and values of rural life with those of city life. Ask them to consider what effect being out of tune with nature may have on city dwellers. (They may become less concerned about the dangers of pollution and waste.)

Teach

Guided Reading

- How does Hubbell make the neighboring dairy farmer come alive? What would be lost if the line of dialogue were related through indirect discourse?
- How did Hubbell determine that the insects flying around the farmer's barn were flies? How are the flies similar to bees? How do they differ?
- Why do beekeepers sometimes use a pollen substitute? Why does Hubbell believe that the substitute isn't worth the expense? **L2**

Literature Model

Expository Writing

In early springtime, the bees' need for pollen may be greater than what is available, and then they will compulsively gather up almost any fine granular material—sawdust, bits of plastic packing material, ashes—whether it is useful to them or not. I often see them at the bird feeder, picking through the wild bird feed. At that time of year, I often get a telephone call from a dairy farmer who lives near one of my beeyards.

"Hey, Sue," he says. "How about coming over and feeding your bees? They're in the calf feed again."

He's always a little embarrassed. The first time he called me, years ago, was on a day in autumn. There were, he insisted, bees flying all around the inside of his milking shed. He didn't want to spray them with insecticide, but he was going to have to do that unless I could lure them out.

It sounded like an odd way for bees to behave, but I drove over to his place. There they were, golden-striped fuzzy insects flying around inside his barn, darting here and there. They looked like bees, but they didn't act like bees, so I captured one in my hand. The creature did not sting me as a honeybee would have done and on close scrutiny its beelike appearance disappeared. Moreover, the insect had only a single pair of wings, not two sets, as a bee has. The two wings, a single pair, puts any insect into the zoological order Diptera (which means two-winged), the order of flies. Honeybees belong to the order Hymenoptera (or membrane-winged), which includes not only all the bees but also wasps, ants and other similar insects.

I wasn't sure which flies these were in the milk barn, because I don't know much about Diptera, but I know that there were a number of fly species that mimic bees in appearance. I showed the farmer the single pair of wings and told him that this and the others in the air were flies, not bees. He was interested, and asked more questions than I could answer. When I got home, I photocopied as much information about bee-mimicking flies as I could find on my bookshelves and sent it to him. Now when he calls he always makes sure that the insect about which he is lodging a complaint is indeed a honeybee.

The first time he found bees in his calf feed he was worried that they were after the calves, and might sting and frighten them. I assured him that the bees were not the least concerned with the calves but were looking for the pollen they needed as food in the springtime. As soon as some pollen-bearing flower bloomed, I told him, the bees would disappear from the calf feed, but in the meantime I'd try giving them a pollen substitute that might satisfy them.

Beekeeping-supply companies sell a commercial pollen substitute made of a combination of protein-rich materials such as soy flour and brewers' yeast. This powder can be mixed with honey to make into patties, which can be squished down between the top bars on the frames of the upper hive bodies. Many beekeepers recommend the feeding of pollen substitute as a regular routine, and for a number of years I made up patties and fed them to all my hives. In some parts of the country where there is not a dependable source of pollen this may

Writing in the Real World

Writing to Discover Oneself

In her afterword to *A Book of Bees,* Hubbell explains how she came to write her first book, *A Country Year:* "I wasn't sure why I was here, and because I am a rational creature and like to know what's going on, I wanted to process what I was doing through my brain cells, to put it into words and see if I could arrive at an understanding of it. I had always written for an audience, but this time I was writing for myself, and what I put on paper over the next couple of years was unlike anything I had written before." Discuss the value of writing as a way of understanding one's own actions.

Literature Model

Vincent van Gogh, *View of Arles with Irises*, 1888

Viewing the Art

Vincent van Gogh, *View of Arles with Irises,* 1888

View of Arles with Irises measures 21¼ by 25½ inches and is in the Rijksmuseum Vincent van Gogh in Amsterdam, the Netherlands. Vincent van Gogh used thick, bold brushstrokes to capture the scene, sometimes squeezing oil paint from the tube directly onto the canvas. In a letter to a friend, the artist described the flowers in the painting as a "sea of yellow with a band of purple iris." You might suggest to students that the vibrant color in the work reflects the Mediterranean sunlight of Arles.

271

Teach

Guided Reading

- What is Hubbell's theory of beekeeping?
- What are Hubbell's results when she puts her theory to practice? **L2**

Literature Model

Ernest Lawson, *Garden Landscape*, ca. 1895

be a good practice, but I have concluded that it is not worth the expense or time here in the Ozarks. Bees prefer the real thing—fresh pollen—and although a day or two in these hills may pass when they can't find any, something usually bursts into bloom and they scorn the substitute, leaving it to molder inside the hives. So I stopped feeding pollen substitute, and find that productivity of my hives is no poorer for doing so.

Indeed, the per-hive yield of honey from my bees has grown greater in what appears to be a direct relationship to the decrease in the number of times I open the hives. The less I disrupt and fiddle with the bees, the more they can concentrate on making honey.

Now when the dairy farmer calls, more as a public-relations gesture then anything else, I go to the health-food store and buy

272   Unit 5 Expository Writing

Viewing the Art

Ernest Lawson, *Garden Landscape,* ca. 1895
An art critic once described the colors used by Canadian impressionist Ernest Lawson (1873–1939) as being composed of "crushed jewels." Ask students to describe how *Garden Landscape* illustrates the well-being that Hubbell expresses at the end of the selection. The 20-by-24–inch oil-on-canvas painting, composed in 1895, hangs in the Brooklyn Museum.

Literature Model

fifty-nine cents' worth of soy flour, take it over to the hives near his place, lift off the outer cover of each hive and sprinkle some of it on the inner cover. I did that a few days ago, and today I stopped by his place to give him a jar of honey as a recompense[10] for the nuisance my bees had caused him.

I asked if the bees had stopped coming to the calf feed.

"Yep. They've left. Thank you kindly for feeding them."

"No trouble. Thank you for calling me and letting me know. I don't like the bees to be a bother to you."

Then I drove over to the hives and lifted up the telescoping covers. The soy flour stood unused on the inner covers, and I shook it off on the grass. The bees had not wanted it. Flowers have begun to bloom somewhere, and the bees, their rear legs wadded with golden pollen, are flying into the hives so heavily loaded they find it hard to stay airborne.

The farmer is happy. The calves are happy. The bees are happy.

I sit down beside the end hive and watch the bees flying in with their loads of pollen, which will assure the development of the thousands of young bees needed to gather nectar and make honey in the months to come.

The sun is shining on my back as I watch, and I can feel its warmth. The air is fragrant. There are flowers in bloom everywhere today.

And I am happy.

---

10 recompense (rek′ əm pens′) something given to make up for an inconvenience

Teach

Guided Reading

- Why does Hubbell sprinkle soy flour only on the hives near her neighbor's farm? Why does she give him a jar of honey?
- What techniques does Hubbell use to convey a sense of well-being within her environment?
- In what environment do you feel a sense of well-being? How would you describe it? Compare Hubbell's environment with the one you described. How are they similar? How are they different? **L2**

Additional Resources

For further stimuli for expository writing, see *Fine Art Transparencies,* 25–28

Listening and Speaking Activities, pp. 15–16

Thinking and Study Skills, pp. 3, 8, 11

Linking Writing and Literature

Assess

Evaluation Rubrics

As your students discuss the selection, either in small groups or as a class, encourage them to begin with a personal response. The student responses on this page might be used as a starting point.

Look for evidence that students
- have read the selection
- can state some of the writer's ideas in their own words
- understand the writer's point of view
- have connected the content to their own knowledge and experiences
- understand the ideas and implications of the selection

Following are possible responses to the discussion questions on this page:
1. The mix of anecdotes and facts makes Hubbell's writing more engaging and more appealing to the general reader.
2. Process explanation: to explain how a bee grows from egg to adult; comparison and contrast: to discuss the differences between bees and the bee-mimicking flies in her neighbor's barn; definition: to explain the meaning of the term *hypopharyngeal glands*
3. The mood is springlike and happy. Hubbell uses action verbs and descriptive sensory language to help create this mood.

Close

Ask students to share their own stories about adventures in the natural world. The stories should convey facts about the subject and hold their classmates' attention.

Expository Writing *(side tab)*

Linking Writing and Literature

Readers Respond to the Model

How does Sue Hubbell convey in-depth information in a lively and appealing way?

Explore Sue Hubbell's exposition by answering these questions. Then read what other students liked about Hubbell's writing.

1. Hubbell mixes personal anecdotes with factual information. How does this mix affect her writing?
2. What different kinds of exposition does Hubbell use in her essay? Give an example of each.

3. How would you describe the mood of this selection? What specific words and images help to create this mood?

What Students Say

I liked the springlike mood the author created through her imagery. I think that even though her writing was informational and documentary-like, the author wrote in first person because she was telling her own experiences. The part I remembered most clearly was about pollen's health benefits. Hubbell stated that some people consider pollen a healthy, positive substance. I found the detail about Ronald Reagan eating pollen amusing, and it held my attention.

Chris Fickes

I liked how Hubbell balanced the social and factual parts of her piece. She obviously has love and admiration for a largely misunderstood insect. Through her facts and stories, she was able to make anyone feel more comfortable around bees. However, if I had written the piece, I don't think that I would have included as many facts about the bees while telling the "bee stories."

Yahna Awazu

UNIT 5 Review

Reflecting on the Unit

Summarize what you have learned in this unit by answering the following questions.

❶ What are six kinds of expository writing, and what is the basic purpose of each?

❷ What are some of the ways cause-and-effect writing can be organized?

❸ What types of graphic organizers can help you organize information for a compare-contrast essay?

❹ How do graphs and charts clarify explanations?

❺ How can you use the words in essay questions to plan your answer?

❻ What steps can you take to improve your performance on essay tests?

Adding to Your Portfolio

CHOOSE A SELECTION FOR YOUR PORTFOLIO Look over the expository writing you have done during this unit. Select a completed piece of writing to put in your portfolio. The piece you choose should show some or all of the following:

- a specific audience and writing purpose
- a well-expressed thesis statement
- supporting details that appeal to readers' level of knowledge and interest
- logical organization and clear connections
- a combination of expository types

REFLECT ON YOUR CHOICE Attach a note to the piece you chose, explaining briefly why you chose it and what you learned from writing it.

SET GOALS How can you improve your writing? What skill will you focus on the next time you write?

Writing Across the Curriculum

MAKE A HISTORY CONNECTION Scan your history textbook for a historical event or occurrence that can be described as a process, such as the building of a stockade or the election of a president. Write a brief essay explaining the process. Be sure to explain any unfamiliar terms.

Review **275**

Unit 5 Review

Review

Reflecting on the Unit

You may have students respond to Reflecting on the Unit in writing or through discussion.

Writing Across the Curriculum

Encourage students to pay special attention to chronological order and cause-and-effect relationships in their essays. Remind them to distinguish the two relationships from one another.

Adding to Your Portfolio

Encourage students to review their expository writing pieces as readers. Suggest that they ask themselves which piece handled the subject matter in the most informative and interesting manner.

Portfolio Evaluation Guidelines

If you grade the portfolio selections, you may want to award two marks—one each for content and form. Explain your assessment criteria before students make their selections.

Commend
- experimentation with creative writing techniques
- clear, concise writing in which the main idea, audience, and purpose are evident
- successful revisions
- work that shows a flair for language

✔ ASSESSMENT OPTIONS

📁 *Tests with Answer Key & Rubrics*
Unit 5 Choice A Test, p. 17
Unit 5 Choice B Test, p. 18
Unit 5 Composition Objective Test, pp. 19–20

💾 *Testmaker*
Unit 5 Choice A Test
Unit 5 Choice B Test
Unit 5 Composition Objective Test

You may wish to administer one of these tests as a mastery test.

📼 *MindJogger Videoquizzes*

Persuasive Writing

Viewing the Art

The parchment and quill pen in the image on this page remind us of the time when the U.S. Constitution was written. The Constitution established the role and nature of the federal government and, with the Bill of Rights, made provision for certain rights and freedoms for citizens. While it is hallowed now, the Constitution was, in its time, a controversial document which was ratified only because of the persuasive efforts of some of the new country's most powerful and eloquent men. This unit will explore some of the techniques which can be used in persuasive writing.
Interpret and Analyze Use the following questions for discussion:
- What is the effect of connecting the quill and parchment to this image of the U.S. Constitution?
- What kind of group might use such an image on a brochure designed to advocate its causes?

Discussing the Quotation

In the speech from which the quotation comes (see page 524 of *Glencoe Literature, Course 5*), Martin Luther King Jr. urges his audience to exercise their First Amendment rights to freedom of assembly and free speech. King delivered the speech in 1968, the night before he was assassinated. Have students review the speech and discuss whether they believe that the United States has met the "challenge to make America what it ought to be" in the intervening years.
Writing Prompt In a brief essay, develop your opinion about our progress in the areas of civil rights and race relations since Dr. King gave his Memphis speech. Use specific evidence to persuade your readers to share your opinion.

> *"Let us rise up tonight with greater readiness. Let us stand with a greater determination. And let us move on in these powerful days, these days of challenge to make America what it ought to be."*

—Martin Luther King, Jr.,

"I've Seen the Promised Land"

276

Resource Manager

Planning Resources
- *Lesson Plans*
- *Block Scheduling*

Transparencies
- *Bellringer*
- *Daily Language Practice*
- *Fine Art*
- *Two-Minute Skill Drill*
- *Writing Process*

Other Print Resources
- *Composition Enrichment*
- *Composition Practice*
- *Composition Reteaching*
- *Cooperative Learning Activities*
- *Glencoe Literature Library*
- *Grammar and Composition Handbook*
- *Grammar Workbook*

- *Listening and Speaking Activities*
- *Sentence-Combining Practice*
- *Tests with Answer Key and Rubrics*
- *Thinking and Study Skills*
- *Writing Across the Curriculum*
- *Writing Assessment and Evaluation Rubrics*
- *Writing in the Real World*

UNIT 6 Persuasive Writing

Writing in the Real World: *Mitchiner, Ross and Kahn* 278

Lesson 6.1 **Understanding Persuasive Writing** 282

Lesson 6.2 **Evidence in Persuasive Writing** 286

Lesson 6.3 **Presenting an Opinion** 290

Lesson 6.4 **Writing a Product Evaluation** 294

Lesson 6.5 **Creating an Ad** 298

Lesson 6.6 **Writing a Letter of Complaint** 302

Lesson 6.7 **Writing about Literature: Reviewing a Nonfiction Book** 306

Writing Process in Action 310

Literature Model: "A Plague on Tennis" by Mark Mathabane 314

Unit 6 Review 319

Objectives

- To recognize and understand the characteristics of persuasive writing
- To recognize and use persuasive appeals in writing
- To demonstrate control over persuasive strategies in writing by presenting an opinion, evaluating a product, creating an ad, writing a letter of complaint, and reviewing a nonfiction book

✔ ASSESSMENT OPTIONS

📁 *Tests with Answer Key & Rubrics*
Unit 6 Choice A Test, p. 21
Unit 6 Choice B Test, p. 22
Unit 6 Composition Objective Test, pp. 23–24

💾 *Testmaker*
Unit 6 Choice A Test
Unit 6 Choice B Test
Unit 6 Composition Objective Test

You may wish to administer either the Unit 6 Choice A Test or the Unit 6 Choice B Test as a pretest.

Key to Ability Levels

L1 Level 1 activities are within the basic range of students.

L2 Level 2 activities are within the ability range of average students.

L3 Level 3 activities are more challenging activities.

📹 **Video**
- *MindJogger Videoquizzes*

💾 **Software**
- *Presentation Plus!*
- *Revising with Style*
- *Testmaker*
- *Writer's Assistant*
- *Writer's Choice Puzzlemaker*

🖥 **Web Sites**
- *writerschoice.glencoe.com*
- *lit.glencoe.com*

Focus

Lesson Overview

Objective
- To develop persuasive advertising

Skills
- making pronouns agree with antecedents; writing an advertisement; evaluating characteristics of persuasive writing

Critical Thinking
- generating new information; analyzing

Listening and Speaking
- discussing; formulating questions; working cooperatively

Bellringer
Daily Language Activity

When students enter the classroom, have this assignment on the board: *What is your favorite commercial? Write a paragraph explaining why it is your favorite.*

Grammar Link to the Bellringer

Have students identify the pronouns used and explain whether the pronouns agree with their antecedents.

See also *Daily Language Practice*

Motivating Activity

Ask students to recall an attention-grabbing magazine or billboard advertisement and describe it to the class. Discuss why the ads were effective. Inform the class that the Media Connection illustrates how ad campaigns are created and shows the research and thought required to create a persuasive campaign.

Persuasive Writing

Writing in the Real World

In persuasive writing, the writer tries to influence the reader to accept an idea, adopt a point of view, or perform an action. Effective persuasive writing is unified by one central idea. Advertisements are great examples of persuasive writing. The ads on this page are part of a campaign for Chicago's Museum of Contemporary Art (MCA). The ads were created by Mitchiner, Ross and Kahn, a Chicago advertising agency.

Membership at the MCA: What Will It Do To You?

by the advertising agency of Mitchiner, Ross and Kahn

Resource Manager

Planning Resources
- *Lesson Plans*

Transparencies
- *Bellringer*
- *Daily Language Practice*
- *Writing Process* 12, 28–32

Other Print Resources
- *Cooperative Learning Activities*
- *Writing Assessment and Evaluation Rubrics*
- *Writing in the Real World,* pp. 21–24

A Writer's Process

Prewriting

Finding the Main Idea

Before developing the MCA ad campaign, the Mitchiner, Ross and Kahn team did some basic homework. They studied campaigns for other art museums and looked at figures showing who visits the MCA. They also went to the museum themselves to see, according to senior art director Steven Wohlwender, "how to get your average Joe to come look at contemporary art."

The main theme for the MCA campaign began with a drawing. "I'd drawn this goofy little face with a strange reaction on it," explains Wohlwender, "based on the people I'd seen at the museum. And Marshall Ross, our creative director, simply said, `What will it do to you?'"

"That question started out being a headline for just one ad, but then Ross said, `This should be the main theme because it works for everything.' And the rest of us saw the light."

Assistant creative director Amy Krouse Rosenthal calls "What will it do to you?" an idea with "legs." That expression means the idea can "walk into" a wide range of media, including brochures, banners, bus posters, and newspaper ads. She adds, "We want the people who see these ads to get off their bottoms, go to the museum, and get zapped in the brain."

The idea generated in Wohlwender's sketch of a goofy face was carried through several design stages and ultimately appeared in a variety of formats, from T-shirts to café table tents.

Teach

Building Background

Warm-up

Have students list examples of persuasive pieces that they have recently read or heard.

Persuasion in Speaking

Discuss how and when persuasion is used. For example, a politician's speech, a sales pitch, a telethon host's monologue, and a sermon are all persuasive.

- What are some characteristics of persuasive speech?
- Have you ever been swayed by another person's point of view? How?

Persuasion in Writing

Discuss any persuasive pieces that students may have read.

- What point was the writer trying to make?
- Were you persuaded by the writer's reasons or examples? Why or why not?

Teach

Discussion Prompts

- Why did the museum have to advertise?
- How did the agency begin the campaign?
- Why was evaluating the competition important?
- What was the next step? Why was it so important?

Real World Connection

Social Studies

Demography, the statistical study of populations, is a social-studies discipline widely applied in the marketplace. Explain that demographic data include age, gender, ethnicity, income, education, area, type of residence, and other factors. Ask students what role demographics played in developing the museum campaign. (It determined the subjects of the photos.)

Point out that part of an advertising agency's professional role includes communicating with different cultural groups within the target audience.

Writing in the Real World

Teach

Discussion Prompts

- How does a catchy phrase help a campaign?
- Some people claim advertisements create a demand for things people don't really need. Do you think a campaign such as the one for the museum would merit such criticism? Why or why not?

Discussion

Initiate a discussion of the Media Connection. You may also want to invite students to talk about

- whether or not they were surprised by the importance of persuasive writing in advertising
- other applications of persuasive writing in the real world they can envision **L2**

Discussion

Discuss with students how long ad campaigns typically run (for months, sometimes for years, taking on many forms). Ask students to list media used for promotional messages and ads. Explain that the main idea is to keep the product and the campaign message in the public eye for as long as possible. **L2**

Additional Resources

 Writing Process Transparencies, 12, 28–32

 Writing in the Real World, pp. 21–24

Cooperative Learning Activities

Persuasive Writing

Drafting
Seeing the Picture

The members of the advertising team decided to use photographs of real faces instead of sketches because they believed photos would be more persuasive than drawings. As Wohlwender puts it, "Photography is real. These people look real. The photographer even picked people off the street and told them to give a reaction as if they were looking at art."

"We wanted to make the ads appeal to as broad a group as possible," said Wohlender. "The museum told us what kind of people they wanted shown in terms of ages and ethnic groups they were targeting. The photographer went out and got ten people in each category. You don't want people who look like models, of course. These people look real. We wanted people looking at any one of these ads to be able to say, `This museum is for me.'"

Revising/Editing
Choosing the Right Words

Every word used in an ad must contribute to persuading the audience. For example, Krouse Rosenthal says the word *you* was crucial to this campaign because "it makes you think about yourself." In selecting words for the campaign, the ad team made a conscious decision to keep the language informal.

For the MCA ad campaign, it was crucial to use humor and informal language.

Krouse Rosenthal explains that if the ads had used lofty language, some readers might have felt excluded from the museum experience.

Publishing/Presenting
Getting the Message Out

As part of the campaign, the MCA sent out a booklet to prospective members filled with funny, irreverent questions relating to the main idea, "What will it do to you?" Wohlwender says, "Usually people will read just one line and throw away a piece of junk mail. We tried to write [the booklet] so people would keep turning the pages."

The ads created for the Museum of Contemporary Art were supposed to run for only a year. Within eight months, however, museum attendance had skyrocketed by 42 percent and membership by 16 percent—rises that represented the biggest leaps in the museum's history. As a result, the ads were slated to run indefinitely.

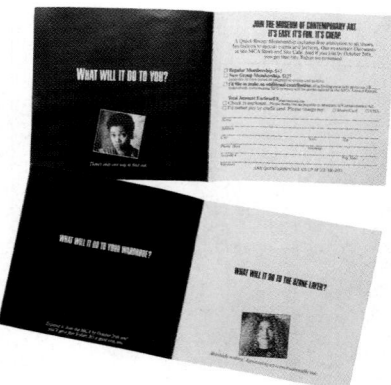

Cooperative Learning

Researching the Teen Market

To better understand how audiences are analyzed for an ad campaign, students can participate in a Think-Pair-Share activity to analyze the teenaged audience. Have students work in pairs to list what distinguishes teenagers from other groups. Next, have partners compare and discuss their lists. Then have the pairs share their ideas with the class. Tell them to save this information for use in future activities.

Examining Writing in the Real World

Analyzing the Media Connection

Deconstruct, or analyze, the ads on pages 278–280 by discussing the following questions.

1. What question do the ads ask? How does each ad answer that question?
2. What is the effect of the word *you* in the ads? Would the word *us* or *them* have the same effect? Why or why not?
3. What is the central idea developed in the ads?
4. In your opinion, what immediate effects do the photographs have? Why?
5. For what reasons do you think these ads were so successful?

Analyzing a Writer's Process

Discuss these questions about the advertising team's writing process.

1. What is the purpose of the MCA ad campaign?
2. How did the advertising team come up with an idea for the campaign?
3. Why did the team decide to use photographs in the ads?
4. What kind of language did the team incorporate in the ads? Why?
5. How did the ad campaign affect attendance and membership?

Grammar Link

Make pronouns agree with antecedents.

A pronoun must agree with its antecedent in gender, number, and person.

> The advertising **team** decided to use photographs . . . because **they** believed . . .

Rewrite each sentence to correct the pronoun use.

1. Our class wants to go to the Museum of Contemporary Art, where you can see an exhibit of Georgia O'Keeffe's paintings.
2. I always rent an audiotape so that you know what to look for when you study a painting.
3. My friend and I plan to visit the museum gift shop, where you can buy prints of your favorite paintings.
4. Many students recognize that you can do firsthand research for a report in a museum.
5. Do you think that someday you'll visit the museum?

See Lesson 17.5, pages 644–648.

Grammar Link

Answers

(Answers will vary.)
1. Our class wants to go to the Museum of Contemporary Art, where we can see an exhibit of Georgia O'Keeffe's paintings.
2. I always rent an audiotape so that I know what to look for when I study a painting.
3. My friend and I plan to visit the museum gift shop where we can buy prints of our favorite paintings.
4. Many students recognize that they can do firsthand research for a report in a museum.
5. (*Correct as written*)

Closing Note

Advertisements for textbooks and trade publications have useful examples of ad campaigns.

Assess

Analyzing The Media Connection

Answers will vary, but might resemble the following:
1. The ads ask people how the museum will affect them. Each ad provides a different answer.
2. *You* makes the ad more personal than would *us* or *them*.
3. The central idea is that a visit to the MCA may give you an exciting, surprising experience.
4. The photographs create curiosity about what art might do.
5. They were simple and funny and appealed to ordinary people.

Analyzing a Writer's Process

1. The purpose of the ad campaign was to get ordinary people to visit the museum.
2. The team did research, visited the museum, and brainstormed about images and words they might use.
3. They used photographs to appeal to a broad audience by showing real people's reactions to art.
4. They used language that was informal and personal, to make the museum seem enjoyable and accessible.
5. The ad campaign helped increase attendance by 42 percent and membership by 16 percent.

See also *Writing Assessment & Evaluation Rubrics.*

Reteaching

Review the three stages of an ad campaign described on page 278.

Enrichment

Have students guess the audience profile of several magazines and then write to request that information from the magazines' marketing directors.

Close

Have students bring to class ads targeted at teenagers and evaluate them. How well do the main-idea headlines "speak" to the audience?

Focus

Lesson Overview

Objective
• To identify common attributes of persuasive writing and to express an opinion with persuasive appeal aimed at a specific audience

Skills
• comparing and contrasting types of persuasive appeals

Critical Thinking
• analyzing; comparing and contrasting

Listening and Speaking
• listening to a persuasive speech; evaluating

Bellringer
Daily Language Activity

When students enter the classroom, have this assignment on the board: *List three persuasive slogans you have heard or read recently.*

Grammar Link to the Bellringer

Have students determine whether their slogans are complete sentences or sentence fragments. Ask them to rewrite the fragments as complete sentences.

See also *Daily Language Practice*

Motivating Activity

Have students share their lists of slogans. Encourage them to discuss what kinds of persuasive writing are published in the newspapers, magazines, or books. Do they include articles on political topics? advertisements? editorials? For what purposes were these pieces written?

LESSON

6.1

Persuasive Writing

Understanding Persuasive Writing

In persuasive writing, you try to convince readers to agree with your opinion and possibly to take action. In the following excerpt, a former Federal Communications Commission chairman appeals to both reason and emotion to persuade broadcasters that television is a "vast wasteland."

> **How would you summarize Minow's opinion in your own words?**

> **What specific examples does Minow use to support his opinion?**

> **In what way does this final question challenge the particular audience to whom Minow spoke?**

Literature Model

When television is bad, nothing is worse. I invite you to sit down in front of your television set when your station goes on the air and stay there without a book, magazine, newspaper, profit-and-loss sheet, or rating book[1] to distract you—and keep your eyes glued to that set until the station signs off. I can assure you that you will observe a vast wasteland.

You will see a procession of game shows, violence, audience participation shows, formula comedies about totally unbelievable families, blood and thunder, mayhem, violence, sadism, murder, Western badmen, Western good men, private eyes, gangsters, more violence and cartoons. And, endlessly, commercials—many screaming, cajoling, and offending. And, most of all, boredom. True, you will see a few things you will enjoy. But they will be very, very few. And if you think I exaggerate, try it.

Is there one person in this room who claims that broadcasting can't do better?

Newton Minow, Address to the Broadcasting Industry

1 rating book: a book that rates TV programs by the number of households viewing them

282   Unit 6 Persuasive Writing

Resource Manager

Planning Resources
• *Lesson Plans*

 Transparencies
• *Bellringer*
• *Daily Language Practice*
• *Fine Art* 29–32
• *Two-Minute Skill Drill*
• *Writing Process* 12, 28–32

 Other Print Resources
• *Composition Enrichment,* p. 456
• *Composition Practice,* p. 45
• *Composition Reteaching,* p. 45
• *Cooperative Learning Activities*
• *Listening and Speaking Activities,* pp. 17, 22–23
• *Sentence-Combining Practice,* pp. 34–35

• *Thinking and Study Skills,* pp. 5, 10, 13
• *Writing Across the Curriculum*
• *Writing Assessment and Evaluation Rubrics*

Recognize Persuasive Writing

When you write persuasively, you express an opinion and try to convince your readers to agree with you. Sometimes you'll want your readers to take action. In persuasive writing, audience is all-important, as the speech about television illustrates. Newton Minow aimed his message at broadcast executives, the very people responsible for television programming.

Every day you see and hear countless persuasive messages: a billboard ad for a popular brand of jeans, a radio spot for a movie the critics are raving about, bumper stickers calling attention to a cause or a candidate. Below are some of the places where you encounter persuasive messages. Can you think of others?

Journal Writing

Persuasive appeals are so widespread that you probably tune many of them out as you go about your business. Think back over the past day, and try to remember all the persuasive appeals you heard or saw. List them in your journal.

Teach

Using the Model

Introduce persuasive writing by asking students to read the literature model and then express their own opinions by writing down one change they feel would improve television (for example, less commercial time or eliminating murders from television dramas). Invite them to share their opinions with the class. In each case, have students identify who would have to be persuaded to make the change. Emphasize that a well-crafted case presented to the right audience can produce positive results. **L2**

Two-Minute Skill Drill

Write this sentence on the board and have students identify which words signal an attempt to be persuasive.

Television executives should bow to the legitimate interests of the concerned majority of citizens and take this inflammatory show off the air.

See also *Two-Minute Skill Drill Transparency 6.1*

Journal Writing Tip

Recalling Obvious appeals are radio and TV advertising, but students should be able to recall that parents, teachers, siblings, or friends tried to persuade them about something.

Teach

Teaching from the Art

Direct students' attention to the section in the corner of the ad that is meant to be returned with a donation. Have students identify the persuasive appeal here. Is it an appeal to reason, emotion, or both? (The details about the variety of life in rainforests appeal to reason, but the reference to human survival appeals to emotion.) **L2**

Making a Pitch

Suggest that a small group prepare a proposal for a new TV program to present to an audience of broadcast executives. Students should decide together on a program concept, vote on one idea, and then write the proposal. Tell students to state the idea as a brief, catchy sentence or phrase. The proposal should consist of supporting details that appeal logically to the executives and point to the show's potential for success. **L3**

Additional Resources

 Writing Process Transparencies, 12, 28–32

 Writing Across the Curriculum

Cooperative Learning Activities

 For further ideas for persuasive writing, see *Fine Art Transparencies,* 29–32

Thinking and Study Skills, pp. 5, 10, 13

Listening and Speaking Activities, pp. 17, 22–23

Sentence-Combining Practice, pp. 34–35

Composition Practice, p. 45

Persuasive Writing

Grammar Tip

When revising a piece of persuasive writing, determine whether the modifiers you have used are vivid and strong enough to support your opinion. For basic information on modifiers, see Lessons 10.4 and 10.5, pages 460–472.

Give Your Persuasive Writing an Edge

Like other types of writing, persuasive writing consists of a topic, a main idea about the topic, and supporting details. However, your main idea in persuasive writing has an edge to it. It's an opinion that you want others to adopt. Therefore, you need to pay special attention to your audience, presenting your supporting ideas in a way that will persuade your audience to accept your opinion.

You can support your opinion with two main kinds of details: appeals to reason and appeals to emotion. To appeal to reason, use facts, statistics, expert opinions, and examples that validate your position. To appeal to emotion, use words that generate strong positive or negative responses. For example, if you want to persuade readers to favor a candidate, you might applaud his "courageous" stand on the issues; if you want to discredit that same candidate, you might attack his "foolhardy" position.

Often you will want to appeal to both reason and emotion in the same piece of persuasive writing. Look at the advertisement below. What kind of appeal does the headline make? What part of the ad appeals to reason? To emotion?

AND ON THE EIGHTH DAY, WE BULLDOZED IT.

Elusive jaguars, rarest orchids, colorful birds-of-paradise.

Rainforests are haven to half of all the plant and animal species on earth. But how much time do they have left?

Fifty thousand rainforest acres are lost each day worldwide. At that rate, the last traces of original, irreplaceable paradise will vanish in a single human lifespan.

To preserve the splendid variety of life we must save the endangered rainforests.

Please support our efforts to conserve a miracle of creation. Tomorrow won't wait.

Save the rainforests and safeguard the survival of half of the species on earth, including our own. Here's my donation of ☐ $25 ☐ $50 ☐ $75 ☐ $100 ☐ _____

NAME _____
ADDRESS _____
CITY _____ STATE _____ ZIP_____

RAINFOREST ACTION NETWORK
300 BROADWAY, SAN FRANCISCO, CA 94133

Public Media Center

Exploring Language

Choosing Words Carefully

Some students may be unaware of certain words' connotations. Explain that reference sources can help writers choose persuasive words. Introduce students to a dictionary that uses clear descriptive labels of style and usage, such as the *Random House Webster's College Dictionary.* Explain the differences between formal, informal, and slang words. Tell students to think twice about using words the dictionary labels *vulgar, disparaging,* or *offensive.* Show advertisements using language that could be easily misconstrued.

Write an Opinion

Express your opinion of the painting below in a brief essay that could be published in an art gallery brochure. Use the details in the painting to support your opinion.

PURPOSE To express and support an opinion
AUDIENCE Visitors to an art gallery
LENGTH 2–3 paragraphs

WRITING RUBRICS To express a convincing opinion in writing, you should

- present your opinion in a main idea statement
- use supporting ideas that appeal to both reason and emotion
- pitch your argument to a particular audience

Viewing and Representing

DECONSTRUCTING MEDIA In a small group, analyze the quality of commercial TV programming. Assign each member to either read a recent article on current TV programming or view different channels for a few hours. Meet to discuss your findings and collaborate on a one-page response to Newton Minow's statements on page 282.

Jonathan Franklin, *Mad Hatters,* 1990

Persuasive Writing

Grammar Link

Avoid sentence fragments in your writing.

A *sentence fragment* is an incomplete sentence punctuated as if it were a complete sentence:

> *Elusive jaguars, rarest orchids, colorful birds-of-paradise.*

Though sentence fragments may be effective in advertising, do not use them in formal writing.

Rewrite to correct the fragments.

1. Television, labeled a "vast wasteland" by Newton Minow.
2. Insulting comedies, violent detective shows, irrelevant talk shows, and endless commercials. The list goes on.
3. There are a few shows that entertain and inform. Such as *Sixty Minutes.*
4. Cable television, supposedly an improvement over network programs.

See Lesson 13.9, pages 557–558.

Listening and Speaking

Present your findings from the Viewing and Representing activity as a persuasive speech. Aim your speech at a particular audience, such as the parents of young children, teachers, or workers in the television industry. Present your completed speech to the class and ask them to identify your intended audience.

6.1 Understanding Persuasive Writing **285**

Assess

Evaluation Rubrics

Write an Opinion

When evaluating students' opinion statements, look for

- a clear topic sentence stating an opinion on the painting
- text directed to gallery visitors
- supporting details from the painting that appeal to emotion and reason

See also *Writing Assessment & Evaluation Rubrics.*

Viewing and Representing

Each written response should

- state a clear opinion on the quality of TV programming
- present supporting facts from research (articles, surveys, etc.)

Listening and Speaking

Each speech should be evaluated in terms of how appropriate its vocabulary, tone, and style are for the intended audience.

Reteaching

📁 *Composition Reteaching,* p. 45

Enrichment

📁 *Composition Enrichment,* p. 45

✏ Use *Fine Art Transparencies,* 29–32, for enrichment activities also.

Close

You might distribute magazines or the day's newspapers to students and check students' ability to identify additional persuasive writing in them.

Grammar Link

Answers
1. Television was labeled . . .
2. This wasteland includes insulting . . .
3. . . . and inform, such as . . .
4. Cable television was supposed to be . . .

Viewing the Art

Jonathan Franklin, *Mad Hatters,* 1990
In *Mad Hatters,* Pablo Picasso's depiction of the cruelties of war is a background for characters suggested by Lewis Carroll's *Alice's Adventures in Wonderland.* Ask students what they think the artist's world represents.

Focus

Lesson Overview

Objective
- To support an opinion with evidence and to evaluate the validity of such evidence

Skills
- marshalling evidence for an opinion; comparing opinions

Critical Thinking
- evaluating; comparing and contrasting

Speaking and Listening
- evaluating television shows

Bellringer
Daily Language Activity

When students enter the classroom, have this assignment on the board: *List the titles of the last five television shows you saw.*

Grammar Link to the Bellringer

Have students identify any collective nouns that appear in their titles.

See also *Daily Language Practice*

Motivating Activity

Ask students how they would respond to the following opinion: "MTV has absolutely no educational value for teens." If students disagree, ask them for evidence to support their opinions. Discuss whether the opinion you quoted could be proved with evidence. (Students should realize that such an opinion is too extreme and too vague to prove; however, citing many examples of MTV content could convince some people to agree with the opinion.)

Persuasive Writing

LESSON
6.2

Evidence in Persuasive Writing

In persuasive writing you need to support your viewpoint with facts and relevant opinions. As you read these two contrasting views of MTV, look for supporting evidence.

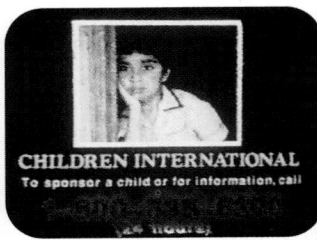

CHILDREN INTERNATIONAL
To sponsor a child or for information, call

Literature Model

> Which of Shales's word choices helps to reinforce his negative opinion of MTV?

MTV is primarily a triumph of marketing. Who would have thought, say, eleven years ago, that TV audiences would sit still for a channel showing nothing but commercials separated by commercials? Those music videos are essentially ads designed to sell records. In between them, MTV places real commercials to sell seven thousand different kinds of jeans and hair glop.

Not for nothing has MTV earned the nickname "Empty-V." Instead of denying that emptiness, however, MTV celebrates it. Members of the viewing audience are frequently assured that they are not to be bothered with matters of consequence. "MTV News," which is shown frequently each day, is "news" about rock stars, pop stars and silly celebrities—puff and fluff spun in the hype mills of Hollywood.

Tom Shales, "MTV Has Shallow Look of Success"

286 Unit 6 Persuasive Writing

Resource Manager

Planning Resources
- *Lesson Plans*

Transparencies
- *Bellringer*
- *Daily Language Practice*
- *Fine Art* 29–32
- *Two-Minute Skill Drill*
- *Writing Process* 12, 28–32

📁 Other Print Resources
- *Composition Enrichment,* p. 46
- *Composition Practice,* p. 46
- *Composition Reteaching,* p. 46
- *Cooperative Learning Activities*
- *Listening and Speaking Activities,* pp. 17, 22–23
- *Sentence-Combining Practice,* pp. 34–35

- *Thinking and Study Skills,* pp. 11, 24–25
- *Writing Across the Curriculum*
- *Writing Assessment and Evaluation Rubrics*

Literature Model

Almost since its inception, MTV has been rightly applauded by a grateful record industry for revitalizing pop music, boosting album sales and creating a thriving new market for home music videos. (MTV helped boost sales of music videos to a record $172.3 million last year, up $55 million from 1989. . . .)

MTV has also been hailed for revolutionizing TV (it is largely credited with inspiring the tone of the "Miami Vice" series), and for making its 1981 slogan "You'll never look at music the same way again," a reality. . . .

Eager to counter the many charges of vacuousness and puffery that have plagued it, MTV has also aired public service programs about political, social and environmental issues, even winning a prestigious Peabody Award for its two-hour retrospective on the '80s, "Decade."

George Varga, "Is It MTV, or Is It 'Empty-V'?"

> **What facts does Varga use to portray MTV in a more positive light?**

Use Facts and Opinions

Persuasive writing is more than just a statement of your opinion. You need to back up your opinion with evidence—facts and opinions that support your viewpoint. Facts are statements, statistics, observations, and examples that can be verified, or proved. Evaluate a fact by answering these questions: Is it accurate? Is it up to date? Is it relevant?

Opinions are personal judgments. They may be supported by facts, or they may be simply personal preferences. Their value depends upon the qualifications of the person stating them. Evaluate an opinion by answering these questions: Is the opinion-giver qualified, with specific knowledge of the subject? Is the opinion-giver biased, with something to gain from supporting a certain viewpoint?

Both facts and opinions can be open to interpretation. Different people draw different conclusions from the same evidence. The key is to decide how valid the evidence is.

> **Prewriting Tip**
>
> Both clustering and brainstorming can help you generate facts and opinions for persuasive writing, but you need to evaluate the evidence you generate.

Journal Writing

What's your opinion on MTV? In your journal, list several facts and opinions that you could use to support your view.

Teach

Using the Model

Show students how Shales uses word choice to present MTV in a negative light by such words and phrases as "silly," "puff and fluff," and "hype mills." Similarly, have students examine how Varga portrays MTV in a positive light by using facts that support his argument, such as MTV's economic impact (boosting album sales). **L2**

Being Critical

Stress the importance of being critical when examining evidence. Emphasize that students should try to determine the author's knowledge and possible bias. Point out that a poor source—an author who is biased or unqualified—is worse than no source. **L1**

Two-Minute Skill Drill

Have students rank these sources according to their value as evidence.

a newspaper article

someone's personal experience

an advertisement

government statistics

a newspaper editorial

See also *Two-Minute Skill Drill Transparency 6.2*

Journal Writing Tip

Drawing Conclusions After students list facts and opinions that support their personal views about MTV, ask them to identify the characteristics of valid evidence (reliable sources, relevant examples, expert opinions, accurate and up-to-date facts). Challenge students to state why each fact or opinion on their list is valid.

Teach

Supporting Evidence

Explain that in legal trials the best kind of evidence to persuade a jury that a defendant is guilty is incriminating evidence in the defendant's possession. Such evidence is far more convincing than opinions that the defendant had a motive for the crime. Tell students to look for evidence that offers solid support for their arguments. **L3**

Additional Resources

 For further stimuli for persuasive writing, see *Fine Art Transparencies,* 29–32.

 Writing Process Transparencies, 12, 28–32

 Cooperative Learning Activities

 Writing Across the Curriculum

 Thinking and Study Skills, pp. 11, 24–25

 Listening and Speaking Activities, pp. 17, 22–23

 Sentence Combining Practice, pp. 34–35

 Composition Practice, p. 46

Persuasive Writing

Grammar Tip

When editing, check that verbs and indefinite pronouns, such as *one* and *some,* agree in number. For more information about indefinite pronouns as subjects, see Lesson 16.7, pages 623–625.

Prepare Arguments

In persuasive writing, an argument is the position you take on an issue, along with the evidence you use to support your position. Often your evidence will include a mix of facts, statistics, expert opinions, and personal opinions that anticipate opposing viewpoints.

The excerpt below is from an ad by the makers of jewel boxes, the plastic packages in which compact discs are sold. The ad writer seeks to convince record companies that jewel boxes are the best packaging for CDs. What evidence supports the position? Is it convincing?

Literature Model

The People's Choice

As the makers and advocates of the jewel box, we believe the best alternative to the longbox already exists. One that's proven internationally—sell CDs in the jewel box, alone.

We're not the only ones who believe this. Peter Gabriel and Raffi are just two of the artists who agree. And with successful "jewel box-only" releases, they've proved the viability of that option.

But most important is the opinion of CD buyers like you—the people who should have the final say in any CD packaging decision. In a recent survey by *CD Review* magazine, they found that 84% of CD buyers preferred the sturdy, plastic jewel box to an alternative, paperboard package. . . .

Environmental Protection

Of course, some argue that an alternative package will be better for the environment. But the facts don't support their position.

Consider that last year alone at least 50 million unsold CDs were returned by retailers. Not a problem with the jewel box—the discs, artwork and booklets can be removed, and the jewel boxes could be re-used or recycled.

But proposed alternative CD packages can't be re-used or recycled, because they're made of paperboard and plastic glued together and pre-printed for just one release. If those 50 million returns were in an alternative package, the packages would have only one place to go—into the garbage.

JAM (Jewelbox Advocates and Manufacturers)

 Less Proficient Readers

MEETING INDIVIDUAL NEEDS

Ensuring Comprehension

To be sure that students understand the ad on this page, ask them to paraphrase it. Before their first reading, have them scan the ad and list troublesome vocabulary words. After they have read it, ask them if they can pick up the meaning of difficult words from their context. If not, have them look up the words before writing their paraphrase.

Review students' work to see that they have understood and included the major points of the ad.

Write an Editorial

Write an editorial for your school newspaper on security measures, testing student athletes for drug use, or some other controversial school issue of your choice.

PURPOSE To express and support an opinion on a school issue
AUDIENCE Readers of the school newspaper
LENGTH 3–4 paragraphs

WRITING RUBRICS To write an effective editorial, you should

- state your position on the issue
- support your position with facts and valid opinions
- anticipate and respond to possible opposing viewpoints

Cross-Curricular Activity

ART The painting on this page is by Mandy Martin, an Australian known for expressing her views on environmental issues through her art. In this painting, she tries to show the negative effect of the mining industry on the environment. Does she succeed? Use observations about the painting along with your personal judgment to write an evaluation of how well the painting fulfills its purpose.

Listening and Speaking

Review copies of your local newspaper and choose an issue of importance to people in your community. Through careful research, develop your own opinion about the topic and prepare a two-minute persuasive speech. Be sure to build a sound argument based on fact and expert opinion. You might want to include quotations from appropriate sources. Present your speech to the class and ask them to evaluate your argument.

Grammar Link

Make collective noun subjects and verbs agree.

A collective noun can be singular or plural. When writing about MTV's *audience*, for example, you would use a singular verb to refer to a group as a whole but a plural verb to refer to group members acting as audiences.

Write the correct form of the verb in parentheses.

1. The crowd (roar, roars) its approval.
2. The crowd (have, has) to pass through the gate, one at a time.
3. The band (is, are) warming up.
4. The band (take, takes) their places on stage.
5. Our whole group (is, are) shocked by the news about the lead singer.

See Lesson 16.4, pages 618–619.

Mandy Martin, *Powerhouse*, 1988

6.2 Evidence in Persuasive Writing **289**

Persuasive Writing

Assess

Evaluation Rubrics

Write an Editorial
Use these criteria when evaluating your students' writing:
- a clear statement of opinion on an issue
- valid, relevant facts and opinions

See also *Writing Assessment & Evaluation Rubrics.*

Cross-curricular Activity
Evaluate student writing using these criteria:
- clear statement of opinion
- support with facts about the painting

Listening and Speaking
Students' speeches should demonstrate an awareness of relevant facts and opinions, using an appropriate vocabulary and tone.

Reteaching
📁 *Composition Reteaching,* p. 46

Enrichment
📁 *Composition Enrichment,* p. 46

🖐 Use *Fine Art Transparencies,* 29–32, for enrichment activities also.

Close

Explain that there are experts who specialize in projecting data in different ways to support different opinions. Encourage students to think about what people can do to guard against being confused by "slippery" statistics.

Grammar Link

Answers
1. roars
2. have
3. is
4. take
5. is

Viewing the Art

Mandy Martin, *Powerhouse,* 1988
An oil painting on canvas, *Powerhouse* measures 90 1/2 by 110 1/4 inches and hangs in Heide Park Art Gallery, Melbourne, Australia.

6.3

Focus

Lesson Overview

Objective
- To predict audience responses and to synthesize facts and opinions into a persuasive argument

Skills
- taking a stand on a topic; predicting readers' responses

Critical Thinking
- analyzing; synthesizing

Listening and Speaking
- discussing

Bellringer
Daily Language Activity

When students enter the classroom, have this assignment on the board: *List all the brand-name objects you can see around you in the room.*

Grammar Link to the Bellringer

Have students analyze nouns and modifiers used in the brand names they listed. What do these words say about the product?

See also *Daily Language Practice*

Motivating Activity

Ask students to imagine a future in which advertisers subsidize teachers' salaries, and in return, teachers perform live commercials in the classroom. What advertisers would be interested in this—computer software companies, for example? Discuss problems and benefits that might result.

Persuasive Writing

LESSON

6.3

Presenting an Opinion

*T*he models below present opposing viewpoints on the issue of high school classes watching commercial television programs. Try to identify the position each writer takes and the audience to which each argument is targeted.

Literature Model

I have no objection to television commercials being shown to a "captive" audience of students in school, especially when the commercials are tastefully done. . . .

The furor over Channel One advertising baffles me. Ads are everywhere in our building and have been for years. The clocks, the No. 2 pencils, the computers, even the footballs have company logos. . . .

The things we use have to be paid for by somebody. Many school systems like mine would never have this kind of equipment except through a program like this.

Betty Berry, *NEA Today*

Summarize Berry's opinion in one sentence.

Literature Model

S chools are marketplaces for ideas, not commercial turf. The opposite concept—that schools should provide a captive audience for commercials "endorsed" by educators—is repulsive. *Educators present all sides of an issue—we don't "sell" one point of view.* . . .

The *Wall Street Journal* reports that American teenagers spent $55 billion in 1988. Harnessing that purchasing power can give an advertiser a big advantage in the marketplace.

Jennifer March, *NEA Today*

Summarize March's opinion in one sentence.

Resource Manager

Planning Resources
- *Lesson Plans*

 Transparencies
- *Bellringer*
- *Daily Language Practice*
- *Fine Art* 29–32
- *Two-Minute Skill Drill*
- *Writing Process* 12, 28–32

Other Print Resources
- *Composition Enrichment*, p. 47
- *Composition Practice*, p. 47
- *Composition Reteaching*, p. 47
- *Cooperative Learning Activities*
- *Listening and Speaking Activities*, pp. 17, 22–23
- *Sentence-Combining Practice*, pp. 34–35

- *Thinking and Study Skills*, pp. 11, 20
- *Writing Across the Curriculum*
- *Writing Assessment and Evaluation Rubrics*

Take a Meaningful Stand

To write persuasively, you must take a stand on a topic you have some knowledge of and then support your position with relevant evidence. For instance, both Berry and March drew on their many years of teaching experience to present specific arguments for and against commercials in classroom programs.

In addition to knowing your subject, you need to make sure that a genuine difference of opinion exists between you and your audience. Taking a stand against pollution would probably not be worth your time, since few people would disagree. Taking a stand in favor of a specific antipollution measure, such as mandatory carpooling, is more controversial since some people may oppose your position. Once you have an arguable topic, express your opinion in a clear thesis statement such as this: Mandatory carpooling regulations should be adopted to ease air pollution.

Examine Your Audience

Knowing your audience is the essence of persuasive writing. After all, you're trying to influence their opinions and sometimes even change their actions. The questions in the chart may help you decide what you need to know about your audience.

Evaluating Your Audience

- What is the current attitude of my audience? Are they likely to agree or disagree? Do they care about the issue, or will I have to overcome their apathy?
- What do they already know about the issue? Do I need to provide background or clear up misconceptions?
- What types of evidence will have the strongest impact on my audience? Will facts and statistics do the job? Should I include informed opinions?
- What do I want my audience to do: change their thinking, take action, or simply recognize the validity of my viewpoint?

Journal Writing

Make notes in your journal about some audiences you could write for, including how your choice of an audience affects your argument. If you presented your opinion about watching commercials in school, what information would appeal to your classmates, your teachers, your parents, and the members of your school board?

Prewriting Tip

Discuss your opinion and your audience with a peer. Ask for ideas about how to get through to the audience you have in mind.

Drafting Tip

For examples of the kinds of details to use to support a position, see Lesson 5.2, pages 224–227.

Teach

Identifying Issues

Ask the class to reflect on the kinds of issues that would move most people to take a stand. To get the discussion going, you might write a range of situations on the board, such as the threat of world war, a proposed tax hike, discrimination, or a rise in neighborhood crime. Ask students on what issues they have taken stands and how they communicated their opinions. Point out that people tend to take stands on issues that directly affect them and that they believe they can actually change. Ask students to think of issues about which they might like to write. **L2**

Two-Minute Skill Drill

Have students rewrite the following bland phrases with vivid modifiers and specific nouns. Then have students incorporate their new phrases into sentences.

1. *some good food*
2. *a nice person*
3. *a rainy day*

See also *Two-Minute Skill Drill Transparency 6.3*

Journal Writing Tip

Classifying Before students indicate which information would appeal to various groups, suggest that they consider the types of information called for in the Evaluating Your Audience guidelines on this student page.

Teach

Using the Model

Point out time structure in the ad copy ("at one time," "in the 1940s and 1950s," "now," "since 1975"). Ask students how this structures the ad's argument (by tracing the threat to and then recovery of the falcon population). Ask students to summarize the argument (the Wildlife Federation has helped to save endangered species) and tell what appeal the ad is making (for readers to join the Wildlife Federation) and what gives the appeal persuasive force (evidence of the success of conservation efforts). **L2**

Organizing Writing

Students who have difficulty organizing their writing can follow the organization shown on the Guidelines for Persuasive Writing chart. Have them use topic sentences that begin "The issue is," "My opinion is," "These are the reasons I hold this opinion," and "In conclusion." **L1**

Additional Resources

Writing Process Transparencies, 12, 28–32

Writing Across the Curriculum
Cooperative Learning Activities

For further ideas for persuasive writing, see *Fine Art Transparencies*, 29–32.
Thinking and Study Skills, pp. 11, 20
Sentence-Combining Practice, pp. 34–35
Listening and Speaking Activities, pp. 17, 22–23
Composition Practice, p. 47

Persuasive Writing

Drafting Tip

As you draft persuasive writing, think about the order of your arguments. You can leave your readers with a stronger impression if you save your best argument for last.

How effective is this headline and why?

What facts does this ad include, and how do they provide strong support for the ad's purpose?

What specific action does this ad call for in its conclusion?

State Your Case

Your success in persuasive writing will depend on stating your case well, and that means organization. Persuasive writing often follows the four-step plan below.

Guidelines for Persuasive Writing			
Introduce the issue	**State your opinion**	**Support your position**	**Draw your conclusion**
Describe the issue, and supply any background needed to help readers understand it.	Take your stand in a clear, direct thesis statement	Present your evidence—facts, opinions, or both—and respond in opposing viewpoints.	End by summarizing your ideas and, if appropriate, giving a clear call to action.

Public-service advertisements often use the approach suggested above to draw attention to a cause or to seek financial support. In your opinion, how well does the following ad make its case?

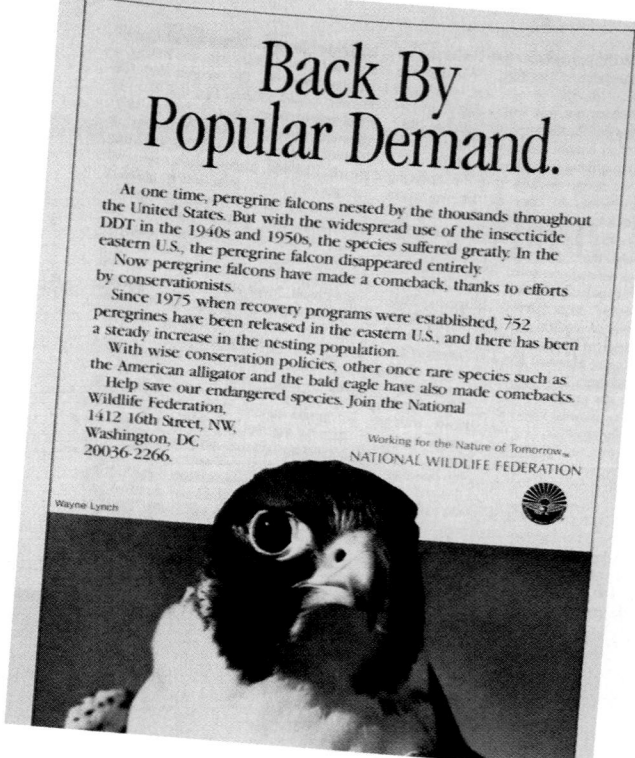

Back By Popular Demand.

At one time, peregrine falcons nested by the thousands throughout the United States. But with the widespread use of the insecticide DDT in the 1940s and 1950s, the species suffered greatly. In the eastern U.S., the peregrine falcon disappeared entirely. Now peregrine falcons have made a comeback, thanks to efforts by conservationists.

Since 1975 when recovery programs were established, 752 peregrines have been released in the eastern U.S., and there has been a steady increase in the nesting population.

With wise conservation policies, other once rare species such as the American alligator and the bald eagle have also made comebacks.

Help save our endangered species. Join the National Wildlife Federation.

1412 16th Street, NW, Washington, DC 20036-2266.

Working for the Nature of Tomorrow™
NATIONAL WILDLIFE FEDERATION

Wayne Lynch

MEETING INDIVIDUAL NEEDS Special Needs

Ordering Arguments

Some students may continue to have difficulty organizing the evidence supporting their opinions. Encourage students to think about the order in which they present their material. Remind students that they will leave their readers with a stronger impression if they leave their most persuasive evidence and strongest arguments to present last.

Write a Letter

Write a letter to your school principal stating your position on this topic: Your school should (should not) receive or continue to receive daily television news broadcasts. As your evidence, use the information below, the information on page 290, and your own ideas.

PURPOSE To write a letter supporting or opposing TV news in the classroom
AUDIENCE Your school principal
LENGTH 2–3 paragraphs

WRITING RUBRICS To write an effective persuasive letter, you should

- explain the issue
- state your position in a thesis statement
- support your position
- draw your own conclusion
- gear your argument to your audience

Pro

___ In exchange for requiring students to watch the television news, with commercials, schools are loaned TV equipment.

___ Many high school students lack knowledge of current events.

___ A study by the producer of the news program found that students who had watched it had a "significantly better" knowledge of world and national events than did other students.

Con

___ The contract requires students to watch the news program every day.

___ When the contract expires, the television equipment must be returned.

___ Schools have no control over what kinds of information and commercials are presented during the broadcasts.

Grammar Link

Use specific nouns and strong modifiers.

Schools are marketplaces for ideas, not commercial turf.

Revise the sentences below, using specific nouns and strong modifiers.

1. Some schools have a lot of things and some don't.
2. School funds should come from many sources.
3. Taxes on many items could be raised.
4. Certain people think that a new tax plan will result in better schools.

See Lesson 10.1, pages 439–444; Lesson 10.4, pages 460–465; and Lesson 10.5, pages 466–472.

Using Computers

Store your facts and opinions in your word-processing program. Enter the information, give it a heading, and box it so that it looks like a note card. Then, organize your notes grouping them under ideas or headings.

Cross-Curricular Activity

EARTH SCIENCE With a partner, draft a letter to the publisher of an environmental newsletter or magazine, presenting a well-supported argument about a current environmental issue. Revise and edit the letter carefully.

6.3 Presenting an Opinion **293**

Assess

Evaluation Rubrics

Write a Letter

When evaluating students' opinion statements, look for writing that

- provides sufficient background information to define the issue of in-school commercial news broadcasts
- clearly states the student's opinion
- uses evidence likely to persuade the principal
- encourages the principal to change his or her thinking or to take a specific action

See also *Writing Assessment & Evaluation Rubrics.*

Using Computers

Rather than boxing their notes to resemble note cards, students might enter their data in an extended outline form. You may wish to have students print out and turn in their notes.

Cross-Curricular Activity

The letters should

- articulate a clear, responsible position on the issue.
- be legible and free of grammatical errors.

Reteaching

Composition Reteaching, p. 47

Enrichment

Composition Enrichment, p. 47

Close

Encourage students to work in small groups, discussing the difference between fact and opinion and what makes an opinion a valid piece of evidence.

Grammar Link

Answers

(Answers will vary, but suggestions are given below.)

1. Affluent schools have better facilities than poorer schools.
2. School revenue should come from a variety of sources.
3. Taxes on luxury items could be increased.
4. Legislators think that a higher tax base will improve schools.

Focus

Lesson Overview

Objective
- To write a product evaluation using appropriate evidence

Skills
- using adverbs and adjectives correctly; organizing comparisons

Critical Thinking
- establishing and evaluating criteria

Listening and Speaking
- formulating questions

Bellringer
Daily Language Activity

When students enter the classroom, have this assignment on the board: *Write a brief evaluation of a product you have used recently that you would not recommend to a friend.*

Grammar Link to the Bellringer

Suggest that students share their evaluations and comment on the strength of their arguments. Have them check their use of adjectives and adverbs that support their argument, such as *good* and *well, careful* and *carefully, correct* and *correctly.*

See also 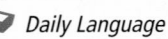 *Daily Language Practice*

Motivating Activity

Ask students what steps they take before buying an expensive item. Discuss advantages of asking friends or consulting an expert when making a purchase. Ask students whether they refer to *Consumer Reports* or a similar publication. (Bring in a copy for the class to examine, if possible.) Explain that the persuasive writing in such publications carries a special responsibility to be accurate and unbiased.

LESSON 6.4

Writing a Product Evaluation

Using persuasive techniques, writers prepare evaluations of a broad range of products and services. Reading a product evaluation such as this one could help you find the right in-line skates.

FREEBLADES Come alive with Freeblades. Cool and in-line.

The article begins by explaining what the product is.

What kind of testing did the evaluators do?

What are the report's recommendations? How might they help a consumer?

Literature Model

The hottest roller skates around don't look much like the skates most grownups remember from their childhood. The hardware most resembles flashy ski boots with a line of plastic wheels down the center of the sole. They're known formally as in-line skates. . . .

We tested nine skates in time trials around a paved running track, in our parking lot, and along some country roads. We also rolled on an exercise treadmill and measured the amount of force needed to keep rolling along. . . .

The hard, molded-plastic boots provide good ankle support—provided you can pull the laces tight enough. That wasn't always easy to do, we found. . . .

Beginners might well look low in the Ratings [of specific models], to skates at less than $100. (Just make sure the boots feel comfortable to you.)

Those skates may not roll quite as easily or rapidly as higher-priced models. But then, you may not want a lot of speed as a beginner. Once the original wheels and bearing wear out, you can swap them for a good set for about $100. Changing wheels is fairly easy.

"In-Line Skates: They Aren't Just for Kids," *Consumer Reports*

Resource Manager

Planning Resources
- *Lesson Plans*

 Transparencies
- *Bellringer*
- *Daily Language Practice*
- *Fine Art* 29–32
- *Two-Minute Skill Drill*
- *Writing Process* 12, 28–32

 Other Print Resources
- *Composition Enrichment,* p. 48
- *Composition Practice,* p. 48
- *Composition Reteaching,* p. 48
- *Cooperative Learning Activities*
- *Listening and Speaking Activities,* pp. 17, 22–23
- *Sentence-Combining Practice,* pp. 34–35

- *Thinking and Study Skills,* p. 25
- *Writing Across the Curriculum*
- *Writing Assessment and Evaluation Rubrics*

Set a Goal

Product evaluations that you write can serve various purposes. You can judge the quality of a particular brand or service; you can compare several brands or services for the purpose of rating them; or you can evaluate the usefulness of a product itself, making a judgment about whether it's worth purchasing *any* brand. Setting a goal at the outset will help you determine what types of evidence you need to gather.

Develop Standards for Evaluation

A product evaluation must be backed up with evidence. You need to develop standards you can use to evaluate the product and then determine how well the product measures up to your standards. *Consumer Reports* evaluates products by running them through a series of tests. You yourself can't conduct that type of evaluation, but you *can* go to product users for evidence. Conduct an informal survey, asking your friends, neighbors, and family to answer questions about the product you plan to evaluate. You can adapt the chart below to fit your product.

Prewriting Tip

A comparison frame can help you organize your evidence for a product evaluation. See Lesson 5.5 on pages 236–239.

TIME

For more about the writing process, see **TIME Facing the Blank Page,** pp. 109–119.

Standards for Evaluating Products	
Price	Is the price reasonable? How does it compare with those of similar products?
Features	What are its most important features? Are any desirable features missing? Are any of its features unnecessary?
Workmanship	Is the product well made? Is anything easily broken?
Design	Is it good-looking? Is it easy to use?

Based on the information from your survey, you can make informed judgments about the product. You can then prepare a written report to help other consumers make the right choices.

Journal Writing

Think of a product you bought recently, and evaluate it according to the standards in the chart above for price, features, quality, and design. Would you have purchased the product if you first had evaluated it according to these standards? Write your answer in your journal.

Teach

Using the Model

Discuss the organization of the Literature Model. Ask students to identify sentences that deal with product definition, types of research conducted, and results from research. Have students summarize the report's recommendations, and ask why readers would be interested in following the advice. (It shows consumers a way to save money.) **L2**

Two-Minute Skill Drill

List these adjectives on the board and have students write the adverbial equivalent of each:

careful   efficient   thoughtful

bad   better   effective

See also *Two-Minute Skill Drill Transparency 6.4*

Journal Writing Tip

Assessing Criteria and Verifying an Evaluation Suggest that students begin by creating an evaluation chart similar to the chart on the student page, based on the criteria listed. Tell them to specify features they are assessing.

Teach

Using Visuals

Tell students that a product evaluator's judgments can be made more persuasive to the reader by including photos or drawings that support the evidence. Point out the photographs on the student page, and explain the difference between an underexposed photograph (one not exposed to light for a sufficiently long time) and a correctly exposed photograph. Ask students to think of other situations in which they might use visuals to make a point. **L2**

Additional Resources

Writing Process Transparencies, 12, 28–32

Writing Across the Curriculum
Cooperative Learning Activities

For further ideas for persuasive writing, see *Fine Art Transparencies,* 29–32.

Thinking and Study Skills, p. 25
Sentence-Combining Practice, pp. 34–35
Listening and Speaking Activities, pp. 17, 22–23
Composition Practice, p. 48

Persuasive Writing

Use Visual Evidence

Photos and other illustrations can add vital information about a product. For example, the *Consumer Reports* evaluation of film-processing services noted that photographers sometimes blame themselves for what are actually problems in processing. To illustrate processing problems, *Consumer Reports* used the following photos as visual evidence.

The film was underexposed in printing, so the print has low contrast and washed-out colors.

Here the film was processed correctly, so the print has sharp edges and bright colors.

Grammar Tip

When editing a product evaluation, check that antecedents of pronouns, such as *this, that, which,* and *it* are clearly stated. For more information about pronoun references, see Lesson 17.6, pages 649–651.

Once you've completed your investigation, you'll need to present your findings. Here are some guidelines you can follow to make your evaluation helpful to your readers.

Writing a Product Evaluation	
Introduce it	What product or service are you evaluating?
State your main idea	Are you judging one product or service? Are you comparing two or more?
Explain your methods	Did you examine the product or service? Did you survey its users?
State your findings	What are your standards? How well did the product or service measure up?
Make a recommendation	Should people buy the product or use the service?

Exploring Language

Choosing Words

Point out that an evaluator must be careful to let the reader know when a statement is a fact and when it is an opinion. List the following phrases on the board and ask students to identify those that refer to the writer's opinions and those that indicate an objective statement, based on research or experiment.

I think   *we discovered*
it seems   *probably*
facts prove   *my friends say*

Write an Evaluation of a Place

Write an article for a travel magazine. Evaluate a place you have visited, such as an amusement park, a museum, or a zoo.

PURPOSE To write an evaluation of a travel destination
AUDIENCE Readers of a travel magazine
LENGTH 3–4 paragraphs

WRITING RUBRICS To write an effective evaluation of a place, you should

- state your main ideas
- identify your standards for evaluating the place
- explain how you gathered your data
- state your findings and make a recommendation
- provide visual evidence if possible

Cross-Curricular Activity

COOPERATIVE LEARNING Work in a small group to evaluate a product or service popular among teenagers—for example, jeans, CD players, or fast-food restaurants. Draw up a list of standards for evaluating your product or service. Then have each member use the standards to conduct an informal survey of friends and classmates. Record individual findings and pool the results of the surveys. Then prepare a product evaluation, having each member write one part of the report.

Grammar Link

Use *good/well* and *bad/badly* correctly.

Good and *bad* are adjectives. They precede nouns and follow linking verbs. Use *well* as an adjective to mean "in good health." Otherwise *well* and *badly* are adverbs and modify action verbs.

Beginners might well look . . . in the ratings . . . swap them for a good set. . . .

Complete each sentence below by adding *good, well, bad,* or *badly.*

1. We have recently been told that butter may be ____ for us.
2. Eating a bucket of unbuttered popcorn is not ____ for you either.
3. Foods saturated with fat or brimming with salt can make you feel ____.
4. Experts debate whether people need vitamins to eat ____.
5. Federal standards for nutrition supplements are enforced ____.

See Lesson 18.5, pages 671–672.

Viewing and Representing

CREATE A BROCHURE Develop a travel brochure using photographs or drawings of a particular place. Consider what visuals would most likely convince others to visit. Label the images with persuasive captions and display your brochure for teachers and classmates to view and evaluate.

Assess

Evaluation Rubrics

Write an Evaluation of a Place
The writer should express clearly the standards used for evaluation, indicate the source of all data, and make a specific recommendation based on his or her findings.

See also *Writing Assessment & Evaluation Rubrics.*

Viewing and Representing
The travel brochures should include attractive visuals and informative captions which make the place seem appealing.

Cross-Curricular Activity
The assignment should show clearly the standards used and indicate the number and variety of people surveyed. Writing done cooperatively should show careful organization and attention to objectivity.

Reteaching
Composition Reteaching, p. 48

Enrichment
Composition Enrichment, p. 48

Close

Discuss how you would set goals, develop standards, and present visual evidence if you were to evaluate a very popular toy or game for a ten-year-old relative.

Grammar Link

Answers
1. bad
2. good
3. bad/good
4. well
5. badly

Focus

Lesson Overview

Objective
- To create an advertisement that will attract attention, arouse interest, create desire, and get action

Skills
- formulating questions; gathering audience information

Critical Thinking
- analyzing

Listening and Speaking
- questioning

 Bellringer

Daily Language Activity

When students enter the classroom, have this assignment on the board: *Write an ad that will help you sell a game or toy you have outgrown.*

Grammar Link to the Bellringer

Ask a partner to read your ad and circle the pronouns. Discuss how each pronoun helps clarify your ad.

See also *Daily Language Practice*

Motivating Activity

Read aloud the following anonymous verse from *It Pays to Advertise:*

    The codfish lays ten thousand eggs,
    The homely hen lays one.
    The codfish never cackles
    To tell you what she's done.
    And so we scorn the codfish,
    While the humble hen we prize,
    Which only goes to show you
    That it pays to advertise.

Ask students what the verse says about why advertising pays. (It gets products noticed and appreciated.)

Persuasive Writing

LESSON 6.5

Creating an Ad

A strong ad is carefully worded to grab the attention of its intended audience. At what audience is the ad below aimed? Do you think it successfully "sells" advertising?

> How does the headline grab your attention?

> The ad appeals to reason and emotion as it answers common arguments against advertising.

> Does the ad present its strongest argument at the end? Support your opinion.

THIS AD IS FULL OF LIES.

LIE #1: ADVERTISING MAKES YOU BUY THINGS YOU DON'T WANT.
Advertising is often accused of inducing people to buy things against their will.

But when was the last time you returned home from the local shopping mall with a bag full of things you had absolutely no use for? The truth is, nothing short of a pointed gun can get *anybody* to spend money on something he or she doesn't want.

No matter how effective an ad is, you and millions of other American consumers make your own decisions. If you don't believe it, ask someone who knows firsthand about the limits of advertising. Like your local Edsel dealer.

LIE #2: ADVERTISING MAKES THINGS COST MORE. Since advertising costs money, it's natural to assume it costs *you* money. But the truth is that advertising often brings prices down.

Consider the electronic calculator, for example. In the late 1960s, advertising created a mass market for calculators. That meant more of them needed to be produced, which brought the price of producing each calculator down. Competition spurred by advertising brought the price down still further.

As a result, the same product that used to cost hundreds of dollars now costs as little as five dollars.

LIE #3: ADVERTISING HELPS BAD PRODUCTS SELL.
Some people worry that good advertising sometimes covers up for bad products.

But nothing can make you like a bad product. So, while advertising can help convince you to try something once, it can't make you buy it twice. If you don't like what you've bought, you won't buy it again. And if enough people feel the same way, the product dies on the shelf.

In other words, the only thing advertising can do for a bad product is help you find out it's a bad product. And you take it from there.

LIE #4: ADVERTISING IS A WASTE OF MONEY. Some people wonder why we don't just put all the money spent on advertising directly into our national economy.

The answer is, we already do.

Advertising helps products sell, which holds down prices, which helps sales even more. It creates jobs. It informs you about all the products available and helps you compare them. And it stimulates the competition that produces new and better products at reasonable prices.

If all that doesn't convince you that advertising is important to our economy, you might as well stop reading.

Because on top of everything else, advertising has paid for a large part of the magazine you're now holding.

And that's the truth.

ADVERTISING.
ANOTHER WORD FOR FREEDOM OF CHOICE.
American Association of Advertising Agencies

Resource Manager

Planning Resources
- *Lesson Plans*

Transparencies
- *Bellringer*
- *Daily Language Practice*
- *Fine Art* 29–32
- *Two-Minute Skill Drill*
- *Writing Process* 12, 28–32

Other Print Resources
- *Composition Enrichment,* p. 49
- *Composition Practice,* p. 49
- *Composition Reteaching,* p. 49
- *Cooperative Learning Activities*
- *Listening and Speaking Activities,* pp. 17, 22–23
- *Sentence-Combining Practice,* pp. 34–35

- *Thinking and Study Skills,* pp. 4, 6, 7
- *Writing Across the Curriculum*
- *Writing Assessment and Evaluation Rubrics*

Get Your Audience's Attention

Advertisements have a clear purpose—to persuade people to buy a product or service or to support a point of view, idea, or candidate. The goals of advertising can be summed up in the acronym AIDA: a good ad must attract *Attention*, arouse *Interest*, create *Desire*, and get *Action*. Study this chart to see how AIDA works.

AIDA	
Attention	Use an attention-getting headline or striking design to draw readers in.
Interest	Present evidence to show why readers should be interested. Use facts and opinions to explain the product's features and show how it's different from the competition—and better.
Desire	Appeal to your readers' reason and emotions to make them want your product.
Action	End with a clear call to action—buy the product, give money to the cause, vote for the candidate.

Create an Audience Profile

You want your ad to succeed, and that means reaching the right audience: those who are likely to use your product, service, or idea. An audience profile gives you the information you need to tailor your ad to the desired audience. All it takes is asking a few simple questions.

Audience Profile	
Age group	How old are the people who might use your product or service?
Education level	Does your product or service appeal to people with a certain level of education?
Buying power	Does your product or service appeal to people with a certain level of income?
Attitudes	What opinions and interests characterize your audience?
Life style	What entertainment characterizes your audience?
Needs	What are the needs of your audience?

Journal Writing

Find a magazine or newspaper ad that you think is effective, and paste it in your journal. Prepare an audience profile for the ad, answering as many questions as you can from the chart above.

Revising Tip

In advertising, a few words go a long way. Keep your message short and to the point.

Teach

Evaluating a Position

Ask students whether they agree with this quotation from Norman Douglas: "You can tell the ideals of a nation by its advertisements." What do the advertisements students see every day say about the ideals of the United States? Ask students to give examples to support their remarks. Discuss how a writer's understanding of an audience's ideals will help him or her to get the audience's attention and create an audience profile. **L2**

 Two-Minute Skill Drill

List these nouns on the board and have students write a possessive pronoun for each.

person   class   friends

children   I   it

See also *Two-Minute Skill Drill Transparency 6.5*

Journal Writing Tip

Confirming Criteria Remind students to review the criteria for an effective ad. The acronym AIDA will help them to answer the chart questions and acquire information for their audience profile.

Teach

Using the Right Word

Ask students to explain how the writer uses words with a double meaning to get the reader's attention in the ad on the student page. (Most readers identify the term "Great Lakes" with the five Great Lakes in the Midwest.) Point out that this use of words will lead most readers to read the rest of the ad, which explains that Idaho's lakes are great in the sense of being magnificent. **L1**

Additional Resources

Writing Process Transparencies, 12, 28–32

Writing Across the Curriculum

Cooperative Learning Activities

For further stimuli for persuasive writing, see *Fine Art Transparencies,* 29–32.

Thinking and Study Skills, pp. 4, 6, 7

Sentence-Combining Practice, pp. 34–35

Listening and Speaking Activities, pp. 17, 22–23

Composition Practice, p. 49

Cross-reference: Dictionary and Thesaurus

For more information about how to determine the connotations of synonyms, refer students to Lesson 24.2, pp. 816–817.

Persuasive Writing

Vocabulary Tip

When looking for the right word, you may want to use a thesaurus. For information about how to use this reference, see Lesson 24.2, pages 816–817.

Grammar Tip

When editing copy for an ad, make sure that a noun of amount, such as *hundreds,* agrees in number with its verb. For more information about verb agreement with special subjects, see Lesson 16.4, pages 618–619.

Choose the Right Words

To arouse your audience's interest and create desire for the product, you need to use the right words. Mark Twain once said, "The difference between the right word and the nearly right word is the same as that between lightning and the lightning bug."

Use Precise Words   Ad writers choose words carefully. Wear Champions running shoes, and you won't just run fast; you'll "glide effortlessly." Devine Cookies aren't simply delicious; they're "honey-sweet and taste-tempting." The Rapmaster isn't just a new radio; it's "a state-of-the-art sound system." Concrete nouns, strong action verbs, and colorful adjectives and adverbs help to create a desire for your product, service, or idea.

Recognize Connotations   You're writing an ad for the Fataway exerciser. Do you promise customers a "scrawny body" or a "lean body"? *Scrawny* and *lean* have similar meanings; both are synonyms of *thin.* But the connotations of the words—their positive or negative associations—are strikingly different. Since persuasive writing appeals to emotion as well as to reason, you can enhance your message by keeping connotations in mind. What word choices help to make the following ad effective?

Words paint an attractive picture of Idaho's lakes and suggest a relaxing travel destination.

Ad writers capitalize on double meanings. How does this ad play on two meanings of "great lakes"?

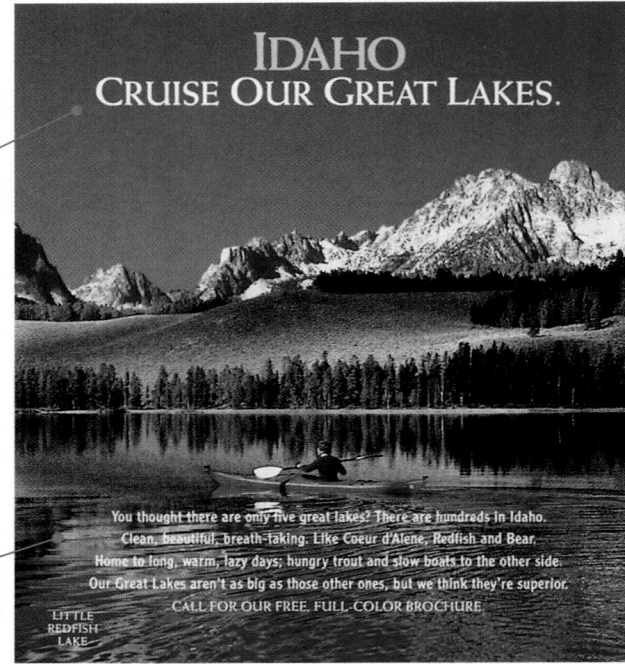

IDAHO
CRUISE OUR GREAT LAKES.

You thought there are only five great lakes? There are hundreds in Idaho. Clean, beautiful, breath-taking. Like Coeur d'Alene, Redfish and Bear. Home to long, warm, lazy days; hungry trout and slow boats to the other side. Our Great Lakes aren't as big as those other ones, but we think they're superior.
CALL FOR OUR FREE, FULL-COLOR BROCHURE.

LITTLE REDFISH LAKE

300   Unit 6 Persuasive Writing

MEETING INDIVIDUAL NEEDS   English Language Learners

Connotations

Students learning English may be unfamiliar with the connotations of some words. To demonstrate the shades of meaning for some words that are not always interchangeable, ask a volunteer to select two or three synonyms for the word *smart* in the thesaurus and look up each synonym in the dictionary to see whether the words have identical connotations. Encourage students to share words with similar connotations from their native languages.

Persuasive Writing

Write an Ad

Write a one-page ad for your local newspaper. You can create an ad for an exhibit of paintings, for a travel agency, a soap, a perfume, a cleaning service, or for a product, service, or idea of your choice.

PURPOSE To create an advertisement
AUDIENCE Readers of the local newspaper
LENGTH 1 page

WRITING RUBRICS To write an effective ad, you should

- appeal to your desired audience
- write an attention-getting headline
- present evidence
- appeal to readers' reason and emotion
- end with a clear call to action
- use precise words with appropriate connotations

Using Computers

Use computer software to create text and visuals for your ad. Present your completed voting ad to the class. Discuss with classmates the persuasive elements in each ad. Which design elements seem to be more persuasive? Explain.

Claude Monet, *Les Coquelicots (Wild Poppies)*, 1873

Cross-Curricular Activity

GOVERNMENT You are working on an advertising campaign urging citizens to register to vote in the upcoming election. Your task is to create an advertisement targeted specifically to people who have just turned eighteen and are eligible to vote for the first time. Write the ad copy and design a full-page ad. Include an appropriate graphic.

Grammar Link

Make indefinite pronouns and the personal pronouns referring to them agree in number and person.

Pronouns referring to indefinite pronouns should be singular if the indefinite pronoun is singular and plural if it is plural. If the gender of a singular indefinite pronoun is unknown, you may wish to rephrase to avoid "he or she."

Rewrite the sentences to make the personal and indefinite pronouns agree.

1. Most of the consumers assume that you cannot be swayed by advertising.
2. Few of the men think that he has been forced to buy products or services against their will.
3. Others of them have purchased an item because he or she was influenced by an ad.
4. Neither of the girls bought this item because they believed the ad.
5. None of us should blame the advertiser, however, if they buy a shoddy product twice.

See Lesson 17.5, pages 644–648.

Grammar Link

Answers

1. . . . that they cannot . . .
2. . . . that they have been . . .
3. . . . because they were . . .
4. . . . because she believed . . .
5. . . . if we buy . . .

Viewing the Art

Claude Monet, *Les Coquelicots (Wild Poppies),* 1873
French Impressionist Claude Monet's 1873 oil painting of poppies in a spacious landscape captures the feeling of a bright summer day. *Les Coquelicots,* 19 1/2 by 25 inches, is at the Musée d'Orsay in Paris.

Assess

Evaluation Rubrics

Write an Ad

When evaluating students' opinion statements, look for writing that
- speaks to a clearly defined audience
- includes an attention-getting headline
- uses precise words
- shows an understanding of the power of appropriate connotations

See also *Writing Assessment & Evaluation Rubrics.*

Cross-Curricular Activity

Each ad should
- be directed toward young adults
- state a message clearly and persuasively
- carry a design and text that work together

Reteaching

Composition Reteaching, p. 49

Enrichment

Composition Enrichment, p. 49

Use *Fine Art Transparencies* 29–32 for enrichment activities also.

Close

Invite students to list the standards they would use if asked to judge ads written to sell a new fast-food product.

Focus

Lesson Overview

Objective
- To compose a letter of complaint that states the problem and proposes a reasonable solution

Skills
- using details effectively; using commas effectively

Critical Thinking
- identifying problems; setting goals

Listening and Speaking
- discussing

Bellringer
Daily Language Activity

When students enter the classroom, have this assignment on the board: *Write a short paragraph that details a complaint you have about a recent purchase or experience.*

Grammar Link to the Bellringer

Have students reread their paragraphs, checking to see that their verb tenses are correct and consistent.

See also *Daily Language Practice*

Motivating Activity

Ask students to think of the last time they had a legitimate complaint about something. Were they excited, angry, calm, wishy-washy, firm? To whom did they complain? Did anyone act on the complaint? Discuss the purpose of legitimate complaints, to whom they should be directed, and effective methods of getting results.

Persuasive Writing

LESSON
6.6

Writing a Letter of Complaint

"Try to imagine how much I care!"

When you write a letter of complaint, you usually want to persuade someone to solve a problem. In the letter below, notice how the writer calmly identifies the problem, offers evidence, and proposes a reasonable solution.

Student Model

> Summarize Reis's complaint in a sentence.

I purchased an automatic dishwasher, model 98765, from B & A Appliance Service Center on April 18. On May 2 the washer began leaking water from the bottom.

Right away, I called B & A and explained the problem. I also explained my warranty, which entitles me to parts and labor for a full year from the purchase date. The next day B & A sent two repairmen, but they were unsuccessful, and the washer still leaked. I called again, and on May 6 the same men came back but still could not fix the washer. On May 8, I received a bill for $59.03 from B & A for parts and labor. I now have called and visited your store on several occasions. Mr. Black, the department manager, insists that I am responsible for paying the bill.

> What evidence does Reis present to justify her complaint?

I am enclosing a copy of my original receipt, my warranty, and the repair bill. I believe I am not responsible for these charges. My washer still leaks, so I request that B & A live up to the terms of the warranty and fix it. If it cannot be fixed, please replace it with another washer of the same make and model. I hope we can come to an agreement on this matter.

> What solution does Reis suggest? Is her suggestion reasonable?

Teresa Reis, Quartz Hill High School, Quartz Hill, California

302 Unit 6 Persuasive Writing

Resource Manager

Planning Resources
- *Lesson Plans*

Transparencies
- *Bellringer*
- *Daily Language Practice*
- *Fine Art* 29–32
- *Two-Minute Skill Drill*
- *Writing Process* 12, 28–32

Other Print Resources
- *Composition Enrichment,* p. 50
- *Composition Practice,* p. 50
- *Composition Reteaching,* p. 50
- *Cooperative Learning Activities*
- *Listening and Speaking Activities,* pp. 17, 22–23
- *Sentence-Combining Practice,* pp. 34–35

- *Thinking and Study Skills,* pp. 2, 24
- *Writing Across the Curriculum*
- *Writing Assessment and Evaluation Rubrics*

Identify the Problem and a Solution

When you write a letter of complaint, you are trying to solve a problem. Your goals are to explain your problem, convince your reader that you have a valid complaint, and propose a reasonable solution. Your letter can follow this simple pattern.

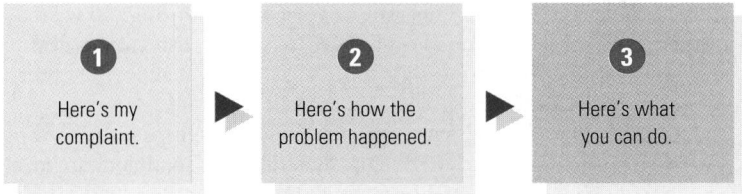

In the model letter on the opposite page, Teresa Reis has presented these three ideas in three paragraphs. Some complaints have a long history, and, therefore, the letter must be longer. Other complaints can be explained in one paragraph. Whatever its length, your letter should have the same three parts.

First open with a clear statement of the problem, usually in a sentence or two. Make it brief but complete. No one can help you without understanding what your problem is.

Next tell your story. In a paragraph or two, explain what happened, describing any previous attempts to correct the problem. This middle section is usually a narrative, so arrange the details in chronological order, the order in which they happened. Include dates and names, but avoid unnecessary details. Enclose any relevant evidence, such as a photocopy of the manufacturer's warranty.

In your final paragraph, explain specifically what you want done. If the solution you propose is a reasonable one, you are likely to get the results you want. The key word here is *reasonable.* A reasonable solution is one that the person or company can agree to without going to an excessive amount of trouble or expense.

Revising Tip

Ask a peer reviewer whether your letter offers adequate evidence and whether your proposed solution is reasonable.

Journal Writing

Set aside a page in your journal. Label the page "Complaints," and keep a running list of ideas for complaint letters. Over a period of time, you may find that the same complaint appears again and again. When that happens, it may be time to compose and mail that letter of complaint.

Teach

Analyzing a Letter

Have students summarize Teresa's complaint. (billed for repairs covered by the warranty; unsatisfactory work) Have them analyze her use of evidence and identify the solution that she suggests. (evidence: her receipt, warranty, and repair bill; solution: that the store cancel the repair charges and either repair or replace the dishwasher) Discuss what makes Teresa's letter persuasive. **L1**

Recognizing Problems

Students might consider stating a case for correction of a social problem. For example, a student might write a sponsor of a TV show to complain about the show's violence. Ask students to list problems that concern citizens today, name an organization to whom they might complain, and state a solution. They might work in groups to write a letter of complaint. **L3**

Journal Writing Tip

Drawing Conclusions Suggest that students divide the "Complaints" page of their journals into three parts—Problem, Chronology, and Solution—and list important details.

Teach

Using Words Carefully

Discuss strategies for achieving a businesslike tone in complaint letters. Write on the board emotionally charged statements such as *I hate your product* or *Your service was lousy* under the heading *EMOTIONAL.* Ask students to write neutral restatements under *BUSINESSLIKE.* Explain that a businesslike tone makes it likely that the receiver will seriously consider the letter. **L2**

Two-Minute Skill Drill

Ask students to select the word or phrase in each row that is appropriate in a business letter.

cool or *attractive*

trash or *of poor quality*

lies or *misleading statements*

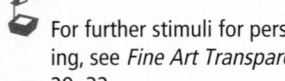 **See also** *Two-Minute Skill Drill Transparency 6.6*

Additional Resources

For further stimuli for persuasive writing, see *Fine Art Transparencies,* 29–32.

Writing Process Transparencies, 12, 28–32

Cooperative Learning Activities

Thinking and Study Skills, pp. 2, 24

Sentence-Combining Practice, pp. 34–35.

Listening and Speaking Activities, pp. 17, 22–23

Composition Practice, p. 50

Persuasive Writing

Presenting Tip

Some complaints fail because they are not directed to the right person. If possible, find out who has the authority to solve your problem, and address your letter to that person.

Grammar Tip

When editing a letter, check that you have used commas correctly. For information about commas in letter writing, see Lesson 21.6, pages 743–751.

Use a Businesslike Tone and Form

When you are writing a letter of complaint, chances are you're angry. Your first impulse may be to strike back with sarcasm, insults, even threats. ("I'll never shop in your stupid store again, and I'll tell all my friends to stay away, too.") To write an effective letter of complaint, you need to keep your emotions under control. Remember, your goal is to get the problem corrected. Your tone of voice comes through in writing just as it does in speech. You're more likely to accomplish your goal if your letter has a calm, businesslike tone. That way, you allow the other side to respond calmly and reasonably as well.

Another way to ensure that your letter will get a sympathetic reading is to use proper form. The letter below illustrates the semiblock form, a popular style for a business letter that will help you get results.

```
                                    123 Washington Way
                                    Irving, NY 12034
                                    July 27, 1992

Sales Manager
Bemus Music Store
1 Trailblazer Way
Portland, OR 97202

Dear Sir or Madam:

   On July 15, I ordered the tape Ice Rink,
by Carrie Carey.  Today it came, but it
broke the first time I played it.
   When I inserted the tape and pushed the
play button on my tape player, I heard the
beginning of the first number, but no more.
When I removed the tape, I could see that
it was broken.  I played some other tapes
to make sure my player had not caused the
problem, but it worked perfectly.
   I am enclosing a copy of the receipt,
and I am returning the defective tape in a
separate package.  Please send me another
copy.

                       Yours truly,

                       Peter Bianco
                       Peter Bianco
```

Enrichment and Extension

Choosing Words

To help students organize their complaint letters, suggest that they include at least one paragraph for each item on the chart. Help them draft a topic sentence for each part of the letter: "My problem is . . . ," "Here is what happened . . . ," "I would like you to. . . ." These paragraph starters will guide students in drafting coherent letters. Students may then revise the wording of each topic sentence to fit the specific details and persuasive goals of the letter.

Write a Complaint Letter

Think about problems with products and services you or members of your family have had. Write a letter of complaint about a problem of your choice or about one listed below. Follow correct business-letter format.

(1) You paid $299 for a new camera. The next week the manufacturer announced that it was discontinuing the model and replacing it with a more advanced one at an introductory price of $250.

(2) You washed a new sweater as directed on the label, but the sweater shrank two sizes.

(3) You and some friends waited to be served in a restaurant for almost an hour. When the food came, it was cold.

PURPOSE To write a letter of complaint
AUDIENCE Person or company
LENGTH 3 paragraphs

WRITING RUBRICS To write an effective letter of complaint, you should

- state the complaint clearly and briefly
- explain what happened
- propose a reasonable solution
- use a businesslike tone
- use correct business-letter form

Listening and Speaking

COOPERATIVE LEARNING In small groups, read aloud your letters of complaint. Discuss and evaluate them for effective argument, clear and concise language, and business-like tone.

Grammar Link

Use the past and past perfect tenses correctly.

Use the past tense to describe an action that was started and completed in the past. Use the past perfect tense to show that a past action began and ended before another past action began.

Write the correct form of each verb in parentheses.

1. By the time I (go) shopping for a cordless phone, I (research) the product in several consumer magazines.
2. However, the sales clerk (convince) me to buy a different model than the one that I (choose).
3. When I (arrive) home, I knew that I (make) a terrible mistake.
4. I (want) these special features long before they (become) popular.

See Lesson 15.3, pages 589–592, and Lesson 15.4, pages 593–595.

Using Computers

The electronic spelling checker in your word processing program can be a great help in proofreading. Be especially careful, though, since your spelling checker won't help you if you've misspelled a proper noun, such as the name of the company, or if you've used the wrong homonym, such as *you're* instead of *your*.

Assess

Evaluation Rubrics

Write a Complaint Letter

When evaluating the opinion statements, make sure students
- address a realistic problem
- follow business-letter format
- use appropriate wording
- include necessary information
- suggest a reasonable solution

See also *Writing Assessment & Evaluation Rubrics.*

Using Computers

Remind students that they should have a peer editor proofread their paper in addition to using the electronic spell check.

Listening and Speaking

Students' presentations should include
- a clear statement of the complaint.
- a sensible proposal for a solution.
- a reasonable tone.

Reteaching

📁 *Composition Reteaching,* p. 50

Enrichment

📁 *Composition Enrichment,* p. 50

Close

Have students summarize what they would look for in a letter of complaint from someone who was trying to persuade them to accept his or her solution to a problem.

6.6 Writing a Letter of Complaint **305**

Grammar Link

Answers
1. went; had researched
2. convinced; had chosen
3. arrived; had made
4. had wanted; became

Persuasive Writing

Focus

Lesson Overview

Objective
- To review a nonfiction book, summarizing its content and effectiveness

Skills
- taking notes; supporting opinions

Critical Thinking
- evaluating; summarizing

Listening and Speaking
- discussing

 Bellringer
Daily Language Activity

When students enter the classroom, have this assignment on the board: *List titles of five books, songs, or films you would recommend to a friend.*

Grammar Link to the Bellringer

Have students review their list of titles for correct punctuation, capitalization, and underlining or italics.

See also *Daily Language Practice*

Motivating Activity

Ask students if they read the endorsements on the cover of a book. Point out that some of these glowing comments are misleading quotes from longer reviews. A review stating "Compared with the author's first book, which was a masterpiece, this book is weak" could appear as "A masterpiece" on the cover. Reading the full review is the best way to find out how the book was evaluated.

WRITING ABOUT LITERATURE

Reviewing a Nonfiction Book

B *ook reviews are a type of product evaluation. The reviewer gives an opinion, supported with evidence, about whether a book is worth a reader's time and money.*

Answer Questions in a Review

Readers ask two basic questions about any nonfiction book: What's it about? and Is it any good? As a reviewer, your job is to answer those questions. Begin by assuming that your readers are unfamiliar with the

---

Resource Manager

Planning Resources
- *Lesson Plans*

 Transparencies
- *Bellringer*
- *Daily Language Practice*
- *Fine Art* 29–32
- *Two-Minute Skill Drill*
- *Writing Process* 12, 28–32

📁 **Other Print Resources**
- *Composition Enrichment*, p. 51
- *Composition Practice*, p. 51
- *Composition Reteaching*, p. 51
- *Cooperative Learning Activities*
- *Listening and Speaking Activities*, pp. 17, 22–23
- *Sentence-Combining Practice*, pp. 34–35

- *Thinking and Study Skills*, p. 25
- *Writing Across the Curriculum*
- *Writing Assessment and Evaluation Rubrics*

book. Summarize the book's contents—its subject and the author's purpose in writing. You may also need to provide background information about the author and subject, though such information isn't always necessary. Reviewers who write for *Rolling Stone*, for example, can assume that their readers have a basic knowledge of rock-and-roll, so they spend less time on background than they would for the general public.

Prepare by Taking Notes

A good nonfiction review says more than whether the reviewer liked the book; it explains why, presenting specific reasons to support its position. The best way to write such a review is to respond to the book as you are reading it. Take notes—in your reader-response journal if you have one—about ideas and opinions. Quote whole sentences that are striking. Also take notes on your own responses: Do you agree or disagree with the author? Are you surprised, angered, encouraged, or discouraged by the book's message? You may wish to reread the book, or key parts of it, to grasp the author's meaning fully. The questions below can help you reflect on your reading.

Journal Writing

You and your friends probably give each other mini-reviews of books, movies, and music. Think about discussions you've had. In your journal explain what information helps you the most in choosing books, movies, and music for yourself.

Grammar Tip

When quoting whole sentences from a book, use quotation marks to set off direct quotes. When summarizing statements in your own words, you do not need quotation marks. For information on how to use punctuation with quotations, see Lesson 21.9, pages 755–757.

Persuasive Writing

6.7

Teach

Summarizing Contents

Summarizing the content of a book is crucial to writing a good review. Ask students to select a familiar nonfiction book about which they will write a summary. Suggest they write a sentence based on each chapter title or section heading. If a book doesn't have chapter titles or section headings, the student can write a sentence summarizing each chapter. Remind students to keep summaries brief. **L1**

 Two-Minute Skill Drill

Write *recommend* on the board and have students list words they find useful when recommending a book. Repeat the activity under the heading *don't recommend*.

See also *Two-Minute Skill Drill Transparency 6.7*

Journal Writing Tip

Establishing Criteria Before students explain what information helps them evaluate reviews, suggest they discuss which types of information they are likely to ignore and which they take seriously.

Teach

Choosing Books to Review

The success of a nonfiction review usually depends on the reviewer's taking a personal interest in the subject. A reviewer often expresses opinions about the quality of the book based on the reviewer's own knowledge of the topic. This personal involvement is one ingredient that makes reviews lively and interesting. Suggest that students review books in subject areas they know and like. **L2**

Additional Resources

 Writing Process Transparencies, 12, 28–32

 Writing Across the Curriculum
Cooperative Learning Activities

 For further ideas for persuasive writing, see *Fine Art Transparencies,* 29–32.

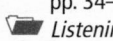 *Thinking and Study Skills,* p. 25
Sentence Combining Practice, pp. 34–35
Listening and Speaking Activities, pp. 17, 22–23
Composition Practice, p. 51

Persuasive Writing

Grammar Tip

When you use the book's title in your review, remember to underscore it to indicate italics. For more about writing titles, see Lesson 21.10 on pages 758–759.

> The first paragraph provides important historical background and an overview of the book's content.

> What details in the review give readers a feel for the liveliness of the author's style?

> Explain the purpose of the last sentence, referring to both its content and its style.

Find a Focus

Once you've finished reading, use your notes to help you write a statement of opinion—a thesis statement—to focus your book review. For a nonfiction book, your statement of opinion will sum up the author's purpose and state whether you recommend the book. Then in the body of the review consider these points: Was the purpose a worthy one? How well did the author achieve it? Should others read the book? In the review below, notice how David Fricke's enthusiasm comes through.

Literature Model

Sam Phillips did not set out to make rock & roll history when he founded Sun Records in 1952. History came to him, walking through the doors of his converted storefront studio, the Memphis Recording Service, in the form of Elvis Presley, Jerry Lee Lewis, Roy Orbison, Johnny Cash and Carl Perkins, among others. But as Colin Escott and Martin Hawkins explain in *Good Rockin' Tonight,* Phillips presided over the birth of rock & roll because he had the instinctive wisdom to recognize the wealth of talent at his doorstep, the indefatigable energy to record as much of it as possible and the discriminating genius to select the pick of the litter to bear Sun's immortal yellow rooster-at-dawn logo. . . .

But the most impressive thing about *Good Rockin' Tonight* is that its narrative drive is every bit as contagious as the music it celebrates. "Long on feel and short on contrivance" is how Escott, in his preface, describes the explosive hybrid of blues, country, gospel and rockabilly that came to be known as the Sun Sound. It is an apt description of the book as well. *Good Rockin' Tonight* reads like a day at Phillips's office, with its breathless parade of frantic farm-boy rockers, blustery blues singers and hillbilly crooners passing daily in front of the Sun microphones. . . .

Phillips . . . wasn't a great businessman; his biggest stars had all left the label by 1963. But the breadth of his vision and the depth of his faith in the music he recorded and released is eloquently documented here. From Sun-rise to Sun-set, *Good Rockin' Tonight* is the last word on the first great rock & roll record label.

David Fricke, "Sam Phillips and the Birth of Rock & Roll,"
Rolling Stone

Exploring Language

Choosing Words

Have students work with partners. Suggest that they bring in copies of books they have enjoyed at some time in their lives and discuss briefly what they liked about the book. Then suggest that they list words they would use to "sell" the book to someone else. For example, the words *mysterious* and *space* might interest a ten-year-old, while an older student would read a book described as "unusual" or "fast-paced."

Write a Book Review

Select a nonfiction book you have read, and write a review of it for your school newspaper. First, consider your audience's knowledge and interest level. Then, make notes about the author's opinions and ideas and about your responses.

PURPOSE To write a book review
AUDIENCE High school students and teachers
LENGTH 1–2 paragraphs

WRITING RUBRICS To write an effective book review, you should

- write a thesis statement summarizing the author's purpose and your opinion of the book
- include your own response to the book

Cross-Curricular Activity

MUSIC Find a review of any nonfiction book about music or musicians. Read the review carefully. Then use the information in the review to write 100–200 words of text for the jacket of the book. If necessary, provide background information about the author and the subject and quote striking sentences from the review.

Viewing and Representing

Look at a number of book jackets in your school library or local bookstore, carefully reading the pertinent text information inside the jackets. Choose a book jacket whose design you do not find appealing and redesign it. Present your book jacket to the class, explaining the reasons for your new design.

Grammar Link

Punctuate and capitalize titles correctly.

BOOK TITLE: *Good Rockin' Tonight*
BOOK REVIEW: "Sam Phillips and the Birth of Rock & Roll"

Write the titles below correctly. Underline the titles that should be italicized.

1. one writer's beginning [book]
2. an electronic job hunt [magazine article]
3. U.S. news & world report [magazine]
4. the charge of the light brigade [short poem]
5. great lady on a white horse [short story]
6. playing through [magazine article]
7. new forces of nationalism [chapter in a book]
8. the world almanac and book of facts [book]
9. the new york times [newspaper]
10. long day's journey into night [play]
11. the new york public library desk reference [book]
12. the rime of the ancient mariner [long poem]
13. a midsummer night's dream [play]
14. a perfect day for bananafish [short story]
15. the waves [book]

See Lesson 20.2, pages 715–721; Lesson 21.9, pages 755–757; and Lesson 21.10, pages 758–759.

Persuasive Writing

Assess

Evaluation Rubrics

Write a Book Review

Student reviews should include these elements:

- information relevant to a teen audience
- a clear thesis statement
- supporting details from the book
- personal response

See also *Writing Assessment & Evaluation Rubrics.*

Cross-Curricular Activity

Students' work should include these elements:

- brief text
- selection of most interesting details to attract attention
- background information if relevant
- significant quotes

Viewing and Representing

Students' redesigned book jackets should
- reflect the students' assessment of the content of the book.
- reflect the tone and substance of the book.

Reteaching

📁 *Composition Reteaching,* p. 51

Enrichment

📁 *Composition Enrichment,* p. 51

Close

Have students list the three elements of a book review that would be most likely to attract their attention.

Grammar Link

Answers

1. *One Writer's Beginnings*
2. "An Electronic Job Hunt"
3. *U.S. News & World Report*
4. "The Charge of the Light Brigade"
5. "Great Lady on a White Horse"
6. "Playing Through"
7. "New Forces of Nationalism"
8. *The World Almanac and Book of Facts*
9. *New York Times*
10. *Long Day's Journey Into Night*
11. *The New York Public Library Desk Reference*
12. *The Rime of the Ancient Mariner*
13. *A Midsummer Night's Dream*
14. "A Perfect Day for Bananafish"
15. *The Waves*

Focus

Lesson Overview

Objective

- To compose a persuasive letter proposing a rule change in a sport or game

Skills

- using the five stages of the writing process: prewriting, drafting, revising, editing, presenting; stating a position; providing evidence; choosing an audience; proofreading

Critical Thinking

- analyzing; synthesizing; main idea; building background; visualizing; making decisions; generating new information

Listening and Speaking

- discussing; evaluating; listening to criticism

Bellringer
Daily Language Activity

When students enter the classroom, have this assignment on the board: *On paper, name a game rule or practice that you disagree with and explain why you feel that way.*

Grammar Link to the Bellringer

Remind students to check their writing for sentence fragments.

See also *Daily Language Practice*

Motivating Activity

Ask students if they have ever attempted to modify the rules of a game while playing it. Encourage students to explain the circumstances and the outcome. Then ask what part persuasion played in their efforts to get others to accept their views.

Persuasive Writing *(sidebar)*

WRITING Online

Visit the Writer's Choice Web site at **writerschoice. glencoe.com** for additional writing prompts.

Persuasive Writing

In preceding lessons, you have learned the techniques of persuasive writing. You have learned about how to present and support an opinion, create an ad, and write a product evaluation and a complaint letter. Now it's time to apply what you've learned. In this lesson you're invited to write a letter persuading someone in authority to change a rule in a game or sport that you enjoy playing or watching.

Assignment

Context

Years of playing or watching have convinced you that a rule change would enhance a certain sport or game. You have decided to write a letter to the people who have the power to change the rules. You want to persuade them to adopt the rule change you propose.

Purpose

To write a brief persuasive essay on a rule change you propose for a sport or game you play or enjoy watching

Audience

The rules committee, governing body, or manufacturer of the sport or game you want to change

Length

1 to 2 pages

The following pages can help you plan and write your letter. Read through them and then refer back to them as you write. However, do not feel tied down by these guidelines. Remember you're in charge of your own writing process.

Resource Manager

Planning Resources
- *Lesson Plans*

Transparencies
- *Bellringer*
- *Daily Language Practice*
- *Writing Process* 12, 28–32

 Other Print Resources
- *Composition Enrichment,* p. 52
- *Composition Practice,* p. 52
- *Composition Reteaching,* p. 52
- *Grammar Workbook,* Lessons 31, 38, 44, 55–57, 66–67, 96–97
- *Sentence-Combining Practice,* pp. 34–35
- *Thinking and Study Skills,* p. 5

- *Writing Assessment and Evaluation Rubrics*

 Software
- *Writer's Assistant*

 Web Sites
- *writerschoice.glencoe.com*
- *lit.glencoe.com*

Writing Process in Action

Prewriting

Should professional football make greater use of instant replays? Should Pin the Tail on the Donkey be changed to Tape the Tail on the Donkey to avoid cruelty to animals? Maybe an idea for a rule change came to mind the minute you read this assignment. If not, the suggestions on the right may help you.

When you have identified a rule change to propose in your letter, spend some time exploring the change to see if it is a reasonable one. Consider potential short- and long-term consequences and the effect of the change on players and spectators.

Once you have chosen your topic, express your position clearly and directly in a thesis statement. Then think about how to approach your audience. You will be writing to the people responsible for the rules of the game, so you know that you won't need to provide background information and clarify terms. You will, however, need to present compelling and convincing evidence to support your position.

When gathering evidence, look for facts and valid opinions. Although facts are generally the stronger kind of evidence, it might be difficult to find hard facts to support your position. Therefore, you may have to cite the opinions of experts who have specific knowledge of your sport or game.

Drafting

In persuasive writing more than in other kinds of writing, your effectiveness depends upon both what you say and how you say it. Choose a tone that is appropriate for the point you want to make. Then, as you write, choose specific words with strong positive or negative connotations to bolster your argument.

Now you are ready to state your case. Begin with an introduction that will create interest in your topic and motivate your audience to read on. Then state your position clearly and precisely. In the model on the next page, note how Mark Mathabane introduces his position on the emergence of power rackets on the professional tennis circuit.

Prewriting Options

- Freewrite about sports and games you know well.
- Ask "What If" questions: What if soccer players could use their hands?
- Brainstorm with classmates.

Prewriting Tip

To gain a better understanding of your audience, use the questions in Lesson 6.3, page 291.

Drafting Tip

For suggestions about using precise words and words with strong connotations, see Lesson 6.5, page 300.

Teach

Prewriting

Developing Ideas for Persuasive Writing

Students may initially draw a blank when asked to recall sports rules. Suggest that students use memory joggers such as skimming sports-page headlines or discussing possible rule changes with a sports fan or coach. **L2**

Drafting

Including Specific Evidence

To impress upon students the value of being specific in the supporting evidence for their arguments, direct their attention to Mathabane's fifth sentence in the third paragraph on page 316. Ask them why "hit the ball at 100 miles an hour" is more effective than "hit the ball hard." (The great speed suggested by the number is far more memorable than "hard" would be.) What does Mathabane accomplish in the next sentence by mentioning specific championship skills? (These references establish him as an expert in the field and give the reader specific information about the alternative to power playing.) By including such specific evidence in their writing, students can establish themselves as "persuasive champions." **L1**

Teach

Revising

Peer Editing

Students can work in writing conferences with peer editors before they revise their writing. Suggest that peer editors respond to the following questions:
- Is the letter directed to the concerns of the intended audience?
- Is the presented evidence relevant?
- Does the argument show a clear understanding of the sport or game?

You may want to duplicate the Peer Response forms in *Writing Assessment & Evaluation Rubrics.* **L2**

Editing

Peer Editing

After students have edited their own work, have them edit another student's writing. Remind them to refer to the Editing Checklist on student page 313. **L2**

Presenting

Before students present their persuasive writing, discuss how to prepare their papers for publication. Emphasize the importance of a neat final draft.

Additional Resources

 Writing Process Transparencies, 12, 28–32

 Thinking and Study Skills, p. 5

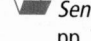 *Sentence-Combining Practice,* pp. 34–35

Composition Practice, p. 52

 Grammar Workbook, Lessons 31, 38, 44, 55–57, 66–67, 96–97

Persuasive Writing

Literature Model

The U.S. Open, America's premier tennis event, is under way and at the end of its two hectic weeks of fierce competition, new champions will be crowned in the men's and women's fields. But one of the hottest controversies on the professional tennis circuit will remain unresolved: the threat to the integrity of the game proposed by the new breed of power rackets. . . . Over the past three or four years, these rackets have transformed the sport of tennis from one of skill and finesse to one of sheer power.

Mark Mathabane, "A Plague on Tennis"

As you provide evidence in support of your position, be sure to respond to opposing viewpoints. Ignoring arguments against your viewpoint makes your case weaker.

Once you have presented your evidence, write a conclusion that puts an exclamation point on your argument. You want your readers to act on your proposal, so you need to leave them with a convincing call to action.

Revising Tip

When revising your letter, you may need to qualify or limit your arguments to avoid generalizations. For example, state that "*Some* experts believe . . . ," not "*Everyone* believes . . ."

Revising

To begin revising, read over your draft to make sure that what you've written fits your purpose and audience. Then have a **writing conference.** Read your draft to a partner or small group. Use your audience's reactions to help you evaluate your work so far. The Revising Checklist can help you and your listeners.

Revising Checklist

- Is my position stated in a clear thesis statement?
- Is the supporting evidence convincing? Have I addressed opposing viewpoints?
- Are the facts and opinions relevant and credible?
- Does the conclusion relate to the evidence?
- Is the tone appropriate?

Enrichment and Extension

Follow-up Ideas
- Set aside a time for students to celebrate the conclusion of their writing projects.
- If students are sending their work out of the classroom for publication or sharing, make sure that photocopies are retained.

Extending Persuasive Writing

Brainstorm with students ways they can use their expertise in persuasive writing in other subject areas, such as history (make a case for a public memorial to a specific event) or science (write an editorial for or against an ecological restoration project).

Editing/Proofreading

Once you are happy with the content of your letter, **proofread** it carefully for errors in grammar, usage, mechanics, and spelling. Use the questions at the right as a guide.

In addition to proofreading, use the list below to assess your letter. When you're satisfied, make a clean copy and proofread it one more time.

Reflection

Make sure your persuasive letter —

✔ focuses on a rule change in a sport or game you know well
✔ addresses potential problems and consequences of the rule change
✔ follows a plan that includes a strong thesis statement and a clear call for action
✔ uses valid evidence and logical reasoning
✔ follows correct grammar, usage, mechanics, and spelling

Publishing/Presenting

You're almost ready to send your letter off to the powers that be. But what if your proposal is rejected? That doesn't have to be the end. How about submitting a letter to the editor of a newspaper or a magazine that is read by fans of the sport or game of your choice?

Editing/Proofreading Checklist

- Have I avoided sentence fragments?
- Do pronouns and antecedents agree?
- Are *good/well* and *bad/badly* used correctly?
- Are the tenses and numbers of my verbs correct?
- Have I checked carefully for possible misspellings?

Proofreading

For proofreading symbols, see page 84. The electronic spelling and grammar checkers in your word processing program can help you edit and proofread your letter.

Journal Writing

Reflect on your writing process experience. Answer these questions in your journal: What do you like best about your persuasive letter? What was the hardest part of writing it? What did you learn in your writing conference? What new things have you learned as a writer?

Assess

Evaluation Rubrics

Use the following criteria to evaluate the students' finished writing. Make sure students' proposed rule changes include

- a well-developed main idea expressed as the reason for the proposed change
- evidence to support the idea—both facts and authoritative opinions
- tone and details appropriate for the audience (authorities in the sport or game)
- a reasoned response to opposing viewpoints
- use of specific words with strong connotations
- a conclusion that includes a clear, convincing call to action

See also *Writing Assessment & Evaluation Rubrics.*

Reteaching

📁 *Composition Reteaching,* p. 52

Enrichment

📁 *Composition Enrichment,* p. 52

Close

Set aside class time for each student to share his or her proposal with the class. Encourage students to question one another. As students defend or explain their positions, remind them that many of the principles of persuasive writing (clear statement of goals, presentation of specific evidence, respect for one's audience) apply to public discourse as well.

Civic Literacy

Effecting Change

Make the point that persuasive writing is one method people use to bring about change in their country, community, or organization. Stress that change is most effectively brought about not by breaking rules but by persuading decision-makers through the democratic process. This includes writing persuasive letters to those in authority and expressing opinions in articles or editorials. Emphasize that the writing and thinking skills students will be practicing in this activity translate into skills of responsible citizenship.

About the Author

When Mark Mathabane watched American tennis pro Arthur Ashe publicly condemn apartheid in 1973, Ashe became Mathabane's hero. Mathabane strove to imitate Ashe—in tennis playing and speaking out on issues.

Focus

Lesson Overview

Objective
- To evaluate the use of persuasive evidence by a professional writer

Skills
- reading comprehension

Critical Thinking
- analyzing; contrasting; making decisions

Listening and Speaking
- discussing; debating

Bellringer
Daily Language Activity

When students enter the classroom, have this assignment on the board: *Complete this sentence:*

I think tennis is a _____ sport because . . .

See also *Daily Language Practice*

Motivating Activity

Ask several students to read their sentences. (Try to get several different opinions.) Ask if they have ever tried to persuade a group of people to agree with their position on an issue. How did they get their point across?

314

A Plague on Tennis

by Mark Mathabane

Mark Mathabane, a black South African, escaped his country's oppressive apartheid system on a tennis scholarship that sent him to the United States. As you read the excerpt below, look for evidence Mathabane uses to support his views on the emergence of power rackets in professional tennis. Then try the activities in Linking Writing and Literature on page 318.

Resource Manager

Planning Resources
- *Lesson Plans*

📑 **Transparencies**
- *Bellringer*
- *Daily Language Practice*
- *Fine Art 29–32*

 Other Print Resources
- *Listening and Speaking Activities, pp. 17, 22, 23*
- *Writing Assessment and Evaluation Rubrics*

 Web Sites
- *writerschoice.glencoe.com*
- *lit.glencoe.com*

Literature Model

The U.S. Open, America's premier tennis event, is under way and at the end of its two hectic weeks of fierce competition, new champions will be crowned in the men's and women's fields. But one of the hottest controversies on the professional tennis circuit will remain unresolved: the threat to the integrity of the game posed by the new breed of power rackets.

A power racket is much bigger than a traditional racket. It's almost two rackets welded together. Its "sweet spot"— the best place for the ball to be struck, in the center of the racket head—is abnormally large.

Over the past three or four years, these rackets have transformed the sport of tennis from one of skill and finesse to one of sheer power. They have removed a compelling reason for players to develop all-round games, as did champions of the past.

"Power-hitters" like Andre Agassi, Ivan Lendl, Jennifer Capriati and Monica Seles typify this change. Some tennis experts, among them the commentator Bud Collins and the champion Jimmy Connors, have gone so far as to call for a ban on power rackets at high levels of competition.

When I took up tennis in the early 1970's the sport was synonymous with wooden rackets. The players I idolized, enjoyed watching, and sought to emulate—Arthur Ashe, Stan Smith and Rod Laver—all relied on wooden rackets to carve out illustrious

The nature of tennis today is, in a word, power.

Persuasive Writing

Charles March Gere, *The Tennis Party,* 1900

Literature Model **315**

Guided Reading

- What is Mathabane's main claim? How does he makes it convincing?
- What are some of the concessions and counterarguments Mathabane makes regarding the power racket? Why do you think he mentions them? **L2**

Viewing the Art

Charles March Gere, *The Tennis Party,* 1900
This painting shows tennis as leisurely, relaxed, and friendly, as opposed to today's fast-paced, rigorous, and highly competitive contests. Gere's *The Tennis Party* is in the Cheltenham Art Gallery and Museum, Cheltenham, Gloucestershire, England.

Teach

Guided Reading

- Why did the author use the image "Armed with rackets that behave like cannons on the court"? Does it seem persuasive to you?

Persuasive Writing

Literature Model

careers and win major championships, including Wimbledon and the U.S. Open.

Their talent and finesse on the court were unmistakable. They served, volleyed and hit ground-strokes flat, sliced or with topspin, and whenever the occasion demanded, they played delicate touch strokes, such as angled drop shots. In sum, they possessed all-round games. They were the closest thing to the "complete player" and a delight for spectators to watch.

The demise of wooden rackets changed all that. The nature of tennis today is, in a word, power. The new rackets can generate so much power in the hands of just about anyone that players of modest abilities are transformed into giant-killers on the court, capable on any given day, usually in the early rounds, of defeating the game's finest.

Are power rackets good for tennis? The weekend player has certainly benefited from them. Their large "sweet spot" can compensate for poor vision, awkward footwork and lapses in concentration. But at the professional level these rackets have had a ruinous effect. After all, the true test of a champion is not whether he or she can hit the ball at 100 miles an hour. Racket control, variety of strokes, footwork, concentration, conditioning and above all, the ability to out-think one's opponent, are the marks of great champions.

. . . most tennis professionals today play predictable, insipid and monotonous tennis.

One need only recall the impeccable styles and court acumen[1] of players like Althea Gibson, Don Budge, Margaret Court, Yvonne Goolagong and Billie Jean King to get the point.

Most tennis fans I know would rather watch the symphonic[2] play that was characteristic of these players than the "boom-boom" tennis matches of their modern replacements. With a few notable exceptions such as John McEnroe, Martina Navratilova, Boris Becker and Zina Garrison, most tennis professionals today play predictable, insipid[3] and monotonous tennis.

Their robotic games are hopelessly lacking in variety. Armed with rackets that behave like cannons on the court, all these players are content to do, all day if need be, is keep firing the same "boom-boom" missiles until their opponents drop dead.

Some people have argued that power rackets are a great equalizer and enable small players like Michael Chang to compete with big, tall players like Boris Becker. I disagree. I believe that a player of Michael Chang's talents can compete with the best using any racket.

I know it's unrealistic to expect a return to wooden rackets. For players and racket manufacturers, there's simply too much money in the new rackets. But one would

316 Unit 6 Persuasive Writing

Cultural Connections

Researching Tennis's Heritage

Make the point that tennis has a rich cultural heritage. Suggest that students research the backgrounds of some of the professionals mentioned in the essay, such as Arthur Ashe, Rod Laver, Althea Gibson, Yvonne Goolagong, Martina Navratilova, and Boris Becker.

Literature Model

hope that for the sake of the lovely sport of tennis, already tarnished by commercialism and unsportsmanlike behavior, professional tennis players and racket makers would curb the mania[4] for more powerful rackets.

Something can be learned from major league baseball's insistence on wooden bats. The rule recognizes that it should be the batter's ability, not the bat, which drives that pitch out of the ball park. The same should apply to tennis. Fans at the U.S.

I know it's unrealistic to expect a return to wooden rackets.

Open and other major tournaments around the world deserve to watch tennis at its best. And the best tennis remains that provided by players with complete games.

1 **acumen** (əkyoo′ mən) shrewdness
2 **symphonic** (sim fän′ ik) harmonious; having all parts combined in a pleasing arrangement
3 **insipid** (in sip′ id) dull and lifeless
4 **mania** (mā′ nē ə) a persistent enthusiasm; a craze

Persuasive Writing

Literature Model **317**

Teach

Guided Reading

- Does Mark Mathabane win you over to his viewpoint in this persuasive piece? Why or why not? Do you think his article will change the minds of tennis fans, tennis professionals, and racket makers? **L2**

Additional Resources

Fine Art Transparencies, 29–32
Listening and Speaking Activities, pp. 17, 22, 23

Writing in the Real World

Genre and Style

This essay states a clear-cut opinion and supports it with evidence, precise language, and personal fervor. The arguments have emotional and rational appeal. The essay does not try to motivate action, but it does try to sensitize readers to the issue and suggest change.

Assess

Evaluation Rubrics

As your students discuss the selection, either in small groups or as a class, encourage them to begin with a personal response. The student responses on this page might be used as a starting point.

Look for evidence that students
• have read the selection
• can state some of the writer's ideas in their own words
• understand the writer's point of view
• have connected the content to their own knowledge and experiences
• understand the ideas and implications of the selection

Some possible responses to the discussion questions on this page:

1. For recreational tennis, Mathabane feels power rackets are a benefit. They can make up for poor vision, footwork, and concentration. On the professional level, he feels that racket has had a ruinous effect on the game.
2. Mathabane provides the following background information: Bud Collins and Jimmy Connors calling for a ban on power rackets; major league baseball's insistence on wooden bats.
3. Facts: the power racket is bigger than the traditional racket; players like Arthur Ashe and Stan Smith used wooden rackets. Opinions: players are transformed into "giant-killers" with the power racket; power rackets "behave like giant cannons."
4. Mathabane calls for major tennis tournaments to insist on wooden rackets.

Close

Invite students to debate the issues raised by Mathabane's piece. Have some defend the "all-round" game of tennis while others advocate the power game. At the end, have the class vote on the issue.

Persuasive Writing

Linking Writing and Literature

Readers Respond to the Model

What central idea unifies Mark Mathabane's writing, and how persuasive is his argument?

Explore Mark Mathabane's persuasive writing by answering these questions. Then read what other students thought about his writing.

1. How does Mathabane view the use of power rackets in recreational tennis? on the professional tennis circuit?
2. What kind of background information does he provide his audience?
3. What are two facts and two opinions Mathabane uses as evidence to support his position?
4. What specific action does Mathabane call for in his conclusion?

What Students Say

❝This selection was about the new power rackets being used in professional tennis matches. I liked that the writer backed up his opinions with more than one fact. I most enjoyed the part where he talked about the finesse earlier tennis players had when they played with the wooden racket. The author seemed very concerned about real tennis fans and the game of tennis itself. I think he must be a true tennis fan because he feels so strongly about this topic. Tennis is my favorite sport, and I agree with the author. It's refreshing to hear this point of view. ❞

Torré Triplett

❝The part that really got my attention was when Mathabane said that the player's ability counts most in the game. I disagree. I think that good sportsmanship and having a good time are more important. If I had written this selection, I would have made this point. I would not recommend this selection to a friend because I disagree with the opinion it expresses. ❞

Maritza Pagán

UNIT 6 Review

Reflecting on the Unit

Summarize what you have learned in this unit by answering the following questions.

1 What are some characteristics of good persuasive writing?

2 Why is knowing your audience so important in this type of writing?

3 When creating an ad, what four goals should you keep in mind?

4 What is an effective three-step plan to follow when writing a letter of complaint?

5 How is a book review like a product evaluation?

Adding to Your Portfolio

CHOOSE A SELECTION FOR YOUR PORTFOLIO Look over the persuasive writing you have done during this unit. Select a completed piece of writing to put in your portfolio. The piece you choose should show some or all of the following:

- a position supported with facts and opinions that have been evaluated
- evidence that appeals to both reason and emotion
- an awareness of the audience to whom the writing is targeted
- a clear thesis statement, supporting details, and a conclusion calling for action
- precisely chosen words with appropriate connotations

REFLECT ON YOUR CHOICE Attach a note to the piece you chose, explaining briefly why you chose it and what you learned from writing it.

SET GOALS How can you improve your writing? What skill will you focus on the next time you write?

Writing Across the Curriculum

MAKE A HISTORY CONNECTION Scan the opinion page in your local and national newspapers. Find an editorial or a letter to the editor on a historical or political topic of interest to you. Read the editorial carefully and then draft a letter composed of two or three paragraphs to the editor of the paper, supporting or opposing the writer's position.

Persuasive Writing

Review

Reflecting on the Unit

You may have students respond to Reflecting on the Unit in writing or through discussion.

Writing Across the Curriculum

Remind students to take a few minutes to outline their opinions before they draft their letters.

Adding to Your Portfolio

As students decide what to include in their portfolios, remind them to choose pieces that show the best use of the persuasive writing elements covered in this unit. Suggest as one criterion that students include pieces that classmates found most persuasive.

Portfolio Evaluation

If you grade the portfolio selections, you might want to award two marks—one each for content and form. Explain your assessment criteria before students make their selections.

Commend
- experimentation with creative prewriting techniques
- clear, concise writing in which the main idea, audience, and purpose are evident
- successful revisions
- work that shows a flair for language

✔ ASSESSMENT OPTIONS

📁 *Tests With Answer Key & Rubrics*
Unit 6 Choice A Test, p. 21
Unit 6 Choice B Test, p. 22
Unit 6 Composition Objective Test, pp. 23–24

💾 *Testmaker*
Unit 6 Choice A Test
Unit 6 Choice B Test
Unit 6 Composition Objective Test

You may wish to administer one of these tests as a mastery test.

📼 *MindJogger Videoquizzes*

Research Paper Writing

Viewing the Art

This photograph shows the magnitude and beauty of the cloud-filled sky near Mount Rainier. A person viewing this photograph might reflect on the scientific details it reveals, such as what the cloud formation might mean in terms of developing weather patterns; or a person might view the photograph metaphorically, considering that life is a challenge filled with enormous forces and offering many possibilities.

Interpret and Analyze Use the following questions for discussion:

- Why might the photographer have chosen this sky and mountain as a subject?
- What feeling toward nature is reflected in this photograph? Explain.
- What topics for research might this photograph inspire?

Discussing the Quotation

The quotation is from George Russell's article, "Colombia's Mortal Agony," on page 355 of *Glencoe Literature,* Course 5. The article describes the death and devastation in Colombia that accompanied the sudden eruption of a long-dormant volcano. Have students discuss how the quotation relates to the conception of nature reflected in the photograph.

Writing Prompt Have students write a brief account of a time when they experienced the power of a natural force, such as a flood, a blizzard, a torrential rainstorm, or severe winds. Have them brainstorm possible research topics that they might develop based on the causes or effects of a natural phenomenon.

"Then came a shower of ash. . . ."

—George Russell, "Colombia's Mortal Agony"

320

Resource Manager

Planning Resources
- *Lesson Plans*
- *Block Scheduling*

Transparencies
- *Bellringer*
- *Daily Language Practice*
- *Two-Minute Skill Drill*

Other Print Resources
- *Grammar and Composition Handbook*
- *Guide to Using the Internet and Other Electronic Resources*
- *Research Paper and Report Writing*
- *Style and Documentation Sourcebook for Writers*
- *Tests with Answer Key & Rubrics*

- *Thinking and Study Skills*
- *Writing Across the Curriculum*
- *Writing Assessment and Evaluation Rubrics*

Video
- *MindJogger Videoquizzes*

UNIT 7

Research Paper Writing

Lesson 7.1 **Prewriting: Planning and Researching**   322

Lesson 7.2 **Prewriting: Outlining**   328

Lesson 7.3 **Drafting**   332

Lesson 7.4 **Citing Sources**   336

Lesson 7.5 **Revising**   342

Lesson 7.6 **Editing and Presenting: A Model Paper**   346

Unit 7 Review   357

Objectives

- To learn to plan, research, and outline a research paper
- To create a draft of a research paper
- To learn and apply the conventions of documenting information and citing sources
- To demonstrate control over the research process by writing, editing, and presenting a research paper

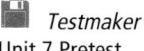

✓ ASSESSMENT OPTIONS

📁 *Tests with Answer Key & Rubrics*
Unit 7 Pretest, pp. 25–26
Unit 7 Mastery Test, pp. 27–28

💾 *Testmaker*
Unit 7 Pretest
Unit 7 Mastery Test

You may wish to administer the Unit 7 Pretest at this point.

Key to Ability Levels

L1 Level 1 activities are within the basic ability range of students.

L2 Level 2 activities are within the ability range of average students.

L3 Level 3 activities are more challenging activities.

321

Software
- *Presentation Plus!*
- *Revising with Style*
- *Testmaker*
- *Writer's Assistant*
- *Writer's Choice Puzzlemaker*

💻 Web Sites
- *writerschoice.glencoe.com*
- *lit.glencoe.com*

Focus

Lesson Overview

Objective
- To plan a research paper

Skills
- drawing schedules; selecting and examining topics; locating information; developing a bibliography; taking notes

Critical Thinking
- identifying main idea; summarizing; decision making; generating new information; categorizing

Listening and Speaking
- note taking; evaluating; discussing

 ## Bellringer
Daily Language Activity

When students enter the classroom, have this assignment on the board: *Write four sentences explaining research you should do before you buy a new car.*

Grammar Link to the Bellringer

Ask students to rewrite their four sentences, combining them into compound or complex sentences and using correct punctuation.

See also *Daily Language Practice*

Motivating Activity

Ask students what people do before buying a car, house, or other substantial purchase. Discuss such things as visiting various car dealers or realtors, comparing prices and features, talking to friends and acquaintances, and making notes. Establish that potential buyers need information about their purchase, and to find it they must conduct an investigation or do research.

 Research Paper Writing

Prewriting: Planning and Researching

*L*ike a detective, the writer of a research paper must search for the facts. You need to gather data and let the evidence lead you to a conclusion.

Evaluation Rubric

By the time you complete Lesson 7.1, you will have
- selected a research paper topic that is neither too broad nor too narrow
- identified a central idea for your paper
- identified appropriate authoritative sources of information
- created complete, accurate source cards
- taken notes from your sources in order to avoid plagiarism

Types of Research Papers

Research papers come in many forms. The following chart lists the most common forms.

Types of Research Papers	
Summary	The writer explores a topic by summing up the opinions of other writers but does not express an opinion about it.
Evaluative	The writer states an opinion and backs it up with evidence found in primary and secondary sources.
Original	The writer does original research on a topic and reports on his or her findings.
Combination	The writer combines approaches, such as evaluating the research of others and then conducting original research.

Draw Up a Schedule

Set a schedule for yourself. A good research paper can't be written in a weekend. The schedule below shows how you might divide your time among the stages of the writing process.

Two Weeks	Two Weeks	One Week	One Week
Planning, researching, and outlining March 28	Drafting April 10	Revising April 24	Editing and presenting May 1

May **8** *paper due!*

Resource Manager

Planning Resources
- *Lesson Plans*

Transparencies
- *Bellringer*
- *Daily Language Practice*
- *Two-Minute Skill Drill*

Other Print Resources
- *Guide to Using the Internet and Other Electronic Resources*
- *Research Paper and Report Writing*, pp. 1–12
- *Style and Documentation Sourcebook for Writers*

- *Thinking and Study Skills*, pp. 4, 24
- *Writing Across the Curriculum*
- *Writing Assessment and Evaluation Rubrics*

Select a Topic

After making a schedule, select a topic. Spend some time in the library skimming books and encyclopedia articles. Researching and writing will be easier if you are curious about the topic you choose and if you find an approximate focus for your paper.

Amy Colleen Bryan, a student at Lexington High School in Lexington, Virginia, was interested in the sinking of the *Titanic* in 1912. Throughout this unit, you will see examples of notes, outlines, and drafts, and Amy's final paper in Lesson 7.6.

Besides your interests, consider what resources are available. If you have only one source on a topic, you will have only one viewpoint. On the other hand, selecting, condensing, and interpreting a mountain of information about a broad topic is difficult. This diagram shows how to identify an appropriate research paper topic.

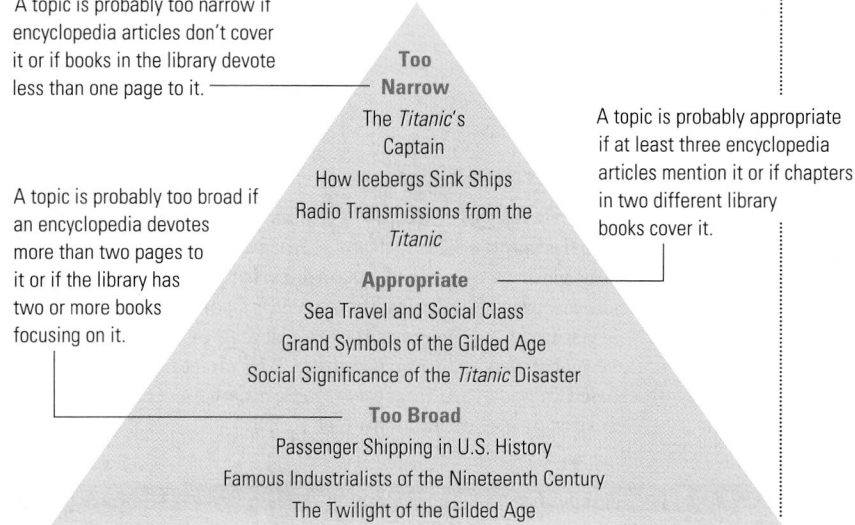

A topic is probably too narrow if encyclopedia articles don't cover it or if books in the library devote less than one page to it.

Too Narrow
The *Titanic's* Captain
How Icebergs Sink Ships
Radio Transmissions from the *Titanic*

A topic is probably appropriate if at least three encyclopedia articles mention it or if chapters in two different library books cover it.

A topic is probably too broad if an encyclopedia devotes more than two pages to it or if the library has two or more books focusing on it.

Appropriate
Sea Travel and Social Class
Grand Symbols of the Gilded Age
Social Significance of the *Titanic* Disaster

Too Broad
Passenger Shipping in U.S. History
Famous Industrialists of the Nineteenth Century
The Twilight of the Gilded Age

Examine the Topic

As you continue to read about your topic, you will begin to determine your central idea. Examine your topic from various points of view. Amy might have considered the following perspectives: How did the owners of the *Titanic* respond to the disaster? What did survivors recall about the sinking? Whom did investigators blame for the tragedy? Don't worry if some angles lead to dead ends. For now just try to think critically about the topic from several perspectives.

> **Drafting Tip**
>
> As you define special terms in your paper, you may want to review the characteristics of a good definition. See Lesson 5.6, pages 240–243.

Teach

Searching for a Topic

To facilitate students' search for a topic, conduct the following Simultaneous Roundtable activity. Working in small groups, each student thinks of a general topic of interest (such as world peace, the American Civil War, or twentieth-century India) and writes it at the top of a piece of paper. Students pass their papers to the right, and each group member adds one or two limited topics below the general topic (United Nations, Battle of Gettysburg, Mahatma Gandhi). When the paper has gone all around the circle, each student should have a list of ideas that may be appropriate for a research paper. **L2**

Visual Thinking

If your students are preparing a research paper for this unit, call attention to the graphic organizer at the bottom of the opposite student page. Give them the final deadline now and suggest they divide their own writing process into the four parts shown on the graphic, allotting the time specified for each part. Remind students that the stages of their process may overlap—researching may continue during drafting, or revising may begin before drafting is completed. **L1**

⇄ Cross-reference: Writing

For instruction and practice of topic selection, refer students to Lesson 2.2, pp. 50–55

Teach

Promoting Discussion

To clarify the distinction between primary and secondary sources, ask students whether they'd rather hear about a friend's vacation experience from the friend directly or from another person who has spoken with the friend. Contrast these reports: (1) Judy says that Molly enjoyed her trip. (2) Molly says, "Hey! I had a great time! I'd go again in a minute! Let me tell you all about it." Lead students to discuss advantages and disadvantages of each type of source. Point out that primary sources are of "primary" importance to historians because these sources, being actual records of the past, provide the most reliable information for research. **L2**

Peer Editing

To ensure completeness and accuracy of bibliographic information in compiling a list of works cited, students can check each other's bibliography cards against their sources in the library. **L1**

Two-Minute Skill Drill

Make a list of the sources you will use to gather information for your research topic.

See also *Two-Minute Skill Drill Transparency 7.1*

(side tab) Research Paper Writing

To set a path for research, identify three to seven questions to answer first. As you answer these questions, you will discover others, as the diagram below shows. Let your central idea guide you in selecting questions.

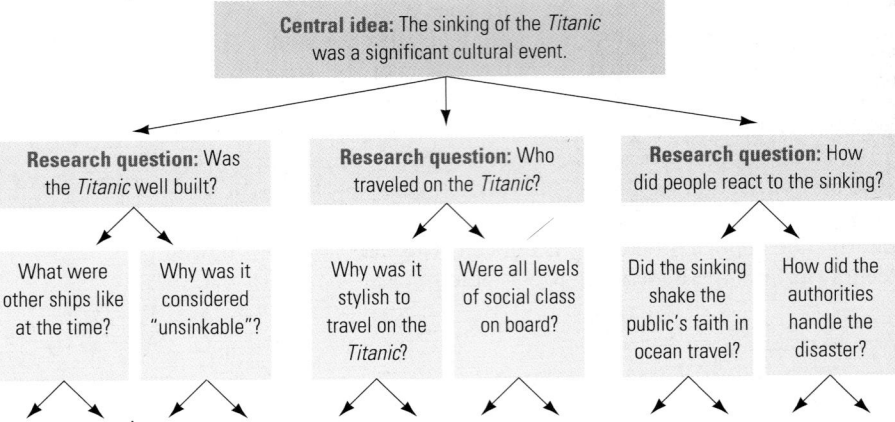

Locate Information

You may use two types of sources—primary and secondary. A **primary** source is a firsthand account of an event, such as a *Titanic* survivor's testimony before Congress. A **secondary** source is a secondhand account, such as an article analyzing the survivor's comments. If possible, use primary sources to give your report a degree of authority that's hard to achieve using only secondary sources. The chart below lists some basic sources used in social studies research. Some of the examples have their own Web sites or are available on CD-ROM.

Sources of Information on Social Studies Topics		
Type	**Definition**	**Examples**
Periodicals	Magazines and journals devoted to history and written for nonscholarly audiences	*American Heritage* focuses on topics in United States history. *Zillions* covers consumer and economic issues of interest to many students.
Reference Books	Specialized works that provide excellent background information on social studies topics	*Encyclopedia of American History* lists and describes events in U.S. history. *Encyclopedia of World History* lists significant world events in chronological order.
News Updates	Publications that provide information on current events and people	*Facts on File* is an up-to-date review of current events. *Current Biography* provides detailed biographies of important people in the news.

MEETING INDIVIDUAL NEEDS — English Language Learners

Using Resources

Encourage students with reading proficiency in another language to make use of resources in the language to gain information on their topics that may not be available in English. Advise them to consult a college or university library in the community for indexes in their topic areas listing pertinent periodicals and books in the language.

Develop a Working Bibliography

As you begin your research, you will need to develop a working bibliography, a record of the books, articles, and other sources you will consult for your paper. Record the publication data for each appropriate source—including the publishing company, city, and date of publication—in a computer file or on a three-by-five-inch index card, as shown below. Number each source file or card in the upper right corner so that when you take notes, you can jot down the number of the source in which you find information. Preparing complete source files or cards now will help you compile your works-cited list at the end of your paper. Write notes to yourself as well, as shown on the magazine source card below.

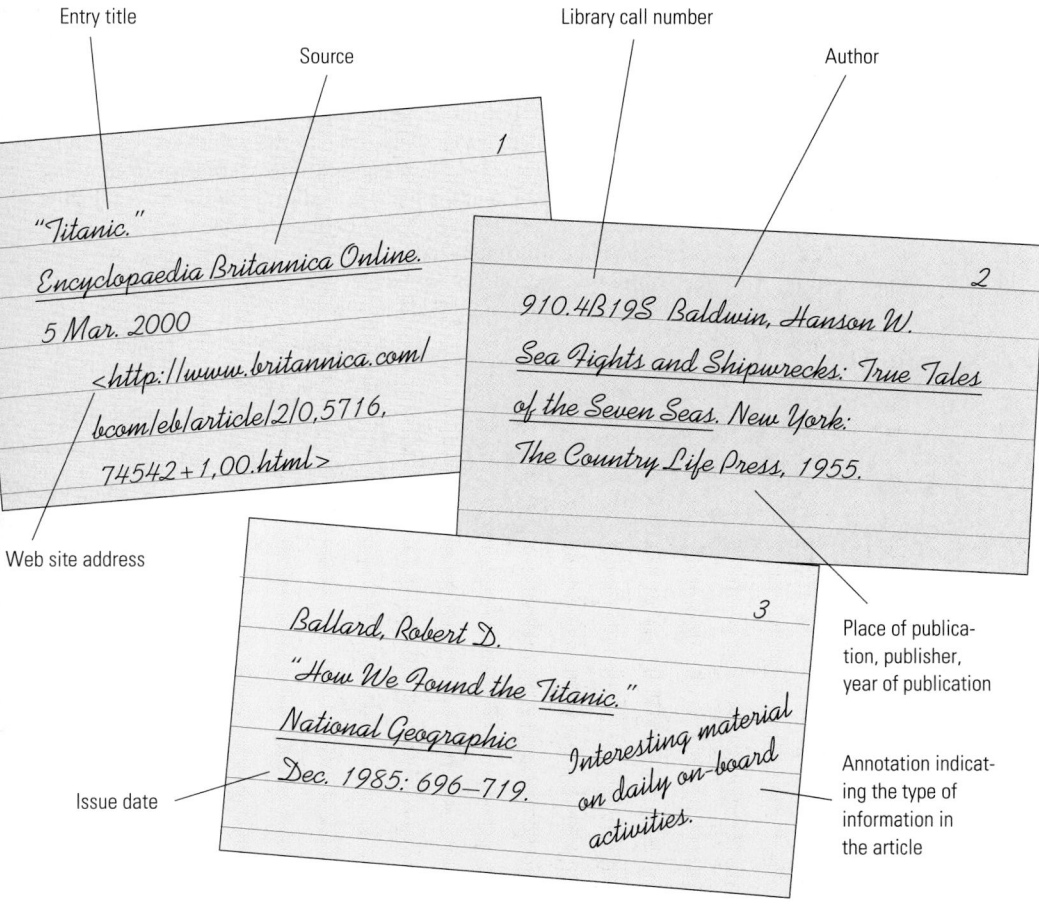

Entry title

Source

Library call number

Author

1

"Titanic."
Encyclopaedia Britannica Online.
5 Mar. 2000
<http://www.britannica.com/
bcom/eb/article/2/0,5716,
74542+1,00.html>

Web site address

2

910.4B19S Baldwin, Hanson W.
Sea Fights and Shipwrecks: True Tales
of the Seven Seas. New York:
The Country Life Press, 1955.

3

Ballard, Robert D.
"How We Found the Titanic."
National Geographic
Dec. 1985: 696–719.

Interesting material on daily on-board activities.

Issue date

Place of publication, publisher, year of publication

Annotation indicating the type of information in the article

Teach

Annotating Bibliography Cards

Encourage students to annotate each source card, as indicated in the lower right corner marginal note on the student page. By mentioning particular features of each source on their cards, students will be able to remember the sources more easily and decide quickly which would provide the most helpful information. **L2**

Researching Cultural Topics

Encourage students to choose a research topic that connects with their own cultural background or a culture that interests them. Culturally related topics can be found for all subject areas. In history, for example, students could investigate their own or a celebrated person's family background, or a past event illustrative of a particular culture. **L2**

Formulating Questions

Invite students to share with the class another project in which they are engaged (sewing a garment, painting a poster). Ask them what questions they had to ask themselves in the preparation stage (questions about materials, techniques they would use, and the project's purpose). What problems would they have had in completing their projects if they'd failed to formulate these questions? **L3**

MEETING INDIVIDUAL NEEDS · English Language Learners

Finding Resource Materials

Students who are not proficient in English may be challenged to find resource materials that they can readily comprehend. You may wish to enlist the aid of a school librarian in preparing a list of possible topics that use easy-to-understand resources. Contemporary topics in newspapers and popular magazines may prove to be the best choices for these learners.

325

Teach

Maintaining Accuracy

Encourage students to paraphrase with care when taking notes. Sloppy note takers can overlook nuances and misrepresent their source material. Remind students that accurately quoting or representing sources is a scholarly responsibility, similar to supplying education and employment information about oneself on applications. If information is not accurate, others could be misled and confusion will result. **L2**

Modeling Note-taking Techniques

Students can benefit from watching you or a fellow student model the note-taking techniques described on this student page, especially good paraphrasing techniques. If possible, demonstrate with materials from a student's own research. Emphasize ways of putting the information in one's own words, such as using incomplete sentences and summarizing without referring to the source. **L1**

Additional Resources

📁 *Writing Across The Curriculum*
📁 *Research Paper and Report Writing*, pp. 1–12
📁 *Thinking and Study Skills*, pp. 4, 24

Grammar Tip

When taking notes, remember to use quotation marks to enclose direct quotes. For more information about quotation marks, see Lesson 21.9, pages 756–757.

Take Notes

Just as you use cards when developing your working bibliography, you can use cards when taking notes. As you find a piece of information that answers one of your research questions, write it on a four-by-six-inch note card. In the upper right-hand corner of the note card, write the number of the source from the working bibliography.

You might want to put your initials by any of your own thoughts that you jot down on note cards. By initialing your own comments, you will be able to keep straight which information comes from other sources and which comes from your own interpretation.

Three ways of taking notes—paraphrasing, summarizing, and writing direct quotations—are shown below.

Original source

Nor did Congress care what happened to Third Class. Senator Smith's *Titanic* investigation covered everything under the sun, including what an iceberg was made of ("Ice," explained Fifth Officer Lowe), but the steerage [another name for Third Class] received little attention. Only three of the witnesses were Third Class passengers. Two of these said they were kept from going to the Boat Deck, but the legislators didn't follow up. Again, the testimony doesn't suggest any deliberate hush-up—it was just that no one was interested.

The British Court of Enquiry

Third-class passengers
Fate of Third Class passengers was not considered important in official inquiries.
—only three Third Class witnesses appeared before Congress; none before British Court of Enquiry.
— no follow-up

8
Third-class passengers
Disaster investigations were thorough, but no one cared about Third Class passengers.
Congress failed to follow up on stories of discrimination against Third Class passengers. British court found no discrimination, although no Third Class passengers testified. Page. 108

Third-class passengers
"Only three of the witnesses were Third Class passengers. Two of these said they were kept from going to the Boat Deck, but the legislators didn't follow up."

Page 108

Summarizing: condensing the main ideas and important details, using your own words.

Paraphrasing: restating the information in your own words.

Direct quotation: writing the passage exactly as it appears in your source and putting it in quotation marks on your card and in your paper.

326 Unit 7 Research Paper Writing

Writing in the Real World

Conducting Research

Encourage students to plan to conduct interviews for part of their research. Remind them to keep a bilingual dictionary at hand to help with any research that they do. Students may find it convenient to use photocopying machines in libraries to make copies of book pages or magazine articles. Students can highlight the pertinent information and then transcribe it onto note cards.

Examine Sources Critically

Because each source you use is written by a person with particular interests, knowledge, and values, be alert to each author's bias. Find sources that approach your topic from different angles. Asking the following questions will help you critically evaluate your sources.

Questions About Sources

1. What is the author's purpose in writing the book or article?
2. Has new information been discovered since the source was written?
3. Are the views of the author often disputed by others knowledgeable on the topic?
4. Would someone from another culture, religious group, economic class, or time period view the events differently?

Grammar Tip

When editing and proofreading, you will be correcting capitalization and punctuation. To make this task easier, be sure to use correct capitalization and punctuation in your notes.

Avoid Plagiarism

Presenting someone else's ideas or expressions as your own is plagiarism, a form of cheating. Even when unintentional, plagiarism is a serious offense. You must give credit to the sources of information you use in your paper. To avoid plagiarism, keep clearly documented notes so you know where you found each piece of information. Lesson 7.4 will teach you how to credit your sources accurately.

7.1   Writing Activities

Skills Practice

1. Write a brief explanation of why each topic below is too broad, too narrow, or about right for a seven-page research paper.

- the Mongol Empire under Genghis Khan
- the controversy over the death penalty
- the childhood of Indira Gandhi
- African independence movements since 1945

2. For each general area, suggest two topics appropriate for a seven-page research paper:

- great leaders in African history
- relations between China and Japan
- cultural diversity in South America
- railroads in United States history

Your Research Paper

Begin the process of writing a research paper, following the directions below.

- Select a research paper topic that interests you and do some preliminary reading to help you narrow the topic appropriately.
- Write at least five research questions.
- Conduct library research and prepare source cards, using the *MLA Handbook for Writers of Research Papers* and the examples on pages 325 and 340 as guides to recording publication information accurately.
- Take legible notes from the sources you've gathered and make sure to properly cite the source of each idea.

7.1 Prewriting: Planning and Researching   **327**

Critical Thinking

Examining Sources

Encourage students to pay close attention to the reliability of an author and to the publication date of a source. Acknowledging opposing points of view is important, but students must first evaluate the author's expertise and reliability.

Assess

Evaluation Rubrics

1. These are explanations:
   - too broad: Genghis Khan's empire was vast and enduring
   - about right: views can be summarized, period limited
   - too narrow: childhood too limited
   - too broad: many nations have emerged
2. These are possibilities:
   - Kwame Nkrumah, Nelson Mandela
   - the 1937 war, Japan and China during World War II
   - the people of Lima or Chile
   - the golden spike, those who built the first railroads

See also Writing Assessment and Evaluation Rubrics.

Your Research Paper

Check research for
- appropriate topic scope
- a clear central idea
- source cards with varied, appropriate sources
- notes with summaries, paraphrases, and direct quotations

Reteaching

Ask students to think of topics that could be researched in each type of information source on page 324.

Enrichment

Suggest that students keep a list of other topics they come across as possibilities for future research papers.

Close

Have students discuss their topic ideas. Through discussion they can help one another shape their ideas into viable topics.

Focus

Lesson Overview

Objective
- To create a working outline and thesis statement for a research paper

Skills
- developing an outline; developing a thesis statement

Critical Thinking
- organizing; classifying; summarizing; analyzing; synthesizing

Listening and Speaking
- discussing

 Bellringer
Daily Language Activity

When students enter the classroom, have this assignment on the board: *Many activities need a game plan to ensure their success. Write a short paragraph giving instructions for a picnic with a group of friends at a local park.*

Grammar Link to the Bellringer

Ask students to share their paragraphs and check that the verb tenses are consistent.

See also *Daily Language Practice*

Motivating Activity

Introduce this lesson with a class discussion about game plans or strategies for winning athletic contests. (A student football player might describe a typical game plan for the sport.) Point out that a game plan can be any long-range strategy to achieve a goal. When the goal is a research paper, writers describe their game plan in a working outline.

Evaluation Rubric

By the time you complete Lesson 7.2, you will have
- made a formal outline or graphic organizer that indicates an appropriate method of organization for your paper
- drafted and revised a thesis statement that provides a clear focus for your writing

---

Prewriting: Outlining

Your rapidly growing pile of note cards is threatening to bury you. What do you do? It's simple. You learn the lesson that military generals throughout history have learned. If you break up your opposition into smaller units, you can quickly take control of the situation.

Develop an Outline

An outline is a summary of the main points and the ideas that support them. Soon after you have begun your research—before your pile of note cards is too big—you can start to outline your paper. Outlining will help you organize your information and further focus your research efforts.

A Working Outline As you take notes, look for ways to classify the facts and ideas you find. For example, look for similar features, such as two facts about the role of an individual in a historical event. Begin to group the note cards as you classify them.

As you make decisions on how to organize your cards, you are developing the information you need to write a working outline. The reasons you use to categorize your cards will become the headings on your working outline. If some cards do not fit under the headings, set them aside. Later you can decide whether to keep or discard them.

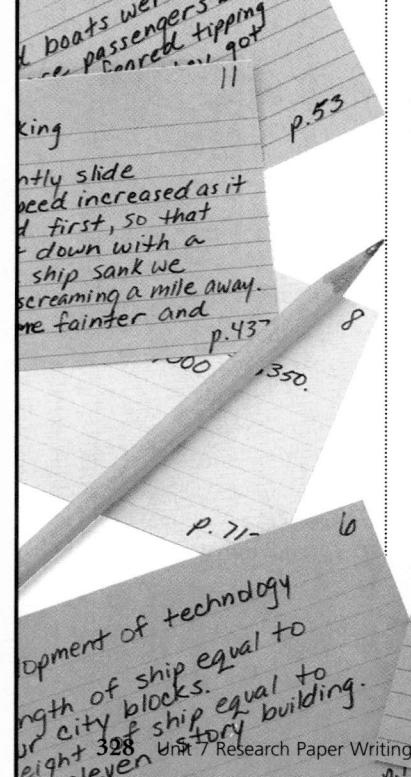

Resource Manager

Planning Resources
- *Lesson Plans*

Transparencies
- *Bellringer*
- *Daily Language Practice*
- *Two-Minute Skill Drill*

Other Print Resources
- *Research Paper and Report Writing,* pp. 13–17
- *Style and Documentation Sourcebook for Writers*
- *Thinking and Study Skills,* pp. 11, 14

- *Writing Across the Curriculum*
- *Writing Assessment and Evaluation Rubrics*

Think of this first outline as a preliminary sketch. As you continue your research, revise your working outline and your central idea to reflect new information. If a heading seems to be less important than it did earlier, make it a subheading or discard it altogether. Try creating your outline on a computer so you can easily make changes as you continue researching. The annotations on the example show how to organize headings and information.

The Impact of the Titanic's Sinking

I. The Gilded Age
   A. Growth of prosperity
   B. Unprecedented wealth for a few people

II. Development of Technology
   A. Titanic symbolized the era
     1. Four blocks long, eleven stories high
     2. Facilities
   B. Trial voyage, 5–11–1911

III. Maiden Voyage, 4–10–1912
   A. Passenger list
     1. Illustrious, wealthy patrons
     2. Modest passengers and poor immigrants
   B. Distinguished crew
   C. Ship considered unsinkable

IV. The Disaster
   A. All iceberg warnings ignored
   B. Iceberg rips 300-foot gash in ship's hull
   C. Rescue calls go out to other ships
   D. Lifeboats lowered
     1. Confusion because drills had never been held
     2. Lifeboats sent off half-filled

Designate main headings by Roman numerals.

Indent subheads under main headings and label with capital letters.

Beneath subheads, further label and indent items.

Never have just one numeral or letter at a given level of organization. For example, if you have a (1), you must have a (2) as well.

Teach

Ordering and Classifying

Encourage students to create each section of their working outline as a mini-outline. They should classify their cards under their main headings and then outline each section. Finally, they can complete their working outline by ordering the pages logically, though the order may change later. **L2**

Using the Model

Tell students to read the example outline on this page and then read the student model on pages 349 through 355 to see how the writer follows the outline. Point out that, while the subtopic of the ship's supposed unsinkability appears only at the end of section III in the outline, references to this supposition appear throughout the student model pages. Ask why. (The writer probably repeated it to underscore the irony of the ship's sinking.) **L2**

Revising Outlines

Some advanced students may tolerate greater flexibility in the outline stage than other students. Tell them to feel free to revise their working outline to accommodate new research. Suggest, however, that they make a copy of any outline or section they abandon—to keep for future reference in case they wish to change back to a previous organization. Encourage them to experiment and assure them that scrapping or revising outlines is a commonplace part of the writing process. **L3**

Teach

Experimenting

Encourage students to experiment with several different organizing methods. Explain that all of the methods described on this student page are logical, in that the writer's main concern in organizing is to ensure that all points logically follow one another. Tell students that the topic they have chosen often suggests the organizing method they should use. What method would students use for the topic Factors Contributing to the Great Depression? (cause and effect) What method would they use for the Battle of Vicksburg? (Chronological order is best.) **L1**

Testing the Thesis Statement

As students draft their thesis statements, encourage them to compare them to their outlines point by point. If all of the outline points support the statements in some way, then the statements are probably appropriate to the topic. If many of the outline points do not support the statements, students should revise their statements. **L2**

Two-Minute Skill Drill

List the main points that must be included in your thesis statement.

📝 **See also** *Two-Minute Skill Drill Transparency 7.2*

Additional Resources

📁 *Writing Across the Curriculum*
📁 *Research Paper and Report Writing,* pp. 13–17
📁 *Thinking and Study Skills,* pp. 11, 14

Research Paper Writing

Three Methods of Organization As you categorize your note cards, begin to consider ways to organize the information within each category. Three of the most common methods of organization are described below. Note that Amy Bryan uses the chronological method in her outline.

Methods of Organization		
Method	**Description**	**Example**
Chronological	Information arranged according to when it happened; often used in papers describing historical changes	A paper surveying China's changing policies under Mao Zedong toward the former Soviet Union
Cause and Effect	Items arranged showing how one development directly influenced another; often used in papers explaining why something happened	A paper analyzing how each new idea led to another during the Industrial Revolution
Cumulative	Items arranged according to how important or how familiar each one is; often used in papers evaluating results	A paper evaluating the impact of the Gulf War of 1991

Prewriting Tip

For further help in developing a thesis statement, you may wish to review Lesson 2.3, pages 57–59.

Develop a Thesis Statement

When you have completed your research, prepare a final version of your outline. You can now rewrite your central idea into a concise thesis statement—a single sentence describing your topic and your approach to it. Although you may change your thesis statement slightly in later stages, it will provide a clear direction for your writing.

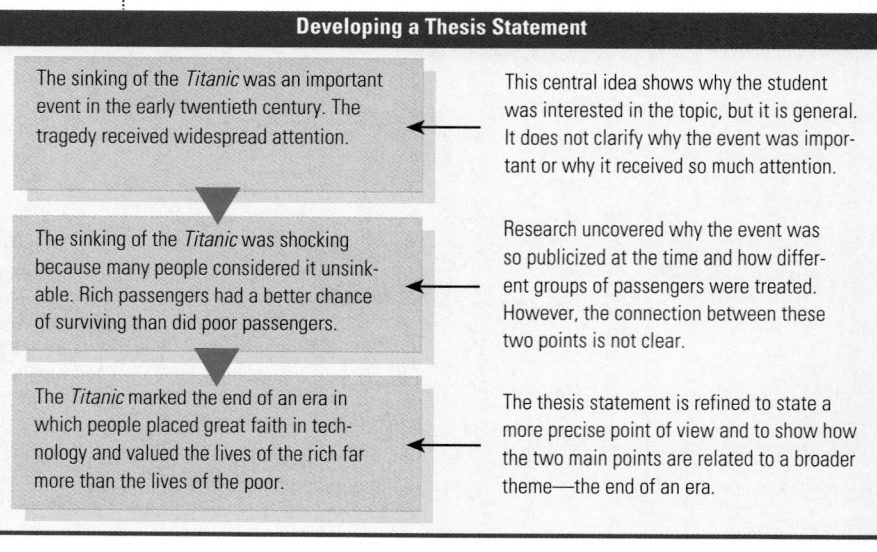

Developing a Thesis Statement

The sinking of the *Titanic* was an important event in the early twentieth century. The tragedy received widespread attention. → This central idea shows why the student was interested in the topic, but it is general. It does not clarify why the event was important or why it received so much attention.

The sinking of the *Titanic* was shocking because many people considered it unsinkable. Rich passengers had a better chance of surviving than did poor passengers. → Research uncovered why the event was so publicized at the time and how different groups of passengers were treated. However, the connection between these two points is not clear.

The *Titanic* marked the end of an era in which people placed great faith in technology and valued the lives of the rich far more than the lives of the poor. → The thesis statement is refined to state a more precise point of view and to show how the two main points are related to a broader theme—the end of an era.

MEETING INDIVIDUAL NEEDS **English Language Learners**

Developing an Outline

Students who are less proficient in English may need to think through and write out their outlines in their primary languages. Then encourage them to translate them into English.

The type of thesis statement you use will depend upon the type of paper you write. The chart below lists some types of thesis statements.

Four Types of Thesis Statements	
Original	Used to demonstrate new information that you have developed
Evaluative	Used when stating your opinion on a topic
Summary	Used when your paper primarily reports the ideas of others
Combination	Utilizes two of the three other categories listed in this chart

7.2 Writing Activities

Skills Practice

1. Create a chronological outline by organizing the statements below under the given headings.

Headings

I.   Pre-Berlin Wall Political Divisions

II. The Wall as a Physical Barrier

III. Beginnings of Reunification

Statements

- The Berlin Wall was erected in 1961.
- After World War II ended in 1945, Berlin was divided and occupied by the four major Allied powers.
- Many people defected from East Germany by escaping to West Berlin in the 1950s.
- The Berlin Wall prevented free movement between East Germany and West Berlin until 1989.
- The Berlin Wall was dismantled in December 1989.
- East Germany was created in 1949.
- In the 1980s, the Soviet Union reduced its influence over East Germany.

2. Organize the following notes into cause-and-effect order.

- Because of trade, Mali prospered.
- Because of scholars, Mali became an intellectual center.
- In the 1300s, the West African kingdom of Mali controlled trade across the Sahara.
- Because of its prosperity, Mali was able to recruit scholars to live there.

3. Write a thesis statement for the outline you developed in 2 above.

Your Research Paper

Continue working on your research paper. Complete the following steps.

- Arrange your note cards in groups according to subject.
- Identify main ideas and use them as the main headings in a formal outline or graphic organizer.
- Complete your outline or graphic organizer, adding subheadings and details.
- Write a thesis statement that states the main idea you will develop in your paper.

7.2 Prewriting: Outlining   **331**

Assess

Evaluation Rubrics

1. Evaluate student headings for these categories:
   - pre–Berlin Wall political divisions (second, third, and sixth points)
   - the Wall as a physical barrier (first and fourth points)
   - beginnings of Reunification (fifth and seventh points)

2. The proper order is
   - third point
   - first point
   - fourth point
   - second point

3. Evaluate statements for this general idea:
   - control of Saharan trade led to Mali's becoming an intellectual center

See also *Writing Assessment and Evaluation Rubrics.*

Your Research Paper

Do the outlines show
- a consistent organization?
- logical flow without gaps?
- correct outline form?

Do the thesis statements exhibit
- a unifying idea stating a truth about the topic?
- clarity?
- concise expression?

Reteaching

Review outline form and hierarchical order—general to specific.

Enrichment

Suggest that students save information they do not use in their outlines for possible future research topics.

MEETING INDIVIDUAL NEEDS English Language Learners

Using Cooperative Groups

Students who are not proficient in reading English will need help reading the activities on student page 331. Set up cooperative groups to work together on this material.

Close

With the class, create an outline on the board. Use a topic that the entire class is familiar with, perhaps one you studied earlier in the year.

Focus

Lesson Overview

Objective
- To draft the initial version of a research paper

Skills
- writing from an outline; writing an introduction and conclusion

Critical Thinking
- drawing conclusions; summarizing; synthesizing

Listening and Speaking
- discussing

Bellringer
Daily Language Activity

When students enter the classroom, have this assignment on the board: *Make an outline of your favorite sport or activity. Include in your outline heads and subheads that capture the fun and excitement of the activity for you. Now think about how you would write a paper based on this outline.*

Grammar Link to the Bellringer

Have students take a second look at the outlines they wrote for the Bellringer activity. Encourage them to think about vivid adjectives and adverbs they could use to express the fun and excitement of the activity.

See also *Daily Language Practice*

Motivating Activity

Mention that Thomas Edison is credited with saying, "Genius is one percent inspiration and ninety-nine percent perspiration." The quote applies to research papers as well. By the drafting stage, students have done most of their research, and they have many ideas about their topics. Now comes the exciting and demanding challenge of putting their initial ideas into organized, written form.

332

Research Paper Writing

Drafting

According to legend, a mid-nineteenth-century historian who lived in London would not begin writing until he had read every book available on the topic he was researching. Today that task would be nearly impossible. So many books—not to mention journals, magazines, newspapers, and Web sites—exist that it would be ambitious to read everything written about even a narrow topic. At some point, like every researcher, you must begin to write.

Evaluation Rubric

By the time you complete Lesson 7.3, you will have
- drafted your research paper, making sure that your ideas logically progress from one idea to the next
- written an interesting introduction that includes your thesis statement
- created a conclusion that integrates your ideas and brings your paper to a close

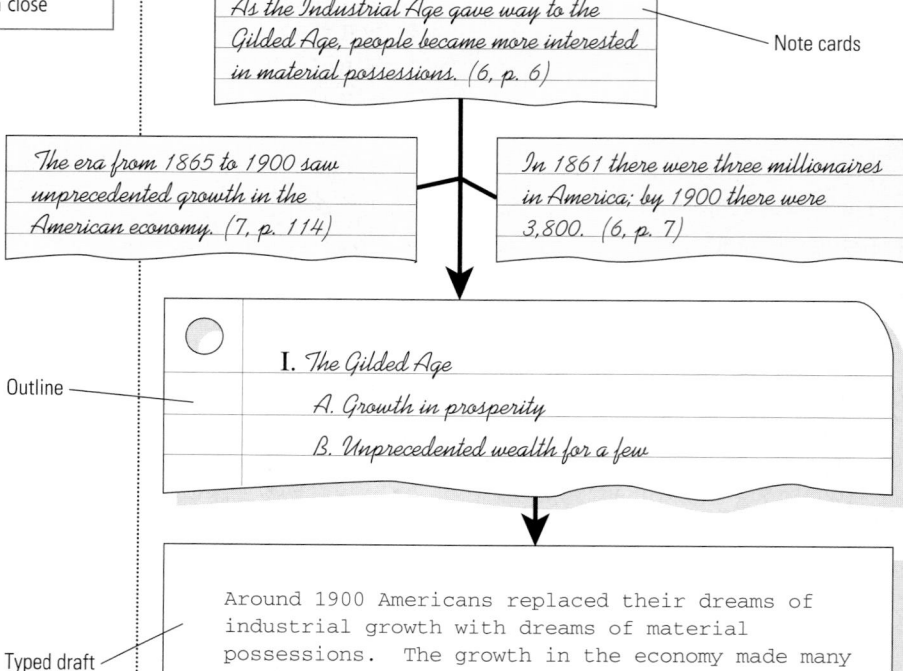

Note cards

> As the Industrial Age gave way to the Gilded Age, people became more interested in material possessions. (6, p. 6)

> The era from 1865 to 1900 saw unprecedented growth in the American economy. (7, p. 114)

> In 1861 there were three millionaires in America; by 1900 there were 3,800. (6, p. 7)

Outline

> I. The Gilded Age
>   A. Growth in prosperity
>   B. Unprecedented wealth for a few

Typed draft

> Around 1900 Americans replaced their dreams of industrial growth with dreams of material possessions. The growth in the economy made many people richer than they had ever been before. There were three millionaires in the United States in 1861, while in 1900 there were 3,800....

Resource Manager

Planning Resources
- *Lesson Plans*

Transparencies
- *Bellringer*
- *Daily Language Practice*
- *Two-Minute Skill Drill*

Other Print Resources
- *Research Paper and Report Writing*, pp. 18–24
- *Style and Documentation Sourcebook for Writers*
- *Thinking and Study Skills*, pp. 22, 24, 27–28

- *Writing Across the Curriculum*
- *Writing Assessment and Evaluation Rubrics*

Use Your Outline and Notes

In writing your first draft, use your outline as a map to guide the direction of your writing. Write at least one paragraph for each main heading in your outline. As shown on the preceding page, you can combine information from several cards to help you state one idea. Keep your ideas flowing logically from one to the next but don't get bogged down by details or trying to find the perfect words to express your ideas. This is only your first draft—you will revise it later.

As you take information from note cards and insert it into your draft, also insert the number of the note card next to the information. You will then have a clear and accurate record of your sources to use in the final version of your paper.

As you write, you may run into some difficulty in handling a large quantity of information. The chart below gives advice for overcoming some problems that commonly occur in the early stages of drafting.

Grammar Tip

Your paper will be more interesting to read if you vary your sentences. Before you revise your first draft, look at examples of sentence structures you might use. See Lessons 13.3 and 13.4, pages 545–548.

Research Paper Writing

Drafting: Problems and Solutions

Problem	Solution
I have a large stack of note cards. How do I handle so many notes?	Read through them and remove anything that duplicates another note or that contains only irrelevant material. Set them aside for possible use later.
I have many notes on some aspects of my topic but very few on others. What should I do?	Conduct more research, or look again at your outline to see if you can write a good paper with the notes you now have. If so, revise your outline.
Do I have to write the first part of the paper first, the second part second, and so on?	Write in whatever way is easiest for you. If you write sections out of sequence, pay close attention when you revise to the transitions between sections and to how forcefully you are building your argument.
How can I overcome writer's block when I sit down to write my first draft?	Don't worry about finding the perfect words. Just get the ideas down. You can always improve your writing in your next revision.
I seem to run out of time before I get very far into my writing. How should I plan my time?	Set aside at least three hours for nothing but writing your paper. Eliminate distractions by going to the library or asking your family not to disturb you.

Teach

Boiling Down Data

Beginning researchers may feel overwhelmed by the prospect of "boiling down" their research data into one coherent paper. Suggest that students make each main topic a mini-paper, devoting at least a paragraph to each subhead. Students might wish to write the mini-paper sections at separate sittings, probably on different days. To help students connect their mini-papers into one paper, review transitions with them, using Lesson 2.7, Drafting: Organizing a Paragraph, pp. 72–75. **L2**

Coping Strategy

To help students with organizational difficulties draft their papers, ask them to make a separate stack of note cards for each main topic, to go through the cards highlighting parts they want to include in their papers, and to put these cards in an order that seems right to them. Assure them that they can change the order whenever they wish. Suggest that students make the main topic into a paragraph and write a sentence for each subhead. Then help them add transitional sentences between paragraphs. **L1**

⇄ Cross-reference: Drafting

For instruction and practice of drafting, refer students to Lesson 2.6, pp. 68–71 and Lesson 2.7, pp. 72–75.

Two-Minute Skill Drill

Write down one common problem in writing a draft and its solution.

📖 **See also** *Two-Minute Skill Drill Transparency 7.3*

Teach

Promoting Discussion

Remind students that their paper's conclusion should hark back to the thesis statement. Read Amy Bryan's thesis on student page 349. Then read her final paragraph on student page 355. Ask how Bryan's conclusion harks back. (It serves to answer the question posed in the thesis statement— "Was the sinking of the *Titanic* really the end of an era?") How is this so? Students should see that the sentences "The sinking of the *Titanic* shocked Americans back to reality" and "It made them retrace their steps and look at the world in a different light" indicate that the disaster did signal the end of an era. Instruct students to make a similarly strong connection between their conclusion and thesis statement. **L2**

Analyzing and Emulating

Advanced students may benefit from analyzing and then emulating introductions created by professional writers. Suggest that students read introductions to feature articles or columns in newspapers and magazines. Challenge students to devise three introductions to their papers, each with a different strategy gleaned from a professional model. **L3**

Additional Resources

📂 *Research Paper and Report Writing*, pp. 18–24

📂 *Thinking and Study Skills*, pp. 22, 24, 27–28

Write an Introduction and a Conclusion

A good paper has an identifiable introduction and conclusion. An effective introduction attracts and holds the reader's attention; it should also contain your thesis statement, which clearly describes the topic or central idea of the paper. A few suggestions for how to start your introduction are shown below. Each describes a way to capture the attention of your readers.

Tips for Writing Introductions	
Summarize	Providing an overview of the main headings in your outline will make your reader comfortable with the topic.
Describe	Include an unusual fact or amusing anecdote about your topic. This will entertain your reader and show your topic from a new perspective.
Pose a Question	If you are writing about the Civil War, for example, ask your reader to imagine what the United States would be like today if the South had won.
Use a Quotation	An eyewitness opinion often is more emotional and gripping than comments by later analysts.
Describe a Scene	In the model paper for this lesson, the writer describes the eerie underwater wreckage of the *Titanic,* transporting the reader to the decks of the once elegant ship.

Your conclusion should pull the paper together and alert the reader that you are finishing your argument. As with the introduction, a conclusion can be written in many different ways. Since it is the last part of your paper, use the conclusion to summarize your main point for your reader. Amy Bryan concludes her paper with a quotation that addresses the question asked in her thesis statement.

Tips for Writing Conclusions
1. Summarize your main points to refresh the reader's memory of your arguments.
2. Reexamine the topic and its effects. Did your opinion on the topic change as you researched it? Did any part of your research surprise you?
3. Consider the future. How does your research put your topic in a new light? What questions for further research can you think of?

MEETING INDIVIDUAL NEEDS English Language Learners

Writing a Draft

Encourage students with less proficiency in English to talk through their introduction and conclusion draft on a tape recorder. Then they can write down what they said. In that way the process of writing in English and getting the flow of the draft will not conflict.

Skills Practice

Use the following outline entries and note cards to write a cohesive paragraph about the early life of former South African president Nelson Mandela. Your audience is a group of seventh-grade students. Use only the entries and note cards that you need to write one good paragraph.

Outline Entries

I. Early years marked Mandela as a leader and a lover of democracy
  A. Adopted by the chief of the Thembu
    1. Listened to many legal cases
    2. Went to school to study law
  B. Suspended from school for leading a student strike
  C. Urged by adoptive father to stop the strike
    1. Father wanted him to become chief of the Thembu
    2. Father had arranged a marriage for him

Note Cards

Mandela's father was the second-most-important leader of the Thembu. On his deathbed, his father asked Chief David Dalindyebo to take Mandela into his care.

The Thembu, though governed by a chief, had a long heritage of democracy. Mandela heard these stories at tribal meetings with his father.

Despite the South African government's attempts to diminish the authority of the tribal leaders, Dalinyebo still heard and decided on many legal issues. Mandela often sat in on the court deliberations.

Chief Dalindyebo was grooming Mandela to become chief of the Thembu.

Mandela went to Fort Hare College in 1938 to get a bachelor of arts degree, the first step toward getting a law degree.

In 1940 the authorities at Fort Hare College decided to lessen the responsibilities of the student council.

- Mandela was a member of the council.
- He led a student strike in protest and was suspended.

Chief Dalindyebo urged him to stop the strike and return to class. The chief also had chosen a wife for Mandela.

Your Research Paper

Draft your research paper, completing the following steps.

- Begin by writing the section about which you feel most confident.
- Using the main and subordinate headings in your outline as a guide, pull information from your note cards. Provide clear transitions from one idea to the next.
- Write an introduction that captures your reader's attention and includes a thesis statement that states the direction your paper will take.
- Write a conclusion that reinforces your thesis and the main points of your paper.

Assess

Writing Activities Evaluation Rubrics

Student paragraphs should include these elements:

- adherence to the outline
- a strong introduction
- smooth transitions between sentences

See also *Writing Assessment and Evaluation Rubrics*.

Your Research Paper

Evaluate the first draft for

- an attention-grabbing introduction that includes a concise, informative thesis statement
- details arranged according to a clear organizing principle
- smooth transitions between sentences and paragraphs
- author names and note card numbers for all sources
- a conclusion that summarizes and drives home important points

Reteaching

Review ordering note cards according to the outline as part of organizing for the drafting stage.

Enrichment

Suggest that students try a spinoff writing project on their topic, such as a letter to an expert in the field.

Close

Have students choose the opening paragraph from an article and explain why it is or is not a good introduction to the article.

Enrichment and Extension

Creative License

Suggest that students write a catchy introduction to intrigue the reader. Refer to Bryan's use of an eyewitness quote on student page 349 and point out its informality. Explain that eyewitness quotes, while they may not follow formal grammar rules, are permissible for getting the reader's attention. Students' writing, however, should follow the rules of correct grammar and usage.

Focus

Lesson Overview

Objective
• To document sources in notes and in a list of works cited

Skills
• documenting appropriately; using proper formats for citations

Critical Thinking
• categorizing; classifying; establishing and evaluating criteria

Listening and Speaking
• discussing

Bellringer
Daily Language Activity

When students enter the classroom, have this assignment on the board: *Write a brief paragraph explaining how you might feel if someone took credit for something you had done.*

Grammar Link to the Bellringer

Ask students to reread their paragraphs looking for any passive voice construction. Have them rewrite passive voice sentences to make them active.

See also *Daily Language Practice*

Motivating Activity

Ask students if someone else has ever claimed credit for their work or ideas. How did the students feel about this? Some students may wish to share their Bellringer paragraphs. Point out that just as they expect to receive credit when others use their ideas, the authors of their sources expect this as well. In addition, you may want to explain your policies on plagiarism or improper documentation. Emphasize that if students have done their own thinking and organizing, acknowledging others' contributions will give their papers added credibility.

LESSON 7.4

Research Paper Writing

Citing Sources

*W*hen did Christopher Columbus first sail to the Americas? The answer is common knowledge: 1492. When did the industrial revolution begin? Not everyone's answer would be precisely the same. When you write a research paper to answer such a question, you must know when to tell your readers where you got your information and when you can assume they know and accept your information.

Document Appropriately

The information you include in your research paper must be properly documented. In other words, you need to identify where you found the information. By citing the sources of all ideas, statements, and quotations that you have used, you allow your reader to judge the validity of the information. For example, information quoted from a respected historical journal will carry more weight than a statement quoted from a television dramatization.

Why Document By citing your sources properly, you acknowledge those people whose ideas you are using. Since they developed the facts, opinions, and analyses that you have borrowed, they deserve a mention in your work.

In addition, by citing your sources properly, you avoid plagiarism—the presentation of someone else's ideas or statements as your own. You should cite your source whether you use the information word for word or you paraphrase it.

What Not to Document While you want to credit others for their work, you don't have to cite the source of common knowledge. Examples of common knowledge include widely accepted facts, such as that the Andes are in South America or that the Magna Carta was signed in 1215. Widely known proverbs, famous quotations, and simple definitions are also common knowledge. The following chart gives examples of statements and whether or not they need documentation.

Evaluation Rubric

By the time you complete Lesson 7.4, you will have
• learned what information in your paper does and does not need to be documented
• chosen an appropriate method for citing your sources
• correctly cited your sources in the body of your paper

Resource Manager

Planning Resources
• *Lesson Plans*

Transparencies
• *Bellringer*
• *Daily Language Practice*
• *Two-Minute Skill Drill*

Other Print Resources
• *Guide to Using the Internet and Other Electronic Resources*
• *Research Paper and Report Writing*, pp. 25–27
• *Style and Documentation Sourcebook for Writers*

• *Writing Across the Curriculum*
• *Writing Assessment and Evaluation Rubrics*

Documenting Your Information		
Type of Information	**Citation?**	**Explanation**
Direct quotation: The sinking of the *Titanic* "signaled the end of the Edwardian era in all its cocky opulence."	Yes	The source of each direct quotation should be given because the words are clearly borrowed from someone else.
Opinion: Americans equated size with security and excess with success.	Yes	This is a paraphrase of another author's conclusions. Sources of conclusions and other opinions should be cited.
Opinion: Completed in 1912, the *Titanic* was considered the most luxurious ship of its day.	No	The luxuriousness of the ship is an opinion widely enough accepted that is common knowledge.
Statistics: The *Titanic* was four city blocks long and eleven stories high.	Yes	Phrasing the measurements in terms familiar to general readers was the work of another writer, so the source should be cited.
Data: The ship sailed out of London and was to reach New York one week later.	No	General information about the trip could be found in several reference Works. None of this information comes from one particular work.

Format Citations Properly

Documenting your sources will be easy if you have accurately completed and numbered your source cards and note cards during the prewriting stage. All the information you need should be right at your fingertips. (If you've missed something, return to the library to find your sources again.)

You can cite your sources in one of three ways: footnotes, endnotes, or parenthetical documentation, which is recommended by the Modern Language Association of America (or MLA). Parenthetical documentation is generally preferred because the reader does not have to search for the citation. The instruction and models in this unit conform to the MLA guidelines; however, check with your teacher and use the method that he or she prefers.

Parenthetical Documentation with a Works-Cited List

A works-cited list is an alphabetized list of the sources that you have used in writing your research paper. In your paper, after each quotation, summary, or paraphrase of information from a source, you must include within parentheses a reference to a source and, when appropriate, a page reference. This citation points readers to the corresponding entry in your works-cited list.

Revising Tip

As you revise your paper and move information from one part of the paper to another, be careful to move the documentation with the information.

Teach

Promoting Discussion

Students will probably know they must document direct quotes but may be unsure about unquoted use of source material. Ask students to explain in their own words what constitutes general information or common knowledge that does not need documentation. If they seem confused, suggest that they discuss a specific case with a peer or someone who is one grade above or below them in school. If that person is acquainted with the information, citation is probably not required. The most problematic instances occur when students paraphrase an author's material. Emphasize that if they didn't think of the idea themselves, they must give the original author credit. Encourage classmates to offer other helpful suggestions about when to cite sources. Suggest that, when in doubt, beginning researchers should supply documentation. **L2**

Thinking Visually

Ask students to cover the center and right-hand columns of the graphic organizer on this student page and try to supply their own explanations of whether or not the information should be documented. Tell them to jot down their explanations and then check to see whether they were correct. **L3**

Two-Minute Skill Drill

Write *citation* on the board and have students look up the word in a dictionary and write a definition for it.

See also *Two-Minute Skill Drill Transparency 7.4*

Teach

Standardizing Styles

Students may find it confusing if they are required to use different methods of documenting sources in the papers they write for different courses. You may wish to discuss this matter with other teachers and reach concensus on how students should document their sources.

Citing Sources

Any scholarly book will document its sources. Inform students that there are both legal and professional reasons for this procedure. Legally, documentation protects writers against charges of plagiarism and libel—defamation of character. Writers who scrupulously cite their sources in effect deny claim to any idea that isn't theirs. Professionally, citing sources is crucial to writers establishing their credibility as scholars. The breadth and specificity of their bibliographies communicate as much about writers' understanding of the subject as their written pieces do. Have students look through books in the classroom or library and find examples of cited sources. **L3**

Research Paper Writing

Drafting Tip

For more information about italicizing (underlining) titles or using quotation marks, see Lessons 21.9 and 21.10, pages 755–759.

When you drafted your paper, taking information from your note cards, you jotted down the corresponding number of the source from which you took the information. Now you can replace those numbers with proper parenthetical documentation. Place the citation as close as possible to the borrowed information. The parenthetical reference usually should be positioned where a pause would naturally occur, such as just before a comma or at the end of a sentence (but before the final period), as shown in this example:

> *In 1861 there were three millionaires in the United States; in 1900 there were 3,800 (Wade 7).*

The examples that follow and Amy Bryan's final draft of her research paper on pages 349–356 provide guidance and models for using parenthetical documentation to cite sources in text.

PARENTHETICAL DOCUMENTATION GUIDELINES

1. (Lord 108)

Put the author's last name and the page reference in parentheses. If you're using two or more works by different authors with the same last name, include the author's first name or initial.

2. (Kingston and Lambert 145)

For a work by two or three authors, put the authors' last names and the page reference in parentheses. If a work has more than three authors, use the last name of the first author, followed by *et al.,* and the page reference: (Kingston et al. 145).

3. (*White Star 110*)

If a source does not have an author, use a shortened form of the title in parentheses. Provide a page reference if possible.

4. (Angier, "Haunting Images" 58)

If you use more than one source by the same author, include the author's last name followed by a comma, the source title or a shortened form of it, and a page reference.

5. (Lord 171–172; *Secrets*)

If you use a piece of information that you found in more than one source, cite each work as you normally would, inserting a semicolon between the entries.

MEETING INDIVIDUAL NEEDS **English Language Learners**

Sequencing

Students who are proficient in a foreign language may be used to a different sequencing of names and dates from that dictated by English documentation. Carefully discuss with students the rules and examples on this and subsequent student pages to ensure they understand the sequencing principles. Emphasize that documentation is a logical and not arbitrary procedure and that citation style should be consistent.

6. (109)

When you use the author's name in the sentence that includes the information you need to document, provide only a page reference in parentheses, as shown in this example: As Walter Lord noted, "The *Titanic* was the last stand of wealth and society in the center of public affection" (109).

7. ("Titanic")

If you use a nonprint source, such as a videocassette, a film, or an article published online (the example above is for an article published by *Encyclopaedia Britannica Online*), name the work in running text or, in parentheses, give readers the information they need to find the complete citation in the works-cited list.

Format Your List of Works Cited

Whichever form of citation you use, at the end of the paper you should include a list of works cited. Unlike your working bibliography, the works-cited list includes only those sources that you use in your final paper. Although you may have consulted many additional sources for background and other general information, these sources should not be included on this final list.

Record the publication information from your source cards, following the formats shown on the next page and in Amy Bryan's works-cited list on pages 355–356. If you use a source that is not modeled in this unit, consult your teacher or the *MLA Handbook for Writers of Research Papers*.

The following are some general tips for formatting works-cited lists.

Formats for Works Cited Entries

1. Arrange entries in alphabetical order according to the author's or editor's last name. Write the name in reverse order—last name first. For works with two or more authors, reverse only the first author's name.

2. If no author or editor is given, alphabetize the entry by the title, disregarding the word *a, an,* or *the* at the beginning of a title.

3. When more than one work by an author is listed, use three hyphens followed by a period rather than repeat the author's name.

4. Begin each entry at the left margin. If an entry runs more than one line, indent every line five spaces after the first.

5. Book and magazine titles should be in italics or else underlined.

6. Article titles should be enclosed in quotation marks.

> **Vocabulary Tip**
>
> When you edit your paper, check the spelling of the names of authors you cite against your list of works cited for possible misspellings.

Teach

Understanding Works Cited

Point out that bibliography items consist of two or three components, each ending with a period: the author, title, and publisher. Ask students to note that components can be made up of several subparts. (Several authors or editors can be listed; both an article title and the title of the magazine, newspaper, or reference work are listed when these apply; the publisher component differs for books and periodicals and may include such information as the place of publication, the name of the publisher, and the copyright year or date of the periodical.)

Suggest that students refer to the models and charts on this and the next student page to find the exact order and format for each component, including use of quotation marks or italics for a title, and punctuation usage between elements. **L2**

Two-Minute Skill Drill

Ask students to write, in a sentence or two, the main information included in a works-cited entry.

➤ **See also** *Two-Minute Skill Drill Transparency 7.4*

MEETING INDIVIDUAL NEEDS **English Language Learners**

Clarifying When to Cite a Source

Remind students that they must cite a source whenever they use words or information that is unique to the source. Commonly known dates or measurements do not require citation, for example, but most opinions and any direct quotations require the citing of a source. Remind students to use the chart on page 337 to determine whether or not a citation is necessary.

Teach

Reviewing Citations

Review the different methods of citation by examining some of the resources students have been using in their research. Examine a variety of citations: those with a sole author, more than one author, or no author or editor; those with more than one work by the same author; and those with more than one source at the same place. Ask students to supply examples of parenthetical documentation and lists of works cited, including citations from professional journals, if available. **L2**

Additional Resources

Research Paper and Report Writing, pp. 25–27

Research Paper Writing

> Use a shortened form of the publisher's name—for example, "Knopf" for "Alfred A. Knopf, Inc." Use the abbreviation "UP" for "University Press." (See the entry under "Bishop" in the chart.)

The chart below shows how to format different types of entries in a works-cited list. Some examples are from Amy Bryan's paper.

Works-Cited Entries	
Source	**Example of Entry**
Book with one author	Baldwin, Hanson W. *Sea Fights and Shipwrecks: True Tales of the Seven Seas.* New York: Country Life Press, 1955.
Book with two or three authors	Kingston, Jeremy, and David Lambert, *Catastrophe and Crisis.* New York: Facts on File, 1979.
Book with no author	*The White Star Triple Screw Atlantic Liners Olympic and Titanic.* New York: Arco, 1970.
Book with an editor but no single author	Kuntz, Tom, ed. *The Titanic Disaster Hearing: The Official Transcripts of the 1912 Senate Investigation.* New York: Pocket Books, 1998.
A selection in an anthology	Bishop, Mrs. H. D. "The *Titanic:* From a Lifeboat, 15 April 1912." *Eyewitness to History* Ed. John Carey. Cambridge: Harvard UP, 1987. 436–437.
Encyclopedia article	"Titanic." *Encyclopedia Americana.* 1998 ed.
Magazine article	Ballard, Robert D. "How We Found the *Titanic. National Geographic* Dec. 1985: 696–719.
Newspaper article	"New Liner *Titanic* Hits an Iceberg" *New York Times* 15 Apr. 1912: A1.
Personal interview	Watkins, Eliza. Personal interview. 30 October 1999.
Lecture, address, or sermon	Baker, Reverend A. B. Sermon. Trinity Church. Princeton, 21 Apr. 1912.
Radio broadcast	"Titanic Photo Book." Narr. Bob Edwards. *Morning Edition.* Natl. Public Radio, WBEZ, Chicago. 15 Apr. 1998.
Online resource	"Titanic." *Encyclopaedia Britannica Online.* 5 Mar. 2000 <http://www.britannica.com/bcom/eb/article/2/0,5716,74542+1,00.html>.
CD-ROM	Garzke, William H. Jr. "Titanic." *The World Book Multimedia Encyclopedia.* Vers. 1.0. CD-ROM Disc 1. Chicago: World Book, 1999.
Personal or professional Web site	*The Virginia Newspaper Project Exhibit of the Titanic.* 11 Nov. 1999 <http://www.lva.lib.va.us/pubserv/vnp/titanic/titanic1.htm>.

Cultural Connections

Checking Spelling

Remind students to carefully check the spelling of all names in their citations. In addition, they should note accents in names and handwrite these marks or use special fonts in their typed or printed copy. Stress the point that the scholarly community embraces a wide variety of cultures and that all scholars share the responsibility of properly spelling source names.

Skills Practice

1. For each piece of information below, tell whether you think source documentation is necessary. Explain the reasons for your answer.

- Kemal Ataturk ruled Turkey from 1923 to 1938.
- Ataturk declared, "Our thoughts and our mentality will become civilized from head to toe."
- According to one historian, Ataturk was more concerned with reforming his country than with increasing his power.
- The status of Turkish women was raised during Ataturk's rule.
- Radical changes instituted by Ataturk threatened to destroy traditional Turkish culture.

2. Each of the following entries from a list of works cited contains two mistakes in punctuation. Copy each entry, correcting the punctuation as you do so.

- Ghareeb, Edmund. *The Kurdish Question in Iraq.* Syracuse, Syracuse UP. 1981.
- "British Views of Disunion." *New York Times:* 8 Feb. 1861:8
- Koch, Adrienne and William Peden, eds. *The Life and Selected Writings of Thomas Jefferson.* New York: The Modern Library, 1944.
- Lih, Lars T. "Gorbachev and the Reform Movement." *Current History* October 1987: 310

3. Using parenthetical documentation, write the citation that would appear in the text for each of the following sources:

- a quotation from page 21 of *Abuse of Power* by Theodore Draper
- a quotation from page 17 of *England Under the Tudors* by G. R. Elton, one of three books by Elton used in the paper
- a quotation from page 100 of *The Mau Mau from Within,* by Donald J. Barnett and Karari Njama
- a quotation from page 19 of an article in *Time* magazine, "Six Minutes," with no author listed

Your Research Paper

Continue working on your research paper by completing the following steps.

- Insert proper documentation within the body of your paper. If you're using parenthetical documentation, replace the note card numbers that correspond to your source cards with a proper citation in parentheses.
- Create a draft of your works-cited list.
- Ensure the accuracy of your documentation and your works-cited list by following the formats outlined in this lesson and in the *MLA Handbook for Writers of Research Papers.*

Assess

Evaluation Rubrics

1. Responses should be based on the chart on student page 337:
- no, widely referenced
- yes, direct quote
- yes, paraphrase
- yes, author's conclusion
- yes, author's conclusion

2. Corrections are as follows:
- Ghareeb, Edmund. *The Kurdish Question in Iraq.* Syracuse: Syracuse UP, 1981.
- "British Views of Disunion." *New York Times* 8 Feb. 1861: 8.
- Koch, Adrienne, and William Peden, eds. *The Life and Selected Writings of Thomas Jefferson.* New York: The Modern Library, 1944.
- Lih, Lars T. "Gorbachev and the Reform Movement." *Current History* Oct. 1987: 310.

3. Correct citations:
- (Draper 21)
- (Elton, *England Under* 17)
- (Barnett and Njama 100)
- ("Six Minutes" 19)

See also *Writing Assessment and Evaluation Rubrics.*

Your Research Paper

Evaluate each student's samples for consistency with the charts on student pages 338–340.

Reteaching

Carefully distinguish between the styles used for citations in the body of the paper and for the list of works cited.

Enrichment

Challenge students to verify the accuracy of a secondary source note by looking it up in the original source.

Close

Have students choose a topic that interests them. Challenge them to make a list of works cited with at least three resource materials.

Cooperative Learning

Using Study Groups

Students with less proficiency in reading may have problems with the activities on this student page. Divide the class into cooperative groups to complete these citation entries together.

Focus

Lesson Overview

Objective
- To revise for word choice, transitions, and presentation of ideas

Skills
- solving first-draft problems

Critical Thinking
- analyzing; evaluating

Listening and Speaking
- discussing

Bellringer
Daily Language Activity

When students enter the classroom, have this assignment on the board: *Rewrite this sentence, substituting more precise words for the general nouns:*

> *The group talked about the problem.*

Grammar Link to the Bellringer

Ask students to revise the Bellringer sentence again by adding prepositional phrases to modify the nouns and verb. Discuss which revision students prefer.

See also *Daily Language Practice*

Motivating Activity

Discuss the importance of revising a research paper. Have volunteers give their opinions as to why revisions might be necessary (to correct mistakes, to express ideas in a clearer fashion). Explain that a first draft of a research paper may contain many good ideas, relevant facts, and authoritative opinions that need only revision to cover the topic in a more precise way.

Research Paper Writing

Evaluation Rubric

By the time you complete Lesson 7.5, you will have
- evaluated your research paper draft for both content and mechanics
- reviewed the paper's organization and reorganized the content to ensure coherence, logical progression, and support for ideas
- refined your writing style to suit the requirements of the research paper and to meet the needs of your audience

Revising

Even the Declaration of Independence, one of the most powerfully written documents in United States history, needed revision. Thomas Jefferson, the Declaration's author, knew what every good writer knows: almost anything you write can be improved through revision. Your first draft is an important beginning, but you should plan to make changes to it.

Resource Manager

Planning Resources
- *Lesson Plans*

Transparencies
- *Bellringer*
- *Daily Language Practice*
- *Two-Minute Skill Drill*

Other Print Resources
- *Grammar and Composition Handbook*
- *Grammar Workbook*
- *Research Paper and Report Writing*, pp. 28–31
- *Style and Documentation Sourcebook for Writers*

- *Thinking and Study Skills*, p. 18
- *Writing Across the Curriculum*
- *Writing Assessment and Evaluation Rubrics*

Improve Your Paper

When you revise your first draft, work on mechanics, word choice, transitions, and presentation of ideas. Remember that in a formal research paper, you should write in a voice and a style that are appropriate to your audience and purpose. The following chart describes problems you may face and offers possible solutions to them.

Revising: Questions and Answers	
Questions	**Identifying What Needs Revising**
Have I given the first draft a clear focus?	Review your thesis statement to be sure it is clearly stated.
Have I accomplished what I set out to do in this paper?	Skim your paper, looking for and deleting irrelevant information. Add ideas that readers might need to follow your reasoning.
Do my paragraphs flow logically and smoothly?	Read the last sentence of each paragraph and the first sentence of the following paragraph. If the flow of ideas is not smooth, add transitions.
Have I used someone else's ideas without credit?	Scan your paper, reading each sentence that does not contain a citation. Add documentation if necessary.
Do my examples and supporting details help clarify my main point?	Replace the questionable examples or details with direct and appropriate ones.
Have I used terms that are not familiar to the average reader?	Scan your paper, picking out specialized terms or unusual words. Review your definitions or explanations of each of these terms or words.
Is my choice of words interesting and appropriate?	Delete redundant words and phrases. If a word is repeated often, find synonyms for it. Replace vague terms with more precise ones.
Are my introduction and conclusion effective?	Read your first and last paragraphs. Each should highlight the main point of the paper.

Using proofreading marks like the ones modeled on the next page saves time during revision and makes your copy easier to read. To review proofreading symbols, see page 92.

7.5 Revising **343**

Research Paper Writing

Drafting Tip

As you revise your paper, try to keep a mental note of the types of changes you make most often. This can help you when you begin drafting another paper.

Revising Tip

For examples of different kinds of supporting details you can use when revising your first draft, see Lesson 2.6, pages 68–71.

Teach

Revising

Point out the amount of revising that was done to the preamble to our Declaration of Independence. Explain that the best writers spend as much or more time revising their work as they do in producing it. Then discuss how students can mark their papers during the drafting stage as a reminder to return to the problems they had with spelling, awkward wording, or ideas that may need more research. **L2**

Using the Computer

Students who use a computer can benefit from saving each version of their paper as a separate file. When making stylistic revisions, writers may delete passages they later want to include or find it difficult to decide whether the current version reads better than its predecessor. By saving different versions with files clearly named to indicate in what order they were created, students can confidently experiment with revisions. Caution students to exercise care in deleting versions, so as not to lose the wrong one. **L2**

Cross-reference: Vocabulary

For instruction and practice on word choice see Lessons 24.2, pp. 816–817, and 25.1, pp. 819–821.

Two-Minute Skill Drill

Have students write five or six specific synonyms for each of the following words:

speak	*nice*
move	*event*

See also *Two-Minute Skill Drill Transparency 7.5*

Teach

Identifying Logical Errors

Suggest that students analyze information and opinions from sources as carefully as they would analyze their own drafts for such logical errors as drawing a conclusion not supported by evidence or letting bias sway one's interpretation of the facts. Students should revise errors in their first drafts. **L2**

Proofreading Symbols

Less able writers may have difficulty remembering and using proofreading symbols. You may want to give them freedom to use any marking system they wish. Also, they may find it easier to start on a section that needs heavy revision. Some writers even cut apart and rearrange pieces of their draft in a better order. **L1**

Additional Resources

📁 *Writing Across the Curriculum*
📁 *Research Paper and Report Writing*, pp. 28–31
📁 *Thinking and Study Skills*, p. 18

Using synonyms avoids repetition of word "Titanic."

Combine sentences to avoid repetition and present related information together.

"Reportedly" is more concise than "it was reported."

Revise to improve the flow of the sentence.

Using pronouns avoids repetition.

Add a phrase to create or improve the transition between paragraphs.

Change verb so the number agrees with the subject.

The ~~Titanic~~ ^ship also ~~had~~ carried a ^distinguished ~~good~~ crew. The captain of the <u>Titanic</u> was Edward Smith, ^and ~~He~~ was a favorite among high-society American. ~~He also~~ ^who had been captain of the <u>Olympic</u>, the <u>Titanic</u>'s sister ship, Upon sailing, ~~it was reported that~~ Second Officer C. H. Lightoller ^reportedly said, "It was clear to everyone on board that we had a ship that was going to create the greatest stir British shipping circles had ever known" (218). When a woman asked a deckhand ~~was~~ ^if the <u>Titanic</u> ^was really "unsinkable," ^he ~~the deckhand~~ replied, "God himself could not sink this ship" (Friedrich 70).

This overconfident attitude was matched by
~~They had~~ perfect weather for the first four days of sailing. Then at 9:00 ^A.M. ~~in the morning~~ on April 14, the <u>Titanic</u> receive^d~~s~~ iceberg warnings from |another ship,| the <u>Coronia</u>. Two more warnings ~~was~~ ^were received that afternoon, yet Captain Smith dismissed all three, He never decreas^ing~~ed~~ the ship's speed of 22 knots or chang^ing~~ed~~ its course. At 7:30 P.M. another ship, the <u>Californian</u>, warned the <u>Titanic</u> of ice.

Revise Your Paper

Certain writing problems are common in research papers. Try exchanging papers with a partner to get another perspective on your work and to provide your partner with feedback. Review the points in the following checklist as you revise your paper.

MEETING INDIVIDUAL NEEDS   English Language Learners

Revising with Peers

Many students who are not familiar with English will not have the English skills to revise their own papers without assistance. You may direct paired students to read each other's papers, keeping in mind the problem-solving chart on student page 345. If a student comes to a problematic part, he or she should call it to the other's attention. Students should consider their partner's comments when revising and attempt to be equally objective in evaluating their own work.

Checklist for Revising a Research Paper

1. How can you strengthen your thesis statement so that it provides a clear focus for the paper?
2. How can your main ideas be better organized to ensure coherence and logical progression? What irrelevant or repetitious ideas can you delete?
3. Which ideas could be better supported with information from sources?
4. How can you strengthen the transitions between ideas and paragraphs?
5. Have you written in a voice and style that is consistent throughout—and is appropriate, given your audience and purpose?
6. Have you varied your sentence structures and used lively verbs so that your paper isn't boring?
7. What technical terms still need to be defined?
8. Which frequently used words can be replaced with appropriate synonyms?
9. Have you cited your sources correctly in the body of your paper?
10. Is your works-cited list accurate, complete, and properly formatted?

Assess

Evaluation Rubrics

Students should make revisions such as the following:

- Substitute *elected* for "to serve," since Roosevelt was the youngest ever to serve.
- Substitute *1981* for "1980."

See also *Writing Assessment and Evaluation Rubrics.*

Your Research Paper

After the student has made revisions, evaluate the second draft to suggest further improvements in focus, organization, clarity, and coherence.

Reteaching

Go over the revising problems on this page, inviting students to write on the board passages that classmates can help to edit.

Enrichment

Ask students to look for logical errors by comparing treatment of the same topic in different sources.

Close

Have the students discuss the importance of revision and the distinction between revising and proofreading.

7.5 | Writing Activities

Skills Practice

Each of the following pairs of statements includes an excerpt from a first draft of a social studies paper and a new bit of information that the writer found after completing the first draft. Use the new information to help you revise the italicized information in each first-draft excerpt.

- **First draft:** In 1960 forty-three-year-old John Kennedy became president of the United States. *As the youngest person ever to serve* as president, he brought great energy to government.

  New information: Theodore Roosevelt was only forty-two years old when, following the assassination of President McKinley, he became president in 1901.

- **First draft:** Jimmy Carter defeated Gerald Ford in the 1976 presidential election. Carter served as president *until 1980.*

  New information: Carter served only one term as president, from 1977 to 1981.

Your Research Paper

Revise your research paper. Complete these steps and use the Checklist for Revising a Research Paper to guide you.

- Clarify your thesis statement if necessary, making sure that it adequately sets a purpose and direction for the paper.
- Evaluate the organization of your draft and decide how you can improve the flow of ideas.
- Conduct additional research if necessary to support your data.
- Strengthen your transitions to ensure that your paper is coherent.

Cooperative Learning

Editing with Peers

Have students arrange for peer editors to read their papers and comment on incorrectly or awkwardly phrased passages. If many revisions are required in the first draft, the peer editor may read it a second time after it is revised. If students receive separate grades for form and content, you should remind peer editors to give equal emphasis to each.

Focus

Lesson Overview

Objective
- To polish and present a completed research paper

Skills
- preparing final copy; presenting a paper

Critical Thinking
- analyzing; relating; making inferences; evaluating; identifying main idea

Listening and Speaking
- informal speaking; questioning; note taking

Bellringer
Daily Language Activity

When students enter the classroom, have this assignment on the board: *Write a short paragraph about the things you must check before handing in the final draft of a paper.*

Grammar Link to the Bellringer

Ask students to check through the paragraph they wrote for the Bellringer to make sure they used complete sentences and avoided fragments and run-ons.

See also *Daily Language Practice*

Motivating Activity

Give students additional incentive to complete their papers by arranging to exhibit the finished papers in some prominent location, such as the library. To encourage students to exhibit their work, issue author's permission forms for students to sign. If more than one of your classes are writing research papers, the exhibit would allow them to view each other's final products. Tell readers to write at least a one-sentence comment on every paper they peruse.

346

Research Paper Writing

LESSON
7.6

Editing and Presenting: A Model Paper

After Thomas Jefferson revised the Declaration of Independence, he commissioned a final version in elegant, flowing handwriting. Although the ideas in the Declaration were powerful, Jefferson still took time to prepare a perfect document that would help him win support for his ideas. To win the most support for your research paper, you should follow Jefferson's example.

Prepare the Final Copy

After you have made your paper as clear, logical, and coherent as you can, focus your attention on editing. Proofread your paper, watching for mistakes in citations, grammar, spelling, punctuation, and word usage. Read your paper aloud to catch mistakes that you might miss by reading silently. Once your research paper is free of errors, you can type or print your final copy. The checklist below can help you remember to examine all the important aspects of your final version.

Evaluation Rubric

By the time you complete Lesson 7.6, you will have

- proofread your paper, identifying and correcting errors in grammar, punctuation, and spelling
- confirmed that every summary, paraphrase, and quotation is properly credited to a source and checked that every source you used is listed in a properly formatted works-cited list
- created a clean final copy that is free of errors and ready to present to your audience

Editing and Presenting Checklist

1. Have I organized my ideas clearly?
2. Have I explained or defined any words that may be unfamiliar to the reader?
3. Have I discussed my topic completely and fairly?
4. Have I checked the paper for missing words or letters?
5. Have I considered the proper meaning of the words I've used?
6. Have I corrected all grammar and punctuation mistakes?
7. Is each word spelled and capitalized correctly?
8. Is the paper neat and easy to read?

Resource Manager

Planning Resources
- *Lesson Plans*

Transparencies
- *Bellringer*
- *Daily Language Practice*

Other Print Resources
- *Research Paper and Report Writing*, pp. 32–35
- *Style and Documentation Sourcebook for Writers*
- *Thinking and Study Skills*, p. 3
- *Writing Across the Curriculum*
- *Writing Assessment and Evaluation Rubrics*

Present Your Paper

Bryan 1

Amy Colleen Bryan
Ms. Meryl Wilk
English Composition
26 April 2000

The *Titanic:*
Was It the End of an Era?

Writer's last name and the page number should appear on each page, one-half inch from the top and one inch from the right edge of the paper.

Writer's name, teacher's name, course name, and date should appear on the first page, one inch from the top of the page and one inch from the left edge of the paper.

The title should be centered on the page.

You may want to create a cover for your paper or enclose it in a special folder. A separate title page should include the title of your paper, your name, your teacher's name, the course name, and the date on which you submit the paper. If you don't have a separate title page, put this information on the first page of your paper, as shown here. The last page of your paper is always the list of works cited.

Give some thought to whether your paper would be enhanced by the use of any visuals, such as copies of photographs or works of art, diagrams, time lines, or charts. These materials may be attached to the end of your paper, before the works-cited list.

Your teacher may ask you to submit a variety of materials along with your final paper. You may be asked to submit your note cards, your final outline (which should not include your introduction and conclusion), or a summary statement. Make sure that you know what's expected of you well in advance of the final due date. You don't want any last-minute surprises!

Teach

Using Model Papers

If students have difficulty following guidelines or verbal instructions for formatting their final drafts, supply them with a model of a properly presented research paper. Encourage them to study the model paper at the end of this lesson. **L2**

Assess

Evaluation Rubrics

1. Students should make the following corrections:
   - . . . is represented by two senators.
   - . . . missionaries and fur trappers.
2. Students should make the following corrections:
   - Depression threw . . .
   - . . . and an experienced soldier.
3. Students should discern the following errors:
   - time confusion—How is one to know what Jefferson would think in another era?
   - lack of connection—What was Gandhi admired for around the world?
   - lack of connection—What does gold in Canada have to do with U.S. mineral wealth?

See also *Writing Assessment and Evaluation Rubrics.*

Research Paper Writing

Skills Practice

1. On a separate paper, rewrite the following sentences to make them clearer.
   - Each of the United States is represented by two people in the Senate.
   - The first Europeans to explore the Great Lakes were missionaries and fur-trapping operations.
2. Copy the following sentences, and correct the problems of word usage and writing style.
   - The Great Depression through millions of people out of work.
   - Andrew Jackson was tough, shrewd, and had experience as a soldier.
3. Read these sentences and identify misleading comments or poorly constructed thoughts.
   - Because his plantation relied on the efforts of enslaved persons, Thomas Jefferson probably would have sided with the Confederates in the American Civil War.
   - Gandhi was beloved by the Indian people because of his nonviolent principles, and he had admirers around the world as well.
   - The purchase of Alaska increased the mineral wealth of the United States, and gold was soon discovered in the Canadian Yukon.

Your Research Paper

As you prepare the final version of your research paper, use the student model on the following pages as a guide. Read the call-out notes in the side column and use the student model to help you understand each note and to answer any questions you find there. Pay special attention to the following strategies:

- Presenting Tip
- Grammar Tip
- Editing Tip

Also, note how the Works Cited list is presented. As you create your own list, refer back to the Formats for Works Cited Entries on page 339 and the examples in the Works-Cited Entries chart on page 340.

Prepare the final version of your research paper, and hand it in to your teacher. Be sure to include any additional materials that your teacher requires.

The *Titanic:*
Was It the End of an Era?

Amy Colleen Bryan

"All around us there was this twisted mass of wreckage and tons of coal spread around. And then there was this lady's shoe. It was incredible, just haunting" (Lemonick 70). On September 1, 1985, marine geologist Dr. Robert Ballard, with the help of U.S. and French researchers, found the *Titanic* 13,000 feet below the surface of the Atlantic Ocean. Using sonar and a robot submarine, Dr. Ballard located the ship about 500 miles south of Newfoundland, where it had sunk seventy-three years before. Thirteen thousand feet below the surface the water is totally black with no marine life and a temperature of 39° F, yet the *Titanic* had been well preserved. It was sitting upright covered with silt, and although it split in half during the sinking, the grand staircase, railings and wooden deck were still intact, the planks still visible. On closer investigation, Ballard's crew found five cases of wine with the corks still in them, china plates, wash basins, chamber pots, and luggage.

Completed in 1912, the *Titanic* was considered the most luxurious ship of its day. The *Titanic* has been called a "monument to the Gilded Age" (Marbach 46) and its sinking "signaled the end of the Edwardian era in all its cocky opulence" (Angier, "*Titanic* Find" 68). Was the sinking of the *Titanic* really the end of an era?

The two decades before World War I have been labeled the Gilded Age for a number of reasons. After the American Civil War, as westward expansion resumed, industry expanded and many Americans discovered wealth for the first time. Around 1900 the optimistic "dream" for industrial growth turned into an optimistic dream for material possessions (Wade 6). Many people were richer than ever before. In 1861 there were three millionaires in the United States; in 1900 there were 3,800 (Wade 7). Americans equated size with security and excess with success (Wade 29). They wanted to expand technologically and materially. They prized business success and placed faith in extravagance. *(continued)*

Remember to underline titles when appropriate in your text and works-cited list; or use italics if you're using a word processing program. (See Lesson 21.10 on pages 758–759 for reminders about appropriate punctuation of titles.)

Bryan grabs her reader's attention by describing vivid scenes of the wreck.

How does this background information help the reader?

Bryan states her thesis as a question she is trying to answer in her paper.

Research Paper Writing

Teach

Using the Model

Direct students' attention to the marginal boxes as a means of analyzing Bryan's paper as a student model:

- The eyewitness quote gets readers' attention and draws them into the paper.
- Readers will be intrigued by envisioning this formal, civilized setting underwater.
- Does Bryan follow through by giving an answer? (yes, at the end—student page 355)

About the Author

Amy Colleen Bryan wrote the model paper in 1989 while she was attending Lexington High School in Lexington, Virginia. It was published by the *Concord Review,* a quarterly review of essays by students of history, in the fall of 1990.

Learning Disabled

Following Instructions

Students with certain kinds of learning disabilities may have difficulty following guidelines or verbal instructions for formatting their final drafts. It might help these students to see a model of a complete paper, including title page, citations, list of works cited, and any other elements you wish them to include. Annotations on the model might also be helpful for these students.

Teach

Using the Model

Ask what transition is being made in the second full paragraph on this student page. (The discussion is shifting from the era's material to technological growth.) How does Bryan use the *Titanic* to discuss this advancement? (She describes the ship as a symbol of turn-of-the-century technology.) What other details on student pages 349–350 illustrate the wealth of the period? (cases of wine; china plates; the number and prominence of millionaires at the time; the number of builders of the *Titanic;* the facilities aboard the ship) **L2**

Promoting Discussion

Ask students to count the number of references to the *Titanic* being unsinkable on this and the following page (four). Why does Bryan include so many? (Doing so underscores the irony of its sinking and the overconfidence of crew and passengers.) **L2**

> Transitions help the reader follow the course of events.

> Why, do you think, did Bryan put the dimensions of the *Titanic* in these terms?

Presenting Tip

Including a diagram or a photograph of the *Titanic* in the final draft would enhance a reader's understanding of the dimensions of the ship.

In the beginning of the 1900s there were no movie, radio, or television stars to idolize, so "the public depended on the socially prominent people for all the vicarious glamour that enriches drab lives" (Lord 109–110). In fact the rich lifestyle of the Gilded Age existed for very few. Those who did fit the description held a wealth almost beyond comprehension, a wealth that has never quite been repeated. The life and fate of the rich and famous received the most attention. John Jacob Astor IV, the richest man in America, possessed thirty million dollars (an amount almost equivalent to $350,000,000 in today's money). Benjamin Guggenheim followed with twenty million and Isidor Straus and George Widener each had ten million (Davie 45).

Besides material growth, the time around 1900 was full of invention and technology, from automobiles to rubberbands (*Secrets*), and it seemed like the *Titanic* was the epitome of this era, symbolizing all that this time had to offer.

Work began on the *Titanic* in 1909 at Harland & Wolff's shipping yards in Belfast, Ireland. It took three thousand men two years to build. When completed, the ship was made of 46,000 tons of steel and measured 882.5 feet long and 105.7 feet high. Comparatively speaking, the *Titanic* was four city blocks long and eleven stories high (Lord 170). The inside of the ship contained facilities ranging from Turkish baths and tennis courts to sun parlors, a theater, and a miniature golf course.

As news of the extravagant technological wonder spread throughout the world, it soon became known as the "unsinkable" *Titanic.* Experts considered the ship "unsinkable" because of its vast size and the strength and stiffness of the floor; the keel, longitudinals, and inner and outer bottoms were greater in size, weight, and thickness than in any other ship; the floor extended up the sides of the ship so as to "frame" it; the whole length of the hull was stiffened by deep web frame girders; the hull was divided into sixteen watertight compartments, four of which could be flooded and the ship would still float; the deck beams were ten inches thick and held to the sides with steel; and the elaborate pipe systems could delay the rise of water ("Experts" 981). The structural stability of the ship, unparalleled for its time, was ready to be tested in open waters.

Real World Connection

Observing

Challenge students to use their imaginations and observation skills to describe an underwater scene like that of the sunken *Titanic,* only with a modern-day vessel. What contemporary objects of passengers and crew might be still intact and in place?

The *Titanic* set sail from Belfast Harbor on May 11, 1911. Her trial voyage lasted eight hours, and upon her return, her builders were confident that she was indeed "unsinkable." She left Southampton at twelve noon on April 10, 1912, on her maiden voyage. She was to reach New York City one week later.

There were approximately 2,207 passengers on board when the *Titanic* left the harbor (Friedrich 70), 706 of whom were immigrants traveling to the United States for the first time (Baldwin 47). About 350 of the biggest names in American and British society were on the first-class list ("*Titanic* in Peril"). These people paid $4,350 for their seven-day trip, an amount almost equivalent to $50,000 in today's money (Ballard 712). The passenger list included General John Jacob Astor IV and his wife; Major Archibald Butt, military aide to President William Howard Taft; John B. Thayer, Vice-President of the Pennsylvania Railroad; Charles M. Hays, President of Grand Trunk Railways in Canada; Mr. And Mrs. Isidor Straus, owners of Macy's Department Store; and J. Bruce Ismay, chairman and managing director of the White Star Line.

The ship also carried a distinguished crew. The captain of the *Titanic* was Edward Smith, who had been a captain of the *Olympic*, the *Titanic's* sister ship, and was a favorite among high-society Americans. Upon sailing, Second Officer C. H. Lightoller reportedly said, "It was clear to everyone on board that we had a ship that was going to create the greatest stir British shipping circles had ever known" (218). When a woman asked a deckhand if the *Titanic* was really "unsinkable," he replied, "God Himself could not sink this ship" (Friedrich 70).

This over-confident attitude was matched by perfect weather for the first four days of sailing. Then at 9:00 A.M. on April 14, the *Titanic* received iceberg warnings from the *Coronia*. Two more warnings were received that afternoon, yet Captain Smith dismissed all three, never decreasing the ship's speed of 22 knots or changing its course. At 7:30 P.M. the *Californian* warned the *Titanic* of ice. Second Operator Harold Bride ignored these signals because he was figuring accounts. Around 9:30 P.M. Commander Lightoller ordered Frederick Fleet to get up in the crow's nest to watch for icebergs. At 11:00 P.M. the *Californian* again warned the *Titanic*

(*continued*)

Bryan converts amounts of money to modern equivalences so the reader can understand their significance.

Grammar Tip

When editing your paper, check that you have used commas correctly. For information about comma usage, see Lesson 21.6, pages 743–751.

What form of organization does Bryan use in describing the voyage?

Teach

Using the Model

Refer students to the marginal boxes.

- Ask what significance Bryan attributes to the first-class fare by converting its dollar amount to a modern equivalent. (It underscores the opulence of the passengers who were able to afford such a sum.)

- Students should discern that the organization is chronological. Ask why Bryan uses this form. (Chronological order conveniently and logically narrates the events leading to the disaster, builds suspense, and communicates how inattentiveness on the part of the crew—due to overconfidence—led, step by step, to the disaster.) **L2**

Using Chronology

To aid students in using chronological organization, direct them to the last paragraph on this student page. Note that the second sentence ("Then at 9:00 A.M. on April 14, . . .") marks the beginning of the paper's chronological organization. Tell them that Bryan switches to this organization to describe the events that led to the sinking of the *Titanic*. Ask the students to skim this and subsequent pages to find other times of day and the events associated with them. Describe why this method of organization is particularly effective in describing these events. (By telling what led up to the disaster in chronological order, Bryan builds suspense and also informs the reader how the crew's disregard of warnings precipitated the disaster.) **L1**

Extension and Enrichment

Inviting a Speaker

Invite as a guest speaker to your class someone who is currently writing or has recently completed a major research paper such as a doctoral dissertation or master's thesis. Ask the visitor to bring examples of materials that he or she used at various stages of the research process and, if available, the final product. In advance of the visit, ask students to prepare questions regarding the stages of the visitor's writing process: topic selection, outlining, drafting, revising, and documentation of sources.

Teach

Using the Model

Direct attention to the first marginal box. Ask students why the eyewitness descriptions are powerful. (They both give vivid, human accounts of the sinking—the first by describing the screams of those on board; the second by detailing the self-protective instinct of the "chap" in the lifeboat who hit the narrator on the head.) **L2**

Evaluating Descriptions

Direct students' attention to the second complete paragraph. Ask them to describe in a word the lifeboat launch arrangements. (confused, disorganized, biased, unfair) Tell them to support the word they chose with evidence from the paragraph. To defend *confused* and *disorganized,* students can point to the random loading of the boats—with boats filled halfway or less. To support *biased* and *unfair,* they can mention that Lifeboat 1 was lowered with more men than women—foregoing the "women and children" priority rule. **L2**

about ice. First Operator Phillips, who relieved Bride, told the *Californian* operator to shut up and leave him alone because he was busy (Baldwin 49). The *Titanic* still steamed full speed ahead at 22 knots.

Up in the crow's nest, at 11:40 P.M., 1300 miles from New York City, Fleet saw an iceberg looming in the distance. The officer on the bridge gave the order to turn the ship hard to starboard. The orders were too late. There was a faint jarring that lasted for ten seconds. The result was a 300-foot gash along the starboard side of the hull. Five water-tight compartments had been flooded, enough to sink the ship. The first wireless call for help went out at 12:15 A.M. The *Virginian,* the *Carpathia,* and the *Baltic* received the call and started for the ship. Evans, the wireless operator for the *Californian,* had turned off his signals and retired to bed fifteen minutes before. Ironically, the *Californian* was less than ten miles from the *Titanic* (Angier, "Haunting" 58).

At 12:45 A.M. the first distress rocket was fired, and the first lifeboat was lowered. Launching arrangements were confused; because no lifeboat drills had been held beforehand, loading was random. Women and children were given first priority along with the first-class passengers in general (Kingston and Lambert 145). Half-filled boats were asked to take more passengers but did not; they feared tipping and sinking once they got into the water (Baldwin 53). Lifeboat 6 had a capacity of sixty-five passengers but left with only twenty-eight (Baldwin 53). Lifeboat 1 had a capacity of forty people but left with only twelve ("*Titanic* Diary"). Two of these passengers were women, the rest men—among them were three millionaires and J. Bruce Ismay.

At 1:40 A.M. the crew fired the last rocket into the air and at 2:05 A.M. lowered the last lifeboat, "collapsible D," into the water. Benjamin Guggenheim and his valet came on deck in full evening dress, saying "We've dressed in our best and are prepared to go down like gentlemen" (Friedrich 70). When Astor tried to board a lifeboat with his wife, he was refused; he told her he would meet her later.

Around 2:10 A.M. the wireless operator sent the last call for help. As the ship sank at 2:20 A.M., Mrs. H. D. Bishop observed from a lifeboat, "It began to slide gently downwards. Its speed increased as it went down head first, so that the stern shot down with a rush. . . . As the ship sank we could

> Eyewitness descriptions carry more power than an analysis from a secondary source.

> Use ellipses to indicate that material has been omitted from quotations.

hear the screaming a mile away. Gradually it became fainter and died away" (437).

Many lifeboats made little attempt to help other survivors in the water. Fireman Harry Senior was swept off the ship as it went down. Later he explained, "I tried to get aboard a boat, but some chap hit me over the head with an oar. There were too many people in her" (435).

The *Carpathia* arrived at dawn to pick up survivors. By 8:50 A.M. the *Carpathia* was headed for New York City with 705 *Titanic* passengers (Lord 171–172; *Secrets*). The total death count was 1,502.

When the news reached American newspapers, the *New York Times* was so confident that the *Titanic* was unsinkable that it carried only a small front page story about the accident ("New Liner"). However, on April 16 when the news was confirmed, the stories filled up the entire front section of the *New York Times* for five consecutive days. New York City swarmed with people trying to find out who had survived. The *New York Times* ran front page stories on the rich and famous who were on board, with an entire article devoted to John Jacob Astor alone; almost as an afterthought the 1,800 others who might have died were listed (Lord 110).

The shock of this calamity raised many questions. Almost immediately after the disaster, both the United States and Great Britain set up investigations. Through these investigations, the injustices that occurred on the *Titanic* that night were made public. These were conditions that would "never get by the social consciousness (or news sense) of today's press" (Lord 108). There were lifeboats for only half the passengers on board, and of the 1,500 people in the water, only 13 were picked up by lifeboats (Kingston and Lambert 145). Greatly debated was the treatment of the second-class, third-class, and steerage passengers. Of the women in first-class, only 4 of 143 drowned (3 by choice); 15 of 93 women in second-class drowned; and 81 of 179 women in third-class drowned. All except 1 of 30 children in first- and second-class survived, but only 23 of the 76 children in steerage survived (Lord 107).

For the most part the third-class passengers had to fend for themselves. Some in third-class thought that access to the lifeboats was a privilege of the first- and second-classes (Lord 108–109). Unbelievably, there was a higher loss of third-class

(continued)

Editing Tip

It is common practice to not italicize the article preceding the title of a magazine or newspaper.

How does this sentence help the reader?

Why is this sentence a helpful lead-in to the paragraph?

Research Paper Writing

Teach

Using the Model

Refer students to the marginal boxes.
- The sentence helps the reader by adding perspective: that is, that the disaster came as a shock to the general public and led to investigations into injustices.
- The sentence is helpful because it summarizes the plight of third-class passengers—they had to "fend for themselves." **L2**

Promoting Discussion

Ask students how the statistics enumerated in the third and fourth paragraphs tell the story of the injustices aboard the *Titanic*. Students can point out numbers and percentages showing discrepancies in survival among different class passengers of men, women, and children. (For example, all except 1 of 30 children in the first and second class survived, as compared with only 23 of the 76 steerage children.) **L3**

Cooperative Learning

Evaluating the Model

Designate Co-op groups for students to analyze the student model as an over-view of research paper writing. Each group could focus on one of the following: the thesis statement's preview of the paper, the organization's structuring of information, the evidence's persuasive power, and the sources' relevance and accuracy. Each group should evaluate the paper's effectiveness in its designated area and give an analytical report to the class.

Teach

Using the Model

Clarify the different kinds of source citations noted in the two marginal boxes.

- A long indented quote can be preceded by a direct reference to the author ("Reverend A. B. Baker said:"). The source can then be cited in the works-cited list. Tell students to affirm this citation by checking the next page.

- In a series of quotes by the same author, a short quote preceded by the author's name can be referenced with parenthetical documentation.

- Point out that Bryan carefully documents the vast differences between the wealthy and less fortunate, and the corresponding treatment given them during the *Titanic* disaster. What is the significance of Lord's quote? (Such unequal treatment of the wealthy and poor would not be tolerated today.) Ask students if they agree with Lord. **L2**

Evaluating Sources

Many readers may not recognize the name Reverend A. B. Baker. What other cues does Bryan give that lend him authority as a speaker? (She tells us that he is a minister, thereby associating him with morality and spiritual leadership. She also tells us that he spoke at Princeton University, a prestigious school.) **L3**

children than first-class men (Lord 108). A steward stationed on the third-class deck testified that some men were kept locked below deck until almost 1:15 A.M. Thirty-four percent of the first-class men were saved, while only eight percent of the second-class and twelve percent of the third-class survived (Davie 45). When lawyers investigated the situation, however, White Star Line was indifferent, as were the press and even Congress. The British enquiry said it found no discrimination (Lord 108).

The investigation procedures for each country were very different but ultimately resulted in the same conclusions. Some recommendations that resulted from the investigations were: life preservers and regulation lifeboats for all passengers on board, lifeboat drills, a wireless operator on duty at all times, and a double-skin for the hull, longitudinal bulkheads, and water-tight decks. The United States and British governments set up the International Ice Patrol and the first International Convention for the Safety of Life at Sea was begun in London in 1913 ("Titanic").

Laws at sea changed, but also Americans realized that in their haste to progress, they had sacrificed safety; in their quest for material possessions, they had forgotten the spiritual. In a sermon given at Princeton University the Sunday after the *Titanic* disaster, Reverend A. B. Baker said:

> Was there not something of self-confidence and self-sufficiency in the contention that it was perfectly safe, that it could outride any ocean storm and come unharmed through any danger to which it might be exposed? . . . It will not do to put our confidence in ships nor in anything that represents the boastful progress of the age.

In this disaster the world had lost a number of the noted wealthy. As a result many Americans changed their view of wealth and success. The *Titanic* was the "last time the special position of First Class was accepted without question" (Lord 109). Many Americans quickly realized that prominent people under stress could be selfish and conceited (Lord 109). As Walter Lord noted, "The *Titanic* was the last stand of wealth and society in the center of public affection" (109). The First World War and later the Depression made sure of that. After the *Titanic* disaster it was more difficult for Americans to be as confident of technology and progress. The *Titanic* "mirrored" the Gilded Age. It had seemed to be the peak of all

Set off any quotations longer than three lines by indenting the entire passage.

Since the author's name is given in the text, only the page number is needed in the citation.

technology, wealth, and luxury. Life after its sinking was never the same.

Many people have tried to pinpoint reasons for the *Titanic* disaster. The chance is one in a million that a ship will hit an iceberg and sink to the ocean floor (Beasley 174). Was this disaster destined by fate? Had people become so sure of themselves that Divine Intervention was needed to put them back in their place?

The Gilded Age was a period of extremes—growing wealth and growing technology. The sinking of the *Titanic* shocked Americans back to reality. It made them retrace their steps and look at the world in a different light, a world where it was harder to be so confident and sure of oneself. Dr. Charles H. Parkhurst tried to explain the reason for this tragedy by saying:

> The two sore spots which really run into one another and which constitute the disease that is gnawing into our civilizations are the love of money and the passion for luxury. These two combined are what sunk the *Titanic* and sent 1500 souls prematurely to their final account ("Religious Views" 939).

Bryan ends her paper with a strong quotation.

Works Cited

Angier, Natalie. "After 73 Years, a *Titanic* Find." *Time* 16 Sep. 1985: 68.

—. "Haunting Images of Disaster." *Time* 23 Sep. 1985: 58.

Baker, Reverend A. B. Sermon. Trinity Church. Princeton, 21 Apr. 1912.

Baldwin, Hanson W. *Sea Fights and Shipwrecks: True Tales of the Seven Seas.* New York: Country Life Press, 1955.

Ballard, Robert D. "How We Found the *Titanic*." *National Geographic* Dec. 1985: 696–719.

Beasley, Lawrence. *The Loss of the* Titanic. London: Philip Allan, 1929.

Bishop, Mrs. H. D. "The *Titanic* From a Lifeboat, 15 April 1912." *Eyewitness to History.* Ed. John Carey. Cambridge: Harvard, 1987. 436–437.

Research Paper Writing

Presenting Tip

In your final works-cited list, cite only those sources from which you actually used information in your research paper. Your teacher may ask you to include a brief annotation for each work cited in which you explain the source's content and usefulness.

Teach

Using the Model

Note that the quotation mentions the "love of money" and the "passion for luxury"—themes which Bryan has consistently tied to her account of the *Titanic* disaster. Make the point that she probably had the quotation in mind as her conclusion when she wrote her thesis statement. Refer students to the thesis statement in the second paragraph of her paper. Note that Bryan reserves her judgment on the "cocky opulence" until her concluding quote, which condemns it as a "disease."

In addition, note that the same author wrote the first two articles referenced in the works-cited list. Remind students that the author's name is omitted from the second entry and is replaced by three hyphens or a dash. Note that one of Bryan's sources is a National Geographic Society video. Encourage students to examine videos as sources for research. Discuss other possible nonprint sources (tapes of radio interviews, lectures, performances, photographs, live interviews). Note the bibliographic components of Bryan's video citation. **L2**

Analyzing the Conclusion

Point out that Bryan's concluding quote is not her summary. The quote is a strong one, which makes a good conclusion, but it needs preparation. The purpose of Bryan's words at the beginning of the paragraph is to start the summary process and prepare us for the concluding quote. **L1**

Additional Resources

📁 *Writing Across the Curriculum*
📁 *Research Paper and Report Writing,* pp. 32–35
📁 *Thinking and Study Skills,* p. 3

Teach

Writing Annotations

Ask students to write a brief annotation for one of Bryan's sources. Discuss the kind of information needed to show the author's credibility and the source's usefulness. **L2**

Reteaching

Lead students to reinforce their outlining skills by condensing the model into outline form.

Enrichment

Suggest that students present summary statements for their research papers to the class.

Close

After students turn in their papers, encourage them to reflect on the project in a class discussion. Ask students which stages of the writing process were most enjoyable, difficult, frustrating, time-consuming, or surprising. What would they do differently next time they get this kind of assignment? What strategies and procedures would they like to remember and use again? Suggest that they write down their perceptions to assist them with their future research assignments.

TIME

For more about the writing process, see **TIME Facing the Blank Page,** pp. 109–119.

Davie, Michael. Titanic: *The Death and Life of a Legend.* New York: Alfred A. Knopf, 1986.

"Experts on the *Titanic* Wreck." *Literary Digest* 11 May 1912: 981.

Friedrich, Otto. "When the Great Ship Went Down." *Time* 16 Sep. 1985: 70.

Kingston, Jeremy, and David Lambert. *Catastrophe And Crisis.* New York: Facts on File, 1979.

Lemonick, Michael D. "Treasures Reclaimed from The Deep." *Time* 2 Nov. 1987: 70.

Lightoller, Commander. Titanic *and Other Ships.* London: Ivor Nicholson and Watson, 1935.

Lord, Walter. *A Night to Remember.* New York: Henry Holt, 1955.

Marbach, William D. "The Sea Gives Up a Secret." *Newsweek* 16 Sep. 1985: 46.

"New Liner *Titanic* Hits an Iceberg." *New York Times* 15 Apr. 1912: A1.

"Religious Views of the *Titanic.*" *Literary Digest* 4 May 1912.

Secrets of the Titanic. Videocassette. Dir. Nicholas Nixon. With Martin Sheen. National Geographic Society Video, 1986, 58 min.

Senior, Harry. "The *Titanic:* A Fireman's Story, 15 April 1912." *Eyewitness to History.* Ed. John Carey. Cambridge: Harvard, 1987. 434–435.

"Titanic." *Encyclopaedia Britannica Online.* 5 Mar. 2000 <http://www.britannica.com/bcom/eb/article/2/0,5716,74542+1,00.html>.

"Titanic Diary." *Encyclopedia Titanica.* Sept. 1996. 4 Mar. 2000 <http://atschool.eduweb.co.uk/phind/lifeboats/boat_01.html>.

"*Titanic* in Peril on Leaving Port." *New York Times* 11 Apr. 1912: A1.

Wade, Wyn Craig. The Titanic—*End of a Dream.* New York: Rawson, Wade, 1979.

UNIT 7 Review

Reflecting on the Unit

Summarize what you learned in this unit by answering the following questions.

1 What are the important elements of planning and researching a paper?

2 How and why do you outline the information gathered during your research?

3 What is the purpose of a thesis statement?

4 What are the important steps to follow when you draft a research paper?

5 How and why should you document information you use in your paper?

6 What techniques can help you revise and present your paper effectively?

Adding to Your Portfolio

Look over the research paper you prepared during this unit and add it to your portfolio. The final draft of your paper should show some or all of the following:

- an appropriate research topic and a useful working bibliography
- a clear thesis statement supported with adequate details
- an effective introduction and a strong conclusion
- clarity, logic, and coherence
- proper documentation of sources

REFLECT ON YOUR CHOICE Write a brief note to explain what you learned from writing your research paper. Attach the note to your paper.

SET GOALS How can you improve your writing? What skill will you focus on the next time you write?

Writing Across the Curriculum

MAKE A SCIENCE CONNECTION One type of research paper is an evaluative paper. In such a paper, the writer states an opinion and backs it up with evidence found in primary and secondary sources. Scan the newspaper, a weekly newsmagazine, or a science journal, and choose an issue or topic that interests you. Draft a central idea statement presenting your opinion on the topic. Locate supporting evidence—facts and educated opinions—in primary and secondary sources. Then outline the contents of the paper and write a thesis statement and opening paragraph for it.

Review **357**

Review

Reflecting on the Unit

You may have students respond to Reflecting on the Unit in writing or through discussion.

Adding to Your Portfolio

Look to see that students have revised and edited their work carefully. Smooth transitions and logical conclusions, as well as correct mechanics, will distinguish thorough work from sloppy work.

Writing Across the Curriculum

Students may find conflicting evidence in their research. Students should discuss significant conflicts in their papers, as omissions of this sort can be inaccurate and misleading.

Portfolio Evaluation

If you grade the portfolio selections, you may want to award two marks—one each for content and form. Explain your assessment criteria before students make their selections. Commend

- experimentation with creative prewriting techniques
- clear, concise writing in which the main idea, audience, and purpose are evident
- successful revisions
- work that shows a flair for language

✔ ASSESSMENT OPTIONS

📁 *Tests with Answer Key & Rubrics*
Unit 7 Pretest, pp. 25–26
Unit 7 Mastery Test, pp. 27–28

💾 *Testmaker*
Unit 7 Pretest
Unit 7 Mastery Test

You may wish to administer the Mastery Test at this point.

📼 *MindJogger Videoquizzes*

Sentence Combining

"The bear in the picture is big. The bear in the picture is brown. The bear in the picture is angry." Writing such as this gets boring, no matter how frightening or interesting the subject is. Brainstorm with students to see how many descriptive elements they can blend into one coherent, grammatical sentence about the photograph, including not only what they see, but what they think about what they see. Tell students that in this unit they will learn about ways to combine thoughts and sentences in order to achieve more variety and complexity in their writing.

Interpret and Analyze Use the following questions for discussion:
- What qualities of the bear are emphasized in the photograph?
- How has the photographer used the camera to emphasize those qualities?

Discussing the Quotation

This quotation is from Robert H. Abel's short story "Appetizer" on page 1024 of *Glencoe Literature,* Course 5. In the short story, which describes an encounter with a brown bear such as the one in the photograph, the author uses various literary techniques to turn what could have been a terrifying event into a very funny narration. Abel also employs sentence-combining techniques to give his story rhythm and variety.

Writing Prompt Ask students to write a paragraph, in short, simple sentences, about a time when they survived a frightening experience. Then have students revise their writing by combining sentences to make their paragraphs more interesting to hear or read. If possible, students should add elements of humor, as Abel did.

"About three minutes after Ms. Bear walked into the cannery, twenty of the twenty-four workers were climbing out . . ."

—Robert H. Abel, "Appetizer"

358

Resource Manager

Planning Resources
- *Lesson Plans*
- *Block Scheduling*

Transparencies
- *Bellringer*
- *Two-Minute Skill Drill*

Other Print Resources
- *Grammar Workbook*
- *Sentence-Combining Practice*
- *Tests with Answer Key and Rubrics*

Video
- *MindJogger Videoquizzes*

Software
- *Presentation Plus!*
- *Revising with Style*
- *Testmaker*
- *Writer's Choice Puzzlemaker*

Web Sites
- *writerschoice.glencoe.com*
- *lit.glencoe.com*

UNIT 8

Sentence Combining

Style Through Sentence Combining 360

Skills and Applications

Lesson **8.1**   **Description** 365

Lesson **8.2**   **Narration** 369

Lesson **8.3**   **Exposition** 373

Lesson **8.4**   **Persuasion** 377

Lesson **8.5**   **Literature Exercises** 381

Objectives

- To develop an understanding of techniques for combining short, simple sentences into longer, more complex ones
- To improve writing style and fluency in description, narration, exposition, and persuasion

✔ ASSESSMENT OPTIONS

📁 *Tests with Answer Key & Rubrics*
Unit 8 Mastery Test, pp. 29–30

💾 *Testmaker*
Unit 8 Mastery Test

Key to Ability Levels

L1 Level 1 activities are within the basic ability range of students.

L2 Level 2 activities are within the ability range of average students.

L3 Level 3 activities are more challenging activities.

359

Focus

Lesson Overview

Objective
- To give students options for combining multiple ideas in various stylistic constructions

Skills
- synthesizing ideas; using coordinating conjunctions and punctuation; using sentence constructions

Critical Thinking
- analyzing; evaluating; decision-making

Listening and Speaking
- discussing

Bellringer
Daily Language Activity

When students enter the classroom, have this assignment on the board: *Combine these three sentences into one sentence:*

The trip was long.
The trip was difficult.
The trip was totally unnecessary.

See also *Daily Language Practice*

Motivating Activity

Discuss students' responses to the Bell-ringer, and write one response on the board. (The trip was long, difficult, and totally unnecessary.) Ask volunteers to explain how combining sentences might improve readability, interest, and meaning.

Style Through Sentence Combining

*W*hat do you have in common with writers such as James Baldwin, Annie Dillard, James Thurber, Amy Tan, and Rudolfo Anaya? Like them, you have a distinctive writing style, a way of communicating your personality. Developing a clear, expressive writing style requires practice, of course. By writing regularly in your journal and trying out different types of writing—poems, essays, stories, letters to the editor—you develop a range of skills. Another excellent approach for developing style is sentence combining.

Unlock Your Style

Sentence combining is a research-tested writing strategy that enables you to explore options, make choices, and develop style. This process of combining short sentences into more complex ones is the focus of this unit. Your goal, however, is not to make long sentences, but to make good ones. Sometimes you will find that longer, more complex sentences enable you to express your ideas with precision and clarity. At other times, shorter is better.

The point is that sentence combining helps you understand your stylistic options. Instead of being locked into one type of sentence and "playing it safe" with a short, choppy style that reads like a first-grade reader, you can make choices as a writer. Practice in combining unlocks your style by making you aware of writing choices.

Learn the Drill

In sentence combining, you express the same information in different ways by using four combining strategies: (1) deleting repeated words; (2) using connecting words; (3) rearranging words; and (4) changing the form of words. Consider this cluster of short, basic sentences to see how they might be combined differently.

Sentence combining is a writing strategy.
The strategy has been tested by research.
It enables students to explore options.
It enables students to make choices.
It enables students to develop style.

Resource Manager

Planning Resources
- *Lesson Plans*

Transparencies
- *Bellringer*
- *Two-Minute Skill Drill*

Other Print Resources
- *Sentence-Combining Practice, pp. 1–35*

As you scan these sentences, your brain goes to work, drawing upon your knowledge of language. You can use the four combining strategies to express these ideas in fewer words. Look at the example below.

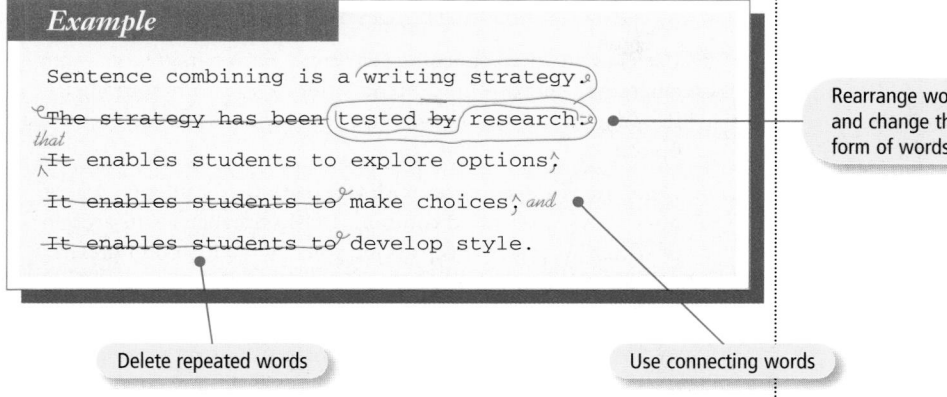

Example

Sentence combining is a (writing strategy.)
~~The strategy has been~~ (tested by research.)
that
~~It~~ enables students to explore options;
~~It enables students to~~ make choices; *and*
~~It enables students to~~ develop style.

Rearrange words and change the form of words

Delete repeated words

Use connecting words

Notice how editing produces the sentence that starts the section headed "Unlock Your Style" on page 360. Note the parallel structure of the three verbs—explore, make, and develop—that makes the sentence effective. But there are many other ways to combine these sentences. Read the ones below aloud, listening to differences in style:

1. Sentence combining is a writing strategy that has been tested by research; as options are explored and choices are made, students develop style.

2. Sentence combining, a writing strategy that has been tested by research, enables students to develop style by exploring options and making choices.

3. Enabling students to explore options, make choices, and develop style, sentence combining is a strategy for writing that has been tested by research.

All of these sentences communicate basically the same message, but each one has a different emphasis. Which is "best"? The answer to that question depends on the *context,* your *purposes* as a writer, and your sense of *audience.* Put simply, your choice of the "best" sentence depends on what sounds right to you.

Follow the Hints

Sentence combining is easy and fun. On the next page are some basic suggestions that you might try as you explore style.

Teach

Using the Four Strategies

Explain to students that they can use the four sentence-combining strategies (p. 360) to emphasize different facts or details in a series of shorter sentences. Point out that each of the three example sentences on this page emphasizes different details.

- Sentence 1 emphasizes that the strategy has been "tested by research" and mentions its use.
- Sentence 2 downplays "tested by research" and emphasizes how the strategy helps students.
- Sentence 3 stresses how students are helped and mentions that the strategy has been "tested by research." **L2**

Choosing a Strategy

Give students a chance to practice choosing a strategy by writing the following sentences on the board:

- A wedding photograph had a burned frame.
- A wedding photograph had its glass shattered.
- A rose vase had been blackened and twisted.
- We found these things in the old house after the fire.

Ask students to emphasize different facts or details in their combined sentences. **L2**

 Two-Minute Skill Drill

Have students combine these sentences into one:

The boy ran quickly down the alley and up to the bus stop.

The boy was long-legged.

The alley was dark, and the bus stop was deserted.

See also *Two-Minute Skill Drill Transparency 8.1*

MEETING INDIVIDUAL NEEDS **Less Proficient Readers**

Cooperative Learning

Students who have difficulty reading might feel frustrated by sentence-combining activities, especially if the activities are presented too often. To help these students gain skill in sentence combining, pair them with students who are proficient in English. It is suggested that such activities be introduced for brief periods a couple of times a week.

Teach

Practicing the Hints

Have students work in pairs or in small groups to complete Exercise A in Lesson 8.1, using the sentence-combining hints on this page. Invite pairs of students to begin working orally and then write down each other's solutions. Oral work helps students hear how clusters of short sentences can be combined to good effect. Go over the answers with them after they have finished the exercise. **L2**

Stressing Quality

Students may need to be reminded that the point of sentence combining is to improve the quality of sentences, not merely to increase their length. Help students discover opportunities for eliminating wordiness as they combine sentences. **L1**

Applying the Strategies

Challenge more proficient students to write a short story or descriptive essay of 2 to 3 pages using short, choppy sentences. Then ask them to revise their work using two of the sentence-combining strategies they have learned and the strategies for style suggested on student page 363. Ask them to read both of their versions aloud when they are finished and to evaluate the strengths and weaknesses of each version. **L3**

Sentence Combining

1. **Whisper sentences to yourself.** As you work with clusters of sentences, try saying them aloud. This process is faster than writing, and it helps you decide on a "best sentence" to write down.

2. **Work with a partner.** By trying out sentences on a partner—and hearing your partner's ideas—you often discover new, interesting ways to solve specific challenges. Feel free to borrow ideas.

3. **Use context when choosing sentences.** Each paragraph has an emerging context—the sentences you have already combined. Reading this context aloud helps you decide on the best sentence option.

4. **Compare your sentences with those of other students.** Seeing how others have solved combining tasks broadens your awareness of sentence options. Keep asking yourself, "Which do I prefer?"

5. **Look for stylistic patterns in your writing.** Calculate the average number of words per sentence; study your sentence openers; listen to rhythms in your style. Try new patterns to stretch yourself.

6. **Take risks.** Learning to make clear, effective sentences also means taking risks and making mistakes. It actually makes *sense* to accept mistakes—even *welcome* them—as you combine sentences. After all, mistakes provide feedback for your language learning. As you learn from them, you develop an expressive style, a voice of personal authority. You come to know yourself as a writer.

As you can see, sentence combining involves the skills of talking to yourself, making judgments, and holding what you say in your short-term memory so that you can transcribe it. These are oral skills as much as they are writing skills. Good writers trust their "inner voices."

Style and Focus Workshop

Looking ahead in this unit, you will find two kinds of sentence combining. The exercises in sections 8.1 through 8.4 present clusters of short sentences, with spaces between the clusters. The exercises in section 8.5, drawn from literature selections in this book, are set up in an unclustered format.

Sections 8.1 to 8.4 give you practice in making descriptive, narrative, expository, and persuasive paragraphs. You can combine each cluster into a single sentence, but you can also leave a cluster partially combined—or combine clusters with others. The idea, always, is to take risks and create the best sentences you can. The exercises on facing pages deal with the same topic or situation. Think of these exercises as "bookends" for the writing you will do. After you have combined sentences, your task is to connect the paragraphs into a longer essay or story. Doing so will help you transfer sentence-combining skills to your own writing.

Section 8.5 invites you to test your skills against those of professional writers. As you do these unclustered exercises, you will need to figure out which ideas logically belong together. After you have done the sentence combining, you can check your version against the author's original. By studying the similarities and differences between the two passages, you will learn a great deal about your own style. Sometimes you will prefer the professional writer's sentences. Why, specifically, are they "better" than yours? However, you will sometimes prefer your own style. Can you build on this writing skill, trying it out in your own stories and essays? Either way, you will learn to write better.

Explore Your Own Style

The whole point of sentence combining practice is to improve your revising and editing skills. Practice in sentence combining helps you see that sentences are flexible tools for thought, not rigid structures cast in concrete. The simple fact that you feel confident in moving sentence parts around increases your control of revising and editing. To acquire this sense of self-confidence—one based on your real competence in combining and revising sentences—you can try strategies like those shown below.

1. **Vary the length of your sentences.** Work for a rhythmic, interesting balance of long and short sentences, remembering that short sentences can be dramatic.

2. **Vary the structure of your sentences.** By using introductory clauses on occasion—and by sometimes tucking information in the middle of a sentence—you can create stylistic variety.

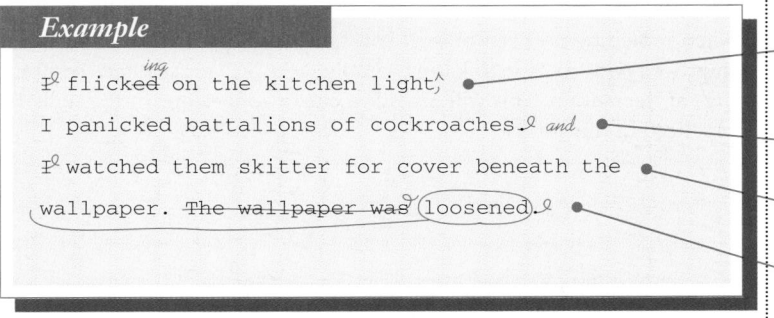

Example

I flicked^(ing) on the kitchen light,
I panicked battalions of cockroaches. and
I watched them skitter for cover beneath the
wallpaper. ~~The wallpaper was~~ (loosened).

Open with an introductory participial phrase by deleting the subject and changing *flicked* to *flicking*.

Use a connecting word.

Create a main clause with a compound predicate.

Delete and rearrange words.

Author's Original Version   Flicking on the kitchen light, I panicked battalions of cockroaches and watched them skitter for cover beneath the loosened wallpaper.

from *Growing Up* by Russell Baker

Style Through Sentence Combining   **363**

Sentence Combining

Teach

Exploring Style

Have students select a piece of writing they have done previously. Ask them to rewrite a portion of their work using the five strategies shown under Explore Your Own Style. Point out that sentence combining offers an opportunity for taking risks with language. Students can become better writers if they explore how different syntactic choices produce sentences of varying quality. Ask volunteers to read their revised portions aloud.

Assess

Evaluation Guidelines

Sentence combining practice helps students improve their revising and editing skills. Check to see that students are confidently moving sentence parts around and experimenting with different styles. Use the following questions:

- Are sentences of varying length?
- Is sentence structure varied?
- Is parallelism employed?
- Do sentences use colons, dashes, semicolons, commas, and parentheses effectively?
- Are sentence patterns sometimes reversed?

Close

How do students think that they might use sentence combining when they edit and revise their own writing? Elicit from students their thoughts about the value of learning to combine sentences. Explain that they will have an opportunity to practice their new skills in Lessons 8.1–8.5.

Sentence Combining

Use **parallelism,** or similar grammatical structure, in the remaining sentence parts. Note how the repeated participial phrases create a consistent, distinctive rhythm.

Use commas to separate phrases in a series.

Delete repeated words.

3. **Use parallelism for emphasis.** Experiment with repeated items in a series—words, phrases, and clauses—to understand how structural patterns work and how you can use them to advantage.

Example

Writers did not have to trudge through town.
~~They were not~~ peddling from canvas bags;
~~They were not~~ defending themselves against angry
dogs; ~~They were not~~ being rejected by surly
strangers.

Author's Original Version   Writers did not have to trudge through town peddling from canvas bags, defending themselves against angry dogs, being rejected by surly strangers.

from *Growing Up* by Russell Baker

4. **Use interruption for emphasis.** Colons, semicolons, dashes, commas, parentheses—all of these are useful tools in your stylistic toolkit. Knowing how to use them well will help you.

5. **Use unusual patterns for emphasis.** That you might sometimes reverse normal sentence patterns may never have occurred to you, but using such a strategy can work—if you know how to do it right.

When it comes time to rework a draft, it's important to apply what you have learned about combining and revising. The same holds true when providing peer response. If you spot a passage that could be improved with stylistic tinkering, simply write *SC* (for sentence combining) in the margin. This will provide a cue to apply some of the skills practiced in this unit.

Description

Exercise A: Playoff Game

Directions Combine each cluster of numbered items into one or more sentences. Combine clusters if you wish.

1.1 The gym was jammed with students.
1.2 The gym was jammed with townspeople.
1.3 The gym was jammed with TV equipment.
1.4 The gym was sweltering.

2.1 Signs festooned the walls.
2.2 The signs were made of butcher paper.
2.3 The signs were huge.
2.4 The walls were cinderblock.

3.1 A hometown band erupted into sound.
3.2 The sound was brassy.
3.3 The sound was discordant.
3.4 Cheerleaders bounded into action.
3.5 They were like marionettes.
3.6 The marionettes were perky.

4.1 They danced in syncopation.
4.2 Their syncopation was well rehearsed.
4.3 They danced from left to right.
4.4 They brought the crowd to its feet.

5.1 Voices chanted in unison.
5.2 The voices were hoarse.
5.3 The voices were excited.
5.4 Voices finally became a chorus.
5.5 The chorus was screaming.
5.6 The chorus had one mind.

6.1 The score was tied.
6.2 It was the fourth quarter.
6.3 There were only minutes left to play.

7.1 Noise rose in crescendo.
7.2 The crescendo was thundering.
7.3 It was like a tidal wave of sound.

Extension What else do you picture happening in this scene? Use your description to link "Playoff Game" to "Final Seconds."

8.1 Description **365**

Grammar Tip

Try opening either cluster 4 or 5 with a participial phrase. For more on participial phrases, see page 527.

Focus

Lesson Overview

Objective
- To give students practice in combining short sentences to express more complex ideas

Skills
- synthesizing ideas; using coordinating conjunctions and punctuation; using sentence constructions

Critical Thinking
- analyzing; evaluating; decision making

Listening and Speaking
- discussing

Practice and Assess

Answers: Exercise A

Answers will vary, but some suggestions follow.

1. The sweltering gym was jammed with students, townspeople, and TV equipment.
2. Festooning the cinderblock walls were huge butcher-paper signs.
3. A hometown band erupted into brassy, discordant sound, and cheerleaders bounded into action like perky marionettes.
4. Dancing from left to right in well-rehearsed syncopation, they brought the crowd to its feet.
5. Hoarse, excited voices chanted in unison, finally becoming a screaming chorus with one mind.
6. With only minutes left to play in the fourth quarter, the score was tied.
7. Like a tidal wave of sound, noise rose in a thundering crescendo.

Resource Manager

Planning Resources
- *Lesson Plans*

Other Print Resources
- *Sentence-Combining Practice,* pp. 1–35

Practice and Assess

Answers: Exercise B

Answers will vary, but some suggestions follow.

1. The high-pitched shriek of a referee's whistle pierced the jeers and groans from local fans.
2. Police and security guards braced themselves for any move that might signal trouble.
3. As the hometown coach chewed a thumbnail and paced restlessly along the sidelines, both teams took positions downcourt to await a foul shot that could decide the conference title.
4. Cocky and grinning, the opposing star toed the foul line, bounced the ball twice, and spun it through his fingertips.
5. He shrugged off the catcalls, barely eyeing the basket.
6. The shot, lofting up in a high, soft arc, dragged the crowd to its feet.
7. Hitting the back of the rim, it bounced against the glass backboard that looked like a rising moon.

Sentence Combining

Directions   Combine each cluster of numbered items into one or more sentences. Combine clusters if you wish.

1.1   A referee's whistle made a shriek.
1.2   The shriek was high-pitched.
1.3   It pierced the jeers.
1.4   It pierced the groans.
1.5   The groans came from local fans.

2.1   Police braced themselves.
2.2   Security guards braced themselves.
2.3   They were braced for any move.
2.4   The move might signal trouble.

3.1   The hometown coach paced restlessly.
3.2   He chewed a thumbnail.
3.3   He was on the sidelines.
3.4   Both teams took positions down court.
3.5   They were awaiting a foul shot.
3.6   It could decide the conference title.

4.1   The opposing star was cocky.
4.2   The opposing star was grinning.
4.3   The opposing star toed the foul line.
4.4   He bounced the ball twice.
4.5   He spun it through his fingertips.

5.1   He shrugged off the catcalls.
5.2   He barely eyed the basket.

6.1   The shot lofted up in an arc.
6.2   The arc was soft.
6.3   The arc was high.
6.4   It dragged the crowd to its feet.

7.1   It hit the back of the rim.
7.2   It bounced against the backboard.
7.3   The backboard was glass.
7.4   The backboard was like a rising moon.

Extension   Describe what you see happening after this scene. Share your text with a writing partner.

Directions Combine each cluster of numbered items into one or more sentences. Combine clusters if you wish.

1.1 The canyon trail crossed logs.
1.2 The trail was shadowy.
1.3 The logs were moss covered.
1.4 It passed through thickets of ferns.

2.1 Wildflowers grew in clumps of yellow.
2.2 Wildflowers grew in clumps of purple.
2.3 The clumps were cheerful.
2.4 The clumps were bright.
2.5 The clumps were along the river's edge.

3.1 Huge boulders lay in the white water.
3.2 The water was rushing.
3.3 They were like hippos.
3.4 The hippos were sleeping.

4.1 The trail finally became a clearing.
4.2 The clearing was grassy.
4.3. It was filled with sunlight.
4.4 It was filled with insects.
4.5 The insects hummed.

5.1 Maple trees swelled with life.
5.2 Aspen tees swelled with life.
5.3 Leaves uncurled from buds.
5.4 The leaves were golden.
5.5 The buds were tiny.

6.1 The sky above was like a hole.
6.2 The sky was cobalt-blue.
6.3 The hole was deep.
6.4 It was rimmed by treetops.

7.1 The air smelled sweet.
7.2 The air smelled fiercely green.
7.3 It was a first taste of spring.

Extension Move farther into the clearing, describing what you see and sense around you. Link your description to "Throwaway."

Vocabulary Tip

In cluster 7, try a *first taste of spring* at the beginning, in the middle, and at the end of the sentence. Which position do you think works best?

Sentence Combining

Practice and Assess

Answers: Exercise C

Answers will vary, but some suggestions follow.

1. The shadowy canyon trail passed through thickets of ferns and crossed moss-covered logs.
2. Cheerful, bright clumps of yellow and purple wildflowers grew along the river's edge.
3. In the rushing white water, huge boulders lay like sleeping hippos.
4. The trail finally became a grassy clearing filled with sunlight and humming insects.
5. Maple and aspen trees swelled with life, their golden leaves uncurling from tiny buds.
6. Above, like a deep hole rimmed by treetops, was the cobalt-blue sky.
7. The air smelled fiercely green and sweet—a first taste of spring.

Practice and Assess

Answers: Exercise D

Answers will vary, but some suggestions follow.

1. At the bottom of a ravine, the rusting car lay abandoned near the stream's edge.
2. Black scabs of oxidized paint had lifted off to reveal blotches of gray primer.
3. The driver's door hung open, permanently ajar, and bullet holes ventilated the windows.
4. Inside under the dash was a *Life* magazine from 1948 and a single shoe, its leather cracked and twisted.
5. Coiled springs pushed through worn fabric seatcovers.
6. Although the car smelled dead, it was now home to mice, birds, and changing seasons.
7. Once its fenders had been stroked and its interior caressed, but that day was long gone.

Additional Resources

📁 *Sentence Combining Practice*, pp. 1–35

Close

Write the following sentence on the board, and ask students what kinds of errors they find:

Like a first taste of spring the air smelled sweet as well as, fiercly green.

Errors include a missing comma (*spring the*), an unnecessary comma (*as,*), a misspelling (*fiercly*).

Corrected version: *Like a first taste of spring, the air smelled sweet as well as fiercely green.*

Directions Combine each cluster of numbered items into one or more sentences. Combine clusters if you wish.

1.1 The car lay rusting.
1.2 The car lay abandoned.
1.3 It was at the bottom of a ravine.
1.4 It was near the stream's edge.

2.1 Scabs of paint had lifted off.
2.2 The scabs were black.
2.3 The paint was oxidized.
2.4 This revealed blotches of primer.
2.5 The primer was gray.

3.1 The driver's door hung open.
3.2 It was permanently ajar.
3.3 Bullet holes ventilated the windows.

4.1 Inside was a single shoe.
4.2 It was under the dashboard.
4.3 Its leather was cracked.
4.4 Its leather was twisted.
4.5 Inside was a *Life* magazine.
4.6 It was from 1948.

5.1 Springs pushed through seats.
5.2 The springs were coiled.
5.3 The seatcovers were worn.
5.4 The seatcovers were fabric.

6.1 The car smelled dead.
6.2 It was now home to mice.
6.3 It was now home to birds.
6.4 It was now home to seasons.
6.5 The seasons changed.

7.1 Once its fenders had been stroked.
7.2 Once its interior had been caressed.
7.3 That day was long gone.

Extension What thoughts does the old car prompt about forgotten lives—or about recycling? Share the text you create with a writing partner.

> ### Vocabulary Tip
>
> As you begin to combine sentences in each cluster, reread your sentence from the cluster before. How does the language in that sentence relate to the new cluster?

Exercise A: Solo

Directions Combine each cluster of numbered items into one or more sentences. Combine clusters if you wish.

1.1 The mood was festive.
1.2 The mood was energetic.
1.3 The mood was focused on homecoming weekend.
1.4 This was felt especially on the dance floor.

2.1 A jazz band had played for two hours.
2.2 The playing was inspired.
2.3 The audience was chanting for more.
2.4 The audience was appreciative.

3.1 The soloist stepped into the lights.
3.2 He mouthed his thanks to the audience.
3.3 He laced his fingers around his trumpet.
3.4 His fingers were long.
3.5 The trumpet was gleaming.

4.1 The applause grew louder.
4.2 The applause grew more enthusiastic.
4.3 He raised the trumpet.
4.4 He grinned at the flashbulbs.
4.5 The flashbulbs were exploding.

5.1 Faces below him shone expectantly.
5.2 The faces were radiant.
5.3 He nodded a cue to the drummer.
5.4 The cue was decisive.
5.5 The drummer was nearby.

6.1 Sound swirled through the room.
6.2 The notes of the solo were crisp and clear.
6.3 The solo was intricate.
6.4 The drum and bass provided a beat.
6.5 The beat was steady and insistent.

7.1 Each player in turn picked up the tune.
7.2 The players were talented.

Extension Narrate what happens next in the "Solo" scenario. Link this narrative to the accompanying "Good Vibrations" exercise.

Grammar Tip

In cluster 3, try using one or two participial phrases (beginning with *stepping, mouthing,* or *lacing*) as modifiers for the base sentence. For more on participial phrases, see page 527.

Focus

Lesson Overview

Objective
• To give students practice in combining short, kernel sentences into longer narrative sentences

Skills
• using proper punctuation; synthesizing ideas

Critical Thinking
• analyzing; evaluating; decision making

Listening and Speaking
• discussing

Practice and Assess

Answers: Exercise A

Answers will vary, but some suggestions follow.

1. For homecoming weekend, the mood was festive and energetic, especially on the dance floor.
2. Although a jazz band had played with inspiration for two hours, the appreciative audience was chanting for more.
3. The soloist stepped into the lights, mouthing thanks to the audience and lacing his long fingers around his gleaming trumpet.
4. As the applause grew louder and more enthusiastic, he raised his trumpet and grinned at the exploding flashbulbs.
5. Radiant faces below him shone expectantly as he nodded a decisive cue to the nearby drummer.
6. The clear, crisp notes of the intricate solo swirled through the room to the steady, insistent beat of the drum and bass.
7. Each of the talented players in turn picked up the tune.

Resource Manager

Planning Resources
• *Lesson Plans*

☞ Other Print Resources
• *Sentence-Combining Practice,* pp. 1–35

Practice and Assess

Answers: Exercise B

Answers will vary, but some suggestions follow.

1. As the music surged and vibrated through the room, it drew in the listeners.
2. Students shuffled their feet in rhythmic patterns on the dusty wax.
3. The bodies of students tapping and swaying to the sound made moving shadows on the walls.

4–5. The boys' tight-lipped faces betrayed concentration as their heads bobbed and dipped while their arms hung loose; but the girls danced with practiced ease, whirling and turning to the irresistible music.

6. On stage the trumpeter closed his eyes and threw himself into the song's windup—a final, triumphant chorus.
7. The musicians took their bows and beamed exultantly at the dancers, who cheered and clapped in unison.

Sentence Combining

Exercise B: Good Vibrations

Directions Combine each cluster of numbered items into one or more sentences. Combine clusters if you wish.

1.1 Music surged through the room.
1.2 Music vibrated through the room.
1.3 It drew in the listeners.

2.1 Students moved their feet in patterns.
2.2 The patterns were rhythmic.
2.3 Students shuffled on the wax.
2.4 The wax was dusty.

3.1 Students tapped to the sound.
3.2 Students swayed with the sound.
3.3 Their bodies made shadows on the walls.
3.4 The shadows were moving.

4.1 The boys betrayed concentration.
4.2 Their faces were tight-lipped.
4.3 Their heads bobbed.
4.4 Their heads dipped.
4.5 Their arms hung loose.

5.1 The girls danced with ease.
5.2 Their ease was practiced.
5.3 They whirled with the music.
5.4 They turned with the music.
5.5 The music was irresistible.

6.1 On stage the trumpeter closed his eyes.
6.2 He threw himself into the song's windup.
6.3 The windup was a final chorus.
6.4 The chorus was triumphant.

7.1 The musicians took their bows.
7.2 The musicians were exultant.
7.3 The musicians beamed at the dancers.
7.4 The dancers cheered in unison.
7.5 The dancers clapped in unison.

Extension What next? Narrate an effective ending for "Solo" and "Good Vibrations." Share your text with a writing partner.

Grammar Tip

In cluster 6 try an appositive—a phrase that describes the song's windup. For more on appositives, see page 525.

Directions Combine each cluster of numbered items into one or more sentences. Combine clusters if you wish.

1.1 Mona reached for the travel alarm clock.
1.2 The travel alarm was palm-sized.
1.3 It was beside her bed.
1.4 She squinted at the numbers.

2.1 A crow screamed on the window sill.
2.2 Its screaming was brazen.
2.3 It welcomed the day's first light.
2.4 The light was a thin skin of gray.
2.5 The skin was on the landscape.

3.1 Each morning the crow did not stay long.
3.2 It stayed only for a few moments.
3.3 The moments were raucous.

4.1 It delivered its message.
4.2 It began a fixed routine.
4.3 It first bounced between the pines.
4.4 It floated to the lawn.
4.5 The lawn was dewy.
4.6 It then fussed over the dumpster.
4.7 The dumpster was next door.

5.1 Its work was finished.
5.2 The crow always spread its feathers.
5.3 The feathers were glossy.
5.4 The feathers were black.
5.5 It always headed east.

6.1 She watched its ritual once again.
6.2 She knew it was time for her work.
6.3 Her work was a run toward town.
6.4 The run was through quiet streets.

7.1 Mona had heard the crow call her name.
7.2 She now needed to get started.

Extension Narrate Mona's getting out of bed in clear, precise detail. Use your narration to link "The Crow" to "Training Run."

Vocabulary Tip

Notice the strong, specific nouns, verbs, and adjectives in each cluster. Do your combined sentences make good use of these words? For more information on strong nouns, verbs, and adjectives, see pages 439, 453, and 460.

Practice and Assess

Answers: Exercise C

Answers will vary, but some suggestions follow.

1. Mona reached for the palm-sized travel alarm beside her bed and squinted at the numbers.
2. A crow screamed brazenly on the window sill, welcoming the day's first light, a thin skin of gray on the landscape.
3. Each morning the crow stayed only for a few raucous moments.
4. It delivered its message and began a fixed routine: first it bounced between the pines and floated to the dewy lawn; then it fussed over the dumpster next door.
5. Its work finished, the crow always spread its glossy black feathers and headed east.
6. She watched its ritual once again and knew it was time for her work—a run toward town through quiet streets.
7. Having heard the crow call her name, Mona now needed to get started.

Practice and Assess

Answers: Exercise D

Answers will vary, but some suggestions follow.

1. The air was cool and still outside; there was no hint of breeze.
2. After bending down to tighten her shoelaces, Mona began her leg stretches, taking time to loosen her calves and thighs, working out any kinks.
3. Then she set off on her usual course—at first an easy jog through the damp grass. She let her body set its own pace.
4. Patches of creamy light filled the sky. She picked up the pace and settled into a loping rhythm.
5. Sweat blossomed on her arms and forehead as her lungs gulped for oxygen.
6. Turning off her usual course and cutting through the town cemetery, she bounded down a crunchy gravel path past faceless stone markers.
7. As Mona finally slowed to a walk, she listened to inner whispers and felt herself being drawn east.

Additional Resources

📁 *Sentence Combining Practice*, pp. 1–35

Close

Write this sentence on the board and ask students to find the errors.

After delivering it's message, it began a fixed routine, first it bounced between the pines and floated to the dewy lawn, then it fussed over the dumpster next door.

Errors: misspelling (*it's*);comma splices (*routine, first; lawn, then*).

Corrected version: *After delivering its message, it began a fixed routine: First it bounced between the pines and floated to the dewy lawn; then it fussed over the dumpster next door.*

Sentence Combining

Directions   Combine each cluster of numbered items into one or more sentences. Combine clusters if you wish.

1.1 Outside the air was cool.
1.2 It was still.
1.3 There was no hint of breeze.

2.1 Mona bent down.
2.2 She tightened her shoelaces.
2.3 She began her leg stretches.
2.4 She took time to loosen her calves.
2.5 She took time to loosen her thighs.
2.6 She took time to work out all the kinks.

3.1 Then she set off on her usual course.
3.2 She jogged easily at first.
3.3 She jogged through the damp grass.
3.4 She let her body set its own pace.

4.1 Patches of light filled the sky.
4.2 The light was creamy.
4.3 She picked up the pace.
4.4 She settled into a rhythm.
4.5 The rhythm was loping.

5.1 Sweat blossomed on her forehead.
5.2 Sweat blossomed on her arms.
5.3 Her lungs gulped for oxygen.

6.1 She turned off her usual course.
6.2 She cut through the town cemetery.
6.3 She bounded down a gravel path.
6.4 The gravel was crunchy.
6.5 She bounded past stone markers.
6.6 The markers were faceless.

7.1 Finally Mona slowed to a walk.
7.2 She listened to inner whispers
7.3 She felt herself being drawn east.

Extension   To complete the story, narrate what happens next. Share your text—"The Crow" plus "Training Run"—with a writing partner.

> ### Grammar Tip
>
> To open cluster 6 with participial phrases, use *turning* and *cutting* as key words. For more on participial phrases, see page 527.

Exposition

Exercise A: Car Culture

Directions   Combine each cluster of numbered items into one or more sentences. Combine clusters if you wish.

1.1 Cars serve practical ends.
1.2 They get us from place to place.
1.3 They also serve as objects of ornament.
1.4 They are much like clothing.

2.1 Cars make statements.
2.2 The statements are about who we are.
2.3 The statements are about what we value.
2.4 They create a "public identity."

3.1 A sports car projects a lifestyle.
3.2 The lifestyle is carefree.
3.3 The lifestyle is romantic.
3.4 A station wagon projects an image.
3.5 The image is family-oriented.

4.1 An economy runabout suggests thrift.
4.2 An economy runabout suggests efficiency.
4.3 It zips nervously through traffic.
4.4 A luxury sedan makes a different statement.
4.5 It guzzles gas.
4.6 It wallows toward its destination.

5.1 Such images shape our thinking.
5.2 They are reinforced by advertising.
5.3 The advertising is relentless.
5.4 They influence how we see others.
5.5 They influence how we see ourselves.

6.1 We may make snap judgments about people.
6.2 The judgments are based on their automobiles.
6.3 We may choose a car to satisfy our fantasies.
6.4 We may choose a car to impress others.

7.1 Judging books by their covers is dangerous.
7.2 So is judging drivers by their cars.

Extension   Write about a personality that *differs* from his or her car (see cluster 7). Relate your text to "Car Culture."

Grammar Tip

In clusters 1, 3, and 4, try several connectors—*but, yet, however, while, although*—before settling on one. For information on the correct punctuation, see pages 740 and 743–747.

Focus

Lesson Overview

Objective

• To give students practice in combining short, kernel sentences into longer expository sentences

Skills

• synthesizing ideas; using correct punctuation

Critical Thinking

• analyzing; evaluating; decision making

Listening and Speaking

• discussing

Practice and Assess

Answers: Exercise A

Answers will vary, but some suggestions follow.

1. Cars serve practical ends by getting us from place to place, but they also serve as objects of ornament, much like clothing.
2. Because cars make statements about who we are and what we value, they create a "public identity."
3. A sports car projects a carefree, romantic lifestyle, whereas a station wagon projects a family-oriented image.
4. An economy runabout suggests thrift and efficiency as it zips nervously through traffic; a gas-guzzling luxury sedan makes a different statement, however, as it wallows toward its destination.
5. Such images—reinforced relentlessly by advertising—shape our thinking and influence how we see ourselves and others.
6. We may make snap judgments about people based on their automobiles, and we may choose a car to impress others or to satisfy our fantasies.
7. Just as judging books by their covers is dangerous, so is judging drivers by their cars.

Resource Manager

Planning Resources
• *Lesson Plans*

📂 Other Print Resources
• *Sentence-Combining Practice,* pp. 1–35

Practice and Assess

Answers: Exercise B

Answers will vary, but some suggestions follow.

1. In contrast to early car buyers, who had one choice of color ("basic black"), today's consumer has many color options.

2. Psychologists contend that car colors can reveal basic personality traits and express "hidden selves."

3. Red, a fire color, appeals to attention-seekers, who may be impulsive or aggressive.

4. Cautious, analytical people often choose brown, whereas active types, who may have an artistic bent, often like yellow.

5. Blue, which is linked with steadiness and consistency, appeals to many introverts—and to some extroverts as well.

6. Safety-conscious drivers who are critical and compulsively neat often choose white.

7–8. Green typically appeals to romantics and intellectuals while black—a "power color"— appeals to sophisticates who are self-confident and wish to be taken seriously.

Sentence Combining

Directions Combine each cluster of numbered items into one or more sentences. Combine clusters if you wish.

1.1 Early car buyers had one choice of color.
1.2 The color was "basic black."
1.3 Today's consumer has many color options.

2.1 Psychologists contend something.
2.2 Car colors can reveal personality traits.
2.3 These traits are basic.
2.4 Car colors can express "hidden selves."

3.1 Red appeals to attention seekers.
3.2 Red is a fiery color.
3.3 They may be impulsive.
3.4 They may be aggressive.

4.1 Cautious people often choose brown.
4.2 The people are analytical.
4.3 Active types often like yellow.
4.4 These types may have an artistic bent.

5.1 Blue is associated with steadiness.
5.2 Blue is associated with consistency.
5.3 It appeals to many introverts.
5.4 It appeals to some extroverts.

6.1 Drivers often choose white.
6.2 The drivers may be critical.
6.3 The drivers may be compulsively neat.
6.4 The drivers may be safety conscious.

7.1 Green typically appeals to romantics.
7.2 Green typically appeals to intellectuals.

8.1 And black is a "power color."
8.2 It appeals to sophisticates.
8.3 The sophisticates are self-confident.
8.4 They wish to be taken seriously.

Extension Based on what you know about cars and colors, write about the kind of car—and color—that you might choose for yourself. Relate what you write to "Car Colors."

Directions   Combine each cluster of numbered items into one or more sentences. Combine clusters if you wish.

1.1 Many of us have heard of cholesterol.
1.2 Its dangers have been widely publicized.
1.3 Few of us know much about it.

2.1 Cholesterol is found in the bloodstream.
2.2 Cholesterol is found in all body tissues.
2.3 It is a fatlike substance.
2.4 It is white and waxy.

3.1 It is used in the outer membrane of cells.
3.2 It is used as a sheath around nerve fibers.
3.3 It is used as a building block for hormones.
3.4 It is clearly essential to life.

4.1 Our bodies convert fats into cholesterol.
4.2 Our bodies convert proteins into cholesterol.
4.3 Our bodies convert carbohydrates into cholesterol.
4.4 Our bodies also ingest it directly from various foods.

5.1 The body manufactures its own cholesterol.
5.2 We don't have to consume it to stay healthy.

6.1 Confusion surrounds cholesterol.
6.2 There are two types of the substance.
6.3 One type is called HDL.
6.4 The other type is called LDL.

7.1 HDL is "helpful" cholesterol.
7.2 LDL is "harmful" cholesterol.

8.1 HDL takes cholesterol back to the liver.
8.2 The cholesterol is in the bloodstream.
8.3 The liver reprocesses or excretes the substance.

9.1 But LDL circulates cholesterol through the body.
9.2 It accumulates on arterial walls.

Extension   Develop a character sketch or dramatic incident to introduce "Cholesterol Facts" and "More Cholesterol Facts."

8.3

Sentence Combining

Practice and Assess

Answers: Exercise C

Answers will vary, but some suggestions follow.

1. Because its dangers have been widely publicized, many of us have heard of cholesterol, but few of us know much about it.
2. Cholesterol, a white and waxy fat-like substance, is found in the bloodstream and in all body tissues.
3. Used in the outer membrane of cells, as a sheath around nerve fibers, and as a building block for hormones, it is clearly essential to life.
4. Our bodies convert fats, proteins, and carbohydrates into cholesterol and also ingest it directly from various foods.
5. Because the body manufactures its own cholesterol, we don't have to consume it to stay healthy.
6–7. Confusion surrounds the two types of cholesterol: HDL ("helpful" cholesterol) and LDL ("harmful" cholesterol).
8–9. HDL takes cholesterol in the bloodstream back to the liver, which reprocesses or excretes the substance, but LDL circulates cholesterol through the body, where it accumulates on arterial walls.

Practice and Assess

Answers: Exercise D

Answers will vary, but some suggestions follow.

1. Many Americans know that cholesterol is found primarily in meat and dairy products.
2. Plant foods, including vegetables, fruits, grains, and nuts, contain no harmful cholesterol.
3. One can decrease cholesterol intake by eating more plant foods and by cutting back on animal products, including meats and poultry, dairy goods, and eggs.
4. Because fat stimulates one's cholesterol production, one must also eat less saturated fat, which is found in both types of foods.
5. Beef, some pork, poultry skin, and whole milk are high in saturated fat, as are coconut oil and palm oil.
6. Finns and Americans have diets that are rich in saturated fat, and both groups have very high cholesterol levels; consequently, they are world leaders in heart disease.
7. The Japanese have diets that are extremely low in saturated fat, and they have the world's lowest levels of cholesterol and heart disease.

Additional Resources

Sentence Combining Practice, pp. 1–35

Close

Write the following passages on the board, and ask students what kind of errors they find:

The body which manufactures it's own cholesterol. We dont have to consume it to stay healthy.

Errors include a sentence fragment, a misspelling (*it's*), and a missing apostrophe (*dont*).

Corrected version: *The body manufactures its own cholesterol, so we don't have to consume it to stay healthy.*

Sentence Combining

Vocabulary Tip

In clusters 4, 5, and 6, try causal connectors such as *because, since, therefore, consequently,* and *so.* For more information on punctuation with causal connectors, see pages 746 and 748.

Exercise D: More Cholesterol Facts

Directions Combine each cluster of numbered items into one or more sentences. Combine clusters if you wish.

1.1 Cholesterol is found primarily in meat.
1.2 Cholesterol is found primarily in dairy products.
1.3 Many Americans know this fact.

2.1 Plant foods contain no harmful cholesterol.
2.2 These foods include vegetables.
2.3 These foods include fruits.
2.4 These foods include grains.
2.5 These foods include nuts.

3.1 One can decrease cholesterol intake.
3.2 This is done by eating more plant foods.
3.3 This is done by cutting back on animal products.
3.4 Animal products include meats and poultry.
3.5 Animal products include dairy goods.
3.6 Animal products include eggs.

4.1 But one must also eat less saturated fat.
4.2 Fat is found in both plant and animal foods.
4.3 Fat stimulates one's cholesterol production.

5.1 Beef is high in saturated fat.
5.2 Some pork is high in saturated fat.
5.3 Poultry skin is high in saturated fat.
5.4 Whole milk is high in saturated fat.
5.5 So is coconut oil.
5.6 So is palm oil.

6.1 Finns and Americans have diets.
6.2 The diets are rich in saturated fat.
6.3 Both groups have very high cholesterol levels.
6.4 This makes them world leaders in heart disease.

7.1 The Japanese have the world's lowest level of cholesterol.
7.2 The Japanese have the world's lowest level of heart disease.
7.3 Their diets are extremely low in saturated fat.

Extension Write a concluding paragraph for "Cholesterol Facts" and "More Cholesterol Facts." Then share your text with a writing partner.

Persuasion

Exercise A: Success Story

Directions   Combine each cluster of numbered items into one or more sentences. Combine clusters if you wish.

1.1 A bald eagle spreads its wing.
1.2 The eagle is white maned.
1.3 Its wings are enormous.
1.4 It soars on the morning wind.

2.1 This predator faced extinction in 1963.
2.2 This predator is magnificent.
2.3 It is America's national bird.
2.4 Only four hundred pairs of eagles remained in 1963.
2.5 The eagles were in the lower forty-eight states.

3.1 America had been home to thousands of bald eagles.
3.2 They were decimated by loss of habitat.
3.3 They were decimated by illegal hunting.
3.4 They were decimated by the use of DDT.

4.1 Eagles were at the top of the food chain.
4.2 They were especially vulnerable to DDT.
4.3 DDT affected their ability to reproduce.

5.1 The ban on DDT gave eagles a chance.
5.2 Breeding programs gave eagles a chance.
5.3 Strict law enforcement gave eagles a chance.
5.4 Their numbers slowly began to build.

6.1 By the mid 1990s, the number of nesting pairs had increased.
6.2 There were about 4,500 in the lower forty-eight states.
6.3 The bald eagle's status was upgraded to threatened.
6.4 It was hoped that by 2000 the bald eagle could be removed from the threatened list.

7.1 Some people feared that removing the bird from the list would expose it to new harms.
7.2 Government acts continue to protect the species.
7.3 The Migratory Bird Treaty Act is one such act.
7.4 The Bald and Golden Eagle Protection Act is another.

Extension   What does the eagle's success story suggest about the spirit of the country it symbolizes? Develop a follow-up paragraph.

8.4 Persuasion   **377**

Grammar Tip

To experiment with subordinate clauses, try using *because* as a connector in cluster 4 and *although* as a connector in cluster 6. For more on subordinate clauses, see page 544.

Sentence Combining

Focus

Lesson Overview

Objective
• To give students practice in combining short, kernel sentences into longer sentences

Skills
• synthesizing ideas; using correct punctuation

Critical Thinking
• analyzing; evaluating; decision making

Listening and Speaking
• discussing

Practice and Assess

Answers: Exercise A
Answers will vary, but some suggestions follow.

1. A white-maned bald eagle spreads its enormous wings, soars on the morning wind, and scans the terrain below.
2. This magnificent predator, which is America's national bird, faced extinction in 1963, when only four hundred pairs of eagles remained in the lower forty-eight states.
3. America had been home to thousands of bald eagles before they were decimated by loss of habitat, illegal hunting, and the use of DDT and other poisons.
4. Because eagles were at the top of the food chain, they were especially vulnerable to DDT, which affected their ability to reproduce.
5. Strict law enforcement, breeding programs, and the ban on DDT gave eagles a chance; their numbers slowly began to build.
6. By the mid 1990s, when the number of nesting pairs had increased to about 4,500 in the lower forty-eight states, the bald eagle's status was upgraded to threatened, and it was hoped that by 2000 the bald eagle could be removed from the threatened list.
7. Some people feared that removing the bird from the list would expose it to new harms, but government acts—such as the Migratory Bird Treaty Act and the

Bald and Golden Eagle Protection Act—continue to protect the species.

Resource Manager

Planning Resources
• *Lesson Plans*

📂 Other Print Resources
• *Sentence-Combining Practice,* pp. 1–35

Practice and Assess

Answers: Exercise B

Answers will vary, but some suggestions follow.

1. Predators are part of the ecosystem on public rangelands, where western ranchers graze their sheep.

2–3. Ranchers lose about 500,000 sheep (5 percent of their flocks) annually to coyotes, wild dogs, and eagles (which feed mainly on fish, small game, and spring lamb).

4. Frustrated by predator attacks and angered by economic losses, some ranchers have fought back by injecting carcasses with illegal poisons.

5. Their targets have mainly been coyotes and dog packs, but they have also killed hundreds of eagles that have ingested the toxic meat.

6. At issue are questions of land use and public policy because ranchers pay for grazing rights and contribute much to local economies.

7. A final point must be underscored: although bald eagles are protected by law, there are serious threats to their safety.

Sentence Combining

Directions Combine each cluster of numbered items into one or more sentences. Combine clusters if you wish.

1.1 Predators are part of the ecosystem.
1.2 The ecosystem is on public rangelands.
1.3 Western ranchers graze their sheep there.

2.1 Ranchers lose about 500,000 sheep annually.
2.2 This is about 5 percent of their flocks.
2.3 The loss is to coyotes.
2.4 The loss is to wild dogs.
2.5 The loss is to other predators.

3.1 These predators include eagles.
3.2 The eagles feed mainly on fish.
3.3 The eagles feed mainly on small game.
3.4 The eagles also dine on spring lamb.

4.1 Some ranchers have fought back.
4.2 They are frustrated by predator attacks.
4.3 They are angered by economic losses.
4.4 They have injected carcasses with poisons.
4.5 The poisons are illegal.

5.1 Their targets have mainly been coyotes.
5.2 Their targets have mainly been dog packs.
5.3 They have also killed hundreds of eagles.
5.4 The eagles have eaten the meat.
5.5 The meat is toxic.

6.1 At issue are questions of land use.
6.2 At issue are questions of public policy.
6.3 Ranchers pay fees for grazing rights.
6.4 Ranchers contribute much to local economies.

7.1 A final point must be underscored.
7.2 Bald eagles are protected by law.
7.3 There are threats to their safety.
7.4 The threats are serious.

Extension Should taxpayers support the losses of ranchers to keep them from resorting to extreme measures? Develop a follow-up paragraph that presents your point of view.

Exercise C: Ozone Problem

Directions Combine each cluster of numbered items into one or more sentences. Combine clusters if you wish.

1.1 We have too much ozone at ground level.
1.2 We have too little ozone in the stratosphere.
1.3 The stratosphere is ten to twenty-five miles above us.

2.1 Both types of ozone are chemically alike.
2.2 One is a dangerous component of smog.
2.3 Smog results from burning fossil fuels.
2.4 The other serves as a natural screen.
2.5 It protects us from the sun's radiation.

3.1 Something is unfortunate.
3.2 The ozone in smog cannot reach the stratosphere.
3.3 It might do some good there.
3.4 It might reduce the greenhouse effect.

4.1 The ozone screen is destroyed by compounds.
4.2 The ozone screen is in the upper atomsphere.
4.3 The compounds are synthetic.
4.4 The compounds are called chlorofluorocarbons (CFCs).

5.1 CFCs have a wide range of industrial uses.
5.2 They serve as coolants for refrigerators.
5.3 They serve as coolants for air conditioners.
5.4 They serve as foaming agents for food packages.
5.5 They serve as foaming agents for mattresses.
5.6 They serve as solvents in microchip production.

6.1 CFCs are released during product use.
6.2 CFCs eventually rise into the stratosphere.
6.3 Radiation breaks them down, releasing chlorine.
6.4 Chlorine has an effect on ozone.
6.5 The effect is devastating.

7.1 CFCs take decades to reach the stratosphere.
7.2 We do not know the full extent of their damage.
7.3 The damage is continuous.

Extension Write a paragraph that introduces "Ozone Problem" by focusing on the problem in an everyday situation.

Vocabulary Tip

To create an adverb in cluster 3, add *-ly* to *unfortunate*. For sentence variety, try opening cluster 6 with *released*.

Practice and Assess

Answers: Exercise C

Answers will vary, but some suggestions follow.

1. We have too much ozone at ground level and too little ozone in the stratosphere, which is ten to twenty-five miles above us.
2. Although both types of ozone are chemically alike, one is a dangerous component of smog, which results from burning fossil fuels, and the other serves as a natural screen that protects us from the sun's radiation.
3. Unfortunately, the ozone in smog cannot reach the stratosphere, where it might do some good by reducing the greenhouse effect.
4. In the upper atmosphere, the ozone screen is destroyed by synthetic compounds called chlorofluorocarbons (CFCs).
5. CFCs have a wide range of industrial uses: they serve as coolants for refrigerators and air conditioners, foaming agents for food packages and mattresses, and solvents in microchip production.
6. Released by human beings, CFCs eventually rise into the stratosphere, where radiation breaks them down, releasing chlorine, which has a devastating effect on ozone.
7. CFCs take decades to reach the stratosphere; consequently, we do not know the full extent of their damage, which is continuous.

Practice and Assess

Answers: Exercise D

Answers will vary, but some suggestions follow.

1. In the ozone layer over Antarctica and the Arctic, NASA has found ominously vast holes.

2. Scientists have predicted that increased radiation will lead to more melanoma, an especially deadly skin cancer, and that it may also damage crops on earth, including plankton in the oceans.

3. Because ozone depletion is a worldwide problem, its solution depends on international cooperation and consumer awareness.

4. Governments must agree to timetables that phase out CFC production, and American consumers must curtail CFC use.

5. Since automobile air conditioners cause most of our CFC emissions, one should deal with service stations that are equipped to recycle CFCs.

6. One should avoid food-packaging products made from plastic foam, such as are often found in fast-food restaurants.

7–8. One should check labels on aerosol cans to ensure the cans are environmentally safe, and one should also choose an energy-efficient refrigerator, which will release fewer CFCs into the atmosphere when it eventually wears out and is discarded.

Independent Practice

Sentence-Combining Practice, pp. 1–35

Close

Write the following sentence on the board, and ask students what kinds of errors they find:

When CFCs are released by human beings, they rise into the stratosphere eventually, radiation breaks them down into chlorine; which has a devastating affect on ozone.

Errors include a comma splice (*eventually, radiation*), incorrect punctuation (*chlorine;*), and a misspelling (*affect*).

Corrected version: *When CFCs are released by human beings, they rise into the stratosphere eventually, and radiation breaks them down into chlorine, which has a devastating effect on ozone.*

Sentence Combining

Directions Combine each cluster of numbered items into one or more sentences. Combine clusters if you wish.

1.1 NASA has found holes in the ozone layer.
1.2 The holes are ominously vast.
1.3 The holes are over Antarctica and the Arctic.

2.1 Scientists have predicted something.
2.2 Increased radiation will lead to more melanoma.
2.3 Melanoma is an especially deadly skin cancer.
2.4 The radiation may also damage crops on earth.
2.5 This damage includes plankton in the oceans.

3.1 Ozone depletion is a worldwide problem.
3.2 Its solution depends on cooperation.
3.3 The cooperation must be international.
3.4 Its solution depends on consumer awareness.

4.1 Governments must agree to timetables.
4.2 The timetables phase out CFC production.
4.3 American consumers must curtail CFC use.

5.1 Air conditioners cause most of our CFC emissions.
5.2 The air conditioners are in automobiles.
5.3 One should go to service stations.
5.4 The stations are equipped to recycle CFCs.

6.1 One should avoid food-packaging products.
6.2 The products are made from plastic foam.
6.3 They are often found in fast-food restaurants.

7.1 One should check labels on aerosol cans.
7.2 This is to ensure that the cans are environmentally safe.

8.1 One should also choose a refrigerator.
8.2 The refrigerator should be energy efficient.
8.3 It will release fewer CFCs into the atmosphere.
8.4 It eventually wears out and is discarded.

Extension Link "Ozone Problem" and "Ozone Solutions" and write a conclusion. Then share your text with a writing partner.

Literature Exercises

Exercise A

Directions   Scan the sentences below, which are adapted from *Blue Highways* by William Least Heat-Moon. Decide which of the numbered sentences belong together, and combine them in your own way. Then compare your sentences with the originals on pages 34–35.

1. It was nearly May.
2. The rain popped.
3. It then stopped.
4. It popped.
5. It stopped.
6. The incline became steeper.
7. Light rain fell steadily.
8. It rolled red dust off the roof.
9. The dust was from the desert.
10. I hadn't hit showers since east Texas.
11. It was good.
12. The pleasant cool turned to cold.
13. I switched on the heater.
14. The headlights glared off the snowbanks.
15. The snowbanks were edging closer to the highway.
16. The highway climbed.
17. The rain became sleet.
18. That's when I began thinking something.
19. I might have made a little miscalculation.
20. I looked for a place to turn around.
21. There was only narrow road.
22. The road was twisted.
23. The sleet got heavier.
24. The headlights were cutting only thirty feet into it.
25. Maybe I could drive above and out of the storm.
26. The wind came up at eight thousand feet.
27. It was rough.
28. It was nasty.
29. It bullied me about the road.

> **Grammar Tip**
>
> Read quickly through all sentences to get a sense of the entire piece before you begin combining.

Focus

Lesson Overview

Objective
- To figure out which ideas belong together
- To combine unclustered sentences into a fluent piece of writing

Skills
- comparing one piece of writing to another similar piece; decision making

Critical Thinking
- using creative thinking; synthesizing; restructuring

Listening and Speaking
- discussing

Practice and Assess

Answers: Exercise A

Answers will vary from the original on pages 34–35, but a suggestion is given below.

It was nearly May, and light rain fell steadily. I hadn't hit showers since east Texas, so it felt good. Rain plopped and rolled red desert dust off the roof. The highway climbed, and the pleasant cool turned to cold. I switched on the heater and noticed that the rain was now sleet. As the incline became steeper, the sleet got heavier; the headlights cut only thirty feet into it. Maybe I could drive above and out of the storm. The wind came up at eight thousand feet, and it bullied me about the twisting road. That's when I began thinking maybe I made a little miscalculation. I looked for a for a place to turn around, but there was only narrow road.

Resource Manager

Planning Resources
- *Lesson Plans*

📂 Other Print Resources
- *Sentence-Combining Practice,* pp. 1–35

Practice and Assess

Answers: Exercise B

Answers will vary from the original on page 105, but a suggestion is given below.

Goose-pimples the size of lemons seemed to pop all over me. My cumulative notebooks were in my knapsack. The first of them described my hearing about the African "*Kin–tay*" in my boyhood. "*Kin–tay*" always said he was kidnapped near his village as he was chopping wood to make a drum.

I showed the interpreter, and he showed and told the *griot*. The *griot* then excitedly told the people, and they grew very agitated. They then formed a human ring, encircling me, dancing and chanting. Perhaps a dozen of the women rushed in toward me carrying their infant babies and thrusting the infants into my arms. I later learned that this conveyed "the laying on of hands. This flesh is part of us. We are you; you are us."

Directions Scan the sentences below. Some are from *My Furthest-Back Person: The African,* by Alex Haley. The numbered sentences are adapted from Haley's original. Decide which of the numbered sentences belong together, and combine them in your own way. Then compare your sentences with the originals on page 105.

About the time the king's soldiers came, the eldest of these four sons, Kunta, when he had about 16 rains, went away from this village to chop wood to make a drum . . . and he was never seen again . . .

1. Goose-pimples seemed to pop all over me.
2. They were the size of lemons.
3. My cumulative notebooks were in my knapsack.
4. The first of them included something.
5. In my boyhood my Grandma told of the African "*Kin-tay.*"
6. In my boyhood Cousin Georgia told of the African "*Kin-tay.*"
7. In my boyhood others told of the African "*Kin-tay.*"
8. Kin-tay always said he was kidnapped near his village.
9. He was chopping wood to make a drum.
10. I showed the interpreter.
11. He showed and told the *griot.*
12. The *griot* excitedly told the people.
13. They grew very agitated.
14. They then formed a human ring.
15. This happened abruptly.
16. They were encircling me.
17. They were dancing.
18. They were chanting.
19. Perhaps a dozen of the women rushed in toward me.
20. They were carrying their infant babies.
21. They thrust the infants into my arms.
22. I later learned something.
23. This conveyed "the laying on of hands."
24. "This flesh is part of us."
25. "We are you."
26. "You are us."

The men hurried me into their mosque, their Arabic praying later being translated outside: "Thanks be to Allah for returning the long lost from among us."

Directions   Scan the sentences below. One comes directly from *The Solace of Open Spaces*, by Gretel Ehrlich. The numbered sentences are adapted from Ehrlich's originals. Decide which numbered sentences belong together, and combine them in your own way. Then compare your sentences with the originals on page 160.

1. Conversation goes on.
2. It sounds like a code.
3. The code is private.
4. A few phrases imply a complex of meanings.
5. You ask directions.
6. You get a list of details.
7. The list is curious.
8. I was trailing sheep.
9. I was told something.
10. "Ride up to that kinda upturned rock."
11. "Follow the pink wash."
12. "Turn left at the dump."
13. "Then you'll see the water hole."

> One friend told his wife on roundup to "turn at the salt lick and the dead cow," which turned out to be a scattering of bones and no salt lick at all.

14. Sentence structure is shortened.
15. It expresses the skin and bones of a thought.
16. Descriptive words are dropped.
17. Even verbs are dropped.
18. A cowboy will say something to a wrangler.
19. The cowboy is looking over a corral.
20. The corral is full of horses.
21. "Which one needs rode?"
22. People hold back their thoughts.
23. It seems to be a dumbfounded silence.
24. Then they erupt with a remark.
25. The remark is perceptive.
26. The remark is excoriating.
27. Language is compressed.
28. It becomes metaphorical.
29. A rancher ended a relationship with one remark.
30. "You're a bad check."
31. This meant that bouncing in and out was intolerable.
32. This meant that even coming back would be no good.

Sentence Combining

Practice and Assess

Answers: Exercise C

Answers will vary from the original on page 160, but a suggestion is given below.

The conversation goes on and sounds like a private code. A few phrases imply a complex of meanings. You ask directions and get a list of curious details. When trailing sheep once, I was told, "Ride up to that kinda upturned rock, follow the pink wash, turn left at the dump, then you'll see the water hole."

Sentence structure is shortened to express the skin and bones of a thought. Descriptive words and even verbs are dropped. A cowboy will say something to a wrangler looking over a corral full of horses: "Which one needs rode?" People hold back their thoughts, creating dumbfounded silence. Then they erupt with a perceptive, excoriating remark. Their language is compressed and becomes metaphorical. One rancher ended a relationship by saying "You're a bad check." This meant that bouncing in and out was intolerable and that even coming back would be no good.

Practice and Assess

Answers: Exercise D

Answers will vary from the original on page 269, but a suggestion is given below.

Each worker bee is covered with stiff hairs that catch the granules as the bee brushes against the flower's anthers. Since the anthers bear pollen, she is soon covered with pollen. She uses her two front pairs of legs to comb the sticky pollen from her body. Then she packs the pollen into baskets located on her rear pair of legs. Soon her legs become heavy with wads of pollen, which she unloads in her hive. House bees arrange the pollen granules into the honeycomb cells around the developing bee larvae, conveniently available to the nurse bees.

The eggs and larvae are there to see, but the oldest brood, with their stomachs full, have spun themselves cocoons. Sealed in their cells by a tough, velvety brown cover and hidden from human eyes, they pupate [develop] within the cocoons and emerge as adults. The entire semicircle of brood is bordered by a ring of pollen-filled cells. Honey surrounds the ring, and as the season progresses, nectar surrounds the ring.

Directions Scan the sentences below. One comes directly from *A Book of Bees*, by Sue Hubbell. The numbered sentences are adapted from Hubbell's original. Decide which numbered sentences belong together, and combine them in your own way. Then compare your sentences with the originals on page 269.

1. Each worker bee is covered with hairs.
2. The hairs are stiff.
3. These hairs catch the granules.
4. The bee brushes against the flower's anthers.
5. The anthers bear pollen.
6. She is soon covered with pollen.
7. She stops to use her two front pairs of legs.
8. She combs the pollen from her body.
9. The pollen is sticky.
10. She packs it into the baskets.
11. The baskets are on her rear pair of legs.
12. Her legs become heavy.
13. The heaviness is wads of pollen.
14. She returns to her hive to unload.
15. House bees arrange the pollen granules.
16. The arrangement is in the honeycomb cells.
17. The cells are around the bee larvae.
18. The larvae are developing.
19. The pollen is available to the nurse bees.
20. The availability is convenient.

> In the springtime, a typical frame of brood—as beekeepers call developing bees—contains a large central semicircle of cells containing eggs and larvae in various stages.

21. The eggs and larvae are there to see.
22. The oldest brood have spun themselves cocoons.
23. Their stomachs are full.
24. They pupate [develop] within the cocoons.
25. They are hidden from human eyes.
26. They are sealed in their cells by a covering.
27. The covering is tough and velvety brown.
28. They will emerge as adults from beneath it.
29. The entire semicircle of brood is bordered by a ring.
30. The ring is of cells filled with pollen.
31. The ring in turn is surrounded by honey.
32. It is surrounded by nectar as the season progresses.

Directions Scan the sentences below. One comes directly from "A Plague on Tennis," by Mark Mathabane. The numbered sentences are adapted from Mathabane's original. Decide which numbered sentences belong together, and combine them in your own way. Then compare your sentences with the originals by Mathabane on page 361.

1. I took up tennis in the early 1970s.
2. The sport was synonymous with wooden rackets.
3. The players all relied on wooden rackets.
4. I idolized the players.
5. I enjoyed watching them.
6. I sought to emulate them.
7. They included Arthur Ashe.
8. They included Stan Smith.
9. They included Rod Laver.
10. The rackets enabled them to carve out illustrious careers.
11. The rackets enabled them to win major championships.
12. The championships included Wimbledon.
13. The championships included the U.S. Open.
14. Their talent on the court was unmistakable.
15. Their finesse on the court was unmistakable.
16. They served and volleyed.
17. They hit groundstrokes flat.
18. They hit groundstrokes sliced.
19. They hit groundstrokes with topspin.
20. The occasion made its demands.
21. They played delicate touch strokes.
22. These included angled drop shots.
23. In sum, they possessed all-around games.
24. They were the closest thing to the "complete player."
25. They were a delight for spectators to watch.
26. The demise of wooden rackets changed all that.
27. The nature of tennis today is expressed in a single word.
28. The word is "power."

The new rackets can generate so much power in the hands of just about anyone that players of modest abilities are transformed into giant-killers on the court, capable on any given day, usually in the early rounds, of defeating the game's finest.

Practice and Assess

Answers: Exercise E

Answers will vary from the original on page 314, but a suggestion is given below.

I took up tennis in the early 1970s when the sport was synonymous with wooden rackets. Players I idolized, enjoyed watching, and sought to emulate—Arthur Ashe, Stan Smith, and Rod Laver—relied on wooden rackets, which enabled them to carve out illustrious careers and win major championships such as Wimbledon and the U.S. Open. Their talent and finesse on the court was unmistakable. They served, volleyed, and hit flat groundstrokes that sliced and had topspin. When the occasion demanded it, they played delicate touch strokes that included angled drop shots. In sum, they possessed all-around games— the closest thing to the "complete player." They were a delight for spectators to watch, but the demise of wooden rackets changed all that. The nature of tennis today is expressed in a single word: power.

Independent Practice

📁 *Sentence-Combining Practice,* pp. 1–35

Close

Encourage students to work in small groups to create the longest sentence they can. Have the groups share their sentences either orally or on the chalkboard and discuss each other's choices of wording.

✔ ASSESSMENT OPTIONS

📁 *Tests with Answer Key & Rubrics*
Unit 8 Mastery Test

💾 *Testmaker*
Unit 8 Mastery Test

You may wish to administer the Unit 8 Mastery Test at this point.

📼 *MindJogger Videoquizzes*

Troubleshooter

Just as a sea urchin can sting you and spoil a nice day at the beach, so can careless errors slip in and ruin your best attempts at writing. To avoid the sea urchin's stings, you have to be cautious and observant. To avoid careless errors—such as run-on sentences, sentence fragments, agreement problems, faulty punctuation—you need to know some basic strategies. This unit will help you avoid the sting of careless errors.

Interpret and Analyze Use the following questions for discussion:

- What effect does this warning sign on a Florida beach achieve by using an old-fashioned script to convey its message?
- Can you think of ways to make this sign more effective and dramatic?

Writing Prompt Create your own poem of advice about some activity you know about—a sport, a hobby, a particular task. Follow Al Young's example and experiment with language and punctuation to make your message more dramatic. Break some rules if that will help, but be ready to explain what effect you achieved by doing so.

386

Resource Manager

Planning Resources
- *Lesson Plans*
- *Block Scheduling*

 Transparencies
- *Bellringer*
- *Two-Minute Skill Drill*

Other Print Resources
- *Grammar and Composition Handbook*
- *Grammar Enrichment*
- *Grammar Practice*
- *Grammar Reteaching*

- *Grammar Workbook*
- *Sentence-Combining Practice*

Video
- *MindJogger Videoquizzes*

UNIT 9

Troubleshooter

*U*se Troubleshooter to help you correct common errors in your writing.

Lesson 9.1   **Sentence Fragment**   *388*

Lesson 9.2   **Run-on Sentence**   *390*

Lesson 9.3   **Lack of Subject-Verb Agreement**   *392*

Lesson 9.4   **Lack of Pronoun-Antecedent Agreement**   *396*

Lesson 9.5   **Lack of Clear Pronoun Reference**   *398*

Lesson 9.6   **Shift in Pronoun**   *400*

Lesson 9.7   **Shift in Verb Tense**   *401*

Lesson 9.8   **Incorrect Verb Tense or Form**   *402*

Lesson 9.9   **Misplaced or Dangling Modifier**   *404*

Lesson 9.10   **Missing or Misplaced Possessive Apostrophe**   *406*

Lesson 9.11   **Missing Commas with Nonessential Element**   *408*

Lesson 9.12   **Missing Comma in a Series**   *410*

387

Objectives

- To learn to identify common errors in writing
- To learn techniques for correcting common errors in writing
- To demonstrate control over grammar and usage conventions by correcting common errors in writing

Key to Ability Levels

L1   Level 1 activities are within the basic ability range of students.

L2   Level 2 activities are within the ability range of average students.

L3   Level 3 activities are more challenging activities.

 Software
- *Presentation Plus!*
- *Writer's Choice Puzzlemaker*

Web Sites
- *writerschoice.glencoe.com*
- *lit.glencoe.com*

Focus

Lesson Overview

Objective

- To recognize various kinds of sentence fragments: those that lack a subject and/or a verb and those that are subordinate clauses

Bellringer
Daily Language Activity

When students enter the classroom, have this assignment on the board: *Write the following sentence fragments as complete sentences:*

Dug a very deep trench.

Cassandra's best quality.

When Diego arrived.

Rainy, windy, and cold.

See also *Daily Language Practice*

Motivating Activity

Discuss with students why the sentence fragments in the Bellringer were confusing. Explain that sentence fragments can make written material hard to understand. This lesson will teach students how to correct any sentence fragments in their writing.

Teach

Cross-reference: Grammar

For instruction and practice of the material in problems 1 and 2, refer students to Lesson 13.9, pp. 557–558.

9.1 Sentence Fragment

Problem 1

Fragment that lacks a subject

> *frag* Jamal is very athletic. Plays a great game of tennis.

SOLUTION   Add a subject to the fragment to make it a complete sentence.

Jamal is very athletic. He plays a great game of tennis.

Problem 2

Fragment that lacks a complete verb

> *frag* Sabra saw a bright light in the sky. A meteor with brilliant colors.
>
> *frag* We can hardly hear ourselves think. Ruth trying out her new set of drums.

SOLUTION A   Add a complete verb or a helping verb to make the sentence complete.

Sabra saw a bright light in the sky. A meteor with brilliant colors was flashing by.

We can hardly hear ourselves think. Ruth is trying out her new set of drums.

SOLUTION B   Combine the fragment with another sentence.

Sabra saw a bright light in the sky—a meteor with brilliant colors.

With Ruth trying out her new set of drums, we could hardly hear ourselves think.

Resource Manager

Planning Resources
- *Lesson Plans*

Transparencies
- *Bellringer*
- *Two-Minute Skill Drill*

Other Print Resources
- *Grammar Enrichment,* p. 23
- *Grammar Practice,* p. 23

Troubleshooter

Problem 3

Fragment that is a subordinate clause

frag José often succeeds. (Because he is persistent.)

frag I am reading a book by Alice Walker. (Who is one of my favorite writers.)

SOLUTION A Combine the fragment with another sentence.

José often succeeds because he is persistent.

I am reading a book by Alice Walker, who is one of my favorite writers.

SOLUTION B Rewrite the fragment as a complete sentence, eliminating the subordinating conjunction or the relative pronoun and adding a subject or other words necessary to make a complete thought.

José often succeeds. He is persistent.

I am reading a book by Alice Walker. She is one of my favorite writers.

Problem 4

Fragment that lacks both a subject and a verb

frag Kate felt ill and left the theater. (Before the end of the movie.)

SOLUTION Combine the fragment with another sentence.

Kate felt ill and left the theater before the end of the movie.

If you need more help in avoiding sentence fragments, turn to Lesson 13.9, pages 557 – 558.

Teach

 Cross-reference: Grammar

For instruction and practice of the material in problems 3 and 4, refer students to Lesson 13.9, pp. 557–558.

Two-Minute Skill Drill

Write this sentence fragment on the board, and have students rewrite it as a complete sentence:

With great agility, Stepanich over the fence.

See also *Two-Minute Skill Drill Transparency 9.1*

Additional Resources

📁 *Grammar Practice,* p. 23
📁 *Grammar Reteaching,* p. 23
📁 *Grammar Enrichment,* p. 23

📖 *Grammar Workbook,* Lesson 31

Close

Have students explain in their own words the four kinds of sentence fragments presented in this **Troubleshooter.** Ask them to check their current writing assignments for similar errors and to correct them.

Focus

Lesson Overview

Objective

- To recognize run-on sentences and to correct them

 Bellringer

Daily Language Activity

When students enter the classroom, have this assignment on the board: *Tell what is confusing about the following sentences and then write them correctly.*

I want to go with you, when are you leaving?

Let's wait Ben isn't here yet.

The old wolf jumped from one ice floe to another and other members of the pack quickly followed her.

See also Daily Language Practice

Motivating Activity

Discuss with students why the sentences in the Bellringer were confusing. Explain that run-on sentences can make written material hard to understand. This lesson will teach students how to avoid or correct run-on sentences in their writing.

Teach

Cross-reference: Grammar

For instruction and practice of the material in problems 1 and 2, refer students to Lesson 13.10, pp. 559–561.

Troubleshooter

9.2 Run-on Sentence

Problem 1

Comma splice—two main clauses separated only by a comma

run-on (Paula told me the answer to the riddle, I have forgotten what she said.)

SOLUTION A Replace the comma with an end mark of punctuation, such as a period or question mark, and begin the new sentence with a capital letter.

Paula told me the answer to the riddle. I have forgotten what she said.

SOLUTION B Place a semicolon between the two main clauses.

Paula told me the answer to the riddle; I have forgotten what she said.

SOLUTION C Insert a coordinating conjunction after the comma.

Paula told me the answer to the riddle, but I have forgotten what she said.

Problem 2

Two main clauses with no punctuation between them

run-on (The lights flickered a few times then they went out.)

SOLUTION A Separate the main clauses with an end mark of punctuation, such as a period or a question mark, and begin the second sentence with a capital letter.

The lights flickered a few times. Then they went out.

 Resource Manager

Planning Resources
- *Lesson Plans*

Transparencies
- *Bellringer*
- *Two-Minute Skill Drill*

Other Print Resources
- *Grammar Enrichment,* p. 24
- *Grammar Practice,* p. 24
- *Grammar Reteaching,* p. 24
- *Grammar Workbook,* Lesson 32

SOLUTION B   Separate the main clauses with a semicolon.

The lights flickered a few times; then they went out.

SOLUTION C   Insert a comma and a coordinating conjunction between the main clauses.

The lights flickered a few times, and then they went out.

9.2

Problem 3

Two main clauses with no comma before the coordinating conjunction

run-on *Ilona would like to own a pet but she is allergic to most animals.*

run-on *My brother just started playing soccer and he wants me to play as well.*

SOLUTION A   Insert a comma before the coordinating conjunction to separate the two main clauses.

Ilona would like to own a pet, but she is allergic to most animals.

My brother just started playing soccer, and he wants me to play as well.

If you need more help in avoiding run-on sentences, turn to Lesson 13.10, pages 559–561.

Troubleshooter

Teach

⇄ Cross-reference: Grammar
For instruction and practice of the material in problem 3, refer students to Lesson 13.10, pp. 559–561.

Two-Minute Skill Drill

Write this sentence on the board, and have students rewrite it correctly.

We arrived in town late at night in the morning our car was covered with snow.

📦 **See also** *Two-Minute Skill Drill Transparency 9.2*

Additional Resources
📁 *Grammar Practice,* p. 24
📁 *Grammar Reteaching,* p. 24
📁 *Grammar Enrichment,* p. 24

📖 *Grammar Workbook,* Lesson 32

Close

Have students explain in their own words the three kinds of run-on sentences presented in this **Troubleshooter.** Ask students to check their current writing assignments for similar errors and to correct them.

Focus

Lesson Overview

Objective
- To recognize and correct errors in subject-verb agreement

Bellringer
Daily Language Activity

When students enter the classroom, have this assignment on the board: *Tell what is confusing about the following sentences and then write them correctly.*

The number of mistakes in John's essay are surprisingly low.

Three months has passed.

See also *Daily Language Practice*

Motivating Activity

Discuss with students why the sentences in the Bellringer were confusing. Explain that lack of subject-verb agreement can make written material hard to understand. This lesson will teach students how to avoid or correct errors in subject-verb agreement.

Teach

Cross-reference: Usage
For instruction and practice of the material in problem 1, refer students to Lesson 16.1, pp. 613–614.

Cross-reference: Usage
For instruction and practice of the material in problem 2, refer students to Lesson 16.2, p. 615.

Cross-reference: Usage
For instruction and practice of the material in problem 3, refer students to Lesson 16.3, p. 616–617.

Troubleshooter

9.3 Lack of Subject-Verb Agreement

Problem 1

A subject that is separated from the verb by an intervening prepositional phrase

> *agr   A complex system of roads* ⟨link⟩ *the two cities.*
> *agr   The sounds of the traffic* ⟨keeps⟩ *her awake.*

Do not mistake the object of a preposition for the subject of a sentence.

SOLUTION   Make the verb agree with the subject, which is never the object of the preposition.

A complex system of roads links the two cities.
The sounds of the traffic keep her awake.

Problem 2

A predicate nominative that differs in number from the subject

> *agr   Grapes* ⟨is⟩ *his favorite snack.*

SOLUTION   Ignore the predicate nominative, and make the verb agree with the subject of the sentence.

Grapes are his favorite snack.

Problem 3

A subject that follows the verb

> *agr   On the wall* ⟨hangs⟩ *two handsome watercolors.*
> *agr   There* ⟨goes⟩ *the last two bicyclists.*

Resource Manager

Planning Resources
- *Lesson Plans*

Transparencies
- *Bellringer*
- *Two-Minute Skill Drill*

Other Print Resources
- *Grammar Enrichment,* p. 28–29
- *Grammar Practice,* p. 28–29
- *Grammar Reteaching,* p. 28–29
- *Grammar Workbook,* Lessons 44–51
- *Sentence-Combining Practice,* p. 16

SOLUTION In an inverted sentence look for the subject *after* the verb. Then make sure the verb agrees with the subject.

On the wall hang two handsome watercolors.
There go the last two bicyclists.

Problem 4

A collective noun as the subject

agr *The soccer team have won consistently.*
agr *The group has different views on the issue.*

SOLUTION A If the collective noun refers to a group as a whole, use a singular verb.

The soccer team has won consistently.

SOLUTION B If the collective noun refers to each member of a group individually, use a plural verb.

The group have different views on the issue.

Problem 5

A noun of amount as the subject

agr *Five dollars are too much for that item.*
agr *Five pennies makes a nickel.*

SOLUTION Determine whether the noun of amount refers to one unit and is therefore singular or whether it refers to a number of individual units and is therefore plural.

Five dollars is too much for that item.
Five pennies make a nickel.

Teach

⬩ **Cross-reference: Usage**

For instruction and practice of the material in problems 4 and 5, refer students to Lesson 16.4, p. 618–619.

🕐 **Two-Minute Skill Drill**

Write this sentence on the board, and have students rewrite it so the subject and verb agree:

The local dental association recommend annual check-ups.

👆 **See also** *Two-Minute Skill Drill Transparency 9.3*

Teach

⇄ **Cross-reference: Usage**

For instruction and practice of the material in problem 6, refer students to Lesson 16.5, p. 620.

⇄ **Cross-reference: Usage**

For instruction and practice of the material in problem 7, refer students to Lesson 16.5, p. 620.

⇄ **Cross-reference: Usage**

For instruction and practice of the material in problem 8, refer students to Lesson 16.5, p. 620.

Troubleshooter

Problem 6

A compound subject that is joined by *and*

agr Copper and zinc (makes) brass.

agr Rice and beans (are) a healthful main dish.

SOLUTION A   If the parts of the compound subject do not belong to one unit or they refer to different people or things, use a plural verb.

Copper and zinc make brass.

SOLUTION B   If the parts of the compound subject belong to one unit or if both parts refer to the same person or thing, use a singular verb.

Rice and beans is a healthful main dish.

Problem 7

A compound subject that is joined by *or* or *nor*

agr Neither my cousins nor my aunt (resemble) her.

SOLUTION   Make the verb agree with the subject that is closer to it.

Neither my cousins nor my aunt resembles her.

Problem 8

A compound subject that is preceded by *many a, every,* or *each*

agr Many a bluejay and robin (have) visited that feeder today.

When *many a, every,* or *each* precedes a compound subject, the subject is considered singular.

SOLUTION Use a singular verb when *many a*, *each*, or *every* precedes a compound subject.

Many a bluejay and robin has visited that feeder today.

Problem 9

A subject that is separated from the verb by an intervening expression

agr *My karate class, as well as Kazuo's swimming class, ~~take~~ place on Saturday.*

Certain expressions, such as *as well as*, *in addition to*, and *together with*, do not change the number of the subject.

SOLUTION Ignore an intervening expression between a subject and its verb. Make the verb agree with the subject.

My karate class, as well as Kazuo's swimming class, takes place on Saturday.

Problem 10

An indefinite pronoun as the subject

agr *Each of the contestants ~~receive~~ a gift.*

Some indefinite pronouns are singular, some are plural, and some can be either singular or plural, depending upon the noun they refer to. (See page 647 for a list of indefinite pronouns.)

SOLUTION Determine whether the indefinite pronoun is singular or plural and make the verb agree.

Each of the contestants receives a gift.

If you need more help with subject-verb agreement, turn to Lessons 16.1 through 16.7, pages 623–625.

Teach

 Cross-reference: Usage

For instruction and practice of the material in problem 9, refer students to Lesson 16.6, pp. 621–622.

Cross-reference: Usage

For instruction and practice of the material in problem 10, refer students to Lesson 16.7, pp. 623–625.

Two-Minute Skill Drill

Write this sentence on the board, and have students rewrite it so that the subject and verb agree:

Bacon and eggs are a favorite breakfast dish for some people.

See also *Two-Minute Skill Drill Transparency 9.3*

Additional Resources

📁 *Grammar Practice*, p. 28–29
📁 *Grammar Reteaching*, p. 28–29
📁 *Grammar Enrichment*, p. 28–29

📕 *Grammar Workbook*, Lessons 44–51

Close

Have students explain in their own words the ten common errors in subject-verb agreement presented in this **Troubleshooter**. Ask them to check their current writing assignments for similar errors and to correct them.

Focus

Lesson Overview

Objective
• To recognize and correct errors in pronoun-antecedent agreement

Bellringer
Daily Language Activity

When students enter the classroom, have this assignment on the board: *Write the following sentences correctly:*

A schoolteacher helps her students learn.

Bert knows that you should always plan ahead.

Neither of the girls will finish their homework early.

See also *Daily Language Practice*

Motivating Activity

Discuss with students why the sentences in the Bellringer were confusing. Explain that pronouns that do not agree with their antecedents can make written material hard to understand. This lesson teaches students to use correct pronoun-antecedent agreement in their writing.

Teach

Cross-reference: Usage
For instruction and practice of the material in problem 1, refer students to Lesson 17.5, pp. 644–648.

Cross-reference: Usage
For instruction and practice of the material in problem 2, refer students to Lesson 17.5, pp. 644–648.

Troubleshooter

9.4 Lack of Pronoun-Antecedent Agreement

Problem 1

A singular antecedent that can be either male or female

ant An attorney must protect (his) clients' interests.

Traditionally a masculine pronoun was used to refer to an antecedent that might be either male or female. This usage ignores or excludes female.

SOLUTION A Reword the sentence to use *he or she, him or her,* and so on.

An attorney must protect his or her clients' interests.

SOLUTION B Reword the sentence so that both the antecedent and the pronoun are plural.

Attorneys must protect their clients' interests.

SOLUTION C Reword the sentence to eliminate the pronoun.

An attorney must protect every client's interests.

Problem 2

A second-person pronoun that refers to a third-person antecedent

ant Isaiah drinks milk because it supplies (you) with calcium and protein.

Be sure not to refer to an antecedent in the third person using the second-person pronoun *you.*

Resource Manager

Planning Resources
• *Lesson Plans*

Transparencies
• *Bellringer*
• *Two-Minute Skill Drill*

Other Print Resources
• *Grammar Enrichment,* p. 33
• *Grammar Practice,* p. 29
• *Grammar Reteaching,* p. 33
• *Grammar Workbook,* Lessons 55–57

SOLUTION A   Use the appropriate third-person pronoun.

Isaiah drinks milk because it supplies him with calcium and protein.

SOLUTION B   Use an appropriate noun instead of a pronoun.

Isaiah drinks milk because it supplies people with calcium and protein.

Problem 3

A singular indefinite pronoun as an antecedent

ant   Each of the mothers brought (their) own child to the zoo.
ant   Neither of the boys at the table finished (their) dinner.

Each, everyone, either, neither, and *one* are singular and therefore require singular personal pronouns.

SOLUTION   Don't be fooled by a prepositional phrase that contains a plural noun. Determine whether the indefinite pronoun antecedent is singular or plural, and make the noun agree.

Each of the mothers brought her own child to the zoo.
Neither of the boys at the table finished his dinner.

If you need more help with pronoun-antecedent agreement, turn to Lesson 16.7, pages 623–625, and Lesson 17.5, pages 644–648.

Troubleshooter

Teach

Cross-reference: Usage

For instruction and practice of the material in problem 3, refer students to Lesson 16.7, pp. 623–625.

Two-Minute Skill Drill

Write this sentence on the board, and have students rewrite it to correct the pronoun-antecedent error:

An athlete works constantly to build his strength and agility.

See also *Two-Minute Skill Drill Transparency 9.4*

Additional Resources

📁 *Grammar Practice,* p. 33
📁 *Grammar Reteaching,* p. 33
📁 *Grammar Enrichment,* p. 33

📖 *Grammar Workbook,* Lessons 55–57

Close

Have students explain in their own words the three kinds of errors in pronoun-antecedent agreement presented in this **Troubleshooter.** Ask them to check their current writing assignments for similar errors in pronoun-antecedent agreement and to correct them.

Focus

Lesson Overview

Objective
- To recognize and correct errors in pronoun references

Bellringer
Daily Language Activity

When students enter the classroom, have this assignment on the board: *Tell what is confusing about the following sentences and then write them correctly.*

They were late for the movie, but it didn't matter.

When the snowflakes hit our faces, they melted.

In some schools, you have free periods every day.

See also *Daily Language Practice*

Motivating Activity

Discuss with students why the sentences in the Bellringer were confusing. Explain that such unclear pronoun references can make written material hard to understand. This lesson will teach students how to use clear pronoun references in their writing.

Teach

Cross-reference: Usage
For instruction and practice of the material in problem 1, refer students to Lesson 17.6, pp. 649–651.

Cross-reference: Usage
For instruction and practice of the material in problem 2, refer students to Lesson 17.6, pp. 649–651.

9.5 Lack of Clear Pronoun Reference

Problem 1

A pronoun reference that is weak or vague

> ref The musicians played, (which) we enjoyed.
>
> ref Economists differ about how to improve the economy, and (that) has led to inconsistent economic policies.
>
> ref The author argues at length that there (is) life on other planets, but (it) is not convincing.

Be sure that *this, that, which,* and *it* have clear antecedents.

SOLUTION A Rewrite the sentence, adding a clear antecedent for the pronoun.

The musicians played several old songs, which we enjoyed.

SOLUTION B Rewrite the sentence, substituting a noun for the pronoun.

Economists differ about how to improve the economy, and their disagreement has led to inconsistent economic policies.

The author argues at length that there is life on other planets, but his theory is not very convincing.

Problem 2

A pronoun that could refer to more than one antecedent

> ref When Nelson gave his father the book, (he) beamed with pleasure.
>
> ref The parents met with the teachers, and (they) asked whether the principal could be present.

Resource Manager

Planning Resources
- *Lesson Plans*

Transparencies
- *Bellringer*
- *Two-Minute Skill Drill*

📂 **Other Print Resources**
- *Grammar Enrichment*, p. 34
- *Grammar Practice*, p. 34
- *Grammar Reteaching*, p. 34
- *Grammar Workbook*, Lesson 58

SOLUTION A Rewrite the sentence, substituting a noun for the pronoun.

When Nelson gave his father the book, the boy beamed with pleasure.

SOLUTION B Rewrite the sentence, making the antecedent of the pronoun clear.

The teachers asked whether the principal could be present at their meeting with the parents.

Problem 3

The indefinite use of *you* or *they*

> *ref* In court (you) are innocent until proved guilty.
> *ref* In that store (they) have some excellent bargains.

SOLUTION A Rewrite the sentence, substituting a noun for the pronoun.

In court defendants are innocent until proved guilty.

SOLUTION B Rewrite the sentence, eliminating the pronoun entirely.

That store has some excellent bargains.

If you need more help in making clear pronoun references, turn to Lesson 17.6, pages 649–651.

Teach

⬉ Cross-reference: Usage

For instruction and practice of the material in problem 3, refer students to Lesson 17.6, pp. 649–651.

Two-Minute Skill Drill

Write this sentence on the board, and have students rewrite it so that the pronoun reference is clear:

The lunch line moves so slowly on Monday, but it is not easy to solve.

👆 **See also** *Two-Minute Skill Drill Transparency 9.5*

Additional Resources

📁 *Grammar Practice,* p. 34
📁 *Grammar Reteaching,* p. 34
📁 *Grammar Enrichment,* p. 34

📕 *Grammar Workbook,* Lesson 58

Close

Have students explain in their own words the three kinds of unclear pronoun references presented in this **Troubleshooter.** Ask them to check their current writing assignments for similar errors and to correct them.

Troubleshooter

399

Focus

Lesson Overview

Objective

• To recognize and correct illogical shifts in person between pronouns

Bellringer

Daily Language Activity

When students enter the classroom, have this assignment on the board: *Write the following sentences correctly:*

Alfredo loves dancing because it gives you an excellent workout.

When one enrolls in a new school, sometimes it's hard for you to make friends right away.

See also Daily Language Practice

Teach

Cross-reference: Usage

For instructions and practice of the material in the problem, refer students to Lesson 17.5, pp. 644–648.

Close

Have students write an explanation of incorrect shifts between pronouns as presented in this **Troubleshooter.** Ask them to check their current writing assignments for such shifts and to correct any errors.

9.6 Shift in Pronoun

Problem

An incorrect shift in person between two pronouns

> pro   *Kenji and Jeanne are going on a trip to the mountains, where* (you) *can hike and breathe fresh air.*
>
> pro   *I like movies that keep* (you) *guessing.*
>
> pro   *When one examines the card catalog,* (you) *find a wealth of information.*

Incorrect pronoun shifts occur when a writer or speaker uses a pronoun in one person and then illogically shifts to a pronoun in another person.

> **SOLUTION A**   Replace the incorrect pronoun with a pronoun that agrees with its antecedent.
>
> **Kenji and Jeanne are going on a trip to the mountains, where they can hike and breathe fresh air.**
>
> **I like movies that keep me guessing.**
>
> **When one examines the card catalog, one finds a wealth of information.**

> **SOLUTION B**   Replace the incorrect pronoun with an appropriate noun.
>
> **Kenji and Jeanne are going on a trip to the mountains, where vacationers can hike and breathe fresh air.**
>
> **I like movies that keep the audience guessing.**

If you need more help in eliminating incorrect pronoun shifts, turn to Lesson 17.5, page 646.

Resource Manager

Planning Resources
• *Lesson Plans*

Transparencies
• *Bellringer*

Other Print Resources
• *Grammar Enrichment,* p. 33
• *Grammar Practice,* p. 33
• *Grammar Reteaching,* p. 33
• *Grammar Workbook,* Lesson 56

9.7 Shift in Verb Tense

Problem 1

An unnecessary shift in tense

shift t   Jan opens the can and savored *the aroma.*
shift t   Otis left the room just as we arrive.

When two or more events occur at the same time, be sure to use the same verb tense to describe both or all events.

SOLUTION

Jan opens the can and savors the aroma.
Otis left the room just as we arrived.

Problem 2

A lack of correct shift in tenses to show that one event precedes or follows another

shift t   By the time the coach sent him in, Julius sat *on the bench for an hour.*

When events being described have occurred at different times, shift tenses to show that one event precedes or follows another.

SOLUTION   Shift from the past tense to the past perfect tense to indicate that one action began and ended before another past action began. Use the past perfect tense for the earlier of the two actions.

By the time the coach sent him in, Julius had sat on the bench for an hour.

If you need more help with shifts in verb tenses, turn to Lesson 15.4, pages 593–595, and Lesson 15.6, pages 598–599.

Focus

Lesson Overview

Objective

- To recognize and correct errors in using verb tenses

Bellringer

Daily Language Activity

When students enter the classroom, have this assignment on the board: *Write the following sentences correctly:*

Casey wandered home and watches television.

The wind roars and bellowed.

After Randall had lost his wallet, he realizes he has no cash for the bus.

See also *Daily Language Practice*

Teach

Cross-reference: Usage

For instruction and practice of the material in problem 1, refer students to lesson 15.6, pp. 598–599.

Cross-reference: Usage

For instruction and practice of the material in problem 2, refer students to lesson 15.4, pp. 593–595.

Close

Have students explain in their own words the two kinds of problems with shifts in verb tense presented in this **Troubleshooter.** Ask them to check their current writing assignments for similar errors and to correct them.

Resource Manager

Planning Resources
- *Lesson Plans*

Transparencies
- *Bellringer*

Other Print Resources
- *Grammar Enrichment,* p. 27
- *Grammar Practice,* p. 26
- *Grammar Reteaching,* p. 26
- *Grammar Workbook,* Lesson 42

Troubleshooter

Focus

Lesson Overview

Objective

• To recognize and correct errors in verb tenses or forms

 Bellringer

Daily Language Activity

When students enter the classroom, have this assignment on the board: *Write the following sentences correctly:*

Tomorrow Sandy and Julie went to the carnival.

Anton knowed it was time to go home.

The canyon has drew many tourists.

See also 📖 *Daily Language Practice*

Motivating Activity

Discuss with students why the original sentences in the Bellringer were confusing. Explain that such incorrect verb tenses or forms can make written material hard to understand. This lesson will teach students how to use verb tenses and forms correctly in their writing.

Teach

🔁 Cross-reference: Usage

For instruction and practice of the material in problems 1 and 2, refer students to Lessons 15.1 and 15.2, pp. 585–588.

9.8 Incorrect Verb Tense or Form

Problem 1

An incorrect or missing verb ending

tense Last Saturday night, I cook for the family.
tense Have you ever want to study modern dance?

SOLUTION Add *-ed* to a regular verb to form the past tense and the past participle.

Last Saturday night, I cooked for the family.
Have you ever wanted to study modern dance?

Problem 2

An improperly formed irregular verb

tense Emilio swinged the bat but missed the ball.
tense Mr. Caruso teached violin lessons.

Irregular verbs form their past tense and past participle in some way other than by adding *-ed*. Memorize these forms, or look them up.

SOLUTION

Emilio swung the bat but missed the ball.
Mr. Caruso taught violin lessons.

Problem 3

Confusion between the past form and the past participle

tense The committee has chose Juana as chairperson.
tense He has broke our school's high-jump record.

Resource Manager

Planning Resources
• *Lesson Plans*

📖 **Transparencies**
• *Bellringer*
• *Two-Minute Skill Drill*

📂 **Other Print Resources**
• *Grammar Enrichment,* p. 25
• *Grammar Practice,* p. 25
• *Grammar Reteaching,* p. 25
• *Grammar Workbook,* Lessons 38–40

SOLUTION Use the past participle form of an irregular verb, not the past form, when you use the auxiliary verb *have*.

The committee has chosen Juana as chairperson.

He has broken our school's high-jump record.

Problem 4

Improper use of the past participle

> *tense* He ⟨*swum*⟩ across the lake.
>
> *tense* The school choir ⟨*sung*⟩ beautifully at the class assembly.
>
> *tense* The bell ⟨*rung*.⟩

The past participle of an irregular verb cannot stand alone as a verb. It must be used with the auxiliary verb *have*.

SOLUTION A Add the auxiliary verb *have* to the past participle to form a complete verb.

He has swum across the lake.

The school choir has sung beautifully at the class assembly.

The bell has rung.

SOLUTION B Replace the past participle with the past form of the verb.

He swam across the lake.

The school choir sang beautifully at the class assembly.

The bell rang.

If you need more help with correct verb forms, turn to Lesson 15.1 and Lesson 15.2, pages 585–588.

9.8 Incorrect Verb Tense or Form **403**

9.8

Troubleshooter

Teach

⇄ Cross-reference: Usage

For instruction and practice of the material in problem 4, refer students to Lessons 15.1 and 15.2, pp. 585–588.

 Two-Minute Skill Drill

Write this sentence on the board, and have students rewrite it to correct the verb tense:

The wind has blew very hard all day.

See also *Two-Minute Skill Drill Transparency 9.8*

Additional Resources

📁 *Grammar Practice,* p. 25
📁 *Grammar Reteaching,* p. 25
📁 *Grammar Enrichment,* p. 25

📕 *Grammar Workbook,* Lessons 38–40

Close

Have students explain in their own words the four kinds of errors in using verb tenses or forms presented in this **Troubleshooter.** Ask them to check their current writing assignments for similar errors and to correct them.

Focus

Lesson Overview

Objective

- To recognize and correct misplaced or dangling modifiers

 Bellringer
Daily Language Activity

When students enter the classroom, have this assignment on the board: *Write the following sentences correctly:*

Chiming the hour, Deirdre heard the carillon.

Chet only has a motorcycle at home.

Vaulting almost high enough, the pole was knocked down.

See also *Daily Language Practice*

Motivating Activity

Discuss with students why the original sentences in the Bellringer were confusing. Explain that misplaced or dangling modifiers can make written material hard to understand. This lesson will teach students how to place modifiers correctly in their writing.

Teach

Cross-reference: Usage

For instruction and practice of the material in problems 1 and 2, refer students to Lesson 18.7, pp. 674–679.

9.9 Misplaced or Dangling Modifier

Problem 1

A misplaced modifier

> *mod* The insects fascinated the children with their long antennae.
>
> *mod* Hanging on the wall, Tamiko saw her painting.
>
> *mod* The cat hissed at the goldfish staring at the fishbowl.

Modifiers that modify the wrong word or seem to modify more than one word in a sentence are called misplaced modifiers.

SOLUTION Move the misplaced phrase as close as possible to the word or words it modifies.

With their long antennae, the insects fascinated the children.
Tamiko saw her painting hanging on the wall.
Staring at the fishbowl, the cat hissed at the goldfish.

Problem 2

The adverb *only* misplaced

> *mod* Sylvia only orders soup as an appetizer.

The meaning of your sentence may be unclear if *only* is misplaced.

SOLUTION Place the adverb *only* immediately before the word or group of words it modifies. Note that each time *only* is moved in the sentence, the meaning of the sentence changes.

Only Sylvia orders soup as an appetizer.
Sylvia orders only soup as an appetizer.
Sylvia orders soup only as an appetizer.

Resource Manager

Planning Resources
- *Lesson Plans*

Transparencies
- *Bellringer*
- *Two-Minute Skill Drill*

Other Print Resources
- *Grammar Enrichment,* p. 37
- *Grammar Practice,* p. 37
- *Grammar Reteaching,* p. 37
- *Grammar Workbook,* Lesson 64

Problem 3

A dangling modifier

mod (By paying attention to the instructions,) the bookcase was assembled easily.

mod (Concerned about making mistakes,) the driving lesson went surprisingly well.

mod (Standing on the mountaintop,) the view was breathtaking.

Dangling modifiers do not logically seem to modify any word in the sentence.

SOLUTION Rewrite the sentence, adding a noun to which the dangling phrase clearly refers. Often you will have to add other words to make the meaning of the sentence clear.

By paying attention to the instructions, Rachel easily assembled the bookcase.

Concerned about making mistakes, Duane felt that his driving lesson went surprisingly well.

Standing on the mountaintop, Ted found the view breathtaking.

If you need more help with misplaced or dangling modifiers, turn to Lesson 18.7, pages 674–679.

Troubleshooter

Teach

⬍ **Cross-reference: Usage**

For instruction and practice of the material in problem 3, refer students to Lesson 18.7, pp. 674–679.

 Two-Minute Skill Drill

Write this sentence on the board, and have students rewrite it to correct the dangling modifier:

Waiting for the water to boil, the teakettle began to steam.

✎ **See also** *Two-Minute Skill Drill Transparency 9.9*

Additional Resources

📁 *Grammar Practice*, p. 37
📁 *Grammar Reteaching*, p. 37
📁 *Grammar Enrichment*, p. 37

📔 *Grammar Workbook*, Lesson 64

Close

Have students explain in their own words the three kinds of misplaced or dangling modifiers presented in the **Troubleshooter.** Ask them to check their current writing assignments for similar errors and to correct them.

Focus

Lesson Overview

Objective
- To recognize and correct errors in the use of possessive apostrophes

 Bellringer
Daily Language Activity

When students enter the classroom, have this assignment on the board: *Write the following sentences correctly:*

Charles favorite dish is chili.

The gerbils cage was left open.

My dog ate all of it's food.

See also *Daily Language Practice*

Motivating Activity

Discuss with students why the sentences in the Bellringer were confusing. Explain that such misplaced or absent possessive apostrophes can make written material hard to understand.

Teach

Cross-reference: Mechanics
For instruction and practice of the material in problems 1, 2, and 3, refer students to Lesson 21.11, pp. 760–762.

Troubleshooter

9.10 Missing or Misplaced Possessive Apostrophe

Problem 1
Singular nouns

poss That ⟨artists⟩ painting is ⟨James⟩ favorite.

SOLUTION Use an apostrophe and an -*s* to form the possessive of a singular noun, even one that ends in -*s*.

That artist's painting is James's favorite.

Problem 2
Plural nouns ending in -*s*

poss The ⟨officers⟩ quarters are in that building.

SOLUTION Use an apostrophe alone to form the possessive of a plural noun that ends in -*s*.

The officers' quarters are in that building.

Problem 3
Plural nouns not ending in -*s*

poss ⟨Womens⟩ shoes are sold on the third floor.

SOLUTION Use an apostrophe and an -*s* to form the possessive of a plural noun that does not end in -*s*.

Women's shoes are sold on the third floor.

Resource Manager

Planning Resources
- *Lesson Plans*

Transparencies
- *Bellringer*
- *Two-Minute Skill Drill*

Other Print Resources
- *Grammar Enrichment,* pp. 30, 51
- *Grammar Practice,* pp. 30, 51
- *Grammar Reteaching,* pp. 30, 51
- *Grammar Workbook,* Lesson 89
- *Sentence-Combining Practice,* p. 10

Problem 4

Pronouns

poss *Anyones* guess is as good as mine.

poss *I see every painting but your's.*

SOLUTION A Use an apostrophe and an *-s* to form the possessive of a singular indefinite pronoun.

Anyone's guess is as good as mine.

SOLUTION B Do not use an apostrophe with any of the possessive personal pronouns.

I see every painting but yours.

Problem 5

Confusion between *its* and *it's*

poss *That car has lost it's front bumper.*

poss *Its always good to try new things.*

The possessive of *it* is *its*. *It's* is the contraction of *it is*.

SOLUTION Do not use an apostrophe to form the possessive of *it*. Use an apostrophe to form the contraction of *it is*.

That car has lost its front bumper.
It's always good to try new things.

If you need more help with apostrophes and possessives, turn to Lesson 17.1, page 638, and Lesson 21.11, pages 760–762.

Troubleshooter

Teach

⬌ Cross-reference: Usage and Mechanics

For instruction and practice of the material in problems 4 and 5, refer students to Lesson 17.1, pp. 637–638, and to Lesson 21.11, pp. 760–762.

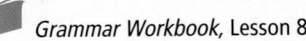

Two-Minute Skill Drill

Write this sentence on the board, and have students rewrite it to correct possessive apostrophe errors:

Jims experiment was better than her's.

See also *Two-Minute Skill Drill Transparency 9.10*

Additional Resources

📁 *Grammar Practice*, pp. 30, 51
📁 *Grammar Reteaching*, pp. 30, 51
📁 *Grammar Enrichment*, pp. 30, 51
📁 *Sentence-Combining Practice*, p. 10

📓 *Grammar Workbook*, Lesson 89

Close

Have students explain in their own words the five kinds of problems with possessive apostrophes presented in this **Troubleshooter.** Ask them to check their current writing assignments for similar errors and to correct them.

Focus

Lesson Overview

Objective
- To recognize when commas are needed to set off nonessential elements

Bellringer
Daily Language Activity

When students enter the classroom, have this assignment on the board: *Write the following sentences correctly:*

Exhilarated the choir prepared for the concert tour.

Kyra whose mother you remember will visit here tomorrow.

Wow did you see that meteor?

See also *Daily Language Practice*

Motivating Activity

Discuss with students why the sentences in the Bellringer were confusing. Explain that when commas are not used to set off nonessential elements, written material can be hard to understand. This lesson teaches students how to use commas to set off nonessential elements in sentences.

Teach

Cross-reference: Mechanics
For instruction and practice of the material in problems 1 and 2, refer students to Lesson 21.6, pp. 743–751.

Troubleshooter

9.11 Missing Commas with Nonessential Element

Problem 1

Missing commas with nonessential participles, infinitives, and their phrases

> com The team defeated trudged wearily to the bus.
> com The waves gleaming in the sunlight pounded the beach.
> com To be sure I have no experience with this kind of problem.

SOLUTION Determine whether the participle, infinitive, or phrase is truly not essential to the meaning of the sentence. If it is not essential, set off the phrases with commas.

The team, defeated, trudged wearily to the bus.
The waves, gleaming in the sunlight, pounded the beach.
To be sure, I have no experience with this kind of problem.

Problem 2

Missing commas with nonessential adjective clauses

> com Kai-chi who comes from Shanghai is studying piano.

SOLUTION Determine whether the clause is truly not essential to the meaning of the sentence. If it is not essential, set off the clause with commas.

Kai-chi, who comes from Shanghai, is studying piano.

Resource Manager

Planning Resources
- *Lesson Plans*

Transparencies
- *Bellringer*
- *Two-Minute Skill Drill*

Other Print Resources
- *Grammar Enrichment*, p. 45
- *Grammar Practice*, p. 45
- *Grammar Reteaching*, p. 45
- *Grammar Workbook*, Lesson 78

Problem 3

Missing commas with nonessential appositives

> *com*   Mr. Lomawaima our anthropology professor will speak on Hopi customs.

SOLUTION   Determine whether the appositive is truly not essential to the meaning of the sentence. If so, set off the appositive with commas.

Mr. Lomawaima, our anthropology professor, will speak on Hopi customs.

Problem 4

Missing commas with interjections and parenthetical expressions

> *com*   Oh I know what you mean.
>
> *com*   Derrick I believe offered to help with the scenery for the play.

SOLUTION   Set off the interjection or parenthetical expression with commas.

Oh, I know what you mean.
Derrick, I believe, offered to help with the scenery for the play.

If you need more help with commas and nonessential elements, turn to Lesson 21.6, pages 743–751.

Troubleshooter

Teach

⇄ Cross-reference: Usage and Mechanics

For instruction and practice of the material in problems 3 and 4, refer students to Lesson 21.6, pp. 743–751.

Two-Minute Skill Drill

Write this sentence on the board, and have students rewrite it so that nonessential elements are set off by commas:

The cavern dark and challenging tempted the explorers.

✎ **See also** *Two-Minute Skill Drill Transparency 9.11*

Additional Resources

📁 *Grammar Practice,* p. 45
📁 *Grammar Reteaching,* p. 45
📁 *Grammar Enrichment,* p. 45

📕 *Grammar Workbook,* Lesson 78

Close

Have students explain in their own words the four kinds of problems caused when commas aren't used to set off nonessential elements. Ask them to check their current writing assignments for similar errors and to correct them.

Focus

Lesson Overview

Objective

• To recognize when commas should be added to separate items in series

Bellringer
Daily Language Activity

When students enter the classroom, have this assignment on the board: *Write the following sentences correctly:*

Trevor's son gurgled sighed and fell asleep against Natalie's shoulder.

Thunder dragged me awake lightning blinded me and I couldn't go back to sleep.

See also *Daily Language Practice*

Teach

Cross-reference: Mechanics

For instruction and practice of the material in the problem, refer students to Lesson 21.6, pp. 743–751.

9.12 Missing Comma in a Series

Problem

Missing commas in a series of words, phrases, or clauses

> *s com*   Birches maples and hemlocks covered the sides of the mountain.
>
> *s com*   The motor sputtered coughed whined and finally died.
>
> *s com*   The ivy crept up the wall around the drainpipe and over the roof.
>
> *s com*   Lila sat nervously, biting her lip frowning and drumming her fingers on the table.
>
> *s com*   The rain stopped the clouds rolled away and the sun came out.

SOLUTION   When there are three or more elements in a series, use a comma after each element, including the element that precedes a conjunction.

Birches, maples, and hemlocks covered the sides of the mountain.

The motor sputtered, coughed, whined, and finally died.

The ivy crept up the wall, around the drainpipe, and over the roof.

Lila sat nervously, biting her lip, frowning, and drumming her fingers on the table.

The rain stopped, the clouds rolled away, and the sun came out.

If you need more help with commas in a series, turn to Lesson 21.6, page 743.

Resource Manager

Planning Resources
• *Lesson Plans*

Transparencies
• *Bellringer*

Other Print Resources
• *Grammar Enrichment*, p. 44
• *Grammar Practice*, p. 44
• *Grammar Reteaching*, p. 44
• *Grammar Workbook*, Lesson 77
• *Sentence-Combining Practice*, p. 3

Proofreading Symbols

⊙	Lieut Brown	Insert a period.
∧	No one came to the party.	Insert a letter or a word.
⋏	The bell rang the students left for home.	Insert a semicolon.
≡	I enjoyed paris.	Capitalize a letter.
/	The Class ran a bake sale.	Make a capital letter lowercase.
⌢	The campers are home sick.	Close up a space.
ⓈⓅ	They visited N.Y. ⓈⓅ	Spell out.
⋀	Sue please help.	Insert a comma.
∩	He enjoyed feild day.	Transpose the position of letters or words.
#	alltogether	Insert a space.
℈	We went to to Boston.	Delete letters or words.
⌄ ⌄	She asked Who's coming?	Insert quotation marks.
/=/	mid January	Insert a hyphen.
¶	"Where?" asked Karl. "Over there," said Ray.	Begin a new paragraph.
⌄	She liked Sarah's glasses.	Insert an apostrophe.

Close

Have students explain in their own words what problems are created when items in series are not separated by commas. Ask students to check their current writing assignments for items in a series that need to be separated by commas, as shown in the **Troubleshooter,** and then have them correct the errors.

Proofreading Symbols   **411**

Business and Technical Writing

Objectives

- To understand the characteristics of effective business letters
- To identify and apply standard formats for business letters
- To write effective business letters
- To understand and apply the rubrics for memos, e-mail, and forms
- To compose effective memos and e-mail
- To complete forms accurately
- To identify effective uses for graphic organizers
- To create effective graphic organizers
- To understand the purposes and characteristics of technical writing
- To write clear abstracts and instructions
- To work collaboratively to produce a research report

✔ ASSESSMENT OPTIONS

📁 *Tests with Answer Key & Rubrics*
Business and Technical Writing Test

💾 *Testmaker*
Business and Technical Writing Pretest

You may wish to administer the Business and Technical Writing Pretest at this point.

Key to Ability Levels

L1 Level 1 activities are within the basic range of students.

L2 Level 2 activities are within the ability range of average students.

L3 Level 3 activities are more challenging activities.

Business and Technical Writing

Contents

Business Letters	*413*
Memos, E-mail, and Applications	*420*
Using the Computer as a Writing Tool	*424*
Technical Writing	*431*
Collaborative Writing in the Business World	*434*

Resource Manager

Planning Resources
- *Lesson Plans*

 Transparencies
- *Writing Process*

📁 **Other Print Resources**
- *Business and Technical Writing Activities*

- *Grammar and Composition Handbook*
- *Guide to Using the Internet and Other Electronic Resources*
- *Tests with Answer Key and Rubrics*
- *Writing Assessment and Evaluation Rubrics*

 Software
- *Presentation Plus!*
- *Revising with Style*
- *Testmaker*

 Web Sites
- *writerschoice.glencoe.com*
- *lit.glencoe.com*

Business Letters

People write business letters to apply for jobs, complain about poor service, order products, say thanks, request help or information, and express opinions. Knowing how to write an effective business letter is a valuable skill—one that you will use your whole life.

Why Write Business Letters?

You will probably write a number of business letters while you are still in high school, perhaps to apply for a job, to request information from businesses or government agencies, or to express your opinions on subjects of interest to you.

Business writing is a special form of expository writing. The most important thing to know about business writing is that it needs to be *efficient*. The reader should be able to grasp the meaning of a business letter quickly and with a minimum of effort. A letter that is long and complicated simply will not be read. You are much more likely to get the results you want if your letter is brief and clearly written.

Business letters use relatively formal language. The style is conversational but polite. Keep in mind that the impression the letter makes on the reader will certainly affect how he or she responds. Correct grammar, spelling, and punctuation are musts.

Business letters are usually single spaced and written on one side of a page only. However, you may double space a very short business letter so that it fills up more of the page. If the letter goes

to two pages, number pages after the first as follows, with the name of the recipient, the date, and the page number, all flush with the left margin and at the top of the page:

```
R. Mandel

10/23/01

Page 2
```

 ## Activity

Bring an example of a business letter to class. In small groups, evaluate your letters. How effective are they? What do the letters have in common? Present the results of your discussion to the rest of the class by creating a set of criteria for an effective business letter.

Styles of Business Letters

Two basic styles are used for most business letters. These are the block style and the modified block style.

quently writes letters on the job and school administrative assistants who write letters or produce correspondence for administrators.

Focus

Lesson Overview

Objectives
- To understand the formats, types, and characteristics of business letters
- To evaluate a variety of business letters
- To write an effective business letter

Critical Thinking
- analyzing
- generalizing

Listening and Speaking
- discussing

 ## Bellringer
Daily Language Activity

When students enter the classroom, have this assignment on the board: *Briefly describe a situation in which you or members of your family might need to write a business letter.*

Grammar Link to the Bellringer

Have volunteers share their descriptions. Select one of the situations described, and ask students what impression the writer would probably want to make. How might errors in grammar and mechanics affect the reader's perception of the writer? Review a few business punctuation basics. (*Examples:* Use a colon after a salutation and a comma after a complimentary closing.)

See also *Daily Language Practice*

Practice and Assess

Evaluation Rubrics

Use the following rubrics to evaluate the criteria that students generate for the activity on student page 413. Business letters should be clear, concise, complete, courteous, correct.

Motivating Activity

Invite a guest speaker to give your class tips about business writing. Candidates for guest speaker might include a parent who fre-

Teach

Technology Tip

Encourage students to word process their business letters. Composing on line makes it easier to format, revise, and save letters as well as create letterhead stationery to project a professional image.

Using the Model

Have students note and discuss the names, sequence, and punctuation of the parts of the model business letter on student page 414. Note that the letter illustrates a standard format for a personal business letter (one that a person writes to a business on his or her own behalf). Point out that business people writing on behalf of their company generally use letterhead stationery that has a preprinted heading.

Business & Technical Writing

Business Letters

Block Style The use of conventional styles or formats in business writing lets readers know exactly what to expect and where to look for important information. The most commonly used style is block format. In this style, all parts of the letter are aligned at the left margin.

Notice that this letter is brief, clear, and carefully organized to meet the needs of the reader. The writer has asked for what she wants in the first paragraph and provided her reader with all the basic information needed to make a decision.

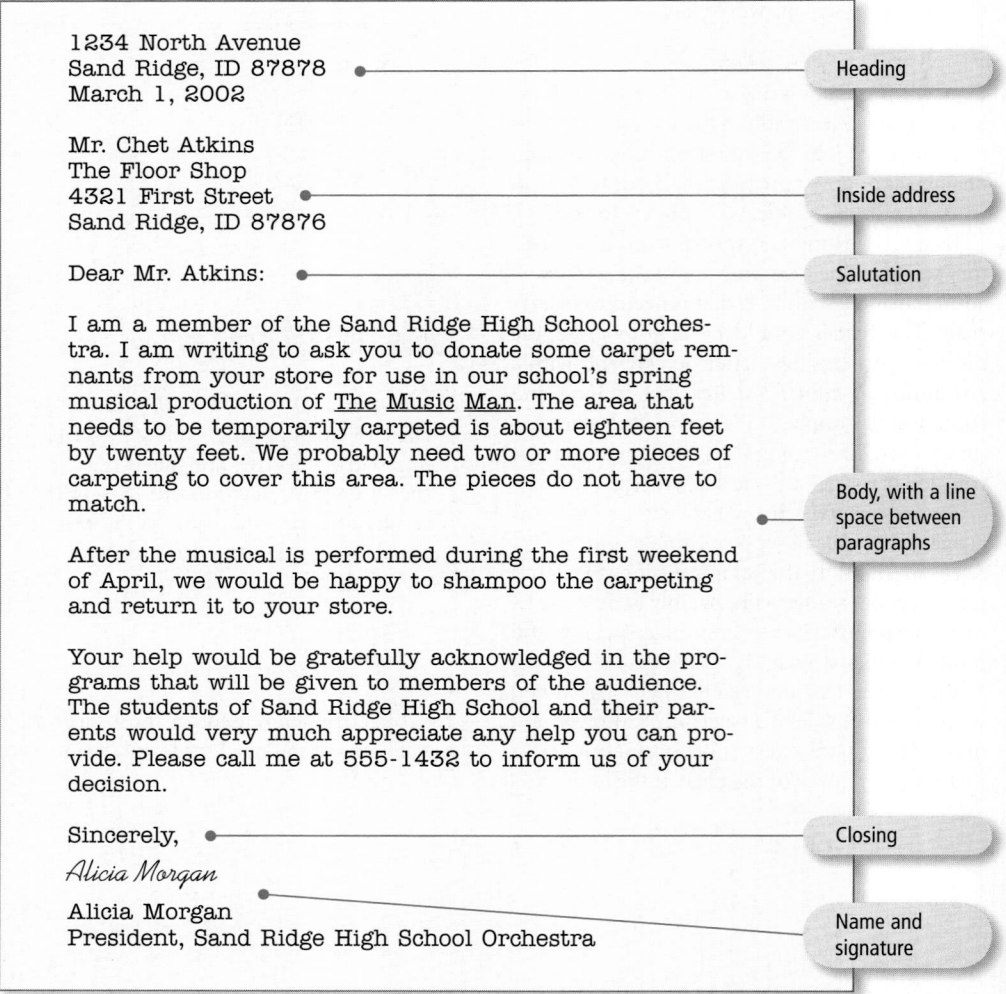

The letter contents:

1234 North Avenue
Sand Ridge, ID 87878
March 1, 2002 — **Heading**

Mr. Chet Atkins
The Floor Shop
4321 First Street
Sand Ridge, ID 87876 — **Inside address**

Dear Mr. Atkins: — **Salutation**

I am a member of the Sand Ridge High School orchestra. I am writing to ask you to donate some carpet remnants from your store for use in our school's spring musical production of <u>The Music Man</u>. The area that needs to be temporarily carpeted is about eighteen feet by twenty feet. We probably need two or more pieces of carpeting to cover this area. The pieces do not have to match.

After the musical is performed during the first weekend of April, we would be happy to shampoo the carpeting and return it to your store.

Your help would be gratefully acknowledged in the programs that will be given to members of the audience. The students of Sand Ridge High School and their parents would very much appreciate any help you can provide. Please call me at 555-1432 to inform us of your decision. — **Body, with a line space between paragraphs**

Sincerely, — **Closing**
Alicia Morgan
Alicia Morgan
President, Sand Ridge High School Orchestra — **Name and signature**

Critical Thinking

Evaluating Purpose

Ask students to identify the purpose of the model letter (to make a request) and to evaluate how well it achieves its purpose. Is the letter clear? Concise? Complete? Courteous? Correct?

Modified Block Format Some writers prefer modified block format. With this format, the date and closing are indented to the right. Paragraphs are indented and do not have a line space between them. Here is the same letter in the modified block format.

1234 North Avenue
Sand Ridge, ID 87878
March 1, 2002

Mr. Chet Atkins
The Floor Shop
4321 First Street
Sand Ridge, ID 87876

Dear Mr. Atkins:

I am a member of the Sand Ridge High School orchestra. I am writing to ask you to donate some carpet remnants from your store for use in our school's spring musical production of <u>The Music Man</u>. The area that needs to be temporarily carpeted is about eighteen feet by twenty feet. We probably need two or more pieces of carpeting to cover this area. The pieces do not have to match.

After the musical is performed during the first weekend of April, we would be happy to shampoo the carpeting and return it to your store. Your help would be gratefully acknowledged in the programs that will be given to members of the audience.

The students of Sand Ridge High School and their parents would very much appreciate any help you can provide. Please call me at 555-1432 to inform us of your decision.

Sincerely,

Alicia Morgan

Alicia Morgan,
President, Sand Ridge
High School Orchestra

> The writer's address and the date are indented.

> Paragraphs are indented.

> The closing is indented and aligned with the return address.

Teach

Technology Tip

Many word-processing programs include functions that automatically format business letters and memos and allow users to create customized templates. Encourage students to make use of these and other on-line formatting aids.

Using the Model

Have students compare and contrast the format of the modified-block business letter with that of the full-block letter on student page 414. Ask students which format they prefer and why. Point out that many business people prefer the full-block style because it takes less time to format but that the modified-block style is also frequently used.

Viewing and Representing

Creating Posters

Encourage students to create posters that illustrate standard ways to format business letters. Have students find examples of effective business letters, create call-outs to identify the parts of the letters, and enlarge the letters on a photocopier. Display the posters on a classroom bulletin board. (Remind students to procure permission to publish letters that are not in the public domain and to change the names and addresses to preserve confidentiality.)

Teach

Using the Model

After students view and analyze the model personal letter on student page 416, have them identify occasions for which it might be appropriate to combine business-letter content with personal-letter style. (*Sample answers:* to thank a business person who provided exceptional service, to offer condolences to a business associate who has suffered a death in the family, to congratulate a business associate on a promotion)

416

Business & Technical Writing

Personal Letter Format Although most business letters are written to strangers, some are more personal. Personal letters are usually handwritten, not typed. They are less formal in format and tone.

> 1234 North Avenue
> Sand Ridge, ID 87878
> March 1, 2002
>
> Dear Uncle Chet,
>
> Do you remember that I play violin in the Sand Ridge High School Orchestra? Well, we have a problem, and we were hoping you could help by donating some carpet remnants from your store.
> This spring the school is producing The Music Man. During practice we found out that it's sometimes hard to hear the singers because the orchestra is too loud. We have to find a way to deaden the music, and we thought putting carpeting on the floor under us might work.
> Do you think you can find some old pieces of carpet that we could use? Everyone here would sure appreciate it. Please give me a call if you can help. We will be happy to shampoo the carpeting and return it to your store after the production is over, and we will acknowledge your help in the program given to members of the audience.
> I look forward to seeing you and Aunt Teri at Mom and Dad's anniversary party.
>
> Love,
> Alicia

The salutation is informal and followed by a comma.

The tone of the body of the letter is informal.

The closing is personal.

416 Business and Technical Writing

Exploring Language

Contrasting Diction

Have students contrast the level of diction of the model business letter on page 415 with that of the model personal letter on page 416. Which letter is more formal? What words and phrases make it so? How does the writer's relationship with the reader influence the level of diction?

Activity

Imagine that you have completed a science project that you would like to enter in a science fair. Locate the name and address of the appropriate organization and write a business letter requesting specific information about procedures for entering, forms that need to be completed, dates and locations, and any other information needed to participate in the fair. Use either the block or modified block style.

PURPOSE To write a business letter requesting information

AUDIENCE Science fair officials

LENGTH 1 page

Writing Rubrics

In writing a letter requesting information, you should

- write clearly and to the point
- state your request in the first paragraph of the letter
- use polite but conversational language
- use correct business letter format
- check your letter for grammar, spelling, and mechanics

Types of Business Letters

People write business letters for many purposes. They may be requesting information or assistance, complaining, expressing an opinion about a product or service, apologizing, or applying for a job. The basic form of the letter remains unchanged regardless of the purpose, but each type of letter will be organized and structured somewhat differently. Your style may also change depending on your purpose.

Request The key to writing a letter requesting information or action is to ask for what you want in the first paragraph and to provide directions to the recipient as to how to respond in the paragraphs that follow. If you are requesting several items, it is helpful to indicate what you want in a bulleted list.

> Please send the following items:
> - two dozen test tubes
> - four Bunsen burners
> - one dozen small beakers
> - six large beakers

Teach

Discussion

Have students read and discuss the material on business letters of request. Remind students that the model letters on student pages 414–416 make requests. Ask students to identify situations for which they might need to write letters of request. (*Sample answer:* to ask a teacher or former employer to write a letter of recommendation on the student's behalf)

Practice and Assess

Evaluation Rubrics

To evaluate the letters that your class writes for the activity on student page 417, apply the Writing Rubrics that follow the activity.

Cooperative Learning

Evaluating Letters

Pair students and ask them to exchange the request letters that they wrote for the activity on student page 417. Have students use the rubrics to evaluate each other's letters. Encourage students to offer each other specific suggestions for revising.

Teach

Discussion

Have students read and discuss the material on business letters of complaint, opinion, and apology. Ask students to identify situations for which they might need to write each type of letter. (*Sample answers:* letter of complaint—to point out a problem that they experienced with a business or service organization and to request some form of restitution; letter of opinion—to express their opinion in a letter to the editor of a school newspaper; letter of apology—to extend a formal apology to an adult)

Teaching Tip

Letters of Complaint

Many students believe that it is acceptable (and effective) to adopt an angry or sarcastic tone when writing letters of complaint. Dispel this notion by reminding students that courteous letters are more likely to result in prompt and satisfactory action. Advise students to avoid using emotionally charged language and to state the facts without making accusations or threats. Together, discuss the "just-the-facts" approach illustrated in the model paragraph of complaint.

Business Letters

Another kind of request, more difficult than placing an order or asking for information, is a personal request for assistance. To write this type of letter, you should:

- acquaint the reader with the basics of the situation
- provide details
- make it easy for the reader to do as you ask

> I am writing to ask if I may change the time of my driving lesson from 7:00 p.m. to 4:00 p.m. My father has been taking me to my lesson, but his work schedule has changed, making it difficult for me to make the 7:00 time. The 4:00 time would allow me to walk to my lesson after school. If you do not have an opening then, please let me know at what other times you have openings so that we can work out a mutually convenient time.

The tone of your letter should be respectful but not pleading or demanding.

Complaint If you are writing to complain about a product or service, first decide what you want the company to do about your complaint. Do you want an apology, a replacement, or a refund?

Explain the problem and ask for exactly what you want in the first paragraph. If your tone is polite, you are more likely to get a positive response. If your letter is formal, you convey to the reader that your complaint is to be taken seriously.

> I recently ordered the enclosed book from your online service. As you can see, the book is damaged. I would like you to send me a replacement as soon as possible.

Opinion When you state your opinion in a letter, your goal is to persuade the recipient to adopt your point of view. Begin by stating what you believe. If you are disagreeing with another point of view, state the opposing position as clearly and as accurately as possible. This strategy avoids giving the impression that you are attacking a point of view that you do not appreciate or understand.

Whenever you express your opinion, your credibility as a writer is especially important. Be sure your facts are correct and your writing is error free.

> I am opposed to the construction of a new strip mall on the north edge of town. I am aware that the town's population is growing and more places to shop are needed. However, there are many buildings in the downtown area that are currently empty. The town should make use of existing buildings rather than spoil the scenic open spaces north of town. Doing so will also help to bring life back to the downtown area and help keep it from becoming run down.

Cultural Connections

Investigating Business Etiquette

Many business professionals communicate face to face and in writing with people whose cultural traditions are different from their own. Have students form small research groups to investigate business etiquette in foreign cultures of their choice. (Direct students to look in cultural guides for business people and to search the Internet by using the key words "business etiquette AND culture.") Have groups present their findings in brief oral reports. Together, discuss how an understanding of different cultures can improve communication.

Note the effort the writer makes to show an understanding of the other point of view. Remember, the more controversial the issue, the more important it is that the tone of the letter be reasonable.

Apology To write an effective apology, never trivialize the concern of the person making the complaint or make excuses. Too often, people who write apologies say things like "I'm very sorry for any inconvenience you experienced," but to the person who bothered to complain, inconvenience is probably much too weak a word to describe the experience. The person complaining also doesn't want to hear about how "busy we were" or how "how hard we try." Apologize, simply and directly.

> You are correct. We checked our files and you were scheduled for a haircut last Thursday. As our way of saying we are sorry, we will not charge you for your next haircut. We are very sorry for the trouble you experienced and are checking our procedures so that we do not make the same mistake again.

Notice that the writer takes the complaint seriously and doesn't offer excuses for the error.

Activity

Write a letter to your school newspaper expressing your opinion about an issue that concerns you. You might write about a traffic problem, the need to clean up the halls, or how to make use of a vacant classroom. Before you write, take some time to investigate the issue and understand the opposing position or positions. Use either a block or a modified block format.

PURPOSE To write a letter expressing an opinion about an issue
AUDIENCE Readers of school newspaper
LENGTH 1 page

Writing Rubrics

To write an effective letter, you should
- state your opinion clearly in a reasonable tone
- provide evidence or reasons to support your opinion
- give a fair picture of the opposing points of view
- use correct business letter form
- check the letter for grammar, spelling, and mechanics

Practice and Assess

Evaluation Rubrics

Encourage students to apply the Writing Rubrics listed after the activity on student page 419 to evaluate their own letters to the editor.

Cross-Reference: Letters to the Editor

To provide instruction and practice in argument and persuasion, refer students to Lesson 6.1 and Lesson 6.2.

Close

Remind students to update their portfolios by including copies of the business letters that they have written. Discuss the value of knowing how to write effective business letters.

Civic Literacy

Solving Problems

Discuss the causes and effects of a community problem that your students would like to see solved. Together, brainstorm ways to alleviate or solve the problem; then have students conduct research to evaluate the feasibility of the solutions. Follow up by having students use their research to write letters to the editor of a community newspaper or newsletter.

Focus

Objectives

- To understand appropriate formats for memos
- To write effective memos
- To understand the elements of e-mail messages
- To demonstrate mastery of the guidelines for filling out forms
- To complete a sample job application form accurately

Critical Thinking

- analyzing
- generalizing
- identifying

Listening and Speaking

- discussing

 Bellringer
Daily Language Activity

When students enter the classroom, have this assignment on the board: *Briefly define what a memo is. In what ways is it similar to a business letter? In what ways is it different?*

See also *Daily Language Practice*

Motivating Activity

Have students share their definitions and lists of similarities and differences. (*Sample definition:* A memo is a brief written interoffice message; that is, a written message intended to be shared among members of the same company, department, or group. *Similarities:* The rubrics that apply to business letters also apply to memos. *Differences:* Memos are formatted differently, are usually more concise, and may be less formal.) Provide students with a variety of models by sharing memos that you have received (and can make public) or by downloading sample memos from a business-writing Web site. Post the memos on a classroom bulletin board.

Memos, E-mail, and Applications

Written business communication can take forms other than formal letters.

Business Memos

People who work in a school, business, or other organization use memos to communicate with one another. Memos share many of the characteristics of the business letter but are usually less formal.

The memo format is designed to be as efficient as possible. The heading is double spaced and contains essential information for the reader, including who wrote the memo and what it is about. The rest of the document is single spaced with a line space between paragraphs. The content is direct and to the point. Typically, a memo is one page or less. It delivers its message immediately and directly.

One of the advantages of the memo format is that the recipient can write his or her response on the memo itself and return it. If you choose, you can end the memo with the word *Response:* or *Comment:* to make it clear that you expect only a quick, handwritten note in response.

To: Committee Chairpersons

From: Lisa Hopkins *LH*

Date: February 4, 2002

Re: Committee Chairpersons Meeting

We need to schedule the quarterly meeting for all of the school's committee chairpersons. Will Thursday afternoon at 3:00 P.M. in the library work for you? Please let me know as soon as possible.

It is important that you make every effort to attend the meeting, since we need to begin discussing plans for the class party. Thank you.

Instead of a signature at the end, the writer initials his or her name in the heading.

Re is an abbreviation for *regarding.* The subject of the memo goes here.

All text is flush left.

There is no closing, since the writer is identified in the heading.

420

E-mail

Of all the forms of business communication, e-mail is by far the most informal. E-mail often reads like a transcript of a conversation.

As e-mail becomes more and more common in business and elsewhere, writers need to analyze their audiences. The use of sentence fragments, colloquial language, and abbreviations may be fine for friends, but they are not appropriate for most business exchanges.

For anyone other than a close friend, an e-mail should be similar to a memo in format and style. The subject line, in fact, is even more important, since busy readers use the subject line to decide whether to open the message.

Clarity and directness are also important. Answering "I can come" to an e-mail may be more puzzling than helpful. If you are answering an e-mail, repeat enough of the original message to remind the recipient of the context, so he or she doesn't have to guess what you are writing about.

Remember that e-mail may not be private. Companies can access the e-mail of employees, and recipients of e-mail can easily forward what you have written. Before you know it, your "private" message may end up on a bulletin board that boasts 250 "hits" a day.

Because you cannot always format an e-mail as you can a letter (and because the format can sometimes be garbled in transmission of the e-mail), more formal communications should be done in a word processing program and e-mailed as an attachment. In most e-mail programs, sending an attachment requires simply that you click on a button marked *attachment,* insert the path and file name, and click OK.

Activity

Pretend you are a member of a student committee that has been asked to make recommendations about the best place to hold a school-sponsored dance or concert. Write a memo to members of the committee asking that they poll classmates and gather their own ideas prior to the first meeting. Be sure to include the date and time of the meeting.

PURPOSE To write a memo
AUDIENCE Committee members
LENGTH 1 page or less

Writing Rubrics

To write an effective memo, you should
- convey your message clearly and concisely
- use the correct memo format
- include all necessary information
- proofread the memo

Practice and Assess

Evaluation Rubrics

To evaluate the memos that your class writes for the activity on student page 421, apply the Writing Rubrics that follow the activity.

Teach

Discussion

Have students read and discuss the material on e-mail. Point out that e-mail is a channel for sending all types of business writing. Although the typical e-mail message box has a subject line that is similar to that of a memo, e-mail is, in fact, used to send letters and reports as well as memos.

Writing in the Real World

E-mail and chatrooms can be excellent tools for motivating reluctant writers and English language learners to express themselves in writing. Surf the Internet to find appropriate pen-pal sites, chatrooms for ELLs, famous-author sites with electronic bulletin boards, and electronic bookstores that encourage readers to review books.

Business and Technical Writing **421**

Listening and Speaking

Call for volunteers who are skilled in uploading and downloading e-mail attachments to give brief "how-to" demonstrations. If possible, have your class meet in the school computer lab, or bring a modem-equipped laptop computer to class.

Business and Technical Writing

Teach

Using the Model

After students read and discuss the material on filling out applications, review together the sample form on student page 422. Discuss why organizations create forms to gather information. (*Sample answers:* Forms are an organized and convenient way to gather standard information. Well-designed forms make it easy to find information quickly.)

CONNECTION

Use the Internet to find a variety of forms for your students to study and complete. Many business and government sites have application forms that can be downloaded or printed out.

Applications

To apply for almost any job, secure a library card, get a driver's license, rent an apartment, open a bank account, or attend a college, you will need to fill out an application. The application conveys an impression of you as a person. Many applicants have been passed over because of typographical or spelling errors on a job application.

Volunteer Application Form

Thank you for considering volunteer work at the Lincoln Animal Shelter.

Name: _____ Date: _____

Address: _____

City: _____ State: _____ ZIP Code: _____

Phone: _____ Fax: _____ E-mail: _____

DOB: _____ SSN: _____

Best time to reach you: _____

Education (circle highest level completed):
7   8   9   10   11   12

Is this experience for school credit?   Yes   No

School Name and address: _____

_____

Why do you want to volunteer? _____

_____

_____

Describe previous volunteer experience. _____

_____

_____

Signature: _____

Callout annotations:
- Be sure that the form is filled out neatly in black ink.
- Abbreviations commonly used on applications include DOB (date of birth) and SSN or SS# (social security number).
- Include hyphens in your social security number.
- If the information asked for does not apply to you, write *n/a* in the blank.

Real World Connection

Creating Forms

Have students create forms that they can use at home, on the job, or in organizations to which they belong. Students might create phone-message forms, checklists for completing tasks, or evaluation forms for gathering opinions.

In completing an application form, read through the entire document before writing anything. Follow instructions carefully.

Neatness counts. If possible, request more than one copy of the form so you can redo it if necessary.

Don't leave blank spaces. If something does not apply, write *n/a* (not applicable) in the space. Blank spaces suggest that you have something to hide or that you did not carefully read the form.

Complete the form in ink, preferably black ink.

Activity

Fill out one or more practice applications. You can obtain blank forms from a local bank, the Registry of Motor Vehicles, the public library, potential employers, or parents. Work in a small group to evaluate and critique each other's work.

PURPOSE To complete at least one sample application
AUDIENCE Your classmates
LENGTH Length of the application(s)

Writing Rubrics

To effectively prepare an application form, you should
- answer each question
- correctly place information on the form
- write neatly and legibly
- check spelling and punctuation

Practice and Assess

Evaluation Rubrics

Encourage students to evaluate their own applications by applying the Writing Rubrics that follow the activity on student page 423.

Close

Remind students to update their portfolios by including copies of assignments that they have completed. Discuss the value of knowing how to write effective memos and e-mail and how to complete forms accurately.

Focus

Objectives
- To practice reading various types of graphic organizers
- To create effective charts and graphs

Skills
- creating computer graphics
- presenting information concisely

Critical Thinking
- analyzing
- organizing

Listening and Speaking
- discussing

Bellringer
Daily Language Activity
When students enter the classroom, have this assignment on the board: *Create an hour-by-hour table that shows how you spend a typical day at school.*

See also *Daily Language Practice*

Motivating Activity
Bring or have students bring to class a variety of graphic organizers from newspapers and magazines. (The national newspaper *U.S.A. Today* and *Time* magazine are useful sources.) Post the graphic organizers on a classroom bulletin board, and ask students to vote on which graphics are the most effective and to explain why.

Using the Computer as a Writing Tool

Computers can be used to research information, create and format documents, and present data graphically. The instructions given for these functions in this section are general; every software program performs some or all of these tasks a little differently. The easiest way to learn these functions is by reading the instruction manual or using the Help menu.

Making Tables and Graphs

Your word processing program can be used to display information and data in tables and graphs. In most cases, you can create either with a few keystrokes.

Tables Tables are used to present facts and figures in an easy-to-read format. Tables organize information into columns and rows. Columns are the vertical elements in a table and rows are the horizontal elements. Cells are the individual boxes that contain data.

To make a table in a word processing program, use the Help menu or the Tables pull-down menu. Then select the number of rows and columns you need. In most cases you will need one "extra" row to provide headings for each of the columns. If necessary, you can insert and delete rows and columns after you have created your table. You can also adjust the appearance of the table by adding borders and shading or color. Here is an example of a table.

Prefix	Meaning	Examples
re-	again	restate, restart
ante-	coming before	anteroom, antecedent
un-	not	unclean, undone
sub-	below	subcommittee, submarine

Graphs While a table can help readers quickly find and compare data, graphs highlight a comparison by showing it pictorially. You can use your word processing program to display information and data in tables or graphs. Keep in mind that in many software programs, graphs are referred to as charts. To learn to use the capabilities of your computer software, read the instruction manual that comes with your software or use the Help menu.

A **bar graph** shows data plotted along two axes. The vertical axis is the Y axis, and the horizontal is the X axis. Bar charts are used to showcase comparisons. The example bar graph shown here compares the number of students enrolled in various science classes. Notice how the size of the bars allow you to quickly rank the classes from smallest to largest enrollment.

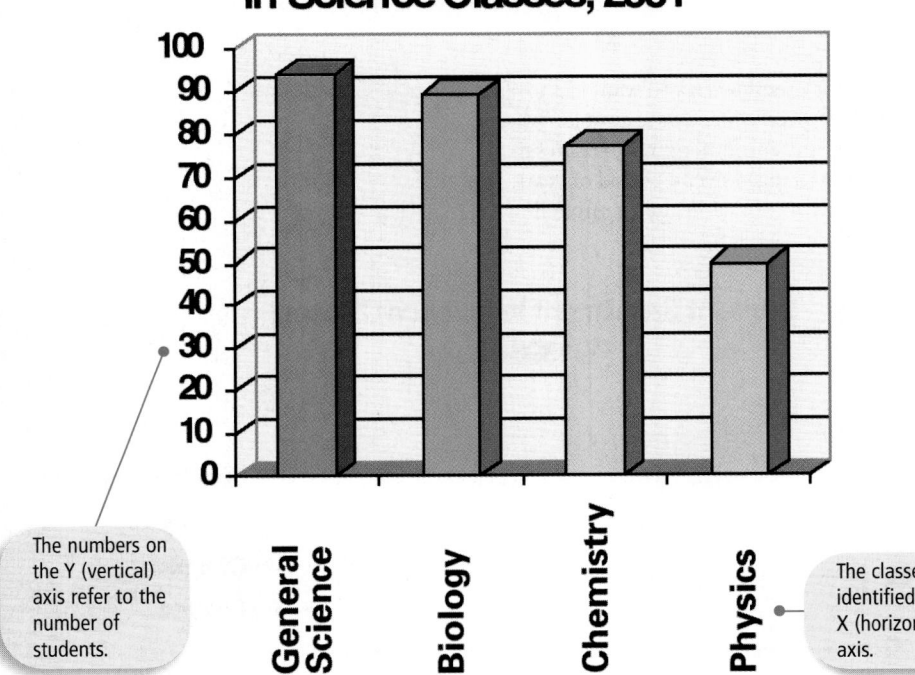

Student Enrollment in Science Classes, 2001

The numbers on the Y (vertical) axis refer to the number of students.

The classes are identified on the X (horizontal) axis.

General Science · Biology · Chemistry · Physics

Teach

Using the Model

Many students have difficulty reading graphic organizers. Carefully review with students how to read the bar graph illustrated on student page 425. Emphasize that bar graphs are used to show comparisons. Point out each axis and its label. If necessary, demonstrate how to find the point at which the two axes intersect.

Viewing and Representing

Creating Bar Graphs

To provide students with practice in creating a bar graph, have them plot their quiz or test scores over a semester or other period of time. Encourage students to create their graphs on computers.

Teach

Circle (Pie) Graphs

Emphasize that circle graphs are often used to express percentages. Point out that while many circle graphs are one-dimensional, the graph illustrated is three-dimensional and viewed from the side.

Line Graphs

As students examine the line graph, point out that line graphs are used to show changes in data over time. Color is often used on line graphs to distinguish one item from another. When color is not used, lines may be dotted or broken to distinguish among data.

Connections Across the Curriculum

Encourage students to scan their textbooks to find examples of the three types of graphic organizers (bar, circle, and line). Divide the class into small groups, and assign each group a different discipline to investigate. Have groups share with the class the organizers that they consider to be the most effective and explain why.

Using the Computer as a Writing Tool

A **circle graph,** or pie chart, shows the relationship of parts to a whole. In the circle graph shown, for example, the complete circle stands for all the students enrolled in a science class. The segments represent the percentage of students in each type of science class.

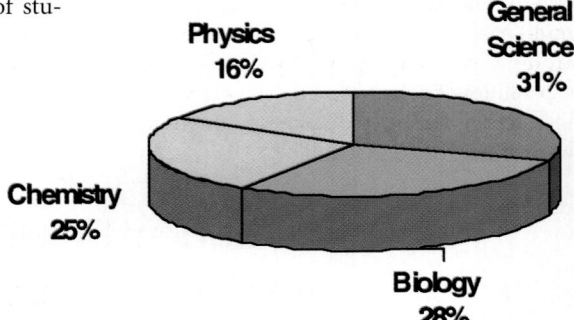

Student Enrollment in Science Classes, 2001

Physics 16%

General Science 31%

Chemistry 25%

Biology 28%

A **line graph** is useful when you want to show changes in data over time. For example, you might show how the enrollment numbers in science classes have changed over a period of years. What trends do you notice in the example line graph?

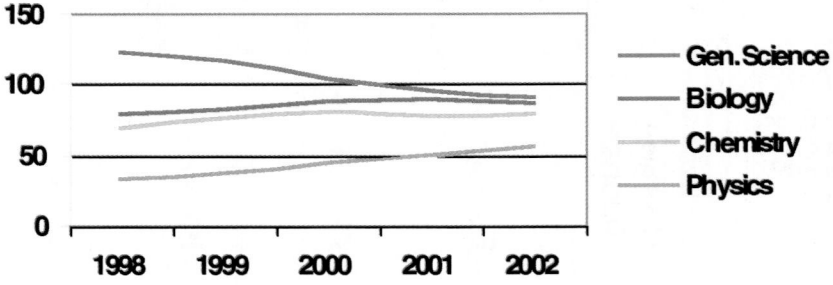

Student Enrollment in Science Classes, 1998-2002

Gen. Science
Biology
Chemistry
Physics

Speaking and Listening

Explaining Computer Graphics

Call for volunteers who are skilled in creating computer graphics to give brief "how-to" demonstrations. If possible, have your class meet in the school computer lab, or bring a lap-top computer to class.

Creating graphs, or charts as they are called in word processing programs, is easy. You can enter data directly in a table designed to work with the charting function. When the data is entered, you choose the kind of chart you want, enter a title and—if needed—a legend, and click OK. The word processor creates the graph for you and inserts it into your document. If you discover a problem once your graph has been inserted into the document, simply double click on the graph to return to the editing function. Usually, you can switch between one type or style of graph and another once the data is entered to see which best conveys the point you are trying to make.

 Activity

Gather statistical data for publication in a magazine. You may choose any topic that interests you. Examples of the kinds of things you might research include the most popular CDs or movies among young adults; the most popular sports among young adults in selected states; or driver's education policies at various high schools across the United States. The possible topics are countless.

Research your topic and write a report that presents the data not only in words but also in at least two different graphic formats: tables, charts, or graphs. Document your sources.

PURPOSE To gather, use, and present data in graphic form
AUDIENCE Readers of a student magazine
LENGTH 2–3 pages

Writing Rubrics

To prepare an effective table, chart, or graph, you should

- choose data that can be presented pictorially
- select a format appropriate for the audience
- present the data using the most effective graphic form
- include a descriptive title, labels, and/or legend
- proofread for accuracy

Business & Technical Writing

Practice and Assess

Evaluation Rubrics

To evaluate students' reports and graphic organizers, use the Writing Rubrics that follow the activity on student page 427.

Business and Technical Writing

Teach

Using the Model

Point out that organization charts show relationships among people or departments. Together, read the organization chart on student page 428 and discuss why companies often provide new employees with organization charts. With input from the class, draw on the board a simple organization chart that shows the chain of command in your school or a school group.

Creating Organization Charts and Flowcharts

Organization charts show how individuals, positions, or departments within an organization are related to one another. Check your Help menu to see if your program has a function or template to help you create organization charts. If your program does not allow you to create them automatically, you can use the drawing tools to make a chart. To make an organization chart, click on the appropriate icons to create boxes and lines similar to those shown in the example chart. You can choose either a vertical (portrait) or horizontal (landscape) orientation from Page Setup in the File menu. Once you have determined a structure, type in the names, titles, and other information you need. The example shows the basic organization of a student government.

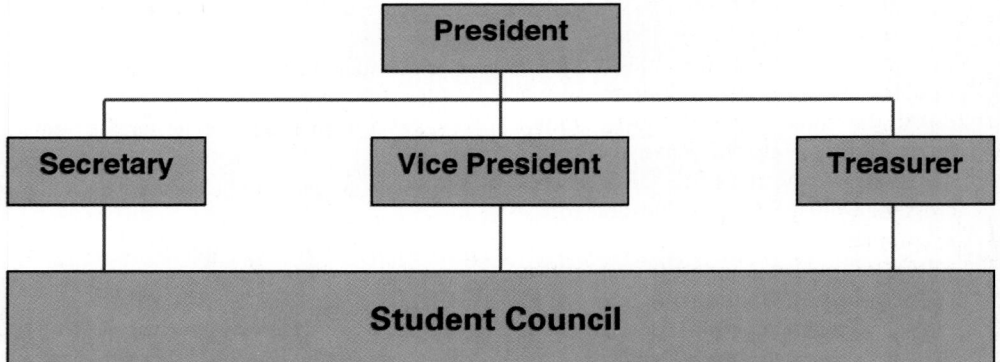

Proposed New Student Government Organization

President

Secretary Vice President Treasurer

Student Council

Be careful not to show too much information in one chart or one box; your information should be easy to see and understand. Start each box the same way. Be sure to include a title for your chart.

Flowcharts highlight a different kind of relationship; they show the stages in a process. They often use arrows to show progress from one step to the next. For flowcharts, be consistent in the kind of information you enter in each box. For example, each box might include a single step or a single action in a process. The example describes how you can use your word processing software to create a flowchart.

How to Create a Flowchart

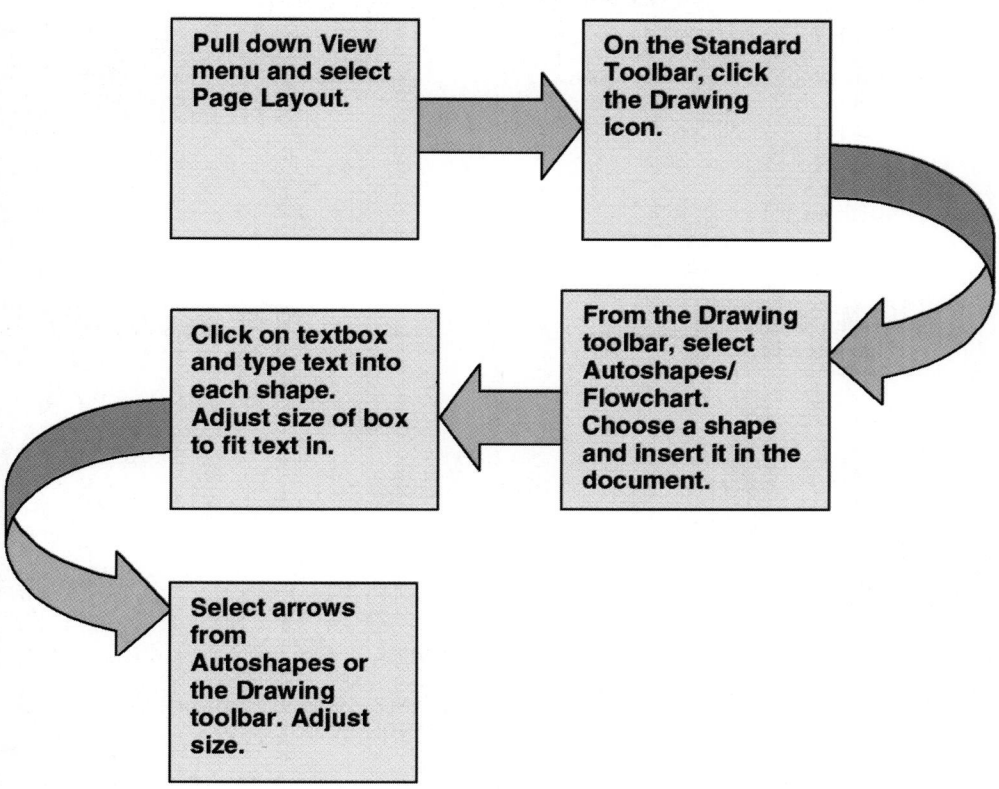

Pull down View menu and select Page Layout.

On the Standard Toolbar, click the Drawing icon.

From the Drawing toolbar, select Autoshapes/ Flowchart. Choose a shape and insert it in the document.

Click on textbox and type text into each shape. Adjust size of box to fit text in.

Select arrows from Autoshapes or the Drawing toolbar. Adjust size.

Teach

Using the Model

Stress that flowcharts show the stages or steps in a process. As a class, read the flowchart on student page 429 and discuss why companies often provide new employees with flowcharts.

Cross-Reference: Flowcharts

To provide further practice in reading flowcharts, refer students to the chart on student pages 110–111, which shows the writing process that *Time* magazine editors and writers follow.

Critical Thinking

Challenge students to analyze how different news media use graphics in their coverage of the same stories. Assign students to watch an evening newscast and to take notes on the subjects covered and the use of graphics and other visuals. The following day, bring a copy of a city newspaper to class and ask students to compare and contrast the lead stories of the TV news program with those on the front page of the newspaper. Are the subjects similar? How do the graphic organizers and other visuals presented in the newspaper compare with those presented by the newcast? How might students account for the similarities and differences?

Business and Technical Writing

Practice and Assess

Evaluation Rubrics

To evaluate students' charts, use the Writing Rubrics that follow the activity on student page 430.

Close

Remind students to update their portfolios by including copies of graphic organizers that they have completed. You might also have students post on a classroom bulletin board graphic organizers that they have created. Encourage students to share strategies that worked especially well for them.

Making an Investment Decision

 Activity

Choose one option:
- Use a computer to make an organization chart showing the structure of your student council or some other school group. Show each level of the organiztion.
- Use a computer to make a flowchart that explains a process with which you are familiar, such as how to do a science experiment, how to set up a VCR, or how to decorate a cake. Show all steps in the process.

PURPOSE To create an organization chart or a flow-chart

AUDIENCE Your teachers and classmates

LENGTH 1 page

Writing Rubrics

To create an effective chart, you should
- identify each step and its place in the process
- write a title for the chart
- use the correct format
- label consistently
- check for accuracy

Technical Writing

Technical writing puts scientific or technical information into language that is easy to read and understand. Accuracy, consistency, clarity, and brevity are important characteristics of technical writing.

Elements of Technical Writing

Accuracy While errors in all kinds of writing are to be avoided, errors can be a calamity in technical writing. Putting a decimal point in the wrong place in a manual written for computer engineers can lead to millions of dollars worth of damage.

Consistency Technical writers and editors use a uniform style, so that words are consistently capitalized and units of measure are the same throughout the document. In some cases, inconsistencies may just be annoying, but in other cases they can spell disaster.

It is also important to be consistent in the names that you give to objects and processes. If your document tells the reader to "rotate" an object, then you should continue to use the word *rotate* rather than synonyms such as *spin, turn,* or *twist*. By doing so, you lessen the chance that your reader might become confused.

Most companies that issue technical documents and reports have a style manual to help writers maintain a consistent style. These manuals deal with such issues as capitalization, abbreviations, punctuation, and how to write numbers and equations.

Clarity Technical writers must be aware of their audience. Language appropriate for an audience of engineers may baffle nontechnical readers. On the other hand, if a document is intended for specialists, translating technical jargon into everyday language will unnecessarily complicate the writing.

Brevity Technical writers know that their readers want to gather relevant information as quickly as possible. Therefore, they often use short sentences, bulleted or numbered lists, and brief paragraphs to convey information. They also divide the text into multiple sections that make it easier to find specific information.

Many technical reports and papers begin with an abstract that summarizes the document in one tightly written paragraph. Many readers rely on abstracts not only to get the information they need but also to help them decide if the document is one they need to read in its entirety.

Technical writers are careful to organize reports so that readers can easily find the sections they need. Tables of contents guide the reader, and chapters are divided into clearly labeled sections. Abstracts provide a quick summary, and appendices include details too cumbersome to be included in the body of the report.

Technical writers also help their readers by presenting as much information as possible in charts, graphs, tables, or other graphic forms.

Focus

Objectives
- To understand the characteristics of technical writing
- To write effective abstracts and instructions

Skills
- presenting information concisely

Critical Thinking
- organizing
- clarifying
- drawing conclusions

Listening and Speaking
- discussing

Bellringer
Daily Language Activity

When students enter the classroom, have this assignment on the board: *List at least three technical manuals or sets of directions that you have used during the past month.*

See also *Daily Language Practice*

Motivating Activity

Encourage students to share their experiences reading technical writing. Together with the class, generate a list of characteristics of effective technical writing. Then compare the items on your list to the items described in Elements of Technical Writing on student page 431.

Business and Technical Writing

Teach

Writing Abstracts

As a class, read and discuss the activity on student page 432. Explain to students that their abstracts should be written in their own words but may include a brief quotation. Review when and how to quote.

Model how to prepare to write an abstract. Remind students that the title, introduction, and subheads of a piece of writing are guides to the main idea and major supporting details. Demonstrate by reading aloud the title, introduction, and headings of student page 431. To give students practice in summarizing, challenge them to write a one-sentence summary of the information provided under the subhead "Accuracy" on student page 431. (*Sample summary:* All information in a piece of technical writing must be accurate.)

Practice and Assess

Evaluation Rubrics

To evaluate students' abstracts, use the Writing Rubrics that follow the activity on student page 432.

Teach

Writing Instructions

Select a simple process with which students are familiar, and with input from the class draw a flowchart of the major stages in the process.

Activity

Suppose that your school newspaper is planning to include brief summaries of computer software reviews. Prepare a summary to submit to your school paper.

Read a review of a piece of new software on the Internet or in a computer magazine and write an abstract of no more than 250 words. The abstract should thoroughly summarize the review, reflecting its major points and conclusions. Be sure to write the abstract in your own words, although you can quote from the original as necessary.

PURPOSE To write an abstract of a software review
AUDIENCE Readers of your high school paper
LENGTH 250 words or less

Writing Rubrics

In writing an effective abstract, you should
- summarize the major points of the original review
- clearly state the conclusion
- write clearly, simply, and succinctly
- proofread your work carefully

Writing Instructions

Instructions are a form of technical writing. In order to give meaningful instructions, you have to understand the process you are describing thoroughly and completely. Then you must recall what it was like not to understand the process so you can explain it to others. In thinking about the process, divide it into clearly delineated steps. Then place those steps in an order that avoids repetition of steps or the need to backtrack. Below are some key recommendations from technical writers of how-to manuals.

Tips for Technical Writing

- Show or describe the finished product so the reader knows the goal.
- List all required parts and tools. You don't want to send the reader down to the basement in the middle of a project because you forgot to mention that your process requires a hot-glue gun or a stapler.
- Label each step clearly: (*Step One: Open the view menu.*)
- Write imperative sentences. (*Select page layout.*)
- Spell out even those steps that you think ought to be obvious. (*Turn on your computer.*)
- Check for errors or omissions by following your directions exactly as they are written.
- Have someone else follow the steps to help you identify instructions that may be confusing or difficult to understand.

We often write or follow instructions in science laboratory classes. The following chart presents an example of instructions that were written for a biology mini-lab.

What happens to plant cells in a hypertonic solution?

Plant tissue is normally rigid or crisp because of the turgor presssure within the cells. When plant cells lose their turgor pressure, the plant wilts. What happens on the cellular level when a plant cell is exposed to hypertonic solution?

Procedure

1. Use forceps to take a leaf from the tip of an *Elodea* sprig, and place it on a slide with a drip of water. Apply a coverslip.
2. Use your microscope to observe it first with low power and then with high power. Draw a cell and its contents.
3. Place a drip of 3% salt solution on the slide near one side of the coverslip. Place a piece of paper towel on the opposite side of the coverslip to draw out the plain water and pull the salt water underneath the coverslip.
4. Observe the cell for a few ninutes and then sketch it.

Activity

Write a brief "how-to" manual to teach your classmates to perform a step-by-step process. Select a process that you know well but which others may not know. Consider such processes as changing a set of spark plugs, adjusting the gears on a racing bike, firing a clay pot, or giving medication to an uncooperative cat or dog.

PURPOSE To write a "how-to" manual
AUDIENCE Your teacher and classmates
LENGTH 2–4 pages

Writing Rubrics

In writing effective instructions, you should
- list tools and equipment needed
- place steps in sequential order
- label each step
- use visuals effectively
- write clearly
- take into account the level of knowledge of the audience
- proofread for vague language and for errors in grammar, usage, and spelling
- test for omissions

Assess

Evaluation Rubrics

To evaluate students' "how to" manuals, apply the Writing Rubrics that follow the activity on student page 433.

Close

Remind students to update their portfolios by including copies of technical writing that they have completed. Discuss the importance of knowing how to read, write, and follow instructions.

Listening and Speaking

Encourage students to use their "how to" manuals as the basis for brief demonstration speeches. Remind speakers to rehearse, paying special attention to their use of nonverbal communication (pitch, rate, and tone of voice; posture; use of gestures; and eye contact with audience). Have students revise and expand on the Writing Rubrics to create a set of criteria by which they might evaluate one another's speeches.

Objectives

- To learn ways to work effectively as part of a team
- To use active listening strategies during small-group discussions
- To work collaboratively to produce a written report

Skills

- presenting information concisely

Critical Thinking

- organizing
- clarifying
- drawing conclusions

Listening and Speaking

- discussing
- active listening

Bellringer

Daily Language Activity

When students enter the classroom, have this assignment on the board: *Recall times when you have worked with others on a project. What are some of the advantages of collaborating? What are some of the potential pitfalls?*

See also *Daily Language Practice*

Motivating Activity

Point out to students that the books they read and the TV programs they watch are the products of teamwork. Together, brainstorm a list of media products that are collaborative efforts (nightly news programs, newspapers and newsmagazines, documentaries, Web sites, and so on). Select one of the products, and identify various team members who collaborate to produce it. (*Sample answer:* TV news program—reporters, camera operators, news writers and editors, anchorpersons). Review the Active Listening Tips on student page 434, and ask how the tips might help team members avoid the pitfalls of collaboration.

— Collaborative Writing in the Business World —

Today, many organizations stress collaboration and teamwork, insisting that employees analyze and solve problems in groups, evaluate each other's performance, and report to management as one voice.

Businesses use teams because people in groups tend to generate more and better ideas than individuals. Creativity is enhanced when people share ideas in open discussion. There are few experiences more satisfying than a team experience in which everyone contributes to create a first-class product. Collaboration can be rewarding and enjoyable if group members work well together.

However, if the participants do not know how to work together effectively, collaborating on a project can be a frustrating and time-consuming process. Also, whenever people work together in groups, there is a risk that those who are more outgoing may silence those who are quiet but have much to contribute.

Active Listening

Working effectively in groups requires active listening. To listen actively:

- Make sure that everyone's point of view is not only heard but also understood.
- Don't interrupt, and try not to disagree until the other person has fully expressed his or her views.
- Ask open-ended questions and paraphrase the answers to be sure you have understood what the other person is saying.
- If necessary, ask follow-up questions to clarify the other person's ideas.

Enrichment and Extension

Encourage students to use the community library or the Internet to find books and articles about teamwork and the roles team members fulfill. Have students use their research to write brief "how to" feature articles for the school newspaper.

Once a group has been assigned a task, it should agree on the purpose and audience. Be as concrete and specific as possible: (For example, *The purpose of this report is to convince students of the dangers of smoking.*) Do not assume everyone understands the rules of group work. Discuss them thoroughly and record the statements the group has mutually agreed to.

Then list the tasks involved in completing the assignment. Discuss the strengths of group members, and assign various aspects of the project based on what each person does best. One person may be especially good at research on the Internet; another may be more knowledgeable about library reference sources; someone may know how to create professional-looking graphics.

Watch out for potential problems within the group. If someone is not pulling his or her weight or is refusing to participate, meet as a group to discuss the problem and find a solution.

Assign portions of the writing to individuals, or have each person draft the entire report and pull the best parts from each individual attempt. Then have the entire group suggest revisions and proofread the final project.

Activity

Working in small groups, create a history of your school, neighborhood, or community. It should show what the place was like in at least three different time periods.

The report may be presented in any manner you choose, but it must be a group project. Focus equally on visual images and words. You may tell the whole story of the place from its beginnings to today or highlight selected periods. Include visual aids to enhance your presentation.

PURPOSE To prepare an oral report about a particular place.
AUDIENCE Classmates
LENGTH 5–10 minutes

Writing Rubrics

To prepare an effective collaborative presentation, you should

- collect enough information to tell a coherent story
- present the information in both words and pictures so your audience can grasp key events easily
- assign tasks based on members' strengths

Assess

Evaluation Rubrics

To evaluate students' collaborative reports, apply the Writing Rubrics that follow the activity on student page 435.

Close

Have group members evaluate the strengths and weaknesses of their group, and ask students to describe what they learned from collaborating on their reports. Remind students to update their portfolios by including copies of writing assignments that they have completed.

✔ ASSESSMENT OPTIONS

Tests with Answer Key & Rubrics
Business and Technical Writing Mastery Test

Testmaker
Business and Technical Writing Mastery Test

MindJogger Videoquizzes

You may wish to administer the Business and Technical Writing Mastery Test at this point.

Grammar, Usage, and Mechanics

Objectives

The units in Part 2 continue to guide students in their development toward becoming effective, confident writers. Throughout these units, students will be asked

- to write clearly and effectively using the conventions and mechanics of English
- to identify parts of speech such as nouns, pronouns, verbs, adjectives, adverbs, prepositions, conjunctions, and interjections
- to analyze sentence construction, including phrases, clauses, and overall sentence structure
- to understand, through sentence diagraming, how the various words and parts of a sentence function together
- to demonstrate control over grammatical elements such as verb tenses, verb forms, subject-verb agreement, pronoun-antecedent agreement, and modifiers
- to produce work that demonstrates the accurate use of the rules of capitalization and punctuation
- to compose more complex sentences that contain gerunds, infinitives, and participles

Viewing the Art

This painting depicts a group of three animals in an idyllic setting. The lush foliage and unusual postures of the three figures points to a mythic, rather than a naturalistic treatment of the subject. In much the same way, writers sometimes depart from strict realism, employing fantasy or imagination to convey their themes.

Interpret and Analyze Use the following questions for discussion:

- How would you describe the relationship among the three figures in the painting?
- Can you see a story in this painting? How would you put the story into words?

"I'm fishing this beautiful stream in Alaska, catching salmon, char and steelhead, when this bear lumbers out of the woods and down to the stream bank."

—Robert H. Abel

436

Resource Manager

Use the following resources to customize your teaching of the units in Part 2.

Planning Resources
- *Lesson Plans*
- *Block Scheduling*

Transparencies
- *Bellringer*
- *Daily Language Practice*
- *Two-Minute Skill Drill*

Other Print Resources
- *Grammar and Composition Handbook*
- *Grammar Enrichment*

- *Grammar Practice*
- *Grammar Reteaching*
- *Grammar Workbook*
- *Sentence-Combining Practice*
- *Spelling Power*
- *Taking Standardized Tests*
- *Tests with Answer Key and Rubrics*
- *Vocabulary Power*

Jan Plaskosinski,
The Animal Kingdom

PART 2

Grammar, Usage, and Mechanics

Unit 10 **Parts of Speech**   *438*

Unit 11 **Parts of the Sentence**   *496*

Unit 12 **Phrases**   *522*

Unit 13 **Clauses and Sentence Structure**   *542*

Unit 14 **Diagramming Sentences**   *574*

Unit 15 **Verb Tenses and Voice**   *584*

Unit 16 **Subject-Verb Agreement**   *612*

Unit 17 **Using Pronouns Correctly**   *636*

Unit 18 **Using Modifiers Correctly**   *662*

Unit 19 **Usage Glossary**   *690*

Unit 20 **Capitalization**   *712*

Unit 21 **Punctuation, Abbreviations, and Numbers** *732*

437

Discussing the Quotation

The quotation comes from "Appetizer," a short story by Robert H. Abel (b. 1941). Discuss the quotation with the class. Ask students to explain if they think the fisherman fears the bear as a dangerous intruder, or if they think he views the bear as a part of the natural setting. Ask students how the relationship among the man, the bear, and the fish in the quotation is similar to or different from the relationship among the animals in the painting. To find out more information about the author and the story from which this quotation was taken, see *Glencoe Literature,* Course 5, page 1017.

Writing Prompt Have students write a short narrative in which they include characters from the quotation and the painting. Have them create a setting for their narrative that is based on the setting in the painting or on the place described in the quotation. Students should proofread their writing for accuracy in spelling and for correct uses of conventions of punctuation and capitalization.

📼 **Video**
• *MindJogger Videoquizzes*

💾 **Software**
• *Interactive Grammar and Language Workbook*
• *Language Arts PASS*
• *Presentation Plus!*
• *Revising with Style*

• *Sentence Diagraming*
• *Testmaker*
• *Vocabulary Power Puzzlemaker*
• *Writer's Choice Puzzlemaker*

💻 **Web Sites**
• *writerschoice.glencoe.com*

Objectives

- To develop an understanding of the eight parts of speech
- To demonstrate control over the parts of speech by identifying their uses and by writing sentences using them effectively

✔ ASSESSMENT OPTIONS

📁 *Tests with Answer Key & Rubrics*
Unit 10 Pretest, pp. 31–32
Unit 10 Mastery Test, pp. 33–34

💾 *Testmaker*
Unit 10 Pretest
Unit 10 Mastery Test

You may wish to administer the Unit 10 Pretest at this point.

Key to Ability Levels

L1 Level 1 activities are within the basic ability range of students.

L2 Level 2 activities are within the ability range of average students.

L3 Level 3 activities are more challenging activities.

UNIT 10 Parts of Speech

Lesson 10.1	**Nouns**	*439*
Lesson 10.2	**Pronouns**	*445*
Lesson 10.3	**Verbs**	*453*
Lesson 10.4	**Adjectives**	*460*
Lesson 10.5	**Adverbs**	*466*
Lesson 10.6	**Prepositions**	*473*
Lesson 10.7	**Conjunctions**	*476*
Lesson 10.8	**Interjections**	*482*
Grammar Review		*484*
Writing Application		*495*

438

Resource Manager

Planning Resources
- *Lesson Plans*
- *Block Scheduling*

📑 **Transparencies**
- *Bellringer*
- *Daily Language Practice*
- *Two-Minute Skill Drill*

📁 **Other Print Resources**
- *Grammar and Composition Handbook*

- *Grammar Enrichment*
- *Grammar Practice*
- *Grammar Reteaching*
- *Grammar Workbook*
- *Sentence-Combining Practice*
- *Tests with Answer Key and Rubrics*

Video
- *MindJogger Videoquizzes*

💾 **Software**
- *Interactive Grammar and Language Workbook*
- *Language Arts PASS*
- *Presentation Plus!*
- *Revising with Style*
- *Testmaker*
- *Writer's Choice Puzzlemaker*

🖥 **Web Sites**
- *writerschoice.glencoe.com*

10.1 | Nouns

■ A **noun** is a word that names a person, a place, a thing, or an idea.

PERSON	woman, man, Juanita Brown, great-grandfather
PLACE	planet, Texas, farm, high school
THING	dolphin, parrot, ivy, bookmark
IDEA	success, affection, freedom, courage

■ A **concrete noun** names an object that occupies space or can be recognized by any of the senses. Concrete nouns are things you can see, hear, taste, touch, smell, or feel.

thorn	stars	thunder	gas	milk
child	drum	velvet	headache	dove

■ An **abstract noun** names an idea, a quality, or a characteristic.

excitement	honesty	innocence	happiness	harmony
truth	bravery	softness	fear	peace

Most nouns can take either a singular or a plural form, depending upon whether they name *one* person, place, thing, or idea or *more than one.*

SINGULAR	desk, bench, sky, wolf, man
PLURAL	desks, benches, skies, wolves, men

The possessive form of a noun can show possession, ownership, or the relationship between two nouns.

SINGULAR POSSESSIVE	PLURAL POSSESSIVE
the **girl's** coat	the **girls'** coats
a **business's** debts	those **businesses'** debts
a **prince's** crown	the **princes'** crowns
a **man's** voice	the **men's** voices

Exercise 1 — Identifying Nouns

Find the twenty nouns that appear in the following paragraph, and write them on your paper.

Musical Flair

[1]When Seiji Ozawa, the colorful principal conductor of the orchestra, performs, the auditorium is usually overflowing. [2]He performs with a stylish blend of intelligence, fierce concentration, and theatricality. [3]As the famed director leads the orchestra through fast, loud, and dramatic passages, his baton flashes like a sword, and his thick mop of black hair bobs furiously up and down. [4]There are no sheets of music on the podium as he conducts because he routinely memorizes the entire score of each work.

10.1 Nouns **439**

Parts of Speech

Focus

Lesson Overview

Objectives
- To identify types of nouns
- To use nouns appropriately in writing

 Bellringer
Daily Language Activity
When students enter the classroom, have this assignment on the board: *List five nouns someone might use in speaking of you.*

See also *Daily Language Practice*

Teach

☑ **Grammar Tip**
Point out that all nouns are alike in one way. They name someone or something. As you discuss kinds of nouns listed on this page, ask students to give additional examples.

Practice and Assess

Answers: Exercise 1
1. Seiji Ozawa, conductor, orchestra, auditorium
2. blend, intelligence, concentration, theatricality
3. director, orchestra, passages, baton, sword, mop, hair
4. sheets, music, podium, score, work

Resource Manager

Planning Resources
- *Lesson Plans*

Transparencies
- *Bellringer*
- *Daily Language Practice*
- *Two-Minute Skill Drill*

📂 **Other Print Resources**
- *Grammar and Composition Handbook*
- *Grammar Enrichment*, p. 1
- *Grammar Practice*, p. 1
- *Grammar Reteaching*, p. 1
- *Grammar Workbook,* Lessons 1, 2

Practice and Assess

Answers: Exercise 2

Answers will vary, but suggestions are provided below.

1. speed	11. scholar
2. sound	12. smile
3. fragrance	13. night
4. taste	14. smell
5. pain	15. fool
6. faithfulness	16. scream
7. perception	17. host
8. digestion	18. firecracker
9. gentleness	19. party
10. communication	20. prize

Answers: Exercise 3

1. lessons	11. churches
2. cheeses	12. concerns
3. taxes	13. stereos
4. boys	14. cities
5. radios	15. children
6. brushes	16. calves
7. halves	17. businesses
8. countries	18. moose
9. aptitudes	19. valleys
10. women	20. envelopes

Answers: Exercise 4

1. my three sisters' bedrooms
2. the men's tailor
3. a friend's misfortune
4. the bus's fumes
5. several galaxies' stars
6. the mice's squeals
7. the wives' trip
8. the video's stars
9. the boy's parents
10. the children's behavior

Parts of Speech

Exercise 2   Supplying Abstract and Concrete Nouns

For each concrete noun in items 1–10, write an abstract noun that names an idea with which the concrete noun can be associated. For each abstract noun in items 11–20, write a concrete noun that has the quality of the abstract noun.

SAMPLE ANSWERS   dancer—grace
redness—tomato

1. quarterback	11. intelligence
2. scream	12. friendliness
3. perfume	13. darkness
4. pepper	14. aroma
5. bruise	15. stupidity
6. dog	16. anger
7. binoculars	17. hospitality
8. teeth	18. noise
9. lamb	19. celebration
10. book	20. luck

Exercise 3   Writing Singular and Plural Nouns

On your paper, write the plural form of each singular noun below. If you need help, consult a dictionary.

1. lesson	11. church
2. cheese	12. concern
3. tax	13. stereo
4. boy	14. city
5. radio	15. child
6. brush	16. calf
7. half	17. business
8. country	18. moose
9. aptitude	19. valley
10. woman	20. envelope

Exercise 4   Writing Possessive Forms of Nouns

On your paper, write each of the following phrases, supplying the possessive form of the italicized noun.

1. my three *sisters* bedrooms	6. the *mice* squeals
2. the *men* tailor	7. the *wives* trip
3. a *friend* misfortune	8. the *video* stars
4. the *bus* fumes	9. the *boy* parents
5. several *galaxies* stars	10. the *children* behavior

MEETING INDIVIDUAL NEEDS   English Language Learners

Using Plurals

Students new to English have great difficulty with nouns that have no plural. They may say, "I have some homeworks to do." Nouns that cannot be counted are called noncount nouns. We cannot say, for example, *one homework, two homeworks.* Noncount nouns fall into relatively well defined groups:
Fluids: water, coffee, milk, oil, blood

Particles: rice, dust, dirt, sand, sugar
Gases: air, steam, oxygen, smoke, smog
Abstractions: beauty, honesty, luck
Phenomena: weather, lightning, gravity
Collections: clothing, garbage, baggage
     Provide students with practice using sentences with noncount nouns.

Exercise 5   Adding Nouns to Categories

On your paper, add one more noun to each group of nouns listed below.

SAMPLE   tulips, roses, carnations, _____
ANSWER   tulips, roses, carnations, peonies

1. lion, gorilla, orangutan, _____
2. hatred, hostility, battle, _____
3. aunt, cousin, great-grandmother, _____
4. plateau, mountain, river, _____
5. neighbors, strangers, merchants, _____
6. justice, democracy, fairness, _____
7. library, theater, convention center, _____
8. Jenny's, Kim's, Mariana's, _____
9. potatoes, noodles, bread, _____
10. mathematics, sociology, anthropology, _____
11. sensitivity, kindness, concern, _____
12. Paris, Buenos Aires, Kuala Lumpur, _____
13. container, plate, dish, _____
14. teacher, doctor, private investigator, _____
15. courage, honor, decency, _____
16. planet, space, solar system, _____
17. insect, bird, reptile, _____
18. defendant, witness, prosecutor, _____
19. possibility, prospect, opportunity, _____
20. Thomas, Derek, Anthony, _____

Exercise 6   Completing Sentences with Nouns

On your paper, complete each sentence by filling in the blanks with nouns. Be sure that your completed sentences make sense.

1. The two _____ bought new _____.
2. The _____ coat was made of _____.
3. The _____ watched a(n) _____.
4. Her _____ seems to be her best _____.
5. Seven _____ sat on the _____.
6. My three _____ moved to a new _____.
7. The _____ shoes were covered with _____.
8. In _____ I enjoy the _____ and the _____.
9. One _____ stood alone on his _____.
10. _____ are at the _____.

Answers: Exercise 5
Answers will vary, but some suggestions are given below.
1. cheetah
2. enmity
3. mother
4. desert
5. secretaries
6. liberty
7. auditorium
8. Maria's
9. pasta
10. economics
11. patience
12. London
13. cup
14. clerk
15. gentleness
16. galaxy
17. mammal
18. judge
19. chance
20. José

Answers: Exercise 6
Answers will vary, but some suggestions are given below.
1. The two ranchers bought new trucks.
2. The cowhand's coat was made of sheepskin.
3. The rancher watched a coyote.
4. Her uncle seems to be her best instructor.
5. Seven magpies sat on the trough.
6. My three cousins moved to a new house.
7. The child's shoes were covered with mud.
8. In Montana I enjoy the antelope and the moose.
9. One ram stood alone on his rock.
10. Crowds are at the airport.

MEETING INDIVIDUAL NEEDS   Less Proficient Readers

Using Possessive Nouns

A major problem for some students is remembering the correct spelling of possessive nouns. Such students have a better chance of remembering the proper possessive form when they think of the apostrophe as standing for something. Explain, therefore, that in the possessive form the apostrophe can be thought of as standing for the phrase *belongs to.* **L1**

Teach

Proper and Common Nouns

☑ **Grammar Tip**

Students sometimes think that a proper noun is a noun with a unique reference. For example, since I have only one mother, then *mother* must be a proper noun. A proper noun, however, is a title or a form of address. For example, *mother* is a proper noun in the sentence *What's for dinner, Mother?* but not in the sentence *I called my mother.*

Practice and Assess

Answers: Exercise 7

1. h	**11.** q
2. d	**12.** r
3. i	**13.** t
4. f	**14.** n
5. a	**15.** k
6. g	**16.** l
7. b	**17.** o
8. c	**18.** p
9. e	**19.** m
10. j	**20.** s

Two-Minute Skill Drill

Have students substitute proper nouns for each of these common nouns:

president   singer
comedian   actor
athlete

👆 **See also** *Two-Minute Skill Drill Transparency 10.1*

Parts of Speech

Proper and Common Nouns

■ A **proper noun** is the name of a particular person, place, thing, or idea.
■ A **common noun** is the general—not the particular—name of a person, place, thing, or idea.

Proper nouns are capitalized, whereas common nouns are not usually capitalized.

TYPE OF NOUN	PROPER NOUNS	COMMON NOUNS
PERSON	Aunt Shirley, Uncle Arnold	relatives
	General Powell, General Lee	generals
PLACE	Atlantic Ocean, Pacific Ocean	oceans
	Mars, Venus, Jupiter	planets
THING	Labor Day, Fourth of July	holidays
	The Lion King, Aladdin	movies
IDEA	Buddhism, Judaism	religions
	Middle Ages, Great Depression	eras

Exercise 7   Matching Proper Nouns with Common Nouns

On your paper, match proper nouns 1–10 on the left with common nouns *a–j* on the right. Then match proper nouns 11–20 with common nouns *k–t.*

1. Santa Fe
2. *National Geographic*
3. Kleenex
4. Shakespeare
5. Denzel Washington
6. Florence Griffith-Joyner
7. Africa
8. the Grand Canyon
9. the Empire State Building
10. Linda Ronstadt
11. Theodore Roosevelt
12. Islam
13. Grammy
14. Canada
15. Chrysler
16. Macintosh
17. Industrial Revolution
18. *Hamlet*
19. David Letterman
20. Mississippi

a. actor
b. continent
c. gorge
d. magazine
e. skyscraper
f. author
g. athlete
h. city
i. tissue
j. singer
k. automobile
l. computer
m. comedian
n. country
o. historical movement
p. play
q. president
r. religion
s. state
t. award

Enrichment and Extension

Choosing Nouns in Composition

Direct students' attention to Unit 3, Descriptive Writing, pp. 120–163. Remind the class that choosing precise and vivid nouns is the essence of effective descriptive writing. Ask students to select descriptive paragraphs from books they are reading and to study each writer's use of nouns in description. Discuss the use of strong nouns as replacements for adjective-noun combinations. Have students summarize the discussion in their journals.

Collective Nouns

■ A **collective noun** names a group.

army	committee	(the) public
team	choir	(a) pride (of lions)

You can consider collective nouns either singular or plural, depending upon the meaning you wish to convey. If a collective noun refers to a group as a whole, it is considered singular. If a collective noun refers to the individual members of a group, it is considered plural. Note the differences in the meaning in the following examples:

SINGULAR	The **committee** wants our attention.
PLURAL	The **committee** have gone their separate ways.
SINGULAR	The **class** likes to read plays.
PLURAL	The **class** takes their seats.

Exercise 8   Identifying Collective Nouns

On your paper, list the five collective nouns in the following paragraph.

Observing the Wonders of Ocean Life

¹After the crew of the merchant ship finish their chores, they love to watch the sea. ²Occasionally at night a swarm of plankton makes the ocean glow softly. ³A young sailor watches in amazement as a pod of feeding whales suddenly breaks the calm surface. ⁴Only a few days earlier, along the coast of California, the sailors had spotted a herd of sea lions frolicking in the waves. ⁵The varied population of the sea never ceases to delight the young sailor.

Exercise 9   Using Plural and Singular Collective Nouns

On your paper, complete the sentences in each pair by writing one of the collective nouns listed below. Indicate how the noun is used by writing *plural* or *singular*.

family	jury	audience	club	people	infantry

1. a. The _____ struggle into their coats after the play.
  b. The _____ applauds when the curtain falls.
2. a. The _____ meets every other Thursday.
  b. The _____ vote for a chairperson and treasurer every two years.
3. a. The _____ plans a vacation.
  b. The _____ each have different chores.
4. a. The _____ disagree on a verdict.
  b. Has the _____ reached a decision?
5. a. _____ have different characteristics.
  b. This _____ has created a great civilization.

Teach

Collective Nouns

☑ **Grammar Tip**

Since collective nouns may be either singular or plural, it is sometimes difficult to know whether to use a singular or plural verb. Usage varies. For example, in British usage, collective nouns are usually used with plural verbs. Whereas Americans would say *Our team has lost,* British speakers would say *Our team have lost.*

⇄ **Cross-reference: Grammar**

For instruction and practice in using collective nouns, refer students to Lesson 16.4, pp. 618–619.

Practice and Assess

Answers: Exercise 8

1. crew
2. swarm
3. pod
4. herd
5. population

Answers: Exercise 9

Answers will vary, but some suggestions are given below.

1. audience (plural)
   audience (singular)
2. club (singular)
   club (plural)
3. family (singular)
   family (plural)
4. jury (plural)
   jury (singular)
5. People (plural)
   people (singular)

Parts of Speech

Enrichment and Extension

Using Collective Nouns

Most collective nouns can be used as either singular or plural words. Have students make up sentences that illustrate both uses of *board, committee, couple, crew, group, staff, herd, majority,* and *minority.* Suggest that students work with partners to share and evaluate their sentences.

Practice and Assess

Answers: Exercise 10

1. proper	11. common
2. collective, common	12. proper
	13. collective, common
3. common	
4. common	14. proper
5. proper	15. collective, common
6. collective, common	
	16. common
7. common	17. proper
8. collective, common	18. common
	19. collective, common
9. collective, common	
10. proper	20. proper

Answers: Exercise 11

Answers will vary, but some possible nouns are given below.
1. Rosa, backpack, gym
2. improvising, band
3. class, ability, contest
4. river, beavers, grass
5. C. S. Lewis, author
6. destruction, concern
7. herd, flock, Africa
8. Michael Jordan, basketball
9. junior class, dance
10. grandfather, Denver, June

Answers: Exercise 12

Sentences will vary. Students should use concrete nouns to convey vivid pictures. Sample:

My favorite place, the living-room couch, is covered with worn green velvet pillows. Strewn about are the latest newspapers and glossy magazines. Illumination comes from a weak lightbulb in the antique lamp on the end table. Its soft green hue and downy texture soothe my frayed senses after a stressful day. It is my own space, my six feet of sanctuary and refuge.

Additional Resources

Grammar Practice, p. 1
Grammar Reteaching, p. 1
Grammar Enrichment, p. 1

Grammar Workbook, Lessons 1, 2

Parts of Speech

Exercise 10 Classifying Common Nouns, Proper Nouns, and Collective Nouns

On your paper, classify each of the following nouns by writing *common, proper,* or *collective*. Some nouns belong in more than one category.

1. Uncle John	11. scout
2. assembly	12. Hilton Hotel
3. uncle	13. chorus
4. juror	14. University of California
5. Cape May	15. class
6. troop	16. manager
7. major	17. Fifteenth Amendment
8. crowd	18. person
9. flock	19. committee
10. Niagara Falls	20. Renaissance

Exercise 11 Completing Sentences with Different Kinds of Nouns

On your paper, complete each sentence by filling in the twenty-five blanks with the kinds of nouns specified in *italic* typeface. Be sure that your completed sentences make sense.

1. *Proper* left her *common* in the *concrete*.
2. The practice of *common* has become popular with the *common collective*.
3. The *common collective* proved its *abstract* at the *common*.
4. Near the *common* I saw three *common* run across the *concrete*.
5. *Proper* is a famous *common*.
6. Environmental *abstract* is a serious *abstract* for anyone who cares about humankind.
7. A *common collective* of zebras and a *common collective* of ostriches are only two of the spectacular sights on the plains of East *proper*.
8. I was thrilled to be able to watch *proper* practice *common* before the game.
9. The *common collective* voted for the *common*.
10. His *common* was born in *proper* on *proper* 4, 1932.

Exercise 12 Creating Sentences with Nouns

Write five sentences about one of your favorite places. Rely especially on concrete nouns to convey a vivid picture of the place.

Close

Ask each student to select a writing sample from his or her portfolio and to revise it by using nouns more effectively and accurately.

10.2 Pronouns

■ A **pronoun** is a word that takes the place of a noun, a group of words acting as a noun, or another pronoun. The word or group of words that a pronoun refers to is called its **antecedent.** A pronoun must agree in number and gender with its antecedent.

> When **she** was still a young girl, Sylvia Plath decided to become a writer. [The pronoun *she* replaces the noun *Sylvia Plath*.]
>
> George Orwell wrote *Animal Farm* and *1984* in the 1940s. **Both** remain immensely popular today. [The pronoun *both* takes the place of the nouns *Animal Farm* and *1984*.]
>
> Phillis Wheatley published **her** first poem at the age of sixteen and soon found **herself** a celebrity. [The pronouns *her* and *herself* take the place of the noun *Phillis Wheatley*.]

There are a limited number of pronouns, about seventy-five, in English. They fall into one or more of the following categories: personal and possessive pronouns, reflexive and intensive pronouns, demonstrative pronouns, interrogative pronouns, relative pronouns, and indefinite pronouns.

Exercise 13   Identifying Pronoun Antecedents

On your paper, write the antecedent of each italicized pronoun.

Emily Dickinson

1. In *her* poems, Emily Dickinson wrote about love, nature, and immortality.
2. "I never saw a Moor" and "They Sky is low—the Clouds are mean" are *both* about nature.
3. For many years, Emily's father did not support *her* interest in poetry.
4. Emily, her brother Austin, and her sister Vinnie grew up in Amherst, Massachusetts. *They* continued to live there as adults.
5. Emily seldom left Amherst. *She* spent many years as a recluse.
6. Some of Emily's acquaintances urged *their* friend to publish her poems.
7. Emily sent a few poems to a poetry critic at *The Atlantic Monthly* and asked for *his* opinion.
8. *They* corresponded until Emily's death in 1886.
9. Emily found beauty in nature and all *its* variations.
10. Emily once wrote of *herself:* "I am small, like the Wren."

Focus

Lesson Overview

Objectives
- To identify types of pronouns
- To use pronouns appropriately in writing

Bellringer
Daily Language Activity

When students enter the classroom, have this assignment on the board: *Read the following passage and identify the pronouns.*

> Tears began streaming down my face too. I pitied him, myself, my family, the rest of black South Africa. Why does apartheid do this to us? . . . Why had it created within my father's heart a granite wall, which had prevented him from expressing feelings of love, care, comprehension, and understanding?
>
> —Mark Mathabane, *Kaffir Boy*

(Answers: *my, I, him, myself, my, us, it, my, him*)

See also *Daily Language Practice*

Practice and Assess

Answers: Exercise 13
1. Emily Dickinson
2. "I never saw a Moor" and "The Sky is low, the Clouds are mean"
3. Emily's
4. Emily, her brother Austin, and her sister Vinnie
5. Emily
6. Some of Emily's acquaintances
7. a poetry critic at *The Atlantic Monthly*
8. Emily and the poetry critic
9. nature
10. Emily

Parts of Speech

Resource Manager

Planning Resources
- *Lesson Plans*

Transparencies
- *Bellringer*
- *Daily Language Practice*
- *Two-Minute Skill Drill*

📁 Other Print Resources
- *Grammar and Composition Handbook*
- *Grammar Enrichment,* p. 2
- *Grammar Practice,* p. 2
- *Grammar Reteaching,* p. 2
- *Grammar Workbook,* Lessons 3, 4

Teach

Personal and Possessive Pronouns

☑ **Grammar Tip**

Possessive pronouns have two forms: one form that is used before a noun and another form that is used alone. Those that are used alone are true pronouns—they stand in place of a noun. Possessive forms used before a noun, however, play the role of noun modifiers. In the sentence *This is her radio, her* modifies *radio.*

Two-Minute Skill Drill

Have students form pairs. First, direct one student to write three sentences, each with a personal and a possessive pronoun. Then have the second student identify each personal pronoun and each possessive pronoun. Students should support their claims as needed and respond appropriately to their peer's review.

👆 **See also** *Two-Minute Skill Drill Transparency 10.2*

Parts of Speech

Personal and Possessive Pronouns

■ A **personal pronoun** refers to a specific person or thing by indicating the person speaking (the first person), the person being spoken to (the second person), or any other person or thing being spoken about (the third person).

Personal pronouns, like nouns, are either singular or plural.

Personal Pronouns		
	Singular	**Plural**
FIRST PERSON	I, me	we, us
SECOND PERSON	you	you
THIRD PERSON	he, him	they, them
	she, her	
	it	

FIRST PERSON	Thomas went with **me** to the game. [*Me* refers to the person speaking.]
SECOND PERSON	Ask Gina to show **you** the article. [*You* refers to the person being addressed.]
THIRD PERSON	**He** gave **them** a poor excuse. [*He* and *them* refer to the persons being discussed.]

Third-person singular pronouns express **genders.** *He* and *him* are masculine; *she* and *her* are feminine; *it* is neuter (neither masculine nor feminine).

The **possessive pronouns** in the following chart take the place of the possessive forms of nouns.

Possessive Pronouns		
	Singular	**Plural**
FIRST PERSON	my, mine	our, ours
SECOND PERSON	your, yours	your, yours
THIRD PERSON	his	their, theirs
	her, hers	
	its	

The first form of each pronoun in the preceding chart can be used before a noun. The second form is used alone, like a noun.

USED BEFORE A NOUN	This is **her** radio.
	Its battery is new.
USED ALONE	This radio is **hers.**

446 Unit 10 Parts of Speech

English Language Learners

MEETING INDIVIDUAL NEEDS

Using Pronouns in Conversations

Pair students new to English with those whose primary language is English. Direct pairs to have a conversation and to note personal and possessive pronouns that their partners use.

Exercise 14   Identifying Personal and Possessive Pronouns

On your paper, list the personal or possessive pronoun in each of the following items. Then identify the pronoun as *personal* or *possessive*.

Ancient Rome

1. The Romans built a forum in the center of each city and used it for public activities.
2. Their houses had little furniture and usually only a single door as protection against thieves.
3. The father of a Roman family had total power over all members of his household.
4. Roman parents selected marriage partners for their children.
5. As a student in a school in ancient Rome, you would have used a wax tablet for writing.
6. Your day would have started before dawn.
7. For entertainment, citizens went to races and bet on a chariot and its driver.
8. Some entertainment was bloody. It involved gladiators fighting to the death.
9. Wealthy people had servants and often sent them to do the shopping.
10. Servants were often enemy soldiers captured in battle. They tended gardens, served meals, and taught the children.
11. Men and women wore a gown called a tunic. It hung to the knees or below.
12. Men dressed in white, but women dyed their clothing various colors.
13. Romans made few scientific discoveries, but they did collect scientific information.
14. Pliny the Elder assembled scientific knowledge of his day.
15. Most Romans lived by farming. They used crop rotation to enrich soil.
16. Romans invented concrete, which provided a strong building material for their structures.
17. Many roads crisscrossed the Roman Empire. They helped hold the empire together.
18. Augustus was the first emperor of Rome. He built an elaborate arch in the middle of town to celebrate a victory in battle.
19. His uncle was Julius Caesar.
20. A Roman woman of noble birth had an important role. She looked after the house and all the servants.

Exercise 15   Using Personal and Possessive Pronouns

Improve the following paragraph by replacing each underlined word or group of words with a personal or possessive pronoun. Write your answers on your paper.

Navajo Chants

¹Two friends and the writer of this article attended a lecture on Native American history and culture. ²The writer's two friends especially enjoyed the lecture, since the lecture was presented by the two friends' mother, who is an expert on the subject. ³The lecturer's

---

Practice and Assess

Answers: Exercise 14

1. it, personal
2. Their, possessive
3. his, possessive
4. their, possessive
5. you, personal
6. Your, possessive
7. its, possessive
8. It, personal
9. them, personal
10. They, personal
11. It, personal
12. their, possessive
13. they, personal
14. his, possessive
15. They, personal
16. their, possessive
17. They, personal
18. He, personal
19. His, possessive
20. She, personal

Answers: Exercise 15

1. I
2. My; it; their
3. Her; me
4. his
5. no change
6. his
7. no change
8. You
9. It

Parts of Speech

Enrichment and Extension

Acting as Pronoun or Adjective?

Say the sentence *This is her radio.* Then ask students whether *her* is a pronoun or an adjective. Allow students to discuss, and then explain as follows: Generally speaking, when there is a difference between a word's form and its function, the word is classified by its function. Thus, *her* is classified as an adjective because it performs an adjectival function in the sentence. Usually, possessives used to modify nouns are classified as adjectives.

Teach

Reflexive and Intensive Pronouns

☑ **Grammar Tip**

Reflexive and intensive pronouns have identical forms but quite different functions. Reflexive pronouns are part of the basic grammar of their sentence: they are objects or predicate nominatives. If they were to be deleted, the sentence would no longer make sense. Intensive pronouns, like appositives, can be deleted without changing the meaning of the sentence.

Two-Minute Skill Drill

Have each student write one sentence with each pair of pronouns, using the second reflexively:

I, myself   *we, ourselves*
you, yourself   *they, themselves*
she, herself

📖 **See also** *Two-Minute Skill Drill Transparency 10.2*

(sidebar, vertical) Parts of Speech

---

comments about the importance of music in Navajo religious ceremonies interested <u>the writer of this article</u>. ⁴Navajo religious ceremonies regularly feature a male singer, or medicine man, who is a highly respected member of <u>the singer's</u> community. ⁵The music is designed to provide healing for tribe members. ⁶The singer has a great responsibility, for <u>the singer's</u> chant (which may take several days to complete) must be performed perfectly. ⁷Otherwise the chant will not carry its healing powers. ⁸<u>The reader of this passage</u> would have loved to hear the demonstration of the Navajo mountain chant. ⁹<u>The demonstration</u> was fascinating.

Reflexive and Intensive Pronouns

You form the reflexive and intensive pronouns by adding *-self* or *-selves* to certain personal and possessive pronouns.

Reflexive and Intensive Pronouns		
	Singular	**Plural**
FIRST PERSON	myself	ourselves
SECOND PERSON	yourself	yourselves
THIRD PERSON	himself, herself, itself	theirselves

■ A **reflexive pronoun** refers, or reflects back, to a noun or pronoun used earlier in the sentence. A reflexive pronoun always adds information.

   I almost exhausted **myself** working for her in the campaign.

   Today, for the first time in months, she is **herself.**

   As a team they have no faith in **themselves.**

■ An **intensive pronoun** adds emphasis to another noun or pronoun.

■ An **intensive pronoun** does not add information to the sentence. If it is omitted, the meaning of the sentence will still be the same.

■ An **intensive pronoun** is often placed directly after its antecedent.

   You **yourself** told me to stop.

   Rita **herself** met us.

However, an **intensive pronoun** may come anywhere in the sentence.

   I baked the bread **myself.**

   We will bake it **ourselves.**

Exploring Language

"Bending-back" Pronouns

Explain that *reflexive* means "bending back." Both reflexive and intensive pronouns "bend back" to refer to the subject of the sentence. Use arrow diagrams like those on the student page to help students understand the role of reflexive and intensive pronouns in sentences. **L1**

Exercise 16 — Identifying Antecedents of Reflexive and Intensive Pronouns

On your paper, write the antecedent of the italicized pronoun in each of the following sentences.

SAMPLE   John Tyler and his wife, Julia, wrote a poem and set it to music *themselves.*

ANSWER   John Tyler and his wife, Julia

Presidents and Their Families

1. During her college years, Pat Nixon supported *herself* as a bank teller and also worked as a movie extra.
2. Mamie Eisenhower and her friends often amused *themselves* by playing cards.
3. To entertain *himself* at his father's inauguration, Charles Taft read a book.
4. The White House *itself* was the focus of much of Jacqueline Kennedy's reading before she actually moved in.
5. Because Gerald Ford *himself* had laryngitis, he asked his wife to extend his congratulations to President-elect Jimmy Carter.

Exercise 17 — Distinguishing Between Reflexive and Intensive Pronouns

On your paper, write the reflexive or intensive pronoun in each of the following sentences. Then identify each pronoun as *reflexive* or *intensive.*

Marie Curie

1. As a child, Marie threw herself into her studies.
2. Learning itself was her passion.
3. By the time she married Pierre Curie, he had already made himself a reputation as a well-known physicist.
4. When working with radioactive compounds, even Marie herself was surprised at how much radioactivity they gave.
5. Recognizing the significance of his wife's work, Pierre convinced himself to abandon his research and help Marie.
6. Marie often had to defend herself from attacks made against her because she was a woman scientist.
7. During World War I, Marie promoted the use of the X-ray machine for medical purposes. The doctors themselves were not immediately convinced of the machine's usefulness.
8. Marie's contribution to science was invaluable, but the work itself may have led to her untimely death.
9. Because so little was known about radioactivity, Marie did not realize that she needed to protect herself from polonium radiation.
10. Did Marie congratulate herself when she was appointed as a delegate to the League of Nations?

Practice and Assess

Answers: Exercise 16
1. Pat Nixon
2. Mamie Eisenhower and her friends
3. Charles Taft
4. The White House
5. Gerald Ford

Answers: Exercise 17
1. herself, reflexive
2. itself, intensive
3. himself, reflexive
4. herself, intensive
5. himself, reflexive
6. herself, reflexive
7. themselves, intensive
8. itself, intensive
9. herself, reflexive
10. herself, reflexive

Exploring Language

Identifying Reflexive or Intensive Pronouns

Explain this simple rule to help students work the exercises on this page: A reflexive pronoun has one or more words between itself and its antecedent. An intensive pronoun usually stands next to its antecedent. **L2**

Teach

Demonstrative Pronouns

☑ **Teaching Tip**

Students often confuse demonstrative pronouns with the same words used as adjectives. The following examples may clarify the difference.

I didn't order that dessert.
I didn't order that.

In the first example, *that* is an adjective because it modifies the noun *dessert.* In the second example, *that* is a demonstrative pronoun because it stands in place of a noun.

Practice and Assess

Answers: Exercise 18

1. myself, intensive
2. itself, reflexive
3. That, demonstrative
4. ourselves, reflexive
5. themselves, reflexive
6. These *or* Those, demonstrative
7. itself, intensive
8. himself, intensive
9. ourselves, reflexive
10. That *or* This, demonstrative

Parts of Speech

This is the hat.

Demonstrative Pronouns

■ A **demonstrative pronoun** points out specific persons, places, things, or ideas.

Demonstrative Pronouns		
SINGULAR	this	that
PLURAL	these	those

■ A **demonstrative pronoun** can come before or after its antecedent. An antecedent may also be understood.

BEFORE ANTECEDENT	**This** is the hat I want.
	These are the potatoes left over from dinner.
AFTER ANTECEDENT	My old shoes are nicer than **those.**
UNDERSTOOD ANTECEDENT	Show me **that** [thing] again.

Exercise 18 **Completing Sentences with Reflexive, Intensive, and Demonstrative Pronouns**

Supply the appropriate reflexive, intensive, or demonstrative pronoun for each blank. On your paper write the pronoun and identify it as *reflexive, intensive,* or *demonstrative.*

Recollecting the Harlem Renaissance

1. Actually, I _____ suggested a field trip to New York City to learn more about Countee Cullen and the Harlem Renaissance.
2. Our class polled _____ to determine whether there was interest in the trip.
3. _____ was the most one-sided vote I had ever seen.
4. We surprised _____ by raising enough money to allow the entire class to spend one day and night in New York.
5. During the 1920s and 1930s, Countee Cullen, Langston Hughes, Zora Neale Hurston, W. E. B. Du Bois, and Jean Toomer all lived and supported _____ in Harlem.
6. _____ are only a few of the hundreds of writers, musicians, and artists who helped make Harlem vibrant.
7. The class set two specific goals: they were to find the site of the historic Cotton Club _____ and to locate the building where Countee Cullen grew up.
8. Our teacher reminded us that Cullen _____ had been a schoolteacher in New York's public schools.
9. After walking four miles, we treated _____ to a picnic in Riverside Park.
10. Back home again, we all said, "_____ was a trip we shall never forget."

Viewing and Representing

Interpreting Visuals

Pointing It Out Call students' attention to the picture on the student page that relates the demonstrative pronoun *this* to the antecedent *hat.* Also call their attention to the arrow diagram that performs the same function. Then provide sentences with demonstrative pronouns and work with students to devise similar graphic aids to show the demonstrative pronoun and its antecedent.

Interrogative and Relative Pronouns

■ An **interrogative pronoun** is used to form questions.

who?   whom?   whose?   what?   which?

Who are those strangers?
Whom should I invite?
Whose did you borrow?
What did you say?
Which of these personal computers shall I buy?

The intensive forms of the interrogative pronouns are *whoever, whosoever, whomever, whichever,* and *whatever.*

Whoever told you that?   **Whatever** did you say?

■ A **relative pronoun** is used to begin a special subject-verb word group called a subordinate clause (see Unit 13).

who   whose   whomever   that   what
whom   whoever   which   whichever whatever

The pilot **who** landed the plane is my cousin. [The relative pronoun *who* begins the subordinate clause *who landed the plane.*]

The plane, **which** landed late, carried our friends. [The relative pronoun *which* begins the subordinate clause *which landed late.*]

| Exercise 19 | Distinguishing Between Interrogative and Relative Pronouns |

On your paper, list the interrogative and relative pronouns that appear in the following sentences, and label each pronoun as *interrogative* or *relative.* (Some sentences have more than one interrogative or relative pronoun.)

Frida Kahlo

¹On a quiz show, I heard the question "Which of the modern Mexican artists had a museum named after her?" ²It was then that I first heard of Frida Kahlo, whose paintings include *The Broken Column.* ³Kahlo, who in her youth was in a highway accident that forced her to abandon her dream of becoming a doctor, became an artist instead. ⁴Whoever sees her work is enchanted by its bright colors and vibrant forms. ⁵It is clear, however, that Kahlo's paintings often contain images of figures in pain. ⁶One might ask, What was it that gave her the strength to continue painting after the accident had left her in constant pain? ⁷After her death in 1954, her husband, Diego Rivera, who was also a celebrated painter, gave Kahlo's home to the Mexican government for use as a museum.

⁸In recent years, much has been written about Frida Kahlo, whose art is now displayed in galleries worldwide. ⁹The book that tells the story of her life with Diego Rivera is especially fascinating. ¹⁰Whoever wrote it must have known both artists well.

Teach

Interrogative and Relative Pronouns

☑ **Grammar Tip**
The nominative pronoun *who* is used for subjects.

Who is in charge here?

The objective pronoun *whom* is used for direct objects or objects of prepositions.

Whom are you meeting today? (direct object)

She is someone about whom I know little. (object of preposition)

Practice and Assess

Answers: Exercise 19
1. which, interrogative
2. that, relative; whose, relative
3. who, that, relative
4. Whoever, relative
5. that, relative
6. what, interrogative; that, relative
7. who, relative
8. whose, relative
9. that, relative
10. Whoever, relative

Parts of Speech

MEETING INDIVIDUAL NEEDS — English Language Learners

Using Correct Word Order

Students new to English sometimes confuse the use of *who* as an interrogative pronoun with its use as a relative pronoun. The use of *who* as an interrogative pronoun requires the verb to appear before the subject: *Who are you?* Students sometimes mistakenly use the same reversed word order in noun clauses. *I know who are you.* Explain the differences in word order of questions and noun clauses.

451

Teach

Indefinite Pronouns

☑ **Teaching Tip**

Students often confuse indefinite pronouns with the same words used as adjectives. The following examples may clarify the difference.

I didn't order another dessert.
I didn't order another.

In the first example, another is an adjective because it modifies the noun *dessert*. In the second example, *another* is an indefinite pronoun.

Practice and Assess

Answers: Exercise 20

1. that, relative
2. her, possessive; anyone, indefinite; who, relative; her, personal
3. This, demonstrative; what, interrogative
4. many, none, indefinite
5. himself, intensive; her, personal
6. he, personal; herself, reflexive
7. whose, relative; they, personal; him, personal
8. our, possessive; everyone, indefinite
9. It, you, I, personal; all, indefinite
10. We, personal; our, possessive; ourselves, reflexive

Evaluation Rubric: Exercise 21

Sentences will vary. Students should use pronouns from the categories studied in this lesson.

Additional Resources

📁 *Grammar Practice,* p. 2
📁 *Grammar Reteaching,* p. 2
📁 *Grammar Enrichment,* p. 2

 Grammar Workbook, Lessons 3, 4

Close

Ask students to choose one long writing sample from their portfolios and to evaluate the use of pronouns in it. Suggest that they make changes wherever necessary.

Parts of Speech

Indefinite Pronouns

■ An **indefinite pronoun** refers to persons, places, or things in a more general way than a noun does.

> Jacob seems to know **everyone** at school. [The indefinite pronoun *everyone* refers to people in general.]
>
> I'm going to bake **something** special. [The indefinite pronoun *something* does not indicate to what it specifically refers.]
>
> We served the bread, not knowing **some** was stale. [The indefinite pronoun *some* has the specific antecedent *bread*.]

Some Indefinite Pronouns				
all	each	many	nothing	somebody
another	either	most	one	someone
any	enough	much	other	something
anybody	everybody	neither	others	
anyone	everyone	nobody	plenty	
anything	everything	none	several	
both	few	no one	some	

Exercise 20 Identifying Different Kinds of Pronouns

(a) On your paper, list in order the 25 pronouns that appear in the following paragraph.

(b) Identify each pronoun as *personal, possessive, reflexive, intensive, demonstrative, interrogative, relative,* or *indefinite.*

The Riddle of the Sphinx

¹The Sphinx was a mythical monster that had the body of a lion and the head of a woman. ²The people of Thebes were under her control, and anyone who met her had to answer a riddle correctly or die. ³This was the riddle: what walks on four legs in the morning, on two legs at noon, and on three legs at night? ⁴Many tried, but none could solve the riddle. ⁵Then Oedipus, himself a Greek hero, confronted her. ⁶When he correctly answered the riddle, the enraged Sphinx threw herself from a cliff. ⁷The people of Thebes, whose deliverance Oedipus had won, were so grateful they made him king. ⁸In our time everyone knows the answer to the riddle. ⁹It is you and I and all of humankind. ¹⁰We crawl on hands and knees as babies, travel on two legs in our youth, and use a cane to support ourselves in old age.

Exercise 21 Creating Sentences with Different Kinds of Pronouns

Write 10 sentences about a favorite meal that you shared with friends or members of your family. Try to use pronouns from all the categories you have studied in this lesson.

10.3 Verbs

■ A **verb** is a word that expresses action or a state of being and is necessary to make a statement.

Business people **work.**
The curtain **closed** too soon.
Artists **are** creative.

A verb has the ability to express time—present, past, and future—by means of *tense.*

PRESENT TENSE	We **hear** a car outside.
PAST TENSE	We **heard** a car outside.
FUTURE TENSE	We **will hear** a car outside.

Exercise 22 Completing Sentences with Verbs

On your paper, write twenty complete sentences by supplying a verb for each blank.

Hawks as Hunters

1. The solitary hawk _____ slowly high above the green valley.
2. It _____ black against the blue sky.
3. Sensing the hawk's presence, the rodents _____ in the grass.
4. Riding rising air currents, the hawk barely _____ its wings.
5. Its flight _____ effortless.
6. With its piercing eyes, the hawk _____ the countryside in search of food.
7. A hawk _____ eight times more acutely than a human being.
8. Some hawks will even _____ at night, catching bats on the wing.
9. Hawks are territorial birds that _____ their nests from other hawks.
10. Most hawks _____ their nests high in trees.
11. Some hawks _____ by themselves or in small flocks.
12. Cooper's Hawks often _____ on telephone poles.
13. The osprey, a type of hawk, _____ fish almost exclusively.
14. Hawks _____ for the slightest movement in the grass below.
15. The red-tailed hawk _____ mainly on small rodents.
16. Many bird watchers _____ Hawk Mountain in Pennsylvania.
17. Experienced bird watchers _____ hawks flying in the distance.
18. Hawks _____ hooked bills and strong talons.
19. Bird watchers _____ different kinds of hawks by their coloring and silhouettes.
20. Hawks _____ larger than most other birds.

10.3 Verbs **453**

Parts of Speech

Focus

Lesson Overview

Objectives
• To identify various types of verbs
• To use verbs effectively in writing

Bellringer
Daily Language Activity

When students enter the classroom, have this assignment on the board: *Identify the action verbs in the following sentence:*

The wind howled furiously, while thunder crashed and lightning flashed across the sky.

See also *Daily Language Practice*

☑ **Teaching Tip**

Check students' understanding of the general concept of tense.

Practice and Assess

Answers: Exercise 22

Answers will vary, but some suggestions are given below.

1. soared	11. fly
2. appeared	12. perch
3. hid	13. eats
4. moved	14. look
5. seemed	15. lives
6. scoured	16. visit
7. sees	17. notice
8. fly	18. possess
9. protect	19. recognize
10. build	20. are

Resource Manager

Planning Resources
• *Lesson Plans*

Transparencies
• *Bellringer*
• *Daily Language Practice*

📂 **Other Print Resources**
• *Grammar and Composition Handbook*
• *Grammar Enrichment,* pp. 3–4
• *Grammar Practice,* pp. 3–4
• *Grammar Reteaching,* pp. 3–4
• *Grammar Workbook,* Lessons 5–7

Teach

Action Verbs

☑ **Grammar Tip**

All verbs are action verbs except for the roughly two dozen linking verbs. It is nearly impossible to define *action* in any useful way. We can define the class of action verbs negatively: action verbs are not linking verbs. Thus, students may find it easier to learn the characteristics of linking verbs first. Then, any verb that doesn't fit the definition of a linking verb must be an action verb.

⇄ **Cross-reference: Composition**

For instruction and practice in using verbs in narrative writing, refer students to Unit 4, Narrative Writing, pp. 164–213.

Parts of Speech

Action Verbs

■ An **action verb** tells what someone or something does.

PHYSICAL ACTION	The huge lineman **lead** the charge through the defense.
MENTAL ACTION	The coaches **plan** the team's strategy before each game.

■ A **transitive verb** is an action verb that is followed by a word or words that answer the question *what?* or *whom?*

Chipmunks **climb** small trees to get at berries and nuts. [The action verb *climb* is followed by the noun *trees*, which answers the question *climb what?*]

■ An **intransitive verb** is an action verb that is *not* followed by a word that answers the question *what?* or *whom?*

Chipmunks also **climb** much of the time simply to escape from their enemies. [The action verb is followed by words that tell *when* and *why.*]

To decide whether a verb in a sentence is transitive or intransitive, ask *what?* or *whom?* after the verb. If the answer is given in the sentence, the verb is transitive. If the answer is not given in the sentence, the verb is intransitive.

Many action verbs can be either transitive or intransitive, depending on how they are used in a sentence.

TRANSITIVE	Jill usually **ate** her sandwich in the cafeteria. [*Sandwich* tells what Jill ate.]
INTRANSITIVE	Jill **ate** right before class today. [*Right before class today* tells when Jill ate.]

Some verbs have only transitive or intransitive uses. A dictionary will indicate how a verb may be used.

 English Language Learners

Making a Verb Chart

Students who are not proficient in English may have trouble with intransitive and irregular verbs. Encourage students to make a chart of verbs. Have them include the present and past forms of each verb.

Understanding Intransitive Verbs

An excellent test of a transitive verb is to see whether the sentence can be turned into a *whom* or *what* question whose answer is the object. Since only transitive verbs have objects, any sentence that can be changed into such a question must contain a transitive verb.

Exercise 23 — Identifying Action Verbs

On your paper, write the action verb that appears in each of the following sentences. Indicate how the verb is used by writing *transitive* or *intransitive*.

Hints for Backpackers

1. Backpackers often carry contour maps on a hike.
2. Contour lines on a map identify the elevation of each spot.
3. Numerals on a contour line tell an area's distance above sea level.
4. On steep slopes, contour lines run close together.
5. Rivers, creeks, and rills always flow downward across the contour lines of a map.
6. Hills and valleys show vividly on a contour map.
7. The abbreviation *BM* (for *bench mark*) indicates the location of a tablet with the exact elevation of that spot.
8. Surveys by the United States Geological Survey place at least two bench mark tablets in each township.
9. Hikers use bench marks for reference.
10. With the help of a contour map, compass, and bench marks, backpackers find the right track.

Exercise 24 — Identifying and Using Transitive and Intransitive Verbs

On your paper, write the verb that appears in each of the following sentences. Label each verb *transitive* or *intransitive*, depending on how it is used in the sentence. Then write five new sentences, using each transitive verb as an intransitive verb and each intransitive verb as a transitive verb.

SAMPLE: I type my poetry assignments for English class.
ANSWER: type, transitive
I type slowly but accurately.

The Challenge of Haiku

1. Most of my classmates wrote poems that rhyme.
2. Barbara and I, however, each composed a haiku—three lines, with seventeen syllables of unrhymed verse.
3. The great Japanese poet Bashō lived in the seventeenth century.
4. The simplicity of Bashō's verses awakened in many readers a love of all poetry, especially haiku.
5. What other poet thought as simply and clearly as Bashō?

Exercise 25 — Creating Sentences with Action Verbs

Choose five of the action verbs that you identified in Exercise 23. For each verb write one sentence.

10.3 Verbs **455**

Parts of Speech

Practice and Assess

Answers: Exercise 23
1. carry—transitive
2. identify—transitive
3. tell—transitive
4. run—intransitive
5. flow—intransitive
6. show—intransitive
7. indicates—transitive
8. place—transitive
9. use—transitive
10. find—transitive

Answers: Exercise 24
Answers will vary, but some suggestions are given below.
1. wrote—transitive; He wrote brilliantly.
2. composed—transitive; I composed without paper.
3. lived—intransitive; He lived a long life.
4. awakened—transitive; We awakened early.
5. thought—intransitive; I thought the idea was fascinating.

Answers: Exercise 25
Answers will vary, but some suggestions are given below.
1. These trucks carry a heavy load.
2. Eleanor can identify all the state capitals.
3. Tell me how to get there.
4. I run best with a partner.
5. The two rivers flow together at this point.

Exploring Language

Recognizing Transitive and Intransitive Verbs
Students who have difficulty thinking abstractly may benefit from acting out or paraphrasing the concepts of the example sentences on page 454. Such an activity will enable students to visualize the difference between transitive and intransitive verbs within the context of a sentence. **L1**

455

Teach

Linking Verbs

☑ **Grammar Tips**

Only linking verbs can be followed by a predicate adjective. Thus, a simple test of linking verbs is to see whether you can place an adjective immediately after the verb.

Explain that the most common linking verb is *be.* Moreover, *be* can replace most other linking verbs and still produce a grammatical sentence with roughly the same meaning. Thus, a quick and highly reliable test is to see whether the verb in question can be replaced with *be.* See *Grammar Reteaching,* p. 4.

Practice and Assess

Answers: Exercise 26

Answers will vary, but some suggestions are given below.
  1. remains
  2. are
  3. seems
  4. feel, grow
  5. appear

Parts of Speech

Linking Verbs

■ A **linking verb** links, or joins, the subject of a sentence (often a noun or pronoun) with a word or expression that identifies or describes the subject. A linking verb does not show action.

The most commonly used linking verb is *be* in all its forms—*am, is, are, was, were, will be, has been, was being.*

> I **am** a musician.
> That singer **is** an artist.
> The days **were** hot.
> Those **are** mosquitoes.

Several verbs other than the forms of *be* can also act as linking verbs.

Other Linking Verbs			
appear	grow	seem	stay
become	look	sound	taste
feel	remain	smell	

> The cake **tastes** good.
> He **grew** taller over the summer.
> She **felt** good about the election results.
> He **seems** better today.

Exercise 26 Completing Sentences with Linking Verbs

On your paper, write a linking verb to complete each sentence below. Try to use as many different linking verbs as possible.

Weather in the Great Lakes

1. The weather around the Great Lakes _____ quite cold in the winter.
2. The summers, however, _____ either cool or very hot.
3. The weather _____ most pleasant in the fall.
4. The days _____ warm even though the nights _____ colder.
5. People _____ happiest about the weather when the sun shines.

Exercise 27 Identifying Linking Verbs

On your paper, write the linking verb that appears in each of the following sentences.

The United States Flag

1. After World War II, the flag of the United States became a familiar symbol around the world.
2. Before the American Revolution, most colonial flags looked similar to the British flag.

456 Unit 10 Parts of Speech

Enrichment and Extension

Writing About People and Events

Have students write a paragraph describing a person or an event that made a great impact on them. Encourage them to pay attention to sentences they write that contain linking verbs. Remind students that describing a person or an object can help them practice the use of linking verbs. After the paragraphs are written, have students trade papers with a partner and check each other's use of linking verbs.

3. The traditional story about Betsy Ross's role in the creation of the first U.S. flag now appears unlikely.
4. Francis Hopkinson, a delegate to the Continental Congress, was probably the designer of the first American flag.
5. The stripes in the flag, an idea from a colonial patriot group's flag, are symbolic of the thirteen original colonies.
6. Though not official, a flag with thirteen stars in a circle is often representative of the nation's early years.
7. The colors red, white, and blue on the flag are traditional.
8. After years of confusion about where to place each new star, the positions of the flag's stars became official by presidential order in 1912.
9. By government regulation, an American flag is part of every public building and school.
10. The U.S. flag is always the flag on the right in a parade or display with other flags.
11. No other flags are more prominent than the U.S. flag.
12. The blue field of stars appears uppermost in any display.
13. Most of these regulations seem helpful for the preparation of official exhibits about the flag's history.
14. A flag with a rattlesnake on it was once a symbol of the American colonies.
15. Many of the state flags, like the U.S. flag, are red, white, and blue.

Exercise 28 **Identifying Action and Linking Verbs**

On your paper, list ten verbs that appear in the following paragraph. Identify each verb as either *action* or *linking*.

Jesse Owens, Gold Medalist

¹Jesse Owens was one of the first superstars in track and field. ²As a junior high school student in Cleveland, Ohio, in the 1920s, Owens sprinted 100 yards in 10 seconds. ³A few years later, he captured the entire nation's attention with a 10.3-second 100-yard dash at East Technical High School. ⁴His fame increased during his years as an athlete at Ohio State University. ⁵Owens's performance in four events on May 25, 1935, seemed extraordinary. ⁶At the age of 22, he shattered world records for the 220-yard dash, the 220-yard low hurdles, and the broad jump. ⁷A new record in a fourth event, the 100-yard dash, was just out of his reach. ⁸Jesse Owens's fame peaked the following year at the 1936 Olympics in Berlin, Germany. ⁹In the presence of the Nazi dictator, Adolf Hitler, Owens won gold medals in four events. ¹⁰Hitler's lack of acknowledgment of the achievements of this famous African American only heightened the world's appreciation of Owens's success.

Parts of Speech

Answers: Exercise 27
1. became
2. looked
3. appears
4. was
5. are
6. is
7. are
8. became
9. is
10. is
11. are
12. appears
13. seem
14. was
15. are

Answers: Exercise 28
1. was—linking
2. sprinted—action
3. captured—action
4. increased—action
5. seemed—linking
6. shattered—action
7. was—linking
8. peaked—action
9. won—action
10. heightened—action

Cooperative Learning

Using Linking Verbs

Provide students with this easy rule for identifying linking verbs other than *be*. Have students work together to create sentences with linking verbs. First, one student should write a sentence. The second student then should replace the linking verb with the correct form of *be*. The sentence should still be grammatically correct. For example:

Yolanda *seems* happy.
Yolanda *is* happy. **L1**

Teach

Verb Phrases

☑ Grammar Tips

There are four families of auxiliary verbs. First is *be,* which occurs in progressive tenses (*He is walking*) and the passive voice (*An accident was reported*). Second is *have,* which occurs in the present perfect (*He has won*) and past perfect (*He had won*) tenses. Third is *do,* which is used for emphasis (*She did win after all*) and with *not* in the absence of other auxiliary verbs (*She didn't win*). The remaining verbs (*can, could, may, might, must, shall, should, will,* and *would*) are the modals.

The modals are used to express permission, obligation, or volition: *I can go; I may go; I must go.* They are also used to express the possibility, probability, or necessity of something's being true or actually happening: *It may rain. It might rain. It must rain.*

Practice and Assess

Answers: Exercise 29

1. (has) been
2. (may) be
3. (can) enjoy; (are) listening
4. (might) hear
5. (must) begin
6. (may) last
7. (has) attracted
8. (can) display; (have) done
9. (could) humble
10. (will) remember

Parts of Speech

Verb Phrases

The verb in a sentence may consist of more than one word. The words that accompany the main verb are called **auxiliary,** or helping, **verbs.**

■ A **verb phrase** consists of a main verb and all its auxiliary, or helping, verbs.

The forms of *be* and *have* are the most common auxiliary verbs. They help the main verb express the various tenses.

I am walking.   **I have walked.**   **I had been walking.**

Auxiliary Verbs	
FORMS OF *BE*	am, is, are, was, were, being, been
FORMS OF *HAVE*	has, have, had, having
OTHER AUXILIARIES	can, could may, might shall, should do, does, did must will, would

In addition to expressing time, the other auxiliary verbs are used to express different shades of meaning.

She **might wait.**   We **would have played.**
He **could win.**   I **must be going.**

Exercise 29   Identifying Verb Phrases

On your paper, write each verb phrase that appears in the following sentences. (Two of the sentences have more than one verb phrase.) Put parentheses around the auxiliary verbs in each phrase. (Words that interrupt a verb phrase are not considered part of the verb phrase.)

San Antonio's April Fiesta

1. For a long time now, the April fiesta has been the highlight of the year in San Antonio.
2. The fiesta may be the world's most enjoyable party, and it attracts visitors from all over.
3. People can enjoy excellent Spanish and Mexican meals while they are listening to delightful music.
4. They might hear country swing, country rock, or Dixieland.
5. The fiesta must begin in front of the Alamo on a Saturday.
6. It may last ten days.
7. Always the highlight, the Battle of Flowers Parade has attracted people since 1891.
8. During the fiesta all of San Antonio's diverse cultures can display themselves and have done so brilliantly over the years.
9. The pomp and lavishness of the fiesta could humble the royalty of Europe.
10. Tourists will long remember the lights, flowers, and music.

MEETING INDIVIDUAL NEEDS   **English Language Learners**

Exploring Verb Phrase Order

Explain to students new to English that the left-to-right word order of a verb phrase is completely fixed. To illustrate, consider a sentence with a relatively long verb phrase; for example, *Javier should have been working.*

Scramble the order of words in the verb phrase: *Javier been should working have.* Ask students to put the words back into their correct order. There is only one possible correct order for a given verb phrase.

Exercise 30   Completing Sentences with Verb Phrases

On your paper, complete the following sentences by replacing each blank with a verb phrase. Be sure that your completed sentences make sense.

Florida

1. Florida _____ the "sunshine state."
2. Because of environmental problems, many native animals in Florida, such as the manatee and the Florida panther, _____ in number.
3. Tourists _____ to Florida by the warm climate, beautiful beaches, and many entertainment centers.
4. With the opening of Disney World, central Florida _____ from a quiet rural area to a world-renowned tourist destination.
5. The Apollo 11 moon rocket _____ from the Kennedy Space Center near Titusville.
6. Each night the beautiful sunset _____ by the many people congregated in Key West's Mallory Square.
7. St. Augustine, the oldest city in America, _____ in 1564.
8. Miami became an important city after railroads _____ to link it with cities farther north.
9. Many ships _____ at the port in Jacksonville.
10. High-technology and electronics industries _____ in the Melbourne–Palm Bay area.

Exercise 31   Completing Sentences with Different Kinds of Verbs

On your paper, complete each sentence in the following paragraph by supplying a verb. The kind of verb to use in each case is indicated in italics. Be sure that your completed sentences make sense.

Hobbies

Because people ¹*action verb* more leisure time than ever before, hobbies ²*verb phrase* in popularity. Preferences for hobbies ³*action verb* greatly from person to person. Whereas some people ⁴*action verb* sculpture, others ⁵*linking verb* most content when they ⁶*verb phrase* an old car. Photography ⁷*action verb* to many people, some of whom ⁸*action verb* darkrooms, where they ⁹*verb phrase* their own film. Hobby stores ¹⁰*action verb* model planes that actually ¹¹*action verb* even though they ¹²*verb phrase* very fragile. People who ¹³*action verb* for a hobby ¹⁴*linking verb* quite pleased when they ¹⁵*verb phrase* their work at an art show. Anyone ¹⁶*verb phrase* a philatelist, which ¹⁷*linking verb* the term for a person who ¹⁸*action verb* stamps. The more a philatelist's collection ¹⁹*action verb*, the more valuable it ²⁰*linking verb*.

Exercise 32   Creating Sentences with Vivid Verbs

On your paper, write five sentences about one of your favorite outdoor activities. Choose very specific action verbs and verb phrases to convey vividly a sense of the activity.

Answers: Exercise 30

Answers will vary, but some suggestions are given below.

1. has been called
2. have been dwindling
3. have been attracted
4. has changed
5. was launched
6. can be seen
7. was founded
8. had arrived
9. have docked
10. have developed

Answers Exercise 31

Answers will vary, but some suggestions are given below.

1. enjoy
2. have increased
3. vary
4. prefer
5. seem
6. are repairing
7. appeals
8. build
9. can develop
10. sell
11. fly
12. seem to be
13. paint
14. are
15. can display
16. can become
17. is
18. collects
19. grows
20. becomes

Answers: Exercise 32

Answers will vary, but some suggestions are given below.

1. My jersey is filthy from sliding into home.
2. Infielders cower when I'm at bat, because I really smack the ball.
3. I fly down the basepath, and sometimes my tendons feel as though they'll pop.
4. I rocket out of first base when I'm stealing second.
5. Sometimes I can barely drag myself home.

Additional Resources

📁 *Grammar Practice*, pp. 3–4
📁 *Grammar Reteaching*, pp. 3–4
📁 *Grammar Enrichment*, pp. 3–4

📖 *Grammar Workbook*, Lessons 5–7

Close

Each student may select a writing sample from his or her portfolio and revise it, using verbs and verb phrases more effectively and accurately. Have students exchange samples and evaluate one another's work.

Focus

Lesson Overview

Objectives

- To identify adjectives, degrees of comparison, and other adjectival forms
- To use adjectival elements effectively in writing

Bellringer

Daily Language Activity

When students enter the classroom, have this assignment on the board: *Read the following sentence and point out the adjectives.*

> And then a small, dry voice, like the voice of someone who has not spoken in a long time, joined our singing: a small, dry, eggshell voice from the other side of the door. . . .
>
> —Dylan Thomas, "A Child's Christmas in Wales"

See also *Daily Language Practice*

Motivating Activity

Ask students to read the above passage without the adjectives. Encourage them to do the same for sentences from readings of their choice. Initiate a discussion of what vivid adjectives add to writing and speaking.

(vertical text) Parts of Speech

HOW

THAT

THE TULIP IS

THE FLORIST
CONSIDERED IT

THE TULIPS,

BEAUTIFUL

THE TULIP IS !

TULIP WON
FIRST PRIZE.

.

.

IN THE
SUNLIGHT,
DANCED IN
THE WIND.

10.4 Adjectives

■ An **adjective** is a word that modifies a noun or pronoun by limiting its meaning.

An adjective may describe a noun or pronoun by answering one of these questions: *What kind? Which one? How many? How much?*

QUESTION	ADJECTIVES	
What kind?	**green** sweater	**sunny** Greece
	tall woman	**pure** joy
Which one?	**this** book	**these** islands
	that child	**those** rules
How many?	**four** oceans	**few** farmers
	many rings	**both** principals
How much?	**more** money	**no** time
	enough salad	**little** patience

Adjectives appear in various positions in the sentence.

How **beautiful** the tulip is!
That **beautiful** tulip won first prize.
The tulip is **beautiful.**
The florist considered the tulip **beautiful.**
The tulips, **beautiful** in the sunlight, danced in the wind.

The words *a, an,* and *the* are special kinds of adjectives called **articles.** *A* and *an* are called **indefinite articles.** *The* is called the **definite article.**

INDEFINITE	We camped near **a** river.
	Kim ate **an** orange.
DEFINITE	We camped near **the** river.
	Kim ate **the** orange.

Forms of Adjectives

Many adjectives have different forms to indicate their degree of comparison. The **positive degree** is the simple form of the adjective. The **comparative degree** compares two persons, places, things, or ideas. The **superlative degree** compares more than two persons, places, things, or ideas.

POSITIVE	COMPARATIVE	SUPERLATIVE
slow	slower	slowest
healthy	healthier	healthiest
strenuous	more strenuous	most strenuous

Comparative adjectives of two or more syllables are usually formed by placing the words *more* or *most* before the positive form.

Resource Manager

Planning Resources
- *Lesson Plans*

 Transparencies
- *Bellringer*
- *Daily Language Practice*
- *Two-Minute Skill Drill*

 Other Print Resources
- *Grammar and Composition Handbook*
- *Grammar Enrichment,* p. 5
- *Grammar Practice,* p. 5
- *Grammar Reteaching,* p. 5
- *Grammar Workbook,* Lesson 8
- *Sentence-Combining Practice,* pp. 4, 11

Identifying Adjectives and the Nouns They Modify

In the following sentences, identify the adjectives and the nouns they modify. Do not include definite and indefinite articles. On your paper, list the words in two columns, one labeled *adjectives* and the other labeled *nouns they modify*.

SAMPLE   Bells are musical instruments that originated in ancient China.
ANSWER   **ADJECTIVES**   **NOUNS THEY MODIFY**
         musical   instruments
         ancient   China

A Short History of Bells

1. Some of the earliest bells had rich ornamentation.
2. Such bells were used originally to provide an atmosphere of mystery to religious ceremonies.
3. It was once thought that ringing a bell would drive away deadly diseases.
4. The Chinese and Japanese decorated temples with bells that made a delicate sound in the slightest breeze.
5. The ancient Goths stirred reluctant soldiers to military order with the ringing of bells.
6. Women in Persia once wore little bells as jewelry.
7. Bells have also been used to warn off a nearby enemy or other danger.
8. The practical Greeks used bells to announce the arrival of fish fresh from the sea.
9. If we heard a bell in a busy supermarket today, we would consider the sound bizarre.
10. In Rome no bells advertised merchandise, but many bells tolled the news when an emperor died.
11. In ancient Greece and Rome, bells were hung on the tomb and funeral carriage of a king.
12. In Burma bells were hung in the pagodas to drive away evil spirits.
13. In Africa healers hung a bell over the doorway of the house of a sick person.
14. The Celts became more famous than the Romans for making melodic chimes.
15. Since the sixth century, Christians have had a great enthusiasm for bells.
16. Bells were once hung in some churches as a protection against violent storms.
17. In Italy special towers, or *campaniles,* were constructed for particularly immense bells.
18. In England a local officer rang a bell to announce a late curfew, a fire, a meeting, or even a certain deadline.
19. A crier in a town would ring a bell to attract a large crowd and then shout the latest news.
20. Today we hear fewer bells because most of them have been replaced by electronic methods of communication.

10.4 Adjectives   **461**

Teach

Forms of Adjectives

Cross-reference: Usage
For instruction and practice in using the comparative forms of adjectives, refer students to Lessons 18.1–18.4, pp. 663–670.

Practice and Assess

Answers: Exercise 33

Adjective	Noun
1. earliest	bells
rich	ornamentation
2. such	bells
religious	ceremonies
3. deadly	diseases
4. delicate	sound
slightest	breeze
5. ancient	Goths
reluctant	soldiers
military	order
6. little	bells
7. nearby	enemy
other	danger
8. practical	Greeks
fresh	fish
9. busy	supermarket
bizarre	sound
10. no	bells
many	bells
11. ancient	Greece, Rome
funeral	carriage
12. evil	spirits
13. sick	person
14. famous	Celts
melodic	chimes
15. sixth	century
great	enthusiasm
16. some	churches
violent	storms
17. special	towers
immense	bells
18. local	officer
late	curfew
certain	deadline
19. large	crowd
latest	news
20. fewer	bells
electronic	methods

English Language Learners

Using *a* and *an*
The use of articles can be one of the most difficult aspects of English grammar for students new to the language. Help these students understand the basic guidelines for using *a* and *an*:
1. Use *a* or *an* the first time a new topic is introduced: *I saw **a** mouse this morning.*
2. Use *a* or *an* in generalizations about nouns: ***An** antelope can thrive in hot, dry climates.*

461

Teach

Proper Adjectives

☑ **Teaching Tip**

Begin this lesson by reviewing the definition of proper nouns. Ask students to give a few examples of proper nouns. Then have them try to turn each proper noun into an adjective and to create a sentence using that proper adjective.

Practice and Assess

Answers: Exercise 34

1. Asian
2. Freudian
3. Georgian
4. Greek, Grecian
5. Turkish
6. Martian
7. Javanese
8. Dickensian
9. Siberian
10. Brazilian
11. Chinese
12. Canadian
13. Shakespearean
14. Maltese
15. Irish
16. Icelandic
17. Jacksonian
18. Hungarian
19. Edwardian
20. European
21. British
22. Bostonian
23. Nepalese
24. Norwegian
25. Parisian

Parts of Speech

Proper Adjectives

■ A **proper adjective** is formed from a proper noun and begins with a capital letter.

> Duke Ellington was an **African American** composer.
> The term ***Victorian Era*** refers to the years 1837 to 1901.

Proper adjectives are often created by adding the following suffixes: *-an, -ian, -n, -ese, -ish,* and *-ic.* In some cases, the noun and adjective forms are the same.

PROPER NOUNS	PROPER ADJECTIVES
Queen Elizabeth I	Elizabethan
Indonesia	Indonesian
Japan	Japanese
Spain	Spanish

Some words that began as proper adjectives have been used for so long that their origins have been forgotten or disregarded. Such words have become **common adjectives** that begin with lowercase letters.

PROPER NOUNS	COMMON ADJECTIVES
Italy	italic
Rome	romantic
Puritan	puritanical
Bohemia	bohemian

Exercise 34 **Forming Proper Adjectives from Proper Nouns**

Write a proper adjective for each proper noun below. Consult a dictionary if necessary.

1. Asia
2. Sigmund Freud
3. King George
4. Greece
5. Turkey
6. Mars
7. Java
8. Charles Dickens
9. Siberia
10. Brazil
11. China
12. Canada
13. William Shakespeare
14. Malta
15. Ireland
16. Iceland
17. Andrew Jackson
18. Hungary
19. King Edward
20. Europe
21. Britain
22. Boston
23. Nepal
24. Norway
25. Paris

Exploring Language

Identifying Adjectives

One easy way to identify adjectives that modify nouns is to ask a question (usually, *which one? how many?* or *what kind?*) about the noun. Only an adjective that modifies a noun can answer the question. For instance, in the phrase *three protons,* the word *three* answers the question *how many?* Therefore, *three* functions as an adjective modifying the noun *protons.* **L2**

Nouns Used as Adjectives

In some cases, nouns are used as adjectives. A noun used as an adjective answers one of these questions: *What kind? Which one?*

NOUNS	NOUNS AS ADJECTIVES
music	**music** critic (What kind of critic?)
city	**city** bus (What kind of bus?)
history	**history** lesson (Which lesson?)
United States	**United States** flag (Which flag?)

Sometimes possessive nouns are used as adjectives.

Kate's parrot   the **river's** source   the **story's** end   **Don's** restaurant

---

Exercise 35   **Identifying Adjectives and Nouns Used as Adjectives**

On your paper, list the adjectives in the following sentences. Do not include definite and indefinite articles. If the adjective is also a noun, write *noun* in parentheses.

SAMPLE   In the early 1900s, there were few laws against child labor.
ANSWER   early, few, child (noun)

Chicago's "Newsies"

1. In the first part of this century, the newspaper business was thriving in Chicago.
2. The newspapers' success was due largely to a sensational style of journalism.
3. A small army of children sold these papers to commuters in the downtown section of the city.
4. These so-called newsies were not street urchins but ordinary kids who wanted to earn a little money after school.
5. They came from every ethnic group in the city.
6. Before the daily supply of papers arrived, the newsies would often play a baseball game.
7. As soon as rush hour began, they went to work.
8. Industrious little hustlers appeared where carefree children had stood.
9. The eager children stationed themselves along streets with the heaviest pedestrian traffic.
10. Some set up shop outside department stores and subway stations.
11. Those newsies who succeeded had a good business sense and an aggressive sales pitch.
12. On a slow day, some of the newsies made up false news headlines to attract customers.
13. The children lived for the great headlines, the large red type that sold editions.
14. The newsies had to anticipate probable sales before they purchased any newspapers.
15. However, they made more money by begging for tips from big spenders.
16. The excitement of street life provided a break from the stuffy classroom.

Viewing and Representing

Drawing Nouns and Adjectives

Students who have trouble with the abstract concept of nouns' use as adjectives may benefit from drawing pictures to illustrate nouns used as nouns and nouns used as adjectives. For example, ask students to draw a picture of a city. Then ask them to draw a picture of a city bus. Use the drawings to help explain how the word *city* can be used as different parts of speech. **L1**

Teach

Nouns used as Adjectives

☑ **Teaching Tip**

Write two sentences on the board to demonstrate how a noun can be used as an adjective.

*Dina's loud **music** disturbed the neighbors. The **music** critic came to the concert.*

Point out that in the first sentence the word *music* is the subject and in the second it modifies the noun *critic*.

Two-Minute Skill Drill

Have students see how many nouns they can list that can also be used as adjectives. Tell them to include a noun to be modified by each adjective.

See also *Two-Minute Skill Drill Transparency 10.4*

Parts of Speech

Practice and Assess

Answers: Exercise 35

1. first, this, newspaper (noun)
2. newspapers' (noun), due, sensational
3. small, these, downtown (noun)
4. These, so-called, street (noun), ordinary, little
5. every, ethnic
6. daily, baseball (noun)
7. rush (noun)
8. Industrious, little, carefree
9. eager, heaviest, pedestrian (noun)
10. department (noun), subway (noun)
11. Those, good, business (noun), aggressive, sales (noun)
12. slow, false, news (noun)
13. great, large, red
14. probable, any
15. more, big
16. street (noun), stuffy
17. Social, children's (noun), serious
18. Few, real, adult (noun)
19. These, industrious

20. successful, business (noun), work (noun), Chicago's (noun)

Teach

Pronouns Used as Adjectives

☑ **Teaching Tip**

Begin by asking students whether they can think of ways to use pronouns as adjectives. If they have trouble, list the following pronouns to help them:

my, your, her, his, its, our, their, that, those, which, what.

Give students five minutes to write a five-sentence paragraph using a pronoun as an adjective in each sentence.

Practice and Assess

Answers: Exercise 36

1. bright, full, clear
2. Dark, old, shadowy, his, much, small, their, honest
3. his
4. his, his, good, rough, unkempt, shady, brown, noisy

Answers: Exercise 37 (p. 465)

1. a, 132
2. These, beautiful, 1,523
3. Major, an, famous, active
4. a, Hawaiian, major
5. no
6. naval
7. Minor, big, great, small, infertile, human
8. Hawaii's
9. its
10. Much, the, Asian

17. Social reformers feared that the children's lifestyle would lead them to serious crime later on.
18. Few boys, however, became real criminals in the adult world.
19. These industrious children raised themselves from poverty to prosperity.
20. Most of them ended up as successful business executives because of the work ethic they had developed on Chicago's streets.

Pronouns Used as Adjectives

Some pronouns can also be used as adjectives. **Possessive adjectives** are possessive pronouns that answer the question *which one?*

There are seven possessive pronouns that can also be used as adjectives: *my, your, her, his, its, our,* and *their.*

> Woody wrecked **his** car in the crash.
> Roller-blading is **our** idea of fun.
> The Millers cultivated **their** garden.
> **Your** photo turned out well.

Demonstrative adjectives are pronouns that answer the questions *which one? how many?* and *how much?*

> She went to **that** concert. They took **those** classes.

Interrogative adjectives are pronouns that are used to ask questions.

> **Which** concert did she hear?
> **What** grade did he get?
> **Whose** party was best?

Exercise 36   Identifying Adjectives and Pronouns Used as Adjectives

On your paper, list the twenty adjectives that appear in the following passage. Count possessive pronouns as well as regular adjectives in this exercise but do not count the words *a, an,* and *the.*

A Farmer and His Land

¹There was a bright, full moon in the clear sky, and the sunset was still shining faintly in the west. ²Dark woods stood all about the old . . . farmhouse, save down the hill, westward, where lay the shadowy fields which John Hilton, and his father before him, had cleared and tilled with much toil—the small fields to which they had given the industry and . . . affection of their honest lives. ³John Hilton was sitting on the doorstep of his house. ⁴As he moved his head in and out of the shadows, . . . one could see his good face, rough and somewhat unkempt, as if he were indeed a creature of the shady woods and brown earth, instead of the noisy town.

From "The Hiltons' Holiday" by Sarah Orne Jewett

MEETING INDIVIDUAL NEEDS   **English Language Learners**

Using *This, That, These, Those*

Students new to English often confuse the demonstrative pronouns/adjectives *this/these* and *that/those*. Explain that the demonstrative adjectives *this* and *these* point out persons and things that are nearby. The demonstrative adjectives *that* and *those* point out persons and things farther away. Ask students to make up sentences referring to people and objects close by and farther away in the classroom.

Exercise 37 Identifying Different Kinds of Adjectives

On your paper, write the twenty-five adjectives, including articles, that appear in the following paragraph.

The Hawaiian Islands

[1]Hawaii is a chain of 132 islands. [2]These beautiful islands extend 1,523 miles. [3]Major islands include Maui, Oahu, and Hawaii, an island that is famous for active volcanoes. [4]Although there are a number of islands, Hawaiian people live only on major ones. [5]Kahoolawe has no inhabitants. [6]It is used only for naval purposes. [7]Minor islands, some only as big as great rocks, are too small and infertile to support human life. [8]Hawaii's population displays a mixture of origins. [9]Diversity is one of its sources of vitality. [10]Much of the population is of Asian descent.

Exercise 38 Expanding Sentences with Adjectives

Rewrite the following sentences, adding at least two appropriate adjectives to each one. In your fifteen sentences, include at least one comparative or superlative adjective, one noun used as an adjective, and one pronoun used as an adjective.

An Audio Demonstration

1. Music filled the showroom of the electronics store.
2. A salesman showed a speaker system to my two friends and me.
3. Though we liked the size and appearance of the speakers, we were obviously more interested in the sound.
4. The salesman played tapes to demonstrate the speakers' power, clarity, and versatility.
5. First, my friends and I listened to a song by Loretta Lynn.
6. Seconds later, we heard the notes of a Mozart piano concerto.
7. When the piano, bass, and drums of an Aretha Franklin song kicked in, we noticed a number of feet beginning to tap.
8. Before long, bodies began to sway, and customers started to mouth the words of the song.
9. I almost expected the singer to appear out of nowhere.
10. My friends and I are fans of soul music from the 1960s and 1970s—especially the music of Aretha Franklin.
11. She has a way of making music that touches the hearts and souls of all people.
12. As much as I loved the sound that came through those speakers, I knew that I would never own them, for their price was astronomical.
13. My speakers at home have problems that I guess I will have to endure a bit longer.
14. I wonder whether that store will ever have a sale on speakers.
15. I'll look for advertisements in the weeks ahead.

Exercise 39 Creating Sentences with Adjectives

Write five sentences about a favorite food. Use at least two descriptive adjectives in each sentence.

10.4 Adjectives **465**

Parts of Speech

Answers: Exercise 38

Answers will vary. Suggestions for the first ten items are given below.

1. Loud music filled the crowded showroom of the electronics store.
2. A young salesman showed a fantastic speaker system to my two best friends and me.
3. Though we liked the size and appearance of the small speakers, we were obviously more interested in the best sound.
4. The knowledgeable salesman played popular music tapes to demonstrate the speakers' great power, clarity, and versatility.
5. First, my two friends and I listened to a country song by Loretta Lynn.
6. Seconds later, we heard the unforgettable notes of a lovely Mozart piano concerto.
7. When the piano, bass, and drums of an Aretha Franklin rhythm-and-blues song kicked in, we noticed a number of eager feet beginning to tap.
8. Before long, many bodies began to sway, and customers started to mouth the familiar words of the song.
9. I almost expected the lively and popular singer to appear out of nowhere.
10. My friends and I are devoted fans of soul music from the 1960s and 1970s—especially the stirring music of Aretha Franklin.

Answers: Exercise 39

Sentences will vary. Sample:
   My favorite food is thin-crust pizza. There's nothing better than a steaming pizza and an action video. Sometimes I like thin-crust pizza with spicy pepperoni. My parents prefer deep-dish spinach pizza. I order my favorite pizza and a large drink.

Additional Resources

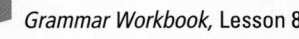

Sentence Combining Practice, pp. 4, 11
Grammar Practice, p. 5
Grammar Reteaching, p. 5
Grammar Enrichment, p. 5

Grammar Workbook, Lesson 8

Close

Ask students to choose a writing sample from their portfolios that they think could benefit from a better use of adjectives. Have them work in small groups to revise the piece, using what they have learned about adjectives in this lesson.

465

Focus

Lesson Overview

Objectives
- To identify adverbs and degrees of comparison
- To use adverbs effectively in writing

Bellringer
Daily Language Activity

When students enter the classroom, have this assignment on the board: *Identify the adverbs in the following passage.*

> It has to be carefully timed: my hearty, boisterous laughter must not come too soon, but neither must it come too late; it must come just at the right spot. . . .
>
> —Heinrich Böll, "The Laugher"

(Answers: *carefully, not, too, soon, neither, too, late, just*)

See also *Daily Language Practice*

Teach

Adverbs That Modify Verbs

☑ Teaching Tip
To identify adverbs that modify verbs, move the adverb to either the beginning or the end of the sentence. For example, *Eventually the train will arrive* may be rewritten *The train will arrive eventually.*

Parts of Speech

" Nothing can stop me now,"

Tom said tirelessly.

10.5 Adverbs

■ An **adverb** is a word that modifies a verb, an adjective, or another adverb by making its meaning more specific.

Adverbs that Modify Verbs

Adverbs add meaning to verbs and verb phrases by answering the questions *when? where? how?* and *to what degree?*

ADVERBS THAT MODIFY VERBS		
QUESTION	VERB	ADVERB
When?	fly	fly **now**
	had arrived	had arrived **early**
Where?	jump	jump **aside**
	was charging	was charging **forward**
How?	argued	argued **effectively**
	will speak	will speak **clearly**
To what degree?	finish	finish **completely**
	would have known	**hardly** would have known

When modifying a verb, an adverb may appear in various positions in relation to the verb.

Eventually the train will arrive at the station.

The train will **eventually** arrive at the station.

The train will arrive at the station **eventually.**

Negative words also function as adverbs modifying verbs.

Adverbs include the word *not* and the contraction *-n't.* Other negative words can also function as adverbs of time, place, and degree.

The cow is **not** in the barn.
The cow is **nowhere** in sight.
I **never** saw a purple cow.
The cow **hardly** chews her cud.

466   Unit 10 Parts of Speech

Resource Manager

Planning Resources
- *Lesson Plans*

📖 Transparencies
- *Bellringer*
- *Daily Language Practice*
- *Two-Minute Skill Drill*

📁 Other Print Resources
- *Grammar and Composition Handbook*
- *Grammar Enrichment,* p. 6
- *Grammar Practice,* p. 6
- *Grammar Reteaching,* p. 6
- *Grammar Workbook,* Lesson 9
- *Sentence-Combining Practice,* p. 13

Exercise 40   Identifying Different Kinds of Adverbs

On your paper, write each of the twenty adverbs in the paragraph below. Then write the verb that each adverb modifies.

SAMPLE   Hercules performed difficult tasks easily because of his strength.
ANSWER   easily—performed

The Labors of Hercules

¹People usually equate the word *Hercules* with physical strength, and today I learned the Greek myth behind the name. ²As a child, Hercules earnestly studied the sports of chariot racing, wrestling, and archery. ³He grew steadily in physical strength but never improved his self-control. ⁴Once he attacked his music teacher in a fit of rage; for this misdeed he was sent off to the countryside by the king of Thebes. ⁵There he lived in the fresh air and increased his strength daily. ⁶As an adult, he still possessed a hot temper and a violent streak. ⁷Then the Greek gods sternly ordered him to perform twelve difficult tasks that had not been completed by anyone else. ⁸He slew a savage lion and brought back its skin as his initial task. ⁹Next he somehow found the land of the Amazons and took away the precious belt of Hippolyta, the queen of the Amazons. ¹⁰Hercules finally tamed his unruly temper, and afterward he became the national hero of Greece. ¹¹We often refer to difficult tasks as "the labors of Hercules."

Exercise 41   Positioning Adverbs That Modify Verbs

Rewrite each of the following sentences, adding the verb-modifying adverb that appears in parentheses. Then write each sentence again, this time placing the same adverb in a different position.

SAMPLE   At the end of the steep trail, we beheld the ruins of Machu Picchu. (finally)
ANSWER   a. At the end of the steep trail, we finally beheld the ruins of Machu Picchu.
          b. Finally, at the end of the steep trail, we beheld the ruins of Machu Picchu.

The Lost City of the Inca

1. The ancient Inca city of Machu Picchu was discovered by an American archeologist in 1911. (surprisingly)
2. Hiram Bingham had searched for the city before finding it. (tirelessly)
3. News of the fabulous discovery began to spread. (soon)
4. Archaeologists had found such a splendid site before. (seldom)
5. The Inca held on to Machu Picchu until the sixteenth century. (tenaciously)
6. The Spanish conquistador Francisco Pizarro conquered the Inca Empire in 1533. (ruthlessly)
7. The sacred city of Machu Picchu was abandoned. (then)
8. It has survived earthquakes and erosion. (fortunately)
9. The world has seen finer stonework than that of Machu Picchu. (never)

10.5 Adverbs   **467**

Practice and Assess

Answers: Exercise 40

1. usually—equate; today—learned
2. earnestly—studied
3. steadily—grew; never—improved
4. Once—attacked; off—sent
5. There—lived; daily—increased
6. still—possessed
7. Then—ordered; sternly—ordered; not—had been completed
8. back—brought
9. Next—found; somehow—found; away—took
10. finally—tamed; afterward—became
11. often—refer

Answers: Exercise 41

Answers will vary, but some suggestions are given below.

1. Surprisingly, the ancient Inca city of Machu Picchu . . . The ancient Inca city of Machu Picchu was discovered, surprisingly, . . .
2. Hiram Bingham had searched tirelessly . . . Tirelessly Hiram Bingham had . . .
3. Soon news of . . . News of the fabulous discovery soon . . .
4. Seldom had archaeologists . . . Archaeologists had seldom . . .
5. Tenaciously the Inca held . . . The Inca held onto Machu Picchu tenaciously . . .
6. Ruthlessly the Spanish . . . The Spanish conquistador Francisco Pizzarro ruthlessly . . .
7. Then the sacred city . . . The sacred city of Machu Picchu was then . . .
8. Fortunately, it has . . . It has fortunately . . .
9. Never has the world . . . The world has never . . .

MEETING INDIVIDUAL NEEDS English Language Learners

Using *Some* and *Any*

Particularly difficult for students new to English is the shift from *some* to *any* in negative sentences. Encourage students to write several sample sentences in their journals, demonstrating the shift.

Teach

Adverbs That Modify Adjectives

 Grammar Tip

Tell students that the addition of the suffix -*ly* usually changes a word's part of speech—from adjective to adverb. For example, the adjective *quick* becomes the adverb *quickly*.

Two-Minute Skill Drill

Write the following adjectives on the board and have students provide an adverb for each that answers the question *to what degree?*

1. *dry*
2. *pale*
3. *vibrant*
4. *sparkling*
5. *difficult*

 See also *Two-Minute Skill Drill Transparency 10.5*

Practice and Assess

Answers: Exercise 42

1. somewhat/recent
2. truly/talented
3. particularly/risky
4. greatly/superior
5. understandably/small
6. very/first
7. extremely/popular
8. quite/amazing
9. much/safer
10. simply/spectacular

Parts of Speech

Adverbs That Modify Adjectives

Adverbs can give additional meaning to adjectives. An adverb that modifies an adjective answers the question *to what degree?*

QUESTION	ADJECTIVE	ADVERB
To what degree?	beautiful	**very** beautiful
	shy	**rather** shy
	optimistic	**unusually** optimistic
	clean	**thoroughly** clean

Adverbs that modify adjectives generally appear directly before the word they modify.

The train is **extremely** late. June felt **rather** weak.

Will pitches **incredibly** fast. My **very** best friend moved.

Exercise 42   Identifying Adverbs That Modify Adjectives

On your paper, list the adverb in each sentence that modifies an adjective. Then write the adjective the adverb modifies.

Hot-Air Ballooning

1. Hot-air ballooning is a somewhat-recent sport craze in the United States.
2. The first flight in history was accomplished by the truly talented Montgolfier brothers at Annonay, France, in 1783.
3. It must have seemed a particularly risky undertaking because this was the first time people had defied gravity.
4. Within a few years, balloonists substituted hydrogen gas for hot air because hydrogen was greatly superior in buoyancy.
5. The world's first air force was an understandably small balloon corps established by the French in 1794.
6. In 1793 Jean Pierre Blanchard made the very first balloon flight in America.
7. As late as the 1930s, balloon flights and races were extremely popular events.
8. In the 1960s, ballooning enjoyed a quite-amazing revival.
9. The new generation of enthusiasts returned to hot air because they determined that it was much safer than hydrogen.
10. To the spectator, balloons look simply spectacular as they float silently over a large city.

Enrichment and Extension

Testing for Adverbs

Point out that a useful test for adverbs is to ask an adverb question (typically beginning with *when, where, how,* or *why*). The answer is almost always an adverb. For example, in the sentence *The train comes Monday, Monday* is an adverb answering the question *When does the train come?* In the sentence *I went home, home* is an adverb answering the question *Where did I go?* **L2**

Adverbs That Modify Adverbs

Sometimes adverbs are used to give extra meaning to other adverbs. An adverb that modifies an adverb answers the questions *to what degree?*

QUESTION	ADJECTIVE	ADVERB
To what degree?	walked **slowly**	walked **quite** slowly
	always wins	**almost** always wins
	call **often**	call **too** often

An adverb that modifies another adverb appears directly before the modified word.

They were **only** partially convinced.   Please speak **more** slowly.
The play ended **somewhat** abruptly.   I know him **very** well.

Exercise 43   **Identifying Adverbs That Modify Other Adverbs**

On your paper, list the adverb in each sentence that modifies another adverb. Then write the adverb that is being modified.

The Bermuda Triangle

1. The tabloid press quite frequently writes about bizarre events in an area known as the Bermuda Triangle.
2. Their stories depict most vividly a long list of strange occurrences that presumably have taken place there.
3. Journalists ask their readers to imagine a line that runs somewhat approximately from Melbourne, Florida, to Bermuda, to Puerto Rico, and back to Florida.
4. They claim that within this triangle a large number of ships and airplanes have too often disappeared under mysterious circumstances.
5. It is known that storms move into this area very quickly.
6. Violent downward air currents occur there more frequently than in other places.
7. Scientists, however, are almost unanimously dubious about such tales.
8. They reiterate rather patiently that no such peculiarities exist.
9. They cannot understand why people nearly always accept hearsay over scientific evidence.
10. Nevertheless, readers of these tales remain convinced that we have just barely begun to understand the menace of the Bermuda Triangle.

Parts of Speech

Teach

Adverbs That Modify Adverbs

Cooperative Learning
Have students work in pairs to complete Exercise 43. Partners should take turns asking and answering the question *to what degree?*

Practice and Assess

Answers: Exercise 43

1. quite/frequently
2. most/vividly
3. somewhat/approximately
4. too/often
5. very/quickly
6. more/frequently
7. almost/unanimously
8. rather/patiently
9. nearly/always
10. just/barely

Cooperative Learning

Connecting with Writing

Challenge students to write an expository paragraph, using adverbs that modify verbs, adjectives, and adverbs, about how to study for a test. Ask students to underline the adverbs they use. After the paragraphs are written, have students switch papers and check each other's use of adverbs. Students should verify whether the adverbs answer the questions *when?, where?, how?,* or *to what degree?*

Teach

Forms of Adverbs

Cross-reference: Usage

For instruction and practice with degrees of comparison in adverbs, refer students to Lessons 18.1–18.2, pp. 663–667.

Practice and Assess

Answers: Exercise 44

Answers will vary, but some suggestions are given below.

1. more thoroughly, most thoroughly; Jan swept the stairs more thoroughly than Sue did, but Roger did his chores most thoroughly of all.
2. more eagerly, most eagerly; He awaited the holiday more eagerly than Sue did; but of all the students, she most eagerly anticipated her visit home.
3. lower, lowest; The plane dipped lower and soon reached its lowest cruising altitude.
4. better, best; I did better on the test than I did last time, but you got the best grade in the class.
5. nearer, nearest; Mario lives nearer me than Sanjay, but Carla is nearest.
6. worse, worst; She played worse this week than usual, but he played the worst of any performer.
7. closer, closest; They sat closer to the speaker than they did yesterday, but we were closest.
8. more angrily, most angrily; That group responded more angrily to the demand, but this group reacted most angrily of all.
9. more quickly, most quickly; I completed my homework more quickly than Joanna, but my dog ate it the most quickly of any meal he's ever had.
10. more curiously, most curiously; Alice looked through the attic more curiously than Jon; Antonia, however, searched through the boxes of heirlooms most curiously of all the grandchildren.

470

Parts of Speech

Forms of Adverbs

Like adjectives, some adverbs have different forms to indicate degree of comparison. The comparative form of an adverb compares two actions. The superlative form of an adverb compares more than two actions.

For adverbs of only one syllable, add *-er* to make the comparative form and *-est* to make the superlative form.

POSITIVE	COMPARATIVE	SUPERLATIVE
plays **hard**	plays **harder**	plays **hardest**
climbed **high**	climbed **higher**	climbed **highest**

When an adverb ends in *-ly*, use the word *more* to form the comparative and *most* to form the superlative.

POSITIVE	COMPARATIVE	SUPERLATIVE
walks **slowly**	walks **more slowly**	walks **most slowly**
smiles **easily**	smiles **more easily**	smiles **most easily**

Some adverbs do not form the comparative and superlative in the regular manner.

POSITIVE	COMPARATIVE	SUPERLATIVE
skates **well**	skates **better**	skates **best**
dances **badly**	dances **worse**	dances **worst**
knows **little**	knows **less**	knows **least**
goes **far**	goes **farther**	goes **farthest**

Exercise 44 **Using Comparative and Superlative Forms of Adverbs**

On your paper, write the comparative and superlative form of each adverb below. Then write a sentence using each of those forms.

SAMPLE hard
ANSWER harder, hardest
He threw the ball harder than Peter, but I threw it hardest of all.

1. thoroughly
2. eagerly
3. low
4. well
5. near
6. badly
7. close
8. angrily
9. quickly
10. curiously

Exploring Language

Avoiding Adverbs in Writing

Students should be advised to avoid adverbs in tag lines when writing dialogue; for example, *he said lovingly* or *she replied coldly*. Remind students that the dialogue and the actions described should reveal characters' personalities and feelings.

Distinguishing Between Adverbs and Adjectives

Some words can be either adverbs or adjectives, depending on how they are used in a sentence. To distinguish between these two parts of speech, remember that an adjective modifies a noun or pronoun, and an adverb modifies a verb, an adjective, or another adverb.

I arrived **late.** (adverb)   She ate **early.** (adverb)
The bus was **late.** (adjective)   She had an **early** date. (adjective)

You can sometimes distinguish an adverb from an adjective by remembering that many adverbs are formed by adding -*ly* to an adjective.

a **rare** ADJ.	book NOUN	a **great** ADJ.	treat NOUN
rarely ADV.	find VERB	**greatly** ADV.	appreciate VERB

Not all words that end in -*ly* are adverbs. Some are adjectives in their own right (*lonely, deadly*), and some are adjectives formed by adding -*ly* to the noun.

NOUN	ADJECTIVE ENDING IN -*LY*
brother	**brotherly** love
state	a **stately** home

Exercise 45   Distinguishing Between Adverbs and Adjectives

On your paper, identify each of the italicized words as an *adverb* or an *adjective*.

Nostalgia

1. My mother often speaks *nostalgically* about her childhood.
2. She and her two sisters enjoyed a *leisurely* existence in a small town.
3. Mother says her town was a *neighborly* place in which to live.
4. Most people she knew cared *little* for expensive cars and exotic vacations.
5. As she was the youngest, Mother was always getting *sisterly* advice from the other two.
6. They lived *close* to a park where the girls loved to skip rope and play jacks.
7. They felt *close* to each other because they got along so well.
8. Every night, the three young girls went to bed very *early.*
9. Their father told them, "The *early* bird catches the worm."
10. Now Mother's life is more *worldly,* but she misses those simpler times.

Teach

Distinguishing Between Adverbs and Adjectives

Cooperative Learning

Have students locate an article from a favorite magazine or newspaper. Ask each student to make a list of adverbs and adjectives found in the article. Then ask pairs of students to trade articles and lists and to write the word that each adverb or adjective modifies.

 Two-Minute Skill Drill

Write the following sentences on the board and ask students to identify the adverbs and adjectives.

1. *The stew cooked slowly all day.*
2. *We arrived late for dinner because of slow traffic.*
3. *Although we arrived late, dinner was ready.*
4. *Everyone agreed to see the late movie instead.*

See also *Two-Minute Skill Drill Transparency 10.5*

Practice and Assess

Answers: Exercise 45

1. adverb	**6.** adverb
2. adjective	**7.** adjective
3. adjective	**8.** adverb
4. adverb	**9.** adjective
5. adjective	**10.** adjective

Parts of Speech

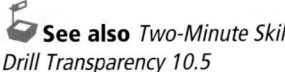 **English Language Learners**

Determining Adjectives and Adverbs

Some students may have trouble distinguishing between adjectives and adverbs. You may wish to complete Exercise 45 in class. To help students distinguish between adverbs and adjectives, encourage them to identify the word that is being modified and to determine its function in the sentence.

Practice and Assess

Answers: Exercise 46

For scoring purposes, students are required to find twenty adverbs. You may treat the twenty-first adverb as a bonus item.

1. still—was
2. Later—attended;
   apparently—planned
3. never—expected
4. very—quickly;
   quickly—distinguished
5. Soon—won;
   exclusively—was studying
6. Subsequently—worked
7. professionally—performed;
   everywhere—received
8. justifiably—called
9. greatly—interested;
   widely—is credited
10. quite—frequent;
    substantially—helped;
    meaningfully—translated
11. hardly—had slowed
12. creatively—developed;
    persistently—worked
13. finally—received

Answers: Exercise 47

Answers will vary, but some suggestions are given below.

1. . . . Min warned hotly.
2. . . . said the carpenter smoothly.
3. . . . the florist said freshly.
4. . . . asked Luis icily.
5. . . . Robin exclaimed sourly.
6. "This knife won't cut anything," Mark said dully.
7. "Have a cracker," offered Kwok crisply.
8. "The sherbet melted," Art moaned softly.
9. "This dish needs some spice," announced Jim blandly.
10. "I feel a breeze," said Linda coolly.

Additional Resources

📁 *Sentence-Combining Practice,* p. 13

📁 *Grammar Practice,* p. 6

📁 *Grammar Reteaching,* p. 6

📁 *Grammar Enrichment,* p. 6

📓 *Grammar Workbook,* Lesson 9

Parts of Speech

Exercise 46 | **Identifying Different Kinds of Adverbs**

On your paper, write each of the twenty adverbs that appear in the following paragraph. Then write the word or words that each adverb modifies.

A Great African American Dancer

¹While she was still a child, Pearl Primus came to the United States from Trinidad. ²Later she attended college in New York and apparently planned to be a doctor. ³She never expected to be a dancer. ⁴Her obvious talent very quickly distinguished her. ⁵Soon she won a scholarship and was studying dance exclusively. ⁶Subsequently, she worked with Martha Graham, Doris Humphrey, and other masters of modern dance. ⁷When she performed professionally, she received rave reviews everywhere for her beautiful dancing. ⁸Critics justifiably called her the finest new dancer of 1943. ⁹Primus was greatly interested in African dance and is widely credited with the introduction of African motifs into American dance. ¹⁰Her quite frequent trips to the Caribbean and Africa helped her substantially, and she translated African dances meaningfully for all audiences. ¹¹At the age of 60 Primus had hardly slowed her pace. ¹²She creatively developed programs for the handicapped and worked persistently on her doctoral degree. ¹³In 1978 she finally received it.

Exercise 47 | **Completing Sentences with Adverbs**

A Tom Swifty is a sentence in which an adverb comments in a humorous way on an action or object mentioned in a quotation. Note the relationship between each adverb and quotation in the following examples:

"I cleaned my room," Leroy said **tidily.**
"This picture has no color," complained Andrea **drably.**

Tom Swifties

Write the Tom Swifties in items 1–5 on your paper, completing each with an adverb that comments on the quotation. Then write five Tom Swifties of your own, using the adverbs provided in items 6–10. Consult a dictionary if necessary.

1. "Don't burn yourself!" Min warned _____.
2. "Nice job of sanding," said the carpenter _____.
3. "These flowers were just picked," the florist said _____.
4. "Is the pond frozen yet?" asked Luis _____.
5. "That lemon made my mouth pucker!" Robin exclaimed _____.
6. dully
7. crisply
8. softly
9. blandly
10. coolly

Close

Review Lesson 10.5 with students. Then have students correct a piece of their writing from their portfolio. Emphasize the importance of checking their drafts carefully to ensure that they are using adverbs correctly. Peer editing can help students understand how to use adverbs correctly.

10.6 Prepositions

■ A **preposition** is a word that shows the relationship of a noun or pronoun to some other word in a sentence.

> The garage is **behind** the house. [*Behind* shows the spatial relationship between the house and the garage.]
>
> The engine purred **after** the adjustment. [*After* tells the time relationship between the purring and the adjustment.]
>
> It started **with** ease. [*With* relates the verb *started* to the noun *ease.*]

Commonly Used Prepositions

aboard	behind	except	opposite	under
about	below	excepting	out	underneath
above	beneath	for	outside	until
across	beside	from	over	unto
after	besides	in	past	up
against	between	inside	pending	upon
along	beyond	into	regarding	with
amid	but*	like	respecting	within
among	by	near	since	without
around	concerning	of	through	
as	despite	off	throughout	
at	down	on	to	
before	during	onto	toward	

*meaning "except"

■ A **compound preposition** is a preposition that is made up of more than one word.

Compound Prepositions

according to	because of	next to
ahead of	by means of	on account of
along with	in addition to	on top of
apart from	in front of	out of
aside from	in spite of	owing to
as to	instead of	

Phrases that begin with a preposition usually end with a noun or pronoun, called the **object of the preposition.**

> He gave me a book **of poetry.**
> Mei Ying sat **next to me.**
> I was talking **with Mei Ying.**

10.6 Prepositions **473**

Focus

Lesson Overview

Objectives
- To identify prepositions and objects of prepositions
- To use prepositional phrases appropriately and effectively in writing

Bellringer
Daily Language Activity

When students enter the classroom, have this assignment on the board: *Read the following passage and identify the prepositions in it.*

> His father's razor was in a blue leather case, hinged at the broad edge and with one hinge broken.
>
> —Leslie Norris, "Shaving"

(Answers: *in, at, with*)

See also *Daily Language Practice*

Teach

☑ Teaching Tip

It is important to stress that a preposition must have an object (called the object of the preposition). Thus, prepositions may be distinguished from phrasal verbs—compound-verb constructions that use preposition-like words—for example: *The doctor called back. I finally told him to come up. We had to call it off. Back, up,* and *off* are not prepositions in these cases because they do not have objects. They are adverbs.

Resource Manager

Planning Resources
- *Lesson Plans*

Transparencies
- *Bellringer*
- *Daily Language Practice*

📁 Other Print Resources
- *Grammar and Composition Handbook*
- *Grammar Enrichment,* p. 7
- *Grammar Practice,* p. 7
- *Grammar Reteaching,* p. 7
- *Grammar Workbook,* Lesson 10
- *Sentence-Combining Practice,* p. 11

Parts of Speech

10.6

Practice and Assess

Answers: Exercise 48

1. of, for, of, in
2. by, of, between
3. By means of, with, through
4. in, from, instead of
5. after, throughout, on, concerning, in
6. During, across, to, around
7. In addition to, onto, in front of
8. Because of, into, on
9. on top of, above
10. as, by

Answers: Exercise 49

Paragraphs will vary, but a sample is given below.

Against my better judgment, I set out to deliver a message for the ancient magician. According to his directions, I was to go to a nearby town. "I left you a map," he had said, "underneath the dining-room table." I found the table and the map near the back door. On top of the map were a huge metal key, a sealed envelope, and written directions. I went outside the house. Between you and me, I wasn't sure I wanted to travel to an unknown town for this strange magician. I began my trip on the highway outside of town. I continued throughout the evening. Suddenly I saw something beyond belief.

Parts of Speech

Exercise 48   Identifying Prepositions

On your paper, list the prepositions that appear in each of the following sentences. Remember that some prepositions are made up of more than one word. (The numeral in parentheses at the end of each item indicates the number of prepositions in that sentence.)

A Special-Effects Pioneer

1. Willis O'Brien, a creator of special effects for the early film industry, pioneered the use of rubber and clay models in movies. (4)
2. Shooting the film frame by frame and changing the position of the model slightly between shots, he created illusionary movement. (3)
3. By means of this method, O'Brien shot an experimental film with a clay dinosaur that "roamed" through a miniature set. (3)
4. Since the dinosaur's movements looked too choppy in this first attempt, O'Brien shot a second version, using dinosaurs made from rubber and metal instead of clay and wood. (3)
5. Six years after this film, which was distributed throughout the United States, O'Brien worked on a full-length movie concerning dinosaurs in a South American jungle. (5)
6. During one scene, a brontosaurus is brought across the ocean to London, where it escapes and runs around the city. (4)
7. In addition to his dinosaur models, O'Brien used scenery painted onto glass panes that he positioned in front of the action. (3)
8. Because of O'Brien's skill, models and sets were transformed into believable monsters and jungles on the movie screen. (3)
9. Years later, another movie showed a giant gorilla on top of the Empire State Building, high above the frightened crowds. (2)
10. This giant gorilla, which we now know as King Kong, was created by O'Brien. (2)

Exercise 49   Using Prepositional Phrases

Use each of the following prepositional phrases in an original sentence. Then combine your sentences into a coherent paragraph or two. You may combine your sentences in any order.

1. according to his directions
2. underneath the dining-room table
3. near the back door
4. on top of the map
5. outside the house
6. between you and me
7. beyond belief
8. throughout the evening
9. on the highway outside of town
10. against my better judgment

474   Unit 10 Parts of Speech

English Language Learners

Identifying Prepositions

Before students do Exercise 48, pair students new to English with students proficient in English. Have the pairs review the prepositions listed on page 473 and work together to complete Exercise 48. After students have completed the exercise, ask them to explain the basis on which they identified the prepositions. Discuss the function of prepositions and emphasize that prepositions qualify relationships.

474

Some words may be used as either prepositions or adverbs. A word is used as a preposition if it has a noun or pronoun as its object. A word is used as an adverb if it does not have an object.

WORD USED AS PREPOSITION	WORD USED AS ADVERB
He left his friends **behind** the stadium.	He left his friends **behind.**
I finally took my boots **off** the step.	I finally took my boots **off.**
The bike is **outside** the garage.	The bike is **outside.**

Exercise 50 Completing Sentences with Prepositions and Adverbs

On your paper, complete each sentence by writing any preposition or adverb that makes sense. Then write whether you used the word as a *preposition* or an *adverb*. Use the charts on page 473 to help you choose appropriate words.

SAMPLE   I lost my balance and fell _____.
ANSWER   over—adverb

White-Water Rafting

1. Our first exposure to white-water rafting was _____ the Nantahala River.
2. The Nantahala is a swift-flowing river _____ Great Smoky Mountains National Park.
3. Friends had told us that nothing else compares to the thrill _____ white-water rafting.
4. Our guide warned us not to leave our life jackets _____.
5. Our equipment was a large rubber raft _____ six long oars.
6. We learned how to direct our raft to the right or left, and even how to turn it completely _____.
7. As we started, we felt very chilly _____ the bright sun.
8. At first we were nervous because we were afraid of tipping the raft _____.
9. Soon we relaxed and began to joke with the people in the raft _____ us.
10. _____ our successful experience this time, we plan to ride an even wilder river in the future.

Exercise 51 Creating Sentences with Prepositions

Choose five prepositions from the lists on page 473. Use each one in a sentence. Add adjectives and adverbs wherever necessary.

Teach

☑ **Teaching Tip**
Remind students that an adverb is a word used to modify a verb, an adjective, or another adverb and that a preposition shows the relation of a noun or pronoun to another word in the sentence.

Practice and Assess

Parts of Speech

Answers: Exercise 50
1. on—preposition
2. in—preposition
3. of—preposition
4. behind—adverb
5. with—preposition
6. around—adverb
7. out of—preposition
8. over—adverb
9. beside—preposition
10. Because of—preposition

Answers: Exercise 51
Sentences will vary. Samples:
1. Tina tossed the ragged old baseball against the brick wall.
2. Between the houses was a colorful garden.
3. Ahead of me in line stood an old friend.
4. I've finished all of today's homework except social studies.
5. Next week, my family and I will be out of town.

Additional Resources
📁 *Sentence-Combining Practice,* p. 11
📁 *Grammar Practice,* p. 7
📁 *Grammar Reteaching,* p. 7
📁 *Grammar Enrichment,* p. 7

 Grammar Workbook, Lesson 10

Close

Have students identify the prepositions and prepositional phrases in one of the longer pieces of writing from their portfolios. Have them make appropriate changes in the use of prepositions to improve their writing.

Focus

Lesson Overview

Objectives

• To identify various types of conjunctions
• To use various types of conjunctions appropriately in writing

 Bellringer
Daily Language Activity

When students enter the classroom, have this assignment on the board: *Tell the function of conjunctions.* (To join words or groups of words)

See also *Daily Language Practice*

Teach

Coordinating Conjunctions

☑ **Teaching Tip**

Often students don't recognize *but, for, nor,* and *yet* as coordinating conjunctions. Students need many examples of sentences containing these words to see that they function as coordinating conjunctions.

🖫 **Cross-reference: Grammar**

For instruction and practice with coordinating conjunctions, refer students to Lesson 13.3, pp. 545–546.

Practice and Assess

Answers: Exercise 52

1. but, and	**5.** or	**9.** but
2. and, for	**6.** and	**10.** nor
3. and	**7.** and, for	
4. yet	**8.** and	

Parts of Speech (side tab)

10.7 Conjunctions

■ A **conjunction** is a word that joins single words or groups of words.

Coordinating Conjunctions

■ A **coordinating conjunction** joins words or groups of words that have equal grammatical weight in a sentence.

Coordinating Conjunctions						
and	but	or	nor	for	yet	so

She designs **and** builds.
He writes in French **but** not in English.
Practice writing, **or** you will never improve.
She had no homework, **nor** did she have basketball practice.

Exercise 52   **Identifying Coordinating Conjunctions**

On your paper, write the coordinating conjunction(s) that appear in each of the following sentences.

Baseball, an Integrated Sport

[1]Many people know something about the history of baseball in our country, but the story of African Americans and baseball is often neglected. [2]The history of African Americans and baseball began sometime during the Civil War, for it was then that black soldiers learned to play the game. [3]In 1885 a group of waiters from the Argyle Hotel in Babylon, New York, met and organized a paid baseball team. [4]All of the team's players were African American, yet they called themselves the Cuban Giants. [5]Their choice, they thought, was to pretend that they were Hispanic or face discrimination. [6]By the turn of the century, African Americans were playing on several college teams in the northern and the western sections of the country. [7]The 1920s was an important era for minorities and baseball, for several African American teams were organized during that decade. [8]Among them were the Homestead Grays, the American Giants, the Kansas City Monarchs, and the St. Louis Stars. [9]The great Jackie Robinson could have chosen to play on an African American team, but in 1947 he joined the Brooklyn Dodgers, becoming the first African American to play in the major leagues. [10]Prejudice didn't deter African American baseball heroes such as Jackie Robinson, nor were they discouraged by the low pay that they received during those early years.

 Resource Manager

Planning Resources
• *Lesson Plans*

🖫 **Transparencies**
• *Bellringer*
• *Daily Language Practice*

📁 **Other Print Resources**
• *Grammar and Composition Handbook*
• *Grammar Enrichment,* p. 8
• *Grammar Practice,* p. 8
• *Grammar Reteaching,* p. 8
• *Grammar Workbook,* Lessons 11, 12
• *Sentence-Combining Practice,* pp. 2, 21–23

Correlative Conjunctions

■ **Correlative conjunctions** work in pairs to join words and groups of words of equal weight in a sentence.

Correlative Conjunctions		
both . . . and	just as . . . so	not only . . . but (also)
either . . . or	neither . . . nor	whether . . . or

The relationship between words or groups of words is emphasized by using correlative conjunctions rather than coordinating conjunctions.

COORDINATING CONJUNCTIONS	CORRELATIVE CONJUNCTIONS
You **and** I must go.	**Both** you **and** I must go.
You **or** I must go.	**Either** you **or** I must go.
	Neither you **nor** I must go.
We saw Tokyo **and** Kyoto.	We saw **not only** Tokyo **but also** Kyoto.

Exercise 53   **Identifying Correlative Conjunctions**

On your paper, write both parts of the correlative conjunctions that appear in the following sentences.

Special-issue Stamps

¹A great many countries issue special stamps either to honor a famous person or to commemorate an important event. ²Some countries print specially priced stamps in order both to celebrate an event and to generate extra funds. ³Either original art or reproductions of famous paintings may decorate the special stamps. ⁴A special 1893 stamp was not only a tribute to the discovery of America but also the first commemorative stamp issued by the United States. ⁵Other stamps have honored both famous leaders and important occasions. ⁶Neither the Apollo space program nor the nation's bicentennial passed without a special stamp. ⁷During the International Year of the Child, another significant event, children's art appeared on both postage stamps and holiday seals. ⁸Neither the American Lung Association, which used children's art on its holiday seals, nor the design sponsors chose the themes for the seals. ⁹Each school chosen to take part decided on its own whether to tell its students exactly what to draw or simply to suggest a holiday theme. ¹⁰Just as these holiday seals celebrated children's art, so the postage stamps from many other countries continue to do so.

Teach

Correlative Conjunctions

☑ **GrammarTip**

Tell students that correlative conjunctions enable writers to express relationships more complex than can be expressed by simply using *and* or *but*. For example, point out that the sample sentence on student page 477 *We saw not only Tokyo but also Kyoto* implies that although any visitor to Japan would naturally see Tokyo, we were fortunate enough to see Kyoto in addition. The word *and* alone does not convey this meaning.

Practice and Assess

Answers: Exercise 53

1. either . . . or
2. both . . . and
3. Either . . . or
4. not only . . . but also
5. both . . . and
6. Neither . . . nor
7. both . . . and
8. Neither . . . nor
9. whether . . . or
10. Just as . . . so

Parts of Speech

MEETING INDIVIDUAL NEEDS   English Language Learners

Joining Clauses with Conjunctions

The correlative conjunction *not only . . . but (also)* has a feature that may confuse students new to English. When *not only . . . but (also)* joins clauses, the first verb in the first clause precedes the subject: *Not only can Mary sing, but she can also dance.* Have students join clauses with different conjunctions, and then introduce *not only . . . but (also)* to show the difference.

Teach

Subordinating Conjunctions

☑ GrammarTip

Point out to students that when a subordinate clause precedes a main clause, they should use a comma after the subordinate clause. When a subordinate clause follows a main clause, a comma may or may not be needed.

Before the storm hit, I brought the clothes in.
I brought the clothes in before the storm hit.

A subordinating conjunction joins two clauses unequally; that is, the dependent clause is subordinated to the main clause.

⇄ Cross-reference: Grammar

For instruction and practice with subordinate clauses, refer students to Lessons 13.5–13.7, pp. 549–555.

Practice and Assess

Answers: Exercise 54

1. Considering that
2. when
3. When
4. Because
5. Before
6. Whereas
7. As soon as
8. while
9. when
10. After

Subordinating Conjunctions

■ A **subordinating conjunction** joins two clauses, or ideas, in such a way as to make one grammatically dependent upon the other.

The idea, or clause, introduced by a subordinating conjunction is considered subordinate, or dependent, because it cannot stand alone as a complete sentence.

We cheered the tall ships **because** they were so glorious.
We cheered the tall ships **when** they arrived.
Whenever the ships sail again, we will want to see them.
We will want to see them **if** they sail again.

Common Subordinating Conjunctions			
after	as though	provided (that)	until
although	because	since	when
as	before	so long as	whenever
as far as	considering (that)	so that	where
as if	if	than	whereas
as long as	inasmuch as	though	wherever
as soon as	in order that	unless	while

Exercise 54   Identifying Subordinating Conjunctions

Write the subordinating conjunction that appears in each sentence below. Remember that some subordinating conjunctions are made up of more than one word.

Harold Krents, a Success Story

1. Considering that Harold Krents was totally blind by his eighth birthday, his achievements are extraordinary.
2. Life is not easy when one's vision is impaired.
3. When he was in high school, Krents's classmates elected him president of his school.
4. Because Krents was brilliant, he was accepted by Harvard.
5. Before he went to college, Krents spent the summer as an arts counselor at camp.
6. Whereas others had difficulty finding their way around the tents in the dark, Krents moved about easily and kept the campers quiet after taps.
7. As soon as he had graduated *cum laude* from Harvard University, Krents was accepted at Harvard Law School.
8. Krents met his future wife while she was reading for visually challenged law students.
9. Krents was very surprised when his draft board mistakenly classified him 1-A.
10. After he heard Krents's story, Leonard Gershe wrote the play *Butterflies Are Free*.

Enrichment and Extension

Identifying and Classifying Conjunctions

Without some instruction or review of the concept of clauses, some students may have difficulty recognizing subordinating conjunctions. Before asking students to identify and classify such conjunctions, check their understanding of the concept of a clause as a unit that contains a subject and a verb and expresses an idea.

Conjunctive Adverbs

■ A **conjunctive adverb** is used to clarify the relationship between clauses of equal weight in a sentence.

Conjunctive adverbs tend to be stronger and more precise than coordinating conjunctions.

| COORDINATING CONJUNCTION | The ships sailed away, **but** they left us with happy memories. |
| CONJUNCTIVE ADVERB | The ships sailed away; **nevertheless,** they left us with happy memories. |

Conjunctive adverbs have several uses:

TO REPLACE *AND*	also, besides, furthermore, moreover
TO REPLACE *BUT*	however, nevertheless, still
TO STATE A RESULT	consequently, therefore, so, thus
TO STATE EQUALITY	equally, likewise, similarly

Exercise 55 Completing Sentences with Conjunctive Adverbs

On your paper, write each of the following sentences, replacing the blank with an appropriate conjunctive adverb that makes the sentence meaningful. In most cases, there is more than one correct answer.

The Early Inuit

1. Some people think that the Inuit are native to Alaska; _____, they actually came from Siberia about five thousand years ago.
2. Some people think the Inuit crossed from Siberia to Alaska by sea; _____, others say that they walked over a land bridge.
3. The early Inuit hunted caribou; _____, they moved often to follow the herds.
4. They lived in one of the coldest, darkest, and most desolate regions of the world; _____, their life was harsh.
5. The Inuit invented many words to describe minute changes in the weather; _____, they had a rich vocabulary of hunting terms.
6. Some Inuit carvings may have magical or religious associations; _____, archaeologists are not certain of this.
7. It is hard to imagine the Inuit without sled dogs; _____, the Inuit learned to train dogs only about nine hundred years ago.
8. The Inuit thought that nothing should be wasted; _____, they made dozens of useful objects from the animals they killed.
9. Traditional Inuit clothing, made from caribou hides and sealskins, is light and warm; _____, it is waterproof.
10. Many people refer to these people as *Eskimos;* _____, the group itself uses the term *Inuit.*

Parts of Speech

Teach

Conjunctive Adverbs

☑ **Teaching Tip**

Many students confuse subordinating conjunctions with conjunctive adverbs. Part of the problem is the confusing term *conjunctive* in the name *conjunctive adverb.* Tell students that unlike true conjunctions, conjunctive adverbs do not link two clauses grammatically; conjunctive adverbs merely show how the meaning of the subordinate clause is related to the meaning of the main clause.

⇄ **Cross-reference: Mechanics**

For instruction and practice in punctuating sentences with conjunctive adverbs, refer students to Lesson 21.6, pp. 743–751.

Practice and Assess

Answers: Exercise 55

Answers will vary, but some suggestions are given below.
1. however
2. however
3. therefore
4. consequently
5. moreover
6. still
7. nevertheless
8. consequently
9. furthermore
10. however

Enrichment and Extension

Categorizing Conjunctions

Have students discuss the kind of relationship indicated by each of these subordinating conjunctions: *after, although, as if, as though, because, before, even though, if, since, so that, unless, until, when, whenever, where, wherever, while.* Help students see that the conjunctions fall into categories such as these:

Time: after, as, before, since, until, when, while
Place: where, wherever
Manner: as, as if, as though
Cause: as, because, since, so that
Concession: although, even though
Condition: if, unless

Practice and Assess

Answers: Exercise 56

1. Because, subordinating
2. While, subordinating
3. both . . . and, correlative
4. When, subordinating
5. Although, subordinating
6. Since, subordinating
7. or, coordinating
8. and, coordinating; and, coordinating
9. Both . . . and, correlative
10. Not only . . . but also, correlative
11. but, coordinating
12. Although, subordinating
13. Just as . . . so, correlative
14. As soon as, subordinating; and, coordinating
15. if, subordinating
16. either . . . or, correlative
17. yet, coordinating
18. After, subordinating
19. and, coordinating; when, subordinating
20. and, coordinating
21. If, subordinating
22. After, subordinating; and, coordinating
23. not only . . . but also, correlative
24. and, coordinating
25. Because, subordinating; and, coordinating

Parts of Speech

Exercise 56 Identifying Different Kinds of Conjunctions

On your paper, write the conjunction in each of the following sentences. Label each conjunction as *coordinating, correlative,* or *subordinating.* Some sentences contain more than one conjunction.

The Constellations

1. Because the earth revolves around the sun, different constellations can be seen at different times of the year.
2. While it can be very helpful in locating constellations, you must learn how to use a star map effectively.
3. Astronomers use both binoculars and telescopes to observe the stars.
4. When you look at a constellation, you may see a planet wandering through it.
5. Although there are eighty-eight constellations, only about two dozen constellations are visible at any time.
6. Since the earth revolves around the sun, some constellations can be seen only during certain seasons.
7. An observer at the North or South Pole can see only one hemisphere of stars.
8. Greeks and Romans named stars after animals and mythological characters.
9. Both Leo and Taurus are constellations named for animals.
10. Not only Orion but also Perseus is a constellation named for a Greek hero.
11. Many people think the Big Dipper is a constellation, but it is actually part of the large constellation called the Great Bear.
12. Although the Little Dipper is small, it contains the most important star in our skies, the North Star.
13. Just as you can use the Big Dipper to find the North Star, so you can use the Big Dipper to find Regulus, the brightest star in the constellation Leo.
14. As soon as you find the Great Square of Pegasus, find Andromeda and Cassiopeia.
15. You may be able to find the Andromeda Nebula, the most distant object visible to the unaided eye, if the night is clear.
16. The constellation Cassiopeia is thought to represent either the mythological queen Cassiopeia or her throne.
17. In the constellation Taurus the Bull, the Pleiades look like a tiny cloud, yet they are actually a group of stars.
18. After you find the Pleiades, look for the star Aldebaran in the bull's head.
19. Night and day are the same length when the sun reaches the bottom of the Pisces constellation.
20. This happens about March 21 and marks the beginning of spring.
21. If you find three bright stars in a straight line, you are looking at Orion.
22. After you spot the belt of three stars, look below it to find the Orion Nebula.
23. Orion has not only the reddish star Betelgeuse but also the bluish white star Rigel.
24. Castor and Pollux are stars in the constellation Gemini.
25. Because Gemini is part of the zodiac, planets wander into the constellation and often put on an impressive show.

Exploring Language

Adverbs and Conjunctions

Conjunctive adverbs and subordinating conjunctions are easily confused because both connect clauses. Explain that one way to tell whether a word is a conjunctive adverb or a subordinating conjunction is to examine the position of the word in its clause. A subordinating conjunction must always be the first word in a clause. A conjunctive adverb, however, can usually be moved to the middle or the end of a clause. **L2**

Exercise 57 | Completing Sentences with Different Kinds of Conjunctions

On your paper, replace each blank with the kind of conjunction stated in parentheses at the end of each sentence.

SAMPLE The country drained by the Flathead River is _____ a valuable ecological area _____ an important recreation area. (correlative conjunction)

ANSWER The country drained by the Flathead River is both a valuable ecological area and an important recreation area.

The Flathead River

1. The Flathead River lies mostly in the United States; _____, its headwaters are in Canada. (conjunctive adverb)
2. The lands drained by the Flathead River are forest, _____ they are populated by about two-thirds of the remaining grizzly bears. (coordinating conjunction)
3. _____ the threatened grizzly bear _____ the Rocky Mountain wolf inhabit the Flathead wilderness. (correlative conjunction)
4. The north fork of the Flathead River is eventually joined by _____ the middle fork _____ the south fork. (correlative conjunction)
5. _____ you visit the North Fork valley, you may meet Mary McFarland, a veterinarian. (subordinating conjunction)
6. From Mary McFarland's window, you can see mountains _____ you turn. (subordinating conjunction)
7. _____ a Dolly Varden trout _____ a rare cutthroat trout is a likely catch along the Flathead River. (correlative conjunction)
8. Otters play along the Flathead River, _____ bald eagles soar overhead. (subordinating conjunction)
9. _____ it leaves the wild country, the Flathead River meanders through rich farmlands into Flathead Lake, west of the Missouri. (subordinating conjunction)
10. _____ the Flathead emerges from the lake, it turns to join the Clark Fork River. (subordinating conjunction)

Exercise 58 | Creating Sentences with Different Kinds of Conjunctions

Think of a favorite room that you have known or read about, in which there are many interesting articles and pieces of furniture. Write several sentences about that room, using as many conjunctions as possible.

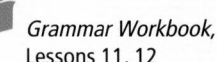

Parts of Speech

Answers: Exercise 57

Answers may vary, but some suggestions are given below.

1. however
2. and
3. Not only, but also
4. both, and
5. If
6. wherever
7. Either, or
8. while
9. After
10. As soon as

Answers: Exercise 58

Sentences will vary. A sample is given below:

I loved my grandmother's back porch because it contained not only an old, comfortable sofa but also pillows and plants galore.

Additional Resources

📁 *Sentence-Combining Practice*, pp. 2, 21–23

📁 *Grammar Practice*, p. 8

📁 *Grammar Reteaching*, p. 8

📁 *Grammar Enrichment*, p. 8

📖 *Grammar Workbook*, Lessons 11, 12

Close

Have students find writing pieces in their portfolios that can be improved by combining sentences. Have them use various kinds of conjunctions and conjunctive adverbs described in this lesson to combine sentences.

Cooperative Learning

Reviewing Conjunctions

As a review, have students write at least five conjunctions on separate notecards. Then ask pairs of students to trade cards and compose a paragraph using each conjunction at least once. Students may wish to share their paragraphs with their partners.

Focus

Lesson Overview

Objectives
- To identify interjections
- To use interjections effectively in writing

Bellringer
Daily Language Activity

When students enter the classroom, have this assignment on the board: *Write a list of ten words that show emotion.*

See also *Daily Language Practice*

Teach

☑ Teaching Tip

Some students will confuse interjections with imperative and exclamatory sentences. Remind students that interjections are not sentences and do not have subjects and verbs.

Practice and Assess

Answers: Exercise 59

Answers will vary, but some suggestions are given below.

1. Hush	**6.** Whew
2. Help	**7.** Golly
3. Good luck	**8.** Oh my
4. Hi	**9.** Hey
5. Wow	**10.** Gee whiz

Parts of Speech

10.8 Interjections

■ An **interjection** is a word or phrase that expresses emotion or exclamation.

An interjection has no grammatical connection to the other words in the sentence and is set off from the other words by an exclamation mark or a comma.

Different emotions are expressed by different interjections.

surprise	**Oh,** didn't you know?
delight	**Ah,** your father knows the recipe.
confusion	**What!** I didn't know that.
pain	**Ouch!** That hurts.
joy	**Wow!** This is great.

Interjections are used mostly in speech. They should be used sparingly in writing.

Exercise 59 — Using Interjections

On your paper, fill each blank in the following items with an appropriate interjection from the following list:

wow	hey	gee whiz	help	hi
oh my	golly	good luck	hush	whew

1. _____, the movie is about to begin.
2. _____! The sink is overflowing.
3. _____! We hope to see you at the finish line.
4. _____, we just moved into the house next door.
5. _____! How did you manage to catch that pass?
6. _____! I'm glad that test is over.
7. _____! What an incredible view there is from here!
8. _____, I wish you'd told me that sooner.
9. _____! Where do you think you're going with my bicycle?
10. _____, what a gorgeous picture that would make!

Resource Manager

Planning Resources
- *Lesson Plans*

Transparencies
- *Bellringer*
- *Daily Language Practice*

📂 Other Print Resources
- *Grammar and Composition Handbook*
- *Grammar Enrichment,* p. 8
- *Grammar Practice,* p. 8
- *Grammar Workbook,* Lesson 12

Exercise 60   Identifying Parts of Speech

On your paper, write the part of speech of the italicized word in each of the following sentences.

Seashells

1. Anyone out for a stroll on a beach may find *wonderful* shells.
2. For even better discoveries, *look* in tidal pools.
3. Seashells are often more *numerous* after a storm.
4. Some seashells are *collectors'* items.
5. Such items are *usually* large, beautiful, and not well known.
6. Seashells, unlike stamps and coins, rarely increase *in* value.
7. *These* are the leading families of collectibles: cones, cowries, volutes, murexes, slit shells, and scallops.
8. Prehistoric people *often* used large univalve shells as pots or ladles.
9. Conch shells were sounded like trumpets, *not only* to call buffalos or warriors *but also* to frighten evil spirits or to accompany a funeral.
10. *Which* Central American people "milked" a particular live seashell for its purple dye?
11. In many ancient cultures cowrie shells were used as money *because* of their small size, beautiful shape, and luster.
12. The Chinese used cowries as *their* money from about 2000 B.C. to 600 B.C.
13. *Ah,* how beautiful are some of the seashells depicted in art!
14. Native Americans made wampum belts from shells of the quahog clam, *and* they used the belts as money or to record important events.
15. Pen shells have a tuft of silky threads with which they anchor *themselves* to the bottom of the sea.
16. Some historians think that Jason's Golden Fleece was material woven from *the* pen shells' silky threads.
17. Shells, especially scallop shells, are often used in the decorative arts; *moreover,* the theme is repeated in architecture.
18. Painted during the *Renaissance,* one of Sandro Botticelli's greatest works depicts Venus being gently blown to shore on the lower half of a fluted shell.
19. *Anyone* can see this painting at the Uffizi Gallery in Florence, Italy.
20. Shells truly *are* one of nature's wonders.

Exercise 61   Using Parts of Speech

On your paper, write a paragraph about a collection or hobby of your choice. Describe the hobby, using at least one example of each of the eight parts of speech. Use as many types of the parts of speech as possible—for example, proper and abstract nouns, subordinating conjunctions, and conjunctive adverbs.

Answers: Exercise 60

1. adjective
2. verb or action verb
3. adjective
4. possessive noun or adjective
5. adverb
6. preposition
7. pronoun or demonstrative pronoun
8. adverb
9. conjunction or correlative conjunction
10. pronoun or interrogative pronoun
11. conjunction or subordinating conjunction
12. pronoun or possessive pronoun or adjective
13. interjection
14. conjunction or coordinating conjunction
15. pronoun or reflexive pronoun
16. article or definite article
17. adverb or conjunctive adverb
18. noun or proper noun
19. pronoun or indefinite pronoun
20. verb or linking verb

Evaluation Rubric: Exercise 61

Check for pronouns, adjectives, adverbs, conjunctions, prepositions, and interjections. Sample:

My hobby may seem strange to some people; nonetheless, it is enjoyable to me. When I first discovered sand painting, I was traveling in the Southwest. I met a woman who was quietly creating abstract paintings. Wow! The colors were beautiful. I was hooked.

Additional Resources

📁 *Grammar Practice,* p. 8
📁 *Grammar Enrichment,* p. 8

📖 *Grammar Workbook,* Lesson 12

Close

As a final activity, review with students the eight parts of speech. Have them choose a piece of writing from their portfolios. Then ask them to identify the parts of speech in three or four sentences.

Teach

About the Literature

Explain that the review contains a passage from chapter 13 of the novel *The Sound of Waves* by Yukio Mishima. The passage is followed by exercises based on related topics. After students read the passage, discuss its characters, setting, and mood. Then ask students to determine which words are, or are not, essential to the meaning of the passage.

Linking Grammar and Literature

Critical Thinking

Ask students to consider the roles played by the highlighted words in the passage. Have them determine which words are essential to the meaning of the passage and which could be eliminated.

✔ ASSESSMENT OPTIONS

📁 *Tests with Answer Key & Rubrics*
Unit 10 Mastery Test, p. 33

💾 *Testmaker*
Unit 11 Mastery Test

PARTS OF SPEECH

The Sound of Waves, by the prolific Japanese writer Yukio Mishima, tells the story of the love between a young boy and girl who live in a fishing village in Japan. World War II has just ended, and the villagers are slowly rebuilding their lives. This scene describes how the women of the island dive for abalone. The passage has been annotated to show the parts of speech covered in this unit.

Parts of Speech (sidebar)

Literature Model

from The Sound of Waves
by Yukio Mishima
translated from the Japanese by Meredith Weatherby

The young girls of the **island** faced the arrival of the diving season with precisely the same heart-strangling feeling city youths have when confronted by a final school-term examinations. Their games of scrambling for pebbles on the bottom of the sea close to the beach, begun during the early years of grade school, first **introduced** them to the art of diving, **and** they naturally became more skillful as their spirit of rivalry increased. But when they **finally** began diving for a living and their carefree games turned into real work, without exception the young girls became frightened, and the arrival of spring meant only that the dreaded summer was approaching.

There **was** the cold, the strangling feeling of running out of breath, the inexpressible agony **when** water forced its way under the water-goggles, the panic and sudden fear of collapsing that invaded the entire body just when an abalone was almost at the fingertips. There were also all kinds of accidents; and the wounds inflicted on the tips of the toes when kicking off against the sea's bottom, with its carpet of sharp-edged shells, to rise to the surface; and the leaden languor **that** possessed the body after it had been forced to dive

Annotations: Common noun · Action verb · Coordinating conjunction · Adverb · Linking verb · Subordinating conjunction · Relative pronoun

---

Resource Manager

Planning Resources
• *Lesson Plans*

📁 **Other Print Resources**
• *Grammar Workbook,* Lessons 1–12; Unit 10 Review; *Cumulative Review*

almost beyond endurance. . . . All these things had become
sharper and sharper in the remembering; the terror had
become all the more intense in the repeating. And often sudden nightmares would awaken the girls from sleep so deep as
seemingly to leave no room for dreams to creep in. Then, in
the dead of night, in the darkness surrounding their peaceful,
dangerless beds, they would peer at the flood of sweat
clenched within their fists.

It was different with the older divers, with those who had
husbands. Coming out of the water from diving, they would
sing and laugh and talk in loud voices. It seemed as though
work and play had become united in a single whole for them.
Watching them enviously, the young girls would tell themselves that they could never become like that, and yet as the
years passed they would be surprised to discover that, without their quite realizing it, they themselves had reached the
point where they too could be counted among those light-
hearted, veteran divers.

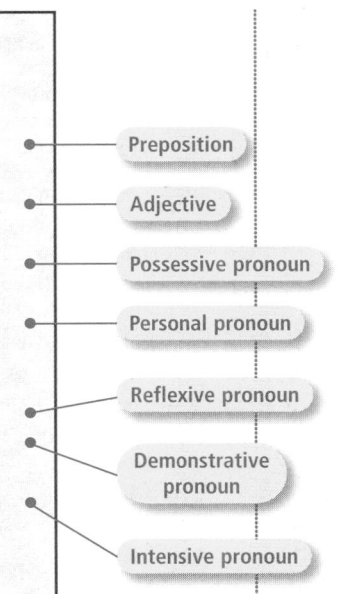

Preposition

Adjective

Possessive pronoun

Personal pronoun

Reflexive pronoun

Demonstrative
pronoun

Intensive pronoun

Parts of Speech

Review: Exercise 1 **Identifying Nouns**

The following sentences elaborate on ideas or images suggested by the passage from
The Sound of Waves. On your paper, identify each noun and write in parentheses
common, proper, or *collective,* depending upon how it is used in the sentence.

1. On one side of the country lies the Pacific Ocean.
2. On the other side is the Sea of Japan.
3. Many islanders depend upon the ocean for jobs.
4. On Song Island the women dive for abalone.
5. The young girls play games at the beach.
6. Crowds scramble for stones at the bottom of the ocean.
7. Sometimes teams compete for prizes.
8. The competition often improves the girls' diving skills.
9. Later the lighthearted contests become work.
10. Do the young women still enjoy their dives?
11. The search for a colony of abalone is no longer a game.
12. Suddenly the new crew of divers fears the cold waters of the Pacific Ocean.
13. Cuts from the sharp edges of the shells are very painful.
14. The young workers also fear the feeling of exhaustion after a dive.
15. In spring the girls dread the start of the new diving season.

Grammar Review   **485**

Practice and Assess

Answers: Exercise 1

1. side (common)
   country (common)
   Pacific Ocean (proper)
2. side (common)
   Sea of Japan (proper)
3. islanders (common)
   ocean (common)
   jobs (common)
4. Song Island (proper)
   women (common)
   abalone (common)
5. girls (common)
   games (common)
   beach (common)
6. Crowds (collective)
   stones (common)
   bottom (common)
   ocean (common)
7. teams (collective)
   prizes (common)
8. competition (common)
   skills (common)
9. contests (common)
   work (common)
10. women (common)
    dives (common)
11. search (common)
    colony (collective)
    abalone (common)
    game (common)
12. crew (collective)
    divers (common)
    waters (common)
    Pacific Ocean (proper)
13. Cuts (common)
    edges (common)
    shells (common)
14. workers (common)
    feeling (common)
    exhaustion (common)
    dive (common)
15. spring (common)
    girls (common)
    start (common)
    season (common)

Practice and Assess

Answers: Exercise 2

For scoring purposes, students are required to find twenty-five pronouns. You may treat the twenty-sixth pronoun as a bonus item.

1. which, itself
2. It, their
3. These, which
4. most, who
5. these, all
6. her, she, herself, which, she
7. this
8. that, who, its
9. Whoever, these, their
10. others, him, their, that

Answers: Exercise 3

Answers may vary slightly, but some suggestions are given below.

1. As the day drew to a close, the young women of Song Island gathered at the harbor, where they often helped the returning fishers.
2. The fishers had been out in their boats all day, hoping to fill them with a good catch.
3. The men still had to transfer their fish to the boat owned by the Fishers' Cooperative.
4. Then they had to pull their heavy boats up onto the beach, where they were kept on wooden frames.
5. The frames were called abacuses because of their shape.
6. The girls dragged the frames down to the shoreline, and the men slipped the frames under the backs of their boats.
7. When the boats were safe for the night, the men and women could go home for their evening meal.
8. Later the men would visit the public baths because they did not have baths in their homes.
9. Once a week, the unmarried young men attended a meeting of the Young Men's Association.
10. There they argued politics and discussed various projects that they thought would be good for civic improvement.

Review: Exercise 2   Identifying Pronouns

The paragraph below describes the Japanese literary tradition from which Yukio Mishima emerged. On your paper, list the twenty-five pronouns used in the paragraph.

[1]The Japanese literary tradition out of which Mishima emerged is itself quite interesting. [2]It reflects many of the characteristics of the Japanese people, such as their love of tradition and sensitivity to nature. [3]These elements occur in the oldest existing manuscripts, which date to the eighth century. [4]During the Heian period (794–1185), most of the people who wrote literature were members of the nobility. [5]Of these, the greatest were women, and the greatest of all was Murasaki Shikibu. [6]In her masterpiece, *The Tale of Genji*, she writes about herself and the court life of which she was a part. [7]Drama and poetry have also played important roles in this literary tradition. [8]The verse form that is known as *haiku* was developed in the 1600s by Matsuo Bashō, who established its strict rules. [9]Whoever reads the best of these is entranced by their ability to stimulate the imagination. [10]In modern Japan, Mishima and others like him have blended their own literary tradition with that of Western culture.

Review: Exercise 3   Using Pronouns Effectively

The paragraph below is based on passages from *The Sound of Waves* that are not reprinted in this textbook. On your paper, rewrite each sentence in the paragraph, substituting pronouns for nouns when a pronoun would make good sense. Do not substitute a pronoun for a noun if the pronoun makes the sentence unclear.

[1]As the day drew to a close, the young women of Song Island gathered at the harbor, where the young women often helped the returning fishers. [2]The fishers had been out in the fishers' boats all day, hoping to fill the fishers' boats with a good catch. [3]The men still had to transfer the men's fish to the boat owned by the Fishers' Cooperative. [4]Then the men had to pull the men's heavy boats up onto the beach, where the boats were kept on wooden frames. [5]The frames were called abacuses because of the frames' shape. [6]The girls dragged the frames down to the shoreline, and the men slipped the frames under the backs of the men's boats. [7]When the boats were safe for the night, the men and women could go home for the men's and the women's evening meal. [8]Later the men would visit the public baths because the men did not have baths in the men's homes. [9]Once a week, the unmarried young men attended a meeting of the Young Men's Association. [10]There the young men argued politics and discussed various projects that the young men thought would be good for civic improvement.

Review: Exercise 4   Identifying Verbs and Verb Phrases

The following sentences are adapted from the literary passage. Write on your paper any simple verbs and any verb phrases that appear in the sentences, and label them accordingly.

SAMPLE   By early morning, the women and girls had assembled on the beach.
ANSWER   had assembled—verb phrase

1. The older women were laughing about the events of the previous evening.
2. The young girls wore more solemn expressions.
3. Some of them might have been remembering their nightmares.
4. Others were probably recalling the carefree dives of earlier years.
5. The women did not waste a moment.
6. They quickly scrambled onto the boats and sailed offshore.
7. Before long the splash of divers in the water could be heard.
8. Then each diver was alone with her thoughts.
9. At noon they would meet again on the beach and eat lunch.
10. After lunch they would return to their daily search for abalone.

Review: Exercise 5   Identifying Transitive and Intransitive Verbs

The following sentences contain verbs that appear in the passage from *The Sound of Waves*. For each item, write *transitive* or *intransitive* on your paper, depending upon the way the italicized verb is used in the sentence.

SAMPLE   The divers *faced* a challenge of enormous proportions.
ANSWER   transitive

1. They *confronted* the difficulty of diving in heavy seas.
2. More experienced divers *introduced* the younger ones to advanced safety precautions.
3. The younger women's excitement *increased* in anticipation of a bold adventure.
4. Each diver *approached* the event with extreme caution.
5. Fear *overwhelmed* some of the young women.
6. The older divers *possessed* experience and a healthy respect for nature.
7. Watching the older women *awakened* an unexpected strength in the younger divers.
8. They all *peered* into the dark water.
9. All of them *clenched* their teeth at the start of the dive.
10. After a strenuous but successful venture, the divers *sang* songs of the sea and laughed.

Answers: Exercise 4

1. were laughing—verb phrase
2. wore—simple verb
3. might have been remembering—verb phrase
4. were recalling—verb phrase
5. did waste—verb phrase
6. scrambled—simple verb
   sailed—simple verb
7. could be heard—verb phrase
8. was—simple verb
9. would meet—verb phrase
   (would) eat—verb phrase
10. would return—verb phrase

Answers: Exercise 5

1. transitive
2. transitive
3. intransitive
4. transitive
5. transitive
6. transitive
7. transitive
8. intransitive
9. transitive
10. transitive

Parts of Speech

Practice and Assess

Answers: Exercise 6

1. fleshy—body; tasty—meal
2. dishlike—shell; gray—mother-of-pearl
3. this—substance; lustrous—substance; fancy—buttons
4. valuable—pearls
5. Handsome—pearls; foreign—objects
6. several—layers
7. entire—process; three—years
8. most—pearls; white—pearls, other—colors
9. artificial—method; pearl—production; Japanese—experimenters
10. this—method; foreign—object; human—hands

Answers: Exercise 7

Answers will vary, but some suggestions are given below.

1. At Garden Beach the female divers prepared to enter the choppy water.
2. Colorful rowboats took the brave women from the shore to deep water.
3. Away from the rocky beach the water was colder.
4. A tall woman wearing a white turban was the first to dive.
5. Taking a huge gulp of air, she plummeted into the dark ocean.
6. On the ocean floor she felt alone and peaceful.
7. Working quickly, the skillful diver grabbed an abalone.
8. A strong push carried her to the surface, where a basket bobbed on a thick rope tied to her waist.
9. A few rapid strokes brought her to the basket, which was soon full of valuable abalone.
10. In seconds the daring diver was ready for another quick descent to the bottom of the ocean.

Parts of Speech

Review: Exercise 6   Identifying Adjectives

The following sentences are about abalone. On your paper, write the adjectives that appear in each sentence. Count pronouns and proper adjectives but do not count the words *a*, *an*, and *the*. After each adjective write a dash and the word that the adjective modifies.

SAMPLE   Abalone is valuable for three reasons.
ANSWER   valuable—abalone; three—reasons

1. The fleshy body, or foot, inside the shell makes a tasty meal.
2. The dishlike shell of the abalone is lined with gray mother-of-pearl.
3. From this lustrous substance fancy buttons are made.
4. Like oysters, abalone can also produce valuable pearls.
5. Handsome pearls develop when foreign objects accidentally lodge inside a shell.
6. The shellfish reacts by coating the object with several layers of mother-of-pearl.
7. The entire process may take three years.
8. Although most pearls are white, other colors are found.
9. Between 1893 and 1919, an artificial method of pearl production was developed by Japanese experimenters.
10. Pearls produced by this method must still grow inside shellfish, but the foreign object is inserted by human hands.

Review: Exercise 7   Expanding Sentences with Adjectives

The following sentences elaborate on ideas suggested by the passage from *The Sound of Waves*. On your paper, rewrite each sentence, adding adjectives in the places indicated by carets. Although there are no specific correct answers, you should base your choices on what you have learned from reading the passage.

SAMPLE   In July the days were ∧ and ∧.
ANSWER   In July the days were warm and sunny.

1. At Garden Beach, the ∧ divers prepared to enter the ∧ water.
2. ∧ rowboats took the ∧ women from the shore to ∧ water.
3. Away from the ∧ beach, the water was ∧.
4. A ∧ woman wearing a ∧ turban was the first to dive.
5. Taking a ∧ gulp of air, she plummeted into the ∧ ocean.
6. On the ocean floor, she felt ∧ and ∧.
7. Working quickly, the ∧ diver grabbed ∧ abalone.
8. A ∧ push carried her to the surface, where a basket bobbed on a ∧ rope tied to her waist.
9. A few ∧ strokes brought her to the basket, which was soon full of ∧ abalone.
10. In seconds the ∧ diver was ready for another ∧ descent to the bottom of the ocean.

Review: Exercise 8   Identifying Adverbs

The sentences below are about octopus fishing, another typical industry of the islands off the coast of Japan. On your paper, write each adverb that appears in these sentences. After each adverb, write a dash and the word that the adverb modifies.

SAMPLE   The fishers headed sleepily toward their boat.

ANSWER   sleepily—headed

1. The master of the boat was always cheerful.
2. Because of his good humor, his two assistants willingly worked for him.
3. Soon the three reached the village's fishing grounds.
4. There they found the other boats from the village.
5. A bitterly cold wind chilled the fishers as they worked.
6. Laboriously the boys pulled heavy traps from the ocean.
7. In twenty traps, they did not find a single octopus.
8. Eventually a full trap was collected.
9. The master and his assistants then grew optimistic.
10. By afternoon they were quite happy with the day's catch.

Review: Exercise 9   Using Adverbs

The following sentences are based on a passage from *The Sound of Waves* that is not reprinted in this textbook. On your paper, rewrite each sentence, substituting an appropriate adverb for the prepositional phrase in italics. The adverb should express the same idea as the prepositional phrase.

SAMPLE   As the fishers left their boats, they laughed and sang *with boisterous energy.*

ANSWER   As the fishers left their boats, they laughed and sang boisterously.

1. A young fisher strolled along the beach *in an unhurried manner.*
2. He was carrying a halibut, which he would *in a short time* deliver to the lighthouse keeper.
3. The boy noticed a girl leaning *in a calm way* against some boat frames.
4. Her manner of dress suggested that she had *at some recent time* been working.
5. The boy regarded her *with curiosity,* for he had never seen her before.
6. The girl stared at the sky *with an intent look.*
7. *In a purposeful way* the boy passed quite near the stranger.
8. He stood before her and started at her *in a rude manner.*
9. *To a surprising degree* the mysterious young woman remained motionless.
10. Finally, the boy turned *in an abrupt manner* and moved on.

Answers: Exercise 8
1. always—cheerful
2. willingly—worked
3. Soon—reached
4. There—found
5. bitterly—cold
6. Laboriously—pulled
7. not—did find
8. Eventually—was collected
9. then—grew
10. quite—happy

Answers: Exercise 9

Answers may vary slightly, but some suggestions are given below.
1. A young fisher strolled along the beach unhurriedly.
2. He was carrying a halibut, which he would shortly deliver to the lighthouse keeper.
3. The boy noticed a girl leaning calmly against some boat frames.
4. Her manner of dress suggested that she had recently been working.
5. The boy regarded her curiously, for he had never seen her before.
6. The girl stared at the sky intently.
7. Purposefully, the boy passed quite near the stranger.
8. He stood before her and stared at her rudely.
9. Surprisingly, the mysterious young woman remained motionless.
10. Finally, the boy turned abruptly and moved on.

Parts of Speech

Grammar Review   **489**

Practice and Assess

Answers: Exercise 10

1. At, about, on
2. before
3. by, of
4. because of, of
5. In, for
6. inside, on
7. to, for, with, on
8. After, in
9. up, at, of
10. above

Answers: Exercise 11

Answers will vary, but some suggestions are given below.

1. As children, they ran joyfully on the rocky island coast.
2. Grabbing pebbles from the ocean floor was a favorite pastime.
3. Gradually their childish games had become contests of skill.
4. When diving turned into their life's work, however, they became frightened of it.
5. During a dive they often felt that they were strangling.
6. Broken shells on the ocean floor rubbed their toes raw.
7. After a dive the girls were exhausted.
8. Did they tell their friends about their nightmares?
9. The older divers did their job without such fears.
10. They usually came up from a dive laughing and talking among themselves.

Parts of Speech

Review: Exercise 10   Identifying Prepositions

The following sentences are based on passages from *The Sound of Waves* that are not reprinted in this textbook. On your paper, list the prepositions that appear in each sentence. Remember that some prepositions are made up of more than one word. (The numeral in parentheses at the end of each item indicates the number of prepositions the sentence contains.)

1. At home the young fisher thought about the girl on the beach. (3)
2. He had never seen her before that day. (1)
3. He was tormented by thoughts of her lovely face. (2)
4. One day, because of high winds, none of the fishing boats left the shore. (2)
5. In his free time, the young man was doing chores for his mother. (2)
6. A few days earlier, she had gathered firewood and left it inside a concrete tower on the mountain. (2)
7. Her son climbed to the tower and looked for the small bundle with his mother's name on it. (4)
8. After a few minutes in the tower, he heard a sound. (2)
9. He hurried up the stone steps and quickly arrived at the top of the tower. (3)
10. There, above the tower, was the girl. (1)

Review: Exercise 11   Completing Sentences with Prepositions

Each of the sentences below elaborates on the passage from *The Sound of Waves*. On your paper, rewrite each sentence, replacing the blank with a preposition that completes the word or phrase in italics and makes sense in the sentence. In some cases, there may be more than one preposition that makes sense.

SAMPLE   The young girls thought fearfully _____ *the diving season.*
ANSWER   The young girls thought fearfully about the diving season.

1. As children, they ran joyfully _____ *the rocky island coast.*
2. Grabbing pebbles _____ *the ocean floor* was a favorite pastime.
3. Gradually their childish games had become contests _____ *skill.*
4. When diving turned into their life's work, however, they became frightened _____ *it.*
5. _____ *a dive* they often felt that they were strangling.
6. Broken shells _____ *the ocean floor* rubbed their toes raw.
7. _____ *a dive* the girls were exhausted.
8. Did they tell their friends _____ *their nightmares?*
9. The older divers did their job _____ *such fears.*
10. They usually came up from a dive laughing and talking _____ *themselves.*

Grammar Review

Review: Exercise 12 **Completing Sentences with Conjunctions**

The following sentences describe Japan, where *The Sound of Waves* is set. On your paper, replace each blank with an appropriate conjunction according to the directions in parentheses. Choose your conjunctions from the list that precedes the exercise. There are more conjunctions listed than you will need.

SAMPLE Japan's geography _____ history are closely intertwined.
(Add a coordinating conjunction.)

ANSWER Japan's geography and history are closely intertwined.

CONJUNCTIONS

and	but	or	nor	for
both . . . and	neither . . . nor			
although	as long as	as soon as	because	if	so that	until

1. Japan is a nation of islands _____ large _____ small.
(Add a correlative conjunction.)
2. There are four main islands _____ many hundreds of smaller ones.
(Add a coordinating conjunction.)
3. Japan's rugged mountains create a beautiful landscape _____ leave farmers little land for cultivation.
(Add a coordinating conjunction.)
4. Thus, _____ Japan's soil is fertile, only a small percentage of it is farmed.
(Add a subordinating conjunction.)
5. _____ the island nation has a long coastline, fishing has always been a popular occupation.
(Add a subordinating conjunction.)
6. In the seventeenth century, Japan almost completely closed its borders to foreigners _____ it could protect itself from outside influence.
(Add a subordinating conjunction.)
7. Japan's rulers were able to maintain a policy of isolation _____ Japanese ports stayed closed to foreign ships.
(Add a subordinating conjunction.)
8. _____ the United States sent Commodore Matthew Perry to open trade with Japan in 1853, Japan was secluded from the outside world for 250 years.
(Add a subordinating conjunction.)
9. The Japanese government had a choice: it could fight Perry's fleet _____ submit peacefully and open its ports.
(Add a coordinating conjunction.)
10. _____ the Meiji Constitution of 1889 modernized Japanese society, Japan became a major world power.
(Add a subordinating conjunction.)

Grammar Review **491**

Parts of Speech

Answers: Exercise 12
Answers will vary, but some suggestions are given below.
1. Japan is a nation of islands both large and small.
2. There are four main islands and many hundreds of smaller ones.
3. Japan's rugged mountains create a beautiful landscape but leave farmers little land for cultivation.
4. Thus, although Japan's soil is fertile, only a small percentage of it is farmed.
5. Because the island nation has a long coastline, fishing has always been a popular occupation.
6. In the 1600s Japan almost completely closed its borders to foreigners so that it could protect itself from outside influence.
7. Japan's rulers were able to maintain a policy of isolation as long as Japanese ports stayed closed to foreign ships.
8. Until the United States sent Commodore Matthew Perry to open trade with Japan in 1853, Japan was secluded from the outside world for 250 years.
9. The Japanese government had a choice: it could fight Perry's fleet or submit peacefully and open its ports.
10. As soon as the Meiji Constitution of 1889 modernized Japanese society, Japan became a major world power.

Grammar Review

Practice and Assess

Answers: Exercise 13

Answers may vary slightly, but some suggestions are given below.

1. Many people think Japan is one large island; however, it is actually hundreds of islands.
2. Much of Japan is steep, mountainous terrain; consequently, arable farmland is scarce.
3. Japan has a meager supply of minerals; nevertheless, it is one of the world's richest nations.
4. Volcanic eruptions take place frequently; moreover, earthquakes are common occurrences.
5. Japanese trees are often cultivated as miniatures; similarly, gardens are often designed as smaller versions of the surrounding landscape.
6. The main island, Honshu, is less than two hundred miles at its greatest width; therefore, no part of Japan is more than one hundred miles from the sea.
7. Few inlets are found on the east coast north of Tokyo; however, south of Tokyo are many of the best harbors.
8. Every valley in Japan has a stream; still, no long navigable rivers exist in Japan.
9. Some scenic Japanese lakes are located in river valleys; nevertheless, most of the lakes are mountain lakes.
10. In the Japanese mountains, there are about 200 volcanoes; however, only about 50 are active.

Answers: Exercise 14
Proofreading

This proofreading activity provides editing practice with (1) the current or previous units' skills, (2) the **Troubleshooter** errors, and (3) spelling errors. Students should be able to complete the exercise by referring to the units, the **Troubleshooter**, and a dictionary. (Note: A run-on sentence counts as one error.)

Error (Type of Error)
1. chief (spelling)
2. father's (singular possessive)
3. concentrate (spelling)
4. painters (plural noun)
   Japanese (proper adjective)

Review: Exercise 13 Rewriting Sentences with Conjunctive Adverbs

The sentences below are about the land of Japan. On your paper, rewrite each sentence, using a conjunctive adverb. Choose your adverbs from the list on page 479.

1. Many people think Japan is one large island; it is actually hundreds of islands.
2. Much of Japan is steep, mountainous terrain; arable farmland is scarce.
3. Japan has a meager supply of minerals but is one of the world's richest nations.
4. Volcanic eruptions take place frequently; earthquakes are common occurrences.
5. Japanese trees are often cultivated as miniatures; gardens are often designed as smaller versions of the surrounding landscape.
6. The main island, Honshu, is less than two hundred miles wide at its greatest width; no part of Japan is more than one hundred miles from the sea.
7. Few inlets are found on the east coast north of Tokyo, but south of Tokyo are many of the best harbors.
8. Every valley in Japan has a stream; no long navigable rivers exist in Japan.
9. Some scenic Japanese lakes are located in river valleys; most of the lakes are mountain lakes.
10. In the Japanese mountains, there are about 200 volcanoes, and only about 50 are still active.

Review: Exercise 14

Proofreading

The following passage describes the artist Andō Hiroshige, whose work appears on the opposite page. Rewrite the passage, correcting the errors in spelling, capitalization, grammar, and usage. Add any missing punctuation. There are twenty-five errors.

Andō Hiroshige

[1]Andō (or Ichiyū-sai) Hiroshige (1797–1858) was the son of a fire-brigade cheif. [2]Shortly after the death of his mother—she died when her son was twelve—Hiroshige inherited his fathers post. [3]He eventually abandoned the position so that he could consentrate on painting, his real love.

[4]Unlike painter's in Europe and America, japanese artists explored a limited number of themes according to strict rules of representation. [5]Hiroshige experiment with a variety of pictorial themes, including portraits and historical scenes, before settling on Landscapes. [6]He focused on this subject throughout his' long and productive life.

[7]Hiroshige's landscapes are gentle lyrical, and subdued in tone. [8]In many of his prints, the stark beauty of the Japanese landscape are softened by a

5. experimented (verb form)
   landscapes (common noun)
6. his (possessive pronoun)
7. gentle, (commas in a series)

human presence. ⁹Peasants trudge home in great drifts of snow or villagers hurry, heads bowed, through a rainstorm. ¹⁰Variations in weather and the Seasons is depicted with care and precision.

¹¹When he was thirty-five, Hiroshige embarked on the more ambitious project of his career. ¹²He begun a series of fifty-five woodblock prints illustrating scenes along the great highway that linked the city of kyoto to Edo (now known as Tokyo). ¹³These prints established Hiroshige as one of the master's of his day. ¹⁴His later pictures of birds and flowers seems tentative and sentimental by comparison.

¹⁵The woodblock prints for which Hiroshige is famous was a technical feat. ¹⁶Each color is printed separately by rubbing paper against the woodblock or by running the block through a press. ¹⁷The first prints, generally the clearest and most subtly colored, becomed the most valuable.

¹⁸*Imagiri Promontory from Maizaka* is typical of Hiroshiges mature style. ¹⁹It's harmonious composition projects a mood of stillness and calm. ²⁰Hiroshige was particularly famous for his deep blues and reds which are subtle yet vivid. ²¹One can imagine in such a scene the diver's described in *The Sound of Waves*.

Andō Hiroshige, *Imagiri Promontory from Maizaka*, 1833

Grammar Review **493**

Parts of Speech

Answers: Exercise 14 (continued)

Error (Type of Error)
8. is softened (subject-verb agreement)
9. snow, (run-on sentence)
10. seasons (common noun)
    are depicted (subject-verb agreement)
11. most ambitious (superlative degree)
12. began (verb form)
    Kyoto (proper noun)
13. masters (plural noun)
14. seem (subject-verb agreement)
15. were (subject-verb agreement)
16. was printed (shift in tense)
17. became (verb form)
18. Hiroshige's (singular possessive)
19. Its (possessive pronoun)
20. reds, (nonessential adjective clause)
21. divers (plural noun)

Viewing the Art

Andō Hiroshige, *Imagiri Promontory from Maizaka*, 1833

In Hiroshige's painting, the serenity of the coastal landscape is enhanced by the graceful shapes of the boats that ply the waters of the bay or rest in the shelter of the harbor. Yukio Mishima uses a similar technique in *The Sound of Waves*. Rather than merely describe the ocean, for example, he enables readers to perceive the sea and its dangers through the eyes of the young divers. This technique gives his descriptions great immediacy and emotional impact.

493

Assess

Answers: Exercise 15
Mixed Review

Answers may vary, but some suggestions are given below.

1. The Japanese writer Yukio Mishima was born in 1925.
2. As a child, Mishima suffered from poor health.
3. At the same time, he was very successful in his schoolwork.
4. At an early age, Mishima became interested in literature.
5. Before he reached his eighteenth birthday, his writing had already been published in a magazine.
6. To conceal his youth, he adopted a pen name.
7. In 1949 writing became a full-time career for Mishima.
8. Mishima wrote *The Sound of Waves* after a trip to Greece.
9. This happy and romantic novel was made into a movie.
10. Yukio Mishima wrote several kinds of works, such as essays and novels.
11. Both Yukio Mishima and Kimitake Hiraoka are names used by the same person.
12. Before his death, Mishima produced forty novels.
13. He enjoyed the Greek Islands; consequently, the story they inspired was his happiest.
14. By the age of sixteen, Mishima had published his first novel.
15. A common theme of his novels is conflict.
16. The novel itself established Mishima as an author.
17. Mishima is a famous writer in Japanese history.
18. We will never know what else he might have written.
19. His work is admired by readers everywhere.
20. Everyone should read Mishima's books.

Close

Have students examine a passage from a novel to find examples of each part of speech shown in the annotated literature model on student pages 484–485.

Parts of Speech

Review: Exercise 15

Mixed Review

The biography of Yukio Mishima below is followed by twenty sentences. Rewrite each one, replacing the blank with an appropriate word. Use the directions in parentheses.

Yukio Mishima

Yukio Mishima is the pen name of Kimitake Hiraoka, one of the most famous writers of modern Japan. Born in 1925, Mishima was weak and sickly as a child. He was highly intelligent, however, and took an interest in literature early in life. His first work was published in 1941, when he was just 16. Because he was so young, he decided to take a pen name. *Confessions of a Mask,* published in 1949, established Mishima's reputation as an author. From that time on, he devoted himself to writing. *The Sound of Waves,* published in 1954, was inspired by a vacation in the Greek islands. This romantic story is the happiest of Mishima's forty novels. Mishima also wrote plays, essays, and short stories. He died in 1970.

1. The _____ writer Yukio Mishima was born in 1925. (Add a proper adjective.)
2. As a child, Mishima suffered from poor _____. (Add a common noun.)
3. At the same time, he was _____ successful in his schoolwork. (Add an adverb.)
4. At an early age, Mishima _____ interested in literature. (Add a linking verb.)
5. _____ he reached his eighteenth birthday, his writing had already been published in a magazine. (Add a subordinating conjunction.)
6. To conceal his youth, he _____ a pen name. (Add an action verb.)
7. _____ 1949 writing became a full-time career for Mishima. (Add a preposition.)
8. Mishima wrote *The Sound of Waves* after a trip to _____. (Add a proper noun.)
9. This happy _____ romantic novel was made into a movie. (Add a coordinating conjunction.)
10. Yukio Mishima wrote _____ kinds of works. (Add an adjective.)
11. _____ Yukio Mishima _____ Kimitake Hiraoka are names used by the same person. (Add a pair of correlative conjunctions.)
12. _____ his death, Mishima produced forty novels. (Add a preposition.)
13. He enjoyed the Greek islands; _____, the story they inspired was his happiest. (Add a conjunctive adverb.)
14. By the age of sixteen, Mishima _____ his first novel. (Add a verb phrase.)
15. A common theme _____ his novels is conflict. (Add a preposition.)
16. The novel _____ established Mishima as an author. (Add an intensive pronoun.)
17. Mishima is a famous writer in Japanese _____. (Add an abstract noun.)
18. We will _____ know what else he might have written. (Add a negative adverb.)
19. _____ work is admired by readers everywhere. (Add a possessive pronoun.)
20. _____ should read Mishima's books. (Add an indefinite pronoun.)

Writing Application

Adverbs in Writing

In this passage from Ralph Ellison's short story "Flying Home," a farmer and his son have come across a pilot who has fallen from a small plane. Notice how Ellison uses adverbs to help convey the pilot's shock and confusion. Examine the passage, focusing especially on the italicized adverbs.

> Sounds come to him *dimly*. . . . He lay rigid, hearing their breathing and trying to weave a meaning between them and his being stretched *painfully* upon the ground. He watched them *warily*, his mind traveling *back* over a painful distance. Jagged scenes, *swiftly* unfolding as in a movie trailer [preview], reeled through his mind, and he saw himself piloting a tailspinning plane and landing and falling from the cockpit and trying to stand. *Then*, as in a great silence, he remembered the sound of crunching bone.

Techniques with Adverbs

Try to apply some of Ralph Ellison's writing techniques when you write and revise your own work.

❶ Use adverbs to clarify actions or behavior. In Ellison's passage, for example, the adverb *painfully* helps explain why the pilot is confused.

WITHOUT ADVERB . . . his being stretched upon the ground . . .

ELLISON'S VERSION . . . his being stretched *painfully* upon the ground . . .

❷ Use adverbs to emphasize a point. Compare the following descriptions of the pilot's memories.

WITHOUT ADVERB Jagged scenes, unfolding as in a movie trailer, reeled through his mind . . .

ELLISON'S VERSION Jagged scenes, *swiftly* unfolding as in a movie trailer, reeled through his mind . . .

❸ Try to choose adverbs that contribute to the mood, or atmosphere, that you are trying to convey.

WITHOUT ADVERBS He watched them, his mind traveling over a painful distance.

ELLISON'S VERSION He watched them *warily*, his mind traveling *back* over a painful distance.

TIME

For more about the writing process, see **TIME Facing the Blank Page,** pp. 109–119.

Parts of Speech

Practice Practice these techniques by revising the following passage, using a separate sheet of paper. Add adverbs in the places indicated with carets (^).

Afternoon teas at Mrs. Chan's apartment are ^ to be missed. Mrs. Chan ^ brings out her finest china and ^ sets it on the kitchen table. Her best cloth napkins are ^ folded at each place. She ^ prepares delicate almond cakes and pork dumplings to serve to her guests. Each woman comes to the tea ^ dressed. The women chat ^, and newcomers are ^ welcome. When tea is over, the guests ^ leave. Everyone ^ agrees to come back next week.

Writing Application **495**

Writing Application

Adverbs in Writing

Have a student read the paragraph aloud without interruption. Ask students to go back and read the paragraph again to themselves, paying particular attention to adverbs. Have them discuss the italicized adverbs in relation to the techniques listed in column two.

Techniques with Adverbs

Discuss the revisions of the sentences on this page to clarify meaning and to correct misuse of adverbs. Then choose another piece of writing—the paragraphs on student pages 492–493, for example. Ask students to revise the sentences in this selection and to discuss their revisions.

Practice

The answers to this challenging and enriching activity will vary. Refer to Techniques with Adverbs as you evaluate student choices.

Sample answer:
Afternoon teas at Mrs. Chan's apartment are not to be missed. Mrs. Chan carefully brings out her finest china and solemnly sets it on the kitchen table. Her best cloth napkins are intricately folded at each place. She usually prepares delicate almond cakes and pork dumplings to serve to her guests. Each woman comes to the tea formally dressed. The women chat quietly, and newcomers are always welcome. When tea is over, the guests reluctantly leave. Everyone enthusiastically agrees to come back next week.

✔ ASSESSMENT OPTIONS

📁 *Tests with Answer Key & Rubrics*
Unit 10 Mastery Test, p. 33

💾 *Testmaker*
Unit 10 Mastery Test

📼 *MindJogger Videoquizzes*

You may wish to administer the Unit 10 Mastery Test at this point.

Objectives

- To learn about the various parts of sentences, including simple and compound subjects and predicates and various kinds of complements
- To demonstrate control over the uses of various kinds of subjects, predicates, and complements by identifying them and writing sentences using them correctly

✔ ASSESSMENT OPTIONS

📂 *Tests with Answer Key & Rubrics*
Unit 11 Pretest, pp. 35–36
Unit 11 Mastery Test, pp. 37–38

💾 *Testmaker*
Unit 11 Pretest
Unit 11 Mastery Test

You may wish to administer the Unit 11 Pretest at this point.

Key to Ability Levels

L1 Level 1 activities are within the basic ability range of students.

L2 Level 2 activities are within the ability range of average students.

L3 Level 3 activities are more challenging activities.

UNIT 11 Parts of the Sentence

Lesson **11.1**	**Simple Subjects and Simple Predicates**	*497*
Lesson **11.2**	**Complete Subjects and Complete Predicates**	*498*
Lesson **11.3**	**Compound Subjects and Compound Predicates**	*500*
Lesson **11.4**	**Order of Subject and Predicate**	*503*
Lesson **11.5**	**Complements**	*506*
Grammar Review		*512*
Writing Application		*521*

496

Resource Manager

Planning Resources
- *Lesson Plans*
- *Block Scheduling*

 Transparencies
- *Bellringer*
- *Daily Language Practice*
- *Two-Minute Skill Drill*

📂 Other Print Resources
- *Grammar and Composition Handbook*
- *Grammar Enrichment*
- *Grammar Practice*
- *Grammar Reteaching*
- *Grammar Workbook*
- *Tests with Answer Key and Rubrics*

📹 **Video**
- *MindJogger Videoquizzes*

💾 Software
- *Interactive Grammar and Language Workbook*
- *Language Arts PASS*
- *Presentation Plus!*
- *Testmaker*
- *Writer's Choice Puzzlemaker*

🖳 **Web Sites**
- *writerschoice.glencoe.com*

11.1 Simple Subjects and Simple Predicates

- A **sentence** is a group of words expressing a complete thought.

  The two basic parts of every sentence are the *subject* and the *predicate*.

- The **subject** is the part of the sentence about which something is being said.

- The **predicate** is the part that says something about the subject.

  Both the subject and the predicate may consist of more than one word.

- The **simple subject** is the key noun or pronoun (or group of words acting as a noun) that tells what a sentence is about.

- The **simple predicate** is the verb or verb phrase that tells something about the subject.

A simple predicate that is a verb phrase consists of the verb and any helping verbs.

SIMPLE SUBJECT	SIMPLE PREDICATE
Condors	soar.
Spring	will come.
Coretta Scott King	is speaking.
Nora	sang.
Breakfast	is served.

You find the simple subject by asking *who?* or *what?* about the verb. For example, in the first sentence above, the noun *condors* answers the question *what soar?* In the second sentence, *spring* answers the question *what will come?*

Exercise 1   Identifying Simple Subjects and Simple Predicates

On your paper, write the simple subject and simple predicate of each sentence. Underline the simple predicate.

1. American teenagers spent about $88 billion in 1993.
2. The amount increased to approximately $99 billion in 1994.
3. The cause for the increase was partly an increase in the number of teenagers in the United States.
4. Money came from parents, jobs, allowances, and gifts.
5. Many teens hold jobs after school, on weekends, and during school vacations.

11.1 Simple Subjects and Simple Predicates   **497**

Parts of the Sentence

Focus

Lesson Overview

Objectives
- To identify simple subjects and simple predicates
- To use simple subjects and predicates appropriately in writing

 Bellringer
Daily Language Activity

When students enter the classroom, have this assignment on the board: *Identify the complete predicate in this sentence: Some chickens discovered an egg-stealing weasel as big as a young cat.*

See also   *Daily Language Practice*

Teach

Cross-reference: Sentence Parts

For help in identifying words that can be used as the subject of a sentence, refer students to Lessons 10.1 and 10.2, pages 439–452. For help in identifying the predicate of a sentence, refer students to Lesson 10.3, page 453.

Practice and Assess

Answers: Exercise 1
1. teenagers/spent
2. amount/increased
3. cause/was
4. Money/came
5. Teens/hold

Close

Have students write three sentences, each with a simple subject and predicate, and underline the predicates.

 Resource Manager

Planning Resources
- *Lesson Plans*

Transparencies
- *Bellringer*
- *Daily Language Practice*

Other Print Resources
- *Grammar and Composition Handbook*
- *Grammar Enrichment,* p. 9
- *Grammar Workbook,* Lesson 13

Focus

Lesson Overview

Objective
- To identify complete subjects and complete predicates

 Bellringer
Daily Language Activity

Use the Bellringer Transparency for Lesson 11.2.

See also *Daily Language Practice*

Teach

☑ **Teaching Tip**

Provide additional guidance in identifying complete subjects and predicates by asking students to verbalize the identification process. Tell students to identify the subject by asking themselves this question: Who (or what) is this sentence about? To identify the predicate, they might ask this question: What statement is made about the subject?

Practice and Assess

Answers: Exercise 2

1. Canobie . . . Hampshire/opened in 1902.
2. Many people/consider . . . States.
3. The . . . grounds/feature . . . lake.
4. Guests . . . park/are . . . riverboat.
5. The . . . park/ is . . . New England.
6. The entire family/will . . . there.
7. Visitors/love . . . horses.
8. Young . . . seekers/ride . . . again.
9. Small children/squeal . . . park.
10. The park/presents . . . long.

Parts of the Sentence

The pieces of the puzzle connect in only one way.

11.2 Complete Subjects and Complete Predicates

In most sentences, the addition of other words and phrases expands or modifies the meaning of the simple subject and the simple predicate.

- The **complete subject** consists of the simple subject and all the words that modify it.
- The **complete predicate** consists of the simple predicate and all the words that modify it or complete its meaning.

COMPLETE SUBJECT	COMPLETE PREDICATE
The condors of California	soar gracefully in the sky.
A welcome spring	will come after a cold winter.
Coretta Scott King	is speaking first.
My sister Nora	sang a lullaby.
A late breakfast	was served at the same time as lunch.

Exercise 2   Identifying Complete Subjects and Complete Predicates

Write the following sentences on your paper. Underline each complete subject once and each complete predicate twice.

Canobie Lake Park

1. Canobie Lake Park in the southeastern section of New Hampshire opened in 1902.
2. Many people consider Canobie Lake Park one of the most beautiful amusement parks in the United States.
3. The pleasant grounds feature tree-lined walkways, flower gardens, and a lake.
4. Guests to the park are especially amused by the 150-passenger paddle-wheel riverboat.
5. The eighty-acre park is regarded as one of the popular entertainment centers in New England.
6. The entire family will find something of enjoyment there.
7. Visitors love the antique carousel with its beautiful hand-carved horses.
8. Young and not-so-young thrill seekers ride the park's four roller coasters again and again.
9. Small children squeal in delight at the costumed characters throughout the park.
10. The park presents high-tech fireworks and musical performances all summer long.

498   Unit 11 Parts of the Sentence

Resource Manager

Planning Resources
- *Lesson Plans*

 Transparencies
- *Bellringer*
- *Daily Language Practice*

📁 **Other Print Resources**
- *Grammar and Composition Handbook*
- *Grammar Reteaching,* p. 9
- *Grammar Workbook,* Lesson 14

Exercise 3   Identifying Subjects and Predicates

On your paper, write each of the following sentences, and draw a vertical line between the complete subject and the complete predicate. Then underline the simple subject once and the simple predicate twice.

SAMPLE ANSWER   <u>One</u> of the most important leaders of the abolitionist movement | <u><u>was</u></u> Frederick Douglass.

Frederick Douglass, Champion of Equality

1. Frederick Douglass dedicated his life to the fight for racial equality.
2. He was born enslaved in Tuckahoe, Maryland, around 1818.
3. Douglass escaped from slavery 1838.
4. The brave young man spoke at an antislavery meeting in Massachusetts in 1841.
5. The enthusiastic reaction to his speech led to a series of lecture engagements.
6. Douglass worked for civil rights for African Americans.
7. His activities included the publication of an antislavery newspaper.
8. President Abraham Lincoln conferred with Douglass during the Civil War.
9. The proud African American served as United States minister to Haiti from 1889 to 1891.
10. The United States owes a great debt to Douglass and his tireless struggle for civil rights.

Exercise 4   Expanding Subjects and Predicates

Expand each of the following sentences by adding words and phrases to both the simple subject and the simple predicate. Write your sentence. Then underline the simple predicate in each sentence. (There are many ways to expand each sentence.)

SAMPLE   Sky darkened.
ANSWER   The previously clear sky <u>darkened</u> suddenly to a furious yellowish-gray.

1. Wind screeched.
2. Rain began.
3. Leaves flew.
4. Trees bent.
5. Windows rattled.
6. Water dripped.
7. Gutters overflowed.
8. Waves crashed.
9. Clouds raced.
10. Sky lightened.

Parts of the Sentence

Teach

☑ Grammar Tip

If any of your students still have difficulty identifying the complete subject in a sentence, explain that the subject names the person, place, thing, or idea that the sentence is about. Words that modify are not part of the simple subject.

Practice and Assess

Answers: Exercise 3

1. Frederick Douglass/dedicated
2. He/was born
3. Douglass/escaped
4. man/spoke
5. reaction/led
6. Douglass/worked
7. activities/included
8. President Abraham Lincoln/conferred
9. African American/served
10. United States/owes

Answers: Exercise 4

Answers will vary, but some suggestions are given below.
1. The relentless wind <u>screeched</u> furiously.
2. A drenching rain soon <u>began</u>.

Additional Resources

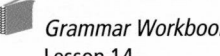 *Grammar Reteaching*, p. 9

Grammar Workbook Lesson 14

Close

Have students discuss the ways in which a simple subject and a simple predicate can be expanded.

MEETING INDIVIDUAL NEEDS   English Language Learners

Choosing Words

Students may have difficulty locating the simple predicate in English sentences if their primary language normally places the simple predicate at the end of sentences. Pair such students with students proficient in English, who can help in identifying simple predicates.

Focus

Lesson Overview

Objectives

- To identify compound subjects and predicates
- To use compound subjects and compound predicates effectively in writing

 Bellringer
Daily Language Activity

Use the Bellringer Transparency for Lesson 11.3.

See also *Daily Language Practice*

Teach

Compound Subjects

☑ **Teaching Tip**

A good way to identify compound subjects joined by *and* is by pronoun substitution. Try replacing a compound subject with *they* or *we*.

Practice and Assess

Answers: Exercise 5

1. Two peach baskets and a gym
2. Two teams and an old soccer ball
3. Nets and backboards
4. men and women
5. Stanford and California

Answers: Exercise 6

Answers will vary, but a suggestion is given below.
- **a.** The team played many soccer games.
- **b.** Ken, Elizabeth, Oskar, Darrel, and Jennifer played many soccer games.

Parts of the Sentence

11.3 Compound Subjects and Compound Predicates

A sentence may have more than one simple subject or simple predicate.

Compound Subjects

■ A **compound subject** is made up of two or more simple subjects that are joined by a conjunction and have the same verb.

The conjunctions most commonly used to join the subjects in a compound subject are *and* and *or*.

> Shall **you** and **I** go to the nature preserve tomorrow?
> **Eagles** and **owls** hunt for food.
> A **cardinal** or a **robin** will be frightened by these hunters.

Correlative conjunctions may be used to join compound subjects.

> Neither the two **eagles** nor the lone **owl** is hunting.
> Both the **eagle** and the **owl** are strong fliers.

When more than two words are included in the compound subject, the conjunction is usually used only between the last two words, and the words are separated by commas.

> **Eagles, owls,** and **vultures** are birds of prey.

Exercise 5 | **Identifying Compound Subjects**

On your paper, write the compound subject in each sentence.

1. Two peach baskets and a gym set the stage for the world's first basketball game in 1891.
2. Two teams and an old soccer ball put the play into motion.
3. Nets and backboards were early additions to the game.
4. Men and women played basketball in the early years of its development.
5. Stanford and California met in 1896 for the first women's intercollegiate match.

Exercise 6 | **Expanding Subjects**

(a) Write five sentences. In each one, use a simple subject and a simple predicate.
(b) Expand each sentence by making the subject compound.

SAMPLE ANSWER
- **a.** Toni Morrison wrote several highly successful novels.
- **b.** Toni Morrison and Alice Walker wrote several highly successful novels.

---

500 Unit 11 Parts of the Sentence

 ## Resource Manager

Planning Resources
- *Lesson Plans*

📀 **Transparencies**
- *Bellringer*
- *Daily Language Practice*

📂 **Other Print Resources**
- *Grammar and Composition Handbook*
- *Grammar Enrichment,* p. 9
- *Grammar Practice,* p. 9
- *Grammar Workbook,* Lesson 15

Compound Predicates

- A **compound predicate** (or **compound verb**) is made up of two or more verbs or verb phrases that are joined by a conjunction and have the same subject.

> Eagles **soar** and **plunge.**
> Suki either **is** here already or **will be** here soon.

In compound verbs that contain verb phrases, the helping verb may not be repeated before the second verb.

> We **have lost** or at least **misplaced** the map.
> Tyrone **will buy** a stamp, **mail** the letter, and **hurry** home.

Some sentences have both a compound subject and a compound predicate.

>   **S**   **S**   **P**   **P**
> **Eagles** and **condors soar** and **plunge** in the sky.

>   **S**   **S**   **P**   **P**
> Either **you** or **I have lost** or **misplaced** the map.

Exercise 7   Identifying Compound Predicates

On your paper, write the compound predicate in each of the following sentences.

Cats

1. Many cats are faithful pets and make friendly companions.
2. Cats seem independent and sometimes resist training.
3. They generally are fed canned food but may prefer fish or meat.
4. Cats are good hunters and prey on small creatures.
5. Cats climb trees, run fast, and walk on narrow ledges.
6. Their pride, however, keeps them from foolish behavior and sometimes makes them stubborn.
7. An arched back with puffed-out fur is caused by fear or initiated by anger.
8. These physical changes make the cat's appearance larger, give the impression of ferocity, and intimidate enemies and prey.
9. Cats usually approach their prey very stealthily and then pounce.
10. The Birman is easy-going, does not stray far, and appears very affectionate and even tempered.

Exercise 8   Expanding Predicates

(a) Write five sentences. In each one, use a simple subject and a simple predicate.
(b) Expand each sentence by making the predicate compound

SAMPLE ANSWER   **a.** The horse jumped the fence.
                    b. The horse jumped the fence and trotted away.

11.3 Compound Subjects and Compound Predicates   **501**

Parts of the Sentence

Teach

Compound Predicates

☑ **Teaching Tip**
Explain how students can tell whether they have a compound predicate or a compound sentence (the latter has two subjects). Then warn students to be careful of this when they write sentences for Exercise 8.

Practice and Assess

Answers: Exercise 7

1. are, make
2. seem, resist
3. are fed, may prefer
4. are, prey
5. climb, run, walk
6. keeps, makes
7. is caused, initiated
8. make, give, intimidate
9. approach, pounce
10. is, does stray, appears

Answers: Exercise 8

Answers will vary, but a suggestion is given below.
   a. The boy asked a question.
   b. The boy asked a question and answered it himself.

MEETING INDIVIDUAL NEEDS   English Language Learners

Cooperative Learning

Pair students beginning to learn English with students proficient in English. Ask the English-proficient students to provide contexts to help beginning English students create oral sentences with compund elements. Suggest a setting, such as a grocery. Ask, What two things might you do in a grocery? (check labels and compare prices)

Practice and Assess

Answers: Exercise 9

1. cultures/built
2. Adena, Hopewell, Mississippians/ were
3. time, effort/were devoted
4. quantities/were
5. builder/carried, transported
6. horses, oxen, carts/assisted
7. Jewelry, pipes/were buried
8. mounds/stand
9. Giant Serpent Mound/resembles, is
10. Monk's Mound/covers, is

Answers: Exercise 10

Answers will vary, but a suggestion is given below.

1. Carly and her sister planted, weeded, and fertilized the garden.

Additional Resources

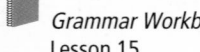 *Grammar Reteaching*, p. 9
Grammar Enrichment, p. 9

Grammar Workbook
Lesson 15

Close

Discuss with students how using compound elements in sentences can make their writing less repetitive and more interesting. Have students write a reminder of this tip in their journal for future reference.

Parts of the Sentence

Exercise 9   Identifying Subjects and Predicates

On your paper, write the simple subject and the simple predicate from each sentence. Underline the simple predicates. Note that some subjects and predicates are compound.

The Mound Builders

1. Several North American cultures built large mounds of earth thousands of years ago and used them as burial places and foundations for buildings.
2. The Adena, the Hopewell, and the Mississippians were the three major groups of mound builders.
3. Much time and much effort were devoted to the construction of each mound.
4. Large quantities of dirt and stone were the primary construction materials of the mound builders.
5. Each mound builder carried loads of dirt on his back and transported them to the burial sites.
6. No horses, oxen, or carts assisted the workers in their difficult task.
7. Jewelry or pipes for the deceased were often buried in the mounds.
8. Many large mounds still stand in the midwestern United States and Canada.
9. The Giant Serpent Mound near Hillsboro, Ohio, resembles a huge, sinuous snake and is approximately a quarter of a mile long.
10. Monk's Mound near Cahokia in southern Illinois covers about sixteen acres and is about one hundred feet high.

Exercise 10   Writing Compound Subjects and Predicates

On your paper, expand each of the following sentences by making both the subject and the predicate compound. (You may need to make other changes, too.)

SAMPLE   Worms crawl.
ANSWER   Worms and insects crawl and hide.

Gardening

1. Carly fertilized the garden.
2. Mulch had covered the ground.
3. A garden rake can break up the soil.
4. Crocuses arrive in early spring.
5. Peonies come in many colors.
6. Lilacs flower in late spring.
7. Cottonwoods spread their seeds widely.
8. Some lilies bloom in late June.
9. Sunlight makes a good garden.
10. Carly starts her garden plans earlier each year.

502   Unit 11 Parts of the Sentence

Enrichment and Extension

Expanding Subjects and Predicates

Ask students to write two paragraphs on a subject of their choice. Afterward, have them review their first drafts to see if they can improve their writing by adding words or phrases to the subject or predicate to make their writing more interesting and to avoid short, choppy sentences. Have students rewrite these sentences in the improved form as part of the revision.

11.4 Order of Subject and Predicate

The subject comes before the verb in most sentences in English. Some exceptions to this normal word order are discussed below.

Commands and Questions

The subject *you* is understood rather than expressed in the case of commands or requests.

    [You] **Jump!**   [You] **Tear** it down.   [You] **Ask** her, please.

Questions frequently begin with a verb or helping verb.

    Is he right?   **Will** you **visit** your cousin?

Other questions often begin with the words *who, what, when, where, why,* or *how.*

    What does she want?   **Why** did he go to the gym?

Notice that the subject generally follows the verb or helping verb.

To find the subject of a question, rearrange words to form a statement.

SUBJECT	PREDICATE
He	is right.
You	will visit your cousin.
She	does want what.
He	did go to the gym why.

Exercise 11   **Identifying Subjects and Predicates in Commands and Questions**

On your paper, write the simple subject and the simple predicate of each of the following sentences. (Remember that the simple predicate may contain one or more helping verbs.) If the sentence is a command, write (*You*) as the subject.

1. Can anyone name three main types of musical instruments?
2. Notice the string instruments, wind instruments, and percussion instruments.
3. Give me an example of a string instrument.
4. What kind of sound does a woodwind make?
5. Beat a drum for a good idea of percussion sound.
6. In what ways are a drum and a xylophone similar?
7. Is a piano a string instrument or a percussion instrument?
8. Study these parts of a saxophone.
9. Do you see the reed in the mouthpiece slot?
10. Watch it carefully.

11.4 Order of Subject and Predicate   **503**

Resource Manager

Planning Resources
- *Lesson Plans*

Transparencies
- *Bellringer*
- *Daily Language Practice*

Other Print Resources
- *Grammar and Composition Handbook*
- *Grammar Enrichment,* p. 9
- *Grammar Workbook,* Lesson 16

11.4

Focus

Lesson Overview

Objective
- To recognize usual subject-predicate word order and to recognize exceptions to this order

 Bellringer
Daily Language Activity

As students enter the classroom, have this assignment on the board: *Jot down what you notice about the subject and predicate in this sentence: Into the room stalked the guilty butler.*

See also *Daily Language Practice*

Teach

Commands and Questions

☑ **Grammar Tip**

Not all commands or questions use inverted order. Often questions that begin with *who* or *what* follow normal word order: *Who answered the question?* The words *who* or *what* are pronouns that may function as subjects.

Practice and Assess

Answers: Exercise 11
1. anyone/Can name
2. (You)/Notice
3. (You)/Give
4. woodwind/does make
5. (You)/Beat
6. drum, xylophone/are
7. piano/Is
8. (You)/Study
9. you/Do see
10. (You)/Watch

Parts of the Sentence

503

Teach

Inverted Order

☑ **Grammar Tip**

One departure from normal word order is inverted order, in which the complete predicate precedes the complete subject.

Another common type of inversion occurs when an adverb or adverb phrase is moved from its normal position in the predicate to a position in front of the subject. The effect is to emphasize the adverb or the adverb phrase—for example: *With a flourish, Holmes produced the missing pearls.* Before analyzing inverted sentences, students should put the elements back into their normal positions.

⇆ **Cross-reference: Usage**

For help with subject-verb agreement in inverted sentences, refer students to Lesson 16.3, p. 616.

Practice and Assess

Answers: Exercise 12

1. The <u>development</u> . . . pictures/ <u>began</u> in the late 1800s.
2. Flexible celluloid <u>film</u>/<u>came</u> from George Eastman . . . inventor.
3. Two <u>machines</u>/<u>were invented</u> . . .
4. <u>Success</u>/<u>came</u> . . .
5. <u>Strips</u> of "moving" pictures/<u>could be seen</u> through . . .
6. Several short <u>films</u>/<u>were made</u> in Edison's studio.
7. Intrigued <u>cutomers</u>/ <u>streamed</u> in and out . . .
8. A new <u>projection machine</u>/<u>was invented</u> by Thomas Armat.
9. The earliest commercial <u>motion pictures</u>/<u>were shown</u> on Armat's projector.
10. A new and popular <u>art form</u>/ <u>came</u> . . .

Parts of the Sentence

Inverted Order

A sentence written in **inverted order,** where the predicate comes before the subject, serves to add emphasis to the subject.

PREDICATE	SUBJECT
Over the mount **soared**	the two **eagles.**
Beyond the eagles **was**	a **condor.**

Remember that a word in a prepositional phrase can never be the subject.

When the word *there* or *here* begins a sentence and is followed by the verb *to be,* the subject generally comes after the predicate. (The sentence appears in inverted order.) Keep in mind that *there* and *here* are almost never the subject of a sentence.

PREDICATE	SUBJECT
There **are**	three **owls** in the nest.
Here **is**	my **sister.**

Exercise 12   Reordering Sentences

On your paper, rewrite each of the following sentences so that the complete subject comes before the predicate. Then underline the simple subject once and the simple predicate twice. (Remember that both subjects and predicates may be compound.)

The Invention of Motion Pictures

1. In the late 1800s began the development of motion pictures.
2. From George Eastman, the American inventor, came flexible celluloid film.
3. There were two machines invented by Thomas Edison for use with George Eastman's new film.
4. With Edison's kinetoscope came a brief success.
5. Through a peephole could be seen strips of "moving" pictures.
6. There were several short films made in Edison's studio.
7. In and out of the Kinetoscope Parlor in New York City streamed intrigued customers.
8. There was a new projection machine invented by Thomas Armat.
9. On Armat's projector were shown the earliest commercial motion pictures.
10. From these early efforts came a new and popular art form.

MEETING INDIVIDUAL NEEDS

English Language Learners

Choosing Words

To help students who are learning English understand sentences written in inverted order, place each word in the following sentence on a separate card:

BEYOND THE EAGLE WAS A CONDOR.

Ask students to rearrange the cards to form this

sentence:

A CONDOR WAS BEYOND THE EAGLE.

Have students discuss the effect of each sentence.

Exercise 13 Analyzing Subjects and Predicates

Copy each of the following sentences, draw a vertical line between the complete subject and the complete predicate, and label each. Then underline the simple subject once and the simple predicate twice. Write *(You)* for an understood subject. Finally, indicate with the letter *C* or *I* those sentences that are either a command *(C)* or written in inverted order *(I)*. (Not all sentences will be labeled *C* or *I*.)

SAMPLE ANSWER
$$\overset{S}{(You)} \mid \overset{P}{\underline{\underline{Look}}} \text{ at that clothing. } \mathbf{C}$$

$$\overset{P}{\text{On the hat rack } \underline{\underline{is}}} \mid \overset{S}{\text{a huge } \underline{sombrero.}} \text{ } \mathbf{I}$$

$$\overset{P}{\text{There } \underline{\underline{are}}} \mid \overset{S}{\text{many beautiful Mexican } \underline{costumes.}} \text{ } \mathbf{I}$$

Traditional Dress in Mexico

1. Some residents of Mexican villages still wear traditional types of clothing.
2. Many of these styles of clothing date back many centuries.
3. Look at the young boy in the cornfield.
4. On his head is a wide-brimmed straw hat, or sombrero.
5. The sombrero serves as excellent protection against the intense Mexican sun.
6. There are several other types of protective clothing for men and women.
7. A poncho, or blanket with a slit in the center for the head, is popular with men in cold or rainy weather.
8. Notice the rebozos, or fringed cotton shawls, covering the heads of those village women near the fountain in the plaza.
9. There are some special costumes for holidays and other occasions.
10. Look at the handsome suits worn by the cowboys, or *charros,* from Guadalajara.
11. Here is an example of a traditional Mexican outfit.
12. The material for the suit of a *charro* may be doeskin or velvet.
13. There are a short jacket, or bolero, and tight pants with gold buttons down the sides of the legs.
14. A shirt, boots with spurs, and a large sombrero complete the costume.
15. Among popular women's costumes is the beautiful *china poblana.*
16. It may have been named for a seventeenth-century Chinese princess.
17. The costume includes a full cotton skirt, a colorful blouse, and a wide sash.
18. There are many people in modern styles.
19. A common shoe is the *huarache.*
20. Many Mexican city dwellers no longer wear traditional clothing.

Parts of the Sentence

Practice and Assess

Answers: Exercise 13

1. Some <u>residents</u> of Mexican villages / still <u><u>wear</u></u> traditional types of clothing.
2. <u>Many</u> of these styles of clothing / <u><u>date</u></u> back several centuries.
3. (You) / <u><u>Look</u></u> at the young boy in the cornfield. C
4. On his head <u><u>is</u></u> / a . . . <u>hat</u>, or <u>sombrero</u>. I
5. The <u>sombrero</u> /<u><u>serves</u></u> as excellent protection . . .
6. There <u><u>are</u></u> / several other <u>types</u> . . . I
7. A <u>poncho</u> . . . / <u><u>is</u></u> popular . . .
8. (You) / <u><u>Notice</u></u> the rebozos . . . C
9. There <u><u>are</u></u> / some special <u>costumes</u> . . . I
10. (You) / <u><u>Look</u></u> at the handsome suits . . . from Guadalajara. C
11. Here <u><u>is</u></u> /an <u>example</u> of a traditional Mexican outfit. I
12. The <u>material</u> for the suit of a *charro* / <u><u>may be</u></u> doeskin or velvet.
13. There <u><u>are</u></u> / a short <u>jacket</u>, or bolero, and tight <u>pants</u> . . . I
14. A <u>shirt</u>, <u>boots</u> with spurs, and a large sombrero / <u><u>complete</u></u> the costume.
15. Among popular women's costumes <u><u>is</u></u> / the beautiful *china poblana.* I
16. <u>It</u> / <u><u>may have been named</u></u> for a seventeenth-century Chinese princess.
17. The <u>costume</u> / <u><u>includes</u></u> a full cotton skirt, a colorful blouse, and a wide sash.
18. There <u><u>are</u></u> / <u>many</u> . . . I
19. A common shoe / <u><u>is</u></u> the *<u>huarache</u>.* I
20. Many Mexican city <u>dwellers</u> / no longer <u><u>wear</u></u> traditional clothing.

Additional Resources

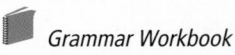 *Grammar Enrichment,* p. 9

Grammar Workbook Lesson 16

Close

Have three or four volunteers write sentences in inverted order on the chalkboard. Have the class discuss the reason for and effectiveness of the inversion.

Enrichment and Extension

Literature

Ask students how inverted order makes the sentence below more dramatic.

There under the mulberry tree stands a man, a dervish unlike those I've seen before.

—Naguib Mahfouz, "A Tale of Our Quarter"

Make sure students note that by placing the verb before the subject and by abruptly beginning the sentence with the adverb *there,* Mahfouz heightens the sense of his making a sudden disclosure.

Focus

Lesson Overview

Objectives
- To identify the four types of complement: direct objects, indirect objects, object complements, and subject complements
- To use various types of sentence complements in writing

Bellringer
Daily Language Activity

When students enter the classroom, have this assignment on the board: *Label the simple subject and simple predicate in this sentence: Careless skaters can injure ankles, kneecaps, and elbows.*

See also *Daily Language Practice*

Teach

Direct Objects

☑ **Grammar Tip**

The term *complement* is applied only to pronouns, nouns, and predicate adjectives. Adverbs and adverb phrases, even when necessary for the meaning of the sentence, are not complements.

Practice and Assess

Answers: Exercise 14
1. won; fame, fortune
2. heard; rumors
3. began; expedition
4. hindered; him
5. located; Inca, empire
6. pleased; explorer
7. captured; Atahualpa
8. gave; quantity
9. killed; ruler
10. conquered; Inca, city

Parts of the Sentence

11.5 Complements

- A **complement** is a word or group of words that completes the meaning of a verb.

The four kinds of complements are *direct objects, indirect objects, object complements,* and *subject complements.*

Direct Objects

- A **direct object** answers the question *what?* or *whom?* after an action verb.

The verb in a sentence usually indicates the action being performed by the subject. That action may be received by or directed toward someone or something: the direct object. Direct objects are nouns, pronouns, or words acting as nouns; and they may be compound. Only transitive verbs have direct objects.

> Roberto bought **tomatoes.** [Roberto bought *what?*]
> Sandra likes **me** very much. [Sandra likes *whom?*]
> Ralph reported his **discovery.** [Ralph reported *what?*]
> Roberto bought plum **tomatoes** and red-leaf **lettuce.** [Roberto bought *what?*]

Exercise 14   **Identifying Direct Objects**

On your paper, write the action verb that appears in each of the following sentences. Then list any direct objects.

Francisco Pizarro, a Spanish Conqueror

1. Francisco Pizarro, a sixteenth-century Spanish explorer, won much fame and fortune for his country.
2. Around 1520 Pizarro heard rumors of a vast and rich empire in the central highlands of South America.
3. In 1524 Pizarro began an expedition to the west coast of South America.
4. Bad weather hindered him in his first visit to the region.
5. In 1528, however, Pizarro located the Inca and their extensive empire.
6. Signs of gold and other riches in the Inca capital of Cuzco pleased the explorer greatly.
7. In 1532 Pizarro captured Atahualpa, a great Inca ruler, in the town of Cajamarca.
8. The Incas gave a vast quantity of gold and silver objects to Pizarro in order to save Atahualpa.
9. In the end Pizarro heartlessly killed the Inca ruler.
10. After the death of Atahualpa, Pizarro conquered the Inca and their capital city.

Resource Manager

Planning Resources
- *Lesson Plans*

Transparencies
- *Bellringer*
- *Daily Language Practice*
- *Two Minute Skill Drill*

Other Print Resources
- *Grammar and Composition Handbook*
- *Grammar Enrichment,* pp. 10–12
- *Grammar Practice,* pp. 10–12
- *Grammar Reteaching,* pp. 10–12
- *Grammar Workbook,* Lessons 17–18

Indirect Objects

■ An **indirect object** answers the question *to whom? for whom? to what?* or *for what?* after an action verb.

In most cases, a sentence can have an indirect object only if it has a direct object as well. The indirect object always appears after the verb and before the direct object.

> We gave **students** awards. [We gave awards *to whom?*]
>
> Trisha gives **homework** her full attention. [Trisha gives her full attention *to what?*]
>
> Angela bought **Soo** and **Gloria** lunch. [Angela bought lunch *for whom?*]

Exercise 15 — Identifying Direct and Indirect Objects

On your paper, write the direct object in each of the following sentences. Then write and underline any indirect objects. (There may be more than one indirect object in a sentence, or there may be none at all.)

Kristi Yamaguchi, Olympic Champion

1. Kristi Yamaguchi, a fourth-generation Japanese American, showed many female athletes and Asian Americans the rewards of dedication.
2. At age four, Yamaguchi started ballet study and ice-skating lessons.
3. She entered her first ice-skating competition at age eight.
4. As a young skater, Yamaguchi won many titles and medals.
5. She gave the audience and judges the best free-skate performance of her career.
6. Yamaguchi completed six triple jumps in this program.
7. At the 1992 Winter Olympics, Yamaguchi brought the United States a gold medal in figure skating.
8. Having won her Olympic gold medal just a month earlier, Yamaguchi provided her hometown a thrill by winning a second consecutive world championship.
9. She joined a professional tour in 1993.
10. Yamaguchi's artistry and athleticism have given her family, her country, and many audiences great pride and much pleasure.

Exercise 16 — Using Direct and Indirect Objects

On your paper, rewrite the following sentences so that each contains both a direct and an indirect object. Write a *D* above each direct object and an *I* above each indirect object.

1. Book groups offer meetings on a regular basis.
2. Members give information about a wide variety of books.
3. One by one, each member tells his or her impressions of the book.
4. Sometimes the members write about the book.
5. Book groups also offer the possibilities of new friendships.

11.5 Complements **507**

Teach

Indirect Objects

☑ **Grammar Tip**

Objects (both direct and indirect) occur only after transitive action verbs. Thousands of transitive verbs can have direct objects but fewer than fifty verbs can be used with indirect objects.

◀ **Cross-reference: Grammer**

For instruction and practice with transitive verbs, refer students to Lesson 10.3, p. 453.

Practice and Assess

Answers: Exercise 15

1. rewards, <u>athletes, Asian Americans</u>
2. study, lessons
3. competition
4. titles, medals
5. performance, <u>audience, judges</u>
6. jumps
7. medal, <u>United States</u>
8. thrill, <u>hometown</u>
9. tour
10. pride, pleasure, <u>family, country, audiences</u>

Answers: Exercise 16

Answers will vary, but some suggestions are given below.
1. Book groups offer readers [I] meetings [D] on a regular basis.
2. Members give one another [I] information [D] about a wide variety of books.
3. One by one, each member tells the group [I] his or her impressions [D] of the book.
4. Sometimes the members write publishers [I] letters [D] about the book.
5. Book groups also offer people [I] the possibilities [D] of new friendships.

Exploring Language

Identifying Indirect Objects

A good way to identify an indirect object is to see whether it can be replaced with a prepositional phrase beginning with *to* or *for*. We can show, for example, that *cat* is the indirect object in the sentence

> *I gave the cat some water.*

We can replace *cat* with the prepositional phrase *to the cat:*

> *I gave some water to the cat.*

Teach

Object Complements

☑ **Grammar Tip**

About forty verbs can be followed by a direct object plus an object complement. Object complements differ from indirect objects in two ways: First, object complements can be predicate adjectives, whereas indirect objects must be nouns. Second, unlike indirect objects, object complements can never be replaced with prepositional phrases.

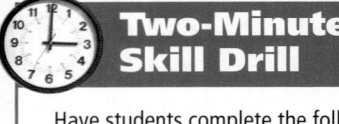

Two-Minute Skill Drill

Have students complete the following sentences with a noun or an adjective:

They named the baby _____.

The fans considered the player

_____.

Everyone found the heat

_____.

✒ **See also** *Two-Minute Skill Drill Transparency 11.5*

Practice and Assess

Answers: Exercise 17

1. masterpieces
2. irreplaceable, priceless
3. delicate, expressive
4. subject
5. interesting
6. popular
7. [no object complement]
8. master
9. subjects
10. fascinating

Answers: Exercise 18

Answers will vary, but some suggestions are given below.

1. theirs; *P*
2. irritating; *A*
3. a golden pond; *N*
4. dangerous; *A*
5. a disadvantage; *N*
6. eerie; *A*

Parts of the Sentence

Object Complements

■ An **object complement** answers the question *what?* after a direct object. This is, it *completes* the meaning of the direct object by identifying or describing it.

You will find object complements only in sentences that contain a direct object *and* include one of the following action verbs or a similar verb that has the general meaning of "make" or "consider":

appoint	choose	elect	prove
call	consider	name	vote

An object complement follows a direct object and may be an adjective, a noun, or a pronoun.

Engineers find plans **essential.** [adjective]

Nations often make their bridges **symbols.** [noun]

The citizens call that privilege **theirs.** [pronoun]

Mozelle considers me a **close friend** and **helpful adviser.** [nouns with modifiers]

Exercise 17   Identifying Object Complements

On your paper, write the object complements that appear in the following sentences. (Two sentences have two object complements, and one sentence has none.)

Japanese Prints

1. Art historians and critics consider many Japanese prints masterpieces.
2. A museum curator calls seventeenth-century Japanese prints irreplaceable and priceless.
3. Some scholars think the early black-and-white prints particularly delicate and expressive.
4. Harunobu, a master of the print, found children a worthy subject.
5. Somehow he rendered the children interesting.
6. An eighteenth-century printmaker, Harunobu, made color prints popular.
7. Some collectors prefer Utamaro's color prints.
8. Many in the art world have named Utamaro a master.
9. Quite often Utamaro made women his subjects.
10. Some artists consider the art of printmaking fascinating.

Exercise 18   Using Object Complements

On your paper, complete the following sentences with object complements. Then write the letter *A, N,* or *P* to identify each object complement as an adjective, noun, or pronoun.

1. The selfish children considered all the toys ____.
2. Drivers found the traffic ____.
3. Sunshine made the meadow ____.
4. The highway patrol called the storm ____.
5. Pilots considered the weather ____.
6. Vacationers thought the fog ____.

MEETING INDIVIDUAL NEEDS **English Language Learners**

Identifying Object Complements

Help students who are learning English recognize object complements by reminding them that the word *complement* means "completer, that which completes." An object complement completes the object. In the sentence *They elected him governor,* the object, *him,* is incomplete without its complement, *governor.* Have students first identify the direct object and then find the word that completes the direct object. That word will be the object complement.

Subject Complements

- A **subject complement** follows a subject and a linking verb and identifies or describes the subject.

The two kinds of subject complements are *predicate monimatives* and *predicate adjectives.*

- A **predicate nominative** is a noun or pronoun that follows a linking verb and points back to the subject to identify it further.

Engineers are **scientists.**

The engineer on this project is **she.**

Although predicate nominatives most often appear in sentences containing forms of the linking verb *be,* a few other linking verbs (for example, *become* and *remain*) can be followed by a predicate nominative.

San Francisco is a **city.**

Monday remains a **holiday** for us.

Tanya became a famous **singer** and **dancer.**

- A **predicate adjective** follows a linking verb and points back to the subject and further describes it.

Engineers are **inventive.**

Engineers must be highly **responsible.**

Predicate adjectives may follow any linking verb.

The hikers had become very **weary.**

The team looks **ready** for the game.

Lena seems **eager** and **determined.**

I feel quite **chilly.**

Exercise 19   **Identifying Predicate Nominatives**

On your paper, write the predicate nominatives that appear in the following sentences. (If a sentence has no predicate nominative, write *none.*)

George Mason

1. George Mason was a statesman during the Revolutionary War era.
2. Born in Virginia, Mason became a brilliant student of law.
3. Mason was not a supporter of slavery.
4. Public officials appreciated Mason's legal genius.
5. Mason's work became the basis for Thomas Jefferson's Bill of Rights.

The trail looked suspicious!

Parts of the Sentence

Teach

Subject Complements

✅ **Teaching Tip**

The complements that follow linking verbs are called subject complements. If the subject complement is a noun or pronoun (as opposed to an adjective), the noun or pronoun is called a predicate nominative, not an object. The term *object* is used only for those nouns and pronouns that follow action verbs.

Vocabulary Link

The basic meaning of *complement* is "that which is necessary to complete something."

🔁 **Cross-reference: Grammar**

For instruction and practice with linking verbs, refer students to Lesson 10.3, p. 453.

 Two-Minute Skill Drill

Have students identify the subject complements in the following sentences:

Jeremy was a lawyer.

After a trip to the doctor, I always feel better.

The book was *Pride and Prejudice.*

📖 **See also** *Two-Minute Skill Drill Transparency 11.5*

Practice and Assess

Answers: Exercise 19
1. statesman
2. student
3. supporter
4. none
5. basis

Exploring Language

Identifying Predicate Nominatives

Explain to students that predicate nominatives (unlike objects) always refer to the subject. One way to identify a predicate nominative is to see whether the noun following the verb "equals" the subject. If it does, then it is a predicate nominative. If the noun following the verb does not "equal" the subject, then it is a direct object. Have students mentally substitute the word *equals* between subject and predicate to help them complete Exercise 19. **L2**

Practice and Assess

Answers: Exercise 20

1. behavior, strange
2. animal, irritable
3. It, *none*
4. animal, normal
5. appearance, *none*
6. actions, *none*
7. (you), *none*
8. animal, restless
9. animal, unfriendly
10. (you), *none*

Answers: Exercise 21

Answers will vary, but some suggestions are given below.

1. place; *predicate nominative*
2. popular; *predicate adjective*
3. festive; *predicate adjective*
4. crisp, fresh; *predicate adjectives*
5. delicious; *predicate adjective*
6. risers; *predicate nominative*
7. none
8. persuasive; *predicate adjective*
9. none
10. customer; *predicate nominative*

Answers: Exercise 22

Answers will vary, but some suggestions are given below.

1. the villain; *PN*
2. glamorous; *PA*
3. ordinary; *PA*
4. exciting; *PA*
5. dull; *PA*

Parts of the Sentence

Exercise 20   Identifying Predicate Adjectives

On your paper, write the simple subject and predicate adjective in each of the following sentences. If a sentence has no predicate adjective, write *none*.

Rabies

1. The behavior of an animal with rabies seems strange.
2. A rabid animal grows irritable.
3. It ventures fearlessly into contact with people.
4. The sick animal looks normal.
5. Its appearance often does not change.
6. The animal's strange actions, not its appearance, should be watched often.
7. Do not go near a strange-acting animal.
8. An animal with rabies feels unusually restless.
9. A normally friendly animal may become unfriendly.
10. Call an authority about a possibly rabid animal.

Exercise 21   Identifying Subject Complements

On your paper, write all the subject complements that appear in the following sentences. Identify each as a *predicate nominative* or a *predicate adjective*. (One sentence has more than one subject complement; other sentences have none.)

The Farmer's Market

1. A farmer's market is a place for the sale of the produce of local farmers.
2. In many communities, these markets have become quite popular.
3. With the eager crowds, colorful stands, and shouting vendors, a farmer's market seems festive.
4. Locally grown fruits and vegetables, arranged on open stands, look crisp and fresh.
5. Breads and rolls, often still warm from the oven, smell delicious.
6. The farmers must be early risers.
7. Many of them sell preserves or handicrafts as well as fruits and vegetables.
8. Their loud sales pitches always sound persuasive.
9. Spend a morning at a farmer's market.
10. Soon you will be a regular customer.

Exercise 22   Using Subject Complements

On your paper, complete each of the following sentences by adding a noun, a pronoun, or an adjective. (You may also add other words.) Write *PN* or *PA* to identify the complement as a predicate nominative or predicate adjective.

1. The most interesting type of character created by Hollywood is _____.
2. The lives of Hollywood-created characters seem _____.
3. In real life, however, most people remain _____.
4. Many of the situations of Hollywood characters appear _____.
5. Compared to these situations, ordinary people's lives look _____.

510   Unit 11 Parts of the Sentence

Enrichment and Extension

Understanding Ambiguity

A classic Marx Brothers gag involves using the verb *call* with two different complement types. Here is the dialogue:

　　Man: Quick, call me a taxi!
　　Groucho: All right, you're a taxi.

Have students explain the two different complements used with *call*. (The man is using an indirect object plus a direct object complement: *Call me a taxi* means "Call a taxi for me." Groucho treats *call* as having a direct object plus an object complement: *Call me a taxi* then means "Call me by the name *taxi*.")

Exercise 23   Identifying Complements (Part 1)

On your paper, write the complements that appear in the following sentences. Next to each complement, write the kind of complement it is: *direct object, indirect object, object complement, predicate nominative,* or *predicate adjective.*

Batik and Tie-dyeing

1. Batik is a method of fabric decoration.
2. The batik artist applies wax to parts of the cloth.
3. The artist then gives the cloth a dye bath.
4. The bath dyes the unwaxed part a vivid color.
5. The part of the cloth with wax resists the dye.
6. This method gives the cloth intricate designs.
7. The colors of batik appear rich and often subtle.
8. The process of tie-dyeing is similar but easier.
9. Common to both of these crafts is the resist-dyeing technique.
10. The tie-dye artist ties string around the cloth in different places.
11. The artist then dyes the fabric a color.
12. The tied areas give the cloth its design.
13. This design often appears random.
14. Usually, the fabric does not resist the dye uniformly.
15. Uneven dyeing makes the final product quite beautiful.

Exercise 24   Identifying Complements (Part 2)

On your paper, write the complements that appear in the following paragraph. Next to each complement, write the kind of complement it is: *direct object, indirect object, object complement, predicate nominative,* or *predicate adjective.*

The Mystery of Lightning

[1]Lightning was mysterious to the ancient Greeks. [2]In fact, for them lightning was a weapon used by their chief god, Zeus. [3]According to mythology, the Greeks gave Zeus the thunderbolt. [4]Many persons today still consider lightning scary. [5]Of course, the reasons for this fear seem sound. [6]During a storm, lightning strikes the earth about one hundred times a second. [7]Sometimes lightning strikes the tallest tree in a field. [8]Lightning may cause fire. [9]In addition, in the United States alone, lightning kills approximately one hundred people every year. [10]Lightning can be both mysterious and dangerous.

Exercise 25   Writing Sentences with Complements

Write four sentences about an environmental concern, such as acid rain, air pollution, noise pollution, deforestation, or oil spills. In each sentence, use at least one of the four kinds of complements: *direct object, indirect object, object complement,* and *subject complement.* Label the complements.

Parts of the Sentence

Practice and Assess

Answers: Exercise 23

1. method—*predicate nominative*
2. wax—*direct object*
3. cloth—*indirect object*
   dye bath—*direct object*
4. part—*direct object*
   color—*object complement*
5. dye—*direct object*
6. cloth—*indirect object*
   designs—*direct object*
7. rich, subtle—*predicate adjectives*
8. similar, easier—*predicate adjectives*
9. Common—*predicate adjective*
10. string—*direct object*
11. fabric—*direct object*
    color—*object complement*
12. cloth—*indirect object*
    design—*direct object*
13. random—*predicate adjective*
14. dye—*direct object*
15. product—*direct object*
    beautiful—*object complement*

Answers: Exercise 24

1. mysterious—*predicate adjective*
2. weapon—*predicate nominative*
3. Zeus—*indirect object*
   thunderbolt—*direct object*
4. lightning—*direct object*
   scary—*object complement*
5. sound—*predicate adjective*
6. earth—*direct object*
7. tree—*direct object*
8. fire—*direct object*
9. people—*direct object*
10. mysterious, dangerous—*predicate adjectives*

Answers: Exercise 25

Answers will vary, but some suggestions are given below.

1. Noise pollution affects many people *(direct object).*
2. Excessive noise causes some people *(indirect object)* headaches *(direct object).*
3. Noise can make people *(direct object)* uneasy *(object complement).*
4. Usually, noise is simply annoying *(subject complement).*

Additional Resources

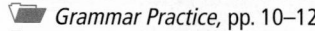 *Grammar Practice,* pp. 10–12
📁 *Grammar Reteaching,* pp. 10–12
📁 *Grammar Enrichment,* pp. 10–12

📓 *Grammar Workbook*
Lessons 17–18

Close

Assign students a passage of reading and have them find and identify the kinds of complements in it.

Teach

About the Literature

Explain that *Palace Walk* is a novel by the Egyptian writer Naguib Mahfouz. The passage reproduced in this review is from Chapter 8 of the novel. Ask a volunteer to read the passage aloud. Have the rest of the class listen, respond, and appropriately evaluate the presentation. In a discussion, students should identify and analyze the characters, the setting, and the mood of the passage. Students should use peer feedback to evaluate their effectiveness in presenting and to set goals for future presentations. Then ask them to focus on the annotated elements of the passage. Explain how each highlighted element functions within the sentence in which it appears. Encourage students to ask questions for clarification and to respond appropriately to classmates' responses.

Linking Grammar and Literature

Ask students to identify the simple subject and the simple predicate in at least five of the sentences in the literary passage. (Have students work with simple sentences; for example: She was leaning her arm on the windowsill.)

✔ ASSESSMENT OPTIONS

📁 *Tests with Answer Key & Rubrics*
Unit 11 Mastery Test, pp. 37–38

💾 *Testmaker*
Unit 11 Mastery Test

You may wish to administer the Unit 11 Mastery Test at this point.

PARTS OF THE SENTENCE

Cairo is the home of Naguib Mahfouz [nä gēb´ mä fooz´]. His novel *Palace Walk* traces the fortunes of a middle-class Cairo family in the years between the two world wars. In this scene, the youngest son of the family, Kamal, is on his way home from school. The passage has been annotated to show some of the parts of the sentence covered in this unit.

Literature Model

from Palace Walk
by Naguib Mahfouz

translated from the Arabic by William Maynard Hutchins and Olive E. Kenny

He reached the pastry shop and stretched out his hand with the small change he had hung on to since morning. He took a **piece** of pastry with the total delight he experienced only on such a sweet occasion. It made him frequently dream of owning a candy store one day, not to sell the candy but to eat it. He continued on his way down al-Husayn Street, **munching** on the pastry with pleasure. He **hummed** and **forgot** he had been a prisoner all day long, not allowed to move, not to mention play or have fun. . . .

On his way, he passed by the tobacco store of Matoussian. He stopped under its sign, as he did every day at this hour, and raised his small eyes to the colored poster of a woman reclining on a divan with a cigarette between her crimson lips, from which rose a curling plume of smoke. She was leaning her arm on the windowsill. The **curtain** was drawn back to reveal a scene combining a grove of date palms and a branch of the Nile. He privately called the woman **Aisha** after his sister, since they both had golden hair and blue eyes. Although he was just going on ten, his admiration for the mistress of the poster was **limitless**. How often he thought of her enjoying life in its most splendid manifestations. How

*Annotation labels:*
- Direct object
- Compound predicate
- Simple subject
- Object complement
- Subject complement (predicate adjective)

Side label: Parts of the Sentence

Resource Manager

Planning Resources
- *Lesson Plans*

📁 Other Print Resources
- *Grammar and Composition Handbook*
- *Grammar Workbook,* Lessons 13–18; Unit 2 Review; Cumulative Review: Units 1–2

often he imagined himself sharing his carefree days in that luxurious room with its pristine view that offered her, in fact both of them, its earth, palms, water, and sky. He would swim in the green river valley or cross the water in the skiff that appeared ghostlike far off in the picture. He would shake the palm trees till the dates fell around him or sit near the beautiful woman with his eyes gazing at her dreamy ones.

He left the vaulted section of the alley for the other half. At the end he could see Palace Walk and the entrance of Hammam al-Sultan. Then his eyes fell on his home's dark green wooden grilles and the large door with its bronze knocker. His mouth opened in a happy smile at the wide variety of amusements this place harbored for him. Soon the boys from all the neighboring houses would run to join him in his wide courtyard, with its several chambers, surrounding the oven room. There would be fun and games and sweet potatoes.

At that moment he saw the Suarès omnibus slowly crossing the street heading for Palace Walk. His heart leaped. Pleasure at his own cleverness filled him. At once he tucked his book bag under his left arm and reached to catch it. He jumped on the back steps, but the conductor did not let him enjoy his pleasure for very long. He came and asked the boy for his fare, giving him a suspicious, challenging look. Kamal told him ingratiatingly that he would get off as soon as it stopped but could not while it was moving. The conductor turned from him and yelled to the driver to stop the vehicle. He was angrily scolding Kamal, but when he looked away the boy seized the opportunity to tread on the instep of his foot, take a swing at him, and hop to the ground. He shot off in flight.

- Indirect object
- Complete predicate
- Simple predicate
- Complete subject
- Sentence beginning with *there*

Parts of the Sentence

Review: Exercise 1   **Identifying Simple Subjects and Predicates**

For each of the following sentences, write the simple subject and simple predicate. Underline the simple predicate.

1. The young boy bought a pastry at a shop on his way home.
2. The tobacco store of Matoussian had a beautiful woman on its sign.
3. Kamal privately called the woman Aisha after his sister.
4. Dreams of a luxurious life filled his imagination.
5. The entrance to Hammam al-Sultan was nearby.

Grammar Review   **513**

Practice and Assess

Answers: Exercise 1
1. boy/bought
2. store/had
3. Kamal/called
4. Dreams/filled
5. entrance/was

Grammar Review

Practice and Assess

Answers: Exercise 2

1. . . . poster/seemed . . . .
2. . . . She/was reclining . . .
3. . . . Nile/could be seen . . .
4. . . . sister/had . . .
5. . . . boy/privately called . . .
6. . . . picture/beckoned. . .
7. . . . poster/looked . . .
8. . . . dates/might . . .
9. . . . life/filled . . .
10. . . . boy/finally . . .

Answers: Exercise 3

Answers will vary, but some suggestions are given below.

1. The pastry shop was located in the middle of the plaza.
2. The storekeeper took the change from Kamal.
3. His precious purchase delighted Kamal.
4. The happy young boy munched on his pastry.
5. The tobacco store was another favorite place.
6. A colorful poster caught his eye.
7. The magnificent room in the poster offered a beautiful view.
8. The alley was located near Palace Walk.
9. Kamal would soon be playing in the large courtyard.
10. The oven room smelled delicious.
11. The Suarès omnibus headed for Palace Walk.
12. Kamal's heart filled with pleasure at his cleverness.
13. Kamal jumped on the back of the bus.
14. The conductor asked for his fare.
15. An ingratiating smile was the boy's response.

Parts of the Sentence

Review: Exercise 2   Identifying Complete Subjects and Predicates

The following sentences are based on the excerpt from *Palace Walk*. Copy each sentence and draw a line between the complete subject and complete predicate.

1. The woman on the poster seemed exotic to the small boy.
2. She was reclining on a divan and leaning her arm on a windowsill.
3. A scene with a grove of date palms and a view of the Nile could be seen behind her.
4. Kamal's sister had blond hair and blue eyes, just like the woman on the poster.
5. The boy privately called the woman Aisha.
6. A life of luxury similar to the view in the picture beckoned to Kamal.
7. The water of the Nile in the poster looked good for a swim or a sail in a skiff.
8. The dates from the palm trees might fall around him and the beautiful woman.
9. Thoughts of this wondrous life filled his mind for many minutes.
10. The young boy finally continued on his way home.

Review: Exercise 3   Writing Sentences with Complete Subjects and Complete Predicates

Each of the following partial sentences elaborates on an idea suggested by the passage from *Palace Walk*. Write either a complete subject or a complete predicate to complete each sentence. Do not repeat the exact wording from the novel. Your sentence should make sense within the context of the passage.

SAMPLE   The young boy _____.
ANSWER   was walking home from school.

1. The pastry shop _____.
2. _____ took the change from Kamal.
3. His precious purchase _____.
4. The happy young boy _____.
5. _____ was another favorite place.
6. _____ caught his eye.
7. The magnificent room in the poster _____.
8. _____ was located near Palace Walk.
9. _____ would soon be playing in the large courtyard.
10. The oven room _____.
11. The Suarès omnibus _____.
12. _____ filled with pleasure at his cleverness.
13. _____ jumped on the back of the bus.
14. The conductor _____.
15. _____ was the boy's response.

Review: Exercise 4   Writing Sentences with Compound Subjects and Compound Predicates

On your paper, write a complete sentence to answer each of the following questions. Begin your sentence with the subject and follow the instructions in parentheses. Underline and label the simple or compound subject and the simple or compound predicate. Draw a line separating the complete subject from the complete predicate.

SAMPLE   What foods gave Kamal great pleasure? (Use a compound subject.)

                   COMPOUND SUBJECT   SIMPLE PREDICATE
ANSWER   <u>Pastry</u> and other <u>sweets</u> | <u>gave</u> Kamal great pleasure.

1. Who lived in the city of Cairo?
   (Use a compound subject.)
2. What two shops were special to Kamal?
   (Use a compound subject.)
3. What did the young boy do after leaving the pastry shop?
   (Use a compound predicate.)
4. What two women had the same coloring?
   (Use a compound subject.)
5. What was the woman in the poster doing?
   (Use a compound predicate.)
6. What could be seen outside the woman's window?
   (Use a compound subject with three different nouns.)
7. What would Kamal and his friends do in Kamal's courtyard?
   (Use a compound predicate.)
8. What are three things Kamal did on his way home?
   (Use a compound predicate with three different verbs.)
9. Who had an unpleasant encounter on the back steps of the bus?
   (Use a compound subject.)
10. What gave Kamal particular pleasure on his walk?
    (Use a compound subject with three different nouns.)
11. What three features of Kamal's house promised amusement?
    (Use a compound subject with three different nouns.)
12. Who might have been riding on the bus with Kamal?
    (Use a compound subject with two different nouns.)
13. What did Kamal do to the conductor when the man turned his head?
    (Use a compound predicate with two different verbs.)
14. How might the passengers have reacted to Kamal's antics?
    (Use a compound predicate with two or three different verbs.)
15. Who would probably be having dinner at Kamal's house that night?
    (Use a compound subject with three different nouns.)

Practice and Assess

Answers: Exercise 4

Answers will vary, but some suggestions are given below.

1. <u>Kamal</u> and <u>Aisha</u>/<u>lived</u> in the city of Cairo.
2. The tobacco <u>store</u> and the pastry <u>shop</u>/<u>were</u> special to Kamal.
3. The young <u>boy</u>/<u>ate</u> pastry and <u>hummed</u> a tune.
4. <u>Aisha</u> and the <u>woman</u> on the poster/<u>had</u> the same coloring.
5. The <u>woman</u> in the poster/<u>was reclining</u> on a divan and <u>smoking</u>.
6. <u>Palms, water</u>, and <u>sky</u>/<u>could be seen</u> outside the woman's window.
7. <u>Kamal</u> and his <u>friends</u>/<u>would play</u> games and <u>eat</u> sweet potatoes in Kamal's courtyard.
8. <u>Kamal</u>/<u>tucked</u> his book bag under his arm, <u>ran</u> to the omnibus, and <u>jumped</u> on the back step.
9. <u>Kamal</u> and the <u>conductor</u>/<u>had</u> an unpleasant encounter on the back steps of the bus.
10. The <u>taste</u> of the pastry, the <u>sight</u> of the woman on the poster, and the <u>freedom</u> from the day's restraints/ <u>gave</u> Kamal particular pleasure on his walk.
11. The large <u>door</u> with its bronze knocker, the wide <u>courtyard</u>, and the oven <u>room</u>/<u>promised</u> amusement.
12. <u>Salespeople</u> and <u>office workers</u>/ <u>might have been riding</u> on the bus with Kamal.
13. <u>Kamal</u>/<u>stepped</u> on the conductor's foot and <u>took</u> a swing at him.
14. The <u>passengers</u>/<u>might glare</u> at Kamal and <u>disapprove</u> of his actions.
15. <u>Kamal</u>, his <u>sister</u>, and his <u>parents</u>/ <u>would</u> probably <u>be having</u> dinner at Kamal's house that night.

515

Practice and Assess

Answers: Exercise 5

1. Through the streets of Cairo walked Kamal.
2. There were fascinating sights, sounds, and smells all around him.
3. There was nothing more wonderful than the excitement and freedom of a stroll through the busy city.
4. Out of one of the shops wafted the luscious aroma of sweet cakes.
5. Into the shop marched the eager boy.
6. Down the busy street proceeded Kamal.
7. There was an enchanting poster above the tobacco store.
8. Into Kamal's head floated thoughts of a luxurious life.
9. Toward him moved a bus, with its promise of new adventure.
10. There was a suspicious conductor on the bus.
11. Toward the boy strode the angry conductor.
12. There was an unpleasant frown on his face.
13. There was a furious glitter in his eyes.
14. Into the angry face smiled the mischievous young boy.
15. From his mouth fell words that were lies.
16. Away from the boy turned the wrathful conductor.
17. There was a curious quiet throughout the bus.
18. Into the silence bellowed the angry man.
19. From the bus hopped the laughing boy.
20. There was a narrow alley nearby, a place to escape.

Parts of the Sentence

| **Review: Exercise 5** | **Writing Inverted Sentences** |

The sentences below are based on the excerpt from *Palace Walk*. On your paper, rewrite each sentence in inverted order, following the instructions in parentheses.

1. Kamal walked through the streets of Cairo. (Begin the sentence with *Through the streets of Cairo.*)
2. Fascinating sights, sounds, and smells were all around him. (Begin the sentence with *There were.*)
3. Nothing was more wonderful than the excitement and freedom of a stroll through the busy city. (Begin the sentence with *There was.*)
4. The luscious aroma of sweet cakes wafted out of one of the shops. (Begin the sentence with *Out of one of the shops.*)
5. The eager boy marched into the shop. (Begin the sentence with *Into the shop.*)
6. Kamal proceeded down the busy street. (Begin the sentence with *Down the busy street.*)
7. An enchanting poster was above the tobacco store. (Begin the sentence with *There was.*)
8. Thoughts of a luxurious life floated into Kamal's head. (Begin the sentence with *Into Kamal's head.*)
9. A bus, with its promise of new adventure, moved toward him. (Begin the sentence with *Toward him.*)
10. A suspicious conductor was on the bus. (Begin the sentence with *There was.*)
11. The angry conductor strode toward the boy. (Begin the sentence with *Toward the boy.*)
12. An unpleasant frown was on his face. (Begin the sentence with *There was.*)
13. A furious glitter was in his eyes. (Begin the sentence with *There was.*)
14. The mischievous young boy smiled into the angry face. (Begin the sentence with *Into the angry face.*)
15. Words that were lies fell from his mouth. (Begin the sentence with *From his mouth.*)
16. The wrathful conductor turned away from the boy. (Begin the sentence with *Away from the boy.*)
17. A curious quiet was throughout the bus. (Begin the sentence with *There was.*)
18. The angry man bellowed into the silence. (Begin the sentence with *Into the silence.*)

19. The laughing boy hopped from the bus.
(Begin the sentence with *From the bus.*)
20. A narrow alley, a place to escape, was nearby.
(Begin the sentence with *There was.*)

Review: Exercise 6   **Writing Sentences with Predicate Nominatives and Predicate Adjectives**

The pairs of words that follow are derived from the passage from *Palace Walk*. For each pair, write a sentence that uses the first word as the subject and the second word as a predicate adjective or a predicate nominative. Do not use the exact wording from the novel, and be sure to add more than just a verb to the pair of words.

SAMPLE   city, home
ANSWER   The city of Cairo was Kamal's home.

1. Kamal, hungry
2. pastry, delicious
3. boy, happy
4. stop, tobacco store
5. person, woman
6. admiration, endless
7. scene, attractive
8. home, place
9. bus, challenge
10. conductor, angry

Review: Exercise 7   **Writing Sentences with Direct and Indirect Objects**

Each of the following groups of words describes an incident related to the passage from *Palace Walk*. Each word is labeled *S* (for *subject*), *DO* (for *direct object*), or *IO* (for *indirect object*). On your paper, write a sentence using these words, but do not use the exact wording from the novel. Try to add modifiers or prepositional phrases to make your sentences more interesting.

SAMPLE   boy (S), merchant (IO), money (DO)
ANSWER   The young boy gave the merchant some money.

1. baker (S), schoolboy (IO), delicacy (DO)
2. sweets (S), Kamal (IO), pleasure (DO)
3. Kamal (S), candy store (DO)
4. poster (S), boy (IO), delight (DO)
5. Kamal (S), woman (IO), affection (DO)
6. Kamal (S), home (DO)
7. home (S), amusements (DO)
8. mother (S), his friends (IO), sweet potatoes (DO)
9. schoolboy (S), bus (DO)
10. conductor (S), Kamal (IO), question (DO)

Practice and Assess

Answers: Exercise 6

1. Kamal felt very hungry after school.
2. The pastry from the shop on al-Husayn Street was delicious.
3. The boy was feeling extremely happy on his walk.
4. His next stop was Matoussian's tobacco store.
5. The person in the poster above the store was a beautiful woman.
6. Kamal's admiration for the woman was endless.
7. The scene in the poster seemed very attractive to Kamal.
8. Still, his home remained the best place of all.
9. The moving bus was a challenge to Kamal.
10. The conductor on the omnibus grew quite angry with Kamal.

Answers: Exercise 7

Answers will vary, but some suggestions are given below.

1. The baker in the pastry shop sold the schoolboy a delicacy.
2. The sweets gave Kamal great pleasure.
3. Kamal wanted a candy store of his own some day.
4. The poster over the tobacco shop gave the boy delight.
5. Kamal offered the beautiful woman in the poster his affection.
6. Kamal loved his home more than anything else.
7. His home offered many amusements.
8. Kamal's mother served his friends sweet potatoes.
9. The schoolboy spotted the bus across the street.
10. The conductor asked Kamal a question about his fare.

Parts of the Sentence

517

Practice and Assess

Answers: Exercise 8

Answers will vary, but some suggestions are given below.

1. The boy considered sweets of any kind a special treat.
2. The store proprietor did not find the mischievous boy funny.
3. Kamal thought the woman in the poster beautiful.
4. The passengers on the bus considered Kamal rude.
5. A friend found the story of Kamal and the conductor funny.

Answers: Exercise 9
Proofreading

This proofreading activity provides editing practice with (1) the current or previous units' skills, (2) the **Troubleshooter** errors, and (3) spelling errors. Students should be able to complete the exercise by referring to the units, the **Troubleshooter**, and a dictionary. (Note: A run-on sentence counts as one error.)

Error (Type of Error)

1. attorney, (nonessential adjective clause)
2. 1890, (run-on sentence)
3. immediately (spelling)
4. painting, which (sentence fragment)
5. his (possessive pronoun)
6. *fauves,* (nonessential appositive)
7. stuck (verb form)
8. Matisse became *or* He became (sentence fragment)
9. techniques (spelling)
10. fluid, (commas in a series)
11. were (subject-verb agreement)
12. said (shift in tense)
13. altogether, (run-on sentence)

Parts of the Sentence

Review: Exercise 8 Writing Sentences with Direct Objects and Object Complements

Each word in the following groups is labeled *S* (for *subject*), *DO* (for *direct object*), or *OC* (for *object complement*). On your paper, write a sentence using these words. Try to add modifiers such as prepositional phrases to make your sentences more interesting.

SAMPLE Kamal (S), walk (DO), fun (OC)
ANSWER Kamal found his walk home from school fun.

1. boy (S), sweets (DO), treat (OC)
2. proprietor (S), boy (DO), funny (OC)
3. Kamal (S), woman (DO), beautiful (OC)
4. passengers (S), Kamal (DO), rude (OC)
5. friend (S), story (DO), funny (OC)

Review: Exercise 9

Proofreading

The following passage describes the artist Henri Matisse, whose painting appears on the opposite page. Rewrite the passage, correcting any errors in spelling, grammar, and usage. Add any missing punctuation. There are twenty-five errors.

Henri Matisse

[1]Born in northern France, Henri Matisse (1869–1954), who intended to become an attorney studied law. [2]He was recovering from illness in 1890 and he decided to amuse himself by painting. [3]He immediatly took to painting. [4]Which became his lifelong passion.

[5]In Paris in 1905, he showed some of his' works to the public at a revolutionary exhibit. [6]Critics labeled Matisse and the other artists in the exhibit *fauves* a French word meaning "wild beasts." [7]The name sticked. [8]Became the movement's unofficial leader.

[9]Matisse worked for years to refine fauvist ideas and technics. [10]His pictures were simple, fluid and colorful. [11]For the fauves and their supporters, color and light was the keys to a painter's power. [12]Sometime during the year of 1908, Matisse says, "What I am after, above all, is expression." [13]As he entered his later years, he frequently abandoned the use of paint altogether and he chose instead to make collages in brilliant hues.

[14]Matisse took his first trip to Morocco in 1912. [15]He was inspired by Africas architecture ancient cultures, and landscape.

Henri Matisse, *The Casbah Gate*, 1912

Practice and Assess

Answers: Exercise 9 (continued)
Proofreading

Error (Type of Error)

14. took (verb form)
15. Africa's (singular possessive)
16. architecture, (commas in a series) produced, (shift in tense)
17. using (spelling)
18. light, (commas in a series)
19. Matisse, (nonessential participial phrase)
20. suggests (subject-verb agreement)
21. picture's (singular possessive) greens, (commas in a series) reflect (subject-verb agreement)
22. raise (subject-verb agreement)

[16]Matisse produces many powerful works in Morocco, including *The Casbah Gate.* [17]He painted the scene, useing brilliant colors. [18]He produced a mood based on color, light and form.

[19]Like the author of *Palace Walk,* Matisse using carefully chosen and rendered details, managed to convey a strong sense of place. [20]The shape of the archway in *The Casbah Gate* suggest the locale. [21]The pictures pale greens pinks, and roses reflects the pure light of the city. [22]Both the passage from *Palace Walk* and the scene in *The Casbah Gate* raises a sense of expectancy, almost as if the viewer were on the edge of a new and glorious adventure.

Grammar Review **519**

Viewing the Art

Henri Matisse, *The Casbah Gate*, 1912
Matisse, like many modern painters, often chose to focus on a few key images, simplifying their forms and heightening their colors. Like Matisse, Naguib Mahfouz chooses his details carefully. Ask students to identify some of the sensory details in Mahfouz's descriptions. What moods do these images suggest?

Answers: Exercise 10
Mixed Review

Answers will vary, but some suggestions are given below.

1. The Egyptian author Naguib Mahfouz was born in the city of Cairo in 1911.
2. There are vivid sketches of Cairo in his books.
3. In Mahfouz's books, the change in Cairo and its people is depicted.
4. Mahfouz describes Egypt's political history and depicts the desperate lives of the oppressed.
5. This talented author has written numerous novels and stories.
6. Because of Mahfouz, the novel and short story have become popular modern genres in Arabic literature.
7. Sixteen Egyptian movies have come from his novels.
8. Winner of the Nobel Prize for Literature in 1988, Mahfouz gives his readers a realistic view of urban Egyptian life.
9. With the translation of his books into English, Mahfouz has become increasingly popular and respected in the United States.
10. Praised as Egypt's finest modern writer, Mahfouz has won high honors.
11. Mahfouz offers his readers detailed images of the luxury longed for by Cairo's impoverished population.
12. These hopes and dreams contrast sharply with the reality of their lives.
13. Mahfouz's words give the reader an accurate picture of Cairo's architecture.
14. Readers from other cultures gain an excellent understanding of twentieth-century Egyptian culture.
15. Students of modern Egyptian culture can enhance their understanding of present-day Egyptian life through reading Mahfouz's work.

Close

Ask students to write a paragraph about a place that was important to them when they were growing up. Instruct them to use a variety of sentence elements: simple and compound subjects, simple and compound predicates, and various objects and complements. Then have them read their paragraphs to the class. Have students discuss how writers can give their writing rhythm and variety by varying the kinds of sentence structures that they use.

520

Parts of the Sentence

Mixed Review

The following sentences describe the life of Naguib Mahfouz. Rewrite each sentence on your paper according to the instructions that appear after each item. Make sure your answers are complete sentences.

Naguib Mahfouz

1. The Egyptian author Naguib Mahfouz was born *in 1911* in the city of Cairo. (Rewrite the sentence so that the phrase in italics, which is part of the complete predicate, appears in another position.)
2. Vivid sketches of Cairo are in his books. (Rewrite to begin with *There are.*)
3. In Mahfouz's books, the change in Cairo is depicted. (Add *and its people* to the complete subject.)
4. Mahfouz describes Egypt's political history. (Add *and depicts the desperate lives of the oppressed* to the complete predicate.)
5. This talented author has written numerous novels. (Add *and stories* to create a second direct object.)
6. Because of Mahfouz, the novel and short story have become modern genres in Arabic literature. (Add *popular* as a modifier of the subject complement.)
7. From his novels have come sixteen Egyptian movies. (Rewrite the sentence so that it begins with the complete subject.)
8. Winner of the Nobel Prize for Literature in 1988, Mahfouz gives a realistic view of urban Egyptian life. (Add *his readers* as an indirect object.)
9. With the translation of his books into English, Mahfouz has become increasingly popular in the United States. (Add *and respected* to create a second predicate adjective.)
10. Praised as Egypt's finest modern writer, Mahfouz has won honors. (Add *high* as a modifier of the direct object.)
11. Mahfouz offers detailed images of the luxury longed for by Cairo's impoverished population. (Add *his readers* to serve as an indirect object.)
12. These dreams contrast sharply with the reality of their lives. (Add another simple subject and a conjunction to form a compound subject.)
13. Mahfouz's words give an accurate picture of Cairo's architecture. (Add *the reader* to provide an indirect object.)
14. Readers from other cultures gain an understanding of twentieth-century Egyptian culture. (Add *excellent* to modify the direct object.)
15. Through reading Mahfouz's work, students of modern Egyptian culture can enhance their understanding of present-day Egyptian life. (Rewrite the sentence so that the complete subject comes before the complete predicate.)

Writing Application

Sentence Patterns in Writing

As you read the following passage from "Through the Tunnel" by Doris Lessing, notice how effectively the author varies the length of her sentences and their word order. Pay particular attention to the italicized sentences.

> *Jerry swam out to the big barrier rock, adjusted the goggles, and dived. . . .*
>
> *Under him, six or seven feet down, was a floor of perfectly clean, shining white sand, rippled firm and hard by the tides.* Two grayish shapes steered there, like long rounded pieces of wood or slate. *They were fish.* He saw them nose toward each other, poise motionless, make a dart forward, swerve off, and come around again. *It was like a water dance.* A few inches above them the water sparkled as if sequins were dropping through it.

Techniques with Sentence Patterns

Try to use Lessing's techniques when you write and revise your work.

❶ Use compound subjects or predicates to tie ideas together.

CHOPPY SENTENCE Jerry swam out to the big barrier rock. He adjusted the goggles. He dived.

LESSING'S VERSION Jerry swam out to the big barrier rock, adjusted the goggles, and dived.

❷ Achieve sentence variety by occasionally inverting word order.

GENERAL SENTENCE ORDER A floor of . . . white sand was under him, six or seven feet down.

LESSING'S VERSION Under him, six or seven feet down, was a floor of . . . white sand . . .

❸ Vary the length of your sentences to maintain the reader's interest. Occasionally use a very short sentence to accent a point.

MONOTONOUS PATTERN Two grayish shapes steered there. They were like rounded pieces of wood or slate. The grayish shapes were fish.

LESSING'S VARIATION Two grayish shapes steered there, like long rounded pieces of wood or slate. They were fish.

TIME For more about the writing process, see TIME Facing the Blank Page, pp. 109–119

Parts of the Sentence

Practice Practice these techniques by revising the following passage, adapted from "Through the Tunnel," combining ideas to create a pleasing variety of sentence lengths.

He put on his goggles. He fitted them tight. He tested the vacuum. His hands were shaking. Then he chose the biggest stone. He slipped over the edge of the rock. He looked up once at the empty sky. He filled his lungs once, twice. Then he sank fast to the bottom with the stone. He let it go. He began to count. No strain was on his lungs.

Writing Application **521**

Writing Application

Sentence Patterns in Writing

You may have students read the paragraph aloud. Read it without interruption and then go back and discuss the italicized complement choices. Discuss these choices in relation to the Techniques with Sentence Patterns.

Techniques with Sentence Patterns

Discuss the techniques described and then see how they are used in another piece of writing—for example, a paragraph or two from the proofreading practice earlier in the review.

Practice

The answers to this challenging and enriching activity will vary. Refer to Techniques with Sentence Patterns as you evaluate student choices. Here is Doris Lessing's actual version.

He put on his goggles, fitted them tight, tested the vacuum. His hands were shaking. Then he chose the biggest stone . . . and slipped over the edge of the rock. . . . He looked up once at the empty sky, filled his lungs once, twice, and then sank fast to the bottom with the stone. He let it go and began to count. . . . There was no strain on his lungs.

—Doris Lessing, "Through the Tunnel"

521

Objectives

- To learn about the various kinds of phrases, including prepositional, appositive, and verbal phrases
- To demonstrate control over the use of various kinds of phrases by identifying them and writng sentences using them effectively

Key to Ability Levels

L1 Level 1 activities are within the basic ability range of students.

L2 Level 2 activities are within the ability range of average students.

L3 Level 3 activities are more challenging activities.

UNIT
12 Phrases

Lesson **12.1**   **Prepositional Phrases**   523

Lesson **12.2**   **Appositives and Appositive Phrases**   525

Lesson **12.3**   **Verbals and Verbal Phrases**   527

Grammar Review   532

Writing Application   541

522

Resource Manager

Planning Resources
- *Lesson Plans*
- *Block Scheduling*

📊 **Transparencies**
- *Bellringer*
- *Daily Language Practice*

📁 **Other Print Resources**
- *Grammar and Composition Handbook*
- *Grammar Enrichment*

- *Grammar Practice*
- *Grammar Reteaching*
- *Grammar Workbook*
- *Sentence-Combining Practice*
- *Tests with Answer Key and Rubrics*

 Video
- *MindJogger Videoquizzes*

💾 **Software**
- *Interactive Grammar and Language Workbook*

- *Language Arts PASS*
- *Presentation Plus!*
- *Revising with Style*
- *Testmaker*
- *Writer's Choice Puzzlemaker*

 Web Sites
- *writerschoice.glencoe.com*

12.1 Prepositional Phrases

- A **phrase** is a group of words that acts in a sentence as a single part of speech.
- A **prepositional phrase** is a group of words that begins with a preposition and usually ends with a noun or pronoun, called the **object of the preposition.**

    I voted **against the idea.** [*Idea* is the object of the preposition *against.*]

    The elevator is necessary **for us.** [*Us* is the object of the preposition *for.*]

    The poet Nikki Giovanni was born **in 1943.** [The date *1943* is the object of the preposition *in.*]

For lists of common prepositions, see page 473.

You may find adjectives and other modifiers appearing between the preposition and its object. Note also that a preposition may have more than one object.

    The elevator goes **to the cool, dark basement.** [adjectives added]

    The elevator goes **to the basement and the penthouse.** [two objects]

A prepositional phrase can act as an adjective or an adverb in a sentence. Used as an adjective, a prepositional phrase modifies a noun or a pronoun. Used as an adverb, it modifies a verb, an adjective, or an adverb.

    Take the elevator **on the right.** [adjective phrase modifying the noun *elevator*]

    Which **of these elevators** is working? [adjective phrase modifying the pronoun *which*]

    After the meeting, you should take this elevator **to the lobby.** [adverb phrases modifying the verb phrase *should take*]

    The elevator is helpful **to us.** [adverb phrase modifying the adjective *helpful*]

    We sometimes work late **last night.** [adverb phrase modifying the adverb *late*]

goes to the cool dark basement.

Phrases

12.1 Prepositional Phrases **523**

Focus

Lesson Overview

Objectives

- To identify adjective and adverb prepositional phrases
- To use prepositional phrases appropriately in writing

Bellringer
Daily Language Activity

When students enter the classroom, have this assignment on the board: *Copy the sentence below and underline the prepositional phrases in it.*

> This was a day <u>for singing</u>, a warm winter day, when the touch <u>of the sun</u> <u>upon the back</u> belied the snow high <u>on distant mountains</u>.
>
> —Juanita Platero and Siyowin Miller, "Chee's Daughter"

See also ✍ *Daily Language Practice*

Teach

☑ Teaching Tip

Students may be confused when one prepositional phrase follows another. The following example may help to clarify the issue. In the sentence *We went home after the movie about skiing,* the adverb prepositional phrase *after the movie* modifies *went.* Following is an adjective prepositional phrase, *about skiing,* that modifies the noun *movie.*

Resource Manager

Planning Resources
- *Lesson Plans*

✍ **Transparencies**
- *Bellringer*
- *Daily Language Practice*

📁 **Other Print Resources**
- *Grammar and Composition Handbook*
- *Grammar Enrichment*, p. 13
- *Grammar Practice*, p. 13
- *Grammar Reteaching*, p. 13
- *Grammar Workbook*, Lesson 19
- *Sentence-Combining Practice*, pp. 11, 13

Practice and Assess

Answers: Exercise 1

1. on the Great Plains
2. From an airplane; of abstract art
3. of modern farming methods
4. in shape
5. along the natural contours; of the land
6. with a variety; of textures; from the plowing
7. around a central water source
8. of bright green
9. on the Great Plains
10. of an unplanned collaboration; between the farmer and nature

Answers: Exercise 2

1. alive—adverb
2. resemble—adverb; works—adjective
3. result—adjective
4. rectangular—adverb
5. plow—adverb; contours—adjective
6. patterns—adjective; variety—adjective; result—adverb
7. pivots—adverb
8. areas—adjective
9. No one—adjective
10. bonus—adjective; collaboration—adjective

Answers: Exercise 3

Answers will vary, but a suggestion is given below.

1. At night, the deep blue lake near our house glimmers in the moonlight.

Answers: Exercise 4

Answers will vary, but a suggestion is given below.

1. The lake near our house (adj.) glimmers in the moonlight (adv.).

Additional Resources

 Grammar Practice, p. 13

Grammar Reteaching, p. 13

Grammar Enrichment, p. 13

Sentence Combining Practice, pp. 11, 13

Grammar Workbook

Phrases

Exercise 1   **Identifying Prepositional Phrases**

On your paper, write each prepositional phrase that appears in the following sentences. (Some sentences have more than one prepositional phrase.)

Art in Nature

1. Great environmental art is alive on the Great Plains.
2. From an airplane, the vast cultivated fields resemble works of abstract art.
3. The varied designs are the result of modern farming methods.
4. The plowed fields are basically hilly and rectangular in shape.
5. Farmers plow along the natural contours of the land.
6. Red, brown, and black patterns with a variety of textures result from the plowing.
7. Irrigation equipment often pivots around a central water source.
8. This technique produces huge circular areas of bright green.
9. No one on the Great Plains has consciously planned these designs.
10. They are the bonus of the collaboration between the farmer and nature.

Exercise 2   **Identifying Adjective and Adverb Phrases**

On your paper, write the word or words each prepositional phrase in Exercise 1 modifies. Then write whether each phrase is acting as an *adjective* or an *adverb*.

Exercise 3   **Expanding Sentences with Prepositional Phrases**

On your paper, copy and expand the following sentences by adding at least one adjective phrase and one adverb phrase to each.

SAMPLE   The loud music blared.
ANSWER   The loud music on the car stereo blared through the open windows.

1. The deep blue lake glimmers.
2. No one told me.
3. The two wild horses galloped.
4. The workers piled up the bricks.
5. The dancers rehearsed tirelessly.
6. The engine stopped suddenly.
7. The Dalmatian and the boxer always run.
8. A strong wind is blowing the papers.
9. That old building collapsed.
10. The geese were flying south.

Exercise 4   **Using Prepositional Phrases in Writing**

On your paper, write five sentences that include prepositional phrases. Underline each prepositional phrase; label it as an *adjective* or an *adverb*.

SAMPLE   The tennis club at school meets on Thursday.
ANSWER   at school, adjective; on Thursday, adverb

MEETING INDIVIDUAL NEEDS   English Language Learners

Showing Relationships

Students whose primary languages are not related to any Indo-European language might have problems with prepositions and prepositional phrases because prepositions may not exist in their native languages. Have these students work with more proficient English speakers in completing Exercises 1 through 4.

12.2 Appositives and Appositive Phrases

- An **appositive** is a noun or a pronoun that is placed next to another noun or pronoun to identify or give additional information about it.

    My friend **Myles** sent me a postcard from England. [The appositive *Myles* identifies the noun *friend.*]

- An **appositive phrase** is an apositive plus any words that modify the appositive.

    Joanne rode a hydrofoil across the English Channel, **the body of water between England and France.** [The appositive phrase, in bold type, identifies *English Channel.*]

Appositives or appositive phrases that are not essential to the meaning of a sentence should be set off by commas.

    Myles's sister **Jean** lives there. [The appositive *Jean* is essential because Myles has more than one sister.]

    Myles's only brother, **Timothy,** now lives in Ireland. [The appositive *Timothy* is not necessary to identify the brother.]

Usually an appositive or appositive phrase follows the noun or pronoun it identifies or explains. Occasionally an appositive phrase precedes the noun or pronoun.

    A **talented artist,** Myles would like to become an illustrator of children's books.

| Exercise 5 | Identifying Appositives and Appositive Phrases |

On your paper, write the appositives and appositive phrases in the following sentences.

1. My cousin Andrea broke her leg.
2. She was visited in the hospital by Dan and Rosalia, two friends from school.
3. During her hospital stay, my mother took Andrea a get-well gift, a very cute toy bear.
4. Andrea stayed in the hospital, Memorial Hospital Center, for two days.
5. On Andrea's cast, her sister Camille drew an appropriate cartoon, a rabbit on skis tumbling down a hill.

Phrases

Focus

Lesson Overview

Objectives
- To identify appositives and appositive phrases
- To use appositives and appositive phrases appropriately in writing

Bellringer
Daily Language Activity

When students enter the classroom, have this assignment on the board: *Add appositives to the following sentence:*
    My best friend was describing his favorite vacation place.

See also *Daily Language Practice*

Teach

☑ **Teaching Tip**

When writing nonrestrictive appositives and appositive phrases, students often omit the second comma, which terminates the phrase. Remind students that commas surround nonrestrictive appositives and appositive phrases just as parentheses enclose parenthetical remarks.

Practice and Assess

Answers: Exercise 5
1. Andrea
2. two friends from school
3. a very cute toy bear
4. Memorial Hospital Center
5. Camille; a rabbit on skis tumbling down a hill

Resource Manager

Planning Resources
- *Lesson Plans*

Transparencies
- *Bellringer*
- *Daily Language Practice*

📂 Other Print Resources
- *Grammar and Composition Handbook*
- *Grammar Enrichment,* p. 14
- *Grammar Practice,* p. 14
- *Grammar Reteaching,* p. 14
- *Grammar Workbook,* Lesson 20
- *Sentence-Combining Practice,* p. 9

Practice and Assess

Answers: Exercise 6

1. the first female justice on the United States Supreme Court—Sandra Day O'Connor
2. a Chinese American—Connie Chung
3. Maria Tallchief—Native American
4. an African American author and university professor—Ntozake Shange; *Betsey Brown*—novel.
5. a teacher and scholar—Jeane Kirkpatrick
6. Margaret Mead—anthropologist
7. a farm wife untrained in art—Anna Mary Robertson Moses; Grandma Moses—painter
8. Althea Gibson—tennis player
9. an American actress—Chita Rivera
10. her novel about China—*The Good Earth*

Answers: Exercise 7

Answers will vary, but a suggestion is given below.

1. My sister's dog Gretchen is a champion.

Additional Resources

 Grammar Practice, p. 14
Grammar Reteaching, p. 14
Grammar Enrichment, p. 14
Sentence Combining Practice, p. 9

Grammar Workbook Lesson 20

Close

Have students write paragraphs on a subject of their choice and use appositives and appositive phrases where appropriate. Have students present their paragraphs.

Phrases

Exercise 6 — Identifying Appositives and Appositive Phrases

On your paper, write the appositive or appositive phrase that appears in each sentence. Then write the noun or pronoun that is identified or expanded by the appositive or appositive phrase. (Two sentences have more than one appositive or appositive phrase.)

Leaders in Their Fields

1. Sandra Day O'Connor, the first female justice on the United States Supreme Court, was appointed by President Reagan.
2. A familiar figure on the evening news was Connie Chung, a Chinese American.
3. The Native American Maria Tallchief became a highly accomplished ballerina.
4. Ntozake Shange, an African American author and university professor, wrote a wonderful novel, *Betsey Brown.*
5. The United States Representative to the United Nations from 1981 to 1985 was Jeane Kirkpatrick, a teacher and scholar.
6. The anthropologist Margaret Meade made her reputation by studying native peoples of the South Pacific.
7. Anna Mary Robertson Moses, a farm wife untrained in art, became the famous painter Grandma Moses.
8. The tennis player Althea Gibson was the first African American to win a national American tennis tournament.
9. Chita Rivera, an American actress, has starred in many movies and musicals.
10. Pearl Buck, who received the Nobel Prize for Literature in 1938, is known for *The Good Earth,* her novel about China.

Exercise 7 — Expanding Sentences with Appositive Phrases

On your paper, expand the following sentences by adding an appositive or an appositive phrase to each one. Be sure to use commas where necessary.

SAMPLE   Matthew Henson went on the first expedition to the North Pole.

ANSWER   Matthew Henson, an African American explorer, went on the first expedition to the North Pole.

1. My sister's dog is a champion.
2. My grandfather is my idol.
3. For my birthday, my cousin gave me a compact disc.
4. Sasha's friends look almost like twins.
5. On Sundays, we always have the same dessert.
6. The film is my favorite.
7. My brother volunteered to read to Elizabeth.
8. Mary preferred to take the old road.
9. My favorite singer is going on tour this summer.
10. Mike will help Mrs. Scott shovel her sidewalk.

MEETING INDIVIDUAL NEEDS — English Language Learners

Identifying an Appositive

Students who are learning English may have difficulty with appositives. Point out that one way to identify an appositive, or to distinguish between an appositive phrase and a relative clause, is to substitute the appositive or appositive phrase for the word it renames. All noun modifiers (including relative clauses) fail this test.

12.3 | Verbals and Verbal Phrases

■ A **verbal** is a verb form that functions in a sentence as a noun, an adjective, or an adverb.

■ A **verbal phrase** is a verbal plus any complements and modifiers.

The three kinds of verbals are *participles, gerunds,* and *infinitives.* All of these types can be expanded into phrases.

Participles and Participial Phrases

■ A **participle** is a verb form that can function as an adjective.

Present participles always end in *-ing.* Although *past participles* often end in *-ed,* they can take other forms as well. Many adjectives commonly used in sentences are actually participles.

The **freezing** rain slowly turned to hail.

The **heated** argument occurred among the **losing** players.

A participle can be used as an adjective or as part of a verb phrase.

PARTICIPLE AS ADJECTIVE   The **married** couple have jobs.
PARTICIPLE IN VERB PHRASE The judge **has married** the couple.

■ A **participial phrase** contains a participle plus any complements and modifiers.

Participial phrases can be used in various positions in a sentence. They always act as adjectives.

Pete Sampras **playing tennis** draws large crowds.

Sampras, **disappointed with his first serve,** vowed to improve his game.

Sitting quietly during one of Sampras's games, his fans watch him intently.

Graciously accepting a trophy from the sponsors, he smiled at the crowd.

In general, a participial phrase at the beginning of a sentence is followed by a comma.

Focus

Lesson Overview

Objectives

• To identify participles and participial phrases, gerunds and gerund phrases, and infinitives and infinitive phrases

• To use various verbals and verbal phrases appropriately in writing

Bellringer
Daily Language Activity

When students enter the classroom, have this assignment on the board: *Write a sentence combining the two sentences below. Begin it with a word ending in -ing.*
   My dog ran swiftly.
   He caught the toy car.

See also Daily Language Practice

Teach

Participles and Participial Phrases

☑ Teaching Tip

A good way to explain participles and participial phrases is by using sentence combining. Thus, *My dog ran swiftly* and *He caught the toy car* can be combined into *Running swiftly, my dog caught the toy car.* The verb of one sentence can be made into a participle (*ran–running*) and used as the basis for a participial phrase. The phrase can then be combined with the second sentence.

Resource Manager

Planning Resources
• *Lesson Plans*

📖 Transparencies
• *Bellringer*
• *Daily Language Practice*

📂 Other Print Resources
• *Grammar and Composition Handbook*
• *Grammar Enrichment,* pp. 15–17
• *Grammar Practice,* pp. 15–17
• Grammar Reteaching, pp. 15–17
• *Grammar Workbook,* Lessons 21, 22, 23
• *Sentence-Combining Practice,* pp. 13, 28

Teach

⇄ Cross-reference: Usage

For additional help in forming present and past participles, refer students to Lesson 15.2, pp. 586–588.

Practice and Assess

Answers: Exercise 8

1. looking for more variety—Americans
2. imported from other lands—goods
3. decorated by hand—silk
4. woven in Ecuador—scarf
5. made by French nuns—veils
6. used for men's shirts—fabrics
7. made in Malaysia—cloth
8. imported from Japan—pearls
9. mined in Australia—gold
10. pierced—ears
11. Embroidered—blouses
12. processed in Italy—Leather
13. mined in Brazil—Aquamarines, topaz
14. crafted by Irish workers—Sweaters
15. interesting—fashions

Answers: Exercise 9

Answers will vary, but a sample is given below.

1. Panting in the midday heat, the <u>dog</u> looked exhausted.

Phrases

Exercise 8 Identifying Participles and Participial Phrases

On your paper, write the participle or the participial phrase that acts as an adjective in each sentence. Then identify the word or words each one modifies.

Fashions from Other Lands

1. Americans looking for more variety often adopt the fashions of other countries.
2. The demand for goods imported from other lands is often great.
3. Chinese textile mills export silk decorated by hand.
4. A wool scarf woven in Ecuador is warm and colorful.
5. Brides prize lace veils made by French nuns.
6. Fine cotton fabrics used for men's shirts come from Egypt.
7. Batik cloth made in Malaysia makes beautiful warm-weather dresses and shirts.
8. Freshwater pearls imported from Japan are used for necklaces and earrings.
9. Rings from gold mined in Australia are prized by American women and men.
10. India exports gold hoops for pierced ears.
11. Embroidered blouses from Mexico contain intricate floral designs.
12. Leather processed in Italy is used in elegant shoes and purses.
13. Aquamarines and topaz mined in Brazil make beautiful jewelry.
14. Sweaters crafted by Irish workers are heavy and durable.
15. Shoppers can find interesting fashions from just about anywhere in the world.

Exercise 9 Writing Sentences with Participial Phrases

Use each of the following phrases in a sentence. Use the phrase as a participle, not as part of a verb phrase. Place your participial phrase as close as possible to the noun or pronoun it modifies. Then underline that noun or pronoun.

SAMPLE limping down the empty road
ANSWER Limping down the empty road, the lost <u>dog</u> looked pathetic.

1. panting in the midday heat
2. whining and whimpering with pain
3. frozen in his tracks
4. broken in two places
5. carrying him home on my shoulders
6. reaching our front porch
7. yelling for someone's help
8. hearing my call
9. sprawled helplessly on the porch floor
10. gathering up the dog in her arms
11. grabbing two soft blankets
12. comforted by our tender care
13. arriving at the veterinarian's office
14. known for his skill with animals
15. wagging his tail with glee

MEETING INDIVIDUAL NEEDS **English Language Learners**

Understanding Verbals

Before teaching verbals and verbal phrases to English Language Learners, be sure they have some familiarity with the uses of English verbs, nouns, adjectives, and adverbs. After reviewing these parts of speech, help them understand that a verbal is derived from a verb (hence the name) and that it can function grammatically as a noun, an adjective, or an adverb. ELL students will benefit by working on Exercises 6–11 in partnership with more proficient users of English.

Gerunds and Gerund Phrases

■ A **gerund** is a verb form that ends in *-ing* and is used in the same way a noun is used.

> **Reading** is my favorite pastime. [gerund as subject]
>
> Dana enjoys **running.** [gerund as direct object]
>
> Jin gives **studying** top priority. [gerund as indirect object]
>
> How much time do you devote to **exercising?** [gerund as object of a preposition]
>
> My preference is **dancing.** [gerund as predicate nominative]
>
> Her hobbies, **skiing** and **hiking,** are strenuous and healthful. [gerunds as appositives]

■ A **gerund** phrase is a gerund plus any complements and modifiers.

> Students are responsible for **mastering their subjects.**

Both a present participle and a gerund end in *-ing.* A present participle is used as an adjective, whereas a gerund is used as a noun.

> **Listening** to the radio, Yusuf worked faster. [present participle]
>
> **Listening** to the radio helps Yusuf work faster. [gerund]

Exercise 10 — Identifying Gerunds and Gerund Phrases

On your paper, list the gerunds and gerund phrases that appear in the following sentences. (Some of the sentences have more than one gerund or gerund phrase.)

The Yanomamo

1. Surviving is a challenge for the Yanomamo, a people from the tropical forests of South America.
2. For centuries, the Yanomamo have lived by raising crops, gathering fruits and nuts, and hunting.
3. Living in remote jungle areas had prevented the Yanomamo from having contact with modern civilization.
4. The Yanomamo look for a way of protecting themselves from the greed of the outside world.
5. Mining and ranching have begun to intrude on the lands of the Yanomamo.
6. Contact with outsiders has endangered the Yanomamo by exposing them to diseases.
7. Contracting unfamiliar illnesses is becoming all too common among the Yanomamo.
8. Coping with an indifferent government is another challenge for them.
9. Fighting to save the environment is one Yanomamo project.
10. Saving their homeland is their goal.

Gerunds

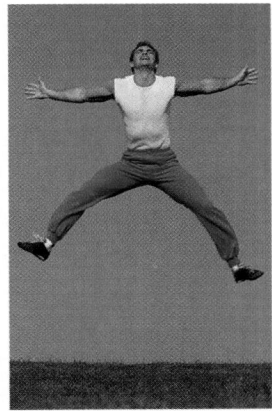

ju*mping*!

Teach

Gerunds and Gerund Phrases

☑ **Teaching Tip**

One way to help students recognize gerunds and gerund phrases is by focusing on their function in the sentence. Gerunds and gerund phrases play all the roles that nouns play: subject, direct object, indirect object, predicate nominative, object of preposition, and appositive. Thus, an *-ing* word used as one of these is *likely* to be a gerund.

Ⓐ **Vocabulary Link**

The term *gerund* comes from a Latin word meaning "to do" or "carry out." The gerund carries over its meaning as a verb to its use as a noun.

Phrases

Practice and Assess

Answers: Exercise 10

1. Surviving
2. raising crops; gathering fruits and nuts; hunting
3. Living in remote jungle areas; having contact with modern civilization
4. protecting themselves from the outside world
5. Mining; ranching
6. exposing them to diseases
7. Contracting unfamiliar illnesses
8. Coping with an indifferent government
9. Fighting to save the environment
10. Saving their homeland

Exploring Language

Applying the *It* Test

Because gerunds and gerund phrases are always nouns and always singular, one test for gerunds and gerund phrases is to replace the gerund phrase with the singular pronoun *it.* The *it* test is especially useful for helping students distinguish between gerunds and present participles, both of which end in *-ing.* For example, in the sentence *We considered flying, flying* can be replaced by *it;* but in the sentence *Flying, we went around the storm clouds,* the participle *flying* cannot be replaced by *it.* Have students practice with sentences such as the ones on this student page. **L2**

Teach

Infinitives and Infinitive Phrases

☑ **Teaching Tips**

Participles are always adjectives, and gerunds are always nouns. Infinitives and infinitive phrases are more difficult to identify because they can function as nouns, adjectives, or adverbs.

Students sometimes confuse infinitives with prepositional phrases that begin with *to*. A simple way to tell them apart is to see whether the word following *to* can be used with the helping verb *will*. If it can, then that word is a verb and the *to* phrase is an infinitive phrase; if it cannot, then the *to* phrase is a prepositional phrase.

Practice and Assess

Answers: Exercise 11

1. to join the American labor movement
2. to change her life
3. to become a union organizer
4. to travel from place to place in a black gown and bonnet
5. to gather evidence for her campaign against child labor
6. to help the garment and streetcar workers
7. to pledge yourselves to stand as one
8. to plead for child labor laws
9. to organize the 1919 steel strike
10. to make a vigorous speech before a camera on her hundredth birthday

Answers: Exercise 12

Answers will vary, but a sample sentence is given below.
1. The square dancers were directed to swing their partners.

Phrases (vertical tab)

Infinitives and Infinitive Phrases

■ An **infinitive** is a verb form that is usually preceded by the word *to* and is used as a noun, an adjective, or an adverb.

When the word *to* appears before the base form of a verb, it is part of the infinitive form of the verb and not a preposition.

To sleep is relaxing. [infinitive as subject]
Every baby needs **to crawl**. [infinitive as direct object]
Her wish is **to succeed**. [infinitive as predicate nominative]
I had a tendency **to doze**. [infinitive as adjective]
He was eager **to rest**. [infinitive as adverb]

■ An **infinitive phrase** contains an infinitive plus any complements and modifiers.

To hike the Appalachian Trail is my sister's dream.
We decided **to dress for the party**.
The committee voted **to appoint Jennifer president**.

Exercise 11 Identifying Infinitives and Infinitive Phrases

On your paper, write the infinitive or infinitive phrase that appears in each of the following sentences. (One sentence has two infinitive phrases.)

Mary Harris Jones, Labor Leader

1. One of the most remarkable figures to join the American labor movement was Mary Harris Jones.
2. In 1880, at the age of 50, Jones decided to change her life.
3. After abandoning her work as a teacher and dressmaker, she proceeded to become a union organizer.
4. Her custom was to travel from place to place in a black gown and bonnet.
5. She worked in the cotton mills of the South to gather evidence for her campaign against child labor.
6. In 1915 she went to New York City to help the garment and streetcar workers.
7. In a speech, she said, "I want you to pledge yourselves . . . to stand as one . . . "
8. She led young millworkers to Washington to plead for child labor laws.
9. Mary Jones helped to organize the 1919 steel strike.
10. Mother Jones, as she was sometimes called, was able to make a vigorous speech before a camera on her hundredth birthday.

Exercise 12 Using Infinitive Phrases

Jot down five action verbs. Then write each one in an infinitive phrase in an original sentence. Underline the infinitive phrases.

English Language Learners

MEETING INDIVIDUAL NEEDS

Marked and Unmarked Infinitives

Most infinitives are used with *to*; some verbs, however, require as their complements infinitives without the *to*—for example: *I made him do it,* not *I made him to do it.* Infinitives used without the *to* are called *unmarked infinitives*. Infinitives used with the *to* are called *marked* infinitives. Students learning English as a second language often incorrectly use the marked infinitive—for example: *I made him to do it.* Have students practice using infinitives with verbs such as *see, watch, hear, make,* and *feel*.

Exercise 13   Identifying Verbal Phrases

On your paper, write the verbal phrases that appear in the following sentences. Write whether each phrase is *participial phrase*, a *gerund phrase*, or an *infinitive phrase*.

Kachina Dolls

1. The word *kachina* is used by the Pueblo peoples in the southwestern United States to name one of the spirit gods.
2. Carving and painting kachina dolls, artists reflect the doll's importance to the people.
3. Used in ceremonies, the dolls are part of the people's beliefs.
4. Raising and planting crops are the most common purposes for ceremonies featuring kachinas.
5. Asking for rain, the people use the dolls.
6. Often, men dressed as kachinas dance in ceremonies.
7. Children watching the dance are not supposed to recognize their fathers dressed as the spirit.
8. Another kachina, a singing kachina, appears on housetops to make announcements.
9. Healing kachinas may be part of ceremonies held for people who are ill.
10. Passing the dolls from one generation to the next, people strengthen the belief in the dolls' powers.
11. Children of the Southwestern pueblos know they are not to play with kachina dolls.
12. Some kachinas bring surprising and exciting gifts to the children, making them feel a part of the ceremonies.
13. The gifts may be fruits and sweets for them to enjoy or toys that remind them of hunting skills.
14. Incorporating their religious beliefs into everyday life is important for the people.
15. In more recent times, artists have begun making kachina dolls to sell to tourists.
16. Some feel that having a singing kachina or a deer kachina may help the buyer understand the purpose of the spirit dolls.
17. Becoming familiar with various spirits may enable a person to respect the beliefs of the native peoples.
18. Many places offering kachinas for sale are approved by the Pueblo peoples.
19. Raising money through sales is important to many communities.
20. However, there are some members of the Southwestern peoples who are reluctant to see their sacred objects sold as souvenirs.

Exercise 14   Using Verbal Phrases

On your paper, write the following verbal phrases in original sentences. Write whether each is used as a *participial phrase*, a *gerund phrase*, or an *infinitive phrase*.

1. collecting money for a canned food drive
2. to set up a contest between classes
3. asking the community
4. to provide a nutritious meal
5. satisfied with the effort

12.3 Verbals and Verbal Phrases   **531**

Practice and Assess

Answers: Exercise 13

1. to name one of the spirit gods (infinitive)
2. Carving and painting kachina dolls (participial)
3. Used in ceremonies (participial)
4. Raising and planting crops (gerund); featuring kachinas (participial)
5. Asking for rain (participial)
6. dressed as kachinas (participial)
7. watching the dance (participial); to recognize their fathers (infinitive); dressed as the spirit (participial)
8. to make announcements (infinitive)
9. held for people who are ill (participial)
10. Passing the dolls from one generation to the next (participial)
11. to play with kachina dolls (infinitive)
12. making them feel a part of the ceremonies (participial)
13. to enjoy (infinitive)
14. Incorporating their religious beliefs into everday life (gerund)
15. making kachina dolls (gerund); to sell to tourists (infinitive)
16. having a singing kachina or a deer kachina (gerund)
17. Becoming familiar with various spirits (gerund)
18. offering kachinas for sale (participial)
19. Raising money through sales (gerund)
20. sold as souvenirs (participial)

Answers: Exercise 14

Sentences will vary. Numbers 2 and 4 are infinitive phrases, 5 is a participial phrase, and 1 and 3 may be used as gerund or participial phrases.

Additional Rescources

📁 *Sentence-Combining Practice,* pp. 13, 28
📁 *Grammar Practice,* pp. 15–17
📁 *Grammar Reteaching,* pp. 15–17
📁 *Grammar Enrichment,* pp. 15–17

📖 *Grammar Workbook Lessons* 21, 22, 23

Close

Have students look through their portfolios for sentences that can be combined using participial, gerund, or infinitive phrases. Ask students to revise their writing and to discuss their changes with a classmate.

531

Teach

About the Literature

After students have read the passage from *The Stuff of Heroes* by Miguel Delibes, initiate a discussion of the contrasts between the two characters in the passage. Then ask students to focus on the highlighted phrases in the passage. Ask them to consider how the sentences in which the phrases appear would sound if the phrases were eliminated.

Linking Grammar and Literature

☑ Teaching Tip

Ask students to identify some of the prepositional phrases that are not highlighted in the passage. (Each sentence in the passage contains at least one prepositional phrase.) You might also ask them to find two additional appositive phrases. (*also leftovers from the Jesuits' departure: Dámaso Valentín and Eduardo Custodio* and *his great passion*)

Critical Thinking

Ask students to write two versions of a paragraph about childhood friends or a related theme. Tell them to use as few phrases as possible in the first version. The second version should contain a variety of phrases, especially prepositional, participial, and appositive phrases. Ask students to form groups to read their paragraphs. Then initiate a discussion about the ways in which phrases can add color and vivid details to prose.

✔ ASSESSMENT OPTIONS

📂 *Tests with Answer Key & Rubrics*
Unit 12 Mastery Test, pp. 41–42

💾 *Testmaker*
Unit 12 Mastery Test

PHRASES

The Stuff of Heroes is about a young boy named Gervasio, who learns about bravery firsthand during the Spanish civil war. Gervasio's family is divided by the conflict, which began in 1936 and lasted for three bitter years. This excerpt from the novel contains a vivid description of two friends of Gervasio's from school. The excerpt, translated from the Spanish, has been annotated to show the kinds of phrases covered in this unit.

Phrases

Literature Model

from The Stuff of Heroes
by Miguel Delibes
translated from the Spanish by Frances M. López-Morillas

In those days the gang gained two new members, also leftovers from the Jesuits' departure: Dámaso Valentín and Eduardo Custodio. Dámaso wore his hair in a brush cut; his thin, elastic lips and the open smiling expression **of his light brown eyes** brought an enormous joie de vivre to the group. The youngest of five brothers, all of whom had left home, he lived **with his widowed mother and two old servants** in the most aristocratic part of town. Perhaps because life was easy for him and his weekly allowance double that of his friends, Dámaso was always smiling, and when he did so he displayed a notched front tooth (souvenir of a childhood fall) which he daintily caressed with the tip of his active red tongue. **An adaptable and generous boy,** he accepted enthusiastically any plan **suggested by his friends** and his prosperity even allowed him to place his small personal properties at the group's disposal. This was the case of the hard rubber ball with which, shortly after they had met him, they began to play after school on the sidewalk that ran alongside the park, **defying the zeal of the municipal guards.**

Annotations (left column labels):
- Prepositional phrase (adjective phrase)
- Prepositional phrase (adverb phrase)
- Appositive phrase
- Participial phrase (past participle)
- Participial phrase (present participle)

Resource Manager

📖 **Transparencies**
• *Lesson Plans*

📂 **Other Print Resources**
• *Grammar and Composition Handbook*
• *Grammar Workbook,* Lessons 19–23; Unit 3 Review; *Cumulative Review:* Units 1–3

Eduardo Custodio was the other; pale, slow, and round-about in speech, with a touch of humor, he suffered from a premature aging that showed in his nearsightedness, his heavy eyelids, his limpness, and a certain stiffness of the legs for which he tried to compensate with tenacity and pride when he played soccer, his great passion. He did not use glasses, and usually combated his myopia by pulling at the outside corner of his eye to make images clearer, and when he went to the movies or some other kind of show he used opera glasses that had belonged to his great-grandmother.

Infinitive phrase

Gerund phrase

| Review: Exercise 1 | Expanding Sentences with Prepositional Phrases |

The following sentences describe an imaginary street scene. Read through the sentences quickly to get an idea of the scene, and then rewrite each sentence, adding at least one prepositional phrase, used as an adjective or an adverb, to each sentence.

SAMPLE   Today was market day.
ANSWER   Today was market day in the small Spanish town.

1. The town had a spacious plaza.
2. The fountain was a gathering place.
3. Farmers brought fresh potatoes and melons.
4. Farmhands arranged their produce.
5. Storekeepers exhibited their wares.
6. Some merchants displayed bundles.
7. Weary teams pulled heavy wagons.
8. Men carefully unloaded the wagons.
9. Fishmongers arranged their freshest fish.
10. The pearly scales gleamed.
11. Weavers exhibited woolen rugs.
12. Each rug had been carefully woven.
13. The leather merchant sold belts.
14. He also sold gloves.
15. A breeze cooled the air.
16. The hot sun cast shadows.
17. Baskets decorated the greengrocer's stall.
18. Wooden crates overflowed.
19. A noisy group assembled.
20. They splashed their hands and ran off.

Phrases

Grammar Review   **533**

Practice and Assess

Answers: Exercise 1

Answers may vary, but some suggestions are given below.

1. The town had a spacious plaza with an elegant fountain.
2. The fountain was a gathering place for the townspeople.
3. Farmers from the countryside brought fresh potatoes and melons.
4. Farmhands arranged their produce in neat piles.
5. Storekeepers exhibited their wares on sturdy tables.
6. Some merchants displayed bundles of colored cloth.
7. Weary teams of horses pulled heavy wagons.
8. Men in heavy work clothes carefully unloaded the wagons.
9. Fishmongers arranged their freshest fish on beds of ice.
10. The pearly scales gleamed in the morning light.
11. Weavers exhibited woolen rugs with intricate designs.
12. Each rug had been carefully woven by a skilled worker.
13. The leather merchant sold belts of sturdy cowhide.
14. He also sold gloves in various sizes.
15. A breeze cooled the air between the canvas walls of the stalls.
16. The hot sun cast shadows across the busy plaza.
17. Baskets of fresh flowers decorated the greengrocer's stall.
18. Wooden crates overflowed with fruits and vegetables.
19. A noisy group assembled by the fountain.
20. They splashed their hands in the cool water and ran off.

Practice and Assess

Answers: Exercise 2

Answers will vary, but some suggestions are given below.

1. Dámaso Valentín, a high-spirited boy, brought to the group great verve, along with a taste of prosperity.
2. He lived with his mother, a widow.
3. Dámaso's family, relatively affluent aristocrats, lived in a house in the nicest part of town.
4. Dámaso's constant smile revealed a notched front tooth, the result of a fall.
5. The others in the group, less affluent boys, could usually count on Dámaso's generosity.
6. After school the group would play on the sidewalk with a hard rubber ball, a possession of Dámaso's.
7. Eduardo Custodio's nearsightedness and stiff legs, middle-aged infirmities, made him seem old before his time.
8. Eduardo played soccer, his great passion, with tenacity.
9. At the movies, he used opera glasses, relics of his great-grandmother's day.
10. In many ways, Eduardo, a slow and cautious boy, was the opposite of the lighthearted Dámaso.
11. While Dámaso was quick, Eduardo, a deliberate and arthritic boy, was slow.
12. At soccer, a game that punishes the slow, Eduardo's self-discipline moved him beyond his limitations.
13. He always played for a goal, proof of his athletic skills.
14. The others admired Eduardo's persistence, a quality that made him one of the best players.
15. Eduardo's dignity, a trait not often found in one his age, earned him respect.
16. Pride kept Eduardo from wearing glasses, a symbol of weakness in his opinion.
17. In sharp contrast to Eduardo was Dámaso, a vibrant and healthy boy.
18. A very different sort of person, Dámaso seemed to float through the ups and downs of daily life.
19. His background, a life of comfort, gave him a favorable view of the world.
20. Dámaso, an easy-going and kindly boy, was immensely likable.

534

| Review: Exercise 2 | Expanding Sentences with Appositives and Appositive Phrases |

The sentences below elaborate on ideas suggested by the passage from *The Stuff of Heroes.* Rewrite each sentence, incorporating the words in parentheses as an appositive or an appositive phrase. Use a comma or commas to set off the appositive or appositive phrase from the rest of the sentence.

SAMPLE   Dámaso and Eduardo were the two new members of the gang. (leftovers from the Jesuits' departure)

ANSWER   Dámaso and Eduardo, leftovers from the Jesuits' departure, were the two new members of the gang.

1. Dámaso Valentín brought to the group great verve, along with a taste of prosperity. (a high-spirited boy)
2. He lived with his mother. (a widow)
3. Dámaso's family lived in a house in the nicest part of town. (relatively affluent aristocrats)
4. Dámaso's constant smile revealed a notched front tooth. (the result of a fall)
5. The others in the group could usually count on Dámaso's generosity. (less affluent boys)
6. After school, the group would play on the sidewalk with a hard rubber ball. (a possession of Dámaso's)
7. Eduardo Custodio's nearsightedness and stiff legs made him seem old before his time. (middle-aged infirmities)
8. Eduardo played soccer with tenacity. (his great passion)
9. At the movies, he used opera glasses. (relics of his great-grandmother's day)
10. In many ways, Eduardo was the opposite of the lighthearted Dámaso. (a slow and cautious boy)
11. While Dámaso was quick, Eduardo was slow. (a deliberate and arthritic boy)
12. At soccer, Eduardo's self-discipline moved him beyond his limitations. (a game that punishes the slow)
13. He always played for a goal. (proof of his athletic skills)
14. The others admired Eduardo's persistence. (a quality that made him one of the best players)
15. Eduardo's dignity earned him respect. (a trait not often found in one his age)
16. Pride kept Eduardo from wearing glasses. (a symbol of weakness in his opinion)
17. In sharp contrast to Eduardo was Dámaso. (a vibrant and healthy boy)
18. Dámaso seemed to float through the ups and downs of daily life. (a very different sort of person)
19. His background gave him a favorable view of the world. (a life of comfort)
20. Dámaso was immensely likable. (an easy-going and kindly boy)

Phrases

Review: Exercise 3   Expanding Sentences with Participial Phrases

The following sentences describe scenes in *The Stuff of Heroes*. Combine the sentences, changing the sentence in parentheses into a participial phrase. Be sure to place the participial phrase near the word that it modifies.

SAMPLE   Dámaso and Eduardo found their school closed.
          (They were beginning the new school year.)
ANSWER   Beginning the new school year, Dámaso and Eduardo found their school closed.

1. The Jesuits shut their schools.
   (The Jesuits were expelled from Spain by the government.)
2. Dámaso and Eduardo sought new friends.
   (Dámaso and Eduardo were feeling self-conscious in their new school.)
3. Gervasio warmly greeted his two new classmates.
   (Gervasio was seeing new faces.)
4. Gervasio's circle of friends gained two new members.
   (The circle of friends was welcoming Dámaso and Eduardo.)
5. Dámaso quickly made friends with everyone.
   (Dámaso was smiling his customary smile.)
6. Dámaso looked sleek and contemporary.
   (Dámaso was wearing his hair in a brush cut.)
7. Dámaso's friends often visited his house.
   (The house was located in an aristocratic part of town.)
8. Dámaso's mother was generous.
   (She was giving him double the weekly allowance of his friends.)
9. The boy had an easy life. (He was experiencing little hardship.)
10. The municipal guards once caught Gervasio's gang.
    (The boys were playing ball on the sidewalk alongside the park.)
11. One of Gervasio's relatives used his influence on the boy's behalf.
    (The relative was conferring with a sergeant of the guards.)
12. The police freed the boys and returned their ball.
    (The police were dropping the charges.)
13. Eduardo Custodio was pale and slow.
    (He was suffering from premature aging.)
14. Eduardo never made excuses for himself.
    (He was often vexed by the stiffness in his legs.)
15. He did not wear eyeglasses. (He was hiding his nearsightedness.)
16. The violence of civil war would soon interrupt the boy's sheltered lives.
    (The violence was provoked by a miners' strike.)

Grammar Review   **535**

Phrases

Practice and Assess

Answers: Exercise 3
Answers will vary.
1. The Jesuits, expelled from Spain by the government, shut their schools.
2. Dámaso and Eduardo, feeling self-conscious in their new school, sought new friends.
3. Seeing new faces, Gervasio warmly greeted his two new classmates.
4. Welcoming Dámaso and Eduardo, Gervasio's circle of friends gained two new members.
5. Smiling his customary smile, Dámaso quickly made friends with everyone.
6. Wearing his hair in a brush cut, Dámaso looked sleek and contemporary.
7. Dámaso's friends often visited his house, located in an aristocratic part of town.
8. Dámaso's mother was generous, giving him double the weekly allowance of his friends.
9. Experiencing little hardship, the boy had an easy life.
10. The municipal guards once caught Gervasio's gang playing ball on the sidewalk alongside the park.
11. Conferring with a sergeant of the guards, one of Gervasio's relatives used his influence on the boys' behalf.
12. The police, dropping the charges, freed the boys and returned their ball.
13. Suffering from premature aging, Eduardo Custodio was pale and slow.
14. Often vexed by the stiffness in his legs, Eduardo never made excuses for himself.
15. Hiding his nearsightedness, he did not wear eyeglasses.
16. The violence of civil war, provoked by a miners' strike, would soon interrupt the boys' sheltered lives.

Grammar Review

Practice and Assess

Answers: Exercise 4

Answers will vary, but some suggestions are given below.

1. Creating a vast colonial empire was Spain's goal at one time.
2. Losing its Latin American colonies set off Spain's decline.
3. Fighting a bloody civil war divided the country before World War II.
4. General Francisco Franco unified Spain by ruling the country as a dictator from 1939 to 1975.
5. Many people opposed Franco for accepting military aid from Hitler.
6. Being ruled by the fascist dictator Franco made Spain an outcast in post-war Europe.
7. Many people in Spain feared returning to the violence of civil war.
8. Restoring the monarchy in 1975 brought political reforms to Spain.
9. King Juan Carlos favored liberalizing Franco's harsh policies.
10. Joining the European Economic Community in 1986 finally made Spain a full participant in Western European society.
11. Participating in free trade with other countries has begun to improve the standard of living in Spain.
12. Franco's opposing the Soviet Union and communism made Spain attractive to the United States during the cold war.
13. By loaning Franco's government millions of dollars, the United States helped Spain during the cold war.
14. Spain helped the United States during the cold war by allowing the United States to set up military bases in Spain.
15. Defending Europe against possible Soviet attack was the purpose of the American military bases in Spain.
16. Joining the United Nations in 1955 improved Spain's standing with other nations.
17. By donating millions of dollars in aid, the United States helped Spain during its time of economic hardship.
18. Undertaking a financial reform program helped pull Spain out of its economic difficulties in the early 1960s.
19. Spain's reward for undergoing financial reform was receiving membership in the European Economic Community.

Phrases

Grammar Review

Review: Exercise 4   Writing Sentences with Gerund Phrases

Each of the following items consists of a question followed by a phrase in parentheses that answers the question. For each item, write a sentence that answers the question, using the words in parentheses as a gerund phrase.

SAMPLE   What helps explain Spain's role in Europe today? (understanding Spanish history)

ANSWER   Understanding Spanish history helps explain Spain's role in Europe today.

1. What was Spain's goal at one time? (creating a vast colonial empire)
2. What set off Spain's decline? (losing its Latin American colonies)
3. What divided the country before World War II? (fighting a bloody civil war)
4. By what means did Franco unify Spain? (ruling the country as a dictator)
5. Many people opposed Franco for what action? (accepting military aid from Hitler)
6. What made Spain an outcast in postwar Europe? (being ruled by a fascist dictator)
7. Many Spaniards feared what turn of events? (returning to civil war)
8. What brought political reforms to Spain? (restoring the monarchy in 1975)
9. What did King Juan Carlos favor? (liberalizing Franco's harsh policies)
10. What finally made Spain a full participant in Western European society? (joining the European Economic Community in 1986)
11. What has begun to improve the standard of living in Spain? (participating in free trade with other countries)
12. What made Spain attractive to the United States during the cold war? (Franco's opposing the Soviet Union and communism)
13. How did the United States help Spain during the cold war? (loaning Franco's government millions of dollars)
14. What did Spain do to help the United States during the cold war? (allowing the United States to set up military bases in Spain)
15. What was the purpose of the American military bases in Spain? (defending Europe against possible Soviet attack)
16. What improved Spain's standing with other nations? (joining the United Nations in 1955)
17. How did the United States help Spain during its time of economic hardship? (donating millions of dollars in aid)
18. What helped pull Spain out of its economic difficulties in the early 1960s? (undertaking a financial reform program)
19. What was Spain's reward for undergoing financial reform? (receiving membership in the European Economic Community)
20. To what can the Spanish people now look forward? (becoming an even more prosperous and respected nation)

20. The Spanish people can now look forward to becoming an even more prosperous and respected nation.

Review: Exercise 5 — Writing Sentences with Infinitive Phrases

The following sentences are based on passages from *The Stuff of Heroes* that are not reprinted in this textbook. Each item consists of a question followed by a phrase in parentheses that answers the question. For each item, write on your paper a sentence that answers the question, using the words in parentheses as an infinitive phrase.

SAMPLE What was Gervasio's childhood dream? (to be a crusader)
ANSWER Gervasio's childhood dream was to be a crusader.

1. What was Gervasio's great desire? (to perform deeds of courage)
2. What did he hope to do? (to battle the enemy)
3. What did these ambitions only manage to do? (to give him goose flesh)
4. What did Gervasio's fervor make his classmates want to do?
   (to laugh at his zeal)
5. When rebels attacked, what was Gervasio's plan?
   (to shoot stones from his slingshot at the attackers)
6. What did Gervasio have to do to become a hero in his own eyes?
   (to participate fully in the battle)
7. What was Gervasio able to do because he began his career as a hero?
   (to feel triumphant)
8. Later, when the civil war broke out, what did Gervasio, Dámaso, and Eduardo volunteer to do? (to join Franco's navy)
9. According to Dámaso, what was the greatest honor? (to die for the cause)
10. What did a torpedo attack force Gervasio to do? (to confront paralyzing fear)
11. What would Gervasio be able to do if he performed courageous deeds?
    (to fulfill a personal goal)
12. What was Gervasio's personal goal? (to prove to himself that he was brave)
13. What did his thoughts of bravery continue to do?
    (to show him how frightened he really was)
14. What did Gervasio's classmates continue to do? (to ridicule his enthusiasm)
15. When he used his slingshot, what was Gervasio's hope? (to have accurate aim)
16. What did Gervasio have to do to gain self-respect? (to fight bravely)
17. As a hero, what would Gervasio have to do? (to take on more responsibility)
18. What did Gervasio, Dámaso, and Eduardo want to do during the civil war?
    (to become sailors)
19. What might be necessary when fighting for a cause?
    (to sacrifice oneself for one's beliefs)
20. What would Gervasio be able to do by engaging in armed conflict?
    (to meet his fear and work through it)

Phrases

Grammar Review **537**

Practice and Assess

Answers: Exercise 5

Answers will vary, but some suggestions are given below.

1. Gervasio's great desire was to perform deeds of courage.
2. He hoped to battle the enemy.
3. These ambitions only managed to give him goose flesh.
4. Gervasio's fervor made his classmates want to laugh at his zeal.
5. When rebels attacked, Gervasio's plan was to shoot stones from his slingshot at the attackers.
6. To become a hero in his own eyes, Gervasio had to participate fully in the battle.
7. Because he began his career as a hero, Gervasio was able to feel triumphant.
8. Later, when the civil war broke out, Gervasio, Dámaso, and Eduardo volunteered to join Franco's navy.
9. According to Dámaso, the greatest honor was to die for the cause.
10. A torpedo attack forced Gervasio to confront paralyzing fear.
11. If he performed courageous deeds, Gervasio would be able to fulfill a personal goal.
12. Gervasio's personal goal was to prove to himself that he was brave.
13. His thoughts of bravery continued to show him how frightened he really was.
14. Gervasio's classmates continued to ridicule his enthusiasm.
15. When he used his slingshot, Gervasio's hope was to have accurate aim.
16. To gain self-respect, Gervasio had to fight bravely.
17. As a hero, Gervasio would have to take on more responsibility.
18. During the civil war, Gervasio, Dámaso, and Eduardo wanted to become sailors.
19. To sacrifice oneself for one's beliefs might be necessary when fighting for a cause.
20. By engaging in armed conflict, Gervasio would be able to meet his fear and work through it.

Practice and Assess

Answers: Exercise 6

Sentences will vary, but some suggestions are given below.

1. Eduardo played soccer with great skill.
2. A boy with enormous joie de vivre, Dámaso was always smiling.
3. The boys played the game suggested by Eduardo.
4. Playing soccer was his great passion.
5. The plan was to play after school.

Answers: Exercise 7
Proofreading

This proofreading activity provides editing practice with (1) the current or previous units' skills, (2) the **Troubleshooter** errors, and (3) spelling errors. Students should be able to complete the exercise by referring to the units, the **Troubleshooter,** and a dictionary.

Phrases

Error (Type of Error)

1. 1908, (introductory participial phrase)
   world's (singular possessive)
2. manufacturer, (nonessential appositive)
3. twenty-three, (introductory participial phrase)
4. believed (spelling)
5. photography, (introductory participial phrase)
   situation, (nonessential appositive)
6. camera, (nonessential appositive)
7. enabled him (pronoun-antecedent agreement)
   quickly, (commas in a series)
8. past, (introductory participial phrase)
9. painter, (introductory participial phrase)
10. Mexico, (commas in a series)
    documentary (spelling)
11. World War II, (introductory participial phrase)
12. Magnum, (nonessential appositive)
13. Cartier-Bresson's (singular possessive)
14. wall, (introductory participial phrase)
    Seville, (nonessential appositive)
15. extraordinary (spelling)
16. hang (subject-verb agreement)

On your paper, write sentences according to the directions that follow. Make your sentences relate to *The Stuff of Heroes*, but do not copy sentences from the passage.

SAMPLE   Write a sentence that includes a prepositional phrase used as an adjective.
ANSWER   The *Stuff of Heroes* is a book about a young boy named Gervasio.

1. Write a sentence using a prepositional phrase that is an adverb.
2. Write a sentence that begins with an appositive phrase.
3. Write a sentence in which a participial phrase modifies the direct object.
4. Make a gerund phrase the subject of a sentence.
5. Write a sentence using an infinitive phrase as a noun.

Proofreading

The following passage describes Henri Cartier-Bresson, the photographer whose work appears on the opposite page. Rewrite the passage, correcting the errors in spelling, grammar, and usage. Add any missing punctuation. There are twenty-five errors.

Henri Cartier-Bresson

¹Born in Chanteloup, France, in 1908 the photographer Henri Cartier-Bresson ranks among the worlds great photojournalists. ²The son of a wealthy thread manufacturer he began drawing and painting when he was very young. ³Recuperating from an illness at the age of twenty-three he discovered photography.

⁴Cartier-Bresson beleived that a photographer should record life as it is, not as the photographer wants it to be. ⁵Disliking the posed pictures common in studio photography he liked to capture the "decisive moment" of a situation the moment in which the essence of a scene is revealed. ⁶During the year of 1933, he bought his first Leica camera a small instrument equipped with a quiet shutter. ⁷This camera enabled you to take photographs quickly easily, and inconspicuously. ⁸Indebted to the great films of the past Cartier-Bresson learned to choose expressive images for his photos. ⁹Trained as a painter he always carried a sketch pad along with his camera.

¹⁰In the decade of the 1930s, Cartier-Bresson documented the lives of people in Mexico worked with the great French film director Jean Renoir, and made his own documentory about Spanish hospitals. ¹¹Captured by the Germans during World War II he escaped from prison on his third attempt. ¹²Later, he helped establish Magnum a photo agency. ➡

Phrases

Henri Cartier-Bresson, *Seville*, 1933

Proofreading
Answers: Exercise 7
(continued)
Error (Type of Error)
17. *Heroes*, (introductory participial phrase)
18. manages (subject-verb agreement)
his (pronoun-antecedent agreement)
19. world's (singular possessive)

¹³*Seville* is typical of Cartier-Bressons documentary style. ¹⁴Taken through a break in a wall the photograph shows a group of children playing in a poor neighborhood in Seville a city in Spain. ¹⁵The composition is extrordinary and seemingly casual. ¹⁶All the elements in the picture hangs in a delicate balance.

¹⁷Writing about the Spanish Civil War in *The Stuff of Heroes* Miguel Delibes describes children who are forced to endure hardships. ¹⁸Each of the boys in Delibes's story manage to survive by creating their own imaginary world. ¹⁹This world mirrors the real worlds conflict, yet it is also full of humor and joy.

Review: Exercise 8

Mixed Review

The biographical sketch of Miguel Delibes [mē gel´ dā lē´ bes] that appears here is followed by ten numbered sentences. Use the facts in the sketch to revise the ten items, following the guidelines that appear in parentheses at the end of each sentence. Be sure to place any phrase you add near the word it modifies.

Viewing the Art

Henri Cartier-Bresson, *Seville*, 1933
This is a masterful example of Henri Cartier-Bresson's philosophy of the "decisive moment." The photographer has captured the precise instant when all the pictorial elements hang in perfect balance. The photograph is also a moving historical document that dramatically foreshadows the Spanish Civil War. If

Cartier-Bresson's portrait is descriptive, it is also non-judgmental. Similarly, Miguel Delibes's descriptions of the young Spanish boys in *The Stuff of Heroes* are clear and precise, yet they are not maudlin.

Practice and Assess

Answers: Exercise 8
Mixed Review

Answers will vary, but some suggestions are given below.

1. Miguel Delibes is a popular and admired novelist of contemporary Spain.
2. Born in the province of Castile, Delibes sets most of his fiction in that region.
3. The Spanish civil war began in 1936.
4. Spain was torn by fighting between fascists and socialists.
5. Delibes volunteered to serve in General Francisco Franco's army during the civil war.
6. After the war, Delibes devoted himself to studying law, business, and journalism.
7. T*he Cypress Casts a Long Shadow*, Delibes's first novel, won the 1947 Nadal Prize.
8. Inspired by this prestigious award, Delibes decided to write more novels.
9. Six of Delibes's works have been translated into English.
10. In *The Stuff of Heroes*, Gervasio is the name of the main character.

Close

Have students look through their portfolios for places where they can improve their writing by using phrases to show relationships between ideas, to add information to sentences, and to vary the rhythm of their writing. Encourage students to revise their writing accordingly.

Phrases

Miguel Delibes

Miguel Delibes is one of Spain's most admired novelists. He was born in 1920 in Valladolid in the province of Castile, and most of his novels are set in that region. During Delibes's youth, Spain was torn by a civil war (1936–1939). General Francisco Franco's Nationalist forces, supported by Nazi Germany and Fascist Italy, battled the leftist Republican forces, which were aided by the Soviet Union. Franco emerged victorious, ruling Spain as a dictator until 1975. During the civil war, Delibes served as a volunteer in Franco's army.

After the war, Delibes earned degrees in law, business, and journalism. His first novel, *The Cypress Casts a Long Shadow,* won the Nadal Prize in 1947. This early success inspired Delibes to become a writer in addition to pursuing an academic career. Six of his many novels and works of nonfiction have been translated into English, including his most popular novel, *El Camino* (1950), published in English as *The Path.* Delibes's novel *The Stuff of Heroes* (1987) is a coming-of-age story based on his experiences as a school boy in Valladolid and as a volunteer in the civil war. Through Gervasio, its main character, the novel explores the meaning of heroism, bravery, and loyalty against the backdrop of divided allegiances within a family and a nation.

1. Miguel Delibes is a popular and admired novelist.
   (Add an adjective prepositional phrase.)
2. Delibes was born in the province of Castile. He sets most of his fiction in that region.
   (Combine the sentences by turning the first sentence into a participial phrase.)
3. The Spanish civil war began. (Add an adverb prepositional phrase.)
4. Spain was torn by something. It was fighting between fascists and socialists.
   (Combine the sentences by turning the second sentence into a gerund phrase.)
5. What did Delibes volunteer to do during the civil war?
   (Respond with a sentence that includes an infinitive phrase.)
6. After the war, Delibes devoted himself to something. He was studying law, business, and journalism.
   (Combine the sentences by turning the second sentence into a gerund phrase.)
7. *The Cypress Casts a Long Shadow* won the 1947 Nadal Prize.
   (Add an appositive phrase.)
8. Delibes was inspired by this prestigious award. Delibes decided to write more novels.
   (Combine the sentences by turning the first sentence into a participial phrase.)
9. Six of Delibes's works have been translated. (Add an adverb prepositional phrase.)
10. In *The Stuff of Heroes,* Gervasio is the name.
    (Add an adjective prepositional phrase.)

Writing Application

Phrases in Writing

William Least Heat-Moon uses many phrases in this passage from *Blue Highways: A Journey Into America*. Read the passage, focusing especially on the italicized phrases.

The highway made an unexpected jog toward Navajo Bridge, *a melding of silvery girders and rock cliffs.* Suddenly, there it was, far below *in the deep and scary canyon of sides so sheer* they might have been cut *with a stone saw,* the naturally silted water turned an unnatural green . . . *by the big settling basin a few miles upriver* called Glen Canyon Dam. Navajo Bridge, *built in 1929 when paved roads began opening the area,* is the only crossing *over the Colorado* between Glen Canyon and Hoover Dam several hundred miles downstream.

Techniques with Phrases

Try to apply some of William Least Heat-Moon's techniques in your own work.

❶ Use prepositional phrases to explain location and to add precision.

GENERAL WORDS Suddenly, there it was, far below . . .

LEAST HEAT-MOON'S VERSION Suddenly, there it was, far below *in the deep and scary canyon* . . .

❷ Consider whether appositive phrases can make your writing more vivid. For example, Least Heat-Moon uses an appositive phrase to help readers picture the Navajo Bridge.

GENERAL WORDS The highway made an unexpected jog toward Navajo Bridge. . . .

LEAST HEAT-MOON'S VERSION The highway made an unexpected jog toward Navajo Bridge, *a melding of silvery girders and rock cliffs.*

❸ Use verbal phrases to improve the flow of your sentences and to show relationships between ideas.

REPETITIVE SENTENCES Navajo Bridge was built in 1929 when paved roads began opening the area. Navajo Bridge is the only crossing . . .

LEAST HEAT-MOON'S VERSION Navajo Bridge, *built in 1929 when paved roads began opening the area,* is the only crossing . . .

> **TIME** For more about the writing process, see TIME Facing the Blank Page, pp. 109–119

Phrases

Practice Practice these techniques by expanding the following paragraph. Use prepositional phrases, appositive phrases, and verbal phrases to make ideas more precise and vivid.

My friends and I stood on the rim of the canyon. The sun was setting. The canyon walls reflected the soft rays. Different shades of red blended into each other. Long shadows crossed the ground. Long shadows hid some of the detail on the canyon's floor. In the distance we could see a small village. An old man rode his horse next to the river. A solitary woman tended a fire. Smoke from the fire rose. A lone eagle soared in and out of the gorge. The only noise I could hear was the slight breeze. It was rustling the leaves on the trees nearby.

Writing Application **541**

Objectives

- To learn about clauses and about simple, compound, complex, and compound-complex sentences
- To demonstrate control over the use of clauses and the various kinds of sentences by identifying them and employing them effectively in writing

✔ ASSESSMENT OPTIONS

📁 *Tests with Answer Key & Rubrics*
Unit 13 Pretest, pp. 43–44
Unit 13 Mastery Test, pp. 45–46

💾 *Testmaker*
Unit 13 Pretest
Unit 13 Mastery Test

You may wish to administer the Unit 13 Pretest at this point.

Key to Ability Levels

L1 Level 1 activities are within the basic ability range of students.

L2 Level 2 activities are within the ability range of average students.

L3 Level 3 activities are more challenging activities.

UNIT
13 Clauses and Sentence Structure

Lesson **13.1** **Main Clauses** 543

Lesson **13.2** **Subordinate Clauses** 544

Lesson **13.3** **Simple and Compound Sentences** 545

Lesson **13.4** **Complex and Compound-Complex Sentences** 547

Lesson **13.5** **Adjective Clauses** 549

Lesson **13.6** **Adverb Clauses** 551

Lesson **13.7** **Noun Clauses** 553

Lesson **13.8** **Four Kinds of Sentences** 556

Lesson **13.9** **Sentence Fragments** 557

Lesson **13.10** **Run-on Sentences** 559

Grammar Review 562

Writing Application 573

542

Resource Manager

Planning Resources
- *Lesson Plans*
- *Block Scheduling*

📖 **Transparencies**
- *Bellringer*
- *Daily Language Practice*
- *Two-Minute Skill Drill*

📁 **Other Print Resources**
- *Grammar and Composition Handbook*

- *Grammar Enrichment*
- *Grammar Practice*
- *Grammar Reteaching*
- *Grammar Workbook*
- *Sentence-Combining Practice*
- *Tests with Answer Key and Rubrics*

📼 **Video**
- *MindJogger Videoquizzes*

💾 **Software**
- *Interactive Grammar and Language Workbook*
- *Language Arts PASS*
- *Presentation Plus!*
- *Revising with Style*
- *Testmaker*
- *Writer's Choice Puzzlemaker*

🖥 **Web Sites**
- *writerschoice.glencoe.com*

13.1 Main Clauses

■ A **clause** is a group of words that has a subject and a predicate and that is used as a part of a sentence.

Clauses fall into two categories: *main clauses*, which are also called *independent clauses*, and *subordinate clauses*, which are also called *dependent clauses*.

■ A **main clause** has a subject and a predicate and can stand alone as a sentence.

There must be at least one main clause in every sentence. Both of the clauses in each of the following examples are main clauses because both can stand alone as sentences.

MAIN CLAUSE	MAIN CLAUSE
Stories entertain,	and people listen.
SUBJECT VERB	SUBJECT VERB

MAIN CLAUSE	MAIN CLAUSE
The author wrote vividly,	but the editor asked for many changes.
SUBJECT VERB	SUBJECT VERB

MAIN CLAUSE	MAIN CLAUSE
The major critics cheered,	and the book sold because of the good reviews.
SUBJECT VERB	SUBJECT VERB

Exercise 1   Identifying Main Clauses

On your paper, copy the following sentences and mark each main clause. Then write *S* below each subject and *V* below each verb. Be sure that each clause you mark can stand alone as a sentence.

SAMPLE ANSWER

The book reached the bookstores, and the advertising campaign began.
    S   **V**   **S**   **V**

1. The publishers advertised, and the bookstore owners responded.
2. The book's cover was a striking design, and the author was pleased.
3. The author toured, and television hosts interviewed her.
4. Sometimes she gave readings, but few people attended.
5. Eventually sales increased, and the author celebrated.

Focus

Lesson Overview

Objectives
- To identify main clauses
- To use main clauses appropriately in writing

Teach

☑ **Grammar Tip**

Read the first example aloud, pausing after each main clause so students can hear the completed clause. Then have volunteers read the other two examples in the same manner. Suggest that students use this technique to help them identify main clauses in sentences.

Practice and Assess

Answers: Exercise 1

Main clauses are in brackets; subjects (S) and verbs (V) are indicated.

1. [The <u>publishers</u> (S) <u>advertised</u> (V)], and [the bookstore <u>owners</u> (S) <u>responded</u> (V)].
2. [The book's <u>cover</u> (S) <u>was</u> (V) a striking design], and [the <u>author</u> (S) <u>was</u> (V) pleased].
3. [The <u>author</u> (S) <u>toured</u> (V)], and [television <u>hosts</u> (S) <u>interviewed</u> (V) her].
4. [Sometimes <u>she</u> (S) <u>gave</u> (V) readings], but [few <u>people</u> (S) <u>attended</u> (V)].
5. [Eventually <u>sales</u> (S) <u>increased</u> (V)], and [the <u>author</u> (S) <u>celebrated</u> (V)].

Close

Have each student write a paragraph. Then have students exchange paragraphs with a partner and identify the main clauses in their partner's writing.

Resource Manager

Planning Resources
- *Lesson Plans*

📂 **Other Print Resources**
- *Grammar and Composition Handbook*
- *Grammar Practice*, p. 18
- *Grammar Workbook*, Lesson 24

Focus

Lesson Overview

Objectives
- To identify subordinate clauses
- To use subordinate clauses correctly in sentences

Bellringer
Daily Language Activity

Use the Bellringer Transparency for Lesson 13.2.

See also *Daily Language Practice*

Teach

☑ Grammar Tip

Explain to students that the best way to distinguish between a main clause and a subordinate clause is to see whether the clause can stand alone outside the sentence. Main clauses can stand alone; subordinate clauses cannot.

Practice and Assess

Answers: Exercise 2
1. subordinate clause
2. subordinate clause
3. main clause
4. subordinate clause
5. main clause
6. subordinate clause
7. subordinate clause
8. main clause
9. subordinate clause
10. subordinate clause

Close

Open a discussion with students about how subordinate clauses contribute to speaking and writing. Ask why the clauses are useful.

544

Clauses and Sentence Structure

13.2 Subordinate Clauses

■ A **subordinate clause** has a subject and a predicate but cannot stand alone as a sentence.

In order for a subordinate clause to make sense, it must be attached to a main clause. Many subordinate clauses begin with subordinating conjunctions or relative pronouns. (Subordinating conjunctions are listed on page 474, and relative pronouns are on page 446.)

MAIN CLAUSE	SUBORDINATE CLAUSE
Stories entertain	because they are amusing.
S V	S V

MAIN CLAUSE
SUBORDINATE CLAUSE
Stories that entertain amuse people.
S   S   V   V

In the first example, the subordinate clause, *because they are amusing,* is attached to the main clause, *Stories entertain.* The subordinate clause is introduced by the subordinating conjunction *because,* which is placed before *they are amusing.* Note that the subordinate clause does not express a complete thought even though it has a subject and a predicate.

In the second example, the subordinate clause comes between the subject and the verb of the main clause. This subordinate clause begins with the relative pronoun *that,* which also serves as the subject of the clause.

Exercise 2   Identifying Clauses

Each of the following sentences has a clause that appears in italics. On your paper, indicate whether the clause is a *main clause* or a *subordinate clause.*

Mahalia Jackson, Gospel Singer

[1]Mahalia Jackson was an African American singer *who became popular worldwide as a performer of gospel music.* [2]*Although she was strongly associated with religious music,* her vocal style was influenced by blues. [3]*Jackson grew up in New Orleans,* where she sang in a church choir. [4]*When she was 16 years old,* Jackson moved to Chicago. [5]*She worked at odd jobs* during the first years that she lived in the city. [6]*Because she possessed a powerful, beautiful voice,* record companies soon offered her contracts. [7]In the 1950s, she gave a series of gospel concerts across the United States *that drew huge audiences.* [8]*Jackson performed internationally* after her United States tours proved so successful. [9]*Although she was a popular gospel star,* Jackson was also very much concerned with politics. [10]*Since she viewed song as an inspiration for peace,* she performed at many civil rights rallies and marches.

Resource Manager

Planning Resources
- *Lesson Plans*

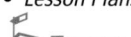
Transparencies
- *Bellringer*
- *Daily Language Practice*

📂 Other Print Resources
- *Grammar and Composition Handbook*
- *Grammar Reteaching,* p. 18
- *Grammar Workbook,* Lesson 24

13.3 Simple and Compound Sentences

■ A **simple sentence** has only one main clause and no subordinate clauses.

A simple sentence may contain a compound subject or a compound predicate or both. The subject and the predicate can be expanded with adjectives, adverbs, prepositional phrases, appositives, and verbal phrases. As long as the sentence has only one main clause, however, it remains a simple sentence.

Stories entertain. [simple sentence]

Stories and riddles entertain. [simple sentence with compound subject]

Stories entertain and amuse. [simple sentence with compound predicate]

Stories and riddles amuse and entertain. [simple sentence with compound subject and compound predicate]

Stories about the Old West entertain adults and children alike. [simple sentence expanded]

■ A **compound sentence** has two or more main clauses.

Each main clause of a compound sentence has its own subject and predicate, and these main clauses are usually joined by a comma and a coordinating conjunction (such as *and, but, or, nor, yet,* or *for*).

MAIN CLAUSE 1	MAIN CLAUSE 2
Stories entertain, and	riddles amuse.
S V	S V

MAIN CLAUSE 1	MAIN CLAUSE 2	MAIN CLAUSE 3
Stories entertain, and	riddles amuse, but	poems delight.
S V	S V	S V

Semicolons may also be used to join the main clauses in a compound sentence.

MAIN CLAUSE 1
Few wild animals live in China's densely populated plains;

MAIN CLAUSE 2
in remoter areas, wildlife is abundant.

Compound Sentence

13.3 Simple and Compound Sentences **545**

13.3

Focus

Lesson Overview

Objectives
- To identify simple and compound sentences
- To use simple and compound sentences in writing

Bellringer
Daily Language Activity
When students enter the classroom, have the following assignment on the board: *Write one sentence that combines the two sentences that follow.*
I wanted to buy a new fish for my aquarium.
I arrived just as the pet store was closing.

See also *Daily Language Practice*

Teach

✓ Teaching Tip
Explain that main clauses introduced by the conjunctions *for* and *yet* are easily confused with subordinate clauses. Here is the difference: main clauses introduced by *for* and *yet* cannot be inverted as subordinate clauses can.

Cross-reference: Mechanics
For practice and instruction in punctuating compound sentences, refer students to Lesson 21.6, pp. 743–751.

Clauses and Sentence Structure

Resource Manager

Planning Resources
- *Lesson Plans*

Transparencies
- *Bellringer*
- *Daily Language Practice*

Other Print Resources
- *Grammar and Composition Handbook*
- *Grammar Practice,* p. 18
- *Grammar Workbook,* Lesson 25
- *Sentence-Combining Practice,* p. 1

Practice and Assess

Answers: Exercise 3

1. simple	6. simple
2. compound	7. compound
3. simple	8. compound
4. compound	9. compound
5. simple	10. simple

Answers: Exercise 4

Answers will vary, but some suggestions are given below.

1. The American painter Grandma Moses was born in 1860.
2. She embroidered all her life but didn't take up painting until the age of 78.
3. Though not formally trained in art, Moses possessed great natural talent.
4. Farm scenes and old-fashioned farm activities are the subjects of her simple, colorful paintings.
5. Moses's talent flourished until her death at the age of 101.

Answers: Exercise 5

Answers will vary, but some suggestions are given below.

1. Grandma Moses was an American painter; she was born in 1860.
2. She embroidered all her life, but she didn't take up painting until the age of 78.
3. Moses had no formal art training, but she possessed great natural talent.
4. Farm scenes and old-fashioned farm activities are her subjects, and her paintings are simple and colorful.
5. Moses's talent flourished; she died at the age of 101.

Additional Resources

 Grammar Practice, p. 18

📁 *Sentence-Combining Practice,* p. 1

 Grammar Workbook, Lesson 25

Close

Encourage students to discuss ways in which using simple and compound sentences will improve their writing.

Clauses and Sentence Structure

Exercise 3   Identifying Simple and Compound Sentences

On your paper, write *simple sentence* or *compound sentence* to identify each sentence. (Remember that a single main clause can have a compound subject and a compound predicate.)

Currier and Ives

1. Nineteenth-century American scenes and customs were recorded and preserved by the firm of Currier and Ives.
2. Nathaniel Currier was a printer, and James Ives was an executive.
3. The two men produced "cheap and popular pictures."
4. Currier favored current events; he produced prints of ships, battles, and news events.
5. Ives had broader interests and generally favored country scenes.
6. Together they published color lithographs depicting every facet of American life.
7. Currier and Ives produced thousands of lithographs, and each print was rich in color and detail.
8. Many prints showed city life, but others depicted life in the country.
9. In the last century, many Americans lived in the country, and many events took place outdoors.
10. Currier and Ives's prints show Americans at work and at play in the nineteenth century.

Exercise 4   Writing Simple Sentences

On your paper, combine each pair of ideas below into a simple sentence. Remember that each sentence must have only one main clause, although the sentence may have a compound subject or predicate.

Grandma Moses

1. Grandma Moses was born in 1860.
   She was an American painter.
2. She embroidered all her life.
   She didn't take up painting until the age of 78.
3. Moses had no formal art training.
   She possessed great natural talent.
4. Farm scenes and old-fashioned farm activities are her subjects.
   Her paintings are simple and colorful.
5. Moses' talent flourished.
   She died at the age of 101.

Exercise 5   Writing Compound Sentences

Use the information in each item from Exercise 4 to write a compound sentence. Remember that each sentence must have two or more main clauses. The clauses may be joined by a comma and a coordinating conjunction—or by a semicolon.

MEETING INDIVIDUAL NEEDS English Language Learners

Identifying Subject and Predicate

Some students may have trouble identifying subject and predicate. Have student pairs take turns writing complete sentences. Then ask students to exchange papers and identify first the simple subject and predicate and then the complete subject and predicate in each sentence.

13.4 Complex and Compound-Complex Sentences

■ A **complex sentence** has one main clause and one or more subordinate clauses.

MAIN CLAUSE
I like Toni Cade Bambara's stories
S V

SUBORDINATE CLAUSE
because they have real-life characters.
   S   V

SUBORDINATE CLAUSE   **MAIN CLAUSE**   **SUBORDINATE CLAUSE**
When I read her stories, I enjoy them because they are true to life.
  S V   **S V**   **S V**

■ A **compound-complex sentence** has two or more main clauses and at least one subordinate clause.

MAIN CLAUSE   **SUBORDINATE CLAUSE**
I read *Frankenstein,* which was written by Mary Shelley,
S V   **S   V**

MAIN CLAUSE
and I wrote a report about it.
  S V

Exercise 6   **Identifying Subordinate Clauses**

On your paper, write the subordinate clause from each of the following sentences. If a sentence has no subordinate clause, write *none.*

1. American pioneers built their houses out of the materials that were readily available.
2. Settlers in heavily forested regions erected log cabins, and newcomers on the treeless plains built sod houses.
3. When they journeyed across the continent, the pioneers lived in their covered wagons.
4. Native Americans of the woodlands built wooden houses, but Native Americans of the Great Plains preferred tepees because they were easy to move.
5. Today Americans who live in the Southwest often build their houses of adobe.

13.4 Complex and Compound-Complex Sentences   **547**

Clauses and Sentence Structure

Focus

Lesson Overview

Objectives
- To recognize complex and compound-complex sentences
- To write using complex and compound-complex sentences

Bellringer
Daily Language Activity
Use the Bellringer Transparency for Lesson 13.4.

See also *Daily Language Practice*

Teach

☑ **Teaching Tip**

Compound-complex sentences can be difficult for students with language-processing impairments or visual-memory problems. To help students process all the information in these longer sentences, review the examples on this page, asking them to explain how they recognize main and subordinate clauses. Point out "clue words," such as subordinating conjunctions and relative pronouns. Suggest students keep a list of "clue words."

Practice and Assess

Answers: Exercise 6

1. that were readily available
2. none
3. When they journeyed across the continent
4. because they were easy to move
5. who live in the Southwest

Resource Manager

Planning Resources
- *Lesson Plans*

Transparencies
- *Bellringer*
- *Daily Language Practice*

📂 **Other Print Resources**
- *Grammar and Composition Handbook*
- *Grammar Enrichment,* p. 18
- *Grammar Workbook,* Lesson 26

Practice and Assess

Answers: Exercise 7

1. When people in New Mexico build their homes (complex)
2. which are made according to an ancient process (complex)
3. who manufacture adobe (complex)
4. After the clay, water, and straw are thoroughly mixed together (complex)
5. that can be used for construction (compound-complex)
6. Once the bricks are dry (complex)
7. that is called stucco (compound-complex)
8. since they remain cool in hot weather (complex)
9. Although adobe is a popular building material in the southwestern United States (complex)
10. If adobe is exposed to frequent rains (complex)

Answers: Exercise 8

Answers will vary, but some suggestions are given below.
1. Some people live in mobile homes, but other people only travel in them. (compound)
2. Many mobile homes have kitchens. (simple)
3. Mobile home owners rent sites at mobile-home parks, which are located in areas determined by the city. (complex)
4. Mobile homes have utilities, which means water, electricity, and gas, so they're much like other kinds of homes. (compound-complex)

Answers: Exercise 9

Answers will vary, but some suggestions are given below.
1. My parents live in Pennsylvania. (simple)
2. My parents live in Pennsylvania, but I live in New York. (compound)
3. My parents live in Pennsylvania, where I grew up. (complex)
4. My parents live in Pennsylvania, where I grew up, but I now live in New York. (compound-complex)

Additional Resources

 Grammar Enrichment, p. 18

Grammar Workbook, Lesson 26

Exercise 7 Identifying Complex and Compound-Complex Sentences

On your paper, write the subordinate clause from each of the following sentences. Indicate whether each sentence is a *complex sentence* or a *compound-complex sentence.*

Adobe Homes

1. When people in New Mexico build their homes, they sometimes use adobe.
2. Adobe is the Spanish name for sun-dried bricks, which are made according to an ancient process.
3. Workers who manufacture adobe mix sandy clay with water and a small amount of straw.
4. After the clay, water, and straw are thoroughly mixed together, the adobe is shoveled into wooden forms and molded into rectangular bricks.
5. The blocks bake in the sun for about two weeks, and the result is strong adobe bricks that can be used for construction.
6. Once the bricks are dry, workers remove the forms.
7. Traditional adobe houses are covered with mud, but modern adobe homes are sometimes covered with a plasterlike material that is called stucco.
8. Many people prefer adobe houses, since they remain cool in hot weather.
9. Although adobe is a popular building material in the southwestern United States, it is not good for very damp or cold areas.
10. If adobe is exposed to frequent rains, the bricks will eventually crumble.

Exercise 8 Writing Simple, Compound, Complex, and Compound-Complex Sentences

Use your own knowledge and the information below to write four original sentences about mobile homes. Write *simple, complex, compound,* or *compound-complex* to identify each sentence you write. (You should write one sentence of each kind.)

Mobile homes are easily moved.
Some people travel in them.
Some people live in them.
They are pulled by cars or trucks.
They became popular during a wartime housing shortage.
They can be connected to utilities.

One quarter of all new single-family dwellings are mobile homes.
Their length varies from 12 to 30 feet.
Communities regulate their placement.
They were once called trailers or caravans.
Sites in mobile-home parks are usually rented.

Exercise 9 Creating Sentences with Various Structures

On your paper, write a simple sentence. Then rework it, making it a compound sentence. Rework the simple sentence again, making it part of a complex sentence. Finally, rework your compound sentence into a compound-complex sentence. Label your four sentences.

(side tab) Clauses and Sentence Structure

Close

Ask students, *Which type of sentence do you use most often in your writing? How could you use each type of sentence to enhance your writing?*

13.5 Adjective Clauses

■ An **adjective clause** is a subordinate clause that modifies a noun or a pronoun.

An adjective clause usually follows the word it modifies.

The horror story **that has always been my favorite** is "The Black Cat."

The writer **whom my sister likes best** is Yoshiko Uchida.

I like a writer **who surprises me.**

Adjective clauses may be introduced by the relative pronouns (*who, whom, whose, that,* and *which*) and by the subordinating conjunctions *where* and *when.*

The Elizabethan Age spans the time **when Elizabeth I ruled.**

That is the house **where I was born.**

At times the relative pronoun is dropped at the beginning of an adjective clause.

This is a story **every science enthusiast should read.** [The relative pronoun *that* has been omitted.]

Some adjective clauses are called *essential clauses,* or *restrictive clauses.* Without them the meaning of the sentence would be unclear.

Edgar Allan Poe is the only American writer **who always fascinates me.** [essential clause]

"The Black Cat" is the story **that I like best.** [essential clause]

Some adjective clauses are *not* needed to make the meaning of the sentence clear. Such clauses are called *nonessential clauses,* or *nonrestrictive clauses.* A nonessential clause is always set off with commas.

Edgar Allan Poe, **who is my favorite author,** wrote "The Black Cat." [nonessential clause]

"The Black Cat," **which was written by Edgar Allan Poe,** is my favorite short story. [nonessential clause]

The word *that* usually introduces an essential clause; the word *which* usually introduces a nonessential clause.

"The Black Cat," **which I like best,** is thrilling. [nonessential clause]

I like a story **that thrills me.** [essential clause]

The detective

who works

under **cover**

was unrecognizable.

Clauses and Sentence Structure

13.5 Adjective Clauses **549**

Focus

Lesson Overview

Objectives
- To identify adjective clauses
- To write adjective clauses and to distinguish between essential and nonessential adjective clauses

Bellringer
Daily Language Activity

Use the Bellringer Transparency for Lesson 13.5.

See also *Daily Language Practice*

Teach

☑ Teaching Tip

Students might be confused about the use of commas with essential and nonessential adjective clauses. Point out that nonessential adjective clauses often merely rename so, like nonrestrictive appositive phrases, they are set off with commas.

⇄ Cross-Reference: Usage

For practice and instruction in choosing the correct relative pronoun, refer students to Lesson 17.4, pp. 642–643.

☑ Teaching Tip

The relative pronoun is a distinctive feature of the adjective clause. Used as objects, however, relative pronouns may be omitted from adjective clauses. For example, in *I found the book I wanted,* the pronoun *that* has been omitted from the adjective clause. Restoring the relative pronoun can help students recognize the clause. See *Grammar Reteaching,* p. 19.

Resource Manager

Planning Resources
- *Lesson Plans*

Transparencies
- *Bellringer*
- *Daily Language Practice*

📁 Other Print Resources
- *Grammar and Composition Handbook*
- *Grammar Enrichment,* p. 19
- *Grammar Practice,* p. 19
- *Grammar Reteaching,* p. 19
- *Grammar Workbook,* Lesson 27
- *Sentence-Combining Practice,* pp. 14, 15, 17

13.5

Practice and Assess

Answers: Exercise 10

1. which is another word for a pen name; pseudonym
2. who lived from 1862 to 1910; Porter
3. which he had founded in Texas in 1894; magazine
4. that was humorous and witty; column
5. that were sympathetic and touching; stories
6. that ended in surprising ways; plots
7. which is a collection of O. Henry's short stories; *The Four Million*
8. [that] many people enjoy; story
9. that is very popular; work
10. who enjoy the unusual and the humorous; Readers

Answers: Exercise 11

1. **a.** that received the most public attention; essential
   b. which went on a six-day mission in June 1983; nonessential
2. **a.** who was flight engineer on the *Challenger;* nonessential
   b. who first entered outer space; essential
3. **a.** that Ride had in astrophysics; essential
   b. which she earned from Stanford University; nonessential
4. **a.** which she had helped design; nonessential
   b. that was 50 feet in length; essential
5. **a.** who have training in specific fields; essential
   b. who are astronauts with training in specific fields; nonessential

Additional Resources

 Grammar Practice, p. 19
Grammar Reteaching, p. 19
Grammar Enrichment, p. 19
Sentence-Combining Practice, pp. 14, 15, 17

Grammar Workbook, Lesson 27

Close

Volunteers may suggest any tips they have for identifying and using adjective clauses.

550

Clauses and Sentence Structure

Exercise 10 Identifying Adjective Clauses and the Words They Modify

On your paper, write the adjective clause that appears in each of the following sentences. Then write the word that the clause modifies. (In one sentence, the relative pronoun has been dropped.)

The Story of O. Henry

1. William Sydney Porter wrote stories under a pseudonym, which is another word for a pen name.
2. Porter, who lived from 1862 to 1910, used the pseudonym O. Henry.
3. Porter contributed a number of articles to a humor magazine, which he had founded in Texas in 1894.
4. He wrote a daily column that was humorous and witty.
5. As O. Henry, Porter published many stories that were sympathetic and touching.
6. He created unusual plots that ended in surprising ways.
7. *The Four Million,* which is a collection of O. Henry's short stories, was published in the year 1906.
8. "The Gift of the Magi" is a story many people enjoy.
9. Another O. Henry work that is very popular is "The Third Ingredient."
10. Readers who enjoy poignant humor will delight in the short stories of O. Henry.

Exercise 11 Identifying Essential and Nonessential Clauses

For each sentence in the pairs below, write the adjective clause and then identify it as an *essential clause* or a *nonessential clause.*

Sally Ride: First U.S. Woman in Space

1. **a.** The 1983 U.S. space mission that received the most public attention was the six-day voyage in June of the *Challenger* space shuttle.
   b. The *Challenger* space shuttle, which went on a six-day mission in June 1983, received much public attention.
2. **a.** Sally Ride, who was flight engineer on the *Challenger,* became the first U.S. woman to enter outer space.
   b. The U.S. woman who first entered outer space was *Challenger* flight engineer Sally Ride.
3. **a.** The background that Ride had in astrophysics helped her qualify for NASA's space program.
   b. Ride's doctorate in astrophysics, which she earned from Stanford University, helped her qualify for NASA's space program.
4. **a.** Sally Ride used a remote-control mechanical arm, which she had helped design, to retrieve a satellite in space.
   b. To retrieve a satellite in space, Sally Ride used the remote-control mechanical arm that was 50 feet in length.
5. **a.** Today's astronauts are people who have training in specific fields.
   b. Today's space program is using mission specialists, who are astronauts with training in specific fields.

550 Unit 13 Clauses and Sentence Structure

Enrichment and Extension

Identifying Essential and Nonessential Clauses

On the board, write sentences with essential and nonessential clauses but without commas, marking the clauses in different colored chalk. Ask students to identify the clauses. Then have students rewrite the sentences, leaving out the clauses.

Discuss how each sentence has changed—whether it still makes sense. Tell students that if the sentence needs the clause, no commas are needed. Have students insert commas where they are needed. **L2**

13.6 Adverb Clauses

■ An **adverb clause** is a subordinate clause that modifies a verb, an adjective, or an adverb. It tells *when, where, how, why, to what extent,* or *under what condition.*

> I studied hard **before I took the test.** [The adverb clause modifies the verb *studied.* It tells *when.*]
>
> I was happy **because I passed the test.** [The adverb clause modifies the adjective *happy.* It tells *why.*]
>
> I can study better **if there is no noise.** [The adverb clause modifies the adverb *better.* It tells *under what conditions.*]

Adverb clauses are introduced by subordinating conjunctions, such as those listed on page 478. Remember that an adverb clause may either precede or follow the main clause. When the adverb clause comes first, separate it from the main clause with a comma. The first example above might have been written as follows:

> **Before I took the test,** I studied hard.

At times words may be left out of an adverb clause. The omitted words, however, are understood, or implied. Adverb clauses from which words are omitted are called *elliptical adverb clauses.*

> She can swim faster **than I [can swim].**
> The news made José happier **than [it made] me [happy].**

Exercise 12 — Identifying Adverb Clauses

On your paper, write the adverb clause that appears in each of the following sentences.

Squanto, Friend of the Pilgrims

1. Although he led a life of hardship, Squanto, a Pawtuxet from Massachusetts, accomplished a great deal.
2. After he was kidnapped by a group of English explorers in 1614, Squanto was taken to Spain.
3. He was taken to Spain so that he could be sold there as an enslaved person.
4. Once the opportunity arose, Squanto escaped to England.
5. As soon as it was safe, Squanto returned home to Massachusetts.
6. When Squanto met the Pilgrims at Plymouth in 1621, they were hungry and discouraged.
7. The Wampanoag were angry because the Pilgrims had taken their corn.
8. Since he spoke fluent English, Squanto became a peacemaker for the two groups.
9. As if that were not enough, Squanto also taught the Pilgrims about corn.
10. No one could have worked more tirelessly than he.

13.6 Adverb Clauses   **551**

Clauses and Sentence Structure

Focus

Lesson Overview

Objectives
- To identify adverb clauses
- To use adverb clauses appropriately in writing

 Bellringer
Daily Language Activity.
Use the Bellringer Transparency for Lesson 13.6.

See also *Daily Language Practice*

Teach

☑ **Grammar Tip**

Like adverbs, adverb clauses can often be moved within sentences. When they appear at the beginning or in the middle of a sentence, they must be set off with commas; however, if an adverb clause occurs at the end of a sentence, a comma is often unnecessary. For example: *Unless she is out of town,* Rosa will attend the meeting. Rosa, *unless she is out of town,* will attend the meeting. Rosa will attend the meeting *unless she is out of town.*

Practice and Assess

Answers: Exercise 12

1. Although he led a life of hardship
2. After he was kidnapped by a group of English explorers in 1614
3. so that he could be sold there as an enslaved person
4. Once the opportunity arose
5. As soon as it was safe
6. When Squanto met the Pilgrims at Plymouth in 1621
7. because the Pilgrims had taken their corn
8. Since he spoke fluent English
9. As if that were not enough
10. than he (worked)

Resource Manager

Planning Resources
- *Lesson Plans*

Transparencies
- *Bellringer*
- *Daily Language Practice*

📂 Other Print Resources
- *Grammar and Composition Handbook*
- *Grammar Enrichment,* p. 20
- *Grammar Practice,* p. 20
- *Grammar Reteaching,* p. 20
- *Grammar Workbook,* Lesson 28
- *Sentence-Combining Practice,* pp. 18–20

Practice and Assess

Answers: Exercise 13

1. when the Puritan settlements began to spread
2. so that they could survive . . . environment
3. when . . . colonists
4. After . . . spy
5. as Metacomet's troops . . . frontier
6. because . . . their homelands
7. if his fighting force had been larger
8. as fiercely as the Puritans (fought)
9. Before he was killed by one of his own men
10. When . . . futility of their efforts

Answers: Exercise 14

Answers will vary, but some suggestions are given below.

1. When they first arrived, . . . in America.
2. . . . Pilgrims because he had learned English.
3. . . . Pilgrims until Puritan settlements spread.
4. So that he could get revenge, . . . to wage war.
5. . . . discouraged because they were outnumbered.
6. After the war ended, . . . the Puritans.
7. . . . steadily once colonists adjusted to America.
8. When they heeded Squanto's advice, . . . lives.
9. . . . decreased as the European population grew.
10. . . . in New England if the Puritan settlements had failed.

Additional Resources

📁 *Grammar Practice,* p. 20
📁 *Grammar Reteaching,* p. 20
📁 *Grammar Enrichment,* p. 20
📁 *Sentence-Combining Practice,* pp. 18–20

 Grammar Workbook, Lesson 28

Close

Have each student write three sentences with adverb clauses—one clause modifying an adjective, one a verb, and one an adverb. Then have students exchange papers and label the word each clause modifies.

Clauses and Sentence Structure

Exercise 13   Identifying Adverb Clauses

On your paper, write the adverb clause that appears in each sentence in the paragraph below. In one of the sentences, the adverb clause is elliptical.

King Philip's War

[1]Metacomet, better known as King Philip, felt threatened when the Puritan settlements began to spread. [2]Like Squanto, in earlier times he had aided the Pilgrims so that they could survive in a harsh new environment. [3]When tensions arose between the Native Americans and the colonists, the colonists forced Metacomet to swear fidelity to the colony. [4]After Metacomet allegedly caused the death of a suspected English spy, three of Metacomet's men were hanged in retaliation. [5]"King Philip's War," a series of battles, began as Metacomet's troops staged raids along the Massachusetts-Connecticut frontier. [6]Metacomet's soldiers were brave because, in their opinion, they were defending their homelands. [7]Metacomet might have been more successful if his fighting force had been larger. [8]The Native Americans fought as fiercely as the Puritans, but the Puritans were better armed and more numerous. [9]Before he was killed by one of his own men, Metacomet had destroyed several towns. [10]When the surviving Native Americans saw the futility of their efforts, they surrendered and the war ended.

Exercise 14   Adding Adverb Clauses to Sentences

On your paper, rewrite each of the following sentences, adding an adverb clause either before or after the main clause. Consult the list of subordinating conjunctions on page 478 for ideas.

SAMPLE   I remember the story of one particular Native American.

ANSWER   Whenever I think about colonial America, I remember the story of one particular Native American.
OR
I remember the story of one particular Native American whenever I think about colonial America.

1. The Pilgrims did not know how to survive in America.
2. Squanto was able to communicate with the Pilgrims.
3. Metacomet had been friendly with the Pilgrims.
4. Metacomet decided to wage war.
5. The Native American troops were discouraged.
6. Life was more secure for the Puritans.
7. New England's population grew steadily.
8. The New England colonists lived longer, healthier lives
9. The Native American population decreased.
10. The Native Americans might still be the only Americans in New England.

13.7 | Noun Clauses

■ A **noun clause** is a subordinate clause used as a noun.

Like a noun or a pronoun, a noun clause can have different functions in a sentence: it can act as a subject, a direct object, an indirect object, an object of a preposition, or a predicate nominative.

NOUN
Farmers often eat home-grown food.
S

NOUN CLAUSE
Whoever lives on a farm often eats home-grown food.
S

NOUN
A drought affects crops.
DO

NOUN CLAUSE
A drought affects whatever grows outdoors.
DO

In the preceding examples, each noun clause forms an inseparable part of the sentence's main clause (the entire sentence).

The following are some of the words that can be used to introduce noun clauses.

how	whatever	which	whoever
that	when	whichever	whose
what	where	who, whom	why

The following are additional examples of noun clauses.

Give **whoever comes to the door** a donation for Farmer's Aid. [indirect object]

This is **how most farmers plant their crops.** [predicate nominative]

Crops are fertilized with **whatever will make them grow fast and strong.** [object of a preposition]

The subordinating conjunction *that* is sometimes dropped at the beginning of a noun clause.

I believe [that] **nobody works harder than farmers.** [The subordinating conjunction *that* is omitted.]

Clauses and Sentence Structure

Focus

Lesson Overview

Objectives
- To identify noun clauses
- To use them appropriately in writing

Bellringer
Daily Language Activity

As students enter the classroom, have the following assignment on the board: *Copy the following sentence and underline the words used as the subject.*

Whoever is coming to the game should arrive by 7 P.M.

See also *Daily Language Practice*

Teach

☑ **Teaching Tip**

A noun clause is always thought of as a unit, or single item, and is therefore always singular.

☑ **Grammar Tip**

A good way to identify a noun clause is to replace it with the pronoun *it* or *somebody*. Since adjective and adverb clauses do not play the role of nouns, they cannot be replaced by pronouns. The pronouns *it* and *somebody* can always replace noun clauses because noun clauses are always singular.

Resource Manager

Planning Resources
- *Lesson Plans*

Transparencies
- *Bellringer*
- *Daily Language Practice*

📁 **Other Print Resources**
- *Grammar and Composition Handbook*
- *Grammar Enrichment*, p. 21
- *Grammar Practice*, p. 21
- *Grammar Reteaching*, p. 21
- *Grammar Workbook, Lesson 29*
- *Sentence-Combining Practice*, pp. 24–25

Practice and Assess

Answers: Exercise 15

1. Whoever has flown a kite; that kite flying can be fun
2. that kites are not only for children
3. What many may not know; that kites have existed for ages
4. where kites were invented
5. that the Chinese military of about two thousand years ago attached bamboo pipes to their kites
6. that the noise from the wind in the pipes panicked the enemy soldiers on the ground below
7. whoever attends
8. What attracts people to this festival
9. That the Hamamatsu festival is popular; what is now a centuries-old tradition
10. that kite flying is an enjoyable activity

Answers: Exercise 16

Answers will vary, but some suggestions are given below.
1. that baseball is America's favorite sport
2. Whoever hits the ball hard
3. How the players hit, run, and field
4. who is safe and who is out
5. what the fans want
6. when the game is delayed
7. whose decision is best
8. where the ball will be thrown
9. whatever he thinks of first
10. which pitcher will start

Clauses and Sentence Structure

On your paper, write the noun clauses that appear in each of the following sentences. (Some of the sentences have two noun clauses each.)

The History of Kites

1. Whoever has flown a kite knows that kite flying can be fun.
2. Few people realize that kites are not only for children.
3. What many may not know is that kites have existed for ages.
4. No one knows for sure where kites were invented, but they probably first appeared in China.
5. Folklorists tell us that the Chinese military of about two thousand years ago attached bamboo pipes to their kites.
6. The result was that the noise from the wind in the pipes panicked the enemy soldiers on the ground below.
7. In Hamamatsu, Japan, the three-day kite-flying festival in early May brings pleasure to whoever attends.
8. What attracts people to this festival is seeing so many brightly painted kites taller than themselves.
9. That the Hamamatsu festival is popular is proved by what is now a centuries-old tradition.
10. Do you agree that kite flying is an enjoyable activity?

Exercise 16   Writing Sentences with Noun Clauses

On your paper, complete the following sentences about baseball by replacing the blanks with noun clauses. Begin each noun clause with the word in parentheses.

SAMPLE   Do you know (why) _____?
ANSWER   Do you know why baseball is America's favorite sport?

Baseball

1. Many people agree (that) _____.
2. (Whoever) _____ can go to first base.
3. (How) _____ is exciting to watch.
4. The umpire decides (who) _____.
5. A fast-paced game with lots of action is (what) _____.
6. Few fans understand (when) _____.
7. The catcher and the pitcher consult about (whose) _____.
8. The batter's biggest worry is (where) _____.
9. His excuse for striking out is (whatever) _____.
10. The coach has decided (which) _____.

MEETING INDIVIDUAL NEEDS   English Language Learners

Using Noun Clauses

Students learning English often mistakenly use question word order in noun clauses. For example, a student might write *I know what is your name* instead of *I know what your name is.* In noun clauses, only the question word is moved in front of the subject.

Exercise 17   Identifying Subordinate Clauses

On your paper, write the subordinate clause in each sentence. Then write *adverb clause, adjective clause,* or *noun clause* to indicate the kind of clause it is.

A Historic Court Decision

¹*Brown* v. *Board of Education of Topeka* was a legal case that changed the face of America's schools. ²What began as a local matter in 1951 had gained national attention by 1954. ³Because his daughter could not attend an all-white school, an African American parent sued the Topeka Board of Education. ⁴Thurgood Marshall, who later became the first African American justice on the Supreme Court, represented the student's father, Oliver Brown. ⁵Marshall was an attorney whom people respected. ⁶In 1954 the Court ruled that segregated schools deprived minorities of an equal education. ⁷Chief Justice Earl Warren declared that segregation violated a citizen's right to equal protection under the law. ⁸After the decision was announced, schools across the country changed their policies. ⁹Many schools adopted a policy of integration, which allowed children of different ethnic backgrounds to learn together. ¹⁰Few Supreme Court cases have had a greater impact on American society than this one.

Exercise 18   Adding Adjective, Adverb, and Noun Clauses to Sentences

On your paper, combine the following pairs of sentences by turning one of them into a subordinate clause. Write the sentence. Then write *adjective clause, adverb clause,* or *noun clause* to identify the kind of clause you created.

SAMPLE   (a) A boomerang is a throwing stick.
              (b) A boomerang was used originally by Australian Aborigines.

ANSWER   A boomerang is a throwing stick that was used originally by Australian Aboringes. (adjective clause)

Boomerangs

1. (a) A boomerang returns to the thrower.
   (b) It rotates horizontally in flight.
2. (a) Early European travelers wrote in their diaries.
   (b) The Aborigines used boomerangs to trap game.
3. (a) The use of boomerangs declined.
   (b) More sophisticated hunting weapons were introduced by the British.
4. (a) Every year the Smithsonian Institution stages a boomerang festival.
   (b) It takes place on the mall in Washington, D.C.
5. (a) The term *boomerang* is sometimes used as a verb.
   (b) It means "to result in harm to the user or doer."

Exercise 19   Writing Subordinate Clauses in Sentences

On your paper, write four original sentences. In the first one, use an adverb clause. In the second one, use an adjective clause. In the third one, use a noun clause as a subject. In the fourth one, use a noun clause as a direct object.

13.7 Noun Clauses   **555**

Clauses and Sentence Structure

Practice and Assess

Answers: Exercise 17

1. that changed . . . system; adjective
2. What began . . . in 1951; noun
3. Because his daughter . . . school; adverb
4. who later . . . Court; adjective
5. whom people . . . skills; adjective
6. that segregated . . . education; noun
7. that segregation . . . law; noun
8. After . . . announced; adverb
9. which allowed . . . together; adjective
10. than this one; adverb

Answers: Exercise 18

Answers will vary, but some suggestions are given below.

1. A boomerang returns to the thrower after it rotates horizontally in flight; adverb clause
2. Early European travelers wrote in their diaries that the Aborigines used boomerangs to trap game; noun clause
3. The use of boomerangs declined when more sophisticated hunting weapons were introduced by the British; adverb clause
4. Every year the Smithsonian Institution stages a boomerang festival, which takes place on the mall in Washington, D.C.; adjective clause
5. When the term *boomerang* is used as a verb, it means "to result in harm to the user or doer"; adverb clause

Answers: Exercise 19

Answers will vary, but some suggestions are given below.

1. When I visited London, I saw a dozen plays.
2. The film that I like best is *ET.*
3. Whoever knows Mercer respects him.
4. I wish that I could speak Japanese.

Close

Have each student write five sentences with noun clauses—one clause acting as subject, one as direct object, one as indirect object, one as object of a preposition, and one as predicate nominative. Have students label the noun clauses, exchange papers, and discuss their efforts.

Additional Resources

 Grammar Practice, p. 21
Grammar Reteaching, p. 21
Grammar Enrichment, p. 21
Sentence-Combining Practice, pp. 24–25

Grammar Workbook, Lesson 29

Focus

Lesson Overview

Objectives

- To identify declarative, imperative, interrogative, and exclamatory sentences
- To use the four types of sentences in writing and to punctuate them correctly

Teach

☑ Grammar Tip

An exclamatory sentence expresses strong feeling and is followed by an exclamation point. An imperative sentence is a command or a request; it has an understood *you* as its subject. Such a sentence is classified as imperative even if it is punctuated with an exclamation point.

Practice and Assess

Answers: Exercise 20

1. interrogative/?
2. exclamatory/!
3. declarative/.
4. declarative/.
5. imperative/.

Answers: Exercise 21

Answers will vary, but some suggestions are given below.
1. Heavy snow blanketed Middleburg today.
2. Use caution when driving.
3. Have you cleared your sidewalk?
4. What a heavy snowfall this is!

Close

Have a sentence bee; call out types of sentences to students in turn.

13.8 Four Kinds of Sentences

■ A **declarative sentence** makes a statement.

> A lion is chasing the ostriches.
> The huge birds run fast.

The declarative sentence is the most frequently used type of sentence. It normally ends with a period.

■ An **imperative sentence** gives a command or makes a request.

> Look at the fleeing ostriches.
> Please take pictures of them.

In an imperative sentence, the subject "you" is understood. An imperative sentence usually ends with a period, but it may end with an exclamation point if it expresses strong emotion.

■ An **interrogative sentence** asks a question.

> What did the lion chase?
> Is the lion chasing the ostriches?

■ An **interrogative sentence** ends with a question mark.

■ An **exclamatory sentence** expresses strong emotion.

> What a good time we had!
> How ferocious the lion looks!

An exclamatory sentence ends with an exclamation point.

Exercise 20 · Identifying and Punctuating Four Kinds of Sentences

On your paper, write *declarative, imperative, interrogative,* or *exclamatory* to identify each sentence below. Then write the correct end mark of punctuation.

1. Have you ever been to an African game park
2. What a wonderful adventure it is
3. Kruger National Park is located in the northeastern part of South Africa, not far from the Limpopo River
4. If you go, you should plan to spend the night in one of the thatch-roofed huts
5. Don't ever get out of your car to take pictures of the elephants

Exercise 21 · Creating Four Kinds of Sentences

On your paper, write four sentences about a recent news story. Use one declarative, one imperative, one interrogative, and one exclamatory sentence. Remember to punctuate each sentence correctly.

Resource Manager

Planning Resources
- *Lesson Plans*

📂 **Other Print Resources**
- *Grammar and Composition Handbook*

- *Grammar Enrichment,* p. 22
- *Grammar Practice,* p. 22
- *Grammar Reteaching,* p. 22
- *Grammar Workbook,* Lesson 30

13.9 Sentence Fragments

■ In general, avoid sentence fragments in your writing. A **sentence fragment** is an error that occurs when an incomplete sentence is punctuated as though it were a complete sentence.

There are three things you should look for when reviewing your work for sentence fragments. First, look for a group of words without a subject. Next, be alert for a group of words lacking a verb, especially a group that contains a verbal rather than a complete verb. Last, make sure that you have not mistaken a subordinate clause for a complete sentence.

You will often be able to correct a sentence fragment by joining it to a main clause that precedes or follows the fragment. At times you may have to add missing words to make a complete sentence.

FRAGMENT	Woodpeckers ate suet from my bird feeder last winter. **Seemed to be particularly fond of it.** [lacks subject]
COMPLETE SENTENCE	Woodpeckers ate suet from my bird feeder last winter, and they seemed to be particularly fond of it.
FRAGMENT	**A large bird with blue feathers eating from the feeder for weeks.** [lacks complete verb]
COMPLETE SENTENCE	A large bird with blue feathers has been eating from the feeder for weeks.
FRAGMENT	I filled the feeder with sunflower seeds. **Which both the jays and the cardinals seem to like.** [has subordinate clause only]
COMPLETE SENTENCE	I filled the feeder with sunflower seeds, which both the jays and the cardinals seem to like.

Professional writers sometimes use sentence fragments. They do so for special effect—to add emphasis or to convey realistic dialogue. They use sentence fragments *carefully* and *intentionally*. In most of the writing you do, however, including your writing for school, you should avoid sentence fragments.

Clauses and Sentence Structure

Focus

Lesson Overview

Objectives
- To understand the difference between sentence fragments and complete sentences
- To identify sentence fragments and to correct them

Bellringer
Daily Language Activity

Use the Bellringer Transparency for Lesson 13.9.

See also 📖 *Daily Language Practice*

Teach

☑ **Teaching Tip**

A quick test for fragments is to try to turn them into questions. Since fragments lack a subject or a complete verb, they will always fail this test.

☑ **Grammar Tip**

The majority of sentence fragments are "afterthoughts" that elaborate, qualify, or exemplify the ideas in the main clause. For instance, a common kind of sentence fragment is an adjective clause punctuated as a complete sentence. This kind of fragment can be easily corrected by joining the adjective clause to the noun that the clause modifies in the preceding sentence.

🔁 **Cross-Reference: Troubleshooter**

For instruction and practice in avoiding sentence fragments, refer students to the **Troubleshooter.**

Resource Manager

Planning Resources
- *Lesson Plans*

📖 **Transparencies**
- *Bellringer*
- *Daily Language Practice*

📁 **Other Print Resources**
- *Grammar and Composition Handbook*
- *Grammar Enrichment*, p. 23
- *Grammar Practice*, p. 23
- *Grammar Reteaching*, p. 23
- *Grammar Workbook*, Lesson 31

Practice and Assess

Answers: Exercise 22

1. complete	6. complete
2. fragment	7. fragment
3. complete	8. complete
4. fragment	9. fragment
5. fragment	10. fragment

Answers: Exercise 23

Answers will vary, but some suggestions are given below.

    With more than 21 million inhabitants, Mexico City is the largest city in the world. Few cities have greater problems related to rapid growth. Once the capital of the Aztec Empire, Mexico City is built on an island in the center of a lake. The arrival of the Spanish surprised the Aztecs. The Spaniards conquered the city because of their superior weapons and their alliances with traditional enemies of the Aztecs. Many residents of modern Mexico City are descendants of the Aztecs or other native groups or of the Spaniards who came to Mexico in the sixteenth century and intermarried with the native population. Modern Mexico City is a vibrant metropolis: a blend . . .

Answers: Exercise 24

Answers will vary, but some suggestions are given below.

1. The Aztec civilization rose . . .
2. The Aztecs were a warlike group . . .
3. They settled on an island in . . .
4. In the thirteenth century, they inhabited the valley of central Mexico.
5. At this time, they also established . . .
6. This empire continued to the time . . .
7. . . . of Tenochtitlán were unsuccessful.
8. Montezuma was preoccupied with conquering war captives . . .
9. Aztec civilization flourished before . . .
10. Upon his arrival, he found a civilization . . .
11. . . . groups that made up the Aztec civilization lived together in peace.
12. These groups grew in political status.
13. They engaged in communal land . . .
14. Together, families worked at irrigating, . . .
15. . . . Cortés defeated the Aztecs . . .

Additional Resources

📁 Grammar Practice, p. 23
📁 Grammar Reteaching, p. 23
📁 Grammar Enrichment, p. 23

558

Exercise 22   **Identifying Sentence Fragments**

On your paper, write whether each numbered item is a *complete sentence* or a *sentence fragment.*

Mexico City

[1]Can you guess which city is the largest in the world? [2]Mexico City, with more than 21 million inhabitants. [3]There are few cities with greater problems related to rapid growth. [4]Once the capital of the Aztec Empire, built on an island in the center of a lake. [5]Then the arrival of the Spanish, surprising the Aztecs. [6]The Spaniards conquered the city because of their superior weapons. [7]Also because of their alliances with traditional enemies of the Aztecs. [8]Many residents of modern Mexico City are descendants of the Aztecs and of other groups native to the area. [9]Or else of the Spaniards who came to Mexico in the sixteenth century and intermarried with the native population. [10]Modern Mexico City: a blend of Native American and Spanish, American and European, modern and traditional.

Exercise 23   **Correcting Sentence Fragments**

Revise the preceding paragraph by correcting each fragment. Wherever possible, combine the fragments with other sentences in the paragraph. You may need to change some words as well.

Exercise 24   **Writing Sentences from Sentence Fragments**

On your paper, write each sentence fragment below to create a complete sentence. You may add or change words as needed. Make sure that your sentences make sense.

The Aztec

1. The Aztec, a native civilization that rose to a position of dominance.
2. A warlike group with an excellent military organization.
3. Settled on an island in Lake Texcoco.
4. In the thirteenth century in the valley of central Mexico.
5. When they established a tribute-collecting empire that included most of present-day Mexico and extended south to what is now Guatemala.
6. Which continued to the time of the Spanish conquest.
7. Montezuma I's attempts to find food for the growing population of Tenochtitlán.
8. Conquering war captives and acquiring luxury goods.
9. Before Hernán Cortés arrived in 1519.
10. A civilization that was flourishing.
11. Despite some discontent with autocratic policies, the many groups that made up the Aztec civilization.
12. As they grew in political status.
13. Communal land ownership with each farm supporting a few families.
14. Worked at irrigating, terracing, and fertilizing the land.
15. Helped by some native groups, Cortés, who defeated the Aztecs in 1521.

 Grammar Workbook, Lesson 31

Close

Ask students to think about sentence fragments they have come across in a book or article. Have them discuss why a writer might have used a fragment instead of a sentence.

13.10   Run-on Sentences

■ Avoid run-on sentences in your writing. A **run-on sentence** is two or more complete sentences written as though they were one sentence.

There are three basic kinds of run-on sentences.

1. The most common type of run-on sentence is a **comma splice.** A comma splice occurs when two main clauses are separated by a comma instead of a period or a semicolon. You can correct a comma splice by replacing the comma with an end mark and starting the new sentence with a capital letter. You can also correct a comma splice by adding a coordinating conjunction.

RUN-ON	Tanya and Naoko are both going to work as camp counselors this summer, they are looking forward to the experience.
CORRECT	Tanya and Naoko are both going to work as camp counselors this summer**.** **T**hey are looking forward to the experience.
CORRECT	Tanya and Naoko are both going to work as camp counselors this summer**,** **and** they are looking forward to the experience.

2. A second type of run-on sentence occurs when two main clauses are written with *no* punctuation between them. To correct this kind of run-on, separate the main clauses with a mark of end punctuation or with a semicolon. Another way to correct the error is by adding a comma and a coordinating conjunction between the main clauses.

RUN-ON	Tanya and Naoko feel the job has many advantages working with children is one of them.
CORRECT	Tanya and Naoko feel the job has many advantages**.** **W**orking with children is one of them.
CORRECT	Tanya and Naoko feel the job has many advantages**;** working with children is one of them.
CORRECT	Tanya and Naoko feel the job has many advantages**,** **and** working with children is one of them.

3. A third type of run-on sentence occurs when the comma is left out before a coordinating conjunction that joins two main clauses. Correct this error by simply adding a comma before the coordinating conjunction.

RUN-ON	They will enjoy what they will be doing and they will be earning money too.
CORRECT	They will enjoy what they will be doing**,** and they will be earning money too.

13.10 Run-on Sentences   **559**

Clauses and Sentence Structure

Focus

Lesson Overview

Objectives
• To identify run-on sentences
• To correct run-on sentences and to avoid using them in writing

Bellringer
Daily Language Activity

Use the Bellringer Transparency for Lesson 13.10.

See also 📖 *Daily Language Practice*

Teach

☑ **Teaching Tip**

Most run-on sentences are the result of the writer's attempt to hold closely related ideas together within the boundaries of a single sentence. Explain to students that this goal can be met by writing properly punctuated compound sentences.

🔁 **Cross Reference: Troubleshooter**

For instruction and practice in avoiding run-on sentences, refer students to **Troubleshooter**, Unit 9, for an alternative presentation of the material in Lesson 13.10.

Two-Minute Skill Drill

Write this run-on sentence on the board and have students suggest ways to correct it.

The climber struggled up a steep ice wall, hanging on with his fingertips, he feared he wouldn't reach the top.

📖 **See also** *Two-Minute Skill Drill Transparency 13.10*

Resource Manager

Planning Resources
• *Lesson Plans*

Transparencies
• *Bellringer*
• *Daily Language Practice*
• *Two-Minute Skill Drill*

📁 **Other Print Resources**
• *Grammar and Composition Handbook*
• *Grammar Enrichment*, p. 24
• *Grammar Practice*, p. 24
• *Grammar Reteaching*, p. 24
• *Grammar Workbook*, Lesson 32

Practice and Assess

Answers: Exercise 25

1. correct
2. run-on sentence
3. run-on sentence
4. correct
5. run-on sentence

Answers: Exercise 26

Answers will vary, but some suggestions are given below.

1. The American artist Georgia O'Keeffe became famous for her paintings of natural objects. Her canvases are stunning.
2. The objects she painted appear huge and overwhelming. Her enlarged flowers and stones seem unique.
3. Her paintings are energetic, strong, and realistic; nevertheless, most of them have an abstract quality.
4. O'Keeffe's colors are bold and startling; for example, a patch of blue and green on a field of white looks stark and compelling.
5. Most of her paintings remain popular with art lovers, for her work is intense, realistic, and unique.
6. O'Keeffe was greatly influenced by the landscape of the American Southwest, and there are many recognizable southwestern images in her paintings.
7. Many people think only of the Southwest when they think of Georgia O'Keeffe, yet she also painted cityscapes.
8. O'Keeffe married the American photographer Alfred Stieglitz; the wedding took place in 1924.
9. Stieglitz operated two art galleries in New York City, and he often displayed his wife's work in them.
10. He also took many photographs of O'Keeffe, and these are well known today.

Clauses and Sentence Structure

Exercise 25   Distinguishing Between Run-ons and Correct Sentences

On your paper, write *run-on sentence* or *correct* to identify each of the following items.

Taos: An Artist Colony

1. Taos, a relatively small town in the north-central section of New Mexico, is one of the oldest settlements in the United States.
2. It was founded in 1615 and it became an important trading center on the Santa Fe Trail during the nineteenth century.
3. An ancient Pueblo village lies north of the town, a Spanish farming center, Ranchos de Taos, lies to the south.
4. Since the early 1900s, Taos has been a noted artist colony and has attracted many well-known artists, including Georgia O'Keeffe.
5. In 1949 O'Keeffe established her home in Taos, its atmosphere and its beautiful scenery inspired some of her finest work.

Exercise 26   Correcting Run-on Sentences

On your paper, write each of the following sentences, correcting the run-ons. Watch for the three types of run-on errors shown on page 559. You may choose from among the several ways of correcting run-ons that you have learned.

Georgia O'Keeffe: An American Artist

1. The American artist Georgia O'Keeffe became famous for her paintings of natural objects, her canvases are stunning.
2. The objects she painted appear huge and overwhelming her enlarged flowers and stones seem unique.
3. Her paintings are energetic, strong, and realistic nevertheless, most of them have an abstract quality.
4. O'Keeffe's colors are bold and startling, a patch of blue and green on a field of white looks stark and compelling.
5. Most of her paintings remain popular with art lovers, her work is intense, realistic and unique.
6. O'Keeffe was greatly influenced by the landscape of the American Southwest and there are many recognizable southwestern images in her paintings.
7. Many people think only of the Southwest when they think of Georgia O'Keeffe yet she also painted cityscapes.
8. O'Keeffe married the American photographer Alfred Stieglitz the wedding took place in 1924.
9. Stieglitz operated two art galleries in New York City and he often displayed his wife's work in them.
10. He also took many photographs of O'Keeffe, these are well-known today.

Enrichment and Extension

Identifying Run-ons

Tell students that a good test for identifying comma splices is to see whether the clauses on either side of a comma can stand alone. If they can, then the clauses are main clauses, and the comma must be replaced with a period, a semicolon, or a comma plus a coordinating conjunction. See Grammar Reteaching, p. 24. **L1**

Exercise 27   Review: Correcting Sentence Fragments and Run-on Sentences

On your paper, write the following items, correcting all sentence fragments and run-on sentences. Write *correct* for any sentences that do not need revision.

Gemstones

1. Gemstones are minerals in crystal form, they occur naturally as chemical elements or compounds.
2. The value of a gem is based on certain properties beauty, durability, and rarity are three of these.
3. Diamonds being the hardest natural substance in the world. They cannot be scratched by any other substance.
4. Two gemstones come from corundum. Which is harder than any other substance except diamonds.
5. The red variety is called ruby and the blue variety is called sapphire.
6. One of the costliest gemstones of all is emerald, which is a kind of beryl.
7. A good emerald stone has a deep green color and is free of flaws. May cost several thousand dollars per carat.
8. The most common of all minerals is quartz. Which may crystallize into such gemstones as citrine, amethyst, tiger eye, and agate.
9. Some gemstones come from living things, among these are pearls, amber, and coral.
10. Gems have continued to fascinate people for ages. Their beauty and value make them among the most exciting and intriguing of objects.

Exercise 28   Review: Correcting Sentence Structure

On your paper, write the following paragraphs, correcting all sentence fragments and run-on sentences.

Lasers

[1]The word *laser* from the expression "light amplification by stimulated emission of radiation." [2]Both radio waves and light waves are forms of energy nevertheless, neither weak radio waves nor weak light waves harms us. [3]Producing and transmitting intense light being the basic purpose of a laser. [4]Either a rare metal or a rare gas used for the intensification of light waves. [5]Chromium and helium were used in early lasers, today various kinds of lamps produce the light that lasers intensify. [6]Electrons and light waves interacting to make the light extremely intense.

[7]Lasers have many practical applications, they are used in everything from surveying equipment to high-tech "smart" weapons. [8]Lasers by eye surgeons and cardiac specialists. [9]In photography, three-dimensional images called holographs produced with lasers. [10]We can thank lasers for the latest developments in the communications revolution, compact discs, videodiscs, and fiber-optic telephone cables are but three examples of laser technology at work.

13.10 Run-on Sentences   **561**

Additional Resources

 Grammar Practice, p. 24
Grammar Reteaching, p. 24
Grammar Enrichment, p. 24

Grammar Workbook, Lesson 32

Practice and Assess

Answers: Exercise 27

Answers will vary, but some suggestions are given below.
1. Gemstones are minerals in crystal form, and they occur . . .
2. The value of a gem is based on certain properties; beauty, durability . . .
3. Diamonds, being the hardest natural substance in the world, cannot . . .
4. Two gemstones come from corundum, which is harder . . .
5. The red variety is called ruby, and the blue variety is called sapphire.
6. correct
7. A good emerald stone . . . is free of flaws; it may cost . . .
8. The most common of all minerals is quartz, which may . . .
9. Some gemstones come from living things; among these . . .
10. correct

Answers: Exercise 28

Answers will vary, but some suggestions are given below.
1. The word *laser* comes from . . .
2. Both radio waves and light waves are forms of energy; nevertheless, neither . . . harm us.
3. Producing and transmitting intense light is the basic purpose of a laser.
4. Either a rare metal or . . . gas is used . . .
5. Chromium and helium . . . lasers; today various kinds of lamps produce the light that lasers intensify.
6. Electrons and light waves interact . . .
7. Lasers have many practical applications; they are used in everything . . .
8. Lasers are used by eye surgeons and cardiac specialists.
9. In photography, three-dimensional images called holographs are produced with lasers.
10. . . . communications revolution. Compact discs, videodiscs, and fiber-optic telephone cables are . . .

Close

Encourage students to share techniques they use to help them avoid run-on sentences and sentence fragments in their own writing.

561

Teach

About the Literature

Explain that the workshop features a passage from book 9, section 3, of Willa Cather's novel, *Death Comes for the Archbishop* and that the literature is followed by exercises based on the novel and on related topics. Have students read the passage and note the complexity of the ideas. Then ask students to focus on the highlighted sentences and clauses in the passage. How do clauses and sentence structure help to communicate the ideas? Do they sharpen our view of the scene or detract from it? Are they essential to our understanding of the scene, or could they be eliminated?

Linking Grammar and Literature

Listening and Speaking

Point out that most of the sentences in the passage consist of a main clause and one or more subordinate clauses. (The only simple sentence in the passage has been highlighted.) Ask students to reread the literature passage aloud and to identify some of the main clauses and subordinate clauses. Then initiate a discussion about how writers can use clauses to vary the rhythms of their sentences and to avoid unnecessary repetition.

✔ ASSESSMENT OPTIONS

📁 *Tests with Answer Key & Rubrics*
Unit 13 Pretest, pp. 43–44
Unit 13 Mastery Test, pp. 45–46

💾 *Testmaker*
Unit 13 Pretest
Unit 13 Mastery Test

UNIT 13

Grammar Review

Clauses and Sentence Structure *(sidebar)*

CLAUSES AND SENTENCE STRUCTURE

Set in the mid-nineteenth century, Willa Cather's novel *Death Comes for the Archbishop* tells the story of Bishop Jean Latour, who has left his parish in France and returned to New Mexico, where he had served as a young man. In this scene, the bishop awakes in the same small room he had lived in years earlier, and he muses about the past. The passage has been annotated to show some of the clauses and sentence structures covered in this unit.

Literature Model

from Death Comes for the Archbishop
by Willa Cather

He felt a great content at being here, where he had come as a young man and where he had done his work. The room was little changed; the same rugs and skins on the earth floor, the same desk with his candlesticks, the same thick, wavy white walls that muted sound, that shut out the world and gave repose to the spirit.

As the darkness faded into the gray of a winter morning, he listened for the church bells,—and for another sound, that always amused him here; the whistle of a locomotive. Yes, he had come with the buffalo, and he had lived to see railway trains running into Santa Fé. He had accomplished an historic period.

In New Mexico he always awoke a young man; not until he rose and began to shave did he realize **that he was growing older.** His first consciousness was a sense of the light dry wind blowing in through the windows, with the fragrance of hot sun and sage-brush and sweet clover; a wind that made one's body feel light and one's heart cry "To-day, to-day," like a child's.

Beautiful surroundings, the society of learned men, the charm of noble women, the graces of art, could not make up

Annotations:
- Adverb clause
- Compound sentence
- Simple sentence
- Noun clause

Resource Manager

Planning Resources
- *Lesson Plans*

📁 **Other Print Resources**
- *Grammar and Composition Handbook*

- *Grammar Enrichment,* pp. 18–24
- *Grammar Practice,* pp. 18–24
- *Grammar Reteaching,* pp. 18–24
- *Grammar Workbook,* Lessons 24–32

to him for the loss of those light-hearted mornings of the desert, for that wind that made one a boy again. He had noticed that this peculiar quality in the air of new countries vanished after they were tamed by man and made to bear harvests. Parts of Texas and Kansas that he had first known as open range had since been made into rich farming districts, and the air had quite lost that lightness, that dry aromatic odor. The moisture of plowed land, the heaviness of labor and growth and grain-bearing, utterly destroyed it; one could breathe that only on the bright edges of the world, on the great grass plains or the sage-brush desert.

That air would disappear from the whole earth in time, perhaps; but long after his day. He did not know just when it had become so necessary to him, but he had come back to die in exile for the sake of it. Something soft and wild and free, something that whispered to the ear on the pillow, lightened the heart, softly, softly picked the lock, slid the bolts, and released the prisoned spirit of man into the wind, into the blue and gold, into the morning, into the morning!

Complex sentence

Adjective clause

Compound-complex sentence

Clauses and Sentence Structure

Review: Exercise 1 **Identifying Main and Subordinate Clauses**

The following sentences are based on the passage from *Death Comes for the Archbishop*. Each sentence contains a clause that appears in italics. On your paper indicate whether the italicized clause is a *main clause* or a *subordinate clause*.

1. *Because Bishop Jean Marie Latour had once lived in the room*, he felt at home there.
2. *The room had changed remarkably little*, even though many years had passed.
3. The furnishings *that he recalled so well* still stood in the room.
4. The bishop awoke, began to shave, and reflected about the land and *why he felt so content there*.
5. The bishop, *who was now an old man*, felt almost like a boy again in his former surroundings.
6. He experienced a feeling of newness and vigor *whenever he breathed the light, dry morning air of New Mexico*.
7. The source of the invigorating air was the country around him, *which was still untamed*.
8. Other places had once produced this remarkable effect, but *they no longer did*.
9. A sense of newness disappeared *after an area was developed*.
10. Although progress brought with it many civilized comforts and pleasures, *it also carried a high price*.

Grammar Review **563**

Teach

☑ Teaching Tip

Ask students to write a paragraph about a journey, using some short sentences that consist of only one main clause and some long sentences with two or more main or subordinate clauses. Remind them that subordinate clauses begin with relative pronouns such as *who* or *which* or with subordinating conjunctions such as *when, as,* or *before.* Then have them read their paragraphs to the class. Ask the class to listen to the rhythms of the sentences. Discuss whether short sentences are always preferable to long ones.

Practice and Assess

Answers: Exercise 1

1. subordinate
2. main
3. subordinate
4. subordinate
5. subordinate
6. subordinate
7. subordinate
8. main
9. subordinate
10. main

Practice and Assess

Answers: Exercise 2

1. complex
2. compound
3. complex
4. complex
5. compound-complex
6. compound
7. compound
8. compound
9. complex
10. compound-complex
11. complex
12. compound-complex
13. compound
14. complex
15. compound-complex
16. compound
17. compound
18. complex
19. complex
20. complex

Review: Exercise 2   Identifying Compound, Complex, and Compound-Complex Sentences

The following sentences provide some background details from the novel *Death Comes for the Archbishop.* On your paper, write whether each sentence is *compound, complex,* or *compound-complex.*

1. In the late 1840s, after the Mexican War, the Catholic Church renewed its interest in New Mexico because the territory had just become part of the United States.
2. Missionaries had been working there since 1500, but control over Church activities was limited.
3. A new bishop could renew the Church there if the right man could be found.
4. A few years after the Mexican War, a young French priest who had just been elevated to the position of bishop was sent to Santa Fe, New Mexico.
5. Bishop Latour was exhausted when he finally arrived in New Mexico, for the trip had taken nearly a year.
6. There was a railroad out of New York, but it ended in Cincinnati, Ohio.
7. From Ohio, Bishop Latour had gone by boat to Galveston on the Texas coast, and then he had traveled across Texas.
8. He needed both strength and flexibility, or he would not succeed in his job.
9. After Bishop Latour had worked effectively in the area for many years, he retired.
10. Now he had come back to New Mexico, for he knew that he would soon die.
11. Willa Cather modeled Bishop Latour on two real priests who had lived in New Mexico during the nineteenth century.
12. John B. Lamy went to Santa Fe as bishop in 1846, and Joseph P. Machebeuf, who later became bishop of Colorado, accompanied Lamy as his able assistant.
13. Lamy instituted extensive reforms, and religious conditions in New Mexico improved greatly during his time there.
14. A few years after his arrival, Lamy built the Cathedral of Saint Francis of Assisi, which stands today in Santa Fe as an impressive landmark.
15. When Cather first visited New Mexico, she was impressed with the history of the Catholic Church in the region, but she didn't have enough facts to write about it.
16. She went back often, for the subject continued to fascinate her.
17. On one trip, she discovered a book about the life of Father Machebeuf; this book inspired her to write her own book.
18. The book also contained detailed information about Bishop Lamy because the two men were colleagues and friends.
19. Father Machebeuf's letters gave Cather a sense of the mood in which these two missionaries accepted the hardships of desert life.
20. She titled *Death Comes for the Archbishop,* the writing of which she called "a happy vacation from life," after a painting by Albrecht Dürer.

Clauses and Sentence Structure

Review: Exercise 3 Writing Sentences with Adjective Clauses

The sentences that follow elaborate on ideas in the passage from *Death Comes for the Archbishop*. On your paper, rewrite each sentence, adding an adjective clause that answers the question in parentheses. Your clause must begin with a relative pronoun (see the list that follows), and it must contain a verb. Your sentence should make sense within the context of the passage but should not use Cather's exact words. There may be more than one answer.

RELATIVE PRONOUNS who whom whose which that

SAMPLE He was a bishop. (What had he done?)

ANSWER He was a bishop who had worked in New Mexico for many years.

1. Bishop Latour was back in New Mexico. (How did he feel about being there?)
2. The old rugs, desk, and candlesticks were still in the room. (From what time did the bishop remember these items?)
3. He took comfort from the solid white walls. (How did the walls make him feel?)
4. He was an aging man. (How did he feel when he came to New Mexico?)
5. The room was cooled by a gentle wind. (What did the wind bring in?)
6. Bishop Latour had almost forgotten his age. (How did his body feel that morning?)
7. He had abandoned many cultural advantages. (How did they compare with the benefits of the desert?)
8. To the bishop, the desert had a special wind. (What was special about the wind?)
9. The air in places like Texas and Kansas had lost its lightness. (What was happening to those places now?)
10. The bishop could find this special air only in open, undeveloped areas. (What could this air do for the bishop?)
11. When he looked around the room, he saw the rugs and skins on the floor. (How did the room look compared to before?)
12. The walls were painted white. (What did the walls do to sound?)
13. He listened to the whistle of the locomotive. (How did the sound of the whistle make him feel?)
14. The sun shone through the window. (How did the sun feel on his skin?)
15. Bishop Latour had once lived in other surroundings. (How did he remember them?)
16. He had enjoyed the society of men. (What sort of men were they?)
17. The special air of the desert floated in on the morning breeze. (What did the air smell of?)
18. The air whispered in his ear. (What qualities did the air have?)
19. His spirit was released. (How had his spirit felt before?)
20. His spirit was caught up in the morning. (What color was the morning?)

Grammar Review **565**

Answers: Exercise 3

Answers will vary.

1. Bishop Latour, who felt very content, was back in New Mexico.
2. The old rugs, desk, and candlesticks, which he remembered from his youth, were still in the room.
3. He took comfort from the solid white walls, which protected him from the outside world.
4. He was an aging man whom New Mexico made young again.
5. The room was cooled by a gentle wind, which brought in the wonderful aromas of the outdoors.
6. Bishop Latour, whose body felt light and eager that morning, had almost forgotten his age.
7. He had abandoned many cultural advantages that he enjoyed less than the desert's benefits.
8. To the bishop the desert had a special wind that made him feel like a boy.
9. The air in places like Texas and Kansas, which were now being farmed, had lost its special quality.
10. The bishop could find this special air, which lightened his spirit, only in open, undeveloped areas.
11. When he looked around the room, which was little changed from before, he saw the rugs and skins on the floor.
12. The walls, which muted sound, were painted white.
13. He listened to the whistle of the locomotive, whose sound always amused him.
14. The sun, which felt hot on his skin, shone through the window.
15. Bishop Latour had once lived in other surroundings, which he also remembered with pleasure.
16. He had enjoyed the society of men who were learned.
17. The special air of the desert, which smelled of sagebrush and clover, floated in on the morning breeze.
18. The air, which was soft and wild and free, whispered in his ear.
19. His spirit, which had been imprisoned, was released.
20. His spirit was caught up in the morning, which was blue and gold.

Practice and Assess

Answers: Exercise 4

Answers will vary, but some suggestions are given below.

1. Bishop Latour felt quite happy because he was back in New Mexico.
2. As the night faded, he listened for church bells.
3. He had first come to New Mexico during an earlier period of the territory's history, before the railroad had arrived.
4. Bishop Latour felt like a young man whenever he awoke in New Mexico.
5. After he rose and began to shave, he realized that he was old.
6. That morning the aging bishop became aware of the fragrant wind when he awoke.
7. The light, dry wind made the bishop feel eager and full of life, as he had felt as a boy.
8. The bracing mornings of the desert had been worth his sacrifice of the comforts of civilization because in the desert he regained his youth.
9. Unfortunately, the air in a new, untamed country lost its freshness and lightness after the area was developed.
10. For example, the dry, fragrant air had changed in parts of Texas and Kansas when the land had been plowed.
11. The bishop's room seemed little changed because it had the same rugs and skins, the same desk, and the same walls.
12. The walls gave repose to the spirit as they muted sound and shut out the world.
13. He was amused because he heard the whistle of a locomotive.
14. The air had lost that dry, fresh fragrance when the land was plowed.
15. It was still quite possible, however, to breathe the special air wherever there were great grass plains or the sagebrush desert.
16. The special air would very likely disappear after the bishop was dead.
17. He had to come back to die in exile because the air had become necessary to him.
18. His heart lightened because something whispered in his ear.
19. The air whispered in his ear as he lay in bed.

Review: Exercise 4 Writing Sentences with Adverb Clauses

The sentences that follow elaborate on ideas suggested by the passage from *Death Comes for the Archbishop*. On your paper, rewrite each sentence, adding an adverb clause that answers the question in parentheses. Your clause must begin with one of the subordinating conjunctions listed below, and it must contain a verb. The sentence should make sense within the context of the passage but should not use Cather's exact words. There may be more than one answer for each item.

SUBORDINATING CONJUNCTIONS

after	as if	in order to	though	whenever
although	because	since	until	where
as	before	than	when	wherever

SAMPLE The room was familiar to Latour. (Why?)
ANSWER The room was familiar to Latour because he had lived there before.

1. Bishop Latour felt quite happy. (Why?)
2. He listened for church bells. (When?)
3. He had first come to New Mexico during an earlier period in the territory's history. (When?)
4. Bishop Latour felt like a young man. (When?)
5. He realized that he was old. (When?)
6. That morning the aging bishop became aware of the fragrant wind from his window. (When?)
7. The light, dry wind made the bishop feel eager and full of life. (To what extent?)
8. The bracing mornings of the desert had been worth his sacrifice of the comforts of civilization. (Why?)
9. Unfortunately, the air in a new, untamed country lost its freshness and lightness. (When?)
10. For example, the dry, fragrant air had changed in parts of Texas and Kansas. (When?)
11. The bishop's room seemed little changed. (Why?)
12. The walls gave repose to the spirit. (How?)
13. He was amused. (Why?)
14. The air had lost that dry, fresh fragrance. (When?)
15. It was still quite possible, however, for one to breathe the fresh, sweet air. (Where?)
16. The special air would very likely disappear. (When?)
17. He had to come back to die in exile. (Why?)
18. His heart lightened. (Why?)
19. The air whispered in his ear. (When?)
20. His spirit was outdoors. (Where?)

566 Unit 13 Clauses and Sentence Structure

20. His spirit was outdoors, wherever the wind blew.

Review: Exercise 5 — Identifying Noun Clauses

The following sentences describe the history of New Mexico. On your paper, write the noun clauses that appear in the sentences. Two of the sentences have two noun clauses each.

1. Whoever is familiar with the Southwest recognizes that New Mexico's history makes it one of the most intriguing states in the country.
2. Does this reference book tell whether the earliest human settlements in New Mexico date from ten thousand years ago or twenty thousand years ago?
3. Pueblos and cliff dwellings were built by whoever originally inhabited the region.
4. How these structures were built can be determined by examining the remaining ruins.
5. What historians also know is that the Navajo and Apache later moved down to New Mexico from the north.
6. The sixteenth century was when the Spanish explorers and Catholic missionaries arrived.
7. The explorers believed that they would find huge amounts of gold in the Americas.
8. Have you read about how the Spaniards treated the Native Americans?
9. What had become part of Mexico's territory in 1821 was ceded to the United States in 1848, after the Mexican War.
10. This history of settlement and conquest tells us why three cultures come together in New Mexico today: Native American, Spanish, and Anglo-American.
11. The history of New Mexico in the nineteenth century is the story of how the area became a United States territory.
12. The opening of the Santa Fe Trail meant that more pioneers could travel to New Mexico.
13. The trading post at Santa Fe was an important stopover for whoever journeyed west along the trail.
14. A major turning point in the Civil War was when the Union troops defeated the Confederates at Glorieta Pass.
15. Why do historians think that the battle of Glorieta was important?
16. That the Union victory kept the Southwest from joining the Confederacy is of major significance.
17. The newly built railroads provided transportation to wherever New Mexicans wanted to go.
18. Why so many settlers poured into New Mexico in the 1890s is a question that has many answers.
19. The increase in population is why New Mexico was admitted to the Union as the forty-seventh state in 1912.
20. What attracts people to this state today is its climate, its scenery, and its rich mix of peoples and cultures.

Grammar Review **567**

Clauses and Sentence Structure

Answers: Exercise 5

1. Whoever is familiar with the Southwest; that New Mexico's history makes it one of the most intriguing states in the country
2. whether the earliest human settlements in New Mexico date from ten thousand years ago or twenty thousand years ago
3. whoever originally inhabited the region
4. How these structures were built
5. What historians also know; that the Navajo and Apache later moved down to New Mexico from the north
6. when the Spanish explorers and Catholic missionaries arrived
7. that they would find huge amounts of gold in the Americas
8. how the Spaniards treated the Native Americans
9. What had become part of Mexico's territory in 1821
10. why three cultures come together in New Mexico today: Native American, Spanish, and Anglo-American
11. how the area became a United States territory
12. that more pioneers could travel to New Mexico
13. whoever journeyed west along the trail
14. when the Union troops defeated the Confederates at Glorieta Pass
15. that the battle of Glorieta was important
16. That the Union victory kept the Southwest from joining the Confederacy
17. wherever New Mexicans wanted to go
18. Why so many settlers poured into New Mexico in the 1890s
19. why New Mexico was admitted to the Union as the forty-seventh state in 1912
20. What attracts people to this state today

Practice and Assess

Answers: Exercise 6

1. exclamatory; New Mexico's history is fascinating.
2. declarative; Was New Mexico annexed to the United States in 1848?
3. interrogative; New Mexico formerly belonged to Mexico.
4. interrogative; Investigate the earliest human settlements in New Mexico.
5. declarative; Did Bishop Latour's first trip to New Mexico take much longer than such a journey would take today?
6. exclamatory; It was a long and difficult journey.
7. imperative; He took a ship from New Orleans to Galveston.
8. exclamatory; Did Latour endure many hardships on the way?
9. interrogative; Latour had to travel through the Rio Grande Valley.
10. declarative; Work hard at your mission.
11. interrogative; How wild and beautiful the landscape was!
12. imperative; He savored the air of this country while he still could.
13. declarative; How the bishop loved the desert!
14. exclamatory; How familiar and comforting did his old room seem?
15. declarative; Feel the gentle wind in the morning.
16. imperative; Will you make your home in the desert, Bishop Latour?
17. exclamatory; Was the air light and fragrant?
18. declarative; Did the bishop know that he had come to the desert to die?
19. interrogative; How the air made the old man feel like a boy again!
20. declarative; Trade the comforts of civilization for something better—your freedom.

Review: Exercise 6   **Writing Four Kinds of Sentences**

The following sentences develop an idea or image suggested by the passage from *Death Comes for the Archbishop*. On your paper, identify each of the following sentences as *declarative, imperative, interrogative,* or *exclamatory.* Then rewrite each sentence in the form noted in parentheses. There may be more than one answer.

SAMPLE   He took the train from New York to Cincinnati.
(Rewrite in the imperative form.)

ANSWER   declarative
Take the train from New York to Cincinnati.

1. How fascinating New Mexico's history is! (Rewrite as a declarative sentence.)
2. New Mexico was annexed to the United States in 1848. (Rewrite as an interrogative sentence.)
3. Did New Mexico formerly belong to Mexico? (Rewrite as a declarative sentence.)
4. Did you investigate the earliest human settlements in New Mexico? (Rewrite as an imperative sentence.)
5. Bishop Latour's first trip to New Mexico took much longer than such a journey would today. (Rewrite as an interrogative sentence.)
6. What a long and difficult journey it was! (Rewrite as a declarative sentence.)
7. Take a ship from New Orleans to Galveston. (Rewrite as a declarative sentence.)
8. How many hardships Latour endured on the way! (Rewrite as an interrogative sentence.)
9. Did Latour have to travel through the Rio Grande Valley? (Rewrite as a declarative sentence.)
10. Bishop Latour worked hard at his mission. (Rewrite as an imperative sentence.)
11. Was the landscape wild and beautiful? (Rewrite as an exclamatory sentence.)
12. Savor the air of this country while you still can. (Rewrite as a declarative sentence.)
13. The bishop loved the desert. (Rewrite as an exclamatory sentence.)
14. How familiar and comforting his old room seemed? (Rewrite as an interrogative sentence.)
15. Latour always felt the gentle wind in the morning. (Rewrite as an imperative sentence.)
16. Make your home in the desert, Bishop Latour. (Rewrite as an interrogative sentence.)
17. How light and fragrant the air was! (Rewrite as an interrogative sentence.)
18. The bishop knew that he had come to the desert to die. (Rewrite as an interrogative sentence.)
19. Did the air make the old man feel like a boy again? (Rewrite as an exclamatory sentence.)
20. He traded the comforts of civilization for something better—his freedom. (Rewrite as an imperative sentence.)

Review: Exercise 7   Correcting Sentence Fragments

The following paragraph describes a scene related to the passage from *Death Comes for the Archbishop*. On your paper, revise the paragraph, correcting sentence fragments by combining sentences, adding words (a subject or a verb), or changing a verb form.

SAMPLE   The man who came to Santa Fe.

ANSWER   The man who came to Santa Fe had lived there before.

¹Waking in his old room, felt happy. ²A white-walled room, filled with familiar furnishings, such as his old rugs, desk, and candlesticks. ³Also familiar sounds floating in from the outside. ⁴For example, the locomotive whistle that always amused him. ⁵Most important of all, however, was the wondrous fresh wind from the desert. ⁶Made him feel young and spirited like a boy. ⁷Actually, an elderly man seeking the wild desert. ⁸Because he could not do without its magic air. ⁹Would that air last forever? ¹⁰Not after the primitive area tamed.

Review: Exercise 8   Correcting Run-on Sentences

On your paper, revise the following sentences, correcting run-ons. Write *correct* if the sentence does not contain run-ons.

SAMPLE   New Mexico's stunning landscapes attract tourists from all over the world its colorful history fascinates scholars from many fields.

ANSWER   New Mexico's stunning landscapes attract tourists from all over the world. Its colorful history fascinates scholars from many fields.

1. New Mexico has been inhabited for at least 10,000 years early rock carvings can still be found near the Sandia Mountains and the present-day town of Folsom.
2. The landscape of New Mexico is varied and spectacular; it includes not only sandy deserts but also snowy mountains, forests, buttes, and mesas.
3. The population has exploded recently yet New Mexico remains one of the least populous states in the country.
4. More than 38 percent of New Mexico's population is of Spanish or Mexican origin, another 9 percent is made up of Navajo, Pueblo, and other Native American groups.
5. New Mexico includes vast open spaces, but nearly three quarters of the total population is concentrated in urban areas such as Albuquerque and Santa Fe.
6. The Spanish first came to New Mexico in search of gold however, missionary work became the main activity in the 1600s.
7. Navajos were treated harshly their relations with the Spanish were often hostile.
8. In 1848 New Mexico was made a U.S. territory, in 1912 it became a state.
9. The railroad reached New Mexico in 1878 and the population began to expand.
10. The architecture, art, and crafts of the area are exceptional, the arts of three cultures have flourished—and often blended—there.

Grammar Review   **569**

10. The architecture, art, and crafts of the area are exceptional. The arts of three cultures have flourished—and often blended—there.

Clauses and Sentence Structure

Answers: Exercise 7

Answers may vary, but some suggestions are given below.

1. Waking in his old room, Bishop Latour felt happy.
2. It was a white-walled room, filled with familiar furnishings, such as his old rugs, desk, and candlesticks.
3–4. Familiar sounds floated in from the outside, such as the locomotive whistle that always amused him.
5–6. Most important of all, however, was the wondrous desert wind that made him feel young and spirited like a boy.
7–8. Actually he was an elderly man seeking the wild desert because he could not do without its magic air.
9. Would that air last forever?
10. No, it would disappear after the primitive area was tamed.

Answers: Exercise 8

Answers will vary, but some suggestions are given below.

1. New Mexico has been inhabited for at least 10,000 years; early rock carvings can still be found near the Sandia Mountains and the present-day town of Folsom.
2. correct
3. The population has exploded recently, yet New Mexico remains one of the least populous states in the country.
4. More than 38 percent of New Mexico's population is of Spanish or Mexican origin. Another 9 percent is made up of Navajo, Pueblo, and other Native American groups.
5. correct
6. The Spanish first came to New Mexico in search of gold; however, missionary work became the main activity in the 1600s.
7. Navajos were treated harshly, and their relations with the Spanish were often hostile.
8. In 1848 New Mexico was made a U.S. territory; in 1912 it became a state.
9. The railroad reached New Mexico in 1878, and the population began to expand.

Practice and Assess

Answers: Exercise 9

Answers will vary, but a suggestion is given below.

1. New Mexico has dozens of fascinating places to visit; they range . . . ancient communities.
2. In the south is Carlsbad Caverns National Park, which contains the largest cavern yet discovered.
3–4. Also in the south is White Sands National Monument, a rare gypsum desert, where the white sand is formed into huge dunes.
5–6. The most spectacular sight . . . balloon fiesta, which takes place in October.
7. North of Albuquerque is Santa Fe, with its many shops, museums, beautiful old mission churches, and stunning opera house.
8. Nearby are the ancient cliff dwellings of the Anasazi people, and slightly higher up is the village of Los Alamos, where the first atomic bomb was developed.
9. Scattered through the state are pueblos in which Native Americans have lived for centuries.
10. The two most populous Native American groups in New Mexico are the Navajo and the Apache; many of them live on large reservations.

Answers: Exercise 10
Proofreading

This proofreading activity provides editing practice with (1) the current or previous units' skills, (2) the **Troubleshooter** errors, and (3) spelling errors. Students should be able to complete the exercise by referring to the units, the **Troubleshooter,** and a dictionary. (Note: A run-on sentence counts as one error.)

Error (Type of Error)

1. was born (verb tense)
2. began (verb form)
3. art, (run-on sentence)
4. taught (verb form)
5. She was (sentence fragment)
6. time, (run-on sentence)
7. realistic; (run-on sentence)
8. her summers (pronoun-antecedent agreement)
9. She moved (sentence fragment)
10. Mexico, (run-on sentence)
11. perspectives, (nonessential adjective clause)

12. skull (spelling)
13. consider (subject-verb agreement)
14. exaggerated (spelling)
15. painted! (End punctuation)
16. Mexico, (nonessential appositive)

570

Grammar Review

Review: Exercise 9   Correcting Sentence Structure

The following paragraph describes places of interest in New Mexico. On your paper, revise the paragraph, correcting sentence fragments and run-on sentences. Some sentences are correct, but you may wish to combine them with other sentences. Try to vary your sentence structure and use correct punctuation.

[1]New Mexico has dozens of fascinating places to visit, they range from lush forests to steep ski slopes, include art museums and ancient communities. [2]In the southern part of the state, Carlsbad Caverns National Park, which contains the largest cavern yet discovered. [3]Also in the south is White Sands National Monument, it is a rare gypsum desert. [4]White sand into huge dunes. [5]The most spectacular sight in Albuquerque is the hot-air balloon fiesta. [6]Takes place in October. [7]North of Albuquerque is Santa Fe, its many shops, museums, beautiful old mission churches, and stunning opera house. [8]Nearby the ancient cliff dwellings of the Anasazi people, slightly higher up is the village of Los Alamos, where the first atomic bomb was developed. [9]Scattered through the state are pueblos, Native Americans have lived there for centuries. [10]The two most populous Native American groups in New Mexico are the Navajo and the Apache and many of them live on large reservations.

Review: Exercise 10

Proofreading

The following passage describes the artist Georgia O'Keeffe, whose painting appears on the opposite page. Rewrite the passage, correcting the errors in spelling, grammar, and usage. Add any missing punctuation. There are twenty-five errors.

Georgia O'Keeffe

[1]Georgia O'Keeffe (1887–1986) is born in Sun Prairie, Wisconsin. [2]When she was only seventeen, she begun her formal training at the Art Institute of Chicago. [3]Two years later, she went to New York City to continue her study of art and she remained in the city for several years. [4]During the winters from 1912 to 1918, she taught school in Texas. [5]Was drawn to its dramatic landscape and enormous skies.

[6]O'Keeffe lived in New York for a time and she made her first paintings of nature there. [7]These paintings were not realistic they were filled with flat patterns and bold colors. [8]O'Keeffe began spending your summers in New Mexico in 1929. [9]Moved there permanently in 1949. [10]She refined her lush, highly abstract style in New Mexico and it was there that she painted her most memorable works. [11]Her landscapes often present unusual perspectives which make the

Clauses and Sentence Structure

viewer feel suspended in air. ¹²Other paintings focus closely on a single image, such as a flower or the weather-beaten skul of an animal.

¹³Many critics in the art world considers O'Keeffe one of the forerunners of American abstract art. ¹⁴She deliberately exagerated the shape, proportion, size, and color of the objects and scenes that she painted. ¹⁵What huge flowers she painted ¹⁶Her paintings, particularly those made in New Mexico have a spiritual quality.

¹⁷*Gate of Adobe Church* (1929) is typical of O'Keeffes abstract style. ¹⁸She captures in this picture which has broad sweeps of color and a simple design, the mood and sense of a place. ¹⁹She paints with uncluttered simplicity which evokes a quiet spirituality an energetic clarity, and a radiant warmth. ²⁰O'Keeffe's strong sense of place is strikingly similar to Willa Cathers. ²¹Indeed, *Death Comes for the Archbishop* is filled with concrete, evocative images of the Southwest ²²Some of the most striking images is evoked by the main character of the novel a French bishop who has returned to New Mexico because he misses the dry, warm wind and the hot sun. ²³Can you feel the hot southwestern sun in this picture

Georgia O'Keeffe, *Gate of Adobe Church,* **1929**

Clauses and Sentence Structure

Answers: Exercise 10 (continued)
Proofreading

Error (Type of Error)
17. O'Keeffe's (singular possessive)
18. picture, (nonessential adjective clause)
19. simplicity, (nonessential adjective clause)
    spirituality, (commas in a series)
20. Cather's (singular possessive)
21. Southwest. (end punctuation)
22. are evoked (subject-verb agreement)
    novel, (nonessential appositive)
23. picture? (end punctuation)

Viewing the Art

Georgia O'Keeffe, *Gate of Adobe Church,* 1929

Both Georgia O'Keeffe and Willa Cather appealed to the senses to create a sense of place. In *Gate of Adobe Church,* O'Keeffe conveys the warmth and openness of New Mexico through her strong, balanced composition and the contrast between the richly textured ocher tones of the church and the cool azure sky.

Ask students to read through Willa Cather's passage from *Death Comes for the Archbishop* and to identify images that appeal to the senses. Which images evoke sounds? smells? touch? sight?

Practice and Assess

Answers: Exercise 11
Mixed Review

Answers will vary, but some suggestions are given below.

1. Willa Cather was born in Virginia in 1873, and her family moved to Nebraska in 1882.
2. In Red Cloud, Nebraska, she lived among European immigrants who were beginning a new life.
3. When Cather attended the University of Nebraska at Lincoln, she began to recognize her talent for writing.
4. She graduated from the university in 1895, and she moved across the continent to Pittsburgh, where she began working on the staff of the *Pittsburgh Leader.*
5. Cather worked next as the principal of a Pittsburgh high school.
6. In 1912 Cather decided that she would become a writer of novels.
7. When did Cather leave her position as managing editor of *McClure's,* the well-known magazine published in New York?
8. Cather was awarded the Pulitzer Prize for her novel *One of Ours* (1922), which deals largely with World War I.
9. Although her early novels were based on her memories of pioneer life, many of her later works focused on the anguish of creative people trapped in small-town life.
10. From 1925 to 1931, she produced four great novels, which were *The Professor's House* (1925), *My Mortal Enemy* (1926), *Death Comes for the Archbishop* (1927), and *Shadows on the Rock* (1931).

Close

Have students look through writing they have done to locate a paragraph that could benefit from sentence combining and especially the addition of subordinate clauses. Have them share their revisions with the class.

Clauses and Sentence Structure

Mixed Review

The items that follow describe the life of Willa Cather. On your paper, revise each item in the manner indicated in parentheses.

SAMPLE   Willa Cather often wrote about pioneers. Cather grew up on the Nebraska frontier. (Combine the sentences by turning the second sentence into an adjective clause beginning with *who.*)

ANSWER   Willa Cather, who grew up on the Nebraska frontier, often wrote about pioneers.

Willa Cather

1. Willa Cather was born in Virginia in 1873. Her family moved to Nebraska in 1882. (Rewrite as a compound sentence.)
2. In Red Cloud, Nebraska, she lived among European immigrants. They were beginning a new life. (Combine the sentences by turning the second sentence into an adjective clause beginning with *who.*)
3. Cather attended the University of Nebraska at Lincoln. She began to recognize her talent for writing. (Combine the sentences by turning the first sentence into an adverb clause beginning with *When.*)
4. She graduated from the university in 1895, and she moved across the continent to Pittsburgh. She began working on the staff of the *Pittsburgh Leader.* (Rewrite as a compound-complex sentence.)
5. Did Cather work next as principal of a Pittsburgh high school? (Rewrite as a declarative sentence.)
6. In 1912 Cather decided something. She would become a writer of novels. (Combine the sentences by turning the second sentence into a noun clause beginning with *that.*)
7. It was then that Cather left her position as managing editor of *McClure's,* the well-known magazine published in New York. (Rewrite as an interrogative sentence.)
8. Cather was awarded the Pulitzer Prize for her novel *One of Ours* (1922). Deals largely with World War I. (Eliminate the fragment by creating a complex sentence.)
9. Her early novels were based on her memories of pioneer life. Many of her later works focused on the anguish of creative people trapped in small-town life. (Combine the sentences by turning the first sentence into an adverb clause beginning with *Although.*)
10. From 1925 to 1931, she produced four great novels. These novels include *The Professor's House* (1925), *My Mortal Enemy* (1926), *Death Comes for the Archbishop* (1927), and *Shadows on the Rock* (1931). (Combine the sentences by turning the second sentence into an adjective clause beginning with *which.*)

Clauses and Sentence Structure

Writing Application

Sentence Structure in Writing

In *Tortuga* Rudolfo A. Anaya uses a variety of sentence types not only to capture the reader's interest but also to develop a pleasing rhythm and an appropriate mood. In the following passage, notice the structure of Anaya's sentences and the kinds of clauses he uses.

I remembered the rainbows of my childhood, beautifully sculptured arches reaching from north to south, shafts of light so pure their harmony seemed to wed the sky and earth. My mother had taught me to look at rainbows, the mantle of the Blessed Virgin Mary she called them. When a summer thunderstorm passed, she would take me out and we would stand in the thin drops which followed the storm. We would turn our faces up to the sky, and the large, glistening drops of rain would pelt our faces. She would open her mouth and hold out her tongue to receive the large, golden drops. She would stir the muddy ponds and pick up the little frogs which came with the rain.

Techniques with Sentence Structure

Try to apply some of Anaya's writing techniques when you write and revise.

❶ Avoid using the same sentence structure repeatedly.

SAME STRUCTURE A summer thunderstorm passed . . . She would take me out . . . We would stand . . .

ANAYA'S VERSION When a summer thunderstorm passed, she would take me out and we would stand . . .

❷ To emphasize some ideas and downplay others, put some ideas into subordinate clauses.

EQUAL ATTENTION We would stand in the thin drops [of rain]. The drops of rain followed the storm.

ANAYA'S VERSION . . . we would stand in the thin drops which followed the storm.

> **TIME**
> For more about the writing process, see TIME Facing the Blank Page, pp. 109–119

Clauses and Sentence Structure

Practice Practice these techniques by revising the following series of sentences and sentence fragments. Decide which ideas to stress and which to downplay. Use a variety of sentences.

I looked out the window of my car. I had stopped. By the side of the road. In the distance, a bare outline of mountain range. All around was the white, alkaline desert. Only the hardiest shrubs and grasses could grow on the desert. The cold winter rain continued. It had been only a drizzle. It had drizzled when I left home. Then the rain had turned icy. It had become more intense. Suddenly the rain stopped, the sun struggling to break through the clouds. The clouds were gray and heavy. Minutes passed. A glorious, glowing rainbow in the east. I sat entranced. The sight reminded me of other rainbows. I had enjoyed rainbows as a child.

Grammar Review **573**

Sentence Structure in Writing

You may have a student read the paragraph aloud. Then have students read it silently without interruption. Have them discuss how the structure of Rudolfo A. Anaya's sentences varies. Also, suggest that students make note of the different kinds of clauses Anaya uses.

Techniques with Sentence Structure

After students have discussed the writing techniques in the passage by Anaya, encourage them to see how those techniques are used in another piece of writing—for example, a paragraph or two from earlier in the review.

Practice

The answers to this challenging and enriching activity will vary. Refer to Techniques with Sentence Structure as you evaluate student choices.

I turned my head and looked out the window of my car, which was stopped by the side of the road. In the distance, I could see a bare outline of a mountain range. All around me was the white, alkaline desert on which only the hardiest shrubs and grasses could grow. The cold winter rain, which had started as a drizzle when I left home, had become more intense, turning into an icy rain. Then quite suddenly the rain stopped, and the sun struggled to break through the heavy gray clouds. Minutes passed, and soon a glorious, glowing rainbow appeared in the east. I sat entranced by the sight, remembering other rainbows that I had enjoyed as a child.

✔ **ASSESSMENT OPTIONS**

📁 *Tests with Answer Key & Rubrics*
Unit 13 Pretest, pp. 43–44
Unit 13 Mastery Test, pp. 45–46

💾 *Testmaker*
Unit 13 Pretest
Unit 13 Mastery Test

📼 *MindJogger Videoquizzes*

You may wish to administer the Unit 13 Mastery Test at this point.

Objectives

- To learn how to identify various sentence components, such as simple and complete subjects and various kinds of complements and modifiers
- To demonstrate control over various sentence components by representing them accurately in sentence diagrams

Key to Ability Levels

L1 Level 1 activities are within the basic ability range of students.

L2 Level 2 activities are within the ability range of average students.

L3 Level 3 activities are more challenging activities.

UNIT
14 Diagraming Sentences

Lesson **14.1**   **Diagraming Simple Sentences**   *575*

Lesson **14.2**   **Diagraming Simple Sentences with Phrases**   *578*

Lesson **14.3**   **Diagraming Sentences with Clauses**   *581*

574

Resource Manager

Planning Resources
- *Lesson Plans*
- *Block Scheduling*

 Transparencies
- *Bellringer*
- *Two-Minute Skill Drill*

📁 **Other Print Resources**
- *Grammar and Composition Handbook*

- *Grammar Enrichment*
- *Grammar Practice*
- *Grammar Reteaching*
- *Grammar Workbook*
- *Tests with Answer Key and Rubrics*

📼 **Video**
- *MindJogger Videoquizzes*

💾 **Software**
- *Interactive Grammar and Language Workbook*
- *Language Arts PASS*
- *Presentation Plus!*
- *Sentence Diagraming*
- *Testmaker*
- *Writer's Choice Puzzlemaker*

 Web Sites
- *writerschoice.glencoe.com*

14.1 Diagraming Simple Sentences

■ **Diagraming** is a method of showing how the various words and parts of a sentence function and relate to the sentence as a whole.

You begin to diagram a sentence by finding the simple subject. After you have found the subject, find the action or linking verb that goes with it. Write the subject and the verb on a horizontal line, called a baseline. Separate the subject and the verb with a vertical line that bisects the baseline. This line indicates the division between the complete subject and the complete predicate.

Senators meet.

subject	*action verb*
Senators	meet

Compound Subjects and Verbs

A compound subject or verb is placed on two horizontal lines, with the conjunction on a dotted vertical line connecting the horizontal lines. To diagram a simple sentence with a compound subject and a compound verb, follow the model diagram below. Note how the compound elements extend from the baseline.

Staffers and senators will meet and decide.

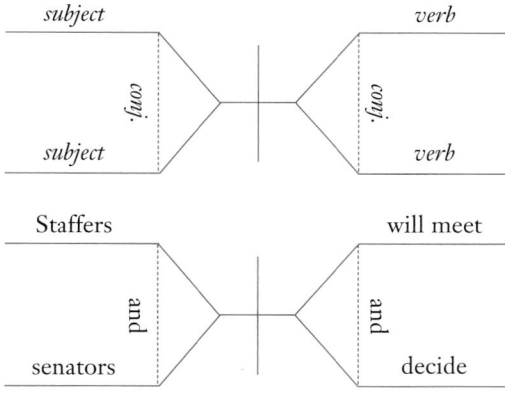

Focus

Lesson Overview

Objectives
- To understand how words function as parts of a sentence
- To represent sentence components correctly in sentence diagrams

 Bellringer
Daily Language Activity

When students enter the classroom, have this assignment on the board: *List and describe the parts of a complete sentence.* (A complete sentence has a subject and a predicate. The subject is the part about which something is being said. The predicate is the part that says something about the subject.)

See also *Daily Language Practice*

Motivating Activity

Write this sentence on the board: *Some dogs bark all night.* Have students tell why this is a simple sentence. (There is only one main clause and no subordinate clause.)

Teach

Compound Subjects and Verbs

☑ **Teaching Tip**

Before students begin diagraming, advise them to move any introductory adverbs or adverb phrases into the predicate part of the sentence.

Resource Manager

Planning Resources
- *Lesson Plans*

📂 **Other Print Resources**
- *Grammar and Composition Handbook*
- *Grammar Workbook,* Lesson 33

Diagraming Sentences

Teach

Direct Objects and Indirect Objects

☑ **Teaching Tip**

Make sure students understand how to distinguish the direct object from the indirect object.

Object Complements

☑ **Teaching Tip**

Point out to students that diagraming an object complement builds on what they learned about diagraming direct and indirect objects.

Subject Complements

☑ **Grammar Tip**

Remind students that a subject complement is a word that identifies or describes a subject. Subject complements often follow some form of the verb *be*.

Adjectives and Adverbs

☑ **Teaching Tip**

Point out that when more than one modifier modifies a single word, the modifiers should appear in the diagram in the same order in which they appear in the original sentence. Adverbs modifying adjectives appear in the diagram before the adjectives they modify.

Two-Minute Skill Drill

Have students diagram the following sentence:

The brown cow jumped over the silver moon.

✎ **See also** *Two-Minute Skill Drill Transparency 14.1*

Diagraming Sentences

Direct Objects and Indirect Objects

To diagram a simple sentence with an indirect object and a direct object, follow the model diagram below.

Experts have given senators advice.

subject	action verb	direct object
		indirect object

Experts	have given	advice
		senators

Object Complements

To diagram a simple sentence with an object complement, follow the model diagram below.

Everyone considered her important.

subject	action verb	direct object	object complement

Everyone	considered	her	important

Subject Complements

To diagram a simple sentence with a subject complement (a predicate nominative or a predicate adjective), follow the model diagram below.

Senators are legislators.

subject	linking verb	subject complement

Senators	are	legislators

MEETING INDIVIDUAL NEEDS — English Language Learners

Understanding Diagraming

Pair students who are learning English with students whose primary language is English. Have pairs work together to determine the parts of each sentence. They can take turns drawing the diagrams and checking one another's work. To assess students' knowledge, you may wish to have them describe their understanding of the function of a sentence diagram. Remind students that a sentence diagram shows the relationships of the words in the sentence to the sentence as a whole.

Senators should be helpful.

| Senators | should be \ | helpful |

Adjectives and Adverbs

To diagram a simple sentence with adjectives and adverbs, follow the model diagram below.

The more experienced senators meet regularly.

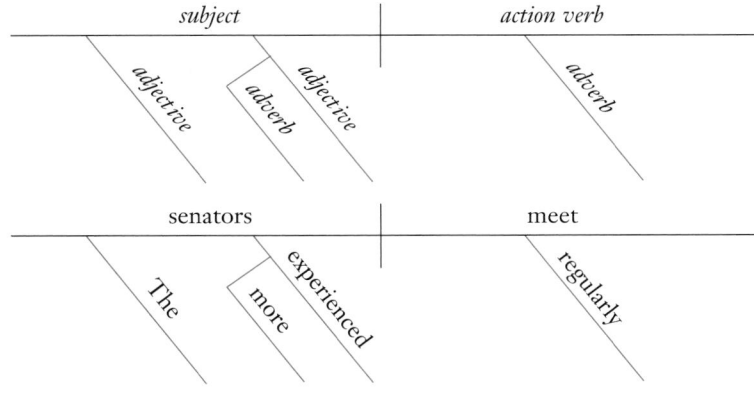

subject | action verb
adjective
adjective
adverb
adverb
senators | meet
The
experienced
more
regularly

Exercise 1   **Diagraming Simple Sentences**

Using the preceding models as a guide, diagram the following sentences.

1. An informed citizen votes thoughtfully.
2. The voters gave the candidate a landslide.
3. Rich and poor elected him president.
4. A president is powerful but may seem hesitant.
5. Newspapers called the election an easy victory.
6. Friends and associates sent the winner their congratulations.
7. The elated president-elect spoke happily.
8. The country was now the primary concern.
9. She felt the responsibility keenly.
10. The future would not be easy.

Close

Have students work in pairs to practice diagraming sentences. Remind them to check each other's work and to discuss any corrections that are needed.

Diagraming Sentences

Practice and Assess

Answers: Exercise 1

1.
2.
3.
4.
5.
6.
7.
8.
9.
10.

Additional Resources

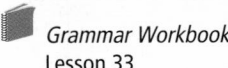

Grammar Workbook
Lesson 33

14.2

Focus

Lesson Overview

Objectives

- To understand how phrases function as parts of a sentence
- To diagram simple sentences with phrases correctly

 Bellringer

Daily Language Activity

When students enter the classroom, have this assignment on the board:
Diagram the following simple sentence:

Leaky pipes cause problems.

Have volunteers explain why they diagramed it the way they did.

See also *Daily Language Practice*

Teach

Prepositional Phrases

☑ **Teaching Tip**

Remind students to connect the prepositional phrase to the word it modifies.

Appositives and Appositive Phrases

☑ **Teaching Tip**

Remind students that an appositive is a noun or pronoun that is placed next to another noun or pronoun to identify or give additional information about it. An appositive phrase contains an appositive and words that modify it.

⇄ **Cross-reference: Grammar**

For instruction and practice on the function of phrases in sentences, refer students to Unit 12, pp. 522–541.

Diagraming Sentences (side tab)

14.2 Diagraming Simple Sentences with Phrases

Prepositional Phrases

Place the preposition on a diagonal line that descends from the word the prepositional phrase modifies. Place the object of the preposition on a horizontal line that joins the diagonal. The diagonal line on which the preposition is placed should extend somewhat beyond the horizontal on which the object of the preposition is placed, forming a "tail."

In their work, carpenters of today use tools with electric power.

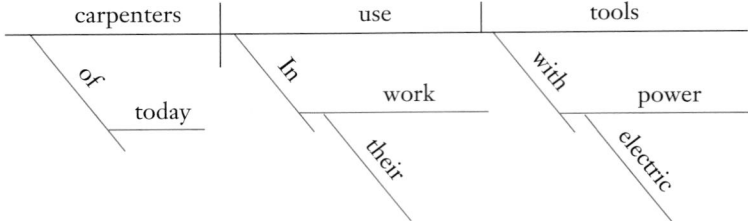

Appositives and Appositive Phrases

Place an appositive in parentheses after the noun or pronoun it identifies. Beneath it add any words that modify the appositive. Any words that modify the noun or pronoun itself, and not the appositive, should be placed directly beneath the noun or pronoun.

Argentina is proud of beautiful Buenos Aires, its cosmopolitan capital.

Resource Manager

Planning Resources
- *Lesson Plans*

📠 **Transparencies**
- *Bellringer*
- *Two-Minute Skill Drill*

📁 **Other Print Resources**
- *Grammar and Composition Handbook*
- *Grammar Workbook,* Lesson 34

Participles and Participial Phrases

The line on which the participle is placed descends diagonally from the word the participle modifies and then extends to the right horizontally. The participle is written on the curve, as shown below. Add any modifiers, objects, and complements to the horizontal line in the same way that you would show the modifiers, objects, and complements of an action verb.

Whistling, the carpenter completed the work, happily driving the last two nails.

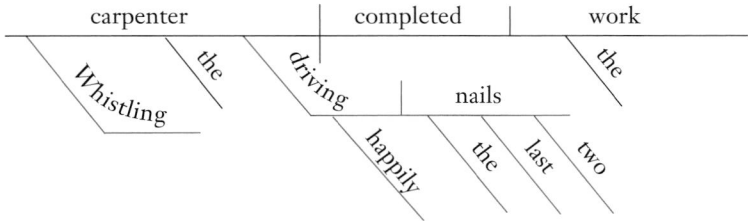

Gerunds and Gerund Phrases

Place a gerund on a "step," and add complements and modifiers in the usual way. Then set the gerund or the gerund phrase on a "stilt," and position the stilt in the diagram according to the role of the gerund in the sentence. (Remember that a gerund can be a subject, a direct object, an indirect object, a predicate nominative, an object of a preposition, or an appositive.)

Mitering is a common way of forming corner joints.

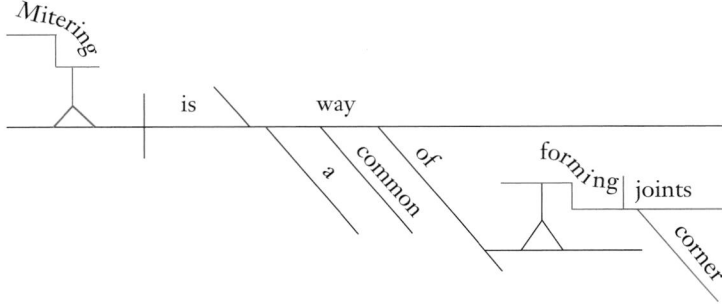

Teach

Participles and Participial Phrases

☑ **Teaching Tip**

Let a student give the definition of a participle (verb form that can function as an adjective). To locate the participle in a sentence, students should ask themselves these adjective questions: *What kind? Which one?*

Gerunds and Gerund Phrases

☑ **Grammar Tip**

Point out that gerunds are verbals. Gerunds are verb forms that end in *-ing* and function as nouns.

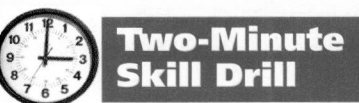 **Two-Minute Skill Drill**

Have a student write a simple sentence on the board, and let a volunteer diagram it. Students should evaluate the diagram and discuss any corrections that may be needed.

👉 **See also** *Two-Minute Skill Drill Transparency 14.2*

Diagraming Sentences

Exploring Language

Making a Chart

Go over the definitions (appositives, gerunds, and participles) that may confuse students. Suggest that students make a chart with the definitions. They can then refer to the chart as they diagram sentences. **L1**

579

Teach

Infinitives and Infinitive Phrases as Adjectives or Adverbs

☑ **Teaching Tip**

Explain to students that when deciding whether the infinitive phrase acts as an adjective or adverb, they should locate the word being modified and ask themselves what the phrase describes.

Infinitives and Infinitive Phrases as Nouns

☑ **Teaching Tip**

Tell students that as a noun, the infinitive phrase is often the subject of the sentence.

Practice and Assess

Answers: Exercise 2

1.

2.

3.

4.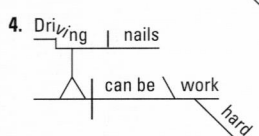

(sidebar) Diagraming Sentences

Infinitives and Infinitive Phrases as Adjectives or Adverbs

When an infinitive or an infinitive phrase is used as an adjective or an adverb, it is diagramed like a prepositional phrase.

Carpenters struggled to meet the deadline.

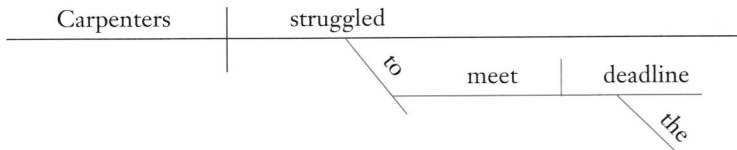

Infinitives and Infinitive Phrases as Nouns

When an infinitive or an infinitive phrase is used as a noun, it is diagramed like a prepositional phrase and then placed on a "stilt" in the subject, direct object, or predicate nominative position.

To work is to know satisfaction.

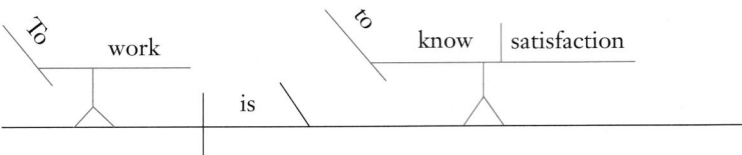

Exercise 2   Diagraming Simple Sentences with Phrases

Using the preceding models as a guide, diagram the following sentences.

1. A plumber from town installed pipes for water.
2. The pipes, copper tubing cylinders, arrived by heavy truck.
3. Several shingles, damaged by the wind, needed repairs.
4. Driving nails can be hard work.
5. To measure accurately is to save work.
6. The trade and craft of carpentry require working with lumber.
7. To build a house is to know joy.
8. Exhausted, the cabinetmaker finished by sanding carefully.
9. Crafting decorative woodwork requires a delicate touch.
10. Roofers, often unappreciated, work carefully to prevent costly leaks.

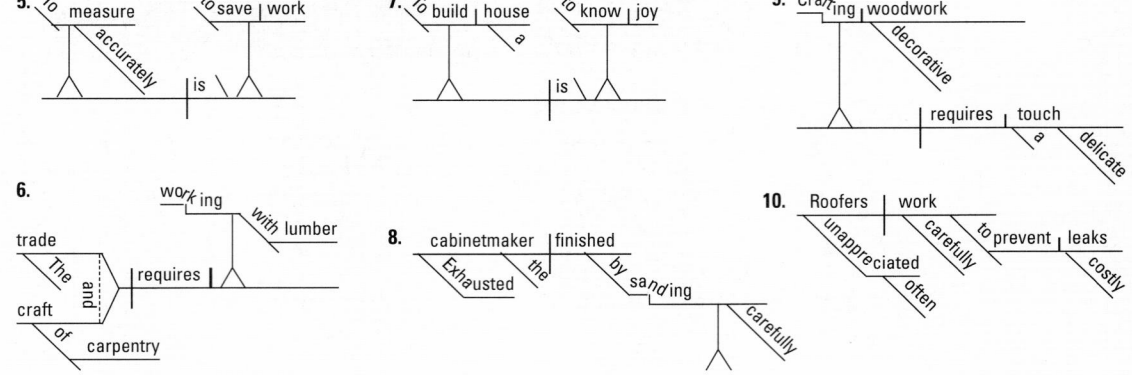

14.3 Diagraming Sentences with Clauses

Compound Sentences

Diagram each main clause separately. If the clauses are connected by a semicolon, use a vertical dotted line to connect the verbs of each main clause. If the main clauses are connected by a conjunction, place the conjunction on a solid horizontal line, and connect it to the verbs of each main clause by vertical dotted lines.

Mechanics like to fix objects, but carpenters must learn to build.

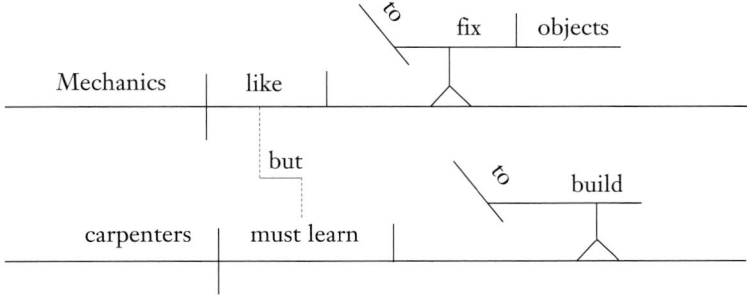

Complex Sentences with Adjective Clauses

Place the main clause in one diagram and the adjective clause beneath it in another diagram. Use a dotted line to connect the relative pronoun or other introductory word in the adjective clause to the modified noun or pronoun in the main clause.

The carpenter whom you hired fixed the shelves that were uneven.

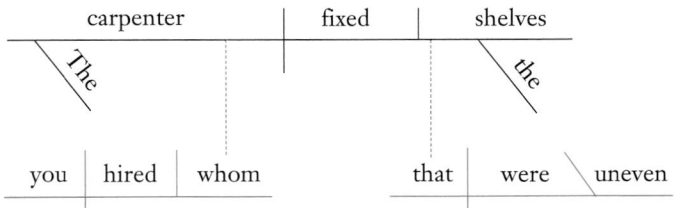

14.3 Diagraming Sentences with Clauses **581**

Focus

Lesson Overview

Objectives
- To see how clauses function as parts of composed and complex sentences
- To diagram compound and complex sentences correctly

 Bellringer
Daily Language Activity

When students enter the classroom, have this assignment on the board: *Write a sentence with a subordinate clause.*
Have volunteers read their sentences aloud and identify the main and subordinate clauses in them.

See also *Daily Language Practice*

Teach

Compound Sentences

☑ **Teaching Tip**

Explain that in compound sentences, each clause is diagramed on a separate horizontal line, following the format of the simple sentence. Connect the clauses with dotted lines.

Complex Sentences with Adjective Clauses

☑ **Teaching Tip**

Explain to students that in a complex sentence with more than one subordinate clause, each clause should be diagramed under the word it modifies. Clauses (whether subordinate or main) are connected with dotted lines rather than solid lines.

Diagraming Sentences (side tab)

Resource Manager

Planning Resources
- *Lesson Plans*

 Transparencies
- *Bellringer*
- *Two-Minute Skill Drill*

 Other Print Resources
- *Grammar and Composition Handbook*
- *Grammar Workbook*, Lesson 35

Teach

Complex Sentences with Adverb Clauses

☑ Teaching Tip

Tell students to ask themselves the *how? when?* and *to what extent?* questions to locate the adverb clause for each sentence.

⇄ Cross-reference: Grammar

For instruction and practice on the function of adverb clauses in sentences, refer students to Lesson 13.6, pp. 551–552.

Complex Sentences with Noun Clauses

☑ Teaching Tip

Remind students that a noun clause has the same function it would have if it were a single noun. You may wish also to remind students of some of the common introductory words that begin noun clauses—for example, *how, that, when, whoever, what.*

⇄ Cross-reference: Grammar

For instruction and practice on the function of noun clauses in sentences, refer students to Lesson 13.7, pp. 553–555.

Diagraming Sentences

Two-Minute Skill Drill

Remind students of the technique of diagraming compound sentences by having them diagram the following sentence.

You bring the coffee, and I will bring the doughnuts.

See also *Two-Minute Skill Drill Transparency 14.3*

Complex Sentences with Adverb Clauses

Place the main clause in one diagram and the adverb clause beneath it in another diagram. Place the subordinating conjunction on a diagonal dotted line, connecting the verb in the adverb clause to the modified verb, adjective, or adverb in the main clause.

Before they cut the wood, carpenters make a design.

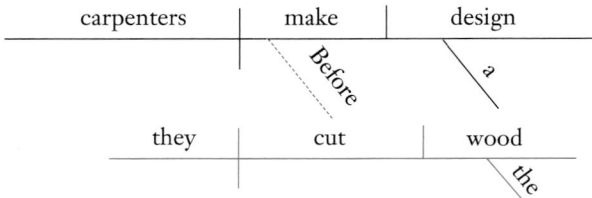

Complex Sentences with Noun Clauses

First decide what role the noun clause plays within the main clause. Is it the subject, direct object, predicate nominative, or object of a preposition? Then diagram the main clause, placing the noun clause on a "stilt" in the appropriate position. Place the introductory word of the clause in the position of the subject, object, or predicate nominative within the noun clause itself. If the introductory word merely begins the noun clause, place it on a line of its own above the verb in the noun clause, connecting it to the verb with a dotted vertical line.

NOUN CLAUSE AS SUBJECT

What that carpenter builds is especially sturdy.

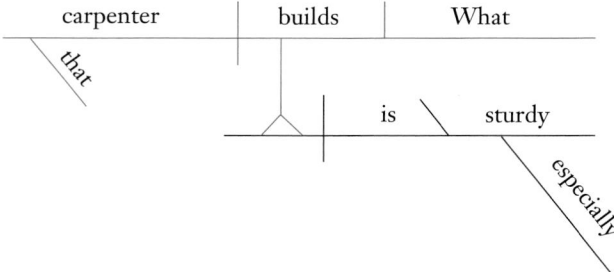

MEETING INDIVIDUAL NEEDS — Gifted and Talented

Diagraming Nursery Rhymes

Invite students to diagram famous lines from nursery rhymes. Have them write suggestions on the board. For example: "Jack Sprat could eat no fat." For further challenge, they could try diagraming a nonsense sentence from a poem such as Lewis Carroll's "Jabberwocky." **L3**

NOUN CLAUSE AS DIRECT OBJECT

We know that the mechanic fixes machines.

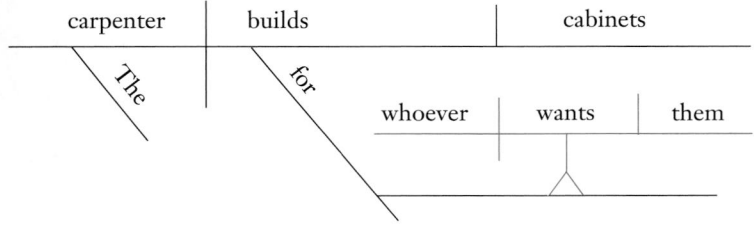

NOUN CLAUSE AS OBJECT OF A PREPOSITION

The carpenter builds cabinets for whoever wants them.

Exercise 3 Diagraming Sentences with Clauses

Using the preceding models as a guide, diagram the following sentences.

1. Carpenters work with wood, and masons work with stone.
2. The wood that we use is yellow pine.
3. When you design a house, you think about spaces.
4. An architectural style is what you must choose next.
5. That tastes in style vary is common knowledge.
6. The colonial style is popular with whoever values tradition.
7. Some people like whatever their neighbors like.
8. Before people move, they decide on a style.
9. When you travel in the West, you see more modern houses.
10. The style that I prefer is really a combination.

14.3 Diagraming Sentences with Clauses **583**

Diagraming Sentences

Practice and Assess

Answers: Exercise 3

1.
2.
3.
4.
5.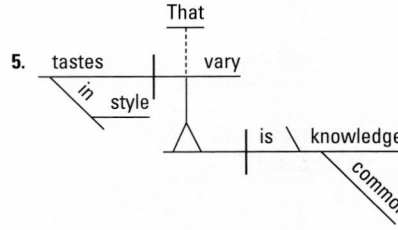

6. Diagram appears in the bottom channel.

7.

583

6.
8.
9.
10.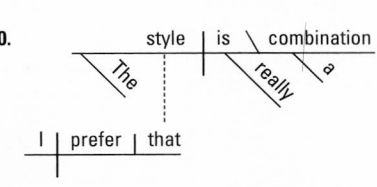

Objectives

- To learn about the tenses and voice of verbs, including the past, past perfect, and future perfect tenses, and active and passive voice

- To demonstrate control over the use of verb tenses and voice by identifying them and by using them correctly and effectively in writing

Key to Ability Levels

L1 Level 1 activities are within the basic ability range of students.

L2 Level 2 activities are within the ability range of average students.

L3 Level 3 activities are more challenging activities.

UNIT 15 Verb Tenses and Voice

Lesson **15.1**	**Principal Parts of Verbs**	585
Lesson **15.2**	**Regular and Irregular Verbs**	586
Lesson **15.3**	**Tenses of Verbs**	589
Lesson **15.4**	**Perfect Tenses**	593
Lesson **15.5**	**Progressive and Emphatic Forms**	596
Lesson **15.6**	**Compatibility of Tenses**	598
Lesson **15.7**	**Voices of Verbs**	600
Grammar Review		602
Writing Application		611

Resource Manager

Planning Resources
- *Lesson Plans*
- *Block Scheduling*

Transparencies
- *Bellringer*
- *Daily Language Practice*
- *Two-Minute Skill Drill*

📁 Other Print Resources
- *Grammar and Composition Handbook*
- *Grammar Enrichment*
- *Grammar Practice*
- *Grammar Reteaching*
- *Grammar Workbook*
- *Tests with Answer Key and Rubrics*

📼 Video
- *MindJogger Videoquizzes*

💾 Software
- *Interactive Grammar and Language Workbook*
- *Language Arts PASS*
- *Presentation Plus!*
- *Testmaker*
- *Writer's Choice Puzzlemaker*

🖥 Web Sites
- *writerschoice.glencoe.com*

15.1 Principal Parts of Verbs

■ All verbs have four **principal parts**—a *base form*, a *present participle*, a *simple past form*, and a *past participle*. All the verb tenses are formed from these principal parts.

Principal Parts of Verbs			
Base Form	**Present Participle**	**Past Form**	**Past Participle**
sail	sailing	sailed	sailed
soar	soaring	soared	soared
work	working	worked	worked
sing	singing	sang	sung
be	being	was, were	been
hit	hitting	hit	hit

You can use the base form (except the base form of *be*) and the past form alone as main verbs. The present participle and the past participle, however, must always be used with one or more auxiliary verbs to function as the simple predicate.

> Carpenters **work.** [base or present form]
>
> Carpenters **worked.** [past form]
>
> Carpenters **are working.** [present participle with the auxiliary verb *are*]
>
> Carpenters **have worked.** [past participle with the auxiliary verb *have*]

Exercise 1   Using Principal Parts of Verbs

Copy and complete each of the following sentences with the principal part of the verb that is indicated in parentheses.

1. Most plumbers ___ hot water heaters.
   (base form of *repair*)
2. Our plumber is ___ the kitchen sink.
   (present participle of *repair*)
3. Last month, he ___ the dishwasher.
   (past form of *repair*)
4. He has ___ many appliances in this house.
   (past participle of *repair*)
5. He is ___ his work.
   (present participle of *enjoy*)

Focus

Lesson Overview

Objectives
- To identify principal parts of verbs
- To use the principal parts of verbs correctly in writing

Bellringer
Daily Language Activity

When students enter the classroom, have this assignment on the board: *Use each of the following verbs in a complete sentence:*

think	*was thinking*
thought	*had thought*

See also *Daily Language Practice*

Teach

📧 **Cross-reference: Troubleshooter**
For instruction and practice in using verbs correctly, refer students to the **Troubleshooter.**

Practice and Assess

Answers: Exercise 1

1. repair	**4.** repaired
2. repairing	**5.** enjoying
3. repaired	

Close

Point out to students that each verb listed in the Bellringer is a form of the verb "to think." Discuss with students the formation of the verb tenses using *think*.

Verb Tenses and Voice

Resource Manager

Planning Resources
- *Lesson Plans*

🖥 **Transparencies**
- *Bellringer*
- *Daily Language Practice*

📁 **Other Print Resources**
- *Grammar and Composition Handbook*
- *Grammar Reteaching*, p. 25
- *Grammar Workbook*, Lesson 36

Focus

Lesson Overview

Objectives
- To identify the forms of regular and irregular verbs
- To use the correct forms of verbs in writing

Bellringer
Daily Language Activity

When students enter the classroom, have this assignment on the board: *Write the past and past participle forms of the following verbs. Then use one form of each verb in a sentence.*

perform   sing   teach

See also *Daily Language Practice*

Motivating Activity

Ask students to write five base forms of verbs on a piece of paper. Then challenge pairs of students to trade lists and to write the past and past participle form of each word without consulting the charts on the student pages.

Teach

Cross-reference: Grammar
For instruction and practice of verb and verb phrases, refer students to Lesson 10.3, pp. 453–459.

Cross-reference: Usage
For instruction and practice in using *lay, lie, sit,* and *set,* refer students to Unit 19, pp. 690–703.

Verb Tenses and Voice

15.2 | Regular and Irregular Verbs

■ A **regular verb** forms its past and past participle by adding -*ed* to the base form.

Regular Verbs		
Base Form	**Past Form**	**Past Participle**
soar	soared	soared
climb	climbed	climbed
ski	skied	skied

When a suffix beginning with a vowel is added to the base form of some regular verbs, the verbs undergo spelling changes.

regulate + **-ed** = regulat**ed**   try + **-ed** = tri**ed**

stop + **-ed** = stopp**ed**   grin + **-ed** = grinn**ed**

■ An **irregular verb** forms its past and past participle in some way other than adding -*ed* to the base form.

Irregular Verbs		
Base Form	**Past Form**	**Past Participle**
be	was, were	been
beat	beat	beaten
become	became	become
begin	began	begun
bite	bit	bitten *or* bit
blow	blew	blown
break	broke	broken
bring	brought	brought
burst	burst	burst
buy	bought	bought
catch	caught	caught
choose	chose	chosen
come	came	come
do	did	done
draw	drew	drawn
drink	drank	drunk
drive	drove	driven
eat	ate	eaten
fall	fell	fallen
feel	felt	felt
find	found	found
fly	flew	flown

Resource Manager

Planning Resources
- *Lesson Plans*

Transparencies
- *Bellringer*
- *Daily Language Practice*
- *Two-Minute Skill Drill*

📂 **Other Print Resources**
- *Grammar and Composition Handbook*
- *Grammar Enrichment,* p. 25
- *Grammar Practice,* p. 25
- *Grammar Workbook,* Lesson 37

Irregular Verbs		
Base Form	**Past Form**	**Past Participle**
freeze	froze	frozen
get	got	got *or* gotten
give	gave	given
go	went	gone
grow	grew	grown
hang	hung *or* hanged	hung *or* hanged
have	had	had
hold	held	held
know	knew	known
lay*	laid	laid
lead	led	led
leave	left	left
lend	lent	lent
lie*	lay	lain
lose	lost	lost
put	put	put
ride	rode	ridden
ring	rang	rung
rise*	rose	risen
run	ran	run
say	said	said
see	saw	seen
set*	set	set
shake	shook	shaken
shrink	shrank *or* shrunk	shrunk *or* shrunken
sing	sang	sung
sink	sank *or* sunk	sunk
sit*	sat	sat
speak	spoke	spoken
spend	spent	spent
spring	sprang *or* sprung	sprung
steal	stole	stolen
swim	swam	swum
swing	swung	swung
take	took	taken
teach	taught	taught
tear	tore	torn
tell	told	told
think	thought	thought
throw	threw	thrown
wear	wore	worn
weave	wove	woven
win	won	won
write	wrote	written

*For more detailed instruction on *lay* versus *lie*, see Unit 19.

*For more detailed instruction on *raise* versus *rise* and *sit* versus *set*, see Unit 19.

15.2 Regular and Irregular Verbs **587**

Teach

Cooperative Learning

Have students form pairs and ask each student to write seven verbs on an index card. The verbs can be regular or irregular. Next, challenge students to exchange cards with their partners and use all the verbs in a narrative that begins *Just last week . . .* Students can share their narratives with the class.

☑ Teaching Tip

With a few exceptions, such as *become* and *begin*, most of the irregular verbs are monosyllabic, and all of them have come to us from Old English rather than from Latin or Old French.

⇄ Cross-reference: Troubleshooter

For instruction and practice in using regular and irregular verbs, refer students to the **Troubleshooter**.

☑ Grammar Tip

Students often confuse the past and the past participle forms of verbs. One way to help them distinguish the two forms is to remind them that only the past participle can follow the helping verb *have*.

Two-Minute Skill Drill

List these base words on the board. Have students write the past participle of each base word.

be	*do*	*hang*
draw	*ride*	*wear*

See also *Two-Minute Skill Drill Transparency 15.2*

English Language Learners

Pronouncing the Past Form of Regular Verbs

Students just beginning to learn English sometimes have trouble pronouncing the regular past-tense ending. Here are the rules:

1. If the verb ends in a voiceless consonant, the *-ed* is pronounced /t/: *looked, helped, watched, dressed, laughed.*

2. If the verb ends in a voiced sound (voiced consonants and all vowels), the *-ed* is pronounced /d/: *believed, enjoyed, grabbed, hugged, tried, moaned, healed.*

3. If the verb ends in either *d* or *t*, the *-ed* is pronounced /d/: *needed, added, seeded, waited, roosted, counted.*

Practice and Assess

Answers: Exercise 2

1. grown
2. gone
3. found
4. became
5. come
6. brought
7. chose
8. began
9. taken
10. given
11. saw
12. lent
13. laid
14. written
15. was
16. caught
17. satisfied
18. knew
19. took
20. thrown

Additional Resources

 Grammar Practice, p. 25

 Grammar Enrichment, p. 25

Grammar Workbook, Lesson 37

Close

Discuss the importance of using correct verb forms and their spellings in writing. Have students write rules and troublesome verbs in their journals for future reference.

Verb Tenses and Voice

Exercise 2 — Using the Principal Parts of Verbs

On your paper, write the principal part of the verb that is indicated in parentheses.

The History of Words

1. The number of words in the English language has _____ over the centuries. (past participle of *grow*)
2. Most words in our language have _____ through changes in spelling or meaning. (past participle of *go*)
3. Etymologists, who study the history of words, have _____ interesting clues to the present meanings of words. (part participle of *find*)
4. Two Latin words meaning "not speaking" _____ the word *infant*. (past form of *become*)
5. An ancient word meaning "blood" has _____ down to us as the word *red*. (past participle of *come*)
6. The word *ketchup* comes from the Malaysian name for a fish sauce that sailors _____ to England in the seventeenth century. (past form of *bring*)
7. Long ago people sometimes _____ their last name on the basis of their profession; it is easy to understand why the names Baker, Carpenter, Miller, Taylor, Wheelwright, and Smith were often selected. (past form of *choose*)
8. Celtic families often _____ their last name with Mac or Fitz, meaning "son of." (past form of *begin*)
9. The name John has _____ various forms in different languages around the world, including Jean, Giovanni, Juan, Hans, and Ivan. (past participle of *take*)
10. The Spanish have _____ us such English words as *brocade, canyon, mosquito, plaza,* and *vanilla*. (past participle of *give*)
11. In the school library, I _____ a dictionary that dealt with the origin of words and phrases. (past form of *see*)
12. My English teacher _____ me his copy of this intriguing reference work. (past form of *lend*)
13. This dictionary _____ to rest many of my misconceptions about language and word usage. (past form of *lay*)
14. The authors of the dictionary have _____ many best-selling references, including the Berlitz language books. (past participle of *write*)
15. One of the authors _____ the advisory editor of a standard dictionary. (past form of *be*)
16. His syndicated newspaper column, "Words, Wit, and Wisdom," has _____ the interest of more than 12 million readers. (past participle of *catch*)
17. The dictionary has _____ my curiosity about the origins of many everyday words and expressions. (past participle of *satisfy*)
18. I never _____ that the abbreviation *COD* stands for "collect on delivery" in the United States and "cash on delivery" in Britain. (past form of *know*)
19. *Hamburger* _____ its name from the city of Hamburg, Germany, and was originally called "Hamburg steak." (past form of *take*)
20. The baseball term *duster* refers to a ball that a pitcher has _____ hard and close to the batter to make the batter step back from the plate. (past participle of *throw*)

MEETING INDIVIDUAL NEEDS

Special Needs

Mastering Tenses

Some students have sequencing problems that hinder their mastery of tenses. Instruct students to review the charts showing principal parts (pp. 585–587). Remind students to look for the column of the requested form (for example, past participle) before proceeding down the chart. Alternatively, you might point out tense forms in the students' own writing so that students can focus on mastering the grammatical principle rather than on reading new material.

Tense of Verbs

■ The **tenses** of a verb are the forms that help to show time.

There are six tenses in English: *present, past,* and *future* and *present perfect, past perfect,* and *future perfect.*

Present Tense

The present tense of any verb other than *be* is the same as the base form of the verb. To form the third-person singular of these verbs, add *-s* or *-es* to the base form.

	SINGULAR	PLURAL
FIRST PERSON	I **play.**	We **play.**
SECOND PERSON	You **play.**	You **play.**
THIRD PERSON	She, he, or it **plays.**	They **play.**
	Ronnie **plays.**	The children **play.**

	SINGULAR	PLURAL
FIRST PERSON	I **am** happy.	We **are** happy.
SECOND PERSON	You **are** happy.	You **are** happy.
THIRD PERSON	She, he, or it **is** happy.	They **are** happy.
	Ronnie **is** happy.	The children **are** happy.

■ The **present tense** expresses a constant, repeated, or habitual action or condition. It can also express a general truth.

> The Hudson River **flows** into the Atlantic. [not just now but always: a constant action]
>
> Jessie **plays** the flute superbly. [now and always: a habitual action]
>
> Uranium **is** radioactive. [a condition that is generally true]

■ The **present tense** can also express an action or condition that exists only now.

> Ronnie **feels** sick. [not always but just now]
>
> I **declare** these games over. [at this very moment]

■ The **present tense** is sometimes used in historical writing to express past events and, more often, in poetry, fiction, and reporting (especially in sports) to convey a sense of "being there."

> Above the crowd, the *Hindenburg* suddenly **bursts** into flame.
>
> I **watch** as my sister **runs** after the ducks and **slips** in the mud.
>
> The pitch **gets** away from the catcher and **bounces** into the fence.

15.3 Tense of Verbs   **589**

Focus

Lesson Overview

Objectives
- To identify the main functions of the present, past, and future tenses
- To use tenses appropriately in writing

Bellringer
Daily Language Activity

When students enter the classroom, have this assignment on the board: *Read the following sentences and identify the verb tenses. Note the use of the present tense to describe an action that occurred long ago.*

> Murdoch, in charge on the starboard side, eyes tragic, but calm and cool, orders boat No. 7 lowered. The women hang back; they want no boat-ride on an ice-strewn sea; the *Titanic* is unsinkable.
>
> Hanson W. Baldwin,
> "R.M.S. *Titanic*"

See also *Daily Language Practice*

Teach

Present Tense

☑ Teaching Tip

A common use for the present tense is to describe or comment on something read. For example, even though *Macbeth* was written hundreds of years ago, we normally use the present tense when we discuss it: *In Macbeth, Shakespeare **deals** with the conflict of light and dark. Macbeth's first words **are** about light and dark weather.*

Verb Tenses and Voice

Resource Manager

Planning Resources
- *Lesson Plans*

Transparencies
- *Bellringer*
- *Daily Language Practice*

🗂 Other Print Resources
- *Grammar and Composition Handbook*
- *Grammar Enrichment,* p. 25
- *Grammar Workbook,* Lessons 38–39

Teach

Past Tense

☑ Grammar Tip

Narratives (such as anecdotes, short stories, novels) are usually written in the past tense. One reason for using the past tense is that the alternative, the present tense, does not convey a sense of immediate present time. The present tense is used for habitual or repeated actions and thus is not well suited for narration, which usually deals with a series of discrete events.

Though occasionally works of fiction are written in present tense (the "historic present"), storytelling in the present tense usually sounds colloquial: *I go up to Main Street and bump into Jake, an old friend of mine.*

Practice and Assess

Answers: Exercise 3

Answers will vary, but some suggestions are given below.

1. She works in the mornings on weekdays.
2. The bells sound louder than usual.
3. Platinum is more precious than gold.
4. Jim says we should wait until tomorrow.
5. Carlos and his sister sing beautifully.
6. Marissa finishes the race with a final burst of energy.
7. They prefer to take their tea on the shaded porch.
8. For entertainment, she reads mysteries.
9. The climate changes with the passing of seasons.
10. The people rarely elect a third-party candidate.

Answers: Exercise 4

Answers will vary, but some suggestions are given below.

I thought about the problem for a week or two and decided that I knew precisely what I would do. I gave it a lot of thought. I chose the simplest solution. Then I took the first step.

As I put on my running shoes, I tried to visualize my competition. In my mind, I moved with dignity and ran a tough race. At the

(sidebar) Verb Tenses and Voice

Past Tense

■ Use the **past tense** to express an action or condition that was started and completed in the past.

The team **defeated** its opponent.
The rivalry **seemed** fierce.
Victory **tasted** sweet.
My friends and I **led** the cheers.

Except for *be*, nearly all verbs—regular and irregular—have just one past-tense form, such as *climbed* or *became*. When you use the past tense of *be*, however, you must choose between the forms *was* and *were*.

	SINGULAR	PLURAL
FIRST PERSON	I **was** happy.	We **were** happy.
SECOND PERSON	You **were** happy.	You **were** happy.
THIRD PERSON	He, she, or it **was** happy.	They **were** happy.

Exercise 3   Using the Present Tense in Sentences

On your paper, write a sentence using each of the following present tense verbs. The content of your sentence should express the kind of present time indicated in parentheses.

SAMPLE   does (now and always)
ANSWER   He does his laundry on Saturdays.

1. works (now and always)
2. sound (just now)
3. is (generally true)
4. says (at this moment)
5. sing (always)
6. finishes (a single sports event)
7. prefer (just now)
8. reads (now and always)
9. changes (generally true)
10. elect (historical present)

Exercise 4   Using the Past Tense in Sentences

On your paper, write two paragraphs. In the first, use the past tense of verbs 1–5; in the second, use the past tense of verbs 6–10. In your paragraphs, use the verbs in any order.

1. give
2. think
3. choose
4. take
5. know
6. beat
7. try
8. run
9. put
10. win

end, I crossed the finish line, beat the other runners, and won the race without even feeling winded!

Future Tense

■ Use the **future tense** to express an action or condition that will occur in the future.

To form the future tense of any verb, use *shall* or *will* with the base form:
I shall talk; you will come.

> I **shall write** my essay tonight.
> Angela **will mail** the application.
> You **will see** me tomorrow.

There are other ways to express future time besides using *shall* or *will*.

1. Use *going to* with the present tense of *be* and the base form of a verb.

   > Angela **is *going to* mail** the application.
   > You **are *going to* see** me tomorrow.

2. Use *about to* with the present tense of *be* and the base form of the verb.

   > I **am *about to* write** my essay.
   > Angela **is *about to* mail** the application.

3. Use the present tense with an adverb or an adverb phrase that shows future time.

   > Frank **sails *tomorrow.***
   > Frank **sails *on the fifteenth of next month.***

Exercise 5 Using Expressions of Future Time

On your paper, write the verb in each sentence below in the future tense. Try to use at least two other ways of expressing future time besides adding *shall* or *will* to the base form of the verb.

India's Classical Dances

1. Two classmates and I presented a report about the classical dances of India.
2. First Chandra spoke about *Bharata natyam*, the sacred Hindu dance form.
3. She described its complex movements for the hands, arms, and torso.
4. Chandra demonstrated several of the hand and arm movements.
5. Then Lan described two other highly stylized Indian dance forms: *kathakali*, a dramatic style from southern India, and *kathak*, an ancient dance from northern India.
6. He told us about the *kathakali*'s link to early Hindu mythology.
7. He also presented a videotape of an authentic performance of *kathakali*, showing the dance's strong rhythms and rapid turns.
8. Then it was my turn to describe *manipuri*, a dignified dance from northeastern India.
9. I taught the students a few of the difficult movements typical of *manipuri* dancers.
10. Finally Chandra danced a pantomime from the *Bharata natyam* tradition.

Verb Tenses and Voice

Teach

Future Tense

☑ **Grammar Tip**

The way the future tense is formed is completely different from the way the present and the past tenses are formed. Both the present and the past tenses are indicated by a distinctive change of the ending or the vowel of the main verb. The future tense is not indicated by any distinctive change in the main verb. Instead, it is indicated by a verb phrase consisting of two verbs: the helping verb *will* or *shall* plus the base form of the main verb.

Practice and Assess

Answers: Exercise 5

Answers may vary, but some suggestions are given below.

1. Two classmates and I are going to present a report . . .
2. First Chandra will speak about *Bharata natyam* . . .
3. She is about to describe . . .
4. Chandra will demonstrate several . . .
5. Then Lan will describe . . .
6. He is going to tell us . . .
7. He is also going to run a videotape . . .
8. Then it will be my turn . . .
9. I shall teach the students . . .
10. Finally Chandra will dance . . .

English Language Learners

Examining Verb Tenses

Students whose first language is not English may have difficulty understanding the formation of tenses in English. Some languages do not express the time of an action through verb tense, and others have more or different tenses than does English. Discuss the way time is expressed (through verb tense or any other way) in their primary languages. Help students understand the tenses in English by having students compare the tenses to similar forms in the students' primary languages or by giving and asking them to think of example sentences.

Practice and Assess

Answers: Exercise 6

Answers will vary, but some suggestions are given below.

Next week is going to be different. I am about to turn over a new leaf. The new regimen begins Monday. I shall finish my homework by eight o'clock, and I shall be in bed by ten. Won't my family be surprised!

Answers: Exercise 7

1. was
2. took
3. leaves
4. will soar (are going to soar; are about to soar)
5. wins
6. became
7. beat
8. found
9. is going to release; is about to release
10. fell
11. know
12. will pose (is about to pose; is going to pose)
13. loses
14. drops
15. oversaw

Additional Resources

 Grammar Enrichment, p. 25

 Grammar Workbook, Lessons 38–39

Close

Suggest that students review some of the writing in their portfolios. Have them explain what tenses a few pieces are in and why that tense was chosen. They should correct any mistakes in verb tense.

Verb Tenses and Voice

Write five statements or predictions about the future. Your sentences may be as realistic or as fantastical as you wish. Remember to vary the ways in which you express future time.

SAMPLE ANSWERS   Film companies are going to produce all-day movies.
In-line skating is about to become the very next craze.
On Friday I fly to Puerto Rico.

Exercise 7   Changing Verb Tenses

Change the tense of the italicized verb in each sentence below, following the directions in parentheses. Write the correct tense on your paper.

1. The local minor league baseball team, the Panthers, *is* one of the least profitable teams in its league. (Change to the past tense.)
2. At that time, two major investors *take* over the ownership and management of the team. (Change to the past tense.)
3. Bill Smith, a former major leaguer, *left* his job as an insurance executive to take over the day-to-day operation of the team. (Change to the present tense.)
4. With a winning record and a whole series of give away programs, the Panthers' profits *soar.* (Change to the future tense.)
5. In 1997 the team *won* their first championship ever. (Change to the present tense.)
6. The Panthers eventually *become* the most consistant winner in their division. (Change to the past tense.)
7. Tom Flowers, the Panthers' former star pitcher, *beats* the World Series winners in his first major league game. (Change to the past tense.)
8. Baseball fans *find* it difficult to buy tickets for the Panthers' final play-off game. (Change to the past tense.)
9. Bill Smith says that the team *will release* their aging shortstop to make room for another player. (Change to another form showing future time.)
10. Early in the regular season, the team *falls* well behind their arch rivals, the Comets. (Change to the past tense.)
11. Real fans *knew* the team's misfortunes might last a bit longer. (Change to the present tense.)
12. They think that the departure of Tom Flowers *poses* a threat to the team's chances. (Change to the future tense.)
13. Every year, the team *lost* several players to the major leagues. (Change to the present tense.)
14. Attendance *dropped* at all the other ballparks in the league. (Change to the present tense.)
15. Even more success came to the management team that *oversees* the Panthers' business operations. (Change to the past tense.)

Enrichment and Extension

Writing Verb Tenses

Have students work in small groups to write sentences using the tenses they have learned about. Each group should think of a verb such as *think* or *know*. Then each student in the group should write four sentences, using the verb in the present, past, and future tenses. Have students exchange papers and discuss one another's sentences.

15.4 Perfect Tenses

Present Perfect Tense

■ Use the **present perfect tense** to express an action or condition that occurred at some *indefinite* time in the past.

To form the present perfect tense, use *has* or *have* with the past participle of a verb: *has studied, have chosen.**

She **has listened** to the recording.
They **have bought** a new home.

The present perfect tense can refer only to past time that is indefinite. You cannot add adverbs such as *yesterday* to make the time more specific.

He **has arrived** from Nebraska.

To refers to completed past time, you usually use the simple past tense.

He **arrived** from Nebraska yesterday.

You can also use the present perfect tense to show that an action or a condition *began* in the past and *continues* into the present. This use usually involves adverbs of time or adverb phrases.

He **has spoken daily** from his campaign headquarters.
Special guards **have remained** at the embassy **around the clock.**

*Do not be confused by the term *present perfect;* this tense expresses past time. Present refers to the tense of the auxiliary verb *has* or *have.*

Exercise 8   Using the Present Perfect Tense

(a) On your paper, rewrite each of the following sentences, changing the verb tense from past to present perfect. (b) Add adverbs or adverb phrases to each sentence to show that an action or condition began in the past and continues into the present.

SAMPLE   We looked for a new car.
ANSWER   **a.** We have looked for a new car.
          b. We have looked for a new car for two weeks.

1. He taught swimming classes.
2. Movie critics praised the film.
3. The state highway was under repair.
4. Our art class studied portrait painting.
5. The towering waves cascaded over the craggy shore.
6. The student council met with the principal.
7. The senior class sponsored a schoolwide fundraising project.
8. Several students served meals at the shelter for the homeless.
9. The counselor drove them to their after-school jobs.
10. Many teachers worked on a special exhibit for the library.

15.4 Perfect Tenses   **593**

Verb Tenses and Voice

Focus

Lesson Overview

Objectives
• To identify the main functions of the perfect tenses
• To use perfect tenses appropriately in writing

 Bellringer
Daily Language Activity

When students enter the classroom, have the following assignment on the board: *What is the verb tense in the following sentence?*

Luis has arrived from Argentina.

See also 📖 *Daily Language Practice*

Teach

Present Perfect Tense

☑ **Teaching Tip**
The form of the helping verb *have*—present, past, or future—determines the perfect tense. The main verb is always in the past participle form: *has met, had met, will have met.*

Practice and Assess

Answers: Exercise 8
Answers will vary, but some suggestions are given below.

1. has taught   6. has met
2. have praised   7. has sponsored
3. has been   8. have served
4. has studied   9. has driven
5. have cascaded   10. have worked

Resource Manager

Planning Resources
• *Lesson Plans*

📖 **Transparencies**
• *Bellringer*
• *Daily Language Practice*
• *Two-Minute Skill Drill*

📁 **Other Print Resources**
• *Grammar and Composition Handbook*
• *Grammar Practice,* p. 26
• *Grammar Reteaching,* p. 26
• *Grammar Workbook,* Lesson 40

Teach

Past Perfect Tense

☑ Grammar Tip

When students focus on the perfect tenses, they may forget that the verb *have*, in addition to being the helping verb required in all perfect tenses, can also be a main verb in its own right. See *Grammar Reteaching*, p. 26.

⬛ Cross-reference: Troubleshooter

For instruction and practice of the material in Lesson 15.4, refer students to the **Troubleshooter**.

Two-Minute Skill Drill

List these words on the board. Have students write a sentence using each verb in the given verb form.

fly (present perfect)

stand (past perfect)

write (past perfect)

See also *Two-Minute Skill Drill Transparency 15.4*

Practice and Assess

Answers: Exercise 9

1. had served
2. had analyzed
3. had made
4. had discussed
5. had stopped
6. had cost
7. had completed
8. had accepted
9. had drafted
10. had organized

Verb Tenses and Voice

April

May

On May 15th I took the job.

June

She had worked as manager.

Past Perfect Tense

■ Use the **past perfect tense** to indicate that one past action or condition began *and* ended before another past action started.

To form the past perfect tense, use *had* with the past participle of a verb: *had guessed, had driven.*

PAST PERFECT	PAST

She **had worked** as manager before I **took** the job. [She worked; she stopped working; I worked.]

PAST	PAST PERFECT

By the time I **arrived,** several actors **had auditioned.** [They auditioned; they finished auditioning; I arrived.]

PAST	PAST PERFECT

Before I **fell,** I **had noticed** the sticky spots on that section of the floor. [I noticed; I stopped noticing; I fell.]

Exercise 9   **Using the Past Perfect Tense**

Decide which verb in each sentence should be in the past perfect tense. Write the past perfect form of that verb on your paper.

1. She served as mayor of our city for years when she decided to run for Congress.
2. Once she carefully analyzed the pros and cons of entering the race, she called a press conference to announce her decision.
3. Although still young for a politician, she wished she made the decision to enter politics earlier.
4. She told the press she already discussed the decision to run for office with her family.
5. By 6:00 P.M. on election day, she stopped in more than a hundred towns throughout her district.
6. By the week that the election was over, her campaign cost much more than she had calculated.
7. By the time she moved to Washington, D.C., she completed the selection of all members of her staff.
8. When she was sworn in, her chief of staff already accepted job applications from hundreds of job hunters.
9. When her old friends visited her in March, the first-year representative already drafted her first piece of legislation.
10. She organized her entire reelection campaign by the time August arrived.

MEETING INDIVIDUAL NEEDS

English Language Learners

Identifying Tenses

To help students new to English distinguish between present, past, and future tenses, have each student say three sentences aloud: one about something that is happening now, one about something that happened yesterday, and one about something that will happen tomorrow. Have other students identify the verbs and verb tenses in the sentences. Encourage students to ask questions for clarification and to respond appropriately.

Future Perfect Tense

■ Use the **future perfect tense** to express one future action or condition that will begin *and* end before another future event starts. To form the future perfect tense, use *will have* or *shall have* with the past participle of a verb: *will have talked, shall have talked.*

> By June I **will have worked** here two months. [Two months will be over before another future event, the coming of June, occurs.]

Exercise 10 Using the Future Perfect Tense

Use each phrase and verb below to write a sentence in the future perfect tense.

SAMPLE   By early May—plant
ANSWER   By early May, I will have planted 100 bulbs.

1. By next Sunday—give
2. Before the beginning of summer—buy
3. By the time I vote for the first time—watch
4. Before Susan's birthday—make
5. By New Year's Day—stop

Exercise 11 Writing the Perfect Tenses

On your paper, write the perfect-tense verb indicated in parentheses after each sentence.

African American Folktales

1. Folklorists _____ African American folktales for years. (present perfect of *collect*)
2. African Americans who _____ to this country as enslaved people later adapted West African folktales to suit the circumstances of their new culture. (past perfect of *come*)
3. The folktales about Brer Rabbit, for instance, grew out of trickster tales that African Americans _____ in their native West Africa. (past perfect of *learn*)
4. In the near future, some variations of West African folktales _____ in this country for more than 200 years. (future perfect of *survive*)
5. The African American inhabitants of the Georgia Sea Islands _____ variations of West African tales for many generations. (present perfect of *tell*)
6. Once African Americans _____ Western religions, they invented many preacher tales. (past perfect of *adopt*)
7. These religious tales _____ many African American ballads and spirituals. (present perfect of *influence*)
8. Writers such as Zora Neale Hurston found inspiration in folktales that _____ themselves into the fabric of African American culture. (past perfect of *weave*)
9. Many blues singers _____ from folktales themes that describe or allude to the hardships inherent in African American life. (present perfect of *take*)
10. It is likely that all American children _____ some African American folktales by the time they grow up. (future perfect of *hear*)

15.4 Perfect Tenses **595**

Practice and Assess

Answers: Exercise 10

Answers will vary, but some suggestions are given below.

1. By next Sunday, Michael will have given five hundred dollars to the charity.
2. Before the beginning of summer, I will have bought forty-nine mosquito-repellent candles.
3. By the time I vote for the first time, I will have watched over one thousand political campaign commercials on television.
4. Before Susan's birthday, she will have made enough cookies to feed an army!
5. By New Year's Day, Mother will have stopped counting her chickens before they're hatched.

Answers: Exercise 11

1. have collected
2. had come
3. had learned
4. will have survived
5. have told
6. had adopted
7. have influenced
8. had woven
9. have taken
10. will have heard

Additional Resources

📁 *Grammar Practice*, p. 26
📁 *Grammar Reteaching*, p. 26

 Grammar Workbook, Lesson 40

Close

Encourage students to review Lesson 15.4 and note any items or exercises that were particularly troublesome. Then discuss with students any problems they might have had. Encourage students to jot down in their journal any helpful hints for the perfect tenses.

Enrichment and Extension

Using Perfect Tenses

Have students locate a story or report they have written or magazine article they have read recently. Ask them to mark or list the verbs and indicate their tenses. Have them rewrite a few of the sentences, changing some of the verb tenses to the past, present, and future perfect tenses.

Focus

Lesson Overview

Objectives
- To identify progressive and emphatic verb forms
- To use progressive and emphatic verb forms appropriately in writing

 Bellringer

Daily Language Activity

When students enter the classroom, have this assignment on the board: *Write a short paragraph about an activity in which you partake. In your writing, try to use a verb form that expresses continuing action.*

See also *Daily Language Practice*

Teach

☑ **Grammar Tip**

The progressive consists of forms of the helping verb *be* plus a verb ending in *-ing* (the present participle).

Practice and Assess

Answers: Exercise 12

1. had (*or* has) been attracting
2. have been coming
3. are settling
4. had been anticipating
5. did have
6. are living
7. had been speaking
8. is becoming
9. were hoping
10. are deciding

Verb Tenses and Voice *(vertical sidebar)*

15.5 Progressive and Emphatic Forms

■ Each of the six tenses has a **progressive** form that expresses a continuing action.

To make the progressive forms, use the appropriate tense of the verb *be* with the present participle of the main verb.

PRESENT PROGRESSIVE	They *are* listening.
PAST PROGRESSIVE	They *were* listening.
FUTURE PROGRESSIVE	They *will be* listening.
PRESENT PERFECT PROGRESSIVE	They *have been* listening.
PAST PERFECT PROGRESSIVE	They *had been* listening.
FUTURE PERFECT PROGRESSIVE	They *will have been* listening.

■ The present and past tenses have additional forms, called **emphatic,** that add special force, or emphasis, to the verb.

To make the emphatic forms, use *do, does,* or *did* with the base form.

PRESENT EMPHATIC	I *do* listen.
PAST EMPHATIC	I *did* listen.

Exercise 12 — Using the Progressive and Emphatic Forms

For each sentence, write the progressive or the emphatic form of the verb in parentheses. Choose the form that makes more sense in the sentence.

Miami's Cuban Community

1. For decades the city of Miami (attract) many visitors from the Caribbean.
2. Since the late nineteenth century, when Miami was first developed as a resort, wealthy Cubans, Venezuelans, and Colombians (come) to Miami on vacation.
3. Today many poor Nicaraguans and Mexicans (settle) in Miami, but the largest Spanish-speaking community in the city is Cuban.
4. Before 1959 few (anticipate) a large influx of Cubans fleeing Castro's new regime.
5. Nevertheless, it is clear now that the Cuban revolution of 1959 (have) a major impact on the population of Miami.
6. Today more than half a million people of Cuban descent (live) in Dade County, where Miami is located.
7. By the year 2000, almost as many people (speak) Spanish as English in Miami and the nearby communities.
8. Bilingualism (become) increasingly common among people who now work here.
9. Many Cubans who fled their homeland (hope) at first to return to their country.
10. Many Cuban Americans, however, (decide) that Miami is now their permanent home.

596   Unit 15 Verb Tenses and Voice

 Resource Manager

Planning Resources
- *Lesson Plans*

 Transparencies
- *Bellringer*
- *Daily Language Practice*

Other Print Resources
- *Grammar and Composition Handbook*
- *Grammar Enrichment,* p. 26
- *Grammar Workbook,* Lesson 41

Exercise 13 Review: Using Verb Tenses and Forms

On your paper, complete each of the following sentences by writing the tense or form indicated in parentheses.

Kwanzaa

1. In 1966 Dr. Maulana Karenga _____ Kwanzaa as a way for African Americans to reflect on and celebrate their rich heritage. (past tense of *create*)
2. Since its inception this nonreligious and nonpolitical holiday _____ worldwide acceptance. (present perfect progressive form of *gain*)
3. Dr. Karenga _____ the annual celebration around African cultural and social experiences, particularly the traditional festival of first fruits. (past perfect tense of *develop*)
4. By the end of the weeklong celebration, African Americans _____ the Nguzo Saba, the Seven Principles of Kwanzaa. (future perfect tense of *observe*)
5. The Seven Principles _____ a set of values that emphasize accountability, reliability, and concern for one another. (present tense of *be*)
6. Prior to December 26, the first day of the celebration, millions of African Americans _____ weeks preparing the basic Kwanzaa symbols. (future progressive form of *spend*)
7. One is the Mkeka, or place mat, which _____ tradition. (present tense of *represent*)
8. Another symbol is Vibunzi, an ear of corn, which _____ to symbolize each child in the family. (present perfect tense of *come*)
9. Estimates indicate that 15 to 18 million people _____ this holiday in recent years. (past progressive form of *celebrate*)
10. Many students _____ to celebrate Kwanzaa along with their traditional religious holidays. (present perfect tense of *choose*)

Exercise 14 Review: Identifying Verb Tenses and Their Uses

On your paper, explain the difference in meaning between the sentences in each of the pairs below. Name the tense(s) used in each sentence.

SAMPLE **a.** Did she live in Washington long?
        b. Has she lived in Washington long?
ANSWER In sentence *a* the action occurred in the past and has ended—past. In sentence *b* the action occurred in the past and is continuing—present perfect.

1. **a.** They went to Utah for vacation.
   b. They have gone to Utah for vacation.
2. **a.** We planned a trip to Virginia to visit friends.
   b. We were planning a trip to Virginia to visit friends.
3. **a.** Marisa did work in New Mexico.
   b. Marisa has worked in New Mexico.
4. **a.** She has been visiting them in Texas.
   b. She visited them in Texas.
5. **a.** Earl is traveling through Colorado.
   b. Earl has been traveling through Colorado.

15.5 Progressive and Emphatic Forms **597**

Practice and Assess

Answers: Exercise 13

1. created
2. has been gaining
3. had developed
4. will have observed
5. are
6. will be spending
7. represents
8. has come
9. were celebrating
10. have chosen

Answers: Exercise 14

Answers will vary, but some suggestions are given below.

1. In sentence *a*, the action occurred in the past and has ended (past). In sentence *b*, the action has occurred in the past and is continuing (present perfect).
2. In sentence *a*, the action occurred in the past and had ended (past). In sentence *b*, the action was continuing in the past (past progressive).
3. In sentence *a*, the action indeed occurred in the past (past emphatic). In sentence *b*, the action occurred at an indefinite time in the past (past perfect).
4. In sentence *a*, the action began in the past and is continuing (present perfect progressive). In sentence *b*, the action occurred in the past and has ended (past).
5. In sentence *a*, the action is occurring continuously in the present (present progressive). In sentence *b*, the action began in the past and is continuing (present perfect progressive).

Additional Resources

 Grammar Enrichment, p. 26

Grammar Workbook, Lesson 41

Close

Remind students that the *-ing* verb ending shows the progressive form. The helping verbs *do, does,* and *did* show the emphatic form.

Focus

Lesson Overview

Objectives
- To identify the tense of verbs and the time relationship of the events the verbs describe
- To ensure that tenses are compatible in writing

Teach

☑ Teaching Tip

An awkward problem in a past-tense narrative is a statement that is not limited to the time of the narrative. *For example: We had dinner at the Café Royal, which was in the old part of town.* Most authorities would recommend shifting the tense of the verb in the subordinate clause to the present tense because was would incorrectly imply that the Cafe Royal is no longer in the old part of town.

Practice and Assess

Answers: Exercise 15
1. had felt
2. gives
3. bought
4. plans
5. teaches

Verb Tenses and Voice

15.6 Compatibility of Tenses

- Do not shift, or change, tenses when two or more events occur at the same time.

| INCORRECT | During the storm the dam **broke,** and the river **reaches** flood level. [The tense shifts from the past to the present.] |
| CORRECT | During the storm the dam **broke,** and the river **reached** flood level. [Now it is clear that both events happened at nearly the same time in the past.] |

- Shift tenses only to show that one event precedes or follows another.

| INCORRECT | By the time the game **ended,** she **bowled** six strikes. [The two past-tense verbs give the mistaken impression that both events—the ending of the game and the bowling of the strikes—happened at the same time.] |
| CORRECT | By the time the game **ended,** she **had bowled** six strikes. [The shift from the past tense (*ended*) to the past perfect tense (*had bowled*) clearly indicates that the bowling of six strikes happened before the game ended.] |

- Keep a statement about a general truth in the present tense even if other verbs are in the past tense.

| CORRECT | Then he **remembered** that Christmas **is** on December 25. |

Exercise 15 Choosing Compatible Tenses

Find the first verb that appears in each sentence below. Then choose and write the correct tense of the second verb in parentheses.

SAMPLE Jaime had jogged daily after school, but he (has found, found) exercising in the evening difficult.

ANSWER found

1. Before Jaime began his morning workouts, he (felt, had felt) sluggish and lazy.
2. Then he remembered that exercise (gives, gave) a person more energy.
3. It has been almost a year since he (had bought, bought) a student membership in the gym.
4. If he has time this summer, he (plans, will have planned) to enroll in a diving class.
5. In the summer, he works at a hotel and also (teaches, will teach) tennis.

Resource Manager

Planning Resources
- *Lesson Plans*

📁 Other Print Resources
- *Grammar and Composition Handbook*
- *Grammar Enrichment,* p. 27
- *Grammar Workbook,* Lesson 42

Exercise 16 — Making Tenses Compatible

First find the two verbs that appear in each of the following sentences. Then rewrite each sentence, making the second verb compatible with the first verb.

Two Opera Stars

1. Victoria de los Angeles was born in Barcelona, Spain, in 1923, where she later had studied music at the Barcelona Conservatory.
2. After she had completed the six-year course at the conservatory in only three years, she makes her concert debut in 1944.
3. Although the public knows her by her stage name, her real name was Victoria Gómez Cima.
4. She took private voice lessons for five years and then wins first prize in an international singing contest in Switzerland.
5. De los Angeles soon discovered that she has offers for concert appearances from all over Europe and America.
6. By the time she made her debut in New York in the fall of 1950, the public already heard many favorable things about her.
7. She had recorded many of her most brilliant roles before she had left the stage in 1969.
8. After she retired from opera, de los Angeles had devoted herself to musical recitals.
9. She began her recitals with operatic arias and was ending them with Spanish flamenco songs.
10. De los Angeles mastered French, Italian, and German and was excelling in each language.
11. Julia Migenes is a popular soprano who gains fame for her memorable performance as Carmen in the film version of the opera.
12. Although she was not nominated for an Oscar, she receives a Grammy for her performance.
13. She appeared in the film with the tenor Placido Domingo, who is performing the role of Don José.
14. The *London Financial Times* called Migenes "mesmerizing" and describes her delivery as "straight and from the heart."
15. Migenes has played many leading roles; two of these will be Jenny in *The Fall of Mahagonny* and the title role in the opera *Lulu*.
16. When the Metropolitan Opera presented *Lulu*, PBS televises it.
17. Migenes will perform at the Kennedy Center where she sang excerpts from her most famous roles.
18. She introduced a program that features popular music, such as French *chansons* and the music of Brecht and Weill.
19. She enjoys performing the music of Leonard Bernstein, who had become one of her favorite composers.
20. Nowadays, Migenes often treats her audiences to several Gershwin songs that will be among her personal favorites.

Verb Tenses and Voice

Practice and Assess

Answers: Exercise 16

Answers will vary, but some suggestions are given below.

1. . . . where she later studied . . .
2. . . . she made her concert . . .
3. . . . name is Victoria . . .
4. . . . then won first prize . . .
5. . . . she had offers . . .
6. . . . public had already heard . . .
7. . . . she left the stage . . .
8. . . . de los Angeles devoted herself . . .
9. . . . and ended them . . .
10. . . . and excelled in each . . .
11. . . . who gained fame . . .
12. . . . she received a Grammy . . .
13. . . . who performed . . .
14. . . . and described her delivery . . .
15. . . . these are Jenny . . .
16. . . . PBS televised it.
17. . . . she will sing excerpts . . .
18. . . . that featured popular music . . .
19. . . . who became . . .
20. . . . that are among . . .

Additional Resources

 Grammar Enrichment, p. 27

Grammar Workbook, Lesson 42

Close

As a review, discuss the importance of verb compatibility. Then ask students to choose a piece of writing from their portfolios to check whether their use of verbs is compatible.

English Language Learners

Checking Tenses

Have students new to English work on the first five items in Exercise 16 as a group and discuss their choices. You should then check and discuss their answer choices with them, and allow them to continue helping each other solve any problems with tenses that they might have.

Focus

Lesson Overview

Objectives
- To identify active and passive voice
- To use the passive voice appropriately in writing

Teach

☑ Teaching Tip

In the active voice, the subject is usually the *agent*, the doer of the action. In the passive voice, the role of the agent is passed to the object of the preposition *by*. In the active sentence *John ate the banana*, John is both the subject and the agent. In the corresponding passive-voice sentence, *The banana was eaten by John*, John is still the agent, but *banana* now plays the role of the subject.

Practice and Assess

Answers: Exercise 17

1. published—active voice
2. is described—passive voice
3. are related—passive voice
4. was told—passive voice
5. depicts—active voice
6. ran—active voice
7. was attended—passive voice
8. granted—active voice
9. tempted—active voice
10. was chosen—passive voice

Verb Tenses and Voice

15.7 Voice of Verbs

■ An action verb is in the **active voice** when the subject of the sentence performs the action.

> The trainer **teased** the lion.

■ An action verb is in the **passive voice** when its action is performed on the subject.

> The lion **was teased** by the trainer.

The active voice is generally stronger, but sometimes the passive voice is preferred or even necessary. Use the passive voice if you do not want to call attention to the performer, if you do not know who the performer is, or if the performer is unimportant.

> The window **was broken.** [You may not want to identify the culprit.]
>
> The roses **were sent.** [You do not know who the sender is.]
>
> All the cards **were sold.** [It doesn't matter who sold them.]

To form the passive voice, use a form of the auxiliary verb *be* with the past participle of the verb. The tense of the auxiliary verb determines the tense of the passive verb.

> The lion **is teased** by the trainer. [present tense, passive voice]
>
> The lion **was being teased.** [past progressive tense, passive voice]
>
> The lion **will have been teased** by the trainer. [future perfect tense, passive voice]

Exercise 17 — Identifying Active and Passive Voice

For each sentence, write the verb and identify its voice as *passive* or *active*.

1. In 1977 Leslie Marmon Silko published *Ceremony,* a powerful novel.
2. In the book, the life of a Native American veteran of World War II is described.
3. Stories about her own Pueblo tribe are often related by Silko.
4. The young Silko was told many stories by her great-aunts and great-grandmother.
5. Silko's writing often depicts the differences between Native American and white cultures.
6. The Bureau of Indian Affairs ran Silko's school in Old Laguna, New Mexico.
7. This school was attended by many children from the nearby Pueblo reservation.
8. The University of New Mexico granted Silko a diploma in 1969.
9. The idea of a career in law initially tempted Silko.
10. Eventually, a career as a writer was chosen by her instead.

Resource Manager

Planning Resources
- *Lesson Plans*

📚 **Transparencies**
- *Bellringer*
- *Daily Language Practice*

📁 **Other Print Resources**
- *Grammar and Composition Handbook*
- *Grammar Practice,* p. 27
- *Grammar Reteaching,* p. 27
- *Grammar Workbook,* Lesson 43

Exercise 18   Identifying and Writing Active and Passive Voice

On your paper, rewrite the sentences below, changing the active voice to the passive or the passive voice to the active. For some passive voice sentences, it may not be necessary to include the performer of the action.

SAMPLE   Several popular folk songs were performed by the band.
ANSWER   The band performed several popular folk songs.

Joan Baez, Folksinger

1. A musical career was launched by Joan Baez in 1960.
2. An entire generation was touched by her music and her message.
3. In the late 1950s, a teaching job was offered by the Massachusetts Institute of Technology to Joan's father, Dr. Alberto Vicio Baez.
4. One evening Joan was taken by her father to a coffeehouse in Cambridge's Harvard Square.
5. For the first time, the songs of some popular young folksingers were heard by Joan.
6. From then on, she focused her attention on the guitar and traditional folk ballads.
7. A music promoter saw her performance in a Cambridge coffeehouse.
8. Joan was booked by the promoter into the Gate of Horn, a club in Chicago.
9. There she was invited by singer Bob Gibson to a folk festival in Newport, Rhode Island.
10. As a result of her solo performance, record deals were offered to Joan by several recording companies.
11. A small recording company called Vanguard was chosen by Joan.
12. During the fall of 1960, several weeks were spent by Joan Baez in a recording studio in New York City.
13. Constant touring followed the success of her first album, a major hit nationwide.
14. The Democratic party asked Joan to a gala for President John F. Kennedy.
15. During the 1960s, their country's involvement in the Vietnam War was protested by many young Americans.
16. The anger and frustration of young Americans from all backgrounds was reflected in the music of Joan Baez.
17. Her lyrics revealed deep feelings about peace and war and injustice.
18. Her audiences were moved by such songs as "Blowing in the Wind" and "We Shall Overcome."
19. In 1966 the Reverend Martin Luther King Jr. was joined by Joan Baez in escorting African American children to their newly integrated school.
20. Many young people joined activist and singer Baez in her efforts for political reform.
21. In 1974 an album of Spanish-language songs was released by Joan.
22. The album featured songs of love and death from Central and South America.
23. Joan dedicated the album to her father.
24. Throughout the years, albums of diverse musical styles, including country and western, have been recorded by Joan.
25. Audiences of all ages are still thrilled by her voice and her music.

15.7 Voice of Verbs   **601**

25. Her voice and music still thrill audiences of all ages.

Additional Resources

 Grammar Practice, p. 27
Grammar Reteaching, p. 27

Grammar Workbook, Lesson 43

20. Activist and singer Baez was joined by many young people in her efforts for political reform.
21. In 1974 Joan released an album of Spanish-language songs.
22. Songs of love and death from Central and South America were featured on the album.
23. The album was dedicated by Joan to her father.
24. Throughout the years, Joan has recorded albums of diverse musical styles, including country and western.

Practice and Assess

Answers: Exercise 18

1. Joan Baez launched her musical career in 1960.
2. Her music and her message touched an entire generation.
3. In the late 1950s, the Massachusetts Institute of Technology offered a teaching job to Joan's father, Dr. Alberto Vicio Baez.
4. One evening Joan's father took her to a coffeehouse in Cambridge's Harvard Square.
5. For the first time, Joan heard the songs of some popular young folksingers.
6. From then on, her attention was focused on guitar and traditional folk ballads.
7. Her performance in a Cambridge coffeehouse was seen by a music promoter.
8. The promoter booked Joan into the Gate of Horn, a club in Chicago.
9. There singer Bob Gibson invited her to a folk festival in Newport, Rhode Island.
10. As a result of her solo performance, several recording companies offered record deals to Joan.
11. Joan chose a small recording company called Vanguard.
12. During the fall of 1960, Joan Baez spent several weeks in a recording studio in New York City.
13. The success of her first album, a major hit nationwide, was followed by constant touring.
14. Joan was asked by the Democratic Party to a gala for President John F. Kennedy.
15. During the 1960s, many young Americans protested their country's involvement in the Vietnam War.
16. The music of Joan Baez reflected the anger and frustration of young Americans from all backgrounds.
17. Deep feelings about peace and war and injustice were revealed in her lyrics.
18. Such songs as "Blowing in the Wind" and "We Shall Overcome" moved her audiences.
19. In 1966 Joan Baez joined the Reverend Martin Luther King Jr. in escorting African American children to their newly integrated school.

Teach

About the Literature

Explain that the review features a passage from J. R. R. Tolkien's *The Fellowship of the Ring* and that the literature is followed by a group of exercises based on Tolkien's novel. Ask a volunteer to read the passage aloud. Have the rest of the class listen, respond, and appropriately evaluate the presentation. In a discussion, students should identify and analyze the characters, the setting, and the mood of the excerpt. Then ask students to focus on the verbs highlighted in the passage. Ask them why they think Tolkien cast most of the passage in the past tense and why he seemed to prefer the active voice to the passive voice.

Linking Grammar and Literature

Cooperative Learning

Ask students to invent a scene from an imaginary novel about fantastic people or creatures, in the manner of *The Fellowship of the Ring.* Suggest that students use a computer when they write and revise. They should cast their narrative entirely in the present tense. Ask pairs of students to read each other's work and discuss whether their narratives are successful in the present tense. Have pairs rewrite their narratives, changing the tense entirely to the past. Have them discuss some of the disadvantages and some of the advantages of writing in the present tense.

Listening and Speaking

Ask students to write a paragraph about an eerie or frightening event, real or fictional. Have them write the paragraph in the active voice. Then ask them to rewrite the paragraph in the passive voice. Have students form groups to read the paragraphs and to discuss the differences they detect between the use of passive voice and the use of active voice.

✔ ASSESSMENT OPTIONS

📁 *Tests with Answer Key & Rubrics*
Unit 15 Mastery Test, pp. 53–54

💾 *Testmaker*
Unit 15 Mastery Test

📼 *MindJogger Videoquizzes*

602

VERB TENSES AND VOICE

Set in the imaginary kingdom of Middle Earth, Tolkien's novel recounts the adventures of a group of hobbits, an ancient, peace-loving race. In this episode, three hobbits—Frodo, Sam, and Pippin—encounter a mysterious horseman. The meeting so disturbs Frodo that he is tempted to call on the powers of his magical ring. The passage has been annotated to show some of the kinds of verbs covered in this unit.

Verb Tenses and Voice

Literature Model

from The Fellowship of the Ring
by J. R. R. Tolkien

Past progressive

Past perfect

Passive voice

Past perfect progressive

Present tense of a regular verb

Past tense of an irregular verb

The sun was beginning to get low and the light of afternoon was on the land as they went down the hill. So far they had not met a soul on the road. This way was not much used, being hardly fit for carts, and there was little traffic to the Woody End. They had been jogging along again for an hour or more when Sam stopped a moment as if listening. They were now on level ground, and the road after much winding lay straight ahead through grassland sprinkled with tall trees, outliers of the approaching woods.

"I can hear a pony or a horse coming along the road behind," said Sam.

They looked back, but the turn of the road prevented them from seeing far. "I wonder if that is Gandalf coming after us," said Frodo; but even as he said it, he had a feeling that it was not so, and a sudden desire to hide from the view of the rider came over him.

"It may not matter much," he said apologetically, "but I would rather not be seen on the road. . . . Let's get out of sight!"

The other two ran quickly to the left and down into a little hollow not far from the road. There they lay flat. Frodo hesitated for a second: curiosity or some other feeling was struggling with his desire to hide. The sound of hoofs drew nearer.

602 Unit 15 Verb Tenses and Voice

Resource Manager

Planning Resources
• *Lesson Plans*

📁 **Other Print Resources**
• *Grammar and Composition Handbook*
• *Grammar Workbook,*
Lesson 36–43; Unit 15 Review;
Cumulative Review: Units 10–15

Just in time he threw himself down in a patch of long grass behind a tree that overshadowed the road. Then he lifted his head and peered cautiously above one of the great roots.

    Round the corner came a black horse, no hobbit-pony but a full-sized horse; and on it sat a large man, who seemed to crouch in the saddle, wrapped in a great black cloak and hood, so that only his boots in the high stirrups showed below; his face was shadowed and invisible.

    When it reached the tree and was level with Frodo the horse stopped. The riding figure sat quite still with its head bowed, as if listening. From inside the hood came a noise as of someone sniffing to catch an elusive scent; the head turned from side to side of the road.

    A sudden unreasoning fear of discovery laid hold of Frodo, and he thought of his Ring. He hardly dared to breathe, and yet the desire to get it out of his pocket became so strong that he began slowly to move his hand. . . . At that moment the rider sat up, and shook the reins. The horse stepped forward, walking slowly at first, and then breaking into a quick trot.

> Past tense of a regular verb

> Active voice

> Verb Tenses and Voice

Practice and Assess

Answers: Exercise 1

1. base form; sink
2. past participle; begun
3. base form; find
4. past form; led
5. past participle; driven
6. past participle; seen
7. past form; went
8. past participle; taken
9. present participle; running
10. past form; caught

Review: Exercise 1   **Identifying Principal Parts**

    The following sentences are based on *The Fellowship of the Ring*. Each sentence contains a verb in one of four forms: (a) the base form, (b) the past form, (c) the present participle, or (d) the past participle. At the end of the sentence is a second verb in parentheses. On your paper, write the form of the verb in italics. Then write the verb in parentheses in the same form as the original verb.

1. Their spirits *fall* at the approach of sunset. (sink)
2. The hobbits had *started* their journey too late in the day. (begin)
3. They *locate* a deserted road over the hill. (find)
4. The road *stretched* toward the dark woods ahead of the hobbits. (lead)
5. Few carts had *traveled* on the road in recent years because of its poor condition. (drive)
6. So far they had not *met* a soul along the road. (see)
7. In the fading light, Frodo and the other hobbits nervously *hurried* down the hill. (go)
8. Each hobbit had *carried* a few belongings from home in a pack on his back. (take)
9. Despite the rough road, they were *jogging* steadily toward the Woody End. (run)
10. Sam *heard* the sound of a horse's hoofs. (catch)

Grammar Review **603**

Grammar Review

Practice and Assess

Answers: Exercise 2

1. had
2. begins
3. thought
4. broke
5. came
6. tells
7. will fly
8. sinks
9. go
10. arose
11. will see
12. wears
13. will speak
14. drew
15. will remember
16. thinks
17. gave
18. take
19. will come
20. feel

Verb Tenses and Voice

Review: Exercise 2   Using the Present, Past, and Future Tenses

Each of the following sentences elaborates on ideas suggested by the passage from *The Fellowship of the Ring*. On your paper, write each verb, changing the tense according to the instructions in parentheses. Use only the present, past, and future tenses; with the exception of *will* to express the future tense, do not use any helping verbs.

SAMPLE   The hobbits *remain* in hiding.
(Change to the future tense.)

ANSWER   will remain

1. Frodo *has* a Ring with magical powers. (Change to the past tense.)
2. Frodo *began* a dangerous journey through the imaginary kingdom of Middle-earth. (Change to the present tense.)
3. Frodo *thinks* admiringly of the powerful wizard Gandalf during his journey. (Change to the past tense.)
4. An unexpected noise *breaks* through the still air. (Change to the past tense.)
5. At the sound of the horseman, a sudden fear *will come* over Frodo. (Change to the past tense.)
6. After a slight hesitation, Frodo *told* the other hobbits of his nervousness. (Change to the present tense.)
7. The hobbits *fly* in different directions. (Change to the future tense.)
8. Frodo *sank* swiftly into a patch of tall grass. (Change to the present tense.)
9. His companions *went* to the left side of the road to find a place to hide. (Change to the present tense.)
10. Curiosity about the approaching horseman soon *will arise* in Frodo. (Change to the past tense.)
11. Before long Frodo *saw* a black horse—no mere hobbit-pony—and its rider. (Change to the future tense.)
12. The looming horseman *wore* a long black cloak and hood. (Change to the present tense.)
13. The horseman *speaks* to no one. (Change to the future tense.)
14. The rider's face *draws* back within the folds of his hood. (Change to the past tense.)
15. Frodo *remembers* the magic Ring in his pocket. (Change to the future tense.)
16. Frodo *will think* about the Ring in his pocket. (Change to the present tense.)
17. The horseman *will give* the horse's reins a shake. (Change to the past tense.)
18. The travelers *will take* greater precautions after this incident. (Change to the present tense.)
19. Perhaps Gandalf *comes* to their assistance. (Change to the future tense.)
20. The hobbits *will feel* nervous during the night. (Change to the present tense.)

Review: Exercise 3   Using the Perfect Tenses

Each of the following sentences is based on passages from *The Fellowship of the Ring* that are not reprinted in this textbook. On your paper, write the italicized verb in the tense indicated in parentheses, using the past participle of the main verb and the appropriate form of the helping verb *have*.

SAMPLE   Before he started his journey, Frodo ∧ his house.
           (past perfect tense of *sell*)
ANSWER   had sold

1. Frodo ∧ the magical Ring that is in his pocket from his uncle Bilbo. (present perfect tense of *inherit*)
2. Bilbo found the Ring in a cave, where Gollum, a wicked creature, ∧ it earlier. (past perfect tense of *lose*)
3. Before Gollum obtained the Ring, it ∧ to Sauron the Great, an evil power. (past perfect tense of *belong*)
4. A brave man named Isildur ∧ the Ring from Sauron's hand, but Isildur later lost the Ring in a river. (past perfect tense of *cut*)
5. Gollum murdered his friend Deagol, who ∧ the Ring from the river bottom. (past perfect tense of *got*)
6. Gandalf, a friendly wizard, ∧ Frodo of the Ring's unusual powers. (present perfect tense of *warn*)
7. Over the course of time, the Ring ∧ greed in each of its possessors. (present perfect tense of *foster*)
8. Gollum and Sauron's followers ∧ for the Ring for many years. (present perfect tense of *search*)
9. By the time the hobbits reach Mount Doom, perhaps some elves ∧ them. (future perfect tense of *help*)
10. Soon the Black Riders, Sauron's enthusiastic followers, ∧ Frodo. (future perfect tense of *attack*)

Review: Exercise 4   Using Verb Tenses in Writing

Choose a story that you have read recently or one that you have seen in the movies or on television. On your paper, write five sentences summarizing the story and describing the main characters. In each sentence, use at least two verbs that are compatible in tense. Write the verbs and label the tenses. Use all six verb tenses in your sentences.

SAMPLE ANSWER   Last Saturday I saw a movie that I had heard about for weeks.
                saw—past tense; had heard—past perfect tense

Verb Tenses and Voice

Practice and Assess

Answers: Exercise 3
1. has inherited
2. had lost
3. had belonged
4. had cut
5. had gotten
6. has warned
7. has fostered
8. have searched
9. will have helped
10. will have attacked

Answers: Exercise 4
Answers will vary, but a suggestion is given below.

Carol will arrive at the party when everyone will already have been there an hour. (will arrive—future tense; will have been—future perfect tense)

Practice and Assess

Answers: Exercise 5

1. The sun has set in the distance, and twilight soon will be coming.
2. An unfamiliar territory does surround the group of adventurous hobbits.
3. For many miles the strange road was winding down a steep hill.
4. Sam was listening to the thunder of a horse's hoofs.
5. The horse was galloping briskly along the road just behind the travelers.
6. Unfortunately, the bend in the road does obscure a view of any approaching rider.
7. The hobbits soon were dashing into hiding places near the edge of the road.
8. Frodo's heart was pounding fiercely against his chest.
9. Before long Frodo was peering over the roots of a tree at the mysterious rider.
10. The horseman's dark and sinister appearance did seem threatening.
11. The rider is bowing his head.
12. The rider's hooded head is turning from one side of the road to the other.
13. The rider is sniffing the air for an elusive scent.
14. After such a ride, dust will be clinging to the horseman's cloak and saddle.
15. The horse will be panting heavily when it stops running.
16. In spite of his anxiety, Frodo does wonder about the identity of the mysterious rider.
17. Frodo will be moving his hand gradually toward the Ring in his pocket.
18. Frodo truly does struggle against his uncontrollable desire for the Ring.
19. Frodo indeed does suspect the motives of the black-cloaked rider.
20. Evidently the horseman is following the hobbits on their journey.

Verb Tenses and Voice

Review: Exercise 5   Using the Progressive and Emphatic Forms

On your paper, rewrite the following sentences, inserting the italicized verb in the form indicated in parentheses. Use the present participle of the main verb with the appropriate tense of the auxiliary verb *be*, or use the base form of the main verb with the appropriate form of *do*.

1. The sun has set in the distance, and twilight soon ∧ . (future progressive form of *come*)
2. An unfamiliar territory ∧ the group of adventurous hobbits. (present emphatic form of *surround*)
3. For many miles, the strange road ∧ down a steep hill. (past progressive form of *wind*)
4. Sam ∧ to the thunder of a horse's hoofs. (past progressive form of *listen*)
5. The horse ∧ briskly along the road just behind the travelers. (past progressive form of *gallop*)
6. Unfortunately, the bend in the road ∧ a view of any approaching rider. (present emphatic form of *obscure*)
7. The hobbits soon ∧ into hiding places near the edge of the road. (past progressive form of *dash*)
8. Frodo's heart ∧ fiercely against his chest. (past progressive form of *pound*)
9. Before long Frodo ∧ over the roots of a tree at the mysterious rider. (past progressive form of *peer*)
10. The horseman's dark and sinister appearance ∧ threatening. (past emphatic form of *seem*)
11. The rider ∧ his head. (present progressive form of *bow*)
12. The rider's hooded head ∧ from one side of the road to the other. (present progressive form of *turn*)
13. The rider ∧ the air for an elusive scent. (present progressive form of *sniff*)
14. After such a ride, dust ∧ to the horseman's cloak and saddle. (future progressive form of *cling*)
15. The horse ∧ heavily when it stops running. (future progressive form of *pant*)
16. In spite of his anxiety, Frodo ∧ about the identity of the mysterious rider. (present emphatic form of *wonder*)
17. Frodo ∧ his hand gradually toward the Ring in his pocket. (future progressive form of *move*)
18. Frodo truly ∧ against his uncontrollable desire for the Ring. (present emphatic form of *struggle*)
19. Frodo indeed ∧ the motives of the black-cloaked rider. (present emphatic form of *suspect*)
20. Evidently, the horseman ∧ the hobbits on their journey. (present progressive form of *follow*)

Review: Exercise 6   Making Tenses Compatible

The following sentences are based on the passage from *The Fellowship of the Ring* and other passages from the novel that are not reprinted in this textbook. On your paper, rewrite the sentence, changing the tense of the italicized verb to a form that makes the tenses of the verbs in the sentence compatible.

SAMPLE   Before the horseman appeared, the hobbits *jumped* into hiding places.
ANSWER   Before the horseman appeared, the hobbits had jumped into hiding places.

1. The mysterious figure sniffed the air as he *pauses* beside Frodo's concealed body.
2. As Frodo longingly *touches* his Ring, he remembered Gandalf's warning.
3. Before he disappeared, Gandalf *explains* the Ring's dangerous powers.
4. To the hobbits' relief, the horse broke into a trot while Frodo *watches*.
5. After the horseman rides away, Frodo *walked* toward his companions.
6. By the time Frodo reached his friends, they *stood* up.
7. The hobbits *discuss* the horseman who had frightened them.
8. Sam's father *saw* a stranger similar to the horseman before the hobbits left on their journey.
9. Frodo knew that the evil creature Gollum *left* his cave months ago in search of the Ring.
10. Frodo wondered whether Sauron *sends* the rider as a spy.

Review: Exercise 7   Changing the Voice of Verbs

The following sentences are based on *The Fellowship of the Ring*. First, identify each sentence as being in the *passive voice* or the *active voice*. Then rewrite each sentence, changing the active voice to the passive or the passive voice to the active.

SAMPLE   The horseman's head was covered by a dark hood.
ANSWER   passive voice; A dark hood covered the horseman's head.

1. The landscape of Middle Earth is described clearly by the novel's author, J. R. R. Tolkien.
2. A gray light bathed the lonely meadow.
3. The grassland around the bumpy road was sprinkled with all trees.
4. The branches of a large tree overshadowed the road.
5. The curvy road was used by few people.
6. The rapid clatter of the horse's hooves alarmed Frodo and his friends.
7. Giant tree roots hid the small hobbits from view.
8. A great black cloak concealed most of the horseman's enormous body.
9. Suddenly Frodo was seized by a desire for his Ring.
10. The trembling hobbits were terrified by the horseman.

Grammar Review   **607**

Practice and Assess

Answers: Exercise 6

1. The mysterious figure sniffed the air as he paused beside Frodo's concealed body.
2. As Frodo longingly touched his Ring, he remembered Gandalf's warning.
3. Before he disappeared, Gandalf had explained the Ring's dangerous powers.
4. To the hobbits' relief, the horse broke into a trot while Frodo watched.
5. After the horseman rides away, Frodo walks toward his companions.
6. By the time Frodo reached his friends, they had stood up.
7. The hobbits discussed the horseman who had frightened them.
8. Sam's father had seen a stranger similar to the horseman before the hobbits left on their journey.
9. Frodo knew that the evil creature Gollum had left his cave months ago in search of the Ring.
10. Frodo wondered whether Sauron had sent the rider as a spy.

Answers: Exercise 7

Answers may vary, but some suggestions are given below.

1. passive; The author, J. R. R. Tolkien, clearly describes the landscape of Middle Earth.
2. active; The lonely meadow was bathed by a gray light.
3. passive; Tall trees sprinkled the grassland around the bumpy road.
4. active; The road was overshadowed by the branches of a large tree.
5. passive; Few people used the curvy road.
6. active; Frodo and his friends were alarmed by the rapid clatter of the horse's hooves.
7. active; The small hobbits were hidden from view by giant tree roots.
8. active; Most of the horseman's enormous body was concealed by a great black cloak.
9. passive; A desire for his Ring suddenly seized Frodo.
10. passive; The horseman terrified the trembling hobbits.

Practice and Assess

Answers: Exercise 8

Answers will vary, but some suggestions are given below.

1. The crimson meadow can be seen through the thick woods.
2. The sun was shining most of the day.
3. The horse has been carrying that rider for a long time.
4. Horrendous sounds did inspire fear in the onlookers.
5. The hobbits will be coming home soon.

Answers: Exercise 9
Proofreading

This proofreading activity provides editing practice with (1) the current or previous units' skills, (2) the **Troubleshooter** errors, and (3) spelling errors. Students should be able to complete the exercise by referring to the units, the **Troubleshooter**, and a dictionary. (Note: A run-on sentence counts as one error.)

Error (Type of Error)

1. London, (nonessential appositive)
   showed (verb form)
2. had already had (compatibility of tenses)
3. met (shift in tense)
   encouraged (compatibility of tenses)
4. man, (run-on sentence)
   married (shift in tense)
5. became (verb form)
6. interest, (run-on sentence)
7. filled (shift in tense)
8. Blake, (nonessential appositive)
9. were destroyed (compatibility of tenses)
10. was found (verb form)
11. landscape (spelling)
    is depicted (sentence fragment)
12. has drawn (verb form)
13. predominate. Some *or* predominate; (run-on sentence)
    fields, (commas in a series)
    Palmer's (singular possessive)

Review: Exercise 8 Using Verb Tense, Form, and Voice

Using details from the passage or your own ideas, write a sentence about each pair of nouns. Use the verb tense, form, or voice indicated in parentheses.

SAMPLE hobbits, road (past perfect progressive)
ANSWER The hobbits had been trudging along the road for an hour.

1. meadow, woods (present tense, passive voice)
2. sun, day (past progressive)
3. horse, rider (present perfect progressive)
4. sounds, fear (past emphatic)
5. hobbits, home (future progressive)

Review: Exercise 9

Proofreading

The following passage describes the artist Samuel Palmer, whose painting appears on the opposite page. Rewrite the passage, correcting the errors in spelling, usage, and grammar. Add any missing punctuation. There are twenty-five errors.

Samuel Palmer

¹Samuel Palmer (1805–1881), the son of a bookseller who lived on the outskirts of London shown an early talent for painting. ²By the time Palmer was fourteen, he has already had works accepted by the Royal Academy in London. ³At the age of seventeen, he meets the artist John Linnell, who encourages him to study European art. ⁴Linnell had a strong personal and professional influence on the young man and Palmer marries Linnell's daughter in 1837. ⁵The relationship between the two men become difficult, however, because of Linnell's bossy and violent personality.

⁶Landscapes were Palmer's chief interest and he painted them with a keen eye. ⁷He fills his notebooks with detailed drawings that expressed a deeply spiritual view of nature. ⁸His view of life was strongly influenced by his friendship with William Blake the visionary English poet and painter. ⁹Unfortunately, when Palmer died, many of his early sketches are destroyed by his son.

¹⁰*Early Morning* was finded among the few early sketches of Palmer's that had not been destroyed. ¹¹The gentle land scape depicted early in the morning. ¹²Palmer has drawed each leaf, stone, and hillock with care and precision. ¹³Rounded shapes predominate, some examples are the oak tree on the left, the cottage roof behind the wheat fields the sloping hills, and even Palmers signature

at the bottom of the canvas. ¹⁴In a hollow below the tree sit a group of people. ¹⁵Some critics beleive that the rabbit might symbolize the abundance of nature.

¹⁶Palmer often drawed his landscapes with a mythological quality, much like the settings in J. R. R. Tolkien's *The Fellowship of the Ring.* ¹⁷He has wove elements of both realism and fantasy into the scene pictured in *Early Morning.* ¹⁸Both Palmer and Tolkien was deeply spiritual men. ¹⁹Both choosed to portray the sanctity of nature and the power of the human spirit.

Samuel Palmer, *Early Morning*, 1825

Review: Exercise 10

Mixed Review

The following sentences describe the life of the author J. R. R. Tolkien [tӓl′ kēn]. Rewrite each sentence, following the instructions in parentheses.

1. As a youth, J. R. R. Tolkien learns Greek and Latin and developed his own alphabet. (Change the first verb to make the tenses compatible.)

Grammar Review **609**

Practice and Assess

**Answers: Exercise 9 (continued)
Proofreading**

Error (Type of Error)
14. sits (subject-verb agreement)
15. believe (spelling)
16. drew (verb form)
17. has woven (verb form)
18. were (subject-verb agreement)
19. chose (verb form)

Verb Tenses and Voice

Viewing the Art

Samuel Palmer, *Early Morning*, 1825
Like *The Fellowship of the Ring,* Samuel Palmer's painting *Early Morning* gives us a window into a gentle and otherworldly place. The painting almost seems to tell a story. Have students work in groups to invent a brief story based on the painting. They could include the rab-bit, the people sitting under the tree, the mythological forest, and the distant village in their tale. Ask students to set their story in early morning, when the air is still cool and the shadows are long. Remind students that verb tenses and voice can help them "paint" a picture.

609

Practice and Assess

Answers: Exercise 10
Mixed Review

1. learned
2. studied
3. had demonstrated
4. Oxford University awarded a scholarship to the gifted young student.
5. His interest in Old English literature was intensified by his studies of *Beowulf,* an early English epic.
6. was gathering
7. do inhabit
8. appeared
9. was grading
10. reflect
11. taps
12. People call Tolkien a "colonizer of dreams."
13. does present
14. has found
15. stole
16. named
17. had been awaiting
18. do believe
19. remains
20. will be delighting

Close

Have students write a short narrative describing a real or imaginary place. During the revision, encourage students to exchange papers and check that they have used the correct tense of each verb and that they have used the active voice.

2. He also studies Finnish, and he invented the imaginary language of Quenya. (Correct the error caused by the use of the present tense.)
3. By the time Tolkien entered college, he already demonstrated an exceptional talent for languages. (Change the second verb to the past perfect.)
4. The gifted young student was awarded a scholarship by Oxford University. (Rewrite the sentence in the active voice.)
5. His studies of *Beowulf,* an early English epic, intensified his interest in Old English literature. (Rewrite the sentence in the passive voice.)
6. While Tolkien was still a student, he already gathered ideas for his future books about a mythological kingdom. (Change the second verb to the past progressive form.)
7. Elves, dwarfs, hobbits, and goblins truly inhabit this kingdom. (Change the verb to the present emphatic form.)
8. *The Hobbit,* the first book that Tolkien wrote about Middle Earth, appears in 1937. (Replace the inappropriate present tense.)
9. The idea of hobbits came to Tolkien as he graded exams at Oxford. (Change the second verb to the past progressive form.)
10. Some scholars think Tolkien's fantasies are reflecting the battle between good and evil in the real world. (Change the second verb from the present progressive to the present.)
11. A reviewer once observed that Tolkien will tap his readers' most common nightmares and fantasies. (Change the second verb to the present tense.)
12. Tolkien is called a "colonizer of dreams." (Change the verb to the active voice.)
13. He presents his readers with a viable alternative to the madness of the real world. (Change the verb to the present emphatic form.)
14. He introduced the word *hobbit,* which find its way into our everyday language. (Change the second verb to make the tenses compatible.)
15. In *The Hobbit,* Bilbo Baggins discovered, or perhaps steals, the One Ring of Power. (Change the second verb to make the tense compatible with that of the first.)
16. The last of the trilogy, which Tolkien names *The Return of the King,* was published in 1956. (Change the first verb to make the tenses compatible.)
17. Readers have been awaiting the publication of the final book for years. (Change the present perfect progressive to the past perfect progressive form.)
18. Critics believe that Tolkien's trilogy is one of the great literary achievements of our time. (Change the first verb to the present emphatic form.)
19. Sixty years later the story of the hobbits does remain profoundly relevant. (Change the verb form to the simple present tense.)
20. Tolkien's epic fantasy classic will delight readers for generations. (Change the verb to the future progressive form.)

Writing Application

Verbs in Writing

In this passage from *Roots: The Saga of an American Family,* Alex Haley explains how he began researching the story of his African American ancestors. As you read, note Haley's use of verbs.

The microfilm rolls *were delivered,* and I turned them through the machine with a building sense of intrigue, viewing in different census takers' penmanship an endless parade of names. After about a dozen microfilmed rolls, I *was beginning* to tire, when in utter astonishment I looked upon the names of Grandma's parents: Tom Murray, Irene Murray . . . older sisters of Grandma's as well—every one of them a name that I'd heard countless times on her front porch.

It *wasn't* that I *hadn't believed* Grandma. You just *didn't* not *believe* my Grandma. It was simply so uncanny actually seeing those names in print and in official U.S. Government records.

Techniques with Verbs

When you write and revise your own work, try to use verbs in some of the ways that Haley uses them.

❶ Use the emphatic form for emphasis or to make a point. Notice how Haley uses the negative for additional emphasis.

UNEMPHATIC VERSION You just believed my Grandma.

HALEY'S VERSION You just *didn't* not *believe* my Grandma.

❷ Use a verb form that correctly conveys your exact meaning. Compare the difference in meaning of these two sentences.

PAST TENSE VERSION After about a dozen microfilmed rolls, I *began* to tire.

HALEY'S VERSION After about a dozen microfilmed rolls, I *was beginning* to tire.

> **TIME**
> For more about the writing process, see TIME Facing the Blank Page, pp. 109–119

Verb Tenses and Voice

Practice Practice these techniques by revising the following passage on a separate sheet of paper. Choose an appropriate tense, form, and voice for each verb in parentheses. Make other changes to the passage that you think are needed.

When Alex Haley was seventeen, he enlisted in the U.S. Coast Guard with the permission of his father. During World War II, he (serve) on a warship. After he (write) adventure stories set on the high seas, he (submit) them to the editors of various magazines. For eight years, Haley (collect) rejection slips. Occasionally one of his stories (purchase) and (publish).

Haley retired from the Coast Guard after serving for twenty years, the last several years as a journalist. Now he (be) ready to begin a full-time career as a writer. He (begin) writing mostly magazine articles. In 1965 Haley (collaborate) on his first book, *The Autobiography of Malcolm X,* which was highly acclaimed. After twelve years of research and travel, Haley (produce) *Roots,* the winner of a special citation awarded by the Pulitzer Prize committee in 1977.

Writing Application **611**

Verbs in Writing

You may have students read the passage aloud. Students should read it without interruption and then go back and discuss the italicized verb choices. Discuss these choices in relation to Techniques with Verbs below.

Techniques with Verbs

Discuss the techniques described and then have students see how the techniques are used in another piece of writing—a paragraph or two from the Proofreading practice on pp. 608–609 or an independent piece of writing. Students can highlight verb choices and determine whether the verb choices were appropriate.

Practice

The answers to this challenging and enriching activity will vary, but a suggestion is given below. Refer to Techniques with Verbs as you evaluate student choices.

When Alex Haley was seventeen, he enlisted in the U.S. Coast Guard with the permission of his father. During World War II, he served on a warship in the South Pacific. He wrote adventure stories set on the high seas and submitted them to the editors of various magazines. For eight years, Haley collected rejection slips. Occasionally, one of his stories was purchased and published.

Haley retired from the Coast Guard after serving for twenty years, working the last several years as a journalist. Now he was ready to begin a full-time career as a writer. He began writing mostly magazine articles. In 1965 Haley collaborated on his first book, *The Autobiography of Malcolm X,* which was highly acclaimed. After twelve years of research and travel, Haley produced *Roots,* the winner of a special citation awarded by the Pulitzer Prize committee in 1977.

> **✔ ASSESSMENT OPTIONS**
>
> 📁 *Tests with Answer Key & Rubrics*
> Unit 15 Mastery Test, pp. 53–54
>
> 💾 *Testmaker*
> Unit 15 Mastery Test
>
> 📺 *MindJogger Videoquizzes*
>
> You may wish to administer the Unit 15 Mastery Test at this point.

Objectives

- To develop an understanding of subject-verb agreement and how it is achieved, even in the presence of intervening phrases, inverted sentences, compound elements, and other special situations
- To demonstrate control over subject-verb agreement by checking and editing exercises and by writing sentences in which subjects and verbs are used correctly in agreement with each other

✔ ASSESSMENT OPTIONS

📁 *Tests with Answer Key & Rubrics*
Unit 16 Pretest, pp. 55–56
Unit 16 Mastery Test, pp. 57–58

💾 *Testmaker*
Unit 16 Pretest
Unit 16 Mastery Test

You may wish to administer the Unit 16 Pretest at this point.

Key to Ability Levels

L1 Level 1 activities are within the basic ability range of students.

L2 Level 2 activities are within the ability range of average students.

L3 Level 3 activities are more challenging activities.

UNIT
16
Subject-Verb Agreement

Lesson **16.1**   **Intervening Prepositional Phrases**   *613*

Lesson **16.2**   **Agreement with Linking Verbs**   *615*

Lesson **16.3**   **Agreement in Inverted Sentences**   *616*

Lesson **16.4**   **Agreement with Special Subjects**   *618*

Lesson **16.5**   **Agreement with Compound Subjects**   *620*

Lesson **16.6**   **Intervening Expressions**   *621*

Lesson **16.7**   **Indefinite Pronouns as Subjects**   *623*

Grammar Review   *626*

Writing Application   *635*

612

Resource Manager

Planning Resources
- *Lesson Plans*
- *Block Scheduling*

🖨 Transparencies
- *Bellringer*
- *Daily Language Practice*
- *Two-Minute Skill Drill*

📁 Other Print Resources
- *Grammar and Composition Handbook*
- *Grammar Enrichment*
- *Grammar Practice*
- *Grammar Reteaching*
- *Grammar Workbook*
- *Tests with Answer Key and Rubrics*

📼 Video
- *MindJogger Videoquizzes*

💾 Software
- *Interactive Grammar and Language Workbook*
- *Language Arts PASS*
- *Presentation Plus!*
- *Testmaker*
- *Writer's Choice Puzzlemaker*

🖥 Web Sites
- *writerschoice.glencoe.com*

16.1 Intervening Prepositional Phrases

■ A verb must agree with its subject in person and number.

Number can be singular or plural. Singular words indicate one and take a singular verb. Plural words indicate more than one and take a plural verb.

To show agreement, most verbs change form only in the present tense: when the subject is third-person singular, an *-s* (or *-es*) is added to the base verb.

SINGULAR	PLURAL
She **learns.**	They **learn.**
He **watches.**	They **watch.**

An exception is the linking verb *be,* which changes form in both the present tense and the past tense.

SINGULAR	PLURAL
The dog **is** happy.	The dogs **are** happy.
The apple **was** sour.	The apples **were** sour.

In order to show agreement with third-person subjects, the auxiliary verbs *be, have,* and *do* change form in verb phrases.

SINGULAR	PLURAL
She **is learning.**	They **are learning.**
She **has gone** home.	They **have gone** home.
Does he **live** in Virginia?	**Do** they **live** in Virginia?

Exercise 1 — Making Subjects and Verbs Agree

On your paper, write the simple subject from each of the following sentences. Then write the verb form in parentheses that agrees with the subject.

The Class Party

1. Chandra, Bill, and Marco (is planning/are planning) the class party.
2. Carla (offers/offer) her house for the party.
3. The class representatives (votes/vote) to have the party on a Saturday.
4. Three students (visits/visit) the mall for ideas on decorating.
5. A teacher (volunteers/volunteer) to chaperone.
6. All class members (plans/plan) to attend the party.
7. They (knows/know) the food will be good.
8. It (is being/are being) made by student volunteers.
9. The volunteers (has been/have been) preparing sample dishes.
10. Everybody's favorite so far (was/were) the vegetarian deep-dish pizza.

16.1 Intervening Prepositional Phrases **613**

Subject-Verb Agreement

Focus

Lesson Overview

Objective

• To achieve subject-verb agreement with an intervening prepositional phrase

Bellringer
Daily Language Activity

Use the Bellringer Transparency for Lesson 16.1.

See also *Daily Language Practice*

Teach

☑ **Grammar Tip**

Students learning English may not have mastered the conjugation of English verbs. Be sure they understand the difference between singular and plural verbs and first-, second-, and third-person verbs.

Practice and Assess

Answers: Exercise 1

1. Chandra, Bill, and Marco/are planning
2. Carla/offers
3. representatives/vote
4. students/visit
5. teacher/volunteers
6. members/plan
7. They/know
8. It/is being
9. volunteers/have been
10. favorite/was

Resource Manager

Planning Resources
• *Lesson Plans*

 Transparencies
• *Bellringer*
• *Daily Language Practice*
• *Two-Minute Skill Drill*

📂 **Other Print Resources**
• *Grammar and Composition Handbook*
• *Grammar Reteaching,* p. 28
• *Grammar Workbook,* Lessons 44–45

Practice and Assess

Answers: Exercise 2

1. report/is	6. longings/seem
2. Keckley/was	7. faith/was
3. daughter/was	8. Keckley/was
4. talents/were	9. opinions/were
5. Keckley/was	10. success/continues

 Cross-reference: Troubleshooter

For an alternative presentation of the material in Unit 16, refer students to the **Troubleshooter.**

Two-Minute Skill Drill

Choose the verb that agrees with each subject.

1. The leaves on the tree (has turned/have turned) gold and red.

2. The oak tree between the two houses (has/have) plenty of acorns.

 See also *Two-Minute Skill Drill Transparency 16.1.*

Additional Resources

📁 *Sentence Combining Practice,* p. 16
📁 *Grammar Reteaching,* p. 28

📔 *Grammar Workbook,* Lessons 44–45

Close

Ask a few volunteers to demonstrate on the board how to make sure subject and verb agree when a prepositional phrase intervenes. Have them read their examples aloud to demonstrate how to check for subject-verb agreement.

Subject-Verb Agreement

■ Do not mistake a word in a prepositional phrase for the subject of a sentence.

The subject of a sentence is never the object of a preposition. The verb must agree with the simple subject of the sentence, not with the object of a preposition.

> The **color** of the roses **pleases** us. [The subject, *color,* is singular; *of the roses* is a prepositional phrase; the verb, *pleases,* is singular because it agrees with the singular subject.]

> The **flowers** for the bouquet **are** pretty. [The subject, *flowers,* is plural; *for the bouquet* is a prepositional phrase; the verb, *are,* is plural because it agrees with the plural subject.]

Exercise 2 **Making Subjects and Verbs Agree When Prepositional Phrases Intervene**

On your paper, write the simple subject in each of the following sentences. Then write the verb form in parentheses that agrees with the subject.

Elizabeth Keckley

1. A report for one of my history classes (is/are) about Elizabeth Keckley, an African American who became the dressmaker for and confidante of First Lady Mary Todd Lincoln.
2. Keckley in her early years (was/were) enslaved in Virginia.
3. A daughter of the family (was/were) fond of Keckley and brought her to St. Louis to live.
4. Keckley's talents in the art of dressmaking (was/were) so considerable that she was able to help support the family.
5. In 1855 Keckley, with the help of loans from her customers, (was/were) able to purchase her freedom.
6. To me, Keckley's irrepressible longings for freedom and dignity (seems/seem) extraordinary.
7. Keckley's faith in herself and in her abilities (was/were) rewarded, for she moved to Washington, D.C., and became the dressmaker of President Lincoln's wife.
8. Keckley, as a personal friend of the Lincolns, (was/were) privy to many family matters at the White House.
9. Her opinions about the White House (was/were) published in 1868 in a book entitled *Behind the Scenes.*
10. The success of this determined woman (continues/continue) to inspire people today.

MEETING INDIVIDUAL NEEDS Less Proficient Readers

Understanding Intervening Phrases

Explain to students that an error in subject-verb agreement sometimes occurs when the verb agrees with the object of a prepositional phrase that modifies the simple subject. A good way to help them eliminate this type of error is to delete the prepositional phrase so that the actual subject is placed next to the verb. See *Grammar Reteaching.* **L1**

16.2 Agreement with Linking Verbs

■ Do not be confused by a predicate nominative that is different in number from the subject. Only the subject affects the number of the linking verb.

The last ***course*** **was** strawberries with cream. [The singular verb, *was,* agrees with the singular subject, *course,* not with the predicate nominative, *strawberries.*]

The main ***courses*** for the dinner **were** a selection of fish dishes. [The plural verb, *were,* agrees with the plural subject, *courses,* not with the predicate nominative, *selection.*]

Baskets of flowers **were** the decoration at the banquet. [The plural verb, *were,* agrees with the plural subject, *baskets,* not with the predicate nominative, *decoration.*]

My favorite ***part*** of musicals **is** the duets. [The singular verb, *is,* agrees with the singular subject, *part,* not with the predicate nominative, *duets.*]

Exercise 3 — Making Linking Verbs Agree with Their Subjects

On your paper, write the simple subject or subjects in each of the following sentences. Then write the form of the verb in parentheses that agrees with the subject.

Modern Circuses

1. For many people the joys of the circus (is/are) a pleasure that they never outgrow.
2. Circuses (remains/remain) a popular form of entertainment in many countries.
3. The circuses of ancient Rome (was/were) actually a group of chariot races performed in a ring.
4. Perhaps the first of the modern circuses (was/were) a one-ring show by Philip Astley, an eighteenth-century horse trainer.
5. In the eighteenth and nineteenth centuries, circus performers (was/were) the elite among popular entertainers.
6. The most exotic part of all circuses (is/are) the wild animals.
7. The feats of an acrobat or a trapeze artist (seems/seem) an impossibility to most of us.
8. A clown's acrobatic leaps (appears/appear) an easy trick, but in fact they are quite difficult to perform.
9. The strains of the calliope (is/are) a joyous sound, don't you think?
10. To me, an irresistible temptation (is/are) the aromas of popcorn and roasted peanuts.

Subject-Verb Agreement

Focus

Lesson Overview

Objective

• To make linking verbs agree with subjects

Bellringer
Daily Language Activity

Use the Bellringer Transparency for Lesson 16.2.

See also *Daily Language Practice*

Teach

Speaking and Listening

Point out that students' sense of how the language sounds might help them decide on the correct subject-verb agreement in sentences with predicate nominatives. Consider how awkward the following incorrect sentence sounds: *The three women was an asset to the club.*

Practice and Assess

Answers: Exercise 3

1. joys/are
2. circuses/remain
3. circuses/were
4. first/was
5. performers/were
6. part/is
7. feats/seem
8. leaps/appear
9. strains/are
10. temptation/is

Close

Ask each student to write a sentence similar to those in Exercise 3. Have pairs of students exchange sentences and choose the correct verb in their partners' sentence.

Resource Manager

Planning Resources
• *Lesson Plans*

Transparencies
• *Bellringer*
• *Daily Language Practice*

🖿 Other Print Resources
• *Grammar and Composition Handbook*
• *Grammar Enrichment,* p. 28
• *Grammar Practice,* p. 28
• *Grammar Workbook,* Lesson 46

Focus

Lesson Overview

Objective
- To identify the subject and agreeing verb in an inverted sentence

 ### Bellringer
Daily Language Activity

When students enter the classroom, have this assignment on the board: *If the following sentence contains an error, rewrite it correctly:*

In the mountains are a clear blue lake.

See also *Daily Language Practice*

Motivating Activity

Discuss the error in the Bellringer sentence. Point out that because the sentence has been inverted, *mountains* has been mistakenly thought of as the subject.

Teach

☑ Teaching Tip

A basic strategy for checking subject-verb agreement in inverted sentences is to put the sentence back into its normal order. For example, change the inverted sentence *By the mills stands an old house* to the normal order, *An old house stands by the mills.*

(side tab: Subject-Verb Agreement)

16.3 Agreement in Inverted Sentences

- In an **inverted sentence**—a sentence in which the subject follows the verb—take care in locating the simple subject and make sure that the verb agrees with the subject.

  Because an inverted sentence often begins with a prepositional phrase, the object of the preposition may easily be mistaken for the subject. In an inverted sentence, however, the subject follows the verb.

                           V   S

  SINGULAR   Near the trees **sleeps** the *camper.*

                           V   S

  PLURAL   Near the trees **sleep** the *campers.*

  Inverted sentences may also begin with the word *there* or *here. There* or *here* is almost never the subject of a sentence.

                   V   S

  SINGULAR   There **is** a *camper* on the mountain.

                 V   S

  Here **comes** the last *runner.*

                 V   S

  PLURAL   There **are** *campers* on the mountain.

                 V   S

  Here **come** the last two *runners.*

  In interrogative sentences, the subject may come after an auxiliary verb. In this case, you will find the subject between the auxiliary verb and the main verb.

                     V   S   V

  SINGULAR   **Does** that *eagle* **live** in the mountains?

                   V   S   V

  PLURAL   **Do** those *mountains* **contain** eagles?

                   V   S   V

  SINGULAR   **Is** the *tent* **pitched** in the right place?

                   V   S   V

  PLURAL   **Are** the *tents* **pitched** in the right place?

 ## Resource Manager

Planning Resources
- *Lesson Plans*

Transparencies
- *Bellringer*
- *Daily Language Practice*

Other Print Resources
- *Grammar and Composition Handbook*
- *Grammar Enrichment,* p. 28
- *Grammar Workbook,* Lesson 47

Exercise 4 — Making Subjects and Verbs Agree in Inverted Sentences

On your paper, write the simple subject in each of the following sentences. Then write the form of the verb in parentheses that agrees with the subject.

Blues from the Delta

1. In many a rock musician (beats/beat) the heart of a blues musician from the region of the United States known as the Mississippi Delta.
2. There (was/were) a dozen or more influential blues musicians born in the Mississippi Delta in the first two decades of this century.
3. In the group work songs of cotton-field workers (lies/lie) the roots of the Delta blues.
4. On the plantations of the Delta (was/were) heard the music of Robert Johnson, Muddy Waters, and John Lee Hooker, among others.
5. (Do/Does) these names seem familiar to you?
6. Unfortunately, there (is/are) few recordings of the very early musical pieces of some of these blues artists.
7. There (was/were) several musicians who carried the blues north, especially to Chicago, in the 1940s and 1950s.
8. (Was/Were) blues singers Howlin' Wolf and Muddy Waters performing in Chicago?
9. In the blues (lives/live) a sense of hope, strength, and survival.
10. In the debt of Delta blues musicians (is/are) artists as diverse as the Rolling Stones, Robert Cray, and Whitney Houston.

Exercise 5 — Using Subject-Verb Agreement

On your paper, write the simple subject in each of the following sentences. Then write the form of the verb in parentheses that agrees with the subject.

SAMPLE There (is/are) much history to be found in Boston and its surroundings.
ANSWERS history is

Bunker Hill

1. One of many famous monuments (stands/stand) above Boston's waterfront.
2. Perhaps the most famous one of the Revolutionary War monuments (is/are) this one on Bunker Hill.
3. South of Bunker Hill and the monument (rises/rise) Breed's Hill.
4. Although the battle fought here was named for Bunker Hill, the true site of the first of many Revolutionary War conflicts (was/were) Breed's Hill.
5. Along the base of Breed's Hill (stretches/stretch) the old battle lines.
6. Among the American leaders in that conflict (was/were) Colonel William Prescott.
7. The hastily organized colonial militiamen (was/were) the "irregular" army that faced the better-organized British force.
8. One outcome of the Battle of Bunker Hill (was/were) the colonists' moral triumph.
9. Several patriotic songs and my favorite poem (is/are) based on the story of the Battle of Bunker Hill.
10. There (is/are) always many tourists at the historical site.

16.3 Agreement in Inverted Sentences 617

Practice and Assess

Answers: Exercise 4
1. heart/beats
2. musicians/were
3. roots/lie
4. music/was
5. names/Do
6. recordings/are
7. musicians/were
8. Howlin' Wolf and Muddy Waters (compound subject)/Were
9. sense/lives
10. artists/are

Answers: Exercise 5
1. One/stands
2. one/is
3. Breed's Hill/rises
4. site/was
5. lines/stretch
6. Colonel William Prescott/was
7. militiamen/were
8. outcome/was
9. songs and poem (compound subject)/ are
10. tourists/are

Additional Resources

 Grammar Enrichment, p. 28

Grammar Workbook, Lesson 47

Close

Have students paraphrase the sentences in the exercises on this page, putting the subject in the first position; for example: *There is some juice in the freezer* becomes *Some juice is in the freezer.* They should make sure that the verb forms they have chosen make sense. Have them read their sentences aloud and evaluate their work.

English Language Learners

Understanding Agreement in Inverted Sentences

In informal situations, many speakers of English use a singular verb form when a sentence begins with *there.* For these speakers, *there is* or *there was* is virtually a fixed phrase. Thus, a sentence like the following sounds completely normal: *There's some people here who want to see you.* You may want to draw special attention to the fact that these fixed phrases are actually two separate words and that the verb must agree with the subject of the sentence.

617

Focus

Lesson Overview

Objective
- To learn how to make verbs agree with special subjects

Bellringer
Daily Language Activity

Use the Bellringer Transparency for Lesson 16.4.

See also *Daily Language Practice*

Teach

Collective Nouns

☑ Grammar Tip

Students may have difficulty determining whether a collective noun is plural or singular. In some cases, they can find clues elsewhere in the sentence. For example, in the sentence *The flock sing in harmony with one another,* the words *with one another* show that *flock* refers to members of a group rather than the group as a whole.

Special Nouns

☑ Teaching Tip

Students can remember that *scissors, pants, binoculars,* and *eyeglasses* are plural because they each have two parts (two blades, for example).

Practice and Assess

Answers: Exercise 6

1. team/was
2. audience/are
3. Diabetes/is
4. headphones/are
5. ethics/were

Subject-Verb Agreement

16.4 Agreement with Special Subjects

Collective Nouns

- A **collective noun** names a group. Consider a collective noun singular when it refers to a group as a whole. Consider a collective noun plural when it refers to each member of a group individually.

SINGULAR	The ***squadron*** of planes **soars.**
PLURAL	The ***squadron*** **land** one at a time.
SINGULAR	The ***crowd*** **cheers.**
PLURAL	The ***crowd*** **rush** to find their seats.

Special Nouns

- Certain nouns that end in *-s,* such as *mumps, measles,* and *mathematics,* take singular verbs.

SINGULAR	***Mathematics*** **interests** many people.

- Certain other nouns that end in *-s,* such as *scissors, pants, binoculars,* and *eyeglasses,* take plural verbs.

PLURAL	The ***scissors*** **were** defective. Your ***pants*** **are** too short.

- Many nouns that end in *-ics* may be singular or plural, depending upon their meaning.

SINGULAR	***Politics*** **is** often interesting. [one subject of interest]
PLURAL	His ***politics*** **are** shameless. [more than one action of a political nature]

Exercise 6   **Making Verbs Agree with Special Subjects**

On your paper, write the simple subject of each sentence. Then write the form of the verb in parentheses that agrees with each subject.

1. The team (was/were) victorious in the state finals.
2. The audience (is/are) expressing their opinions about the play.
3. Diabetes (is/are) a disorder of the body's insulin production.
4. The headphones (is/are) on the table.
5. His ethics (was/were) questioned by the local newspaper.

Resource Manager

Planning Resources
- *Lesson Plans*

 Transparencies
- *Bellringer*
- *Daily Language Practice*

📁 Other Print Resources
- *Grammar and Composition Handbook*
- *Grammar Enrichment,* p. 29
- *Grammar Practice,* p. 29
- *Grammar Workbook,* Lesson 48

Nouns of Amount

■ When a noun of amount refers to a total that is considered as one unit, it is singular. When it refers to a number of individual units, it is plural.

SINGULAR	Four *dollars* **is** a fair price. [one amount]
PLURAL	Four *dollars* **lie** on the sidewalk. [four individual bills]
SINGULAR	Two *months* **is** the waiting period. [one unit of time]
PLURAL	Two *months* **have gone** by. [two individual time periods]

Titles

■ A title is always singular, even if a noun within the title is plural.

SINGULAR	*Little Women* **delights** readers of all ages.
SINGULAR	*Cakes and Bagels* **is** my favorite bakery.

Exercise 7   Making Verbs Agree with Special Subjects

On your paper, write the simple subject in each sentence. Then write the form of the verb in parentheses that agrees with the subject.

Traditional Japanese Sports

1. After two hours, the audience at this demonstration of Japanese sports still (wears/wear) expressions of interest on their faces.
2. In traditional Japanese sports, each team (obeys/obey) strict rituals and rules.
3. More than 1,000 years (has/have) passed since Japanese men began to wrestle in the style known as sumo.
4. Statistics (confirms/confirm) that the average weight of a sumo wrestler is 300 pounds.
5. Fifteen feet (is/are) too far for the average person to throw or push a man weighing several hundred pounds, yet sumo wrestlers routinely perform this feat.
6. *Graceful Giants* (is/are) a good title for a sumo-wrestling film.
7. My binoculars (helps/help) me to appreciate the precise movements of the judo wrestlers.
8. While watching the sword game called *kendo,* a crowd of American spectators (is/are) apt to wonder at the significance of the stylized gestures.
9. Now a family of five (presents/present) individual demonstrations of *kyudo,* or Japanese archery.
10. The whole family (has/have) extraordinary poise and skill.

16.4 Agreement with Special Subjects **619**

16.4

Subject-Verb Agreement

Teach

Nouns of Amount

⮂ **Cross-reference: Mechanics**

For information regarding the spelling out of numbers at the beginning of a sentence, refer students to Lesson 21.14, pp. 769–771.

Titles

⮂ **Cross-reference: Mechanics**

For a discussion of the italicization of titles, refer students to Lesson 21.10, pp. 758–759.

Practice and Assess

Answers: Exercise 7

1. audience/wear
2. team/obeys
3. years/has *or* have
4. Statistics/confirm
5. feet/is
6. *Graceful Giants*/is
7. binoculars/help
8. crowd/is
9. family/present
10. family/has

Additional Resources

📁 *Grammar Practice,* p. 29
📁 *Grammar Enrichment,* p. 29

📖 *Grammar Workbook,* Lesson 48

Close

When trying to determine whether a special noun is singular or plural, students can try to substitute *that* or *they* for the word in question. If *that* makes sense, then the word is singular. If *they* fits, then the word is plural. In some cases, the noun may be singular or plural.

English Language Learners

MEETING INDIVIDUAL NEEDS

Understanding Time, Money, and Distance

Expressions of time, money, and distance usually require singular verbs. Students new to English often use plural verbs with these expressions because the nouns have plural forms.

Here are some examples that require singular verbs.
Time: *Two hours for lunch is too long.*
Money: *Ten dollars is the asking price.*
Distance: *Five miles is too far to walk.*

Focus

Lesson Overview

Objective
- To correctly identify the number of compound subjects and to make verbs agree

Bellringer
Daily Language Activity

Use the Bellringer Transparency for Lesson 16.5.

See also *Daily Language Practice*

Teach

☑ Teaching Tip

A diagram may help students distinguish between the rules in sentences containing subjects joined by *and* and subjects joined by *or*. Write the following formulas on the board, and add examples:

subject *and* subject: plural verb

subject *or* subject: verb depends on second subject

Practice and Assess

Answers: Exercise 8

1. are   **4.** interests
2. have   **5.** has
3. explain

Close

Ask students to explain in their own words why a compound subject takes a singular verb when preceded by *each, every,* or *many a.*

Agreement with Compound Subjects

(side tab: Subject-Verb Agreement)

Compound Subjects Joined by *And*

■ A compound subject that is joined by *and* or *both . . . and* is plural unless its parts belong to one unit or they both refer to the same person or thing.

PLURAL   The ***lawyer*** *and* the ***client*** **are** conversing.
Both the ***book*** and the ***movie*** **are** enjoyable.

SINGULAR   ***Ham*** *and* ***eggs*** **costs** two dollars. [The compound subject is a single unit.]
Her ***husband*** *and* ***partner*** **consults** her. [One person is both husband and partner.]

Compound Subjects Joined by *Or* or *Nor*

■ With compound subjects joined by *or* or *nor* (or by *either . . . or* or *neither . . . nor*), the verb always agrees with the nearer subject.

PLURAL   *Neither* the ***lawyer*** *nor* the ***clients*** **are** talking.
Either the ***lawyer*** *or* the ***clients*** **are** talking.

SINGULAR   *Either* the ***lawyer*** *or* the ***client*** **is** talking.
Neither the ***lawyers*** *nor* the ***client*** **is** talking.

Many a, Every, and *Each* with Compound Subjects

■ When *many a, every,* or *each* precedes a compound subject, the subject is considered singular.

SINGULAR   *Many a* ***man, woman,*** and ***child*** **knows** hunger.
Every ***eagle, owl,*** and ***parrot*** **fascinates** me.
Each ***eagle*** and ***owl*** **is** soaring.

Exercise 8   **Making Verbs Agree with Compound Subjects**

On your paper, write the correct form of each verb in parentheses.

1. The writer and his researcher (is/are) working together.
2. Neither the editor nor her assistants (has/have) read the manuscript.
3. Both the book and the article (explains/explain) an important historical event.
4. Every history book, article, and biography by that author (interests/interest) me.
5. Either the biographies or the history book (has/have) won a prize.

Resource Manager

Planning Resources
- *Lesson Plans*

 Transparencies
- *Bellringer*
- *Daily Language Practice*

📂 Other Print Resources
- *Grammar and Composition Handbook*
- *Grammar Enrichment,* p. 29
- *Grammar Practice,* p. 29
- *Grammar Workbook,* Lesson 49

16.6 | Intervening Expressions

Certain expressions, such as *accompanied by, as well as, in addition to, plus,* and *together with,* have a meaning that is similar to that of *and,* but they do not form a compound subject. These intervening expressions introduce phrases that modify the subject but do not change its number.

SINGULAR	**Snow,** as well as sleet and ice, **makes** driving difficult.
PLURAL	**Sunshine and warm weather,** in addition to a day off, **lift** the spirit.

■ If a singular subject is linked to another noun by an intervening expression, such as *accompanied by,* the subject is still considered singular.

SINGULAR   **Water,** in addition to food, **is** essential on a camping trip.
The **father,** as well as his daughter, **is arriving.**
Rain, accompanied by wind and thunder, **is** predicted for tomorrow.
Practice, plus talent, **makes** perfect.
The **movie,** together with the book, **tells** a compelling story.

The couple, along with a chaperone, is going to the prom.

Exercise 9 — Making Subjects and Verbs Agree When Expressions Intervene

On your paper, write the simple subject of each sentence, as well as the form of the verb in parentheses that agrees with the subject.

The Cabots

1. John Cabot's life, as well as his voyages, (is/are) somewhat of a mystery to historians.
2. John Cabot, as well as his son Sebastian, (was/were) sent to explore the Americas.
3. Before Columbus's voyage, John Cabot, plus other navigators, (was/were) planning a westward voyage to Asia.
4. John, accompanied by 18 men, (was/were) scheduled to sail from England in 1497.
5. Five ships in the royal fleet, in addition to John's ship, (was/were) prepared to leave on a second voyage in 1498.
6. A crew mutiny, together with a lack of supplies, (appears/appear) to have doomed the voyage.
7. In 1525 Sebastian Cabot, accompanied by three Spanish vessels, (was/were) expected to develop trade with the Orient.
8. However, Cabot, as well as all his men, (was/were) diverted by news of great wealth in South America.
9. Unfortunately, three years, plus tremendous effort, (was/were) wasted, and Cabot was blamed for the failed expedition.
10. Sebastian Cabot, as well as his father, never (seems/seem) to have attained his exploration goals.

16.6 Intervening Expressions   **621**

Subject-Verb Agreement

Focus

Lesson Overview

Objective
- To use correct subject-verb agreement in sentences with intervening expressions

🔔 **Bellringer**
Daily Language Activity
Use the Bellringer Transparency for Lesson 16.6.

See also ✒ *Daily Language Practice*

Teach

☑ **Teaching Tip**
A good way to show students that an intervening expression is not part of a compound subject is to remove the actual subject. The remaining words—the intervening expression—cannot stand alone as a simple subject. For example, we cannot paraphrase the sentence *Water, in addition to food, is essential on a camping trip* as *In addition to food is essential on a camping trip.*

Practice and Assess

Answers: Exercise 9
1. life/is
2. John Cabot/was
3. John Cabot/was
4. John/was
5. ships/were
6. mutiny/appears
7. Sebastian Cabot/was
8. Cabot/was
9. years/were
10. Sebastian Cabot/seems

Resource Manager

Planning Resources
- *Lesson Plans*

✒ **Transparencies**
- *Bellringer*
- *Daily Language Practice*
- *Two-Minute Skill Drill*

📖 **Other Print Resources**
- *Grammar and Composition Handbook*
- *Grammar Enrichment,* p. 29
- *Grammar Workbook,* Lesson 50

Practice and Assess

Answers: Exercise 10

1. was		6. was	
2. was		7. was	
3. remain		8. were	
4. was		9. were	
5. were		10. was	

Answers: Exercise 11

Answers will vary, but some suggestions are given below.

1. Peanut butter and jelly, with a glass of milk, tastes good every time.
2. Neither the plaintiff nor the defendants, tired from the trial, feel better.
3. Both the *Times* and the *Chronicle*, eager to sell papers, cover the topic.
4. Either Mother or her cousin, in addition to Derek, helps us with that.
5. Many a soldier and sailor, off at war, dreams of coming home.
6. Every boy and girl, full of hope, comes to watch the event.
7. Each book and article, written by a scientist, appeals to many readers.
8. Players as well as coaches love to win.
9. Helmets, together with knee pads, protect athletes from injury.
10. Flowers, in addition to crepe paper, remain our favorite decoration.

Additional Resources

 Grammar Enrichment, p. 29

Grammar Workbook, Lesson 50

Close

Remind students that in the sentences in this lesson, the intervening phrase always modifies the noun. They are, therefore, adjective phrases. Discuss how the intervening phrases contribute to the sentences. Read some of the sentences aloud to help students hear how the intervening phrases work.

Subject-Verb Agreement

Exercise 10   Making Verbs Agree with Their Subjects

On your paper, write the correct form of each of the verbs in parentheses.

Struggle for Independence

1. Peru, in addition to other regions of South America, (was/were) ruled by Spain from the 1530s until early in the nineteenth century.
2. The famous Venezuelan Simón Bolívar, as well as the leaders José de San Martín and Antonio José de Sucre, (was/were) foremost in the fight for South American independence.
3. Bolívar's imagination and skills as a military tactician (remains/remain) highly regarded by historians today.
4. This statesman and soldier (was/were) also the author of two great political tracts, *El Manifesto de Cartagena (The Manifesto of Cartagena)* and *La Carta de Jamaica (The Letter from Jamaica).*
5. Napoleon Bonaparte's European victories over Spain, in addition to the unrest in South America, (was/were) crucial in weakening Spain's power around the globe.
6. Between 1808 and 1819, many a devastating battle and dizzying shift of power (was/were) witnessed on the continent of South America.
7. After neither the United States nor Great Britain (was/were) willing to provide military aid, Bolívar successfully appealed to Haiti in 1815 for money and weapons.
8. Neither flooded flatlands nor ice-covered mountains (was/were) able to stop Bolívar's army from ambushing and defeating the Spanish in New Granada in 1819.
9. In later years, Colombia and Peru (was/were) ruled by a dictatorship imposed by the Liberator, as Simón Bolívar became known.
10. Unfortunately, neither Bolívar's parents nor his wife (was/were) alive to witness his triumphs.

Exercise 11   Writing Sentences with Compound Subjects and Intervening Expressions

On your paper, write 10 sentences, using one of the following items as the subject of each sentence. Make each subject agree with a present-tense verb.

1. peanut butter and jelly
2. neither the plaintiff nor the defendants
3. both the *Times* and the *Chronicle*
4. Mother or her cousin
5. many a soldier and sailor
6. every boy and girl
7. each book and article
8. players as well as coaches
9. helmets, together with knee pads,
10. flowers, in addition to crepe paper,

MEETING INDIVIDUAL NEEDS   English Language Learners

Setting off Intervening Phrases

Students for whom English is a second language may be confused by intervening phrases. Explain that commas that set off an intervening expression indicate that the expression is "extra" and not part of the subject. Have students come to the board and work on some of the exercises. Have them bracket the intervening phrase and then determine the correct verb form to use by looking at the subject.

16.7 Indefinite Pronouns as Subjects

■ A verb must agree in number with an indefinite pronoun subject.

Indefinite pronouns can be singular or plural, as indicated on the following chart.

Indefinite Pronouns			
Always Singular	each anything nothing everything one something	everyone either someone anyone no one	nobody everybody neither somebody anybody
Always Plural	several many	few	both
Singular or Plural	some most	all none	any

Singular indefinite pronouns take singular verbs. Plural indefinite pronouns take plural verbs.

SINGULAR   When we checked, ***everything*** **was** as it should be.
                 Someone at the door **wants** to talk to you.
PLURAL   ***Many*** in my class **are** good in Spanish.
                 Several of my friends **were** at the party.

As indicated on the chart, some indefinite pronouns can be singular or plural, depending upon the nouns to which they refer.

SINGULAR   ***All*** of the money **is** gone. [*All* refers to *money,* a singular noun.]
                 Most of the cake **was** gone by noon. [*Most* refers to *cake,* a singular noun.]
PLURAL   ***All*** of the children **want** dessert. [*All* refers to *children,* a plural noun.]
                 Most of the students **were** in favor of the field trip. [*Most* refers to *students,* a plural noun.]

Subject-Verb Agreement

Focus

Lesson Overview

Objective
• To make verbs agree with indefinite pronouns used as subjects

Bellringer
Daily Language Activity

When students enter the classroom, have the following assignment on the board: *What is the difference between the words or phrases* everyone, every person, *and* all people?

See also *Daily Language Practice*

Motivating Activity

Explain that while the words and phrases in the Bellringer all refer to a plural number of people, the first two are singular in form and the third is plural.

Teach

☑ **Teaching Tip**

The chart on this student page is absolutely necessary. Be sure students understand the relationship between the chart and the rest of the page. Ask students to copy the chart into their journals so that they may refer to it when they edit.

Two-Minute Skill Drill

Correct the following sentences to make the indefinite pronoun and verb agree.

Everyone were invited to the party.

All of us was late in arriving.

See also *Two-Minute Skill Drill Transparency 16.7*

Resource Manager

Planning Resources
• *Lesson Plans*

Transparencies
• *Bellringer*
• *Daily Language Practice*
• *Two-Minute Skill Drill*

Other Print Resources
• *Grammar and Composition Handbook*
• *Grammar Reteaching,* p. 29
• *Grammar Workbook,* Lesson 51

Practice and Assess

Answers: Exercise 12

1. Most/are
2. Someone/needs
3. Everyone/wants
4. Some/say
5. No one/expects
6. Both/protect
7. Several/are
8. few/are
9. Anyone/has
10. all/consider

Answers: Exercise 13

Answers will vary, but some suggestions are given below.

1. Everyone loves cabbage.
2. Several are growing in my garden.
3. Few grow successfully in this area.
4. Nobody knows why.
5. One is growing in my neighbor's yard.
6. Many of my seeds are from his plants.
7. Anything grows in his garden.
8. Either of the two students has the potential for leadership.
9. Both of us love to cook.
10. Anybody learns cooking through practice.

Answers: Exercise 14

Answers will vary, but some suggestions are given below.

1. Some of my garden is in bloom. Some of the flowers are colorful.
2. All of the acting seems poor. All of the props look phony.
3. Any of the music pleases me. Any of the songs are delightful.
4. Most of my time is scheduled. Most of my activities relate to sports.
5. None of the funding is available. None of my friends like drama.

Subject-Verb Agreement

Exercise 12   Making Verbs Agree with Indefinite Pronoun Subjects

On your paper, write the simple subject of each sentence and the form of the verb in parentheses that agrees with the subject.

Consumer Regulation

1. Most of us (is/are) consumers.
2. Someone (needs/need) to inform consumers about product safety and quality.
3. Everyone (wants/want) to save money.
4. Some of the people (says/say) we need better standards and more product regulation.
5. No one (expects/expect) poor quality products.
6. Both of these agencies (protects/protect) consumers.
7. Several of today's advertising claims (is/are) credible.
8. Despite all the new products manufactured each year, few (is/are) recalled.
9. Anyone with complaints (has/have) the opportunity to write or call the Better Business Bureau.
10. Not all of the consumers (considers/consider) Ralph Nader the symbol of consumer protection.

Exercise 13   Writing with Indefinite Pronoun Subjects

On your paper, write 10 sentences, using one of the following indefinite pronouns as the subject of each sentence. Make each subject agree with a present-tense verb.

SAMPLE   each
ANSWER   Each of the teachers has a master's degree.

1. everyone
2. several
3. few
4. nobody
5. one
6. many
7. anything
8. either
9. both
10. anybody

Exercise 14   Writing with Indefinite Pronoun Subjects

For each indefinite pronoun listed below, write two sentences, using the pronoun as the subject of both sentences. In the first sentence of each pair, use a singular present-tense verb. In the second sentence, use a plural present-tense verb.

SAMPLE   none
ANSWER   (a.) None of the pudding is for me.
        (b.) None of the fans are happy with the call.

1. some
2. all
3. any
4. most
5. none

MEETING INDIVIDUAL NEEDS   **Learning Disabled**

Paraphrasing Indefinite Pronouns

One way to help students remember that *each, either,* and *neither* are singular is to encourage students to paraphrase these indefinite pronouns with the word *one: each one, either one,* and *neither one,* respectively. See *Grammar Reteaching,* p. 29, for further reference. With the class, discuss a number of sample sentences for each of the troublesome pronouns. **L1**

Exercise 15 — Writing Sentences with Indefinite Pronoun Subjects

On your paper, write a paragraph about something funny or amusing that happened to you or someone else. Use at least five indefinite pronouns as subjects. Make each subject agree with a present-tense verb.

Exercise 16 — Correcting Errors in Subject-Verb Agreement

The following sentences contain twenty errors in subject-verb agreement. Locate the sentences with errors and rewrite those sentences using the correct verb form. (Not every sentence has an error.)

The Circus

1. In the center of the field are a large circus tent, as well as cages of animals.
2. The crowd buy their tickets, and soon each of the animals are led from the cages.
3. One little boy, accompanied by his parents, stare in astonishment at a large bear.
4. On the grass is people eating picnic lunches.
5. There is dishes piled with chicken.
6. Bread and butter seems to be a part of everyone's meal.
7. In most cases, the dessert course of these lunches are made with fruit.
8. Suddenly someone shouts, "Here comes the performers!" and this nineteenth-century American circus begin.
9. The originator of modern circuses was the Englishman Philip Astley.
10. In eighteenth-century Europe, neither traveling troops of acrobats nor the traditional county fair were able to compete with Astley's circus.
11. The diversity of acts were amazing to the audience.
12. Gymnastics was one of Astley's most popular spectacles.
13. Many of Astley's circuses were established during his lifetime.
14. Although much has changed, circuses remain a major event in most towns today.
15. Many a young boy and girl have been delighted by the exotic animals and amazing performers of a circus.
16. All of the circuses today seems to travel from place to place.
17. Most still has animal acts, although some of them have eliminated these shows.
18. For me, animals, together with a good clown, is the heart of the circus.
19. Every trained elephant, dog, and large cat fascinate me.
20. Most of the people in the audience of a circus agree with me.
21. The audience usually cheer loudest for a good animal act.
22. The origin of circuses, according to my encyclopedia, were in ancient Rome.
23. There, a circus was a stadium; today, a circus are both a public entertainment and a circular arena.
24. In the United States, Phineas T. Barnum, one of the greatest promoters, were responsible for opening the first circus, the "Greatest Show on Earth."
25. The most famous circus of all such spectacles were probably the one Barnum formed when he merged with a rival and established Barnum and Bailey.

16.7 Indefinite Pronouns as Subjects   **625**

Practice and Assess

Answers: Exercise 15

Answers will vary, but some suggestions are given below.

Everyone in the house is fast asleep. No one hears the new kitten scrambling out of its basket . . .

Answers: Exercise 16

1. In the center of the field is a large circus tent . . .
2. . . . soon each of the animals is led from the cages.
3. One little boy, accompanied by his parents, stares . . .
4. On the grass are people eating picnic lunches.
5. There are dishes piled with chicken.
6. correct
7. In most cases the dessert course of these lunches is made with fruit.
8. Suddenly someone shouts, "Here come the performers!" . . . circus begins.
9. correct
10. . . .the traditional county fair was able . . .
11. The diversity of acts was amazing to the audience.
12. correct
13. correct
14. correct
15. Many a young boy and girl has been delighted . . .
16. All of the circuses today seem to travel . . .
17. Most still have animal acts . . .
18. . . . animals, together with a good clown, are the heart of the circus.
19. Every . . . fascinates me.
20. correct
21. The audience usually cheers loudest . . .
22. The origin . . . was in ancient Rome.
23. . . . today, a circus is both a public entertainment and a circular arena.
24. . . . Phineas T. Barnum . . . was responsible for opening. . .
25. The most famous circus of all such spectacles was probably . . .

Additional Resources

 Grammar Reteaching, p. 29

Grammar Workbook, Lesson 51

Close

Give students a disorganized list of all the indefinite pronouns named on page 623. Ask students to identify the number of each indefinite pronoun without looking at the chart. Encourage them to review some sample sentences to help them.

Teach

About the Literature

After students have read the passage from Amos Oz's *Elsewhere, Perhaps,* discuss how the author's use of inverted sentences and other sentence types adds variety and a logical flow to his sweeping description of the landscape. Then ask students to focus on the highlighted examples of subject-verb agreement. Point out that careful writers always pay attention to subject-verb agreement, as it helps to make their writing clear and polished. The exercises that follow are based on this passage and related topics.

Linking Grammar and Literature

Speaking and Listening

Ask pairs of students to list a series of nouns, some singular and some plural, and a series of verbs in their base form. Have them exchange papers and discuss which nouns could match with each verb to form sentences. Then ask partners to say their sentences aloud, listening for agreement between the subjects and the verbs. Encourage them to develop the ability to *hear* the correct usage.

Cooperative Learning

Ask students to work together to identify some or all of the nonhighlighted verbs in the passage from *Elsewhere, Perhaps.* Ask them to determine whether each verb is singular or plural. Then have them identify the subject with which each verb agrees. Have students discuss why subject-verb agreement is particularly important in sentences with compound predicates.

✔ ASSESSMENT OPTIONS

📁 *Tests with Answer Key & Rubrics*
Unit 16 Mastery Test, pp. 57–58

💾 *Testmaker*
Unit 16 Mastery Test

You may wish to administer the Unit 16 Mastery Test at this point.

UNIT 16 Grammar Review

SUBJECT-VERB AGREEMENT

In his novel *Elsewhere, Perhaps,* the Israeli author Amos Oz captures the contradictions of contemporary life in his native country. Set on a kibbutz, or collective farm, near the Israeli frontier, the novel describes how a small, close-knit group copes with the threat of enemy fire and with the individuals' own conflicting dreams and desires. The passage, which has been translated from the Hebrew, has been annotated to show some examples of subject-verb agreement covered in this unit.

(sidebar, vertical: Subject-Verb Agreement)

Agreement between a singular noun subject and the singular verb *does break* with a plural object of a preposition intervening between subject and verb

Agreement between a plural indefinite pronoun subject and the plural form of *be*

An inverted sentence with agreement between a singular noun subject and the singular form of *stretch*

Literature Model

from Elsewhere, Perhaps
by Amos Oz
translated from the Hebrew by Nicholas de Lange

You see before you the kibbutz of Metsudat Ram: Its buildings are laid out in strict symmetry at one end of the green valley. The tangled foliage of the trees does not break up the settlement's severe lines, but merely softens them, and adds a dimension of weightiness.

The buildings are whitewashed, and most of them are topped with bright red roofs. This color scheme contrasts sharply with that of the mountain range, which completely blocks the view to the east, and at the foot of which the kibbutz lies spread. The mountains are bare and rocky, cut by zigzagging ravines. With the sun's progress their own shadows spill gradually down these folds, as if the mountains are trying to relieve their desolation with this melancholy shadow play.

Along the lower terraces on the slope stretches the border between our land and that of her enemies.

This border, prominently marked on the maps with a thick green line, is not visible to the observer, since it does not correspond to the natural boundary between the lush green valley and the bleak, bare mountains. The soil of Israel

626 Unit 16 Subject-Verb Agreement

Resource Manager

Planning Resources
• *Lesson Plans*

📁 Other Print Resources
• *Grammar and Composition Handbook*
• *Grammar Workbook,* Lessons 44–51; Unit 7 Review; Cumulative Review: Units 1–7

overflows the limits of the valley and spreads up the lower slopes toward the barren heights. So the eye and the mind— or, more precisely, geology and politics—come to be at odds with one another. The kibbutz itself stands some two miles from the international frontier. We cannot define the distance more precisely without entering into the blood-stained controversy over the exact location of this line.

The landscape, then, is rich in contrasts, contrasts between appearances and reality and also inner contrasts within the appearances. These can be described only by the term "contradiction." There is a kind of enmity between the valley, with its neat, geometrical patchwork of fields and the savage bleakness of the mountains. Even the symmetrical architecture of Kibbutz Metsudat Ram is no more than a negation of the grim natural chaos that looks down on it from above.

> Agreement between a compound noun subject and the plural form of *come*

> An inverted sentence with agreement between a singular noun subject and the singular form of *be*

Review: Exercise 1 **Making Subjects and Verbs Agree When Prepositional Phrases Intervene**

Each of the following sentences elaborates on the passage from *Elsewhere, Perhaps.* Rewrite each sentence on your paper, following the directions in parentheses. In some cases, you will need to change the form of the verb to make the sentence correct; in other cases, the verb will remain the same.

SAMPLE   The description of the scene offers many contrasts. (Change *description* to *descriptions.*)

ANSWER   The descriptions of the scene offer many contrasts.

1. The fertile soil of the valley supports several kinds of trees. (Change *soil* to *soils.*)
2. The mountains near the building sites are quite barren. (Change *sites* to *site.*)
3. The ravine on the mountainside creates many shadows. (Change *ravine* to *ravines.*)
4. The red of the rooftop shines brightly. (Change *rooftop* to *rooftops.*)
5. The white walls of the structures glisten in the sun. (Change *structures* to *structure.*)
6. The scene to the east offers only mountains. (Change *scene* to *scenes.*)
7. The views in other directions include much farmland. (Change *views* to *view.*)
8. At Metsudat Ram, the people farm the land. (Move the prepositional phrase so that it comes directly after the subject.)
9. Fear of the enemy haunts the kibbutz dwellers. (Change *the enemy* to *enemies.*)
10. Near the mountains, the border separates the kibbutz from enemy lands. (Move the first prepositional phrase so that it comes directly after the subject.)

Grammar Review   **627**

Practice and Assess

Answers: Exercise 1

1. The fertile soils of the valley support several kinds of trees.
2. The mountains near the building site are quite barren.
3. The ravines on the mountainside create many shadows.
4. The red of the rooftops shines brightly.
5. The white walls of the structure glisten in the sun.
6. The scenes to the east offer only mountains.
7. The view in other directions includes much farmland.
8. The people at Metsudat Ram farm the land.
9. Fear of enemies haunts the kibbutz dwellers.
10. The border near the mountains separates the kibbutz from enemy lands.

Grammar Review

Practice and Assess

Answers: Exercise 2

Answers will vary, but some suggestions are given below.

1. A river through the valley provides clear, pure water.
2. The foliage on the trees makes a beautiful sight.
3. Wildflowers with colorful blooms grow here and there.
4. People from the kibbutz farm the land.
5. The rich soil in this area produces abundant crops.
6. Cows from the farm graze in the valley.
7. The mountain above the farm is bare and rocky.
8. Ravines on the mountain's surface make a zigzag design.
9. The colors of the mountain contrast with those of the valley.
10. The landscape of this area presents many such contrasts.

Answers: Exercise 3

1. The subject of *Elsewhere, Perhaps* is Israeli kibbutz dwellers.
2. The kibbutz's inhabitants are a fictional creation.
3. The characters' names are pure invention.
4. The novel's setting is the northern farmlands.
5. These communities remain a dangerous place to live.
6. The kibbutz dwellers' neighbors are often the enemy.
7. These details about Metsudat Ram are mostly description.
8. The description becomes a study in contrast.
9. The contrasts are a reflection of the novel's conflicts.
10. The book's main focus is the private struggles of the characters.

Grammar Review

Grammar Review

Review: Exercise 2 Writing Sentences with Intervening Prepositional Phrases

The following sentences describe a landscape similar to the one in the passage from *Elsewhere, Perhaps.* On your paper, rewrite each sentence, adding an appropriate prepositional phrase in the place indicated by the caret and choosing the correct form of the verb in parentheses.

1. A river ∧ (provides/provide) clear, pure water.
2. The foliage ∧ (makes/make) a beautiful sight.
3. Wildflowers ∧ (grows/grow) here and there.
4. People ∧ (farms/farm) the land.
5. The rich soil ∧ (produces/produce) abundant crops.
6. Cows ∧ (grazes/graze) in the valley.
7. The mountain ∧ (is/are) bare and rocky.
8. Ravines ∧ (makes/make) a zigzag design.
9. The colors ∧ (contrasts/contrast) with those of the valley.
10. The landscape ∧ (presents/present) many such contrasts.

Review: Exercise 3 Making Linking Verbs Agree with Their Subjects

Each of the following sentences describes *Elsewhere, Perhaps.* On your paper, rewrite each sentence, following the directions in parentheses. If necessary, change the number of the linking verb.

1. The subject of *Elsewhere, Perhaps* is Israeli kibbutz life. (Change *life* to *dwellers.*)
2. The kibbutz's inhabitants are fictional characters. (Change *fictional characters* to *a fictional creation.*)
3. The kibbutz's name is pure invention. (Change *kibbutz's name* to *characters' names.*)
4. The novel's setting is northern Israel. (Change *northern Israel* to *the northern farmlands.*)
5. The kibbutz remains a dangerous place to live. (Change *The kibbutz* to *These communities.*)
6. The kibbutz dwellers' neighbors are often enemies. (Change *enemies* to *the enemy.*)
7. This passage about Metsudat Ram is mostly description. (Change *This passage* to *These details.*)
8. The descriptions become a study in contrast. (Change *descriptions* to *description.*)
9. The contrasts are reflections of the novel's conflicts. (Change *reflections* to *a reflection.*)
10. The book's main conflicts are the private struggles of the characters. (Change *conflicts* to *focus.*)

Practice and Assess

Review: Exercise 4 — Making Subjects and Verbs Agree in Inverted Sentences

Each of the following sentences describes the kibbutz of the passage from *Elsewhere, Perhaps.* First, write each sentence on your paper, choosing the correct form of the verb in parentheses. Then write each sentence in inverted order, making any necessary adjustments to the verb.

SAMPLE   Metsudat Ram (is/are) near the Golan Heights.
ANSWER   Metsudat Ram is near the Golan Heights.
             Near the Golan Heights is Metsudat Ram.

1. The kibbutz (stands/stand) near the Syrian border.
2. The settlement (sprawls/sprawl) among the trees.
3. The buildings (lies/lie) in a symmetrical pattern.
4. The kibbutz (shines/shine) in white and red.
5. The mountains (is/are) near the kibbutz.
6. The people (lives/live) beside the mountain.
7. Several ravines (cuts/cut) across the mountain.
8. Rich soil (spreads/spread) up the lower slopes.
9. Dark and eerie shadows (looms/loom) on the mountainside.
10. The Syrian frontier (winds/wind) along the terraces.

Review: Exercise 5 — Making Verbs Agree with Special Subjects

The following sentences are about a family touring Jerusalem, Israel. First, on your paper write the subject in each sentence and then the form of the verb in parentheses that agrees with that subject.

SAMPLE   A family (is/are) on tour in Israel not by itself but with a group.
ANSWER   family is

1. Three weeks (has/have) passed since the family arrived in Israel.
2. Measles (is/are) the reason the youngest child had to stay home.
3. The group (learns/learn) many facts about Jerusalem from the tour guide.
4. Forty-two square miles (is/are) the city's total area.
5. Statistics (shows/show) that the city has benefited from a multitude of pilgrims and tourists.
6. *Interesting Sights in Jerusalem* (is/are) the name of the book the guide recommends to the group.
7. The majority (wants/want) to see the Old City in East Jerusalem before viewing the more modern West Jerusalem.
8. The family (goes/go) off in opposite directions to see different parts of the city.
9. Binoculars (is/are) handy for surveying areas of the Old City.

Answers: Exercise 4
1. The kibbutz stands near the Syrian border. Near the Syrian border stands the kibbutz.
2. The settlement sprawls among the trees. Among the trees sprawls the settlement.
3. The buildings lie in a symmetrical pattern. In a symmetrical pattern lie the buildings.
4. The kibbutz shines in white and red. In white and red shines the kibbutz.
5. The mountains are near the kibbutz. Near the kibbutz are the mountains.
6. The people live beside the mountain. Beside the mountain live the people.
7. Several ravines cut across the mountain. Across the mountain cut several ravines.
8. Rich soil spreads up the lower slopes. Up the lower slopes spreads rich soil.
9. Dark and eerie shadows loom on the mountainside. On the mountainside loom dark and eerie shadows.
10. The Syrian frontier winds along the terraces. Along the terraces winds the Syrian frontier.

Answers: Exercise 5
1. weeks/have
2. Measles/is
3. group/learns
4. miles/is
5. Statistics/show
6. *Interesting Sights in Jerusalem*/is
7. majority/want
8. family/go
9. Binoculars/are

Practice and Assess

Answers: Exercise 5 (continued)

10. feet/is
11. feet/is
12. congregation/gathers
13. hours/fly
14. group/disagree
15. crowd/is
16. throng/buys (*or* buy)
17. thousand/is
18. Economics/is
19. group/enjoys
20. "The People of Jerusalem"/is

Answers: Exercise 6

1. The Mediterranean Sea lies off Israel's borders.
2. Jordan borders Israel.
3. Saudi Arabia and Egypt are also among Israel's neighbors in the Middle East.
4. Tel Aviv and Jerusalem are multilingual cities in Israel.
5. Many a tourist and historian visits Israel each year.
6. Virtually every Israeli city and village has a rich history.
7. The Dead Sea also attracts many visitors.
8. Hot, dry summer weather helps to create a pleasant climate.
9. Desert irrigation has produced many farmlands.
10. Tourism and agriculture are vital to Israel's economy.

10. Approximately 40 feet (is/are) the height of the stone walls surrounding the Old City.
11. One hundred sixty feet (is/are) the length of the Wailing Wall, the holiest Jewish shrine in Jerusalem.
12. A congregation of Christian pilgrims (gathers/gather) outside the Church of the Holy Sepulcher.
13. Two hours (flies/fly) by as they tour the Dome of the Rock, an ancient mosque.
14. The group (disagrees/disagree) over what to do the next day.
15. The crowd in the *souks,* or markets, (is/are) definitely another sight worth seeing in the Old City.
16. The throng in the narrow streets (buys/buy) souvenirs in the small, dark shops.
17. Seventeen thousand (is/are) the approximate number of students attending Hebrew University in Jerusalem.
18. Economics (is/are) one of the most important subjects taught there.
19. The tour group also (enjoys/enjoy) viewing the Knesset, the Israeli parliament.
20. "The People of Jerusalem" (is/are) a magazine article that describes the city's three populations—Jewish, Moslem, and Christian.

Review: Exercise 6   Making Verbs Agree with Compound Subjects

Each of the following sentences describes the nation of Israel. On your paper, rewrite each sentence, following the directions in parentheses. Make any necessary adjustments to the form of the verb and to any other words.

SAMPLE   Haifa is among Israel's largest cities. (Add *and Tel Aviv* to the complete subject.)

ANSWER   Haifa and Tel Aviv are among Israel's largest cities.

1. The Mediterranean Sea and the Dead Sea lie off Israel's borders. (Delete *and the Dead Sea* from the complete subject.)
2. Jordan and Syria border Israel. (Delete *and Syria* from the complete subject.)
3. Saudi Arabia is also among Israel's neighbors in the Middle East. (Add *and Egypt* to the complete subject.)
4. Tel Aviv is a multilingual city in Israel. (Add *and Jerusalem* to the complete subject.)
5. Many a tourist visits Israel each year. (Add *and historian* to the complete subject.)
6. Virtually every Israeli city has a rich history. (Add *and village* to the complete subject.)
7. The Dead Sea and the Rift Valley also attract many visitors. (Delete *and the Rift Valley* from the complete subject.)
8. Hot, dry summer weather and fairly mild winters help to create a pleasant climate. (Delete *and fairly mild winters* from the complete subject.)
9. Desert irrigation and swamp drainage have produced many farmlands. (Delete *and swamp drainage* from the complete subject.)
10. Tourism is vital to Israel's economy. (Add *and agriculture* to the complete subject.)

Review: Exercise 7   Making Subjects and Verbs Agree When Expressions Intervene

The following sentences are about Hebrew, the language in which Amos Oz writes. On your paper, rewrite each sentence, correcting any errors in subject-verb agreement. If the sentence contains no errors, write *correct*.

1. Hebrew, together with Arabic, are spoken in Israel.
2. Yiddish, in addition to Hebrew, are the language of some Israeli authors.
3. The German language, plus the Hebrew alphabet and some Slavic words, form the basis of Yiddish.
4. Jewish traditions from Eastern Europe, as well as the Jewish culture of the Mediterranean countries, have influenced the manner in which Hebrew is pronounced.
5. The chief difference between Eastern European and Mediterranean Hebrew, in addition to the sound of certain vowels, lie in the way some words are pronounced.
6. Hebrew, as well as Arabic, is a Semitic language.
7. This pair of languages, together with Aramaic, have common roots.
8. Ancient Egyptian, plus several modern Ethiopian tongues, is distantly related to the Semitic languages.
9. The Hebrew alphabet, unlike the English alphabet, includes only consonants.
10. The letters of the alphabet, together with symbols used to indicate the vowels, forms words that can be sounded out phonetically.

Review: Exercise 8   Making Verbs Agree with Indefinite Pronoun Subjects

The following sentences describe Israel's collective communities, or *kibbutzim* (the plural of *kibbutz*), as well as Israel's cooperative communities, or *moshavim* (the plural of *moshav*). On your paper, rewrite each sentence, replacing the indefinite pronoun in italics with the pronoun in parentheses. If necessary, change the number of the verb.

1. *Some* of the kibbutz members raise crops or livestock. (Several).
2. *Many* of the other members run small businesses for kibbutz residents. (Some)
3. *All* are welcome to join a kibbutz. (Anyone)
4. *Each* of the kibbutz residents shares in ownership of the collective's property. (All)
5. *Most* of Israel's farmers live in cooperative communities called moshavim. (Many)
6. In a moshav, *all* of the families own a separate plot of land. (each)
7. *Both* of these kinds of communities involve group effort. (Either)
8. *Many* in the group are ready and willing to contribute. (Everybody)
9. *None* are allowed to shirk responsibilities. (No one)
10. *Each* of these kinds of communities is important to the Israeli economy. (Both)

Grammar Review   **631**

Practice and Assess

Answers: Exercise 7

1. Hebrew, together with Arabic, is spoken in Israel.
2. Yiddish, in addition to Hebrew, is the language of some Israeli authors.
3. The German language, plus the Hebrew alphabet and some Slavic words, forms the basis of Yiddish.
4. correct
5. The chief difference between Eastern European and Mediterranean Hebrew, in addition to the sound of certain vowels, lies in the way some words are pronounced.
6. correct
7. This pair of languages, together with Aramaic, has common roots.
8. correct
9. correct
10. The letters of the alphabet, together with symbols used to indicate the vowels, form words that can be sounded out phonetically.

Answers: Exercise 8

1. Several of the kibbutz members raise crops or livestock.
2. Some of the other members run small businesses for kibbutz residents.
3. Anyone is welcome to join a kibbutz.
4. All of the kibbutz residents share in ownership of the collective's property.
5. Many of Israel's farmers live in cooperative communities called moshavim.
6. In a moshav, each of the families owns a separate plot of land.
7. Either of these kinds of communities involves group effort.
8. Everybody in the group is ready and willing to contribute.
9. No one is allowed to shirk responsibilities.
10. Both of these kinds of communities are important to the Israeli economy.

Subject-Verb Agreement

Practice and Assess

Answers: Exercise 9

1. No one/works
2. Everything/is
3. Each/labors
4. Everyone/receives
5. Most/are
6. Most/is
7. all/Are
8. none/Have
9. all/Do
10. all/Does

Answers: Exercise 10
Proofreading

This proofreading activity provides editing practice with (1) the current or previous units' skills, (2) the **Troubleshooter** errors, and (3) spelling errors. Students should be able to complete the exercise by referring to the units, the **Troubleshooter,** and a dictionary. (Note: A run-on sentence counts as one error.)

Error (Type of Error)

1. Stashow, (nonessential participial phrase)
2. was (verb tense)
3. studied (spelling)
4. to (spelling)
5. Israel), (nonessential appositive)
6. were (subject-verb agreement)
7. New York, (run-on sentence)
8. began (verb form)
9. has been (subject-verb agreement)
10. has been (subject-verb agreement)
11. are (subject-verb agreement)

Review: Exercise 9 Making Verbs Agree with Indefinite Pronoun Subjects

The following sentences are about Israel's kibbutzim and moshavim. On your paper, write the subject and the correct form of the verb in parentheses for each sentence.

1. No one on the kibbutzim (work/works) for personal profit.
2. Everything on a kibbutz, except personal possessions, (is/are) collectively owned.
3. Each of the members (labors/labor) to capacity.
4. Everyone (receives/receive) according to need.
5. Most of the rooms in the kibbutz (is/are) communal.
6. Most of each community (is/are) cooperatively owned.
7. (Is/Are) all of the kibbutzim entirely agricultural?
8. (Has/Have) none established manufacturing industries?
9. (Does/Do) all of the children attend school?
10. (Does/Do) all of this moshav belong to its residents?

Review: Exercise 10

Proofreading

The following passage describes the artist Elias Newman, whose painting is reproduced on the opposite page. On your paper, rewrite the passage, correcting the errors in spelling, grammar, and usage. Add any missing punctuation. There are twenty errors.

Elias Newman

[1]Elias Newman was born in 1903 in the Russian-ruled city of Stashow located in Poland. [2]When he is ten, Newman and his family immigrated to the United States. [3]Growing up in New York City, he studied at the National Academy of Design and the Educational Alliance Art School.

[4]Newman traveled too Europe and the Middle East in 1925. [5]He lived for four years in Palestine (now Israel) a country for which he felt a great kinship. [6]During Newman's stay there, Jerusalem and Tel Aviv was the sites of his solo exhibitions.

[7]Newman returned to New York but he also became involved in the art community of Rockport, Massachusetts, where he had a summer studio. [8]In addition, he begun working with the New York Artists' Equity Association, a leading organization of artists in America. [9]One of Newman's great contributions to the arts have been his work to raise funds for artists in financial need.

[10]Newman's other main endeavor, in addition to helping artists, have been his art. [11]His landscapes of Palestine is among his most famous works. [12]Using water-

Elias Newman, *Wadi Musserara*, 1926

Practice and Assess

Answers: Exercise 10 (continued)

Error (Type of Error)
12. creates (subject-verb agreement)
13. Newman's (singular possessive)
14. has included (subject-verb agreement)
15. suggests (subject-verb agreement)
16. convey (subject-verb agreement)
17. become (subject-verb agreement)
18. passage (spelling)
    has (subject-verb agreement)
19. buildings, (commas in a series)

Subject-Verb Agreement

colors and oil pigments, he create simple and forceful paintings. ¹³One critic said of Newmans work, "It has an elusive richness and a depth that may well be part of Palestine's experience." ¹⁴Newman's career have included more than a hundred one-person exhibitions, and he has received many awards.

¹⁵*Wadi Musserara* suggest the light and color of a rural landscape in the Middle East. ¹⁶The elements of the landscape conveys movement and design. ¹⁷The green field and plants in the foreground of this painting becomes a directional device to lead the viewer's eyes first to the meandering river and then into the arid hills far in the background.

¹⁸The pasage from Amos Oz's novel *Elsewhere, Perhaps* have as its setting an Israeli landscape very similar to the one depicted in Newman's painting. ¹⁹Oz's description of the whitewashed buildings bare mountains, and "zigzagging ravines" could very well be a caption for Newman's work.

Grammar Review **633**

Viewing the Art

Elias Newman, *Wadi Musserara*, 1926
In *Wadi Musserara*, Elias Newman contrasts the green and fertile lowlands with the barren hills in the distance. The perspective in the painting is exaggerated; the fields seem to tilt at strange angles. The twists and turns of the river give the painting dramatic tension.

In the opening scene of *Elsewhere, Perhaps,* Amos Oz, like Newman, uses contrasts to create dramatic tension. Explain that some of the contrasts are visual and others are historical or psychological. Ask students to discuss any contrasts they observe in *Wadi Musserara.*

Practice and Assess

Answers: Exercise 11
Mixed Review

1. Amos Oz/numbers
2. author/was
3. Most/has
4. He and his wife and children/have
5. home/is
6. name/means
7. Most/takes
8. relationship/is
9. understanding/comes
10. *Touch the Water*/depicts
11. Each/has
12. *My Michael*/is
13. novels/are
14. Many/form
15. part/has
16. element/is
17. writer/is
18. conflicts/are
19. community/has
20. Oz/writes
21. Politics/has
22. Israelis and readers/have
23. *My Michael, Elsewhere, Perhaps*/has
24. Amos Oz/has
25. novels/are

Close

On the board, write sentences with two verb choices and have students determine the agreement.
Samples:
1. *All of us (long/longs) for happiness.*
2. *There (is/are) a lot of details to complete.*

Review: Exercise 11

Mixed Review

The following sentences describe the life of Amos Oz. For each sentence, write on your paper the subject and the appropriate form of the verb in parentheses.

Amos Oz

1. Amos Oz, together with Nobel Prize winner Shmuel Yosef Agnon, (numbers/number) among Israel's best-known writers of fiction.
2. The author of *Elsewhere, Perhaps* (was/were) born in 1939 in Jerusalem.
3. Most of Oz's life since his teenage years (has/have) been lived in a kibbutz.
4. He and his wife and children (has/have) recently moved from northern Israel.
5. Their home (is/are) now in Israel's southern desert lands.
6. Amos Oz's last name, though not his birth name, (means/mean) "strength" in Hebrew.
7. Most of Oz's fiction (takes/take) place in modern Israel.
8. The relationship between Jews and Arabs (is/are) a dominant concern in Oz's work.
9. From his kibbutz experiences (comes/come) his clear understanding of human conflicts and emotions.
10. *Touch the Water,* as well as Oz's earlier novel *Elsewhere, Perhaps,* (depicts/depict) kibbutz life.
11. Each of these books (has/have) won praise from critics.
12. The most successful of Oz's novels (is/are) *My Michael,* which describes the psychological turmoil of an Israeli wife in a troubled marriage.
13. Oz's poetic novels (is/are) a reflection of the struggles of Israeli life.
14. Many of Oz's own experiences on a kibbutz (forms/form) the basis of his literary work.
15. A large part of Oz's literary earnings (has/have) been given to Kibbutz Hulda.
16. There (is/are) an element of religious poetry running through each of Oz's novels.
17. Oz's favorite writer of all American writers (is/are) Herman Melville.
18. The conflicts in Israel (is/are) the setting for many of Oz's stories.
19. The Jewish community (has/have) praised Oz's novels and short stories.
20. Oz, in addition to several other noted authors, (writes/write) all of his books in Hebrew.
21. Politics (has/have) played an important role in Oz's life.
22. Both Israelis and readers around the world (has/have) learned about life on a kibbutz.
23. Neither *My Michael* nor *Elsewhere, Perhaps* (has/have) been made into a motion picture.
24. Amos Oz, along with Isaac Bashevis Singer, (has/have) written stories about specifically Jewish topics.
25. The novels of Amos Oz (is/are) the topic for discussion in class today.

Subject-Verb Agreement

Writing Application

Subject-Verb Agreement in Writing

In this passage about the cable channel MTV, Tom Shales demonstrates correct subject-verb agreement. Examine the passage, focusing especially on the italicized subjects and verbs.

> Not for nothing *has MTV earned* the nickname "Empty-V." Instead of denying that emptiness, however, MTV celebrates it. *Members* of the viewing audience *are* frequently *assured* that they are not to be bothered with matters of consequence. *"MTV News,"* which is shown frequently every day, *is* "news" about rock stars, pop stars and silly celebrities—puff and fluff spun in the hype mills of Hollywood.

Techniques with Subject-Verb Agreement

Try to apply some of Tom Shales's writing techniques when you write and revise.

❶ In inverted sentences, remember that the subject follows the verb.

NON-INVERTED SENTENCE MTV has earned the nickname "Empty-V" not for nothing.

SHALES'S CORRECT USE Not for nothing has MTV earned the nickname "Empty-V."

❷ Be alert to prepositional phrases and other expressions that fall between a subject and its verb.

INCORRECT USE Members of the viewing audience is frequently assured. . . .

SHALES'S CORRECT USE Members of the viewing audience are frequently assured . . . .

❸ Remember that certain nouns that end in -s take singular verbs.

INCORRECT USE "MTV News," which is shown frequently each day, are "news" . . .

SHALES'S CORRECT USE "MTV News," which is shown frequently each day, is "news" . . .

TIME
For more about the writing process, see TIME Facing the Blank Page, pp. 109–119

Practice Apply these techniques and others you have learned in this unit by revising the following paragraph. On your paper, rewrite the paragraph, filling each blank with a verb in the present tense. Make other changes too. Write at least one sentence as an inverted sentence.

The islands known as the West Indies _____ in the Caribbean Sea. Trinidad and Tobago, the southernmost nation in the island chain, _____ the home of a type of music known as calypso. During the carnival held each February, many of the country's calypso singers _____ before a large crowd. Most of their music _____ improvised lyrics, and many of the lyrics _____ satirical. Each of the calypso singers _____ a distinct style, and all of them _____ how to please an audience. There _____ many recordings of calypso music. Both tourists and residents _____ recordings of the music to enjoy later. Nothing _____ more memorable about the island republic of Trinidad and Tobago than its calypso music.

Writing Application **635**

Subject-Verb Agreement in Writing

You may have students read the paragraph without interruption and then go back and discuss the italicized subject and verb choices. Discuss these choices in relation to the Techniques with Subject-Verb Agreement.

Techniques with Subject-Verb Agreement

Discuss the techniques described in the student edition. Then invite students to see how these techniques are used in another piece of writing—for example, a paragraph or two from the Proofreading practice on pp. 632–633.

Practice

The answers to this challenging and enriching activity will vary. Refer to the Techniques with Subject-Verb Agreement as you evaluate student choices.

Sample:
In the Caribbean Sea lie the islands known as the West Indies. Trinidad and Tobago, the southernmost country in the island chain, is the home of a type of music known as calypso. During the carnival held each February, many of the country's calypso singers perform before a large crowd. Most of their music includes improvised lyrics, and many of the lyrics are satirical. Each of the calypso singers has a distinct style, and all of them know how to please an audience. There exist many recordings of calypso music. Both tourists and residents purchase recordings of the music to enjoy later. Nothing is more memorable about the island republic of Trinidad and Tobago than its calypso music.

✔ ASSESSMENT OPTIONS

📁 *Tests with Answer Key & Rubrics*
Unit 16 Mastery Test, pp. 57–58

💾 *Testmaker*
Unit 16 Mastery Test

📼 *MindJogger Videoquizzes*

Objectives

- To develop an understanding of pronouns and the ability to use the correct case and pronoun-antecedent agreement
- To demonstrate control over pronoun case and pronoun-antecedent agreement by completing exercises and by writing sentences in which pronouns are used appropriately and correctly

---

✔ ASSESSMENT OPTIONS

📁 *Tests with Answer Key & Rubrics*
Unit 17 Pretest, pp. 59–60
Unit 17 Mastery Test, pp. 61–62

💾 *Testmaker*
Unit 17 Pretest
Unit 17 Mastery Test

You may wish to administer the Unit 17 Pretest at this point.

Key to Ability Levels

L1 Level 1 activities are within the basic ability range of students.

L2 Level 2 activities are within the ability range of average students.

L3 Level 3 activities are more challenging activities.

UNIT 17

Using Pronouns Correctly

Lesson **17.1**	**Case of Personal Pronouns**	*637*
Lesson **17.2**	**Pronouns with and as Appositives**	*639*
Lesson **17.3**	**Pronouns After *Than* and *As***	*641*
Lesson **17.4**	***Who* and *Whom* in Questions and Subordinate Clauses**	*642*
Lesson **17.5**	**Pronoun-Antecedent Agreement**	*644*
Lesson **17.6**	**Clear Pronoun Reference**	*649*
Grammar Review		*652*
Writing Application		*661*

636

Resource Manager

Planning Resources
- *Lesson Plans*
- *Block Scheduling*

 Transparencies
- *Bellringer*
- *Daily Language Practice*
- *Two-Minute Skill Drill*

📁 **Other Print Resources**
- *Grammar and Composition Handbook*

- *Grammar Enrichment*
- *Grammar Practice*
- *Grammar Reteaching*
- *Grammar Workbook*
- *Tests with Answer Key and Rubrics*

📺 **Video**
- *MindJogger Videoquizzes*

💾 **Software**
- *Interactive Grammar and Language Workbook*

- *Language Arts PASS*
- *Presentation Plus!*
- *Testmaker*
- *Writer's Choice Puzzlemaker*

💻 **Web Sites**
- *writerschoice.glencoe.com*

17.1 Case of Personal Pronouns

- Pronouns that are used to refer to persons or things are called **personal** pronouns.

- Personal pronouns have three **cases,** or forms, called **nominative, objective,** and **possessive.** The case of a personal pronoun depends upon the pronoun's function in a sentence (whether it is a subject, an object, a complement, or a replacement for a possessive noun).

Study the chart to recall the case forms of the different personal pronouns.

Personal Pronouns			
Case	Singular Pronouns	Plural Pronouns	Function in Sentence
NOMINATIVE	I, you, she, he, it	we, you, they	subject or predicate nominative
OBJECTIVE	me, you, her, him, it	us, you, them	direct object, indirect object, or object of preposition
POSSESSIVE	my, mine, your, yours, her, hers, his, its	our, ours, your, yours, their, theirs	replacement for possessive noun(s)

Exercise 1   **Identifying Pronoun Case**

On your paper, write each personal pronoun in the sentences below. Then tell what case each is, and how it functions in the sentence.

> **SAMPLE**   My father and I took him to a basketball game last Saturday afternoon.
>
> **ANSWER**   My—possessive, replacement for possessive noun; I—nominative, subject; him—objective, direct object.

1. We arrived early so that he could see the players shoot practice shots.
2. Our seats put Dad, him, and me near the half-court line.
3. One player smiled at us as she stopped to tie her shoes.
4. She knew that they would be playing their biggest game of the season that day.
5. He held up his pennant and waved it excitedly at her.

17.1 Case of Personal Pronouns   **637**

Using Pronouns Correctly

Focus

Lesson Overview

Objectives
- To identify the three cases of personal pronouns
- To use all three cases of pronouns appropriately in writing

 Bellringer
Daily Language Activity
Use the Bellringer Transparency for Lesson 17.1.

See also ✏ *Daily Language Practice*

Teach

Vocabulary Link
The word *nominative* comes from the Latin word for "name." The nominative case of pronouns always names the subject of a sentence or a clause.

Practice and Assess

Answers: Exercise 1
1. We—nominative, subject
   he—nominative, subject
2. Our—possessive, replacement for possessive noun
   him—objective, direct object
   me—objective, direct object
3. us—objective, object of preposition
   she—nominative, subject
   her—possessive, replacement for possessive noun
4. She—nominative, subject
   they—nominative, subject
   their—possessive, replacement for possessive noun
5. He—nominative, subject
   his—possessive, replacement for possessive noun
   it—objective, direct object
   her—objective, object of preposition

Resource Manager

Planning Resources
- *Lesson Plans*

✏ **Transparencies**
- *Bellringer*
- *Daily Language Practice*
- *Two-Minute Skill Drill*

📂 **Other Print Resources**
- *Grammar and Composition Handbook*
- *Grammar Enrichment,* p. 30
- *Grammar Practice,* p. 30
- *Grammar Reteaching,* p. 30
- *Grammar Workbook,* Lesson 52

Teach

☑ **Teaching Tip**

Show students how to check for proper case in compound subjects and objects by dropping the proper nouns and conjunctions from this sentence: *Al and (I, me) saw Ed and (she, her).*

Two-Minute Skill Drill

Have students identify the case of each personal pronoun in the following sentence (pronouns are underlined).

I had all but rid <u>my</u> mind of the thoughts that jostled in <u>it</u> when <u>I</u> saw the man approaching <u>us</u>, and <u>my</u> grandfather and I exchanged glances.

—Tayeb Salih, *A Handful of Dates*

See also *Two-Minute Skill Drill Transparency 17.1*

Practice and Assess

Answers: Exercise 2

1. she, I   4. me
2. he   5. her, me
3. He

Additional Resources

📁 *Grammar Practice,* p. 30
📁 *Grammar Reteaching,* p. 30
📁 *Grammar Enrichment,* p. 30

📖 *Grammar Workbook,* Lesson 52

Close

Have students write sentences using pronouns of all three cases. Ask students to exchange papers with a partner and to identify the case of each pronoun in their partner's sentences.

Using Pronouns Correctly

Use these rules to avoid errors with the case of personal pronouns.

1. Use the nominative case for a personal pronoun in a compound subject.
   Ann and **I** play tennis.   **She** and **I** are equally matched.

2. Use the objective case for a personal pronoun in a compound object.
   Ann challenged Juan and **her**.   She talked to Sue and **me**.

   Hint: When choosing the correct pronoun in a sentence with a compound subject or object, it is helpful to say the sentence to yourself without the conjunction and the other subject or object.

   The ball bounced toward Ann and me.

3. After a form of the linking verb *be,* use the nominative case of a personal pronoun.
   The winner was **he**.   Ann hoped that it would be **she**.

   Today this rule is changing. In informal speech, people often use the objective case after a form of the linking verb *be;* they say *It's me* or *It was him.* Some authorities even advise using the objective case in informal writing to avoid appearing pretentious. In formal writing, however, always use the nominative case after a form of the verb *be.*

4. Do not spell possessive pronouns with apostrophes.
   This paddle is **yours**.   The table is **ours**.

   Remember that *it's* is a contraction for *it is.* You should not confuse *it's* with the possessive pronoun *its.*
   It's my watch that is lying on the dresser.
   Its band must be replaced.

5. Use possessive pronouns before gerunds (*-ing* verb forms used as nouns).
   Your singing relaxes the baby.   He is amused by **my** talking.

Exercise 2   **Choosing the Correct Case Form**

For each sentence, write the correct personal pronoun from each pair in parentheses.

Satchel Paige, a Legendary Pitcher

1. When Marisa offered to help me with my report on a famous athlete, (she/her) and (I/me) chose Satchel Paige, one of the greatest baseball pitchers of all time.
2. It was (he/him) who became one of the first African Americans in the American League.
3. (He/Him) and Jackie Robinson were among the first African American athletes to play for major-league teams.
4. What impressed Marisa and (I/me) is that Paige never gave up.
5. To (she/her) and (I/me), Paige and his fellow African American players are true heroes.

638   Unit 17 Using Pronouns Correctly

Listening and Speaking

Learning Pronoun Patterns

For many students, it is less important to remember the names of the cases than to recognize when to use each case. Teach patterns by reading sentences like those in Exercise 2 aloud, emphasizing the correct terms as you repeat each one. **L1**

17.2 Pronouns with and as Appositives

■ Use the nominative case for a pronoun that is in apposition to a subject or a predicate nominative.

The candidates, **she** and **Mr. Gomez,** will run for that office. [*Candidates* is the subject.]

The candidates are two people from our district, **Ms. Pierce** and **he.** [*People* is the predicate nominative.]

■ Use the objective case for a pronoun that is in apposition to a direct object, an indirect object, or an object of a preposition.

The crowd favored the local pair, **Hilda** and **her.** [*Pair* is the direct object.]

I gave my friends **Floyd** and **him** a ticket. [*Friends* is the indirect object.]

The officials talked to both groups of players, **them** and **us.** [*Groups* is the object of the preposition *to.*]

■ When a pronoun is followed by an appositive, choose the case of the pronoun that would be correct if the appositive were omitted.

We athletes want to win the cash prize. [*We* is the correct form because *we* is the subject of the sentence.]

It was **we athletes** who practiced for such long hours. [*We* is the correct form because *we* is the predicate nominative.]

The school awarded **us athletes** a handsome trophy. [*Us* is the correct form because *us* is the indirect object.]

The prize was divided evenly among **us athletes.** [*Us* is the correct form because *us* is the object of the preposition *among.*]

Hint: When you are confused about which pronoun to use, try saying the sentence aloud without the appositive.

Focus

Lesson Overview

Objectives
• To identify pronouns used as appositives
• To use the correct case when pronouns are used as or with appositives

Bellringer
Daily Language Activity

When students enter the classroom, have the following assignment on the board: *Write a sentence explaining why the pronouns in the following sentences are correct.*

The best runners, Sheila and she, lined up first.

We cheered the best runners, Sheila and her.

See also Daily Language Practice

Using Pronouns Correctly

Teach

☑ Teaching Tip
Whenever a pronoun used as an appositive merely renames the noun, the pronoun is set off with commas. If the reader needs the appositive to identify the noun, then no commas are used. In this respect, the punctuation of pronouns used as appositives is similar to the punctuation of restrictive and nonrestrictive adjective clauses.

☒ Cross-reference: Writing
For instruction and practice in combining sentences to make writing concise, refer students to Unit 8, pp. 358–385. Remind students that using appositives with personal pronouns is a good way to combine sentences and to make writing concise.

Resource Manager

Planning Resources
• *Lesson Plans*

Transparencies
• *Bellringer*
• *Daily Language Practice*
• *Two-Minute Skill Drill*

📁 **Other Print Resources**
• *Grammar and Composition Handbook*
• *Grammar Enrichment,* p. 31
• *Grammar Practice,* p. 31
• *Grammar Reteaching,* p. 31
• *Grammar Workbook,* Lesson 53

Practice and Assess

Answers: Exercise 3

1. he
2. her
3. him
4. we
5. me

Answers: Exercise 4

1. We
2. she
3. I
4. she
5. us
6. us
7. him
8. her
9. us
10. We, him
11. we
12. me, him
13. us
14. her, us
15. We, I

Additional Resources

 Grammar Practice, p. 31
Grammar Reteaching, p. 31
Grammar Enrichment, p. 31

Grammar Workbook, Lesson 53

Close

Review with students how to decide whether a pronoun in apposition should be in the nominative or the objective case.

Using Pronouns Correctly

Exercise 3　Using Pronouns with and as Appositives

For each sentence in the following paragraph, write the correct pronoun from the pair in parentheses.

An Artistic Triumph

¹In 1959 two New York City theater critics, Brooks Atkinson and (he/him), praised *A Raisin in the Sun,* Lorraine Hansberry's play about the struggles of an African American family. ²The acting by the stars, Sidney Poitier, Diana Sands, Ruby Dee, and (she/her), was widely applauded. ³The play was also praised by two famous American playwrights. Tennessee Williams and (he/him). ⁴Even today (we/us) young actors are very fortunate to be able to work with such a well-written script. ⁵The character of Beneatha, a young girl searching for her identity, had a great impact on one young actor, (I/me).

Exercise 4　Using Pronouns Correctly with and as Appositives

For each of the following sentences, write the correct personal pronoun from each pair in parentheses.

The Game of Tennis

1. (We/Us) American tennis players claim that tennis was invented in the United States.
2. Jason and (she/her) told us that modern tennis was first played in Britain.
3. In preparing a report for our social studies class, the research team, Owen, Majorie, and (I/me), discovered that the ancestor of tennis was a twelfth-century French handball game.
4. It was two student teachers, Ms. Liu and (she/her), who pointed us to the right sources.
5. It was a surprise to (we/us) hard-working researchers to learn that a version of the French game, called real tennis, is still played in Britain today.
6. Apparently Major Walter Clopton Wingfield, an English gentleman, introduced modern lawn tennis at a party on his estate in 1873—a fact that intrigued (we/us) investigators.
7. We learned from Claire and (he/him) that the game was brought to America in 1874 by Mary Ewing Outerbridge, who had learned to play during a visit to Bermuda.
8. An article found by two of our school librarians, Ms. Denver and (she/her), said that the tennis court was originally shaped like an hourglass.
9. The chief librarian, Mr. Wolfe, also gave (we/us) researchers several articles that made our report a resounding success.
10. (We/Us) proud students sent a copy of our report to our advisors Ms. Denver, Ms. Bueno, and (he/him).
11. The librarians and (we, us) students decided to submit the report to a student research contest.
12. Entry forms were filled out by Owen and (I, me) and co-signed by teachers Ms. Bueno and (he, him).
13. A letter came in about six weeks to (we, us) anxious researchers.
14. It was addressed to Mr. Wolfe and (she, her), as well as to (we, us).
15. (We, Us) three—Marjorie, Owen, and (I, me)—had won third prize.

Listening and Speaking

Checking for Pronoun Errors

To help students check for pronoun errors in compound appositives with nouns, ask them to listen to edited sentences to see what sounds correct. Use sentences 2, 4, 7, 8, 10, and 14 from Exercise 4 and ask students to cross out the noun in the compound appositive as well as the noun it refers to. The pronoun will stand alone as the subject or object and the appropriate form should sound correct to most English speakers when the sentence is read aloud. **L1**

17.3 Pronouns After *Than* and *As*

■ In elliptical adverb clauses using *than* and *as*, choose the case of the pronoun that you would use if the missing words were fully expressed.

> You finished the puzzle faster than **he.** [The nominative pronoun *he* is the subject of the complete adverb clause *than he finished the puzzle.*]

> The movie frightened John as much as **them.** [The objective pronoun *them* is the direct object of the complete adverb clause *as much as it frightened them.*]

Some sentences can be completed with either a nominative or an objective pronoun, depending on the meaning intended.

> Tony angered Dana more than I [angered her].

> Tony angered Dana more than [he angered] me.

In informal speech, people often use the objective rather than the nominative form in sentences, such as *My sister is six years younger than me.* In your writing, however, you should be careful to use the correct case.

Exercise 5 **Using the Correct Pronoun After *Than* and *As***

Each sentence contains an italicized word or group of words. Write on your paper the correct pronoun to substitute for the words in italics.

SAMPLE Polar bears are more maternal than *other animals.*
ANSWER they

The Good Mother

1. Mother polar bears seem to take parenting more seriously than *some other animals.*
2. Few animals provide as much parental care as *mother polar bears.*
3. Nothing is as important to polar bear cubs as *their mother.*
4. The mother polar bear needs to care for herself as well as *the cubs.*
5. After one-and-a-half years, the cubs will be as independent as *their mother.*
6. In the meantime, they are more dependent on their mother than *many animals.*
7. When the cubs are born, their eyes are not yet open, and the cubs are not as large as *one of their mother's paws.*
8. It will be years before the cubs are as large as *their mother.*
9. A fully grown polar bear may weigh well over nine hundred pounds—as much as *five large people.*
10. The adult polar bear hunts and eats fish as skillfully as *seals.*

17.3 Pronouns After *Than* and *As* **641**

Using Pronouns Correctly

Focus

Lesson Overview

Objective
• To use the correct case of a pronoun following *than* or *as* in elliptical clauses

🔔 **Bellringer**
Daily Language Activity
Use the Bellringer Transparency for Lesson 17.3.

See also 👆 *Daily Language Practice*

Teach

☑ **Teaching Tip**
Tell students that the case of a pronoun is not determined by *than* or *as* but by the pronoun's function inside the expanded adverb clause. If the pronoun is the subject of its expanded clause, use the nominative case; otherwise, use the objective case.

Practice and Assess

Answers: Exercise 5

1. they   6. they
2. they   7. it
3. she   8. she
4. them   9. they
5. she   10. they

Close

Have students write five sentences using the correct pronoun case following *than* and *as.* Ask them to exchange their work with a partner and to discuss and correct any errors they find. Work with students who have difficulty understanding the concept.

Focus

Lesson Overview

Objective

• To use *who* and *whom* appropriately in questions and subordinate clauses

Bellringer
Daily Language Activity

When students enter the classroom, have the following assignment on the board: *Study the following sentence and explain why* who *rather than* whom *is used to introduce the subordinate clause.*

> Most of all he was tired of cousin Sara, who insisted on treating him like an idiot invalid.
>
> —Barbara Kimenye, *The Winner*

(*Who* is the nominative form and is appropriate because it is the subject of the clause.)

See also *Daily Language Practice*

Teach

☑ Teaching Tip

Who and *whom* are used in two kinds of subordinate clauses. They are used in adjective clauses—*I met the man whom everyone knows*—and in noun clauses—*I know who lives next door.* The form of *who* or *whom* is determined solely by the pronoun's function within its own subordinate clause.

Using Pronouns Correctly

Who will receive my letter?

To **whom** it may concern.

Who and Whom in Questions and Subordinate Clauses

■ Use the nominative pronoun *who* for subjects.

Who called this morning? [*Who* is the subject of the verb *called.*]

Tell us **who is in charge here.** [*Who* is the subject of the noun clause *who is in charge here.*]

■ Use the objective pronoun *whom* for the direct or indirect object of a verb or verbal or for the object of a preposition.

Whom are you telling? [*Whom* is the direct object of the verb *are telling.*]

Whom did she want to tell? [*Whom* is the direct object of the verbal *to tell.*]

Whom did you give the report? [*Whom* is the indirect object of the verb *did give.*]

Jaime asked her **whom** she had seen at the party. [*Whom* is the direct object of the verb *had seen* in the noun clause *whom she had seen at the party.*]

Bette Bao Lord is a writer about **whom** I know very little. [*Whom* is the object of the preposition *about* in the adjective clause *about whom I know very little.*]

When a question contains an interrupting expression, such as *do you think,* it helps to omit the interrupting phrase to determine whether to use *who* or *whom.*

Who do you think gave the best oral report? [Think: *Who* gave the best oral report? *Who* is the subject of the verb *gave.*]

Whom do you think you are asking? [Think: *Whom* are you asking? *Whom* is the direct object of the verb *are asking.*]

When speaking informally, people often use *who* instead of *whom* in sentences like *Who are you calling?* In writing and in formal speech, you should distinguish between *who* and *whom.*

Resource Manager

Planning Resources
• *Lesson Plans*

Transparencies
• *Bellringer*
• *Daily Language Practice*

📁 **Other Print Resources**
• *Grammar and Composition Handbook*
• *Grammar Enrichment,* p. 32
• *Grammar Reteaching,* p. 32
• *Grammar Workbook,* Lesson 54

Exercise 6   Choosing *Who* or *Whom*

For each sentence in the following paragraphs, write on your paper the correct pronoun from the pair in parentheses.

Stories from Greek Mythology

a. ¹(Who/Whom) do you think the Greeks honored as the goddess of agriculture? ²Hades, (who/whom) ruled the underworld, admired Persephone, the daughter of Demeter, and he kidnapped her. ³Persephone, (who/whom) Hades made queen of the underworld, could not escape. ⁴Demeter, (who/whom) had grown angry at the loss of her daughter, refused to allow any crops to grow. ⁵Hades was persuaded by Zeus, (who/whom) the gods must obey, to let Persephone return for part of each year so that the crops would grow.

b. ¹(Who/Whom) did you say was the supreme architect and inventor of his time, according to Greek mythology? ²King Minos of Crete kept a terrible monster called the Minotaur, for (who/whom) he commanded Daedalus, a skilled craftsman, to build a labyrinth where the monster could safely be kept. ³King Minos was delighted with Daedalus, (who/whom) he would not allow to leave Crete lest Daedalus reveal the secret of the labyrinth he had designed. ⁴Daedalus therefore used feathers and wax to build wings for himself and his son, Icarus, (who/whom) Daedalus warned not to fly too close to the sun. ⁵Icarus, (who/whom) was a vain and foolish boy, ignored his father's warning and did fly too near the sun; consequently, the wax in the wings melted, causing him to fall to his death in the sea.

Exercise 7   Using *Who* or *Whom* in Sentences

On your paper, write the correct word *who* or *whom,* to complete each sentence.

The Pueblo, a Native American People

1. Reuben and his older sister, Lara, _____ is a college professor, visited several Pueblo villages in Arizona and New Mexico last summer.
2. Reuben, for _____ the trip was a dream fulfilled, had saved money to pay his way.
3. He had been interested in these Native Americans, _____ many others also admire, for a long time.
4. His sister, _____ he had begged to take him on this trip, studies Native Americans.
5. The Pueblo, _____ are an ancient people, actually consist of several different groups, each speaking a different language.
6. Besides the Hopi, Acoma, Laguna, Taos, and Tewa nations, there is the Zuñi group, for _____ one of the Pueblo languages is named.
7. According to Reuben's sister, _____ many Native Americans honor for her scholarly work, the Pueblo are best known for their large adobe dwellings.
8. Their conquerors, the Spanish, _____ the Pueblo grudgingly tolerated, named the people after their dwellings (*pueblo* is the Spanish word for "village").
9. _____ do you think is the Pueblo individual Reuben most admires?
10. He admires Popé, the leader _____ drove the Spanish off the Tewa lands in 1680.

17.4 *Who* and *Whom* in Questions and Subordinate Clauses   **643**

Teach

☑ Grammar Tip

Tell students that a good test for the correct use of *who* and *whom* in subordinate clauses is to turn the clause into a separate sentence and substitute a personal pronoun for *who* or *whom.* For example, the subordinate clause in the sentence *The girl (who, whom) you talked with today phoned* can be changed to *You talked with her today.* Since the new sentence calls for a personal pronoun in the objective case, *her,* the original sentence calls for the objective *whom.*

Practice and Assess

Answers: Exercise 6

a	b
1. Whom	**1.** Who
2. who	**2.** whom
3. whom	**3.** whom
4. who	**4.** whom
5. whom	**5.** who

Answers: Exercise 7

1. who	**6.** whom
2. whom	**7.** whom
3. whom	**8.** whom
4. whom	**9.** Who
5. who	**10.** who

Additional Resources

📁 *Grammar Reteaching,* p. 32
📁 *Grammar Enrichment,* p 32

📘 *Grammar Workbook,* Lesson 54

Close

Go over students' responses to a few of the exercises, and ask volunteers to explain their choices to the class.

MEETING INDIVIDUAL NEEDS   English Language Learners

Understanding Reversed Order

Often students learning English as a second language confuse the two different uses of *who* and *whom.* The use of *who* and *whom* in questions requires that the verb be in front of the subject—for example: *Who is he?* Students often mistakenly transfer this same reversed word order to noun clauses: *I know who is he.* Students learning English should be made aware of the differences in word order in questions and subordinate clauses.

Focus

Lesson Overview

Objectives

- To learn to make pronouns agree with their antecedents in number, gender, and person
- To demonstrate pronoun-antecedent agreement in writing

Bellringer
Daily Language Activity

Use the Bellringer Transparency for Lesson 17.5.

See also *Daily Language Practice*

Teach

Agreement in Number and Gender

☑ **Teaching Tip**

Explain to students that people often avoid a forced choice of masculine or feminine singular pronouns by substituting the gender-neutral plural pronouns *they, them,* or *their.* Unfortunately, this solution usually creates an agreement problem in number. For example, *A skier must keep his legs strong and limber* may incorrectly become *A skier must keep their legs strong and limber.* This problem is particularly common with "generic" nouns. Probably the simplest solution is to shift the generic noun from singular to plural: *Skiers must keep their legs strong and limber.*

⧉ Cross-reference: Troubleshooter

For instruction and practice in pronoun-antecedent agreement, refer students to the **Troubleshooter.**

17.5 Pronoun-Antecedent Agreement

- An **antecedent** is the word or group of words to which a pronoun refers or that a pronoun replaces. All pronouns must agree with their antecedents in number, gender, and person.

Agreement in Number and Gender

- A pronoun must agree with its antecedent in number (singular or plural) and gender (masculine, feminine, or neuter).

The antecedent of a pronoun may be a noun, another pronoun, or a phrase or clause acting as a noun. In the examples that follow, the pronouns appear in bold type and their antecedents appear in bold italic type:

Emily Brontë published **her** novel, *Wuthering Heights,* in 1847. [singular feminine pronoun]

Emily, Charlotte, and *Anne Brontë* published **their** collected poems in 1846. [plural pronoun]

Langston Hughes published **his** first volume of poetry, *The Weary Blues,* in 1926. [singular masculine pronoun]

Simon J. Ortiz and *Diana Chang* have also published poems that reflect **their** backgrounds. [plural pronoun]

The *spruce,* because of **its** soft wood, is used to make paper. [singular neuter pronoun]

Spruce and *aspen* are economical to raise because of **their** rapid growth. [plural pronoun]

When the gender of the antecedent is not known or when it may be either masculine or feminine, a masculine pronoun has traditionally been used.

A *skier* must keep **his** legs strong and limber.

This usage has changed, however, and many people now prefer to use gender-neutral wording. If you do not wish to use a masculine pronoun, you can frequently reword the sentence in one of three ways: (1) by using *he or she, his or her,* and so forth, (2) by using a plural pronoun, or (3) by eliminating the pronoun.

A *performer* must understand **his** role.

A *performer* must understand **his or her** role.

Performers must understand **their** roles.

A *performer* must understand a role. [no pronoun]

Resource Manager

Planning Resources
- *Lesson Plans*

Transparencies
- *Bellringer*
- *Daily Language Practice*
- *Two-Minute Skill Drill*

📁 Other Print Resources
- *Grammar and Composition Handbook*
- *Grammar Enrichment,* p. 33
- *Grammar Practice,* p. 33
- *Grammar Reteaching,* p. 33
- *Grammar Workbook,* Lesson 55

Agreement in Person

■ A pronoun must agree in person with its antecedent.

Do not use the second-person pronoun *you* to refer to an antecedent in the third person. Use either an appropriate third-person pronoun or a suitable noun.

POOR	Richard and Clara are going to a store where you can buy brand-name clothing at reasonable prices.
BETTER	Richard and Clara are going to a store where **they** can buy brand-name clothing at reasonable prices.
BETTER	Richard and Clara are going to a store where **shoppers** can buy brand-name clothing at reasonable prices.

When the antecedent of a pronoun is another pronoun, the two pronouns should agree in person. Avoid shifting pronouns unnecessarily, as from *they* to *you*, *I* to *you*, or *one* to *you*.

POOR	**They** spent several days in Rome, where ~~you~~ could sense history along every street.
BETTER	**They** spent several days in Rome, where **they** could sense history along every street.
POOR	**I** learned that ~~you~~ cannot see all of Rome in two days.
BETTER	**I** learned that **I** cannot see all of Rome in two days.
POOR	If **one** reads newspapers, ~~you~~ will understand current events.
BETTER	If **one** reads newspapers, **one** will understand current events.
BETTER	If **you** read newspapers, **you** will understand current events.

Exercise 8   Making Pronouns and Antecedents Agree

On your paper, complete the following sentences by replacing each blank with an appropriate possessive pronoun. Then write the antecedent of each pronoun that you supply.

Pablo Neruda, Chilean Poet

¹Like any poet who understands _____ life and times, Pablo Neruda touched deep emotional chords. ²At the age of twelve, he met Gabriela Mistral, a famous Chilean poet, who introduced him to some of _____ favorite authors. ³Both Neruda and Mistral have been honored for _____ achievements; both poets won the Nobel Prize for Literature. ⁴When I read Neruda's beautiful verses about the forests and glaciers of southern Chile, I renewed _____ vow to visit Chile someday. ⁵My brother and I want to take a trip to Isla Negra; _____ intention is to visit the house in which Pablo Neruda lived for many years.

17.5 Pronoun-Antecedent Agreement   **645**

Using Pronouns Correctly

Teach

Agreement in Person

☑ **Grammar Tip**

Remind students that revision is a vital part of the writing process. When revising their writing, they should check to be sure the pronoun *you* is not used to refer to an antecedent in the third person and that two pronouns always agree in person when one is the antecedent of the other. Have students look over their recent writing assignments to find any sentences that need this kind of revision.

Two-Minute Skill Drill

Have students study the sentence below. Ask them to identify the pronouns and the word or words to which they refer.

Although my grandmother lived out her long life in the shadow of Rainy Mountain, the immense landscape of the continental interior lay like memory in her blood.

—N. Scott Momaday
The Way to Rainy Mountain

(my—the speaker; her—the speaker's grandmother)

✎ **See also** *Two-Minute Skill Drill Transparency 17.5*

Practice and Assess

Answers: Exercise 8

1. his *or* her *or* his or her—poet
2. her—Gabriela Mistral
3. their—Neruda and Mistral
4. my—I
5. our—my brother and I

MEETING INDIVIDUAL NEEDS   English Language Learners

Translating Pronouns

Help students who are learning English to compile a list of English pronouns along with their equivalents in the students' primary languages. Have students translate some of the sentences used as examples in this lesson into their primary languages, noting how pronouns change to accommodate differences in number, gender, and person.

645

Practice and Assess

Answers: Exercise 9

Answers will vary, but some suggestions are given below.

1. People who are good at making pottery may like to test their skills by learning to make *raku*, a kind of Japanese earthenware.
2. For centuries a handful of Japanese *raku* artists have been perfecting their craft and passing it down from generation to generation.
3. Students who wish to learn to make *raku* will find that the art tests their patience . . .
4. The potter throws his or her *raku* bowls, dries them and paints them with glaze, and then fires them one by one in a kiln until they are red-hot.
5. *Raku* experts may also take their glowing pots from the kiln and throw them into cold water to crack the glaze, but in the process their pots often shatter.

Answers: Exercise 10

Answers will vary, but some suggestions are given below.

1. The ancient Greeks . . . day. They ate . . . at sunset.
2. Men and women in ancient Greece wore tunics. They wore a brown one for work, but they wore a bleached one . . .
3. There were three social classes in Athens, where a person might . . .
4. The women in ancient Greece led a more restricted life than the men did. The women spent a great deal of their time . . .
5. Children in the city of Athens attended school, where they learned to wrestle, handle weapons, sing, read, and write.
6. The ancient Greeks were the first to develop the idea of democracy, and they encouraged citizens to play an active role . . .
7. Only citizens could participate in government. The ancient Greeks usually denied a person citizenship unless his or her father was a citizen.
8. A person could not own land in ancient Greece unless he or she was a citizen.
9. The people of ancient Greece valued learning. They could hear the world's . . .

In each of the following sentences, find each personal pronoun and its antecedent. (Some sentences have more than one personal pronoun.) Then revise the sentence in one or more ways to correct the problem or problems in pronoun-antecedent agreement.

The Art of Raku

1. A person who is good at making pottery may like to test their skills by learning to make *raku*, a kind of Japanese earthenware.
2. For centuries a handful of Japanese *raku* artists have been perfecting his craft and passing it down from generation to generation.
3. Students who wish to learn to make *raku* will find that the art tests his patience, for the ceramics often break.
4. The potter throws their *raku* bowls, dries them and paints them with glaze, and then fires them one by one in a kiln until they are red-hot.
5. A *raku* expert may also take their glowing pots from the kiln and throw them into cold water to crack the glaze, but in the process their pots often shatter.

On your paper, rewrite each of the following items, eliminating the inappropriate use of *you* by substituting a third-person pronoun or a suitable noun or nouns. You may also have to change other words.

Life in Ancient Greece

1. The ancient Greeks ate only two meals a day. You ate in midmorning and then again at sunset.
2. Men and women in ancient Greece wore tunics. They wore a brown one for work, but you wore a bleached one for special occasions.
3. There were three social classes in Athens, where you might be a citizen, an enslaved person, or a resident alien.
4. The women in ancient Greece led a more restricted life than the men did. You spent a great deal of your time in the home.
5. Children in the city of Athens attended school, where you learned to wrestle, handle weapons, sing, read, and write.
6. The ancient Greeks were the first to develop the idea of democracy, and they encouraged you to play an active role in government.
7. Only citizens could participate in government. The ancient Greeks usually denied you citizenship unless your father was a citizen.
8. A person could not own land in ancient Greece unless you were a citizen.
9. The people of ancient Greece valued learning. You could hear the world's finest orators, philosophers, and poets there.
10. The Greeks were dominant in the eastern Mediterranean for several centuries. You could hardly travel anywhere without seeing their influence.

10. The Greeks were dominant in the eastern Mediterranean for several centuries. A person could hardly travel anywhere without seeing their influence.

Agreement with Indefinite Pronoun Antecedents

■ In general, use a singular personal pronoun when the antecedent is a singular indefinite pronoun, and use a plural personal pronoun when the antecedent is a plural indefinite pronoun.

Indefinite Pronouns				
Always Singular	each	everyone	nobody	anything
	either	everybody	nothing	someone
	neither	everything	anyone	somebody
	one	no one	anybody	something
Always Plural	several	few	both	many
	others			
Singular or Plural	some	all	any	most
	none			

Neither of the men wants to drive **his** car to work.

Each of the girls rides **her** bicycle to school.

Several of the neighbors make **their** commute by train.

Note that the number of the personal pronouns is not affected by the plural nouns in the prepositional phrases—*of the men, of the girls*. The personal pronouns *his* and *her* are singular because *neither* and *each*, their antecedents, are singular. When speaking, however, people often use the plural pronoun *their* in such sentences.

INFORMAL *Neither* of the men drove **their** cars to work.

Use gender-neutral wording when no gender is specified.

Everyone should ride **his or her** bicycle to school.

If you find the sentence above a bit awkward, the best solution may be to reword the sentence. You might replace the singular indefinite pronoun with a plural one or with an appropriate noun, or you might omit the personal pronoun altogether.

All should ride **their** bicycles to school.

All students should ride **their** bicycles to school.

Everyone should ride a bicycle to school. [no pronoun]

Teach

Agreement with Indefinite Pronoun Antecedents

☑ Grammar Tip

Many students have a problem with the indefinite pronouns *everyone* and *everybody* because they seem to be plural in meaning but singular in number. It may help students to remember that *everyone* and *everybody* generally mean "each separate individual." Suggest that they think of *every* as meaning "each" rather than "all."

Cooperative Learning

Many of the indefinite pronouns are compound words—words made up of two shorter words—for example: *anybody, everybody, nobody,* and *somebody.* Have small groups of students list other compound indefinite pronouns that follow this pattern. Then have the groups write their own definitions of the words *any, every, no,* and *some,* and compare their definitions with those in a dictionary. Have the groups share their results with the class.

⇄ Cross-reference: Grammar

For instruction and practice in indefinite pronouns, refer students to Lesson 10.2, pp. 445–452.

⇄ Cross-reference: Usage

For instruction and practice with singular and plural indefinite pronouns, refer students to Lesson 16.7, pp. 623–625.

Using Pronouns Correctly

Exploring Language

Locating Indefinite Pronouns

Have students circle indefinite pronouns and underline their antecedents in a short newspaper or magazine article. Have them explain in writing why the pronouns and antecedents agree. Ask students to work with partners to review and check each other's work on the articles. **L3**

Practice and Assess

Answers: Exercise 11

1. their	6. their
2. their	7. his
3. his or her	8. his or her
4. his	9. their
5. his or her	10. his

Answers: Exercise 12

Answers will vary, but some suggestions are given below.

1. . . . are known for the splendor of their sculptures.
2. correct
3. . . . played their own prominent role . . .
4. . . . had a statue of its guardian spirit.
5. All of the children . . . protected by their own spirit figure.
6. . . . with their naturalistic representations of royal figures and their attendants . . .
7. correct
8. . . . with his legs crossed.
9. . . . the women made pottery while the men created sculptures.
10. Anyone studying African sculpture can discover the majestic . . .

Additional Resources

 Grammar Practice, p. 33
Grammar Reteaching, p. 33
Grammar Enrichment, p. 33

 Grammar Workbook, Lesson 55

Close

Ask students to review each of the rules for pronoun-antecedent agreement taught in this lesson. Have them write sample sentences of their own illustrating each rule.

Using Pronouns Correctly

Exercise 11   Making Pronouns Agree with Indefinite Pronoun Antecedents

Write the singular or plural personal pronoun that correctly completes each sentence.

The Reign of Italian Opera

1. Nearly all of the audiences in eighteenth-century Europe selected opera as _____ first choice of contemporary music.
2. Most of the European composers in the 1700s used Italian librettos, or poetic text, in _____ music.
3. Each of the writers used language and melody to give _____ characters depth.
4. One of the male playwrights introduced comic situations in _____ operas.
5. Each of Goldoni's characters stated _____ point of view at the end of each comic act.
6. Few of the French intellectuals gave _____ approval to Italian opera until the comic opera *La serva padrona* was presented in Paris.
7. One of the French aristocrats wanted _____ government to censor the Italian operas.
8. Almost everyone wanted _____ city to build beautiful new opera theaters in the eighteenth century.
9. Several of the nobility held _____ private parties in the large halls of the Italian opera theaters.
10. In the nineteenth century, Guiseppe Verdi wrote _____ greatest masterpieces for Italian-style opera.

Exercise 12   Making Pronouns Agree with Indefinite Pronoun Antecedents

On your paper, write *correct* for each sentence that is correct. Then revise each incorrect sentence to make it correct. Most sentences can be revised in several ways.

African Sculpture

1. Many of the societies in Africa are known for the splendor of its sculptures.
2. Very few of the traditional African sculptors made their figures and masks from stone; most used wood, ivory, clay, and different metals.
3. Practically all of the sculptures in an African society played its own prominent role in the life of the people.
4. All the households of the Ijo people of Nigeria had a statue of their guardian spirit.
5. All of the children of the Teke people of the Congo River valley would be protected by his own spirit figure.
6. Some of the Yoruba people's ancient brass sculptures with its naturalistic representations of royal figures and their attendants fascinated archaeologists.
7. Almost all of the traditional societies in Africa created statues to honor their dead.
8. When portrayed in a statue, each of the kings of the Kuba tribe would sit stiffly with their legs crossed.
9. Many of the central African societies followed a tradition in which its women made pottery while its men created sculptures.
10. Anyone studying African sculpture can discover for themselves the majestic beauty that was part of the daily lives of African people.

MEETING INDIVIDUAL NEEDS   Less Proficient Readers

Making Indefinite Pronouns Agree

Some students may have difficulty remembering that *each, either,* and *neither* are singular. Explain to students that one way to remember that these pronouns are singular is to think of them as being followed by *one* (each *one,* either *one,* neither *one*). **L1**

17.6 Clear Pronoun Reference

■ Make sure that the antecedent of a pronoun is clearly stated and that a pronoun cannot possibly refer to more than one antecedent.

Vague and Ambiguous Pronoun Reference

Do not use the pronouns *this*, *that*, *which*, and *it* without a clearly stated antecedent.

VAGUE	Luisa is a fine athlete, and **this** was obvious from her gymnastic feats. [What was obvious from her gymnastic feats? Her athletic ability was obvious, but the words *athletic ability* have not been specifically mentioned.]
CLEAR	Luisa is a fine athlete, and **her athletic ability** was obvious from her gymnastic feats.
VAGUE	Katrina and Yuki were arguing, **which** started from a misunderstanding. [What started from a misunderstanding? An argument started, but *argument* does not appear in the sentence.]
CLEAR	Katrina and Yuki were having an argument, **which** started from a misunderstanding.
VAGUE	Earl wants to be a doctor because **it** interests him. [What interests him? Medicine does, but *medicine* has not been specifically mentioned.]
CLEAR	Earl wants to be a doctor because **medicine** interests him.

If a pronoun seems to refer to more than one antecedent, either reword the sentence to make the antecedent clear or eliminate the pronoun.

UNCLEAR ANTECEDENT	When the apples fell among the leaves, **they** were hidden. [Which word is the antecedent of *they*? Were the apples or the leaves hidden?]
CLEAR ANTECEDENT	The apples were hidden when **they** fell among the leaves.
NO PRONOUN	When the apples fell among the leaves, **the apples** were hidden.
NO PRONOUN	The fallen apples were hidden among the leaves.

Luisa is a fine athlete, and was obvious from her gymnastic feats.

Using Pronouns Correctly

Focus

Lesson Overview

Objectives
- To identify pronouns and their antecedents
- To ensure that the antecedents of all pronouns are clear and unambiguous

Bellringer
Daily Language Activity

When students enter the classroom, have the following assignment on the board: *Rewrite this sentence so the pronoun reference is clear:*

> *If you've finished taking the stereo speakers out of the boxes, throw them into the garbage.*

See also *Daily Language Practice*

Teach

Vague and Ambiguous Pronoun Reference

☑ Teaching Tip

The pronoun *which* requires a specific noun as its antecedent. In spoken English *which* is often used without an antecedent to mean "all of the above," as in the sentence *I closed the blinds, which made the room dark. Which* refers to the entire action of closing the blinds, not just to the noun *blinds.* In formal written English, the use of *which* to refer to an entire clause, idea, or concept is considered incorrect.

Resource Manager

Planning Resources
- *Lesson Plans*

📘 Transparencies
- *Bellringer*
- *Daily Language Practice*
- *Two-Minute Skill Drill*

📂 Other Print Resources
- *Grammar and Composition Handbook*
- *Grammar Enrichment*, p. 34
- *Grammar Practice*, p. 34
- *Grammar Reteaching*, p. 34
- *Grammar Workbook*, Lesson 58

Teach

Indefinite Use of Pronouns

☑ Grammar Tip

The demonstrative pronouns *this, that, these,* and *those* are often used in a vague way to refer to a previous idea without making clear which aspect of the idea the writer means. For example, *She was not invited to the dance. This made her sad.* A good way to avoid this problem is to expand the demonstrative pronoun with a noun or a noun phrase that clarifies the reference: *She was not invited to the dance. This rejection made her sad.*

⇄ Cross-reference: Troubleshooter

For further instruction and practice on clear pronoun reference, refer students to the **Troubleshooter.**

Practice and Assess

Answers: Exercise 13

Answers will vary, but some suggestions are given below.
1. People call medieval art Gothic because . . .
2. . . . but these cathedrals became increasingly ornate.
3. . . . these windows told religious stories.
4. The builders of Gothic cathedrals used flying buttresses . . .
5. Painters who illustrated Gothic manuscripts sometimes depicted royal families.

Answers: Exercise 14

Answers will vary, but some suggestions are given below.
1. In most industrial societies, people are affected . . .
2. People can feel anxious . . . and this anxiety affects . . .
3. The Alexanders felt anxious about spending so much money when they went on vacation with the Harrises last summer.
4. My brother Richard suffered a great deal of stress when he beat his best friend . . .

Using Pronouns Correctly

Indefinite Use of Pronouns

■ Avoid the indefinite use of the pronouns *you* and *they.*

INDEFINITE	In areas that get little rain, **you** must irrigate the crops.
CLEAR	In areas that get little rain, **farmers** must irrigate the crops.
INDEFINITE	In some companies, **they** do not work on Fridays during the summer months.
CLEAR	In some companies, **employees** do not work on Fridays during the summer months.

Exercise 13   Replacing Unclear Pronoun References

On your paper, rewrite each sentence to eliminate the use of the unclear pronoun reference. The pronoun you should replace is indicated in italics.

Gothic Art

1. *You* call medieval Italian art Gothic because the Goths invaded Italy during the Middle Ages.
2. Gothic cathedrals originally had simple lines, but *they* became increasingly ornate.
3. Gothic architects used stained-glass windows, and *they* told religious stories.
4. In Gothic cathedrals, *they* used flying buttresses, stone structures against the outside walls, to help support the vaulting.
5. When painters illustrated Gothic manuscripts, *they* sometimes depicted royal families.

Exercise 14   Making Pronoun References Clear

On your paper, rewrite the following sentences, making all pronoun references clear. In some cases, you may choose to eliminate the pronoun entirely.

Coping with Stress

1. In most industrial societies, they are affected by stress.
2. People can feel anxious about both joyful and sad events, and this affects their health.
3. The Alexanders went on vacation with the Harrises last summer, and they felt anxious about spending so much money.
4. When my brother Richard beat his best friend in a tennis tournament, he suffered a great deal of stress.
5. Richard's spectacular performance at the tournament made him feel guilty, and this surprised everyone.
6. When Mrs. Wong told Carrie that the company they worked for was closing, she became depressed.
7. When a family moves to a new city, it can cause anxiety.
8. In psychology books, they often discuss stress.
9. When doctors recommend that patients maintain a good diet and exercise to alleviate stress, they know it will help.
10. Scientists are evaluating the effects of stress on health, and it will have much impact on the medical profession.

---

5. . . . and this reaction surprised everyone.
6. . . . Carrie became depressed.
7. . . . the new environment can cause anxiety.
8. In psychology books, experts often discuss . . .
9. Doctors who recommend . . . exercise know that this regimen will help alleviate stress.
10. . . . and their findings will have much impact . . .

Review: Using Pronouns Correctly

On your paper, rewrite the following sentences, eliminating any mistakes in the use of pronouns. Each item has one error.

Special Effects

1. My brother Roy and me know much about special effects.
2. Each of us has their own special area of knowledge.
3. Desmond told me that they made the cyclone in *The Wizard of Oz* with a tube of fabric moved by a wind machine.
4. Whom did you say made the shark robots for *Jaws?*
5. One robot was used for side views of the shark, while another was used for the famous close-ups of it's jaws.
6. Actors depend upon special makeup to change their appearance, which most people take for granted.
7. In *Driving Miss Daisy,* the stars grow thirty years older; them aging so believably is partly due to great makeup.
8. No one was more surprised than me to discover that the very first movies had special effects.
9. *A Trip to the Moon* was made by the Lumière brothers; it was them who first used special effects to simulate space travel.
10. I guess my favorite special effect occurs during the moment in *Star Wars* when you see the spaceship reach the speed of light.
11. *Star Wars* was made by filmmaker George Lucas, who we all recognize as a trailblazer in the field of special effects.
12. What makes each of his films so remarkable is their use of computer animation.
13. The special-effects breakthroughs in *The Abyss* and *Terminator 2* seemed remarkable to we film buffs, Roy and me.
14. George Lucas is also one of the innovators whom is involved in making computer games of his films.
15. X-Wing is a space-combat simulator. The player pilots his or her Rebel Alliance craft against Darth Vader's Imperial Forces, which is a lot of fun.
16. The game is produced in 3-D, and their sound effects respond to the player who makes the choices.
17. Do you remember Princess Leia, who had a high-pitched voice? It is her whose whiny commands the game simulates.
18. I, who love computer games, am grateful to George Lucas for him creating this game.
19. Games of the future will let we players move more dramatically and control the actions of their characters more completely.
20. No one could be happier than I to hear that everyone will, in effect, be able to direct the outcome of their own game.

Practice and Assess

Answers: Exercise 15

Answers will vary, but some suggestions are given below.
1. My brother Roy and I . . .
2. Each of us has a special . . .
3. Desmond told me that the cyclone in *The Wizard of Oz* was made with . . .
4. Who did you say . . .
5. . . . close-ups of its jaws.
6. . . . a fact that most people take for granted.
7. . . . their aging so believably is . . .
8. . . . more surprised than I . . .
9. . . . it was they who first . . .
10. . . . when the spaceship reaches . . .
11. . . . George Lucas, whom we . . .
12. . . . is its use . . .
13. . . . to us film buffs . . .
14. . . . innovators who is . . .
15. . . . Forces; the game is a lot of fun.
16. . . . and its sound effects . . .
17. . . . It is she whose whiny commands . . .
18. . . . his creating this game.
19. . . . will let us players . . .
20. . . . the outcome of his or her own game.

Additional Resources

 Grammar Practice, p. 34
Grammar Reteaching, p. 34
Grammar Enrichment, p. 34

 Grammar Workbook, Lesson 58

Close

Ask student volunteers to make up sentences with pronoun-reference errors and write them on the board for their classmates to discuss and correct.

MEETING INDIVIDUAL NEEDS English Language Learners

Teaching the Correct Use of *You*

Remind students with little exposure to formal English that the use of *you,* meaning "everybody" or "people in general," is not acceptable in formal written English. Unfortunately, there is no simple substitute for this meaning of *you.* (That is, assuming that the British English *one,* as in *One must irrigate the crops* is out of the question. Although *one* is grammatical, it seems stilted to many Americans.) Usually the whole sentence containing this use of *you* must be rewritten to avoid the problem.

Teach

About the Literature

Explain that the passage is from Chapter 1 of William Conton's novel *The African* and is followed by exercises on related topics. Ask a volunteer to read the passage aloud. Have the rest of the class listen, respond, and appropriately evaluate the presentation. In a discussion, students should identify and analyze the characters, setting, and mood. Students should use peer feedback to evaluate their effectiveness in presenting and to set goals for future presentations.

Linking Grammar and Literature

Critical Thinking

Ask students to focus on the high-lighted pronouns in the passage and determine whether a noun could be substituted for each. Have them discuss why Conton chose to use a pronoun instead of a noun in each case.

✔ ASSESSMENT OPTIONS

📂 *Tests with Answer Key & Rubrics*
Unit 17 Pretest, pp. 59–60
Unit 17 Mastery Test, pp. 61–62

💾 *Testmaker*
Unit 17 Pretest
Unit 17 Mastery Test

You may wish to administer the Unit 17 Pretest at this point.

UNIT 17 Grammar Review

USING PRONOUNS CORRECTLY

Written by the West African writer and teacher William Conton, *The African* tells the story of a young man named Kisimi Kamara, who excels in his studies in West Africa and England and launches a successful political career. In this passage, which has been annotated to show some of the kinds of pronouns covered in this unit, Kisimi describes the village where he grew up.

Using Pronouns Correctly

Literature Model

from The African
by William Conton

Pronoun in the nominative case used as a subject

Pronoun in the possessive case

The pronoun *us* is followed by the appositive *children*. As the object of a preposition, the pronoun appears in the objective case.

Pronoun *who* in the nominative case used as the subject of *looked*

My name is Kisimi Kamara.

I was born at the height of a rainy season, in the village of Lokko in the British West African colony of Songhai. My father cultivated an acre of tired red soil round our hut and fished a near-by muddy stream, wringing from these unimpressive resources a livelihood which most of the other villagers regarded as enviable. I was the second son and the fifth child in a family of eleven, and my childhood was consequently quite unspoilt. . . .

We lived right on the main road; and, it being the first house you came across as you entered the village, now and then a car or lorry would draw up to obtain water for a hissing radiator or for parched throats, or to buy some of my mother's goods. That was always a tremendous event for us children. We grew to tell quite a long way ahead, from the note of the engine, whether or not the driver was looking for somewhere to stop; and we would race out to inspect with solemn awe the wheezing machines we believed to be possessed of some mighty spirit, the conjuring up of which had been done in a distant land called Britain. The supercilious drivers who looked so knowingly under bonnets and chassis

652 Unit 17 Using Pronouns Correctly

Resource Manager

Planning Resources
• *Lesson Plans*

📂 **Other Print Resources**
• *Grammar and Composition Handbook*
• *Grammar Workbook,* Lessons 52–58; Unit 8 Review; Cumulative Review: Units 1–8

during the halt we thought of as a type of high priest, ministering to this spirit; and we would hand them a leaking kerosene tin of muddy well-water with almost as much reverence as a server passing the bishop the holy water. The dust-covered passengers, however, we somehow despised rather than envied; for they seemed so helpless and unhappy, whether they were in the first-class compartment beside the driver, or in the second-class behind.

In fact not one of us would have allowed himself to be carried a yard away from home in any mechanical contraption of any kind. Our world was then a supremely secure one; and we felt instinctively that those flying lorries, with their cloaks of red dust billowing behind them, came from another world that was not nearly so secure or safe; that they were in some way harbingers of evil. . . .

The village we all loved so well consisted of perhaps twenty mud houses grouped in compounds on either side of the main road. Each compound contained four or five houses arranged in a hollow square. One of these compounds, the biggest by far, was the chief's. His was the only house with corrugated iron roofing. Not even his wives' houses in the same compound had this luxury.

> The pronoun *they* in the nominative case is used as a subject. The pronoun agrees in number with its antecedent, *passengers*.

> Pronoun in the objective case used as the object of a preposition

> Agreement in number and gender between the possessive pronoun *his* and its antecedent, *chief's*

Review: Exercise 1   Choosing the Correct Pronoun Case

The following sentences elaborate on ideas suggested by the passage from *The African*. Write each sentence on your paper, replacing each italicized word or group of words with an appropriate pronoun. Note that the sentences are written, as the passage is, from Kisimi Kamara's first-person point of view.

1. Of the children in our household, the second-oldest son was *Kisimi*.
2. Despite our meager resources, many villagers envied *Kisimi* and my family.
3. The acre of land that surrounded the family hut was *my family's property*.
4. Similarly, the land around our neighbors' huts was *our neighbor's property*.
5. My father tried to make the soil productive, but *my father's* struggles had little effect.
6. Unfortunately, the tired red soil had lost much of *the soil's* fertility.
7. The best house in the village belonged to the chief, for it was *the chief* who wielded the greatest power.
8. Our neighbors and *my family* lived on the main road that led through the village.
9. Visitors to our village were rare, but it was not *the visitors* who fascinated us.
10. It was their vehicles that fascinated my brothers and *Kisimi*.

Grammar Review   **653**

Practice and Assess

Answers: Exercise 1

1. Of the children in our household, the second-oldest son was I.
2. Despite our meager resources, many of the other villagers envied me and my family.
3. The acre of land that surrounded the family hut was ours.
4. Similarly, the land around our neighbors' huts was theirs.
5. My father tried to make the soil productive, but his struggles had little effect.
6. Unfortunately, the tired red soil had lost much of its fertility.
7. The best house in the village belonged to the chief, for it was he who wielded the greatest power.
8. Our neighbors and we lived on the main road that led through the village.
9. Although visitors to our village were rare, it was not really they who fascinated us.
10. It was their vehicles that fascinated my brothers and me.

Practice and Assess

Answers: Exercise 2

1. me
2. she
3. they
4. We
5. I
6. me
7. correct
8. she
9. her
10. him

Answers: Exercise 3

1. Because I was able to go to school, I was luckier than they.
2. Since all the students were interested in new things, helping out in the teacher's home appealed to me as much as to them.
3. No volunteers were ever more eager than we.
4. No one, however, was more anxious to help out than I.
5. The sea of volunteers surprised no one more than her.
6. When Miss Schwartz chose me, no one was happier than I.
7. Few students in the village school did as well as I.
8. The schools in the capital were much larger than they.
9. The prospect of attending secondary school in the capital pleased no one more than us.
10. When my father left with me for my new school in the capital, no one was more proud than he.

Review: Exercise 2 — Using Pronouns Correctly with and as Appositives

The following sentences are based on passages from *The African* that are not reprinted in this textbook. For each sentence, determine whether the italicized pronoun appears in the proper form. If it does not, write the pronoun as it should appear. If it is used properly, write *correct*. Note again that the sentences are written from Kisimi Kamara's point of view.

SAMPLE The villagers, my parents and *them,* worked hard to feed their families.
ANSWER they

1. My mother devoted much attention to her children, my eight brothers and sisters and *I.*
2. Two members of the family, my elder brother and *her,* ran a small shop in the village.
3. All the men of the village, my father and *them,* fished and cultivated the land.
4. *Us* children were not all able to attend school, for some had to stay home and work.
5. The students, my friends and *me,* enjoyed special status.
6. An American missionary named Miss Schwartz taught the pupils, my friends and *I.*
7. Learning English was important to *us* students, for we knew that it would help us.
8. The two American missionaries, Miss Schwartz and *her,* lived in a bungalow.
9. A Scotsman named Jim Anderson often brought these Americans, Miss Schwartz and *she,* news from district headquarters.
10. I listened to the conversations of these English speakers, the two women and *he.*

Review: Exercise 3 — Using Pronouns After *Than* and *As*

Rewrite each sentence below, substituting the correct pronoun for the words in italics. Note that the sentences are written from Kisimi Kamara's point of view.

SAMPLE The children who could not attend school were less fortunate than *Kisimi.*
ANSWER The children who could not attend school were less fortunate than I.

1. Because I was able to go to school, I was luckier than *most other village children.*
2. Since all the students were interested in new things, helping out in the teacher's home appealed to me as much as to *the other students.*
3. No volunteers were ever more eager than *the other students and Kisimi.*
4. No one, however, was more anxious to help out than *Kisimi.*
5. The sea of volunteers surprised no one more than *Miss Schwartz.*
6. When Miss Schwartz chose me, no one was happier than *Kisimi.*
7. Few students in the village school did as well as *Kisimi.*
8. The schools in the capital were much larger than *the small village schools.*
9. The prospect of attending secondary school in the capital pleased no one more than *Kisimi and the other students.*
10. When my father left with me for my new school in the capital, no one was more proud than *my father.*

Review: Exercise 4   Choosing *Who* or *Whom*

The following sentences are about Sierra Leone, the West African nation where William Conton has spent most of his life. For each sentence, write the correct pronoun from the pair in parentheses.

1. Sierra Leone was named by Pedro de Sintra, a Portuguese explorer (who/whom) we know lived in the fifteenth century.
2. De Sintra, (who/whom) every schoolchild in Sierra Leone studies, named the country Serra Lyoa, or Lion Mountains.
3. (Who/Whom) did you say are the modern inhabitants of Sierra Leone?
4. There are many people for (who/whom) Sierra Leone is home.
5. The Sierra Leone Creoles, (who/whom) many linguists have studied, are descendants of formerly enslaved people who returned to their native Africa.
6. The Creoles, (who/whom) make up about 2 percent of Sierra Leone's population, developed their own language, Krio.
7. Based on English, Krio also contains African words spoken by the many groups (who/whom) settled in Sierra Leone.
8. Natives of Sierra Leone, each of (who/whom) may speak a different language, often use Krio to communicate when they get together.
9. The many people in the country (who/whom) speak English, the official language of Sierra Leone, also communicate in English.
10. Do you know (who/whom) controlled Sierra Leone during the colonial period?
11. Sierra Leone's people, (who/whom) Britain ruled for more than a century, won their independence in 1961.
12. (Who/Whom) did you tell that the country is bordered on the west by the Atlantic Ocean?
13. I don't know (who/whom) knew that the highest mountain in Sierra Leone is 6,390 feet high.
14. Subsistence farmers (who/whom) produce maize and rice make up a substantial portion of the rural population.
15. Cocoa and coffee are agricultural exports that are profitable for those farmers (who/whom) have larger farms.
16. To (who/whom) do you think go the profits from the export of diamonds and iron?
17. Major population groups include the Mende, Temne, Limba, and Susu, all of (who/whom) are indigenous to the region.
18. Members of the house of representatives, (who/whom) are elected by the people, come from all groups in the country.
19. Did you tell me (who/whom) the first president of the country was?
20. Does anyone in this class know (who/whom) was the most recently elected president of Sierra Leone?

Answers: Exercise 4

1. who
2. whom
3. Who
4. whom
5. whom
6. who
7. who
8. whom
9. who
10. who
11. whom
12. Whom
13. who
14. who
15. who
16. whom
17. whom
18. who
19. who
20. who

Practice and Assess

Answers: Exercise 5

Answers will vary, but some suggestions are given below.

1. My brothers and I spent our youth in a small African village called Lokko in the British West African colony of Songhai.
2. My father's friends farmed their own land and reaped from it a meager harvest.
3. The women in the village spent their days cooking, sweeping, washing, and caring for their children.
4. She also spent many of her waking hours pounding rice.
5. At the end of the day, my parents slept in their hammocks, which hung from the veranda roof.
6. The baby in our family was carried on our mother's back.
7. My mother hoped that her children would receive a good education.
8. My teacher, Miss Schwartz, did her best to teach us English.
9. Our studies were important to us because they gave us a chance for a better future.
10. The students wanted to go to the capital, where they could study in a big secondary school.
11. The houses in our village had walls made of mud.
12. Only chiefs could have their houses covered with corrugated iron roofing.
13. An occasional driver along the road might pull his or her car into the village for water.
14. Children who spotted a car or truck would quickly tell their friends.
15. I never wanted to put my body into those strange vehicles.

Using Pronouns Correctly

Review: Exercise 5　　Making Pronouns and Antecedents Agree

Each sentence below contains an example of pronoun-antecedent agreement. On your paper, rewrite the sentences according to the directions given in parentheses, changing the pronouns if necessary. In some cases, you will also have to change the form of the verb or another word. Note that the sentences are written from Kisimi Kamara's point of view.

SAMPLE　　The village compounds have their huts arranged in a square. (Change *The village compounds* to *My family's compound.*)

ANSWER　　My family's compound has its huts arranged in a square.

1. I spent my youth in a small African village called Lokko in the British West African colony of Songhai. (Change *I* to *My brothers and I.*)
2. My father farmed his own land and reaped from it a meager harvest. (Change *My father* to *My father's friends.*)
3. My mother spent her days cooking, sweeping, washing, and caring for her children. (Change *My mother* to *The women in the village.*)
4. She and my sister also spent many of their waking hours pounding rice. (Change *She and my sister* to *She.*)
5. At the end of the day, my father slept in his hammock, which hung from the veranda roof. (Change *my father* to *my parents.*)
6. The babies of the village were carried on their mothers' backs. (Change *The babies of the village* to *The baby in our family.*)
7. Our mothers hoped that their children would receive a good education. (Change *Our mothers* to *My mother.*)
8. Our teachers, Miss Schwartz and Miss Costello, did their best to teach us English. (Change *Our teachers, Miss Schwartz and Miss Costello* to *My teacher, Miss Schwartz.*)
9. English was important to us because it gave us a chance for a better future. (Change *English* to *Our studies.*)
10. I wanted to go to the capital, where I could study in a big secondary school. (Change the first *I* to *The students.*)
11. A house in our village had its walls made of mud. (Change *A house* to *The houses.*)
12. Only the chief had his house covered with corrugated iron roofing. (Change *Only the chief had* to *Only chiefs could have.*)
13. Drivers along the road might pull their cars into the village for water. (Change *Drivers* to *An occasional driver.*)
14. A child who spotted a car or truck would quickly tell his or her friends. (Change *A child* to *Children.*)
15. We never wanted to put our bodies into those strange vehicles. (Change *we* to *I.*)

Review Exercise 6 — Making Pronouns Agree with Indefinite Pronoun Antecedents

The following sentences are about the storytelling tradition of West Africa. Each sentence contains an example of pronoun-antecedent agreement. Rewrite the sentences according to the directions in parentheses, changing the pronouns if necessary. In some cases, you will also have to change the verb. (See page 647 for a list of singular and plural indefinite pronouns. Remember that some pronouns may be either singular or plural, depending upon the context.)

SAMPLE Each of the storytellers has his or her favorite stories. (Change *Each* to *All.*)
ANSWER All of the storytellers have their favorite stories.

1. Most of the folktales from West Africa have their roots in oral tradition.
   (Change *Most* to *Many.*)
2. All of these stories involve their characters in exciting events.
   (Change *All* to *Each.*)
3. In addition, each of the tales has its educational aspects.
   (Change *each* to *several.*)
4. Much of this body of traditional storytelling also has its historical significance.
   (Change *Much* to *Most.*)
5. Many of West Africa's people call their storytellers *griots*.
   (Change *Many* to *Some.*)
6. People in a rural village give their warmest welcome to a visiting storyteller.
   (Change *People* to *Everyone.*)
7. Most of the children are glad when a griot comes to entertain them.
   (Change *Most* to *Each.*)
8. No one in the village can deny a fascination with the griot's tales.
   (Change *No one* to *Few.*)
9. Each of the storytellers usually asks listeners to join in his or her performances.
   (Change *Each* to *All.*)
10. The listeners and the griot enjoy their roles a great deal.
    (Change *The listeners and the griot* to *Both.*)
11. Most of the griots travel from village to village telling their stories.
    (Change *Most* to *Each.*)
12. Some of the tales have their origin in stories told generations ago.
    (Change *Some of the tales* to *Either this tale or that.*)
13. Each one of the griots tells the stories in his or her own way.
    (Change *Each one* to *All*)
14. A good storyteller incorporates gestures into his or her storytelling.
    (Change *A good storyteller* to *Many storytellers.*)
15. Have most of this storyteller's tales found their way into print?
    (Change *tales* to *body of work.*)

Using Pronouns Correctly

Answers: Exercise 6
Answers will vary, but some suggestions are given below.
1. Many of the folktales from West Africa have their roots in oral tradition.
2. Each of these stories involves its characters in exciting events.
3. In addition, several of the tales have their educational aspects.
4. Most of this body of traditional storytelling also has its historical significance.
5. Some of West Africa's people call their storytellers *griots*.
6. Everyone in a rural village gives his or her warmest welcome to a visiting storyteller.
7. Each of the children is glad when a griot comes to entertain him or her.
8. Few in the village can deny their fascination with the griot's tales.
9. All of the storytellers usually ask listeners to join in their performances.
10. Both enjoy their roles a great deal.
11. Each of the griots travels from village to village telling his or her stories.
12. Either this tale or that has its origin in stories told generations ago.
13. All of the griots tell the stories in their own ways.
14. Many storytellers incorporate gestures into their storytelling.
15. Has most of this storyteller's body of work found its way into print?

Practice and Assess

Answers: Exercise 7

Answers will vary, but some suggestions are given below.

1. In a small African village, Kisimi Kamara was born into a large family, making him an unspoiled child.
2. Although the Kamaras had poor land, their livelihood was envied by other families.
3. The dust stirred up by cars driving down dry mud roads must have surprised the children at first.
4. As the drivers examined their broken-down cars, the children watched, perplexed by the mechanisms under the hood.
5. Kisimi's father, like the village chief, had a mud house, but the chief's roof was made of corrugated iron.

Answers: Exercise 8
Proofreading

This proofreading activity provides editing practice with (1) the current or previous units' skills, (2) the **Troubleshooter** errors, and (3) spelling errors. Students should be able to complete the exercise by referring to the units, the **Troubleshooter**, and a dictionary. (Note: A run-on sentence counts as one error.)

Error (Type of Error)
1. was born (verb form)
2. she and (subject pronoun)
3. kitchen, (run-on sentence)
   and she (subject pronoun)
4. her family (possessive pronoun)
5. writers, (commas in a series)
6. skillets, (commas in a series)
7. businessman (spelling)
   who (subject pronoun)
   plantation's (singular possessive)
8. its simple power (pronoun-antecedent agreement)

Review: Exercise 7   Correcting Vague or Ambiguous Pronoun References

The following sentences are based on ideas in the passage from *The African*. Each sentence contains a vague or an ambiguous pronoun reference. On your paper, rewrite each sentence to eliminate the unclear pronoun reference. You may have to change only one or two words, or you may find it necessary to revise the entire sentence.

1. Kisimi Kamara was born into a large family in a small African village, which made him an unspoiled child.
2. They had poor land, but other families found the Kamaras' livelihood enviable.
3. Cars stirred up dust as they drove down the dry mud roads, and that must have surprised the children at first.
4. The children watched as the drivers examined their broken-down cars, and they were perplexed by the mechanisms under the hood.
5. Kisimi's father and the village chief both had mud houses, but his roof was made of corrugated iron.

Review: Exercise 8

Proofreading

The following passage describes the artist Clementine Hunter, whose work is reproduced on the opposite page. Rewrite the passage, correcting the errors in spelling, grammar, and usage. Add any missing punctuation. There are twenty-five errors.

Clementine Hunter

[1]The African American artist Clementine Hunter (1887–1988) was borned at the Hidden Hill Plantation near Cloutierville, Louisiana. [2]When she was fifteen, her and her parents moved to nearby Melrose Plantation. [3]She worked in the kitchen and her father and her worked in the cotton fields as well. [4]When Hunter and she family arrived in Melrose, the plantation was being restored. [5]It soon became a monument to a vanishing way of life, attracting writers artists, and tourists.

[6]Hunter made her first paintings on window shades, jars, gourds, skillets and other objects. [7]A French businesman named François Mignon, whom visited Melrose in 1938, grew interested in the place and eventually became the plantations' resident librarian. [8]Mignon noticed one of Hunter's paintings and was astonished at their simple power.

[9]Mignon became Hunters mentor and supporter. [10]Her continued to produce works documenting plantation life—it's harvests, holidays, baptisms and funer-

Answers: Exercise 8 (continued)
Proofreading

Error (Type of Error)
9. Hunter's (singular possessive)
10. She (subject pronoun)
    its (possessive pronoun)
    baptisms, (commas in a series)
11. abstract, (run-on sentence)
12. fabric (spelling)
13. designs (spelling)
    brought her (object pronoun)
14. She sold (sentence fragment)
15. She was (subject pronoun)
16. world, (run-on sentence)
17. *African,* (nonessential appositive)
18. who (subject pronoun)
    around them (pronoun-antecedent agreement)

Clementine Hunter, patchwork quilt, 1938

als. ¹¹Her style was abstract and she cared little for proportion or perspective. ¹²In the quilt on the opposite page, Hunter stitched together small swatches of fabrik to produce a lively scene of rural life.

¹³Clementine Hunter's skillful use of simple materials and uncluttered dezigns brought she great success. ¹⁴Sold nearly all of her works. ¹⁵Her was presented with an honorary doctorate of fine arts from Northwestern State University in Natchitoches, Louisiana, in 1986.

¹⁶Hunter grew up in poverty in a small, self-contained world and she recorded what she experienced in rich detail. ¹⁷Kisimi Kamara, the narrator of William Conton's *The African* also spent his youth in a poor and confined world, yet he found great beauty in it. ¹⁸Both Hunter and Kisimi Kamara, whom is much like Conton, were keen observers of the world around him.

Viewing the Art

Clementine Hunter, Patchwork Quilt, 1938
Hunter's quilt could almost be read as a series of snapshots—pictures of bygone days in the rural South. Like Hunter, William Conton strives to record the sights and sounds of the place where he grew up. Both Hunter and Conton are historians, with histories personal and deeply felt. Ask students to imagine painting a picture of the vivid sights and sounds in Conton's native village. Have students discuss any similarities and differences observed in the ways in which Conton and Hunter created their images.

Practice and Assess

Answers: Exercise 9
Mixed Review

1. who
2. they
3. its
4. whom
5. he
6. he
7. his
8. their
9. he
10. who
11. His
12. he
13. his
14. his
15. Who
16. he
17. he
18. she
19. her
20. its

Close

Discuss correct pronoun usage that students have difficulty remembering or understanding. Have students brainstorm to find ways to remember and ways to test correct usage.

Using Pronouns Correctly

Review: Exercise 9

Mixed Review

The following sentences describe aspects of William Conton's life and work. For each sentence, choose the proper pronoun from the pair in parentheses, and write it on your paper.

William Conton

1. William Conton, (who/whom) we know was born in the tiny West African nation of Gambia, has spent most of his life in Sierra Leone.
2. Readers enjoy Conton's fiction, from which (you/they) can learn a great deal about West African life.
3. Most of Conton's short fiction made (its/their) first appearance in West African journals.
4. Conton's novel *The African* describes the life of an ambitious young man named Kisimi Kamara, (who/whom) Conton resembles in many ways.
5. For example, both Conton and (he/him) went to college in England.
6. Both men, (he/him) and Conton, returned to West Africa in the 1950s, when many independence movements in Africa were growing.
7. Neither of the two West African men was unaffected by (his/their) experiences during those exciting years.
8. All of the people living at that time had (his/their) own vivid stories to tell.
9. Despite the similarities between the author and Kisimi, Conton had a more privileged upbringing than (he/him).
10. Conton was the son of an Anglican minister (who/whom) encouraged him to read at an early age.
11. (His/Him) having such a strong interest in writing no doubt stems from his early love of books.
12. As the child of a rural farm family, Conton's character Kisimi is far less sophisticated than (he/him).
13. Each of the men, Conton and the character Kisimi, nevertheless accomplished many of (his/their) ambitions.
14. Much of Conton's reputation is due to (his/him) holding high office in Sierra Leone.
15. (Who/Whom) do you think served as Sierra Leone's minister of education?
16. The minister of education was none other than (he/him), William Conton.
17. For that reason, Conton had little time to be a prolific author; nevertheless, in Sierra Leone few writers are as famous as (he/him).
18. In 1949 Conton married Bertha Thompson; (she/her) and Conton met when he was teaching in Freetown, the capital of Sierra Leone.
19. In fact, education was the chosen field of both Contons, William and (she/her).
20. The culture of West Africa owes some of (its/it's) richness to the vivid writings of William Conton.

Writing Application

Personal Pronouns in Writing

In the following excerpt from her novel *Song of Solomon*, author Toni Morrison tells about a landlord named Macon Dead and a man named Sonny. As you read, notice the many personal pronouns and focus especially on how the author avoids unclear pronoun references.

Macon Dead dug in *his* pocket for *his* keys, and curled *his* fingers around *them*, letting *their* bunchy solidity calm *him*. *They* were the keys to all the doors of *his* houses (only four true houses; the rest were really shacks), and *he* fondled *them* from time to time as *he* walked down Not Doctor Street to *his* office. At least *he* thought of it as *his* office, and even painted the word OFFICE on the door. But the plate-glass window contradicted *him*. In peeling gold letters arranged in a semicircle, *his* business establishment was declared to be Sonny's Shop. Scraping the previous owner's name off was hardly worth the trouble since *he* couldn't scrape *it* from anybody's mind.

Techniques with Personal Pronouns

Try to apply some of Toni Morrison's writing techniques when you write.

❶ Use pronouns to avoid repetition of names and words.

REPEATED WORDS . . . dug in his pocket for his *keys*, and curled his fingers around the *keys*, letting the *keys'* bunchy solidity . . .

MORRISON'S VERSION . . . dug in his pocket for his *keys*, and curled his fingers around *them*, letting *their* bunchy solidity . . .

❷ Make sure each pronoun you use has a clear antecedent.

UNCLEAR ANTECEDENT . . . *his* business establishment was declared to be Sonny's Shop. Scraping *his* name off was hardly worth the trouble . . .

MORRISON'S VERSION . . . *his* business establishment was declared to be Sonny's Shop. Scraping *the previous owner's* name off was hardly worth the trouble . . .

TIME
For more about the writing process, see TIME Facing the Blank Page, pp. 109–119

Using Pronouns Correctly

Practice Apply the techniques above by revising the following passage on a separate sheet of paper. The passage has been adapted from *Song of Solomon*. Eliminate awkward repetition by using personal pronouns, but also be certain that all your pronoun references are clear.

When Mrs. Bains closed the door, Macon Dead went back to the pages of Macon's accounts book, running Macon's fingertips over the figures and thinking with the unoccupied part of Macon's mind about the first time Macon had called on Ruth Foster's father. Macon had had only two keys in Macon's pocket then, and if Macon had let people like the woman who had just left have such people's way, Macon wouldn't have had any keys at all.

Personal Pronouns in Writing

Have a student read the paragraph aloud without interruption. Then have students go back and read it again to themselves, paying particular attention to the italicized pronoun choices. Discuss these choices and the application of the Techniques with Pronouns.

Techniques with Personal Pronouns

Discuss the techniques described and apply them to another piece of writing—for example, a paragraph or two from the Proofreading practice on student pages 658–659.

Practice

The answers to this challenging and enriching activity will vary. Refer to Techniques with Personal Pronouns as you evaluate student choices. Sample answer:

When Mrs. Bains closed the door, Macon Dead went back to the pages of his accounts book. Running his fingertips over the figures, he thought with the unoccupied part of his mind about the first time he had called on Ruth Foster's father. Macon had had only two keys in his pocket then. If he had let people like Mrs. Bains have their way, he wouldn't have had any keys at all.

✔ ASSESSMENT OPTIONS

📁 *Tests with Answer Key & Rubrics*
Unit 17 Pretest, pp. 59–60
Unit 17 Mastery Test, pp. 61–62

💾 *Testmaker*
Unit 17 Pretest
Unit 17 Mastery Test

📼 *MindJogger Videoquizzes*

You may wish to administer the Unit 17 Mastery Test at this point.

Objectives

- To gain an understanding of how modifiers work, with an emphasis on the three degrees of comparison, irregular comparisons, and the use of *good, well, bad* and *badly*.
- To demonstrate control over modifiers by completing exercises and writing sentences which employ them effectively and which avoid such problems as incomplete comparisons, double negatives, and dangling modifiers.

✔ ASSESSMENT OPTIONS

📂 *Tests with Answer Key & Rubrics*
Unit 18 Pretest, pp. 63–64
Unit 18 Mastery Test, pp. 65–66

💾 *Testmaker*
Unit 18 Pretest
Unit 18 Mastery Test

You may wish to administer the Unit 18 Pretest at this point.

Key to Ability Levels

L1 Level 1 activities are within the basic ability range of students.

L2 Level 2 activities are within the ability range of average students.

L3 Level 3 activities are more challenging activities.

UNIT
18 Using Modifiers Correctly

Lesson **18.1**   **The Three Degrees of Comparison**   *663*

Lesson **18.2**   **Irregular Comparisons**   *666*

Lesson **18.3**   **Double Comparisons**   *668*

Lesson **18.4**   **Incomplete Comparisons**   *670*

Lesson **18.5**   ***Good* or *Well; Bad* or *Badly***   *671*

Lesson **18.6**   **Double Negatives**   *673*

Lesson **18.7**   **Misplaced and Dangling Modifiers**   *674*

Grammar Review   *680*

Writing Application   *689*

Resource Manager

Planning Resources
- *Lesson Plans*
- *Block Scheduling*

📋 **Transparencies**
- *Bellringer*
- *Daily Language Practice*
- *Two-Minute Skill Drill*

📂 **Other Print Resources**
- *Grammar and Composition Handbook*
- *Grammar Enrichment*
- *Grammar Practice*
- *Grammar Reteaching*
- *Grammar Workbook*
- *Tests with Answer Key and Rubrics*

 Video
- *MindJogger Videoquizzes*

💾 **Software**
- *Interactive Grammar and Language Workbook*
- *Language Arts PASS*
- *Presentation Plus!*
- *Revising with Style*
- *Testmaker*
- *Writer's Choice Puzzlemaker*

🖥 **Web Sites**
- *writerschoice.glencoe.com*

18.1 The Three Degrees of Comparison

- Most adjectives and adverbs have three degrees of comparison: the positive, or base, form; the comparative form; and the superlative form.
- The **positive** form of a modifier cannot be used to make a comparison. (This form appears as the entry word in a dictionary.)
- The **comparative** form of a modifier shows two things being compared.
- The **superlative** form of a modifier shows three or more things being compared.

POSITIVE	The mechanic's hands are **rough**. The canary sang **happily**.
COMPARATIVE	The mechanic's hands are **rougher** than mine. My canary sang **more happily** than my neighbor's canary.
SUPERLATIVE	Of the three, his hands are **roughest**. The orange canary sang **most happily** of all.

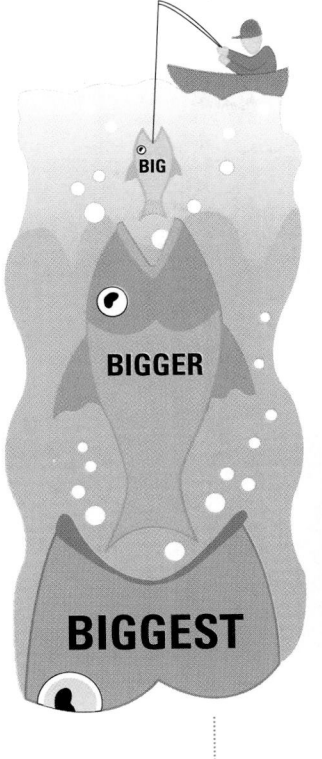

BIG

BIGGER

BIGGEST

Using Modifiers Correctly

Exercise 1 — Identifying Degrees of Comparison

Write the comparative adjectives and adverbs in the following sentences on your paper. Then indicate the degree of comparison by writing *comparative* or *superlative* after each one.

Early Egyptian Rulers

1. The ancient Egyptians believed that their leaders would rule more wisely than other rulers.
2. One of the most capable rulers was Hatshepsut, the first woman leader in history and a strong leader.
3. One of her more daring acts was wearing full pharaohic regalia, including a false beard.
4. Hatshepsut's successor, Thutmose III, was more aggressive and set out on a harsh policy of conquest.
5. Pharaoh Amenhotep IV tried even harder than Thutmose to strengthen the powers of the throne, but Amenhotep worked hardest at changing religion.

Focus

Lesson Overview

Objectives
- To identify positive, comparative, and superlative forms of adjectives and adverbs
- To use them appropriately in writing

Bellringer
Daily Language Activity

When students enter the classroom, have this assignment on the board: *Write a sentence in which you use a modifier to compare two or more things. For example, "My book is newer than yours."*

See also Daily Language Practice

Motivating Activity

Ask students to identify any comparative or superlative forms they used in their Bellringer sentences. Have volunteers write the positive, comparative, and superlative forms of their words on the chalkboard.

Practice and Assess

Answers: Exercise 1
1. more wisely, comparative
2. most capable, superlative
3. more daring, comparative
4. more aggressive, comparative
5. harder, comparative
   hardest, superlative

Resource Manager

Planning Resources
- *Lesson Plans*

Transparencies
- *Bellringer*
- *Daily Language Practice*
- *Two-Minute Skill Drill*

Other Print Resources
- *Grammar and Composition Handbook*
- *Grammar Enrichment*, p. 35
- *Grammar Reteaching*, p. 35
- *Grammar Workbook*, Lesson 59

Teach

☑ Grammar Tips

An amusing exception to the use of the superlative for comparing three or more things is the expression *Put your best foot forward.*

An interesting construction in English uses the article *the* with two comparative forms, as in *The more, the merrier* and *The bigger they are, the harder they fall.*

Cross-reference: Grammar

For instruction and practice with adjectives and adverbs, refer students to Lessons 10.4–10.5, pp. 460–472.

Two-Minute Skill Drill

Have students write the comparative and superlative forms of the following words: *big, flat, fast, wonderful, terrible, thankfully.*

✎ **See also** *Two-Minute Skill Drill Transparency 18.1*

Using Modifiers Correctly

Using The Three Degrees

■ In general, for one-syllable modifiers add *-er* to form the comparative and *-est* to form the superlative.

sweet, sweet**er,** sweet**est**
This is the **sweetest** apple I have ever tasted.

For some words, spelling changes occur when you add *-er* and *-est.*
sad, sa**dder,** sa**ddest**
blue, blu**er,** blu**est**
easy, eas**ier,** eas**iest**

Sometimes it may sound more natural to use *more* and *most* instead of *-er* and *-est* with one-syllable modifiers.
sour, **more** sour, **most** sour
That was the **most sour** lemon I have ever tasted.

■ For most two-syllable adjectives, add *-er* to form the comparative and *-est* to form the superlative.

gentle, gentl**er,** gentl**est**
The black dog is **gentler** than the brown one.

happy, happ**ier,** happ**iest**
My dog is the **happiest** one in the neighborhood.

Use *more* and *most* if *-er* and *-est* sound awkward.
helpful, **more** helpful, **most** helpful
No one was **more helpful** than Rita.

■ For adverbs ending in *-ly,* always use *more* and *most* to form the comparative and superlative degrees.

quickly, **more** quickly, **most** quickly
I am able to run **more quickly** in cold weather.

■ For modifiers of three or more syllables, always use *more* and *most* to form the comparative and superlative degrees.

delicious, **more** delicious, **most** delicious
I think pears are **more delicious** than apples.

■ *Less* and *least,* the opposite of *more* and *most,* can also be used with most modifiers to show comparison.

Rosa is **less talkative** than Daryl.
Bea is the **least talkative** person I know.

English Language Learners

Using *More* and *Most*

Students learning English may have difficulty knowing when to use *more* and *most* with adjectives or adverbs and when to add the endings *-er* and *-est.* (In general, English speakers add *-er* and *-est* to shorter adjectives and adjectives native to English and use *more* and *most* before longer adjectives and adjectives derived from French and Latin words.) Provide students learning English with practice saying sets of words such as
quickly, more quickly, most quickly
beautiful, more beautiful, most beautiful.

Exercise 2 — Using Degrees of Comparison

Write the word or words that would complete the following sentences with the correct degree of comparison of the modifier in parentheses. (You may need to use the positive degree as well as the comparative and superlative.)

The Early Civilizations of the Middle East

1. Civilizations rose _____ in the Middle East than they did in most parts of the world. (early)
2. More than 5,000 years ago, the _____ civilizations known to historians developed in that region. (old)
3. For the approximately 2,000 years that the Sumerians ruled Mesopotamia, religion played an _____ role. (important)
4. Among the _____ Sumerian deities were Inanna, goddess of love and war, and Nanna, the moon god. (important)
5. To honor their deities, the Sumerians built _____ shrines and temples. (grand)
6. It is believed that thousands of workers labored hard for years to build the _____ temple in the empire. (grand)
7. In artists' sketches, each story was _____ in area than the one directly beneath it. (small)
8. The top story of the temple, which dominated the entire city, was the _____ of all the stories. (small)
9. The Babylonian empire, which succeeded the Sumerian, was _____ than the Sumerian empire. (strong)
10. Hammurabi, a famous leader, issued a single code of law that centralized the government _____ than it had been centralized under Sumerian rule. (tightly)
11. The code regulated trade and commerce _____ than ever before. (precisely)
12. The code also provided _____ regulations than before for marriage and divorce. (strict)
13. Punishments for violating the laws in the code were harsh, and the _____ penalty of all was death. (harsh)
14. Babylonia fell to the Assyrians, who were the _____ rulers ever to control Mesopotamia. (harsh)
15. The Assyrians were the _____ warriors on horseback. (fast)
16. Within their vast empire, the Assyrians built a _____ system of communication. (speedy)
17. Encompassing almost all of the Fertile Crescent, the Chaldean empire may have been the _____ of all the Middle Eastern empires. (large)
18. One famous leader, Nebuchadnezzer, constructed _____ fortifications and buildings. (impressive)
19. None was _____ than his own elaborate palace with its lush hanging gardens. (impressive)
20. These gardens, known as one of the seven wonders of the world, were built in Babylon, the _____ city in all of Mesopotamia. (famous)

Using Modifiers Correctly

Practice and Assess

Answers: Exercise 2

1. earlier	**11.** more precisely
2. oldest	**12.** stricter
3. important	**13.** harshest
4. most important	**14.** harshest
5. grand	**15.** fastest
6. grandest	**16.** speedy
7. smaller	**17.** largest
8. smallest	**18.** impressive
9. stronger	**19.** more impressive
10. more tightly	**20.** most famous

Additional Resources

 Grammar Reteaching, p. 35

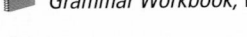 *Grammar Enrichment*, p. 35

Grammar Workbook, Lesson 59

Close

Have students compare their answers for Exercises 1 and 2. Encourage them to discuss any differences with a small group of classmates.

Remind students that comparisons can help writers vividly describe people, places, or things. Using degrees of comparison can make descriptions all the more specific. Have students look through their portfolios for passages of description that can be improved by using degrees of comparison.

Exploring Language

Using Absolute Adjectives

A number of adjectives do not have comparative or superlative forms. These are *absolute* adjectives—adjectives whose meaning does not permit degrees of comparison. For example, *unique* is an absolute adjective. You say *a unique gem* but not *the most unique gem*. Have students work in small groups to think of other examples of absolute adjectives. **L2**

Focus

Lesson Overview

Objectives
- To identify irregular forms of comparison
- To use them correctly in writing

 Bellringer
Daily Language Activity

When students enter the classroom, have this assignment on the board: *If a friend says, "This is my best coat," how many coats does your friend have?*

See also *Daily Language Practice*

Teach

A Vocabulary Link

Many people confuse *farther* and *further*. *Farther* means "more far." *Further* is usually used to mean "more," "additional," or "later." For example, *He had no further questions. The swimming pool is closed until further notice. There is no further reason for acting now.*

☑ Teaching Tip

Students may want to copy the chart on this page into their writing journals and to keep it for reference.

Practice and Assess

Answers: Exercise 3

1. oldest	**6.** worse
2. worst	**7.** best
3. best	**8.** more
4. better	**9.** further
5. less	**10.** farther

Using Modifiers Correctly

18.2 Irregular Comparisons

A few modifiers have irregular forms.

Modifiers with Irregular Forms of Comparison		
Positive	**Comparative**	**Superlative**
good	better	(the) best
well	better	(the) best
bad	worse	(the) worst
badly	worse	(the) worst
ill	worse	(the) worst
far (distance)	farther	(the) farthest
far (degree, time)	further	(the) furthest
little (amount)	less	(the) least
many	more	(the) most
much	more	(the) most

Exercise 3 — Making Correct Comparisons

Complete the following sentences with the correct degree of comparison of the modifier in parentheses. (The positive degree is used in four sentences.)

SAMPLE Lea's drawings are _____ than mine. (imaginative)
ANSWER more imaginative

The Art of Drawing

1. Drawing is one of the ____ art forms of all. (old)
2. Even though they drew on some of the ____ surfaces, prehistoric people created colorful images on rock or clay. (bad)
3. During the Middle Ages, parchment was one of the ____ drawing surfaces available. (good)
4. Partly because silk wore ____ than other materials, Eastern artists often used it as a drawing surface. (well)
5. Since the 1400s artists have preferred using paper, which costs ____ than parchment. (little)
6. Though they worked in ____ conditions than present-day artists, artists of centuries ago produced excellent drawings. (bad)
7. Leonardo da Vinci and Michelangelo were among the ____ artists of the High Renaissance. (good)
8. Rembrandt and Goya produced ____ drawings than many of their contemporaries. (much)
9. Many people believe that Pablo Picasso advanced the cause of art ____ than any other artists of this century. (far)
10. Today people will travel ____ than ever to see exhibits of his work. (far)

Resource Manager

Planning Resources
- *Lesson Plans*

Transparencies
- *Bellringer*
- *Daily Language Practice*

📂 Other Print Resources
- *Grammar and Composition Handbook*
- *Grammar Enrichment*, p. 35
- *Grammar Practice*, p. 35
- *Grammar Workbook*, Lesson 60

Exercise 4 — Writing Correct Comparisons

Write the word or words that could complete the following sentences with the correct degree of comparison of the modifier in parentheses.

SAMPLE Belinda is the _____ cyclist in our school. (fast)
ANSWER fastest

Babe Zaharias, All-Around Athlete

1. Many people consider Mildred "Babe" Didrikson Zaharias the _____ all-around athlete of this century. (good)
2. Babe Zaharias excelled in _____ sports than any other athlete, male or female. (many)
3. Of all the sports in which she participated, she was _____ in basketball, track and field, golf, skating, and lacrosse. (outstanding)
4. Zaharias rose to national fame _____ than most other athletes of her generation. (quickly)
5. In high school, she held numerous track-and-field records and was the _____ female basketball player in the country. (fine)
6. During the 1932 summer Olympics, held in Los Angeles, Zaharias performed _____ than ever before, breaking several world records. (good)
7. From 1940 to 1950, she achieved the goal of establishing herself as the country's _____ golfer, winning every possible United States and British title (successful)
8. Zaharias, who won the U.S. Open in 1948, 1950 and 1954, could drive a golf ball _____ than most other golfers. (far)
9. Despite a major operation, Zaharias still played _____ than any other competitor in the 1953 National Women's Open. (skillfully)
10. When Babe Didrikson Zaharias died in 1956, the country lost one of the _____ of all athletes. (talented)

Exercise 5 — Writing Sentences That Make Comparisons

Select five of the irregular modifiers from the list on page 666. Write a sentence for each, using the positive and comparative degrees of the modifier.

SAMPLE far
ANSWER Chen can throw the ball quite <u>far</u>, but Bernice can throw it <u>farther</u>.

Practice and Assess

Answers: Exercise 4
1. best
2. more
3. most outstanding
4. more quickly
5. finest
6. better
7. most successful
8. farther
9. more skillfully
10. most talented

Answers: Exercise 5

Sentences will vary, but each sentence should include the positive and comparative forms of one of the irregular modifiers on page 666. For example,

Ben is a good cook, but Sarah is a better cook than Ben.

Our softball coach has little patience, but our soccer coach has less.

Additional Resources
📁 *Grammar Practice*, p. 35
📁 *Grammar Enrichment*, p. 35

📕 *Grammar Workbook*, Lesson 60

Close

Have students share, discuss, and correct the sentences they wrote for Exercise 5.

Have students work in pairs to practice irregular comparative forms. The first student should say a sentence using the positive form of a modifier in the chart on page 666. The second student should respond with a sentence using the comparative or superlative form of that modifier.

MEETING INDIVIDUAL NEEDS
English Language Learners

Using Comparisons

Students learning English may have difficulty with *few* and *little*. *Few* is used with nouns that can be counted: *I have a few questions. Little* is used with nouns that cannot be counted: *I'll have a little soup.* (See p. 440 of the Teacher's Edition for a discussion of these nouns.) Provide examples of nouns used with *few* (*cookies, books, tickets*) and *little* (*hope, ice cream, fog*) and have students practice them.

Focus

Lesson Overview

Objectives
- To identify double comparisons
- To avoid them in writing

Bellringer
Daily Language Activity

When students enter the classroom, have this assignment on the board: *Tell what is wrong with this sentence:*

It is the most fairest way.

See also *Daily Language Practice*

Teach

☑ Teaching Tip
When writing hurriedly, students may use double comparisons. Remind them to read over their writing to catch such errors.

Practice and Assess

Answers: Exercise 6
1. . . . one of the ablest statesmen . . .
2. Churchill's star shone brightest . . .
3. . . . endure greater hardships . . .
4. One of the happiest sights . . .
5. . . . gave clearer speeches . . .
6. . . . one of the liveliest writers . . .
7. . . . the least careful student . . .
8. . . . one of the fittest leaders . . .
9. . . . had a quieter side . . .
10. . . . with higher esteem.
11. The United States was closer . . .
12. . . . the strongest friendship . . .
13. . . . one of their toughest challenges.
14. What was the fairest way . . .
15. Even better . . .

Using Modifiers Correctly *(side tab)*

18.3 Double Comparisons

■ Do not make a double comparison by using both *-er* or *-est* and *more* or *most*.

INCORRECT	Texas is ~~more~~ bigger than Oklahoma.
CORRECT	Texas is bigger than Oklahoma.
INCORRECT	That is the ~~most~~ funniest joke I have ever heard.
CORRECT	That is the funniest joke I have ever heard.

Exercise 6   **Correcting Double Comparisons**

Write the correct form of the comparison in each of the following sentences.

Winston Churchill, British Statesman

1. Today we recognize Sir Winston Churchill as one of the most ablest statesmen in world history.
2. Churchill's star shone most brightest when he was Great Britain's prime minister during World War II.
3. His courage, eloquence, and faith in victory inspired the British to endure more greater hardships than they had ever before known.
4. One of the most happiest sights during the war was Churchill himself, a cigar in his mouth and two fingers raised in a victory salute.
5. Although he had stuttered as a boy, Churchill gave more clearer speeches than any other leader of his time.
6. Churchill was also one of the most liveliest writers of the day.
7. As a schoolboy, however, he had been the least carefulest student in his class.
8. Physically, Churchill was one of the most fittest leaders of the war.
9. He loved the rough, active life of a soldier, but he also had a more quieter side, which he expressed in some of his excellent paintings.
10. No other British leader of this century is regarded with more higher esteem.
11. The United States was more closer to entering the war than had seemed possible a year before.
12. Churchill and President Roosevelt developed the most strongest friendship of any wartime leaders.
13. Meeting in Yalta in 1945, Churchill and Roosevelt faced one of their most toughest challenges.
14. What was the most fairest way to divide control of postwar Europe?
15. Even more better than his postwar speeches was Churchill's six-volume series, *The Second World War*, which won him a Nobel Prize.

668   Unit 18 Using Modifiers Correctly

Resource Manager

Planning Resources
- *Lesson Plans*

Transparencies
- *Bellringer*
- *Daily Language Practice*

🖅 Other Print Resources
- *Grammar and Composition Handbook*
- *Grammar Enrichment,* p. 36
- *Grammar Workbook,* Lesson 61

Exercise 7   Correcting Comparisons

Rewrite the following sentences, correcting the comparisons. If a sentence needs no correction, write *correct*.

Family Dogs

1. Dad had said that bringing two puppies into the house would be the goodest move our family could make.
2. When he brought them home from the animal shelter, the collie weighed littler than the shepherd.
3. Now the collie is more heavier than the shepherd.
4. Dad chose the collie because it had the sadder eyes of all the dogs at the shelter and he felt sorry for it.
5. The shepherd caught his eye because it had the most prettiest markings.
6. Both dogs have the most sweetest dispositions imaginable.
7. They are more happiest when they are right by our sides.
8. Raising two puppies is hardest than raising just one.
9. When one acts frisky, the other seems to act even friskiest.
10. With two dogs to care for, I have most responsibilities than before.
11. To give them the better care possible, I have had to give up pleasures I once enjoyed.
12. The situation is even badder when one of the dogs is ill.
13. The iller the dog feels, the more time someone must spend with it.
14. The shepherd appears to be in best health than the collie.
15. Since I am the most oldest of three children, it is my responsibility to walk the dogs every morning.
16. Sometimes I wish that the dogs were least playful on their morning walks around our neighborhood.
17. Whenever I am feeling weary, they seem to feel especially adventurous.
18. Then they try to run faster than ever before, dragging me along with them for blocks at a time.
19. I think that each day both dogs try to run further than the day before.
20. Last week, the shepherd ran off for the gooder part of the morning.
21. No one was happiest than I when he finally returned home.
22. The shepherd, whose sense of smell is more acuter than the collie's, was attracted by picnic leftovers in the park.
23. These leftovers were tastiest treats than his regular canned dog food.
24. In recent months, the dogs have become more easiest to train than they were when we first got them.
25. Their training is going the best than before.
26. Now they respond to simple commands most readily than before.
27. Of the two, the collie is gooder behaved than the shepherd.
28. The shepherd is the most stubbornest dog that I have ever known.
29. Sometimes the shepherd is least cooperative than a mule.
30. Raising two young dogs has definitely been entertaining and has brought this family closest together than ever before.

18.3 Double Comparisons **669**

Using Modifiers Correctly

Practice and Assess

Answers: Exercise 7

1. . . . the best move our family could make.
2. . . . the collie weighed less than the shepherd.
3. . . . heavier than the shepherd.
4. . . . the saddest eyes of all the dogs . . . .
5. . . . the prettiest markings.
6. . . . the sweetest dispositions imaginable.
7. They are happiest . . .
8. . . . harder than raising just one.
9. . . . the other seems to act even friskier.
10. . . . more responsibilities than before.
11. . . . the best care . . .
12. The situation is even worse . . . .
13. The worse the dog feels, ...
14. . . . in better health than the collie.
15. Since I am the oldest of three children . . . .
16. . . . less playful on their morning walks.
17. correct
18. . . . run faster than ever before, . . .
19. . . . run farther than the day before.
20. . . . for the better part of the morning.
21. No one was happier than I . . . .
22. . . . is more acute than the collie's . . . .
23. . . . were tastier treats . . .
24. . . . easier to train than when . . . .
25. Their training is going better than before.
26. . . . more readily than before.
27. . . . better behaved than the shepherd.
28. . . . most stubborn dog that . . . .
29. . . . is less cooperative . . .
30. . . . closer together than before.

Additional Resources

 Grammar Enrichment, p. 36

Grammar Workbook, Lesson 61

Close

Discuss the idea that many adjectives and adverbs of three syllables or more form their comparative and superlative degrees with *more* and *most*. Students might enjoy thinking of longer adjectives and adverbs, adding *-er* or *-est* to these words, writing silly sentences using the resulting comparative and superlative forms.

MEETING INDIVIDUAL NEEDS   **English Language Learners**

Using Comparisons

Students just learning English may not realize that although adjectives and adverbs in the comparative form cannot be modified by *more*, they can be modified by *much* and by certain other adverbs. Provide practice with sentences such as the following: *Texas is much bigger than Oklahoma. He's playing much worse than usual.*

Focus

Lesson Overview

Objective
- To identify and avoid incomplete comparisons

 Bellringer
Daily Language Activity

Use the Bellringer Transparency for Lesson 18.4.

See also *Daily Language Practice*

Teach

☑ **Teaching Tip**
When drafting, students are more likely to make incomplete comparisons. Remind them to check for this kind of error when proofreading.

Practice and Assess

Answers: Exercise 8

¹ . . . than in that of any other country.
² . . . than with anyone else. ³ . . . than by any other tradition. ⁴ . . . than any other music.
⁵ . . . than those of American folk music.
⁶ . . . softer than those of a steel-stringed guitar. ⁷ . . . the dancer's role is just as important as the singer's. ⁸ . . . than those of a ballerina. ⁹ . . . than any other performers.
¹⁰ . . . than anything else.

Additional Resources
📁 *Grammar Practice*, p. 36
📁 *Grammar Enrichment*, p. 36
📙 *Grammar Workbook,* Lesson 61

Close

Ask volunteers to make up sentences that may or may not contain incomplete comparisons.

18.4 Incomplete Comparisons

■ Do not make an incomplete or unclear comparison by omitting *other* or *else* when you compare one member of a group with the group.

| UNCLEAR | Crayfish are more like lobsters than any animal. |
| CLEAR | Crayfish are more like lobsters than any **other** animal. |

| UNCLEAR | She reads more books than anyone. |
| CLEAR | She reads more books than anyone **else.** |

Make sure that you are comparing like things.

UNCLEAR	The population of Texas is greater than Oklahoma. [One state's population is being compared illogically with everything about another state.]
CLEAR	The population of Texas is greater than **that of Oklahoma.**
CLEAR	The population of Texas is greater than **Oklahoma's.** [The word *population* is understood after *Oklahoma's.*]

UNCLEAR	The duties of a traffic officer are more complex than a game warden. [The duties of a traffic officer are being compared illogically with a person, namely, a game warden.]
CLEAR	The duties of a traffic officer are more complex than **those of a game warden.**
CLEAR	The duties of a traffic officer are more complex than **a game warden's.**

Exercise 8 **Making Complete Comparisons**

Rewrite each of the following sentences to correct the incomplete comparison.

The Art of Flamenco

¹Since discovering flamenco music, I have become more interested in the culture of Spain than in any other country. ²Flamenco songs and dance are associated more closely with the Gypsies of southern Spain than with anyone. ³Flamenco may have been influenced more by medieval Arabic music than by any tradition. ⁴After listening to a performance of flamenco music, I am now convinced that flamenco is more dramatic than any music. ⁵The rhythmic patterns of flamenco music are more complex and elaborate than American folk music. ⁶The tones of a flamenco guitar's nylon strings are softer than a steel-stringed guitar. ⁷In a flamenco performance, the dancer's role is just as important as the singer. ⁸The gestures of a flamenco dancer are more extravagant than a ballerina. ⁹As flamenco dancers whirl, strut, and strike dramatic poses, they exude more passion than any performer. ¹⁰If I could, I would rather learn flamenco dancing than anything.

Resource Manager

Planning Resources
- *Lesson Plans*

📂 **Transparencies**
- *Bellringer*
- *Daily Language Practice*

📁 Other Print Resources
- *Grammar and Composition Handbook*
- *Grammar Enrichment*, p.36
- *Grammar Practice*, p. 36
- *Grammar Workbook,* Lesson 61

18.5 | *Good* or *Well*; *Bad* or *Badly*

■ Always use *good* as an adjective. *Well* may be used as an adverb of manner telling how ably something is done or as an adjective meaning "in good health."

Natalie is a **good** speaker. [adjective]

Anita feels **good** today. [adjective after a linking verb]

Daniel speaks **well.** [adverb of manner]

Mr. Chong is not **well** right now. [adjective meaning "in good health"]

Always use *bad* as an adjective. Therefore, *bad* is used after a linking verb. Use *badly* as an adverb. *Badly* almost always follows an action verb.

The machine made a **bad** copy. [adjective]

The air smelled **bad.** [adjective following a linking verb]

I felt **bad** about your losing the race. [adjective following a linking verb]

His cut is bleeding **badly.** [adverb following an action verb]

Exercise 9 | **Choosing the Correct Modifier**

Write *good, well, bad,* or *badly* to complete each sentence.

Training a Dog

1. Generally it is _____ to begin training a dog when it is about eight weeks old.
2. In order to respond to training, a dog must feel _____ and be in good shape.
3. To train a dog successfully, owners need a great deal of patience and ready access to a _____ training manual.
4. For large or ill-behaved dogs, professional obedience training can result in pets whose temperaments are _____.
5. Some dog owners do not understand that if they communicate _____, their pet will not obey.
6. Communicating _____ means issuing simple, direct commands in a consistent manner.
7. Because repetition only confuses a dog, it is _____ to give a command only once.
8. It is best to speak firmly and clearly—not loudly—when reprimanding a dog that has behaved _____.
9. Both physical and verbal abuse are _____ for a dog; abuse creates fear in an animal but does not make it behave well.
10. Experts agree that nearly all dogs are eager to please their masters and feel _____ when they misbehave.

Using Modifiers Correctly

Focus

Lesson Overview

Objectives

- To identify *good* and *bad* as adjectives, and *badly* as an adverb; to understand the meaning of *well* when used as an adjective or an adverb
- To use these terms correctly in writing

 Bellringer
Daily Language Activity

When students enter the classroom, have the following assignment on the board: *Choose the appropriate word from the words in parentheses in the following sentence: The students felt (good, well) because they had done (good, well) on their final exams.*

See also 📖 *Daily Language Practice*

Teach

☑ **Grammar Tip**

Well can be either a predicate adjective following a linking verb or an adverb following an action verb. As a predicate adjective, *well* means "healthy," as in *Sally looks well.* As an adverb, *well* has a wide range of meanings but basically means "in a good, effective, or proper manner," as in *Sally sings well.*

Practice and Assess

Answers: Exercise 9

1. good	**6.** well
2. well *or* good	**7.** good
3. good	**8.** badly
4. good	**9.** bad
5. badly	**10.** bad

Resource Manager

Planning Resources
- *Lesson Plans*

📖 **Transparencies**
- *Bellringer*
- *Daily Language Practice*

📁 **Other Print Resources**
- *Grammar and Composition Handbook*
- *Grammar Enrichment,* p. 36
- *Grammar Workbook,* Lesson 62

Teach

Cross-reference: Grammar

For instruction and practice with action and linking verbs, refer students to Lesson 10.3, pp. 453–459.

Practice and Assess

Answers: Exercise 10

1. well	6. well
2. well	7. bad
3. well	8. bad
4. badly	9. good
5. bad	10. badly

Answers: Exercise 11

1. . . . more like human beings than any other animal.
2. . . . more complex than that of a cat.
3. . . . wired as well as a dog's brain.
4. . . . fuller than those of cats.
5. . . . have stronger emotions than do cats.
6. correct
7. . . . as great as those of human beings.
8. . . . more than anything else . . .
9. correct
10. . . . more copies than one about dogs.

Additional Resources

 Grammar Enrichment, p. 36

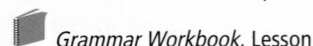 *Grammar Workbook*, Lesson 62

Close

Have students compare and discuss their answers to Exercises 9, 10, and 11. Suggest that the class as a whole try to resolve any differences of opinion.

Using Modifiers Correctly

Exercise 10   **Using the Correct Modifier**

For each sentence, write the correct modifier in parentheses. Then write whether the modifier is used as an *adjective* or an *adverb*.

A Dog's Life

1. Elizabeth Marshall Thomas writes (good/well).
2. Her surprise best-seller, *The Hidden Life of Dogs*, speaks (good/well) of dogs.
3. The theme of her book is that dogs do many things as (good/well) as human beings.
4. There are, of course, things that dogs do (bad/badly) or cannot do at all.
5. Some critics of Thomas's book claim that she condones dogs' behavior even when it is (bad, badly).
6. Thomas believes that dogs live (good/well) if their lives are filled with love and intellectual pursuits.
7. According to Thomas, dogs have a "conscience" and feel (bad/badly) about some of the things they do.
8. Thomas's dog Koki skulked around the house for days because Koki knew that she had been (bad/badly).
9. On the other hand, if a dog feels (good, well) about its behavior, it is likely to show this by acting happy.
10. When one of her dogs acts (bad/badly), Thomas usually finds a logical explanation for its behavior.

Exercise 11   **Correcting Comparisons**

Rewrite each of the following sentences, correcting the incomplete or incorrect comparison. If a sentence contains no errors, write *correct*.

Dogs and Cats

1. I believe that dogs are more like human beings than any animal.
2. I'm convinced that the brain of a dog is more complex than a cat.
3. A cat's brain doesn't seem to be wired as good as a dog's brain.
4. Dogs lead lives that are fuller than cats.
5. Dogs seem to have more stronger emotions than cats do.
6. Cats seldom, if ever, feel bad about things they have done, even when someone is reprimanding them.
7. Dogs' emotional needs may be as great as human beings.
8. What dogs seem to want more than anything is the company of other dogs.
9. What cats want is good food, preferably mice.
10. If someone wrote a book about cats, the book would probably sell even more copies than dogs.

MEETING INDIVIDUAL NEEDS   English Language Learners

Choosing an Adjective or Adverb

Students learning English may have trouble when using adverbs with action verbs because several common adverbs have the same form as adjectives. For example, *fast* can be an adjective as in *He is a fast runner* or an adverb as in *She runs fast*. Provide students with plenty of practice in hearing adverbs of this type used correctly.

18.6 Double Negatives

DON'T

NEVER

■ In general, do not use a double negative, two negative words in the same clause. Use only one negative word to express a negative idea.

INCORRECT	I didn't see ~~no~~ accident.
CORRECT	I did**n't** see **any** accident.
INCORRECT	He doesn't know nothing about my plans.
CORRECT	He does**n't** know **anything** about my plans.
CORRECT	He knows **nothing** about my plans.
INCORRECT	She ~~never~~ tells no lies.
CORRECT	She **never** tells **any** lies.
CORRECT	She tells **no** lies.
INCORRECT	We haven't hardly eaten our breakfasts.
CORRECT	We have **hardly** eaten our breakfasts.

Exercise 12   **Avoiding Double Negatives**

Rewrite the following sentences, eliminating the double negative in each.

Boa Constrictors

1. Boa constrictors do not inject no venom into their prey.
2. Still, I would not want no boa constrictor for a pet.
3. Boa constrictors kill birds and rodents by not allowing them no air.
4. Once captured in the boa constrictor's coils, a bird or rodent cannot do nothing.
5. The boa constrictor is big, but it cannot be compared with no anaconda, or python.
6. Boa constrictors cannot swallow no cows, horses, or people.
7. After a meal, these snakes do not eat nothing for a week or more.
8. Often they do not do nothing; they just sleep and digest their food.
9. Boa constrictors can survive for many months without no food at all.
10. Unlike many other snakes, boa constrictors never lay no eggs.
11. Though my friend Jeremy has one, I wouldn't want no boa constrictor for a pet.
12. There aren't scarcely any snakes that appeal to me.
13. Jeremy shouldn't never have brought his boa constrictor to school.
14. He thought it wouldn't never escape from its bag.
15. He didn't have no clue where the snake was after it escaped.
16. First he pretended that he didn't know nothing about all the commotion.
17. He couldn't hardly keep pretending for long, though.
18. There wasn't nobody in the class who didn't know he had the snake with him.
19. Jeremy hadn't hardly expected to become a school celebrity.
20. He won't bring no snakes to school again anytime soon.

Using Modifiers Correctly

Resource Manager

Planning Resources
• *Lesson Plans*

📂 **Other Print Resources**
• *Grammar and Composition Handbook*
• *Grammar Reteaching,* p. 36
• *Grammar Workbook,* Lesson 63

Focus

Lesson Overview

Objective
• To learn to avoid double negatives

🔔 **Bellringer**
Daily Language Activity

Use the Bellringer Transparency for Lesson 18.6.

See also 📖 *Daily Language Practice*

Teach

☑ **Teaching Tip**

Remind students that it is acceptable to have two negatives in the same sentence if they are in separate clauses—for example, *Since you didn't answer the phone, I didn't think you were home.*

Practice and Assess

Answers: Exercise 12

Answers may vary, but some suggestions are given below.

1. . . . do not inject venom into their prey.
2. . . . I would not want a boa constrictor . . .
3. . . . by not allowing them any air.
4. . . . a bird or rodent can do nothing.
5. . . . it cannot be compared with an anaconda . . .
6. . . . cannot swallow cows, . . .
7. . . . do not eat anything for a week or more.
8. Often they do nothing; . . .
9. . . . can survive . . . with no food at all.
10. Unlike many other snakes, boa constrictors never lay eggs.
11. . . . I wouldn't want a boa . . .
12. There are scarcely any snakes that . . .
13. Jeremy should never have brought . . .
14. He never thought it would escape . . .
15. He didn't have a clue where . . .
16. . . .that he knew nothing about . . .
17. He could hardly keep pretending . . .
18. There was nobody . . . who didn't know . . .
19. Jeremy had hardly expected . . .
20. He won't bring any snakes . . .

Close

Have students compare and discuss their sentences for Exercise 12.

Focus

Lesson Overview

Objective
- To identify incorrectly placed modifiers and modifiers that are not logically modifying any word in the sentence

Bellringer
Daily Language Activity

When students enter the classroom, have the following assignment on the board: *Change the position of the word <u>only</u> in the following sentence to express different meanings: Only the boys washed the dishes.*

See also *Daily Language Practice*

Teach

Misplaced Modifiers

☑ Teaching Tip

Depending on where *only* is positioned, the Bellringer sentence can mean that the boys but not the girls washed dishes, that the boys washed but did not dry the dishes, or that the boys washed dishes but not the pots and pans.

Practice and Assess

Answers: Exercise 13

1. Dumping more water . . . state
2. correct
3. Howling through mountain passes
4. Built in the 1960s
5. correct

Using Modifiers Correctly

18.7 Misplaced and Dangling Modifiers

- Place modifiers as close as possible to the words they modify in order to make the meaning of the sentence clear.

Misplaced Modifiers

Modifiers that modify the wrong word or seem to modify more than one word in a sentence are called **misplaced modifiers.** Moving the modifier as close as possible to the word it modifies or revising the sentence will correct this problem.

MISPLACED	**Proceeding with care,** we stood at the foot of the mountain and watched the determined mountain climbers. [participial phrase incorrectly modifying *we*]
CLEAR	We stood at the foot of the mountain and watched the determined mountain climbers **proceeding with care.** [participial phrase correctly modifying *mountain climbers*]
MISPLACED	The mountains delight many visitors **in their autumn splendor.** [prepositional phrase incorrectly modifying *visitors*]
CLEAR	The mountains **in their autumn splendor** delight many visitors. [prepositional phrase correctly modifying *mountains*]

Exercise 13   Identifying Misplaced Modifiers

Write the misplaced modifier in each sentence. If a sentence is correct, write *correct*.

1. Dumping more water on an already flooded state, California is hit by still another torrential rainstorm.
2. The winter storm battering northern California for days has worked its way down the coast to the southern counties.
3. Howling through mountain passes, a highway winding through the Sierra Nevada is forced to shut down due to heavy winds.
4. Built in the 1960s, officials estimated that three months would be needed to rebuild a bridge.
5. Most meteorologists attributed the storm to a recurring Pacific weather phenomenon known as El Niño.

Resource Manager

Planning Resources
- *Lesson Plans*

📁 **Transparencies**
- *Bellringer*
- *Daily Language Practice*

📂 **Other Print Resources**
- *Grammar and Composition Handbook*
- *Grammar Enrichment*, p. 37
- *Grammar Practice*, p. 37
- *Grammar Reteaching*, p. 37
- *Grammar Workbook*, Lesson 64

Dangling Modifiers

Dangling modifiers do not modify any word in the sentence. By supplying a word that the dangling phrase can sensibly modify, you can easily correct this error.

DANGLING	**Digging in the field,** a Native American village was found. [participial phrase logically modifying no word in the sentence]
CLEAR	**Digging in the field,** archaeologists found a Native American village. [participial phrase modifying *archaeologists*]
DANGLING	**After digging for months,** the find was all the more satisfying. [prepositional phrase logically modifying no word in the sentence]
CLEAR	**After digging for months,** the archaeologists deemed the find all the more satisfying. [prepositional phrase modifying *archaeologists*]
DANGLING	**Feeling proud of our find,** our dinner that night was a celebration. [phrase cannot modify a possessive form]
CLEAR	**Feeling proud of our find,** we made our dinner a celebration. [rewrite supplies a word for phrase to modify]

Placement of *Only*

■ Place the adverb *only* immediately before the word or group of words it modifies.

The meaning of your sentence may be unclear if *only* is positioned incorrectly.

UNCLEAR	Bertina **only** has breakfast on Sunday. [Does she have just one meal on Sunday. Does she skip breakfast every day but Sunday? Is Bertina the only person (in a group) who has breakfast on Sunday?]
CLEAR	Bertina has **only** breakfast on Sunday. [She does not have lunch or dinner.]
CLEAR	Bertina has breakfast **only** on Sunday. [She does not have breakfast on any other day.]
CLEAR	**Only** Bertina has breakfast on Sunday. [No one else (in Bertina's house) has breakfast on Sunday.]

Teach

Dangling Modifiers

☑ **Teaching Tip**

The most common type of dangling modifier is a participial phrase. A participial phrase must modify a main clause. A participial phrase is said to dangle when there is no noun in the main clause that it can logically modify. For example, in the sentence *Digging in the field, a Native American village was found,* the participial phrase *digging in the field* is a dangling modifier because it cannot logically modify the nearest noun, *village.*

Remind students that when a participial phrase is used at the beginning of a sentence, the phrase must modify the subject of the sentence.

⤢ **Cross-reference: Grammar**

For instruction and practice with prepositional and participial phrases, refer students to Lessons 12.1 and 12.3, pp. 523–524 and 527–531.

⤢ **Cross-reference: Troubleshooter**

For instruction and practice with misplaced and dangling modifiers, refer students to the **Troubleshooter.**

MEETING INDIVIDUAL NEEDS | English Language Learners

Rephrasing Sentences

Students learning English may have difficulty rephrasing sentences to correct misplaced or dangling modifiers. It may help these students to pair them with students whose first language is English as they complete the exercises in this unit. Remind pairs of students to read sentences aloud to each other.

Practice and Assess

Answers: Exercise 14

1. Looking for adventure, dangling
2. correct
3. correct
4. Ranging in difficulty from Class I to Class IV, dangling
5. Unlike an amusement-park ride, misplaced
6. Interested in glaciers and icebergs, dangling
7. correct
8. Filled . . . dangers, misplaced
9. only, misplaced
10. correct

Answers: Exercise 15

Answers will vary, but some suggestions are given below.

1. Driving carefully down the road to the park, I avoided the accident.
2. Riding my bike in the park, I saw two squirrels.
3. Searching for wildflowers, I found poison ivy instead.
4. Using a net, we caught a butterfly.
5. Alex and Maria saw two birds making a nest for their young in a big tree near the parking lot.
6. Carmen dreams only of being a forest ranger; . . . .
7. Because of their huge size and strength, grizzly bears are feared by many backpackers and campers in the park.
8. Only Myung knows . . . .
9. Stuck fast on the hook, the fish that I caught in the lake was hard for me to remove.
10. After planning for months, we were pleased that the outing was a big success.

Using Modifiers Correctly

Exercise 14   Identifying Misplaced and Dangling Modifiers

Write any incorrect modifier in the following sentences. Then write *misplaced* or *dangling* to identify the kind. If a sentence contains no errors, write *correct*.

SAMPLE   Renting huge rafts, rivers become accessible to city people.
ANSWER   Renting huge rafts—misplaced

Outdoor Adventures

1. Looking for adventure, white-water rafting, mountain climbing, and bungee jumping have become popular vacation activities.
2. Adventure travel, now a billion-dollar industry, has grown rapidly in recent years.
3. Thousands of people sign up for rafting trips through the Grand Canyon each year.
4. Ranging in difficulty from Class I to Class IV, knowledgeable river guides lead inexperienced rafters.
5. Unlike an amusement-park ride, rafters often find their trip down the rapids unpredictable and strenuous.
6. Interested in glaciers and icebergs, the untouched wilderness of the Yukon territory can be very appealing.
7. Some tourists enjoy watching the mountain gorillas with sloping heads and dense black fur that make their home in central Africa.
8. Filled as they are with hidden dangers, some vacationers find ice climbing and rock climbing especially challenging.
9. Climbers in the best physical shape should only climb glaciers.
10. Extremely vigorous outdoor adventures push people to their physical limits.

Exercise 15   Correcting Misplaced and Dangling Modifiers

Rewrite the following sentences, correcting the misplaced or dangling modifier in each.

A Day in the Park

1. Driving carefully down the road to the park, the accident was avoided.
2. I saw two squirrels riding my bike in the park.
3. Searching for wildflowers, poison ivy was found instead.
4. We caught a butterfly using a net.
5. Making a nest for their young, Alex and Maria saw two birds in a big tree near the parking lot.
6. Carmen only dreams of being a forest ranger; she knows it is what she wants to be, and no other career interests her.
7. Because of their huge size and strength, many backpackers and campers in the park fear grizzly bears.
8. Myung only knows which trail leads to the waterfall; he won't tell anyone else where it is.
9. Stuck fast on the hook, I had trouble removing the fish that I caught in the lake.
10. After planning for months, the outing was a big success.

Exploring Language

Recognizing Dangling Participles

One way to recognize a dangling participle is to turn a participial phrase at the beginning of a sentence into a complete sentence. The subject of the main clause should also be the subject of the new sentence. For example, the participial phrase at the beginning of *Walking to school,*

Sally found a dollar can be made into the sentence *Sally walked to school.* If this new sentence is logical, then the participial phrase is a legitimate modifier of the subject. If it is not, then the participial phrase is dangling. **L2**

Exercise 16 — Correcting Misplaced and Dangling Modifiers

Rewrite the following sentences, correcting the misplaced or dangling modifiers in each.

Toni Morrison, Novelist

1. During her childhood in Lorain, Ohio, Toni Morrison was surrounded by poor, hardworking people and steel mills with little opportunity to get ahead.
2. Finishing high school with honors, Howard University in Washington, D.C., accepted Morrison as an undergraduate.
3. Constantly on the road during the summer, her acting talent shone in the productions of the university's theater troupe.
4. Attending graduate school at Cornell University, William Faulkner and Virginia Woolf were the subjects of her thesis.
5. Graduating in 1955, jobs in education and publishing followed.
6. Until 1969, when her novel *The Bluest Eye* was published, Morrison had edited only books, not written them.
7. In *The Bluest Eye,* a young girl is described by Morrison wishing for blue eyes exactly like Shirley Temple's.
8. With the curious name of Milkman Dead, Morrison created a powerful character in her third novel, *Song of Solomon.*
9. Becoming increasingly aware of his family heritage, the author convincingly pictures Milkman Dead.
10. Some critics liked Morrison's novel *Tar Baby,* but others said that the characters only were stereotypes.
11. Described by some as the last classic American writer, one critic put Morrison in a category with Poe, Twain, and Faulkner.
12. Only *Beloved* was the book written by Morrison to win the Pulitzer Prize.
13. *Song of Solomon* only won the National Book Critics Circle Award.
14. Having won such prestigious literary awards, Princeton University offered Morrison a teaching position.
15. Morrison wrote *Jazz,* angry at the injustices experienced by African American women.
16. After many months of writing, it was published.
17. Heartbreaking and powerful, readers were mesmerized by the story woven by Morrison.
18. Writing with passion, the main characters in *Jazz* formed a triangle of jealousy, murder, and redemption.
19. With their daring themes and lyrical passages, readers admire Toni Morrison's novels.
20. Given for distinguished literary work of an idealistic nature, in 1993 Morrison won the Nobel Prize for Literature.

17. Readers were mesmerized by the heartbreaking and powerful story Morrison wove.
18. Writing with passion, Morrison formed a triangle of jealousy, murder, and redemption with the main characters in *Jazz.*
19. Readers admire Toni Morrison's novels with their daring themes and lyrical passages.
20. In 1993 Morrison won the Nobel Prize for Literature, given for distinguished literary work of an idealistic nature.

Practice and Assess

Using Modifiers Correctly

Answers: Exercise 16

Answers will vary, but some suggestions are given below.

1. During her childhood in Lorain, Ohio, Toni Morrison was surrounded by steel mills and by poor, hardworking people with little opportunity to get ahead.
2. Finishing high school with honors, Morrison was accepted as an undergraduate by Howard University in Washington, D.C.
3. Her acting talent shone in the productions of the university's theater troupe, constantly on the road during the summer.
4. Attending graduate school at Cornell University, Morrison chose William Faulkner and Virginia Woolf as the subjects of her thesis.
5. Following her graduation in 1955, she held jobs in education and publishing.
6. Until 1969, when her novel *The Bluest Eye* was published, Morrison had only edited books, not written them.
7. In *The Bluest Eye,* Morrison describes a young girl wishing for blue eyes exactly like Shirley Temple's.
8. In her third novel, *Song of Solomon,* Morrison created a powerful character with the curious name of Milkman Dead.
9. The author convincingly pictures Milkman Dead becoming increasingly aware of his family heritage.
10. Some critics liked Morrison's novel *Tar Baby,* but others said that the characters were only stereotypes.
11. One critic put Morrison, described by some as the last classic American writer, in a category with Poe, Twain, and Faulkner.
12. *Beloved* was the only book written by Morrison to win the Pulitzer Prize.
13. Only *Song of Solomon* won the National Book Critics Circle Award. Or *Song of Solomon* won only the National Book Critics Circle Award.
14. Having won such prestigious literary awards, Morrison was offered a teaching position at Princeton University.
15. Angry at the injustices experienced by African American women, Morrison wrote *Jazz.*
16. After many months of writing, Morrison got the book published.

Practice and Assess

Answers: Exercise 17

Answers may vary, but some suggestions are given below.

1. Planning ahead, many parents have begun their search for the right summer program for their children.
2. Knowing how difficult the decision is, parents collect as much information as possible.
3. Though sometimes overwhelming, information helps narrow the choices.
4. Often unsure of their decision-making ability, children need help sorting out the possibilities.
5. Various programs, many of them free, are available at public libraries and recreational centers throughout the county.
6. Some programs offered by county agencies have a residency requirement and a small nonresident surcharge.
7. Empty during summer months, college dormitories provide housing for some programs.
8. Children can find any kind of camp suited to their interests.
9. There are nature camps, history camps, and even astronomy camps designed for aspiring astronauts.
10. Only students with experience in digital photography can enroll in the animation program at the computer arts camp.

Answers: Exercise 18

Answers may vary, but some suggestions are given below.

[1]correct [2]Apprenticeship is probably a better way . . . . [3]Apprentices never gain practical skill. . . . [4]As their training progresses, they learn various job skills well. [5]After about four years—longer for some trades . . . . [6]Then the wages received by these skilled workers are better than those received by the unskilled workers. [7]. . . more crowded . . . than any other field. [8]correct [9]Having varying interests, people find some . . . [10]correct [11]correct [12]Sometimes you will find that the best thing . . . [13]Colleges today train a growing number of artists and craftspeople not wanting to miss out on a college education. [14]Nevertheless, many people believe that only the close relationship . . .

Exercise 17 Adding Modifiers to Sentences

Revise the following sentences, adding modifiers as indicated in parentheses.

Summer Programs

1. Many parents have begun their search for the right summer program for their children. (Add *planning ahead.*)
2. Parents collect as much information as possible. (Add *knowing how difficult the decision is.*)
3. Information helps narrow the choices. (Add *though sometimes overwhelming.*)
4. Children need help sorting out the possibilities. (Add *often unsure of their decision-making ability.*)
5. Various programs are available at public libraries and recreational centers throughout the county. (Add *many of them free.*)
6. Some programs have a residency requirement and a small nonresident surcharge. (Add *offered by county agencies.*)
7. College dormitories provide housing for some programs. (Add *empty during summer months.*)
8. Children can find any kind of camp. (Add *suited to their interests.*)
9. There are nature camps, history camps, and even astronomy camps. (Add *designed for aspiring astronauts.*)
10. Students with experience in digital photography can enroll in the animation program at the computer arts camp. (Add *only* to make clear that others cannot enroll.)

Exercise 18 Correcting Modifiers

The following paragraphs contain 10 errors in the use of modifiers. Rewrite the paragraphs, correcting the errors.

Apprenticeships

[1]Going to college is a good way to train for some, but not all, kinds of work. [2]Apprenticeship is probably a more better way to train to be a carpenter, for example. [3]Apprentices never gain no practical skill without on-the-job experience. [4]As their training progresses, they learn various job skills good. [5]After about four years—more longer for some trades and not so long for others—they become experts. [6]Then the wages received by these skilled workers are better than the unskilled workers.

[7]The construction industry is more crowded with registered apprentices than any field. [8]There are many different occupations that require apprenticeship. [9]Having varying interests, some fields are more attractive than others. [10]Apprenticeship programs have entrance exams and minimum age and education requirements. [11]If you want to become an apprentice, the best thing you can do is find out about your chosen field while you are still in school. [12]Sometimes you will find that the most good thing to do is to finish college first. [13]Not wanting to miss out on a college education, colleges today train a growing number of artists and craftspeople. [14]Nevertheless, many people believe that the close relationship between master and apprentice only can provide suitable training.

Exercise 19   Correcting Modifiers

Rewrite the following sentences, correcting any errors in the use of modifiers.

Arthurian Sites

1. My summer vacation was more better than any I ever took before.
2. While traveling in England, places associated with King Arthur were my primary destinations.
3. Located on the coast of Cornwall, our tour guide pointed out King Arthur's legendary birthplace at Tintagel.
4. When I learned that no one really knows where King Arthur was born—or even whether he actually lived—I felt badly.
5. I didn't let nothing keep me from seeing Cadbury Castle, which may have been the real Camelot.
6. Are the Arthurian sites in Glastonbury more numerous than any other city in England?
7. Standing at King Arthur's legendary grave site, the ruins of Glastonbury Abbey surrounded me.
8. I missed visiting the possible sites of Sir Lancelot's northern castle, because I didn't feel good.
9. Hanging in the hall at Winchester Castle, I gazed intently at what is supposed to be the table top of the Round Table.
10. My tour of Arthurian sites provided me with the most fondest memories of my vacation.

Exercise 20   Writing Correct Comparisons

Write 10 sentences, following the directions given in each of the items below.

SAMPLE   Use the comparative of *happy* as an adverb.
ANSWER   I worked *more happily* after I realized that I was almost finished.

1. Use the comparative form of *tiny* to compare the size of two objects.
2. Use the superlative of *little* (meaning amount) as an adjective.
3. Use the modifiers *good* and *well* following the appropriate kinds of verbs.
4. Use the comparative of *far* to compare distance.
5. Compare two games or activities of your choice, using the superlatives of *good* and *bad*.
6. Write a sentence comparing the population of New York with the population of Oregon.
7. Use the comparative form of the modifier *many*.
8. Express the same idea in two sentences. In one, use the negative *never*; in the other, use *ever*.
9. Use the modifier *only* to explain that you have art class one morning a week.
10. Use the participial phrase *reviewing all the grammar* in a sentence.

18.7 Misplaced and Dangling Modifiers   **679**

Additional Resources

📁 *Grammar Practice*, p. 37
📁 *Grammar Reteaching*, p. 37
📁 *Grammar Enrichment*, p. 37

📖 *Grammar Workbook*, Lesson 64

Close

Invite students to create humorous examples of dangling modifiers—for example,

Flying in the air, the girl captured the escaped pigeon.

Practice and Assess

Answers: Exercise 19

Answers will vary, but some suggestions are given below.

1. My summer vacation was better than any I ever took before.
2. While traveling in England, I made places associated with King Arthur my primary destinations.
3. Our tour guide pointed out . . . Tintagel, located on the coast of Cornwall.
4. . . . or even whether he actually lived—I felt bad.
5. I didn't let anything keep me from seeing Cadbury Castle, ...
6. Are the Arthurian sites in Glastonbury more numerous than those in any other city in England?
7. Standing at King Arthur's legendary grave site, I was surrounded by . . . Abbey.
8. Because I didn't feel good (or well), I missed . . .
9. I gazed intently at what is supposed to be the table top of the Round Table that was hanging in the hall at Winchester Castle.
10. My tour of Arthurian sites provided me with the fondest memories of my vacation.

Answers: Exercise 20

Answers will vary, but some suggestions are given below.

1. My room is tinier than yours.
2. Of the three children, the baby is the least trouble.
3. The speaker looked good and enunciated well.
4. Jeff lives farther from school than I do.
5. Of all my friends, I am best at chess and worst at football.
6. The population of New York is greater than that of Oregon.
7. I have more seashells than you do.
8. Mary never makes a mistake. Mary doesn't ever make a mistake.
9. I have art class only one morning a week.
10. Reviewing all the grammar, we prepared for the test.

Using Modifiers Correctly

Teach

About the Literature

Explain that the review features a passage from chapter 8 of Mark Helprin's *A Soldier of the Great War*. The passage is followed by exercises based on related topics. Ask a volunteer to read the passage aloud. Have the rest of the class listen, respond, and appropriately evaluate the presentation. In a discussion, students should identify and analyze character, setting, and mood. Students should use peer feedback to evaluate their effectiveness in presenting and to set goals for future presentations.

Linking Grammar and Literature

Critical Thinking

Ask students to consider the roles that the highlighted modifiers play. As they read, they should ask themselves questions such as the following: Do the modifiers add more information to the sentences? Do they set up a contrast or a comparison? Do they enhance the tone and the rhythm of the writing?

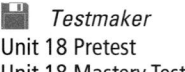

ASSESSMENT OPTIONS

📂 *Tests with Answer Key & Rubrics*
Unit 18 Pretest, pp. 63–64
Unit 18 Mastery Test, pp. 65–66

💾 *Testmaker*
Unit 18 Pretest
Unit 18 Mastery Test

You may wish to administer the Unit 18 Pretest at this point.

USING MODIFIERS CORRECTLY

Alessandro Giuliani, the hero of Mark Helprin's epic novel *A Soldier of the Great War*, is a young Italian student whose life is turned upside down by World War I. In this passage, which has been annotated to show some of the kinds of modifiers covered in this unit, Alessandro is returning on foot from Germany to his family estate in Rome.

Using Modifiers Correctly

> ## Literature Model
>
> #### *from* A Soldier of the Great War
> ##### *by Mark Helprin*
>
> H e crossed six ridges, each **higher** than the one preceding it, before he came to the point where he would not see trees until he was in Italy, and when he cleared the forest he was confronted by a world of glaciated mountains. In the dusk, they were a dusty-rose color and the distance to them appeared so vast that he thought it would take a month to reach them, but it was only a trick of light and shadow, and they were neither as **far** nor as high as they seemed to be.
>
> Here and there in the snow-covered pastures were hay-filled cabins where he could find shelter from the wind. He sought the one **farthest** from any farmhouse or village and closest to the great glacier upon which he would soon be walking. Several hours after dusk he stopped at the end **of the meadows**, in a place where the glacier was so close that he could feel the rivers of cold air that flowed from it and carried its sounds—the muffled sound of a locked wheel skidding on a steel rail, thunder-like cracks, a barely perceptible rumble, as if from a giant piece of furniture being pulled slowly across a rough floor. . . .
>
> He awoke at midnight, shivering so **violently** that he found it difficult to get to his feet. He buttoned his clothes tight, bloused his pants in his socks, put on every item of wool he could find, and burst out the door, almost falling

Comparative form of the adjective *high*

Positive form of the adjective *far*

Superlative form of the adjective *far*

Correctly placed prepositional phrase modifying *end*

Positive form of the adverb *violently*

680   Unit 18 Using Modifiers

Resource Manager

Planning Resources
• *Lesson Plans*

📂 **Other Print Resources**
• *Grammar and Composition Handbook*
• *Grammar Workbook,* Lessons 59–64; Unit 9 Review; Cumulative Review: Units 1–9

down the slope that descended to the tongue of the glacier. The moon was down, his head throbbed, and his fingers were too stiff for him to have opened his food even had he been warm enough to try to eat.

He had to use both axes. The crampons were not necessary, and he would never have been able to strap them on anyway. *After struggling up a short fractured ice wall by pulling himself forward with his arms,* he was on the glacier. It rose gradually toward a line of mountains that then shot straight into the sky like the spray of a wave exploding through a sinkhole. With luck he would have a moon or a sky clear enough to let the starlight through, and with more than luck he would reach the peaks by daylight.

> Correctly placed phrases modifying *he*

Review: Exercise 1   **Making Correct Comparisons**

The following sentences describe World War I and Alessandro Giuliani's involvement in it. For each sentence, write the proper comparative or superlative form of the modifier in parentheses.

1. World War I was called the Great War because _____ men fought and died in it than in any other war up to that time. (many)
2. The nations that fought in World War I assembled the _____ number of soldiers and armaments ever seen. (great)
3. Before the war, Alessandro joined the navy in the belief that wars were fought _____ at sea than on land. (safely)
4. Ironically, he was then sent to fight in the naval infantry and survived some of the _____ battles of all. (dangerous)
5. Alessandro later deserted when German and Austrian forces shattered the Italian front lines; it was Italy's _____ defeat of all in the war. (bad)
6. Desertion was usually punished by the _____ penalty of all: death by firing squad. (severe)
7. The Italian army chose to punish Alessandro's desertion _____ than usual, however; he was simply sent back to fight the Austrians. (harshly)
8. After he was taken prisoner by the Austrians, Alessandro fared _____ than other prisoners did. (good)
9. After Austria's collapse, Alessandro slipped cautiously through enemy lines amid the _____ confusion imaginable. (bad)
10. Every step Alessandro took toward the glacier led him _____ from the enemy and closer to his homeland and to freedom. (far)

Grammar Review   **681**

Practice and Assess

Answers: Exercise 1
1. more
2. greatest
3. more safely
4. most dangerous
5. worst
6. most severe
7. less harshly
8. better
9. worst
10. farther

Practice and Assess

Answers: Exercise 2

1. correct
2. On the lower slopes, many varieties of trees flourish, but the highest slopes are almost bare of vegetation.
3. The taller peaks attract many competent climbers; among them were the characters Alessandro and his friend Rafi.
4. Making his escape from an Austrian prison, Alessandro chose the straightest path to Italy and his home.
5. Alessandro climbed until he was higher than the tree line and within sight of the glaciers.
6. A glacier is a slowly moving river of ice and snow that stays frozen even on the hottest summer days.
7. There are more than a thousand glaciers in the Alps; the largest is the 16-mile-long Aletsch Glacier.
8. The riskiest part of Alessandro's escape from Austria was his crossing a vast glacier at night.
9. Sharp-spiked crampons give climbers a firmer foothold on the ice than plain climbing boots do.
10. correct
11. The glacier on which he climbed was in a warmer climate than many other glaciers.
12. correct
13. Glaciers become larger when more snow falls and smaller when snow melts.
14. correct
15. The steeper the slope, the faster a glacier generally moves.
16. Many glaciers in the Alps are mountain glaciers that begin on the highest slopes.
17. correct
18. The movement causes the mass to become further compacted into glacier ice.
19. The slowest glacier moves about an inch a day; the most rapid one, several hundred feet.
20. correct

Review: Exercise 2 Correcting Double Comparisons

Some of the following sentences elaborate on scenes from *A Soldier of the Great War* that are not reprinted in this textbook. Other sentences describe the Alps and glaciers. For each sentence, write the correct comparison. If a sentence contains no errors, write *correct*.

1. The Alps are probably better known than any other mountains in the world.
2. On the lower slopes of the Alps, many varieties of trees flourish, but the most highest slopes are almost bare of vegetation.
3. The more taller peaks attract many competent climbers; among them were the characters Alessandro and his friend Rafi.
4. Making his escape from an Austrian prison, Alessandro chose the most straightest path to Italy and his home.
5. Alessandro climbed until he was more higher than the tree line and within sight of the glaciers.
6. A glacier is a slowly moving river of ice and snow that stays frozen even on the most hottest summer days.
7. There are more than a thousand glaciers in the Alps; the most largest is the 16-mile-long Aletsch Glacier.
8. The most riskiest part of Alessandro's escape from Austria was his crossing a vast glacier at night.
9. Sharp-spiked crampons give climbers a more firmer foothold on the ice than plain climbing boots do.
10. More skillful than most amateur climbers, Alessandro chose not to wear crampons and used only his two ice axes to climb onto the glacier.
11. The glacier on which he climbed was in a more warmer climate than many other glaciers.
12. Glaciers are found both in polar regions and also in more temperate climates.
13. Glaciers become larger when more snow falls and more smaller when snow melts.
14. A glacier moves more slowly when it reaches an area that is less steeply sloped.
15. The steeper the slope, the more faster a glacier generally moves.
16. Many glaciers in the Alps are mountain glaciers that begin on the most highest slopes.
17. When compressed into a granular mass by more snow on top, the old snow starts to slide slowly down the slope.
18. The movement causes the mass to become more further compacted into glacier ice.
19. The slowest glacier moves about an inch a day; the most rapidest one, several hundred feet.
20. Climbing on glaciers is often more dangerous than climbing on rock.

Using Modifiers Correctly

Review: Exercise 3 **Correcting Incomplete and Unclear Comparisons**

The following sentences describe World War I and Italy's involvement in it. Rewrite each sentence, correcting any errors of incomplete or unclear comparison. Some of the sentences can be revised in more than one way. If a sentence contains no errors, write *correct*.

SAMPLE World War I shaped Alessandro's life more than any event.
ANSWER World War I shaped Alessandro's life more than any other event.

1. The First World War, which involved all the major powers of Europe as well as the United States, produced carnage greater than any previous war.
2. The use of aircraft, tanks, and machine guns made the Great War more impersonal than any war.
3. Some observers believed that British and French soldiers fought more bravely than anyone.
4. The Central Powers—Germany, Austria-Hungary, and the Ottoman Empire—were united as much by geography as by anything.
5. When fighting began in May 1915, Italy's army was less prepared than France or Britain.
6. For months the Alps, more than any place in Europe, were the site of many battles between the Italian and the Austrian forces.
7. The Isonzo River, in northern Italy, was the site of more battles than any other location on the Italian front.
8. After a devastating battle in 1917, Italy's position was weaker than Austria.
9. The Italian offensive of 1918 forced an Austrian retreat more successfully than had any Italian attacks.
10. By the time World War I ended in 1918, Italy had sustained a million casualties, more than in any war in its history.
11. More civilians were affected by World War I than by war.
12. Technological innovations made survival on the battlefront more difficult than earlier wars.
13. Bigger and better battleships and submarines revolutionized naval warfare.
14. Chemical warfare, more devastating than any form of warfare, was introduced.
15. Was the cost of rebuilding Europe higher than the war?
16. Italy's Prime Minister Vittorio Orlando, a delegate to the Paris peace conference, opposed the peace plan more than any delegate.
17. Italy's primary goal was more nationalistic than the other Allies.
18. Italy wanted control of the former Austrian territories more than anything.
19. Orlando took a greater interest in the punishment of Germany than in any other issue discussed at the peace conference.
20. The Italian delegation only walked out of the peace negotiations.

Answers: Exercise 3

Answers may vary, but suggestions are given below.

1. The First World War, which involved all the major powers of Europe as well as the United States, produced carnage greater than that of any previous war.
2. The use of aircraft, tanks, and machine guns made the Great War more impersonal than any previous war.
3. Some observers believed that British and French soldiers fought more bravely than anyone else.
4. The Central Powers—Germany, Austria-Hungary, and the Ottoman Empire—were united as much by geography as by anything else.
5. When the fighting began in May 1915, Italy's army was less prepared than that of France or Britain.
6. For months the Alps, more than any other place in Europe, were the site of many battles between the Italian and the Austrian forces.
7. correct
8. After a devastating battle in 1917, Italy's position was weaker than Austria's.
9. The Italian offensive of 1918 forced an Austrian retreat more successfully than had any other Italian attack.
10. By the time World War I ended in 1918, Italy had sustained a million casualties, more than in any other war in its history.
11. More civilians were affected by World War I than by any previous war.
12. Technological innovations made survival on the battlefront more difficult than it had been in earlier wars.
13. correct
14. Chemical warfare, more devastating than any other form of warfare, was introduced.
15. Was the cost of rebuilding Europe higher than the cost of the war?
16. Italy's Prime Minister Vittorio Orlando, a delegate to the Paris peace conference, opposed the peace plan more than did any other delegate.
17. Italy's primary goal was more nationalistic than that of the other Allies.
18. Italy wanted control of the former Austrian territories more than anything else.
19. correct
20. Only the Italian delegation walked out of the peace negotiations.

Practice and Assess

Answers: Exercise 4

1. good—adjective
2. well—adverb
3. badly—adverb
4. well—adverb
5. well—adverb
6. well—adverb
7. badly—adverb
8. bad—adjective
9. badly—adverb
10. good—adjective

Answers: Exercise 5

Answers may vary, but some suggestions are given below.

1. Most novice climbers don't know anything about the basics of mountaineering.
2. Hiking is the least perilous type of mountaineering; it is no riskier than walking.
3. Rock climbing and ice climbing should not be undertaken by any beginner without expert supervision.
4. Mixed climbing, a combination of rock climbing and ice climbing, is not meant for novices either.
5. correct
6. It would be unusual for beginning climbers not to feel jitters when they start.
7. Except when climbing on ice or snow, no more than two climbers should ever be tied together on a single rope.
8. Climbing instructors never waste any time before explaining the proper use of pitons and carabiners in securing the rope.
9. correct
10. Most careful climbers do not have serious mishaps.

Using Modifiers Correctly

Review: Exercise 4   Choosing the Correct Modifier

The following sentences describe a mountain-climbing expedition that Alessandro and his friend Rafi took before Alessandro enlisted in the Italian navy. For each sentence, write the correct form of the modifier in parentheses. Then write whether the modifier is used as an *adjective* or an *adverb*.

1. Leaving the train, Alessandro and Rafi felt (good/well) about the next day's climb.
2. They carried enough equipment to ensure that the expedition would go (good/well).
3. A novice climber, Rafi needed Alessandro's expertise (bad/badly) to keep him safe.
4. Soon, however, Rafi was climbing safely and (well/good).
5. The climbers deftly hammered small spikes, called pitons, into the cliff, for it was essential that the pitons hold (good/well).
6. Once the pitons seemed to have been placed in the rock (good/well), the climbers snapped clips—carabiners—to the pitons.
7. The safety line they slung through the carabiners would not snag (bad/badly) on outcroppings of rock.
8. With Alessandro in the lead, they inched up the face of the cliff, sidestepping any footholds that looked (bad/badly).
9. Their muscles were aching (bad/badly) as they hammered pitons into the cliff.
10. Since they were feeling (good/well) about the day's work, they rested and planned the next day's climb.

Review: Exercise 5   Correcting Double Negatives

Rewrite each sentence, eliminating any double negatives. If a sentence contains no errors, write *correct*.

1. Most novice climbers don't know nothing about the basics of mountaineering.
2. Hiking is the least perilous type of mountaineering; it is not no riskier than walking.
3. Rock climbing and ice climbing should not be undertaken by no beginner without expert supervision.
4. Mixed climbing, a combination of rock climbing and ice climbing, is not meant for novices neither.
5. Climbers not wearing boots with cleated rubber soles should not begin the ascent.
6. It would be unusual for beginning climbers not to feel no jitters when they start.
7. Except when climbing on ice or snow, no more than two climbers should never be tied together on a single rope.
8. Climbing instructors never waste no time before explaining the proper use of pitons and carabiners in securing the rope.
9. Nonclimbers never have any idea of the tight teamwork climbers must develop.
10. Most careful climbers do not have hardly any serious mishaps.

Review: Exercise 6 — Correcting Misplaced Modifiers

The following sentences describe the scene from *A Soldier of the Great War* that follows the passage featured in this workshop. Rewrite each sentence, correcting misplaced modifiers. If a sentence has no errors, write *correct*.

SAMPLE   Shining silently in the cold night air, Alessandro gazed at the stars.
ANSWER   Alessandro gazed at the stars shining silently in the cold night air.

1. Alessandro was constantly on the lookout for dangerous crevasses walking across the glacier.
2. Possibly obscuring deep chasms, he avoided any thin patches of snow.
3. The bleak vista lay before this lonely man stretching into miles of darkness.
4. The danger of crevasses recently cut into the glacier haunted the soldier.
5. He ran across the icy surface burning with fierce determination.
6. Perfectly hidden from view by a snowdrift, Alessandro narrowly avoided a pair of crevasses.
7. Alessandro leaped into the air beyond the point of feeling fear.
8. Alessandro completely lost all sense of time falling into a wide canyon.
9. Miraculously, he landed on a soft bed of snow in a kneeling position.
10. When he found that he had only survived by a miracle, he began to laugh.

Review: Exercise 7 — Correcting Dangling Modifiers

The following sentences are based on the passage from *A Soldier of the Great War*. Rewrite the sentences, correcting each dangling modifier. In some cases you may need to reword the entire sentence. If a sentence contains no errors, write *correct*.

SAMPLE   After crossing six ridges, trees did not appear again until he was in Italy.
ANSWER   After crossing six ridges, he did not see trees again until he was in Italy.

1. Leaving the forest, a world of glaciated mountains stretched toward the horizon.
2. Rising vast in the distance, Alessandro was amazed by the mountains' immensity.
3. Tricked by the play of light and shadow, the mountains seemed distant to him.
4. Surveying the snow-filled pastures, hay-filled cabins dotted the landscape.
5. Offering shelter from the wind, Alessandro chose the cabin farthest from any settlement.
6. After walking for several hours after dusk, Alessandro stopped at the edge of the meadows.
7. Feeling the rivers of cold air, the proximity of the glacier was certain.
8. Rumbling almost imperceptibly, he was awed by its tremendous power.
9. Hoisting his body upward, the ice wall was scaled only with great difficulty.
10. Given a combination of luck and skill and perseverance, the peaks would be reachable by daylight.

Grammar Review   **685**

Answers: Exercise 6

Answers may vary, but some suggestions are given below.
1. Walking across the glacier, Alessandro was constantly on the lookout for dangerous crevasses.
2. He avoided any thin patches of snow possibly obscuring deep chasms.
3. The bleak vista, stretching into miles of darkness, lay before this lonely man.
4. correct
5. Burning with fierce determination, he ran across the icy surface.
6. Alessandro narrowly avoided a pair of crevasses perfectly hidden from view by a snowdrift.
7. Beyond the point of feeling fear, Alessandro leaped into the air.
8. Falling into a wide canyon, Alessandro completely lost all sense of time.
9. Miraculously, he landed in a kneeling position in a soft bed of snow.
10. When he found that he had survived only by a miracle, he began to laugh.

Answers: Exercise 7

Answers will vary, but some suggestions are given below.
1. Leaving the forest, he found a world of glaciated mountains stretching toward the horizon.
2. Alessandro was amazed by the mountain's immensity rising vast in the distance.
3. Tricked by the play of light and shadow, Alessandro thought the mountains were distant.
4. Surveying the snow-filled pastures, he saw hay-filled cabins dotting the landscape.
5. Seeking shelter from the wind, Alessandro chose the cabin farthest from any settlement.
6. correct
7. Feeling the rivers of cold air, Alessandro was certain of the glacier's proximity.
8. Hearing almost imperceptible rumbles, he was awed by its tremendous power.
9. Hoisting his body upward, he scaled the ice wall only with great difficulty.
10. Given a combination of luck and skill and perseverance, he would reach the peaks by daylight.

Practice and Assess

Answers: Exercise 8

Answers may vary slightly, but some suggestions are given below.

1. Making their plans early, Alessandro and Rafi began their preparations for their mountain climbing expedition.
2. Wanting to be sure they had nourishment for their journey, they packed lightweight, high-energy foods.
3. Rafi, who was not used to such heights, was an inexperienced climber, but Alessandro was ready to help him.
4. Novice climbers climbing alone could easily lose their footing and very possibly their lives.
5. Not knowing how much Rafi remembered, Alessandro reviewed the use of pitons and carabiners with Rafi.
6. Because he was more competent, Alessandro was in the lead, and Rafi followed behind him.
7. By letting Alessandro go first, Rafi could watch his climbing strategies and copy them.
8. Checking their footholds carefully, Alessandro and Rafi inched their way up the face of the first cliff.
9. The expedition that they had dreamed about for so long was more of a physical challenge than the two men had first believed.
10. The two men were extremely pleased at the progress they had made in a day filled with challenges.

Answers: Exercise 9
Proofreading

This proofreading activity provides editing practice with (1) current or previous units' skills, (2) the **Troubleshooter** errors, and (3) spelling errors. Students should be able to complete the exercise by referring to the units, the **Troubleshooter,** and a dictionary. (Note: A run-on sentence counts as one error.)

Error (Type of Error)
1. (1830–1902) at the age of two was brought by his parents to . . . (misplaced modifier)
2. twenty-three, he (sentence fragment)
3. returned (verb tense)
4. Becoming interested in landscape painting, he . . . (misplaced modifier)

Review: Exercise 8   Adding Modifiers to Sentences

The following sentences describe Alessandro and his friend Rafi's mountain-climbing expedition. Rewrite the sentences, adding modifiers as indicated in parentheses. (There will be more than one way to rewrite some sentences.)

1. Alessandro and Rafi began their preparations for their mountain climbing expedition. (Add *making their plans early.*)
2. They packed lightweight, high-energy foods. (Add *wanting to be sure they had nourishment for their journey.*)
3. Rafi was an inexperienced climber, but Alessandro was ready to help him. (Add *who was not used to such heights.*)
4. Novice climbers could easily lose their footing and very possibly their lives. (Add *climbing alone.*)
5. Alessandro reviewed the use of pitons and carabiners with Rafi. (Add *not knowing how much Rafi remembered.*)
6. Alessandro was in the lead, and Rafi followed behind him. (Add *because he was more competent.*)
7. Rafi could watch Alessandro's climbing strategies and copy them. (Add *by letting him go first.*)
8. Alessandro and Rafi inched their way up the face of the first cliff. (Add *checking their footholds carefully.*)
9. The expedition was more of a physical challenge than the two men had first believed. (Add *that they had dreamed about for so long.*)
10. The two men were extremely pleased at the progress they had made in a day. (Add *filled with challenges.*)

Review: Exercise 9

Proofreading

The following passage describes the artist Albert Bierstadt, whose painting appears on the opposite page. Rewrite the passage, correcting the errors in spelling, grammar, and usage. Add any missing punctuation. There are twenty-five errors.

Albert Bierstadt

[1]Born in Germany, Albert Bierstadt (1830-1902) was brought by his parents at the age of two to New Bedford, Massachusetts. [2]When he was twenty-three. [3]He returns to Germany to study painting. [4]He often traveled to Switzerland and Italy and made countless sketches of mountain landscapes becoming intrested in landscape painting.

Albert Bierstadt, *Sunrise on the Matterhorn,* **after 1875**

⁵Bierstadt returned to New Bedford in 1857 and the next year he joined a surveying expedition to the Rocky Mountains. ⁶Their size and beauty overwhelmed him, he made many pencil and oil sketches. ⁷When he was twenty-nine, moved to New York City and set up a studio there. ⁸His huge landscape paintings commanded higher prices than those of anyone.

⁹His training in Europe maked him a master at drawing and oil sketching. ¹⁰Making preliminary sketches from nature, his works were completed in the studio.

¹¹Like many of his fellow artists, the unspoiled grandeur of the West was a frequent subject of Bierstadt's paintings. ¹²His romantic paintings of the West become a symbol of national pride.

¹³Famous for his unusual technique, Bierstadt's paintings combined enormous scale with the delicatest suggestions of light and shadow. ¹⁴The painting on this page which was based on sketches made during his travels through the Alps, is typical of his' style. ¹⁵The delicately lit peek looks least real than the trees in the foreground.

¹⁶The hero in Mark Helprin's story crosses the Swiss Alps wanting bad to return home. ¹⁷Here Bierstadt portrays one of the most grand of all the Swiss mountins the Matterhorn. ¹⁸Does the painting remind you of Helprin's description of the "trick of light and shadow" that can make the Alps appear to be more distanter and more unreachable than they really are?

Grammar Review **687**

Using Modifiers Correctly

Answers: Exercise 9 (continued)
Proofreading

Error (Type of Error)

5. 1857, (run-on sentence)
6. him. He *or* him; *or* him, and (run-on sentence)
7. twenty-nine, he moved (sentence fragment)
8. anyone else (incomplete comparison)
9. made (verb form)
10. nature, he completed his works in (dangling modifier)
11. artists, Bierstadt used the unspoiled grandeur of the West as a frequent subject of his paintings. (dangling modifier)
12. became (verb form)
13. technique, Bierstadt combined [Delete *paintings.*] (dangling modifier) most delicate (incorrect superlative degree)
14. page, (nonessential adjective clause) his (possessive pronoun)
15. peak (spelling) less real (comparative degree)
16. Wanting . . . home, the hero . . . Alps. (misplaced modifier) badly (adverb)
17. the grandest (superlative degree) mountains (spelling) mountains, (nonessential appositive)
18. more distant (double comparison)

Viewing the Art

Albert Bierstadt, *Sunrise on the Matterhorn* (after 1875)

Sunrise on the Matterhorn recalls the great European landscape paintings of the nineteenth century. Like the English painter John Constable, Bierstadt romanticizes nature and invests it with spiritual qualities. Like Bier- stadt, Mark Helprin is a romantic. As the romantic writers of the nineteenth century did before him, he celebrates both nature and the individual. Ask students to discuss those elements of *Sunrise on the Matterhorn* that they think reflect the romantic atmosphere that Helprin has created.

Practice and Assess

Answers: Exercise 10
Mixed Review

Sentences will vary, but some suggestions are given below.

1. Helprin performed well both as a scholar and as a soldier before turning to a literary career.
2. After settling in Brooklyn, Helprin made writing his primary pursuit.
3. The *New Yorker* magazine did not accept any of the first twelve stories that Helprin submitted.
4. The reviews of his third book, *Ellis Island and Other Stories,* were more positive than those of his first book, *A Dove of the East and Other Stories.*
5. To Helprin most romantic fantasies are more vivid than most realistic tales.
6. Of all of Helprin's books, only *Ellis Island and Other Stories* received the National Jewish Book Award.
7. Helprin's novel *Winter's Tale* describes the exploits of a flying horse racing over frozen winter landscapes.
8. The heroes of Helprin's novels are adventurers with great courage and virtue who defeat evil beings.
9. In *Winter's Tale,* the hero is pursued by creatures called Short Tails, who are more evil than anyone else.
10. A skilled mountain climber, Helprin often depicts in his novels courageous mountaineers on treacherous slopes.

Close

Write the following sentence on the board:
The commuters climbed aboard the bus.

Have the students communicate two or more different moods by using different modifiers in this sentence. For example:

Talking and laughing, the excited commuters climbed quickly aboard the bus.

Dragging their feet and their briefcases, the exhausted commuters climbed wearily aboard the bus.

Direct students to share their sentences with a partner. Each pair can then select one of their sentences to share with the class.

Mixed Review

Read the following brief biography of Mark Helprin. Then rewrite the sentences that follow it, correcting any errors in the use of modifiers. If you need to obtain information to complete your sentences, consult the biography.

Mark Helprin

Born in 1947 in New York City, Mark Helprin attended Harvard University, earning a bachelor's degree in 1969 and a master's degree in Middle Eastern studies in 1972. He then joined the Israeli armed forces, where he served in the infantry and in an elite unit of the air force. After further study at Princeton and Oxford universities, he moved to Brooklyn and began to write fiction. Helprin submitted a dozen stories to the *New Yorker* magazine before two stories were finally accepted at once. In 1975 he published *A Dove of the East and Other Stories;* two years later his first novel appeared. *Ellis Island and Other Stories* won the National Jewish Book Award in 1982, and Helprin was also awarded the prestigious Prix de Rome by the Institute for Arts and Letters. Helprin published his popular novel *Winter's Tale* in 1983. *A Soldier of the Great War* was published in 1991.

1. Helprin performed good as both a scholar and a soldier before turning to a literary career.
2. After settling in Brooklyn, writing became his primary pursuit.
3. The *New Yorker* magazine did not accept none of the first twelve stories that Helprin submitted.
4. The reviews of his third book, *Ellis Island and Other Stories,* were more positive than his first book, *A Dove of the East and Other Stories.*
5. Generally speaking, to Helprin most romantic fantasies are more vivider than most realistic tales.
6. Of all of Helprin's books, *Ellis Island and Other Stories* only received the National Jewish Book Award.
7. Racing over frozen winter landscapes, Helprin's novel *Winter's Tale* describes the exploits of a flying horse.
8. The heroes of Helprin's novels are adventurers who defeat evil beings with great courage and virtue.
9. In *Winter's Tale,* the hero is pursued by creatures called Short Tails, who are eviller than anyone.
10. A skilled mountain climber, Helprin's novels often depict courageous mountaineers on treacherous slopes.

Using Modifiers Correctly

Writing Application

Modifiers in Writing

Good writers use modifiers correctly and position them carefully to make their meaning clear. Notice, for example, the use of the italicized modifiers in this passage from "Tuesday Siesta," a short story by Gabriel García Márquez that has been translated into English by J. S. Bernstein.

> *Keeping to the protective shade of the almond trees,* the woman and the girl entered the town without disturbing the siesta. They went directly to the parish house. The woman scratched the metal grating *on the door* with her fingernail, waited a moment, and scratched again. An electric fan was humming inside. They did not hear the steps. They *hardly* heard the slight creaking of a door, and immediately a cautious voice, right next to the metal grating. . . .

Techniques with Modifiers

Try to apply some of García Márquez's techniques when you write and revise.

❶ Place modifiers as close as possible to the words they modify.

MISPLACED MODIFIER Keeping to the protective shade of the almond trees, *the town . . .*

GARCÍA MÁRQUEZ'S VERSION Keeping to the protective shade of the almond trees, *the woman and the girl . . .*

❷ Will moving a modifier make your meaning clearer? Compare the two positions of the prepositional phrase *on the door.*

CONFUSING PLACEMENT *On the door,* the woman scratched the metal grating with her fingernail . . .

GARCÍA MÁRQUEZ'S VERSION The woman scratched the metal grating *on the door* with her fingernail . . .

❸ Try not to create double negatives, especially with *hardly* and *scarcely.*

DOUBLE NEGATIVE They *couldn't hardly* hear the slight creaking . . .

GARCÍA MÁRQUEZ'S VERSION They *hardly* heard the slight creaking . . .

TIME For more about the writing process, see TIME Facing the Blank Page, pp. 109–119

Using Modifiers Correctly

Practice

On your paper, practice these techniques by revising the following paragraphs.

Born in Aracataca, Colombia, many of Gabriel García Márquez's stories and novels are set in small Latin American towns. *One Hundred Years of Solitude* portrays the history of the remote town of Macondo, one of the most popular books ever published in the Spanish-speaking world. Many critics, symbolizing the turbulence of Latin American politics, think Macondo and the people living there eccentric.

Magical and at times surreal, the author has a distinct writing style. After winning the Nobel Prize in literature, many new readers from all over the world were attracted to García Márquez. The author, who, in my opinion, doesn't have no patience for human rights abuses, has also won praise worldwide for his humanitarian efforts.

Writing Application **689**

Writing Application

Techniques with Modifiers

Discuss the revisions of the sentences on this page to clarify meaning and to correct misuse of modifiers. Then choose another piece of writing—the paragraphs on student pages 686–687, for example—and have students discuss their revisions of the sentences in this selection.

Practice

The answers to this challenging and enriching activity will vary. Refer to Techniques with Modifiers as you evaluate student choices. Sentences should be revised so that modifiers appear close to the words they modify.

Sample:
Born in Aracataca, Colombia, the writer Gabriel García Márquez set many of his stories and novels in small Latin American towns. *One Hundred Years of Solitude,* one of the most popular books ever published in the Spanish-speaking world, portrays the history of the remote town of Macondo. Many critics think that Macondo and the eccentric people who live there symbolize the turbulence of Latin American politics.

The author has a distinctive writing style which has been described as magical and at times surreal. After García Márquez won the Nobel Prize in literature, many new readers from all over the world were attracted to his writings. The author, who, in my opinion, has no patience for human rights abuses, has also won praise worldwide for his humanitarian efforts.

✔ ASSESSMENT OPTIONS

📁 *Tests with Answer Key & Rubrics*
Unit 18 Pretest, pp. 63–64
Unit 18 Mastery Test, pp. 65–66

💾 *Testmaker*
Unit 18 Pretest
Unit 18 Mastery Test

📼 *MindJogger Videoquizzes*

You may wish to administer the Unit 18 Mastery Test at this point.

689

Objectives

- To develop an understanding of and an ability to recognize and correct common usage problems, including the confusion of certain similar words, such as *accept* and *except,* and the use of incorrect words and terms, such as *irregardless* and *this here.*
- To demonstrate control over usage problems by editing sentences using the Usage glossary to find answers to specific usage problems.

✔ ASSESSMENT OPTIONS

📂 *Tests with Answer Key & Rubrics*
Unit 19 Pretest, pp. 67–68
Unit 19 Mastery Test, pp. 69–70

💾 *Testmaker*
Unit 19 Pretest
Unit 19 Mastery Test

You may wish to administer the Unit 19 Pretest at this point.

Key to Ability Levels

L1 Level 1 activities are within the basic ability range of students.

L2 Level 2 activities are within the ability range of average students.

L2 Level 3 activities are more challenging activities.

UNIT

19 Usage Glossary

Usage Glossary	*691*
Grammar Review	*704*
Writing Application	*711*

690

Resource Manager

Planning Resources
- *Lesson Plans*
- *Block Scheduling*

 Transparencies
- *Bellringer*
- *Daily Language Practice*
- *Two-Minute Skill Drill*

📂 **Other Print Resources**
- *Grammar and Composition Handbook*

- *Grammar Enrichment*
- *Grammar Practice*
- *Grammar Reteaching*
- *Grammar Workbook*
- *Tests with Answer Key and Rubrics*

📺 **Video**
- *MindJogger Videoquizzes*

💾 **Software**
- *Interactive Grammar and Language Workbook*
- *Language Arts PASS*
- *Presentation Plus!*
- *Testmaker*
- *Writer's Choice Puzzlemaker*

 Web Sites
- *writerschoice.glencoe.com*

19 Usage Glossary

Certain usages of English are preferred by most educated speakers and writers. The glossary in this unit presents some aspects of preferred usage that are particularly troublesome. It shows you how to choose between words that are often confused, and it advises you to avoid certain words and expressions when you are speaking or writing for school or business.

a, an The article *a* is used when the word that follows begins with a consonant sound: *a ticket.* Words that begin with a sounded *h* or the "yew" sound are thus also preceded by *a: a hurricane, a eulogy, a uniform.* The article *an* is used when the word that follows begins with a vowel sound or an unsounded *h: an umbrella, an hour.*

a lot, alot This expression, which means "a large amount," should always be written as two words. Some authorities advise that you avoid it completely in formal English.

    A lot of television programs show too much violence.

a while, awhile An article and a noun form the expression *a while.* Often the preposition *in* or *for* precedes *a while,* forming a prepositional phrase. The single word *awhile* is an adverb.

    She'll speak in **a while.**
    She'll speak for **a while.**
    She'll speak **awhile** before showing the filmstrip.

accept, except *Accept* is a verb meaning "to receive" or "to agree to." *Except* is occasionally used as a verb or a conjunction, but much more frequently it is used as a preposition meaning "but."

    Miki will **accept** the invitation to lunch.
    The restaurant is open every day **except** Monday. [preposition]

affect, effect *Affect* is a verb meaning "to cause a change in" or "to influence." *Effect* as a verb means "to bring about" or "to accomplish." As a noun *effect* means "result" or "that which has been brought about."

    Daily exercise will **affect** your health. [verb meaning "cause a change in"]
    Daily exercise will **effect** a positive change in your health. [verb meaning "bring about"]
    Daily exercise will have a good **effect** on your health. [noun meaning "result"]

Usage Glossary **691**

Focus

Lesson Overview

Objective

- To understand the difference between words that are often confused and to know that certain words and expressions should be avoided in formal English

🔔 Bellringer
Daily Language Activity

When students enter the classroom, have this assignment on the board: *Why is an used in the passage below instead of a?* (Answer: *An* precedes a vowel sound.) *Why is accepted used instead of excepted?* (Answer: *Accepted* is a verb meaning "agreed to.")

See also 📖 *Daily Language Practice*

> It had always been an unprogressive school, so the Mission authorities decided to send a young and energetic man to run it. Obi accepted this responsibility with enthusiasm.
>
> —Chinua Achebe, "Dead Men's Path"

Teach

☑ Teaching Tip

Effect is seldom used as a verb. The real problem is that students confuse the verb *affect,* "to cause a change," with the noun *effect,* "result." Here is a mnemonic trick that may help students remember that *effect* is a noun: Remember the phrase *the effect.* Only nouns can follow the definite article, and the *e* in *the* reminds us that the noun *effect* begins with the letter *e.*

Resource Manager

Planning Resources
- *Lesson Plans*

📖 **Transparencies**
- *Bellringer*
- *Daily Language Practice*
- *Two-Minute Skill Drill*

📂 **Other Print Resources**
- *Grammar and Composition Handbook*

Teach

☑ **Teaching Tip**

To introduce students to the difference between standard and nonstandard English, invite them to look up the words *ain't* and *alright* in a dictionary. Ask them to study any usage notes given with the word and to explain the word's use or misuse in their own words.

☑ **Grammar Tip**

Point out that *all ready* in the example sentence functions as a predicate adjective, whereas *already* functions as an adverb.

⇄ **Cross-reference: Dictionary**

Point out that a dictionary is a good source for discovering the accepted usage of a word. Even though some dictionaries might list *alright* as a word, they also indicate that it is a disputed spelling. For more information on how to use the dictionary, see Unit 24, Using Dictionaries, pp. 811–817.

ain't   *Ain't* is never used in formal speaking or writing unless you are quoting the exact words of a character or real person. Instead of using *ain't*, say or write, *I am not; she is not;* and so on.

all ready, already   *All ready,* written as two words, is an adjective phrase that means "completely ready." *Already,* written as one word, is an adverb that means "before" or "by this time."

> Lloyd was **all ready** to go at seven o'clock, but his friends had **already** left without him.

all right, alright   The expression *all right* should be written as two words. Although some dictionaries acknowledge the existence of the single word *alright,* this spelling is not generally accepted as correct.

> I hope the baby is **all right.**

all the farther, all the faster   These are informal expressions. It is much better to use *as far as* and *as fast as* in speaking and writing.

> Reno was **as far as** I wanted to go.
> Is this **as fast as** you can walk?

all together, altogether   *All together* means "in a group." *Altogether* is an adverb meaning "completely" or "on the whole."

> The actors joined hands and took a bow **all together.**
> **Altogether** it was a very good play.

amount, number   *Amount* and *number* both refer to quantity, but *amount* refers to nouns that cannot be counted, and *number* refers to nouns that can be counted.

> A huge **amount** of lava spurted from the erupting volcano.
> A **number** of volcanoes are still active today.

bad, badly   See Unit 18.

being as, being that   Although these expressions sometimes replace *because* or *since* in informal conversation, you should always avoid them in formal speaking and writing.

> **Because** bears are hibernators, they sleep during the winter.
> **Since** the movie has already started, let's come back later.

692   Unit 19 Usage Glossary

Listening and Speaking

Using *A* and *An*

Students new to English may have difficulty with the indefinite articles *a* and *an.* Have students say words with and without an initial /h/ sound, such as *harp* and *honor,* to hear when to use *a* and when to use *an.* **L1**

beside, besides   *Beside* means "located at the side of." *Besides* is ordinarily used to mean "in addition to."

>The cat sat **beside** the refrigerator.

>**Besides** losing my gloves, I lost two buttons from my coat.

between, among   *Between* should generally be used when comparing one person or thing with another person or thing or with an entire group.

>It was difficult to choose **between** ice cream and pudding for dessert. [Two desserts are compared.]

>What is the difference **between** this opera and others by Verdi? [One opera is compared with the entire group of Verdi's operas.]

Among is generally used to show a relationship in which more than two persons or things are considered as a group.

>Tim's great-grandfather had lived **among** the Iroquois.

Exercise 1   **Making Usage Choices**

On your paper, write the correct word or expression from each pair in parentheses.

George Washington, Our First President

1. General George Washington fought with great determination for (a/an) independent United States.
2. As leader of the Continental Army, Washington tried to make sure his troops were (alright/all right), even though a great (number/amount) of them had poor health and low spirits.
3. Washington's courage and determination to win (affected/effected) his soldiers, improving their morale.
4. After his stunning victory, Washington rested (a while/awhile) at home at Mount Vernon on the Potomac River.
5. When delegates from the states met (all together/altogether) to write the Constitution, they chose Washington from (among/between) all the delegates to be their leader.
6. Washington was asked to (accept/except) the office of president after the vote of the first Electoral College.
7. President Washington was (all ready/already) widely known and respected when he took office.
8. As the first president of the United States, Washington did (a lot/a lot) to shape the duties of his office and to (affect/effect) a responsive administrative system to lead the nation forward.
9. (Beside/Besides) showing strong leadership, Washington went (all the farther/as far as) he could go to mold the young nation into a strong republic.
10. It (ain't/is not) at all surprising that the capital of the United States was named in honor of Washington.

Usage Glossary   **693**

Usage Glossary

Teach

☑ Teaching Tip

As stated on student page 692, *amount* is used with a class of nouns that name things that normally cannot be counted, like *lava.* Typical nouns that fall into this class are fluids (*a large amount of water*), materials (*a large amount of lumber*), gases (*a large amount of oxygen*), and particles (*a large amount of dust*). Nouns that cannot be counted are often called *noncount* nouns.

Most nouns, however, name things that can be counted—for example, one apple, two apples. These nouns are often called *count* nouns.

Practice and Assess

Answers: Exercise 1

1. an
2. all right, number
3. affected
4. awhile
5. all together, among
6. accept
7. already
8. a lot, effect
9. Besides, as far as
10. is not

Exploring Language

Using Prepositions

Have students give a brief oral description of something in the classroom, using the prepositions *beside, among, between,* and *underneath.* Suggest that students begin their sentences with a prepositional phrase (for example, *Beside the bookcase . . .*).

Teach

☑ **Teaching Tip**

In addition to *bring* and *take*, a number of other verb pairs have the meaning of movement toward or away from the speaker. For example, *go* means "move away from the speaker," and *come* means "move toward the speaker."

⇄ **Cross-reference: Usage**

For instruction and practice in the different forms of the irregular verb *lend*, refer students to Lesson 15.2, p. 587.

Listening and Speaking

Point out to students that although *can* is sometimes used in place of *may* in informal speech, a distinction should be made when speaking or writing formally. For more information about speaking and listening, see Unit 29, Listening and Speaking, pp. 882–889.

Usage Glossary

borrow, lend, loan   *Borrow* is the opposite of *lend*. The verb *borrow* means "to take something with the understanding that it must be returned." The verb *lend* means "to give something with the understanding that it will be returned." *Loan* should be used as a noun. Although *loan* may be used as a verb, *lend* is the preferred usage.

> Mari wants to **borrow** Victor's bicycle. [verb]
> Victor will **lend** her the bicycle if she puts air in the tires. [verb]
> Mari asked her aunt for a **loan** so she could buy a bicycle. [noun]

bring, take   *Bring* means "to carry from a distant place to a closer one." *Take* means "to carry from a nearby place to a more distant one."

> **Bring** the dog when you come to our house on Saturday.
> Don't **take** the dog when you go to the Bradleys'.

can, may   *Can* implies the ability to do something. *May* implies permission to do something or the possibility of doing it.

> You **may** go skiing this weekend if you **can** find a place to rent the necessary equipment.

can't hardly, can't scarcely   These expressions are considered double negatives, since *hardly* and *scarcely* by themselves have a negative meaning. Do not use *hardly* and *scarcely* with *not* or *-n't*.

> Juliana **can hardly** believe that she is taller than both her mother and her brother.
> I **can scarcely** hear my television program when my neighbor plays the drums.

could of, might of, must of, should of, would of   The helping verb *have*, not the preposition *of*, should follow *could, might, must, should,* or *would*.

> I **could have** danced all night.
> I **might have** won the singing award if I had not lost my voice the day before.

different from, different than   The expression *different from* is generally preferred to *different than*.

> Square dancing is **different from** ballroom dancing.

694   Unit 19 Usage Glossary

Exploring Language

Using the Glossary

Ask students to write sentences that include the words listed below. Have them use the Usage Glossary if they need help with a word's correct usage. **L2**

- *bring* and *take*
- *borrow* and *lend*
- *farther* and *further*
- *different from*
- *doesn't* and *don't*
- *emigrate* and *immigrate*

doesn't, don't   *Doesn't* is a contraction, or shortened form, of *does not* and is used with *she, he, it,* and singular nouns. *Don't* is a contraction of *do not* and is used with *I, you, we, they,* and plural nouns.

> My mother is one commuter who **doesn't** mind long bus rides.

> Most subway riders **don't** expect comfort.

emigrate, immigrate   *Emigrate* means "to leave one country to settle in another." *Immigrate* means "to enter a country in order to live there permanently." With *emigrate* use *from,* and with *immigrate* use *to* or *into.*

> Roberto will **emigrate** from Mexico this spring.

> He will **immigrate** to the United States.

farther, further   Use *farther* to refer to physical distance. Use *further* to refer to degree or time.

> Compact cars can go **farther** on a gallon of gasoline than full-sized cars can.

> Argue no **further**—I will do as you suggest!

Exercise 2   **Making Usage Choices**

On your paper, write the correct word or expression from each pair in parentheses.

Abraham Lincoln, a President of the People

1. As a young man, Abraham Lincoln had to (borrow/lend) money in order to open a store.
2. (Because/Being that) Lincoln always dealt fairly with people, he earned the nickname Honest Abe.
3. As president, Lincoln (could of/could have) isolated himself, but his style was (different from/different than) that of his predecessors.
4. If I had to choose (between/among) the Gettysburg Address and Lincoln's second inaugural address, I would choose the second inaugural address as the better speech.
5. Other issues (beside/besides) slavery divided the North and the South.
6. Toward the end of Lincoln's first term, the Civil War was going (badly/bad) for the North.
7. Many people who (emigrate/immigrate) to this country know all about Lincoln.
8. I (can't hardly/can hardly) believe that a great man like Lincoln was assassinated.
9. (Can/May) we borrow this biography of Lincoln? Ted (doesn't/don't) know where ours is.
10. Ann will (bring/take) the biography with her to my house on Sunday.

Teach

Vocabulary Link
Knowing the etymology of *emigrate* and *immigrate* may help students remember which word to use in a given sentence. Both are based on the Latin verb *migrare,* "to move." The *e-* in *emigrate* comes from *ex-* ("out of"); the *im-* in *immigrate* comes from *in-* ("into").

Cross-reference: Writing
For instruction and practice in using apostrophes with contractions such as *doesn't* and *don't,* refer students to Lesson 21.11, pp. 760–762.

Practice and Assess

Answers: Exercise 2
1. borrow
2. Because
3. could have, different from
4. between
5. besides
6. badly
7. immigrate
8. can hardly
9. May, doesn't
10. bring

Usage Glossary

Cooperative Learning

Using *Doesn't* and *Don't*
Pair less-proficient students with more-advanced learners to construct sentences using the contractions *doesn't* and *don't* according to the grammar rules on page 695. The more-advanced partners can read students' work and explain how to check for subject-verb agreement when using the contractions.

Teach

☑ **Teaching Tip**

Few and *fewer* modify count nouns; *little* and *less* modify noncount nouns. For a discussion of count and noncount nouns, see the commentary on teaching *amount* and *number* on p. 693 of the Teacher's Edition.

☑ **Teaching Tip**

Many verbs use adverbs or adverb phrases to complete their meaning. Some verbs—verbs of motion—use adverb phrases of movement: *We walked into the store.* In informal speech *into* is often contracted to *in: We walked in the store.* This phrase actually refers only to the area within the store, not to the act of walking from the outside to the inside.

⮂ **Cross-reference: Vocabulary**

For instruction and practice in how prefixes and suffixes affect word meaning, refer students to Unit 25, Vocabulary, pp. 818–826.

Usage Glossary

fewer, less   *Fewer* is generally used to refer to things or qualities that can be counted. *Less* is generally used to refer to things or qualities that cannot be counted. In addition, *less* is sometimes used with figures that are regarded as single amounts or single quantities.

> Why did **fewer** people come to this year's gallery opening than last year's?
>
> There is **less** space in the new building than there was in the old one.
>
> The rent in the new gallery is **less** than 400 dollars a month. [The money is treated as a single sum, not as individual dollars.]

good, well   See Unit 18.

had of   The word *of* should not be used between *had* and a past participle.

> I wish I **had known** that you were ill.

hanged, hung   When your meaning is "put to death by hanging," use *hanged.* In all other cases use *hung.*

> Although Benedict Arnold escaped punishment for his treachery in the American Revolution, his messenger, John André, was caught and **hanged** as a spy.
>
> Clara **hung** her oil painting in a prominent place in the school auditorium.

in, into   Use *in* to indicate location "inside" or "within" a place. Use *into* to indicate movement or direction to a place, generally from the outside to a point within.

> The onions were **in** the stew.
>
> The chef put the roast **into** the oven.

irregardless, regardless   Both the prefix *ir-* and the suffix *-less* have negative meanings. When they are used together, they produce a double negative, which is incorrect. Therefore, you should use *regardless* rather than *irregardless.*

> **Regardless** of the heat, the workers at the steel mill remained on the job.

this kind, these kinds   Because *kind* is singular, it is modified by the singular from *this* or *that. This* and *that* should also be used with the nouns *sort* and *type* (*this type, that type, this sort, that sort*). When the plural *kinds* is used, the plural form *these* or *those* modifies it. *These* and *those* should be used with the plural nouns *sorts* and *types.*

Exploring Language

Identifying/Correcting Errors

Write the following sentences on the board. Have students identify the usage problem in each sentence. Then ask them to use the information on page 696 to solve the problem and to correct each sentence.

- There are less whales than there used to be. (*fewer*)
- They rollerblade good. (*well*)
- If only I had of remembered my keys. (Delete *of.*)
- My, those roses smell really well. (*good*)

This kind of exercise is challenging.

These kinds of exercises are easy.

That sort of fruit is delicious.

Those sorts of fruits are delicious.

Exercise 3   Making Usage Choices

On your paper, write the correct word or expression from each pair in parentheses.

Theodore Roosevelt, a Man of Determination

1. Theodore Roosevelt's ancestors (emigrated/immigrated) from Holland during the 1640s, (bringing/taking) their belongings with them.
2. Roosevelt fought so (good/well) in the Spanish-American War that he gained national attention.
3. Many of President Roosevelt's policies were (different from/different than) those of his predecessor, William McKinley.
4. Roosevelt's conservation efforts went (farther/further) than those of any previous president; he (could have/could of) been an influence on nature groups.
5. An enthusiastic leader, Roosevelt put a great deal of energy (in/into) his work.
6. (These kind/These kinds) of qualities made Theodore Roosevelt a good president, (regardless/irregardless) of his faults.
7. If I (had/had of) known more about President Roosevelt, I might have seen the merit in much that he did.
8. Even those people who criticize Roosevelt (doesn't/don't) deny his great determination.
9. Theodore Roosevelt wrote no (less/fewer) than forty books.
10. Hunting trophies (hanged/hung) on the walls of his home.
11. Roosevelt was a president who had an unforgettable (effect/affect) on the people of the country.
12. They (could hardly/couldn't hardly) ignore his bravery.
13. Because he kept right on talking after he was shot while making a speech, people (accepted/excepted) him as a hero.
14. Some critics believe that Roosevelt (took/brought) many imperialistic viewpoints to the presidency.
15. Others say those viewpoints were not so (different from/different than) what many politicians of his day believed.

lay, lie   *Lay* means "to place" or "to put" something down. It always takes a direct object. *Lie* means "to recline" or "to be positioned"; it does not take an object.

Lay the bar of soap on the edge of the sink.

I like to **lie** under a warm blanket in the winter.

Occasionally there is confusion in sorting out the principal parts of these verbs. Notice the similarities and differences between the two.

Usage Glossary (sidebar)

Teach

Cross-reference: Grammar

For instruction and practice in demonstrative pronouns and their functions in a sentence, refer students to Lesson 10.2, p. 450.

Practice and Assess

Answers: Exercise 3

1. emigrated, taking
2. well
3. different from
4. further, could have
5. into
6. These kinds, regardless
7. had
8. don't
9. fewer
10. hung
11. effect
12. could hardly
13. accepted
14. brought
15. different from

Exploring Language

Using *Hanged*

Write the passage at the right on the board. Ask more advanced students to explain why *hanged* is used instead of *hung* as the past-tense form of *hang*. (Here *hanged* means "put to death by hanging.")

The man who was engaged in being hanged was apparently about thirty-five years of age.

—Ambrose Bierce, "An Occurrence at Owl Creek Bridge"

Teach

⇄ Cross-reference: Writing

Direct students' attention to Unit 3, Descriptive Writing, pp. 120–163. Remind the class that the function of imagery is to appeal to the reader's senses. One kind of imagery is the simile, a comparison (using the words *like* or *as*) between two seemingly unlike things. The use of similes can help make descriptions more vivid and more memorable.

☑ Grammar Tip

As can be a preposition, as in *He posed as a secret agent. As* may be preferable to *like* when preceding an elliptical clause: *She treated him as [she would treat] a son.*

Usage Glossary

BASE FORM	lay	lie
PRESENT PARTICIPLE	laying	lying
PAST FORM	laid	lay
PAST PARTICIPLE	laid	lain

He **laid** the bar of soap on the edge of the sink this morning.

Last night I **lay** under my warm blanket and slept soundly.

He had **laid** his toothbrush down beside the soap.

I have **lain** under those wonderful blankets on every chilly night.

learn, teach   *Learn* means "to gain knowledge." *Teach* means "to instruct" or "to give knowledge to."

I **learned** to speak Swahili.

My sister Midori **teaches** organic chemistry at Yale.

leave, let   *Leave* means "to go away" or "to depart." *Let* means "to allow" or "to permit."

Lian had to **leave** the auditorium.

The usher **let** her use the house telephone.

With the word *alone,* however, you may use either *let* or *leave.*

Leave me alone.   **Let** me alone.

like, as   Use *like,* a preposition, to introduce a prepositional phrase. Use *as,* a subordinating conjunction, to introduce a subordinate clause. Many experts believe that *like* should not be used before a clause in formal English.

Kathleen sings **like** an angel.

Maya thinks **as** I do in this matter.

loose, lose   Use the adjective *loose* when you mean "free," "not firmly attached," or "not fitting tightly." Use the verb *lose* when you mean "to have no longer," "to misplace," or "to fail to win."

That button is so **loose** I'm afraid I will **lose** it.

passed, past   *Passed* is the past and the past participle form of *to pass. Past* is used as an adjective, a noun, a preposition, or an adverb.

The challenger in the race **passed** the leader. [verb]

I paid many bills this **past** month. [adjective]

San Antonio is a city with an interesting **past.** [noun]

Make a sharp right turn **past** the bank. [preposition]

When did the bus drive **past?** [adverb]

698   Unit 19 Usage Glossary

⬤ MEETING INDIVIDUAL NEEDS   English Language Learners

Using *Lay* and *Lie*

For students new to English, the distinction between *lie* and *lay* may be particularly confusing. Model for students the word *lay* as the past participle of *lie* (Yesterday, I lay on the sofa) and as the present form of the verb *lay* (Lay that book on the table).

precede, proceed   Use *precede* when you mean "to go or come before." Use *proceed* when you mean "to continue" or "to move along."

In a dictionary, the entry for *airplane* **precedes** that for *airship*.

An airplane can **proceed** at a faster speed than an airship.

raise, rise   The verb *raise* means "to cause to move upward" or "to lift up." It always takes an object. The verb *rise* means "to get up" or "to go up." It is an intransitive verb and never takes an object.

We will **raise** the flag at six o'clock tomorrow morning.

They will **rise** at seven o'clock for exercise.

reason is, because   *Because* means "for the reason that." Therefore, do not use *because* after *reason is*. Use either *reason is that* or *because* alone.

The **reason** Leroy entered the marathon **is that** he enjoys long-distance running.

Leroy entered the marathon **because** he enjoys running.

respectfully, respectively   Use *respectfully* to mean "with respect." Use *respectively* to mean "in the order named."

The basketball champion shook the president's hand **respectfully.**

Ann and Arlene are my aunt and cousin, **respectively.**

says, said   *Says* is the third-person singular of the verb *say*. *Said* is the past tense of *say*. Do not use *says* when you mean *said*.

Enrique always **says** that he is just an average pianist.

Last week my teacher **said** I was ready to perform in public.

sit, set   *Sit* means "to be seated." It rarely takes an object. *Set* means "to put" or "to place," and it generally takes an object. When *set* is used to mean "the sun is going down," it does not take an object.

Before a show starts, many people find it hard to **sit** quietly.

The stage manager **set** the flowers on the mantelpiece.

The lighting designer saw to it that the sun **set** in a blaze of color.

than, then   *Than* is a conjunction. Use it in comparisons and to show exception.

Winston is more athletic **than** Carl.

The winner is none other **than** last year's champion, Rashida.

Usage Glossary   **699**

Usage Glossary (sidebar tab)

Teach

☑ Teaching Tip

There are several pairs of verbs *(lay, lie; raise, rise;* and *set, sit)* that have a special historic relationship to one another. The first verb in these three pairs is a causative verb—one whose basic meaning involves causing something to happen. For example, to *lay something* is "to cause it to *lie"*; to *raise something* is "to cause it to *rise"*; to *set something* is "to cause it to *sit.*"

Perhaps the easiest causative verb to explain is *fell* in the pair *fell, fall*. To *fell a tree* is "to cause it to *fall.*"

⇄ Cross-reference: Grammar

For instruction and practice in the present and past tenses of verbs, refer students to Lesson 15.3, pp. 589–592.

⇄ Cross-reference: Writing

Direct students' attention to Unit 5, Expository Writing, pp. 214–275. Remind the class that this kind of writing involves many cause-and-effect relationships. Impress on students that they should avoid repetitious prose by using either *because* or *the reason is that*, but not *the reason is because.*

Exploring Language

Using the Glossary

For those students still having difficulty using the glossary, help them complete the first few items of each exercise. Show them how they can find the correct answer by looking in the Usage Glossary under the word or words in each item or exercise. **L1**

Teach

Speaking and Listening

Remind students that some words sound strikingly similar to other words, especially in informal speech. Have students listen to the somewhat subtle difference between the words *than* and *then* in order to help them spell and use the two words correctly.

Two-Minute Skill Drill

Ask students to complete the following sentences by choosing the correct word in parentheses.

1. You don't need to (raise, rise) from your seat to answer.
2. (Sit, Set) your books on the desk.
3. Your dog is smaller (than, then) mine

See also *Two-Minute Skill Drill Transparency 19*

Practice and Assess

Answers: Exercise 4

1. that
2. learn
3. These kinds
4. raised
5. passed
6. lay
7. As
8. let
9. proceed
10. lose

Usage Glossary

Then is an adverb and is mostly used to refer to time. *Then* is also used to mean "soon afterward," "the time mentioned," "at another time," "for that reason," "in that case," and "besides."

> Sam was an inexperienced cook **then.**
> You bowl first, and **then** it will be my turn.
> By **then** we will be experts.
> If you won't try it, **then** I will.

this here, that there   Do not use *here* and *there* after *this* and *that*.

> I want to look at **this** newspaper.
> Please hand me **that** lantern.

where at   Do not use *at* after *where*.

> **Where** is Salt Lake City?

who, whom   See Unit 17.

Exercise 4 ▪ Making Usage Choices

On your paper, write the correct word or expression from each pair in parentheses.

John F. Kennedy, a Vibrant Leader

1. One reason John F. Kennedy is still admired is (because/that) he showed exceptional leadership qualities.
2. As a young man, Kennedy toured Europe, talking to heads of state to (learn/teach) their political views.
3. (These kind/These kinds) of situations helped prepare Kennedy for the presidency.
4. When Kennedy took office, he (raised/rised) the nation's morale with his inaugural address.
5. Kennedy declared that "the torch has been (passed/past) to a new generation of Americans."
6. Much of his charm (lay/laid) in his fine speaking ability.
7. (Like/As) you would expect from people interested in the arts, the Kennedys invited many performers to the White House.
8. During the missile crisis, Kennedy refused to (leave/let) the Soviet Union keep missiles on the island of Cuba.
9. Kennedy's decision to (precede/proceed) with a naval blockade of Cuba was a difficult one.
10. It was painful for Americans to (loose/lose) such a young and vibrant leader.

700   Unit 19 Usage Glossary

Exploring Language

Working Independently

Some students may complete all these exercises independently using the Usage Glossary to determine correct usage of the words. When they have finished, you may wish to review those items that students had problems understanding. **L3**

Exercise 5   Making Usage Choices

On your paper, write the correct word or expression from each pair in parentheses.

Franklin Roosevelt, a President During Hard Times

1. Many people (said/says) that Franklin Roosevelt was a great president.
2. After being stricken with polio in 1921, Roosevelt had to work harder (than/then) ever to maintain an active life.
3. (This/This here) paralysis struck when he was thirty-nine.
4. Warm Springs, Georgia, was (where he took treatments/where he took treatments at).
5. Roosevelt did not (set/sit) idly during the Depression.
6. People (who/whom) had lost everything looked to Roosevelt for hope.
7. The Tennessee Valley Authority and the Works Progress Administration were, (respectively/respectfully), a natural resources corporation and an employment program.
8. After Pearl Harbor was attacked, Roosevelt, (then/than) in his third term, led the country into World War II.
9. In February 1945 at Yalta, Roosevelt and Winston Churchill met with Joseph Stalin, with (who/whom) they planned Germany's defeat and its postwar occupation.
10. After Roosevelt's death on April 12, 1945, President Truman (respectively/respectfully) proclaimed a national day of mourning.

Exercise 6   Make Usage Choices

On your paper, write the correct word or expression from each pair in parentheses.

Puerto Rico, Past and Future

1. When Christopher Columbus reached Puerto Rico in 1493, the Arawak (already/all ready) inhabited the island.
2. Columbus and the Spanish explorer Ponce de León landed on the island in 1493 and 1508, (respectfully/respectively).
3. (Awhile/A while) after Ponce de León founded the island's first Spanish colony, he became its governor.
4. Spain ceded Puerto Rico to the United States in 1898, but nineteen years (passed/past) before Puerto Rico was designated a U.S. territory.
5. In 1952 (a/an) effort to establish the Commonwealth of Puerto Rico was approved by the citizens and government leaders of both Puerto Rico and the United States.
6. Since then the debate (between/among) Puerto Ricans has been about whether the island should be a commonwealth, an independent nation, or a state.
7. For decades, more Puerto Ricans have lived in the city of San Juan (then/than) in any other community on the island.
8. (Irregardless/Regardless) of the problems that occurred after World War II, Puerto Rico has one of the highest standards of living among the Caribbean islands.
9. Due to urbanization, (fewer/less) Puerto Ricans live in rural areas.
10. Perhaps (farther/further) debate about Puerto Rican statehood is inevitable.

Usage Glossary   **701**

Usage Glossary

Practice and Assess

Answers: Exercise 5
1. said
2. than
3. This
4. where he took treatments
5. sit
6. who
7. respectively
8. then
9. whom
10. respectfully

Answers: Exercise 6
1. already
2. respectively
3. Awhile
4. passed
5. an
6. among
7. than
8. Regardless
9. fewer
10. further

Cooperative Learning

Solving Grammar Questions

Divide the class into groups, pairing students new to English with more proficient students. Have a group member use the Usage Glossary to make up a question about usage for the group to answer. Then have the other group members find the answer in the glossary. Tell students to use only the Usage Glossary to make up their questions. **L1**

Practice and Assess

Answers: Exercise 7

1. a lot
2. aren't
3. number
4. can
5. different from
6. Besides
7. taught
8. loose
9. lies
10. different from
11. as far as
12. Because
13. this
14. could have
15. well
16. These kinds
17. number
18. beside
19. lie
20. borrow

Exercise 7   Making Usage Choices

On your paper, write the correct word or expression from each pair in parentheses.

Native American Place Names

1. I have found that (a lot/alot) of Americans don't know that many place names are derived from Native American languages.
2. If you (ain't/aren't) sure about the derivation of a place name, see if it is explained in a dictionary or an encyclopedia.
3. The (amount/number) of place names in the United States is more than 3.5 million.
4. We (can/may) make a list of Native American place names in our state.
5. Many place names aren't very (different than/different from) their source words.
6. (Beside/Besides) adopting tribal names, such as Dakota and Delaware, as place names, settlers often adopted descriptive Native American words, such as *yaphank,* which means "river bank" in Algonquian.
7. My trip to Meddybemps, Maine, (learned/taught) me two things: that the name comes from an Algonquian word meaning "plenty of alewives" and that an alewife is a type of small fish.
8. A (loose/lose) translation of the Ojibway word *kichi* is "big"; Kichi Lake, in Minnesota, received its name from the Ojibway word.
9. *Nebraska* is a Sioux word that means "a wide, flat river"; the word refers to the Platte River, which (lays/lies) in the southern part of the state.
10. Although the names of Pennawa Creek, Florida, and Penacook, New Hampshire, look similar, their meanings—"turkey" and "sloping place"—are quite (different from/different than) each other.
11. The Mississippi River is not as long as the Nile River or the Amazon River; the Gulf of Mexico is (all the farther/as far as) the Mississippi River goes.
12. (Because/Being as) so many Cherokee were forced to migrate to Oklahoma during the nineteenth century, Cherokee is a common place name in that state.
13. A town in Oklahoma is called Pawhuska; (this/this here) word means "white hair."
14. I've learned that the word *ponca* comes from *pa-bonga,* meaning "sacred leader," but I don't know how it (could have/could of) become the name of a town.
15. The Native Americans of Acoma, which is located on a mile-high mesa in New Mexico, named their pueblo (good/well); *acoma* means "sky city."
16. (These kind/These kinds) of place names appear to be among the oldest names in North America.
17. The large (amount/number) of lakes in Minnesota may be why the Dakota used the words *minne,* meaning "water," and *sota,* meaning "reflection of sky upon water," to name the region.
18. The banks (beside/besides) the Olentangy River in central Ohio are streaked in red; hence, the river has an Algonquian name meaning "place where paint is found."
19. The hills for which Massachusetts was named (lie/lay) near Massachusetts Bay.
20. May I (borrow/loan) your book so that I can research the name Nippersink?

Cooperative Learning

Writing Sentences for Usage

Have students work in pairs to make ten sentence frames. The words needed to complete each sentence frame should be in parentheses. Ask student pairs to exchange papers with another pair and complete the sentence frames with the correct usage of the word. Students should include the glossary page number where the answer can be found. Give students this example to help them set up their sentence frames.

- I found a tulip (*between, among*) the daffodils. **L2**

Exercise 8   Making Usage Choices

On your paper, write the correct word or expression from each pair in parentheses.

Spirituals

1. The first time I heard a spiritual, I was surprised by the (affect/effect) the music had on me.
2. I had heard that spirituals were known as sorrow songs, yet I didn't find the music (all together/altogether) sad.
3. In fact, the inspirational lyrics and haunting melody made my spirits (raise/rise).
4. My friends agree that these songs don't make them feel (bad/badly) but, rather, inspired and hopeful.
5. When I decided to do some research on spirituals, the first thing I did was to go (in/into) the library's audio room.
6. I then (preceded/proceeded) to locate such songs as "Go Down, Moses," "Michael, Row the Boat Ashore," and "Steal Away."
7. I decided to (sit/set) all my research books on the table and concentrate on the music.
8. Even now, I (can hardly/can't hardly) believe how inspiring I found these songs of hardship and faith in religious salvation.
9. If you listen closely to a spiritual, you (can/may) hear how the verses alternate with a refrain.
10. The lyrics of some spirituals express the singers' desire to have the cruel world (leave/let) them alone.
11. I listened to a tape of the singers Dock Reed and Vera Hall, (who/whom) researchers recorded in the 1930s and 1940s.
12. The recording was made with primitive equipment, so the sound quality is (alright/all right) but not excellent.
13. Before starting my research, I (had/had of) thought that spirituals originated in America.
14. Some people (doesn't/don't) believe spirituals originated here, since there are African elements in many of them.
15. Spirituals did not achieve international popularity until the Jubilee Singers, an American group from Fisk University, (brought/took) their act to Europe in the 1870s.
16. It (must of/must have) been quite an experience to hear those powerful songs sung by such beautiful voices.
17. By the early twentieth century, the spiritual had begun to be treated (like/as) a true artistic form: songs were published and performed by choral groups and symphony orchestras.
18. African Americans such as Paul Robeson and William Grant Still were (accepted/excepted) around the world as fine performers of spirituals.
19. The reason spirituals are an important part of our musical heritage is (because/that) they have influenced many other types of music, from folk to gospel.
20. Last week my friend Jeanine (says/said) that she would be going to the library to learn more about spirituals.

Practice and Assess

Answers: Exercise 8

1. effect
2. altogether
3. rise
4. bad
5. into
6. proceeded
7. set
8. can hardly
9. can
10. leave or let
11. whom
12. all right
13. had
14. don't
15. took
16. must have
17. as [Note: *As* is considered correct here because what follows is an elliptical clause. Nonetheless, a student may justifiably choose *like*.]
18. accepted
19. that
20. said

Close

Review with students how to use the Usage Glossary to find answers to their usage questions. Point out to students that they can use this glossary while they are writing, editing, or revising any writing assignments throughout the school year.

Cooperative Learning

Editing Previous Works

Invite students to use the Usage Glossary to edit a recently written composition, checking the glossary to resolve any questions they might have about standard usage. Have students work in groups of three or four, reviewing each other's work to see whether all the usage questions have been resolved. **L2**

Teach

About the Literature

Explain that the review features quotations about nature followed by usage items covered in the glossary. Ask a volunteer to read the quotations aloud. Have the rest of the class listen, respond, and evaluate whether the oral reading was appropriate for the content of each quotation. Student readers should use feedback to evaluate their effectiveness in presenting and to set goals for future presentations.

Next, ask students to focus on the highlighted words. Then ask them to try to formulate a rule governing the usage of each item.

Linking Grammar and Literature

Cooperative Learning

Ask groups of students to write a paragraph about nature, incorporating at least five of the following pairs of terms: *accept* and *except, affect* and *effect, borrow* and *lend, can* and *may, doesn't* and *don't, farther* and *further, good* and *well, leave* and *let, raise* and *rise,* and *than* and *then.* Then have each group read their paragraph aloud to the class. Encourage students to discuss whether the usage items are used correctly.

☑ Teaching Tip

Ask students to look up in the Usage Glossary each of the highlighted terms in the quotations. Discuss the rule, if there is one, that governs the usage of each particular item. Explain that while improper usage may be acceptable in everyday speech, it is usually unacceptable in formal writing. Point out that most writers strive to make proper usage choices.

UNIT 19 Grammar Review

USAGE GLOSSARY

The following quotations deal with different aspects of our relationship with nature. Conflicts with nature, the need for harmony with nature, and the wonders of nature are all discussed by poets and novelists. The quotations, some of which appear in translation, have been annotated to show usage items covered in this unit.

Usage Glossary

> **Literature Model**
>
> ## Quotations About Nature
>
> *The articles* a *used before a word beginning with a consonant and* an *used before a word beginning with an unsounded* h
>
> • To see a World in a Grain of Sand
> • And a Heaven in a Wild Flower,
> • Hold Infinity in the palm of your hand
> And Eternity in an hour.
>
> From "Auguries of Innocence" by William Blake
>
> *May used to suggest possibility*
>
> • It may be that the stars of heaven appear fair and pure simply because they are so far away from us, and we know nothing of their private life.
>
> From *The Romantic School* by Heinrich Heine, translated from the German
>
> *The intransitive verb* lie
>
> • The whole secret of the study of nature lies in learning how to use one's eyes.
>
> From *Nouvelles Lettres d'un Voyageur* by George Sand, translated from French
>
> *The conjunction* than *used in a comparison*
>
> • I like trees because they seem more resigned to the way they have to live than other things do.
>
> From *O Pioneers!* by Willa Cather
>
> *Doesn't used with a singular pronoun*
>
> • Something there is that doesn't love a wall,
> The sends the frozen-ground-swell under it
> And spills the upper boulders in the sun,
> And makes gaps even two can pass abreast.
>
> From "Mending Wall" by Robert Frost

704 Unit 19 Usage Glossary

Resource Manager

Planning Resources
• *Lesson Plans*

Other Print Resources
• *Grammar and Composition Handbook*
• *Grammar Workbook,* Lessons 65–69; Unit 10 Review; Cumulative Review: Units 1–10

> Surrounded by the voracity of nature, Aureliano and Amaranta Ursula continued cultivating the oregano and the begonias and defended their world with demarcations of quick lime, building the last trenches in the age-old war *between* man and ant.
>
> From *One Hundred Years of Solitude* by Gabriel García Márquez, translated from the Spanish by Gregory Rabassa

The preposition *between* used to show a relationship between two elements

> Mankind's true moral test, its fundamental test (which lies deeply buried from view), consists of its attitude towards those *who* are at its mercy: animals.
>
> From *The Unbearable Lightness of Being* by Milan Kundera, translated from the Czech by Michael Henry Heim

The relative pronoun *who* in the nominative case because it is the subject of a clause

Review: Exercise 1   Making Usage Choice

The following sentences describe the seasons of the year. On your paper, write the correct word or expression from each parentheses.

1. In many areas of this country, each season—spring, summer, autumn, or winter—is (different from/different than) every other season.
2. There is however, (less/fewer) difference in the seasons in the southern United States than in other regions.
3. In the spring, the geese fly by the thousands across the prairie sky, (emigrating/immigrating) from their southern winter habitat.
4. Thawing snow fills the streams and rivers with (a lot/alot) of water, sometimes bringing on flooding.
5. The warmth of summer (affects/effects) all plant life, bringing green lawns, buzzing insects, and brightly colored flowers.
6. By June most people have (hanged/hung) their sweaters and jackets back in the closet and are eagerly anticipating the hot summer months.
7. Warm summer weather invites youngsters everywhere to jump (in/into) swimming pools.
8. Summer (proceeds/precedes) the coming of autumn, when the weather usually turns cooler.
9. I wish you (could of/could have) seen the brilliant orange, red, and yellow colors of the autumn leaves in Vermont this year.
10. In the winter, all trees (accept/except) the evergreens are bare, brisk winds blow, winter storms leave a white carpet of snow, and streams and rivers freeze solid into thick layers of ice.

Grammar Review   **705**

Usage Glossary

Teach

☑ **Grammar Tip**

Review with students the usage of *who* and *whom*. Remind them that *who* can be used as the subject of a clause but never as an object. *Whom,* on the other hand, can be used as an object but never as the subject of a clause.

Practice and Assess

Answers: Exercise 1

1. different from
2. less
3. emigrating
4. a lot
5. affects
6. hung
7. into
8. precedes
9. could have
10. except

Practice and Assess

Answers: Exercise 2

1. Because
2. altogether
3. teach
4. number
5. Regardless
6. affected
7. respectively
8. Where
9. lose
10. already

Answers: Exercise 3

1. This
2. farther
3. as
4. lies
5. a
6. Farther
7. fewer
8. that
9. rise
10. among

Usage Glossary

Review: Exercise 2   Making Usage Choices

The following sentences describe endangered and extinct animals. On your paper, write the correct word or expression from each parentheses.

1. (Because/Being as) dinosaurs are so popular, people flock to museums to see their skeletons.
2. Dinosaurs roamed the earth for 120 million years (all together/altogether).
3. I wish someone would (learn/teach) me more about dinosaurs.
4. The (number/amount) of dinosaur species that populated the earth was greater than I had imagined.
5. (Irregardless/Regardless) of how many dinosaurs there once were, they all became extinct.
6. Many animals are (affected/effected) adversely when their habitat is altered.
7. The black rhinoceros and the giant panda, which roam over sub-Saharan Africa and China, (respectively/respectfully), are both endangered.
8. (Where at/Where) do grizzly bears, lynxes, and red wolves live?
9. If people are not careful, they might (loose/lose) these animals permanently.
10. Far too many animals have (already/all ready) become extinct, thus diminishing the world's biological resources and sometimes upsetting the delicate balance of nature.

Review: Exercise 3   Making Usage Choices

The following sentences discuss topics related to astronomy. On your paper, write the correct word or expression from each parentheses.

1. (This here/This) machine is a telescope, which is used to view the moon, stars, comets, planets, and other celestial bodies.
2. Scientists will travel (farther/further) than most other people will to get a good view of a total eclipse of the sun.
3. Earth revolves around the sun, just (like/as) the other eight major planets of our solar system do.
4. Our solar system (lies/lays) within one swirling arm of the Milky Way galaxy.
5. The Milky Way acquired its name from our view of it as (a/an) hazy, luminous, milk-like band of stars enveloping the night sky.
6. (Farther/Further) in space, beyond the Milky Way, lie perhaps 100 billion other galaxies.
7. The Milky Way galaxy alone has no (fewer/less) than 200 billion stars.
8. The reason stars appear to twinkle is (that/because) the turbulent motion of Earth's atmosphere distorts the light that comes from them.
9. The sun and the moon appear to (rise/raise) and set in the sky.
10. Perhaps one day we will be able to travel easily (between/among) the stars.

Review: Exercise 4 — Making Usage Choices

The following sentences relate to the study of ocean life. On your paper, write the correct word or expression from each parentheses.

1. Some people believe that life (don't/doesn't) exist in the icy depths of the oceans.
2. Oceanographers, however, (can't hardly/can hardly) enumerate the various kinds of life found in the oceans of the world.
3. You must (bring/take) special equipment with you when you explore the ocean depths.
4. (Beside/Besides) being the home of fish and mammals of normal size, the oceans are home for plankton, which are microscopic animals and plants.
5. On a television documentary I saw the other day, an oceanographer (says/said) that *plankton* is a Greek word meaning "wandering."
6. Plankton drifts through the upper levels of the sea rather (than/then) in the depths.
7. (These kind/These kinds) of living organisms become food for other marine life.
8. My cousin, (who/whom) I believe is an expert on ocean life, told me that many deep-sea fish have fantastic shapes.
9. I (should of/should have) joined my cousin on her last deep-sea adventure.
10. My cousin said that she always thought my idea of a deep-sea adventure was to (sit/set) my fishing line in the water and wait for a fish to bite.

Review: Exercise 5 — Making Usage Choices

The following sentences describe rain forests. On your paper, write the correct word or expression from each parentheses.

1. Many people feel that it is not (alright/all right) to exploit rain forests.
2. If care is not taken to preserve these forests, they will be gone after (a while/awhile).
3. Some plants seem to thrive (irregardless/regardless) of where they grow.
4. Plants that grow (well/good) on the forest floor are the same kind as those that thrive in dimly lighted buildings.
5. Far below the forest's green canopy, the ground is interlaced with streams and rivers formed in times (passed/past).
6. No one knows the exact (number/amount) of plants and insects in the rain forest.
7. If you travel to a rain forest, you will want to (bring/take) a camera with you to record on film the beauty of the extraordinary scenery.
8. I was able to capture the exquisite detail of the plants because my friend had (loaned/lent/borrowed) me a special, high-resolution camera.
9. Only after several years of training (can/may) a nature enthusiast identify many of the different forms of wildlife in a rain forest.
10. As I (preceded/proceeded) through the forest on my last visit, I encountered a band of monkeys rapidly making their way through the treetops.

Practice and Assess

Usage Glossary

Answers: Exercise 4

1. doesn't
2. can hardly
3. take
4. Besides
5. said
6. than
7. These kinds
8. who
9. should have
10. set

Answers: Exercise 5

1. all right
2. a while
3. regardless
4. well
5. past
6. number
7. take
8. lent
9. can
10. proceeded

Practice and Assess

Answers: Exercise 6

Sentences will vary. Samples:
- Mom said the dinner we made for her was especially good.
- Dan plays the piano extremely well.

Answers: Exercise 7
Proofreading

This proofreading activity provides editing practice with (1) the current or previous units' skills, (2) the **Troubleshooter** errors, and (3) spelling errors. Students should be able to complete the exercise by referring to the units, the **Troubleshooter,** and a dictionary. (Note: A run-on sentence counts as one error.)

Error (Type of Error)

1. Tiffany, a gem (nonessential appositive)
2. accepted (usage)
3. Tiffany's (singular possessive) past (usage)
4. this art (usage) was that the or This art movement came into being because. . . . (usage)
5. natural (spelling)
6. different from other (usage)
7. windows like the (usage)
8. opaque glass, (commas in a series)
9. would have contained (usage) more than (usage)
10. beading, (run-on sentence)
11. set (usage)
12. An increasing (usage) increasing number of (usage)
13. effects (usage)
14. explore (subject-verb agreement)
15. separate (spelling) yet we long (pronoun-antecedent agreement)
16. conflict between (usage) is reflected (subject-verb agreement) Tiffany's (singular possessive) window, (nonessential adjective clause) altogether (usage)

Usage Glossary

Review: Exercise 6 Writing Sentences with Correct Word Usage

Choose five of the pairs of words below. For each pair, write a sentence using each word.

bring/take	between/among
good/well	in/into
doesn't/don't	bad/badly
who/whom	lay/lie
fewer/less	farther/further

SAMPLE **a.** Our yard has *fewer* weeds this year than our neighbor's yard has.

ANSWER **b.** We have had *less* rainfall this year than we've had in several years.

Review: Exercise 7

Proofreading

The following passage describes the life and work of Louis Comfort Tiffany, whose stained-glass window is reproduced on the opposite page. Rewrite the passage, correcting the errors in spelling, grammar, and usage. Add any missing punctuation. There are twenty-five errors.

Louis Comfort Tiffany

[1]Louis Comfort Tiffany (1848–1933) was the son of Charles Lewis Tiffany a gem merchant and the founder of the famed Tiffany and Company, manufacturers of fine silverware. [2]The younger Tiffany became excepted as a designer of distinctive glass. [3]Louis Tiffanys' designs reflected the Art Nouveau style of the passed, particularly the late nineteenth century. [4]The reason this here art movement came into being was because the handcrafting of objects was being revitalized as a reaction against the intense industrial activity of the late 1800s. [5]The movement toward handcrafted objects was meant to give naturel beauty and artistic impact to ordinary objects. [6]Art Nouveau was different than other art forms because it characteristically used rounded edges and iridescent colors.

[7]Louis Tiffany began his career making stained-glass windows as the one shown on the opposite page. [8]He used many kinds of colored glass, including opaque glass opalescent glass, and "satin glass," which was developed around 1880. [9]Each piece of glass generally would of contained more then a single color or kind of decoration. [10]The glass pieces were joined together with lead beading and then they were framed in a variety of ways. [11]In the work on the next page, Tiffany sat a natural outdoor scene in a stylized wooden frame.

[12]A increasing amount of artists and writers of this age struggled to "get back to nature." [13]They hoped to counteract the affects of industrialists, who were

Louis Comfort Tiffany, *Autumn Landscape*, 1923

scavenging the land for raw materials. **¹⁴**The literary quotations in this review explores our relationship to nature. **¹⁵**We seprate ourselves from nature in our homes and our buildings, and yet you long to act naturally. **¹⁶**This conflict among human ways and the ways of nature are reflected in Tiffanys stylized window which celebrates nature in an all together self-conscious, highly crafted way.

Grammar Review   **709**

Viewing the Art

Louis Comfort Tiffany,
Autumn Landscape, 1923

The pointed arches of the Tiffany window above echo the shape of stained-glass windows in Gothic cathedrals. Medieval architects believed that light filtering through stained-glass windows symbolized heavenly light. Literature, like the visual arts, is full of symbols.

Ask students to identify symbols of the natural world in both the Tiffany window and the quotations featured in this review. (Examples: a grain of sand, a wild flower, the stars, trees, ants) Have students discuss similarities and differences between the window and the quotations.

Practice and Assess

Answers: Exercise 8
Mixed Review

1. as
2. further
3. an
4. among
5. Because
6. immigrated
7. whom
8. besides
9. doesn't
10. accept
11. respectively
12. fewer
13. as far as
14. could hardly
15. passed
16. that
17. affected
18. took
19. sets
20. altogether

Close

Have students discuss their most common usage errors and the tips they found most helpful in this unit. Then have them check their current writing assignments for errors and make corrections.

710

Usage Glossary

Review: Exercise 8

Mixed Review

The following sentences provide information about authors. On your paper, write the correct word or expression from each parentheses.

1. Writers often focus on nature, (like/as) many other artists do.
2. Knowing the details of an author's life can help a reader (farther/further) understand that person's writings.
3. In addition to being a poet, the English Romantic author William Blake was also (a/an) artist and illustrator of his own works.
4. The nineteenth-century German composer Robert Schumann had to choose (between/among) many of Heinrich Heine's poems when he was composing the song cycle *Poet's Love*.
5. (Being that/Because) George Sand was troubled by the poor treatment of women in her time, she often wrote about social injustice.
6. Willa Cather frequently wrote about people who had (emigrated/immigrated) to the United States to farm the prairie lands of the Midwest.
7. Robert Frost, (who/whom) many people admire, won four Pulitzer Prizes for his lyrical poetry, most of which describes the people and landscapes of New England.
8. Frost's work, (besides/beside) being highly romantic, also contains much irony.
9. The reading public probably (doesn't/don't) know that Nobel Prize-winning author Gabriel García Márquez founded an organization for human rights.
10. The poet and novelist Milan Kundera agreed to (accept/except) French citizenship in 1980, after his political writings cost him his Czechoslovakian citizenship.
11. As a young man, Blake admired Michelangelo and Dürer, artists of Italy and Germany, (respectfully, respectively).
12. In his later years, Blake created (less/fewer) poems than in his youth.
13. Earning a law degree was (as far as/all the farther) Heine went in his law career.
14. One (couldn't hardly/could hardly) call Sand a conventional woman of her time.
15. Many years (past/passed) before critics recognized Sand's literary stature.
16. The reason Cather wrote about pioneers is (because/that) she lived among them during her childhood in rural Nebraska.
17. Cather's love of the American landscape greatly (effected/affected) her writing.
18. When Robert Frost went to England in 1912, he (took/brought) with him vivid memories of his native land.
19. In *One Hundred Years of Solitude*, García Márquez (sets/sits) the family saga in the fictional town of Macondo, a place much like his own hometown in Aracataca, Colombia.
20. Strains of pessimism keep Kundera's novels from being (all together/altogether) humorous.

Writing Application

Word Usage in Writing

The following passage from "The Most Beautiful Place on Earth" by Edward Abbey contains words that writers sometimes use incorrectly. Read the passage, concentrating on the italicized words.

> The view is open and perfect *in* all directions *except* to the west where the ground *rises* and the skyline is only a few hundred yards away. Looking toward the mountains I *can* see the dark gorge of the Colorado River five or six miles away, carved through the sandstone mesa, though nothing of the river itself down inside the gorge. Southward, on the far side of the river, lies the Moab valley *between* thousand-foot walls of rock, with the town of Moab somewhere on the valley floor, too small to be seen from here. Beyond the Moab valley is more canyon and tableland stretching away to the Blue Mountains fifty miles south.

Techniques with Nouns

Try to use these words correctly when you write and revise your own work.

❶ *Except* is most frequently used as a preposition meaning "but." It should not be confused with the verb *accept,* meaning "to receive" or "to agree to."

INCORRECT USE The view is open and perfect in all directions *accept* to the west . . .

ABBEY'S USE The view is open and perfect in all directions *except* to the west . . .

❷ The verb *rise,* which means "to get up" or "to go up," never takes an object. It should not be confused with *raise,* which always takes an object.

INCORRECT USE to the west where the ground *raises* . . .

ABBEY'S USE to the west where the ground *rises* . . .

TIME
For more about the writing process, see TIME Facing the Blank Page, pp. 109–119

Usage Glossary

Practice

Practice correct usage by rewriting the following passage, using a separate sheet of paper. Choose the correct word from each pair in parentheses.

The most beautiful place in my city is a large park where I can ride my bike on weekends. Some cities have nothing (accept/except) block after block of high-rise buildings, so I think I'm lucky to live close to a green, wooded area. Every Saturday morning, as soon as the sun (rises/raises), I'm off on my bike along the trail that winds through the park. At one point the path divides, and it's always hard to decide (among/between) the two forks. One leads (in/into) dark, secluded woods. The other goes (passed/past) an area that the city rents out to people who want to (rise/raise) their own vegetables. One of the women (who/whom) gardens there always offers me one of her luscious red tomatoes. I say politely, "No, thanks," but one of these days I just (can/may) (except/accept) her generous gift. The only thing missing on these Saturday outings is someone to talk to. I'm hoping that my classmate Justin will buy a bike. (Among/Between) all my friends, he's the one who would most enjoy Saturday mornings in the park.

Writing Application **711**

Writing Application

Word Usage in Writing

Encourage students to read the passage silently. Then discuss the italicized words, using the guidelines listed in the Usage Glossary on pp. 690–703.

Techniques with Word Usage

Discuss the techniques described in the Usage Glossary for choosing between a pair of troublesome words or expressions. Then discuss how they are used in the Proofreading exercise on student page 708.

Practice

Refer to Techniques with Word Usage as you evaluate student choices. Ask students to refer to the Usage Glossary as they complete the Practice exercise.

1. except
2. rises
3. between
4. into
5. past
6. raise
7. who
8. may
9. accept
10. Among

✔ ASSESSMENT OPTIONS

📁 *Tests with Answer Key & Rubrics*
Unit 19 Mastery Test, pp. 69–70

💾 *Testmaker*
Unit 19 Mastery Test

📼 *MindJogger Videoquizzes*

You may wish to administer the Unit 19 Mastery Test at this point.

Objectives

- To develop an understanding of capitalization rules, including those which govern the uses of capital letters in sentences of various kinds and in situations involving proper nouns and adjectives
- To demonstrate control over capitalization rules by completing exercises and writing sentences which illustrate correct use of capitals in a variety of situations

Key to Ability Levels

L1 Level 1 activities are within the basic ability range of students.

L2 Level 2 activities are within the ability range of average students.

L2 Level 3 activities are more challenging activities.

UNIT
20 Capitalization

Lesson **20.1**   **Capitalization of Sentences**   *713*

Lesson **20.2**   **Capitalization of Proper Nouns**   *715*

Lesson **20.3**   **Capitalization of Proper Adjectives**   *722*

Grammar Review   *726*

Writing Application   *731*

Resource Manager

Planning Resources
- *Lesson Plans*
- *Block Scheduling*

 Transparencies
- *Bellringer*
- *Daily Language Practice*
- *Two-Minute Skill Drill*

📁 **Other Print Resources**
- *Grammar and Composition Handbook*

- *Grammar Enrichment*
- *Grammar Practice*
- *Grammar Reteaching*
- *Grammar Workbook*
- *Tests with Answer Key and Rubrics*

📼 **Video**
- *MindJogger Videoquizzes*

💾 **Software**
- *Interactive Grammar and Language Workbook*

- *Language Arts PASS*
- *Presentation Plus!*
- *Testmaker*
- *Writer's Choice Puzzlemaker*

Web Sites
- *writerschoice.glencoe.com*

20.1 | Capitalization of Sentences

■ Capitalize the first word of every sentence.

> **T**raditionally, a comedy ends with a marriage between the principal characters.
>
> **H**ave you read her latest novel?

Capitalizing Quotations

■ Capitalize the first word of a direct quotation that is a complete sentence.

> **R**obert E. Lee once wrote, "**D**uty is the sublimest word in our language."
>
> "**H**appiness lies not in the mere possession of money," he observed. "**I**t lies in the joy of achievement."

The first word of a quotation should not be capitalized unless the entire quotation can stand as a complete sentence or begins with a capital in the original text.

> The ecologist reminded the audience to save "**t**he air, the water, the animals, and the trees."

An indirect quotation should not be capitalized. An **indirect quotation,** often introduced by *that,* does not repeat a person's or a document's exact words.

> Amendment VI of the U.S. Constitution states that **a**ccused persons have the right to a speedy trial.

Exercise 1   Capitalizing Sentences and Quotations

On your paper, rewrite the following sentences, correcting any errors in capitalization.

The Words of Thomas Paine

1. writer and political theorist Thomas Paine wrote, "it is the object only of war that makes it honorable."
2. he pointed out that those who expected to reap the blessings of freedom must "Undergo the fatigue of supporting it."
3. "every spot of the Old World is overrun with oppression," wrote Paine in *Common Sense.* "freedom hath been hunted round the globe."
4. Paine observed that In its best state government was a necessary evil and that In its worst state, government was intolerable.
5. "Suspicion is the companion of mean souls," Paine wrote, "And the bane of all good society."

20.1 Capitalization of Sentences   **713**

Capitalization

Focus

Lesson Overview

Objective
• To identify and capitalize correctly direct quotations and words within parentheses

Teach

Capitalizing Quotations

☑ **Teaching Tip**
Students often have difficulty distinguishing between direct and indirect quotations. Remind them that the word *that* is often used to introduce an indirect quotation. Indeed, when the word *that* follows a verb such as *say* or *state,* it almost always introduces an indirect quotation. Ask students for examples of indirect quotations.

Practice and Assess

Answers: Exercise 1
1. Writer, "It
2. He, "undergo
3. "Every, "Freedom
4. in its best, in its worst
5. "and

Resource Manager

Planning Resources
• *Lesson Plans*

📁 **Other Print Resources**
• *Grammar and Composition Handbook*
• *Grammar Enrichment, p. 38*
• *Grammar Practice, p. 38*
• *Grammar Workbook, Lesson 70*

Practice and Assess

Answers: Exercise 2

1. One line . . . asks, "What happens to a dream deferred?"
2. In 1934 Chiang Kai-shek (he was the Chinese . . . leader) . . . "artistically."
3. Helen Keller said that one can never . . .
4. correct
5. In his moving . . . Joseph said, "From where the sun now stands I will fight no more forever."
6. correct
7. Golda Meir (she was a prime minister of Israel) said, "To deny oneself . . . "
8. Marian Anderson once said . . . (She meant that greed encourages conflict.)
9. correct
10. Anaïs Nin wrote, "One handles truths like dynamite."

Answers: Exercise 3

Answers will vary. Students should capitalize the first word of sentences that stand alone within parentheses. They should not capitalize sentences within parentheses that are contained within other sentences. They should capitalize the first word of a sentence within quotation marks.

Additional Resources

 Grammar Practice, p. 38
Grammar Enrichment, p. 38

 Grammar Workbook, Lesson 70

Close

Have students choose any sentence they corrected in Exercise 2 and explain their corrections in writing.

Capitalization

Capitalizing with Parentheses

■ Capitalize the first word of a sentence in parentheses that stands by itself. Do not capitalize a sentence within parentheses that is contained within another sentence.

> Webster's first dictionary encouraged a distinctive American spelling of British words. (**F**or instance, the British word *honour* was replaced by the American word *honor.*)

> A major cotton-producing state in the antebellum South (*antebellum* means "before the war") was Georgia.

Exercise 2 — Capitalizing Sentences and Quotations

On your paper, rewrite any of the following sentences that have errors in capitalization, correcting the errors. Write the word *correct* if a sentence has no errors.

1. one line of Langston Hughes's poem "Dream Deferred" asks, "what happens to a dream deferred?"
2. In 1934 Chiang Kai-shek (He was the Chinese Nationalist leader) said that the Chinese people would improve the nation if they could live "Artistically."
3. Helen Keller said that One can never consent to creep when one feels an impulse to soar.
4. Emerson argued, "Nothing is at last sacred but the integrity of your own mind."
5. in his moving speech of surrender, the Nez Percé leader Chief Joseph said, "from where the sun now stands I will fight no more forever."
6. Abraham Lincoln said that Frederick Douglass was "the most meritorious man of the nineteenth century." (He must have been impressed with Douglass's strong leadership.)
7. Golda Meir (She was a prime minister of Israel) said, "to deny oneself various comforts is also easier in talk than in deed."
8. Marian Anderson once said that when there is money, there is fighting. (she meant that greed encourages conflict.)
9. The first line of Gabriela Mistral's poem "Rocking" is "The sea rocks her thousands of waves."
10. Anaïs Nin wrote, "one handles truths like dynamite."

Exercise 3 — Using Capitalization in Writing

On your paper, write a short paragraph about the philosophy of Benjamin Franklin as expressed in the maxims he published in *Poor Richard's Almanack.* In your paragraph include the quotes below, either as direct or indirect quotations. Make sure that your sentences are capitalized correctly.

1. "But dost thou love life, then do not squander time, for that's the stuff life is made of."
2. "Lost time is never found again."
3. "Early to bed, and early to rise, makes a man healthy, wealthy, and wise."
4. "He that lives upon hope will die fasting."
5. "Laziness travels so slowly, that poverty soon overtakes him."

Viewing and Representing

Using Visuals

Ask students to work together to create a sheet summarizing the capitalization rules taught in this unit. This sheet could be displayed on a bulletin board and used when students review and edit their work. Next use each student's own writing to illustrate the capitalization rules. Use a highlighter to emphasize each capitalized letter, and have students take turns explaining why the capitalization is necessary. **L1**

20.2 Capitalization of Proper Nouns

■ Capitalize a proper noun.

A common noun should not be capitalized unless it is the first word of a sentence. In proper nouns composed of several words, do not capitalize articles, coordinating conjunctions, and prepositions of fewer than five letters within a proper noun.

1. **Names of individuals**

John **F. K**ennedy	**G**randma **M**oses
Kareem **A**bdul-**J**abbar	**S**hirley **C**hisholm
Rita **M**oreno	**S**andra **D**ay **O'C**onnor
Uncle **S**am	**T**oshio **M**ori

2. **Titles of individuals**

■ Capitalize titles used before a proper name and titles used in direct address.

President Lincoln	**G**overnor Pete Wilson
Queen Elizabeth II	**C**ardinal O'Connor
Chief Tecumseh	Yes, **G**eneral. [direct address]

■ In general, do not capitalize titles that follow a proper name or are used alone.

At the White House, the **p**resident greeted Alberto Fujimori, the **p**resident of Peru.

■ In general, capitalize a title that describes a family relationship when it is used with or in place of a proper name.

Dear **C**ousin Yuki,	*but*	My **c**ousin Yuki sews.
Did you see **F**ather?		my husband's **f**ather
Won't you write, **U**ncle?		What did your **u**ncle write?
A few days later, **M**other wrote to us.		My **m**other arrived yesterday.

3. **Names of ethnic groups, national groups, and languages**

African **A**mericans
Apaches
Americans
Chinese
Spanish
Russian

20.2 Capitalization of Proper Nouns   **715**

Focus

Lesson Overview

Objectives
- To distinguish between common and proper nouns
- To capitalize proper nouns correctly in writing

 Bellringer
Daily Language Activity

When students enter the classroom, have this assignment on the board: *List reasons for capitalizing the word* grandmother *in the second sentence but not in the first.*

1. *My grandmother speaks three languages.*
2. *I asked Grandmother how to say "good-bye" in Arabic.*

See also Daily Language Practice

Motivating Activity

Invite students to use other family terms in oral sentences. Have the class determine whether the noun is common or proper and whether it requires capitalization.

Teach

☑ **Teaching Tip**
Remind students that when a family term is preceded by a possessive personal pronoun (*my, our, your, his, her, their, its*) and is not followed by a proper name, the term is generally used as common noun and thus does not require capitalization. When a family term is not preceded by a possessive pronoun, it is used as a proper noun and should be capitalized. See *Grammar Reteaching,* p. 38.

Capitalization

 Resource Manager

Planning Resources
- *Lesson Plans*

Transparencies
- *Bellringer*
- *Daily Language Practice*
- *Two-Minute Skill Drill*

📁 **Other Print Resources**
- *Grammar and Composition Handbook*
- *Grammar Enrichment,* p. 39
- *Grammar Practice,* p. 39
- *Grammar Reteaching,* p. 38
- *Grammar Workbook,* Lesson 71

Teach

⇄ **Cross-reference: Grammar**
For instruction and practice with common and proper nouns, refer students to Lesson 10.1, pp. 439–444.

Practice and Assess

Answers: Exercise 4

1. Governor George Pataki
2. Senator Nancy Kassebaum
3. Uncle Paul and his father
4. the Populist party
5. correct
6. Brown University
7. Secretary of State Thomas Jefferson
8. Federal Trade Commission
9. Sign here, Admiral.
10. correct
11. Bell Atlantic Corporation
12. Nelson Mandela, the president of South Africa
13. Georgia O' Keeffe
14. Pope Constantine
15. Chief Justice William Rehnquist
16. What did you say, Grandma?
17. Boy Scouts of America
18. First City Bank
19. Swahili
20. Japanese Americans

Capitalization

   4. **Names of organizations, institutions, political parties and their members, and firms**

   Environmental **P**rotection **A**gency
   Knights of **C**olumbus
   Ohio **S**tate **U**niversity
   the **C**ongress
   General **M**otors
   a **D**emocrat
   the **R**epublican party

   Do not capitalize the word *party*. Common nouns such as *court* or *university* are also not capitalized unless they are part of a proper noun.

   Kim has to appear in **d**istrict **c**ourt today.
   Their case is now before the **C**ourt of **A**ppeals for the **F**ederal **C**ircuit.
   Teresa visited the **U**niversity of **T**exas.
   Teresa enjoyed her visit to the **u**niversity.

Exercise 4 **Capitalizing Names and Titles**

On your paper, rewrite the following names, titles, and sentences, adding capital letters as necessary. Write *correct* if the item is already capitalized correctly.

1. governor george pataki
2. senator nancy kassebaum
3. uncle paul and his father
4. the populist party
5. the community college
6. brown university
7. secretary of state thomas jefferson
8. federal trade commission
9. Sign here, admiral.
10. traffic court
11. bell Atlantic corporation
12. nelson mandela, the president of South Africa
13. georgia o'keeffe
14. pope constantine
15. chief justice william rehnquist
16. What did you say, grandma?
17. boy scouts of America
18. first city bank
19. swahili
20. japanese americans

MEETING INDIVIDUAL NEEDS **English Language Learners**

Listing Proper Nouns
Help students who are still learning English to compile a list of proper nouns in English and the students' first language. Then have them translate some sentences from this lesson into their primary language and discuss whether the nouns are also proper in their language.

5. Names of monuments, bridges, buildings, and other structures

Tomb of the **U**nknown **S**oldier
Delaware **M**emorial **B**ridge
Empire **S**tate **B**uilding
Sears **T**ower
Grand **C**oulee **D**am
the **T**aj **M**ahal

6. Names of documents, awards, and laws

the **D**eclaration of **I**ndependence   an **O**scar
Treaty of **V**ersailles   **S**herman **A**ntitrust **A**ct
Nobel **P**rize   **C**ivil **R**ights **A**ct of 1968
the **M**agna **C**arta   **F**ourteenth **A**mendment

Do not capitalize short prepositions that appear as part of the name.

7. Trade names

A **F**ord
Crest toothpaste
Kraft cheese
Sanka

8. Geographical terms

■ Capitalize the names of continents, countries, states, counties, and cities, as well as the names of specific bodies of water, topographical features, regions, and streets.

Africa   **R**ocky **M**ountains
Brazil   **G**reat **R**ift **V**alley
Kentucky   **M**ojave **D**esert
Essex **C**ounty   **L**ong **I**sland
Denver   **T**ropic of **C**ancer
Pacific **O**cean   **S**outheast **A**sia
Lake **E**rie   **P**ennsylvania **A**venue
Snake **R**iver   **F**orty-second **S**treet
Midwest   **C**entral **A**merica

9. Names of planets and other celestial bodies

Jupiter   **A**lpha **C**entauri   the **M**oon
Venus   the **L**ittle **D**ipper   the **S**un
Polaris   the constellation **P**isces

Teach

Recognizing Proper Nouns

Students may be confused by the fact that one word can be used as both a lowercased common noun and a capitalized title—for example: *I met the governor at the rally. I met Governor Smith at the rally. Can you explain your view on this issue, Governor?* Point out that the lowercase form is used when the word stands alone, other than in direct address, or when it follows rather than precedes the proper noun, as in *Jeremiah Smith, the governor, was at the rally.* **L2**

⇄ Cross-reference: Writing

Direct students' attention to Unit 2, The Writing Process, pp. 40–108. Remind the class that an important part of proofreading is looking for errors in capitalization.

Capitalization

 Two-Minute Skill Drill

Ask students to copy the following list, capitalizing wherever necessary.

president harry truman
my white house
vietnamese americans
columbia university
the south
my great-grandmother

Discuss students' answers, asking students to explain the choices they made.

✍ **See also** *Two-Minute Skill Drill Transparency 20.2*

Cultural Connections

Investigating Rules of Capitalization

Foreign languages use different rules of capitalization. For example, the names of the months are not capitalized in Spanish. Have students look through grammar texts of foreign languages taught at their school to find other differences in capitalization or punctuation.

Teach

⇄ **Cross-reference: Writing**

Direct students' attention to Unit 5, Expository Writing, pp. 214–275. Point out that the rules on this page are most applicable to expository writing in the subject areas of social studies and science.

Practice and Assess

Answers: Exercise 5

1. Washington, D.C., is located on the Potomac River.
2. The capital city was built on land ceded to Congress by Virginia and Maryland.
3. An engineer from France, Pierre Charles L'Enfant, designed and partly laid out the city with the help of Benjamin Banneker, an African American surveyor.
4. D.C. stands for the District of Columbia.
5. Its avenues are named after the states; Pennsylvania Avenue is one of the most famous.
6. The central point of the design of the city was the Capitol.
7. Tourists come from all over the world to visit such famous attractions as the Washington Monument, the Vietnam Veterans Memorial, and the National Air and Space Museum.
8. The Senate's working copy of the Treaty of Versailles is housed in the National Archives.
9. A rough draft of the Declaration of Independence is on display at the Library of Congress.
10. Tourists stand in line for hours to tour the White House and possibly catch a glimpse of the president and his family.
11. They also take time to visit George Washington's home at Mount Vernon, which is located several miles south of the city.
12. In warm weather, many tourists spend time boating and fishing on nearby Chesapeake Bay.
13. Class trips from high schools in the North, South, East, and West visit Washington in the spring.
14. Many people enjoy the Cherry Blossom Festival.

15. Still others drive to the beaches along the Atlantic Ocean to enjoy the sun and sand.

Capitalize *earth* only when the word refers to the planet, but in that case, do not use the definite article, *the.*

Mercury, Venus, and Earth are the planets closest to the Sun.
There will be an eclipse of the Moon at midnight.
We looked from the sky above to the earth below.

10. Compass points

■ Capitalize the words *north, east, south,* and *west* when they refer to a specific area of the country or the world or when they are part of a proper name. Do not capitalize them when they merely indicate direction.

the South	*but*	south Florida
East Grand Rapids		east of Grand Rapids
North Dakota		north Texas

Exercise 5   **Capitalizing Proper Nouns**

On your paper, rewrite the following sentences, correcting capitalization errors.

Visiting Washington, D.C.

1. Washington, D.C., is located on the potomac river.
2. The capital city was built on land ceded to congress by virginia and maryland.
3. An engineer from france, Pierre Charles L'Enfant, designed and partly laid out the city with the help of Benjamin Banneker, an african american surveyor.
4. D.C. stands for the district of columbia.
5. Its avenues are named after The states; pennsylvania avenue is one of the most famous.
6. The central point of The design of The city was the Capitol.
7. Tourists come from all over the world to visit such famous attractions as the Washington monument, the Vietnam veterans memorial, and the national air and space museum.
8. The senate's working copy of the treaty of Versailles is housed in the national archives.
9. A rough draft of the declaration of independence is on display at the library of Congress.
10. Tourists stand in line for hours to tour the white house and possibly catch a glimpse of the president and his family.
11. They also take time to visit George Washington's home at Mount Vernon, which is located several miles South of the city.
12. In warm weather, many tourists spend time boating and fishing on nearby chesapeake bay.
13. Class trips from high schools in the north, south, east, and west visit Washington in the spring.
14. Many people enjoy The cherry blossom festival.
15. Still others drive to the beaches along the atlantic ocean to enjoy the Sun and sand.

Capitalization

11. **Names of most historical events, eras, and calendar items**

Boston **T**ea **P**arty	the **R**enaissance
Persian **G**ulf **W**ar	**T**hanksgiving **D**ay
Battle of **G**ettysburg	**T**ang **D**ynasty
French **R**evolution	**F**ourth of **J**uly

A historical period referring to a general span of time should not be capitalized.

the **f**ifteenth century	the **s**ixties
the **m**edieval **p**eriod	**t**urn of the **c**entury

■ Capitalize the days of the week and the months of the year, but do not capitalize the names of the seasons (*spring, summer, autumn, fall, winter*).

They will be here all **s**ummer, beginning the first **S**aturday in **J**uly.

12. **Religious terms**

■ Capitalize names of deities, religions and their denominations and adherents, words referring to a supreme deity, and religious books and events.

God	**S**outhern **B**aptist **C**onvention
Allah	**B**uddhists
the **L**ord	**Q**ur'an
Judaism	**B**ible
Hinduism	**E**aster
Christianity	**Y**om **K**ippur

13. **Names of ships, planes, trains, and spacecraft**

USS *Independence*	*Silver Meteor*
Air Force One	*Columbia*

14. **Names of school courses**

■ Capitalize only those school courses that are the name of a language or the title of a specific course. Do not capitalize the name of a subject.

Japanese	*but*	a **f**oreign **l**anguage
Economics 101		**e**conomics
Advanced **C**alculus		**c**alculus

Capitalization

Teach

⇄ Cross-reference: Mechanics

For more information on italics and their use with proper nouns, refer students to Lesson 21.10, pp. 758–759.

Writing in the Real World

Using Capitalization Rules

Provide each student with a newspaper article that includes various types of capitalized words. Have students list the words. Beside each word, they should write the number of the corresponding rule listed in their book that explains why the word is capitalized. Have students exchange papers and check each other's answers. **L2**

Teach

⬌ **Cross-reference: Mechanics**

For more information on how quotation marks and italics are used with titles of works, refer students to Lesson 21.9, pp. 755–757, and Lesson 21.10, pp. 758–759.

Practice and Assess

Answers: Exercise 6

1. University of Texas—name of institution
2. Hillary Rodham Clinton—name of individual
3. the Golden Gate Bridge—name of bridge
4. the *New York Times*—title of newspaper
5. Laotians, Scots, Turks—names of ethnic groups
6. Captain McShane—title of individual
7. Aunt Marilyn and my uncle Jack—titles of individuals
8. a Republican—member of political party
9. the Atlantic Charter—name of organization
10. The Pure Food and Drug Act—name of law
11. Apple Computer, Inc.—name of firm
12. Pulitzer Prize—name of award
13. the first Monday in October—calendar items
14. the northwestern United States—geographical term
15. First District Court—name of institution
16. Appalachian Mountains—geographical term
17. the Reformation and Renaissance—names of historical periods
18. the Big Dipper—name of celestial body
19. World History II and my history class—names of school courses
20. New Testament—title of biblical section
21. "The Star-Spangled Banner"—title of song
22. Wheaties cereal—trade name
23. correct
24. USS *Constitution*—name of ship
25. Sunset Boulevard in Hollywood, California—geographical term

Capitalization

15. Titles of works

The Pearl [novel]
Washington Post [newspaper]
Grolier Encyclopedia [reference book]
"The Monkey's Paw" [short story]
Song of Myself [poem]
"America the Beautiful" [song]
Beauty and the Beast [movie]
Calla Lily with Red Roses [work of art]
Much Ado About Nothing [play]
Out of Africa [memoir]

Always capitalize the first and last words of a title or subtitle. Capitalize all other words except articles, coordinating conjunctions, and prepositions of fewer then five letters.

■ Capitalize articles (*a, an,* and *the*) at the beginning of a title only when they are part of the title itself. It is common practice not to capitalize (or italicize) articles preceding the title of a newspaper or a periodical. Do not capitalize (or italicize) the word *magazine* unless it is part of the title of a periodical.

"The Open Boat"   *but*   the *Post-Dispatch*
"A Christmas Carol"   a *Time* magazine article

| **Exercise 6** | **Capitalizing Proper Nouns and Explaining Why** |

Write the following items, adding capital letters where necessary. For each item, explain why you did or did not add capital letters.

SAMPLE   gulf of mexico
ANSWER   Gulf of Mexico—name of a specific body of water

1. university of texas
2. hillary rodham clinton
3. the golden gate bridge
4. the *new york times*
5. laotians, scots, turks
6. captain McShane
7. aunt marilyn and my uncle jack
8. a republican
9. the atlantic charter
10. the pure food and drug act
11. apple computer, inc.
12. pulitzer prize
13. the first monday in october
14. the northwestern united states
15. first district court
16. appalachian mountains
17. the reformation and renaissance
18. the big dipper
19. world history II and my history class
20. new testament
21. "the star-spangled banner"
22. wheaties cereal
23. Labor Day
24. uss *constitution*
25. Sunset Boulevard in hollywood, california

720   Unit 20 Capitalization

Exercise 7   Capitalizing Sentences and Proper Nouns

On your paper, rewrite the following sentences, correcting capitalization errors.

The Chippewa People

1. In my history class, I learned about the Chippewas, who were once among the most powerful culture groups of north America.
2. In canada chippewas are known as ojibways; both names are derived from a word that describes the group's traditional moccasins.
3. The chippewas, the ottawas, and the potawatomis—all members of a governing body called the Council of Three Tribes—lived peacefully near the shores of lake Superior for several hundred years.
4. During the Seventeenth Century, the chippewas fought and defeated the sioux to the West, the Kickapoos to the South, and the iroquois to the East.
5. The Chippewas fought with the french against the british in the 1760s, yet they sided with the british in the american revolution.
6. By 1871, when the United States congress stopped making treaties with native americans, the Chippewas and the government had signed forty-two Treaties.
7. In the Winter of 1973, the leaders of an organization called the american indian movement seized a piece of federal land in north dakota; it was the site on which the battle of wounded knee had been fought in 1890.
8. The language of the chippewas is related to several other languages still spoken today, including algonquian, cheyenne, arapaho, shawnee, and cree.
9. Perhaps the most famous chippewa was not a real person at all; rather, he was the hero of Henry wadsworth longfellow's poem *hiawatha*.
10. Today, tens of thousands of chippewas live in cities in the midwest and canada.
11. They also live on Reservations in the provinces of manitoba and ontario in canada.
12. The leech lake reservation is a well-known Chippewa Community in minnesota.
13. For years, a medicine man living in south Dakota has been a spiritual leader for many Chippewas.
14. One of the first questions young people ask him is "what is a native american?"
15. This respected man, whose name is leonard crow dog, says Being a native american is to be spiritual. (another well-known modern-day medicine man is Pete Catches.)
16. One of the most prolific Chippewa writers is the Poet Gerald Vizenor, author of the highly acclaimed book *white earth chippewa*.
17. Responding to Native American activism, congress passed a number of laws, including the indian education act of 1972.
18. According to president Richard Nixon, the primary objective of the legislation was "To strengthen the Indian's sense of autonomy without threatening his sense of community."
19. In a poignant poem called "indian," a student at cloquet junior high school reveals what it is like to be a Chippewa today.
20. This poem and other poems and essays written by young Native Americans have been published in a book called *rising voices*.

20.2 Capitalization of Proper Nouns   **721**

Practice and Assess

Answers: Exercise 7

1. In my history class . . . of North America.
2. In Canada Chippewas are known as Ojibways . . .
3. The Chippewas, the Ottawas, and the Potawatomis . . . Lake Superior
4. During the seventeenth century, the Chippewas . . . the Sioux to the west, the Kickapoos to the south, and the Iroquois to the east.
5. . . . with the French against the British . . . with the British in the American Revolution.
6. . . . Congress . . . Native Americans, the Chippewas . . . treaties.
7. In the winter . . . the American Indian Movement seized . . . land in North Dakota . . . the Battle of Wounded Knee . . .
8. . . . Chippewas is related to . . . Algonquian, Cheyenne, Arapaho, Shawnee, and Cree.
9. . . . Chippewa was . . . the hero of Henry Wadsworth Longfellow's poem Hiawatha.
10. . . . Chippewas live in . . . the Midwest and Canada.
11. . . . on reservations in the provinces of Manitoba and Ontario in Canada.
12. The Leech Lake Reservation . . . Chippewa community in Minnesota.
13. . . . in South Dakota . . . .
14. . . . "What is a Native American?"
15. . . . Leonard Crow Dog, . . . being a Native American is to be spiritual. (Another . . . .
16. . . . the poet . . . *White Earth Chippewa*.
17. . . . Congress passed . . . the Indian Education Act of 1972.
18. . . . President Richard Nixon, . . . "to strengthen . . . ".
19. . . . "Indian," a student at Cloquet Junior High School reveals . . . .
20. . . . book called *Rising Voices*.

Additional Resources

📁 *Grammar Practice*, p. 39
📁 *Grammar Reteaching*, p. 38
📁 *Grammar Enrichment*, p. 39

 Grammar Workbook, Lesson 71

Close

Review students' responses to a few of the exercises, and ask volunteers to explain the reasons they capitalized the words they did.

Capitalization

Focus

Lesson Overview

Objective
• To identify and capitalize proper adjectives

Bellringer
Daily Language Activity

When students enter the classroom, have this assignment on the board: *Change the following proper nouns into proper adjectives: Rome, China, Mexico, Poland.*

See also *Daily Language Practice*

Teach

☑ Teaching Tip

Nouns that proper adjectives modify are not usually capitalized: *German car.*

Practice and Assess

Answers: Exercise 8

Answers will vary, but some suggestions are given below.
1. Italian leather
2. Victorian furniture
3. Southwestern pottery
4. Swedish students
5. Alaskan pipeline
6. Saturday morning
7. Buddhist temple
8. Boston clam chowder
9. Passover meal
10. Grammy winner
11. Marxist philosophy
12. Dickensian characters
13. Latin American writers
14. Taiwanese industry
15. Chicago basketball

Capitalization

20.3 Capitalization of Proper Adjectives

■ Capitalize proper adjectives (adjectives formed from proper nouns).

The following are some of the kinds of proper adjectives that should be capitalized:

1. Adjectives formed from names of people

Elizabethan literature	**S**hakespearean actor
Jeffersonian principles	**N**ewtonian physics
Machiavellian character	**A**ristotelian philosophy

2. Adjectives formed from place names and names of national, ethnic, and religious groups

Roman candle	**A**frican **A**merican leaders
Chinese checkers	**P**uerto **R**ican heritage
Irish linen	**J**ewish history

Many proper nouns do not change form when used as adjectives.

Senate majority	**O**scar-winning performance
New **Y**ork debut	**R**embrandt exhibit
Vietnam veteran	**W**hite **H**ouse statement

Some proper adjectives that are in common use are no longer capitalized.

venetian blinds	**r**oman numerals

Exercise 8 — Forming Proper Adjectives

Form a proper adjective from each of the proper nouns listed below. Consult a dictionary if you need help. On your paper, write the adjective plus a noun that the adjective could modify.

SAMPLE Israel
ANSWER Israeli music

1. Italy
2. Queen Victoria
3. Southwest
4. Sweden
5. Alaska
6. Saturday
7. Buddhism
8. Boston
9. Passover
10. Grammy
11. Karl Marx
12. Charles Dickens
13. Latin America
14. Taiwan
15. Chicago

Resource Manager

Planning Resources
• *Lesson Plans*

 Transparencies
• *Bellringer*
• *Daily Language Practice*

📂 Other Print Resources
• *Grammar and Composition Handbook*
• *Grammar Enrichment,* p. 39
• *Grammar Practice,* p. 39
• *Grammar Reteaching,* p. 39
• *Grammar Workbook,* Lesson 72

Exercise 9   Capitalizing Proper Adjectives

On your paper, rewrite the following sentences, correcting capitalization errors. Write the word *correct* if a sentence has no errors.

Marisol Escobar, Sculptor

1. Marisol Escobar was born into a wealthy venezuelan family living in Paris.
2. The name *Marisol* is a combination of the spanish words *mar y sol,* meaning "sea and sun."
3. Even at a young age, Marisol was fascinated by central and south american art.
4. She was especially drawn to aztec and mayan art.
5. Art critics describe Marisol's work as a cross between modern art and Folk art.
6. Many of her wood and clay figurines are pre-Columbian in style.
7. Her work is displayed in several famous european museums.
8. Some of her more whimsical pieces are in the collections of various american museums.
9. A Marisol Exhibit in Washington, D.C., featured wooden caricatures of well-known public figures, including the british royal family.
10. Today Marisol is a new york city Resident who spends most of her time creating new art.

Exercise 10   Capitalizing Proper Adjectives and Proper Nouns

On your paper, rewrite the following sentences, correcting capitalization errors.

Gordon Parks

1. A kansas native, Gordon parks has become one of america's most productive and versatile artists.
2. At the age of twenty-five, Parks decided to move to the chicago area and become a Professional photographer.
3. After holding a successful one-man Photography exhibit, parks served in the military in Europe in the united states office of war information.
4. Returning to the United States after world war II, Parks worked as a filmmaker for a new jersey oil company.
5. Soon afterward, *life* magazine hired parks as a Staff Photographer.
6. In the field of photography, parks's awards include magazine photographer of the year (1961) and Syracuse university's newhouse award.
7. Parks has also published such novels as *the learning tree,* an Autobiographical work called *A Choice Of Weapons,* and a book about photography entitled *a Poet And His Camera.*
8. Parks is also a composer, and his musical work entitled *first concerto for piano and orchestra* won favorable reviews.
9. When he directed a movie version of *the Learning Tree* for Warner brothers, parks established himself as the first African american film director at a major hollywood studio.
10. At a white house ceremony in 1988, this distinguished new york resident was honored by president Reagan as one of the twelve recipients of the national medal of arts.

10. At a White House ceremony . . . distinguished New York resident was honored by President Reagan . . . the National Medal of Arts.

Practice and Assess

Answers: Exercise 9

1. Marisol Escobar was born into a wealthy Venezuelan family living in Paris.
2. The name *Marisol* is a combination of the Spanish words *mar y sol,* meaning "sea and sun."
3. Even at a young age, Marisol was fascinated by Central and South American art.
4. She was especially drawn to Aztec and Mayan art.
5. Art critics describe Marisol's work as a cross between modern art and folk art.
6. correct
7. Her work is displayed in several famous European museums.
8. Some of her more whimsical pieces are in the collections of various American museums.
9. A Marisol exhibit in Washington, D.C., featured wooden caricatures of well-known public figures, including the British royal family.
10. Today Marisol is a New York City resident who spends most of her time creating new art.

Answers: Exercise 10

1. A Kansas native, Gordon Parks . . . one of America's most productive and versatile artists.
2. . . . the Chicago area and become a professional photographer.
3. . . . one-man photography exhibit, Parks served . . . in the United States Office of War Information.
4. . . . after World War II, Parks . . . for a New Jersey oil company.
5. Soon afterward, *Life* magazine hired Parks as a staff photographer.
6. . . . Parks's awards include Magazine Photographer of the Year (1961) and Syracuse University's Newhouse Award.
7. . . . *The Learning Tree,* an autobiographical work called *A Choice of Weapons,* . . . *A Poet and His Camera.*
8. . . . work entitled *First Concerto for Piano and Orchestra* won favorable reviews.
9. . . . *The Learning Tree* for Warner Brothers, Parks established himself as the first African American director of a film at a major Hollywood studio.

Practice and Assess

Answers: Exercise 11

Answers will vary, but some suggestions are given below. Students should include a variety of capitalized proper nouns and proper adjectives in their dialogue. In addition, all sentences and quotations should be capitalized.

While I'm here in New York, I would like to see the Statue of Liberty and Niagara Falls.

When you visit San Francisco, you must see Golden Gate Park, Fisherman's Wharf, Mission Dolores, and Chinatown.

Suggest that students work with partners to compare and evaluate their answers.

Capitalization

Summary of Capitalization Rules	
Capitalize	**Do Not Capitalize**
He told us to turn to page 506 for the rules of capitalization. (There was no page 506.)	He told us to turn to page 506 (there was no page 506) for the rules of capitalization.
She said, "He liked it very much."	She said that he liked it very much.
Attorney General Janet Reno	My attorney advised me.
Will Grandmother visit us?	My grandmother is eighty years old.
Ohio State University	a university in Ohio
Joslyn Art Museum	the art museum in our city
Dial soap, Crest toothpaste	Buy soap and toothpaste.
the First Amendment	The committee added an amendment to the bill.
Atlantic Ocean, Times Square, Eighth Street	the square at the end of the street overlooking the ocean
Jupiter, Venus, Mars, Earth	the planets
the American Civil War	The country was on the verge of a civil war.
Qur'an, Easter Sunday	sacred book, holiday
German, Art History II	foreign language, history
Senator Barbara Mikulski	the senator from Maryland
President Jimmy Carter	a former president
First District Court	criminal court
South Pacific	south of Honolulu
the Stone Age	the fifth century
"The Birthmark"	a short story
Friday, April	summer, winter

Exercise 11   Using Correct Capitalization in Your Writing

Imagine that you are visiting a friend in another state. On your paper, write several sentences of dialogue between you and your friend, discussing the places you would like to visit. Use a variety of proper nouns and proper adjectives. Capitalize all sentences, direct quotations, and proper nouns and adjectives correctly.

Exploring Language

Consulting a Dictionary

Adjectives derived from proper nouns may or may not be capitalized. Sometimes both forms are considered correct: *French fries* and *french fries*. Advise students to consult a dictionary when in doubt about whether to capitalize adjectives derived from proper nouns. Ask students to work in pairs to find other examples of adjectives which may or may not be capitalized. Have them report to the class on any examples they find. **L2**

Exercise 12   Identifying Correct Capitalization

On your paper, write the letter of the one item that is correctly capitalized in each of the following pairs.

1. **a.** Countee cullen said, "good poetry is a lofty thought beautifully expressed."
    b. Countee Cullen said, "Good poetry is a lofty thought beautifully expressed."

2. **a.** the Supreme court
    b. the Supreme Court

3. **a.** the chair of the Joint Chiefs of Staff, General John Shalikashvili
    b. the chair of the joint chiefs of staff, general John Shalikashvili

4. **a.** In what year did President Lincoln sign the Emancipation Proclamation?
    b. In what year did president Lincoln sign the emancipation proclamation?

5. **a.** Gabriela Mistral was the first latin american writer to win the nobel prize for literature.
    b. Gabriela Mistral was the first Latin American writer to win the Nobel Prize for literature.

6. **a.** Diana Chang wrote the novel *The Only Game in Town.*
    b. Diana Chang wrote the novel *the Only Game in Town.*

7. **a.** I took American History II and a course in mathematics at Stanford University.
    b. I took American History II and a course in Mathematics at Stanford university.

8. **a.** Hindu shrine
    b. hindu shrine

9. **a.** Even though the calendar says otherwise, many people consider Memorial Day to be the beginning of the summer season.
    b. Even though the calendar says otherwise, many people consider memorial day to be the beginning of the Summer season.

10. **a.** Explore the southwest.
    b. Explore the Southwest.

11. **a.** I read the article in *the St. Louis Post-dispatch.*
    b. I read that article in the *St. Louis Post-Dispatch.*

12. **a.** We met Jim Thompson, the former Governor of Illinois.
    b. We met Jim Thompson, the former governor of Illinois.

13. **a.** Hello, Officer.
    b. Hello, officer.

14. **a.** He said that the concert was sold out.
    b. He said that The concert was sold out.

15. **a.** He reminded us that Earth is the planet between venus and mars.
    b. He reminded us that Earth is the planet between Venus and Mars.

Capitalization

Practice and Assess

Answers: Exercise 12
  1. b
  2. b
  3. a
  4. a
  5. b
  6. a
  7. a
  8. a
  9. a
  10. b
  11. b
  12. b
  13. a
  14. a
  15. b

Additional Rescources
 Grammar Practice, p. 39
Grammar Reteaching, p. 39
Grammar Enrichment, p. 39

Grammar Workbook, Lesson 72

Close

Ask students to review each of the rules for capitalization taught in this lesson, and have them suggest sample sentences of their own illustrating each rule. Ask students to discuss those rules they have the most trouble with and to suggest strategies for remembering them.

Teach

About the Literature

Ask a volunteer to read aloud the passage from Chapter 22 of Bruce Chatwin's *In Patagonia.* Have the rest of the class listen, respond, and appropriately evaluate the presentation. In a discussion, students should identify and analyze the characters, the setting, and the mood of the passage. Students should use peer feedback to evaluate their effectiveness in presenting and to set goals for future presentations. Finally, ask students to focus on the capitalized words in the passage.

Linking Grammar and Literature

☑ Teaching Tip

Discuss with students whether the meaning of the passage would be as clear if the writer had not thought carefully about which words needed to be capitalized. Ask students to discuss the pros and cons of having a standard of capitalization and encourage students from other cultures to discuss capitalization rules that apply to their primary languages. Finally, ask students to write a brief essay summarizing their views on the matter.

✔ ASSESSMENT OPTIONS

📁 *Tests with Answer Key & Rubrics*
Unit 20 Mastery Test, pp. 73–74

💾 *Testmaker*
Unit 20 Mastery Test

CAPITALIZATION

The British writer Bruce Chatwin spent several months walking through southern Chile and Argentina, and *In Patagonia* resulted from that journey. In this passage, Chatwin describes one of Patagonia's more famous residents, the outlaw Butch Cassidy. The passage has been annotated to show some of the rules of capitalization covered in this unit.

Literature Model

from In Patagonia
by Bruce Chatwin

Butch Cassidy, in those years, was drover, horse-wrangler, mavericker, part-time bank-robber, and leader of men; the sheriffs feared him most for the last of these accomplishments. In 1894 they gave him two years in the Wyoming State Penitentiary for stealing a horse he hadn't stolen, valued at five dollars. The sentence soured him to any further dealing with the law. And, from 1896 to 1901, his Train Robbers' Syndicate, better known as The Wild Bunch, performed the string of perfect hold-ups that kept lawmen, Pinkerton detectives and the railroad in perpetual jitters. The stories of his antics are endless; breathless rides along the Outlaw Trail; shooting glass conductors from telegraph poles; or paying a poor widow's rent by robbing the rent man. The homesteaders loved him. Many were Mormons, outlawed themselves for polygamy. They gave him food, shelter, alibis. . . . Today he would be classed as a revolutionary. But he had no sense of political organization.

Butch Cassidy never killed a man. Yet his friends were seasoned killers; their murders drove him to fits of remorse. He hated having to rely on the deadly aim of Harry Longabaugh, the Pennsylvania German with evil blue eyes and a foul temper. He tried to go straight, but there was too much on his Pinkerton card and his pleas for amnesty went unheard. Each new robbery spawned another and added years to his sentence. The costs of operating became unbearable.

Sidebar labels:
- Person's name
- Name of an institution
- Name of an organization
- Trade name
- Name of a religious group
- First word of a sentence
- Name of an ethnic group

Capitalization

726   Unit 20 Capitalization

Resource Manager

Planning Resources

- *Lesson Plans*

📁 Other Print Resources

- *Grammar and Composition Handbook*
- *Grammar Workbook,* Lessons 70–72; Unit 11 Review; Cumulative Review: Units 1–11

In the fall of 1901 Butch met the <u>Sundance Kid</u> and his girl, Etta Place, in <u>New York</u>. She was young, beautiful and intelligent, and she kept her men to heel. Her Pinkerton card says she was a school teacher in Denver; one rumor has it she was the daughter of an <u>English</u> remittance man called George Capel, hence Place. Under the names of James Ryan and <u>Mr.</u> and <u>Mrs.</u> Harry A. Place, the "family of 3" went to operas and theaters. (<u>T</u>he Sundance Kid was a keen Wagnerian.) They bought Etta a gold watch at Tiffany's and sailed for Buenos Aires on <u>S.S. *Soldier Prince*</u>. On landing they stayed at the Hotel Europa, called on the <u>**Director of the Land Department,**</u> and secured 12,000 acres of rough camp in Chubut.

"Are there any bandits?" they asked. They were glad to hear there were none.

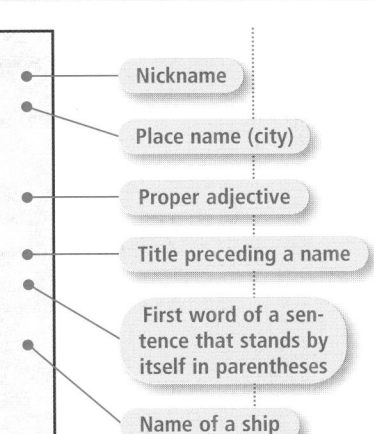

Nickname

Place name (city)

Proper adjective

Title preceding a name

First word of a sentence that stands by itself in parentheses

Name of a ship

Capitalization

Review: Exercise 1   **Capitalizing Sentences**

On your paper, rewrite the following sentences about Butch Cassidy, correcting any errors in capitalization. If a sentence has no errors, write *correct.*

1. Robert Leroy Parker (Also known as Butch Cassidy) borrowed his nickname from a friend named Mike Cassidy.
2. the same friend also taught Parker many of his "outlaw" skills. (Mike Cassidy was a hired hand on the Parker ranch.)
3. By 1892 Butch Cassidy was well known throughout the West as a Horse Thief.
4. Cassidy's motto was that He would never rob a person with whom he had "Broken bread."
5. When Cassidy asked for a pardon, the Wyoming governor said, "will you give me your word that you'll go straight?"
6. "can't do that," Cassidy said. He did promise, however, that he would never again "molest the state of Wyoming."
7. Years later, a friend told the governor that. He should have made Cassidy promise to leave Utah alone as well.
8. the Sundance Kid (His real name was Harry Longabaugh) was a dead shot and had a "Foul temper."
9. When asked whether he would ever give himself up to the law, Longabaugh answered, "they'll never take me alive."
10. Interestingly, Cassidy's Pinkerton file described him in this way: "He is a gentlemanly sort of man."

Practice and Assess

Answers: Exercise 1

1. Robert Leroy Parker (also known as Butch Cassidy) borrowed his nickname from a friend named Mike Cassidy.
2. The same friend also taught Parker many of his "outlaw" skills. (Mike Cassidy was a hired hand on the Parker ranch.)
3. By the year 1892, Butch Cassidy was well-known throughout the West as a notorious horse thief.
4. Cassidy's motto was that he would never rob a person with whom he had "broken bread."
5. When Cassidy asked for a pardon, the Wyoming governor said, "Will you give me your word that you'll go straight?"
6. "Can't do that," Cassidy said. He did promise, however, that he would never again "molest the state of Wyoming."
7. Years later, a friend told the governor that he should have made Cassidy promise to leave Utah alone as well.
8. The Sundance Kid (his real name was Harry Longabaugh) was a dead shot and had a "foul temper."
9. When asked whether he would ever give himself up to the law, Longabaugh answered, "They'll never take me alive."
10. correct

Practice and Assess

Answers: Exercise 2

1. Butch Cassidy grew up on a ranch near Bryce Canyon, Utah, and . . . dime novels about Jesse James.
2. correct
3. In the nineteenth century, the Pinkerton Agency did work similar to . . . Federal Bureau of Investigation.
4. The Cassidy gang . . . Union Pacific Railroad.
5. Trying to escape, . . . Republican senator from Nevada.
6. Joe Lefors, portrayed in Paramount's movie *Butch Cassidy and the Sundance Kid,* pursued them.
7. . . . the North American outlaws . . . on a Patagonian ranch.
8. correct
9. . . . Bolivian mine.
10. . . . they found Butch and Sundance dead, one wearing Etta's Tiffany watch.

Answers: Exercise 3
Proofreading

The proofreading activity provides editing practice with (1) the current or previous unit's skills, (2) **Troubleshooter** errors, and (3) spelling errors. Students should be able to complete the exercise by referring to these units, the **Troubleshooter,** and a dictionary. (Note: A run-on sentence counts as one error.)

Error (Type of Error)

1. The (first word in sentence)
   France (proper noun)
2. Daguerre's (singular possessive)
3. Daguerre (proper noun)
   vapor (spelling)
4. English (proper adjective)
   Fox (proper noun)
5. Talbot's (singular possessive)
6. Not (first word in sentence)

Capitalization (vertical text)

On your paper, rewrite the following sentences about Butch Cassidy, correcting any errors in capitalization. If a sentence has no errors, write *correct.*

1. Butch Cassidy grew up on a ranch near Bryce canyon, utah, and spent much of his spare time reading Dime Novels about Jesse James.
2. Cassidy's reputation as the Robin Hood of the West was probably exaggerated but not wholly unjustified.
3. In the Nineteenth Century, the Pinkerton Agency did work similar to that done today by the federal bureau of investigation.
4. The Cassidy Gang accidentally blew up thousands of dollars during a holdup of the union Pacific railroad.
5. Trying to escape, they mistakenly stole horses belonging to a republican senator from nevada.
6. Joe lefors, portrayed in paramount's movie *Butch Cassidy and the Sundance kid,* pursued them.
7. For three years, the north American outlaws lived quietly on a patagonian Ranch.
8. Cassidy knew that Argentina, Peru, and the Amazonian nations were not Jeffersonian republics: if caught, he would have no assurances of legal rights or due process.
9. Cassidy gave himself away in 1908 when he stole a mule during the theft of a payroll for a bolivian Mine.
10. After dozens of soldiers attacked the outlaws' hut, they found butch and sundance dead, one wearing Etta's tiffany watch.

Review: Exercise 3

Proofreading

The following passage discusses photography in general and the photograph of Butch Cassidy's Wild Bunch shown on the opposite page. On your paper rewrite the passage, correcting the errors in spelling, capitalization, grammar, and usage. Add any missing punctuation. There are twenty-five errors.

Early Photography

[1]the evolution of photography was given a boost in 1837 by Louis-Jacques-Mandé Daguerre of france. [2]Daguerres' process involved the exposure of a polished silver plate to the vapors of iodine (this process formed a sensitive layer of silver iodide). [3]After exposing the plate in the camera, daguerre developed the image with mercury vaper.

[4]The announcement of Daguerre's discovery spurred an english photographer named Henry fox Talbot to develop his own photographic process, which used a paper negative. [5]The photographic process we use today is based on Talbots

negative-to-positive principle. ⁶not merely a technical expert, Talbot had an eye fox beauty and composition as well. ⁷According to the Art historian kenneth Clark, "fox Talbot was the first photographer who could properly be called a great artist."

⁸Indeed, the significance of the Photographic camera at first seemed more artistic than practical but it soon has far-reaching effects in many areas. ⁹For the first time in history, the World was made visible and accessible. ¹⁰Photography changed our view of ourselves and the World around us. ¹¹Because there was now a precise means to show what things looked like, science and teknology flourished. ¹²Communication was also affected by the advent of Photography: magazine and newspaper reporting became more pictorial.

¹³The photograph shown here of butch Cassidy and his gang was taken in 1901 during the final days of Americas Wild west—a period that began after the Civil war. ¹⁴Butch Cassidy was a charming character with an easy smile but he was an outlaw, nonetheless. ¹⁵Cassidys gang received the name the Wild Bunch because of the uproar they caused while unwinding in town after a hard day of rustling. ¹⁶Do you find it ironic to see the members of the Gang sitting in such a serene and genteel pose?

Photographer unknown, *Butch Cassidy and the Gang*, 1901

Capitalization

Answers: Exercise 3 (continued)
Proofreading

Error (Type of Error)
7. art (common adjective)
   Kenneth (proper noun)
   Fox (proper noun, first word in direct quotation)
8. photographic (common adjective)
   practical, (run-on sentence)
9. world (common noun)
10. world (common noun)
11. technology (spelling)
12. photography (common noun)
13. Butch (proper noun)
    America's (singular possessive)
    West (proper noun)
    War (proper noun)
14. smile, (run-on sentence)
15. Cassidy's (singular possessive)
16. gang (common noun)

Viewing the Art

Butch Cassidy and the Gang, 1901
Computer technology now enables photographers to manipulate their images with ease, but until recently photographs were considered historic documents. A photograph preserved a particular place and time, thus shaping our opinion of it. Nonfiction writers, like photographers, strive to record the world objectively. Yet they may still have a point of view. Ask students to discuss what point of view the photograph of Butch Cassidy's gang seems to reflect. Do they think the photographer was sympathetic to the outlaws or critical of them?

Grammar Review

Practice and Assess

Answers: Exercise 4
Mixed Review

1. In the early sixties, Bruce Chatwin walked away from a "brilliant future" at Sotheby's . . .
2. At Sotheby's, Chatwin attributed his expertise . . . scant knowledge of Chinese porcelain.
3. . . . termed "a horror of things" and quit . . . the *London Sunday Times.*
4. He announced his departure with a telegram . . .
5. . . . (Two of the most popular are the semifictional *The Songlines,* about Australia, and *In Patagonia*).
6. . . . World War II, when his father was a naval officer.
7. . . . such as being arrested (in Africa), . . . did not dull Chatwin's appetite for travel.
8. Chatwin's Himalayan trek convinced him that a person's true home is on the road, . . .
9. correct
10. . . . of legendary tales, myths, and strange truths.
11. Chatwin described Patagonia as "the uttermost part of the earth."
12. . . . in South America, where the Darwinian . . . "survival of the fittest" had been formulated.
13. . . . to a distant cousin, Captain Charles Amherst Milward, whose ship sank at . . . the Strait of Magellan.
14. . . . in Chilean Patagonia, Milward found . . . a prehistoric animal, a toothless mammal.
15. correct
16. . . . third-class ship.
17. . . . the book *In Patagonia* without . . . Milward's daughter Monica Barnett, who lived in Lima, Peru.
18. Chatwin won the 1982 Whitbread Award for his books *The Viceroy of Ouidah* and *On the Black Hill.*
19. correct
20. . . . in a *New Yorker* magazine review, "touches on the epic."

Review: Exercise 4

Mixed Review

On your paper, rewrite these sentences about Bruce Chatwin, correcting any errors in capitalization. If a sentence has no errors, write *correct.*

1. In the early Sixties, Bruce Chatwin walked away from a "Brilliant future" at Sotheby's, a fine-arts auction house.
2. At Sotheby's, Chatwin attributed his expertise in part to his scant knowledge of chinese porcelain.
3. In time he developed what he termed "A horror of things" and quit his job to write for the *london Sunday times.*
4. he announced his departure with a Telegram stating that he had "gone to Patagonia for six months."
5. Chatwin's strength was writing travel books. (two of the most popular are the semifictional *The songlines,* about australia, and *In Patagonia.*)
6. Chatwin's love of travel began during world war II, when his Father was a naval Officer.
7. Even harrowing experiences as being arrested (in Africa), being harassed, or catching tropical diseases did not dull Chatwin's appetite for travel.
8. Chatwin's himalayan trek convinced him that A person's true home is on the road, not in a house.
9. Chatwin's keen eye made him the pride of his publisher, Viking Press.
10. Chatwin's world was a confusing place full of Legendary tales, Myths, and strange truths.
11. Chatwin described Patagonia as "The uttermost part of the Earth."
12. He was fascinated by this southernmost place in south America, where the darwinian theory of the "survival of the fittest" had been formulated.
13. He owed his interest in Patagonia to a distant cousin, captain Charles Amherst Milward, whose ship sank at the entrance to the strait of Magellan.
14. In a cave in chilean Patagonia, Milward found the frozen remains of a Prehistoric animal, a toothless mammal.
15. The sea captain shipped the skins and bones he recovered from the ice to England, where he sold them to the British Museum.
16. Chatwin returned from Patagonia on a third-class Ship.
17. He acknowledged that he could not have written the book *in Patagonia* without the help of Milward's Daughter Monica Barnett, who lived in lima, Peru.
18. Chatwin won the 1982 whitbread award for his books *the Viceroy Of Ouidah* and *On the Black Hill.*
19. He also received the Hawthornden Prize in Great Britain.
20. "Chatwin's studied style," wrote John Updike in a *New Yorker* Magazine review, "Touches on the epic."

Writing Application

Capitalization in Writing

William Least Heat-Moon, a Native American of Sioux ancestry, chronicled his journey across the less-traveled roads in *Blue Highways: A Journey into America*. As you read the passage below, pay special attention to his use of capitalization.

West of the gorge lay verdant rangeland, much of it given to a buffalo herd maintained by the **A**rizona **G**ame **C**ommission; the great beasts lifted their heads to watch me pass, their dark, wet eyes catching the late sun. To the north rose the thousand-foot butt end of the **V**ermillion **C**liffs; the cliffs weren't truly vermillion, but contrasting with the green valley in the orange afternoon light, they seemed so.

Capitalization Techniques

Like William Least Heat-Moon, you should apply the rules of capitalization when you write and revise your own work.

TIME

For more about the writing process, see TIME Facing the Blank Page, pp. 109–119

❶ Capitalize proper nouns that name specific topographical features or monuments. Do not capitalize common nouns or adjectives unless they are part of a proper noun.

PROPER NOUN Vermillion Cliffs

COMMON NOUNS AND ADJECTIVES cliffs, vermillion

❷ Capitalize the names of organizations.

PROPER NOUN Arizona Game Commission

COMMON NOUN game commission

❸ Do not capitalize *north, south, east, west* when they indicate direction, except as the first word in a sentence.

INCORRECT VERSIONS west of the gorge lay verdant rangeland . . . To the North rose the thousand-foot butt end . . .

LEAST HEAT-MOON'S CORRECT VERSIONS West of the gorge lay verdant rangeland . . . To the north rose the thousand-foot butt end . . .

Practice On your paper, revise the paragraph below to make 25 changes in capitalization.

Arizona

As a result of the treaty of Guadalupe Hidalgo in 1848, mexican lands North of the gila river became part of the territory of new Mexico. A southern section of land was added by the so-called Gadsden purchase in 1853. Arizona, which became the forty-eighth state in 1912, is rich in legend and american folklore. Tombstone was the site of the west's most famous gunfight (This battle took place at the O.K. Corral), and it was in Arizona that chief Geronimo surrendered after 25 years of fighting, today, the State is home to 14 native American groups living on 20 Reservations. (the largest reservations are the navajo, hopi, Fort Apache, and Papago reservations.) Throughout the year, especially in the Spring, tourists come to experience first-hand the scenic beauty of Arizona and to visit such natural wonders as the grand canyon, the Petrified Forest, and the painted desert. The Hoover dam and the reconstructed london Bridge are also popular attractions.

Writing Application **731**

Writing Application

Capitalization in Writing

Have students silently read the paragraph in their book. Then ask them to look back at the capitalization of words in relation to the guidelines mentioned in Techniques with Capitalization.

Techniques with Capitalization

Direct students to the proofreading exercise on pp. 728–729. Ask whether any of the rules discussed in this part of the lesson apply to the words in the last proofreading paragraph. You might point out that *West* is capitalized here because it is included in the name of an era. *Wild Bunch* is the name of a group and therefore is also capitalized.

Practice

The answers to this challenging and enriching activity will vary. Refer to Techniques with Capitalization as you evaluate student choices.

✔ **ASSESSMENT OPTIONS**

📁 *Tests with Answer Key & Rubrics*
Unit 20 Mastery Test, pp. 73–74

💾 *Testmaker*
Unit 20 Mastery Test

📼 *MindJogger Videoquizzes*

You may wish to administer the Unit 20 Mastery Test at this point.

Close

Have students write original sentences to illustrate the capitalization of proper nouns, proper adjectives, sentences in quotations, and sentences within parentheses.

Objectives

- To develop an understanding of the correct use of punctuation, abbreviations, italics, and the writing of numbers and numerals
- To demonstrate control over rules that govern the use of various punctuation marks and other conventions by completing exercises

✔ ASSESSMENT OPTIONS

📁 *Tests with Answer Key & Rubrics*
Unit 21 Pretest, pp. 75–76
Unit 21 Mastery Test, pp. 77–78

💾 *Testmaker*
Unit 21 Pretest
Unit 21 Mastery Test

You may wish to administer the Unit 21 Pretest at this point.

Key to Ability Levels

L1 Level 1 activities are within the basic ability range of students.

L2 Level 2 activities are within the ability range of average students.

L3 Level 3 activities are more challenging activities.

UNIT
21 Punctuation, Abbreviations, and Numbers

Lesson **21.1**	**The Period**	*733*
Lesson **21.2**	**The Exclamation Point**	*734*
Lesson **21.3**	**The Question Mark**	*735*
Lesson **21.4**	**The Colon**	*737*
Lesson **21.5**	**The Semicolon**	*740*
Lesson **21.6**	**The Comma**	*743*
Lesson **21.7**	**The Dash**	*752*
Lesson **21.8**	**Parentheses**	*753*
Lesson **21.9**	**Quotation Marks**	*755*
Lesson **21.10**	**Italics (Underlining)**	*758*
Lesson **21.11**	**The Apostrophe**	*760*
Lesson **21.12**	**The Hyphen**	*763*
Lesson **21.13**	**Abbreviations**	*766*
Lesson **21.14**	**Numbers and Numerals**	*769*
Grammar Review		*772*
Writing Application		*779*

732

Resource Manager

Planning Resources
- *Lesson Plans*
- *Block Scheduling*

 Transparencies
- *Bellringer*
- *Daily Language Practice*
- *Two-Minute Skill Drill*

📁 **Other Print Resources**
- *Grammar and Composition Handbook*

- *Grammar Enrichment*
- *Grammar Practice*
- *Grammar Reteaching*
- *Grammar Workbook*
- *Sentence-Combining Practice*
- *Tests with Answer Key and Rubrics*

📼 **Video**
- *MindJogger Videoquizzes*

💾 **Software**
- *Interactive Grammar and Language Workbook*
- *Language Arts PASS*
- *Presentation Plus!*
- *Revising with Style*
- *Testmaker*
- *Writer's Choice Puzzlemaker*

 Web Sites
- *writerschoice.glencoe.com*

21.1 The Period

■ Use a period at the end of a declarative sentence and at the end of a polite command.

DECLARATIVE SENTENCE	My father came to America when he was not yet twenty-one**.**
	—Yoshiko Uchida
POLITE COMMAND	Look in the story for five quotations from Uchida**.**
	Please read them aloud.

Identifying Use of the Period

Identify each of the following sentences that should end with a period by writing *declarative* or *command* on your paper. If a sentence is neither a declarative sentence nor a polite command, write *no period.*

Japan's Natural Features

1. Read the following sentences carefully
2. You will learn many fascinating facts about Japan
3. Did you know that Japan is an island country in the Pacific
4. Locate Japan on the world map
5. Japan is made up of four large islands and many smaller ones
6. Mountains and hills cover most of the country
7. These beautiful landforms have long been a source of inspiration to poets and painters throughout the world
8. Please open your books to the section about Japan's highest and most famous mountain peak, Mount Fuji, or Fujiyama
9. Mount Fuji is on Honshu, Japan's largest and most heavily populated island
10. Can you find Mount Fuji on your map
11. An inactive volcano, Mount Fuji last erupted in 1707
12. The volcano rises 12,388 feet above sea level
13. In winter, snow covers the mountain's rugged peak
14. In summer thousands of tourists climb the mountain for a view of the crater
15. Consider now how Japan's breathtaking mountains are both an asset and a problem
16. The Japanese Alps attract tourists to the country, thus aiding the economy
17. However, the mountain range covers so much land area that the coastal regions are overcrowded
18. Only one-seventh of Japan's land is suitable for farming
19. How have the Japanese compensated for this scarcity of farmland
20. They farm efficiently and cultivate high-yielding crops, such as rice

21.1 The Period   **733**

Punctuation, Abbreviations, and Numbers

Focus

Lesson Overview

Objective
• To use periods correctly in declarative sentences and polite commands

Bellringer
Daily Language Activity
When students enter the classroom, have this assignment on the board: *Count the number of sentences in a recent piece of your writing. How many of the sentences end with a period? How many end with some other punctuation mark?*

See also ✎ *Daily Language Practice*

Practice and Assess

Answers: Exercise 1

1. command	11. declarative
2. declarative	12. declarative
3. no period	13. declarative
4. command	14. declarative
5. declarative	15. command
6. declarative	16. declarative
7. declarative	17. declarative
8. command	18. declarative
9. declarative	19. no period
10. no period	20. declarative

Close

Discuss how declarative sentences differ from polite commands. Then call out examples of declarative sentences and polite commands. Ask students to identify the sentence types.

Resource Manager

Planning Resources
• *Lesson Plans*

📖 **Transparencies**
• *Bellringer*
• *Daily Language Practice*

📁 Other Print Resources
• *Grammar and Composition Handbook*
• *Grammar Enrichment,* p. 40
• *Grammar Practice,* p. 40
• *Grammar Reteaching,* p. 40
• *Grammar Workbook,* Lesson 73

Focus

Lesson Overview

Objective

• To use exclamation points to show strong feeling and indicate a forceful command

Bellringer
Daily Language Activity

When students enter the classroom, have this assignment on the board: *Write two sentences that end with exclamation points.*

See also *Daily Language Practice*

Practice and Assess

Answers: Exercise 2

1. exclamation point
2. period
3. period
4. exclamation point
5. period
6. exclamation point
7. period
8. exclamation point
9. exclamation point
10. period
11. period
12. period
13. exclamation point
14. period
15. exclamation point
16. exclamation point
17. period
18. period
19. period
20. exclamation point
21. period
22. period
23. period
24. exclamation point
25. period

Close

Have students write a brief dialogue using sentences that require periods and exclamation points.

Punctuation, Abbreviations, and Numbers

21.2 The Exclamation Point

■ Use an exclamation point to show strong feeling and indicate a forceful command.

> What a colorful garden**!**
> How exciting the game is**!**
> Pay attention**!**

■ Use an exclamation point after an interjection expressing a strong feeling.

> Wow**!**   Ouch**!**

Exercise 2   **Identifying Use of the Exclamation Point**

The following items are declarative sentences, polite and forceful commands, interjections, or exclamatory phrases. Identify the correct type of punctuation for each item by writing *period* or *exclamation point* on your paper.

1. How noisy this class is
2. Please pay attention to the presentation on Japanese arts
3. Many Japanese paintings portray the beauty of life in Japan
4. What rich colors the artists used
5. Color priming from wood blocks is very popular
6. Look out
7. We'll pass around this modern wood-block print by Umetaro Azechi
8. Wow
9. What a gorgeous screen painting
10. Japanese sculpture is also outstanding
11. The sculptors worked mostly with wood
12. Please note that some sculptors also used bronze and clay
13. Such fascinating music
14. Traditional Japanese music is made with gongs, drums, flutes, and *samisens* (banjo-like instruments)
15. Oh, my goodness
16. How beautiful Japanese architecture is
17. Most of the houses are small, simple, and unpainted
18. Everyone, please listen now
19. Japanese drama is also worth mentioning
20. How very lively *kabuki* drama is
21. By comparison, the *No* drama is slow-moving
22. The actors in a *No* play often wear special masks to represent emotions
23. *Kabuki* dance-dramas are more popular than *No* because they are easier to understand
24. What a surprise
25. Japanese men have traditionally played women's roles in *kabuki* drama

734   Unit 21 Punctuation, Abbreviations, and Numbers

Resource Manager

Planning Resources
• *Lesson Plans*

 Transparencies
• *Bellringer*
• *Daily Language Practice*

📁 **Other Print Resources**
• *Grammar and Composition Handbook*
• *Grammar Enrichment,* p. 40
• *Grammar Practice,* p. 40
• *Grammar Reteaching,* p. 40
• *Grammar Workbook,* Lesson 73

21.3 The Question Mark

■ Use a question mark to indicate a direct question.

Was W. E. B. Du Bois born in 1868 or 1869**?**

Should I ask my history teacher**?**

Who knows the answer**?**

Do not place a question mark after a declarative sentence that contains an indirect question.

My friend asked whether W. E. B. Du Bois was born in 1868 or 1869.

I wondered whether I should ask my history teacher.

He asked whether anybody knew the answer.

| Exercise 3 | Identifying Use of the Question Mark |

The following items are either direct questions or declarative sentences that contain an indirect question. Identify the correct type of punctuation for each item by writing *period* or *question mark* on your paper.

World Languages

1. How many languages are spoken in the world today
2. My friend asked our Spanish teacher whether she knew how many languages exist today
3. Señora Lopez wondered how anyone could know the answer to that question
4. Do you know that estimates have varied from 3,000 to 10,000 languages
5. How can we possibly count all the languages, plus the dialects within each language
6. More important, what actually counts as a language
7. Our teacher asked whether we realized how difficult it is to complete a linguistic survey throughout the world
8. How can linguists stay current when languages are constantly dying or being discovered
9. A linguist would want to know what factors were considered in the survey
10. The question of how many languages are spoken worldwide does not have a simple answer
11. Have you heard the theory that most of the languages spoken today are descended from one ancient language
12. Linguists hotly dispute whether the theory is valid
13. Some scholars ask how there can be so many similar words without a shared ancestral language
14. Is it ever possible to verify or disprove such a theory
15. Did you know that "baby" words such as *papa* and *mama* are common to many languages in the world

Focus

Lesson Overview

Objective
• To use question marks to punctuate direct questions

Bellringer
Daily Language Activity

When students enter the classroom, have this assignment on the board: *Insert the correct end punctuation for each sentence in the following passage.*

> Would it not be wiser to write the book down to the average reader's level, reserving for some later work the great "effects" into which she had thrown all the fever of her imagination(**?**) The thought was sacrilege(**!**) . . . The manuscript should be sent as it was(**.**)
>
> —Edith Wharton, "April Showers"

See also *Daily Language Practice*

Practice and Assess

Answers: Exercise 3

1. question mark	9. period
2. period	10. period
3. period	11. question mark
4. question mark	12. period
5. question mark	13. period
6. question mark	14. question mark
7. period	15. question mark
8. question mark	

Resource Manager

Planning Resources
• *Lesson Plans*

Transparencies
• *Bellringer*
• *Daily Language Practice*

Other Print Resources
• *Grammar and Composition Handbook*
• *Grammar Enrichment,* p. 40
• *Grammar Practice,* p. 40
• *Grammar Reteaching,* p. 40
• *Grammar Workbook,* Lesson 73

Punctuation, Abbreviations, and Numbers

Teach

Cross-reference: Grammar

For instruction and practice with four kinds of sentences, refer students to Lesson 13.8, p. 556.

Practice and Assess

Answers: Exercise 4

Only end punctuation is given.

1. .	6. .
2. !	7. .
3. .	8. ?
4. ?	9. .
5. ?	10. ?

Answers: Exercise 5

Only end punctuation is given.

1. ?	6. !
2. .	7. .
3. .	8. ?
4. .	9. ?
5. .	10. .

Additional Resources

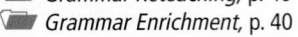 *Grammar Practice*, p. 40

Grammar Reteaching, p. 40

Grammar Enrichment, p. 40

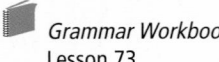 *Grammar Workbook*
Lesson 73

Close

Have students find examples of direct and indirect questions, polite commands, and declarative sentences in magazine and newspaper articles.

Punctuation, Abbreviations, and Numbers

Exercise 4   Using End Punctuation (Part 1)

Rewrite the following sentences, adding periods, exclamation points, and question marks where they are needed.

Major-League Baseball

1. Major-league baseball has often been called the national game of the United States
2. What an exciting sport it is
3. I asked how many fans crowd into baseball parks each year
4. How many more Americans, do you suppose, watch the games on television
5. How did such a popular sport get its start
6. Children in colonial Boston were probably the first to use bases with bat-and-ball games
7. Note that these colonial games probably developed from the English sport of cricket, a bat-and-ball game in which each team defends its wicket
8. Should we credit Abner Doubleday for originating the game
9. In 1839 in Cooperstown, New York, Doubleday developed a diamond-shaped field with four bases and named the game *baseball*
10. Did you know that the National Baseball Hall of Fame and Museum opened in Cooperstown one hundred years later

Exercise 5   Using End Punctuation (Part 2)

Rewrite the following sentences, adding periods, exclamation points, and question marks where they are needed.

Willie Mays, a Great Baseball Player

1. Baseball fans are forever arguing about who the greatest baseball player was. Which player would you choose.
2. Many people would name Willie Mays as an all-time great player.
3. In 1951 Mays entered major-league baseball as a center fielder for the New York Giants and quickly became a hero to the fans.
4. For years there was a spirited rivalry in New York involving Mays, the Yankees' Mickey Mantle, and the Dodgers' Duke Snider
5. When the Giants moved to San Francisco, Mays electrified the fans there as well
6. He will always be remembered as a fearless base runner and an exceptionally gifted fielder. What a fantastic catch he made in the 1954 World Series
7. Many people wonder whether there will ever be another outfielder as spectacular as Mays
8. Mays's hitting statistics were also impressive. Do you know that he hit 660 home runs and had a career batting average of 0.302
9. How many players have hit more homers than Mays did Only Babe Ruth and Hank Aaron have.
10. In 1979 Mays was elected to the National Baseball Hall of Fame. Some still wonder why the vote was not unanimous

736   Unit 21 Punctuation, Abbreviations, and Numbers

Exploring Language

Identifying Direct Questions

Tell students that many verbs have as their direct objects noun clauses beginning with *if, whether, how,* or the *wh-*words (*when, whether, where, what, why,* and so on). These kinds of objects are called *indirect questions*. Students sometimes mistake indirect questions for direct questions. Point out that direct questions always begin with a verb or an interrogative pronoun. **L2**

21.4 The Colon

Colons to Introduce

1. Lists

■ Use a colon to introduce a list, especially after a statement that uses such words as *these*, *the following*, or *as follows*.

> My grandparents' garden contains **these** flowers: camellias, pansies, peonies, tulips, marigolds, and chrysanthemums.

> Perform **the following** operations to start a car with a stick shift: (1) step on the clutch, (2) put the car into first gear, and (3) turn the ignition key.

> Maria's class schedule is **as follows:** English, history, and math.

If a list immediately follows a verb or a preposition, do not use a colon to introduce it.

> The author Alice Walker **writes** poetry, articles, essays, and fiction. [The list follows the verb *writes*.]

> Do not leave for your trip **without** your toothbrush, toothpaste, comb, and brush. [The list follows the preposition *without*.]

2. Illustrations or restatements

■ Use a colon to introduce material that illustrates, explains, or restates the preceding material.

> You can see how bitterly cold the winters are in Alaska: On a windy morning your breath freezes into ice crystals in front of you.

A complete sentence following a colon is capitalized.

3. Quotations

■ Use a colon to introduce a long or formal quotation. A formal quotation is often preceded by words such as *these*, *the following*, or *as follows*.

> Lincoln began the Gettysburg Address with **these** famous words: "Fourscore and seven years ago our fathers brought forth on this continent a new nation . . . "

When poetry quotations take up more than one line and prose quotations take up more than several lines, they generally appear below the introductory statement and are indented.

> Stephen Crane makes this admission in his poem "Truth":
> For truth was to me
> A bread, a wind . . . .

21.4 The Colon **737**

Focus

Lesson Overview

Objective

• To use colons to introduce lists, illustrations, restatements, and quotations; to use colons between hour and minute in expressions of time, between chapter and verse in Bible references, and after a salutation in a business letter

 Bellringer
Daily Language Activity

When students enter the classroom, have this assignment on the board: *Write a list of common greetings used in business letters and friendly letters.*

See also *Daily Language Practice*

Motivating Activity

Have students call out some of the greetings they wrote. Focus their attention on the punctuation used after the salutations of business letters. Explain that in this lesson they will examine the use of the colon.

Teach

Colons to Introduce

☑ **Grammar Tip**

In sentences with lists, students often mistakenly use a colon between the verb and its complement—for example: *The list included: coffee, bread, and eggs.* For the colon to be used correctly, it must follow a complete sentence or what serves as one: *The list included these items: coffee, bread, and eggs. Examples: red, yellow, and blue.*

 Resource Manager

Planning Resources
• *Lesson Plans*

Transparencies
• *Bellringer*
• *Daily Language Practice*

Other Print Resources
• *Grammar and Composition Handbook*
• *Grammar Enrichment*, p. 41
• *Grammar Practice*, p. 41
• *Grammar Reteaching*, p. 41
• *Grammar Workbook*, Lesson 74

Practice and Assess

Answers: Exercise 6

1. In our literature class, we memorized famous lines by these writers: T. S. Eliot, Emily Dickinson, Edgar Allan Poe, and Federico García Lorca.
2. Noted architect Frank Lloyd Wright once made the following observation: "What is needed most in architecture today is the very thing that is most needed in life—integrity."
3. correct
4. correct
5. In "The Still Voice of Harlem," Conrad Kent Rivers writes the following: "I am the hope of your unborn."
6. This famous sentence is from a book by Stephen Crane: "He wishes that he, too, had a wound, a red badge of courage."
7. An old Native American saying goes something like this: "When you were born, you cried and the world rejoiced. Live your life in such a manner that when you die, the world cries and you rejoice."
8. correct
9. Poet Walt Whitman was referring to the death of Abraham Lincoln when he wrote the following lines: . . .
10. Consider the following observation by Mother Teresa: "If you judge people, you have no time to love them."
11. Robert Frost once compared poets and baseball pitchers: . . .
12. correct
13. The Declaration of Independence lists these unalienable rights: . . .
14. The artist Georgia O'Keeffe explained her purpose in these words: . . .
15. . . . before her death: Only six poems . . .

(sidebar) Punctuation, Abbreviations, and Numbers

Exercise 6   Using Colons Correctly

On your paper, rewrite each of the following sentences, adding colons where they are needed. If a sentence has no errors, write *correct.*

Famous Words

1. In our literature class, we memorized famous lines by these writers T. S. Eliot, Emily Dickinson, Edgar Allan Poe, and Federico García Lorca.
2. Noted architect Frank Lloyd Wright once made the following observation "What is needed most in architecture today is the very thing that is most needed in life—integrity."
3. Physicist Albert Einstein placed great value on imagination: He believed that imagination is more important than knowledge.
4. According to the Italian poet Petrarch, five great enemies to peace are avarice, ambition, envy, anger, and pride.
5. In "The Still Voice of Harlem," Conrad Kent Rivers writes the following "I am the hope of your unborn."
6. This famous sentence is from a book by Stephen Crane "He wishes that he, too, had a wound, a red badge of courage."
7. An old Native American saying goes something like this "When you were born, you cried and the world rejoiced. Live your life in such a manner that when you die, the world cries and you rejoice."
8. Abolitionist Theodore Parker defined the American ideal as a government of *all* the people, by *all* the people, for *all* the people.
9. Poet Walt Whitman was referring to the death of Abraham Lincoln when he wrote the following lines

   O powerful western fallen star!
   O shades of night—O moody, tearful night!
   O great star disappeared—O the black murk that hides the star!
   O cruel hands that hold me powerless—O helpless soul of me!
   O harsh surrounding cloud that will not free my soul.

10. Consider the following observation by Mother Teresa "If you judge people, you have no time to love them."
11. Robert Frost once compared poets and baseball pitchers "Both have their moments. The intervals are the tough things."
12. Addressing a Wellesley College commencement, Barbara Bush, wife of then-president George Bush, made this remark: "Somewhere out in this audience may even be someone who will one day follow in my footsteps and preside over the White House as the President's spouse. I wish him well!"
13. The Declaration of Independence lists these unalienable rights life, liberty, and the pursuit of happiness.
14. The artist Georgia O'Keeffe explained her purpose in these words "I had to create an equivalent for what I felt about what I was looking at—not copy it."
15. Emily Dickinson, one of the most quoted of all poets, was little known before her death only six poems were published in her lifetime.

Exploring Language

Understanding Colon Use

Work with students to assess their understanding of colon placement. Ask them to find examples of the use of the colon in other pieces of writing. Remind students that colons are not used after verbs or prepositions. You may wish to write a few examples of incorrect and correct colon use to build students' awareness.

Other Uses of Colons

■ Use a colon between the hour and the minute of the precise time, between the chapter and the verse in biblical references, and after the salutation of a business letter.

5:45 P.M.	1 Kings 11:1–13
8:30 A.M.	Madam:
Proverbs 8:22–31	Dear Sir:

Exercise 7   Using the Colon

Rewrite the following sentences, adding colons where they are needed. Two items will need two colons.

Quotations

1. "There are two times in a man's life when he should not speculate when he can't afford it and when he can."

    —Mark Twain
2. The Chinese philosopher Lao-Tse described his "three treasures" as follows

    The first is deep love,
    The second is frugality,
    And the third is not to dare to be ahead of the world.
3. Dear Company Officers

    Please send me the following a prospectus, a copy of your annual report, and an application form.
4. Toni Morrison says the following about her work "I always know the ending; that's where I start."
5. Dorothy Parker asked to have this epitaph engraved on her tombstone "Excuse my dust."
6. A haiku by Ezra Pound follows

    The petals fall in the fountain
    the orange-colored rose-leaves,
    their ochre clings to the stone.
7. These famous words are engraved on the Statue of Liberty "Give me your tired, your poor . . ."
8. The following quotation appeared in Eleanor Roosevelt's autobiography, *This Is My Story* "No one can make you feel inferior without your consent."
9. After he stepped onto the moon on July 20, 1969, astronaut Neil Armstrong spoke these words at 4 17 P.M. "That's one small step for a man, one giant leap for mankind."
10. In reading Genesis 21 1-21, keep in mind that *Sarah* means "princess" and *Isaac* means "laughter."

Teach

Other Uses of Colons

☑ **Teaching Tip**

Work through some of the sentences in Exercise 7 with students. As you do so, review the rules for using colons. Have students restate the rules.

Practice and Assess

Answers: Exercise 7

1. "There are two times in a man's life when he should not speculate: when he can't afford it and when he can."

    —Mark Twain
2. The Chinese philosopher Lao-Tse described his "three treasures" as follows: . . .
3. Dear Company Officers: Please send me the following: . . .
4. Toni Morrison says the following about her work: "I always know the ending . . ."
5. Dorothy Parker asked to have this epitaph engraved on her tombstone: "Excuse my dust."
6. A famous haiku by Ezra Pound follows: . . .
7. These famous words are engraved on the Statue of Liberty: "Give me your tired, your poor . . ."
8. The following quotation appeared in Eleanor Roosevelt's autobiography, *This Is My Story:* "No one can make you feel inferior without your consent."
9. After he stepped onto the moon on July 20, 1969, astronaut Neil Armstrong spoke these words at 4:17 P.M.: "That's one small step for a man, one giant leap for mankind."
10. In reading Genesis 21:1–21, keep in mind that *Sarah* means "princess" and *Isaac* means "laughter."

Additional Resources

📁 *Grammar Practice,* p. 41
📁 *Grammar Reteaching,* p. 41
📁 *Grammar Enrichment,* p. 41

 Grammar Workbook
Lesson 74

Close

Have students look at a piece of their own writing in which they may have used colons. Encourage them to correct any mistakes, using the rules they learned in this lesson.

Focus

Lesson Overview

Objective

- To use semicolons to separate main clauses and items in series that already contain commas

Bellringer
Daily Language Activity

Use the Bellringer Transparency for Lesson 21.5.

See also *Daily Language Practice*

Teach

Semicolons to Separate Main Clauses

☑ **Grammar Tip**

Explain that between two closely related main clauses a semicolon is better than a period because it indicates the close relationship.

Practice and Assess

Answers: Exercise 8

1. . . . family; she . . .
2. . . . United States; nevertheless, . . .
3. . . . friend; she . . .
4. . . . color; however, . . .
5. . . . situations; for example, . . .

Punctuation, Abbreviations, and Numbers

21.5 The Semicolon

Semicolons to Separate Main Clauses

- Use a semicolon to separate main clauses that are not joined by a coordinating conjunction (*and, but, or, nor, yet,* or *for*).

> The acting and directing ability of Orson Welles is considered phenomenal, **and** his film *Citizen Kane* is still studied and appreciated.

> The acting and directing ability of Orson Welles is considered phenomenal; his film *Citizen Kane* is still studied and appreciated.

- Use a semicolon to separate main clauses joined by a conjunctive adverb (such as *however, therefore, nevertheless, moreover, furthermore,* and *consequently*) or by an expression such as *for example* or *that is.*

A conjunctive adverb or an expression such as *for example* is usually followed by a comma.

> In her youth Mary Cassatt was strongly discouraged from any artistic endeavors; nevertheless, she later became one of America's foremost painters.

> Many of her associates were world-famous artists; for instance, she was strongly influenced by the great French painters Edgar Degas and Edouard Manet.

Exercise 8   **Using Semicolons with Main Clauses**

On your paper, write each of the following sentences correctly, adding semicolons where necessary.

Mary Cassatt, American Artist

1. Mary Cassatt was born in 1844 to a wealthy Pittsburgh family she later studied at the Pennsylvania Academy of Art.
2. Cassatt's father wanted her to remain in the United States nevertheless, she moved to Paris, France.
3. Edgar Degas became her close friend she relied on him for guidance and counseling.
4. Cassatt's paintings are Impressionist in color however, her delicacy of line resembles that of Japanese prints.
5. Cassatt became famous for her paintings of mothers and children in everyday situations for example, she depicted mothers holding, hugging, and bathing their children.

740   Unit 21 Punctuation, Abbreviations, and Numbers

Resource Manager

Planning Resources
- *Lesson Plans*

 Transparencies
- *Bellringer*
- *Daily Language Practice*

🖿 Other Print Resources
- *Grammar and Composition Handbook*
- *Grammar Enrichment,* p. 42
- *Grammar Practice,* p. 42
- *Grammar Reteaching,* p. 42
- *Grammar Workbook,* Lesson 75

Semicolons and Commas

- Use a semicolon to separate the items in a series when these items contain commas.

  Notable abolitionists were Harriet Beecher Stowe, who wrote *Uncle Tom's Cabin*; Frederick Douglass, who spoke out against slavery; and Harriet Tubman, who led many slaves to freedom through the Underground Railroad.

- Use a semicolon to separate two main clauses joined by a coordinating conjunction when such clauses already contain several commas.

  Leonardo da Vinci pursued a wide range of subjects, including mathematics, music, astronomy, and engineering; but he always returned to his primary interest, which was, of course, art.

Exercise 9   Using Semicolons in Sentences with Commas

On your paper, rewrite the following sentences, adding semicolons where they are needed.

The Arts in Renaissance Italy

1. The Medici family, especially "Lorenzo the Magnificent," became the most famous patrons of the arts in Renaissance Italy, and they summoned poets, philosophers, and artists to the city of Florence.
2. Artists such as Leonardo da Vinci, Michelangelo, and Sandro Boticelli reflected the spirit of the Medici court, for they tried to portray a world of beauty, grace, and nobility.
3. Botticelli's *La Primavera* depicts Venus, who is the goddess of love, Zephyr, who portrays the warm wind of spring, Flora, who is transformed into spring, Mercury, who holds the symbol of medicine, and the three Graces, who symbolize poetry, art, and music.
4. The famous painter Leonardo da Vinci is also considered a great sculptor, architect, and scientist, yet no existing sculptures and buildings, nor any specific inventions, can be attributed to him.
5. Michelangelo's most famous achievements include *The Last Judgment*, a fresco that covers the altar wall of the Sistine Chapel, the dome for St. Peter's Church in Rome, which he designed, and his sculptures *Evening* and *Dawn* on the tomb of Lorenzo de Medici.

Teach

Semicolons and Commas

☑ **Grammar Tip**

Tell students that the following transition words may be used after a semicolon: *however, nevertheless, accordingly, consequently, for example, furthermore, therefore.*

Practice and Assess

Answers: Exercise 9

1. The Medici family, especially "Lorenzo the Magnificent," became the most famous patrons of the arts in Renaissance Italy; and they summoned poets, philosophers, and artists to the city of Florence.
2. Artists such as Leonardo da Vinci, Michelangelo, and Sandro Botticelli reflected the spirit of the Medici court; for they tried to portray a world of beauty, grace, and nobility.
3. Botticelli's *La Primavera* depicts Venus, who is the goddess of love; Zephyr, who portrays the warm wind of spring; Flora, who is transformed into spring; Mercury, who holds the symbol of medicine; and the three Graces, who symbolize poetry, art, and music.
4. The famous painter Leonardo da Vinci is also considered a great sculptor, architect, and scientist; yet no existing sculptures and buildings, as well as no specific inventions, can be attributed to him.
5. Michelangelo's most famous achievements include *The Last Judgment,* a fresco that covers the altar wall of the Sistine Chapel; the dome for St. Peter's Church in Rome, which he designed; and his sculptures . . .

Exploring Language

Linking Clauses with Semicolons

Make sure students understand that an independent clause has a subject and a verb. Clauses in some compound sentences can be joined by semicolons. To check whether the semicolon is used properly to join main clauses, students should make sure that the parts on either side of the semicolon can stand alone as complete sentences. Note that the second sentence may begin with a conjunctive adverb (*however, moreover, thus,* or the like). **L2**

Practice and Assess

Answers: Exercise 10

Semicolons should appear after the following words, as shown.

1. prosecuted;/banished;
2. *Finn;*
3. music;
4. *Mavra;/Pulcinella;*
5. Russia;/France;
6. Stravinsky;
7. instruction;
8. readers;
9. Mexicans;
10. musicians;
11. amusement;
12. instruction;
13. role;
14. delighting;
15. scenes;/actor;
16. plagiarist;
17. further;
18. totalitarianism;
19. change;
20. art;

Additional Resources

 Grammar Practice, p. 42
Grammar Reteaching, p. 42
Grammar Enrichment, p. 42

Grammar Workbook
Lesson 75

Close

Let students work with a partner in the following timed activity. Give students one minute to search through the Media Connections or Literature Models to find a sentence using a semicolon. Have them suggest another way of punctuating the sentence and tell which punctuation is better and why they think so.

Exercise 10   Using the Semicolon

On your paper, rewrite the following sentences, adding semicolons where they are needed.

The Purpose of Art: To Instruct or Delight?

1. "Persons attempting to find a motive in this narrative will be prosecuted persons attempting to find a moral in it will be banished persons attempting to find a plot will be shot."
2. Mark Twain attached the preceding notice to *Huckleberry Finn* he felt that too much analysis made art less enjoyable.
3. "The trouble with music appreciation in general is that people are taught to have too much respect for music they should be taught to love it instead." —Igor Stravinsky
4. Among Stravinsky's compositions are the operas *Oedipus Rex, The Rake's Progress,* and *Maura* the ballets *Petrouchka, The Firebird,* and *Pulcinella* and three symphonies.
5. Stravinsky lived in Saint Petersburg, Russia Paris, France and the United States.
6. Oscar Wilde agreed with Twain and Stravinsky he said that art should be pleasurable rather than instructive.
7. On the other hand, some writers and artists try to combine pleasure with instruction they seek to teach and delight simultaneously.
8. Simon Ortiz, who is of Acoma Pueblo descent, does not write simply to entertain his readers rather, he wants to impart knowledge about his heritage.
9. In his art, Diego Rivera portrays the hard life experienced by some Mexicans he also shows the arrogance of their oppressors.
10. Capturing the imagination of their public is enough for most painters, writers, and musicians other creative people, wanting to raise consciousness, use art to instruct.
11. Leo Tolstoy once observed that art was neither a pleasure nor an amusement instead, art was a great matter.
12. By contrast, Pablo Picasso was unconcerned with art's role in instruction his only concern was that his paintings evoke emotion.
13. French painter Georges Braque also placed great emphasis on art's emotional role for example, he felt that art was created to disturb.
14. Still other creative people believe art has purposes beyond instructing or delighting in fact, they regard art as revolutionary.
15. Many artistic people have agreed that art inspires revolution, including Paul Gauguin, a painter of South Seas scenes, Jean-Louis Barrault, the French actor, and Mihajlo Mihajlov, a Russian writer.
16. Gauguin said art was either a revolutionist or a plagiarist it could not be otherwise.
17. Barrault went a step further he regarded art as a permanent revolution
18. Mihajlov stated that art was a direct challenge to communist totalitarianism consequently, one true artist was more dangerous than any political adversary.
19. Walter Savage Landor agreed that art creates change he regarded every great writer as a great reformer.
20. British writer John Ruskin provided an eloquent definition of art he defined good art as that in which the hand, the head, and the heart of the artist go together.

Enrichment and Extension

Using Semicolons in Sentences

Have students do the following:
1. Write a sentence joining two independent clauses with a semicolon.
2. Write a sentence using semicolons to separate items (in series) that also contain commas.
3. Write a sentence joining two independent clauses and a transition word, such as *however* or *nevertheless.*
4. Write a sentence joining two independent clauses and another transition word.

21.6 The Comma

As you study the rules for comma usage, remember that "separating" elements means placing a comma between two equal elements and that "setting off" an element means putting commas *before* and *after* it.

Commas in a Series and with Coordinate Adjectives

■ Use commas to separate three or more words, phrases, or clauses in a series.

Alaska, Texas, and California are our three largest states.
The movie was long, dull, and humorless.
They have traveled on land, by sea, and in the air.
I enjoy reading stories, writing articles, and listening to poetry.
Preheat the oven, beat the eggs, and sift the flour.

When the items are separated by conjunctions, commas are unnecessary.
The movie was long and dull and humorless.

Nouns used in pairs (*eggs and bacon, salt and pepper*) are considered single units and are not separated by commas. The paired nouns are set off from the other nouns or groups of nouns in a series.
The storm brought thunder and lightning, high winds, and heavy rain.

■ Place a comma between coordinate adjectives that precede a noun.

Adjectives that are **coordinate** modify the same noun to an equal degree. You can tell whether adjectives in a sentence are coordinate by reversing their order or putting the word *and* between them. If the sentence sounds right, then the adjectives are coordinate.
It was a warm, starry, fragrant evening.

Avoid placing a comma between adjectives that precede a noun if they sound strange with their order reversed or with *and* between them. In general, do not use a comma between adjectives that describe size, shape, age, color, and material.
The big old oak desk stood in one corner of the room.

Some, but not all, of the adjectives in a series may require commas between them.
A noisy, dusty Japanese truck roared down the street.

21.6 The Comma **743**

Focus

Lesson Overview

Objective
• To use commas to separate and set off elements in a sentence

 Bellringer
Daily Language Activity
When students enter the classroom, have this assignment on the board: *Write a sentence listing your favorite hobbies or sports.*
See also *Daily Language Practice*

Motivating Activity
Have a student read a paragraph or a letter that has had all the commas removed. Point out how difficult the passage was to read and understand without commas. Then ask several students to read their sentences. Ask the class to tell where the commas should be placed.

Teach

Commas in a Series and with Coordinate Adjectives

☑ **Grammar Tip**
Students may not understand the difference between commas that separate and commas that set off. Commas that separate play the joining role of *and*. Commas that set off play the role of parentheses: they surround an element and separate it from the rest of the sentence.

Resource Manager

Planning Resources
• *Lesson Plans*

Transparencies
• *Bellringer*
• *Daily Language Practice*
• *Two-Minute Skill Drill*

Other Print Resources
• *Grammar and Composition Handbook*
• *Grammar Enrichment,* pp. 43–47
• *Grammar Practice,* pp. 43–47
• *Grammar Reteaching,* pp. 43–47
• *Grammar Workbook,* Lessons 76–83
• *Sentence-Combining Practice,* pp. 1, 3, 5, 9, 18–22, 30

Teach

Commas and Compound Sentences

🔵 Vocabulary Link

The term *comma* derives from a Greek verb meaning "to cut." Commas were once used to "cut off," or mark, the end of a sentence; today they "cut off" parts of sentences.

Practice and Assess

Answers: Exercise 11

1. Hispanic culture is complex, diverse, and rich in many . . .
2. It has been a vibrant, vital part of American life ever since Spanish friars settled in the Southwest . . .
3. People may think Hispanic culture is Spanish, but it has also been influenced by Latin American . . .
4. The influence of Aztec culture can be seen in the popular, striking paintings of Carlos Almaraz, a Mexican American.
5. Almaraz's paintings combine beauty, oddness, power, and . . .
6. Music from the Spanish-speaking Caribbean islands—Cuba, the Dominican Republic, and Puerto Rico— sparkles with rhythms brought to the Americas by . . .
7. correct
8. Hispanic literature is also popular, and English translations of Hispanic books are eagerly sought.
9. The works of the Mexican poet Octavio Paz, the Colombian novelist Gabriel García Márquez, and the Argentine novelist Julio Cortázar have influenced American writers.
10. There is no doubt that Hispanic culture will continue to influence, enrich, and enliven American life.

Commas and Compound Sentences

■ Use commas between the main clauses in a compound sentence.

A comma should be placed before a coordinating conjunction (*and, but, or, not, yet,* or *for*) that joins two main clauses.

> I told Eartha what he said, and she advised me to forget it.
> I picked up the clay jar carefully, yet it crashed to the floor.

When two very short, closely linked main clauses are connected by a coordinating conjunction, you may omit the comma between them unless it is needed to avoid confusion.

> Alicia opened the door and Manuel came in. [clear]
> Alicia opened the door for the dog and the cat ran out. [confusing]
> Alicia opened the door for the dog, and the cat ran out. [clear]

Exercise 11   Using the Comma (Part 1)

Rewrite the following sentences, adding commas where they are needed. For the sentence that needs no comma, write *correct*.

Hispanic Culture

1. Hispanic culture is complex diverse and rich in many historical traditions.
2. It has been a vibrant vital part of American life ever since Spanish friars settled in the Southwest in the sixteenth century.
3. People may think Hispanic culture is Spanish but it has also been influenced by Latin American and Caribbean cultures.
4. The influence of Aztec culture can be seen in the popular striking paintings of Carlos Almaraz, a Mexican American.
5. Almaraz's paintings combine beauty oddness power and tranquillity—qualities found in Aztec art.
6. Music from the Spanish-speaking Caribbean islands—Cuba the Dominican Republic and Puerto Rico—sparkles with rhythms brought to the Americas by enslaved people.
7. The lively, syncopated rhythms have been borrowed by such popular American rock groups as the Talking Heads.
8. Hispanic literature is also popular and English translations of Hispanic books are eagerly sought.
9. The works of the Mexican poet and essayist Octavio Paz the Colombian novelist Gabriel García Márquez and the Argentine novelist Julie Cortázar have influenced many American writers.
10. There is no doubt that Hispanic culture will continue to influence enrich and enliven American life.

Exploring Language

Determining Whether a Comma Is Necessary

To help students determine whether a comma is required before a coordinating conjunction that joins two clauses, have them try using a period in place of a comma. (Note that the second sentence will begin with a coordinating conjunction.) If the result is two complete sentences, tell students that the clauses can be joined with a comma and a coordinating conjunction. **L2**

Commas and Nonessential Elements

1. Participles, infinitives, and their phrases

■ Use commas to set off participles, infinitives, and their phrases if they are not essential to the meaning of the sentence.

> He read, engrossed, until the doorbell broke his concentration.
> I am not very thirsty, to tell the truth.

If participles, infinitives, and their phrases are essential to the meaning of a sentence, do not set them off with commas.

> The girl watching us is my sister. [The participial phrase tells which girl.]
> To study my notes would not help you much. [The infinitive phrase is used as the subject of the sentence.]

2. Adjective clauses

■ Use commas to set off a nonessential adjective clause.

A nonessential (nonrestrictive) clause provides additional information about a noun. Considered an extra clause, it does not change the meaning of a sentence but adds to it. It is therefore set off with commas.

> Jackson Pollock, who was an American painter, was born in 1912. [*Who was an American painter* is a nonessential clause.]

Do not use commas with an essential adjective clause. An essential (restrictive) clause gives necessary information about a noun and is thus needed to convey the exact meaning of the sentence.

> One of the few American writers whom she read was Langston Hughes. [*Whom she read* is an essential clause.]

3. Appositives

■ Use commas to set off an appositive if it is not essential to the meaning of a sentence.

A nonessential (nonrestrictive) appositive provides additional information and is therefore set off with commas.

> Lucha Corpi, teacher and author, has published many poems.
>
> A historic city, New Orleans was originally settled by the French. [The appositive, *A historic city*, precedes the subject.]

An essential (restrictive) appositive is not set off with commas because it gives necessary information about a noun.

> Both the *Iliad* and the *Odyssey* are traditionally attributed to the poet Homer. [The appositive, *Homer*, identifies the poet.]

Teach

Commas and Nonessential Elements

☑ **Teaching Tip**

One way for students to distinguish between essential and nonessential adjective clauses is to ask a *who* question about the noun being modified. If the answer requires the noun together with its adjective-clause modifier, the adjective clause is essential. If the *who* question can be answered meaningfully by the noun alone, the adjective clause is nonessential.

⇄ **Cross-reference: Grammar**

For instruction and practice in using participles, infinitives, and their phrases, refer students to Lesson 12.3, pp. 527–531. For adjective clauses, refer students to Lesson 13.5, pp. 549–550. For appositives, refer students to Lesson 12.2, pp. 525–526.

 Two-Minute Skill Drill

Have students add commas to the following sentences.

1. Cara likes apples bananas and strawberries.
2. Tyrone our best student aced the test.
3. Traci tried on the dress and she asked the clerk to find a matching necklace.

✎ **See also** *Two-Minute Skill Drill Transparency 21.6*

Enrichment and Extension

Writing with Nonessential Elements

Have students write a sentence. Then ask them to exchange sentences with a partner. Have the partner add a phrase or clause to the sentence. Ask the partners to look at the addition, determine whether it is essential or nonessential, and punctuate it correctly.

Teach

Commas with Interjections, Parenthetical Expressions, and Conjunctive Adverbs

☑ **Grammar Tip**

Parenthetical expressions are like commentaries on the truth or importance of the sentence. These commentaries play no grammatical role in the sentence.

Practice and Assess

Answers: Exercise 12

1. Thousands of pioneers from China, lured by reports of riches, rushed . . .
2. Gold Mountain, the name these Chinese immigrants gave California, tells more . . .
3. The seven-thousand-mile journey across the Pacific Ocean, which often took more than three months, drained . . .
4. correct
5. Chinese miners did receive wages; nevertheless, the amount they received was . . .
6. On the bright side, the Chinese miners, tireless laborers, often succeeded where others . . .
7. They often worked in abandoned mines, hoping to find what previous miners had overlooked.
8. correct
9. These Chinese miners, determined to succeed, persisted despite the severe hardships they faced.
10. To succeed in the United States was, to tell the truth, far more difficult than they had imagined.

Punctuation, Abbreviations, and Numbers

Commas with Interjections, Parenthetical Expressions, and Conjunctive Adverbs

■ Use commas to set off interjections (such as *oh* and *well*), parenthetical expressions (such as *on the contrary, on the other hand, in fact, by the way, to be exact,* and *after all*), and conjunctive adverbs (such as *however, moreover,* and *consequently*).

Yes, I hope to build my own home one day.

The beautiful and historic city of Philadelphia, in fact, is three centuries old.

After all, we did the best we possibly could under extraordinarily difficult circumstances.

We drank two bottles of orange juice last night; consequently, we did not have enough left to make the punch today.

She intended to use the money to buy an expensive stereo, nonetheless.

Exercise 12   Using the Comma (Part 2)

Rewrite the following sentences, adding commas where they are needed. For the two sentences that need no commas, write *correct*.

Chinese Pioneers

¹Thousands of pioneers from China lured by reports of riches rushed to California after gold was discovered there in 1848. ²Gold Mountain the name these Chinese immigrants gave California tells more about their expectations than it tells about the reality they found. ³The seven-thousand-mile journey across the Pacific Ocean which often took more than three months drained the pioneers both physically and financially. ⁴Chinese men who had arranged passage on credit found themselves in debt to the steamship company for several years. ⁵Chinese miners did receive wages; nevertheless the amount they received was usually less than that paid to non-Asian miners.

⁶On the bright side the Chinese miners tireless laborers often succeeded where others had failed. ⁷They often worked in abandoned mines hoping to find what previous miners had overlooked. ⁸There they sifted through gravel heaps to extract the last traces of gold dust that the others had failed to notice. ⁹These Chinese miners determined to succeed persisted despite the severe hardships they faced. ¹⁰To succeed in the United States was to tell the truth far more difficult than they had imagined.

MEETING INDIVIDUAL NEEDS

Gifted and Talented

Moving Expressions

One of the characteristics of parenthetical expressions is that they can be moved around in a sentence rather freely. They can be in an initial position, in a final position, or next to the verb. Challenge students to write the same sentence three ways: with a parenthetical expres-

sion in the initial position, in the final position, and beside the verb. (For example: *In fact,* Philadelphia is three centuries old. Philadelphia is three centuries old, *in fact*. Philadelphia, *in fact,* is three centuries old.) **L3**

Commas with Introductory and Antithetical Phrases

1. Prepositional phrases

■ A comma after a short introductory prepositional phrase is not incorrect, but the only time it is necessary is if the sentence might be misread without the comma.

> Among those running, women were well represented. [The comma is needed to prevent misreading.]

> Before the election the candidates will participate in two debates. [A comma would not be wrong but is not needed.]

■ Use a comma after a long prepositional phrase or after the final phrase in a succession of phrases.

> During the coldest part of winter, she caught a bad cold.

> On the first Wednesday after the first Monday of each month, our book group meets.

If the prepositional phrase is immediately followed by a verb, do not use a comma.

> Among the candidates in the race for mayor were three women from our part of the city.

2. Participles and participial phrases

■ Use commas to set off introductory participles and participial phrases.

> Gesturing forcefully, the speaker held her audience spellbound.

> Running after my cats, I sprained my ankle.

3. Antithetical Phrases

■ Use commas to set off an antithetical phrase.

In an **antithetical phrase,** a word such as *not* or *unlike* qualifies what comes before it.

> Alaska, not Texas, is the largest state in the United States of America.

> Australia, unlike New Zealand, is an island that is considered a continent.

Punctuation, Abbreviations, and Numbers

Teach

Commas with Introductory and Antithetical Phrases

A Vocabulary Link

Students may not understand the term *antithetical. Antithetical* is the adjective form of *antithesis,* "the exact opposite."

Antithetical phrases and clauses are usually set off from the rest of a sentence with commas, as a nonessential element, so that readers will understand that what comes next in the sentence will be counter to what they might expect.

☑ Grammar Tip

Students sometimes confuse a noun clause used as a subject with an introductory clause, and they set the noun clause off from the rest of the sentence with a comma. A good way to avoid this error in punctuation is to see whether the words following the comma can stand alone. If they can, the comma is correct; if they cannot, a comma should not be used.

Two-Minute Skill Drill

Read aloud the following sentence and ask students where they would place a comma.

About an hour and a half north of Beijing we come to the Great Wall. . . .

—Rudolfo Anaya, "A Chicano in China"

See also *Two-Minute Skill Drill Transparency 21.6*

Enrichment and Extension

Eliminating Commas

Challenge students to rewrite the example sentences on student page 747 so that no commas or fewer commas are needed. Have students compare their sentences with the examples to determine which version is easier to understand.

Teach

Commas and Adverb Clauses

⇄ **Cross-reference: Grammar**
For instruction and practice in using adverb clauses, refer students to Lesson 13.6, pp. 551–552.

Practice and Assess

Answers: Exercise 13

1. Throughout the long history of art, only a few artists can be said to have changed the course of painting.
2. correct
3. Because Jasper Johns and Robert Rauschenberg have influenced each other, it is interesting to compare their work.
4. Putting aside their traditional training, both artists preferred to work with abstract images.
5. Their finished works, although they were carefully planned and executed, sometimes look haphazard.
6. In the middle of a splash of paint and beside a scrap of newspaper, Rauschenberg placed a light bulb.
7. Confused by such unusual combinations, art critics have held differing opinions ever since they first attempted to interpret Rauschenberg's work.
8. Although the critics were puzzled at first, they eventually realized that the everyday objects Rauschenberg used took on new meanings in his work.
9. The use of everyday objects by both artists was meant to be symbolic, not absurd.
10. Everyday articles such as light bulbs and brooms became mysterious and beautiful things, unlike ordinary light bulbs and brooms.

Punctuation, Abbreviations, and Numbers

Commas and Adverb Clauses

■ Use commas to set off all introductory adverb clauses.

Because it was a beautiful day, we decided to have a picnic.

■ Use commas to set off internal adverb clauses that interrupt the flow of a sentence.

Our outing, although it was well planned, did not run smoothly.

In general, do not set off an adverb clause at the end of a sentence. (If the clause is parenthetical or the sentence would be misread without the comma, however, the clause should be set off.)

We went home early even though we weren't tired.

Exercise 13 Using the Comma (Part 3)

Rewrite the following sentences, adding commas where they are needed. If a sentence is correct, write *correct*.

Jasper Johns and Robert Rauschenberg

1. Throughout the long history of art only a few artists can be said to have changed the course of painting.
2. One candidate might be Jasper Johns because many critics consider him to be the most influential of modern artists.
3. Because Jasper Johns and Robert Rauschenberg have influenced each other it is interesting to compare their work.
4. Putting aside their traditional training both artists preferred to work with abstract images.
5. Their finished works although they were carefully planned and executed sometimes look haphazard.
6. In the middle of a splash of paint and beside a scrap of newspaper Rauschenberg placed a light bulb.
7. Confused by such unusual combinations art critics have held differing opinions ever since they first attempted to interpret Rauschenberg's work.
8. Although the critics were puzzled at first they eventually realized that the everyday objects Rauschenberg used took on new meanings in his work.
9. The use of everyday objects by both artists was meant to be symbolic not absurd.
10. Everyday articles such as light bulbs and brooms became mysterious and beautiful things unlike ordinary light bulbs and brooms.

Exploring Language

Identifying Clauses

Ask students to explain the distinction between a clause and a phrase: a clause contains a subject and a verb; a phrase does not. Although all introductory adverb clauses should be set off with a comma, introductory adverb phrases are often set off with a comma only when they are particularly long or when a comma is necessary to prevent misreading. **L2**

Additional Uses of Commas

1. Titles of people

■ Use commas to set off titles when they follow a person's name.

    Maria Lopez, Ph.D.   George Allen, governor of Virginia

    Alberta Jones, D.D.S., will address us.

2. Addresses, geographical terms, and dates

■ Use commas to separate the various parts of an address, a geographical term, or a date.

    Lancaster County, Pennsylvania, is known for its farms.

    Please forward my mail to 6390 West Nassau Circle, Englewood, CO 80110, until Thursday, June 20, 1996.

    Tuesday, April 1, 1996, was the day I won the scholarship.

Use the following forms for letter writing:

    6390 West Nassau Circle
    Englewood, CO 80110
    April 1, 1995

If only the month and the day or the month and the year are given, do not use commas.

    July 4   July 1776

3. References

■ Use commas to set off the parts of a reference that direct the reader to the exact source.

    Refer to John Steinbeck's *The Pearl*, pages 37–47.

    We rehearsed act 2, scene 3, of Lorraine Hansberry's *A Raisin in the Sun*.

4. Direct address

■ Use commas to set off words or names used in direct address.

    Carlo, are you sure that you can get tickets for the game?

    Remain in your seats, students, until the lecture is over.

    Please don't forget to call me tomorrow, Anna.

Punctuation, Abbreviations, and Numbers

Teach

Additional Uses of Commas

Cooperative Learning

Have students work in small groups to create an invitation to a real or imaginary event, making sure the date and address are punctuated correctly.

⬌ Cross-reference: Grammar

For instruction and practice with capitalizing geographical terms and dates, refer students to Lesson 20.2, pp. 715–721.

Two-Minute Skill Drill

Have students add commas to the following sentences.

1. Trying hard to stop biting her nails Mrs. Maldonado started chewing gum.
2. Jason like Alex loves Oshkosh Wisconsin.
3. Well I can't believe I have to wait until September 4 for my new couch!

See also *Two-Minute Skill Drill Transparency 21.6*

Exploring Language

Using Commas in Direct Address

Words or names used in direct address are always set apart from the rest of a sentence. Let students know that a good test of whether a word or name should be set off with commas is to see whether it can be deleted from the sentence. If it can be, then the term is most likely being used in direct address and requires a comma. **L1**

Teach

☑ **Grammar Tip**

The grammar of tag questions is complex. First, the tag often reverses the positive or negative meaning of the main sentence; that is, if the main sentence is positive, the tag is usually negative. Second, the verb in the tag comes before the subject, as in questions. Third, the verb in the tag repeats the first auxiliary verb (or the verb *be*) in the main sentence, if there is one. If the verb in the main sentence does not contain an auxiliary verb or the verb *be*, the tag uses the verb *do*. Finally, the subject of the tag is a personal pronoun that refers to the subject in the main sentence.

Practice and Assess

Answers: Exercise 14

714 Williams Road
Charlottesville, Virginia 22901
September 12, 1997
Dear Greta,
    How have you been? . . . Our new address is 62 Channing Way, Cranbury, NJ 08512. . . .
        . . . You haven't already found a copy of it, have you, Greta? The original speech was published in the September 9, 1963, edition of *Newsweek*, page 21. You can use it for your English assignment, can't you?
    On August 23, 1963, there was an important civil rights march in Washington, D.C. The march was led by Dr. Martin Luther King Jr., who was a church leader and a political activist. . . . He organized a boycott of the segregated bus system of Montgomery, Alabama, in December 1955.
    I hope the speech and this information will be helpful to you, Greta.
                    Your friend,
                    Tamara

5. **Tag questions**

■ Use commas to set off a tag question.

    A tag question—such as *shouldn't I?* or *have you?*—suggests the answer to the statement that comes before it.
        You checked your baggage, didn't you?
        You haven't read that book, have you?
        I should return the book to the library, shouldn't I?

6. **Letter writing**

■ Place a comma after the salutation of an informal letter and after the closing of all letters.

    Dear Juan,   Dear Aunt Miriam,
    Sincerely,   Love,

| **Exercise 14** | **Using the Comma** |

Rewrite the following letter, adding commas where they are needed. (Twenty corrections are needed altogether.)

                    714 Williams Road
                    Charlottesville VA 22901
                    September 12 1997

Dear Greta
    How have you been? I hope that you and your family are in good health. Did I write last time that we are moving? Our new address is 62 Channing Way Cranbury NJ 08512. I hope we will be all moved in by the first of next month.
    I am enclosing a copy of the famous speech you requested. You haven't already found a copy of it have you Greta? The original speech was published in the September 9 1963 edition of *Newsweek* page 21. You can use it for your English assignment can't you?
    On August 23 1963 there was an important civil rights march in Washington D.C. The march was led by Dr. Martin Luther King Jr. who was a church leader and a political activist. Dr. King believed in nonviolent protest and put his beliefs into practice. He organized a boycott of the segregated bus system of Montgomery Alabama in December 1955.
    I hope the speech and this information will be helpful to you Greta.

                    Your friend
                    Tamara

Listening and Speaking

Using Inflection in Questions

Point out that in speaking, a rise in tone or pitch usually indicates a question. Americans tend to give the highest tone or pitch to the final word of a question; other English speakers sometimes put their querying note earlier. Have students practice asking each other questions and listening for the querying note.

Misuse of Commas

Do not use a comma before a conjunction that connects a compound predicate or a compound subject.

INCORRECT	The quarterback threw the ball$_x$ and then slipped.
CORRECT	The quarterback threw the ball and then slipped.
INCORRECT	The quarterback$_x$ and the running back are good athletes.
CORRECT	The quarterback and the running back are good athletes.

If two main clauses are not part of a series, do not use a comma alone to join them. Remember to add a coordinating conjunction or use a semicolon.

INCORRECT	The North Carolina state flag is red, white, blue, and gold$_x$ the state flower is flowering dogwood.
CORRECT	The North Carolina state flag is red, white, blue, and gold, and the state flower is flowering dogwood.
CORRECT	The North Carolina state flag is red, white, blue, and gold; the state flower is flowering dogwood.

A comma should not be used between a subject and its verb or between a verb and its complement.

INCORRECT	What she thought fit to do$_x$ was beyond me.
CORRECT	What she thought fit to do was beyond me.
INCORRECT	On our vacation we will bring$_x$ our tent, snack food, and beach clothes.
CORRECT	On our vacation we will bring our tent, snack food, and beach clothes.

Exercise 15   Using Commas Correctly

Each item contains one or more examples of incorrect comma usage. On your paper, rewrite each sentence to make it correct. You may need to delete commas, use a semicolon in place of a comma, or add a coordinating conjunction with the comma.

The Fascinating World of Seashells

1. The enormous diversity among seashells, makes them one of nature's most delightful creations.
2. Seashells come in all different sizes, and have spectacular patterns.
3. Some shells are fragile and easily broken, others are solid and sturdy.
4. What some people do not know, is that a shell is the outer skeleton of a soft-bodied animal known as a mollusk.
5. The five main classes of shells are, gastropods, bivalves, tusk shells, chitons, and cephalopods.

Teach

Misuse of Commas

⇄ **Cross-reference: Grammar**

For instruction and practice in using compound predicates, main clauses, and subjects, verbs, and complements, refer students to Lesson 11.3, pp. 500–502; Lesson 13.1, p. 543; and Lessons 11.1, p. 497; 11.2, pp. 498–499; and 11.5, pp. 506–511.

Practice and Assess

Answers: Exercise 15

1. The enormous diversity among seashells makes them one of nature's most delightful creations.
2. Seashells come in all different sizes and have spectacular patterns.
3. Some shells are fragile and easily broken; others are solid and sturdy.
4. What some people do not know is that a shell is the outer skeleton of a soft-bodied animal known as . . .
5. The five main classes of shells are gastropods, bivalves, tusk shells, chitons, and cephalopods.

Additional Resources

📁 *Sentence-Combining Practice,* pp. 1, 3, 5–9, 18–22, 30
📁 *Grammar Practice,* pp. 43–47
📁 *Grammar Reteaching,* pp. 43–47
📁 *Grammar Enrichment,* pp. 43–47

📔 *Grammar Workbook* Lessons 76–83

Close

Have students name ways commas are used. Then challenge them to write a paragraph that contains as many types of commas as possible.

Exploring Language

Avoiding Misuse of Commas

Students often add commas in compound predicates because they intuitively supply the understood subject of the second predicate. They mentally create a main clause that they then punctuate as though it existed on paper. For example, in the sentence *The quarterback threw the ball* *and then slipped,* writers mentally add the understood subject and then use a comma before this second predicate. Have students practice writing and punctuating sentences with compound predicates. **L1**

Focus

Lesson Overview

Objective
• To use dashes to signal change and to indicate emphasis

Teach

☑ Teaching Tip
A good test of the correct use of dashes is to delete the information that the dashes set off. If the remaining sentence retains its basic meaning, then the dashes were properly used. If the remaining sentence has lost crucial information, then the dashes were incorrectly used.

Practice and Assess

Answers: Exercise 16
Answers show the words each dash separates.
1. Washington—he . . . militia—assumed
2. site—so . . . thought—located
3. soldiers—if . . . that—had
4. huts—simple . . . cabins—for
5. long—snow . . . early—and
6. soldiers—already . . . hungry—soon
7. Forge—an . . . everyone—dragged
8. Forge—a . . . soldiers—played
9. Washington—he . . . devotion—also
10. Washington—he . . . error—emerged

Close

Ask volunteers to write their sentences for Exercise 16 on the board. Ask the class to comment on any sentences in which they disagree on the way dashes were used.

Punctuation, Abbreviations, and Numbers

21.7 The Dash

On a typewriter, indicate a dash with two hyphens (--). On a computer, you may be able to make an actual dash. Refer to the manual of your word processing program for instructions.

A comma, semicolon, colon, or period should not be placed either before or after a dash.

1. Dashes to signal change
■ Use a dash to indicate an abrupt break or change in thought within a sentence.

What was it—I paused to think—what was it that so unnerved me in the contemplation of the House of Usher?

— Edgar Allan Poe

2. Dashes to emphasize
■ Use a dash to set off and emphasize supplemental information or parenthetical comments.

The crowd marveled as fifty pounds were lifted by the circus performer—using one finger.

The circus performer—using one finger—lifted fifty pounds.

Exercise 16   Using the Dash

On your paper, rewrite the following sentences, adding dashes where needed.

Forging Steel at Valley Forge

1. On July 3, 1775, George Washington he had served as commander-in-chief of the Virginia militia assumed command of the Continental Army.
2. One winter the army camped at Valley Forge, an easily defensible site so many people thought located 15 miles from Philadelphia.
3. Few soldiers if indeed they could be called that had ever heard of Valley Forge.
4. Washington himself designed the huts simple log cabins for his troops.
5. That winter was long snow fell early and bitterly cold.
6. The soldiers already exhausted, freezing, and hungry soon found themselves barefoot.
7. Life in Valley Forge an unbearable nightmare for everyone dragged on.
8. Yet Valley Forge a place where boys became men and men became soldiers played a crucial role in the war.
9. The unwavering commitment shown by General Washington he worked alongside his men and earned their devotion also inspired the troops.
10. Washington he developed his military skill by trial and error emerged from his defeat at Valley Forge with a well-trained and loyal army.

752   Unit 21 Punctuation, Abbreviations, and Numbers

Resource Manager

Planning Resources
• *Lesson Plans*

📂 Other Print Resources
• *Grammar and Composition Handbook*
• *Grammar Enrichment,* p. 48
• *Grammar Practice,* p. 48
• *Grammar Reteaching,* p. 48

• *Grammar Workbook,* Lesson 84
• *Sentence-Combining Practice,* pp. 8–9

752

21.8 Parentheses

■ Use parentheses to set off supplemental material.

Parentheses, like commas and dashes, are used to set off supplemental material. Commas are used to set off material that is closely related to the rest of the sentence. Dashes are used not only to set off—but also to emphasize—material that abruptly interrupts the sentence. Parentheses are used to set off material that is incidental to the main statement but is nevertheless important enough to include.

Minnesota **(**named after the Dakota Sioux word meaning "cloudy water"**)** was explored by French scouts.

1. With complete sentences

If a complete sentence within parentheses is contained within another sentence, it is not capitalized and requires no period. If a complete sentence stands by itself within parentheses, both a capital letter and a period are required.

As gold and silver mining waned **(m**ining declined in the 1870s**)**, cattle became Nevada's principal source of revenue.

Nebraska contains two of the widest and flattest rivers in the country: the Missouri River and the Platte River. **(T**he name *Nebraska* comes from the Native American word *nibrathka,* meaning "flat water."**)**

2. With a comma, semicolon, or colon

■ Always place a comma, semicolon, or colon *after* the closing parenthesis.

Although Death Valley may appear barren (it is often called a desert**),** many plants and animals flourish there.

Pioneer towns had few women (more than half the population of Seattle were bachelors**);** in 1864, however, a settler brought a group of widows and orphans to Seattle.

Washington State is the site of these fur-trapping posts (all built before 1833**):** Spokane, Walla Walla, and Nisqually.

Focus

Lesson Overview

Objective

• To use parentheses to set off supplemental material

Bellringer
Daily Language Activity

When students enter the classroom, have this assignment on the board: *Add a new phrase or clause (enclosed in parentheses) to the following sentence:*

Nicole glanced nervously at the door.

See also *Daily Language Practice*

Motivating Activity

Ask students to share their Bellringer additions. Discuss how the use of parentheses changed the tone or content of the sentence.

Teach

◀ Vocabulary Link

The term *parentheses* comes from a Greek word meaning "to put something next to something else." Since parentheses occur in pairs, we often use the word in the plural. (The singular is *parenthesis.*)

☑ Teaching Tip

When parentheses are used to set off lengthy material, students sometimes forget to use the closing parenthesis. Suggest to students that when they are proofreading, they always look for the closing parenthesis as soon as they encounter an opening parenthesis.

Resource Manager

Planning Resources
• *Lesson Plans*

Transparencies
• *Bellringer*
• *Daily Language Practice*

📁 **Other Print Resources**
• *Grammar and Composition Handbook*
• *Grammar Enrichment,* p. 48
• *Grammar Workbook,* Lesson 85
• *Sentence-Combining Practice,* pp. 6–8

Practice and Assess

Answers: Exercise 17

1. Anne Frank wrote a remarkable diary about her life in Amsterdam during World War II. (She and her family were born in Germany but had moved to Holland before the war.)
2. The diary—addressed to an imaginary friend named Kitty—has been published in over thirty languages.
3. Anne, her parents, an older sister, and four friends—eight persons in all—went into hiding during the Nazi occupation of the Netherlands.
4. Their hiding place was an unused section of an office building. (In Dutch their secret apartment was called *het achterhuis,* which means "the house in the back.")
5. The eight persons hidden in the apartment had to avoid making any noise. (How could they have remained so quiet for so long?)
6. The diary (begun in June 1942 and ended in August 1944) covers Anne's life from the age of thirteen to that of fifteen—a significant period in a girl's life.
7. One entry tells how pleased she was (who wouldn't be?) to find out that a boy she liked also liked her.
8. Another entry reveals that she felt that her hopes could not compete with "the ever approaching thunder"—the misery and destruction sweeping through Europe.
9. When Anne and the others were eventually discovered and taken prisoner, the diary was left behind. The diary was later found—along with some short stories and sketches—and was published in 1947.
10. Anne Frank died in the concentration camp at Bergen-Belsen, Germany, in March 1945. (She was not even sixteen.)

Additional Resources

 Sentence-Combining Practice, p. 6–9
 Grammar Enrichment, p. 48

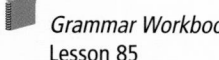 Grammar Workbook
Lesson 85

. With a question mark or exclamation point

■ Place a question mark or an exclamation point *inside* the parentheses if it is part of the parenthetical expression.

> There is a city named Clinton (named after American statesman De Witt Clinton**?)** in almost every state.

> Many names have been suggested for the Black Hills of South Dakota (surprisingly, they were almost named the Purple Mountains**!).**

■ Place a question mark or an exclamation point *outside* the parentheses if it is part of the entire sentence.

> Did you visit the famous cowpoke capitals of the Old West (Dodge City, Cimarron, Wichita, and Abilene**)?**

> How surprised I was to find out that the Alamo was originally a Franciscan mission (the Mission of San Antonio de Valero**)!**

Exercise 17 Using the Dash and Parentheses

Rewrite the following sentences, adding dashes and parentheses where they are needed. Use the marks of punctuation indicated in parentheses at the end of each sentence.

The Story of Anne Frank

1. Anne Frank wrote a remarkable diary about her life in Amsterdam during World War II. She and her family were born in Germany but had moved to Holland before the war. (parentheses)
2. The diary addressed to an imaginary friend named Kitty has been published in over thirty languages. (dashes)
3. Anne, her parents, an older sister, and four friends eight persons in all went into hiding during the Nazi occupation of the Netherlands. (dashes)
4. Their hiding place was an unused section of an office building. In Dutch their secret apartment was called *het achterhuis,* which means "the house in the back." (parentheses)
5. The eight persons hidden in the apartment had to avoid making any noise. How could they have remained so quiet for so long? (parentheses)
6. The diary begun in June 1942 and ended in August 1944 covers Anne's life from the age of thirteen to that of fifteen a significant period in a girl's life. (parentheses, dash)
7. One entry tells how pleased she was who wouldn't be? to find out that a boy she liked also liked her. (parentheses)
8. Another entry reveals that she felt that her hopes could not compete with "the ever approaching thunder" the misery and destruction sweeping through Europe. (dash)
9. When Anne and the others were eventually discovered and taken prisoner, the diary was left behind. The diary was later found along with some short stories and sketches and was published in 1947. (dashes)
10. Anne Frank died in the concentration camp at Bergen-Belsen, Germany, in March 1945. She was not even sixteen. (parentheses)

Close

Ask students to copy a paragraph from a selection or passage in their text. Have them add parenthetical material such as descriptions, directions, or comments. Invite them to exchange papers with a partner to check their use of parentheses.

Punctuation, Abbreviations, and Numbers

Quotation Marks for Direct Quotations

■ Use quotation marks to enclose a direct quotation.

Place quotation marks only around the quoted material.

Introductory or explanatory remarks may be set off from the actual quotation with a comma.

> The Mexican American poet Marina de Bellagente wrote, **"You cannot put a fence around the planet earth."**

> **"I celebrate myself, and sing myself,"** wrote Walt Whitman.

(For the use of colons to introduce quotations, see page 737.)

■ When a quotation is interrupted by explanatory words such as *he said* or *she wrote*, use two sets of quotation marks.

Each part of the quotation should be separated from the interrupting phrase with two marks of punctuation, such as two commas or a comma and a period. The second part of the quotation should begin with a capital letter if it is a complete sentence.

> **"Luis Tiant,"** Reggie Jackson once declared, **"is the Fred Astaire of baseball."**

> **"I never think of the future,"** wrote Albert Einstein. **"It comes soon enough."**

Quotation marks should not be used in an indirect quotation.

ORIGINAL QUOTATION	**"I never intended to become a run-of-the-mill person,"** said Barbara Jordan.
INDIRECT QUOTATION	Barbara Jordan said that she never intended to become a run-of-the-mill person.

■ Use single quotation marks around a quotation within a quotation.

> My instructor replied, **"Sarah Bernhardt said, 'An artiste with short arms can never, never make a fine gesture.'"**

■ In writing dialogue, begin a new paragraph and use a new set of quotation marks every time the speaker changes.

> **"What grade you in now, Raymond?"**

> **"You got anything to say to my brother, you say it to me,** Mary Louise Williams of Raggedy Town, Baltimore.**"**

> **"What are you, his mother?"** sasses Rosie.

> —Toni Cade Bambara

"I never intended to become a run-of-the-mill person."

Barbara Jordan said that she never intended to become a run-of-the-mill person.

Punctuation, Abbreviations, and Numbers

Focus

Lesson Overview

Objective
• To use quotation marks to enclose direct quotations, titles of short works, and unusual expressions

🔔 Bellringer
Daily Language Activity

When students enter the classroom, have this assignment on the board: *Write a favorite quotation.*

See also 📖 *Daily Language Practice*

Motivating Activity

Invite students to share their quotes. Point out that quotes and dialogue can make writing more interesting to read. Write one of their quotations on the board. Use it as a lead-in to discuss how quotations should be punctuated.

Teach

Quotation Marks for Direct Quotations

☑ Teaching Tip
Some students have difficulty distinguishing between direct and indirect quotations. Tell them that an indirect quotation can always be recognized if one inserts *that* in front of it. For example, *She said she was ready* can be read as *She said that she was ready.* In contrast, *that* cannot be added to direct quotations. We would not say, for example, *She said, that "I am ready."*

Teach

Quotation Marks with Other Marks of Punctuation

☑ Grammar Tip

A good way to tell whether question marks and exclamation points go inside or outside quotation marks is to take the direct quotation out of the sentence and see how it would be punctuated if it stood alone. If it would be punctuated with a question mark or an exclamation point, that mark of punctuation should go within the quotation marks. If the new sentence would be punctuated with a period, then the question mark or exclamation point should go outside the quotation marks.

Cooperative Learning

Ask students to pair up and take turns interviewing each other about an issue of interest to both. Have one partner write the other's comments. Then have partners work together to punctuate the quotations correctly.

A Vocabulary Link

The term *quote* comes from the Latin word meaning "how many." Related words are *quota* and *quotient*.

Two-Minute Skill Drill

Have students rewrite the following as direct quotations.

1. Hari said the life of a teenager can be incredibly hard.

2. Anneliese wondered whether she would be elected class president.

See also *Two-Minute Skill Drill Transparency 21.9*

Punctuation, Abbreviations, and Numbers

Quotation Marks with Other Marks of Punctuation

1. **With a comma or a period**

■ Always place a comma or a period *inside* closing quotation marks.

  "Everything had its wonders, even darkness and silence**,"** wrote Helen Keller, who was blind and deaf from a young age.

  Gwendolyn Brooks has said, "Poetry is life distilled**."**

2. **With a semicolon or a colon**

■ Always place a semicolon or a colon *outside* closing quotation marks.

  Lorraine Hansberry wrote "On Summer"**;** this essay tells how her feelings about the season changed over the course of her life.

  There are two Spanish verbs that mean "to be"**:** *ser* and *estar.*

3. **With a question mark or an exclamation point**

■ Place the question mark or exclamation point *inside* the closing quotation marks when it is part of the quotation.

  My friend asked, "How did you persuade your mother**?"**
  My father kept saying, "That's incredible**!"**

■ Place the question mark or exclamation point *outside* the closing quotation marks when it is part of the entire sentence.

  Why did he say, "This is only the beginning"**?**
  How wonderful that she will print your story "Winter"**!**

If both your sentence and the quotation at the end of your sentence need a question mark (or an exclamation point), use only one question mark (or exclamation point) placed *inside* the quotation marks.

  When did she ask, "Will the car be fixed in time**?"**
  I ran when he yelled, "Come quickly**!"**

Do not use a comma after a quotation that ends with a question mark or exclamation point.

  "That's incredible**!"** my father said yet again.

Exploring Language

Shifting Tenses

Indirect quotations often confuse students. When the main clause is in the past tense, the verb tense in the indirect quotation uniformly shifts back.

• If the verb in the quotation is in the present tense, the verb in the indirect quotation should be in the past.

• If the verb in the quotation is in the past tense, the verb in the indirect quotation should be in the past perfect tense.

• If the verb in the quotation uses a present-tense modal, the verb in the indirect quotation should shift to the corresponding past-tense form. **L2**

Quotation Marks with Titles and Unusual Expressions

1. With titles of short works

■ Use quotation marks to enclose titles of short works, such as short stories, short poems, essays, newspaper and magazine articles, book chapters, songs, and single episodes of a television series.

"Chee's Daughter" [short story]

"The Road Not Taken" [poem]

"On Summer" [essay]

"Welform Reform Debated" [newspaper article]

"Climates of the Earth" [chapter]

"America the Beautiful" [song]

"A Stranger Comes to Town" [episode in a television series]

2. With unusual expressions

■ Use quotation marks to enclose unfamiliar slang and other unusual or original expressions.

My roommate calls clumps of dust "dust bunnies."

Exercise 18　Using Quotation Marks

Rewrite the following sentences, adding quotation marks where they are needed. For the sentences that need no changes, write *correct*.

Albert Einstein

1. Albert Einstein's uncle taught him algebra. It is a merry science, he told the boy. When the animal that we are hunting cannot be caught, we call it *x*.
2. The young Einstein was often called oddball.
3. One of Einstein's teachers is supposed to have said to him, Your presence in this class destroys the respect of the students; and someone else apparently told him, You will never amount to anything, Einstein.
4. I am a horse for a single harness, Einstein later said, not cut out for tandem or teamwork.
5. Einstein published a paper called The Influence of Gravity on the Propagation of Light.
6. If Einstein's theory should prove correct, said physicist Max Planck, he will be considered the Copernicus of the twentieth century.
7. Was it in 1916 that Einstein published his paper General Theory of Relativity?
8. Einstein believed—amazingly so at the time—that time and space could disappear!
9. In the 1950s, Einstein said he was ready to introduce his unified field theory, in which gravitation, electromagnetism, and subatomic phenomena are explained in one set of laws.
10. The most incomprehensible thing about the world is that it is comprehensible, said Einstein.

Teach

Quotation Marks with Titles and Unusual Expressions

☑ **Teaching Tip**

Caution students about overusing quotation marks with unusual expressions. Stress that the expressions should be unfamiliar or truly unusual.

Practice and Assess

Answers: Exercise 18

1. Albert Einstein's uncle taught him algebra. "It is a merry science," he told the boy. "When the animal that we are hunting cannot be caught, we call it *x*."
2. The young Einstein was often called "oddball."
3. One of Einstein's teachers is supposed to have said to him, "Your presence in this class destroys the respect of the students"; and someone else apparently told him, "You will never amount to anything, Einstein."
4. "I am a horse for a single harness," Einstein later said, "not cut out for tandem or teamwork."
5. Einstein published a paper called "The Influence of Gravity on the Propagation of Light."
6. "If Einstein's theory should prove correct," said physicist Max Planck, "he will be considered the Copernicus of the twentieth century."
7. Was it in 1916 that Einstein published his paper "General Theory of Relativity"?
8. correct
9. correct
10. "The most incomprehensible thing about the world is that it is comprehensible," said Einstein.

Additional Resources

📁 *Sentence-Combining Practice,* p. 26
📁 *Grammar Practice,* p. 49
📁 *Grammar Reteaching,* p. 49
📁 *Grammar Enrichment,* p. 49

 Grammar Workbook
Lessons 86, 87

Close

Have students work in pairs to make up a dialogue between two persons on some topic of interest to students. Ask them to use what they have learned in this lesson to be sure they have punctuated their quotations correctly.

Focus

Lesson Overview

Objective
- To use italics (underlining) for titles, foreign words, and words and other items used to represent themselves

Bellringer
Daily Language Activity

When students enter the classroom, have this assignment on the board: *Write the title of your favorite book, play, film, television series, painting, or sculpture.*

See also *Daily Language Practice*

Motivating Activity

Tell students that every title they named should be italicized or underlined. Ask students to share their titles and list them on the board. Then discuss and categorize the items. Invite students to identify other names or titles that should be italicized.

Teach

Italics for Titles and Foreign Words

☑ **Grammar Tip**

Deciding when to use italics (underlining) and when to use quotation marks for titles may seem like a subjective decision. A simple test is to ask whether the title is a part of a larger work or collection. If it is, the title is enclosed in quotation marks. If the title refers to a work that is self-contained, the title is italicized. Titles of songs and poems, however, are enclosed in quotation marks.

Punctuation, Abbreviations, and Numbers

21.10 Italics (Underlining)

Italic type slants upward and to the right. (*This is printed in italics.*) On a typewriter or in handwriting, indicate italics by underlining. (<u>This is underlined.</u>) On a computer you can actually use italic type. Refer to your software manual for help.

Italics for Titles and Foreign Words

1. With titles

■ Italicize (underline) titles of books, lengthy poems, plays, films and television series, paintings, and sculptures, and long musical compositions. Also italicize the names of newspapers and magazines, ships, trains, airplanes, and spacecraft.

The Color Purple [book]	*Appalachian Spring* [ballet]
The People, Yes [long poem]	the *Baltimore Sun* [newspaper]
Macbeth [play]	*Newsweek* [magazine]
On the Waterfront [film]	U.S.S. *Constitution* [ship]*
The Civil War [television series]	*Yankee Clipper* [train]
American Gothic [painting]	*Air Force One* [airplane]
Venus de Milo [sculpture]	*Sputnik I* [spacecraft]

*Do not italicize abbreviations such as U.S.S. in the name of a ship.

■ Italicize (underline) and capitalize articles (*a, an, the*) written at the beginning of a title only when they are part of the title itself. It is common practice not to italicize (underline) the article preceding the title of a newspaper or a magazine. Do not italicize the word *magazine* unless it is part of the title of a periodical.

The Red Desert	but	the *Boston Globe*
A Farewell to Arms		a *Reader's Digest* magazine

2. With foreign words

■ Italicize (underline) foreign words and expressions that are not used frequently in English.

> Because Einstein was unconventional as a child, he was considered an **enfant terrible.**

Do not italicize such words if they are commonly used in English.

> Apple pie **á la mode** is my favorite dessert.

Resource Manager

Planning Resources
- *Lesson Plans*

📠 **Transparencies**
- *Bellringer*
- *Daily Language Practice*

📂 **Other Print Resources**
- *Grammar and Composition Handbook*
- *Grammar Enrichment,* p. 50
- *Grammar Practice,* p. 50
- *Grammar Reteaching,* p. 50
- *Grammar Workbook,* Lesson 88

Italics with Words and Other Items Used to Represent Themselves

■ Italicize (underline) words, letters, and numerals used to represent themselves.

> Why does the author of that poem use the word **essence** instead of **life**?

> While I was carefully proofreading my essay, I noticed that the **i** and the **t** were reversed in the title.

> In order to complete the mathematical equation, I needed to find the values of **s** and **y**.

Exercise 19   Using Italics

Rewrite the following sentences, underlining the parts that should be italicized.

Noteworthy Americans

1. Lorene Cary's book Black Ice is a memoir of the author's experiences as one of the first African American students at St. Paul's, a boarding school in New Hampshire.
2. When Will I See You Again, painted by Martin Wong, realistically depicts an image from the artist's neighborhood.
3. Américo Paredes, a professor who has also served as editor of the Journal of American Folklore, has written about Mexican proverbs, or dichos.
4. Paredes points out that although the formal word for proverb in Spanish is refrán, many Mexican Americans use the word dichos, meaning "sayings."
5. Mary Tyler Moore has been successful on television in her highly popular comedy series The Mary Tyler Moore Show and later in movies as the star of such films as Ordinary People.
6. A short-lived magazine of the late 1980s was Lear's, created by Frances Lear for women age forty and older.
7. Novelist N. Scott Momaday won a Pulitzer Prize for his book House Made of Dawn in 1969, but he is perhaps best know for The Way to Rainy Mountain, a collection of stories and legends of the Kiowa people.
8. The well-known American composer Aaron Copland was awarded the Pulitzer Prize for his ballet score Appalachian Spring and later received an Academy Award for his film score for The Heiress.
9. Mark Harris once wrote an entire comic novel that consisted of correspondence supposedly composed on a defective typewriter; the work lacked the letter f throughout.
10. The Puerto Rican artist Arnaldo Roche Rabell's emotional and expressionistic style is evident in such paintings as Blind Dreams and You Tell Me If This Is Not an Omen.

Teach

Italics with Words and Other Items Used to Represent Themselves

Listening and Speaking

One difference between oral and written language is the role of emphasis. In the unplanned rush of the spoken language, speakers rely to a great extent on emphasis to make their points clear. In the written language, however, good writers use exclamation marks and italics sparingly. A student who uses exclamation marks or italics (underlining) excessively may be trying to transcribe oral language.

Practice and Assess

Answers: Exercise 19

Only the items that should be italicized appear below.

1. *Black Ice*
2. *When Will I See You Again*
3. *Journal of American Folklore; dichos*
4. *refrán; dichos*
5. *The Mary Tyler Moore Show; Ordinary People*
6. *Lear's*
7. *House Made of Dawn; The Way to Rainy Mountain*
8. *Appalachian Spring; The Heiress*
9. *f*
10. *Blind Dreams; You Tell Me If This Is Not an Omen*

Additional Resources

📁 *Grammar Practice*, p. 50
📁 *Grammar Reteaching*, p. 50
📁 *Grammar Enrichment*, p. 50

📕 *Grammar Workbook*
Lesson 88

Close

Ask students to write a paragraph containing at least three items that should be italicized. Tell students not to underline the items. Then have them exchange paragraphs with a partner and insert the correct underscoring.

759

Focus

Lesson Overview

Objective

• To use apostrophes with possessives, contractions, and special plurals

Bellringer

Daily Language Activity

When students enter the classroom, have this assignment on the board: *Rewrite the following sentences, adding apostrophes where they are needed.*

• *The two lionesses cubs roamed freely.*

• *Kirbys dog ran away.*

• *The doctors hands were steady as he made the incision.*

See also *Daily Language Practice*

Teach

Apostrophes with Possessives

☑ Teaching Tip

Tell students that the possessive apostrophe shows meaning in a visual way. That is, there is no way to distinguish aurally among forms such as *princesses, princess's,* and *princesses';* although the three forms have distinctly different meanings, they are all pronounced alike. Accordingly, writers who tend to write by ear rather than by sight have difficulty learning to use the apostrophe correctly.

21.11 The Apostrophe

Apostrophes with Possessives

1. **Pronouns**

■ Use an apostrophe and *-s* for the possessive of a singular indefinite pronoun.

An apostrophe should not be used with any possessive pronouns.

one**'s** time	*but*	**his** duty
somebody else**'s** clothes		**its** paws

2. **Singular nouns**

■ Use an apostrophe and *-s* to form the possessive of a singular noun, even one that ends in *-s.*

the man**'s** collar	Mexico**'s** landscape
the dress**'s** hem	George Burns**'s** humor
The heiress**'s** instructions	Dickens**'s** novels
the fox**'s** lair	Max**'s** father

Some exceptions to this rule do exist, however. When forming the possessive of ancient proper nouns that end in *-es* or *-is,* the name *Jesus,* and expressions that contain sibilants (*s* sounds) close together, such as *appearance'* sake and *goodness'* sake, add an apostrophe only.

Aristophanes**'** plays	Jesus**'** followers
Isis**'** temple	Xerxes**'** army

3. **Plural nouns ending in** *-s*

■ Use an apostrophe alone to form the possessive of a plural noun that ends in *-s.*

purple mountains**'** majesty	the Hawaiian Islands**'** charm
the gloves**'** size	the *Ladies**'** Home Journal*

4. **Plural nouns not ending in** *-s*

■ Use an apostrophe and *-s* to form the possessive of a plural noun that does not end in *-s.*

the men**'s** department	Women**'s** Medical Center
the deer**'s** antlers	the geese**'s** eggs

Resource Manager

Planning Resources

• *Lesson Plans*

Transparencies

• *Bellringer*
• *Daily Language Practice*
• *Two-Minute Skill Drill*

📂 Other Print Resources

• *Grammar and Composition Handbook*
• *Grammar Enrichment,* p. 51
• *Grammar Practice,* p. 51
• *Grammar Reteaching,* p. 51
• *Grammar Workbook,* Lesson 89
• *Sentence-Combining Practice,* p. 10

5. Compound nouns

■ Put only the last word of a compound noun in the possessive form.

> my mother-in-law**'s** camera
> the district attorney**'s** victory
> the heir apparent**'s** throne
> the surgeon general**'s** warning

6. Phrases

■ In a phrase or combination of names, add an apostrophe and -s to the last word only.

> the President of the United States**'s** inauguration
> the director from Hollywood**'s** last movie
> Chief Medicine Crow of Montana**'s** delegation

7. Joint possession versus individual possession

■ If two or more persons (or partners in a company) possess something jointly, use the possessive form for the last person named.

> Shiro and Suki**'s** home
> Bernum and Bailey**'s** Circus
> Gilbert and Sullivan**'s** operettas

■ If two or more persons (or companies) possess an item (or items) individually, put each one's name in the possessive form.

> Jorge Amado**'s** and Jorge Luis Borges**'s** novels
> Mozart**'s** and Beethoven**'s** music

8. Expressions of time and money

■ Use a possessive form to express amounts of money or time that modify a noun.

It is also correct to express the modifier as a hyphenated adjective. When that is done, the possessive form is not used.

> five dollar**s'** worth   *but*   a five-dollar contribution
> one minute**'s** pause   a one-minute pause
> a day**'s** journey   a one-day journey
> six day**s'** rest   a six-day rest

Punctuation, Abbreviations, and Numbers

Teach

☑ Grammar Tips

Remind students that the spelling of the plural possessive of a noun ending in -*y* is based on the plural form of the noun. For example, the plural possessive form of *spy* is *spies'*, and the plural possessive of *boy* is *boys'*.

Although an apostrophe is used to form the plural of numbers that appear as numerals (*10's*), it is not used when a century and a decade are expressed as a single unit, as in the *1950s*.

Two-Minute Skill Drill

Rewrite each phrase to make it possessive.

1. the film of Spike Lee
2. the guild of the directors
3. the audiences of the three films
4. the screenplay of Jamil and Barbara

📖 **See also** *Two-Minute Skill Drill Transparency 21.11*

⇄ Cross-reference: Grammar

For instruction and practice in using possessive pronouns and indefinite pronouns, refer students to Lesson 10.2, pp. 445–452.

MEETING INDIVIDUAL NEEDS
English Language Learners

Identifying Possessive Nouns

Students who are new to the English language may have trouble with possessive nouns. Explain that a good way to tell whether a noun is possessive (and thus requires an apostrophe) is to determine whether it can be paraphrased as the answer to a *whose* question. Any noun answering a *whose* question must be a possessive. An additional benefit of this test is that the answer often makes clear whether the possessive noun is singular or plural.

Teach

Apostrophes with Contractions and Special Plurals

☑ **Teaching Tip**

Students may mistakenly use the apostrophe before the contracted forms of not. For example, they may write *does'nt* instead of *doesn't* and *do'nt* instead of *don't*. Students who make this error may be using the apostrophe to separate words rather than to show missing letters. They may be thinking of *I'm, you're,* and *it's,* where the missing letters are at the beginning of the second word in the contraction.

Practice and Assess

Answers: Exercise 20

¹Let's imagine that we are compiling a list of actors' and actresses' names. . . . ²Under the *c*'s we'd include Kevin Costner, a popular contemporary actor, and Claudette Colbert, a brilliant actress of the thirties and forties. ³We mustn't forget to include Bill Cosby's name, because he's essential. ⁴He and Whoopi Goldberg would probably appear on everybody's list of excellent performers. ⁵We would also include Graham Greene. . . . ⁶Under the *m*'s I'd expect to see a good many names. ⁷My friend Max's choice is Pat Morita. . . . ⁸Then there's Rita Moreno, whose role as Anita in United Artists' *West Side Story* earned her wide praise. ⁹After an hour's time we would have a much longer list, including Julia Roberts's and Susan Sarandon's names. ¹⁰My friend James's first choice is Tom and Dick Smothers, one of show business's best comedy teams from the past.

Additional Resources

📁 *Grammar Practice,* p. 51
📁 *Grammar Reteaching,* p. 51
📁 *Grammar Enrichment,* p. 51
📁 *Sentence-Combining Practice,* p. 10

📖 *Grammar Workbook,* Lesson 89

Punctuation, Abbreviations, and Numbers

Apostrophes with Contractions and Special Plurals

1. With contractions

■ Use an apostrophe in place of letters omitted in contractions.

A **contraction** is a word formed from two words that have been combined by omitting one or more letters. Contractions are generally formed from a subject and a verb or a verb and an adverb.

	formed from	
I'm		I am
you're		you are
it's		it is, it has
doesn't, don't		does not, do not

■ Use an apostrophe in place of the omitted numerals of a year.

the World Series of '83   the fall television season of '97

2. With special plurals

■ Use an apostrophe and *-s* to form the plural of letters, numerals, symbols, and words used to represent themselves.

Only the letter, numeral, symbol, or word should be italicized (underlined), not the apostrophe or the *-s*.

Your *a*'s are indistinguishable from your *o*'s.

All of the *8*'s had been typed as *3*'s.

Exercise 20   **Using the Apostrophe**

Rewrite the following sentences, adding apostrophes where they are needed and *-s* wherever necessary.

American Performers

¹Lets imagine that we are compiling a list of actors and actresses names for a biographical dictionary of American performers. ²Under the cs wed include Kevin Costner, a popular contemporary actor, and Claudette Colbert, a brilliant actress of the thirties and forties. ³We mustnt forget to include Bill Cosbys name, because hes essential. ⁴He and Whoopi Goldberg would probably appear on everybodys list of excellent performers. ⁵We would also include Graham Greene, the Native American performer who received critical acclaim for his performance in *Dances with Wolves.* ⁶Under the ms Id expect to see a good many names. ⁷My friend Maxs choice is Pat Morita, whose performance in *The Karate Kid* movies entertained audiences everywhere. ⁸Then theres Rita Moreno, whose role as Anita in United Artists *West Side Story* earned her wide praise. ⁹After an hours time we would have a much longer list, including Julia Roberts and Susan Sarandons names. ¹⁰My friend James first choice is Tom and Dick Smothers, one of show business best comedy teams from the past.

Close

Have students write a two-paragraph review of a film they have seen recently. Remind them to use apostrophes correctly when showing possession and forming contractions.

21.12 | The Hyphen

Hyphens with Prefixes

Hyphens are not usually used to join a prefix to a word. The following are some exceptions:

■ Use a hyphen after any prefix joined to a proper noun or a proper adjective. Use a hyphen after the prefixes *all-*, *ex-* (meaning "former"), and *self-* joined to any noun or adjective.

pre-Columbian	all-encompassing
un-American	ex-governor
mid-August	self-addressed
post-World War I	self-employed

■ Use a hyphen after the prefix *anti-* when it joins a word beginning with *i-*. Also use a hyphen after the prefix *vice-*, except in *vice president*.

anti-inflationary	vice-principal
anti-inflammatory	vice-chancellor

■ Use a hyphen to avoid confusion between words beginning with *re-* that look alike but are different in meaning and pronunciation.

re-count the ballots	*but*	recount a story
re-lay the tiles		relay the message
re-mark the papers		remark on her condition

Exercise 21   Using Hyphens with Prefixes

On your paper, rewrite the following sentences, adding hyphens where they are needed.

The American Revolution

1. The desire for selfgovernment among British colonists grew steadily during the preRevolutionary War period.
2. Antimonarchy and antiimperialist forces prevailed, and the Continental Congress prepared for allout war with Britain.
3. Not only was the British army considered the best allaround fighting force, but it also had the support of the proBritish Iroquois Confederacy.
4. At first British leaders remarked disdainfully that most American soldiers were self-taught.
5. After carefully recreating their government, the exBritish colonies became the United States of America.

21.12 The Hyphen   **763**

Punctuation, Abbreviations, and Numbers

Focus

Lesson Overview

Objective
- To use hyphens with prefixes, in compound words, in numbers, and in divided words

Bellringer
Daily Language Activity

Use the Bellringer Transparency for Lesson 21.12.

See also   *Daily Language Practice*

Teach

Hyphens with Prefixes

☑ **Teaching Tip**

Explain that the prefix *anti-* requires a hyphen only when followed by a capitalized word or by a word that begins with *i-*. This rule prevents spelling words with two successive *i*'s.

Practice and Assess

Answers: Exercise 21

1. The desire for self-government among British colonists grew steadily during the pre-Revolutionary War period.
2. Antimonarchy and anti-imperialist forces prevailed, and the Continental Congress prepared for all-out war with Britain.
3. Not only . . . the best all-around fighting force, but . . . the pro-British Iroquois Confederacy.
4. At first British leaders remarked disdainfully that most American soldiers were self-taught.
5. After carefully re-creating their government, the ex-British colonies became the United States of America.

Resource Manager

Planning Resources
- *Lesson Plans*

Transparencies
- *Bellringer*
- *Daily Language Practice*
- *Two-Minute Skill Drill*

☞ Other Print Resources
- *Grammar and Composition Handbook*
- *Grammar Practice*, p. 52
- *Grammar Reteaching*, p. 52
- *Grammar Workbook*, Lesson 90
- *Sentence-Combining Practice*, p. 5

Teach

Hyphens with Compounds

☑ Teaching Tip

One of the most confusing areas of English spelling is determining how to spell compound words. For example, how should we spell *firefighter*—as one word, as a hyphenated word, or as two words? Tell students that answers to such questions can be found by consulting a current dictionary, especially an unabridged edition.

Note, however, that recently coined compounds are almost always spelled as two words. Thus, if the compound is not listed in the dictionary, students should assume it is spelled as two words.

☑ Grammar Tip

Tell students that when the word *from* is used at the beginning of a span of years, *to* is preferred to a hyphen between the years: *from 1884 to 1903,* not *from 1884–1903.*

Also note that although a hyphen is used on a typewriter to indicate a span, printed material makes use of a short dash that is slightly longer than a hyphen.

Punctuation, Abbreviations, and Numbers

Two-Minute Skill Drill

Insert hyphens where necessary to change the following word combinations into compound words.

1. self + starter
2. far + reaching
3. half + truth
4. mayor + elect

📖 **See also** *Two-Minute Skill Drill Transparency 21.12*

Hyphens with Compounds

1. Compound adjectives

■ Use a hyphen in a compound adjective that precedes a noun.

When a compound adjective follows a noun, it is usually not hyphenated.

up-to-the-minute news	*but*	The news was up to the minute.
a nine-year-old boy		The boy was nine years old.
a well-educated girl		The girl is well educated.

An expression is not hyphenated when it is made up of an adverb ending in *-ly* and an adjective.

a happily married couple	the beautifully prepared dinner
a mainly green interior	the amazingly bright child
a nicely decorated house	the perfectly grand day

2. Compound numbers

■ Hyphenate any spelled-out cardinal or ordinal compound number up to ninety-nine or ninety-ninth.

forty-five	eighty-eighth
twenty-first	sixty-seventh

3. Fractions used as adjectives

■ Hyphenate a fraction used as an adjective or as a noun.

two-thirds majority	two-thirds of the members
one-half liter	one-half of a liter
one-eighth mile	one-eighth of a mile

4. Connected numerals

■ Hyphenate two numerals to indicate a span.

pages 354-392	1884-1903
April 1-6	15th-16th centuries

MEETING INDIVIDUAL NEEDS — English Language Learners

Using a Dictionary

If students new to English are unsure how to spell compound words or words with prefixes or suffixes, refer them to a dictionary. Many dictionaries group words with common prefixes (*non-, un-*) into free-standing lists.

Hyphens to Divide Words at the End of a Line

When a word must be divided at the end of a line, it should be divided between syllables or pronounceable parts. If you are unsure of the correct place to divide a word, check your dictionary.

- In general, if a word contains two consonants occurring between two vowels or if it contains a double consonant, divide the word between the two consonants.

rep-resentative	skip-per
fluc-tuate	insig-nificant
impor-tant	big-gest

- If a suffix has been added to a complete word that ends in two consonants, divide the word after the two consonants.

track-ing	black-est
roll-ing	full-est

Exercise 22 **Using Hyphens**

Hyphens must be added to seven of the following sentences. On your, paper rewrite those sentences, adding the hyphens where they are needed. If a sentence contains only words that need no hyphens, write *correct*. Then make a list of all the italicized words, showing where each would be divided if it had to be broken at the end of a line.

Looking at Statistics

1. Statistics can tell us an extraordinarily broad *spectrum* of things about Americans.
2. In 1830, for instance, nearly three fourths of the U.S. population lived on family farms; today one in *fifty* Americans lives on a farm.
3. There is a clear cut trend toward *urban* living.
4. A look at the *almanac* reveals the wide ranging salaries of United States governors—going from just under $56,000 to well over $100,000 a year.
5. During a period of fifty years (1935 1985), the average annual income of a person *working* in the United States jumped from less than $500 to nearly $14,000.
6. American women, however, continue to earn less than men; on average, for every *dollar* that a man earns, a woman earns sixty nine cents.
7. By the year 2000, the number of Asian Americans and Native Americans in the work force is *expected* to experience a two thirds increase.
8. Whereas most Americans work for others, a significant *number* of adults are self employed.
9. The fast growing Hispanic population is having a great impact on American *culture* and society.
10. One widely known statistic is that more and more African Americans are *holding* public office.

Teach

Hyphens to Divide Words at the End of a Line

☑ **Teaching Tip**

Tell students that one-syllable words (*weigh*) should not be divided and words that contain hyphens (*son-in-law*) should be divided at the hyphens.

Punctuation, Abbreviations, and Numbers

Practice and Assess

Answers: Exercise 22

1. correct; spec-trum
2. correct; fif-ty
3. There is a clear-cut trend toward urban living. (ur-ban)
4. A look at the almanac reveals the wide-ranging salaries of United States governors—going from just under $56,000 to well over $100,000 a year. (al-ma-nac)
5. During a period of fifty years (1935–1985), the average annual income of a person working in the United States jumped from less than $500 to nearly $14,000. (work-ing)
6. American women, however, continue to earn less than men; on average, for every dollar that a man earns, a woman earns sixty-nine cents. (dol-lar)
7. By the year 2000, the number of Asian Americans and Native Americans in the work force is expected to experience a two-thirds increase. (ex-pect-ed)
8. Whereas most . . . for others, a significant number of adults are self-employed. (num-ber)
9. The fast-growing Hispanic population is having a great impact on American culture and society. (cul-ture)
10. correct; hold-ing

Additional Resources

📁 *Grammar Practice*, p. 52
📁 *Grammar Reteaching*, p. 52
📁 *Sentence-Combining Practice*, p. 5

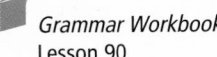 *Grammar Workbook*
Lesson 90

Close

Provide students with a list of words to divide. Have them estimate, by counting syllables, where the word breaks will occur. Then have them check a dictionary to see whether they are correct.

765

Focus

Lesson Overview

Objective

- To recognize and use the correct form of abbreviations

 Bellringer

Daily Language Activity

When students enter the classroom, have this assignment on the board: *List some common abbreviations you use every day.*

See also *Daily Language Practice*

Teach

Capitalization of Abbreviations

☑ **Teaching Tip**

Certain expressions used in formal writing may sometimes be written as abbreviations with periods. For example, *i.e.* is an abbreviation of *id est; e.g.,* of *exempli gratia; viz.,* of *videlicet; ca.* or *c.,* of *circa; cf.,* of *confer;* and *etc.,* of *et cetera.*

Ⓐ **Vocabulary Link**

The term *abbreviation* comes from a Latin verb meaning "to shorten." It is related to the English word *brief.*

Punctuation, Abbreviations, and Numbers

21.13 Abbreviations

Abbreviations are shortened forms of words. They are used to save space and time and to avoid wordiness. For example, it is more concise and easier to write 800 B.C. than to write *800 years before the birth of Christ.* Periods follow most abbreviations. For guidance on how to write a particular abbreviation, check a dictionary.

- If an abbreviation occurs at the end of a sentence that would ordinarily take a period, do not add an additional closing period

    I am going to Washington, **D.C.**

- If an abbreviation occurs at the end of a sentence that ends with a question mark or an exclamation point, use the period for the abbreviation *and* the second mark of punctuation.

    Have you been to Washington, **D.C.?**
    I can't wait to go to Washington, **D.C.!**

Capitalization of Abbreviations

- Capitalize abbreviations of proper nouns.

    Dwight **D.** Eisenhower
    135 Claremont **Ave.**
    U.S. Department of Labor

The names of many organizations and agencies, whether pronounced letter by letter or as words, are abbreviated by using the initial letters of the complete name without periods.

    NAACP   YMCA   CIA   FCC   UN   NATO

Capitalize these abbreviations related to historical dates:

A.D. (*anno Domini*), "in the year of the Lord" (since the birth of Christ); place before the date: **A.D.** 66

B.C. (before Christ); place after the date: 336 **B.C.**

B.C.E. (before the common era; equivalent to *B.C.*); place after the date: 1000 **B.C.E.**

C.E. (common era; equivalent to *A.D.*); place after the date: 60 **C.E.**

A.M. (*ante meridiem*), "before noon"; place after exact times: 2:45 **A.M.**

P.M. (*post meridiem*), "after noon"; place after exact times: 10:30 **P.M.**

 Resource Manager

Planning Resources
- *Lesson Plans*

 Transparencies
- *Bellringer*
- *Daily Language Practice*

📂 **Other Print Resources**
- *Grammar and Composition Handbook*
- *Grammar Practice,* p. 52
- *Grammar Workbook,* Lesson 91

State Abbreviations

In ordinary prose, spell out state names. When addressing mail, however, use the abbreviations of state names that appear in the list below. (*Note:* No comma appears between the state postal abbreviation and the number in a zip code.)

Alabama	**AL**	Montana	**MT**
Alaska	**AK**	Nebraska	**NE**
Arizona	**AZ**	Nevada	**NV**
Arkansas	**AR**	New Hampshire	**NH**
California	**CA**	New Jersey	**NJ**
Colorado	**CO**	New Mexico	**NM**
Connecticut	**CT**	New York	**NY**
Delaware	**DE**	North Carolina	**NC**
Florida	**FL**	North Dakota	**ND**
Georgia	**GA**	Ohio	**OH**
Hawaii	**HI**	Oklahoma	**OK**
Idaho	**ID**	Oregon	**OR**
Illinois	**IL**	Pennsylvania	**PA**
Indiana	**IN**	Rhode Island	**RI**
Iowa	**IA**	South Carolina	**SC**
Kansas	**KS**	South Dakota	**SD**
Kentucky	**KY**	Tennessee	**TN**
Louisiana	**LA**	Texas	**TX**
Maine	**ME**	Utah	**UT**
Maryland	**MD**	Vermont	**VT**
Massachusetts	**MA**	Virginia	**VA**
Michigan	**MI**	Washington	**WA**
Minnesota	**MN**	West Virginia	**WV**
Mississippi	**MS**	Wisconsin	**WI**
Missouri	**MO**	Wyoming	**WY**

The zip code form for the District of Columbia, for use on envelopes only, is **DC.**

Exercise 23   Using Abbreviations

On your paper, write the abbreviations for the italicized words or phrases in the following sentences. If an abbreviation should not be used, write *correct.*

1. The *Young Men's Christian Association* has been promoting family and recreational activities since *anno Domini* 1881.
2. The *United States* Capitol is located in Washington, D.C.
3. One zip code for Fargo, *North Dakota,* is 58103.
4. The *Federal Aviation Administration* establishes regulations for airline companies.
5. Many Americans begin work at 9:00 *ante meridiem* and end at 5:00 *post meridiem.*

21.13 Abbreviations   **767**

Punctuation, Abbreviations, and Numbers

21.13

Teach

State Abbreviations

☑ **Grammar Tip**

Periods have traditionally been used with abbreviations in the English system. The trend today, however, is away from the use of periods in abbreviations, particularly in scientific writing. Abbreviations for units of the metric system, which is used in most scientific writing, are rarely seen with periods.

☑ **Teaching Tip**

Point out that in a personal letter it is appropriate to use a state abbreviation in the address. In other forms of writing, such as expository writing, students should spell out the name of a state. For example, in a paper on the tourist trade in Florida, students should always spell out the state's name.

Practice and Assess

Answers: Exercise 23
1. YMCA; A.D.
2. U.S. *or* correct
3. correct
4. FAA *or* correct
5. A.M.; P.M.

MEETING INDIVIDUAL NEEDS   English Language Learners

Listing Common Abbreviations

Because many of the abbreviated words used in this lesson may be unfamiliar to students new to English, provide students with a list of words that are commonly abbreviated. Encourage students to copy the list into their journals. Suggest that they highlight the periods in the abbreviations so that they remember to include them.

767

Teach

Abbreviations of Titles and Units of Measure

☑ **Teaching Tip**

Scientific and technical abbreviations are normally used without periods—for example, *AM* (amplitude modulation), *cps* (cycles per second), *DC* (direct current), and *RF* (radio frequency).

Practice and Assess

Answers: Exercise 24

1. Gov. *or* correct
2. Mr.
3. Dr.
4. correct
5. ml *or* correct

Additional Resources

 Grammar Practice, p. 52

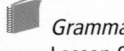 *Grammar Workbook*
Lesson 91

Close

Ask students to discuss why some words are usually abbreviated.

Punctuation, Abbreviations, and Numbers

Abbreviations of Titles and Units of Measure

1. Personal titles

■ Use abbreviations for some personal titles.

Certain titles, including *Mrs., Mr., Ms., Sr.,* and *Jr.,* are almost always abbreviated. Professional and academic titles, such as *Dr., M.D.,* and *B.A.,* are also usually abbreviated. When they are used before a full name, the titles of government and military officials and members of the clergy are frequently abbreviated.

Mrs. Elizabeth Dole	**Gov.** Tommy Thompson
Ms. Amy Tan	**Sen.** Carol Mosely-Braun
Dr. Joseph Fernandez	**Rev.** Jesse Jackson

2. Units of measure

■ Abbreviate units of measure used with numerals in technical or scientific writing but not in ordinary prose.

In the list below, the abbreviations stand for plural as well as singular units:

ENGLISH SYSTEM		METRIC SYSTEM	
ft.	foot	**cg**	centigram
gal.	gallon	**cl**	centiliter
in.	inch	**cm**	centimeter
lb.	pound	**g**	gram
mi.	mile	**kg**	kilogram
oz.	ounce	**km**	kilometer
pt.	pint	**l**	liter
qt.	quart	**m**	meter
tbsp.	tablespoon	**mg**	milligram
tsp.	teaspoon	**ml**	milliliter
yd.	yard	**mm**	millimeter

Exercise 24 **Using Abbreviations (Part 2)**

Write the abbreviations for the italicized words or phrases in the following sentences. If no abbreviation should be used, write *correct.*

1. *Governor* Nellie Tayloe Ross of Wyoming, elected in 1924, was the first woman to hold that office in any state.
2. Among the guests were *Mister* Diaz and his daughters.
3. *Doctor* C. Everett Koop was the surgeon general during George Bush's administration.
4. The pitcher stood 60 *feet* 6 *inches* from the batter and glanced at first base.
5. Add 20 *milliliters* of water to the formula.

Enrichment and Extension

Abbreviating Names

Have students provide the full names: AFL-CIO (American Federation of Labor and Congress of Industrial Organizations), BMW (Bavarian Motor Works), EEC (European Economic Community), IBM (International Business Machines), NBA (National Basketball Association), NBC (National Broadcasting Company), NSF (National Science Foundation), OPEC (Organization of Petroleum Exporting Countries), PBS (Public Broadcasting Service), and UNESCO (United Nations Educational, Scientific, and Cultural Organization).

21.14 Numbers and Numerals

In ordinary prose, some numbers are written out in words, and some are expressed in figures. Numbers that are expressed in figures are known as *numerals*.

Numbers Spelled Out

■ In general, spell out cardinal and ordinal numbers that can be written in one or two words.

> The Senate consists of **one hundred** members—**two** senators from each of the **fifty** states.

> The building is **sixty-eight** feet tall.

> Juanita was the **thirty-sixth** person waiting in line for concert tickets.

■ Spell out any number that occurs at the beginning of a sentence.

> **Two thousand twenty-eight** people were at the concert.

> **Twenty-nine** students are in our class.

Exercise 25 Using Numbers

On your paper, rewrite the following sentences, spelling out numbers where necessary.

The Inca Empire

1. The Inca Empire dominated the Andes region of South America for more than 1/3 of a century.
2. 2,200 miles of Pacific coastline were controlled by the Incas.
3. The 8th Inca ruler was the first to be called *Sapa Inca,* meaning "emperor."
4. 150 miles a day was not an uncommon distance for a team of Inca runners carrying messages throughout the empire.
5. The mighty Inca Empire was destroyed in only 3 years by the Spanish explorer Francisco Pizarro.
6. In 1531 Pizarro made his 3rd expedition to Peru, determined to conquer the rich and powerful Inca Empire.
7. 180 men went with Pizarro when he sailed from Panama to Peru.
8. At the start of his expedition, Pizarro had only 27 horses and 2 pieces of artillery.
9. Pizarro and his men were the 1st Europeans to reach the interior of Peru and confront the Inca ruler.
10. Within 50 years of the Spanish conquest, there was little trace of the once-glorious Inca civilization.

21.14 Numbers and Numerals **769**

Focus

Lesson Overview

Objective
• To spell out numbers of one or two words and to use numerals for numbers of more than two words and for amounts, dates, times, and addresses

 Bellringer
Daily Language Activity

When students enter the classroom, have this assignment on the board: *Spell out the following numbers: 29; 2,000; and 5,000,000.*

See also *Daily Language Practice*

Teach

Numbers Spelled Out

☑ **Teaching Tip**

The most commonly followed convention for spelling out numbers is to spell out whole numbers from one to ninety-nine and the same numbers when followed by the words *hundred, thousand, million,* and so on: *seven hundred, twelve thousand, eighty million.*

Practice and Assess

Answers: Exercise 25

Only the spelled-out numbers appear below.
1. one third
2. Two thousand two hundred
3. eighth
4. One hundred fifty
5. three
6. third
7. One hundred eighty
8. twenty-seven; two
9. first
10. fifty

Punctuation, Abbreviations, and Numbers

Resource Manager

Planning Resources
• *Lesson Plans*

 Transparencies
• *Bellringer*
• *Daily Language Practice*
• *Two-Minute Skill Drill*

📂 **Other Print Resources**
• *Grammar and Composition Handbook*
• *Grammar Enrichment,* p. 52
• *Grammar Workbook,* Lesson 92

Teach

Numerals

☑ Teaching Tip

In scientific writing, all numbers are usually expressed in figures: *3 cubic feet, 120 volts, 2 miles, 4 meters.*

ⒶVocabulary Link

The term *numeral* comes from the Latin word for *"number."* English has borrowed many related words—for example, *number, numerical,* and *numerous.*

☑ Grammar Tip

In a complete street address, numbered streets and avenues are written in numerals if the number is greater than ten: *123 West 25th Street.* When referring to a street and not to an address on the street, spell out the name of the street: *I live on West Twenty-fifth Street.*

Two-Minute Skill Drill

List these numbers on the board. Ask students to spell out the numbers that should be spelled out.

24,800,000	3:00
8th century	85
10.7 grams	

✎ **See also** *Two-Minute Skill Drill Transparency 21.14*

Punctuation, Abbreviations, and Numbers

Numerals

■ In general, use numerals to express numbers that would be written in more than two words.

> The Homestead Act allowed each farmer to claim **160** acres.
>
> The speed of light is **186,000** miles per second.

When a large number can be written as a mixed number followed by the word *million* or *billion,* the numeral should appear in decimal form.

> The television station was purchased for **$86.5 million.**

■ If some numbers of a category can be written out while other related numbers should appear as numerals, use all numerals.

> Of the **435** members of the House of Representatives, **50** were newly elected.

1. **Money, decimals, and percentages**

■ Use numerals to express amounts of money, decimals, and percentages.

$19.50	**2.5** pounds
$6.25 million	**57** percent

If an amount of money can be expressed in one or two words, however, it should be spelled out.

seventy-six cents	**sixty thousand** dollars

2. **Dates and time**

■ Use numerals to express the year and day in a date and to express the precise time with the abbreviations *A.M.* and *P.M.*

> The First Continental Congress met on September **5, 1774.**
>
> The president was to meet the ambassador at **3:15** P.M.

Spell out expressions of time that do not use *A.M.* or *P.M.*

> The ambassador's meeting was scheduled for **three** o'clock.

■ To express a century when the word *century* is used, spell out the number. Likewise, to express a decade when the century is clear from the context, spell out the number.

> The greatest decade of the **twentieth** century was the **twenties.**

■ When a decade is expressed as a single unit, use numerals followed by *-s.*

> The **1920s** were known as the Jazz Age.

MEETING INDIVIDUAL NEEDS English Language Learners

Expressing Time

Students new to English may have difficulty with expressions of time. Remind students that they should never use the words *morning* or *evening* with A.M. or P.M. For example, it would be redundant to write *8 A.M. in the morning.*

3. Addresses

■ Use numerals for streets and avenues numbered above ten and for all house, apartment, and room numbers. Spell out numbered streets and avenues with numbers of ten or under.

526 West **111th** Street   **52** South **Ninth** Street
Apartment **6D**   Room **8**
18 East **12th** Avenue   **866 Third** Avenue

4. References

■ Use numerals to express page, line, act, and scene numbers and the like.

Look on pages **9** and **24** for references to Arthur Ashe.
Read paragraphs **3** and **4** on page **360** of my Chinese cookbook.
We danced in scenes **1** and **2** of the community ballet.

Exercise 26   **Using Numbers and Numerals**

Write out the following sentences, making any necessary changes in the use of numbers and numerals.

Wilma Rudolph, Sprinter

1. One of the fastest female runners of the 20th century, Wilma Rudolph won 3 gold medals at the 1960 Olympic games.
2. Besides placing 1st in the women's one-hundred-meter and two-hundred-meter dashes, she pushed her team to victory in the women's four-hundred-meter relay.
3. Rudolph's feat is all the more astonishing because she was not able to walk until she was 8.
4. Her birth weight was low, well under 5 pounds, and she suffered from a series of illnesses that left her, at the age of 4, without the use of her left leg.
5. By the time Rudolph entered high school, she had recovered so well that she excelled in basketball; in 1 year she scored eight hundred three points in 25 games.
6. At the Millrose Games in nineteen hundred sixty-one, she ran the 60-yard dash in six and nine-tenths seconds; she broke that world record 2 weeks later.
7. 11.3 seconds was her time in the one-hundred-meter dash at the 1960 Olympics— a time she bettered by one tenth of a second on July nineteen, 1961, when she set the women's world record.
8. At 5 feet 11 inches and one hundred thirty pounds, Rudolph was tall yet extraordinarily graceful.
9. After her Olympic victory, she toured Europe, greeting 1,000s of people and traveling more than two thousand miles.
10. During the nineteen sixties Rudolph retired from running while still in her 20s; she then devoted herself to developing track-and-field teams for girls.

Practice and Assess

Answers: Exercise 26

1. One of the fastest . . . of the twentieth century, Wilma Rudolph won three gold medals at the 1960 Olympic games.
2. Besides placing first in the women's one-hundred-meter and two-hundred-meter dashes, she pushed her team to victory in the women's four-hundred-meter relay.
3. Rudolph's feat is all the more astonishing because she was not able to walk until she was eight.
4. Her birth weight was low, well under five pounds, and she suffered from a series of illnesses that left her, at the age of four, without the use of her left leg.
5. . . . in one year she scored 803 points in twenty-five games.
6. At the Millrose Games in 1961, she ran the sixty-yard dash in 6.9 seconds; she broke that world record two weeks later.
7. Eleven and three-tenths seconds was her time in the one-hundred-meter dash at the 1960 Olympics— a time she bettered by one tenth of a second on July 19, 1961, when she set . . .
8. At five feet eleven inches and 130 pounds, Rudolph was tall . . .
9. After her Olympic victory, she toured Europe, greeting thousands of people and traveling more than two thousand miles.
10. During the 1960s Rudolph retired from running while still in her twenties . . .

Additional Resources

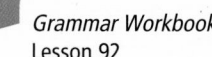 *Grammar Enrichment,* p. 52

Grammar Workbook
Lesson 92

Close

Have students write a paragraph of at least six sentences, using some numbers that are spelled out and some written as figures. Students should also include some of the following: dates, time, money, percentages, and decimals.

Punctuation, Abbreviations, and Numbers

Teach

About the Literature

The passage from *One Writer's Beginnings* by Eudora Welty is taken from part 2 of the memoir. Explain that the review contains a passage followed by exercises on related topics. After students have read the passage, discuss its characters, setting, and mood. Then ask students to determine which highlighted punctuation marks are, or are not, essential to the meaning of the passage.

Linking Grammar and Literature

Critical Thinking

Ask students to focus on the use of semicolons in the literature passage. Guide them to see that some of the long sentences can be easier to deal with if the semicolons are viewed as periods. Then ask students to examine the use of dashes and parentheses in the passage.

✔ ASSESSMENT OPTIONS

📂 *Tests with Answer Key & Rubrics*
Unit 21 Mastery Test, pp. 77–78

💾 *Testmaker*
Unit 21 Mastery Test

PUNCTUATION

Eudora Welty has spent most of her long and productive life in Jackson, Mississippi, where she was born in 1909. This seemingly sheltered life has not been without risk, for "all serious daring starts from within," as she says in her memoir, *One Writer's Beginnings*. In this excerpt from that book, she reminisces about her father's family and alludes to her mother's, the Andrewses. The passage has been annotated to show some of the rules of punctuation covered in this unit.

Punctuation, Abbreviations, and Numbers

Semicolon to separate main clauses

Dash to indicate a change in thought

Period at the end of a declarative sentence

Colon to introduce a restatement

Apostrophe to indicate a contraction

Question mark to indicate a question

Commas to separate elements in a series

Apostrophe and -*s* to indicate the possessive forms of *father*

Comma to separate two main clauses that are joined by a coordinating conjunction

Literature Model

from One Writer's Beginnings
by Eudora Welty

The Weltys were originally German Swiss; the first ones to come to this country, back before the Revolutionary War here, were three brothers, and the whole family is descended from them, I understand—it seems to hark back to German fairy-tale tradition.

My father is not the one who told me this: he never happened to tell us a single family story; could it have been because he'd heard so many of the Andrews stories? I think it was rather because, as he said, he had no interest in ancient history—only the future, he said, should count. At the same time, he was exceedingly devoted to his father, went to see him whenever he could, and wrote to him regularly from his desk at home; I grew up familiar with seeing the long envelopes being addressed in my father's clear, careful hand: Jefferson Welty, Esquire. It was the only use my father made of the word; he saved it for his father. I took "Esquire" for a term of reverence, and I think it stood for that with him; we were always aware that Daddy loved him.

An English Welti, who spelled his name thus, with an *i*, wrote to me once from Kent, in curiosity, after an early book of mine had appeared over there; he asked me about my

772   Unit 21 Punctuation, Abbreviations, and Numbers

Resource Manager

Planning Resources
• *Lesson Plans*

📂 **Other Print Resources**
• *Grammar and Composition Handbook*
• *Grammar Workbook*, Lessons 73–92; Unit 12 Review; Cumulative Review: Units 1–12

name. My father, who had never told us anything, had died, and this was before my mother set herself as she did later to looking into records. Mr. Welti knew about the whole throng of them, from medieval times on, and the three brothers who set forth to the New World from German Switzerland and settled from Virginia westward over Pennsylvania, Ohio, and Indiana before the Revolutionary War. "I expect you know," wrote the British Mr. Welti, "that one unfortunate Welty fell at Saratoga."

The only part of his letter that would have interested my father is that about the St. Gotthard Tunnel and the Welty who pushed it through. The fact that this same Welty had been President of Switzerland seven times running would have caused him to say "Pshaw!", his strongest expletive. (That my mother's strongest exclamation was "Pshaw!" too rather took away some of its force for both of them.)

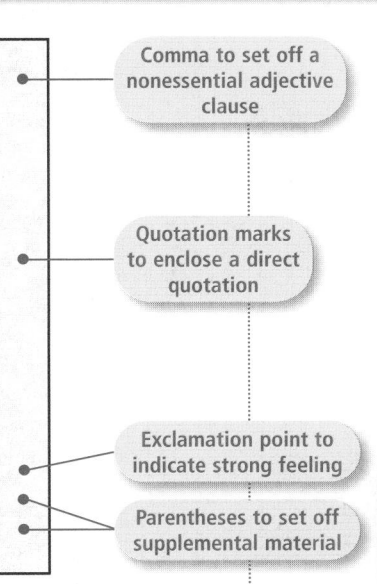

> Comma to set off a nonessential adjective clause

> Quotation marks to enclose a direct quotation

> Exclamation point to indicate strong feeling

> Parentheses to set off supplemental material

Punctuation, Abbreviations, and Numbers

Review: Exercise 1   Using End Punctuation

The following sentences describe some of Eudora Welty's early teachers. On your paper, rewrite each item, correcting any errors in end punctuation. If an item contains no errors, write *correct.*

1. Don't most people vividly remember at least one teacher from their childhood. One of Eudora Welty's most memorable teachers was Miss Duling.
2. Can you imagine a prim woman, wearing a black-and-white checked dress, a long red sweater, black stockings, and black high-top shoes. Wow.
3. What a perfectionist Miss Duling seemed to Eudora?
4. Miss Duling was intolerant of excuses and pretensions. The governor's daughter, named Lady Rachel, was just plain Rachel to Miss Duling.
5. Miss Duling asked the Mississippi legislature to compete in a spelling match with her fourth-grade class?
6. Who won the spelling match. Welty hints that the class did.
7. Miss Eyrich, Welty's physical-education teacher, was also memorable.
8. How her booming commands terrorized reluctant runners?
9. Mrs. McWillie, a stern fourth-grade teacher, once overhead Welty and a friend using improper grammar.
10. The furious Mrs. McWillie asked which of the girls had used an incorrect verb form? Why, she even threatened to report them to the principal.

Practice and Assess

Answers: Exercise 1

1. Don't most people vividly remember at least one teacher from their childhood? One of Eudora Welty's most memorable teachers was Miss Duling.
2. Can you imagine a prim woman, wearing a black-and-white checked dress, a long red sweater, black stockings, and black high-top shoes? Wow!
3. What a perfectionist Miss Duling seemed to Eudora!
4. Miss Duling was intolerant of excuses and pretensions. The governor's daughter, named Lady Rachel, was just plain Rachel to Miss Duling.
5. Miss Duling asked the Mississippi legislature to compete in a spelling match with her fourth-grade class.
6. Who won the spelling match? Welty hints that the class did.
7. correct
8. How her booming commands terrorized reluctant runners!
9. correct
10. The furious Mrs. McWillie asked which of the girls had used an incorrect verb form. Why, she even threatened to report them to the principal!

Practice and Assess

Answers: Exercise 2

1. Eudora Welty's parents valued reading; therefore, they purchased books that would delight as well as instruct.
2. Books in the Welty library included those by the following authors: Mark Twain, Ring Lardner, and Charles Dickens.
3. correct or . . . early age; in fact, . . .
4. *Our Wonder World,* one of Welty's favorite sets of books, contained legends about Robin Hood and King Arthur, fairy tales by H.C. Anderson, and fables by Aesop.
5. One critic describes Welty's *One Writer's Beginnings* as follows: "This splendid little book will itself be remembered and used and loved."

Answers: Exercise 3

1. The Mississippi writer William Faulkner is considered to be among the greatest authors of the twentieth century.
2. Faulkner, who won a Nobel Prize in 1949, wrote a saga about life in Yoknapatawpha County.
3. He depicts in these books that feature the Snopes family as protagonists a changing South.
4. The Southern author whom I enjoy most is Alice Walker.
5. Alice Walker, whose most famous book is *The Color Purple,* writes about African Americans.
6. Yes, Flannery O'Connor did grow up in Georgia.
7. O'Connor, by the way, depicts eccentrics and outcasts.
8. She writes about a character who is called The Misfit.
9. Carson McCullers, another Georgian, depicts an isolated café owner and a hearing-impaired person in one of her novels.
10. One of the most famous of McCullers's works, *The Member of the Wedding,* focuses on a lonely Southern girl.

Punctuation, Abbreviations, and Numbers

Review Exercise 2 Using Colons and Semicolons

The following sentences tell about Eudora Welty's love of reading. On your paper, rewrite each sentence, correcting any errors in the use of colons and semicolons. If a sentence contains no errors, write *correct.*

1. Eudora Welty's parents valued reading: therefore, they purchased books that would delight as well as instruct.
2. Books in the Welty library included those by the following authors; Mark Twain, Ring Lardner, and Charles Dickens.
3. Welty was exposed to books at an early age: books were a favorite gift in her household.
4. *Our Wonder World,* one of Welty's favorite sets of books, contained: legends about Robin Hood and King Arthur, fairy tales by H. C. Anderson, and fables by Aesop.
5. One critic describes Welty's *One Writer's Beginnings* as follows, "This splendid little book will itself by remembered and used and loved."

Review: Exercise 3 Using the Comma (Part 1)

The following sentences describe Southern writers. Rewrite each sentence, adding the material in parentheses in the place indicated by the caret. If the material is *not* essential to the meaning of the sentence, add commas. If it is essential, do not add commas.

SAMPLE   Writers∧have contributed greatly to the body of memorable American literature. (who are from the South)

ANSWER   Writers who are from the South have contributed greatly to the body of memorable American literature.

1. The Mississippi writer∧is considered to be among the greatest authors of the twentieth century. (William Faulkner)
2. Faulkner∧wrote a saga about life in Yoknapatawpha County. (who won a Nobel Prize in 1949)
3. He depicts in these books∧a changing South. (that feature the Snopes family as protagonists)
4. The Southern author∧is Alice Walker. (whom I enjoy most)
5. Alice Walker∧writes about African Americans. (whose most famous book is *The Color Purple*)
6. ∧Flannery O'Connor did grow up in Georgia. (Yes)
7. O'Connor∧depicts eccentrics and outcasts. (by the way)
8. She writes about a character∧. (who is called The Misfit)
9. Carson McCullers∧depicts an isolated café owner and a hearing-impaired person in one of her novels. (another Georgian)
10. ∧*The Member of the Wedding* focuses on a lonely Southern girl. (one of the most famous of McCullers's works)

Review: Exercise 4 Using the Comma

The following sentences describe the Southern settings used by some American writers. On your paper, rewrite each sentence, adding or deleting commas where necessary.

1. The South is often the setting in works written by Eudora Welty Harper Lee and Walker Percy.
2. Lee grew up in Alabama and she used a small, Southern town as the setting for her only novel *To Kill a Mockingbird.*
3. *To Kill a Mockingbird* won a Pulitzer Prize in 1961; subsequently it was made into a movie.
4. By the way the main characters in *To Kill a Mockingbird* seem much like the young Eudora Welty and her father.
5. Walker Percy grew up in Birmingham, Alabama but his novels are set in various locales throughout the South.
6. Although Percy called his view of the world "cold-eyed" and "despairing" his books are popular.
7. Percy's first novel, *The Moviegoer,* is about a young affluent New Orleans stockbroker searching for a new direction in his life.
8. His settings create a mood that is at once grotesque, and humorous, and disturbing.
9. Writers such as Zora Neale Hurston, Alice Walker and Truman Capote left the South but the region remained a presence in their writing.
10. For example Capote's "A Christmas Memory" is a story set in Monroeville Alabama.

Review: Exercise 5 Using the Dash and Parentheses

The following sentences are about the Saint Gotthard Tunnel, which one of Welty's ancestors helped build. Rewrite each sentence, adding dashes or parentheses where needed. Use the marks of punctuation indicated in parentheses at the end of each sentence.

1. The masonry-lined tunnel it is more than nine miles long connects Andermatt to Airolo in the Swiss Alps. (dashes)
2. Did you know that the tunnel, at its highest point of elevation, is 3,786 feet 1,154 meters above sea level? (parentheses)
3. The project after a decade of construction was finally completed in 1882; it was part of the Saint Gotthard Railway. This line connects Lucerne, Switzerland, to Milan, Italy. (dashes, parentheses)
4. The tunnel was costly in human terms hundreds lost their lives during its construction; it was also a financial burden the company almost went bankrupt several times. (two pairs of parentheses)
5. This tunnel a massive undertaking cut the traveling time between Milan and Lucerne to ten hours. (dashes)

Answers: Exercise 4

1. The South is often the setting in works written by Eudora Welty, Harper Lee, and Walker Percy.
2. Lee grew up in Alabama, and she used a small Southern town as the setting for her only novel, *To Kill a Mockingbird.*
3. *To Kill a Mockingbird* won a Pulitzer Prize in 1961; subsequently, it was made into a movie.
4. By the way, the main characters in *To Kill a Mockingbird* seem much like the young Eudora Welty and her father.
5. Walker Percy grew up in Birmingham, Alabama, but his novels are set in various locales throughout the South.
6. Although Percy called his view of the world "cold-eyed" and "despairing," his books are popular.
7. Percy's first novel, *The Moviegoer,* is about a young, affluent New Orleans stockbroker searching for a new direction in his life.
8. His settings create a mood that is at once grotesque, humorous, and disturbing.
9. Writers such as Zora Neale Hurston, Alice Walker, and Truman Capote left the South, but the region remained a presence in their writing.
10. For example, Capote's "A Christmas Memory" is a nostalgic story set in Monroeville, Alabama.

Answers: Exercise 5

1. The masonry-lined tunnel—it is more than nine miles long—connects Andermatt to Airolo in the Swiss Alps.
2. Did you know that the tunnel, at its highest point of elevation, is 3,786 feet (1,154 meters) above sea level?
3. The project—after a decade of construction—was finally completed in 1882; it was part of the Saint Gotthard Railway. (This line connects Lucerne, Switzerland, to Milan, Italy.)
4. The tunnel was costly in human terms (hundreds lost their lives during its construction); it was also a financial burden (the company almost went bankrupt several times).
5. This tunnel—a massive undertaking—cut the traveling time between Milan and Lucerne to ten hours.

Answers: Exercise 6

1. Welty loved listening to music: first, lullabies like "Rock-a-Bye Baby" and, later, selections from the opera *Carmen.*
2. Using today's slang, someone might call Eudora's mother's avid reading "totally awesome"; she read everything from novels such as *Jane Eyre* to scientific works.
3. "Eudora is going to be a writer," we can imagine one of her teachers saying, "because she loves fine literature."
4. Welty learned the meaning of words such as somnambulist by watching *The Cabinet of Dr. Caligari* and other films.
5. Welty relates that the first book she ever bought was *In April Once,* by William Alexander Percy, a Mississippi poet. The first poem in the volume was entitled "Home."

Answers: Exercise 7

1. *One Writer's Beginnings* is about Eudora Welty's early life.
2. Both parents' love for her was steady but unindulgent; it's apparent in the book.
3. Their children's success in life is partially due to the Weltys' high regard for education.
4. correct
5. Grandma Andrews (Mrs. Welty's mother) must have been pleased with her son-in-law's adoration of her daughter.

Answers: Exercise 8
Proofreading

This proofreading activity provides editing practice with (1) the current or previous units' skills, (2) the **Troubleshooter** errors, and (3) spelling errors. Students should be able to complete the exercise by referring to the units, the **Troubleshooter,** and a dictionary. (Note: A run-on sentence counts as one error.)

Error (Type of Error)

1. • Boston, (geographical term)
2. • six (one-word number)
   • six, (introductory adverb clause)
3. • Cambridge, where (sentence fragment)
4. • nineteen (one-word number)
   • nineteen, (introductory adverb clause)
5. • there, (introductory participial phrase)
   • illustrator (spelling)
   • periodical, (nonessential appositive)

| **Review: Exercise 6** | Using Quotation Marks and Italics |

These sentences are based on other parts of Welty's memoir. On your paper, rewrite each one, adding quotation marks or italics (underlining) when necessary.

1. Welty loved listening to music: first, lullabies like Rock-a-Bye Baby and, later, selections from the opera Carmen.
2. Using today's slang, someone might call Eudora's mother's avid reading totally awesome; she read everything from novels such as Jane Eyre to scientific works.
3. Eudora is going to be a writer, we can imagine one of her teachers saying, because she loves fine literature.
4. Welty learned the meaning of words such as somnambulist by watching The Cabinet of Dr. Caligari and other films.
5. Welty relates that the first book she ever bought was In April Once, by William Alexander Percy, a Mississippi poet. The first poem in the volume was entitled Home.

| **Review: Exercise 7** | Using the Apostrophe |

Rewrite each of the following sentences, adding or deleting apostrophes where necessary. If a sentence has no errors, write *correct*.

1. *One Writers' Beginnings* is about Eudora Welty's early life.
2. Both parent's love for her was steady but unindulgent; its apparent in the book.
3. Their children's success in life was partially due to the Weltys high regard for education.
4. Welty also describes the trip to her Grandma Andrews's house in West Virginia.
5. Grandma Andrews (Mrs. Weltys' mother) must have been pleased with her son-in-law's adoration of her daughter.

| **Review: Exercise 8** |

Proofreading

The following passage describes the artist Winslow Homer, whose painting appears on the opposite page. Rewrite the passage, correcting the errors in spelling, usage, and grammar. Add any missing punctuation. There are twenty-five errors.

Winslow Homer

[1]American artist Winslow Homer (1836–1910) was born in Boston Massachusetts. [2]When he was 6 his family moved to the nearby town of Cambridge. [3]Where Homer first developed a love for the outdoors. [4]By the time he was 19 Homer had apprenticed himself to a Boston lithographer. [5]Uninspired by the work there he became a free-lance illustrater for *Ballou's Pictorial,*

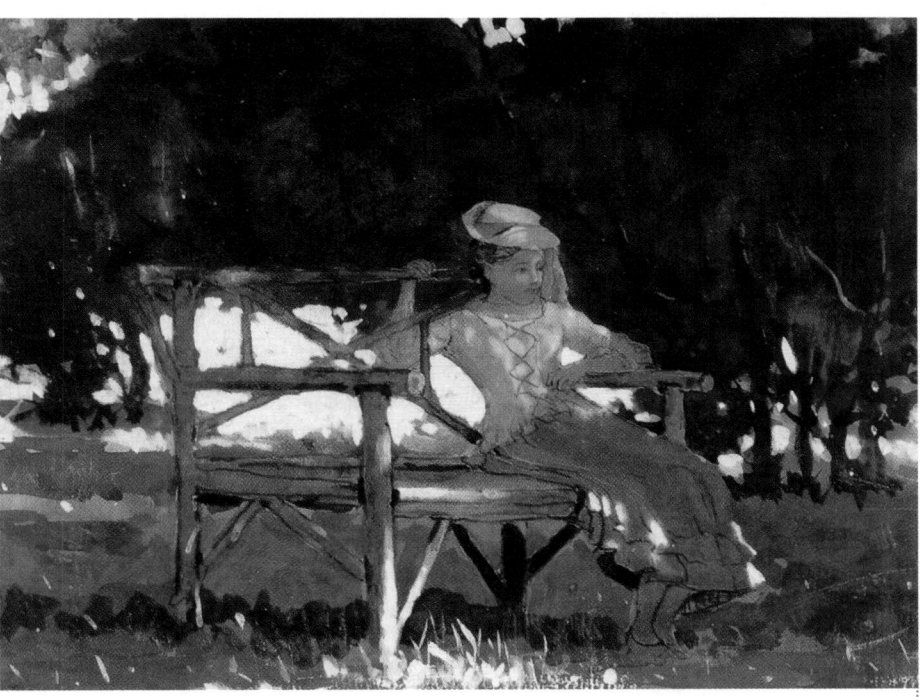

Winslow Homer, *Girl on a Garden Seat,* 1878

**Answers: Exercise 8
Proofreading
(continued)**

Error (Type of Error)

6. • 1859, (run-on sentence)
   • continued (verb tense)
7. • began, (introductory adverb clause)
8. • well-drawn (compound adjective)
   • exaggeration (spelling)
9. • ended, (introductory adverb clause)
10. • Homer's (singular possessive)
11. • watercolors, (nonessential appositive)
12. • strokes, (introductory participial phrase)
    • shadow, (commas in a series)
13. • nature, (nonessential participial phrase)
    • accurately (spelling)
14. • predominate, (nonessential adjective clause)
15. • They are powerful (sentence fragment)
16. • Welty's relatives (singular possessive)
17. • prosperous. She or prosperous; or prosperous, and (run-on sentence)

a Boston periodical and for *Harper's Weekly,* a New York magazine. [6]He moved to New York in 1859 and he continues to make illustrations for *Harper's Weekly.*

[7]When the Civil War began *Harper's Weekly* sent Homer to Virginia to document the fighting along the front lines. [8]His well drawn illustrations of the war were accurate and lacked heroic exageration.

[9]After the war ended Homer turned to painting scenes of contemporary country life. [10]The painting above is typical of Homers work after the war. [11]Like many of his paintings, it was executed in watercolors a medium in which he excelled. [12]Using only a few brush strokes he was able to convey an entire world of light, shadow and color. [13]Homer's paintings always reflected his love of nature recording life acurately without being sentimental. [14]His nature scenes, where the land and sea predominate are very popular. [15]Powerful examples of Homer's trust in nature.

[16]It is easy to imagine that either Eudora Welty or one of Weltys' relatives is depicted in the painting above. [17]The portrait shows a young woman who is prosperous she symbolizes all the young women of her time and class.

Grammar Review   **777**

Viewing the Art

Winslow Homer, *Girl on a Garden Seat,* 1878

In *Girl on a Garden Seat,* Winslow Homer has captured the perfect ease of a summer day. The viewer can almost feel the cool shadows and hear the lazy buzzing of insects. The painting is nostalgic, but it is not sentimen-tal. Ask students to reexamine Homer's *Girl on a Garden Seat* and to suggest an entry the girl might make in her diary when she returns to her home.

Practice and Assess

Answers: Exercise 9
Mixed Review

1. The author Eudora Welty was born in 1909 in Jackson, Mississippi (the state's capital).
2. Her parents, who valued reading, purchased books . . .
3. Welty first attended a women's college in Mississippi, but she graduated . . .
4. In 1936 Welty published her first short story, "Death of a Traveling Salesman"; moreover, she followed it quickly . . .
5. "Place," Welty once said, "has the most delicate control over character." She then discussed the role of setting in the fiction of William Faulkner, Emily Brontë, and Thomas Mann.
6. Welty's characters—sometimes labeled with the word *grotesque*— evoke . . .
7. Among the memorable characters in Welty's stories are these: Phoenix Jackson, in "A Worn Path"; Leota, in "Petrified Man"; and Marian, in "A Visit of Charity."
8. After reading the story "A Worn Path," some readers have asked, "Is Phoenix's grandson really dead?"
9. Another character, the narrator of "Why I Live at the P.O.," vividly describes her eccentric relatives.
10. Welty's novel *The Optimist's Daughter* won a Pulitzer Prize in 1973. (Its main characters resemble her parents.)
11. Her ancestors on her father's side (who were of German-Swiss background) arrived in America . . .
12. Welty's father said that he was not interested in ancient history.
13. However, her father did keep in touch with his own father, Jefferson Welty, Esquire, for whom . . .
14. "It was the only use my father made of the word; he saved it for his father," wrote Welty in her memoir, *One Writer's Beginnings.*
15. As a result, Welty always held the term *Esquire* in great respect.
16. After her father died, an English Welti, who spelled his name with an *i*, told Welty about . . .

Review: Exercise 9

Mixed Review

The following sentences are about Eudora Welty and her family. Rewrite each sentence, correcting all errors in punctuation.

1. The author, Eudora Welty, was born in 1909 in Jackson, Mississippi (the state's capital.
2. Her parents who valued reading purchased books for their children.
3. Welty first attended a womens' college in Mississippi: but she graduated from the University of Wisconsin.
4. In 1936 Welty published her first short story "Death of a Traveling Salesman:" moreover she followed it quickly with two collections of stories.
5. "Place", Welty once said, "has the most delicate control over character; she then discussed the role of setting in the fiction of William Faulkner, Emily Brontë and Thomas Mann.
6. Welty's characters sometimes labeled with the word grotesque evoke the atmosphere of the small-town South.
7. Among the memorable characters in Welty's stories are these; Phoenix Jackson, in "A Worn Path," Leota, in "Petrified Man," and Marian, in "A Visit of Charity".
8. After reading the story *A Worn Path*, some readers have asked, "Is Phoenix' grandson really dead"?
9. Another character the narrator of "Why I Live at the P.O.", vividly describes her eccentric relatives.
10. Welty's novel "The Optimist's Daughter" won a Pulitzer Prize in 1973. (It's main characters resemble her parents)
11. Her ancestors on her fathers side who were of German Swiss background) arrived in America before the Revolutionary War.
12. Weltys' father said that "he was not interested in ancient history."
13. However her father did keep in touch with his own father, Jefferson Welty Esquire, for whom he had a deeply felt regard.
14. "It was the only use my father made of the word he saved it for his father," wrote Welty in her memoir *One Writer's Beginnings*.
15. As a result Welty always held the term Esquire in great respect.
16. After her father died an English Welti, who spelled his name with an i told Welty about her ancestors.
17. Three Welty brothers left German Switzerland for the Americas, and settled in Virginia Pennsylvania Ohio and Indiana before the Revolutionary War.
18. Welty said her father would have been interested in the following information one Welty helped push through construction of the St. Gotthard Tunnel.
19. Whenever her mother, and her father, became excited, they would exclaim "Pshaw"
20. Welty wrote of both her fathers family, and her mothers.

17. Three Welty brothers left German Switzerland for the Americas and settled in Virginia, Pennsylvania, Ohio, and Indiana before the Revolutionary War.
18. Welty said her father would have been interested in the following information: one Welty . . . the St. Gotthard Tunnel.
19. Whenever her mother and her father became excited, they would exclaim, "Pshaw!"
20. Welty wrote of both her father's family and her mother's.

Writing Application

Colons and Commas in Writing

In the following passage from *Blue Highways: A Journey into America*, William Least Heat-Moon describes the fear of being stranded in a snowstorm while attempting to drive across rural America. His careful use of colons and commas enlivens the experience. Examine the passage, focusing on the punctuation in the italicized items.

I wondered how long I might have to stay in the Breaks before I could drive down. *The cold didn't worry me much: I had insulated the rig myself* and slept in it once when the windchill was thirty-six below. I figured to survive if I didn't have to stay on top too long. Why hadn't I listened to friends who advised carrying a CB? *The headline showed darkly:* FROZEN MAN FOUND IN AVALANCHE. The whole night *I slept and woke, slept and woke, while the hail fell like iron shot, and thunder slammed around, and lightning seared the ice.*

Techniques with Colons and Commas

Try to apply some of Least Heat-Moon's techniques when you write and revise.

1 When introducing information that explains preceding material, use a colon for emphasis and economy of style.

WITHOUT COLON The cold didn't worry me much because I had insulated the rig myself . . .

LEAST HEAT-MOON'S STYLE The cold didn't worry me much: I had insulated the rig myself . . .

2 Use commas to vary sentence length and to set off ideas. Least Heat-Moon's sentence is less choppy but still emphasizes each separate occurrence.

WITHOUT COMMAS I slept and woke. I slept and woke. The hail fell like iron shot. The thunder slammed around. Lightning seared the ice.

LEAST HEAT-MOON'S STYLE I slept and woke, slept and woke, while the hail fell like iron shot, and thunder slammed around, and lightning seared the ice.

TIME
To find more suggestions about using details and emotions, see the **TIME** *Facing the Blank Page*, pages 109–119.

Practice On your paper, revise the following passage, correcting all punctuation errors.

Called a pine snake east of the Mississippi the bullsnake puts on quite a show when it feels threatened. The snake swells up. It hisses loudly. It vibrates its tail. It lunges toward the enemy. Be on your guard The snake is not merely bluffing. It bites. Fortunately, it's bite is not poisonous and a person will recover from one physically, if not emotionally. Bullsnakes are sometimes referred to as a farmer's best friend. They eat large numbers of mice, rats, and gophers that consume crops. These snakes live primarily in these dry habitats open pinewoods and   sandhills and brushlands and de serts. They are also found on grass covered prairies.

Writing Application   **779**

Punctuation, Abbreviations, and Numbers

Colons and Commas in Writing

Have students read the passage in their books silently. Then discuss the passage in terms of the points mentioned in Techniques with Colons and Commas, in the second column.

Techniques with Colons and Commas

Review and discuss the techniques with students. Make sure they recognize the effects of colon and comma use in William Least Heat-Moon's writing. Then draw students' attention to Welty's use of the colon in the second paragraph of the passage on page 772. The second and third paragraphs of the passage show Welty's careful use of commas.

Practice

The answers to this challenging and enriching activity will vary. Refer to Techniques with Punctuation as you evaluate student choices.

Sample:
The bullsnake, called a pine snake east of the Mississippi, puts on quite a show when it feels threatened. The snake swells up, hisses loudly, vibrates its tail, and lunges toward the enemy. Be on your guard: the snake is not merely bluffing; it bites! Fortunately, its bite is not poisonous, and a person will recover physically from one, if not emotionally. Bullsnakes are sometimes referred to as "a farmer's best friend." They eat large numbers of mice, rats, and gophers that consume crops. These snakes live primarily in dry habitats—open pinewoods, sandhills, brushlands, and deserts. They are also found on grass-covered prairies.

Resources and Skills

Objectives

The units in Part 3 continue to guide students in their development toward becoming effective, confident writers. Throughout these units, students will be asked

- to develop an appreciation of the richness and diversity of English
- to use writing to ask questions, refine topics, and clarify ideas
- to use the library to organize and compile information from primary and secondary sources including electronic resources
- to analyze context to figure out the meanings of unfamiliar words and to develop a stronger vocabulary
- to produce legible work that reflects an understanding of basic spelling rules
- to use writing as a study tool to clarify, organize, and remember information
- to learn strategies for answering a wide variety of objective test questions
- to analyze, appreciate, and evaluate oral performances and presentations
- to prepare, organize, and present informative and persuasive oral messages
- to understand and interpret visual messages
- to analyze and critique the significance of media messages
- to draw on technology in the process of writing

Viewing the Art

This painting presents a portrait of a young woman bedecked with elaborate clothing and jewelry. Her posture, with bejeweled hand on hip, and her sad, aloof facial expression, suggest a haughtiness of demeanor.
Interpret and Analyze Use the following questions for discussion:
- What overall impression of this woman do you think the artist wishes to convey?
- What details in the painting might you use in an imaginative story or biography?

"Around her neck she wore strings of false pearls, on her arms bracelets of imitation gold, and combs set with glass jewels."

780

—**Guy de Maupassant**

Resource Manager

Use the following resources to customize your teaching of the units in Part 3.

Planning Resources
- *Lesson Plans*
- *Block Scheduling*

Transparencies
- *Bellringer*
- *Daily Language Practice*
- *Two-Minute Skill Drill*

Other Print Resources
- *Guide to Using the Internet and Other Electronic Resources*
- *Listening and Speaking Activities*
- *SAT-9 Preparation and Practice*
- *Spelling Power*
- *Style and Documentation Sourcebook for Writers*
- *Taking Standardized Tests*
- *TerraNova Preparation and Practice*
- *Tests with Answer Key & Rubrics*

- *The Iowa Tests Preparation and Practice Workbook*
- *Thinking and Study Skills*
- *Viewing and Representing Activities*
- *Vocabulary and Spelling Strategies and Practice*
- *Vocabulary Power*

Portrait of a Woman,
17th Century

PART 3

Resources and Skills

Unit 22 **History and Development of English**   *782*

Unit 23 **Library Resources**   *798*

Unit 24 **Using Dictionaries**   *811*

Unit 25 **Vocabulary**   *818*

Unit 26 **Spelling**   *827*

Unit 27 **Study Skills**   *835*

Unit 28 **Taking Tests**   *846*

Unit 29 **Listening and Speaking**   *882*

Unit 30 **Viewing and Representing**   *890*

Unit 31 **Electronic Resources**   *901*

781

Discussing the Quotation

This quotation, which comes from "The False Gems," a short story by Guy de Maupassant (b. 1850), describes some of the items decorating the figure of a woman. Discuss the quotation with the class. Ask students what the author's choices of words, such as *false pearls, imitation gold,* and *glass jewels* suggest to them. Then ask students what these words might reveal about a character who would wear such items. To find out more information about the author and the story from which this quotation was taken, see *Glencoe Literature,* Course 5, page 289.

Writing Prompt Have students write a character sketch for a woman based on the details revealed in Maupassant's quotation and in the portrait of the woman. Have students take turns reading their sketches to the class.

 Video
• *MindJogger Videoquizzes*

💾 **Software**
• *Presentation Plus!*
• *Testmaker*
• *Vocabulary Power Puzzlemaker*
• *Writer's Choice Puzzlemaker*

🖥 **Web Sites**
• *writerschoice.glencoe.com*

UNIT 22

Objectives

- To become familiar with the origins of the English language both spoken and written, its relation to other Indo-European languages, and its development from Old English to Modern English
- To show an understanding of the history of English by using reference materials to research word origins, by compiling and analyzing lists of words with distinctive uses such as acronyms and jargon terms, and by writing brief reports

✓ ASSESSMENT OPTIONS

📁 *Tests with Answer Key & Rubrics*
Unit 22 Pretest, pp. 79–80

💾 *Testmaker*
Unit 22 Pretest

You may wish to administer the Unit 22 Pretest at this point.

Key to Ability Levels

L1 Level 1 activities are within the basic ability range of students.

L2 Level 2 activities are within the ability range of average students.

L3 Level 3 activities are more challenging activities.

UNIT 22 History and Development of English

Lesson 22.1	How Language Began	783
Lesson 22.2	From Speaking to Writing	786
Lesson 22.3	Indo-European Language Family	789
Lesson 22.4	Old and Middle English	792
Lesson 22.5	Modern English	795

782

Resource Manager

Planning Resources
- *Lesson Plans*
- *Block Scheduling*

 Transparencies
- *Bellringer*
- *Daily Language Practice*

 Other Print Resources
- *Tests with Answer Key and Rubrics*
- *Vocabulary and Spelling Strategies and Practice*

 Video
- *MindJogger Videoquizzes*

💾 **Software**
- *Presentation Plus!*
- *Testmaker*
- *Vocabulary Power Puzzlemaker*
- *Writer's Choice Puzzlemaker*

 Web Sites
- *writerschoice.glencoe.com*

22.1 How Language Began

Walk along a busy street in any major metropolitan area—New York, London, Mexico City, Tokyo—and look at the signs in the storefronts you pass. Chances are you'll see signs in a variety of languages from many different parts of the world. Where did all these languages come from? How did language itself originate? No one knows for sure, but linguists, people who study the history and development of languages, have proposed some interesting theories.

Bow-Wow's and Yo-he-ho's

According to the bow-wow theory, language may have begun when people imitated the sounds they heard in the natural world. Imagine some early hunter returning to his family group after discovering a pond alive with ducks. The hunter communicates his discovery by making a quacking sound. The other hunters in the group nod excitedly and grab their weapons. Was this the first sign of the ability to form words having meanings?

22.1 How Language Began   **783**

Resource Manager

Planning Resources
• *Lesson Plans*

Transparencies
• *Bellringer*
• *Daily Language Practice*

Other Print Resources
• *Vocabulary and Spelling Strategies and Practice*

Focus

Lesson Overview

Objective
• To become familiar with and appreciate the history and development of the English language

Skills
• using reference materials; taking notes

Critical Thinking
• synthesizing

Listening and Speaking
• discussing

Bellringer
Daily Language Activity

When students enter the classroom, have this assignment on the board: *List five words whose origins you think might be interesting.*

See also *Daily Language Practice*

Teach

Theorizing About Language Origins

Discuss some theories on the origin of human language, calling on students to point out similarities and differences among the theories. Ask students which theory they think is most plausible and why no one theory explains the richness of our languages. What other explanations can students suggest? Could a combination of these theories satisfactorily explain the origin of language? Students might enjoy giving their theories clever names, such as those on the chart on page 784. **L3**

History and Development of English

Practice and Assess

Evaluation Rubrics
Exercise 1
Answers will vary. They should exhibit the following characteristics:
- a clear reference to the animal being studied
- a description of the animal's method of communication or the method of communication being taught to the animal
- some indication of the researchers' conclusions or the effectiveness of the experiment

Additional Resources
Vocabulary and Spelling Practice

Close

Ask students to suggest words that have entered the English language recently. What part has technology played in the development of these new words? Have students write a paragraph giving their opinions as to how their generation has added new words to the English lexicon. Ask students to check their paragraphs for errors before handing them in.

History and Development of English

Theories of Language Origin			
The Gesture Theory argues that gestures were accompanied by sounds that eventually came to mean what the gesture meant.	**The Ding-Dong Theory** states that primitive people instinctively reacted to every sensory experience with a specific vocal expression.	**The Pooh-Pooh Theory** suggests that language arose from instinctive emotional cries expressing pain, joy, disappointment, anger, and so on.	**The Musical Theory** proposes that language arose from song or that speech and music developed together.

A second attempt to account for the origin of language is referred to as the yo-he-ho theory. A fourteenth-century French scholar named Noiré observed that when people engage in hard physical labor—moving a heavy rock, for example—part of the effort involves trapping air in the lungs by closing the vocal cords. During brief moments of relaxation, the vocal chords open, and involuntary grunting and groaning noises are made. Noiré suggested that these sounds may have evolved into words that meant "heave" or "lift."

Other theories of language origin have been proposed, such as the four listed and described in the Theories of Language Origin chart. None of these theories accounts for the complexity and richness of human languages. Still, each theory suggests a possible explanation for how people learned to talk to one another.

A Mother Tongue?

Since the late 1700s, linguists have known that certain languages are closely related to other languages, indicating these differing languages developed from a common source. Did all languages originate from one common language—a "mother tongue"? Is it possible that the earliest humans in one part of the African continent created a language that, through contact with other groups of people elsewhere, slowly spread throughout the world? Or did different varieties of human speech begin in different places on the earth with different people? Again, we don't know. What we do know is that a very long time ago, human communication became human language.

Exercise 1

For some years, scientists have attempted to teach chimpanzees to "speak" human language through typing, sign language, and other methods. Other scientists have tried to decode the "language" of dolphins, whales, and other creatures. Investigate one of these attempts at human-animal communication and write a brief report. Present your report to the class.

MEETING INDIVIDUAL NEEDS **English Language Learners**

Using Sources
Students with limited English proficiency may find reading expository English especially difficult. Help them to complete the exercise by referring them to high-interest, easy reading sources for their chosen topic. Consult the school or local public librarian for titles, or suggest that students consult the librarian.

Wordworks

ACRONYMS

From *A* to *Z*

In this fast-paced society of ours, it seems everything has speeded up. We have bullet trains, supersonic airliners, 150-mph sports cars, and instant satellite and e-mail communications. We even have a speeded-up language, thanks to acronyms. Acronyms are words formed from the initial letters of other words that make up a phrase. Acronyms can make communicating quicker, easier, and more creative.

Acronyms can take two forms. One type of acronym is a word that is pronounced as a sequence of letters. Examples include *LA* (*L*os *A*ngeles), *CD* (*c*ompact *d*isc), *SUV* (*s*port-*u*tility *v*ehicle), and *DJ* (*d*isc *j*ockey).

A second type of acronym is pronounced not as a sequence of letters but as a word. These acronyms are usually formed by using the first letter of each word in a phrase: *swat* (*s*pecial *w*eapons *a*nd *t*actics). Other acronyms you're

probably familiar with include *scuba* (*s*elf-*c*ontained *u*nderwater *b*reathing *a*pparatus), *radar* (*ra*dio *d*etection *a*nd *r*anging), and *laser* (*l*ight *a*mplification by *s*timulated *e*mission of *r*adiation).

Genuine acronyms develop as a natural process of abbreviation. Reverse acronyms, however, are deliberately created. For example, during World War II, the U.S. Navy created a special force of women to perform volunteer work. The navy called the women *Waves* and said the acronym stood for women accepted for volunteer emergency service. It is thought, however, that the navy first came up with the clever name and then created a phrase to support it. That's how reverse acronyms work.

The French bullet train, or *train à grande vitesse* (TGV)

 Game (Great Acronym-Making Endeavor)

Try your hand at creating reverse acronyms. First choose a word; this will be your acronym. Then work out a phrase that supports the acronym. Here are two examples from *The Oxford Guide to Word Games*, by Tony Augarde: shovel (sharp hand-operated vertical earth lifter) and brain (box retaining assorted interesting notions). You might want to use the title of a film: Jaws (just a white shark). Share your reverse acronyms with your classmates.

History and Development of English

 Wordworks **785**

Civic Literacy

Using Acronyms in Government

Among the most avid users of acronyms is the United States government. Encourage students to begin a search for political, scientific, and military acronyms that are part of the government's working vocabulary. From newspapers, newscasts, and government publications, students can compile a list that includes the acronyms, their meanings, and examples of how they are used.

Focus

Lesson Overview

Objective
• To understand the origin and formation of acronyms

Skills
• using creative thinking

Critical Thinking
• analyzing

Listening and Speaking
• reporting

Teach

Discussion

Have students read *Wordworks,* p. 785, and discuss the following questions: How do acronyms and reverse acronyms develop? How do they become part of standard English?

Researching Acronyms

Explain that many acronyms such as *radar, scuba,* and *laser* are words that may no longer be thought of as acronyms. Ask students to look up *COD* and *AWOL* and report on what these acronyms stand for. In what field did they originate? (COD—collect on delivery, mailing and delivery; AWOL—absent without official leave, military). **L2**

Practice and Assess

Evaluation Rubrics Game

Answers may vary but should meet these criteria:
• The acronym should be an existing word that relates to the subject of the phrase.
• The acronym should be made by combining the first letters of every word or each important word in a related phrase.

Close

Challenge small groups of students to produce sentences that contain as many acronyms as possible.

Focus

Lesson Overview

Objective
• To understand how written forms of language developed

Skills
• comparing and contrasting

Critical Thinking
• categorizing

Listening and Speaking
• discussing

 Bellringer
Daily Language Activity

When students enter the classroom, have this assignment on the board: *Make a list of five languages. Put an asterisk by any that you think use an alphabet other than the one used in English.*

See also *Daily Language Practice*

Teach

Making Word Pictures

Some students may need a concrete example of difficulties that writing in hieroglyphics can present. To demonstrate, you may want to ask volunteers to play a game in which a picture must stand for at least one complete word. Students will soon discover how difficult it is to communicate a word such as *startle* or *season* with a single symbol. To show the progression to cuneiform, suggest that students illustrate parts of words. **L2**

History and Development of English

22.2 From Speaking to Writing

Browse through an international bookstore and you'll see books written in many languages using different writing systems. Choose one book written in Chinese, another in Japanese, and a third in Greek, and what will you find? Each of these languages uses a different type of writing system.

Chinese is written using a logographic writing system: each character (there are about fifty thousand of them) represents an entire word. Japanese uses a writing system called a syllabary: each of the approximately fifty characters represents a syllable, or a group of sounds. Greek, like English, uses an alphabet: each of the twenty-four characters in the Greek alphabet represents a sound. All of these writing systems enable people to write what they say and read what they've written. Although these systems have vastly different numbers of characters, each system is capable of expressing a world of ideas.

Three Writing Systems		
Chinese Logography	**Japanese Syllabary**	**Greek Alphabet**
文	こ と ば	λόγος
	ko to ba	l o g o s
wén, "character"	kotoba, "language"	logos, "word"

Picture Writing

Did people always have writing systems? No. In fact, although spoken language probably originated several hundred thousand years ago, language scholars think that the first fully developed writing system got its start much later—about 5,500 years ago—with hieroglyphs, or picture writing.

Hieroglyphs were pictures that represented objects or ideas rather than words or sounds. This type of writing emerged in many parts of the world at about the same time. You may have seen illustrations of the Egyptian hieroglyphs of northern Africa, in photographs of Egyptian tombs. However, the Hittites, the earliest inhabitants of what is now the country of Turkey, also used hieroglyphs. And half a world away, in Central America, the Maya used hieroglyphic writing to record important information about science, religion, and other aspects of their culture.

Resource Manager

Planning Resources
• *Lesson Plans*

Transparencies
• *Bellringer*
• *Daily Language Practice*

📁 **Other Print Resources**
• *Vocabulary and Spelling Strategies and Practice*

Sounds and Symbols

Picture writing, however, proved cumbersome and limiting. Over time, the pictures became streamlined, enabling complex information to be conveyed more efficiently. In Sumer, an ancient region in what is now southeastern Iraq, cuneiform symbols underwent this kind of streamlining.

Cuneiform consisted of about six hundred wedge-shaped symbols. At first, these symbols represented objects and ideas. At some point, however, some of the symbols came to be associated with specific sounds as well. For example, the cuneiform arrow symbol represented the object "arrow." The word for "arrow" was pronounced *te*, so the arrow symbol came to represent the syllable *te* in all the words in which that syllable occurred, regardless of their meaning. Cuneiform was changing from a logography to a syllabary.

We Get Letters

Another milestone in the development of writing systems took place along the coasts of what are now Syria, Lebanon, and Israel. By 1000 B.C. the Phoenicians, the people who inhabited the coastal region, had developed a great trading and manufacturing civilization. Their society demanded a written language that was easy to use and learn. So the Phoenicians slowly adapted their existing writing system, finally arriving at one that included just twenty-two characters. Each character in the system represented a single consonant sound. By 900 B.C., the Phoenicians had created an alphabet.

The Greeks further refined the Phoenician alphabet by adding characters that represented vowel sounds. This Greek alphabet proved so useful for expressing and communicating ideas that it has remained virtually unchanged for nearly three thousand years. All of the alphabets in use in Europe today have their origins in the Greek alphabet.

Cuneiform, 1800 B.C.

Exercise 1

Collect a variety of books, newspapers, or magazines that use different writing systems for a class display. You may find examples from reading materials in your home, or you may be able to photocopy examples at your community library. You may also be able to obtain examples from the Internet. Try to find examples of Cyrillic, Hebrew, Japanese, Latin, Chinese, Arabic, and Greek writing. Create a chart to display your findings.

History and Development of English

Practice and Assess

Evaluation Rubrics
Exercise 1

Student responses will vary. Allow students to work alone or in groups. Encourage students to make use of librarians, teachers, friends, and family members in their search for examples of writing systems. You may want to ask students to write a short description of any examples they bring. Evaluation could be based on evidence that students grasp these basic differences among various writing systems:

- Chinese uses logography.
- Japanese uses a syllabary.
- Cyrillic, Hebrew, Latin, Arabic, and Greek use alphabets.

Additional Resources
Vocabulary and Spelling Practice

Close

Invite students to create their own systems of writing and to write messages. Volunteers can describe their systems and put their messages on the chalkboard for the class to decipher.

Connections Across the Curriculum

History

The earliest known writings are those discovered on stone walls. For thousands of years stone was a primary writing surface for records intended to be kept permanently. Over time, written records were made more transportable by the use of stone tablets, wood, bark, leather, and papyrus. Not until 3,500 years after the beginning of hieroglyphic writing was paper invented.

Focus

Lesson Overview

Objective
- To become familiar with malapropisms

Skills
- identifying and creating malapropisms

Critical Thinking
- analyzing

Listening and Speaking
- discussing

Teach

Discussion

Have students read *Wordworks,* p. 788, and discuss the following questions: What is a malapropism? Give an example of a malapropism with a humorous effect.

Creating Malapropisms

Ask students to invent malapropisms. Suggest that they start with an ordinary sentence and then choose a key word to replace with a word that sounds similar and is the same part of speech. This allows the sentence to make grammatical sense while taking on a new and humorous meaning. Students can exchange papers and rewrite one another's sentences. **L3**

Practice and Assess

Answers: Excuse Me?

1. accelerated
2. dialect
3. boll weevils
4. mandolin
5. facet
6. parcel

Close

Invite students to name recent books or movies and change a word in the title into a malapropism—for example, *The Sick Sense.*

Wordworks

MALAPROPISMS

Pullet Surprises

Have you ever unintentionally misused a word with humorous results, as in the following bloopers?

Rich? He's a malted [multi] millionaire!

The ancient city of Pompeii was buried in moldy [molten] lava.

These humorous mistaken uses of words are known as malapropisms, from the French expression *mal à propos,* meaning "not appropriate."

In 1775 playwright Richard Sheridan popularized the notion of malapropisms in *The Rivals* through the character of Mrs. Malaprop, who humorously bungled the English language with such utterances as "She's as headstrong as an allegory [alligator] on the banks of the Nile."

Today, malapropisms are also called Pullet Surprises, after a statement in a student essay from Miss Amsel Greene's high school writing class: "In 1957, Eugene O'Neill won a Pullet Surprise [Pulitzer Prize]." Pullet Surprises, according to Miss Greene, are "marvels of ingenuity and logic," like these:

"The doctor prescribed milk of amnesia [magnesia]."

"The flood damage was so bad they had to evaporate [evacuate] four cities."

"So, until next week — Adios, amoebas."

History and Development of English

ACTIVITY — Excuse Me?
See if you can figure out and correct these malapropisms.

1. They put her in an exhilarated class.
2. We couldn't understand his Scottish derelict.
3. The cotton crop was ruined by bold weasels.
4. He plays both guitar and mandarin.
5. She gave him a diamond that sparkled at every faucet.
6. He sent the package by partial post.

788 Unit 22

Listening and Speaking

Understanding Malapropisms and Comedy

Most malapropisms are funnier when heard than when seen in print, and many humorists deliberately misuse words to get laughs. Ask students which malapropisms they have heard comedians use. Then have students work independently or with partners to prepare brief comedy routines. Remind the class to listen carefully in order to catch each malapropism.

22.3 Indo-European Language Family

Have you ever investigated your family tree to discover who your ancestors were? If so, what did you find? Some people have been surprised to discover a famous—perhaps infamous—relative perched on one of the tree's branches. Family trees are sometimes literally drawn as trees, with branches representing family groups and leaves representing individuals. This diagram shows relationships clearly.

It may surprise you to discover that languages have family trees too—in the sense that languages are related to one another, perhaps with a common source. English, for example, is a member of the Indo-European language family, which is shown on the next page. This vast language family includes most of the languages of Europe as well as those of Iran and India.

As the language tree shows, English belongs to a branch of Indo-European known as Germanic. English shares its linguistic history with the other Germanic tongues, including Yiddish, which derives from Middle High German and is spoken today by eastern European Jews and their descendants in many parts of the world. Another Germanic language is Afrikaans, a language spoken by some white South Africans. Afrikaans derives from Dutch, which was the language of the first white Europeans to settle in South Africa.

The Indo-European languages are believed to have a single "parent" language, although no such parent has yet been found. Language scholars think it is unlikely that direct evidence of this language will ever be found.

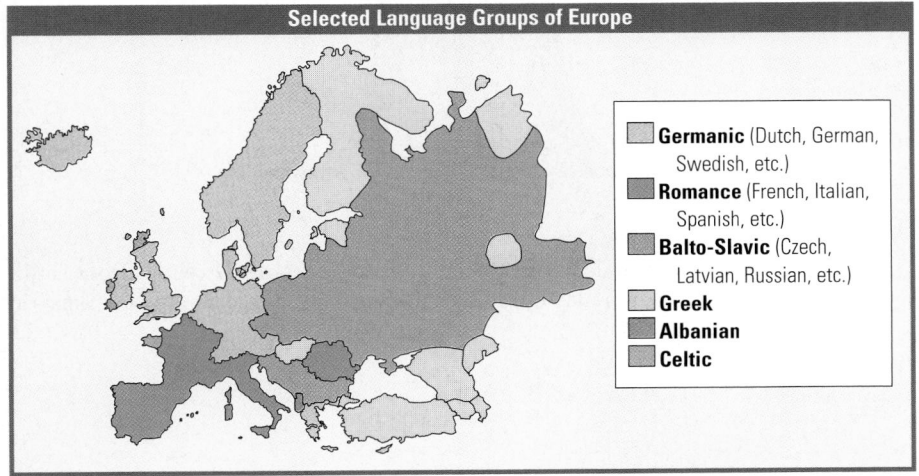

Selected Language Groups of Europe

- **Germanic** (Dutch, German, Swedish, etc.)
- **Romance** (French, Italian, Spanish, etc.)
- **Balto-Slavic** (Czech, Latvian, Russian, etc.)
- **Greek**
- **Albanian**
- **Celtic**

22.3 Indo-European Language Family   **789**

History and Development of English

Focus

Lesson Overview

Objective
- To trace the roots of languages

Skills
- locating language groups; tracing language origins

Critical Thinking
- visualizing; analyzing

Listening and Speaking
- discussing

Bellringer
Daily Language Activity

When students enter the classroom, have this assignment on the board: *Draw a family tree. Include yourself and your closest relatives.*

See also *Daily Language Practice*

Teach

Locating Language Groups

Help students interpret the information on the map showing where Indo-European languages are spoken today. Explain that each language branch is represented by a different color. Ask students which color covers the largest area (purple) and which main language branch is represented by that color (Balto-Slavic). What language branch is most confined in area? (Albanian, in red) Encourage students to compare this map with an atlas or wall map of Europe to name the countries where the language spoken is related to English. **L1**

Resource Manager

Planning Resources
- *Lesson Plans*

Transparencies
- *Bellringer*
- *Daily Language Practice*

Other Print Resources
- *Vocabulary and Spelling Strategies and Practice*

Practice and Assess

Answers: Exercise 2

Parent languages and their descendants are as follows:

- Latin: French, Italian, Spanish, Romanian, Portuguese
- Eastern Slavic: Ukrainian, Russian, White Russian

Branches are as follows:

- Sanskrit: Indo-Iranian
- Icelandic: Common Germanic
- Latvian: Balto-Slavic

Additional Resources

📁 *Vocabulary and Spelling Practice*

Close

Ask students whether anything on these pages indicates that the "geography" of languages reflects historical events. (the map on p. 789) Lead a discussion of the Roman conquest of the area now known as Italy, France, Spain, and Portugal, which is reflected in Romance (Latin-derived) languages being spoken in these countries today.

Common Germanic — West (High — German, Yiddish; Low — Flemish, Dutch — Afrikaans); North (Old Norse — Icelandic, Norwegian); East — Gothic; Danish; Swedish; Anglo-Frisian — English, Frisian

Indo-Iranian — Iranian; Indic — Sanskrit (Marathi; Hindi; Bengali)

Italic — Latin — French, Italian, Spanish, Romanian, Portuguese

Balto-Slavic — Baltic (Latvian, Lithuanian); Slavic — West (Polish, Czech, Slovak, Polabian); East (Russian, Ukrainian, White Russian); South (Serbo-Croatian)

Albanian; Armenian; Tocharian; Anatolian; Greek; Celtic

Indo-European Language Family

Exercise 2

Study the Indo-European language tree. Which languages are descended from Latin? Eastern Slavic? To what branch of the Indo-European language family does Sanskrit belong? Icelandic? Latvian?

Enrichment and Extension

Understanding Dead Languages

Discuss with students the concept of "dead" languages. Explain that normally a language changes as new words are added or meanings are changed, but some languages on the tree are no longer spoken by a community of people. Even though languages such as Latin and Sanskrit are still read and understood by many people, no group speaks Latin or Sanskrit as its native or everyday language. A language that is no longer spoken is considered "dead" because it no longer changes.

Wordworks

IDIOMS

Don't Have a Cow, Man!

You're walking to algebra class one day, and a friend introduces you to Michel, a newly arrived French foreign exchange student. He speaks some English, but he still has a lot to learn. As you're talking, you suddenly realize you're going to be late for class. "Yikes! Michel, I gotta go. If I'm late for algebra again, Mr. Kim will have a cow!" You expect a laugh from your new friend, but instead Michel gives you a puzzled look. Why?

Time flies!

Well, you used an idiom, a phrase whose real meaning cannot be understood by putting together the meanings of the individual words that make up the phrase.

Some of our most colorful idioms have fascinating histories. *Eat humble pie* means "to be forced to admit a mistake or to accept insult or shame." In medieval England, the master of the manor was the only one allowed to hunt game. When he shot a deer, he kept the meat and gave the innards, or "umbles," to his servants, who would make pies from them. *Eat humble pie* meant being forced to accept the least desirable food.

Buy a pig in a poke means "to buy something sight unseen." Centuries ago in England, a farmer would carry a piglet to market in a sack, or *poke*. Dishonest farmers might substitute a stray cat for the valuable piglet and then sell it to some trusting person who did not bother to check out what he was buying.

ACTIVITY

Test Your Idiom IQ

With a partner, see if you can match each of the idioms in the left column with its correct definition in the right column.

1. Sow wild oats	A. To work very hard
2. Put your shoulder to the wheel	B. To do foolish or bad things as a young person
3. Off-the-cuff	C. To move to another city or area
4. Pull up stakes	D. By the rules
5. Throw in the towel	E. To be humiliated
6. Johnny-come-lately	F. To become angry and cause a scene
7. Put on the dog	G. To give up
8. According to Hoyle	H. A newcomer
9. Lose face	I. Unplanned or prepared
10. Raise Cain	J. Make a flashy display

History and Development of English

Wordworks **791**

English Language Learners

MEETING INDIVIDUAL NEEDS

Learning Idioms

Idioms add to the difficulty of learning a new language. What puzzling expressions have students heard and how did they figure out the meanings? Suggest that students keep idiom journals and share new expressions with their families.

Cross-reference: Writing

For a writing situation in which students might use colorful idioms, refer students to Lesson 3.1, pp. 126–131, and Lesson 4.4, pp. 184–187.

Focus

Lesson Overview

Objective
• To understand idioms

Skills
• defining and identifying idioms

Critical Thinking
• recalling

Listening and Speaking
• informal speaking

Teach

Discussion

Have students read *Wordworks*, p. 791, and discuss the following questions: What is a *sitting duck?* (an easy target) Is the phrase an idiom or is it meant to be taken literally?

Identifying Idioms

Group students into teams. Give them five minutes in which to make a list of common idioms that are used at school. To get them started, suggest several contexts in which the idioms might be heard (teachers in classes, sports teams, clubs, band, etc.). When time is up, compare lists. What idioms did the teams have in common? **L2**

Practice and Assess

Answers: Test Your Idiom IQ

1. B	6. H
2. A	7. J
3. I	8. D
4. C	9. E
5. G	10. F

Close

Have students work in cooperative groups to compile a dictionary of common English idioms. Then bring the groups together. If each group mentioned the same idioms, compare definitions.

Focus

Lesson Overview

Objective
- To understand the development of the English language

Skills
- analyzing data from a time line; researching word origins

Critical Thinking
- evaluating

Listening and Speaking
- listening to Middle English; informal speaking

Bellringer
Daily Language Activity

When students enter the classroom, have this assignment on the board: *Think of two foods that you like to eat mixed together. What happens to the original ingredients when you combine them?*

See also *Daily Language Practice*

Motivating Activity

As a class, have students brainstorm for words that contain a common root, such as *port* or *scribe,* and make a list on the chalkboard. Students may use a dictionary to find other words containing that root and to find word meanings. Discuss changes in the root's meaning with different uses.

Teach

Understanding a Time Line

The time line across the student book pages shows major periods of English language development and the events that helped bring about these language changes. Have students point out specific events and discuss the linguistic changes that resulted. **L2**

22.4 Old and Middle English

Can you read these three lines of poetry? They're from *Beowulf,* one of the most famous poems in the English language.

Hafa nu ond geheald husa selest
gemyne mærþo, mægen-ellen cyð,
waca wið wraþum!

Yes, *Beowulf* is written in English—Old English, the earliest form of the English that is spoken today by people in many areas of the world.

Old English was the language of the inhabitants of Britain from about A.D. 449 to 1100. The Celts had been living in Britain under Roman rule for several centuries when Rome withdrew its legions to battle invading barbarians back home. The Celts were left defenseless against a series of invasions by the Picts and Scots from the north and west; Germanic-speaking Saxons, Angles, and Jutes from western Europe; and the Scandinavians. Britain soon became Engla Land, "land of the Angles," and the principal language was largely West Germanic with Scandinavian and Latin influences. This language was Old English.

Old English had three important characteristics. First, it was an inflected language. That means Old English nouns, pronouns, and adjectives had case endings to indicate their function in a sentence—for example, subject or object.

Second, nouns as well as pronouns had grammatical gender. A noun was masculine, feminine, or neuter. Adjectives and certain other modifiers had three sets of endings, and each was used with a noun of a specific gender.

From Old to Middle English

History and Development of English

597 Pope Gregory I orders Christian missionaries to Britain to convert the heathens. Monks open schools and teach Latin. Latin words relating to learning and religion enter English: *master* (*magister*), *candle (candela), temple (templum).*

| 100 B.C. | A.D. 400 | 500 | 600 | 700 |

55 B.C. Julius Caesar invades Britain and claims it for the Roman Empire. Latin vocabulary is introduced into Celtic.

A.D. 449 At the Celts' request, Germanic Saxons, Angles, and Jutes arrive to defeat the Picts and Scots. The conquerors then turn on the Celts, subjugating them. Celtic is gradually replaced by the Germanic languages of the invaders.

792 Unit 22 History and Development of English

Resource Manager

Planning Resources
- *Lesson Plans*

Transparencies
- *Bellringer*
- *Daily Language Practice*

Other Print Resources
- *Vocabulary and Spelling Strategies and Practice*

Finally, Old English was characterized by irregular word formation. There were many ways to form the plurals of nouns and the past tense of verbs.

Middle English

By about 1100, enough cumulative changes had occurred to signal the beginning of a great transitional period for English. This period, Middle English, lasted until about 1450.

How did Middle English differ from Old English? Read these lines from Geoffrey Chaucer's "The Nun's Priest's Tale," written in Middle English.

We alle desiren, if it might bee,
To han housbondes hardy, wise, and free.

This text is much easier to understand than the Old English of *Beowulf*. The changes were more than just cosmetic, however. Compared with Old English, Middle English was grammatically simpler. Grammatical gender began to disappear, as did inflected case endings. Irregular verb forms gave way to regular forms, and the addition of *-s* to a noun became the standard for forming plurals. Unfortunately, these changes were not applied to all words. That's why we still have irregular verbs and plurals today. *Oxen*, the irregular plural for ox, dates back to Old English and is still in use today!

Exercise 3

Look up each of the following words in a dictionary. Write the word as it was formed in Old or Middle English and the language from which English borrowed the word. Look in the front of your dictionary for an explanation of abbreviations.

1. city (Middle English)
2. priest (Old English)
3. adjourn (Middle English)
4. ugly (Middle English)
5. school (Old English)
6. altar (Old English)

1066 William the Conqueror (right) defeats King Harold II at the Battle of Hastings, ushering in a period of French domination over the affairs of England. Many French words relating to government enter English: *authority (auctorité), liberty (liberté), pardon (pardoner),* and *verdict (verdit).*

| 800 | 900 | 1000 | 1100 | 1500 |

865 A large Viking army invades England. Decades of raids follow, and Vikings conquer half the country. Vikings contribute many words to English, including *law (log), skin (skinn), sky (sky),* and *die (deyja).*

1100 The Old English period ends and Middle English begins. English grammar begins to undergo simplification.

History and Development of English

22.4 Old and Middle English **793**

Teach

Understanding Changes

Remind students that words in a language reflect the experiences of a society. The words *cow* and *hog* came from the Old English spoken by farmers who worked with the animals, while *beef* and *pork* came from Old French, spoken by the Norman rulers to whom such meat was served. **L3**

Practice and Assess

Answers: Exercise 4

1. *cite,* from Old French, originally from Latin
2. *preost,* from Latin
3. *ajournen,* from Old French
4. *ugli,* uglike (meaning "frightful") from Old Norse uggligr
5. *scol,* from Latin
6. *altar,* from Latin

You may wish to carry the activity further by asking group members to locate their assigned items in a college dictionary or an unabridged dictionary to find the date of the earliest recorded use of the word.

Additional Resources
📁 *Vocabulary and Spelling Practice*

Close

Remind students that English was originally an inflected language, but that it has been simplified. Ask them to consider whether English should be simplified further; for example, should irregular verbs and plural forms be eliminated?

Listening and Speaking

Hearing Chaucer's Words

If possible, obtain recordings of the Middle English and Modern English versions of Geoffrey Chaucer's *Canterbury Tales* from the school or public library. Ask students which Middle English words they recognize. Suggest that they make a list of some of the Middle English words. Discuss how Middle English pronunciation differs from that of Modern English.

Focus

Lesson Overview

Objective
• To become familiar with weasel words

Skills
• collecting weasel words

Critical Thinking
• recalling; analyzing

Listening and Speaking
• discussing; informal speaking

Teach

Discussion

Have students read *Wordworks,* p. 794, and discuss the following questions: What is the meaning of the term *weasel word?* Where are students likely to find weasel words?

Using Weasel Words

Students might be surprised to discover that they themselves carefully choose "weasel words" in certain situations. For example, have they ever told a parent that they had started cleaning their rooms when all they had done was clear off a chair to sit down? Ask students to name other instances when they have consciously used weasel words. **L2**

Practice and Assess

Evaluation Rubrics
Weasel Watch

Answers will vary, but should indicate that students understand that weasel words are carefully selected by speakers in order to deceive without actually lying. Responses may include one or more of the examples given in the activity.

Close

Read an advertisement aloud and have students identify and explain the reason for each weasel word.

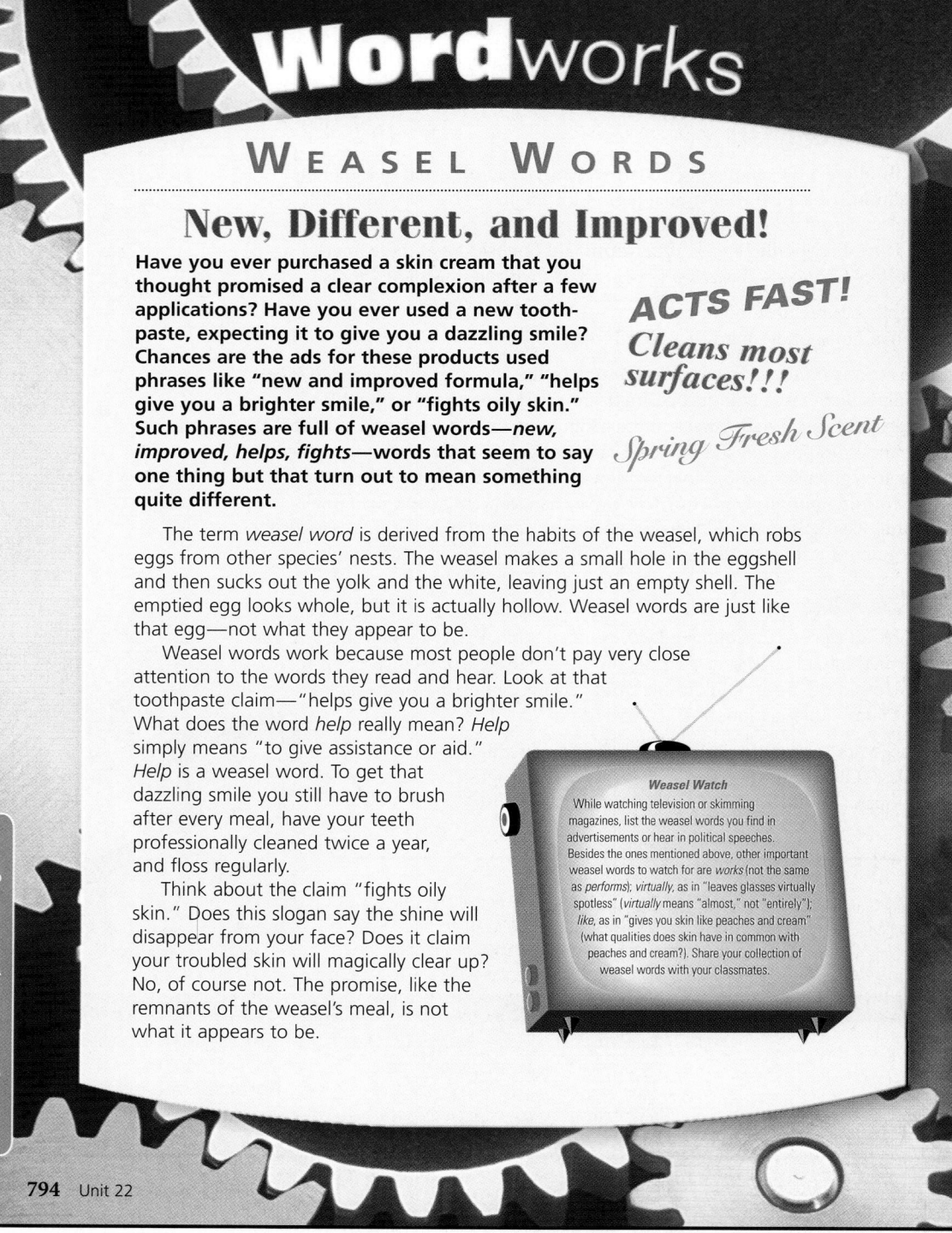

Wordworks

WEASEL WORDS

New, Different, and Improved!

Have you ever purchased a skin cream that you thought promised a clear complexion after a few applications? Have you ever used a new toothpaste, expecting it to give you a dazzling smile? Chances are the ads for these products used phrases like "new and improved formula," "helps give you a brighter smile," or "fights oily skin." Such phrases are full of weasel words—*new, improved, helps, fights*—words that seem to say one thing but that turn out to mean something quite different.

ACTS FAST!
Cleans most surfaces!!!

Spring Fresh Scent

The term *weasel word* is derived from the habits of the weasel, which robs eggs from other species' nests. The weasel makes a small hole in the eggshell and then sucks out the yolk and the white, leaving just an empty shell. The emptied egg looks whole, but it is actually hollow. Weasel words are just like that egg—not what they appear to be.

Weasel words work because most people don't pay very close attention to the words they read and hear. Look at that toothpaste claim—"helps give you a brighter smile." What does the word *help* really mean? *Help* simply means "to give assistance or aid." *Help* is a weasel word. To get that dazzling smile you still have to brush after every meal, have your teeth professionally cleaned twice a year, and floss regularly.

Think about the claim "fights oily skin." Does this slogan say the shine will disappear from your face? Does it claim your troubled skin will magically clear up? No, of course not. The promise, like the remnants of the weasel's meal, is not what it appears to be.

> **Weasel Watch**
> While watching television or skimming magazines, list the weasel words you find in advertisements or hear in political speeches. Besides the ones mentioned above, other important weasel words to watch for are *works* (not the same as *performs*); *virtually*, as in "leaves glasses virtually spotless" (*virtually* means "almost," not "entirely"); *like*, as in "gives you skin like peaches and cream" (what qualities does skin have in common with peaches and cream?). Share your collection of weasel words with your classmates.

History and Development of English

794 Unit 22

Enrichment and Extension

Trapping Weasel Words

Ask pairs of students to select an excerpt from a newspaper editorial or a letter to the editor and circle the weasel words. Have them rewrite the excerpt, substituting an objective term or phrase for each circled word. Ask students to share their work in small groups and write a brief comparison of the strengths of excerpts that use weasel words and those that do not. Remind students to support their comparison with examples and clearly stated reasons.

22.5 Modern English

By the 1590s, when William Shakespeare asked the famous question that begins his "Sonnet 18," the transition from Middle English to modern English had taken place.

> SHall I compare thee to a Summers day?
> Thou art more louely and more temperate:
> Rough windes do ſhake the darling buds of Maie,
> And Sommers leaſe hath all too ſhort a date:
> Sometime too hot the eye of heauen ſhines.

With the exception of some words such as *thee, thou,* and *hath,* Shakespeare's vocabulary could easily be mistaken for contemporary English. In fact, aside from some spelling, vocabulary, and pronunciation changes that would take place over the next century or two, the language spoken in Shakespeare's time was essentially the English we speak today.

Modern English, as the English spoken after 1450 is called, continued the trends of Middle English. English was no longer an inflected language—word order, not case endings, determined the function of words in sentences. Grammatical gender was gone—modifiers no longer needed gender endings to match the gender of the nouns they modified. And thanks to a marvelous new invention, standardization was beginning to take hold of the language.

Prior to the mid-1400s, all written English was handwritten. Then around 1440, Johannes Gutenberg and some associates began using movable raised type on a printing press. In 1476 William Caxton built and began operating the first printing press in England, and English hasn't been the same since.

Printed matter was now available to a much wider audience than ever before. Because London was the center of England's printing industry, the Londoners' ways of speaking and writing soon spread throughout the country. Pronunciation and spelling became more standardized. There were still inconsistencies in written English, but printers were doing their best to bring order to the language.

Contemporary English

None of the changes that transformed Old English into modern English happened overnight. The evolution of a language is a slow process, and often changes aren't even noticed until decades or centuries later.

Even now, the English you speak continues to evolve. New words have entered the vocabulary from foreign sources: *tai chi* and *feng shui* from Chinese, *caffe latte* and *paparazzi* from Italian, and *ayatollah* from Persian.

History and Development of English

Focus

Lesson Overview

Objective
- To understand and identify changes in the English language

Skills
- tracking language shifts

Critical Thinking
- analyzing

Listening and Speaking
- discussing

 Bellringer
Daily Language Activity

When students enter the classroom, have this assignment on the board: *List five words or phrases that you consider outdated (for example: a phrase a parent or older person uses that you would not use).*

See also Daily Language Practice

Teach

Using Unabridged Dictionaries

An unabridged dictionary may be intimidating to some students. You may wish to copy and bring in a few pages to explain how to use it. Help students locate the words *meat* and *starve.* Discuss the first definition of each word and the date when that meaning was first recorded. (Students should find that *meat* originally referred to all types of food; its first recorded use was A.D. 900. *Starve* originally meant "to die"; its first recorded use was A.D. 1000.) **L2**

 Resource Manager

Planning Resources
- *Lesson Plans*

Transparencies
- *Bellringer*
- *Daily Language Practice*

Other Print Resources
- *Vocabulary and Spelling Strategies and Practice*

Practice and Assess

Evaluation Rubrics
Exercise 4

Responses will vary widely, but the categories into which students place words should demonstrate their understanding of the variety of ways by which language changes. From time to time, the class could discuss what they've been recording in their Language Watch files.

Additional Resources

📁 *Vocabulary and Spelling Practice*

⇌ Cross-reference: Vocabulary and Spelling

For tips on defining and spelling new, unfamiliar words, refer students to Lessons 25.1, pp. 819–821; 25.2, pp. 822–826; and 26.1, pp. 828–832.

Close

Invite students to project how they think the grammar, vocabulary, or pronunciation of English will have changed by the time they are seventy-five years old.

Middle English
"Whan that Aprille with hise shoures soote
The droghte of March hath perced to the roote . . ."

Modern English
"O Gertrude, come away!
The sun no sooner shall the mountains touch
But we will ship him hence."

Contemporary English
"Roger, Houston. I copy. Over."

New technology, new ideas, and other innovations demand the creation of new words: *infomercial, euro, search engine, hyperlink, morph.* Some existing words have taken on new meanings: *mouse, rap, network.*

Grammatical shifts are also taking place. The verb *read,* for example, is sometimes used as a noun today: *Barbara Kingsolver's new book is a good read.* The noun *audible* (which originally was an adjective meaning "able to be heard" but took on a new meaning in football as "a new play called at the line of scrimmage") has now been transformed into a verb: *The quarterback audibilized his way out of a potential loss of yardage.*

One fact about the English language is certain. English is a living language, always changing, always growing. Perhaps several hundred years from now, language scholars will look back at the early decades of the twenty-first century and conclude that important changes were taking place in English during this time.

Exercise 4

You can keep track of some of the changes taking place in the English language. Create several pages called "Language Watch" in your journal or another notebook. Label individual pages "New Words," "Existing Words with New Meanings," "Current Slang," "New Acronyms," and "Grammar Shifts." Whenever you run across a word that fits one of these categories—in your reading, in talking with friends, as you listen to radio or television, and so on—add it to your "Language Watch" files, and date the entry.

796 Unit 22 History and Development of English

History and Development of English

Real World Connection

Determining Television's Effect

Encourage students to discuss how television is affecting spoken English today, much as the printing press affected the language in fifteenth-century England. Point out that many Americans speak a regional dialect, such as the various southern dialects or the New England or northeastern dialects. Ask students to discuss the dialect they hear on national newscasts or on programs that are broadcast on major networks. Ask them who or what sets the standard for our language.

Wordworks

JARGON

Clips and Red Dogs

The exasperated supervisor hands a sheaf of papers to her young assistant and says, "Try a new slug, and a new cutline, too. And see if you can come up with a new head." What is this person talking about? Fishing with a cutline and slugs? Or maybe one boxer slugging another? Or is it science fiction? "We're ready for the head transplant, doctor."

In this case, *slug* doesn't have anything to do with slimy sea creatures or with punching somebody out. *Slug, cutline,* and *head* are newspaper jargon, the specialized language used by newspaper people. A *slug* is a story name, a *cutline* is a caption, and a *head* is a headline.

Most trades and professions have their own kind of jargon, or specialized language. Doctors use jargon. Lawyers use it. Auto mechanics, educators, and engineers use it. Even football players use jargon, such as the words you may have recognized in the title above and in the cartoon.

Jargon often sounds like gibberish to people outside the profession. But jargon can enable people within a specialized group to communicate quickly and clearly. Take, for example, this exchange between two medical professionals:

"Her vitals are failing. BP is low. Start an IV and order an MRI. Call Code Blue!"

Confusing? Maybe to you. But when a patient's life is hanging in the balance, it's much quicker than saying:

"This patient is in danger. We're having trouble detecting a pulse and respiration. Her blood pressure rate is falling. Let's inject her arm with an intravenous tube and then order a magnetic resonance image. Call immediately for an emergency team and a cart with resuscitator and other equipment."

Name That Profession!

How many kinds of jargon can you recognize? For each of the following examples of jargon, name the field or profession in which it is used. Then explain what the jargon means. Use a dictionary if necessary.

1. RBI
2. differential
3. tort
4. hacker
5. cross-check
6. stet

History and Development of English

Wordworks **797**

Less Proficient Readers

Understanding Jargon

Make sure students are clear on the concept of jargon. Suggest that they make a list of unfamiliar terms and consult a dictionary as to their meanings. You might also suggest that they consult computer manuals, sports dictionaries, and other specialized reference books for definitions. They can probably find these books in the local library.

Focus

Lesson Overview

Objective
• To become familiar with jargon

Skills
• finding and defining jargon

Critical Thinking
• categorizing; defining

Listening and Speaking
• discussing

Teach

Discussion

Have students read *Wordworks,* p. 797, and discuss the following questions: What are some examples of school jargon? When should one avoid the use of jargon?

Practice and Assess

Answers: Name That Profession!

1. baseball; runs batted in
2. auto mechanics; a differential gear; an arrangement of gears which allows two axles in the same line to turn at different speeds
3. law; a wrongful act for which a civil suit can be brought
4. computers; computer hobbyist/fanatic
5. hockey; one player blocking another with his body
6. publishing; proofreading mark showing that canceled matter should be printed as it appeared originally

Close

Invite students to think of a word or phrase that is jargon, write it in a sentence, and see if the class can decipher its meaning.

Objectives

- To learn about classification systems used in libraries
- To learn about the various sections of libraries
- To learn how to search for periodicals, reference sources, and other library materials
- To demonstrate control over library skills by using systems to find information

✔ ASSESSMENT OPTIONS

📁 *Tests With Answer Key & Rubrics*
Unit 23 Pretest, pp. 83-84

💾 *Testmaker*
Unit 23 Pretest

You may wish to administer the Unit 23 Pretest at this point.

Key to Ability Levels

L1 Level 1 activities are within the basic ability range of students.

L2 Level 2 activities are within the ability range of average students.

L3 Level 3 activities are more challenging activities.

UNIT 23 Library Resources

Lesson 23.1 **Arrangement of a Library** 799

Lesson 23.2 **Locating Books and Other Library Materials** 801

Lesson 23.3 **Searching for Periodicals** 806

Lesson 23.4 **Using Reference Sources** 808

798

Resource Manager

Planning Resources
- *Lesson Plans*
- *Block Scheduling*

 Transparencies
- *Bellringer*
- *Daily Language Practice*

📁 **Other Print Resources**
- *Guide to Using the Internet and Other Electronic Resources*
- *Tests with Answer Key & Rubrics*

- *Thinking and Study Skills*
- *Vocabulary and Spelling Strategies and Practice*

 Video
- *MindJogger Videoquizzes*

💾 **Software**
- *Presentation Plus!*
- *Testmaker*
- *Writer's Choice Puzzlemaker*

🖥 **Web Sites**
- *writerschoice.glencoe.com*

23.1   Arrangement of a Library

Libraries today offer numerous services. You can do research for a term paper, take out a book to read for pleasure, borrow a video or a CD, use the Internet, find out about events in your community, and much more.

Understanding Classification Systems

Libraries organize books on the shelves by *call numbers,* which can be thought of as addresses for the books on the shelves. Call numbers are based on classification systems. Most public and school libraries use the Dewey decimal system, while most university and very large libraries use the Library of Congress system.

Dewey Decimal System

In 1876 librarian Melvil Dewey divided the world of knowledge into ten broad categories, which are still in use today. Under the Dewey decimal system, books are organized according to the following numerical system:

Dewey Decimal System		
Category Numbers	**Major Category**	**Examples of Subcategories**
000–099	General works	Encyclopedias, bibliographies
100–199	Philosophy	Ethics, psychology
200–299	Religion	Theology, mythology
300–399	Social sciences	Law, political science, education
400–499	Language	Dictionaries, foreign languages
500–599	Sciences	Chemistry, astronomy, mathematics
600–699	Technology	Medicine, engineering, agriculture
700–799	Arts	Painting, music, theater, sports
800–899	Literature	Poetry, plays, essays
900–999	History and geography	Ancient history, biography, travel

These general categories are subdivided further into subcategories; for example, under the broad heading, technology, which comprises all the 600s, the 620s are engineering books.

Books are shelved numerically by Dewey decimal number and then alphabetically by author. For example, books on the history of the *Titanic* will be shelved in 910.453, but the book by Steven Biel will be filed before the one by Paul Quinn.

Focus

Lesson Overview

Objective
- To become familiar with the classification systems of libraries

Skills
- identifying the classification systems used in the libraries; learning how to use different classification systems

Critical Thinking
- visualizing; classifying

Bellringer
Daily Language Activity

When students enter the classroom, have this assignment on the board: *List the steps you would take to locate a book about soccer in the school library.*

See also *Daily Language Practice*

Motivating Activity

Ask students to discuss a time when they had difficulty finding a book in the library. What type of book were they looking for? If they were finally able to locate the book, how did they do so? What kind of catalog system did they use?

Library Resources

Resource Manager

Planning Resources
- *Lesson Plans*

Transparencies
- *Bellringer*
- *Daily Language Practice*

📂 **Other Print Resources**
- *Thinking and Study Skills,* pp. 6–7
- *Vocabulary and Spelling Strategies and Practice*

Teach

Connecting the Catalog to the Book

Show students a library copy of a book represented in a card or computer catalog. Help students identify the call number on the book's spine, as well as other bibliographic information on the title and copyright pages. Then help them locate that information on the card or computer catalog entry. **L1**

Classifying New Areas in the Dewey Decimal System

Point out that since 1876, when Melvil Dewey created his system, many new, specialized areas of knowledge have been developed, such as computer technology. Invite students to name other areas of knowledge that Dewey could not have foreseen (space exploration, electronics, radiation). Are there categories in Dewey's system that can accommodate this new knowledge? **L3**

Using the Library of Congress Classification System

Help students become familiar with the Library of Congress Classification System. Have them study the chart on the student page. Then ask students to identify the category letter they would use to find the following books:

- *Art of the American Indian Frontier* (N: fine arts)
- *Women of Science* (Q: science)
- *Great Civil War Heroes* (C–F: history) **L2**

Close

Ask students to discuss various methods they have used to locate books: card catalogs, computer catalogs, Dewey decimal numbers on the shelves. Which method do they prefer? Why?

Library Resources

Public libraries usually do not use call numbers for fiction. Sometimes fiction books are designated by the letter *F* or the abbreviation *Fic* or by the type of novel; for example *SciFi,* or *YA* for young adult. Fiction books are filed alphabetically by the author's last name. If a library has several books by the same author, they are shelved alphabetically by title.

Library of Congress Classification

The Library of Congress (LC) system is used mostly by larger libraries. The LC classification system divides all knowledge into twenty-one general categories. Each category is assigned a letter, as shown on the chart.

Like the Dewey decimal system, the LC has subcategories, identified by additional letters and numbers.

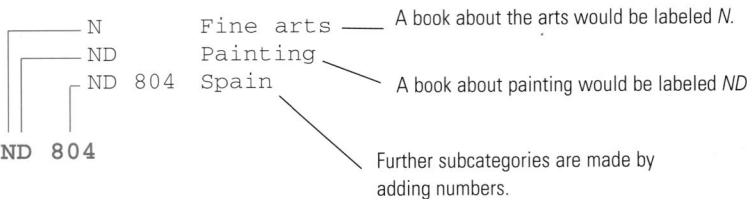

Library of Congress Classification System			
Category Letter	**Major Category**	**Category Letter**	**Major Category**
A	General works	N	Fine arts
B	Philosophy, psychology, religion	P	Language and literature
		Q	Science
C–F	History	R	Medicine
G	Geography, anthropology, recreation	S	Agriculture
		T	Technology
H	Social sciences	U	Military science
J	Political sciences	V	Naval science
K	Law	Z	Bibliography and library science
L	Education		
M	Music		

Special Sections Many libraries group special categories of books, such as reference, biographical, local history, and oversize books, in separate collections. The catalog display screen will direct you to those areas.

An *R* or *Ref* identifies a reference book. You would look for this book in the reference area.

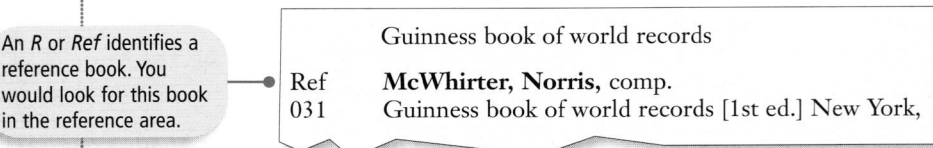

Guinness book of world records

Ref **McWhirter, Norris,** comp.
031 Guinness book of world records [1st ed.] New York,

800 Unit 23 Library Resources

English Language Learners

Using the Dewey Decimal System

Some students may need help identifying the kinds of books that belong in each major category of the Dewey system. First, select a book title from each of the categories and see whether students can place the book in its correct category. Then ask volunteers to name a book they're currently reading and have them challenge the rest of the class to identify its category.

23.2 Locating Books and Other Library Materials

How do you locate a book, video, or compact disc when visiting the library? Use the online catalog to find a complete listing of the library's holdings (all the materials that the library owns). Online catalogs allow you to search by author, title, subject, or keyword, among other options. The most direct way to search is a title search. Keep in mind that some books may have the same title. To be certain the record you have found is for the book you want, make sure that it is written by the correct author. If you want to know all the works by that author in the library, enter the author's name. Always use the last name first. For example, if you want to know which books by Willa Cather the library owns, you type in *Cather, Willa*. The computer will show you a numbered list of all the books by Cather that are in the collection. The list will be alphabetical by title. Remember that the articles *the*, *a*, and *an* at the beginning of titles are skipped and not alphabetized.

When you search by subject in a library, you must use the specific word or phrase selected by the Library of Congress. For example, if you key in *Japanese Cooking* for a subject, you will find nothing because the heading actually should read "Cookery—Japan." If you find no results for your search, always use the same term in a keyword search. The keyword search will find many books on your topic; in fact too many, because it will pull up titles of songs and books and parts of books. To solve this problem, scan the titles retrieved until you find one that seems like it might be on your topic. Open that record and search for the book's Library of Congress subject headings. Then go back and do a subject search under that heading to find materials on your topic.

SEARCH TIP

❶ **DOUBLE-CHECK THE SPELLING** If you type *mathmatics* for *mathematics*, you will find nothing on that subject.

❷ **TRY SYNONYMS FOR YOUR WORDS**

❸ **THE COMPUTER WILL ALSO ALLOW YOU TO LIMIT YOUR SEARCH BY DATE OF PUBLICATION** You can also limit by format—for example, searching only for videos or only for books.

❹ **EACH TIME YOU FIND A BOOK ON YOUR TOPIC, PRINT OUT THE CALL NUMBER** That way you won't forget it by the time you reach the shelves.

Library Resources

Focus

Lesson Overview

Objective
- To become familiar with the organization of a library

Skills
- identifying the sections of a library; naming the resources found in each section

Critical Thinking
- visualizing; classifying

Listening and Speaking
- questioning; discussing

 Bellringer
Daily Language Activity
When students enter the classroom, have this assignment on the board: *List three places in the library where you might find information about ancient Egypt.*

See also 📖 *Daily Language Practice*

Motivating Activity
Ask students to imagine that archaeologists in the year A.D. 10,000 have unearthed a large city from the ancient American civilization, dating back to the early 2000s. One of the archaeologists' greatest finds is an intact library. Ask students to list what they think the archaeologists could learn about this ancient civilization based on the contents of a representative library. Have them compare their lists in a discussion.

Resource Manager

Planning Resources
- *Lesson Plans*

📖 **Transparencies**
- *Bellringer*
- *Daily Language Practice*

📁 **Other Print Resources**
- *Thinking and Study Skills,* pp. 6–7
- *Vocabulary and Spelling Strategies and Practice*

Teach

Navigating the Online Catalog

If possible, ask students to explore the many features of the library's online catalog, including how to limit searches by date, language, type of material, and branch or library location. Have them explore other capabilities of the catalog, including how to create a list of selected titles and how to export this list to other e-mail locations. Ask them to report on their findings. **L3**

Subject Headings

To practice doing subject searches on an online catalog, ask students to search for a book by subject, not by title or author. If their first heading doesn't retrieve the title, ask them to try other possible subject headings. If those fail, ask students to do a keyword search. Ask them to keep track of the number of steps it took to find their book and to note the number of materials their library has under the headings they used. Ask them to share their results with the class. **L2**

Library Resources

Sample Search Result

Screen One   If you are searching for a book on the subject of *canyons*, select *Subject* and hit the *Enter* key.

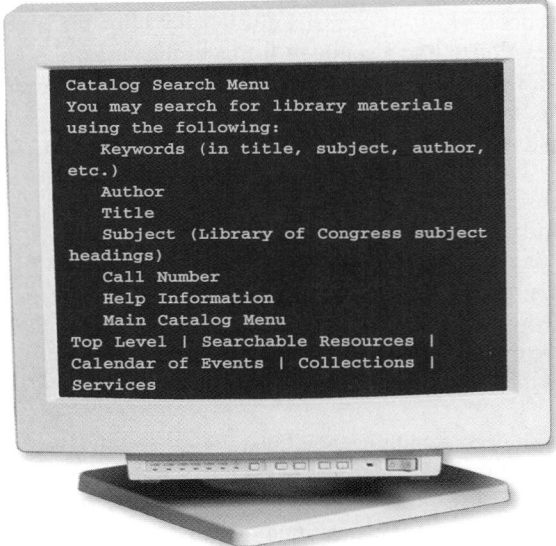

```
Catalog Search Menu
You may search for library materials
using the following:
    Keywords (in title, subject, author,
etc.)
    Author
    Title
    Subject (Library of Congress subject
headings)
    Call Number
    Help Information
    Main Catalog Menu
Top Level | Searchable Resources |
Calendar of Events | Collections |
Services
```

Screen Two   The second screen provides the Library of Congress subject headings that include the word *canyons*. In this case, you might choose category 6, which includes guidebooks for canyons of the southwestern United States.

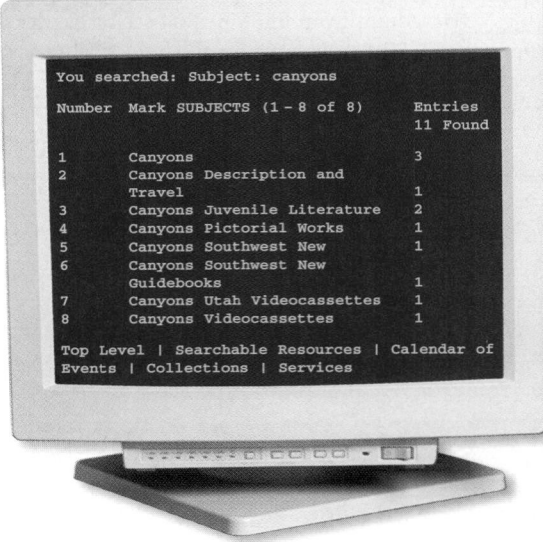

```
You searched: Subject: canyons

Number  Mark SUBJECTS (1 - 8 of 8)       Entries
                                         11 Found

1          Canyons                       3
2          Canyons Description and
           Travel                        1
3          Canyons Juvenile Literature   2
4          Canyons Pictorial Works       1
5          Canyons Southwest New         1
6          Canyons Southwest New
           Guidebooks                    1
7          Canyons Utah Videocassettes   1
8          Canyons Videocassettes        1

Top Level | Searchable Resources | Calendar of
Events | Collections | Services
```

Exploring Language

Synonyms and Searching

Students should be reminded of how important trial and error is to library research. When an online subject retrieves no materials, students should be encouraged to try related terms. Before your class begins to search for materials at the library, have them pick several possible research topics. Under these topics, have them write down words or phrases that mean almost the same thing. Next have them share their papers in a small group to see if other students can think of any more synonyms for the original topics.

Screen Three Category 6 brings you the following reference. Note that this final display provides specific information about the book, including title, author, call number, subject headings, publisher, date, number of pages, price, and whether the book is a first edition.

```
Previous Record/Next Record/Return to Browse/ Another
Search/New Search/Request Item

You searched: Subject: canyons

Author        Annerino, John.
Title         Canyoneering : how to explore the canyons
              of the great Southwest
ISBN          0811727009
CALL NUMBER   796.51 An
STATUS        CHECK SHELVES
Edition       1st ed.
Imprint:      Mechanicsburg, PA : Stackpole Books, c1999.
Description   xxii, 154 p. : ill., maps ; 21 cm.
Subject       Canyons — Southwest, New — Guidebooks.
Cost          $14.95

      Top Level | Searchable Resources | Calendar of
Events | Collections | Services
```

Exercise 1

Use the catalog to find one book on each of the following topics. List the author, title, call number, and publication date for each book you find.

1. Space exploration
2. Pompeii
3. Celtic mythology
4. Black holes
5. Collected works of Edgar Allan Poe
6. Triathlons
7. Biography of Nelson Mandela
8. African American poetry
9. Polar exploration
10. History of jazz

Teach

Connecting the Catalog and Library Materials

Gather a selection of various library items: a reference book, a nonfiction circulating book, a Young Adult novel, a music compact disc, a video. Using one or two samples, point out the title, author, date, type of medium, and call number and show how these compare to the record about the item in the online catalog. Now ask the students to look up each of the library items and look for the same kind of information for the other materials. **L2**

Practice and Assess

Answers: Exercise 1

Answers will vary, but they should be spot-checked to make sure students have included all the requested information.

Library Resources

Internet Connection

The Library of Congress's web catalog is available over the Internet at URL http://catalog.loc.gov. Because the Library of Congress catalogs most books in this country, most of its records give both the Dewey Decimal number and the Library of Congress Classification number. This Website is a good place for students to see how the two systems differ.

Teach

Exploring the Library

Take students on a tour of your school or community library. Point out the available resources and allow students to look them over. Emphasize that the librarian is trained to help locate specific information and that most librarians are happy to assist. Ask students to discuss occasions on which they have asked librarians for assistance. **L1**

Discovering the Library's Resources

Encourage students to create and label a map of their school or community library, with the locations of various reference sources, including reference books, photo archives, and periodicals. Does the library have computers? Is there a time limit for using them? Are the reference works in one section, or divided into departments? Ask students to compare the different arrangements they may have discovered in different libraries. **L2**

Library Resources

Sections of a Library

Learning about the organization of a library will help you use its many resources efficiently. Most school and public libraries are organized into the same general sections. The map below shows these sections.

Circulation Desk To apply for a library card or to check out or return materials, stop at the circulation desk. This desk is also the place where any books that you have requested will be held for you.

Young Adult and Children's Sections Books and materials that appeal to teens and to young children are kept in the young adult and children's sections.

Stacks Shelves in the library are called stacks. Here, you find both fiction and nonfiction books, in separate sections. Nonfiction books are works about a specific subject—for example, psychology, economics, music, or technology. They are fact-based rather than imaginative. Fiction books, including novels and short stories, are considered works of the imagination. Although poems and plays are imaginative works also, they may be shelved under "Literature" in the nonfiction section.

804 Unit 23 Library Resources

Enrichment and Extension

History

The ancient Mesopotamians were the first to establish libraries of clay tablets. Assyrian King Sennacherib, who ruled Mesopotamia from 704 to 681 B.C., kept a library of clay tablets in his palace. The most famous library of ancient times was developed in the 200s B.C. in Alexandria, Egypt.

The Alexandrian Library contained more than 400,000 papyrus scrolls, the largest collection in the ancient world. Eventually the library had a copy of every scroll known by its administrators to exist.

Reference Section Available here are reference materials, which include encyclopedias, dictionaries, almanacs, and atlases. These cannot be checked out of the library. Librarians will show you how to use these resources and help you formulate an effective search strategy.

Audiovisual Materials The audiovisual (AV) department offers a wealth of multimedia sources. Included in the AV section are videos, compact discs, audiocassettes, and even circulating computer software. Many audiovisual departments have listening rooms, where library users can try out different materials.

Periodicals Section Current magazines and newspapers are stored in the periodicals section. You can also find bound and microfilm copies of older magazines and newspapers.

Online Resources Depending on the individual library, computer indexes and electronic databases may be found in the reference section and/or in the periodicals section. In some libraries, these electronic resources are networked throughout the library and are available on most computers. Most libraries have a special section for Internet computers.

Exercise 2

In which section of a library might you find these items?

1. *Africa: A Biography of the Continent*
2. *Premiere* magazine
3. *Mozart's Requiem* (a compact disc)
4. *Encyclopedia of Endangered Species*
5. *The Joy Luck Club* (a novel)

23.2 Locating Books and Other Library Materials **805**

Library Resources

Teach

Young Adult Librarians

Many librarians specialize in working with teenagers. These librarians, known as Young Adult or YA librarians, sponsor teen programs, order books and other materials for young people, and gather reading lists for this age group. Invite a Young Adult librarian to your classroom to discuss the facilities that your school or community library offers. Ask the librarian to bring along books and other materials to show the class.

Practice and Assess

Answers: Exercise 2

1. nonfiction stacks
2. periodicals
3. audio-visual
4. reference
5. fiction stacks

Additional Resources

📁 *Vocabulary and Spelling Strategies and Practice*
📁 *Thinking and Study Skills*, pp. 6–7

Close

Encourage the class to speculate on the library resources a student of the future might use to find information about young people's lives today. They might start by discussing what things are important in their lives and then deciding what sections of the library might hold that information in the future.

MEETING INDIVIDUAL NEEDS

Less Proficient Readers

Talking Books and Videos

Encourage students who have trouble with reading to check out the library's Books on Tape or Books on CD collection. Many libraries collect both nonfiction and fiction titles in these formats. Encourage students to check out both a Book on Tape and a printed copy of the book and try to read along to the recorded tape. This will help students learn about pronunciation, inflections, and the rhythms of English prose.

Focus

Lesson Overview

Objective
- To learn how to use newspaper and periodical indexes

Skills
- using indexes to locate magazine, journal, and newspaper articles

Critical Thinking
- generating new information; classifying

Speaking and Listening
- evaluating

Bellringer
Daily Language Activity
When students enter the classroom, have this assignment on the board: *List one newspaper and two magazines in which you could find current information about cancer research.*

See also *Daily Language Practice*

Motivating Activity
Ask students what sections of the newspaper and what magazines they like to read. Then ask them to discuss what topics they might be likely to research in current newspapers or magazines.

Teach

Finding a Reference
Provide students with a list of topics, such as science, the arts, politics, and sports. Invite students to choose one of the topics. Then help them look through the *Readers' Guide to Periodical Literature* to find articles that would provide information on their chosen topic. **L2**

Library Resources

23.3 Searching for Periodicals

Until the early 1990s, almost all searching for magazine and newspaper articles was done by using printed indexes, and then by searching either bound periodicals or microforms (copies of magazines and newspapers stored on film). Today, magazine searches can be done electronically on the Internet and on various databases. A database is a collection of electronic files that are easily retrieved by a computer. However, if you are searching for older information, such as a magazine source from the early 1980s or before, you still need to search the older way. Scan for your topic in a bound copy of *The Readers' Guide to Periodical Literature* and then follow your citation to the correct issue of the magazine in the periodical section.

But often you will search online. Most libraries provide two different types of electronic databases: general periodical ones, and ones specific to a subject. *The Electric Library,* which searches newspapers, general magazines, maps, and TV and radio transcripts, is an example of a general periodical database. *Social Issues Resource* is an example of a database that is focused on one main subject area, sociology and current social problems.

All databases share common features. Most offer the option to do a basic search or a more advanced search. Each has a query screen. On it you key in your search term(s)—either one word, or a search phrase. Some databases allow you to search by subject, but for many databases the *default* setting (the one that appears first) is a keyword search. The *refine* option lets you limit your search by date. It also lets you do a new search with a more specific search term. Many databases allow you to use natural language—you ask the question the way you would ask a friend. Some databases will let you limit your search to full-text articles only. Some will let you limit your search to one format only, such as maps.

After your search is finished, check the display results carefully. Note if the results are displayed in chronological order or by order of *relevancy.* *Relevancy* means that the search results share a close logical relationship with your topic. The one with the closest relationship will be listed first, and so on.

Sample Periodical Search

This search was done using a database called *MasterFILE Premier,* which searches current magazines and newspapers. The researcher, looking for information on connections between the Internet and radio, has used the keywords "internet and radio" and has limited the search to periodicals published between January 1999 and October 1999.

Resource Manager

Planning Resources
- *Lesson Plans*

 Transparencies
- *Bellringer*
- *Daily Language Practice*

Other Print Resources
- *Thinking and Study Skills,* pp. 6–7
- *Vocabulary and Spelling Strategies and Practice*

Sample Screen Examine the first ten references that came up for this search. An *X* indicates *Full Text*—that is, the entire text of the article is available.

```
Records (1 to 10) of 349
Mark Full Text          Select Result For More Detail
  X   How CBS Is Bartering Its Way Into the Dot.com World.; By:
Kover, Amy., Fortune, 09/27/99, Vol. 140 Issue 6, p312, 2p, 1c
Full Page Image
      X   Print's power play.; By: Kerwin, Ann Marie., Advertising
Age, 1999 Special Issue, Vol. 70 Issue 39, p72, 1p, 1c
  X   Domain-name registry sites pump up ads.; By: Gilbert,
Jennifer., Advertising Age, 09/20/99, Vol. 70 Issue 39, p44, 2p,
1bw
  X   Web key in CBS, Viacom merger.; By: Garrity, Brian.,
Billboard, 09/18/99, Vol. 111 Issue 38, p5, 2p
  X   Egil keeps groove alive via TV, radio, label.; By: Nowinski,
Amanda., Billboard, 09/18/99, Vol. 111 Issue 38, p33,1/3p, 1bw
      Old Media Get a Web Windfall.; By: Hwang, Suein S., Wall Street
Journal Eastern Edition, 09/17/99, Vol. 234 Issue 55, pB1, 0p, 1bw
      Watching the Web.; By: Petersen, Andrea., Wall Street Journal -
Eastern Edition, 09/16/99, Vol. 234 Issue 54, pB11, 0p
      MTV Networks Unit Sues Imagine Radio Founders.; Wall Street
Journal - Eastern Edition, 09/15/99, Vol. 234 Issue 53, pB9, 0p
  X   Radio Ad Specialist Tunes in to Net Niche.; By: Littman,
Margaret., Crain's Chicago Business, 09/13/99, Vol. 22 Issue 37,
p14, 2/5p, 1c
  X   Fun. (cover story); By: Pappas, Ben. and Schifrin, Matthew.
and Berentson, Ben. and Solan, Joshua. and Manzo, Emily and
Nathan, Adit. and Leitzes, Adam., Forbes, 09/13/99, Vol. 164
Issue 6, p105, 1p, 2c
      (1 to 10) of 349  Refine Search  Print/  Email/  Save
```

Look over your display results carefully. The display screen gives you important information about each article, including the title, author, source, date of publication, length, and availability of photographs or other graphics. The abbreviations *c* and *bw* stand for *color* or *black-and-white* images.

Exercise 3

Look at the sample screen and answer these questions.

1. Which of these periodicals did a cover story on this topic? Why might a cover story be more valuable than just any story?
2. How many of these articles have full text available?
3. You have only one hour to finish researching your report. In what ways might you refine your search?
4. You need to illustrate your report. Which of these articles has a full page image? Is the image in color or in black and white?

Teach

Databases and the Internet
Advise students that while periodical databases are still good places to search for current news topics, the Internet can offer even more timely, if less detailed, information. To compare the two venues for searches, have students pick a current topic from a newspaper and search it first on the Internet and then on a periodical database. Ask them which gave more timely information. Which provided more detailed information? Which was easier to search? Why? **L3**

Practice and Assess

Answers: Exercise 3
Parts of some answers will vary.
1. *Forbes.* Cover stories get more attention than others.
2. Six
3. Students might suggest other terms, such as "e-mail."
4. The first item, in *Fortune.*

Additional Resources
📁 *Vocabulary and Spelling Strategies and Practice*
📁 *Thinking and Study Skills,* pp. 6–7

Close

Ask students to discuss their experiences using periodical and newspaper indexes. Invite students to discuss any difficulties they have had using the indexes. What advice would they give first-time index users?

Library Resources

MEETING INDIVIDUAL NEEDS **English Language Learners**

Using the *Readers' Guide*
Introduce students from other countries to English-language magazines they might enjoy reading, such as teen-oriented, sports, and hobby magazines. Choose magazines that are indexed in the *Readers' Guide to Periodical Literature.* Have the students browse through sample issues and choose one feature. Then help them locate their chosen article in the *Readers' Guide.*

Focus

Lesson Overview

Objective
- To become familiar with general reference sources and learn how to use them

Skills
- identifying and using general library reference resources; identifying and selecting information from different parts of books

Critical Thinking
- contrasting; generating information

Listening and Speaking
- oral reporting; discussing

Bellringer
Daily Language Activity

When students enter the classroom, have this assignment on the board: *Where would you look to find the following information about the city of Bogotá, Colombia?*

- *its population*
- *its annual rainfall*
- *the names of its three largest rivers*
- *the kinds of music played there*
- *its most popular sport*

See also *Daily Language Practice*

Motivating Activity

Invite students to discuss the kinds of information that would be valuable to include in reference texts. When might students need to know this kind of information?

Explain to students that in this lesson they'll be learning about where to locate a wide range of reference information that they can use for school reports and other projects.

Library Resources

Libraries offer many reference sources to answer all types of questions and in all subject areas. Today these reference sources are almost always available in both print formats and online. General reference works will satisfy many of your research needs. They do not take much time to survey and they provide excellent background information. If you do not locate what you need, you may have to move on to more specialized reference sources.

General Reference Works

General reference works include sources such as encyclopedias, dictionaries, atlases, and yearbooks. Online versions of these sources are available and may provide video, film, and audio clips in addition to traditional text and photos.

General Reference Sources	Examples
Encyclopedias include general information on a variety of topics.	*World Book Encyclopedia* (print), *Britannica Online*, *Encyclopedia Americana* (print and online), *Encarta* (online)
Almanacs provide statistics, lists, and detailed coverage of last year's events.	*Times/Information Please Almanac* (print and online), *World Almanac* (print)
Atlases are collections of maps. They often include special maps on climate, land use, history, and other topics. **Gazetteers** are geographical dictionaries.	Atlases: *Times Atlas of the World* (print), *History Atlas of North America* (print), *The World Factbook* (online) Gazetteers: *Merriam-Webster's Geographical Dictionary* (print), *Columbia Gazetteer of the World* (print), *The U.S. Gazetteer* (online)
Biographical Reference Works give life histories of noteworthy individuals.	*Current Biography* (print), *Dictionary of American Biography* (print), *Biography Index* (online), *Literature Resource Center* (online)

The Internet

Your public library will also provide access to the Internet, a valuable reference tool. The Internet provides information on any subject—text, images, sound, and video, as well as a way to contact experts. Since it provides the most current news, the Internet can be your first source for any late-breaking news. It also provides full text of speeches, laws, and excerpts of many books. On the Internet, you can search the catalogs of world-class libraries, such as the Library of Congress and the New York Public Library.

Resource Manager

Planning Resources
- *Lesson Plans*

Transparencies
- *Bellringer*
- *Daily Language Practice*

Other Print Resources
- *Thinking and Study Skills,* pp. 6–7
- *Vocabulary and Spelling Strategies and Practice*

Search Engines Since there are so many Internet sites, the best way to find useful information on the Internet is by using a *search engine*. Search engines send out software agents called *spiders* that search every link they can find. If you do not find any usable sources with one search engine, try some others. They each search the Internet differently, and no single search engine will search comprehensively.

Online Libraries Online libraries on the Internet are important reference sources. They offer links to many information sources that can answer your specific reference questions. One advantage of these sites is that they are available twenty-four hours a day. You can connect from home if you have access to a computer and a modem. A disadvantage of these sites is that there are no librarians available to help you find the information you need quickly. Examples of excellent online reference sites include *The Internet Public Library*, sponsored by the School of Information at the University of Michigan, and *Thor: The Virtual Reference Desk +*, the online resource site of Purdue University Library.

Evaluating Internet Sources The Internet is not a perfect research tool, however. Much information on the Internet is unreliable. Always evaluate what you see when you scan a Web site for information. Ask yourself whether it is current, and if it was put there by a reliable source. In addition, check more than one source on the Internet to see if the information corresponds. Many libraries list recommended Web sites, which are ideal starting places for Internet research. (See Unit 7, "Research Paper Writing," page 320, for guidance on evaluating sources and detecting bias.) For any Web site you use, ask yourself the following questions.

1. Is the material authoritative? Who sponsors this site? Is it a government agency, a business promoting its own products, a nonprofit organization, or a private individual? The most reliable sites are sponsored by the government, universities, libraries, and similar reliable organizations.

2. How current is the information? A site that has not been updated for three years may be too old for your purposes.

3. Look over the screens. Are there many errors, misspellings, typos? If so, the person may also have been careless with the accuracy of the information.

4. Is the site easy to navigate? Or are you lost in a sea of words and images?

5. Are there links to other helpful sites? Although it isn't absolutely necessary, the linking feature is an important and useful addition.

Teach

Using Reference Works

Provide students with a single type of reference source, such as an encyclopedia or a biographical dictionary. Give them a list of several pieces of information they might find in the resource and have them choose one. Help them search for the information by showing them how to find items listed alphabetically and explaining such features as the table of contents, glossary, copyright page, and index (if applicable). **L1**

Searching the Internet

One problem with Internet searches is retrieving too much information, much of which may not be relevant to the topic. To avoid this problem, advise students to enclose their search phrase in quotation marks. If they search for "Houston Astros," they will find only sites that use that phrase, as opposed to all sites with *Houston* and all sites with *Astros,* which would be the case if they did not enclose the phrase in quotation marks. **L2**

⬱ Cross-reference: Writing

For information on how and when students should use the title and copyright pages in doing research work, refer students to Lesson 7.4, pp. 336–341.

Library Resources

23.4 Using Reference Sources **809**

Civic Literacy

Understanding Government

Encourage students to investigate the types of reference publications available from government agencies or in government repositories in libraries. Individual students might obtain samples of reference documents and present them to the class or report on the types of information available in various publications. Invite students to discuss the reasons a government might be interested in producing such publications and their value to the citizens who use them.

Teach

Navigating the Internet

For students who find navigating the Internet confusing, advise them to start their research by using *Yahoo!* as their search engine. *Yahoo!* offers defined subject categories that allow for a logical search. Its subject directories are also very detailed so they provide many subcategories to search. *Yahoo!* is also a great search engine to choose when students are having difficulty selecting a research topic. **L1**

Practice and Assess

Answers: Exercise 4

Answers will vary, depending on the resources available in local libraries.

Answers: Exercise 5

Answers will vary, depending on resources available locally.

Additional Resources

📁 *Vocabulary and Spelling Strategies and Practice*

📁 *Thinking and Study Skills,* pp. 6–7

Close

Ask students to describe various reference works and the information provided by each. Which three works would they expect to use most frequently in the next year?

✔ ASSESSMENT OPTIONS

📁 *Tests With Answer Key & Rubrics*
Unit 23 Mastery Test, pp. 85-86

💾 *Testmaker*
Unit 23 Mastery Test

📼 *MindJogger Videoquizzes*

You may wish to administer the Unit 23 Mastery Test at this point.

Library Resources

Online Search Terms

Abstract   A summary of an article or information source.

Database   A collection of information resources which can be searched electronically. Some databases, such as Biography Index, only search a specific subject; others, such as Nexus/Lexus or the Electric Library, search all subjects.

Discussion Groups   An online location where you can ask questions or discuss problems and current events. Discussion groups on the Internet exist on almost every topic, such as the environment, pets, music, and sports.

Full Text   Indication that all of the article is present online. However, sometimes full-text articles do not include charts and graphics.

Hit   The term for a successful result after you have searched online.

Internet   A computer network is composed of many smaller computer networks. The Internet is the largest computer network in the world.

Relevancy   In computer searching, how closely your search results answer your search query. Many databases and search engines display results in a hierarchy from the most relevant to the least. These relevancy relationships are usually given in percentages.

Search Engine   Computer software that browses the Internet for places where your words appear. Examples are Yahoo, Goober, Lycos, and Ask Jeeves.

URL   (Universal Resource Locator) An address for a Web site. It contains the computer name, directory name, and name of the Web page.

World Wide Web   The part of the Internet that provides information in various formats, including print, sound, photos, graphics, and video. Links allow you to move from place to place.

Exercise 4

Use general reference works to answer the following questions. Use at least one encyclopedia, one almanac or yearbook, one atlas, and one biographical reference work. After each answer, indicate the reference source you used.

1. Where was Madeleine Albright born?
2. Who won the Nobel Peace Prize last year?
3. When did Brazil win its independence?
4. What is the average temperature in Bombay, India, in January?

Exercise 5

Ask your librarian to recommend two search engines. On both search engines, look for references for the same topic—a topic from one of your classes. Are there differences in the information you found on each search engine? Which of the two search engines would you prefer to use if you were doing research for a term paper? Why? What are some of the most promising references you found? Explain. Report on your findings to the class.

Enrichment and Extension

Using CD-ROMs

Many traditional reference sources such as encyclopedias, dictionaries, and atlases are now available in a CD-ROM format. Local, state, and federal government agencies and many city and university libraries now offer information on-line through the Internet. Encourage students to familiarize themselves with these new technologies.

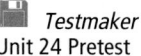
UNIT
24 | Using Dictionaries

Lesson **24.1**   **General Dictionaries**   *812*

Lesson **24.2**   **Using a Thesaurus**   *816*

Objectives

- To develop an understanding of how dictionaries are organized and of the kinds of information they contain
- To learn to use original style and dictionary style thesauruses
- To demonstrate the ability to use dictionaries and thesauruses effectively

✔ ASSESSMENT OPTIONS

📁 *Tests with Answer Key & Rubrics*
Unit 24 Pretest, pp. 87–88

💾 *Testmaker*
Unit 24 Pretest

You may wish to administer the Unit 24 Pretest at this point.

Key to Ability Levels

L1 Level 1 activities are within the basic ability range of students.

L2 Level 2 activities are within the ability range of average students.

L3 Level 3 activities are more challenging activities.

811

Resource Manager

Planning Resources
- *Lesson Plans*
- *Block Scheduling*

 Transparencies
- *Bellringer*
- *Daily Language Practice*

📁 **Other Print Resources**
- *Tests with Answer Key & Rubrics*
- *Vocabulary and Spelling Strategies and Practice*

 Video
- *MindJogger Videoquizzes*

💾 **Software**
- *Presentation Plus!*
- *Testmaker*
- *Vocabulary Power Puzzlemaker*
- *Writer's Choice Puzzlemaker*

 Web Sites
- *writerschoice.glencoe.com*

Focus

Lesson Overview

Objectives
- To understand and use the information in a dictionary

Skills
- understanding dictionary entries; using the dictionary to answer a variety of questions

Critical Thinking
- analyzing; evaluating

Listening and Speaking
- giving a presentation

Bellringer
Daily Language Activity

When students enter the classroom, have this assignment on the board: *List four or five kinds of information you could find in a dictionary.*

See also *Daily Language Practice*

Motivating Activity

Have students tell where they would look to find the origin of a word (in a dictionary). Then have them share and discuss their lists of information that can be found in a dictionary. (They would find pronunciations, definitions, information about places and about famous people, conversion tables for measurements.)

Explain that in this lesson, they will examine the kinds of information they can find in a dictionary.

Using Dictionaries

General Dictionaries

A dictionary is an alphabetical listing of words with their definitions, called entries. Most dictionaries of the English language fall into one of three categories—unabridged, college, school—based on their size and comprehensiveness. The characteristics of each type of dictionary are shown at the bottom of this page.

The Main Entries

Look at the sample dictionary page on page 813 to familiarize yourself with the organization of entries in a dictionary. Two features of the page, the guide words and the pronunciation key, help you find and understand dictionary entries.

Types of Dictionaries

Unabridged Dictionaries   250,000 or More Entries

Characteristics
- Extensive word histories
- Detailed definitions
- May be in several volumes
- Found mostly in libraries

Examples
- *Random House Dictionary of the English Language*
- *Webster's Third New International Dictionary*
- *Oxford English Dictionary*

College Dictionaries   About 150,000 Entries

Characteristics
- Detailed enough to answer most questions on spelling or definitions
- Widely used in schools, homes, and businesses

Examples
- *Random House Webster's College Dictionary*
- *American Heritage Dictionary of the English Language*
- *Webster's New World Dictionary*

School Dictionaries   90,000 or Fewer Entries

Characteristics
- Definitions based on students' backgrounds
- Emphasizes common words

Examples
- *Macmillan Dictionary*
- *Webster's School Dictionary*

Resource Manager

Planning Resources
- *Lesson Plans*

 Transparencies
- *Bellringer*
- *Daily Language Practice*

📂 **Other Print Resources**
- *Thinking and Study Skills*, p. 7
- *Vocabulary and Spelling Strategies and Practice*

kaolin / keep

Guide words indicate the first and last entry on the page
kaolin/keep

The first entry on the page is **kaolin**.

The last entry on the page is **keep**.

Pronunciation key uses well-known words to indicate how to interpret the pronunciation symbols
at; **ā**pe; **cär**; **e**nd; **mē** . . .

at; āpe; cär; end; it; īce; hot; ōld; fôrk; wood; ŏŏ; out; up; ūse; turn; sing; thin; this; zh in treasure; a in ago, taken, pencil, lemon, circus   561

Homographs Two or more words that are spelled the same but have different meanings and histories are listed as separate entries. Such words are called homographs. For example, *sole* could mean "the bottom of a foot," "acting alone," or "a type of fish." Since these three meanings are so distinct from each other, sole is listed as a main entry three times. Each is labeled with a small, raised number. Notice the different meanings and histories of *real*[1] and *real*[2] shown on the next page.

Entry Information Most often you probably look up a word to find a definition. However, entries also provide other information, such as

- correct hyphenation of words with more than one syllable
- pronunciations
- preferred spellings when alternate forms of words are acceptable
- inflected forms of the main entry word, such as plurals, adverbs, or adjectives
- part or parts of speech
- cross-references to synonyms, words with the same or similar meanings, and to antonyms, words with opposite meanings

24.1 General Dictionaries   **813**

Study the Characteristics

Explain to students that the chart on the opposite student page shows the relative size and characteristics of each type of English-language dictionary. Point out that the difference in the number of entries in the three types of dictionaries is an indication of the completeness of each dictionary. Then explain that the more complete dictionaries contain all the information in a school dictionary, plus additional information. Then ask: Which type of dictionary would you use to find the most detailed history of the word *dictionary*? (an unabridged dictionary) **L2**

Compare Dictionaries

Have students work in small groups to create a chart to compare the types of information in unabridged, college, and school dictionaries. Suggest that they investigate the kinds of information found in other types of dictionaries, for example, a biographical dictionary, a gazetteer, and a bilingual dictionary. Ask each group to share its chart with another group to compare findings. **L3**

Using Dictionaries

MEETING INDIVIDUAL NEEDS
English Language Learners

Using the Pronunciation Key

Students who are less fluent in spoken English may need help with the pronunciation key. Using a classroom dictionary, write two or three words from the key, along with their phonetic pronunciations. Ask students to write on the board several other English words that contain the same sounds and pronounce them aloud. Correct any mispronunciations.

Teach

Understanding Meanings

Make sure all students understand the meaning of the word *etymology*, and the information provided in the etymology portion of an entry. Stress that etymology notes show the many languages that have contributed to the English language spoken today. Students may enjoy challenging one another to identify words based on their etymology. List several words on the board. Ask volunteers to look up a word, read the etymology note aloud, and see if the class can identify the word on the board to which the note relates. **L2**

Creating a Dictionary

Make the idea of using a dictionary more manageable by advising students to create their own dictionaries in their writing journals with a list of their personal spelling difficulties and easily confused words. Suggest that students keep this list in a place where they will have ready access during editing, such as inside the back cover. **L1**

⬌ Cross-reference: Grammar

For more information on comparative forms of modifiers and the correct usage of modifiers, see Lesson 18.1, pp. 663–665; Lesson 18.2, pp. 666–667; Lesson 18.5, pp. 671–672; and the Unit 18 Review, pp. 680–688.

Using Dictionaries

Etymology   Many entries also include an etymology, which is the history of a word. For example, the word *telephone* comes from two Greek words—*tele* ("far off, afar") and *phone* ("voice, sound"). From etymologies you can also learn when a word is derived from another, such as *atomic* from *atom.*

Look at the following dictionary entry for *real* to review the elements of an entry.

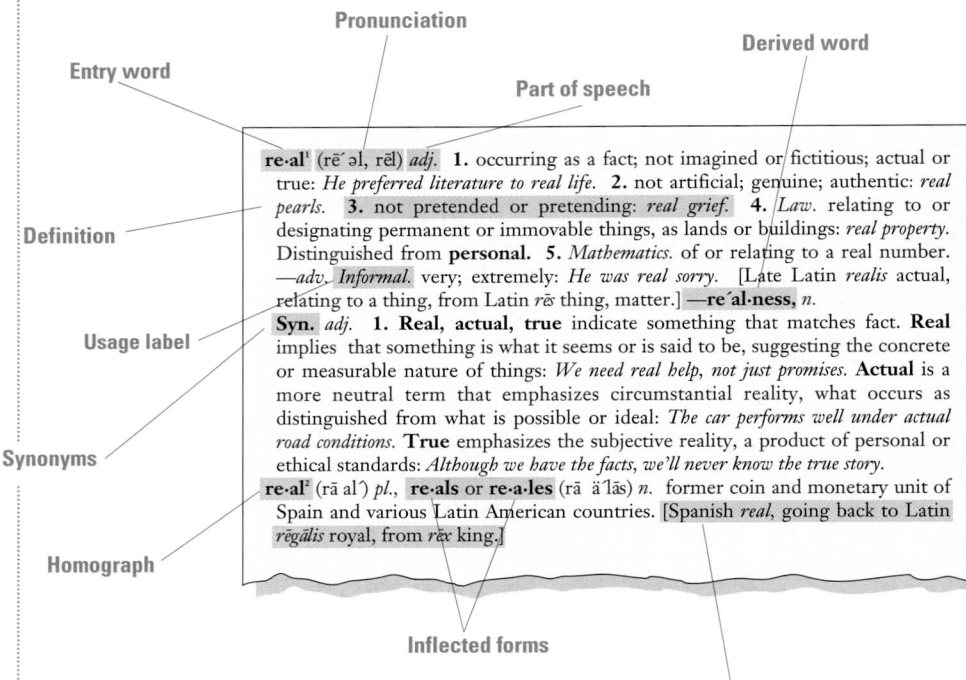

Usage Guidelines   A dictionary entry also provides you with guidelines on usage, meaning the way words are used in different contexts. Labels identify situations in which the word can be used appropriately. For example, the definition of the word *dig* that means "to understand" is labeled "slang." This usage label tells you that this meaning of *dig* does not belong to standard English.

Many dictionaries include a phrase or a sentence illustrating the use of a particular definition of a word. In some dictionaries these phrases and sentences are quotations from actual pieces of writing, in which case the dictionary may also identify the writer and the date of the place.

Common usage labels are described in the table located at the top of the next page.

Enrichment and Extension

Giving a Presentation

Call on student volunteers to act as sales representatives of a major dictionary publisher. Provide each representative with a different type of dictionary. Ask representatives to prepare and give a presentation explaining the usefulness of the dictionary and describing its important features. After the presentations, allow time for potential customers (other class members) to ask questions.

Usage Information in Dictionary Entries

Type of Information	Description	Example
Capitalization	Indicates when a particular meaning of a word needs to be capitalized	**confederate . . . 2. Confederate.** citizen or supporter of the Confederate States of America.
Special field usage	Identifies a definition used only in a particular activity or area of study	**travel . . . 7.** *Basketball.* To walk or run illegally while holding the ball.
Regional usage	Indicates words with special meanings in certain geographical areas.	**submarine . . . 3.** *Chiefly Northeastern and North Midland U.S.* a hero sandwich.
Usage note	Provides guidelines for using (or not using) words in particular situations	**oyez . . . ▲** used to announce that court is in session and to ask for silence.
Out-of-date usage	Labels words as archaic (used only in special contexts) or obsolete (no longer used)	**transport . . . 4.** *Archaic.* to kill.

Special Sections

Many dictionaries also include special sections, such as a biography section listing famous people and a geography section describing cities, countries, and other places.

Accessing Dictionaries on Computers

Today, many dictionaries are available on compact disc (CD-ROM). You can also access dictionaries on the Internet. Online dictionaries allow you to enter a search word to find the definition. For some words, you also get an illustration. Online dictionaries also offer features such as help with spelling, word games, language tips, and amusing facts about words. Some online dictionary services allow you to access many general and specialized dictionaries in one search.

Exercise 1

Use a school or college dictionary to answer the following questions.

1. Who was Haile Selassie?
2. What are the past and past participle of *tread*?
3. Is *theater* or *theatre* the preferred American spelling?
4. What are the origins of the homographs spelled *bow*?
5. What synonyms or antonyms are given for *spectator*?

Using Dictionaries

Practice and Assess

Answers: Exercise 1

1. the former emperor of Ethiopia
2. The past tense is *trod* and past participle is *trodden* or *trod*.
3. *Theater* is the preferred American spelling.
4. All homographs spelled *bow* are from Old English, except one that is Danish in origin and refers to the forward end of a ship.
5. Answers will vary, depending on the dictionary consulted. Synonyms include *onlooker* and *observer;* antonyms include *performer* and *entertainer.*

Additional Resources

📁 *Vocabulary and Spelling Strategies and Practice*
📁 *Thinking and Study Skills,* p. 7

Close

Suggest that students investigate the dictionaries, both print and electronic, which they have access to at school or in their community. Have them make a list of other kinds of dictionaries they find.

Enrichment and Extension

Viewing a Dictionary on Disc

The *Oxford English Dictionary,* one of the most complete and authoritative sources on word histories, is available on compact disc (CD-ROM) to be used in conjunction with a computer. The user inserts the disc and types the word to be searched. The entry is then displayed on the computer screen. Many libraries have this service.

Focus

Lesson Overview

Objective
• To understand the uses of a thesaurus

Skills
• locating synonyms in a thesaurus; determining exact meanings of synonyms and using them correctly

Critical Thinking
• comparing; contrasting; relating meanings

Speaking and Listening
• discussing

Bellringer
Daily Language Activity

When students enter the classroom, have this assignment on the board: *List two words—a noun, and an adjective —that you might use to describe someone and then list a synonym for each word.*

See also *Daily Language Practice*

Teach

Using Two Kinds of Thesauruses

To help students understand how to use a thesaurus, ask them to use both an original-style thesaurus and a dictionary-style thesaurus to locate a common word with a variety of meanings, such as *character.* Students should compare the entries and explain how they differ. Lead a discussion about the advantages and disadvantages of each type of thesaurus. **L3**

Using Dictionaries

24.2 Using a Thesaurus

One special type of dictionary is a book of synonyms, also known as a thesaurus. Such a book can help a writer find colorful, precise words about any given subject. The best-known thesaurus is *Roget's,* first developed by a British doctor, Peter Mark Roget, in 1852. Roget grouped together words related to the same basic concept, such as *improvement,* into categories. He then developed an index to the categories. Thesauruses exist today both in this original form and an updated, dictionary form.

You can also access thesauruses electronically—on CD-ROMs, on the Internet, and even on some word processing software.

Original Form

Using Roget's original thesaurus is a simple two-step process. First, you look up a word in the index to find the category under which it is listed. Then you look up the category to find synonyms for the word. For example, look at the following thesaurus entries for the word *change.*

> The index lists many categories for change. Category 139 lists synonyms for the meaning *alteration.*

> **change**
> *n.* alteration 139
> alternate 149.2
> conversion 145.1
> differentiation 16.4
> petty cash 835.19
> substitution 149.1

> Category 139 lists synonyms for change that mean *alteration.*

> Commonly used words are printed in boldface type.

> **139. CHANGE**
> .1 NOUNS **change, alteration, modification; variation,** variety, difference, diversity, diversification; **deviation,** diversion, **divergence; switch, turn,** turnabout, about-face, **reversal,** flip-flop [informal]; apostasy, defection, change of heart; **shift,** transition, **modulation,** qualification; **conver -sion, renewal,** revival, revivification; remaking, reshaping, re-creation, redesign, restructuring; realignment, **adaptation, adjustment,** accommodation, fitting.

Resource Manager

Planning Resources
• *Lesson Plans*

Transparencies
• *Bellringer*
• *Daily Language Practice*

📂 **Other Print Resources**
• *Thinking and Study Skills,* p. 7
• *Vocabulary and Spelling Strategies and Practice*

Dictionary Form

A variation of Roget's original system is even simpler to use. A thesaurus in dictionary form presents words in alphabetical order. A regular word entry is followed by a few synonyms and cross-references to one or more related major categories, as in the entry for *grow*.

> **grow,** *v.* raise, plant, sow (FARMING);
> vegetate, germinate, sprout (PLANT LIFE);
> fill out, wax, accumulate (INCREASE).

If you can't find an appropriate synonym under the regular entry, try one of the major categories, which are in parentheses. Under a major category entry you will find nouns, verbs, adjectives, and adverbs all related to one main idea. Major categories include cross-references to antonyms. The following excerpt shows the entry for *increase*.

Major category

INCREASE—*N.* **increase,** raise, rise, boost, step-up; addition, increment, accrual, access.

Synonyms for increase

  growth, surge, swell, rise, accretion; accumulation, overgrowth, spread.
  [*abnormal bodily enlargement*] giantism, gigantism, elephantiasis, acromegaly.
  V. **increase,** enhance, aggrandize, augment, add to, heighten, aggravate, intensify, step up, raise, lift, boost, up; multiply, propagate, redouble, magnify, exaggerate, maximize, lengthen.

Subcategories

  grow, surge, swell, fill out, inflate; wax, accumulate, rise, skyrocket; overgrow, overrun, spread.
  expand, distend, dilate, inflate, swell, develop, extend, spread, stretch, widen; enlarge, pad, amplify, bulk.
  enlarge on (*a subject, etc.*), amplify, develop, dilate on, elaborate on, expand, expatiate on, extend.

Cross-references to other major categories

  Adj. **increasing,** etc. (see *Verbs*); accretive, crescent, crescive, incremental, increscent, addititious, cumulative, accumulative.
  See also ADDITION, EXAGGERATION, SPREAD, SWELLING.
Antonyms—See DECREASE, DEDUCTION.

Cross-references to antonyms

Exercise 2

Use a thesaurus to find two synonyms for each word below. Then write an original sentence to illustrate the meaning of each synonym. You may wish to check the exact meaning of each word in a dictionary before you use it in a sentence. Share your sentences with the class.

1. want (verb)
2. angry (adjective)
3. hold (verb)
4. like (verb)
5. near (adverb)
6. deny (verb)
7. throw (verb)
8. good (adjective)
9. condemn (verb)
10. place (noun)

24.2 Using a Thesaurus **817**

Using Dictionaries

Cooperative Learning

Finding Synonyms
Divide students into small groups to complete Exercise 2. Groups should choose a topic into which all words in the exercise would fit (such as pet peeves or bad habits). The group then divides up the list so that every student has two or three words to look up in a thesaurus. After finding synonyms, each student uses them in sentences about the chosen topic. Afterward, they rejoin the group and work together to organize their sentences into a paragraph.

INTRODUCING

UNIT 25

Objectives

- To build vocabulary by analyzing the specific and general context in which unfamiliar words are found
- To build vocabulary by making word lists and diagrams to analyze the prefixes, roots, and suffixes of familiar and unfamiliar words

✓ ASSESSMENT OPTIONS

📁 *Tests with Answer Key & Rubrics*
Unit 25 Pretest, pp. 91–92

💾 *Testmaker*
Unit 25 Pretest

You may wish to administer the Unit 25 Pretest at this point.

Key to Ability Levels

L1 Level 1 activities are within the basic ability range of students.

L2 Level 2 activities are within the ability range of average students.

L3 Level 3 activities are more challenging activities.

UNIT 25 Vocabulary

Lesson 25.1 **Building Vocabulary**   *819*

Lesson 25.2 **Word Parts**   *822*

818

Resource Manager

Planning Resources
- *Lesson Plans*
- *Block Scheduling*

🖨 Transparencies
- *Bellringer*
- *Daily Language Practice*

📁 Other Print Resources
- *Tests with Answer Key & Rubrics*
- *Vocabulary and Spelling Strategies and Practice*
- *Vocabulary Power*

📹 Video
- *MindJogger Videoquizzes*

25.1 Building Vocabulary

Most words that you know you learned through active conversation and through listening and reading. One way to learn new words is by analyzing the passage in which they appear.

Analyzing Specific Context Clues

You can often figure out the meaning of a word from its context— the words and sentences surrounding an unfamiliar word. The following chart describes five different context clues and lists the words that help you interpret those clues. In the Example column, clue words are in bold type. Unfamiliar words and the context that helps you interpret the meaning of those words are in italics.

Interpreting Clue Words		
Type of Context Clue	**Clue Words**	**Example**
Definition: The meaning of the unfamiliar word is stated in the sentence.	which means also known as in other words or	The course emphasized *demography*, **which means** *the study of changes in human population*.
Example: The meaning of the unfamiliar word is explained through other illustrations.	for instance such as for example like	He was the president's *amanuensis*; **for instance**, he *took dictation and copied manuscripts*.
Comparison: The unfamiliar word is similar to a familiar word or phrase.	likewise also similarly as	Consuela had a height *phobia*; **likewise**, she *feared caves*.
Contrast: The unfamiliar word is the opposite of a familiar word or phrase.	however but on the contrary unlike	We were *pertinacious* about the topics; **however**, we were *flexible* about the time of the meeting.
Cause and Effect: The unfamiliar word describes a cause in a sentence in which the effects are understood.	therefore since because when as a result	Otis was typically *loquacious*; **therefore**, the rest of us were unusually *quiet*.

Vocabulary

Focus

Lesson Overview

Objective
- To use context and word analysis as vocabulary-building strategies

Skills
- identifying meanings of unfamiliar words

Critical Thinking
- analyzing; synthesizing

Listening and Speaking
- discussing

Bellringer
Daily Language Activity

When students enter the classroom, have this assignment on the board: *List three ways you can figure out the meanings of unfamiliar words you come across during reading.*

See also *Daily Language Practice*

Motivating Activity

Discuss why readers should take time to figure out unfamiliar words. Point out that there are other benefits of a large vocabulary besides the obvious ones at school. How would a large vocabulary help in a job interview or with friends and family? Stress that the goal of vocabulary building is not using big words, but rather using the most appropriate words in each case.

Students may be surprised to learn that most people know over 3,000 words when they begin kindergarten and as many as 30,000 words when they finish college. This lesson will provide students with methods to increase their word power.

Resource Manager

Planning Resources
- *Lesson Plans*

📚 **Transparencies**
- *Bellringer*
- *Daily Language Practice*

📁 **Other Print Resources**
- *Vocabulary and Spelling Strategies and Practice*

Teach

Using Context Clues

Have students practice using context clues by playing "frobrish." Present a "frobrish" example by saying aloud a sentence in which you have replaced a key word with a nonsense word—for example, "Class, take out your pencils and put your books under your chairs so we can start the frobrish." Discuss with students the apparent meaning of *frobrish* (test or quiz) and the clues that helped them define the word. Then divide the class into teams. Have each team member compose a "frobrish" sentence. Teams take turns reading a member's sentence and challenging other teams to figure out the meaning of the nonsense word. Remind students to identify the word's part of speech and a logical synonym of the word. **L2**

Identifying Word Meanings

Obtain one copy of the Lewis Carroll poem "Jabberwocky" for each pair of students. Let partners discuss nonsense words in the poem and work together to identify their parts of speech and to suggest meanings based on the general context of the poem. Have partners take turns writing a new sentence using one or more of the nonsense words, and challenging the other partner to "translate" the sentence according to the meanings they have identified. **L3**

⬌ Cross-reference: Writing

For situations in which a writer might use context clues to help readers understand new words, refer students to Lesson 5.1, pp. 220–223, and Lesson 5.6, pp. 240–243.

Vocabulary

Analyzing the General Context

What if there are no specific context clues to help you figure out an unfamiliar word? Often you can deduce a meaning of a word because you know other words that appear with it, as in the following sentence: The bowl contained apples, oranges, plantains, cherries, and plums. You may not know that plantains are a fruit similar to bananas. However, because the other items in the list are fruits, you might assume that plantains are a type of fruit.

Sometimes you can begin to figure out the meaning of a word by determining its part of speech. You can use this approach even if practically no words are familiar. For instance, Lewis Carroll began his poem "Jabberwocky" with these two lines: "'Twas brillig, and the slithy toves / Did gyre and gimble in the wabe." Even though Carroll made up most of the words, you can still begin to figure out their meanings.

Start with the word *toves*. You know that *toves* is the subject of the sentence because it is performing some kind of action— "the slithy toves did gyre and gimble in the wabe." The article *the* provides another clue; *the* appears only before nouns. From these two clues, you can figure that *toves* is a noun. In fact, given the plural *-s* ending, *toves* probably means "more than one tove."

Another way to figure out an unfamiliar word's part of speech is to compare the sentence in which it appears to similar sentence constructions. Look at the sentence "'Twas brillig," which means "It was brillig." *Brillig* follows a verb of being, *was*, and could therefore be a noun or an adjective. Think of other times when you have used or read a similar sentence construction. *Brillig* might describe the weather—"It was chilly"—or indicate the time of year—"It was spring."

Remembering Words You've Learned

Increasing your vocabulary improves your reading and writing skills and your chances of scoring well on standardized tests. The following tips will help you remember new words you encounter.

Connections Across the Curriculum

History

The English language began in England around the fifth or sixth century. From languages used by invading Jutes, Angles, and Saxons of Germany and Denmark, various Old English dialects evolved and were in use as "Old English," or Anglo Saxon, until the beginning of the twelfth century.

The Anglo-Saxon language had a vocabulary of about 50,000 words. Today the English language has over 600,000 words—more than any other language. Many of those words are borrowed from other languages.

1. **Write** down new words in a notebook. Just writing the word will help you remember it.

2. **Check** the meaning and pronunciation of the new word in a dictionary. Looking up a word helps you learn its meaning. Include this information in your notebook.

3. **Relate** the new word to words you already know. Associating its spelling or meaning with a familiar word makes a new word easier to remember.

4. **Practice** using the word in your writing and conversation. Using the word repeatedly is the best way to remember it.

Exercise 1

Each of the following passages contains an italicized word that may be unfamiliar. Determine the meaning by examining the context. Look for the context clues described in the chart on page 819. Write the italicized word and its meaning. Then indicate the strategy used in each case by writing *definition*, *example*, *comparison*, *contrast*, or *cause and effect*.

1. Television in the 1950s portrayed a *homogeneous* national population; however, the United States actually included a number of different ethnic groups.
2. Our biology teacher told us to rely only on *empirical* evidence—that is, our careful observations and experiments.
3. The beginning of Beethoven's *Sonata Pathétique* is to be played in *grave* tempo—like a funeral march, only slower.
4. Early tribes were usually *nomadic*, but because of the development of agriculture, some tribes stayed in one place.
5. The defenders of the western bridge were undefeatable, and since the defense of the eastern bridge was also *insurmountable*, the attacking forces gave up.
6. The woman was a true *miser*; for instance, she never donated to charities and spent very little money on presents.
7. At the fall of Berlin, *anarchy*, or complete disorder, prevailed until Allied forces took control.
8. Our creative writing teacher instructed us to use a *pseudonym* to hide our real identities. I chose "Lian Chen" as my pen name.
9. Do not keep *volatile* substances in places where they will be exposed to extremely high temperatures, because they may explode.
10. The World Trade Center and the Empire State Building are among New York City's tallest *edifices*.

25.1 Building Vocabulary **821**

Practice and Assess

Answers: Exercise 1

1. homogeneous: completely mixed, having the same consistency throughout; contrast
2. empirical: based on or derived from experience, experiment, or observation; definition
3. grave: slow and serious; comparison
4. nomadic: moving from place to place, wandering; contrast
5. insurmountable: unable to be overcome or defeated; comparison
6. miser: stingy person; example
7. anarchy: complete disorder; definition
8. pseudonym: fictitious or false name, especially one used by an author to conceal true identity; definition, example
9. volatile: changeable, unpredictable, unstable, easily disturbed; cause and effect
10. edifices: buildings—especially impressive ones; example

Additional Resources
Vocabulary and Spelling Strategies and Practice

Close

Ask students to each write a sentence that contains a context clue for one of its words. They should then replace the word the clue relates to with a nonsense word, trade sentences with a partner, and discuss whether they can figure out the meanings of each other's sentences.

Technology Tip

Using Software Programs
Several software programs have been created specifically for vocabulary development. There are also a number of word games designed for use on the personal computer.

Focus

Lesson Overview

Objective

• To expand vocabulary by analyzing the parts of unfamiliar words

Skills

• understanding word roots, prefixes, and suffixes

Critical Thinking

• analyzing

Listening and Speaking

• discussing

Bellringer
Daily Language Activity

When students enter the classroom, have this assignment on the board: *What root word do the following underlined words have in common?*

The actor <u>autographed</u> the <u>photograph</u> of himself.

What do you think this root word means? List other words that include this same root word.

See also 📖 *Daily Language Practice*

Teach

Creating a Graphic

Discuss the spider diagrams on this student page. You may wish to point out that the root can be at the beginning, in the middle, or at the end of a word and still be considered its root. Draw a spider diagram on the board; in the center write a root such as *equa* or *vis*. Ask the class to brainstorm words that contain those combinations of letters (such as *equal, equator, equate; visual, visor, invisible*). Then ask students to define the root based on their knowledge of the words in which it appears. **L2**

Vocabulary

25.2 Word Parts

Another way to figure out the meaning of a word is by analyzing its parts. The main part of a word is its **root**. When the root is a complete word, it is sometimes called a **base word**. The root or base word is often combined with a **prefix** (a word part attached to the beginning of a word), a **suffix** (a word part attached to the end of a word), or another root to form a different word.

Consider a word you already know—*unbreakable*—and look at its parts. Added to the base word *break* are the prefix *un-* and the suffix *-able*. The prefix *un-* means "not." The suffix *-able* means "capable of." Therefore, *unbreakable* means "not capable of being broken."

Word Roots

While prefixes and suffixes can give hints about a word's meaning, the most important clue is the root. The following diagram shows several words that have been formed from the Latin root *spec*. From what you know about the words given, what do you think *spec* means?

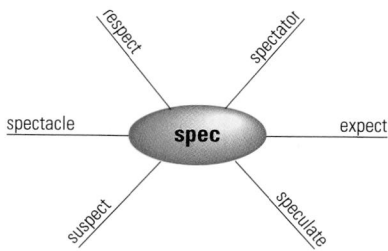

As you might have figured out, *spec* means "to look at." The next diagram shows several words. See if you can figure out which root the following words share and the meaning of the root.

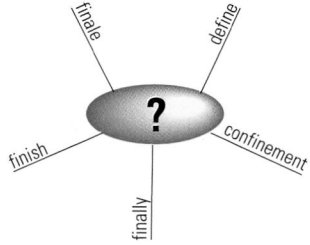

The root of each of these words is *fin*. What do you think *fin* means? All the words relate to some kind of ending, like *finish, finale*, and *finally*, or limitation, like *define* and *confinement*. Therefore, you can deduce that *fin*

Resource Manager

Planning Resources
• *Lesson Plans*

📖 **Transparencies**
• *Bellringer*
• *Daily Language Practice*

📁 **Other Print Resources**
• *Vocabulary and Spelling Strategies and Practice*

means "end" or "limit." The root *fin* comes from Latin. Nearly half of modern English general vocabulary comes from either Latin or French. Many other roots come from Greek or Anglo-Saxon words.

When you are trying to determine the meaning of a new word, think of words that might share a root with it. The meanings of these other words might give you clues to the meaning of the unfamiliar word. The following chart lists some common roots and some words that share them.

Analyzing Word Roots		
Words	**Meanings**	**Roots**
aqueduct aquarium	means of moving water tank of water	*aqua* means "water"
astronaut astronomy	traveler among stars study of stars	*astro* means "stars"
biology autobiography	study of living things story of a person's life written by that person	*bio* means "life"
century centimeter	a hundred years measurement equal to one hundredth of a meter	*cent* means "hundred"
chronological synchronize	arranged in time order cause to happen at the same time	*chron* means "time"
democracy epidemic	rule by the people rapidly spreading among many people	*dem* or *demo* means "people"
geology geocentric	study of the earth measured from center of the earth	*geo* means "earth"
anonymous pseudonym	with no name known or acknowledged pen name	*nym* means "name"
agoraphobia monophobia	fear of open spaces fear of being alone	*phobia* means "fear"
portable transport	capable of being carried to carry across	*port* means "carry"
inscribe scribble	to write or mark on to write messily	*scrib* means "write"
constrict stringent	draw together; bind strict; severe	*string* or *strict* means "bind"
unique unified	one-of-a-kind joined into one	*uni* means "one"
revive vivisection	bring back to life operation on a living animal for science	*viv* means "live" or "alive"

Teach

Building on Root Words

Divide the class into four or five groups for a Simultaneous Roundtable activity. Each group should choose a different root to write at the top of a sheet. Each group member then gets a minute to write as many words containing the root as possible. At the end of the time limit, students pass the sheets to the next person, who does the same thing. The group with the most words wins. **L2**

Combining Roots, Prefixes, and Suffixes

Demonstrate how roots, prefixes, and suffixes can be used as building blocks to create words. Write the root *port* on the board and explain that it means "carry." Add the prefix *re-* to it and ask students to discuss the meaning of the word *report*. Then do the same with the suffix *-er*. Then combine *port* with both the prefix and the suffix. Next, write on the board the prefixes *de-*, *ex-*, and *im-* and the suffixes *-ed*, *-able* and *-ment*. Ask students to create as many words as they can by combining these prefixes or suffixes or both with the root *port*. **L1**

Vocabulary

Connections Across the Curriculum

History

Both Latin and Greek have greatly influenced English. In some cases, English contains two words with similar meanings, but one originated in Greek and the other in Latin. For example, among words relating to the stars, *astral* and *astronomy* come from a Greek root, and *stellar* comes from Latin. To refer to our world, we have *universe* (Latin) and *cosmos* (Greek).

823

Teach

Discussing Prefixes

To demonstrate that prefixes add flexibility and precision to language, ask students to consider what would happen if the prefix *dis-* did not exist in the English language. To express the concept of the words shown on the chart would require the use of an additional word or words ("not honest," "do not trust"). What if the prefix *de-* did not exist? The words listed here (such as *demote*) would not exist in any form. Ask students to discuss how they would express the idea represented by each word on the list without using prefixes. **L2**

⇄ Cross-reference: Spelling

For instruction and practice of spelling rules that apply when adding prefixes to words, refer students to Lesson 26.1, pp. 828–832.

Vocabulary

Prefixes

Prefixes are important tools for building, and learning, new words. Prefixes change the meaning of words, sometimes drastically. Certain prefixes, such as *un-* and *in-*, can even reverse the meaning of a root.

The following chart lists other prefixes and their meanings. You will see that some prefixes can have more than one meaning. Note how some prefixes can change the meaning of a word.

Analyzing Prefixes		
Words	**Meanings**	**Prefixes**
amoral atypical	without morals not typical	*a-* means "without" or "not"
coauthor colead	write together lead together	*co-* means "together"
contradict contrary	to act in opposition opposed	*contra-* means "opposed"
demote deduction	move down in rank conclusion drawn from reasoning	*de-* means "from" or "down"
dishonest distrust	not honest lack of trust	*dis-* means "lack of" or "not"
emit expel	send out drive out	*e-* and *ex-* mean "out"
illegal immoral insignificant irregular	not legal not moral not significant not regular	*il-*, *im-*, *in-*, and *ir-* mean "not"
international interject	among nations to throw between	*inter-* means "among" or "between"
microscopic microwave	invisible to the naked eye very short electromagnetic wave	*micro-* means "small"
misplace mistreat	put in wrong place treat badly	*mis-* means "wrong" or "bad"
monochromatic monogamy	of one color marriage with one mate	*mono-* means "one"
prearrange preliminary	to arrange beforehand coming before the main action	*pre-* means "before"
replay recall	to play again to call back	*re-* means "again" or "back"
submerge subzero	to place under water below zero	*sub-* means "under" or "below"

MEETING INDIVIDUAL NEEDS ## Less Proficient Readers

Visualizing Word Parts

Help students visualize the concept of base words, prefixes, and suffixes. Make a set of flashcards using index cards. On one card write the prefix *un-*. On another write the suffix *-able*. Write base words such as *break, bend, speak, manage,* and *mention* on separate cards. Demonstrate how a base word card paired with a prefix or suffix card forms a word, such as *unbreakable.* Students may take turns combining cards to make words. Encourage students to make and use additional prefix and suffix cards.

Suffixes

Suffixes are letters added to the ends of words to create new words with new meanings. Many suffixes also change the original word's part of speech. Remember the example of *unbreakable* at the beginning of this lesson? When added to the verb *break,* the suffix *-able* forms a new word with a new part of speech, the adjective *breakable.* With certain words, the spelling of the original word may change slightly when a suffix is added, as with *forgivable* (*forgive* + *-able*).

The following chart lists other suffixes, their meanings, and the parts of speech they form. See if you can figure out the meaning of the suffix by looking only at the first two columns in the table.

Analyzing Suffixes			
Words	**Meanings**	**Suffixes**	**Part of Speech Formed**
occupant dependent commandant	one who occupies one who depends one who commands	*-ant* and *-ent* mean "one who does an action"	Concrete noun
boredom freedom	state of being bored condition of being free	*-dom* means "state" or "condition"	Abstract noun
shorten quicken enliven	to cause to be short to cause to be quick to cause to be lively	*-en* means "to cause to be"	Verb
fearful hopeful	full of fear full of hope	*-ful* means "full of"	Adjective
crystallize minimize	to become a crystal to make minimal, or smaller	*-ize* means "to become" or "to make"	Verb
hopeless treeless effortless	without hope without trees without effort	*-less* means "without"	Adjective
quickly slowly	in a quick manner in a slow manner	*-ly* means "in the manner or way mentioned"	Adverb
kindness fondness darkness	state of being kind state of being fond quality of being dark	*-ness* means "quality" or "state"	Abstract noun
furious joyous	full of fury full of joy	*-ous* means "full of"	Adjective

Teach

Inventing Words

Challenge students to invent and define new words by combining roots with prefixes or suffixes from the charts on student pages 823–825. An example would be *viveless,* meaning "without life." Encourage students to be playful and imaginative in their inventions. Some may want to use a single root with different prefixes and suffixes to make several new words. For an added challenge, students can invent words such as *intervive-dom* (the condition of being between lives) that contain both a prefix and a suffix. **L3**

⬤ Cross-reference: Grammar

For instruction and practice with adjectives and adverbs formed by adding suffixes, refer students to Lessons 10.4, pp. 460–465, and 10.5, pp. 466–472.

Vocabulary

Cooperative Learning

Listing Words with Common Suffixes

Have students form small groups. Each group member should choose one of the suffixes from the chart on student page 825 and write it at the top of a sheet of paper. Then give students one minute to list as many words as possible that include the suffix. Have students pass their papers to the next group member, repeating the process until the sheets have been circulated around the entire group. Invite students to share their word listings with the class.

Practice and Assess

Answers: Exercise 2

1. *phil* means "love of"
2. *crat* means "member of a specified class or governing body" or "advocate of a certain way of ruling"
3. *photo* means "light"
4. *ben* means "good"
5. *mort* means "death"

Answers: Exercise 3

1. coworkers
2. postwar recessions
3. misspelled
4. inefficient study habits
5. reexamined

Answers: Exercise 4

1. quickens
2. fearless
3. popularize
4. parking attendant
5. willingness

Additional Resources

📁 *Vocabulary and Spelling Strategies and Practice*

Close

Review the chart on student page 819 and diagrams on page 822. Ask students to explain these strategies for defining unfamiliar words.

Vocabulary

Exercise 2

Divide into groups of three, and have each member in a group write down the meaning of one word from each of the following groups of words. Use a dictionary if necessary. After you share your definitions, decide as a group what root the words share and what the root means.

1. philosophy, bibliophile, philanthropy
2. autocratic, technocrat, bureaucratic
3. photophobia, photography, photosynthesis
4. beneficial, benevolent, benefactor
5. mortician, immortality, mortuary

Exercise 3

Rewrite each of the following sentences, replacing the underlined words with a single word that uses a prefix. You may want to change the word order in some cases.

1. Cooperating with <u>workers with whom you are employed</u> makes work more enjoyable.
2. Many countries have experienced recessions <u>after a war.</u>
3. The journalist <u>spelled incorrectly</u> the senator's name.
4. Students can improve their grades by changing study habits that are <u>not efficient.</u>
5. When a doctor recommends surgery, many patients decide to be <u>examined again</u> by another doctor.

Exercise 4

Rewrite each of the following sentences, replacing the underlined words with a word that uses a suffix. You may want to change the word order in some cases.

1. Jon noticed that when he runs, his heartbeat <u>is made quick.</u>
2. The hero of the tale, Beowulf, is <u>without fear.</u>
3. Mel Allen and Red Barber both helped <u>to make popular</u> radio broadcasting of baseball.
4. As she left the garage, Joan gave her car keys to the <u>one who attended to</u> parking.
5. The eyewitness showed <u>a state of being willing</u> to cooperate with the police investigators.

MEETING INDIVIDUAL NEEDS — English Language Learners

Reviewing Prefixes and Suffixes

Exercises 3 and 4 may be particularly difficult for students who are new to the English language. Suggest they refer back to the charts containing prefixes and suffixes on pages 824 and 825. Make sure students understand which word or words in each underlined phrase should be replaced by a suffix or prefix and which word is the base word. Review the exercises together, pointing out any word order changes that occur.

UNIT 26 | Spelling

Lesson 26.1 **Improving Your Spelling**   *828*

Lesson 26.2 **Spelling Difficult Words**   *833*

Objectives

- To develop an understanding of basic spelling rules and their exceptions and of a simple process to help spell new words
- To learn to identify and spell difficult words and to learn strategies for spelling frequently misspelled and easily confused words
- To demonstrate control over various spelling rules, processes, and strategies by using them to complete exercises and to write effectively

✔ ASSESSMENT OPTIONS

📂 *Tests with Answer Key & Rubrics*
Unit 26 Pretest, pp. 95–96

💾 *Testmaker*
Unit 26 Pretest

You may wish to administer the Unit 26 Pretest at this point.

Key to Ability Levels

L1 Level 1 activities are within the basic ability level of students.

L2 Level 2 activities are within the ability range of average students.

L3 Level 3 activities are more challenging activities.

827

Resource Manager

Planning Resources
- *Lesson Plans*
- *Block Scheduling*

 Transparencies
- *Bellringer*
- *Daily Language Practice*

📂 **Other Print Resources**
- *Listening and Speaking Activities*
- *Spelling Power*
- *Tests with Answer Key & Rubrics*
- *Vocabulary and Spelling Practice*

 Video
- *MindJogger Videoquizzes*

💾 **Software**
- *Presentation Plus!*
- *Testmaker*
- *Writer's Choice Puzzlemaker*

🖥 **Web Sites**
- *writerschoice.glencoe.com*

Focus

Lesson Overview

Objective
- To learn to spell words that follow basic spelling rules

Skills
- spelling words with *ie* and *ei*; spelling unstressed vowels; spelling words that end in *-cede*, *-ceed*, and *-sede*; adding prefixes and suffixes; identifying words by category and using rules to form plurals

Critical Thinking
- analyzing; synthesizing

Listening and Speaking
- listening for special clues

Bellringer
Daily Language Activity

When students enter the classroom, have this assignment on the board: *Make a short list of the words you have the most trouble spelling.*

See also *Daily Language Practice*

Motivating Activity

Discuss words that students have difficulty spelling. What makes these spellings hard to remember? Do any of the words use *ie* or *ei*, require a doubled final consonant, or end in *-ceed*, *-cede*, or *-sede*? You may wish to make a list of troublesome words that can be kept on the board for reference.

Spelling

26.1 Improving Your Spelling

As a writer, you want readers to understand your ideas. Using correct spelling in your writing will enable your readers to focus on what you have to say. One of the best ways to become a good speller is to be an avid reader; the more you see a word, the better you will remember it.

You can improve your spelling in other ways too. First, you can learn some basic rules that will help you spell correctly. Second, you can pay attention to spelling patterns in order to take better guesses as you try to spell new words. Third, you can check your spelling with an authoritative source.

Basic Spelling Rules

The following rules, examples, and exceptions will help you master the spellings of many words.

Spelling *ie* and *ei* Many writers find the rules for certain combinations of letters, like *ie* and *ei*, difficult to remember. One helpful learning strategy is to develop a rhyme to remember a rule. Look at the following rhyme for the *ie* and *ei* rule.

Rule		Examples
Put *i* before *e*,	→	achieve, chief, lien
except after *c*,	→	conceit, receive, ceiling
or when sounded like *a*, as in *neighbor* and *weigh*.	→	eighth, reign, sleigh, freight, veil, neigh

Exceptions
seize, leisure, weird, height, either, forfeit, protein

Spelling *-cede*, *-ceed*, and *-sede* Because various letters in the English spelling system are sometimes pronounced the same way, it is often easy to make slight spelling errors between two different letters. The similarity of pronunciation between *c* and *s* accounts for the confusion in spelling words ending in *-cede*, *-ceed*, and *-sede*. Because there are only four exceptions, however, you should be able to memorize them.

Resource Manager

Planning Resources
- *Lesson Plans*

Transparencies
- *Bellringer*
- *Daily Language Practice*

Other Print Resources
- *Listening and Speaking Activities*, pp. 5–6
- *Vocabulary and Spelling Strategies and Practice*

Rule	Examples
Spell the *sēd* sound as *cede*. →	concede, recede, intercede

Exceptions
One word uses *-sede* to spell the *sēd* sound: *supersede*.
Three words use *-ceed* to spell the *sēd* sound: *proceed, exceed, succeed.*

Spelling Unstressed Vowels   Notice the vowel sound in the second syllable of the word *or-i-gin*. This is the unstressed vowel sound, and it can be spelled several ways. Dictionary respellings use the schwa symbol (ə) to indicate it. To help spell words with unstressed vowels correctly, try thinking of a related word in which the syllable containing the vowel sound is stressed. The chart below shows examples of this process.

Spelling Unstressed Vowels		
Unknown Spelling	**Related Word**	**Word Spelled Correctly**
leg_l	le**gal**ity	legal
fant_sy	fan**tas**tic	fantasy
host_le	hos**til**ity	hostile
opp_site	op**pose**	opposite

Adding Prefixes   When adding a prefix to a word, keep the original spelling of the word. If the prefix forms a double letter, keep both letters.

dis + appear = disappear   ir + regular = irregular
mis + direct = misdirect   co + operate = cooperate

Suffixes and the Silent *e*   Many English words end in a silent letter *e*. Sometimes the *e* is dropped when a suffix is added. The following chart shows when to keep and when to drop the *e*.

Adding Suffixes to Words with Silent *e*	
Rule	**Examples**
When adding a suffix that begins with a consonant to a word that ends in silent *e*, keep the *e*.	place + -ment = placement rare + -ly = rarely
Common exceptions	awe + -ful = awful judge + -ment = judgment (*continued*)

Teach

Rhyming Rules

Encourage students to memorize the "i before e" rule by stressing the rhymes. Point out that this simple rhyme is a mnemonic device, or cue, that can help them remember the rule. Do students know other tricks for remembering how to spell certain words? For example, the sentence "A rat in the house might eat the ice cream" helps some people recall how to spell *arithmetic*. Students may enjoy sharing other devices for remembering spelling rules and exceptions. **L2**

Identifying Accented Syllables

Some students may need help identifying which syllable is accented. Speak a few words aloud, gently tapping out the syllables and slapping the desk vigorously on the accented syllable. You may want to offer students an opportunity to do the same. Then work with students to help them suggest several additional examples for each rule listed on this page. **L1**

Spelling

English Language Learners

Spelling Unstressed Vowels

Students acquiring English may have difficulty with the unstressed vowel sound. For practice, list on the board the words outside parentheses: *drama* (dramatic); *anesthetize* (anesthetic); *continent* (continental); *migratory* (migrate); *democracy* (democratic); *symbol* (symbolic); *atom* (atomic); *symphony* (symphonic). Instruct students to say each word and identify the unstressed vowel. Work with students on the strategy in the chart, helping them think of related words.

Teach

Making a Spelling Chart

On the board develop a spelling chart. First, write the column headings Double Final Consonant and Do Not Double Final Consonant. Students can work through the list of spelling rules for adding suffixes. After making a row for each rule, students should suggest words that fit the rules and explain under which column each word should go. Students may find it helpful to copy the chart in their journals or notebooks. **L2**

Conducting a Spelling Bee

Divide the class into two teams and distribute index cards to the class, three or four per student. Ask students to write out words, one to a card, telling which rule or rules from this unit apply to each word's spelling. Collect the cards, keeping them separate by team. Use these words for a modified spelling bee, challenging teams with the opposite team's words. Each speller in turn must identify the appropriate rule and correctly spell the word. You may want to add excitement by allowing students to use their books, but limiting them to one minute to locate the rule and spell the word. **L3**

Spelling

Adding Suffixes to Words with Silent *e*	
Rule	**Examples**
When adding a suffix that begins with a vowel or *y* to a word that ends in silent *e*, usually drop the *e*. **Common exceptions**	excite + -able = excitable shine + -y = shiny *mile + -age = mileage*
When adding a suffix that begins with *a* or *o* to a word that ends in *ce* or *ge*, keep the *e* so the word will retain the soft *c* or *g* sound.	change + -able = changeable trace + -able = traceable
When adding a suffix that begins with a vowel to a word that ends in *ee* or *oe*, keep the *e*.	agree + -able = agreeable canoe + -ing = canoeing

Suffixes and the Final *y*   When adding a suffix to a word that ends in a consonant + *y*, change the *y* to *i*. Do not change the *y* to *i* when the suffix begins with *i*.

try + ed = tried   copy + ing = copying

When adding a suffix to a word that ends in a vowel + *y*, keep the *y*.

joy + ous = joyous   convey + ed = conveyed

Doubling the Final Consonant   When adding a suffix to a word, you sometimes need to double the final consonant before adding the suffix. Double the consonant when adding a suffix that begins with a vowel to a word that ends in a single consonant preceded by a single vowel, if the original word

- is a one-syllable word: dip + ing = dipping; stop + age = stoppage

- has an accent on the last syllable, and the accent remains there after the suffix is added: occur + ence = occurrence

- is a prefixed word based on a one-syllable word: reset + ing = resetting

Based on the preceding rule, you would not double the final consonant when

- the accent is not on the last syllable: develop + ing = developing

- the accent shifts when the suffix is added: refer + ence = reference

- the final consonant is preceded by two vowels: train + ing = training

- the final consonant is preceded by another consonant: remind + er = reminder

- the word ends in a consonant and the suffix begins with a consonant: reck + less = reckless

830   Unit 26 Spelling

Exploring Language

History

Before the invention of the printing press, spelling varied from region to region in England, depending on the scribes who copied manuscripts. Widespread use of the printing press in the late fifteenth and early sixteenth centuries helped standardize spelling. Since that time, even though pronunciation has changed, spelling has tended to remain frozen in the form it took when printing first began. Thus, we have words such as though, bough, thought, through, and rough, all with the *-ough* spelling but pronounced very differently.

Adding -*ly* When adding -*ly* to a word that ends in a single *l*, keep the *l*. When the word ends in a double *l*, drop one *l*. When the word ends in a consonant + *le*, drop the *le*.

real + ly = really   dull + ly = dully   terrible + ly = terribly

Adding -*ness* When adding -*ness* to a word that ends in *n*, keep the *n*.

sullen + ness = sullenness   keen + ness = keenness

Forming Compound Words When joining a word that ends in a consonant to a word that begins with a consonant, keep both consonants.

after + noon = afternoon   key + board = keyboard

Forming Plurals English nouns form plurals in many ways. Most nouns simply add *s*. The following chart shows other ways of forming plural nouns and some common exceptions to the patterns.

General Rules for Plurals		
If the Noun Ends In	**Then Generally**	**Examples**
ch, s, sh, x, or *z*	add -*es*	wish → wishes crutch → crutches
a consonant + *y*	change *y* to *i* and add -*es*	cannery → canneries baby → babies
a vowel + *y*	add -*s*	day → days key → keys
a vowel + *o*	add -*s*	studio → studios stereo → stereos
a consonant + *o*	generally add -*es*	potato → potatoes cargo → cargoes
Common exceptions	but sometimes add -*s*	*silo → silos halo → halos*
f or *ff* **Common exceptions**	add -*s* change *f* to *v* and add -*es*	reef → reefs *leaf → leaves*
lf	change *f* to *v* and add -*es*	half → halves wolf → wolves
fe	change *f* to v and add -*s*	life → lives knife → knives

A few plurals are exceptions to the rules listed on the previous page or present some other special problem, but they are easy to remember. The following chart lists these plurals and some examples.

Teach

Charting Plural Rules

The chart General Rules for Plurals will help students remember common spelling rules. Discuss the rules on the chart, asking students to come up with additional examples. Students may find it helpful to copy a simplified version of the chart into their notebooks or journals. Encourage them to include some examples of their own. **L1**

Getting to the Roots

Challenge some students to use a dictionary to find the correct singular form for these commonly used plurals from the Greek and Latin: *data, media, bacteria* (*datum, medium, bacterium*); and the plural forms for these singular words: *matrix, metamorphosis, hypothesis* (*matrices, metamorphoses, hypotheses*). Ask students to research the plural rules for these words and words like them, and share them with the class. **L3**

Exploring Language

Using Electronic Dictionaries

Electronic, hand-held spelling dictionaries, similar to pocket calculators, are available. On an alphabetical keyboard the user enters the word in the way he or she believes it is spelled. The correct spelling (or spellings if several words are similar to the misspelling entered) then shows on the display screen. The speller is small enough to fit in a book bag.

Teach

Forming Plurals

You may wish to have students list several more examples of each rule, including any exceptions they can think of. Then ask students to choose an item of clothing they are wearing or an item from their pockets, purses, or book bags and spell the plural of the name of the item. Can they tell which spelling rule is used in making the word plural? **L2**

Developing Strategies

After students read the section on learning to spell new words and scan the next lesson on spelling difficult words, have them compare the words listed on these three pages with the class list of difficult words that was written on the board at the beginning of the unit. Encourage students to identify the parts of their difficult words that cause problems for them. Do students have trouble remembering whether to use an *s* or a *c*, whether to double consonants or use a single consonant? Brainstorm some mnemonic devices they might use to remember how to spell these troublesome words. For example, spelling *all right* as one word is all wrong; a *buffet* is a *b*oard *u*sed *f*or *f*eeding *e*ager *t*urtles. **L2**

Spelling

Special Rules for Plurals	
Special Case	**Examples**
To form the plural of proper names, add either *-s* or *-es*.	D'Amico ➤ D'Amicos Sanchez ➤ Sanchezes
To form the plural of one-word compound nouns, follow the general rules for plurals.	penknife ➤ penknives blackberry ➤ blackberries
To form the plural of hyphenated compound nouns or compound nouns of more than one word, generally make the most important word plural.	father-in-law ➤ fathers-in-law attorney general ➤ attorneys general
Some nouns have irregular forms. These nouns do not follow any rules.	man ➤ men ox ➤ oxen
Some nouns have the same singular and plural form.	series ➤ series deer ➤ deer

Learning to Spell New Words

As you read, note unfamiliar words and words that you recognize but that look hard to spell. As you write, pay attention to any words that you have difficulty spelling. Then try the process shown below.

Say It
Look at the printed word, and say it aloud. Then say it again, pronouncing each syllable correctly.

Visualize It
Picture the word in your mind. Avoid looking at it printed or written on the page. This will help you memorize what the word looks like.

Write It
Look at the printed word, and write it. Then write it again, without looking at the printed word.

Check It
Check what you have written against the printed word. Did you spell the word correctly? If not, try the process again.

Remember that the dictionary is a source for finding the correct spelling of words. You might ask, How can I look up a word if I don't know how to spell it? Frequently you will be able to spell enough of the beginning of a word to find it in the dictionary. If you don't find a word in the first place you look, think of other probable spellings. Once you have located the correct spelling of a word, use the process described above to learn the word.

Viewing and Representing

Visual Thinking

The flow chart illustrates the process for learning to spell individual words. You may wish to have students go through the process several times, using the flow chart for difficult words.

Exercise 1

In each group of words, find the one word that is misspelled. Write the word correctly. Cite the rule that applies to the spelling of the word. If the word is an exception to a rule, note that as well.

1. yield, freight, concieve
2. exceed, supercede, accede
3. sincerely, responsiveness, engagment
4. sheriffes, scarves, thieves
5. headdresses, stone crabs, commander in chiefs

26.2 Spelling Difficult Words

One very useful strategy for learning difficult words is to develop a personal word list. What words do you frequently misspell? Include those words in your personal word list. Study the words, using the four-step process you learned in Lesson 26.1, page 832.

Developing memory devices is another helpful strategy for learning to spell difficult words. Imagine, for example, that you have trouble remembering if the word *tomorrow* has one *m* or two. You might think of the sentence "Tom will arrive tomorrow" to help you remember that *tomorrow* begins with the letters *t-o-m*.

Frequently Misspelled Words

Following is a list of words that many people often misspell. Which words on the list do you have difficulty spelling?

Words Often Misspelled			
accidentally	conscientious	immediate	precede
accommodate	conscious	incidentally	prevalent
advertisement	definite	jewelry	proceed
allot	descent	laboratory	receipt
all right	discipline	library	recommend
arctic	elementary	maintenance	rhythm
attendant	eligible	mischievous	schedule
ballet	embarrass	misspell	separate
business	fascinating	niece	technique
cafeteria	February	occasion	technology
canceled	foreign	original	theory
canoe	forty	pageant	traffic
changeable	government	pastime	usually
colonel	height	pharmacy	variety
commercial	hippopotamus	physical	villain

26.2 Spelling Difficult Words **833**

Practice and Assess

Answers: Exercise 1

1. *Concieve* should be *conceive*: Put *i* before *e*, except after *c*, or when sounded like *a*.
2. *Supercede* should be *supersede*: Spell the *sēd* sound as *-cede*. Supersede is the single exception spelled *-sede*.
3. *Engagment* should be *engagement*: When adding a suffix that begins with a consonant to a word that ends in silent *e*, keep the *e*.
4. *Sheriffes* should be *sheriffs*: If the noun ends in *ff*, add *-s*.
5. *Commander in chiefs* should be *commanders in chief*: To form the plural of hyphenated compound nouns or compound nouns of more than one word, generally make the most important word plural.

Additional Resources

📁 *Vocabulary and Spelling Strategies and Practice*

📁 *Listening and Speaking Activities, pp. 5–6*

Close

Have students form small groups, and have each group write a paragraph using as many troublesome spelling words as possible.

Focus

Lesson Overview

Objective

- To identify words that are frquently misspelled and words that are easily confused

Skills

- spelling frequently misspelled and easily confused words

Resource Manager

Planning Resources
- *Lesson Plans*

 Transparencies
- *Bellringer*
- *Daily Language Practice*

📁 **Other Print Resources**
- *Listening and Speaking Activities, pp. 5–6*
- *Vocabulary and Spelling Strategies and Practice*

Critical Thinking
- classifying

Listening and Speaking
- discussing

833

Bellringer
Daily Language Activity

When students enter the classroom, have this assignment on the board: *Find the misspelled words from this list and spell them correctly:* presede, labratory, February, fasinating, embarrass (precede, laboratory, fascinating)

See also *Daily Language Practice*

Teach

Writing Sentences

Challenge students to write as many complete sentences as possible using pairs of easily confused words. For example, "I accept your excuse for missing class, except for the part about being kidnapped by space aliens." Encourage students to be imaginative and humorous. You may wish to impose a five-minute time limit. **L3**

Cross-reference: Writing

For instruction and practice in checking for frequently misspelled words, see Lesson 2.9, pp. 82–85.

Practice and Assess

Answers: Exercise 2

1. capital
2. stationery
3. effects
4. lose
5. accept

Additional Resources

Vocabulary and Spelling Strategies and Practice

Listening and Speaking Activities, pp. 5–6

Cross-reference: Dictionary

For instruction and practice in determining the correct usage of homophones, see Lesson 24.1, pp. 812–815.

Close

Working in pairs, students can quiz each other on the spellings of troublesome words provided in the lesson.

Easily Confused Words

Some words are easily confused because they contain similar sounds. Other confusing words are homophones, words that have the same pronunciation but different meanings and spellings. Study the following list of easily confused words. Are there any words on the list that you confuse?

Words Often Confused	
accept	to agree to take; to assume; to approve: We accept your plan.
except	but; to omit: I remembered everything except my ticket!
affect	to influence; to act upon: I'm sure the book will affect her.
effect	a result: What effect did the movie have on him?
formally	politely; officially; according to custom: We addressed him formally.
formerly	previously: The principal was formerly a teacher.
lose	to misplace; to drop: Did you lose your assignment?
loose	free; not confined; not tight: My clothes are loose since I lost 10 pounds.
passed	moved through or by; completed satisfactorily: I passed you in the hall.
past	the time before the present; ended; over: You can't change the past.
principal	the head of a school; first; main: My principal concern is for the victims.
principle	a basic truth; a rule of conduct: The principle of fair play is important.
stationary	fixed; unmoving: The plane appeared stationary in the sky.
stationery	writing paper and envelopes: Rhonda preferred simple stationery.
than	in comparison with: You studied harder today than yesterday.
then	at that time; next: He did his chores, and then he played soccer.

Exercise 2

For each sentence below, determine which word in parentheses correctly completes the sentence.

1. Is Mexico City or Acapulco the (capital/capitol) of Mexico?
2. That store sells (stationery/stationary) of every color.
3. What were the (affects/effects) of the tornado?
4. Put your money away, or you may (loose/lose) it.
5. Will you (accept/except) this gift?

Spelling

UNIT 27 | Study Skills

Lesson 27.1 **Studying Effectively** 836

Lesson 27.2 **Reading Graphs and Diagrams** 842

Objectives

- To become familiar with various study techniques, including note taking, memory strategies, and critical reading techniques
- To learn to interpret various types of charts, graphs, and diagrams
- To demonstrate an understanding of how best to use a variety of study skills and strategies and to use and interpret various graphic forms

✓ ASSESSMENT OPTIONS

📂 *Tests with Answer Key & Rubrics*
Unit 27 Pretest, pp. 99–100

💾 *Testmaker*
Unit 27 Pretest

You may wish to administer the Unit 27 Pretest at this point.

Key to Ability Levels

L1 Level 1 activities are within the basic ability range of students.

L2 Level 2 activities are within the ability range of average students.

L3 Level 3 activities are more challenging activities.

835

Resource Manager

Planning Resources
- Lesson Plans
- Block Scheduling

 Transparencies
- Bellringer
- Daily Language Practice

📂 **Other Print Resources**
- Listening and Speaking Activities
- Tests with Answer Key & Rubrics
- Thinking and Study Skills
- Vocabulary and Spelling Strategies and Practice

 Video
- MindJogger Videoquizzes

💾 **Software**
- Presentation Plus!
- Testmaker
- Writer's Choice Puzzlemaker

🖥 **Web Sites**
- writerschoice.glencoe.com

Focus

Lesson Overview

Objective
• To develop effective study skills for reading and remembering information

Skills
• taking notes; using study time wisely; using SQ3R and mnemonic devices; identifying fact and opinion

Critical Thinking
• recalling; analyzing; evaluating

Listening and Speaking
• discussing; questioning

 Bellringer
Daily Language Activity

When students enter the classroom, have this assignment on the board: *You need an A on your next exam in [subject]. List the study skills and learning strategies that will help you attain this goal.*

See also *Daily Language Practice*

Motivating Activity

Ask how many days there are in April. Some students may begin reciting a version of this rhyme:

"Thirty days has September,
April, June, and November."

Encourage discussion of mnemonic devices students use to help them remember things.

Explain that in this lesson students will learn about mnemonic devices and other reading and remembering techniques that can help make their study time more effective.

27.1 Studying Effectively

Some students seem able to study and remember large amounts of material in short periods of time. Why? Part of the answer lies in how effectively students use appropriate study strategies.

Taking Notes in Class

Taking notes during class discussions and lectures can help you remember what you hear. While taking notes, you think about and rephrase the information.

Outlining Your Notes   One common and very useful way of organizing notes is the modified outline form. Like the outline you might write for a research paper (see Lesson 7.2 in Composition, pages 328–331), notes in outline form summarize the main ideas and supporting details of a lecture. However, unlike formal outlines that you write, your notes need not follow precise guidelines about parallel structure or number of entries. By highlighting the main ideas and the relationships among them, an outline makes reviewing the material easy.

Recognizing Signals   Signal words, such as *first*, *most importantly*, *on the other hand*, and *finally*, indicate important information or point out relationships among ideas. Such words help you know what to write down.

The speaker's voice and gestures also provide clues. By suddenly speaking more loudly or quickly, or by punctuating a point with an emphatic sweep of the hand, the speaker may be signaling an important point.

Identify the main idea first; indent supporting information underneath it.

To write down information quickly, use phrases, symbols, and abbreviations.

Write down each key term and its definition.

Plate Tectonics
    the study of the formation & movement of plates
Plates
    rigid sections of the earth's crust
Boundaries of plates
    earthquakes & volcanoes
    3 types of plate boundaries
        converging — plates coming together
        diverging — plates separating
        transform fault — plates sliding past each other

Resource Manager

Planning Resources
• *Lesson Plans*

 Transparencies
• *Bellringer*
• *Daily Language Practice*

📁 Other Print Resources
• *Listening and Speaking Activities*, pp. 1–2
• *Thinking and Study Skills*, pp. 5, 8–9, 12, 14, 17, 34–38

Using Study Time Wisely

Most studying occurs outside of class. Whether in study hall, in a library, or at home, you want to make the most of your study time.

Recognizing Your Learning Style   You can improve your studying by identifying how you learn best. People learn in a variety of ways—by reading, discussing, writing, drawing diagrams, and so on. If you learn best by discussion, meet with a friend to talk about your schoolwork. If you learn best by writing, try rewriting the lesson you are studying.

Preparing to Study   Planning your study time wisely lets you make the most effective use of each minute. Here are some tips to help.

Tips on Planning Your Study Time
1. Study at the same time and place each day. Doing so makes studying a habit; your mind will be prepared when the time comes.
2. Update your list of assignments and due dates weekly. This will help you stay aware of what you need to accomplish.
3. Break down long assignments into stages. Many assignments include researching, reading, and writing stages.
4. Estimate the amount of time each stage of each assignment will require.
5. Don't plan to study one subject for too long. Many students find that changing subjects every thirty to forty-five minutes keeps their minds fresh.

Studying Effectively   When you actually sit down to study, you can increase your efficiency by following the guidelines listed below.

Tips on Studying
1. Set objectives for each study session. Identifying what you want to read, write, or learn helps you focus your efforts.
2. Take notes while reading. The act of writing down information helps you remember it.
3. Create tables, charts, or diagrams. Seeing information in a different form can help you understand and remember it better.
4. Begin your study session with the hardest assignment. This way you can tackle the toughest work while you are freshest.
5. Summarize what you've learned at the end of each study session. (See Lesson 1.2 in Composition, pages 12–15, for information on keeping a learning log.)

Study Skills

Teach

Taking Notes

Point out to students that the model at the bottom of student page 836 shows how one might outline important ideas while listening to a lecture. Ask how the note taker identifies main ideas. (The student begins at the left and uses beginning capital letters.) How are subordinate ideas shown? (They are indented and begin with lowercase letters.) Ask what shortcuts note takers might take to jot down important ideas quickly. (They might use phrases, symbols, and abbreviations.) **L2**

Identifying Learning Styles

Some students will have difficulty identifying their ideal learning styles. Ask them to recall situations in which they learned something especially easily. Explain that the techniques used in those situations—perhaps working with a friend or drawing a diagram—are probably part of the students' preferred learning style. Let students know that while there is no best way to learn, each student should try to study in the ways that seem most effective for him or her. **L1**

MEETING INDIVIDUAL NEEDS

English Language Learners

Paraphrasing Ideas

Help students who are learning English understand that a paraphrase is a restatement of an idea in one's own words. Check students' understanding of the terms used in Tips on Planning Your Study Time and Tips on Studying on student page 837 by asking them to paraphrase and provide examples for each tip.

Teach

Skimming, Scanning, and In-depth Reading

To help students consider when they might use each method of reading, create a chart on the board with the headings *Skim, Scan,* and *In-depth*. Have students brainstorm specific situations in which they might use each reading method. Write their responses under the appropriate heads on the chart. For example, to study for a quarterly science test, students might skim to review main ideas, scan to review key terms, and use in-depth reading only for limited sections they have had difficulty understanding. To prepare an oral presentation on material previously covered in history class, students might scan to find interesting details and suitable examples. **L2**

Cross-reference: Writing

For research and writing situations in which students may use the three reading techniques, refer students to Lesson 7.1, pp. 322–327.

Study Skills

Reading and Remembering

Knowing what your purposes are when you read and keeping track of how well you've understood what you've read are two critical study skills. Match your strategies to your purposes and use whatever methods you need to be sure that understanding does not break down. As with most skills, there are a variety of strategies to help you accomplish your purposes.

Three Ways to Read   Before you begin to read, think about what information you want to learn from the material. Do you want a general idea of the topics covered? Are you looking for a specific fact or definition? Or do you want to learn everything in the passage? The highlighted text that follows shows the information you would learn from reading a passage in three different ways: skimming, scanning, and in-depth reading.

Skimming is glancing over the text to identify main ideas by reading chapter and lesson titles, words in bold or italic type, and topic sentences.

Scanning is glancing over the text in search of specific information by looking for key words.

In-depth reading is reading over the text carefully to absorb new ideas and facts.

Family and Government   Promoting order was Confucius's principal concern. He believed that everyone had a proper role in society. If each person would accept that role and perform the related duties, social and political disorder would end.

Individuals, Confucius taught, should live according to principles of **ethics** — good conduct and moral judgment. Ethics began with respect for family, especially elders, and reverence for the past and its traditions. Ethics should govern each person's behavior in these five primary relationships: ruler and subject, parent and child, husband and wife, old and young, friend and friend.

Each reading style is useful for certain times. Here are a few suggestions for when each style might be appropriate:

- **Skimming** is useful when you're previewing material for a general overview, determining main ideas or an author's purpose, or deciding whether a book covers a subject you're interested in.
- **Scanning** is useful when you're reviewing key terms, looking for a detail to support an opinion, or searching for specific information.
- **In-depth reading** is useful when you're reading for the first time and learning new concepts, or when you're evaluating the information presented or preparing to explain the information to someone else.

Real World Connection

Reading on the Job

Ask students to identify jobs in which one might have to do a lot of reading, such as a business person, computer programmer, doctor, teacher, banker, paralegal, or social worker. Ask which method or methods of reading—skimming, scanning, or in-depth reading—people in the suggested professions might be called upon to use and why. To show the importance of reading skills in the workplace, you might invite parents to speak to the class about the amount and kinds of reading they are required to do in order to perform their jobs effectively.

The SQ3R Method   An effective method for learning and remembering written information is known as SQ3R. The name comes from the steps in the process: survey, question, read, record, and review. Applying this method can help you remember what you read. Look at the chart at the top of the next page to find out how to use this method in your studying.

Survey	Question	Read	Record	Review
Preview the material by skimming. Read heads, highlighted terms, and the first sentence of each paragraph. Look at all pictures and graphs.	Ask questions about the material. Your questions might begin with *who, what, when, where, why,* and *how.*	Read the selection carefully. Identify the main idea of each section. Take notes and add questions to your list.	Write answers to your questions without looking at the text. Make brief notes about additional main ideas or facts.	Check your answers in the text. Continue to study the text until you can answer all questions

Mnemonic Devices   Rhymes, sayings, or words, called mnemonic devices, help you recall basic information and can also help you remember what you study. The list below gives some examples. By looking for patterns in what you study, you can develop your own mnemonic devices.

Common Mnemonic Devices	
Purpose	**Word or Phrase**
To remember that the order of scientific classification of living things is *kingdom, phylum, class, order, family, genus,* and *species*	*King Philip came over from Germany Saturday.*
To remember that the person who runs a school is a principal, not a principle	*A principal is a pal.*
To remember that the lines of the treble clef are the notes *E, G, B, D,* and *F*	*Every good boy deserves fudge.*
To help you interpret centigrade temperatures	30° is hot, 20° is nice; 10° is cool, 0° is ice.
To remember that the order of the planets from the sun is *Mercury, Venus, Earth, Mars, Jupiter, Saturn, Uranus, Neptune,* and *Pluto*	*My very excellent mother just served us nine pickles.*
To remember that the order of colors in the spectrum is *red, orange, yellow, green, blue, indigo,* and *violet*	Roy G. Biv
To remember that the five Great Lakes are *Huron, Ontario, Michigan, Erie,* and *Superior*	homes

27.1 Studying Effectively   **839**

Study Skills

Teach

Using SQ3R

To help students understand the SQ3R method, have them turn to a page in this book that has not yet been covered. As a class, work through each step shown on the flow chart on this page. Ask individuals to read aloud each heading, caption, and the first sentence in each paragraph on the page of text. On the board, list questions students suggest about the content of the page. Instruct them to read the page and then answer the questions without referring to the text. Finally, have them check their answers against the text. **L1**

Creating Mnemonic Devices

Work with students to prepare a list of information that may be difficult to remember, such as major systems of the body, classifications of animals, or important explorers of the Age of Exploration. Some students may name more personal information, such as phone numbers or birthdays of friends and family members. Invite students to propose mnemonic devices such as rhymes, acronyms, or sentences that might help them remember this information. **L2**

Listening and Speaking

Recording and Listening

Some students may find it useful to experiment with a tape recorder to see how well they learn by listening. If possible, ask students to record a speech or lecture in one of their classes, taking notes at the same time. Ask them to report what they learned by listening to the recording later. Did they find that they got the major points the first time? Did they miss anything important?

Teach

Separating Fact from Opinion

Have students read the section Evaluating What You Read on this page. Divide the class into small groups and distribute copies of an editorial or a letter to the editor. Have members of the groups work together to identify each statement as a fact or an opinion, discussing evidence, lack of evidence, or clue words to support their evaluations. Bring the class together to discuss each group's findings. **L3**

Listing Facts and Opinions

You may want to give advanced students an opportunity to use critical reading skills in outside reading. Ask students to choose an issue that is of interest to them. Examples of issues include raising the age limit for driving or increasing the length of the school year. Encourage students to locate and read a newspaper or magazine article on the subject of interest. Students should list the facts and the opinions they find in the article. Have them write how opinions are supported in the article as well as how each fact might be verified. **L3**

Cross-reference: Writing

For situations in which students analyze writing samples and use the facts to support their own opinions, refer them to Lesson 6.1, pp. 282–285; Lesson 6.2, pp. 286–289; and Lesson 6.3, pp. 290–293.

Study Skills

Evaluating What You Read

Another study tool is critical reading. In critical reading, you might ask yourself questions such as the following: Is this statement true? Are these connections logical? Do I agree with the values underlying this writer's viewpoint? Remember that even well-researched and carefully considered writing can contain mistakes or reflect an author's bias.

Identifying Facts and Opinions   One step in evaluating writing is recognizing the difference between fact and opinion. A fact is a statement that can be verified or proved true. The proof of a statement might come from direct experience—something you saw or experienced yourself—or from an authoritative source, such as a reference book or a quotation from an expert on the subject.

An opinion is a personal judgment. Since opinions are expressions of someone's beliefs or feelings, they cannot be proved either true or false. Opinions can provide useful information, but to be valid they should be supported by evidence.

The following chart shows examples of facts and opinions and how to separate them from each other.

Distinguishing Facts from Opinions	
Statement	**Fact or Opinion**
1. Sammy Sosa was the first baseball player to hit sixty homeruns in two consecutive years.	1. Fact: It is easy to confirm through newspapers and reference books that Sammy Sosa was the first baseball player to hit the sixty homerun mark in two consecutive years—1998 and 1999.
2. Sammy Sosa is the best baseball player of the twentieth century.	2. Opinion: While facts might be used to support or oppose this idea, it is a matter of one's personal view. It cannot be proved true.
3. The Hubble Space Telescope was launched on April 24,1990, aboard the space shuttle *Discovery*.	3. Fact: Reference books, newspapers, and newsmagazines can provide evidence to support this statement.
4. Manufacturers' carelessness caused severe flaws in the Hubble Telescope mirror.	4. Opinion: Although some experts have presented evidence to support this idea, other experts remain unconvinced of the connection.

Interpreting and Evaluating Figurative Language   Writers sometimes express ideas using figurative language, a word or phrase used in an imaginative, rather than literal, sense. Similes, metaphors, and idioms are

English Language Learners

Using Clue Words to Determine Fact or Opinion

Students acquiring English may need extra support to make judgments about whether written material conveys facts or opinions. Point out specific clue words that might help them identify opinions. For example, adjectives—such as *excellent, lovelier, as wonderful, more terrifying,* or *greediest*—can be used to convey a personal judgment. Point out that these words express feelings or reactions and are clue words that indicate that an opinion is being expressed.

examples of figurative language. For example, in a U.S. history textbook, you might read Theodore Roosevelt's advice on United States foreign policy: "Walk softly and carry a big stick." He meant that the United States should be cautious in foreign affairs but willing and able to use a powerful military. Be attuned to figurative language so that you can pick up on the subtleties of the materials you read. You will be better able to evaluate an author's message.

Exercise 1

Reorganize the following notes into a modified outline. Use abbreviations and symbols when possible.

Types of reptiles: between six and seven thousand species of reptiles are alive today; most of these are classified into one of four orders

Squamata includes lizards, such as iguanas and Gila monsters, and snakes, including pythons, rattlesnakes, and garter snakes

Chelonia includes reptiles with shells, such as turtles and tortoises; some live on land, others in fresh water, others in salt water; all members of this order lay their eggs on land

Crocodylia includes reptiles such as crocodiles and alligators, also caimans and gavials; crocodiles have longer, thinner snouts than alligators; unlike alligators, the fourth tooth on their lower jaw is visible when their mouths are closed

Rhynchocephalia includes tuatara; these reptiles look like lizards, but are more closely related to dinosaurs; they live off the coast of New Zealand

Exercise 2

Use the SQ3R method to study a lesson that your teacher assigns. Then write a paragraph analyzing whether or not the SQ3R method helped you.

Exercise 3

Identify at least two facts and two opinions in the following paragraph.

The slider is a major-league baseball pitcher's best friend. To the batter, the pitch looks like a fast ball. Even the pitcher's motion is the same as the motion for throwing the fast ball, so there's no hint about what's coming up. The ball will start out in a straight, easy-to-hit line toward the center of the plate. Then, suddenly and unexpectedly, the ball changes direction. It doesn't change much, mind you, just enough to turn solid hits into foul balls, pop-ups, and easy grounders. It's not surprising that every hitter hates the slider and every pitcher can't wait to serve one up.

Practice and Assess

Evaluation Rubrics

Exercise 1
Outlines may vary somewhat. A sample follows.

Reptiles—3 ord., 6,000 spec.
    Squamata
        lizards
            iguanas
            Gila monsters
        snakes
            pythons
            rattlesnakes
            garter snakes
    Chelonia
        have shells
            turtles
            tortoises
        live—land, fresh/salt water
        lay eggs on land
    Crocodilia
        crocodiles
            pointed snouts
            show more teeth with mouth
                closed than do alligators
        alligators
        caimans
        gavials

Exercise 2
Paragraphs will vary but should show that students have used all five steps of the SQ3R process.

Answers: Exercise 3
Opinions: first and last sentences (clues: best friend; every . . . hates; every . . . can't wait); Facts: all other sentences

Additional Resources
📂 *Thinking and Study Skills,* pp. 5, 8–9, 12, 14, 17, 34–38
📂 *Listening and Speaking Activities,* pp. 1–2

Close

Remind students that there are many strategies they can use to develop effective study skills. Invite them to share the strategies they have found effective as well as ones they find interesting and plan to try.

Focus

Lesson Overview

Objective
- To learn about graphs and diagrams and how to interpret them

Skills
- interpreting graphs and diagrams

Critical Thinking
- analyzing; comparing

Listening and Speaking
- discussing

Bellringer
Daily Language Activity

When students enter the classroom, have this assignment on the board: *List kinds of information you often find represented in a table, graph, chart, or diagram.*

See also *Daily Language Practice*

Motivating Activity

Divide the class into small groups. Give each group a different issue of a newspaper or news magazine. Have the members of each group circle all the tables, graphs, charts, and diagrams they find in their issue. Urge them to review the information represented in each graphic. Then invite each group to share their findings with the class.

Explain that this lesson teaches students about various graphics and how to interpret the data in them.

Study Skills

27.2 ## Reading Graphs and Diagrams

Writers often use charts, diagrams, tables, and other graphics to present information. By using a graphic, writers can also make relationships between ideas easy to see. A clear graphic usually has the following components:

- title—a phrase that summarizes the main topic of the graphic
- labels—words or phrases that show the organization of the information in the graphic
- data—words or numbers that provide the actual information in the graphic

Tables

Tables present large amounts of information. They are often used to compare one or more characteristics of a list of similar items. For example, a box score for a baseball game lists each player's name and the number of hits, at bats, and runs batted in for each. At a glance, you can see who had the most hits, who had none, and so forth.

The table below shows the population of four major cities in the United States between 1850 and 1996. Notice how easily you can compare the changes in these cities.

Populations of Four Major Cities in the United States, 1850–1996					
City	1850	1900	1950	1990	1996
New York	696,115	3,437,202	7,891,957	7,322,564	7,380,906
Los Angeles	1,610	102,479	1,970,358	3,485,557	3,553,638
Chicago	29,963	1,698,575	3,620,962	2,783,726	2,721,547
Houston	2,396	44,633	596,163	1,637,859	1,744,058

You can read most tables horizontally (across) or vertically (down). By looking across the row labeled "New York," you can see how the population of that one city changed over time. By looking down the column labeled "1950," you can compare the population of all four cities in one year.

Pie Charts

Tables can show characteristics of several items, but pie charts, sometimes called circle graphs, focus on the parts that make up one whole item. In a pie chart, each slice of the pie represents one part of the whole. A pie chart easily and quickly shows you how big the slices are in relation to each other.

Resource Manager

Planning Resources
- *Lesson Plans*

 Transparencies
- *Bellringer*
- *Daily Language Practice*

Other Print Resources
- *Listening and Speaking Activities,* pp. 1–2
- *Thinking and Study Skills,* pp. 5, 8–9, 12, 14, 17, 34–38

Because they are mathematical parts of a whole, percentages are often shown in pie charts. In the pie chart shown here, the circle represents the entire world population in 1988. Each slice shows a specific region's population as a percentage of the world's total population.

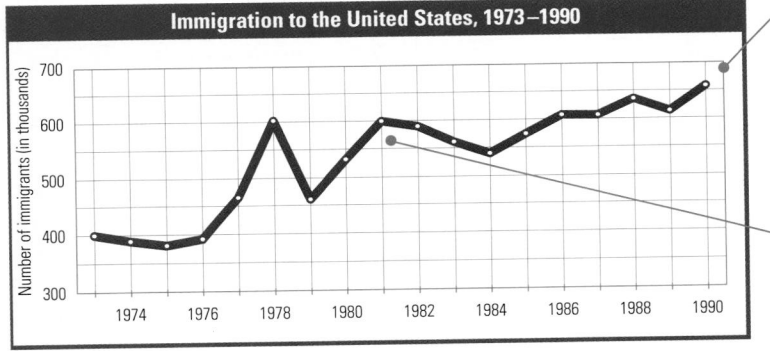

WORLD POPULATION, 1988

Oceania 1%
North America 8%
South America 6%
Africa 12%
Europe 13%
Asia 60%

North America is represented by a slice that is 8 percent of the whole pie chart, the same as its portion of the world's population.

Asia is 60 percent of the whole pie chart—and 60 percent of the world's total population.

Line Graphs

Line graphs can show changes over a period of time. You will often see them in books, magazines, or other news media to show trends or variations in statistics.

To read a line graph, first look at the labels on the axes. The axes are the main vertical line and main horizontal line that make up the graph. The labels tell you what is being compared and the time interval over which the data is being reported.

On the following graph, the vertical axis shows the number of immigrants entering the United States. The horizontal axis shows the year.

Immigration to the United States, 1973–1990

Number of immigrants (in thousands)
700
600
500
400
300

1974 1976 1978 1980 1982 1984 1986 1988 1990

The line's highest point indicates that immigration was highest in 1990.

In 1981 the line intersects at 597. Because the data is given in thousands, this means that about five hundred ninety-seven thousand immigrants arrived in 1981.

Tree Diagrams

Unlike the previously discussed graphics, tree diagrams rarely show numerical data. Instead, they show relationships between things or ideas.

27.2 Reading Graphs and Diagrams **843**

Study Skills

Teach

Reading a Table

Call on volunteers to read aloud the title and labels on the table on student page 842. Ask what information is contained in each column and row. Be sure students understand how to use the column labels (across the top) and row labels (at the left) to locate information in the table. Then provide practice by asking for the following information:

- the population of Los Angeles in 1900 (102,479)
- the city with the second largest population in 1950 (Chicago) and in 1990 (Los Angeles)
- the two cities in which the population declined between 1950 and 1990 (New York and Chicago) **L2**

Reading a Pie Chart and Line Graph

Point out that the pie chart and line graph (student page 843) illustrate two ways in which various types of data can be organized. Explain that pie charts allow readers to see comparisons quickly, as in the case of manufactured goods in the North and South. Point out that a line graph gives an immediate view of when changes were great and small. Call attention to the flatness of the line between 1986 and 1987, two years in which immigration was almost the same. **L2**

Enrichment and Extension

Creating a Line Graph

Ask students to use the data in the table on page 842 to create a line graph showing the changes in Chicago's population from 1900 to 1996. Remind them to make clear what the vertical and horizontal axes represent and to create reasonable gradations for the population figures. If possible, encourage students to use a computer progam to construct their graphs.

Teach

Creating a Tree Diagram

Remind students that a tree diagram usually begins with one main idea. The relationship of other ideas to the main idea is shown by the placement of information in the diagram. Use the diagram on page 844 to demonstrate placement of ideas. Point out the various levels of subordination: first the major divisions (Drama, Nonfiction, Fiction, Poetry), then the subdivisions (Tragedy, Essay, Novel, Epic, etc.), and then the division of History into still smaller categories.

Encourage students to create tree diagrams of their own, using information from other subject areas. Biology students might classify organisms and history students might illustrate the branches of the U.S. government. Urge students to discuss their completed diagrams. **L2**

Creating a Time Line

A simple time line based on familiar facts can help students who find graphic representations confusing. Ask students to depict their own lives on a time line. Remind them that the space between events on a time line should be proportional to real time. Explain that line segments can be any size and scale, but one scale (such as one inch equals one year) must be used consistently. **L1**

⇄ Cross-reference: Composition

For more information on using graphs and diagrams, refer students to Lesson 5.7, pp. 244–247.

Study Skills

Sentence diagrams are a form of tree diagram. They show how words in a sentence relate to one another. An organizational chart for a company is another example of a tree diagram. To see an example of a tree diagram, turn to Lesson 22.3, page 790.

Tree diagrams usually begin with one main idea. In this example, the main idea is literature. Closely related ideas are linked to the main idea by branches that connect to the center line. Ideas related directly to the branching ideas and indirectly to the main idea are connected to the branches. The branches can continue on, with each idea leading to others.

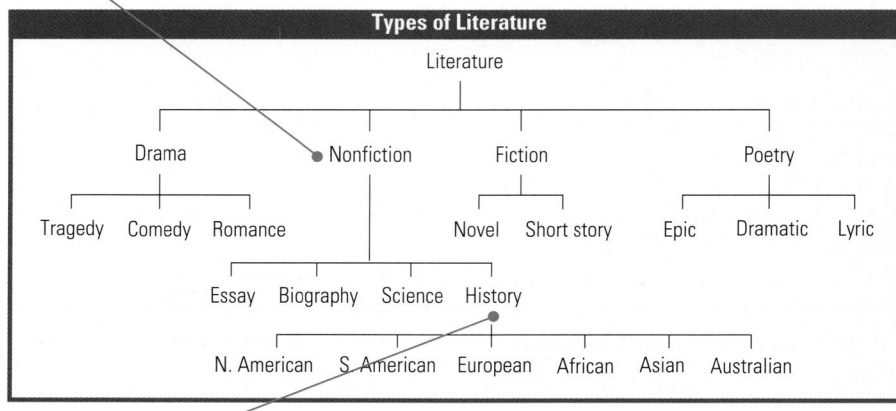

Nonfiction is a type of literature, so it branches off the main idea.

History is a type of nonfiction literature. You can divide it further into smaller categories.

Scales

A scale is a line segment divided into categories that represents a specific distance, time, or quantity in the real world. A thermometer is a scale that measures temperature. In mathematics, scales demonstrate relationships among numbers. For example, a scale might show the relationship between positive and negative integers on a number line.

Map Scales Scales are commonly used on maps. A map scale tells you that a certain number of inches or centimeters on the map represents a specific number of miles or kilometers. By finding the number of inches between Boston and Denver on a map of the United States, for example, you can determine the number of miles or kilometers between the two cities.

One inch on the map equals 250 miles.

The top line of the scale indicates miles. The bottom line indicates kilometers.

Real World Connection

Using U.S. Measurements

Students who are accustomed to the metric system of measurement may have difficulty with the measures used in the United States. Creating a map of the classroom or some other familiar area will allow such students to explore the relationship between American units of measure and actual size. Students may work together on a single map or different students may map the same area, each using a different scale, such as one centimeter equals one meter and one inch equals one foot.

Time Line A time line shows events during a given period of time by representing time as a line. The space between the events on the time line is proportional to the amount of time that passed between the events. For example, a line segment three inches long could represent a period of three hundred years, with one inch equaling one hundred years.

Time lines are often used to show key events leading up to a major event. The time line below shows developments in space exploration.

The title indicates the subject and time period covered.

Each mark on the time line indicates one year.

The space between two events reflects the time that passed between them.

Exercise 4

Answer each of the following questions about graphs and diagrams studied in this lesson.

1. Which type of graph or diagram would best show changes in the cost of a college education over the last thirty years? Why?
2. Which type of graph or diagram would best show what portion of a twenty-four hour day you spend sleeping, going to school, eating meals, and doing other daily activities? Why?
3. Which type of graph or diagram would best compare the average high temperature, average low temperature, and average precipitation in ten U.S. cities? Why?
4. Which type of graph or diagram would you use to show the relationships among different types of foods? Why?
5. Which type of graph or diagram would you use to show the order in which various forms of music, such as classical, jazz, blues, and rock-and-roll, developed? Why?

Exercise 5

Find and copy two different graphics from books, newspapers or newsmagazines, or create a graphic of your own, using information from a current news source. Write a short statement identifying and explaining the information in the graphics you found or in the one you created. Share your visual representations with the class and explain the illustrated information.

27.2 Reading Graphs and Diagrams **845**

Study Skills

Practice and Assess

Answers: Exercise 4

1. A line graph is best for showing changes over time, such as the increase in the cost of college education, because the rising and falling of the line will indicate increases and decreases in costs from year to year.
2. A pie chart is best for showing how the parts (activities) make up one whole unit (a day).
3. A table is best for comparing several characteristics (average high temperature, average low temperature, and average precipitation) for several items (ten U.S. cities).
4. A tree diagram works well for showing the relationships among things such as foods, since it allows for the division of foods into various categories.
5. A time line shows development of events over time, such as the order in which forms of music developed.

Evaluation Rubric
Exercise 5

Responses will vary, but students should name the source of each graph and be able to correctly describe or summarize what it shows.

Additional Resources

📁 *Thinking and Study Skills,* pp. 5, 8–9, 12, 14, 17, 34–38
📁 *Listening and Speaking Activities,* pp. 1–2

✓ ASSESSMENT OPTIONS

📁 *Tests with Answer Key & Rubrics*
Unit 27 Mastery Test, pp. 101–102

💾 *Testmaker*
Unit 27 Mastery Test

📼 *MindJogger Videoquizzes*

You may wish to administer the Unit 27 Mastery Test at this point.

Close

Have students list the types of graphic organizers discussed in this lesson. Then ask them to discuss ways in which they might use each type in their school work or everyday life.

Objectives

- To learn about test preparation time lines and techniques for answering objective test items
- To identify and practice test-taking strategies
- To practice test-taking techniques and strategies by responding to practice exercises

✓ ASSESSMENT OPTIONS

📂 *Tests with Answer Key & Rubrics*
Unit 28 Pretest, pp. 103–104

💾 *Testmaker*
Unit 28 Pretest

You may wish to administer the Unit 28 Pretest at this point.

Key to Ability Levels

L1 Level 1 activities are within the basic ability range of students.

L2 Level 2 activities are within the ability range of average students.

L3 Level 3 activities are more challenging activities.

Taking Tests

Lesson **28.1**   **Preparing for Classroom Tests**   *847*

Lesson **28.2**   **Preparing for Standardized Tests**   *851*

Lesson **28.3**   **Standardized Test Practice**   *857*

846

Resource Manager

Planning Resources
- *Lesson Plans*
- *Block Scheduling*

🖥 **Transparencies**
- *Bellringer*
- *Daily Language Practice*

📂 **Other Print Resources**
- *SAT-9 Preparation and Practice*
- *Taking Standardized Tests*

- *Tests with Answer Key & Rubrics*
- *Thinking and Study Skills*

📼 **Video**
- *MindJogger Videoquizzes*

💾 **Software**
- *Presentation Plus!*
- *Testmaker*
- *Writer's Choice Puzzlemaker*

💻 **Web Sites**
- *writerschoice.glencoe.com*

28.1 Preparing for Classroom Tests

On exam day, you walk into class at the appointed hour. How do you feel? Overwhelmed and panicky? Or confident and relaxed? How you feel and how you perform have a lot to do with how well prepared you are for the test. The following time line suggests steps you can take in preparing for a test.

How to Prepare for a Test

10 **Ten days or more before the test**
Find out about the test. By writing down any information your teacher provides about the test—when it will be given, what it will cover, and so on—you can plan your study time effectively.

8 **Eight days before the test**
Gather your information. Review your textbook, quizzes, homework assignments, class notes, and handouts. By keeping all of your papers in one folder, you'll save time gathering study materials.

6 **Six days before the test**
Test yourself. Develop your own study questions about main ideas and important details, and practice answering them. Writing down your answers allows you to check what you have learned.

4 **Four days before the test**
Form study groups. Meet with members of your class to review material. Try to answer one another's study questions. Explaining information to a peer is one of the best ways to learn the material.

2 **Day before the test**
Sleep well the night before a test. Spreading your study time over several days will give you enough confidence to go to bed at your regular time the night before a test.

Day of the test
Eat a good breakfast. Students who eat a full meal the morning of a test usually score higher than those who don't. Eating well helps you remain alert during the test.

TEST

Taking Tests

Focus

Lesson Overview

Objective
- To become familiar with test preparation time lines and techniques for answering objective test items

Skills
- using and developing a time line in preparing for tests; analyzing objective test items

Critical Thinking
- analyzing; synthesizing

Listening and Speaking
- discussing; listening and responding to questions

🔔 Bellringer
Daily Language Activity
When students enter the classroom, have this assignment on the board: *Jot down a few ideas about how you prepare for an important classroom test.*

See also *Daily Language Practice*

Motivating Activity

Discuss with students various kinds of tests they have taken and how they feel about taking tests. Ask them what they know about college entrance exams such as SAT or ACT and what kinds of tests they think employers might give job applicants. Explain that they will be taking tests throughout their high-school careers and will continue to need test-taking skills whether they choose college or a job after high school.

Resource Manager

Planning Resources
- *Lesson Plans*

📄 **Transparencies**
- *Bellringer*
- *Daily Language Practice*

📁 **Other Print Resources**
- *Taking Standardized Tests*
- *Thinking and Study Skills,* pp. 2, 17, 24, 35–36, 39–40

Teach

Creating a Personal Time Line

Explain to students that the vertical time line on student page 847 represents a "countdown" to test-taking day. Discuss with them why the tasks in the time line need to be completed in the listed order. Ask students how they would combine tasks if they had only six days for test preparation. Then have them develop a time line for their next test, using the model in their texts with any adaptations they feel are necessary. Have students share their time lines with the class. **L2**

Analyzing Multiple-choice Test Items

Invite students to describe the problems they encounter when answering multiple-choice items on tests. Ask them what they could do to choose the best response if all possible responses seem correct. Then read aloud the sample test item on student page 848 and discuss all the responses. Next have students work in pairs to write sample multiple-choice items. Have them present the items to the class members for analysis. **L1**

Taking Tests

Taking Objective Tests

Many of the tests you take during high school will be objective tests. These tests ask for very specific information about material you've studied.

The most common type of objective test item is multiple choice. Each item includes a specific question or an incomplete sentence, and four or five responses. You are to pick the response that best answers the question or that best completes the sentence. When selecting the best response, consider the following tips.

Tips for Answering Multiple-Choice Items

1. Read the item carefully. You need to know what information you are looking for.

2. Read all the responses provided. Even if the first response seems almost correct, a later response may be better.

3. Eliminate any responses that are clearly incorrect. This helps you focus your attention on the responses that might be correct.

4. Be cautious about choosing responses that contain absolute words—*always, never, all,* or *none*. Since most statements have exceptions, absolute statements are often incorrect.

The following item might appear on an earth science test. As you read it, focus on what information is being asked for and how you would select the correct answer.

> Note that the item calls for "first clues." Choice *a* is accurate, but since it does not list "first clues" it is incorrect.

> Since this statement includes the words *all* and *perfectly,* you should select it only if you are sure it is correct.

> This statement is incorrect because it is factually wrong. The answer is *c*.

```
What were the first clues that led scientists
to believe that the continents of the earth
were once connected as a single landmass?
a. Alfred Wegener, a German meteorologist,
   proposed the theory of continental drift.
b. Scientists found that all continents could
   be fitted together perfectly like a puzzle.
c. Similarities in ancient climates, fossils,
   and rock structures seemed to link separate
   landmasses.
d. Scientists discovered ancient historical
   records describing a giant landmass called
   Pangaea.
e. all of the above
```

MEETING INDIVIDUAL NEEDS   Less Proficient Readers

Reading Questions Carefully

Stress the importance of reading questions carefully, particularly for students for whom a language barrier might present additional problems. Write the following questions on the board: "Which of these animals is not a vertebrate? Which of these animals is a vertebrate?" Ask how these two questions are different. Then discuss with students what would happen if they did not read the question carefully.

The chart below describes other types of objective test items and provides some suggestions for answering them.

Tips for Answering Objective Test Items		
Type of Item	**Example**	**Tips**
True-False	_____ Soil erosion on the earth's surface is a natural process unaffected by human activities.	If any part of the item is false, the correct answer is "false." Since the last phrase of this item is wrong, the answer is "false."
Short Answer	Why is the planet Venus known as Earth's twin?_____	Use complete sentences to help you write a clear response. "Venus is almost exactly the same size as Earth."
Fill-in	The most important prophet of the _____ faith was Muhammad.	After completing the sentence, read it again to check that your answer is grammatically correct. In the example, "Islamic," not "Islam," would be the correct answer.
Matching	_____ an Indian leader who emphasized nonviolence _____ a German leader who led the Nazi party _____ a Chinese leader who led a communist revolution _____ an American leader who started the New Deal a. Mao Zedong b. Mohandas Gandhi c. Franklin Roosevelt d. Adolf Hitler	Note in the directions whether some responses can be used more than once or are not used at all. Quickly read each list to become familiar with the choices. Do easy items first to limit the number of choices for the difficult ones.

Teach

Developing and Answering Questions

Divide students into small groups for a cooperative activity. Assign each group a topic and material with which all students are familiar, such as a unit recently covered in this book. Have each group member choose a category from the chart on this page and develop questions covering the assigned material. Ask the groups to compile their questions and challenge the class with them. Tell class members answering the questions to explain why they believe their answers are correct.

Then have students tell which categories of questions they found easiest to answer. Discuss any strategies students developed for preparing questions and how these strategies might be used to help them answer different types of questions. **L2**

Answering Objective Test Items

Review the tips for answering each of the different types of objective test items on the student page. Encourage students to relate problems they have in answering these types of test items. Have the class give suggestions for possible ways of solving these problems. **L1**

Taking Tests

Listening and Speaking

Preparing Multiple-choice Questions

Select a brief passage from a textbook for another class and prepare three multiple-choice questions based on the material. Call on a good oral reader to read the passage to the class, asking students to take notes on the material being read. Then read aloud or write the three questions on the board. Ask the class to answer the questions and discuss what they looked for in each question and how they arrived at the correct answer.

Practice and Assess

Answers: Exercise 1

1. b. The landscape is barren.
2. d. experience extreme humidity in the summer.
3. False. The part of the Arabian Peninsula called the Empty Quarter (not the whole peninsula) is about the size of Texas.
4. The Arabian Shield is a mass of igneous and metamorphic rock; the sedimentary region includes both humid coast lines and hot, dry desert.
5. Red Sea, Persian Gulf

Additional Resources

 Taking Standardized Tests

Thinking and Study Skills, pp. 2, 17, 24, 35–36, 39–40

Close

Ask students to recall occasions when they were especially nervous or exceptionally confident when they took a test. Have students discuss possible reasons for the differences.

Taking Tests

Using Time Wisely

Because test time is usually limited, you will need to use your time efficiently. First, read the directions carefully. If any are unclear, ask questions. Respond to each item on the test, answering the easier ones first. Skip difficult items rather than dwelling on them. When you have answered the easier items, go back and answer hard items that you skipped earlier. Save some time to review your test before handing it in.

Exercise 1

Read the paragraph below, and use your test-taking strategies to help you answer the questions that follow.

The Arabian Peninsula is a wedge of land of about one million square miles between the Red Sea and the Persian Gulf. The peninsula is made up of two distinct geological regions. In the west is the Arabian Shield, made up of a huge mass of igneous and metamorphic rock. To the north, east, and south lies the sedimentary region, once submerged in seas in geologic times, subsequent to the formation of the shield. As part of the sedimentary region, the southern coasts and the coasts of the Red Sea and the Persian Gulf experience extreme humidity, particularly in summer. Much of the interior of the peninsula, however, is hot and dry. Drifting sand dunes cover most of the southeastern part of the peninsula. This area, about the size of Texas, is so barren that it is called the Empty Quarter.

1. Why is part of the Arabian Peninsula called the Empty Quarter?
   a. It is completely uninhabited.
   b. The landscape is barren.
   c. Drifting sand dunes make travel dangerous.
   d. none of the above
2. The sedimentary region of the Arabian Peninsula
   a. includes the Arabian Shield.
   b. is always hot and dry.
   c. is made of a huge mass of igneous and metamorphic rock.
   d. experiences extreme humidity in the summer.
3. True or false: The Arabian Peninsula is about the size of Texas.
4. Contrast the two regions that make up the Arabian Peninsula.

   _____

   _____

5. The Arabian Peninsula is located between the _____ _____ and the _____
   _____.

Enrichment and Extension

Practicing Test-taking Skills

Informal tests often appear in magazines and newspapers. For example, sports magazines might have tests such as "Test Your Sports IQ"; *Reader's Digest* usually has a vocabulary test, "How to Increase Your Word Power." Encourage students to try taking these tests to practice their test-taking skills and learn useful information.

28.2 Preparing for Standardized Tests

Along with the exams that you take in each class, you will often take standardized tests—tests designed to measure your general knowledge, abilities, and interests. They are called standardized because the results are compared with those of other students around the country who have taken the test. The performance of a large group of students provides a standard by which to measure individuals who take the test.

The Purpose of Standardized Tests

You might take a standardized test for one of several reasons. The chart below lists and describes the basic types of standardized tests.

Three Types of Standardized Tests		
Type	**Purpose**	**Examples**
Ability	Ability tests use questions about different subject areas to evaluate your general learning skills and to predict how well you will do in college.	Stanford-Binet tests Preliminary Scholastic Aptitude Test (PSAT)
Achievement	Achievement tests measure your knowledge in specific content areas, such as American history or algebra.	Tests of Achievement and Proficiency
Aptitude	Aptitude tests discover your individual talents and interests. They can help you choose an educational program and a career suited to your needs.	Differential Aptitude Test

Types of Items

You can prepare for standardized tests by reviewing general areas of knowledge, such as English usage and grammar, math, science, and social studies—areas that the tests usually cover. In addition, you can prepare for tests by learning about the types of questions presented. The following pages show examples of commonly used formats for test items and hints for answering each kind.

28.2 Preparing for Standardized Tests **851**

Focus

Lesson Overview

Objective
- To identify and practice test-taking strategies

Skills
- identifying kinds of tests; identifying types of test items; learning test-taking tips

Critical Thinking
- analyzing; synthesizing; defining and clarifying

Listening and Speaking
- discussing; establishing and evaluating criteria

 Bellringer
Daily Language Activity

When students enter the classroom, have this assignment on the board: *List the various kinds of tests you have taken and how you prepared for them.*

See also *Daily Language Practice*

Motivating Activity

Discuss the differences between a class exam in a specific subject and a standardized test. Ask students to explain which type of test they think is most difficult and which they are most confident about. Ask students when they are likely to encounter standardized tests in the future. (Students should mention college entrance exams and employment tests.)

Taking Tests

 Resource Manager

Planning Resources
- *Lesson Plans*

Transparencies
- *Bellringer*
- *Daily Language Practice*

Other Print Resources
- *Taking Standardized Tests*
- *Thinking and Study Skills,* pp. 2, 17, 24, 35–36, 39–40

Teach

Preparing for Testing

Use the chart on student page 851 to guide students in a discussion of the basic types of standardized tests they might encounter. **L2**

Understanding What You Read

Some students may need additional help determining what to look for in order to answer reading comprehension questions. Work through the sample test on pages 852–853 with these students. Ask them to read each question and discuss what they will need to look for to answer it. To answer question 2, for example, students should look for specific activities of the House of Wisdom as they read the passage. Point out that the questions rarely use the exact words found in the passage. For example, if a passage gives background information about some individual scholars, the question may ask whether the scholars' backgrounds were different or similar. Ask students to look for words that might tell whether or not the scholars were being paid (*salaried, earnings, in return for*). **L1**

⬆ Cross-reference: Study Skills

For tips on signal words and selecting the appropriate reading style for different reading tasks, refer students to Lesson 27.1, pp. 836–841.

Taking Tests

Reading Comprehension   The objective of reading comprehension items is to measure your ability to understand what you read. You will be presented with a passage and asked a series of questions—usually multiple-choice—about it. All of the information you need to respond will be in the passage. Skimming the questions before you read the passage will help you know what to look for. However, you should read the passage completely before answering any questions. Read the passage below, and answer the questions that follow.

> According to Muslim tradition, the ʾAbbasid caliph al-Maʾ-mun (mah MOON) founded the House of Wisdom at Baghdad in A.D. 830. This research center specialized in the translation into Arabic of Greek, Persian, and Indian scientific texts. It was believed that al-Maʾ-mun staffed the center with salaried Christian, Jewish, and Muslim scholars who used Arabic to share ideas from different intellectual traditions. These scholars were thought to have performed scientific experiments and mathematical calculations, carefully studying and building upon the ideas of the ancients. The House of Wisdom, therefore, served as a catalyst for many mathematical and scientific achievements in the Islamic world.

> To answer this question, you need to pick out the main idea of the passage. Since *d* summarizes the entire passage, it is the correct answer.

1. Which of the following would be the best title for this passage?
   a. Islamic Translation
   b. Islamic Scholars
   c. Abbasid caliph Maʾmun
   d. The House of Wisdom
   e. none of the above

> Answer *a* seems correct, but never answer a question until you have read all the choices. Since *b*, *c*, and *d* seem correct also, the correct answer is *e*.

2. The House of Wisdom scholars
   a. were paid for their efforts
   b. translated scientific texts into Arabic
   c. had different backgrounds
   d. based their work on the ideas of previous scholars
   e. all of the above

Enrichment and Extension

Identifying the Uses of Tests

By identifying what students have learned in defined areas, achievement tests help identify teaching strategies to use for both individuals and groups of students. Ability tests were once called IQ tests because they were believed to measure a person's intelligence. These tests are actually predictors. By giving a combined estimate of ability to develop a level of skill or knowledge, ability tests help predict how well a person will do academically. Aptitude tests can help students make wise career choices based on their particular interests and talents.

3. The point of view shows that the author
a. doubts the existence of the House of Wisdom
b. is objective about the subject
c. has contempt for the ancient sciences
d. is biased in favor of Islamic achievements
e. believes that science is the most important area of study

> Since the author avoids praising or condemning the information, *b* is the correct answer.

Synonyms   Tests that ask you to identify synonyms require you to select from a list of words one that is closest in meaning to another given word. Look for the best choice; no two words have exactly the same meanings. Study the example below.

_____ perimeter
a. circle
b. middle
c. direction
d. circumference

> All of the choices describe space in some way. Only *d* describes the distance around, so it is the correct response.

Sentence Completion   This type of test item is designed to assess your ability to complete sentences with logical and grammatically correct words. You generally need to choose one or more missing words from a list to complete a sentence. Consider the following example.

The paralysis of his leg, rather than _____ his expectations, actually _____ his drive to succeed.
a. lowering/heightened
b. redefining/acknowledging
c. limiting/lessened
d. clouding/confused

> Identify the relationship between the first and the last parts of the sentence.

> The words "rather than" and "actually" suggest that the two parts express opposite ideas. The words in *a* are the only pair that are opposites.

Items Testing English Skills

Standardized tests often include sections that evaluate your knowledge of written English. Items might ask you to identify usage problems, grammatical errors, and incorrect sentence constructions.

Teach

Using Prefixes, Roots, and Suffixes

You may wish to include the following example of how prefixes, roots, or suffixes can be used as clues in recognizing synonyms. Draw students' attention to the word *circumference*. They should know that the prefix *circum-* means "around," as does the prefix *peri-*. Using this information, students should be able to choose *circumference* as the synonym for *perimeter*, even if they are not familiar with either word. **L2**

⬄ Cross-reference: Thesaurus

For information on using a thesaurus to locate synonyms, refer students to Lesson 24.2, pp. 816–817.

Taking Tests

Cooperative Learning

Thinking of Synonyms

Assign partners for a Think-Pair-Share activity. Give two to three minutes for individual students to think of synonyms. Then have the partners meet, discuss their ideas, and use a thesaurus to develop the synonyms they chose into three test questions like the one under the Synonyms heading on student page 853. Students may exchange their papers with another pair and answer each others' questions of students.

Teach

Correcting Sentences

Students may encounter sentences that include conjunctions or pairs of words that suggest relationships. Write on the board a list of words or word pairs such as *however*, *and*, *because*, *thereafter*, *either/or*, and *not only/but also*. Ask students to make up sentences using these words and then explain the relationship suggested by the words. You may also want to review the section on using context clues in Unit 25, Building Vocabulary, pages 819–821. **L3**

Cross-reference: Usage

For a listing of words that are often confused in English usage, such as *affect* and *effect*, refer students to Lesson 26.2, pp. 833–834.

English Usage Tests of English usage often ask you to identify a variety of mistakes in the following areas:

- grammar
- spelling
- capitalization
- subject-verb agreement
- pronoun references
- improper word choice

Often English usage items include a sentence in which several words or phrases are underlined. Each underlined part is lettered. You are to identify the part of the sentence that includes an error and mark the corresponding letter on your answer sheet. Many items include a choice *e*, which states that the sentence contains no error. Following is a typical example.

> The word "affect" is incorrect; the correct word would be "effect."

```
The fall of the Berlin Wall has had a positive
    a                        b
affect on the human struggles around the world
  c                                  d
for freedom and peace. no error
                         e
```

Sentence Correction In these items, you will be given a sentence with one section underlined and choices for replacing the section. Choice *a* usually is identical to the section in the sentence; choose it if the sentence is without error. The other choices suggest other ways to word the section. Tests often include common errors such as wordiness, lack of parallel construction, and awkward wording. Try the following example.

> Identify the problem in the underlined section. In this example the two parts in the section are not parallel.

```
Ms. Sanchez's plan for redesigning the city's
public transportation system is finan-
cially feasible and has a sound structure.
```

a. is financially feasible and has a sound structure

b. has good financial feasibility and has a good structure

c. is financially feasible and sound in structure

d. is financially feasible and structurally sound

> Find the choice that corrects the problem you identified. Choice *d* is correct because its structure is parallel.

Taking Tests

Enrichment and Extension

Using Computer Software

A variety of educational computer software programs have been produced to help students prepare for standardized tests such as the ACT and SAT. This software is available for most types of computers.

Analogies While vocabulary items test your knowledge of word meanings, analogies test your ability to see the relationships between word meanings. An analogy item may contain a pair of words separated by a colon, and four or five other pairs of words. You are to choose the pair with the same relationship as the first pair. Here is an example.

```
praise : insult ::
a. admire : like
b. waste : devour
c. chide : encourage
d. provide: redistribute
e. entertain: study
```

Identify the relationship: *praise* is the opposite of *insult*.

Identify the pair showing the same relationship: *chide* is the opposite of *encourage*. Therefore, *c* is the correct answer.

To improve your scores on analogies tests, develop your vocabulary. See Unit 25, pages 818–826, for tips on building your vocabulary. In addition, practice identifying the relationship between two items. Following are some of the common relationships used on analogies tests.

Analogy Relationships	
Type	**Examples**
Cause and effect—one word causes or is the result of the other word	tornadoes : damage boredom : yawn
Opposites—one word is the opposite of the other word	happy : sad poor : rich
Users—one word uses or is used by the other word	doctor : stethoscope mechanic : wrench
Synonyms—the two words share a general meaning	elated : happy ready : prepared
Time sequence—one word comes before or after the other word	lunch : dinner sunset : sunrise
Characteristic—one word is a characteristic of the other word	leopard : carnivorous steel : hard
Category—one word is a specific item in the general category of the other word	broccoli : vegetable jazz : music

Standardized tests are sometimes given outside of regular class time. You may need to register to take some tests, such as college entrance exams. If so, register early to ensure that you can take the test on the day you need. In addition, follow the tips in the chart below.

28.2 Preparing for Standardized Tests **855**

Taking Tests

Teach
Making Analogies

Some students may not understand the use of colons and double colons in the structure of a standard analogy question. Explain that the single colon between the two words stands for *is to* and indicates a relationship between the two words; the double colon between the two pairs of words stands for *as* or *in the same way that* and indicates that the words in the second pair have the same relationship to each other as the words in the first pair have. To help students verbalize the relationship, have them read the sample analogy aloud using the words: "praise *is to* insult *as* chide *is to* encourage." Students might also read the analogy by replacing the first colon with the words that describe the relationship, the double colon with *as*, and the final colon with the same words used for the first colon. This reading will show clearly whether or not the relationships are the same. **L2**

Reteaching Analogies

Write the following on the chalkboard. Have students use the chart on student page 855 to name each kind of analogy.
- *sweet:sour* (opposites)
- *predator:eagle* (category)
- *herbs:herbivorous* (characteristics)
- *apathy:indifference* (synonym)
- *twilight:midnight* (time sequence) **L2**

Developing a Sample Test

Have students work in small groups to develop a sample test, using two questions of each type. Have each group exchange tests with another group and answer that group's test questions. **L3**

MEETING INDIVIDUAL NEEDS **English Language Learners**

Writing Analogies

Students who are not familiar with English may need to practice with analogy items with less complex vocabulary than that used in the lesson. Work with students to name additional examples of the relationship listed on the chart on student page 855 using very familiar, concrete items such as bread:flour, shoes:leather; cloth:cotton, candles:wax; pencil:paper, hammer:nail; needle:thread, and computer:disc.

855

Practice and Assess

Answers: Exercise 2
1. d
2. a
3. c
4. c
5. c

Additional Resources
📁 *Taking Standardized Tests*
📁 *Thinking and Study Skills,* pp. 2, 17, 24, 35–36, 39–40

Close

Discuss with students the kinds of tests teachers typically give in their other classes. Ask them what strategies they think they can use to study for these tests, based on what they have learned in this unit.

Tips for Taking Standardized Tests

1. Show up ready for the test. Try to arrive early so you can relax before beginning.
2. Sleep and eat well before the test. Get enough sleep the night before the test so that you are well rested. Eat a good breakfast so you don't get hungry during the test.
3. Pace yourself during the test. You usually have a limited amount of time to take the test, so don't get stalled on hard items. Skip them and move on.
4. Repeatedly compare the item numbers in your test booklet and answer sheet. Be careful to put your answers on the proper lines.
5. If time permits, check your answers. If you are not penalized for guessing, fill in answers for any items you might have skipped.

Exercise 2

Use the test-taking strategies described in this lesson to help you complete the following items. Write your answers on a separate piece of paper.

1. Which of the following is the best synonym for *analogous*?
   a. different
   b. representative
   c. incongruous
   d. alike
   e. agreeable

2. Choose the word that best completes the sentence below.
   _____ his many hours of hard work at the computer, he realized that his progress was insignificant.
   a. Despite
   b. Because of
   c. Through
   d. Besides
   e. By

3. Examine the sentence below and decide if it contains an error in standard English usage. Mark the correct letter.

   All the students who attended the assembly were instructed
   to leave his or her books in the cafeteria. no error
   a ... b ... c ... d ... e

4. Decide whether the underlined portion of the sentence below needs correcting. Pick the best correction from the choices that follow.

   As public outrage over contaminated foods becomes stronger, people who will demand more organically grown vegetables and fruits.
   a. people who will demand
   b. people that will demand
   c. people will demand
   d. people demanding
   e. people who have demanded

5. Choose the pair of words whose relationship is most similar to the following pair.

   paintings : frame ::
   a. photographs : margin
   b. brooms : handle
   c. spectacles : rim
   d. faces : hair
   e. globe : universe

Enrichment and Extension

Using Test Preparation Books
Students may locate a standardized-test preparation book at the library and complete a sample test in each category discussed.

28.3 Standardized Test Practice

INTRODUCTION

The following pages of exercises have been designed to familiarize you with the standardized writing tests that you will take during the school year. These exercises are very similar to the actual tests in how they look and what they ask you to do. Completing these exercises will not only provide you with practice, but also will make you aware of the areas you might need to work on.

These writing exercises—just like the actual standardized writing tests—are divided into three sections.

Sentence Structure   In this section, pages 858 to 865, you will be given short passages in which some of the sentences are underlined. Each underlined sentence is numbered. After you finish reading each passage, you will be asked questions about the underlined sections. The underlined sections will be either incomplete sentences, run-on sentences, correctly written sentences that should be combined, or correctly written sentences that do not need to be rewritten. You will need to select, from the four choices that you are given, which best rewrites the sentences if they contain mistakes.

Usage   In this section, pages 866 to 873, you will also be asked to read short passages. However, in these exercises, a word or words in each passage will be omitted and a numbered blank space will be in their place. After reading the passage, you will need to determine which of the four provided words or groups of words best fits in each numbered space.

Mechanics   Finally, in the third section, pages 874 to 881, you will be asked to read short passages that have parts that are underlined. You will need to determine if, in the underlined sections, there is a spelling error, capitalization error, punctuation error, or no error at all.

Writing well is a skill that you will use for the rest of your life. You will be able to write more accurate letters to your friends and family, better papers in school, and more interesting stories. You will be able to express yourself and your ideas more clearly and in a way that is interesting and engaging. These exercises should help to improve your writing and to make you comfortable with the format and types of questions you will see on standardized writing tests.

Standardized Test Practice

One way you may wish to use this section of *The Writer's Choice,* is to have students complete an exercise or a series of exercises in an environment that resembles a testing environment. Students should be encouraged to work slowly and carefully. After students have completed the assigned exercises, you may want to go over the answers with students. You can explain the correct answers and review the grammar skills being tested.

Not covered in these test practices is the section in many standardized test situations that requires students to write a composition based on a provided topic. In this section, students are tested on their ability to write clear, concise and persuasive compositions. You may want to assign topics to your students and have them write one or two page compositions so that they get practice for this section. When assigning a topic, choose subjects that require the student to have an opinion and to write convincingly as to why their opinion is valid. When advising students on how to prepare for the composition section, tell students that employing the following strategies may not only earn a higher grade on the test, but may also result in good writing skills: use specific examples to illustrate your point, organize your argument in a logical manner, carefully choose words that effectively and descriptively state your thoughts and opinion, be consistent in style and purpose throughout the composition. These are some of the ways that students can create interesting, persuasive and clearly written compositions.

Students are often anxious about taking standardized tests. Part of a teacher's responsibility is to provide support and instruction and to assure students that thorough preparation will enable them to meet the challenges of the test.

Taking Tests

Resource Manager

Planning Resources
- *Lesson Plans*

Other Print Resources
- *Taking Standardized Tests*
- *Thinking and Study Skills,* pp. 2, 17, 24, 35–36, 39–40

Standardized Test Practice

Tested Objective

- To recognize appropriate English usage and sentence structure within the context of a written passage

Answers and Analyses

1. **C** Students should recognize that the first sentence is actually a phrase and cannot stand on its own. The correct answer begins with the adverbial form of *ironic* and combines the sentences by setting off the relative pronoun *though* with commas.

2. **F** The underlined portion is a run-on sentence. Two complete sentences are put together with only a comma. These sentences are properly linked by the relative pronoun *which,* creating two dependent clauses.

3. **D** The underlined portion is a complete sentence and therefore the answer is *correct as is.* Two independent clauses are linked by the proper conjunction, *because.*

THE
PRINCETON
REVIEW **Test-Taking Tip**

Students should have a solid understanding of the meaning of a clause. A clause has a subject and a verb. Clauses are either dependent or independent. An independent clause has a subject and a verb and can stand on its own. A dependent (or subordinate clause) cannot stand on its own. It is dependent on the rest of the sentence to complete its meaning.

Standardized Test Practice

Read each passage. Some sections are underlined. The underlined sections may be one of the following:

- Incomplete sentences
- Run-on sentences
- Correctly written sentences that should be combined
- Correctly written sentences that do not need to be rewritten

Choose the best way to write each underlined section and mark the letter on your paper. If the underlined section needs no change, mark the choice "Correct as is."

Bears are known as animals that hibernate. <u>Ironically, though. Bears do not actually hibernate.</u> In fact,
(1)
they fall into a deep sleep during the winter. There are several factors that make a bear's sleep different from true hibernation. <u>Most important may be the bear's body temperature, it remains relatively constant compared to that of true hibernators.</u> A bear's body temperature will drop from 100 degrees to 93 degrees during its "hibernation." A true hibernator will have a body temperature that is the same temperature as the surrounding environment. <u>Small animals can hibernate because their bodies warm and cool quickly.</u> Bears
(3)
are large animals, so it requires a lot of energy for them to change body temperature.

---

1 A It is ironic, though, bears do not actually hibernate.
  B Ironically, though that bears do not actually hibernate.
  C Ironically, though, bears do not actually hibernate.
  D Correct as is

2 F Most important may be the bear's body temperature, which remains relatively constant compared to that of true hibernators.
  G Most important may be the bear's body temperature. Remaining relatively constant compared to that of true hibernators.
  H Most important, the bear's body temperature, which remains relatively constant compared to that of true hibernators.
  J Correct as is

3 A Small animals doing this hibernation because their bodies warm and cool quickly.
  B Small animals can hibernate. Because their bodies warm and cool quickly.
  C Small animals can hibernate because their bodies warm. And cool quickly.
  D Correct as is

Tucson's Six-Finger Fred was such a good thief that many said he could never be caught. In 1896, he robbed sixteen banks and seven jewelry stores. However, an anonymous letter put the police on his trail. In February 1897, he was almost caught in his hideout. But, Fred escaped the police yet again. In the fall of 1897, the great Brazil Topaz came through Tucson, authorities were sure Six-Finger Fred would try to steal it. They put the jewel under close guard. The jewel was safe all night.

They put the Topaz in a black felt bag and loaded it onto a wagon bound for California. However, when they opened the bag in San Francisco, the Topaz was gone! In its place was a lump of coal and a note that read, "Better luck next time, S-F F."

1 A Tucson's Six-Finger Fred being such a good thief. Many said he could never be caught.
B Tucson's Six-Finger Fred was such a good thief, many said he could never be caught.
C Tucson's Six-Finger Fred being such a good thief, that many said he could never be caught.
D Correct as is

2 F However, an anonymous letter put the police on his trail to catch him in February 1897, when he was in his hideout.
G However, an anonymous letter put the police on his trail, and in February 1897, he was almost caught in his hideout.
H An anonymous letter put the police on his trail. In February 1897, he was almost caught in his hideout however.
J By February 1897, police almost caught him in his hideout, and they also had an anonymous letter.

3 A In the fall of 1897, the great Brazil Topaz came through Tucson, and authorities being sure Six-Finger Fred would try to steal it.
B In the fall of 1897, the great Brazil Topaz coming through Tucson. And authorities were sure Six-Finger Fred would try to steal it.
C In the fall of 1897, the great Brazil Topaz came through Tucson, and authorities were sure Six-Finger Fred would try to steal it.
D Correct as is

STOP

Standardized Test Practice

Answers and Analyses

1. D The answer is *correct as is* because the two clauses are linked by the relative pronoun *that.*
2. G Students should recognize that the underlined portion includes two complete sentences that should be combined to create a smoother, more logical expression of connecting facts.
3. C Students should recognize that the underlined portion contains a run-on sentence. The correct answer combines the two independent clauses with the proper conjunction, *and.*

  Test-Taking Tip

Remind students that one important way in which sentences are linked is with conjunctions. The coordinating conjunction connects equal parts of sentences. Encourage students to make a list of coordinating conjunctions: *and, but, for, nor, so, yet.*

  Test-Taking Tip

Remind students of correlative conjunctions. These conjunctions connect clauses or phrases (like coordinating conjunctions), but they are composed of two conjunctions (both—and, either—or, neither—nor, not only—but, also).

859

Standardized Test Practice

Tested Objective

- To recognize appropriate English usage and sentence structure within the context of a written passage

Answers and Analyses

1. **C** Explain to students that the underlined portion contains a run-on sentence because two complete sentences are linked only by a comma. The correct answer combines the two independent clauses with the conjunction *and*.
2. **J** Students should recognize that the underlined portion is a complete, grammatically correct sentence. Commas correctly link the clauses and there are no unnecessary pronouns.
3. **B** The two sentences are correct, but will read more smoothly if combined. The correct answer combines the two by creating a subordinate clause beginning with the relative pronoun *which* that modifies *architecture*.
4. **H** The first sentence is a subordinate clause. It depends on the second clause for its meaning. The correct answer properly combines the two dependent clauses by removing the unnecessary pronoun *that*.

 Test-Taking Tip

Make sure students know that a complete sentence has a subject and verb and states a complete thought.

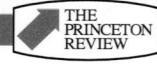 **Test-Taking Tip**

Suggest to students that when they read the answer choices, they make sure the meaning of the original sentence or sentences is retained.

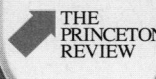

Standardized Test Practice

Read each passage. Some sections are underlined. The underlined sections may be one of the following:

- Incomplete sentences
- Run-on sentences
- Correctly written sentences that should be combined
- Correctly written sentences that do not need to be rewritten

Choose the best way to write each underlined section and mark the letter for your answer. If the underlined section needs no change, mark the choice "Correct as is."

   Nathan stood with his family, watching the plane taxi to the gate. His brother Daniel was finally coming home. <u>Daniel had been studying in Italy for the last eight months, Nathan couldn't wait to hear all about it.</u> (1) No one in Nathan's family had ever been to Europe. <u>Just last year, while a freshman at college, Daniel had accepted a scholarship to study abroad.</u> (2) Daniel, an art major, would study with the masters. <u>Architecture</u> (3) <u>was his main interest. He had written a paper on the Sistine Chapel and received admission to the special program.</u>

---

1 A Daniel had been studying in Italy for the last eight months. Nathan waiting to hear all about it.

  B Daniel studying in Italy for the past eight months. And Nathan couldn't wait to hear all about it.

  C Daniel had been studying in Italy for the past eight months, and Nathan couldn't wait to hear all about it.

  D Correct as is

2 F Just last year, while a freshman at college, Daniel had accepted something, it was a scholarship to study abroad.

  G Just last year, while a freshman at college. Daniel had accepted a scholarship to study abroad.

  H Just last year, while a freshman at college, Daniel had accepted. A scholarship to study abroad.

  J Correct as is

3 A Architecture was his main interest, and he had written a paper on the Sistine Chapel, and he had received admission to the special program.

  B Architecture was his main interest, and after writing a paper on the Sistine Chapel, he received admission to the special program.

  C Architecture, which was his main interest, had written a paper on the Sistine Chapel and received admission to the special program.

  D Architecture was his main interest while he had written a paper on the Sistine Chapel and received admission to the special program.

4 F Studying famous works of art in their native lands. An extraordinary way to learn.

  G Studying famous works of art in their native lands being an extraordinary way to learn.

  H Studying famous works of art in their native lands was an extraordinary way to learn.

  J Correct as is

860 Unit 28 Taking Tests

Standardized Test Practice

Opening night had finally arrived. Joseph had an important job. Joseph operated the spotlight. <u>Standing above the theater in a booth, Joseph watched the audience file into its seats. He watched the musicians enter the orchestra pit.</u> It was going to be a great show. <u>Joseph could hear the crowd murmuring with excitement, he could sense that it was almost time to begin.</u> The house lights were turned off. That was Joseph's cue. <u>When the applause died down. He flipped the switch on the spotlight.</u> A woman stepped onto the stage and into the light. <u>Joseph knew the performance would be perfect even before the actress spoke her first line.</u>

(1) ... (2) ... (3) ... (4)

1 A Standing above the theater in a booth, Joseph watched the audience file into its seats while he watched the musicians enter the orchestra pit.

B Joseph watched the audience file into its seats and the musicians enter the orchestra pit standing above the theater in a booth.

C Standing above the theater in a booth, Joseph watched the audience file into its seats and the musicians enter the orchestra pit.

D Standing above the theater in a booth, Joseph watched the audience file into its seats because the musicians enter the orchestra pit.

2 F Joseph could hear the crowd murmuring with excitement and he could sense. That it was almost time to begin.

G Joseph could hear the crowd murmuring with excitement and he could sense that it was almost time to begin.

H Joseph could hear the crowd murmuring with excitement. And he could sense that it was almost time to begin.

J Correct as is

3 A When the applause died down, he flipped the switch on the spotlight.

B The applause died down since he flipped the switch on the spotlight.

C The applause. It died down when he flipped the switch on the spotlight.

D Correct as is

4 F Joseph knowing the performance would be perfect even before the actress spoke her first line.

G A perfect performance. Joseph knew it even before the actress spoke her first line.

H Joseph knew the performance would be perfect. Even before the actress spoke her first line.

J Correct as is

STOP

28.3 Standardized Test Practice **861**

Standardized Test Practice

Answers and Analyses

1. C Explain to students that the underlined sentences are grammatically correct. However, since the subject of the first sentence is also the subject of the second sentence, they will read more smoothly if combined into one sentence. The correct answer removes the second, repeated subject (*he*) and verb (*watched*) and combines the sentences with the conjunction *and*. Point out to students that the sentence begins with a dependent clause.

2. G Students should recognize that this is a run-on sentence because it is two sentences combined with only a comma. The correct answer simply combines the two independent clauses with the proper conjunction, *and*.

3. A The underlined section contains a dependent clause, or sentence fragment, beginning with *When the applause,* and a complete sentence. The correct answer properly links the two clauses with a comma, making their relationship clear.

4. J The sentence is correct as is because it properly combines an independent and dependent clauses.

THE PRINCETON REVIEW **Test-Taking Tip**

Make sure that students can identify and use the subordinating conjunction. Subordinating conjunctions connect independent and dependent clauses. Encourage students to make a list of subordinating conjunctions: *after, because, except that, when, before, until, while, since, as.*

Tested Objective

- To recognize appropriate English usage and sentence structure within the context of a written passage

Answers and Analyses

1. **D** Students should recognize that the underlined section is a complete sentence and is correct as is.
2. **F** The underlined portion contains two sentence fragments. The correct answer combines the two fragments by simply removing the period separating them.
3. **D** Correct as is.

 Test-Taking Tip

Point out to students that with questions in which the sentences are correct but could be improved if made into one sentence, there is never a *Correct as is* option. Why is this? Because the sentences are, in fact, grammatically correct. However, they will read more smoothly if combined.

Standardized Test Practice

Read each passage. Some sections are underlined. The underlined sections may be one of the following:

- Incomplete sentences
- Run-on sentences
- Correctly written sentences that should be combined
- Correctly written sentences that do not need to be rewritten

Choose the best way to write each underlined section and mark the letter for your answer. If the underlined section needs no change, mark the choice "Correct as is."

Adaptive radiation is a term that many scientists use to describe one way in which species arise. Adaptive
(1)
radiation can occur when the members of a species in one area adapt to local surroundings and become different from those in other areas. The result is that one species. Becomes two or more. For example, at least
(2)
thirteen different species of finch have developed on Ecuador's Galapagos Islands, each with a beak adapted to local foods. The ground finch has a strong beak, while the cactus finch has a long, thin beak. Each bird
(3)
adapted to the food nearby. They eventually developed into distinct species.

---

1 A Adaptive radiation is a term that many scientists use. To describe one way in which species arise.

 B Adaptive radiation is a term that many scientists use it describes one way in which species arise.

 C Adaptive radiation is a term that many scientists use. Describing one way in which species arise.

 D Correct as is

2 F The result is that one species becomes two or more.

 G The result is that one species, becoming two or more.

 H The result that is one species, it becomes two or more.

 J Correct as is

3 A Each bird adapted to the food nearby distinct species eventually developing into.

 B Each bird adapted eventually developing into, because of the food nearby.

 C Each bird adapted to the food nearby, eventually distinct species being developed.

 D Correct as is

Wilbur and Orville Wright built one of the first airports. They did this in 1900. The Wright Brothers
(1)
have been credited with inventing the airplane. This first "airport" was actually just a shelter at Kitty Hawk,
North Carolina, where the Wright Brothers conducted their flying experiments. Kitty Hawk was the perfect
(2)
place for these experiments, it was a barren stretch of sand.

Later, the Wright Brothers moved their "airport" to Kill Devil Hills near a high dune that proved a good
launching place. On December 17, 1903, Wilbur Wright succeeded in making the first manned, sustained,
powered flight.
(3)

1 A Wilbur and Orville Wright built one of the first airports because it was 1900.

B In 1900, Wilbur and Orville Wright built one of the first airports, and that's when they first built it.

C Wilbur and Orville Wright built in 1900 one of the first airports.

D In 1900, Wilbur and Orville Wright built one of the first airports.

2 F Kitty Hawk was the perfect place for these experiments because it was a barren stretch of sand.

G Kitty Hawk was the perfect place for these experiments, it being a barren stretch of sand.

H Kitty Hawk was the perfect place for these experiments. It was a barren stretch of sand.

J Correct as is

3 A On December 17, 1903, Wilbur Wright in making the first manned, sustained, powered flight.

B On December 17, 1903, Wilbur Wright succeeded in making the first manned, sustained flight, and he also succeeded in making the first powered flight.

C On December 17, 1903, Wilbur Wright succeeded in making the first. He made manned, sustained, powered flight.

D Correct as is

STOP

Standardized Test Practice

Answers and Analyses

1. D Students should recognize that the sentences are grammatically correct, but since they start with the same subject and verb (in the second sentence the subject is replaced by the subject pronoun *they*, and the entire predicate is replaced by the verb *did* and the pointing pronoun *this*), the sentences should be combined. The correct answer turns the second sentence into an introductory prepositional phrase: *In 1900.*

2. F Students should recognize that the underlined sentence is a run-on because two independent clauses are joined with only a comma. The correct answer combines the two with the proper coordinating conjunction *because.*

3. D Explain to students that the sentence is correct as is because the prepositional phrase *On December 17, 1903* introduces the main, independent clause creating a compound, complex sentence.

THE PRINCETON REVIEW **Test-Taking Tip**

Make sure that students can identify a run-on sentence. A run-on sentence is comprised of two complete sentences put together without punctuation or with only a comma. Encourage students to read some sample run-on sentences out loud. Is it hard to read the entire sentence without a pause?

THE PRINCETON REVIEW **Test-Taking Tip**

Encourage students to come up with ways to correct run-on sentences either by making them into two complete sentences, or by removing some words to shorten them.

Standardized Test Practice

Tested Objective

- To recognize appropriate English usage and sentence structure within the context of a written passage

Answers and Analyses

1. **C** Explain to students that even though the original sentences are correct, their relationship to each other is better expressed when they are combined. The correct answer combines the sentences with the conjunction *because.* The phrase, *years ago,* now introduces the sentence and correctly modifies *when the job was more difficult.*

2. **H** This question asks students to combine two correctly written sentences in order to make their meanings clearer. The correct answer expresses the relationship between the sentences with the conjunction *because.*

3. **A** In this question, students are again asked to combine two complete sentences with a conjunction. The correct answer links the two sentences, and their ideas, closer together with the conjunction *and.* Explain to your students how choice B incorrectly uses *when,* thereby distorting the original meanings of the sentences.

 Test-Taking Tip

Remind your students to keep an eye out for any mention of dates or time frames in order to ensure that they modify the correct action. Also remind students to preserve a logical relationship between the clauses in a sentence, especially when they are linked by a conjunction or relative pronoun.

Standardized Test Practice

Read each passage. Some sections are underlined. The underlined sections may be one of the following:

- Incomplete sentences
- Run-on sentences
- Correctly written sentences that should be combined
- Correctly written sentences that do not need to be rewritten

Choose the best way to write each underlined section and mark the letter for your answer. If the underlined section needs no change, mark the choice "Correct as is."

Radio sportscasters make listeners at home feel that they are actually at the event. <u>This job was much more difficult years ago. Radio announcers were often not even at the game.</u> (1) In the early days of radio, live broadcast signals could not travel as far as they do today. <u>Some games were played in remote parts of the country. Announcers had to recreate the game for listeners who could not receive the signal.</u> (2) They did this in an interesting way. <u>Sportscasters received updates by telegraph. They used these updates to fuel their broadcasts.</u> (3)

---

1 A This job was much more difficult when radio announcers were often not even at the game years ago.

B Radio announcers were often not even at the game years ago since this job was much more difficult.

C Years ago, this job was much more difficult because radio announcers were often not even at the game.

D Years ago, radio announcers were often not even at the game because this job was much more difficult.

2 F Some games were played in remote parts of the country, so announcers had to recreate the game for listeners. Who could not receive the signal.

G Some games were played in remote parts of the country, then announcers had to recre-ate the game for listeners who could not receive the signal.

H Because some games were played in remote parts of the country, announcers had to recreate the game for listeners who could not receive the signal.

J Correct as is

3 A Sportscasters received updates by telegraph, and they used these updates to fuel their broadcasts.

B Sportscasters received updates by telegraph when they used these updates to fuel their broadcast.

C Fueling their broadcasts were the updates that the sportscasters received by telegraphs.

D Sportscasters received updates by telegraph and these updates were used to fuel broadcasts.

Cathy sells antique glassware, she keeps it in her basement. During a hurricane last year, many towns in
(1)
Cathy's area were flooded. Some even declared a state of emergency. People were advised to stay inside their
(2)
houses. Roads were blocked off. Cathy kept many boxes of antique vases and glasses in her basement.

It was after the hurricane passed. Cathy had to wash the glass, which had gotten dirty in the flooded
(3)
basement. Cathy set up several barrels of water in her yard, some with soapy water and some with clean

rinsing water. She must have washed several thousand glasses!

1 A Cathy sells antique glassware that she keeps
in her basement.

   B Cathy selling antique glassware. She keeps
it in her basement.

   C Cathy sells antique glassware. that she
keeps in her basement.

   D Correct as is

2 F People were advised to stay inside their
houses, because roads were blocked off.

   G People were advised to stay inside their
houses that the roads were blocked off.

   H People were advised to stay inside their
houses, and roads were blocked off.

   J Roads being blocked off and people being
advised to stay inside their houses.

3 A It was after the hurricane passed, and
Cathy had to wash the glass, and they had
gotten dirty in the flooded basement.

   B After the hurricane passed, Cathy had to
wash the glasses, which had gotten dirty in
the flooded basement.

   C It was after the hurricane passed because
Cathy had to wash the glass, which had
gotten dirty in the flooded basement.

   D After the hurricane passed, Cathy had gotten dirty in the flooded basement washing
the glass.

STOP

Standardized Test Practice

Answers and Analyses

1. A Students should recognize the original as a run-on sentence. The correct answer combines the clauses with the relative pronoun *that* and eliminates the unnecessary pronoun *it*.

2. H The underlined section contains two correct sentences that will read better when combined. The correct answer uses the conjunction *and* to join the independent clauses without changing their meaning, as is incorrectly done in choices F and G.

3. B Students should recognize that the two sentences should be combined. The correct answer combines the sentences by changing the first into a modifying phrase by removing the unnecessary pronoun and verb (*it was*).

Test-Taking Tip

Even if the original sentences are incorrect, tell students to try to imagine the best way of expressing the idea they are trying to convey before looking at the answer choices. Tell them to always make sure the answer choice they select preserves the original *meaning* of the sentences.

Test-Taking Tip

Have your students take note of which form of a verb is used, and let that guide them towards keeping the verb tense constant throughout the sentence. This can help them quickly eliminate wrong answers.

Standardized Test Practice

Tested Objective
- To recognize appropriate English usage within the context of a written passage

Answers and Analyses

1. **B** Students should recognize that the verb tense in this sentence needs to be consistent with the tense of the verbs in the sentences before and after it. The correct answer uses the present tense form *operates,* which agrees with the subject *compass.*

2. **H** This question asks for the correct verb tense. Since the passage is describing how magnets function in the present tense, the correct answer uses the present tense of the verb in the passive voice, *is attracted.*

3. **B** The question asks students to supply the superlative adjective, which describes the most or best of something. The correct answer, *quickest,* describes the fastest of all the possible routes home. Remind students that answer choice A, *quicker,* would be used only to compare two routes home.

4. **H** Student should recognize that this question asks them to provide a comparative adverb, one that modifies how you can perform an action—in this case, *reading a map.* The correct answer uses the comparative phrase *more clearly* to express how this action can be done with a *compass in hand.*

Test-Taking Tip

Have your students check the verbs surrounding a verb tense question for clues about which form of the verb to use. Remind them that consistency of verb tense is required within a sentence.

Standardized Test Practice

Read each passage and choose the word or group of words that belongs in each space. Mark the letter for your answer.

> If you have ever played with two bar magnets, you probably discovered that the ends with opposite charges attract one another. A compass ___(1)___ under this basic scientific principle. The needle of a compass is actually a tiny, lightweight magnet. This magnet ___(2)___ to the Earth's magnetic field. Like a bar magnet, the Earth has two oppositely charged poles. The south end of the compass needle is therefore attracted to the Earth's North Pole. This is why a compass needle always points due north. A compass is a very useful device, often providing lost travelers with the ___(3)___ route home. You may find that you can read a map ___(4)___ with a compass in hand.

1 A operate
  B operates
  C will operate
  D has operated

2 F will be attracted
  G was attracted
  H is attracted
  J had been attracted

3 A quicker
  B quickest
  C most quick
  D most quickest

4 F clear
  G most clear
  H more clearly
  J clearliest

Louis Pasteur developed the process now known as pasteurization in the mid-1800s. __(1)__ discovered that many diseases and infections are caused by microorganisms. Some of these microorganisms __(2)__ in fluids, including the milk we drink. When milk is pasteurized, it is heated for a specific period of time. This process __(3)__ most bacteria and other harmful microorganisms. Pasteurization also __(4)__ to keep food fresh and prevent spoilage. Before Louis Pasteur introduced pasteurization to the world, many people contracted diseases from milk and other food products.

1 **A** You
   B We
   C They
   D He

2 **F** are found
   G found
   H had been found
   J will be found

3 **A** killed
   B is killing
   C kills
   D has killed

4 **F** help
   G helps
   H helped
   J had helped

STOP

Standardized Test Practice

Answers and Analyses

1. **D** The question asks students to provide the correct pronoun. Explain to your students how they must examine the pronoun's antecedent in order to determine which pronoun to use. The correct answer uses the singular third person pronoun *He,* because the antecedent is *Louis Pasteur.*

2. **F** Students should recognize this question as a verb tense question. The passage requires consistency in the present, so the correct answer is the present plural form of *to find,* (*are found*). Explain to your students that choice G, *found,* would be correct if not for the structure of the sentence.

3. **C** The question asks students to provide the correct verb form. The correct answer uses the simple present, *kills,* to describe what action the process performs on bacteria.

4. **G** Again, the student is asked to provide the proper verb form. The correct answer is *helps,* because the verb must agree with the subject *pasteurization,* and since the sentence before requires the present tense (*kills*).

 THE PRINCETON REVIEW **Test-Taking Tip**

Encourage students to review the basic parts of speech, such as the pronoun. Pronouns stand in for nouns. Which pronoun to use depends on which noun the pronoun is replacing and what function it has in the sentence. If the noun is the subject of the sentence, use a personal pronoun (*I, you, he, she, it, we,* and *they*). One way to identify subjects is to ask, "Is the word doing something or performing an action?" If the answer is yes, the word is the subject of the sentence.

Standardized Test Practice

Tested Objective

- To recognize appropriate English usage within the context of a written passage

Answers and Analyses

1. **C** The question asks students to distinguish between noun and verb forms. The correct answer requires a plural noun. A singular noun would be preceded by an article—*a* or *the*. Therefore, the correct answer is *viewers*.

2. **F** Students should recognize this question as testing verb form. The correct answer needs to agree with the subject *fireflies,* and must be in the present tense. The passage has used the present tense throughout, so *float* is correct.

3. **B** This question asks students for the correct form of the possessive pronoun. Remind students to check carefully for the pronoun's antecedent, which is *fireflies,* so the correct form of the possessive pronoun is *their.*

4. **G** Students should recognize that this question asks them for a comparative adjective to make the comparison between the *multitude of different patterns.* The correct answer compares two nouns, *some* (*patterns*) and *other* (*patterns*). Therefore, the comparative adjective takes the form *more complex.*

 Test-Taking Tip

Suggest to students that before looking at the answer choices, they come up with an answer in their heads. If they go directly to the answer choices, they could more easily confuse themselves.

Standardized Test Practice

Read each passage and choose the word or group of words that belongs in each space. Mark the letter for your answer.

Have you ever stood out in a field on a summer evening and watched the fireflies twinkle in the moonlight? Fireflies do not perform this spectacle for the benefit of human __(1)__. The fireflies' glow is actually part of a complex mating ritual. With over fifty species of fireflies, it is difficult for fireflies to find the appropriate mate. Male fireflies __(2)__ through the air, flashing specific patterns. On the ground, female fireflies of the same species respond with __(3)__ own corresponding pattern. This is how the male firefly knows it is safe to land. Depending on how many species are in the air, you may see a multitude of different patterns. Some are __(4)__ than others.

1 **A** viewer
  B views
  C viewers
  D viewed

2 **F** float
  G floated
  H had floated
  J will float

3 **A** our
  B their
  C your
  D its

4 **F** complex
  G more complex
  H most complex
  J complexer

Throughout history, ____(1)____ farmers have had to find ways to protect their crops from birds and other pests. The American farmers of the eighteenth century used scarecrows. These straw men looked realistic enough to frighten animals away. The ancient Egyptians also devised a clever way to defend ____(2)____ fields. Using four poles, they suspended large nets over nearby trees. When a flock came to roost, the net ____(3)____, capturing the birds.

Early Japanese farmers ____(4)____ on a different trick. They would hang dirty rags and fish skeletons from sticks and would place these sticks out in the field and set them on fire. The smell was enough to drive the birds and animals away.

1 A imagine
  B imaginative
  C imagined
  D imagination

2 F your
  G its
  H their
  J our

3 A has been dropped
  B is dropped
  C was dropped
  D have been dropped

4 F relied
  G will rely
  H are relying
  J rely

Standardized Test Practice

Answers and Analyses

1. **B** This question asks students to provide the adjectival form of a word. Explain to your students that the correct answer must modify *farmers; imaginative* is the adjective required.

2. **H** Students should recognize that the question is asking for the possessive form of a pronoun. Since the antecedent is *Egyptians,* the third person plural form *their* is required.

3. **C** The question asks students for the correct verb tense. Since the sentence before it uses *suspended,* and the sentence itself uses the simple past *came,* the correct answer is the past form of *to drop—was dropped.*

4. **F** The question asks students for the correct verb tense. Since the past tense is used throughout the passage, the correct answer is the past form of *to rely— relied.* Point out to your students that the subject *Early Japanese farmers,* which refers to something in the past, is another clue that the past tense is required.

 Test-Taking Tip

Remind your students that irregular verbs do not use the suffix *-ed* to create the past tense.

 Test-Taking Tip

Encourage students to review subject-verb agreement. In a sentence, the form of the verb needs to agree with the subject. This means that if the sentence has a singular subject (*I, the man*) it should also have a singular verb (*I ran, the man climbed the stairs*). If the subject is plural, the verb must agree with it.

869

Standardized Test Practice

Standardized Test Practice

Tested Objective

- To recognize appropriate English usage within the context of a written passage

Answers and Analyses

1. **B** Students should recognize that the sentence requires a verb. Clues for verb tense can be found in the sentences surrounding the blank. In the previous sentence, the verb *saw* is the simple past, and the sentence itself uses the verb *wondered,* so the correct answer is the simple past form of *to manage—managed.*

2. **H** The question asks for the correct form of the pronoun. Since the antecedent is *computers,* a plural noun, the correct answer is *them.*

3. **C** Students are asked to compare two nouns with a comparative adjective. The correct answer, *more beautiful,* compares the *grandfather's handwriting* with *Hector's scribbles.* Point out to your students that the word *than* is a hint that they are being asked to compare two items.

4. **H** Students should understand that the sentence requires a verb. Since past tense has been used throughout the passage and the subject is *grandfather,* a singular noun, the correct answer is *was taught,* the passive form of the simple past tense of *to teach.* Remind your students that *teach* is an irregular verb.

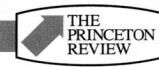
THE PRINCETON REVIEW | Test-Taking Tip

Remind your students of the most common suffixes and the forms of the word they can create (*-ful* for an adjective; *-ion* for a noun; *-ly* for an adverb; *-es* for some plural nouns)

Read each passage and choose the word or group of words that belongs in each space. Mark the letter for your answer.

While perusing an old family scrapbook, Hector noticed several handwritten letters. He wondered how people ____(1)____ without computers. He could not imagine life without ____(2)____. Fascinated, Hector read all of the letters, paying attention to the penmanship. Everybody in his family seemed to have beautiful handwriting.

Hector asked his grandfather about it. "Why is your handwriting ____(3)____ than my scribbles?"

Hector's grandfather explained that he ____(4)____ penmanship at school. "You don't need to write as much as I did," said Grandfather, "because you do your homework on the computer and you only send e-mail."

1 **A** will manage
  B managed
  C managing
  D had been managed

2 **F** it
  G us
  H them
  J you

3 **A** beautifulest
  B most beautiful
  C more beautiful
  D beauty

4 **F** has been taught
  G is taught
  H was taught
  J were taught

Standardized Test Practice

Standardized Test Practice

Answers and Analyses

Have you ever admired the stamp on a letter you received? You might consider becoming a philatelist. A philatelist is someone who collects and ___(1)___ postage stamps. Each country issues ___(2)___ own stamps. The United States releases over a hundred different stamps a year.

Of the thousands of images, some of the ___(3)___ are of historical figures, animals, sports stars, or popular cultural heroes. A stamp collection can be organized according to country, theme, or type. Some people ___(4)___ to the beauty of stamps, while others are interested in their history and monetary value. The next time that you see a stamp on a letter, consider cutting it out and starting your own collection.

1 A will study
  B is studying
  C studies
  D has studied

2 F his
  G our
  H your
  J its

3 A most popular
  B more popularly
  C popularly
  D popular

4 F will be attracted
  G was attracted
  H has been attracted
  J are attracted

1. C The question asks students for the correct form of the verb. Since the first part of the sentence uses the present tense *collects,* the correct answer must also be in the present tense, *studies.*

2. J Students should recognize that the sentence requires a possessive pronoun. Since the antecedent is *Each country,* which is singular, the correct answer is the singular third person *its.* Explain to your students the difference between the possessive pronoun *its* and the contraction *it's.*

3. A The question asks students to provide a superlative adjective to modify *images.* Since they are asked to compare more than two nouns in *thousands of images,* the correct answer is *most popular.*

4. J Students should recognize that the sentence requires a verb. By examining the verbs surrounding the blank, students can see that *are interested* is the passive form of the past tense. Therefore, the correct answer, which also agrees with the plural subject *Some people,* is *are attracted.*

THE PRINCETON REVIEW **Test-Taking Tip**

Make sure students are familiar with indefinite pronouns such as *each, some,* and *any,* and make sure they know whether to use the singular or plural form of the verb with each indefinite pronoun.

Standardized Test Practice

Tested Objective

- To recognize appropriate English usage within the context of a written passage

Answers and Analyses

1. **C** The question requires students to supply an adjective comparing more than two time periods. The correct answer is the superlative adjective *earliest*. Explain to your students that choice A, *most earliest,* is redundant in its superlatives because you do not need to add both *-est* and *most* to make a comparative adjectival phrase.

2. **H** Students should recognize that the sentence requires a verb. The context and meaning of the sentence calls for the present tense. The bridge still exists, therefore it *stretches*. The verb in the following sentence (*is open*) is also in the present tense.

3. **D** Students should recognize the need for a verb in the appropriate verb tense. Here, the clue comes in the form of a date, *May of 1997*. Since this is a date in the past, the correct answer is the past form of *to complete*—(*completed*). Explain to students that the passive form of the past tense is needed because the bridge is the receiver of the action.

4. **F** The question asks students to identify the correct pronoun. Since the antecedent is a plural noun, *owners,* the correct pronoun is the plural subject pronoun, *They*. Explain to your students that the pronoun case *Them* can not serve as the subject of a sentence.

THE PRINCETON REVIEW | **Test-Taking Tip**

Suggest that students break down the sentences into their different parts: the subject, verb, and object. They can use this method to figure out what type of word the blank space requires. What is the missing element?

Standardized Test Practice

Read each passage and choose the word or group of words that belongs in each space. Mark the letter for your answer.

> Since humanity's ___(1)___ days, bridges have been built to make getting from one place to another possible. The world's longest bridge over ice-covered water, called the Confederation Bridge, ___(2)___ from Prince Edward Island to New Brunswick in the Canadian northeast. The 12.9 kilometer bridge ___(3)___ in May of 1997 and is open 24 hours a day, seven days a week.
>
> Safety considerations played a major role in the design of the bridge. The owners of the bridge made sure that it was curved in order to keep drivers alert. ___(4)___ also included 7,300 road drains to keep precipitation from collecting on the bridge.

1 **A** most earliest
   B more earliest
   C earliest
   D earlier

2 **F** stretched
   G had stretched
   H stretches
   J will stretch

3 **A** completes
   B completed
   C had completed
   D was completed

4 **F** They
   G Them
   H Us
   J She

Standardized Test Practice

One of the biggest problems facing cartographers, or people who make maps, is the fact that the Earth is round. Since a flat map, called a projection, can't ___(1)___ show the curved surface of the Earth, it will always distort the way the Earth looks to some extent. Some projections, including the very ___(2)___ Mercator projection, show things in more or less their real shape, but distort their relative sizes. Others, such as the Lambert projection, show the continents in more or less ___(3)___ relative sizes, but are forced to distort their shapes.

You can tell how much distortion a map has by looking at its lines of latitude and longitude. The latitude lines should be parallel and equal distances apart. Longitude lines should be farther apart at the equator, and should ___(4)___ poles.

1 A more accurate
   B accurate
   C accurately
   D most accurater

2 F commonly
   G common
   H more commoner
   J most commonly

3 A their
   B your
   C its
   D our

4 F converge
   G had converged
   H was converging
   J converged

Standardized Test Practice

Answers and Analyses

1. C Students are asked to identify the correct adverbial form of the word *accurate*. The answer choice must modify the verb *show*. The correct answer choice is *accurately*. Explain to your students that answer choice B, *accurate*, is the adjectival form of *accurate*.

2. G Students are asked to identify the correct adjectival form of the word *common*. The correct answer must modify the noun phrase *Mercator projection*. Since the answer is not an adverb, because it does not modify a verb, and since the word is not making a comparison, the correct answer is *common*.

3. A Students should recognize this as a possessive pronoun question. Since the antecedent is *continents,* a plural noun, the possessive form of the pronoun is *their*.

4. F The question asks students to provide the proper verb tense. Since the previous sentences describe *the map* in the present, *should be,* the correct answer should be in the same tense: *should converge.*

THE PRINCETON REVIEW **Test-Taking Tip**

Encourage your students to review the superlative adjective and comparative adjective. Superlatives describe the most or best of something. The superlative is created with the word *most + the adjective.* The comparative adjective compares two things with each other. For one-syllable words such as *fast,* a comparative adjective is formed by adding *-er* to the adjective (*faster*), a superlative, by adding *-est.*

Standardized Test Practice

Tested Objective

- To proofread for spelling, punctuation, and capitalization errors within the context of a written passage

Answers and Analyses

1. B Students should recognize a capitalization error. *Summer* does not require capitalization because it is not a proper noun.

2. F The error is one of spelling. *Informative* is spelled incorrectly.

3. B The error is one of capitalization. Since the *United States Defense Department* is a proper noun naming a specific institution, each of its words should be capitalized.

4. F Students should recognize that there is a spelling error in the underlined section. *Shopping* requires two *p*s.

5. D The underlined portion is correct as written. There are no errors.

6. F *Deside* is spelled incorrectly. The correct spelling is *decide.*

THE PRINCETON REVIEW | Test-Taking Tip

Remind students that compass headings—north, south, east, west, etc.—are capitalized only when they indicate specific regions. The rule is capitalize locations, but not directions.

THE PRINCETON REVIEW | Test-Taking Tip

Suggest to your students that they make a list of the kinds of words that need to be capitalized. Some examples: proper names (people, places, organizations), days of the week, months of the year, book titles.

874

Standardized Test Practice

Read each passage and decide which type of error, if any, appears in each underlined section. Mark the letter for your answer.

Every summer, <u>kids attend Edward's Summer camp to learn</u> how to use the Internet. Many of them have
(1)
never used the computer for more than playing video games. At the camp they <u>learn to use the many info-</u>
<u>mative sites on the Internet.</u> They also learn about the origins of the Internet.
(2)

<u>The Internet was originally created in 1983 by the United States defense department</u> and was further
(3)
developed by the National Science Foundation. At first, only researchers and scientists used this network.
Now the Internet connects millions of computers. It is used <u>for banking, publishing, business, and even</u>
<u>shoping.</u> Students use it to research papers, and many people write to each other <u>through e-mail because it</u>
(4)
<u>is faster than regular mail.</u>
(5)

By the end of the summer, many of the kids will have built their own web sites by using a programming
code called HTML. <u>Some will even deside that the Internet can be more fun than video games!</u>
(6)

---

1 A Spelling error
  B Capitalization error
  C Punctuation error
  D No error

2 F Spelling error
  G Capitalization error
  H Punctuation error
  J No error

3 A Spelling error
  B Capitalization error
  C Punctuation error
  D No error

4 F Spelling error
  G Capitalization error
  H Punctuation error
  J No error

5 A Spelling error
  B Capitalization error
  C Punctuation error
  D No error

6 F Spelling error
  G Capitalization error
  H Punctuation error
  J No error

Standardized Test Practice

Bicycles are a great means of transportation and <u>also a source of pleasure for many people. Actually,</u> it
(1)
was not always so easy to ride a bicycle. <u>The first two-wheeled rider-propelled machine appeared in 1818.</u> It
(2)
was made of wood and the seated rider moved simply by pushing his feet along the ground.

The most practical early version of the bicycle <u>was invented by the michaux family of Paris in the 1860s.</u>
(3)
Its iron and wood construction and lack of springs earned it the nickname "boneshaker." It was driven by
pedaling cranks on the axle of the front wheel. To increase the distance it covered for each turn of the
cranks, the front wheel was enlarged. <u>In england, this bicycle was popularly referred to as a "penny-far-
(4)
thing."</u> The nickname <u>came from the smallest and largest british coins of the time</u> and referred to the small
(5)
and large wheels of the bicycle.

<u>In fact the bicycle would be reinvented several times more</u> before becoming the quick and sturdy two-
(6)
wheeler we know today.

1 A Spelling error
   B Capitalization error
   C Punctuation error
   D No error

2 F Spelling error
   G Capitalization error
   H Punctuation error
   J No error

3 A Spelling error
   B Capitalization error
   C Punctuation error
   D No error

4 F Spelling error
   G Capitalization error
   H Punctuation error
   J No error

5 A Spelling error
   B Capitalization error
   C Punctuation error
   D No error

6 F Spelling error
   G Capitalization error
   H Punctuation error
   J No error

STOP

28.3 Standardized Test Practice **875**

Standardized Test Practice

Answers and Analyses

1. D The sentence is correct as written. There are no errors.
2. H Students should recognize that there is a punctuation error in the underlined section. The sentence contains a list of adjectives that must be separated by commas. The corrected sentence would have a comma after *two-wheeled.*
3. B The question asks students to capitalize a proper noun. *Michaux*, the family name, should be capitalized.
4. G This question asks students to capitalize a geographical name. *England* should be capitalized.
5. B Students should recognize that there is an error in capitalization. *British* should be capitalized because it is a proper adjective.
6. H The underlined portion contains a punctuation error. The introductory phrase, *in fact,* should be set off by a comma.

THE PRINCETON REVIEW   **Test-Taking Tip**

Remind students of the basic rules for commas. Commas are used to separate two independent clauses connected by conjunctions (*and, but, or,* etc.); to separate items in a list or a series of words; to separate an introductory phrase or clause from the independent clause; to set off words or phrases that interrupt the sentence; and to separate a direct quotation from surrounding comments.

Standardized Test Practice

Tested Objective

- To proofread for spelling, punctuation, and capitalization errors within the context of a written passage

Answers and Analyses

1. **B** Students should recognize a capitalization error. *Industry* should not be capitalized because it is not a proper noun.
2. **H** Students should recognize that the underlined section contains a punctuation error. Items in a list should be separated by commas. The corrected sentence would have a comma after *editing*.
3. **A** The underlined section contains a spelling error. *Candadate* is spelled incorrectly. The correct spelling is *candidate*.
4. **J** The underlined portion is correct as written. There are no errors.

THE
PRINCETON
REVIEW   **Test-Taking Tip**

Explain to your students that words with double consonants are often misspelled in these types of writing tests. Try to come up with a short list of words that fit this description (examples: *disappear, arrival, roommate*).

THE
PRINCETON
REVIEW   **Test-Taking Tip**

A review of other common spelling errors may be useful. For example, forgetting to drop the *e* when adding the *-ing* suffix to some verbs (*abusing, forgiving*).

Standardized Test Practice

Read each passage and decide which type of error, if any, appears in each underlined section. Mark the letter for your answer.

Mr. Louis Alvarez
First Class Publishing
301 Rio Grande
Austin, TX 78701

Dear Mr. Alvarez:

It was a pleasure meeting you yesterday. The tour of your <u>office was very informative; I really enjoyed</u>
<u>learning about the publishing Industry.</u> As I mentioned to you, I am interested in many <u>aspects of the pub-</u>
(1)
<u>lishing business, including editing marketing, and sales.</u>
(2)

I hope you will <u>continue to consider me as a strong candadate for the position at your company.</u> A sum-
(3)
mer internship with a professional publishing house is a wonderful opportunity. It is a <u>chance for me to</u>
<u>gain firsthand knowledge as well as valuable life experience.</u>
(4)

Thank you for your consideration.

Sincerely,

Marcia Dooley

1 A Spelling error
  B Capitalization error
  C Punctuation error
  D No error

2 F Spelling error
  G Capitalization error
  H Punctuation error
  J No error

3 A Spelling error
  B Capitalization error
  C Punctuation error
  D No error

4 F Spelling error
  G Capitalization error
  H Punctuation error
  J No error

Standardized Test Practice

The ancient greeks held the first Olympic Games centuries ago. Their Olympics were much different
(1)
from the Games of today. For example, the ancient Olympics had fewer events. Some of these events
included the following, boxing, running, chariot racing, and wrestling. The Pentathlon, one of its most
(2)
famous contests, actually combined five different events. Of all the compatitions, perhaps the most difficult
(3)
was the armored race. In this event, Olympic athletes ran the length of the stadium while wearing a full suit
of armor. This armor could weigh as much as sixty pounds. There are images of the ancient Olympic
(4)
Games on the pottery and other artwork of the period.

1 A Spelling error
   B Capitalization error
   C Punctuation error
   D No error

2 F Spelling error
   G Capitalization error
   H Punctuation error
   J No error

3 A Spelling error
   B Capitalization error
   C Punctuation error
   D No error

4 F Spelling error
   G Capitalization error
   H Punctuation error
   J No error

Standardized Test Practice

Answers and Analyses

1. B The question contains a capitalization error. *Greeks* should be capitalized.
2. H Students should recognize that a punctuation error occurs in the underlined section. A colon must be placed at the beginning of a list. The corrected sentence would have a colon before *boxing*.
3. A The underlined section contains a spelling error. *Competitions* is spelling incorrectly.
4. J The sentence is correct as written. There are no errors.

 Test-Taking Tip

On writing tests such as these, there are only three types of errors to look for: spelling, punctuation, and capitalization. Encourage students to first read the text with only spelling errors in mind. If no error is found, they should reread the text with only capitalization errors in mind. Finally, if no errors are found, they should reread the text one last time for punctuation errors. If your students narrow their focus, these questions may become easier for them.

Standardized Test Practice

Tested Objective

- To proofread for spelling, punctuation, and capitalization errors within the context of a written passage

Answers and Analyses

1. **C** Students should recognize a punctuation error. *Code breaking* is an appositive for *cryptography,* so it needs to be set off by commas.
2. **G** The question contains an error in capitalization. *War* should be capitalized in *Second World War.*
3. **A** The underlined section contains a spelling error. The correct spelling is *obsessive.*
4. **J** The underlined portion is correct as written. There are no errors.
5. **A** The underlined section contains a spelling error. The correct spelling is *hypothesis.*
6. **G** Students should understand that the underlined section contains a capitalization error. *Japanese,* a proper adjective, should be capitalized.

THE PRINCETON REVIEW Test-Taking Tip

It might be useful to review the rules for using quotation marks with students. Quotation marks should be placed around direct quotations. Quotation marks always come in pairs. Make sure your students find an opening and closing quotation mark when someone is speaking in the text. A comma appears within the quotation marks to separate the quote from explanatory words that follow: for example, "I like chocolate cake," said Francis. Commas do not appear if the quotation ends with an exclamation point or a question mark: for example, "Would you like to be my partner?" she asked.

Standardized Test Practice

Read each passage and decide which type of error, if any, appears in each underlined section. Mark the letter for your answer.

Cryptography, or <u>code breaking is a highly important aspect of wartime strategy.</u> Although they work
(1)
far from the battle, code breakers are central players in any army.

One of the most <u>brilliant code breakers in the Second World war was Commander</u> Joseph J. Rochefort.
(2)
He worked in Pear Harbor, Hawaii. <u>He was obsesive about his work, and went</u> for long periods without eat-
(3)
ing or sleeping in order to break the Japanese codes.

In 1942, Rochefort realized that the piece of <u>Japanese code "AF" really meant Midway Island. However,</u>
(4)
his superiors were not sure he was right, so Rochefort designed an experiment to test his <u>hypathesis. He told</u>
(5)
<u>the people on Midway to send</u> a message out about water trouble on the island. He knew the Japanese
would intercept the message and decode it easily. The <u>next day he picked up a japanese transmission about</u>
(6)
water trouble on AF. He knew he was right.

1 A Spelling error
  B Capitalization error
  C Punctuation error
  D No error

2 F Spelling error
  G Capitalization error
  H Punctuation error
  J No error

3 A Spelling error
  B Capitalization error
  C Punctuation error
  D No error

4 F Spelling error
  G Capitalization error
  H Punctuation error
  J No error

5 A Spelling error
  B Capitalization error
  C Punctuation error
  D No error

6 F Spelling error
  G Capitalization error
  H Punctuation error
  J No error

Standardized Test Practice

Native to Tasmania and southern and eastern australia, the platypus is a strange animal indeed. It is a
(1)
mammal, but it lays eggs. It has dense fur, like a beaver's, and has a bill that resembles a duck's. The platypus
(2)
is a semi-aquatic animal. The platypus lives in a long burrow, which it digs by the banks of rivers. With its
flat tail and webbed feet, the platypus is very agile in the water. Useing its elongated snout, the platypus can
stir up the mud at the rivers bottom where it finds food. The platypus subsists on a diet of worms shellfish,
(4)   (5)
and insects. A shy animal by nature, the platypus is rarely observed in the wild.

1 A Spelling error
  B Capitalization error
  C Punctuation error
  D No error

2 F Spelling error
  G Capitalization error
  H Punctuation error
  J No error

3 A Spelling error
  B Capitalization error
  C Punctuation error
  D No error

4 F Spelling error
  G Capitalization error
  H Punctuation error
  J No error

5 A Spelling
  B Capitalization
  C Punctuation
  D No error

28.3 Standardized Test Practice **879**

Standardized Test Practice

Answers and Analyses

1. B The question asks students to capitalize a geographic name. *Australia* should be capitalized. Explain to your students that *southern* and *eastern* do not need to be capitalized because they are merely directional parts of a geographic description.

2. J The underlined portion is correct as written. There are no errors.

3. A *Useing* is spelled incorrectly. The correct spelling is *Using.*

4. H Students should recognize a punctuation error. The corrected sentence would place an apostrophe before the *s* in *rivers* to show possession.

5. C This question asks students to punctuate the items in a list. The corrected portion would include a comma after *worms,* thereby separating the items in a list with commas.

THE PRINCETON REVIEW | **Test-Taking Tip**

Remind students that a colon is a punctuation mark that means *as follows.* Use colons when making lists. For example, I learned three important lessons on my last job: meet deadlines, work hard, and retain a sense of humor.

Standardized Test Practice

Tested Objective

- To proofread for spelling, punctuation, and capitalization errors within the context of a written passage

Answers and Analyses

1. A *bellowd* is spelled incorrectly. The correct spelling is *bellowed*. Remind your students that the suffix *-ed* is added to regular verbs to place them in the past tense.
2. H Students should recognize that the underlined section contains a punctuation error. To set off the adverbial clause, a comma should be added after *tight*.
3. C Students should recognize a punctuation error. Spoken words and direct speech need to be surrounded by quotation marks. The underlined portion should read *"All is well down here."*
4. F *fourty* is spelled incorrectly. The correct spelling is *forty*.
5. B The question asks students to recognize a capitalization error. *Iron* should not be capitalized because it is an adjective describing *the ladder*.
6. J The underlined portion is correct as written. There are no errors.
7. B Students should recognize a capitalization error. Since *Bullhorn Gold Company* is a proper noun, each of its words should be capitalized.

THE
PRINCETON
REVIEW **Test-Taking Tip**

Remind your students to capitalize the first word of a direct quotation.

Standardized Test Practice

Read each passage and decide which type of error, if any, appears in each underlined section. Mark the letter for your answer choice on your paper.

"Look out below!" George bellowd loudly as he tossed the rope down into the hole. Once his end of the
(1)   (2)
rope was tight he leaned toward the opening of the mine and listened carefully.

"All is well down here, called the foreman from deep inside the mine. He had climbed the fourty feet to
(3)   (4)
the bottom of the well earlier in the day and had been working ever since. However, when he had tried to
(5)
climb back up the Iron ladder that was fixed to the wall of the mine, one of the supports had broken. He

had been waiting for George to arrive with a rope that was sturdy enough to get him out of the Bullhorn
(6)   (7)
Gold company's mine.

Slowly the foreman reached the mouth of the mine, struggling, with George's help, to hoist himself out onto the ground.

---

1 A Spelling error
  B Capitalization error
  C Punctuation error
  D No error

2 F Spelling error
  G Capitalization error
  H Punctuation error
  J No error

3 A Spelling error
  B Capitalization error
  C Punctuation error
  D No error

4 F Spelling error
  G Capitalization error
  H Punctuation error
  J No error

5 A Spelling error
  B Capitalization error
  C Punctuation error
  D No error

6 F Spelling error
  G Capitalization error
  H Punctuation error
  J No error

7 A Spelling error
  B Capitalization error
  C Punctuation error
  D No error

Standardized Test Practice

Lila slowly opened her jewelry box and peeked inside <u>cautiosly</u> at the contents. Since she had been a
(1)
child <u>growing up in the mountains of colombia, she had dreamt of having</u> her very own emeralds. <u>For gen-</u>
(2)   (3)
<u>erations her family had worked as gem stone cutters',</u> but <u>had been too poor to afford any of the prescious</u>
(4)
<u>stones for themselves.</u>

"I almost can't <u>believe that you are real," she whispered to the stones. You are too lovely</u> and too perfect
(5)
to belong in my jewelry box." Lila paused as she thought about how the stones had come to be in her possession. <u>Her Father had saved every spare penny for many years to buy these stones</u> for Lila as a gift.
(6)
Yesterday, the <u>day before Lila was to be married, her father had given her two emerald earrings.</u> Now, as she
(7)
prepared to leave for the church, she took the gems out and put them on.

1 A Spelling error
   B Capitalization error
   C Punctuation error
   D No error

2 F Spelling error
   G Capitalization error
   H Punctuation error
   J No error

3 A Spelling error
   B Capitalization error
   C Punctuation error
   D No error

4 F Spelling error
   G Capitalization error
   H Punctuation error
   J No error

5 A Spelling error
   B Capitalization error
   C Punctuation error
   D No error

6 F Spelling error
   G Capitalization error
   H Punctuation error
   J No error

7 A Spelling error
   B Capitalization error
   C Punctuation error
   D No error

STOP

28.3 Standardized Test Practice **881**

Standardized Test Practice

Answers and Analyses

1. A *cautiosly* is misspelled. The correct spelling is *cautiously*.

2. G Students should recognize this as a capitalization error. The geographic name *Colombia* should be capitalized. Explain to your students that *mountains* does not need to be capitalized because it does not refer to a particular place or geographic name.

3. C The question asks students to recognize a punctuation error. *Cutters'* is not a possessive, so there is no need for the apostrophe. It is simply a plural noun.

4. F *prescious* is spelled incorrectly. The correct spelling is *precious*.

5. C This question asks students to correctly punctuate a spoken phrase. A spoken phrase must be surrounded by quotation marks. The corrected version would read *"You are too lovely and too perfect to belong in my jewelry box."*

6. G This question asks students to recognize a capitalization error. *Father* does not need to be capitalized because it does not stand unmodified as a substitute for the person's name. The possessive prounoun *Her* should modify a lowercase *father*.

7. D The underlined portion is correct as written. There are no errors.

 Test-Taking Tip

Point out to students that on writing tests like these, they should not assume that just because an underlined portion consists of punctuation, it is incorrect.

✔ ASSESSMENT OPTIONS

📁 *Tests with Answer Key & Rubrics*
Unit 28 Mastery Test, pp. 105–106

💾 *Testmaker*
Unit 28 Mastery Test

📼 *MindJogger Videoquizzes*

You may wish to administer the Unit 28 Mastery Test at this point.

Objectives

- To develop the ability, by following guidelines and applying new strategies, to listen and speak effectively, to work in groups, and to conduct an interview
- To learn and apply criteria for evaluating spoken messages that are either persuasive or literary
- To present oral reports prepared for by listening actively and by working in groups; to prepare for, draft, and deliver a formal speech; and to write an account of an interview that students have conducted themselves

Key to Ability Levels

L1 Level 1 activities are within the basic ability range of students.

L2 Level 2 activities are within the ability range of average students.

L3 Level 3 activities are more challenging activities.

Listening and Speaking

Lesson 29.1	Listening Effectively	883
Lesson 29.2	Speaking Effectively	887
Lesson 29.3	Working in Groups	891
Lesson 29.4	Conducting an Interview	892

882

Resource Manager

Planning Resources
- *Lesson Plans*
- *Block Scheduling*

 Transparencies
- *Bellringer*
- *Daily Language Practice*

📁 **Other Print Resources**
- *Listening and Speaking Activities*
- *Tests with Answer Key and Rubrics*
- *Thinking and Study Skills*

 Video
- *MindJogger Videoquizzes*

💾 **Software**
- *Presentation Plus!*
- *Testmaker*
- *Writer's Choice Puzzlemaker*

 Web Sites
- *writerschoice.glencoe.com*

29.1 Listening Effectively

Your ability to listen effectively can help you be more successful in school, sports, jobs, and personal relationships. Studies show that the average person comprehends only about half of what he or she hears and remembers only about half of that. In this lesson, you'll learn how to improve your listening comprehension.

Listening Actively

Whether you're listening to a friend, a coach, or a teacher, you need to do more than just hear what the person says. Only by listening actively will you be able to understand, interpret, and respond to what you hear. The chart below shows some important types of active listening. Keep in mind, however, that these types of listening cannot really be neatly separated. For any particular situation, you will probably need to use a combination of these types of listening.

Types of Listening

Type	Example
Empathic listening: understanding and responding to another's feelings	Participating in an informal conversation with a friend who needs advice
Critical listening: separating facts from opinions and evaluating the speaker's message	Listening to a persuasive message such as a political speech or a commercial
Reflective listening: identifying main ideas and thinking about their implications	Listening to an informational message, such as a history lecture
Appreciative listening: enjoying and interpreting a performance	Listening to a spoken performance of a short story

Even though particular listening situations differ greatly, you can still benefit from understanding general strategies for active listening. The following chart presents such strategies.

Active Listening Strategies

Prepare to Listen

- **Eliminate physical distractions.** Make yourself comfortable and put away whatever you're working on.
- **Clear your mind of other thoughts.** Don't think about your schedule for the day or what you're going to do over the weekend.
- **Adopt a positive attitude and an open mind about what you are going to hear.** Don't prejudge the speaker or jump to conclusions about the message before you have listened to everything the speaker has to say. *(continued)*

Focus

Lesson Overview

Objective
- To learn strategies for effective listening

Skills
- listening; interpreting visual cues; summarizing

Critical Thinking
- analyzing; evaluating

Listening and Speaking
- listening attentively; questioning; listening to persuasive and literary presentations; discussing

Bellringer
Daily Language Activity

When students enter the classroom, have this assignment on the board: *Write a list of tips for good listening.*

See also *Daily Language Practice*

Motivating Activity

Ask about half of the students to share their lists from the Bellringer assignment with the class. Discuss their ideas with these students. Then ask students in the other half of the class to summarize the discussion they just heard.

Listening and Speaking

Resource Manager

Planning Resources
- *Lesson Plans*

Transparencies
- *Bellringer*
- *Daily Language Practice*

Other Print Resources
- *Listening and Speaking Activities*
- *Thinking and Study Skills, p. 34*

Teach

Charting Listening Types

Direct students' attention to the Types of Listening chart on student page 883. To help them remember and better understand the different types, discuss the definitions. Then have students come up with examples of their own. Encourage them to copy a simplified version of the chart into their notebooks or journals. **L2**

Active Listening Strategies

- **Identify the situation and the types of listening called for.** Does the situation call mainly for emphatic, critical, reflective, or appreciative listening?

Listen to the Message

- **Focus your attention on what the speaker is saying.** Don't jump ahead and think about what you want to say next.
- **Maintain your concentration by finding something of interest in the message.** Don't doodle, daydream, constantly look around, or become impatient for the speaker to finish.
- **Take notes if the situation calls for it.** Note taking is often useful for classroom presentations, speeches, and interviews.

Interpret the Message

- **Summarize the message.** Identify the purpose of the message and the main ideas or themes.
- **Reflect on what you hear.** Ask yourself: Does this information sound reasonable? Does it conflict with anything else I know?

Respond to the Message

- **Ask questions.** Clarify ideas and terms you don't understand and ask questions that relate to the topic.
- **Discuss the message.** Compare your interpretation with the interpretations of others.
- **Assess the message.** What significance or consequences does the message have for you or for others?

Analyzing and Evaluating What You Hear

The Active Listening Strategies on pages 883–884 can help you understand and interpret the messages you hear. But in certain situations, you'll want to do even more. Some situations—such as persuasive messages and performances of poems, short stories, plays, and other literary works—require you to critically analyze and evaluate what you hear.

How to Evaluate Persuasive Messages   You hear many persuasive messages—from friends, teachers, and parents; on the radio or television; and from a variety of other sources. Some of these messages are reasonable and worth acting on; others are not. How do you decide? Review Unit 6 Persuasive Writing on page 276. You can also use the following questions to analyze and evaluate persuasive messages.

Evaluating Persuasive Messages

- **Purpose.** What is the purpose of the message? In other words, what is the speaker trying to get people to do?
- **Audience.** To what audience is the message targeted?
- **Facts/opinions.** What are the facts and what are the opinions in the message? Do the facts support the opinions or claims? What necessary facts or opinions are missing?
- **Errors in reasoning.** Does the message contain errors in reasoning, such as over-generalization?
- **Persuasive techniques.** What kinds of persuasive techniques—such as loaded language, celebrity testimonial, and exaggeration—are used in the message? How does the message appeal to people's emotions?
- **Values and biases.** What values or biases does the message reflect? How do these values compare to yours?
- **Your opinion.** After analyzing the message, form your opinion. Do you agree, disagree, or need more information?

How to Evaluate Literary Performances Some literary works, such as poems and plays, are intended to be read aloud or performed. But even short stories and essays sometimes come alive more fully in a performance than in a silent reading. You can use the following questions both to assess literary performances and to improve your own performance of literary works.

Evaluating Literary Performances

- **Voice qualities.** Does the performer effectively use such voice qualities as volume, stress, tone, and pronunciation to present the work?
- **Body language.** Does the performer use body language—including posture, eye contact, facial expressions, gestures, and movements—to engage the audience and bring the work to life?
- **Literary elements.** What element of the literary work—such as character development, plot, imagery, rhyme, or figurative language—does the performance emphasize? What is the effect of this element?
- **Your rating.** How would you rate the performer's interpretation of the literary work? Why?

Practice and Assess

Evaluation Rubrics

Exercise 1 (p. 886)

Students should demonstrate effective use of the Active Listening Strategies by including the following:

- a brief description of the purpose of the message and a list of its main ideas
- specific comparisons or conflicts with information from other sources
- specific examples of the significance and consequence of the message

Exercise 2 (p. 886)

Responses will vary, but students' oral reports should clearly answer at least one question from each of the seven categories listed in the Evaluating Persuasive Messages chart on student page 885. As part of the exercise, instruct students to evaluate each oral report. In their notebooks, have students check off which evaluation categories each student was able to address.

Listening and Speaking

Practice and Assess

Evaluation Rubrics

Exercise 3

On their critique forms, for both the poem they performed and the poem they listened to, students should evaluate the performers' voice qualities, body language, and ability to convey one or more literary elements. Students' comparisons should include reasons why a performance was more or less successful. Students' lists of goals should indicate ways in which they can become more effective listeners as well as speakers.

Exercise 4

Students' evaluations should focus on the voice qualities of the performer and on one or more literary elements emphasized by the performer in the taped reading. Students should do more than simply rate the performer in each category. They should support their opinions with details drawn from the performance.

Additional Resources

 Listening and Speaking Activities
 Thinking and Study Skills, p. 34

Close

Ask students to name professions in which good listening and speaking are important. If students respond with only obvious careers like teaching, selling, and law, help them realize that most jobs require these skills.

Listening and Speaking

Exercise 1

Practice the Active Listening Strategies as you listen to an in-depth news program, a panel discussion, or an interview of a public figure on radio or television. Prepare and present an oral report on what you heard. Your report should include the following:

- a summary of the purpose of the message and the main ideas
- your reflections on the message
- a description of the significance or consequences of the message

Exercise 2

Listen to a television commercial that you like and use the questions in the Evaluating Persuasive Messages chart to write an analysis and evaluation of the commercial. Present your report orally to the class.

Exercise 3

Use the Evaluating Literary Performances chart to create a critique form. Then work with a partner to videotape each other performing a poetry reading. Watch the videotape and complete a critique form for both your performance and your partner's. Compare your evaluations with those of your partner. Make a list of goals for yourself for future presentations.

Exercise 4

Obtain an audiotape or videotape that contains a poetry or short story reading. Listen actively to the presentation and then fill out a critique form evaluating the performance.

29.2 Speaking Effectively

Think of some recent situations when you had to use your speaking skills. Have you spoken to a friend on the phone recently? Have you presented a report for one of your classes? Have you given anyone directions? Have you made a speech? Different types of speaking require different skills. In this lesson, you'll learn how to speak effectively when talking informally and when making formal speeches.

Speaking Informally

You speak informally all the time. Whether telling your friends about a television show you saw, explaining the causes of World War I when called on in class, or giving directions to the supermarket, you are speaking informally. In informal speaking, you do not usually plan what you will say, and often others do as much talking as you. The chart describes some typical informal speech situations.

Tips for Informal Speaking		
Type	**Description**	**Hint**
In-person and phone conversations	Conversations are the most common and least formal speaking situations. Subjects are usually spontaneous and varied, and each party both listens and speaks. A phone conversation, however, usually has a more defined purpose.	Letting others speak without interruption helps encourage participation of all those engaged in the conversation. A phone conversation will be more effective if you explain your reason for calling. Be sure to call at a time that is convenient for the person you are phoning and keep the call to a reasonable length.
Announcements	Announcements provide brief, important information about events, meetings, projects, and other such occurrences. Announcements should be clear and give all necessary details.	Encouraging questions after the announcement helps to ensure that you have clearly communicated the necessary information.
Giving directions or instructions	Providing directions or instructions usually involves an explanation of a procedure or process.	Present your points as a series of logical steps. Speak slowly and be sure the listener understands. Encourage the listener to ask questions. You might even ask questions yourself to help your listener understand.

29.2 Speaking Effectively **887**

Resource Manager

Planning Resources
- *Lesson Plans*

 Transparencies
- *Bellringer*
- *Daily Language Practice*

📁 **Other Print Resources**
- *Listening and Speaking Activities*
- *Thinking and Study Skills*, p. 34

Listening and Speaking

Focus

Lesson Overview

Objective
- To prepare for and deliver a formal speech

Skills
- applying tips on informal speaking; preparing and delivering a formal speech

Critical Thinking
- generating new information; relating to an audience

Listening and Speaking
- informal speaking; formal speaking

🔔 ## Bellringer
Daily Language Activity

When students enter the classroom, have this assignment on the board: *Recall a good speech you've heard. List reasons why you enjoyed it.*

See also *Daily Language Practice*

Motivating Activity

Ask students to recall times when they have been a speaker and to describe the ways listeners responded. For example, when giving a demonstration, could the student tell whether listeners were able to follow the steps? Did listeners ask questions or indicate confusion in any way?

Teach

Giving Informal Speeches

Divide the class into groups of six, and have the groups suggest a list of topics, such as class elections, sports rules, or how to make something. Students should take turns giving informal speeches, making sure to cover the types of informal speech described in the chart on student page 887: conversation, announcement, and direction or instruction giving. Other group members should observe and make a list of suggestions to help each speaker improve his or her style. **L2**

Teach

Narrowing the Topic

Emphasize the importance of narrowing the topic of the speech. As a general rule, the shorter the time allotted for the speech, the narrower the topic should be. Have students brainstorm speech topics; then work with them to narrow each topic and develop a thesis statement. **L2**

Preparing a Speech

Some students will need help dealing with the stress of preparing for and giving a formal speech. Such an assignment would need scaling down for some students. Review the seven steps in preparing and delivering a speech described on student pages 888–890. Help students choose a familiar, concrete topic; organize their time to do the research; and organize the information for their speech. Explain that, as with the similar five-stage writing process, any steps in the process may be repeated. **L1**

◄ Cross-reference: Writing

For more information on the close connection between the speech-development process and the writing process, refer students to Lesson 2.1, pp. 46–49.

Preparing and Delivering Formal Speeches

Formal speeches are prepared, rehearsed, and then delivered at a pre-arranged place and time. Preparing a formal speech involves many of the same steps as writing a research paper or a persuasive essay. However, a speech actually involves more steps, as outlined here.

Think About Purpose and Audience Once you have a topic, decide on your purpose for making the speech. Do you want to persuade your audience, inform them, or entertain them? You may end up doing all three—an audience that is entertained is more likely to listen attentively, and an audience that hears solid evidence is more likely to be persuaded. Write a clear statement of your purpose, such as "I want to persuade my audience to participate in our community's recycling program."

After clearly defining your purpose, identify your audience. What age group and economic class do they belong to? Do they live in a large city, a suburb, or a small town? Determine what your audience knows about the topic, even interviewing some of them if possible. What concerns or preconceived ideas do they have? What misinformation might you need to correct? Then think about the kind of language that fits your audience. You may need to tailor your vocabulary to your audience and explain any technical terms.

Research the Topic Do library and Internet research to gather facts, examples, and experts' opinions on your topic. Conduct polls and interviews when appropriate. Study the information you gather and write a clear statement of your thesis. Then select accurate, relevant evidence and examples from reliable sources to support your thesis.

Organize an Outline Choose a pattern of organization that fits your information and your purpose. Outline your information using your thesis as the controlling idea. At this point, consider whether visual aids might be useful.

Draft and Revise Use your outline as a guide to draft your speech, following the standard structure of an introduction, a body, and a conclusion. If you are preparing a persuasive speech, review the appropriate appeals and rhetorical strategies for persuasive writing on pages 310–313.

In your introduction, think of a way to grab your audience's attention. You might consider one of the methods listed in the following chart.

Methods for Introductions	
Tell a compelling story	Two years ago, my older brother was riding in a car that was hit by a drunk driver.
Ask an intriguing question	If you could change one thing about yourself, what would it be?
Use an interesting quote	There is a saying by the Chinese philosopher Confucius that applies to learning: "I hear and I forget. I see and I remember. I do and I understand."
State an amazing fact or statistic	Americans are using up a disproportionate amount of the world's resources. The United States alone consumes 25 percent of the world's energy.

In your conclusion, you might provide an interesting twist that sums up your speech. For example, if you began with a question, you might state it again and give the answer. Whatever method you use, always strive for a strong finish that drives home your message.

Revise your speech, just as you would any other work of informative or persuasive writing. Read your speech out loud and make further changes so that it flows smoothly. You have to be able to say what you write. If your sentences are too long, shorten them. If you stumble over a group of words, change them.

Prepare Materials Some speakers read from manuscript pages; others speak from an outline or note cards. Some even memorize their speeches. If you are not required to use a particular method, choose the method that works best for you and your situation. If you read your speech, prepare a double- or triple-spaced manuscript with wide margins. If you choose to speak from an outline or note cards, use your written speech to prepare these materials. Underline topic sentences, number supporting points, and transfer the ideas to an outline or note cards. Number manuscript pages, outline pages, or note cards at the top.

Practice and Deliver Your Speech Practice your speech in front of a mirror. Ask a friend or relative to listen to your speech or to videotape it. As you rehearse, pay attention to the points listed in the following chart. Even if you read your speech, be sure to make frequent eye contact with your audience, especially at the beginning and end of sentences.

Teach

Delivering a Panel Presentation

Assign a small group of students to deliver an informative panel presentation. Panel members should use the techniques for working in groups to choose a topic. Each student will then research and prepare one portion of the presentation. Encourage panel members to liven up their speeches with humor or personal anecdotes and to use charts and graphs where appropriate. Make one student responsible for organizing the presentation of the material. **L3**

Listening and Speaking

29.2 Speaking Effectively **889**

English Language Learners

Practicing Speeches

Students who are new to the English language may be apprehensive about oral presentations. Encourage students to check the dictionary for pronunciations and to practice saying unfamiliar words aloud. Students may want to write important points in phrases on their note cards. Assign partners with whom students can practice. A partner more familiar with English could coach the student and help with correct idioms and pronunciations. As they speak, students should choose two or three friendly faces in the audience with whom to make eye contact.

Practice and Assess

Evaluation Rubrics

Exercise 5

Students' speeches should show careful work in all verbal and nonverbal techniques listed in the Guidelines for Delivering a Speech chart on student page 890. Students' evaluations should show that they have analyzed the purpose, audience, facts and opinions, errors in reasoning, persuasive techniques, and biases of each speech before having rendered an opinion.

Additional Resources

📁 *Listening and Speaking Activities*
📁 *Thinking and Study Skills, p. 34*

Close

Remind students that they are likely to engage in some form of speaking each day. Ask them to use their own words to restate the tips on making informal or formal speeches.

Listening and Speaking

Guidelines for Delivering a Speech

Verbal Techniques

- **Volume.** Speak loudly enough so that everyone in the audience can hear you.
- **Pronunciation.** Speak clearly, pronouncing all the words.
- **Pace.** Speak at a moderate speed, but vary the rate and use pauses to convey your meaning.
- **Tone.** Speak in a lively tone.
- **Emphasis.** Stress important words and ideas.

Nonverbal Techniques

- **Posture.** Stand up tall with your head straight.
- **Eye contact.** Make eye contact with people throughout your audience.
- **Facial expressions and gestures.** Vary your facial expressions to reflect what you are saying and use natural gestures to reinforce your ideas.
- **Visual aids.** If appropriate for your topic, use charts, diagrams, graphs, or video clips to enhance your speech and convey important information.

Invite questions and comments   When you complete your speech, ask if there are any questions or comments. Answer questions honestly and respectfully. Use this question-and-answer period to correct misunderstandings, to repeat points that your listeners may have missed, and to learn what you could have made clearer in your speech.

Exercise 5

Following the guidelines provided in this lesson, prepare, practice, and deliver a brief persuasive speech in which you propose a solution to a problem in your school or community. Apply the Active Listening Strategies presented on pages 883–884 as you listen to the speeches of your classmates and use the questions in Evaluating Persuasive Messages on page 885 to provide feedback for each speaker.

Technology Tip

Videotaping Oral Reports

Many families have portable video recorders or camcorders. This equipment is useful for students who are preparing an oral report. While practicing, they can record their presentation. They can then view it immediately, make adjustments to the presentation based on the review, and continue to practice, recording and reviewing each time until the speech is just right.

29.3 Working in Groups

You participate in many groups—families, classes, study groups, teams, clubs or organizations, and work groups. To contribute in positive ways to any of these groups, you need good listening and speaking skills as well as an understanding of how to function in a group.

In a study group or discussion group, members typically have definite roles, such as group leader, recorder, and participants. The group leader guides the discussion and keeps the group focused on the topic or task. The recorder takes notes and records decisions. The participants contribute ideas, respond to the ideas of others, and vote on decisions. A group operates most effectively if members follow guidelines like those listed in the chart below.

Guidelines for Working in a Group

- **Be prepared.** Complete any assigned reading or research before the group meets.
- **Focus on the issue.** Don't bring up unrelated topics.
- **Listen actively.** Make an effort to understand each person's viewpoint and don't interrupt when someone is speaking.
- **Show respect.** Recognize that each person has something worthwhile to contribute. An effective group draws upon the different strengths of its members.
- **State your ideas clearly and concisely.** Don't talk on and on so that others have little chance to speak.
- **Respond constructively to the ideas of others.** Explain why you agree or disagree with someone's idea, providing reasons or evidence.
- **Encourage everyone to participate.** If someone has not spoken, ask for his or her opinion.

Exercise 6

Form a small group and choose a group leader and a recorder. Hold an informal, twenty-minute discussion on the following questions: What are high schools doing to deal with the rise in teenage violence? What *should* they be doing? After the discussion, evaluate how well your group functioned, based on the Guidelines for Working in a Group. Then give a brief summary of your discussion to the rest of the class.

Listening and Speaking

29.3 Working in Groups **891**

Focus

Lesson Overview

Objective

- To follow guidelines in order to work successfully with a group

 Bellringer
Daily Language Activity

When students enter the classroom, have this assignment on the board: *Recall an experience working in a study group. List changes in behavior that would have helped the group to work more successfully.*

See also *Daily Language Practice*

Practice and Assess

Evaluation Rubrics

Exercise 6

Students should rate how well their group followed each of the seven guidelines listed in the Guidelines for Working in a Group chart on student page 891. Students could use the ratings Excellent, Good, or Needs Improvement to evaluate their group's performance, but their evaluations should give specific explanations for their opinions. Students' summaries should indicate not only what conclusions they made but how they came about them.

Additional Resources

- *Listening and Speaking Acitivities*
- *Thinking and Study Skills,* p. 34

Close

Ask students to describe problems they might encounter when working with a group. How might these problems be resolved?

Resource Manager

Planning Resources
- *Lesson Plans*

Other Print Resources
- *Listening and Speaking Activities*
- *Thinking and Study Skills,* p. 34

Focus

Lesson Overview

Objective

- To learn how to conduct an effective interview

Skills

- preparing interview questions; asking and responding to interview questions; listening actively; using feedback to set goals for improving one's performance in an interview

Critical Thinking

- generating questions; analyzing; synthesizing; evaluating

Listening and Speaking

- asking questions; listening actively

 Bellringer
Daily Language Activity

When students enter the classroom, have this assignment on the board: *Think of a person you would like to learn more about. Write a list of the questions you would most like that person to answer.*

See also *Daily Language Practice*

Teach

Preparing for an Interview

Invite a representative from a student or local newspaper to give a presentation on how to prepare for and how to conduct oneself during an interview. You might also select a few students to perform a model interview with and to receive constructive criticism from the representative. The audience could then evaluate how well the students prepared and how actively the students listened. **L2**

Listening and Speaking (sidebar tab)

29.4 Conducting an Interview

Listening and speaking skills are also crucial in conducting interviews, which is a valuable way of gathering information. The following guidelines will help you conduct an effective interview.

Guidelines for Interviewing

Prepare for the Interview

- Research the subject and learn about the person you will interview.
- Prepare a list of five or more *who, what, where, when, why,* and *how* questions. Avoid questions that require just a yes or no answer. For example, instead of *Do you agree with this idea?* ask *What do you think of this idea?*
- If you plan to tape the interview, make sure your tape recorder works. If you plan to take notes, make sure you bring along two pens that work and a pad of paper as well as your list of interview questions.

Listen Actively During the Interview

- Take notes or tape-record the interview. Ask for the correct spelling of the person's name and of any unfamiliar places or terms the person uses.
- If necessary, ask the person to explain or repeat statements you do not understand.
- Ask intelligent follow-up questions.
- At the end of the interview, thank the person.

Follow Up after the Interview

- As soon as possible after the interview, write a full account of everything you remember, referring to your notes or your tape.
- If necessary, contact the person to clear up any points of confusion.
- Write the person a thank-you letter.

 Resource Manager

Planning Resources
- *Lesson Plans*

Other Print Resources
- *Listening and Speaking Activities*

Sample interview notes

Note the date of the interview.

Nov. 16, 2000
Interview with Elena Paz, Owner of Paz Landscape Architects

- college major — sociology
- couldn't get job that she enjoyed in that field
- took an interest in landscape architecture
- got entry-level job in landscape architecture business
- went back to school to study landscape architecture
- graduated and started own business
- after much hard work, business became extremely successful
- has just created a Web page for her business

Verify the spelling of the person's name and the company name.

Jot down just a few words to capture questions and answers. These words will jog your memory when you write up a full account of the interview later.

Exercise 7

Interview a parent or another adult about his or her occupation, following the guidelines given in this lesson. Write a full account of your interview and ask the person to check the account for accuracy. Also ask the person to give you feedback on how you conducted the interview. Share highlights of your interview in a brief oral report to the class.

Practice and Assess

Evaluation Rubrics

Exercise 7

Students' accounts of their interviews should include accurate information and should show that they were courteous, that they avoided asking only yes-no questions, and that they asked intelligent follow-up questions whenever possible. Students' oral reports should include the name of the interviewee, his or her occupation, and at least one telling quote from the interview. In addition, students should demonstrate an ability to compress information concisely.

✔ ASSESSMENT OPTIONS

📁 *Tests with Answer Key & Rubrics*
Unit 29 Mastery Test, pp. 109–110

💾 *Testmaker*
Unit 29 Mastery Test

📼 *MindJogger Videoquizzes*

You may wish to administer the Unit 29 Mastery Test at this point.

Close

Remind students that, when applying for college or for a job, the tables will be turned and they will be the interviewees rather than the the interviewers.

Listening and Speaking

Listening and Speaking

Conducting an Interview

Have student volunteers explain to the class how the listening and speaking techniques discussed throughout this unit can help the class conduct better interviews. Which do they feel are the most important points to remember when conducting an interview? Then have students form pairs, and ask each student, in turn with their partner, to conduct an interview on their partner's favorite extracurricular activity. After the class has completed their interviews, encourage them to discuss the pleasures and pitfalls of interviewing.

INTRODUCING

UNIT 30

Objectives

- To develop an understanding of how elements of visual design can be used to convey messages
- To learn to analyze and criticize visual messages in various media
- To create and produce effective videos and Web pages

✓ **ASSESSMENT OPTIONS**

📂 *Tests with Answer Key & Rubrics*
Unit 30 Pretest

💾 *Testmaker*
Unit 30 Pretest

You may wish to administer the Unit 30 Pretest at this point.

Key to Ability Levels

L1 Level 1 activities are within the basic ability range of students.

L2 Level 2 activities are within the ability range of average students.

L3 Level 3 activities are more challenging activities.

UNIT 30 Viewing and Representing

Lesson 30.1   **Understanding Visual Messages**   *895*

Lesson 30.2   **Examining Media Messages**   *902*

Lesson 30.3   **Making Your Own Media Messages**   *905*

894

Resource Manager

Planning Resources
- *Lesson Plans*
- *Block Scheduling*

 Transparencies
- *Bellringer*
- *Daily Language Practice*

📂 **Other Print Resources**
- *Tests with Answer Key & Rubrics*
- *Viewing and Representing*

▭ **Video**
- *MindJogger Videoquizzes*

💾 **Software**
- *Presentation Plus!*
- *Testmaker*
- *Writer's Choice Puzzlemaker*

 Web Sites
- *writerschoice.glencoe.com*

894

30.1 | Understanding Visual Messages

Think of the last time you watched television, listened to a radio broadcast, saw a feature film at a theater, or visited a Web site as part of your research for a school project. In each case, you were turning to mass media for entertainment or information. In many cases, what you see and hear in mass media presentations will not only entertain and inform you, but will also persuade you in one way or another. Whether you realize it or not, media presentations help shape your attitudes, values, and behavior. They not only reflect your culture, but they also help create it.

Developing *media literacy*—the ability to understand, interpret, analyze, and critique media messages as well as create your own—will help you recognize the ways media messages might influence your thinking and your life. The goal of this unit is to help you gain such media literacy.

Interpreting Visual Design

With the exception of radio, all the mass media send visual messages. Being aware of the techniques used in developing visual messages will help you to interpret the messages you see and to understand and analyze the ideas that are presented. To understand the design of a visual image such as a photograph or illustration, you examine its *composition*, or arrangement of elements. The following chart lists some basic elements in the composition of a photograph or illustration. Although the actual effect of an element depends on the overall context of the picture, as you will see in the chart, various effects can be achieved by manipulating each element.

Elements of Visual Design

Element	Example	Some Possible Effects
Shape	Circle	Suggests wholeness, lovableness, softness
	Square	Suggests firmness, stability
	Triangle	Suggests unity, balance, or tension
Line Lines can be real (the edge of a building) or implied (a person's gaze). Lines can be used to direct a viewer's attention or to suggest a mood or theme.	Straight lines	Point or lead to something
	Curved lines	Suggest motion, warmth
	Vertical lines	Suggest dignity, status, power
	Horizontal lines	Suggest peace, stillness
	Diagonal lines	Suggest tension, energy

Viewing and Representing

Focus

Lesson Overview

Objectives
- To develop an understanding of how elements of visual design can be used to convey messages in the mass media

Skills
- interpreting visual designs; analyzing visual techniques and messages

Critical Thinking
- interpreting; analyzing

Listening and Speaking
- discussing; informal speaking

 Bellringer
Daily Language Activity
When students enter the classroom, have this assignment on the board: *List three types of mass media and a specific example of each one.*

See also 🎵 *Daily Language Practice*

Motivating Activity

Have students share their lists of types and examples of mass media. Ask them to discuss what the term *media literacy* might mean ("the ability to understand, interpret, analyze, and critique media messages"). Ask students to consider how developing such skills might help readers, viewers, consumers, and citizens.

 Resource Manager

Planning Resources
- *Lesson Plans*

📂 **Other Print Resources**
- *Viewing and Representing*

Teach

Using the Chart

Discuss the Elements of Visual Design chart. Then, using the text related to the photograph on page 897 of the student edition as a starting point, call on volunteers to use the chart to identify and interpret the message of the photo. Ask students to consider how the visual message might be altered if the photographer had directed the students to strike a more formal pose, to dress differently, or to assume more serious facial expressions. **L1**

Elements of Visual Design (cont.)		
Element	**Example**	**Some Possible Effects**
Color or Tone	Cool colors (blue, green, gray)	Convey calm, emotional distance
	Warm colors (red, yellow, orange)	Convey energy, vibrancy, warmth
	Bright colors	Convey joy, action, excitement
	Subdued or pastel colors	Suggest innocence, softness, serenity
	Light tones	Create happy, playful mood
	Dark tones	Convey sadness, mystery, dullness
Texture	Smooth, flat	Might suggest emptiness or something modern and streamlined
	Rough, woven	Might convey wholesomeness, naturalness, a feeling of home
	Silky, shiny	Creates sense of luxury
Positioning of subjects The positions of figures grouped together can show how the artist views their relationships to one another.	Center of frame	Conveys stability
	Top of frame	Conveys importance, power
	Bottom of frame	Conveys inferiority, weakness
Light A viewer's eye naturally travels to the most lighted area.	Bright light	Draws the eye to a specific area; creates a cheerful mood
	Dim light or shadows	Creates a sense of mystery or doom
Space	Large space around subject	Draws attention to subject; isolates details; can create a sense of openness, vastness, emptiness, loneliness
	Little space around subject	Makes subject seem dominating, overwhelming

To understand how elements of visual design work together in a photograph, study this picture of two high school students, which appeared in a magazine feature story about the lives of teenagers. Several items in the picture show aspects of teen culture—school books, a decorated school locker,

MEETING INDIVIDUAL NEEDS · Gifted and Talented

Illustrating the Graph

Ask students with exceptional visual talents and interests to compose a photograph which uses the same elements as the photo on page 897— two teenagers, a school setting, teen fashions—to project a different impression. Have students display their works and conduct a discussion of how their use of different elements of visual design altered the message and mood of the material.

and popular styles of the time, including athletic shoes and flared jeans. Those items alone inform viewers about teen life. However, the photographer has used certain techniques to send a stronger message. Note how the diagonal lines created by the students' legs draw the viewer into the picture. The subdued lighting and predominance of muted tans and browns add a feeling of warmth and softness to the picture. And the students' position in the center of the frame with lots of space around them, together with the students' relaxed poses and smiling faces, combines to create a positive portrait of friendly, happy teenagers who have an equal, easy-going relationship.

A viewer might look at this photograph and think that the photographer simply shot a realistic portrait of these two teenagers. But the photographer made a conscious decision about where to shoot the picture, what elements to include and exclude, how to position the students, and what facial expressions to try to capture. If the photographer had chosen instead to use very dim light and capture the students scowling instead of smiling, the resulting photograph would have conveyed a completely different impression. Every photograph presents one view of a subject from a particular perspective.

Teach

Point of View

Point out that in the photo on this page, the students' faces are at eye-level with the viewer, encouraging the viewer to identify with them. Have students discuss the effect the photographer might have achieved by shooting the picture from above or below eye level of the subjects. Use the discussion to emphasize the ways in which manipulation of various elements of design and composition can alter the meaning and tone of a visual image.

Viewing and Representing

30.1 Understanding Visual Messages **897**

Viewing and Representing

Interpreting Visuals

Ask students to bring to class copies of photographs which they believe illustrate the effects of some of the elements on the Elements of Visual Design chart on pages 895–896. Have a few volunteers display their photos and present a brief analysis of how the visual elements have been used to achieve certain meanings or effects. Have all students write a brief description of their photos and share their pictures and interpretations in a small group.

Practice and Assess

Teach

Space Research

Encourage volunteers to do some research, in print or electronic sources, about John Glenn and his relationship to and achievements with the U.S. space program. After students have completed Exercise 1, these volunteers could report on their findings, discussing the ways in which the photo captures visually what the historical record revealed. **L3**

Viewing and Representing

Exercise 1

Use the Elements of Visual Design chart to describe the effects of lines, shapes, positioning of subjects, color, light, and space in this 1998 photograph of John Glenn's return into space at the age of seventy-seven. Summarize the ideas that the photograph conveys about the relationships among people, their heroes, and technology in U.S. culture.

 Cultural Connections

Reading Visuals

Ask students with knowledge of different cultures to bring to class some pictorial representation of that culture. It might be a picture of a traditional art work, a photograph of a cultural event, or photographs of traditional clothing. Have students explain how the use of color, light, tone, texture, and other visual elements combine to convey something about the values of the culture.

Film Techniques

The basic elements of visual design apply to the media of motion pictures and videos as well as to photographs and illustrations. In addition, motion picture and television directors—even the creators of video games—use a wide variety of film techniques to tell stories and to convey messages. The following chart describes some of these techniques and the effects they can have.

Basic Film Techniques		
Technique	Example	Possible Effects
Camera angle	High (looking down)	Minimizes status of subject
	Low (looking up)	Emphasizes status of subject
	Straight-on (eye level)	Puts viewer on equal level with subject; promotes identification with subject
Camera shots	Close-up (magnified view)	Promotes identification with subject
	Long shot (wide view)	Establishes relationship between characters and a setting
	Reaction shot	Shows effect of one character on another or of an event on a character
Lighting	High-key (bright, even)	Creates cheerful, optimistic mood
	Low-key (producing shadows)	Creates gloomy, eerie mood
	Lit from above	Subject seems to glow with significance
	Lit from below	May raise audience apprehension
Movement	Slow motion	Emphasizes movement and heightens drama
	Blurred motion	Suggests speed, confusion, or dreamlike state
Editing (selection and arrangement of scenes)	Sequence of short shots	Builds tension, creates a rushed mood
	Sequence of long shots	May convey a feeling of stability
Special effects	Artwork and miniature models	Can be filmed to appear real
	Computer enhancement	Can create composite images or distort qualities of a character or scene
Background music		Evokes audience's emotional response, sets mood, reinforces theme

Teach

Interpreting Film Techniques

Using the introduction to the Basic Film Techniques chart on this page as a starting point, invite students to suggest listed elements which they have noticed in popular movies and television programs. Point out that television and movie directors rely on many of the elements of visual design listed on the chart on pages 895–896. In addition, they employ techniques not available to artists and still photographers, such as camera movement, special effects, and sound—in the form of dialogue and background music. **L2**

Analyzing Film Techniques

Ask students to suggest the names of some popular television shows or movies which make extensive use of film techniques for dramatic effect. Ask students to analyze how the use of visual techniques helps build suspense, fear, comedy, identification with a character, or other effects. Were the techniques used effectively? How did they extend the message sent by the dialogue, action, and setting? How, if at all, did background music contribute to the total effect? **L2**

Viewing and Representing

Enrichment and Extension

Writing in the Reel World

Direct students to sources, both print and electronic, in which they might find reviews of recent movies. Ask students to find reviews which pay special attention to some of the Basic Film Techniques listed on the chart. Have students report on how the reviewers evaluated these techniques and, if possible, how the students' own appraisals compared with those of reviewers. **L3**

Teach

Analyzing Effects

Direct students' attention to the movie still shown on this page of the student edition. Use the information in the text as a starting point to guide students through an analysis of the movie still, based on the Elements of Visual Design and the Basic Film Techniques charts. Ask them how director Steven Spielberg might have achieved different effects if he had chosen different positions or lighting, directed the actors to use different facial expressions, or otherwise changed or re-arranged elements. **L2**

Creating Impressions

Lead a discussion in which students identify current television or movie stars who have cultivated a particular persona in most of their parts. (Arnold Schwarzenegger and Kate Winslett might be used as examples.) Ask students to discuss what elements of each star's visual image—clothing, posture, facial expressions, and other such traits—contribute to that persona.

Viewing and Representing

Examine the elements of visual design and the film techniques used in this still from the movie *Jurassic Park* (1993). This reaction shot shows the characters' amazement as they wake up to see a brachiosaur grazing on the leaves of a tree in which they had slept. Sunlight streams onto the characters from above and behind, lighting up their faces and casting shadows on the tree. The shadows and the blue and green colors of the tree dominate the picture, creating a slightly eerie though calm mood. The characters' bodies form a circle within the radiating branches of the tree, emphasizing the close relationship that has developed between them after their escape from a *Tyrannosaurus rex*. Because of the straight-on camera angle and the long shot, the viewer identifies with the characters' situation. These design elements and film techniques combine to help engage the audience with the characters, who have bonded through a harrowing experience and have kept their ability to be awed by a wonder of nature. Like many scenes in the movie, this one was created using special effects, including a fifty-foot model tree.

Viewing the Art

About the Artist

Stephen Spielberg decided at age eleven that he wanted to make movies. His professional debut as a director came on television, where his early work included efforts on *Rod Serling's Night Caller* and *Columbo.* The incredible success of *Jaws* (1975) established him as a successful director, and subsequent box-office hits like

E.T., Schindler's List, and *Jurassic Park* have only solidified his hold on the American movie-going public. His mainstream popularity is in some ways ironic, since Spielberg has said he "never felt part of the majority. . . . I always felt like I never belonged to any group that I wanted to belong to."

Study the still below from the movie *Jurassic Park*. Use the Elements of Visual Design and Film Techniques charts to help you identify at least three elements or techniques used in the scene and to analyze their effects. Share your analysis in a brief oral report to the class.

30.1 Understanding Visual Messages   **901**

Practice and Assess

Answer: Exercise 2

Answers will vary, depending on students' perceptions. To enhance and extend interpretations, have students first work in small groups to develop analyses of the movie still shown on page 901 of the student edition. Once the groups have analyzed the still based on its obvious components, have each group report on its conclusions to compare and contrast its views with others'.

Close

Ask students to work in small groups to compile lists of scenes from recent movies or television shows which illustrate the use of some of the Basic Film Techniques listed on the chart on page 899. Encourage students to think of examples in which the techniques effectively produced the effect listed on the chart. Have each group synthesize its discussion and report to the class.

Enrichment and Extension

Reviewing Techniques

If possible, show a video of a classic literary work to illustrate some of the Film Techniques covered in this lesson. Classic film versions of *Wuthering Heights, Great Expectations,* and *David Copperfield,* for example, employ many of the visual techniques described here. VCR technology makes it possible to pause or employ slow-motion to help emphasize the techniques.

Focus

Lesson Overview

Objectives
- To analyze and deconstruct media messages
- To understand how media messages can be employed to influence behavior and values

Skills
- comparing and contrasting; deconstructing media messages; identifying and evaluating persuasive techniques

Critical Thinking
- interpreting; analyzing; critiquing

Listening and Speaking
- discussing; informal speaking

Bellringer
Daily Language Activity
When students enter the classroom, have this assignment on the board: *List three examples of movies or television shows that seem to be "realistic."*

See also *Daily Language Practice*

Motivating Activity
Have students share their lists of "realistic" movies and programs and discuss various examples to see whether there is general agreement about them. Lead students to understand that although many such programs appear realistic at some levels, each is carefully constructed to reveal a particular point of view: the director's, the writer's, the advertiser's, the artist's. What is left out is as important as what is kept in, and a given subject—a city, a profession, a person's life, a historical event—can render different messages, depending on the point of view. Point out that this lesson will help students to deconstruct, or analyze, media messages and understand and evaluate the perspective that each one reveals.

Viewing and Representing

30.2 Examining Media Messages

Photographs, movies, and television programs typically seem to capture scenes from life just as they are. For example, although the photograph on page 897 seems realistic, it represents only a portion of the high school student population in the country. Not all students wear athletic shoes and flared jeans. Keep in mind that all media messages are constructed for a purpose and show only a particular view of life from one perspective. Even in a documentary that you might consider strictly factual, a director has made many decisions about how to shoot scenes, what information to include and exclude, and what effects to strive for. To fully understand what you see and how it can influence you, you need to be able to analyze, or **deconstruct,** media messages. This lesson will help you develop that skill.

Identifying Media Genres

Every day you are exposed to a variety of forms of media. These forms, or genres, can be grouped into four main types: print, broadcast, film, and Internet. *Print media* include newspapers, magazines, fliers, books, product packaging, and other materials that convey messages through printed words and images. *Broadcast media* consist of radio and television, in which sounds alone or both sounds and moving images are transmitted to a wide public audience. *Film media* include movies and videotapes, which also consist of sounds and moving images. The *Internet* contains a wide variety of Web sites that consist of some combination of printed words, still and moving images, and sounds.

The form of a media message can affect its meaning and how you interpret or respond to it. For information on a specific topic, you might choose between several types of presentation depending on the kind and amount of information you need. For example, for a quick look at the main news events of the day, you might turn to a newspaper. Another quick source could be a news service on the Internet, which would have links to other articles related to the news items that catch your attention. However, you might gain a fuller appreciation of the impact of a news event—for example, of civil unrest somewhere else in the world—from watching a TV newscast than you would from reading about it in a newspaper article. The moving images on TV have a strong impact and often arouse a stronger emotional response than print does. To learn more in depth about the causes of the problem, you could refer to a book or view a film documentary. Imagine that the United States was involved in a war and you gained all your information about events from the newspaper. How might your view of events and reactions be different than if you watched the live TV news coverage? Which source might give you more comprehensive information? Which might make you feel more personally involved?

902   Unit 30 Viewing and Representing

Resource Manager

Planning Resources
- *Lesson Plans*

Other Print Resources
- *Viewing and Representing*

Exercise 3

Watch a TV newscast for coverage of a foreign war or conflict and take notes on what you learn. Then check the Internet and read a newspaper to find coverage of the same event. Create a chart comparing and contrasting the coverage in the different media, the impressions you gain from each, and the impact that each has on you.

Analyzing Media Messages

As you look critically at a media message—whether it's a print advertisement, an online research resource, or a popular movie—you need to analyze how and why it was created. The following chart describes how to deconstruct a media message.

How to Analyze a Media Message		
Identify	**By Asking Yourself**	**Example**
source	Who made this? How does the source affect the message?	A dairy industry organization sponsors an ad in a national newsmagazine promoting the nutritional value of milk.
purpose	Why was the message made? Is it meant to inform, entertain, or persuade?	The purpose of the ad is to persuade people to buy milk. Another purpose seems to be to inform people about nutritional benefits of milk.
target audience	Who is the message intended for? How has the content been shaped to appeal to the intended audience?	The ad is targeted to middle-aged adults. It shows the middle-aged cast of a popular TV sitcom drinking milk. The middle-aged audience should relate well to the show's cast.
main idea or theme	What is the intended message?	Men and women should drink three glasses of milk each day to get enough calcium in their diet.
design elements and/or film techniques	How are design elements or film techniques used to communicate a message or manipulate a viewer's response?	The actors in the photo are bathed in a golden light that makes them appear healthy, warm, and lovable.

Practice and Assess

Answers: Exercise 3
Answers will vary, depending on the events and the sources used by students. In general, the immediacy and visual impact of television coverage might be contrasted with the greater depth and background often found in print coverage. Students' references to Internet sources should include some evaluation of the credibility of the sources and the accuracy of the information.

Teach

Analyzing Media Messages

Bring to class examples of print advertisements which illustrate some of the techniques and approaches suggested in the chart on pages 903–904. Have students discuss the purpose and effectiveness of celebrity endorsements, for example, or the use (or misuse) of glittering generalities and logical fallacies. **L2**

Viewing and Representing

Viewing and Representing

Pictures into Words
Ask students to find print ads which employ few or no words to convey their messages. Ask students to identify and analyze the purpose, the targeted audience, the main appeal, and the main idea or theme of the ad. Some students might expand their searches to include television ads which use little or no dialogue.

Teach

Comparing and Contrasting Media

Point out that each type, or *genre,* of media may employ different features. Newspaper stories can be illustrated with photographs, diagrams, and maps. A television news story on the same subject might also employ moving pictures, on-site commentary, and sound. Internet news sources can provide "up-to-the-minute" coverage. Ask students to explore the coverage of a current event, in newspapers and magazines, on radio and television, and on the Internet. Lead a discussion of the characteristics of the coverage in each medium, and the strengths and weaknesses of each.

Practice and Assess

Answers: Exercise 4

Students' analyses should demonstrate an understanding of such terms as persuasive techniques, glittering generalities, logical fallacies, symbols, and celebrity testimonials, and demonstrate how meanings are communicated through elements of design. Students' print ads should be visually persuasive and should clearly communicate their messages with appropriate elements of design.

Answers: Exercise 5

Answers will vary but should reflect students' understanding of the purposes of various media forms and their examination of how media messages affect one's perception of reality.

Viewing and Representing

How to Analyze a Media Message (cont.)		
Identify	**By Asking Yourself**	**Example**
elements that reflect a specific culture	What cultural values and assumptions are reflected in this presentation?	Good health and youthful looks are important. People would like to look and act like attractive actors.
persuasive techniques glittering generalities	Does the message make sweeping claims that are impossible to support?	The ad implies that everyone who drinks milk will be as glamorous and look as young and healthy as the actors do.
logical fallacies	Are the statements in the message logical, or are there errors in logic?	The argument that people need calcium in their diet is based on fact, but drinking milk is not the only way to get this nutrient.
symbols	Does the message use symbols that stand for popular ideas or values?	Milk itself is a symbol of health and youth.
celebrity testimonial	Do admired celebrities add to the message or endorse the product?	The ad uses celebrities to endorse a product.

Exercise 4

Use the questions in the How to Analyze a Media Message chart to write an analysis of a print ad targeted to teenagers. Then create a print ad of your own promoting the same product or service and write an explanation of the techniques you use in your ad.

Exercise 5

In a small group, discuss the influence that such media as TV shows and commercials, movies, magazines, and radio programs have had on your ideas about the following topics:

- romantic love
- the importance of physical beauty and standards of beauty
- the importance of material success to a person's happiness
- the kinds of things you want to own and buy

After your discussion, choose one of these topics and write an editorial in which you give your opinion on the media's effects on your perceptions and those of your classmates.

904 Unit 30 Viewing and Representing

MEETING INDIVIDUAL NEEDS — English Language Learners

Cultural Connections

Encourage students with knowledge of and experiences with other cultures to discuss how the topics in Exercise 5 are covered in the media of other countries. Ask them to compare and contrast the messages, techniques, and values conveyed in the U.S. media with those in their own cultures.

30.3 Making Your Own Media Messages

A good way to understand media messages and the decisions behind them is to produce your own media presentation. This lesson provides guidelines for producing two forms of media messages: videos and Web pages.

Making a Video

The creation of a video requires the skills and cooperation of several people. Depending on the topic of your video and the way you choose to present it, you might need people to fill any or all of these roles:

- **Director:** coordinates the activities of the group members and supervises the filming of the video
- **Researcher:** finds background information on the topic and the interviewees
- **Scriptwriter:** writes and revises the script
- **Storyboard designer:** prepares a series of simple sketches of each video scene to go along with the dialogue or narration
- **Interviewer:** prepares questions to ask the interviewees and conducts the interviews
- **Narrator:** reads the script during the filming
- **Camera operator:** films the interviews and other shots

Some members of your production team may take on two or more roles. For example, the scriptwriter might also function as the researcher and narrator. Making a video provides an opportunity to try out different roles and learn new skills.

Consider the elements of visual design and the film techniques described in the first section of this unit as you plan and produce your video. Make sure that you have a clear focus for your video and that you can summarize that focus in a paragraph. The following chart provides additional guidelines for carrying out a video project.

TIPS ON PRODUCING A VIDEO

1. Begin by brainstorming. In your group, discuss these questions: What is the purpose and focus of the video? Who are the intended viewers? What do they already know or think about the subject? What information do we need to find out? What scenes will we shoot? You may want to have a group member write down these questions and the answers as they arise in the discussion. *(continued)*

Viewing and Representing

Focus

Lesson Overview

Objectives
- To produce media messages, including videos and Web sites

Skills
- using various technologies; creating media messages

Critical Thinking
- analyzing; visualizing

Listening and Speaking
- discussing; asking and answering questions; informal speaking

Bellringer
Daily Language Activity

When students enter the classroom, have this assignment on the board: *List three techniques used by photographers, movie and television directors, and advertisers to create specific effects in media messages.*

See also *Daily Language Practice*

Motivating Activity

Ask students to share their lists of techniques and discuss how they relate to the charts on previous pages. Encourage students to think of examples of photographs, scenes from movies or television programs, or advertisements which employ each technique.

Resource Manager

Planning Resources
- *Lesson Plans*

Other Print Resources
- *Viewing and Representing*

Teach

Building Production Teams

Divide the class into groups and ask each group to organize itself into a production team, based on the roles suggested in the Making a Video feature on page 905 of the student edition. Compose the teams carefully, to insure that each team includes students with the necessary talents and interests to produce a video. Encourage students to refer to the charts on pages 895–896 and 899 for ideas regarding techniques and approaches. **L2**

Taking the Tips

Review the Tips on Producing a Video with students, making sure they understand each suggestion and providing explanations and examples as necessary. Ask volunteers to provide examples of a story board, for example, and make sure students understand basic concepts, like the different effects achieved by long and close camera shots. **L1**

Practice and Assess

Answer: Exercise 6

Responses will vary, depending on the equipment available and the energy and sophistication of the students. The finished product should reveal a basic understanding of some of the techniques and approaches covered in this unit.

Viewing and Representing

TIPS ON PRODUCING A VIDEO

2. Use a storyboard to help in planning. A storyboard provides a blueprint for shooting your video. It consists of simple sketches of the sequence of scenes you will shoot, with the dialogue or narration for each scene. You want your video to tell a story—so create a beginning, middle, and end. Include scenes that set the stage, show the location, or provide details that enrich the story.

3. Vary your scenes. Mix long camera shots that show a location with closer shots that focus on a single subject. Shoot from different angles and heights to achieve different effects. Vary the length of the shots you take as well.

4. Work with good lighting. Shoot in strong light—outside during daylight or inside near windows and with all the lights on. Set up your own lights if necessary.

5. Shoot with editing in mind. To make it easier to edit scenes later, leave a little room before and after each scene by letting the camera run. Reshoot scenes that don't turn out well.

6. Create a polished final product with careful editing. At the editing stage, you can eliminate bad footage, add music and sound effects, and insert titles. You also can mix short cuts and long cuts to achieve the pacing you want.

7. Ask for viewer feedback. After you present your video, ask the audience to fill out a questionnaire or participate in a discussion to give you feedback. Ask viewers to state the main idea of your video and to comment on how effectively it was conveyed. In addition, elicit their comments on the pacing, the camera techniques, and the audio and visual quality.

Exercise 6

Working in a small group, choose one of the following video projects to undertake:
- a six-minute documentary designed for adults, describing a contemporary fad
- a movie review show for teenagers
- an instructional program for people who do not use computers on how to produce fliers or books on a computer

Decide on a topic and agree on roles for each group member. Then work together to plan, write, shoot, and edit your video. After presenting the video to the class, hold a discussion to gather feedback from your audience.

Creating a Web Site

You can create a Web page that incorporates photographs, graphics, text, and even sound using a software program or hypertext mark-up language (HTML). A good Web site is attractive, informative, and easy to follow. The following guidelines will help you design a Web site that meets those standards.

Viewing and Representing

Staging a Video Festival

When production groups have completed Exercise 6, organize a video festival at which the class can show their projects to other audiences, including other classes. Have students develop a review check list to be distributed to all viewers and collected by each production team to get reactions to their work.

Guidelines for Developing a Web Site

1. **Begin with a clear purpose.** Identify your intended audience and make sure you have something useful to share. Your home page, or main page, should convey what the site is about in a way that gets viewers' attention.

2. **Plan your site.** View other sites on your topic or similar topics and brainstorm ideas about what to include. Design a layout for each page that is logical and easy to follow. Create a flowchart showing how the pages of your site will be connected.

3. **Keep the design simple and consistent.** Use only a few colors and fonts for your site. Unify the pages by using the same background color and by repeating a logo or icon that identifies your site. Avoid a busy background that detracts attention from your message. Keep key design features consistent on all the pages.

4. **Be sure the site is quick to download.** Viewers will give up if your home page takes too long to download. Keep the images small enough and few enough so that the page downloads quickly. For the same reason, don't embed music on the home page. Instead, put the music on a linked page.

5. **Make the site easy to navigate.** Use a clear, simple navigation scheme on all your pages. Make all your pages accessible from your home page within four or fewer clicks.

6. **Keep the text short and easy to read.** Break up information into short and medium-length sections and put the sections on linked pages. Use a font that is easy to read and a background color that provides enough contrast for reading ease. Carefully proofread and correct all text.

7. **Test your site and revise it.** Ask your friends or classmates to visit your site and test how well it works. Make a form similar to the one below and ask them to complete it.

Evaluating a Web Site

Characteristic	Comments
Location: Do search engines find it using logical searches?	
Ease of Use: Does the site download quickly? Can you navigate the site easily? Do all the images download?	
Design: Is the site visually appealing? Are colors, fonts, photos, and other graphic elements used effectively?	
Content: Is the information easy to understand and useful?	

Exercise 7

Working again in a small group, rethink your video project and turn it into a Web site. Ask classmates to visit your site and complete an evaluation form similar to the one above. Use the responses you receive to revise and improve your site.

30.3 Making Your Own Media Messages **907**

Viewing and Representing

Teach

Finding Model Sites

If possible, call up or display printouts of Web sites that you feel are particularly effective and appropriate as models. Lead a discussion of the features which make the sites attractive and useful. Call on volunteers to suggest other models and have them explain the features which make the sites informative, entertaining, and user-friendly.

Practice and Assess

Answer: Exercise 7

Students' Web sites should, if possible, incorporate graphics, text, and sound. The site should be attractive, informative, and easy to follow and should reflect an understanding of the guidelines provided on student page 907.

Close

Discuss the results of both media projects, inviting students to share their ideas about the techniques they employed and the results they achieved. Ask them to discuss how their knowledge of techniques employed in the mass media might affect their behavior as readers, viewers, consumers, and citizens.

✓ ASSESSMENT OPTIONS

📁 *Tests with Answer Key & Rubrics*
Unit 30 Mastery Test

💾 *Testmaker*
Unit 30 Mastery Test

📼 *MindJogger Videoquizzes*

You may wish to administer the Unit 30 Mastery Test at this point.

MEETING INDIVIDUAL NEEDS — Special Needs

Cooperative Learning

Not all students will be familiar with the Internet or the functions and purposes of Web sites and pages. When composing the production teams for this lesson, make sure these students are teamed with more technologically-experienced students who can serve as teachers and guides. Help all students see how they can contribute creative ideas and approaches, even if they lack technical expertise.

Objectives

- To use technology to prepare for, draft, and revise written material
- To use technology to compile and organize information
- To use technology to design written material and represent information visually
- To develop strategies for analyzing information in visual media
- To create, revise, and evaluate multimedia projects

✔ ASSESSMENT OPTIONS

📁 *Tests with Answer Key & Rubrics*
Unit 31 Pretest

💾 *Testmaker*
Unit 31 Pretest

You may wish to administer the Unit 31 Pretest at this point.

Key to Ability Levels

L1 Level 1 activities are within the basic ability range of students.

L2 Level 2 activities are within the ability range of average students.

L3 Level 3 activities are more challenging activities.

UNIT

31 Electronic Resources

Lesson **31.1** **Electronic Resources and the Writing Process** *909*

Lesson **31.2** **Research and Resources** *913*

Lesson **31.3** **Communicating Visually** *917*

Lesson **31.4** **Visual Analysis** *921*

Lesson **31.5** **Producing in Multimedia** *924*

908

Resource Manager

Planning Resources
- *Lesson Plans*
- *Block Scheduling*

📁 **Other Print Resources**
- *Guide to Using the Internet and Other Electronic Resources*
- *Tests with Answer Key & Rubrics*

 Video
- *MindJogger Videoquizzes*

💾 **Software**
- *Presentation Plus!*
- *Testmaker*
- *Writer's Choice Puzzlemaker*

 Web Sites
- *writerschoice.glencoe.com*

31.1 Electronic Resources and the Writing Process

Writing well is a process that requires much editing and revision. A computer with word processing software has many advantages over writing on paper with pencil or pen. A computer allows you to write and revise without time-consuming recopying. You can move words, sentences, or paragraphs from one place to another with a few mouse movements. You can store copies of many versions of your work or, if you prefer, you can keep your work on the same file—adding, deleting, correcting, and revising until you're satisfied with what you've written.

Generating Ideas

Often the hardest part of writing is thinking of a good idea. The choices are endless, and a blank computer screen can be intimidating. Are there topics that you have enjoyed writing about previously? Use one of these topics as a starting point. Or think about something on your mind that you might want to explore through writing. If you are completely out of ideas, the following list of writing formats might spark some creative thoughts.

- Song
- Questions
- Description
- Explanation
- Letter
- Critique or review
- Proposal
- Endorsement
- Newspaper article
- Opinion column
- Script or play
- Poem
- Character sketch
- Short story
- Essay

Collaborating with one or more other students is also a great way to jump-start your creative juices. You might even collaborate with a pen pal via e-mail over the Internet. You and a collaborator could decide to write a two-person play, with each of you writing his or her own part. Or you might want to write a piece debating an issue, each of you taking one side of the issue.

Begin by brainstorming. On an electronic file, compile a list of random thoughts or questions that you can revise as your plans take shape. In fact, you might find it useful to start a special electronic file for your writing ideas. Call the document "Writing Ideas" and add to it whenever you get a new idea. Look through the file when you're in search of something to write about.

At the prewriting stage, you should also consider your purpose and your audience. What do you hope to accomplish? For example, will you write an essay that will appeal to your fellow students or are you trying to impress your teacher? Do you want to provide a comprehensive guide to the restaurants in town or write a review of one specific restaurant? Do you wish to

Electronic Resources

Focus

Lesson Overview

Objective
- To use technology to organize, draft, and revise an article

Skills
- brainstorming; gathering information; planning; drafting; editing; revising

Critical Thinking
- analyzing; synthesizing; evaluating

Listening and Speaking
- collaborating to generate ideas and published texts; discussing

 Bellringer
Daily Language Activity

When students enter the classroom, have this assignment on the board: *Make a list comparing the benefits of writing with pen and paper to the benefits of writing on a word processor.*

See also *Daily Language Practice*

Motivating Activity

Ask student volunteers to share their lists from the Bellringer assignment with the rest of the class. Invite the rest of the class to summarize the benefits listed by the volunteers and to suggest more benefits. Remind students that writing is more than simply penmanship or typing but is a process with several stages. Explain further that electronic resources such as e-mail and Web sites can also aid in that process.

 Resource Manager

Planning Resources
- *Lesson Plans*

 Other Print Resources
- *Guide to Using the Internet and Other Electronic Resources*

Teach

Avoiding Plagiarism

Explain to students that, while dragging and dropping text from their notes and other sources may make the writing process easier, it also makes plagiarizing easier to do unintentionally. Go over with students some examples of plagiarism, such as those discussed in the *MLA Handbook for Writers of Research Papers,* and remind them that it is necessary to properly cite sources of information. **L2**

enlighten your readers, persuade them, entertain them, or do you have some combination of purposes? With your audience and purpose in mind, you will be better able to define your project.

Finding Information

If you are really stuck for ideas, the Internet may be a source of inspiration. Surf the Net and see what Web sites appeal to you. Is there something you would like to share with other students? There are sites that publish student writing. Perhaps they are looking for a certain type of submission that you can try your hand at. With a little luck, you can be an Internet author.

Once you have a topic, you can use the Internet as an informational resource. Information from the Internet can be downloaded to your hard drive or printed out directly to your printer and saved as reference material. Information can even be cut and pasted directly into your project document. Don't forget to include the source of each item you download. You may need to credit that source in your paper, especially if you rely on it extensively or quote from it. You can learn more about citing Internet resources on pages 336–341.

You'll also want to evaluate the information you find on the Internet. Anyone can start a Web site and claim to be an expert on some topic. You must decide whether the information you find can be trusted and is worth using. Don't be misled by a flashy, elaborate Web site. Think about what's on it. Is the information useful to you? Does it appear to be accurate? Can you confirm it from a second source? Is the writer a recognized authority on the topic?

Planning and Organizing

As you begin planning and organizing a piece of writing, word processing is a great asset. Most programs allow users to work with more than one document open at a time. Thus, if you have a separate document for your prewriting notes, you can keep it open while you are writing your first draft. Then you will be able to drag and drop material from the notes into your draft. You can also easily copy the thoughts you have into a new file and expand them into an outline. Make each main idea a heading and then drop and drag the details under the main ideas they relate to. As you work, you may think of other details you can add.

Also think about your introduction and conclusion. The introduction can state the thesis that the paper supports, with the conclusion summarizing your arguments. Or the introduction can be a quotation or story that sets the mood. As a result of the ease of editing, word processing encourages you to experiment with different ideas. If you write something terrific that does not fit your current piece of writing, save the work in a separate file for use at another time.

Writing the Paper

Once you have created your outline, with main ideas and the details that support the main ideas, you can begin drafting the body of the paper.

Drafting   You might want to begin drafting your piece by simply expanding your outline. Try turning your main ideas and supporting details into sentences. Then keep expanding as needed. Don't worry about including too much. You can cut out what isn't necessary during the revising stage. Anything that doesn't work can be easily dropped, replaced, or revised.

Revising and Editing   Read your work over carefully. Have you gotten all your ideas across? Do your arguments make sense? Then use your word processing software to help fine tune the writing. Most word processing programs have a spelling checker. In a few seconds, this tool will check the spelling of every word in a document. However, remember that a spelling checker can only identify words that are in the computer's memory as correctly spelled words. If you use a wrong word but the word is correctly spelled, the spelling checker will not know the word is wrong. The program may also question proper names and foreign words even when they're correctly spelled. There's no substitute for a careful personal proofreading.

The ability to include headers and footers is available as part of many programs. With these tools, you can include the title of the piece, your name, the date, and the page number either at the top of every page (header) or at the bottom of the page (footer). Don't confuse a footer with a footnote, which provides your reader with a reference for the resources you use to write the paper. Many word processing programs also provide you with the ability to insert automatic footnotes and endnotes, a very handy tool when you need to write a research report.

Publishing   Word processing programs offer you many options for dressing up your work. You can experiment with different fonts, make words **bold** or *italic* or ***bold and italic,*** change the size of the type, add bulleted items, and put lists into columns. Most programs also allow you to add illustrations and graphic elements—photos, artwork, graphs, and maps—to your work.

Many word processing programs also include some of the features of more-complex desktop publishing programs. These features will allow you to design professional-looking reports, newsletters, and brochures. They may

Technology Tip

Among the advantages of using a computer for writing is a word processor's ability to produce macros. A **macro** is a single instruction that stands for a sequence of operations. For example, suppose you were writing a report in which you knew you would have to repeatedly type "Perry's Victory and International Peace Memorial National Monument." You could create a time-saving macro in which one keystroke would produce all eight words, properly spelled and capitalized. Check out your word processor's ability to create macros. It could save your fingers a bit of work.

Electronic Resources

Teach

Checking a Spelling Checker

Have students use a word processor to draft an opinion piece suitable for their school newspaper. After the students have completed their first draft, have them exchange printouts of their papers with a partner to check the spelling of their partner's paper. Then have students use the word processor to run a spelling check of their first draft and compare the results. They should notice that while the word processor may be more consistent in catching some mistakes, they can catch mistakes the word processor can't. Suggest to students that by learning the word processor's limits they can become better proofreaders. **L2**

Cross-reference: Writing

For instruction and practice on writing footnotes, refer students to Lesson 7.4, pp. 336–341.

MEETING INDIVIDUAL NEEDS   **Gifted and Talented**

Using Grammar Checkers

Encourage students with above-average skills in the English Language to write a brief report on the grammar check feature of their word processor for the benefit of the entire class. Students' reports should examine the criteria word processors use to check grammar, compare these criteria to the rules learned in this textbook, advise when to follow the suggestions of the word processor, and suggest alternative ways to fix sentences.

Practice and Assess

Evaluation Rubrics

Exercise 1

Student articles will vary but should be geared to a fifth- or sixth-grade audience. Articles should provide enough information that a fifth- or sixth-grader could feel confident doing the following:
- opening a new document
- dragging and dropping text
- selecting a format
- printing and saving a finished document

Student articles should also suggest how the word processor is used in all the stages of the writing process covered in this lesson.

Close

Ask students to summarize what they have learned about using a word processor as part of the writing process.

Electronic Resources

include predesigned templates with attractive layouts you can use or adapt to meet your personal needs and tastes. Working with classmates, you can collaborate to produce an attractive collection of class writings or to start a school literary magazine.

Exercise 1

Working with a few classmates, write an article about using word processing for school work. Base the article on the software you currently use. Your audience is fifth- or sixth-grade students who are familiar with computers but have not yet used such software.

31.2 Research and Resources

Research is an important part of all writing—from history reports to novels about rabbits. Research is the tool that helps you provide the most accurate information possible and furnishes information to help you make your stories believable and your essays authoritative. Your school or local library is a terrific place to start looking for information. Online resources are accessible through the click of a mouse button. For many topics, Internet resources rival—and may even exceed in importance—such traditional resources as books, magazines, and newspapers. If you want to learn about an upgrade for a particular piece of computer software, for example, the Internet is your best bet for the most up-to-date information.

The Internet

Think of the Internet as an enormous web that stretches around the world and has no center—hence the term *World Wide Web*. There are distinct components: business, education, and government, for example. A site's URL (uniform resource locator, or Net address) will tell you the type of organization that created a particular Web site. (See the Technology Tip on this page.) Sites offer information and resources, and specific software programs help you navigate through hundreds of millions of Web pages to find what you need.

You also have the ability to communicate within the Web through e-mail, chat rooms, and newsgroups. Thus, there is a world of information available to those who are willing to search.

E-mail Electronic mail, or e-mail, is one of the most-used features of the Internet. E-mail allows you to exchange messages with anyone else in the world who has an e-mail account. You can even send the same e-mail to many different people at the same time. E-mail is available twenty-four hours a day, seven days a week, and can be sent and received almost instantaneously. You can correspond with an expert on a topic you hope to write about and include the expert's answers to your questions in your paper. Remember, however, that not everyone is available instantly. Thoughtful responses take time, so you will need to allow a few days for people to respond to your requests. Following is list of a few sites where you can find answers to your questions or information about where you can find answers. Note that none of these sources will do your homework for you, but they can give you valuable advice to help you do it.

Technology Tip

You've no doubt heard radio or television ads giving Internet addresses ending in "dot-com.") The *.com* ending indicates a commercial (for-profit) business. Here are a few more common endings:

.edu (educational organization)

.org (nonprofit organization)

.gov (government)

.mil (military)

Sites outside the United States use a two-letter ending that indicates the country of origin. For example,

.br (Brazil)	*.ng* (Nigeria)
.ca (Canada)	*.sy* (Syria)
.fr (France)	*.vn* (Vietnam).

Focus

Lesson Overview

Objectives
• To use the Internet and other electronic resources to gather information

Skills
• collaborating; compiling information using technology

Critical Thinking
• analyzing; comparing and contrasting; evaluating

Listening and Speaking
• discussing

Bellringer
Daily Language Activity

When students enter the classroom, have this assignment on the board: *Think of a hobby you'd like to learn more about. Write three or four questions about the hobby to be answered by using the Internet.*

See also *Daily Language Practice*

Motivating Activity

Have volunteers share the questions they wrote down in the Bellringer activity. Ask students more familiar with the Internet to explain to the class how the volunteers might go about finding answers.

Electronic Resources

Resource Manager

Planning Resources
• *Lesson Plans*

Other Print Resources
• *Guide to Using the Internet and Other Electronic Resources*

Teach

Evaluating Web Sites

Ask students to explore a topic of interest to them using each of the five Web sites listed in the chart on student page 914. Have them try to find the same information on each Web site. Then have them write a brief report on their searches. Ask them to include their evaluations of the following for each Web site:

- the ease of the search
- the attractiveness of the site's design
- the amount and accuracy of the information **L2**

Site	Web Address (URL)
Answers.Com	http://www.answers.com
Homework Central	http://www.homeworkheaven.com
Infoplease	http://www.infoplease.com
Kids Search Tools	http://www.rcls.org/ksearch.htm
StudyWeb	http://www.studyweb.com

Chat Rooms Imagine a clubhouse where a different discussion is occurring in each room. You can come and go as you please. Chat rooms are like clubhouses, except in chat rooms people communicate via written computer communication rather than by voice. Chat rooms are areas of the Internet where people who have similar interests gather.

There are thousands of chat rooms, hundreds just for teens alone. Some of these teen chat rooms are devoted to general teen discussions, others to specific topics like dating or school work. Since chat rooms are on the World Wide Web, you can often find interesting discussions among young people from many different countries. A Web search will lead you to chat rooms on almost any topic you can think of. Once in a chat room, you can participate in the discussion or just observe. To take part, you simply type a statement or question into your computer. Others in the chat room can respond to you from their computers.

Before you become active in a chat room, you should always look for and read carefully the chat room's membership requirements, rules and regulations, and list of FAQ's (frequently asked questions). Doing so will keep you from asking questions that have been asked and answered previously.

Newsgroups There are newsgroups devoted to discussions of thousands of topics—for example, the uses of particular software programs or computer games, teen concerns, discussions about popular recording artists or movie or TV stars. Like a chat room, newsgroups bring together people with a similar interest. Newsgroups, however, do so via e-mail rather than in real-time discussions. You can send an e-mail with a comment or a question to the group. Your message goes out to all group members, which may be hundreds of people. Any member can respond to you. Newsgroups provide a great way of learning from people who know more about a topic than you do.

Enrichment and Extension

Have students use the Internet to locate reviews of three movies they have seen recently. Ask them to compare the opinions of at least two reviewers who have seen the same three movies as the student. Then have them present to the class a brief oral report summarizing their comparisons of the two reviewers and recommending one. For this activity, encourage students to use partners more familiar with the Internet to guide them in their search.

1. Compose an e-mail message and send it to five people you know. Ask each one to provide you with the URL, or Internet address, of one or more favorite Web sites. Investigate each site and start a list of sites that you think are worth visiting often.
2. Use a search engine to find a chat room that interests you. Visit it and report to the class on what you find.

CD-ROMs and DVDs

While the Internet has loads of information, you often have to sift through a multitude of data to find what you want. Software packages or CD-ROMs (compact disc read-only memory) have been created that contain comprehensive information on specific topics. These CD-ROMs include encyclopedias, dictionaries, atlases, and a variety of other helpful references, many of which contain video clips, animation, and sound as well as text. Check with your school or local library, which may have a collection of such disks that you can consult for your research projects.

DVDs (digital video discs) are a more recent technology. It would take about eight CDs to hold as much information as a single side of a DVD. The storage capacity of a DVD is so great that an entire full-length motion picture can be stored on a single disc. In addition, the video and audio qualities are superior to those of other data storage software. DVDs with feature films are already widely accepted. Because of their huge capacity, they are likely to eventually replace CD-ROMs for computer data storage, software programs, and games.

Finding and Tracking Sites

The best way to find the specific information you want on the Internet is through a search engine. Type one or more keywords into a search engine and within seconds you'll get a list of dozens (or even thousands) of sites that may contain the information you need. On most search engines, brief descriptors will help you sift through the hits for those most likely to help you. The use of well-chosen keywords will keep you from getting too many irrelevant sites.

Your browser will let you keep track of the sites you have visited and would like to return to. (These sites are called Bookmarks or Favorites, depending on which browser you use.) Think of them as an address book for online content. If you think you may want to return to a site, all you need do is pull down the Bookmarks (or Favorites) menu and select the command that will save the site's URL for you. To return to the site, you pull down the menu again and select its name.

Electronic Resources

Practice and Assess

Evaluation Rubrics

Exercise 2

1. Students should demonstrate that they know how to send messages via e-mail. Their lists should include for each site a brief summary of the site's contents and reasons why the site is worth visiting.
2. Students should indicate in their reports which search engine they used and which chat room they visited. Their reports should also describe the topics discussed in the chat room and the kinds of people who participate in the discussion. Students should also give information about the style and tone of the chat room discussion.

Practice and Assess

Evaluation Rubrics

Exercise 3

Students' answers will vary. They should indicate who their favorite author is, which search engine they used, and at what Internet sites they found their answers. Have them include the URLs of each site.

Close

Have students suggest other ways the Internet might be used. Remind them of its uses in other courses of study, such as history or biology.

Exercise 3

Choose a favorite author and use a search engine to find one or more Internet sites devoted to that author and his or her works. Use the sites to answer the following questions about the author you chose.

- When was his/her first book published?
- How many books did he/she publish?
- What was the longest time span between published books?
- What other writers were writing at the same period of time?

31.3 Communicating Visually

Have you ever noticed that some documents are so dense and wordy that you have a headache when you look at them? Such documents are packed with words. There are no headings and no breaks between paragraphs; it is hard to distinguish among the different ideas that are presented. In fact, you can barely read such documents. They are poorly designed because the publisher did not take readability into account.

Everything from the style and size of the font, or letters, to the size of the margins and the length of the page contribute to the appeal of a document. As a writer you should try to make your writing easy to read as well as interesting.

Different Forms, Different Styles

The many different forms of writing have different styles. The form of haiku is very specific—three lines of verse containing five, seven, and five syllables respectively. Newspaper pieces usually have multiple narrow columns with a headline followed by a byline. The headline is bold and centered; it jumps out from the page. The stories usually have very short paragraphs, sometimes as short as a single sentence. Newspaper articles may also contain photographs with a caption and charts, graphs, or maps.

With a word processing program, design elements such as headers, font style, and alignment can be accessed from the tool bars at the top of the window. These elements make your writing readable. However, too many different styles can make your writing as difficult to get through as a piece that has no distinguishing characteristics.

Focus

Lesson Overview

Objectives
- To design written material for specific audiences
- To learn about design elements
- To use technology to enhance written work with graphics

Skills
- using design elements such as typefaces and graphics; communicating information visually

Critical Thinking
- analyzing; evaluating

Listening and Speaking
- discussing

Electronic Resources

Bellringer
Daily Language Activity

When students enter the classroom, have this assignment on the board: *Read the following line of verse from "Those Winter Sundays" by Robert Hayden:*

Sundays too my father got up early . . .
Write down which word or words you think should be italicized for emphasis and why.

See also *Daily Language Practice*

Motivating Activity

Have students discuss their responses to the Bellringer activity. Focus their attention on how the meaning appears to change when different words are emphasized.

Resource Manager

Planning Resources
- *Lesson Plans*

Other Print Resources
- *Guide to Using the Internet and Other Electronic Resources*

Practice and Assess

Evaluation Rubrics

Exercise 4

Students' redesigned writing will vary but should show that they understand, and can make appropriate use of, the rules bulleted on student page 918. Students should make clear what their intended audience is and why their design is suited to it. You might also recommend that they point to aspects of their design throughout their presentation to communicate with their audience more effectively.

Electronic Resources

Does this page look like it would be easy to read?

There are specific style guides that provide rules of usage and instructions on how to write well. Many of these guides are also available on the Internet. Following are several simple rules to get you started.

- Keep the style simple.
- Do not use too many fonts. For most of your writing, one font for your main text and one font for headings is enough. If you are producing something more elaborate, such as a brochure or a Web page, you might consider using more.
- Use generous margins. Margins of one to one-and-a-half inches left, right, top, and bottom will frame your text nicely.
- **Bold**, underlining, and *italics* indicate extra importance, but don't overdo these elements. If you try to make everything look important, nothing will be emphasized.
- Bulleted lists (like this one) or numbered lists can help make your ideas stand out.

Exercise 4

Look through your portfolio for a piece of your writing you particularly like. Use word processing software to redesign the presentation for a particular audience. Suit the design to your intended audience. Share your design and your thoughts about it with your classmates.

Listening and Speaking

Ask students to use a word processor to redesign the text of a newspaper column, speech, or passage of literary prose so that most people reading it would know how to speak it. Encourage students to make use of as many of the typeface and formatting features offered on their word processor as they need. Have other students in the class read the text aloud. Then ask the entire class to discuss whether the new design was successful and why.

Graphics and Writing

Visual images—photographs, artwork, graphs, charts, and tables—enhance your writing. It is easy to imagine the joy of winning a sports championship, but a photo of the enthusiastic faces of the team shows how they cherish their triumph. Images also help with difficult explanations. You could write that ice cream consumption varies considerably from season to season. You could then state the percentages for each season. However, a graph like the one on this page provides all that information much more vividly.

Color-coding parts of a graph makes the parts stand out more clearly. In the ice cream pie chart, it is easy to identify the different seasons since each is a distinct color. On a computer with graphing software, or with your word processing program if the program includes a graphing function, you can enter data into a table and convert the data into several types of graphs.

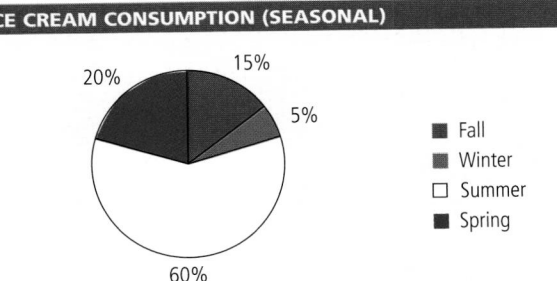

ICE CREAM CONSUMPTION (SEASONAL)

- 15%
- 5%
- 60%
- 20%

- ■ Fall
- ■ Winter
- □ Summer
- ■ Spring

Word processing software allows you to include all kinds of graphic elements within your written text. Check your software to see what options you have for the creation of tables, graphs, and other artwork. The Help function of the program will help you learn to use these tools. Simply create a graphic image and then copy and paste your image into your written text in the same way that you copy and paste text.

Graphic Explanations

Graphics can help you make clear some concepts and processes that are difficult to explain in words. Notice how clearly the family tree on page 920 shows that children with four different last names are all cousins descended from great grandparents Mary and Paul Smith. (The letter *m* in the diagram stands for "married." Each generation of children is shown below the parents.)

Teach

Analyzing Graphs

Show students a variety of charts, tables, maps, and other graphics culled from books, magazines, newspapers, and Web sites. Ask students to examine components most informational graphs have in common, such as the title, the key, explanatory notes, and the graphic itself. Have students discuss whether certain kinds of information are suited to certain kinds of graphs and why. Ask them also to evaluate the clarity and accuracy of the graphs by considering design elements such as color, scale, layout, and typeface. Have students note in particular any graphs that attempt to persuade by distorting scale or setting important information in small print. **L2**

Practice and Assess

Evaluation Rubrics

Exercise 5

1. Graphs will vary in form and content. Students, however, should make use of the table-formatting and graphics features of their word processor. Graphs should also be accurate and labeled properly and contain all the information necessary to be understood.
2. Tables should include a title and a key to abbreviations and should use only the number of rows and columns necessary to present the information. Students should also select sizes of rows, columns, and type that enhance legibility.

Close

Ask students to discuss when it is helpful and appropriate to use graphic explanations in their writing and when it is not. (Graphics may help to explain information about quantities, categories, and spatial relationships; graphics may interrupt the flow of narrative or expository prose.)

Choosing the right kind of graphic is important. Charts and tables can help you sort and organize information in various ways. Your class schedule at school is a chart. It is divided into days and times; your classes are written into the slots. However, your class schedule would be extremely confusing if you tried to graph it as a pie chart. Graphs are excellent choices for comparing items that can be counted with numbers or percentages.

The best way to gain a better understanding of the power of graphics is to experiment. Try creating different graphics with the same information. This will help you see the difference and to better understand how various concepts can be best illustrated.

Exercise 5

1. Gather some data about your school, your class, or a group within your class. Use computer software to convert your data into a graph.
2. Create a table in your word processing program and use it to organize information about ten of your favorite movies. Include at least four categories of information, such as title, year of release, featured stars, and director. You might also want to rate each film. Name the categories in headings at the top of your table.

Electronic Resources

31.4 Visual Analysis

Have you ever thought about how you get your information? Do you read a newspaper or magazines? Do you watch the news on television? Do you listen to something other than music on the radio? Do you look for news and other information on the Internet?

Have you ever tried to **deconstruct** the media? *Deconstruct* means "take apart." For example, have you tried to take apart the content of a news story or a television comedy so that you could look at how each part works and how the parts work together to transmit messages to you?

Technology and the Visual Media

Movies, television, and television commercials have several important similarities. They all hope to capture and hold your attention. Some even want you to suspend your belief in reality and enter the visual world they have created. These visual productions contain many of the same elements as a story. They are set in a particular time and place. They (even most commercials) have a plot and characters. Like books and other writings, they cover everything from reality-based news reports and documentaries to science fiction.

Movies and television also provide viewers with experiences they might not otherwise have. Technology has made these experiences all the more realistic. Wearing special 3-D glasses in an enormous theatre, you can watch swimmers scuba dive off the Great Barrier Reef and feel like you are there. With advanced stereo sound projection, you can almost feel the reverberation as bombs drop during a World War II movie. With a superior script, you can feel and share the stirring emotions of a great drama.

Technology has caused a revolution in television and movie production. Satellites allow pictures to be broadcast from halfway around the world. Computers blur the lines between fantasy and reality. You watch on television car chases between the police and fugitives as they actually happen. Animals seem to talk, and animated characters share the screen with real actors.

As computers and software become more sophisticated, what they create becomes more believable. Watch an old science fiction movie and you can almost see that the space ships were plastic models shot at close range. Yet, when you watch more-recent movies, the computer-generated aliens look as real as the actors.

Since many people tend to believe what they see, visual productions have a relatively easy time capturing the audience's imagination.

Focus

Lesson Overview

Objectives
- To deconstruct messages in a variety of visual media

Skills
- critical viewing of visual representations

Critical Thinking
- analyzing; drawing conclusions; evaluating

Listening and Speaking
- discussing

 Bellringer
Daily Language Activity

When students enter the classroom, have this assignment on the board: *List five different kinds of media, such as television and newspapers, that you use every day.*

See also Daily Language Practice

Motivating Activity

Have students share their responses to the Bellringer, and ask them to tell which media they prefer and why. Extend the discussion to consider more broadly the purposes and audiences of and the content found in various media.

Electronic Resources

 Resource Manager

Planning Resources
- *Lesson Plans*

Other Print Resources
- *Guide to Using the Internet and Other Electronic Resources*

Teach

Analyzing an Ad

Select a television ad appropriate for a classroom setting that does not immediately announce the product being sold or message being given, and show the students the beginning portion of the ad. Have students discuss what the atmosphere and tone of the ad is, how the visual images and sound contribute to that atmosphere and tone, and what audience the ad would appeal to. Then ask them to infer what product the ad is selling or what message it's communicating. Show the remainder of the ad, then discuss whether the ad fulfilled their expectations of it and why. You might extend the discussion by having students speculate about the advertiser's intentions. **L2**

Electronic Resources

The Medium and the Message

Different forms of writing have different lengths in which they can tell their story. A poem may only be several lines, while a novel can go on for hundreds of pages. Likewise television ads tend to last between fifteen and sixty seconds, while most television shows are thirty to sixty minutes in length. A feature film has the luxury of telling its story in two hours or more. The amount of time available has an impact on the plot and character development in a story and on the depth of detail in a documentary. The longer you have, the more in-depth you can go. As with poetry, however, the requirements of a shorter form mean that you must be more exacting in what you produce.

Sights and Sounds

Next time you watch a movie or a television program, pay attention to the set. Notice the amount of detail the set designer has included in order to make that set as believable as possible. In a kitchen set, not only is there food in the refrigerator, but there may be crumbs on the counter, silverware in the dish drain, and a credit card bill on the counter. It looks like a kitchen in anyone's home.

Once you are aware of the surroundings, listen carefully to the soundtrack. Notice how the music varies depending on the emotions the scene tries to evoke. Notice also the sounds added to the scene, other than the actors' voices. Sounds and music are a tremendous tool for setting the mood and manipulating the emotions of the audience.

Lastly, the angle of the camera and the choice of shots affect the storytelling process. The longer the camera dwells on a character's face, the more emotion an actor can show. If the cinematographer zooms in on a subject, that subject takes on greater significance. The camera is the mechanism advancing the story. Are the individual shots long or short? Rapid cutting of a series of short shots can add to the excitement of the scene.

Critical Viewing

Many of the skills you learned for critiquing other people's writing can be applied to the visual realm. Compare the plots of a sixty-second television commercial, a thirty-minute television show, and a movie. Were the characters or actors believable? Did the story capture your attention? How many characters were in each? How many different scenes were there? How many different cuts of the camera? What was the critical turning point of the plot? How did the musical score accentuate this action? Were all the plot twists resolved?

Not many of us evaluate the visual stories in movies, television, and commercials. We tend to watch placidly, without noticing how the filmmaker is manipulating the story. In addition, uninvolved participants and channel surfers seldom realize that even slapstick comedy may have a message.

Learn to watch television and movies with a more critical eye. What is the producer trying to sell you? What message is the program conveying? What effects made a movie especially entertaining? If a news story is particularly compelling, ask yourself whether the most important element was the interviewer's technique, the subject matter, or the visuals. Find ways to use similar techniques in your own work.

Exercise 6

Compare a thirty-second television commercial, a thirty-minute television show, and a movie. Ask yourself such questions as:

- Who made each of them and for what purpose?
- How many characters were in each?
- How many different scenes were there?
- About how many shots did each have in a half-minute period?
- How was the camera used in each?
- How were music and sound effects used?
- What rhythms did the editing create?
- How did all these elements combine to produce one or more messages?
- What messages did you detect?

Working in a small group, discuss and compare your findings and conclusions.

Practice and Assess

Evaluation Rubrics

Exercise 6

Students should answer the bulleted questions, and their conclusions should demonstrate an understanding of the concepts covered in this lesson. Students should also encourage participation within their group.

Close

Ask students to consider and discuss the various media found on the Internet. You might ask them, for example, to consider what the differences are between reading a newspaper online and in print, or between viewing artwork online and in a gallery.

Electronic Resources

Focus

Lesson Overview

Objective
- To learn about multimedia techniques and how to apply them to a topic
- To create a multimedia ad campaign

Skills
- collaborating; outlining/storyboarding; using multimedia presentation software

Critical Thinking
- analyzing; evaluating

Listening and Speaking
- discussing

 Bellringer

Daily Language Activity

When students enter the classroom, have this assignment on the board: *Write a brief paragraph describing how elements of moviemaking such as background music, camera angles, special effects, and lighting affect the mood of movies. Cite examples from specific movies if possible.*

See also *Daily Language Practice*

Motivating Activity

Record a scene from a movie that makes intelligent use of sound and image. First, show students the scene with the sound turned off. Ask students to discuss the action on the screen and the mood the visuals, such as camera angle and lighting, create, and have them infer the main idea. Ask them also what sound or music they might expect to accompany the scene and, if the characters on screen appear to be speaking, what the dialogue might be. Then show the scene with the sound turned on. Have students discuss the ways in which the addition of sound altered their perception of the scene. Remind them that a movie is only one kind of multimedia presentation.

Electronic Resources

31.5 Producing in Multimedia

Multimedia is the merging of written text (the written word), sound (speech, music, sound effects), and images (photos, graphics, video clips) into a single presentation. Productions can be as relatively low-tech as a slide show with a tape recorder or as high-tech as your own Web page with video and audio clips. Some multimedia productions are created to be viewed in a linear fashion, as the author assembled it. Others productions include hyperlinks that allow the user to choose the paths they want to take. Presentation and hypertext software packages can help you create a multimedia production, and you can begin with just a little help from the program itself.

Following are three relatively easy ways to create a multimedia production.

Camera, slide or overhead projector, screen, and tape recorder.	Use 35-mm slides or overhead transparencies for the visuals (text and images). Use a tape recorder for narration, music, or other sounds.
Computer with speakers, monitor, and a microphone	Use presentation software to create a computer-based slide show combining text, graphics, images, and sound.
Computer with speakers, monitor, and a microphone. Also useful: digital camera, video camera, scanner (to scan and digitize images)	Use a hypertext program to combine text, graphics, images, and sound to create a series of "cards" that can be viewed in a sequence.

Multimedia Techniques

If multimedia is the merging of text, sound, and images, the possibilities of what you can create and how you create it are almost endless. You could create an animated flipbook with text captions and an accompanying soundtrack that is played on a tape recorder. Or you could create a DVD that details the history of moviemaking.

In multimedia, as in writing, different subjects lend themselves to different forms. A multimedia production about the history of your hometown might start with several old photos, perhaps accompanied by an interview with a historian or one of the town's founders. More pictures showing the town's gradual development could be followed by video footage of the town as it currently looks and your own reflections presented in text and words.

Resource Manager

Planning Resources
- *Lesson Plans*

Other Print Resources
- *Guide to Using the Internet and Other Electronic Resources*

If you have a great deal of historical information, you might provide links to sidebar stories that users can explore as they wish. You would probably want to use presentation software to create this production and allow users some freedom in following paths of their choice.

By comparison, if you are doing a biography of one of the town's founders, you could choose to create a more linear story, beginning with the founder's birth and moving chronologically into the present. You could also use presentation software for this production so that you could incorporate digitized still photos, slides, home movies, and sound. However, you might require that the user go through the production sequentially, in the order you created it.

Creating a Project

Presentation software provides you many tools with which to create a multimedia production. Start by thinking about the look and feel of your project. Is your goal to entertain, to inform, or to persuade? Who is your audience—people around your age, older people, young children? Or will the audience be a mixed audience? Once you've determined your purpose and audience, choose an appropriate background for your slide template. (Multimedia software programs generally call each different screen a *slide* or a *card*. We'll refer to the different screens as slides.) If each slide is presented on the same background, there will be consistency throughout the presentation. On the other hand, if your topic calls for variety or distinct segments, you can vary the backgrounds and the templates.

Next you can add a few simple hyperlinks to your template. Arrows can be inserted that the user can click on to move from slide to slide. Another hyperlink might take your user back to the first slide—the title slide, or "home." The presentation software makes adding these features fairly simple. The software program's Help function helps you put your presentation together and does the programming for you.

After completing the background, you'll need to set up fields for your text and graphics. A field is an area you define into which you can add either text or images.

Teach

Using Multimedia Software on the Web

Familiarize yourself with multimedia software by viewing Web sites for HyperStudio and HyperCard. Training and workshop materials for HyperStudio, for instance, can be accessed from its site, as can example works by students of various ages. You might suggest that students view these sites, or you might help them publish their own multimedia presentations on the Web. **L3**

Electronic Resources

925

Teach

Using a Storyboard

Ask students to suggest topics suitable for a multimedia presentation, and write the topics on the board. Divide the students into small groups, and have each group select a topic. Instruct the groups to plan a multimedia presentation by creating a storyboard chart like the one on student page 926. When the groups have finished making their charts, have the groups explain them to the rest of the class. Encourage the rest of the class to suggest ways that the groups can improve their charts. **L2**

This sample slide background is one possible design. The number of ways you can use the space on a slide is limited only by your imagination.

Next, script what you want to say. You might want to start drafting your script with word processing software. After you've completed and revised the script, you can cut and paste the text into the appropriate slides. Another alternative is to storyboard your multimedia presentation. Create a table with separate columns for slide number, text, sounds, and images. Each row of your table will describe one slide in your presentation.

Storyboard: Making a Multimedia Presentation			
Segment	Text	Sounds	Images
1	Title: Making a Multimedia Presentation by Jesse Sanchez	Music: to come (something lively)	Opener artwork: sample slide
2	None	Narration: Anyone can make a multimedia presentation.	Photo of me at the computer
3	None	All you need is a computer, presentation software, and an idea.	Photo of presentation software box

Think of each slide as a separate part of an outline, with no more than one main idea per slide. Remember not to overload the production with extras (too much information, too many colors, too many different things happening in each segment). If the images are particularly powerful, you may not need any text. Likewise, you may use a narrator and not need any written text. Start with a title slide. At the end of the presentation, include a slide (or more if needed) to credit your sources.

Presentation software usually has word processing and slide show tools. The word processing tools—such as the variety of fonts and the spelling checker—are similar to what you are familiar with. You will also have the choice of how you want the show to progress, for example, by adding fades or dissolves between slides.

Evaluating a Project

You have spent countless hours creating a multimedia project that you think is great. How can you be sure? Use the following checklist for evaluating your project.

✔ Does the project flow?
✔ Are the ideas easy to understand?
✔ Will users be able to navigate through all the links?
✔ Are there too many fancy cuts and fades that could distract the user?
✔ Have I achieved my purpose and addressed my audience?

Once you have gone through your presentation yourself, set up a dress rehearsal with a friend. First create an evaluation sheet. Then have your friend go through the production. Since multimedia is ultimately viewed by an audience, collaborating with a friend is probably the best way to make sure you have accomplished your goal. Often what an author thinks is obvious is not obvious to the viewer. You may have left out information or provided too much information. Listen to your reviewer's comments and try not to take criticism personally. Remember your friend is helping you. You might also want to view other people's work and note what you like or dislike. Adapt ideas you like to your own project. Like everything, being a good multimedia producer takes practice.

Exercise 7

Working with a group, create an ad campaign for a favorite movie. Plan presentations for a variety of media: print, radio, television, and billboards. Prepare for personal appearances on talk shows with group members playing the host and the star guests.

Practice and Assess

Evaluation Rubrics

Exercise 7
Student presentations should include the name and a brief summary of the movie being advertised and should demonstrate that the students have considered all the questions in the project evaluation checklist on student page 927. You could also ask each group to prepare a similar checklist so that the rest of the class can provide feedback.

Close

Remind students that they can find many examples of multimedia on the Internet. Encourage them to explore sites for information as well as inspiration for future projects.

✔ ASSESSMENT OPTIONS

📁 *Tests with Answer Key & Rubrics*
Unit 31 Mastery Test

💾 *Testmaker*
Unit 31 Mastery Test

📼 *MindJogger Videoquizzes*

You may wish to administer the Unit 31 Mastery Test at this point.

Electronic Resources

---

*inter*NET CONNECTION

Encourage students to use e-mail as part of their collaborations on multimedia projects. If your school has a computer lab, you might hold a computer tutorial there. Show students how to send and copy e-mail, as well as how to attach files to e-mail. Then suggest that they include you on the list of message recipients for all e-mail related to their projects. You might also welcome students to use e-mail to ask you any questions about their projects that fellow students can't answer.

WRITING AND LANGUAGE GLOSSARY

This glossary will help you quickly locate grammatical and other terms useful for writers.

A

Abstract noun. *See* Noun.

Active voice. A verb is in the **active voice** if the subject of the sentence performs the action.

Adjective. A word that modifies a noun or pronoun by limiting its meaning. An adjective may tell *what kind, which one, how many,* or *how much.*

> The **positive degree** is the simple form of the adjective.
> The **comparative degree** compares two persons, places, things, or ideas.
> The **superlative degree** compares more than two persons, places, things, or ideas.

Adjective clause. A dependent clause that modifies a noun or pronoun. *See also* Clause.

Adverb. A word that modifies a verb, an adjective, or another adverb by making its meaning more specific. Adverbs tell *how, when, where,* and *to what degree.*

> The **comparative** form of an adverb compares two actions. (*more quickly, better*) The **superlative** form compares three or more actions. (*most quickly, best*)

Adverb clause. A dependent clause that modifies a verb, an adjective, or an adverb. *See also* Clause.

Allusion. A reference in a composition to a well-known character, place, or situation from a work of literature, music, or art or from history.

Analysis. The act of breaking down a subject into its separate parts to determine its meaning.

Anecdote. A short story or incident, usually presented as part of a longer narrative.

Antecedent. *See* Pronoun.

Appositive. A noun or a pronoun placed next to another noun or pronoun to identify or give additional information about it. (My cousin *Lonnie* is going to Guatemala this summer.)

Argument. A statement, reason, or fact for or against a point; a composition intended to persuade.

Article. The adjectives *a, an,* and *the.* **Indefinite articles** (*a* and *an*) refer to one of a general group of persons, places, or things. The **definite article** (*the*) indicates that the noun is a specific person, place, or thing.

Audience. The person(s) who reads or listens to what the writer or speaker says.

Auxiliary verb. *See* Verb.

B

Bias. A tendency or inclination that prevents impartial consideration of an idea; a quality to consider when producing or evaluating persuasive writing.

Bibliography. A list of the books, articles, and other sources used as reference sources in a research paper.

Body. The central part of a composition that communicates the main idea identified in the introduction.

Bookmarks/Favorites. The feature on many Web browsers that allows the user to save addresses of Internet sites so that the sites can be accessed quickly.

Brainstorming. A group activity in which people generate as many ideas as possible without stopping to judge them.

C

Case. The form of a noun or pronoun that is determined by its use in a sentence. A noun or pronoun is in the **nominative case** when it is used as a subject or after a linking verb, in the **objective case** when it is used as an object, and in the **possessive case** when it is used to show possession.

Cause-and-effect development. A kind of organization that involves examining the reasons for actions or events and the results of those actions.

Character. An individual involved in the plot of a work of fiction. **Round characters** have different traits, some of which may be contradictory. **Flat characters** are those which display one dominant trait. **Static characters** do not change. **Dynamic characters** show development in the course of a story.

Characterization. The techniques a writer uses to reveal character. Characterization may be **direct,** revealed through the description of the character and the character's own words and actions, or **indirect,** revealed through what other characters think and say about the character.

Chronological order. The arrangement of events in order of time.

Clarity. The quality of a piece of writing that makes it easy to understand.

Clause. A group of words that has a subject and a predicate and is used as part of a sentence. Clauses fall into two categories: **independent clauses,** which are also called **main clauses,** and **dependent clauses,** which are also called **subordinate clauses.**

An **independent clause** has a subject and a predicate and can stand alone as a sentence. A **dependent clause** is one that cannot stand alone as a sentence. It may be restrictive or nonrestrictive.

A **nonrestrictive clause,** also called a **nonessential clause,** is one that is not needed to make the meaning of a sentence clear. (Mae Jemison, *who comes from Chicago,* gained fame as an astronaut.)

A **restrictive clause,** also called an **essential clause,** is essential to the meaning of a sentence. (A free doughnut will be given to everyone *who arrives before 9* A.M.)

Cliché. An overused expression. (*quiet as a mouse*)

Climax. The point of greatest emotional intensity, interest, or suspense in the plot of a narrative.

Clustering. A technique for generating writing ideas, which involves writing a word, circling it, and surrounding it with other words and phrases.

Coherence. The quality of a paragraph or composition in which sentences are clearly and logically connected; also called cohesiveness.

Cohesive writing. A type of writing in which sentences and paragraphs are logically connected to one another.

Collaboration. The process of working with others on writing or other projects.

Collective noun. *See* Noun.

Colloquialism. A casual, colorful expression used in everyday conversation.

Common noun. *See* Noun.

Comparative degree. *See* Adjective; Adverb.

Compare-and-contrast development. A type of organization used in expository writing that examines similarities and differences in order to find relationships and draw conclusions.

Complement. A word or phrase that completes the meaning of a verb. The four basic kinds of complements are **direct objects, indirect objects, object complements,** and **subject complements.**

Conceptual map. A graphic device that develops a central concept by surrounding it with examples or related ideas in a weblike arrangement.

Conclusion. A restatement or summing up of the ideas in a composition that brings it to a definite close.

Conflict. The struggle between opposing forces that lies at the center of the plot in a story or drama.

Conjunction. A word that joins single words or groups of words.
  Coordinating conjunctions (*and, but, or, nor, for, yet*) join words or groups of words that are equal in grammatical importance.
  Correlative conjunctions work in pairs to join words and groups of words of equal importance.
  Subordinating conjunctions join a dependent idea or clause to a main clause.

Conjunctive adverb. An adverb used to clarify the relationship between clauses of a compound sentence. (The team lost the game last night; *consequently,* they will not play in the tournament.)

Connotation. The thoughts and feelings associated with a word, rather than its dictionary definition.

Constructive criticism. Comments on another person's writing made with the intention of helping the writer improve a particular draft.

Context. The words and sentences that come before and after a specific word and help to explain its meaning.

Coordinating conjunction. *See* Conjunction.

Correlative conjunction. *See* Conjunction.

Credibility. The quality of a speaker or writer that makes that person's words believable.

Critical analysis. The consideration of the elements of a literary work to examine, organize, evaluate, or draw conclusions about them.

Declarative sentence. A sentence that makes a statement.

Deconstructing. Breaking down into component parts, or analyzing.

Deductive reasoning. A way of thinking or explaining that begins with a general statement or principle and applies that principle to specific instances.

Definite article. *See* Article.

Denotation. The dictionary definition of a word.

Dependent clause. *See* Clause.

Descriptive writing. Writing that uses sensory details to convey a dominant impression of, for example, a setting, a person, an animal, and so on.

Desktop publishing. The use of computer programs to format and produce a document that may include written text, graphics, and/or images.

Dialect. A variation of a language spoken by a particular group of people. A dialect may be regional (based on location) or ethnic (based on cultural heritage).

Dialogue. The conversation between characters in a story, play, or novel.

Diction. A writer's choice of words and the arrangement of those words in phrases, sentences, or lines of a poem.

Documentation. Identification of the sources used in writing research or other informative papers, usually in the form of endnotes or footnotes, or using parenthetical documentation.

Drafting. One of the steps in the writing process; the transforming of thoughts, words, and phrases into sentences and paragraphs.

E

Editing. One of the steps in the writing process in which a revised draft is checked for standard usage, varied sentence structure, and appropriate word choice.

Editorial. An article in a newspaper or other form of media that expresses a personal opinion about a subject of current or general interest.

Either-or reasoning. A logical fallacy that limits possibilities to two opposite choices, ignoring other valid possibilities.

Elaboration. The support or development of a main idea with facts, statistics, sensory details, incidents, examples, or quotations.

Ellipsis. A mark of punctuation, consisting of three spaced periods, that indicates the omission of one or more words.

E-mail. Short for electronic mail; messages, usually text, sent from one person to another by way of computer.

Emphatic form. *See* Verb tense.

Essential clause. A subordinate clause that cannot be omitted without changing the intended meaning of a sentence.

Evaluation. Making a judgment about the strengths and weaknesses of a draft in content, organization, and style.

Evidence. Facts or examples from reliable sources that can be used to support statements made in speaking or writing.

Exclamatory sentence. A sentence that expresses strong or intense emotion.

Explanatory writing. *See* Expository writing.

Expository writing. A kind of writing that aims at explaining an idea or presenting a process; also called informative or explanatory writing.

Expressive writing. Writing that emphasizes and conveys the writer's feelings.

F

Fact. A piece of information that can be verified from direct experience or from an authoritative source.

Feedback. The response a listener or reader gives a speaker or writer about his or her work.

Fiction. Literature in which situations and characters are invented by the writer.

Figurative language. Words used for descriptive effect that express some truth beyond the literal level. Figures of speech such as similes, metaphors, or personification are examples of figurative language.

Foreshadowing. Clues that hint at events that will occur later in the plot.

Formal language. Language that uses correct grammar and omits slang expressions and contractions. It is especially common in nonfiction writing that is not personal.

Freewriting. Writing for a specific length of time without stopping or limiting the flow of ideas.

Future perfect tense. *See* Verb tense.

Future tense. *See* Verb tense.

G

Generalization. A statement that presents a conclusion about a subject without going into details or specifics.

Genre. A division of literature. The main literary genres are prose, poetry, and drama. Each of these is further divided into subgenres.

Gerund. A verb form that ends in *-ing* and is used as a noun.

Glittering generality. An attractive claim based on insufficient evidence.

Graphic organizer. A visual way of organizing information; types of graphic organizers include clustering, graphs, tables, time lines, and tree diagrams.

H

Home page. The location on a Web site by which a user normally enters the site. A typical home page may explain the site, summarize the content, and provide links to other sites.

Hyperlink. A highlighted or underlined phrase or word on a Web page that, when clicked, moves the user to another part of the page or to another Web page.

Hypertext. Links in some text that can be clicked with a mouse to take the user to another document or to a different section in the same document.

I

Idea map. *See* Cluster.

Idiom. A word or phrase that has a special meaning different from its standard or dictionary meaning. (*In the same boat* is an idiom that means "having the same problem.")

Imagery. Language that emphasizes sensory impressions that can help the reader of a literary work to see, hear, feel, smell, and taste the scenes described in the work.

Imperative sentence. A sentence that makes a request or gives a command.

Independent clause. *See* Clause.

Inductive reasoning. A way of thinking or explaining that arrives at a conclusion by examining a series of examples.

Infinitive. A verb form that usually begins with the word *to* and functions as a noun, adjective, or adverb in a sentence.

Informative writing. *See* Expository writing.

Intensifier. An adverb that emphasizes an adjective or another adverb. (*very* important, *quite* easily)

Interjection. A word or phrase that expresses emotion or exclamation. An interjection has no grammatical connection to other words.

Internet. A worldwide computer network that allows users to link to any computer on the network electronically for social, commercial, research, and other uses.

Interpretation. An explanation of the meaning of a piece of writing, a visual representation, or any other type of communication.

Interrogative sentence. A sentence that asks a question.

Interview. A question-and-answer dialogue that has the specific purpose of gathering up-to-date or expert information.

Intransitive verb. *See* Verb.

Introduction. The beginning part of a composition, in which a writer identifies the subject and gives a general idea of what the body of the composition will contain.

Inverted order. The placement of a predicate before the subject in a sentence. In most sentences in English, the subject comes before the predicate.

Irregular verb. *See* Verb tense.

J–L

Jargon. Special words and phrases used by a particular trade, profession, or other group of people.

Journal. A personal notebook for freewriting, collecting ideas, and recording thoughts and experiences.

Learning log. A journal for clarifying ideas about concepts covered in various classes.

Lexicon. A wordbook or dictionary.

Listing. A technique used in generating ideas for writing.

Literary analysis. The act of examining the different elements of a piece of literature in order to evaluate it.

Logical fallacy. An error in reasoning often found in advertising or other persuasive writing. *See* Glittering generalities; Either-or reasoning.

M

Main clause. *See* Clause.

Main idea. *See* Thesis statement.

Media. The forms of communication used to reach an audience; newspapers, radio, TV, and the Internet reach large audiences and so are known as mass media.

Memoir. A type of narrative nonfiction that presents an account of an event or period in history, emphasizing the narrator's personal experience.

Metaphor. A figure of speech that compares seemingly unlike things without using the word *like* or *as.* (The girl's aloof *manner* was her *armor* against snubs.)

Mood. The feeling or atmosphere that a writer creates.

Multimedia presentation. The presentation of a piece of writing accompanied by other media, such as music, video, and visual art.

N

Narrative writing. A type of writing that tells about events or actions as they change over a period of time and often includes story elements such as character, setting, and plot.

Nominative pronoun. *See* Pronoun case.

Nonessential clause. A clause that adds information but is not absolutely needed to express the meaning of the sentence.

Nonfiction. Prose writing about real people, places, and events.

Nonrestrictive clause. *See* Nonessential clause.

Noun. A word that names a person, a place, a thing, an idea, a quality, or a characteristic.
An **abstract noun** names an idea, a quality, or a characteristic.
A **collective noun** names a group of people or things.
A **common noun** names a general type of person, place, thing, or idea, characteristic, or quality.

A **proper noun** names a particular person, place, thing, or idea.

Noun clause. A dependent clause that functions as a noun.

Number. The form of a noun, pronoun, or verb that indicates whether it refers to one (**singular**) or to more than one (**plural**).

O

Objective pronoun. *See* Pronoun case.

Onomatopoeia. A word with a sound that suggests its meaning. (*buzz, clink, pop*)

Opinion. A belief or attitude that cannot be proven true or false. Readers and writers should clearly distinguish opinion from fact.

Oral tradition. Literature that passes by word of mouth from one generation to the next. Oral tradition often reflects the cultural values of a people.

Order of importance. A way of organizing details in a paragraph or composition from least to most or most to least important.

Organization. A system of ordering ideas.

Outline. A systematic arrangement of main and supporting ideas, using Roman numerals, letters, and numbers for a written or an oral presentation.

P

Paragraph. A unit of writing that consists of related sentences.

Parallelism. The use of a series of words, phrases, or sentences that have similar grammatical form.

Paraphrase. A restatement of an idea in different words that retains the meaning, tone, and general length of the original.

Parenthetical documentation. A specific reference to the source of a piece of information; it is placed in parenthesis directly after the information appears in a piece of writing.

Participle. A verb form that can function as an adjective. Present participles always end in *-ing*. Although past participles often end in *-ed*, they can take other forms as well.

Passive voice. The form of a verb used when the subject of the sentence receives the action of the verb.

Peer response. The suggestions and comments provided by peers, or classmates, about a piece of writing or another type of presentation.

Personal writing. Writing that expresses the writer's own thoughts and feelings.

Personification. A figure of speech that gives human qualities to an animal, object, or idea.

Perspective. *See* Point of view.

Persuasive writing. Writing that aims at influencing a reader's opinion and actions.

Phrase. A group of words that acts as a single part of speech in a sentence.
    A **prepositional phrase** consists of a preposition, its object, and any modifiers of the object. A **verb phrase** consists of one or more auxiliary verbs followed by a main verb.

Plagiarism. The dishonest presentation of another's words or ideas as one's own.

Plot. The series of events that follow one another in a story, novel, or play.

Poetry. A form of literary expression that emphasizes the line as the unit of composition. Traditional poetry contains emotional, imaginative language and a regular rhythm.

Point of view. The perspective, or angle, from which a story is told. Most writing is done from a first-person, third-person limited, or third-person omniscient point of view.

Portfolio. A collection of various pieces of writing, which may include finished pieces and works in progress.

Positive degree. *See* Adjective.

Possessive pronoun. *See* Pronoun case.

Predicate. The verb or verb phrase and any of its modifiers that make an essential statement about the subject of a sentence.

Preposition. A word that shows the relationship of a noun or pronoun to some other word in the sentence.

Presenting. The last step in the writing process, which involves sharing the final writing product with others.

Prewriting. The first step in the writing process, which includes deciding what to write about, collecting ideas and details, and making an outline or a plan. Prewriting strategies include brainstorming, clustering, word webs, and freewriting.

Prior knowledge. The facts, ideas, and experiences that a writer, reader, or viewer brings to a new activity.

Progressive form. *See* Verb tense.

Pronoun. A word that takes the place of a noun, a group of words acting as a noun, or another pronoun. The word or group of words that a pronoun refers to is called its **antecedent.**

Pronoun case. A personal pronoun refers to a specific person or thing. Personal pronouns have three **cases**—nominative, objective, and possessive. *See also* Case.

Proofreading. The last part of the editing process that involves checking work to discover typographical and spelling errors.

Propaganda. Information aimed at influencing thoughts and actions; it is usually of a political nature and may contain distortions of truth.

Prose. Writing that is similar to everyday speech and written language, as opposed to poetry and drama.

Publishing. The preparation of a finished piece of writing, often using available technology, so that it can be presented to a larger audience.

Purpose. The aim of writing, which may be to express, discover, record, develop, reflect on ideas, problem solve, entertain, influence, inform, or describe.

Regular verb. *See* Verb tense.

Representation. A way in which information or ideas are presented to an audience.

Research. Locating information on a topic from a variety of sources.

Restrictive clause. *See* Essential clause.

Review. An analysis and interpretation of a subject presented through the mass media.

Revising. The stage of the writing process in which a writer goes over a draft, making changes in content, organization, and style in order to improve it. Revision techniques include adding, elaborating, deleting, combining, and rearranging text.

Root. The part of a word that carries the main meaning.

Run-on sentence. Two or more sentences or clauses run together without appropriate punctuation.

S

Sensory details. Words that appeal to the senses—sight, hearing, taste, smell, and feeling; important element of descriptive writing, especially of poetry.

Sentence. A group of words expressing a complete thought. Every sentence has a **subject** and a **predicate.** Sentences can be classified by function or by structure.

> A **simple sentence** has only one main clause and no subordinate clauses.
> A **compound sentence** has two or more main clauses.
> A **complex sentence** has one main clause and one or more subordinate clauses.
> A **compound-complex sentence** has two or more main clauses and at least one subordinate clause. *See also* Declarative sentence; Exclamatory sentence; Imperative sentence; Interrogative sentence.

Sentence variety. The use of different types of sentences to add interest to writing.

Setting. The time and place in which the events of a story happen.

Simile. A figure of speech that compares two unlike things, using the word *like* or *as*. (The clouds looked *like* melted marshmallows.)

Spatial order. The arrangement of the details of a setting according to their location—for example, from left to right or from top to bottom.

Standard English. The most widely used and accepted form of the English language.

Style. The writer's choice and arrangement of words and sentences.

Subordinate clause. *See* Clause.

Subordinating conjunction. *See* Conjunction.

Summary. A brief statement of the main idea of a composition.

Superlative degree. *See* Adjective, Adverb.

Supporting evidence. *See* Evidence.

Suspense. A literary device that creates growing interest and excitement leading up to the climax or resolution of a story. A writer creates suspense by providing clues to the resolution without revealing too much information.

Symbol. An object, a person, a place, or an experience that represents something else, usually something abstract.

T

Tense. *See* Verb tense.

Theme. The main idea or message of a piece of writing.

Thesis statement. A one- or two-sentence statement of the main idea or purpose of a piece of writing.

Time line. A line, usually horizontal, divided into equal segments, each of which represents a specific interval of time; a helpful device for organizing events in chronological order.

Time order. The arrangement of details based on when they occurred.

Tone. A reflection of a writer's or speaker's attitude toward a subject.

Topic sentence. A sentence that expresses the main idea of a paragraph.

Transition. A connecting word or phrase that clarifies relationships between details, sentences, or paragraphs.

U–V

Unity. The quality of a composition in which all the sentences and paragraphs support one main idea.

URL. The standard form of an Internet address; stands for Uniform Resource Locator.

Venn diagram. A graphic organizer consisting of two or more overlapping circles; used to compare items that have both similar and different traits.

Verb. A word that expresses action or a state of being and is necessary to make a statement.

Verbal. A verb form that functions in a sentence as a noun, an adjective, or an adverb. The three kinds of verbals are gerunds, infinitives, and participles. *See* Gerund; Infinitive; Participle.

Verb phrase. *See* Phrase.

Verb tense. The tense of a verb indicates when the action or state of being occurs. The **present tense** names an action that happens regularly. The **past tense** names an action that has happened, and the **future tense** names an action that will take place in the future.

All verb tenses are formed from the four principal parts of a verb: a base form *(swim)*, a present participle *(swimming)* a simple past form *(swam)* and a past participle *(swum)*. A **regular verb** forms its simple past and past participle by adding *-ed* to the base form. *(jump, jumped, jumped)* An **irregular verb** forms its past and past participle in some other way. *(drive, drove, driven; begin, began, begun)*

In addition to present, past, and future tense, there are three perfect tenses: present perfect, past perfect, and future perfect. The **progressive form** of a verb expresses a continuing action with any of the six tenses. To make the progressive forms, use the appropriate tense of the verb *be* with the present participle of the main verb. The **emphatic form** adds special force, or emphasis, to the present or past tense of a verb. For the emphatic form, use *do, does,* or *did* with the base form.

Voice. The distinctive use of language that conveys the writer's or narrator's personality to the reader. Sentence structure, word choice, and tone are elements that communicate voice.

W

Web site. A location on the World Wide Web that can be reached through links or by accessing a Web address, or URL. *See* URL.

Word processing. The use of a computer for the writing and editing of written text.

World Wide Web. A global system that uses the Internet and allows users to create, link, and access fields of information. *See* Internet.

Writing process. The series of stages or steps that a writer goes through to develop ideas and to communicate them.

GLOSARIO
DE ESCRITURA Y LENGUAJE

Este glosario permite encontrar fácilmente definiciones de gramática inglesa y términos que usan los escritores.

 A

Abstract noun/Nombre abstracto. *Ver Noun.*

Active voice/Voz activa. Forma verbal usada cuando el sujeto de la oración realiza la acción.

Adjective/Adjetivo. Palabra que modifica, o describe, un nombre (*noun*) o pronombre (*pronoun*), limitando su significado. Un adjetivo indica *qué tipo, cuál, cuántos* o *cuánto*. Los adjetivos aparecen en varias posiciones en la oración.

> **Positive degree/Grado positivo.** Forma simple del adjetivo.
> **Comparative degree/Grado comparativo.** Adjetivo que compara a dos personas, lugares, cosas o ideas.
> **Superlative degree/Grado superlativo.** Adjetivo que compara más de dos personas, lugares, cosas o ideas.

Adjective clause/Proposición adjetiva. Proposición dependiente que modifica un nombre o pronombre. *Ver también Clause.*

Adverb/Adverbio. Palabra que modifica a un verbo, adjetivo u otro adverbio, haciendo que su significado sea más específico. Los adverbios responden a las preguntas *cómo, cuándo, dónde, de qué manera* y *qué tan seguido* sucede algo.

> **Comparative/Comparativo.** Compara dos acciones (*more quickly, better*; en español: *más rápido, mejor*).
> **Superlative/Superlativo.** Compara tres o más acciones (*most quickly, best;* en español: *el más rápido, lo mejor*).

Adverb clause/Proposición adverbial. Proposición dependiente que modifica un verbo, un adjetivo o un adverbio. *Ver Clause.*

Allusion/Alusión. Referencia en un texto escrito a un personaje, lugar o situación muy conocidos de una obra literaria, musical, artística o histórica.

Analysis/Análisis. Acción de descomponer un tema o escrito en distintas partes para encontrar su significado.

Anecdote/Anécdota. Narración breve o incidente que se presenta como parte de una narrativa más larga.

Antecedent/Antecedente. *Ver Pronoun.*

Appositive/Apositivo. Nombre colocado junto a otro para identificarlo o agregar información sobre él. (Mi prima *Lupe* va a ir a Guatemala este verano.)

Argument/Argumento. Afirmación, razón o hecho en favor o en contra de algún comentario; texto escrito que trata de persuadir.

Article/Artículo. Nombre dado a las palabras *a, an* y *the* (en español: *un, uno/a, el, la*). *A* y *an* son artículos **indefinidos** (*indefinite articles*), que se refieren a cualquier cosa de un grupo. *The* es un artículo **definido** (*definite article*); indica que el nombre al que precede es una persona, lugar o cosa específicos.

Audience/Público. Persona (o personas) que lee o escucha lo que dicen un escritor o un hablante.

Auxiliary verb/Verbo auxiliar. *Ver Verb.*

B

Bias/Tendencia. Inclinación a pensar de cierta manera que impide la consideración imparcial de una idea; importante de considerar al producir o evaluar un texto persuasivo.

Bibliography/Bibliografía. Lista de los libros, artículos y otras fuentes que se utilizan como referencia en una investigación.

Body/Cuerpo. Parte central de una composición que comunica la idea principal identificada en la introducción.

Bookmarks/favorites/Marcadores/favoritos. Característica de muchos buscadores de red que permiten guardar direcciones de Internet para entrar a ellas rápidamente.

Brainstorming/Lluvia de ideas. Actividad de grupo por medio de la cual se generan ideas al hacer una lista de todo lo que se nos ocurre sin evaluarlo.

C

Case/Caso. Forma de un nombre o pronombre que se determina por su uso en la oración. El nombre o pronombre está en caso **nominativo** (*nominative case*) cuando se utiliza como sujeto o después de un verbo copulativo; en caso **acusativo** y **dativo** (*objective case*) cuando recibe la acción del verbo; y en caso **posesivo*** (*possessive case*) cuando se utiliza para indicar posesión o propiedad.

Cause and effect development/Desarrollo de causa y efecto. Técnica de organización que examina las razones y los resultados de las acciones.

Character/Personaje. Individuo presentado en la trama de una obra de ficción.

Round character/Personaje redondeado. El que tiene una variedad de características, algunas de las cuales pueden ser contradictorias.

Flat character/Personaje plano. El que tiene una característica dominante.

Static character/Personaje estático. El que no cambia.

Dynamic character/Personaje dinámico. El que se desarrolla a lo largo de la narración.

Characterization/Caracterización. Técnicas que utiliza un escritor para crear sus personajes. Puede ser **directa,** por medio de descripción y de las palabras del personaje, o **indirecta,** por medio de lo que dicen de él otros personajes.

Chronological order/Orden cronológico. Organización de detalles de acuerdo con el tiempo en que sucedieron los acontecimientos o acciones.

Clarity/Claridad. Cualidad de un escrito que lo hace fácil de entender.

Clause/Proposición. Grupo de palabras que consta de sujeto y predicado y que se usa como parte de una oración.

Independent clause/Proposición independiente. También llamada **proposición principal** (*main clause*); tiene sujeto y predicado y hace sentido por sí misma.

Dependent clause/Proposición dependiente. También llamada **proposición subordinada** (*subordinate clause*); tiene sujeto y predicado pero depende de la proposición principal. La proposición dependiente puede ser:

Restrictive o **essential clause/Proposición restrictiva** o **esencial,** que es necesaria para el significado de la oración. **Nonessential** o **nonrestrictive clause/Proposición** o **esencial o no restrictiva,** que no es necesaria para entender el significado de la oración.

Cliché/Cliché. Expresión usada con demasiada frecuencia (*blanco como la nieve*).

Climax/Clímax. Momento donde ocurre la mayor intensidad emocional, interés o suspenso en la trama de una narración.

Clustering/Agrupamiento. Técnica para generar ideas que consiste en escribir una palabra, ponerla dentro de un círculo y rodearla con otras palabras y frases.

Coherence/Coherencia. Cualidad de un párrafo o composición en que las oraciones tienen una relación clara y lógica; también se llama cohesión.

Cohesive writing/Escritura coherente. Tipo de escritura en que las oraciones y párrafos están lógicamente relacionados entre sí.

Collaboration/Colaboración. Proceso de trabajar en equipo para escribir un texto o realizar un proyecto.

Collective noun/Nombre colectivo. *Ver Noun.*

Colloquialism/Expresión coloquial. Expresión informal y pintoresca que se utiliza en la conversación diaria.

Common noun/Nombre común. *Ver Noun.*

Comparative degree/Grado comparativo. *Ver Adjective; Adverb.*

Comparison-and-contrast development/Desarrollo por comparación y contraste. Técnica de organizar ideas, señalando sus similitudes y diferencias a fin de ver relaciones y sacar conclusiones.

Complement/Complemento. Palabra o frase que completa el significado de un verbo en una oración. En inglés hay cuatro clases básicas de complementos: **directo** (*direct object*), **indirecto** (*indirect object*), **de objeto** (*object complement*) y **predicativo** (**atributo**) (*subject complement*).

Conceptual map/Mapa conceptual. Recurso gráfico que desarrolla un concepto central rodeándolo con ejemplos o ideas relacionadas a manera de red.

Conclusion/Conclusión. Afirmación que resume las ideas de una composición, antes de ponerle punto final.

Conflict/Conflicto. Lucha entre dos fuerzas opuestas que constituye el elemento central de la trama en un cuento u obra de teatro.

Conjunction/Conjunción. Palabra que une dos palabras o grupos de palabras.

Coordinating conjunction/Conjunción coordinante. Las palabras *and, but, or, nor, for, yet* (*y, pero, o, no, para, aun*) unen palabras o grupos de palabras que tienen igual importancia gramatical.
Correlative conjunction/Conjunción correlativa*. Las palabras *both . . . and, just as . . . so, not only . . . but also, either . . . or, neither . . . nor* (*tanto . . . como, así como, no sólo . . . sino, o . . . o*) son palabras en pares que vinculan palabras o frases de igual importancia.
Subordinate conjunction/Conjunción subordinante. Une una idea u proposición subordinada con la proposición principal.

Conjunctive adverb/Adverbio de coordinación. Adverbio para aclarar la relación entre las proposiciones de una oración compuesta. (El equipo perdió anoche; *por lo tanto,* no jugará en las finales.)

Connotation/Connotación. Pensamientos y sentimientos relacionados con una palabra, más que con su definición de diccionario.

Constructive criticism/Crítica constructiva. Comentario sobre lo que escribe otra persona, con la intención de ayudar a que mejore el borrador.

Context/Contexto. Palabras y oraciones que vienen antes y después de una palabra y ayudan a explicar su significado.

Coordinating conjunction/Conjunción coordinante. *Ver Conjunction.*

Correlative conjunction/Conjunción correlativa*. *Ver Conjunction.*

Credibility/Credibilidad. Cualidad de un hablante o escritor que hace creer sus palabras.

Critical analysis/Análisis crítico. Consideración de los elementos de una obra literaria para examinarlos, organizarlos, evaluarlos o sacar conclusiones sobre ellos.

D

Declarative sentence/Oración afirmativa. Oración que declara algo.

Deconstructing/Desensamblar. Separar en componentes o analizar.

Deductive reasoning/Razonamiento deductivo. Pensamiento o explicación que parte de una afirmación o principio generales y los aplica a casos específicos.

Definite article/Artículo definido. *Ver Article.*

Denotation/Denotación. Definición de una palabra que da el diccionario.

Dependent clause/Proposición dependiente. *Ver Clause.*

Descriptive writing/Escritura descriptiva. Tipo de escritura que da detalles sensoriales para comunicar una impresión predominante de un escenario, persona, animal, etcétera.

Desktop publishing/Edición por computadora. Uso de programas de computadora para formar un documento con texto escrito, gráficas y/o imágenes.

Dialect/Dialecto. Variedad de lenguaje hablado que usa un grupo particular. Un dialecto puede ser regional (de un lugar) o étnico (de un grupo cultural).

Dialogue/Diálogo. Conversación entre personajes en un cuento, obra o novela.

Diction/Dicción. Palabras que escoge un escritor y cómo las utiliza en frases, oraciones o versos.

Documentation/Documentación. Identificación de las fuentes que se emplean para escribir un documento u otros textos informativos; generalmente se ponen como notas al pie, al final del texto o entre paréntesis.

Drafting/Borrador. Paso del proceso de escritura; transformación de ideas, palabras y frases a oraciones y párrafos.

E

Editing/Edición. Paso del proceso de escritura en que se revisa que el borrador corregido tenga un lenguaje estándar, una estructura sintáctica variada y la elección adecuada de palabras.

Editorial/Editorial. Artículo en un periódico u otro medio que expresa las ideas personales y la opinión del escritor.

Either-or reasoning/Razonamiento excluyente. Falacia lógica que limita las posibilidades a dos alternativas opuestas sin tomar en cuenta otras posibilidades válidas.

Elaboration/Elaboración. Sustento o desarrollo de una idea principal con hechos, estadísticas, detalles sensoriales, incidentes, anécdotas, ejemplos o citas.

Ellipsis/Puntos suspensivos. Signo de puntuación que consiste en dejar tres puntos con espacios iguales para indicar que se están suprimiendo una o varias palabras.

E-mail/Correo electrónico. Abreviatura de correo electrónico; mensajes, generalmente textos, que se envían por computadora.

Emphatic form/Forma enfática. *Ver Verb tense.*

Essential clause/Proposición esencial. Proposición subordinada que no puede omitirse sin cambiar el significado de una oración.

Evaluation/Evaluación. Juicio sobre las fallas y los aciertos de un texto en borrador en cuanto a contenido, organización y estilo.

Evidence/Evidencia. Datos o ejemplos de fuentes confiables que sirven para sustentar afirmaciones escritas o habladas.

Exclamatory sentence/Oración exclamativa. Oración que expresa una emoción fuerte o repentina.

Explanatory writing/Texto explicativo. *Ver Descriptive text.*

Expository writing/Texto descriptivo. Tipo de escritura que informa al público presentando información y explicando conceptos e ideas; también llamada escritura informativa o explicativa.

Expressive writing/Texto expresivo. Texto que realza y transmite los sentimientos del escritor.

F

Fact/Hecho. Información que puede comprobarse a partir de la experiencia directa o de una fuente reconocida.

Feedback/Retroalimentación. Respuesta del escucha o lector al mensaje de un hablante o escritor.

Fiction/Ficción. Literatura donde las situaciones y los personajes son inventados por el escritor.

Figurative language/Lenguaje figurado. Palabras usadas con un efecto descriptivo que expresa una verdad más allá del nivel literal. Los tropos, como el símil, la metáfora y la personificación, son ejemplos de lenguaje figurado.

Foreshadowing/Presagio. Pistas o claves que utiliza un autor para advertir a los lectores de los acontecimientos que ocurrirán más adelante en la narración.

Formal language/Lenguaje formal. Lenguaje que utiliza una gramática correcta y omite contracciones y expresiones coloquiales. Es adecuado para textos de no ficción, que no son de carácter personal.

Freewriting/Escritura libre. Búsqueda de ideas escribiendo durante un tiempo determinado, sin detenerse ni limitar el flujo de ideas.

Future tense/Tiempo futuro. *Ver Verb tense.*

Generalization/Generalización. Afirmación que presenta una conclusión acerca de un tema sin entrar en detalles específicos.

Genre/Género. Clasificación literaria o de otro medio. Los principales géneros literarios son la prosa, la poesía y el drama. Cada uno se divide en subgéneros.

Gerund/Gerundio. Verboide que termina en *-ing* y se usa como nombre (en inglés).

Glittering generality/Generalización deslumbrante. Afirmación atractiva sin pruebas suficientes.

Graphic organizer/Organizador gráfico. Manera visual de organizar la información, como el agrupamiento, las tablas, las gráficas, las redes y los árboles de ideas.

H

Home page/Página principal. Página por medio de la cual un usuario entra normalmente a un sitio de Web. Por lo general, explica el sitio, resume el contenido y proporciona vínculos con otros sitios.

Hyperlink/Hipervínculo. Oraciones o palabras sombreadas o subrayadas en una página en red que al activarse con un clic conectan al usuario con otra parte de la página o con otra página de la red.

Hypertext/Hipertexto. Vínculos en algunos textos que con el clic del ratón el usuario llega a otro documento o a una sección distinta del mismo documento.

I

Idea map/Mapa de ideas. *Ver Cluster.*

Idiom/Modismo. Palabra o frase cuyo significado es diferente del significado estándar o de diccionario. (*Hacer la vista gorda* es un modismo que significa "pasar por alto".)

Imagery/Imaginería. Lenguaje que describe impresiones sensoriales para que el lector de un texto literario pueda ver, oír, sentir, oler y gustar las escenas descritas.

Imperative sentence/Oración imperativa. Oración que exige u ordena algo.

Independent clause/Proposición independiente. *Ver Clause.*

Inductive reasoning/Razonamiento inductivo. Pensamiento o explicación que parte de varios ejemplos para llegar a una afirmación general.

Infinitive/Infinitivo. Verboide que comienza con la palabra *to* (en español termina en -*ar*, -*er* o -*ir*). En inglés se usa como sustantivo, adjetivo o adverbio en la oración.

Informative writing/Texto informativo. *Ver Descriptive text.*

Intensifier/Intensificador. Adverbio que refuerza un adjetivo u otro adverbio (*very* important, *quite* easily; *muy* importante, *bastante* fácil).

Interjection/Interjección. Palabra o frase que expresa emoción o exclamación. No tiene relación gramatical con las demás palabras.

Internet/Internet. Red mundial computarizada que permite comunicarse electrónicamente con cualquier computadora de la red para buscar información social, comercial, de investigación y de otro tipo.

Interpretation/Interpretación. Explicación del significado de un texto, de una representación visual o de cualquier otro tipo de comunicación.

Interrogative sentence/Oración interrogativa. Oración que hace una pregunta.

Interview/Entrevista. Diálogo a base de preguntas y respuestas cuyo propósito es obtener información actualizada o de expertos.

Intransitive verb/Verbo intransitivo. *Ver Verb.*

Introduction/Introducción. Sección inicial de un texto en la que el escritor identifica el tema y da la idea general de lo que contendrá el cuerpo del mismo.

Inverted order/Orden invertido. Colocación del predicado antes del sujeto. En la mayoría de las oraciones en inglés, el sujeto va antes del predicado.

Irregular verb/Verbo irregular. *Ver Verb tense.*

J-L

Jargon/Jerga. Terminología peculiar de una profesión, comercio u otro grupo de personas.

Journal/Diario. Libreta personal en la que con

toda libertad se anotan ideas, pensamientos y experiencias.

Learning log/Registro de aprendizaje. Diario para aclarar ideas sobre conceptos tratados en varias clases.

Lexicon/Léxico. Diccionario.

Listing/Lista. Técnica para generar ideas a partir de las cuales se escribe un texto.

Literary analysis/Análisis literario. Examen de las diferentes partes de una obra literaria a fin de evaluarla.

Logical fallacy/Falacia lógica. Error de razonamiento que se encuentra con frecuencia en publicidad o en escritos persuasivos. *Ver Glittering generality; Either or reasoning.*

M

Main clause/Proposición principal. *Ver Clause.*

Main idea/Idea principal. *Ver Thesis statement.*

Media/Medios. Formas de comunicación usadas para llegar a un público. Los periódicos, la radio, la televisión y la Internet llegan a públicos muy grandes, por lo que se conocen como medios de comunicación masiva.

Memoir/Memoria. Tipo de narrativa de no ficción que presenta el relato de un hecho o período de la historia, resaltando la experiencia personal del narrador.

Metaphor/Metáfora. Tropo que compara dos cosas aparentemente distintas sin usar las palabras *like* o *as* (*como*). (*Él es una roca.*)

Mood/Atmósfera. Sentimiento o ambiente de un texto escrito.

Multimedia presentation/Presentación multimedia. Uso de una variedad de medios como video, sonido, texto escrito y artes visuales para presentar ideas e información.

N

Narrative writing/Narrativa. Tipo de escritura que narra sucesos o acciones que cambian con el paso del tiempo; por lo general tiene personajes, escenario y trama.

Nominative pronoun/Pronombre nominativo. *Ver Pronoun case.*

Nonessential clause/Proposición no esencial. Proposición que agrega información pero que no es absolutamente necesaria para expresar el significado de la oración.

Nonfiction/No ficción. Literatura que trata sobre personas, sucesos y experiencias reales.

Nonrestrictive clause/Proposición no restrictiva. *Ver Nonessential clause.*

Noun/Nombre (o sustantivo). Palabra que nombra a una persona, lugar, cosa, o a una idea, cualidad o característica.

> **Abstract noun/Nombre abstracto.** Nombra una idea, una cualidad o una característica.
> **Collective noun/Nombre colectivo.** Nombra un grupo de personas o cosas.
> **Common noun/Nombre común.** Nombra a cualquier persona, lugar, cosa o idea.
> **Proper noun/Nombre propio.** Nombra a una persona, lugar, cosa o idea específica.

Noun clause/Proposición nominal Proposición dependiente que se usa como nombre.

Number/Número. Forma del nombre, pronombre o verbo que indica si se refiere a uno (**singular**) o a más de uno (**plural**).

Objective pronoun/Pronombre personal de complemento directo o indirecto. *Ver Pronoun case.*

Onomatopoeia/Onomatopeya. Palabra o frase que imita o sugiere el sonido que describe (*rattle, boom;* en español: *pum, zas*).

Opinion/Opinión. Creencia o actitud; no puede comprobarse si es falsa o verdadera.

Oral tradition/Tradición oral. Literatura que se transmite de boca en boca de una generación a otra. Puede representar los valores culturales de un pueblo.

Order of importance/Orden de importancia. Forma de acomodar los detalles en un párrafo o en otro texto escrito según su importancia.

Organization/Organización. Sistema para ordenar las ideas.

Outline/Esquema. Organización sistemática de ideas principales y secundarias con números romanos, letras y números arábigos para una presentación oral o escrita.

Paragraph/Párrafo. Una unidad de texto que consta de oraciones relacionadas.

Parallelism/Paralelismo. Uso de una serie de palabras, frases y oraciones que tienen una forma gramatical similar.

Paraphrase/Parafrasear. Reformulación de un pasaje en palabras diferentes que conservan el significado, el tono y la longitud general del original.

Parenthetical documentation/Documentación parentética. Referencia específica a la fuente de la información que se pone entre paréntesis directamente después de ésta.

Participle/Participio. Verboide que se usa como adjetivo. El participio presente siempre termina en *-ing* y el participio pasado por lo general termina en *-ed.*

Passive voice/Voz pasiva. Forma verbal usada cuando el sujeto de una oración recibe la acción del verbo.

Peer response/Respuesta de compañeros. Sugerencias y comentarios que dan los compañeros de clase sobre un texto escrito u otro tipo de presentación.

Personal writing/Escritura personal. Texto que expresa los pensamientos y sentimientos del autor.

Personification/Personificación. Tropo que da cualidades humanas a un animal, objeto o idea.

Perspective/Perspectiva. *Ver Point of view.*

Persuasive writing/Texto persuasivo. Tipo de escritura, generalmente de no ficción, encaminado a llevar al lector a aceptar el punto de vista del escritor mediante la lógica, la emoción, la súplica o la sugestión.

Phrase/Frase. Grupo de palabras que funcionan como unidad en una oración.

Prepositional phrase/ Frase preposicional. Consta de una preposición, su objeto y cualquier modificador del objeto; puede funcionar como adjetivo o adverbio.

Verb phrase/ Frase verbal. Consta de uno o más **verbos auxiliares** (*auxiliary verbs*) seguidos del verbo principal (*main verb*).

Plagiarism/Plagio. Presentación deshonesta de palabras o ideas ajenas como si fueran propias.

Plot/Trama. Serie de sucesos en secuencia en un cuento, novela u obra de teatro.

Poetry/Poesía. Forma de expresión literaria compuesta por versos. La poesía tradicional contiene un lenguaje emotivo e imaginativo y un ritmo regular.

Point of view/Punto de vista. Relación del narrador con la historia. La mayoría de las obras están escritas en primera persona, tercera persona, o tercera persona omnisciente.

Portfolio/Portafolio. Colección de obras creativas que representan el logro de un artista o escritor.

Positive degree/Grado positivo. *Ver Adjective.*

Possessive pronoun/Pronombre posesivo. *Ver Pronoun case.*

Predicate/Predicado. Verbo o frase verbal y sus modificadores que hacen una afirmación esencial sobre el sujeto de la oración.

Preposition/Preposición. Palabra que muestra la relación de un nombre o pronombre con otra palabra en la oración.

Presenting/Presentación. Último paso del proceso de escritura que implica compartir con otros lo que se ha escrito.

Prewriting/Preescritura. Primer paso del proceso de escritura: decidir sobre qué se va a escribir, reunir ideas y detalles, y elaborar un plan para presentar las ideas; usa estrategias como lluvia de ideas, organizadores gráficos, notas y registros.

Prior knowledge/Conocimiento previo. Hechos, ideas y experiencias que un escritor, lector u observador lleva a una nueva actividad.

Progressive form/Durativo. *Ver Verb tense.*

Pronoun/Pronombre. Palabra que va en lugar del nombre; grupo de palabras que funcionan como un nombre u otro pronombre. La palabra o grupo de palabras a que se refiere un pronombre se llama **antecedente** (*antecedent*).

Pronoun case/Caso del pronombre. Forma del pronombre que se determina por su uso en la oración. El pronombre está en caso **nominativo** (*nominative case*), en caso **acusativo** y **dativo** (*objective case*) y en caso **posesivo*** (*possessive case*), dependiendo de su función en la oración. *Ver también Case.*

Proofreading/Corrección de pruebas. Último paso del proceso editorial en que se revisa el texto en busca de errores tipográficos y de otra naturaleza.

Propaganda/Propaganda. Información encaminada a influir en los pensamientos o acciones; en general es de naturaleza política y puede distorsionar la verdad.

Prose/Prosa. Escritura que se diferencia de la poesía por su similitud con la dicción y los ritmos del lenguaje común.

Publishing/Publicación. Presentación de una obra escrita terminada mediante el uso de la tecnología, para darla a conocer a un público amplio.

Purpose/Finalidad. Objetivo de la escritura: expresar, descubrir, registrar, desarrollar o reflexionar sobre ideas, resolver problemas, entretener, influir, informar o describir.

 R

Regular verb/Verbo regular. *Ver Verb tense.*

Representation/Representación. Forma en que se presenta información o ideas al público.

Research/Investigación. Proceso de localizar información sobre un tema.

Restrictive clause/Proposición restrictiva. *Ver Essential clause.*

Review/Reseña. Análisis e interpretación de un tema presentado por lo general a través de los medios de comunicación masiva.

Revising/Revisión. Paso del proceso de escritura en que el autor repasa el borrador, cambia el contenido, la organización y el estilo para mejorar el texto. Las técnicas de revisión son agregar, elaborar, eliminar, combinar y reacomodar el texto.

Root/Raíz. Parte de una palabra que contiene el significado principal.

Run-on sentence/Oración mal puntuada. Dos o más oraciones o proposiciones seguidas, cuyo significado es confuso debido a su inadecuada puntuación.

S

Sensory details/Detalles sensoriales. Lenguaje que apela a los sentidos; los detalles sensoriales son elementos importantes de la escritura descriptiva, sobre todo en la poesía.

Sentence/Oración. Grupo de palabras que expresa un pensamiento completo. Cada oración tiene **sujeto** (*subject*) y **predicado** (*predicate*). Las oraciones se clasifican según su función o según su estructura:

Simple sentence/Oración simple. Consta de una sola proposición principal y no tiene proposiciones subordinadas.
Compound sentence/Oración compuesta. Tiene dos o más proposiciones principales.
Complex sentence/Oración compleja. Formada por una proposición principal y una o más proposiciones subordinadas.
Compound-complex sentence/Oración compuesta-compleja. Consta de dos o más proposiciones principales y por lo menos una proposición subordinada. *Ver también Declarative sentence; Exclamatory sentence; Imperative sentence; Interrogative sentence.*

Sentence variety/Variedad de oraciones. Uso de diferentes tipos de oraciones para agregar interés al texto.

Setting/Escenario. Tiempo y lugar en que ocurren los sucesos de un cuento, novela u obra de teatro.

Simile/Símil. Tropo que compara dos cosas esencialmente distintas, usando las palabras *like* o *as* (*como*).

Spatial order/Orden espacial. Forma de presentar los detalles de un escenario según su ubicación: de izquierda a derecha o de arriba hacia abajo.

Standard English/Inglés estándar. La forma más ampliamente usada y aceptada del idioma inglés.

Style/Estilo. Forma en que un escritor elige y organiza las palabras y oraciones.

Subordinate clause/Proposición subordinada. *Ver Clause.*

Subordinating conjunction/Conjunción subordinante. *Ver Conjunction.*

Summary/Resumen. Breve explicación de la idea principal de una composición.

Superlative degree/Grado superlativo. *Ver Adjective; Adverb.*

Supporting evidence/Sustento. *Ver Evidence.*

Suspense/Suspenso. Recurso literario que genera interés y emoción para llegar al clímax o desenlace de una historia. Un escritor crea suspenso al proporcionar pistas sobre el desenlace pero sin revelar demasiada información.

Symbol/Símbolo. Objeto, persona, lugar o experiencia que representa algo más, por lo general, abstracto.

T

Tense/Tiempo. *Ver Verb tense.*

Theme/Tema. Idea o mensaje principal de una obra escrita.

Thesis statement/Exposición de tesis. Exposición de la idea principal o finalidad de una obra en una o dos oraciones.

Time order/Orden temporal. Organización de detalles en un texto escrito según el momento en que ocurrieron.

Tone/Tono. Reflejo de la actitud del escritor o hablante hacia un sujeto.

Topic sentence/Oración temática. Oración que expresa la idea principal de un párrafo.

Transition/Transición. Palabra o frase de enlace que aclara las relaciones entre los detalles, oraciones o párrafos.

U-V

Unity/Unidad. Integridad de un párrafo o composición; coherencia entre todas las oraciones o párrafos para expresar o sustentar una idea principal.

URL/URL. Forma estándar de una dirección de Internet. (Son iniciales de *Uniform Resource Locator.*)

Venn diagram/Diagrama de Venn. Representación visual que consta de dos círculos que se traslapan, usado para comparar dos cosas con características comunes y diferentes.

Verb/Verbo. Palabra que expresa acción o estado y que es necesaria para hacer una afirmación.

Verbal/Verboide. Forma del verbo que funciona como nombre, adjetivo o adverbio en la oración. Los verboides son: participio *(participles)*, gerundio *(gerunds)* e infinitivo *(infinitives). Ver Gerund; Infinitive; Participle.*

Verb phrase/Frase verbal. *Ver Phrase.*

Verb tense/Tiempo verbal. El tiempo de un verbo indica cuándo ocurre la acción.

> **Present tense/Presente.** Indica una acción que sucede regularmente.

> **Past tense/Pasado.** Indica una acción que ya sucedió.

Future tense/Futuro. Indica una acción que va a suceder.

En inglés todos los tiempos verbales están formados por las cuatro partes principales del verbo: base derivativa *(base form)* *(swim, nadar)*, participio presente *(present participle)* *(swimming, nadando)*, pretérito simple *(simple past form)* *(swam, nadó)* y participio pasado *(past participle)* *(swum, nadado)*.

Un **verbo regular** *(regular verb)* forma su pretérito simple y su participio pasado agregando la terminación *-ed* al infinitivo. Los verbos que forman su pretérito y participio pasado de otra forma se llaman **verbos irregulares** *(irregular verbs)*.

Además de los tiempos presente, pasado y futuro hay tres tiempos perfectos: presente perfecto *(present perfect)*, pretérito perfecto *(past perfect)* y futuro perfecto *(future perfect)*.

Cada uno de los seis tiempos tiene una forma **durativa** *(progressive form)* que expresa acción continua.

> **Emphatic form/Forma enfática.** Agrega fuerza especial, o énfasis, al tiempo presente o pasado de un verbo. Para la forma enfática se usa *do, does,* o *did* con el infinitivo.

Voice/Voz. Uso del lenguaje que transmite al lector la personalidad del escritor o narrador. La estructura de la oración, la elección de las palabras y el tono son elementos que comunican la voz.

W

Web site/Sitio Web. Sitio de World Wide Web que puede ser alcanzado mediante vínculos o una dirección Web o URL. *Ver también* URL; *World Wide Web.*

Word processing/Procesador de palabras. Programa de computadora para escribir y editar un texto.

World Wide Web/World Wide Web. Sistema global que usa Internet y permite a los usuarios crear, vincularse y entrar a campos de información. *Ver también Internet.*

Writing process/Proceso de escritura. Serie de pasos o etapas por los que atraviesa un escritor para desarrollar sus ideas y comunicarlas.

*Este término o explicación solamente se aplica a la gramática inglesa.

INDEX

A

A, an, 691
A lot, alot, 691
A while, awhile, 691
Abbreviations, 766–768
  capitalization of, 766
  defined, 766
  punctuation of, 766
  of states, 767
  of titles of people, 768
  of units of measure, 768
Ability tests, 851
Abstract, of paper, 810
Abstract noun, 439–444, 933
Accept, except, 691, 833
Achievement tests, 851, 857–881
Acronyms, 785
Action verbs, 454–455
Active listening
  in class, 883–884
  in collaborative writing, 434
  interpreting nonverbal clues, 883
  to television and radio, 884
  to evaluate, 884–886
Active voice, of verbs, 600–601, 928
Ad campaign
  audience for, 299
  Case Study in, 278–279
  creation of, 298–301
  drafting, 280
  prewriting, 279
  word choice in, 300
Addresses
  commas in, 749
  numerals in, 771
Adjective clauses, 549–550, 928
  commas to set off, 409, 745
  diagraming, 572
Adjectives
  articles as, 460
  commas in a series, 743
  common, 462
  comparative form of, 460–461,
    663–665, 928
  comparisons, 666–670
  compound, 764
  coordinate, 743
  definition of, 460

demonstrative, 464
diagraming, 577
effective use of, 465
fractions used as, 764
infinitives and infinitive phrases
  as, 530, 580
interrogative, 464
nouns as, 463
as object complement, 508
participial phrases as, 527
participles as, 527
positive form of, 461, 663–665
possessive, 464
predicate, 509–510
prepositional phrases as, 523–524
pronouns as, 464
proper, 462
superlative form of, 460–461,
  663–665, 928
Adverb clauses, 551–552
  commas to set off, 748
  diagraming, 583
  elliptical, 551, 641
Adverbs
  comparative form of, 470,
    663–665, 928
  comparisons, 666–670
  conjunctive, 479, 746, 930
  definition of, 466, 928
  diagraming, 577
  infinitives and infinitive phrases
    as, 531, 580
  as intensifier, 932
  kinds of, 467, 469, 472
  position in sentence, 467
  positive form of, 470, 663–665,
    928
  prepositional phrases as,
    523–524
  superlative form of, 470,
    663–665, 928
Advertising, 278–281, 298–301
Affect, effect, 691, 833
Agreement. *See* Pronoun-
  antecedent agreement;
  Subject-verb agreement
Ain't, 692
Airplanes, capitalizing names of,
  719

All ready, already, 692
All right, alright, 692
All the farther, all the faster, 692
All together, altogether, 692
Allusion, 928
Alphabet development, 787
Alphabetical order, in a
  thesaurus, 816–817
American Heritage, 812
Among, between, 693
Amount, nouns of, 393
Amount, number, 692
Analogies, on standardized tests,
  884–885
Analysis, 928
  critical, 930
  literary, 933
And, and subject-verb agreement,
  396, 620
Anecdotes, 188–191, 928
  literature model for, 188–189
  in narrative writing, 190–191
Annotations, writing, 19
Antecedent. *See also*
  Pronoun-antecedent agreement, definition of, 445
Antithetical phrases, commas to
  set off, 747
Antonyms, in thesaurus, 817
Apostrophes
  in contractions, 762
  correcting missing or mis-
    placed, 406–407
  with possessives, 406–407,
    439–440, 761–762
  with special plurals, 762
Appendix, 810
Applications, 421–422
Appositive phrases, 525
  commas with, 745
  diagraming, 578
  essential, 409, 527
  nonessential, 409, 527
Appositives
  commas to set off, 745
  definition of, 928
  diagraming, 578
  pronouns with and as, 639–640

Aptitude tests, 851
Argument
    definition of, 928
    formal, 288, 888–890
    in persuasive writing, 289
Art, list of works herein. *See* xxvii
Art, writing topics in, 19, 27, 231,
    239, 297
Articles, 460, 928
As, like, 697
As, personal pronouns following,
    641
Audience
    analysis of, for advertising, 299
    definition of, 928
    for book review, 307
    in expository writing, 227
    identifying, 57
    importance of, 87
    in persuasive writing, 285, 291
Audiovisual materials, in library,
    799, 805
Auxiliary verbs, 458–459
Awards, capitalizing names of, 717

B

Bad, badly, 671
Bar graphs, 245–246
Base words, 822
Be
    conjugation of, 589,
    as helping verb, 458, 585, 596
    as linking verb, 456
    passive voice, 600
    principle parts, 585
    and progressive form of verbs,
    595
Because, reason is, 699
Being as, being that, 692
Beside, besides, 693
Between, among, 693
Bias, 287, 928
Bible, references to, 739
Bibliography
    in book, 810
    definition of, 928
    working, in research paper,
    325–326
Biography section, in dictionary,
    815
Biology, writing topics in, 173,
    199, 289
Body
    of business letter, 304, 414, 415,
    416

definition of, 920
    of research paper, 911
Bookmarks/favorites, 929
Books, parts of, 801–802
Borrow, lend, loan, 694
Borrowed words, 795–796
Brainstorming, 52, 55, 59, 172,
    187, 243, 257, 287, 929
Bridges, capitalizing names of,
    717
Bring, take, 694
Buildings, capitalizing names of,
    717
Business letters, 304, 413–419, 739
    styles of, 413–416
    types of, 417–419

C

Calendar items, capitalizing
    names of, 719
Call number, 801, 803
Can, may, 694
Can't hardly, can't scarcely, 694
Capital, capitol, 833
Capitalization
    of abbreviations, 766
    of compass points, 718
    correcting, 326
    of proper adjectives, 722–725
    of proper nouns, 722–725
    of sentences, 713–714
Capitol, capital, 833
Cases of pronouns
    defined, 637, 929, 935
    nominative, 637, 935
    objective, 637
    possessive 446, 637, 935
Cause and effect
    as context clue, 819
    order, 73, 75, 235
    testing for, 233
    transitions showing, 74, 234
Cause-and-effect development
    definition of, 221, 929
    exploring relationships in, 234
    guidelines for, 234
    literature model for, 232
    organization of, 233
Character, 175, 258, 929
Characterization, 21, 25, 44,
    148–150, 151, 184–186, 187,
    194, 204–211, 212, 213,
    258–260, 929
Charting, 171, 173

Chronological order, 73, 75, 143,
    172, 178, 231, 929
Clarity, 930
Classification
    compare and contrast, 221,
    236–238
    defined, 221
    drafting, 219, 238
    in logical order, 229
    prewriting, 218
    presenting, 220, 250
    revising, 230
    as strategy for writing, 221
Classification systems, in library,
    799–800
Clauses
    adjective, 549–550, 581, 929
    adverb, 551–552, 583, 929
    dependent, 470–471, 549, 929
    diagraming, 581–583
    essential, 549, 745, 929, 931
    independent, 929
    main, 543, 929
    nonessential, 408, 549, 745, 929
    nonrestrictive, 929
    noun, 553–554, 582, 935
    restrictive, 929
    semicolons to separate main,
    710–711
    subordinate, 544, 929
Cliché, 929
Climax, in story, 180–181, 194,
    250, 929
Closing, of business letter, 304
Clustering, 53, 55, 255, 287, 929
Coherence, 76–80, 929
Cohesive writing, 929
Collaborative learning. *See*
    Cooperative Learning
Collaborative writing, business,
    434–435, 929
Collective nouns, 443, 929
    and subject-verb agreement,
    393, 618
Colloquialism, 930
Colons
    in biblical references, 708
    to introduce illustrations or
    restatements, 707
    to introduce lists, 707
    parentheses with, 753
    quotation marks with, 707
    before quotations, 707
    after salutation of business
    letter, 709
    in time expressions, 709

Combining sentences. *See*
    Sentence combining
Comma fault, 559, 720
Comma splice, 390, 529
Commas
    in addresses, 749
    with adjective clauses, 745
    with adverb clauses, 748
    with antithetical phrases, 747
    with appositives, 745
    and compound sentences, 545,
        744
    with conjunctive adverbs, 746
    and coordinate adjectives, 743
    in dates, 749
    and direct address, 749
    in geographical terms, 749
    with infinitives, 745
    with interjections, 409, 746
    in letter writing, 750
    missing, with nonessential
        adjective clause, 408
    missing in a series, 410
    misuse of, 751
    with nonessential appositives,
        409, 745
    with nonessential clauses, 408
    with nonessential elements, 745
    with nonessential phrases, 408,
        745, 747
    with parentheses, 753
    with parenthetical expressions,
        409, 746
    with participles, 745
    after participles and participial
        phrases, 745, 747
    after prepositional phrases,
        747
    quotation marks with, 725–726
    with references, 749
    and semicolons, 741
    in series, 410, 743
    and tag questions, 750
    with titles of people, 749
Common noun, 442, 444, 933
Commonplace books, 16, 19, 39
    annotations in, 39
    writing in, 39
Communication
    and audience, 56–58
    electronic, 917–920
    giving and receiving info, 886
    group discussions, 891
    interviewing, 64–66
    nonverbal, 886
    verbal, 887–891

Companies, capitalizing names of,
    716
Comparative form, of modifiers,
    460–461, 470, 663–665, 928
Compare-and-contrast writing
    chart, 238
    comparison frames, 237
    definition of, 221
    essay, 258–261
    feature-by-feature organization,
        238
    literature model for, 236
    organization, 73
    prewriting, 237
    subject-by-subject organization,
        238
    Venn diagrams in, 236
    See also Expository writing
Comparing and contrasting,
    236–239, 930
Comparison
    bad versus *badly*, 671–672
    comparative degree, 663–664,
        928
    as context clue, 819
    double, 668–669
    good versus *well*, 669–672
    incomplete, 670
    irregular, 666
    of modifiers, 460–461, 663–771
    other or *else*, 670
    positive degree, 663–664, 928
    regular, 664
    superlative degree, 663–664, 928
Comparison frame, 237, 295
Compass points, capitalization of,
    718
Complaint letter, 302–305
    form for, 304
    tone in, 304
Complements
    definition of, 930
    direct objects as, 506, 576
    indirect objects as, 507, 576
    object, 508, 576
    subject, 509, 576
Complete predicate, 498
Complete subject, 498
Complex sentence, 547–548, 936
    diagraming, 581–583
Complication, in fictional
    narrative, 176
Composition. *See specific types of
    writing*; Paragraphs; Writing
    process
Compound adjectives, 764

Compound-complex sentence,
    547–548, 936
Compound direct object, 506
Compound indirect object, 507
Compound numbers, 764
Compound object, personal
    pronouns in, 619
Compound object of preposition,
    523, 638
Compound objective comple-
    ment, 508
Compound predicate, 500–502
Compound prepositions, 473
Compound sentences, 545–546,
    936
    and commas, 545, 744
    and coordinating conjunction,
        476
    diagraming, 581
Compound subject
    diagraming, 501–502, 575
    personal pronoun in, 500
    and subject-verb agreement,
        394–395, 620
Computer. *See* Using computers
Computer data bases, 810
Conceptual map, 930
Conclusions
    definition of, 930
    in essay tests, 256
    in expository writing, 221
    in personal writing, 172
    in research paper, 334
Concrete details, 70
Concrete nouns, 439, 441
Conflict, 930
Conflict analysis
    model for, 196, 198
    in narrative writing, 199
    prewriting, 197
    recognizing conflict, 197
    writing, 198
Conjugation of verbs, 589
Conjunctions
    coordinating, 476, 545, 930
    correlative, 477, 930
    definition of, 476, 930
    subordinating, 478, 544, 930
Conjunctive adverbs, 479, 930
    commas with, 746
Connected numerals, 764
Connotations, 300, 930
Constructive criticism, 930
Context, 930
Context clues
    cause-and-effect, 819

comparison, 819
contrast, 819
definitions, 819
examples, 819
Contractions
apostrophes in, 762
Contrast
as context clue, 819
transitions showing, 76
Cooperative Learning, 11, 19, 55, 59, 71, 89, 93, 131, 138, 147, 187, 199, 223, 231, 243, 285
Coordinate adjectives, and commas, 743
Coordinating conjunction, 476, 545, 930
in forming compound sentences, 500
Correlative conjunctions, 477, 930
Could of, might of, must of, should of, would of, 694
Creative Writing, 25–26, 144–147, 174–179, 180–183, 184–187, 188–189
Credibility, 930
Critical analysis
analyzing conflict, 196–199
analyzing point of view, 90–93
analyzing setting in a short story, 148–151
comparing and contrasting literature works, 258–261
definition of, 930
drafting, 92
plot summary, 192–195
responding to imagery in poetry, 144–147
responding to a short story, 24–27
reviewing nonfiction books in, 306–308
using a reader-response journal in, 20–22
Critical listening, 883–887
Critical thinking
analyzing conflict, 196–199
analyzing setting, 148–151
comparing and contrasting, 236–239
evaluating, 77
identifying cause and effect, 232–235
organizing details, 53–62, 180–181
questioning, 65

See also Compare-and-contrast writing; Critical analysis, Order of importance
Criticism, constructive, 930
Cross-curricular writing
in art, 63, 289
in biology, 173, 257
in geography, 75, 163, 179
in government, 301
in history, 75, 151, 191, 261, 275, 319
in journalism, 23
in music, 49, 309
in science, 39, 173, 239, 257, 357
in social studies, 108

D

Dangling modifiers, 404, 675,
Dashes, 752
Database, 810
Dates
commas in, 749
numerals to express, 738
Decimals, numerals to express, 770
Declarative sentences, 556, 773, 930
Deconstructing, 930
Deconstructing media, 63, 110–119, 131, 902–904
Deductive reasoning, 93
Definite article, 460
Definitions
as context clues, 819
in dictionary, 814
writing effective, 240–243, 322
Degrees of comparison, 928
Demonstrative adjectives, 464
Demonstrative pronouns, 450
Denotation, 930
Dependent clauses, 470–471, 544, 929
Descriptive writing, 122–125, 126–131, 930
adding energetic verbs to, 136–139
analyzing setting for short story in, 148–151
drafting, 124, 154
editing, 124, 155
literature models in, 126, 127, 128, 132, 137, 141, 142, 156–161
observing and taking notes in, 132–134

order of importance, 128
organizing details in, 127–128
portfolio in, 163
precise words in, 301
presenting, 155
prewriting, 123–124, 152–153
responding to imagery in poetry, 144–147
revising, 154
sentence combining in, 365–368
spatial order, 128
topic sentence in, 129
vantage points in, 140–143
Desktop publishing, 88, 930
Details
adding to descriptive writing, 134
adding supporting, 70
in drafting a paragraph, 68
listing, in topic exploration, 60–61
organizing, in descriptive writing, 127–128
in persuasive writing, 284
sensory, 936
Development
cause-and-effect, 929
compare-and-contrast, 930
Dewey decimal system, 800–801
Diagraming, sentences, 574–577
Diagrams, in prewriting, 14, 141
Dialect, 930
Dialogue
definition of, 931
editing, 186
guidelines for writing, 186
literature model in, 184–185
methods of using, 186
punctuation of, 186, 755
reasons for using, 184, 185
revising, 185
writing, 85, 185, 187
Diction, 931
Dictionary
biography section in, 815
on computer, 815
definition of, 812
entry information in, 813
etymology in, 814
general, 812–815
geography section in, 815
homographs in, 813
main entries in, 812–813
types, 812
usage guidelines in, 814–815
Different from, different than, 694

Direct address, and commas, 749
Direct object, 506
   diagraming, 576
   noun clause as, 553
   whom as, 642
Direct quotations, 186
   capitalization of, 713
   in a news story, 250
   in note taking, 326
   punctuation of, 757–758
   quotation marks for, 757
Discussion groups, online, 810
Documentation, 336–339, 341,
   931, 934. *See also*
   Bibliography; Endnotes;
   Footnotes; Works-cited list
Documents, capitalizing names
   of, 717
Doesn't, don't, 695
Double comparisons, 668
Double negatives, 27, 273
Drafting, 47, 49, 95, 108
   in ad campaign, 280
   adding details in, 70–71
   in critical analysis, 92
   definition of, 931
   in descriptive writing, 125, 154
   in expository writing, 218,
     263–264
   in formal speech, 889
   in investigative report, 44
   in narrative writing, 167–168,
     201–202
   organizing paragraphs in,
     68–74, 75
   in personal writing, 5–6, 29–30
   in persuasive writing, 311–312
   problems and solutions, 333
   in research paper, 332–335
   TIME Facing the Blank Page,
     109, 110, 114–115
   in writing process, 49, 95–96
   in Writing Process in Action,
     29–30, 95–96, 154, 201–202,
     263–264, 311–312
   writing topic sentence in, 69
Drawing Conclusions, 287

E

Each, and subject-verb
   agreement, 394
Editing, 49, 50, 97, 108, 930
   checking spelling in, 87
   correcting sentence errors in, 83
   in descriptive writing, 124, 155

for double comparisons, 238
   in investigative report, 44
   in narrative writing, 168, 203
   in nonfiction book review,
     306–309
   in personal writing, 31
   in persuasive writing, 280, 313
   proofreading in, 84
   research paper, 345–347
   TIME Facing the Blank Page,
     109, 111, 118
   in writing process, 44, 49, 108
   in Writing Process in Action
     lessons, 31, 97, 155, 203, 265,
     313
   See also Proofreading; Revising
Editorial, 930
Effect, affect, 691, 833
Either-or reasoning, 930
Electronic resources, 909–927
   finding information with, 910
   generating ideas with, 909–910
   organizing with, 910
   planning with, 910
   producing in multimedia,
     924–927
   for research, 806–807, 913–916
   thesaurus, 139, 261
   visual analysis, 921–923
   visual communication,
     907–908, 917–920
   writing a paper with, 911–912
   writing process and, 909–912
Elliptical adverb clauses, 551, 641
Elaboration, 931
Ellipsis, 931
E-mail, 421, 931
Emigrate, immigrate, 695
Emphatic forms, 596, 937
End marks
   exclamation point, 734
   period, 733
   question mark, 735
   and quotation marks, 755
Endnotes, 337
English language
   acronyms in, 785
   contemporary, 795–796
   formal, 413
   history and development of,
     783–784, 786–788, 789,
     792–794, 795–797
   idioms in, 791
   informal, 791
   jargon in, 797
   malapropisms in, 788

Middle, 792–793
   Modern, 795
   Old, 792–793
   standard, 936
   technical, 431–433, 796, 797
   weasel words in, 794
   See also Vocabulary; Words
English usage, on standardized
   tests, 853–854
Eras, capitalizing names of, 719
Essay test answers, 252–257
   conclusion in, 256
   key words in, 254, 257
   organizing, 255
   previewing, 253
   proofreading, 256
   thesis statement for, 255
   time management in, 253
Essays, 252–257. *See also* Critical
   analysis; Expository writing
Essential appositives, 409, 527
Essential clauses, 549, 745, 929,
   931
Ethnic groups, capitalizing names
   of, 715
Etymology, in dictionary, 814
Evaluation, 839–840, 884–886,
   931
Every, and subject-verb
   agreement, 394
Evidence, in speaking or writing,
   286–289, 931
   facts as, 287, 931
   literature models for, 286, 287
   opinions as, 287
Examples, as context clues, 819
Except, accept, 691, 833
Exclamation point, 734
   to end exclamatory sentence,
     546
   parentheses with, 754
   quotation marks with, 756
Exclamatory sentences, 556, 734,
   931
Experience maps, 10
Expository writing, 931
Expository writing
   comparing and contrasting,
     236–239, 247, 264
   definition of, 931
   drafting, 218, 263–264
   editing, 219, 265
   to inform and explain, 220–223
   knowing audience, 224–227
   literary compare-and-contrast,
     258–259

literature models in, 220, 222, 224, 226, 228, 232, 236, 240, 248, 258–259, 266–273
portfolio, 275
presenting, 218, 265
prewriting, 217, 263
process explanation, 228–230
revising, 218, 264–265
sentence combining, 373–376
Expressions, quotation marks with unusual, 757
Expressive writing, 931
Eyewitness report, 42–45

F

Facts
    definition of, 931
    distinguishing, from opinions, 840
    in persuasive writing, 287
Fallacy, logical, 933
Farther, further, 695
Feedback, 931
Fewer, less, 696
Fiction
    conflicts in, 197
    definition of, 931
    plot, 175, 192–195
    point of view, 175
    theme, 175, 188–190
    using anecdotes in, 190
Fictional narratives
    characters in, 175
    complications in, 176
    developing, 174–178
    finding an idea for, 177
    organizing, 180–182, 183
    plot in, 175
    point of view in, 175
    resolution in, 176
    setting in, 175
Figurative language
    imagery, 226, 931
    metaphor, 933
    personification, 934
    simile, 936
Fill-in tests, 849
Film techniques, 899–901
Fine art, list of works herein. *See* xxvii
First draft, evaluating, 77–78
First person point of view, 90, 93, 172
First-person pronoun, 645
Footnotes, 337

Foreshadowing, 148, 931
Form, emphatic, 937
Formal arguments, 288, 888–890
Formal language, 931
Formal outline, 330
Formal speeches, 888–890
Formally, formerly, 834
Fractions, used as adjectives, 764
Freewriting, 11, 17, 46, 48, 49, 50, 51, 53, 54, 55, 59, 75, 89, 93, 151, 173, 183, 931
Full text, online, 810
Future perfect tense, 595, 937
Future tense, 591, 937

G

Gender
    pronoun-antecedent agreement in, 396
    of pronouns, 446
Generality, glittering, 932
Genres of literature, 932
Geographical terms
    commas in, 749
Geography, writing topics in, 139, 174
Geography section, in dictionary, 815
Generalization, 932
Gerunds and gerund phrases, 529
    diagraming, 579, 932
Glittering generality, 794, 864, 885, 932
Glossary, 928–937
Good, well, 671
Government documents, 809
Grammar. *See also specific topic*
Grammar Link, 7, 11, 15, 19, 23, 27, 45, 49, 55, 59, 63, 67, 71, 75, 81, 85, 89, 93, 125, 131, 135, 139, 143, 147, 151, 169, 173, 179, 183, 187, 191, 195, 199, 219, 223, 227, 231, 235, 239, 243, 251, 257, 261, 281, 285, 289, 293, 297, 301, 305, 309
Graphic organizers
    bar graphs, 245, 425
    clustering, 53, 929
    conceptual map, 930
    definition of, 932
    in exposition, 244–247
    flowcharts, 428
    line graphs, 246, 426
    map scales, 843

organization charts, 428
    pie charts, 246, 425, 842–843
    scales, 844–845
    tables, 424, 842
    time lines, 845
    tree diagrams, 844
Graphs, 425–426
Groups
    procedures in, 891–892
    role of members in, 891
Guidelines, 130, 138, 150, 172, 188, 234, 242, 251, 256, 260, 292, 832, 837, 890

H

Had of, 696
Hanged, hung, 696
Heavenly bodies, capitalizing names of, 717
Helping verbs, 458
Historical events, capitalizing names of, 719
History, writing topics in, 151, 195
Hit, online, 810
Holey, wholly, holy, 834
Home page, 932
Homographs, in dictionary, 813
Homonyms, 247
Humanities Index, 808
Hung, hanged, 696
Hyperlink, 932
Hypertext, 932
Hyphens
    in compound adjectives, 764
    to divide words at the end of a line, 765
    in numbers, 764
    with prefixes, 763

I

Idea map, 53, 54, 932. *See also* Conceptual map
Idea tree, 62, 63
Idioms, 791, 932
Illustrations, colons to introduce, 737
Imagery, responding to, in poetry, 144–147, 932
Imperative sentences, 556, 932
Importance
    organizing by, 73, 75, 128, 934
    transitions showing, 74
    See also Order of importance
In, into, 696

Incomplete comparisons, 670
Indefinite articles, 460
Indefinite pronouns, 452
  pronoun-antecedent agreement
    with, 397, 647, 648
  and subject-verb agreement,
    395, 623–625
Independent clauses, 543, 929
In-depth reading, 838
Index, 948
Indirect object, 507
  diagraming, 576
  whom as, 642
Indirect quotations, 186, 755
Indo-European language
  families, 789–791
Inductive reasoning, 932
Infinitives and Infinitive phrases,
  530, 580
  as adjectives, 530
  as adverbs, 531, 580
  commas to set off, 745
  defined, 531, 932
  diagraming, 580
  distinguished from preposi-
    tional pronoun, 531
  as noun, 531
  as verbal, 531
Informal speeches, 887–888
Information
  handling, in research paper,
    332
  locating, for research papers,
    324, 910
  sources, 327, 910, 913–916
Informative writing, *See*
  Expository writing
Inside address, of a business letter,
  304
Institutions, capitalizing names of,
  716
Intensifier, 932
Intensive pronouns, 448
Interjections, 482, 932
  commas with, 434, 736
Internet, as research tool, 805,
  810, 932
Interpretation, 932
Interrogative adjectives, 464
Interrogative pronouns, 451
Interrogative sentences, 556
  word order in, 600, 932
Intervening expressions, and
  subject-verb agreement,
  621–622
Interviewing

definition of, 932
  in prewriting, 64–67
  steps in, 66
Intransitive verbs, 454–455, 937
Introduction
  definition of, 933
  in research paper, 330, 334
  writing, 434
Inverted order, 933
Investigative report, 42–45
  drafting/revising, 44
  editing/presenting, 44
  lead in, 45
  prewriting, 43–44
Irregardless, regardless, 696
Irregular comparisons, 666
Irregular verbs, 586–587, 937
Italics
  with foreign words, 758
  with titles of trains, ships, air-
    craft, spacecraft, 758
  for titles of works, 758
  with words, letters, or numbers
    used to represent themselves,
    759
It's, its, 407, 638

Jargon, 797, 933
Journal Writing, 4–7, 8–10, 11, 13,
  17, 21, 25, 38, 39, 47, 51, 54,
  57, 61, 65, 69, 73, 77, 79, 87,
  91, 127, 129, 133, 136, 141,
  145, 148, 171, 175, 177, 181,
  185, 189, 193, 197, 203, 221,
  225, 229, 232, 237, 241, 245,
  249, 253, 259, 263, 265, 283,
  287, 291, 295, 299, 303, 307,
  311, 933
  commonplace books in, 16–19,
    39
  experimenting in, 11
  format for, 10
  learning log in, 12–15, 39
  reader-response journals in,
    20–23, 27, 39
  types of entries in, 10
Journalism, writing topics in, 23,
  139

Knowledge, prior, 935

Language. *See also* English
    language
  acronyms in, 785
  alphabet development, 787
  beginnings of, 783–784
  bow-wow theory of, 783–784
  capitalizing name of, 715
  contemporary, 795–796
  figurative, 931
  formal, 931
  idioms, 791
  imagery in, 932
  Indo-European families,
    789–790
  jargon, 797
  malapropisms, 788
  mother tongue in, 784
  picture writing, 786–788
  weasel words, 794
  yo-he-ho theory of, 783–784
Laws, capitalizing names of, 714
Lay, lie, 697
Lead, in an investigative report, 45
Learn, teach, 698
Learning log, 12–15, 38, 39, 933
Leave, let, 698
Lend, loan, borrow, 644
Less, fewer, 696
Letter writing
  business, 304, 701, *See also* Bus.
    and Tech. Wrt. Hbk.
  commas in, 750
  of complaint, 302–305
Letters
  forming plural of, 762
  italics with, 759
Lexicon, 933
Library
  arrangement of a, 799–800
  call number, 801, 803
  classification systems, 799–800
  Dewey decimal system, 799–800
  Library of Congress classifica-
    tion system, 800
  locating book in, 801–805
  online catalog, 803–805
  sources of information in,
    808–805
  special sections in, 800
Library of Congress
    classification, 800
Like, as, 698
Line graphs, 246, 843
Linking verbs, 456–457

personal pronoun after, 638
subject-verb agreement with, 615
Listening
  appreciative, 883
  critical, 883
  empathic, 883
  reflective, 883
  See also Active Listening; Speaking
Listing, 7, 29, 60–61, 63, 75, 93, 135, 139, 177, 181, 217, 263, 933
Lists, colons to introduce, 737–738
Literary analysis. *See* Writing about literature
Literary, comparing and contrasting, 258–260
  guidelines for writing, 260
  literature for, 258–259
  making point in, 260
  selecting focus for, 259
Literary genres, 932
Literature. For a complete list of works here in, see p. xxv
Literature, responding to, 38, 107, 162, 212, 274, 318
  See also Writing about literature
Literature, types of
  compare-and-contrast, 258–260
  evaluation, 259–260
  strategies for responding to, 188–290, 192, 194, 258, 260
Logical fallacy, 933

M

Magazine articles
  capitalization of titles, 720
  in list of works cited, 339
  punctuation of titles, 758
Magazine writing, 109–119
Magazines, as reference source, 806–807
Main clauses, 543, 929
Main idea
  in paragraph, 69, 79
  and unity, 76, 79
  See also Thesis statement; Topic sentence
Malapropisms, 788
Many a, and subject-verb agreement, 394–395
Map scales, 844
Mapping, 10, 171, 173, 304

Matching tests, 849
Mathematics, writing topics in, 15
May, can, 694
Measure, abbreviations of units of, 768
Mechanics
  capitalization, 713–725
  punctuation, abbreviations, and numbers, 733–771
  Troubleshooter, 388–411
  See also Capitalization; Punctuation
Media, 933
Media Connection, 4, 39, 42–43, 108, 122–123, 163, 166–167, 213, 216–217, 275, 278, 319
Media genres, identifying, 902–903
Media messages
  analyzing, 903–904
  creating, 904–907
  examining, 902–904
Memoir, 933
Memos, business, 420
Metaphor, 933
Middle English, 792–793
Might of, must of, should of, would of, could of, 694
Misplaced modifiers, 404, 675–679
Mixed imagery, 145–146
MLA Handbook for Writers of Research Papers, 339, 341
Mnemonic devices, 839
Modern Language Association, 337
Modified (semi) block form, for business letters, 304
Modifiers
  dangling, 404, 675–679
  diagraming, 577
  Grammar Review on, 680–688
  irregular, 666
  misplaced, 404, 675–679
  See also Adjectives; Adverbs
Money, numerals to express, 738
Monuments, capitalizing names of, 717
Mood and setting, 148–150, 933
Mother tongue, 784
Multimedia, 924–927, 933
Multiple-choice tests, 848
Music, writing topics in, 9
Must of, might of, should of, would of, could of, 694

N

Names, personal, 715
Narrative writing
  analyzing conflict in, 199
  anecdotes in, 188–191
  conflict analysis, 196–199
  definition of, 933
  dialogue in, 184–187
  drafting, 167–168, 201–202
  editing, 168, 203
  fictional narratives, 174–182
  finding a story, 167–168
  fine-tuning a story, 167
  literature models in, 170, 174–175, 182, 184–185, 188–189, 201, 204–211
  organizing a fictional narrative, 180–181
  performing a story, 168
  personal experience, 170–173
  plot summary, 192–195
  portfolio in, 213
  presenting, 168, 203
  prewriting, 165, 201
  revising, 167, 202
  sentence combining in, 369–372
National groups, capitalizing names of, 715
Negative words, as adverbs, 466
Negatives, double, 673
New York Times Index, 808
News articles, 248–250, 806–807
  adding details, 250
  adding quotations to, 250
  five *w*'s and *h* in, 249
  getting facts for, 249
  guidelines for writing, 250
  writing effective leads for, 249
Newspapers
  in library, 806–807
  as reference source, 806–807
Nominative case for personal pronoun, 637–638, 935
Nominatives, predicate, 509
Nonessential appositives, commas with, 408, 525
Nonessential clauses, 549, 929, 933
  commas with, 469, 745
Nonessential elements, commas with, 745
Nonessential phrases, commas with, 468, 745
Nonfiction
  anecdotes in, 188–189

book review, 306–309
  definition of, 933
  editing, 308
Nonrestrictive clauses, 549, 929
Nonverbal clues, interpreting,
  883–884
Nor, and subject-verb
  agreement, 382
Note cards, for research paper,
  326–327
Note taking, 133
  in class, 836
  for descriptive writing, 134
  in interview, 65–66
  for research paper, 326, 328–329
  as study skill, 836
Noun clauses, 553–554, 582
  defined, 553, 934
  diagraming, 582
  introductory words for, 553
  special, 553
  as subject, 553–555
Nouns, 439
  abstract, 439–440, 928
  as adjectives, 463
  collective, 393, 443–444, 618,
    933
  common, 442–444, 933
  compound, 832
  concrete, 439–440
  definition of, 439
  effective use of specific, 444
  gerunds as, 529
  infinitives and infinitive
    phrases as, 530
  as object complement, 508
  possessive form of, 439–440
  proper, 442, 444, 715, 934
  singular or plural, 439–440, 443
Nouns of amount, 393
  and subject-verb agreement,
    393, 619
Number, amount, 692
Numbers, 769, 934
  forming plural of, 762
  hyphens in, 764
  pronoun-antecedent agreement
    in, 644
  spelled out, 769
Numbers as numbers, italics with,
  728
Numerals, 738, 770–771

Object complements, 508

diagraming, 576
Object of preposition, 523–524
  noun clause as, 553
  whom as, 642
Objective case for personal
  pronouns, 638–639, 929
Observation, in descriptive
  writing, 133
Old English, 792–793
Omniscient point of view, 91, 93
Online catalog, in library,
  803–805
Online libraries, 809
Online resources, 805
Onomatopoeia, 934
Opinions
  distinguishing, from facts, 840,
    934
  evaluating audience, 291
  finding a topic, 291
  guidelines for presenting, 292
  literature models, 286, 287, 292,
    294
  in persuasive writing, 287, 293
  prewriting, 291
Or, and subject-verb agreement,
  394
Oral tradition, 166–169, 934
Order, inverted, 933
Order of ideas
  cause-and-effect, 73, 78, 235,
    923, 929
  chronological, 73, 75, 143, 172,
    179, 231, 929
  compare-and-contrast, 73, 930
  by importance, 73, 75, 128
  methods of, 330
  spatial, 73, 75, 936
Order of importance
  cause-and-effect explanation,
    232–234
  definition of, 934
  description, 128
  evaluation, 296
  literary analysis, 149, 309
  personal essay, 14
  persuasive essay, 292
  and writing process, 73
Organization, system of, 934
Organizations, capitalizing names
  of, 716
Outline, 23
  correct form for, 329
  definition of, 934
  developing, 328–330
  for fictional narrative, 180–181

notes, 836
  use of a computer in, 235
  in writing a research paper,
    328–331, 333

Paragraphs
  cause-and-effect order in, 73
  chronological order in, 73
  coherence of, 81
  compare-and-contrast order
    in, 73
  definition of, 68, 934
  drafting, 68–71
  geography writing topics in, 75
  linking ideas in, 74
  literature models for, 68, 70, 74
  main idea, 79
  order of importance in, 73
  organizing, 72–74
  revising, 230
  spatial order in, 73
  topic sentence in, 69
  transitions for, 74
  types of supporting details for,
    70
Parallelism, 358–360, 934
Paraphrasing, in note taking,
  362, 934
Parentheses
  capitalization of sentence in,
    714
  with other marks of punctua-
    tion, 753
  to set off supplemental mate-
    rial, 753
Parenthetical documentation,
  337–339, 934
Parenthetical expressions,
  commas with, 709, 745
Participles and participial phrases
  as adjectives, 527
  commas to set off, 646, 648
  definition of, 934
  diagraming, 579
  past, 402–403, 585
  present, 585
Parts of speech
  adjectives, 460–464
  adverbs, 466, 468–472
  conjunctions, 476–479
  Grammar Review on, 484–495
  interjections, 482
  nouns, 439, 442–443
  prepositions, 473, 475, 493

pronouns, 443–446, 450–452
verbs, 453–454, 456, 458
Passed, past, 698, 834
Passive voice, of verbs, 934
Past participles, 402–403, 585
distinguishing between past form and, 404–405, 937
improper use of, 405, 937
Past perfect tense, 594, 937
Past tense, 590, 937
Peer editing, 30, 76–79, 187, 230, 243, 291
Peer response, 934
Percentages, numerals to express, 770
Periodical indexes, 806
Periodicals, in library, 806–807
Periods
in abbreviations, 766
to end declarative sentences, 556, 733
to end imperative sentences, 556
quotation marks with, 755
Person, pronoun-antecedent agreement in, 644
Personal experience narrative, 170–173
Personal pronouns, 446
nominative case for, 637–638
objective case for, 637–638
possessive case for, 637
after *than* and *as,* 641
Personal writing
in commonplace book, 16–19, 39
definition of, 934
drafting, 5–6, 29–30
editing, 31
journal writing, 8–11, 39
learning log, 12–14, 39
literature models, 8, 24, 32, 37
portfolio for, 39
prewriting, 5, 24
in a reader-response journal, 20–23, 39
responding to a short story, 24–27
revising, 31
for self-discovery, 11
Personification, 934
Persuasive appeals
distinguishing fact from opinion, 287
recognizing bias, 287
Persuasive writing

ad campaigns as, 278–280, 298–301
arguments in, 287
audience, 285, 291
complaint letters as, 302–305
definition of, 283, 934
details, 284
drafting, 5–6, 29–30, 296, 311–312
editing, 280, 313
effective definitions, 243
elements of, 284
evidence, 286–289
facts, 287
guidelines for, 293
literature models, 282, 286, 287, 288, 290, 294, 314, 316
opinion, 287
portfolio, 319
preparing arguments for, 288
presenting, 280, 313
presenting an opinion, 285, 290–293
prewriting, 279, 287, 289, 311
product evaluation, 294–297
review of nonfiction book as, 309
revising, 284, 312
sentence combining in, 377–380
stating a case in, 292
taking a stand in, 291
Photo-realism, 243
Phrases
adjective, 523
adverb, 523
appositive, 525, 578
definition of, 934
gerund, 529, 579
infinitive, 530, 580
participial, 525–526, 579, 745, 747
verb, 457–458, 934
verbal, 527–528
Picture writing, 786
Pie charts, 246, 842–843
Plagiarism, 322, 327, 336, 934
Planets, capitalizing names of, 717
Plot, 169, 259, 934
Plot diagram, 181
Plot summary
definition of, 193
model for, 192–193, 194
revising, 194
writing, 194, 195
Plurals

apostrophes with, 760, 762
compound nouns, 832
figures, letters, signs, and words representing themselves, 762
irregular nouns, 832
regular nouns, 439, 831
Poetry, responding to imagery in, 144, 147
definition of, 934
"poetry ideas," 146, 147
types of responses, 145
Point of view
analyzing, 90–93
choosing, 175
definition of, 935
first-person, 90, 93, 172
identifying, 90–91
third-person limited, 90, 91, 93
third-person omniscient, 90, 91, 93
Political parties, capitalizing names of, 716
Portfolios, writing in, 39, 108, 163, 213, 275, 319, 357, 935
Positive form, of modifiers, 461, 663–665, 928
Possessive case
adjectives before nouns, 463–464
compound words, 761
defined, 929
distinguished from contractions, 638
indefinite pronouns, 760
individual possession, 761
joint possession, 761
nouns, 760
personal pronouns, 760, 935
punctuating, 760
words indicating time, 761
Possessive nouns, 439–440
as adjectives, 463
Possessive pronouns, 407, 446–447
as adjectives, 463
Possessives, apostrophes with, 406–407, 760–761
Precede, proceed, 699
Predicate adjectives, 509–510
diagraming, 576
Predicate nominatives, 509
noun clauses as, 553
and subject-verb agreement, 392
Predicate nouns, 392
Predicate pronouns, 509

Predicates
   complete, 498–499, 935
   compound, 500–502
   position in sentence of,
      503–505
   simple, 497
   See also Verbs
Prefixes, 824–825, 829
   hyphens with, 763
Preposition, object of the, 473,
   523–526, 553, 642
Prepositional phrases
   as adjectives, 523–524
   as adverbs, 523–524
   commas after, 747
   definition of, 523, 934
   diagraming, 578
   intervening, and subject-verb
      agreement, 392, 395
   object of preposition, 473, 523
Prepositions
   compound, 473
   definition of, 473, 935
   list of common, 473
Present participles, 585
Present perfect tense, 593
Present tense, 589, 937
Presenting, 48, 49, 97, 108
   in class publications, 89
   definition of, 935
   in descriptive writing, 155
   in expository writing, 265
   in formal speech, 889–890
   in narrative writing, 203
   options, for publishing, 86, 87
   in persuasive writing, 313
   poster display in, 135
   research paper, 347–348
   in storytelling, 168
   TIME Facing the Blank Page,
      109, 111, 119
   in writing process, 49, 107
   in Writing Process in Action
      lessons, 31, 97, 155, 203, 265,
      313
Prewriting, 46, 49, 95, 108, 935
   in ad campaign, 278
   "What if" questions in, 311
   brainstorming in, 52, 53, 55, 59,
      95, 153, 169, 172, 187, 191,
      219, 243, 257, 263, 281, 287,
      293, 297, 301, 311
   charting, 171, 173
   choosing point of view in, 175
   clustering in, 53, 54, 55, 255,
      287

commonplace books in, 16–19
comparison-contrast diagram
   in, 238
comparison frame in, 295
in conflict analysis, 197
in descriptive writing, 123–124,
   152–153
developing main idea statements in, 58
diagrams in, 14, 141, 181, 238
examining parts in, 62
experience maps in, 10, 29
exploring topic in, 60–62, 63
in expository writing, 217, 263
finding topic in, 50–55
in formal speech, 889
freewriting in, 10, 17, 29, 46, 48,
   49, 50, 51, 53, 54, 55, 59, 89,
   93, 95, 151, 153, 173, 183,
   263, 311
idea map in, 53, 54
idea tree in, 62, 63
identifying audience in, 57
identifying purpose in, 56
interviewing in, 64–66
in investigative report, 43–44
learning logs in, 12–14
listing in, 7, 29, 61–61, 63, 65,
   93, 135, 139, 177, 179, 229,
   263
looping in, 54, 55
mapping in, 11, 171, 173
in narrative writing, 167, 201
narrowing focus in, 54
outlining in, 23
in personal writing, 5–6, 29–30
in persuasive writing, 279, 287,
   291, 311
plot diagram in, 181
product evaluation in, 295
purpose and audience in, 59
questioning in, 61
in reader-response journals,
   20–22
researching and collecting
   information in, 62, 322–331
in writing process, 29, 95, 153,
   201, 263, 311
TIME Facing the Blank Page,
   109, 110, 112–113
in Writing Process in Action
   lessons, 29, 95, 153, 201, 263,
   311
Primary sources, 322, 324, 334,
   352
Principal parts of verbs, 585

Principal, principle, 834
Principle, principal, 834
Prior knowledge, 935
Proceed, precede, 699
Process explanation, 228, 231
   checklist for, 229
   literature model of, 228
   prewriting, 230
   writing, 228–230
Product evaluation, 294–296
   literature model of, 294
   prewriting, 295
   writing a, 297
Progressive forms of verbs, 596,
   937
Prompts. *See* Writing prompts
Pronoun-antecedent agreement
   correcting problems with, 396,
      397, 644, 646
   with indefinite pronoun
      antecedents, 647, 648
   in number and gender, 644
   in person, 645
Pronoun reference, 398–399,
   644–646
Pronouns
   ambiguous reference with, 645
   antecedent for, 444, 644–646,
      935
   as adjectives, 464
   as appositives, 639–640
   case of, 637–638
   definition of, 445, 935
   demonstrative, 450
   Grammar Review on, 652–660
   indefinite, 452, 647, 650–651
   indefinite use of, 650–651
   intensive, 448–449
   interrogative, 451
   lack of clear reference with, 398,
      399, 649
   as object complement, 508
   person of, 645
   personal, 446, 637–638
   possessive, 446–447, 637
   reflexive, 448–449
   relative, 451
   shift in, 400
   as subjects, 637, 642
   use of, before gerunds, 620
   with and as appositives, 639
   See also Pronoun-antecedent
      agreement
Proofreading
   definition of, 935
   essay question answer, 256

symbols for, 84
TIME Facing the Blank Page, 109, 111, 118
See also Editing; Revising
Propaganda, 935
Proper adjectives, 462
   capitalization of, 722–723
Proper nouns, 442, 444
   abbreviation of, 766, 934
   capitalization of, 715–721
   commas with, 749
   forming plurals of, 831
   forming possessive of ancient, ending in *-es* or *-is*, 729
Prose, 935
Publishing, 935
   TIME Facing the Blank Page, 109, 111, 119
   Writing in the Real World, 6, 86–89, 155, 168, 218, 280
   See also Presenting
Punctuation
   apostrophe, 760–762
   colon, 737–739
   comma, 743–751
   dash, 752
   exclamation point, 734
   hyphen, 763–765
   italics, 758–759
   parentheses, 753–754
   period, 733
   question mark, 735
   quotation marks, 755–757
   semicolon, 741–742
Purpose for writing
   to analyze, 20–23, 935
   to describe, 126–131, 935
   to express yourself, 8–11, 935
   identifying, 56, 935
   to inform, 228–231, 935
   to persuade, 285, 935
   to tell a story, 170–173, 935

Q

Question mark, 735–736
   to end interrogative sentences, 616
   parentheses with, 754
   quotation marks with, 567
Questions
   asking, in interview, 65–66
   asking, in topic exploration, 61
   tag, 750
   who versus *whom* in, 642
   See also Interrogative sentences

Quotation marks
   and commas, 755
   with dialogue, 755
   for direct quotations, 755
   with indirect quotations, 755
   with other marks of punctuation, 756
   Quotation within a quotation, 755
   with titles of short works, 757
   with unusual expressions, 757
Quotations
   capitalization of first word of, 713
   colons to introduce, 737
   direct, 186
   indirect, 186

R

Raise, rise, 699
Reader-response journal, writing in, 20–23, 27, 39
Readers' Guide to Periodical Literature, 806–807
Reading comprehension, on standardized tests, 851–852
Reading styles, 838
Reason is, because, 699
Reasoning
   deductive, 930
   either-or, 931
   inductive, 932
Reference materials, in library, 808–810
Reference works
   almanacs, yearbooks, atlases, 808
   computer databases, 810
   dictionaries, 808
   encyclopedias, 808
   government documents, 809
   in libraries, 802, 808–810
   magazines as, 806–807
   periodical indexes, 806
   periodicals as, 805, 806–807
   Readers' Guide to Periodical Literature as, 806–807
   thesaurus as, 137
   See also Library
References
   commas to set off, 749
   numerals in, 771
Reflecting, 31, 97, 155, 203, 265, 313
Reflexive pronoun, 448–449
Regardless, irregardless, 696

Regular verbs, 586, 937
Relative clauses. *See* Subordinate clauses
Relative pronoun, 451
   to introduce adjective clause, 549
   to introduce noun clause, 543
Relevancy, online, 810
Religious terms, capitalizing, 719
Representation, 935
Research, electronic, 806–807, 913–916, 935
Research paper
   avoiding plagiarism in, 327
   bibliography cards, 325
   citing sources in, 336–341
   conclusion in, 334
   drafting, 332–335
   editing, 346–347
   endnotes in, 337
   final copy of, 346–347
   footnotes in, 337
   introduction in, 330, 334
   locating information for, 324
   organization for, 330
   outlining, 328–331, 333
   parenthetical documentation in, 337–339
   in portfolio, 357
   presenting, 347–348
   prewriting, 322–331
   quotations in, 326
   research process in, 322–324
   revising, 342–344
   selecting topic for, 323
   source materials for, 324, 327
   student model of, 348–356
   taking notes for, 326, 328–329
   thesis statement in, 330
   types of, 322
   working bibliography for, 325–326
   Works-cited list, 339–340
   writing electronically, 911–916
Resolution, in fictional narrative, 176
Respectfully, respectively, 699
Responding to imagery in poetry, 144–147
Responding to literature. *See* Literature, responding to
Responding to Writing in the Real World, 7, 45, 125, 163, 219, 281
Response from readers, 38, 107, 162, 261, 274, 318, 934

Restatements, colons to introduce, 737
Restrictive clauses, 536, 929
Review, 935
Revising, 5–6, 44, 45, 96, 935
    anecdotes, 190, 191
    for common errors, 408–410
    descriptive writing, 124, 154
    dialogue, 185
    for exact verbs, 137
    expository writing, 218, 264–265
    formal speech, 889
    for misplaced or dangling modifier, 404–405, 675–679
    narrative writing, 167, 202
    paragraphs, 79–81
    personal writing, 30–31
    persuasive writing, 284, 312
    plot summary, 194
    for pronoun-antecedent agreement, 396–397
    for pronoun reference, 398–399
    research papers, 342–344
    for run-on sentences, 390–391
    for sentence fragments, 388–389
    for sentence variety, 333
    for shift in pronoun, 400
    for subject-verb agreement, 392–395, 613–614
    TIME Facing the Blank Page, 109, 111, 116–117
    for unity and coherence, 76–81
    for verb tense or form, 401–403
    in writing process, 49, 96–97
    in Writing Process in Action lessons, 30, 96, 154, 202, 264, 312
    See also Editing; Proofreading
Rise, raise, 699
Roget's, 816
Role playing, 11
Root words, 822–824, 935
Rubrics. See Writing rubrics
Run-on sentences, 559–561, 935
    correcting, 390–391

S

Said, says, 699
Salutation, colon after, 739
Says, said, 699
Scales, reading, 844–845
Scanning, 838
School courses, capitalizing names of, 719

Science, writing topics in, 173
Script, formatting interview as, 67
Search engines, 809, 810
Secondary sources, 322, 324, 325
Semicolons
    and commas, 741
    to join main clauses in compound sentence, 545
    parentheses with, 753
    quotation marks with, 756
    to separate main clauses, 740
Sensory details, 936
Sensory images, in descriptive writing, 131
Sentence combining, 360–385
    in descriptive writing, 365–368
    in expository writing, 373–376
    literature-based activities and, 381–385
    in narrative writing, 369–372
    in persuasive writing, 377–380
Sentence fragments, 557–558, 561
    correcting, 388–389
Sentences
    capitalization of, 713–714
    complex, 547–548, 564, 581–583, 936
    compound, 545–546, 581, 936
    compound-complex, 547–548, 936
    correcting errors in, 83
    declarative, 556, 733, 735, 930
    definition of, 936
    diagraming, 574–583
    effective use of, 333
    exclamatory, 556, 734, 931
    imperative, 556, 932
    interrogative, 556, 735, 932
    position of adverb in, 467
    position of subject and verb in, 503–505
    run-on, 390–391, 559–561, 935
    simple, 545–546, 936
    subjects of, 497
    topic, 129
    Troubleshooter for, 388–391
    variety in, 333, 936
Sentence-writing exercises, 442, 449, 452, 454, 459, 465, 472, 490–492, 495, 499, 512–513, 514, 515, 516, 535, 543, 577, 580, 583, 604, 605–606, 648
Series, commas in, 410, 473
Set, sit, 699

Setting, 175, 259, 936
    analyzing, in a short story, 148–151
    uses of, 148
Sexist language, correcting, 396, 644
Ships, capitalizing names of, 719
Short-answer tests, 849
Short story
    analyzing setting in, 148–151
    character in, 24
    plot in, 24
    responding to, 23–27
    setting in, 24
    theme in, 24
Should of, might of, must of, would of, could of, 694
Signal words, recognizing, 836
Simile, 226, 936
Simple predicates, 497
Simple sentences, 545–546, 936
Simple subjects, 497
Sit, set, 699
Skimming, 836
Slang, 243
Social studies paper, revising, 344, 345
Sounds of language, 787
Source cards, for research paper, 322, 324, 325, 327
Spacecraft, capitalizing names of, 719
Spatial order, 72, 75, 128, 936
Speaking, 887–891
    style, 890
    in writing conference, 30, 96, 154, 202, 264, 312
Speeches
    formal, 888–890
    informal, 887–888
Spelling
    basic rules for, 828–832
    difficult words, 832–833
    in editing process, 84
    learning, of new words, 832
    list of frequently misspelled words, 833–834
SQ3R study method, 838–839
Standard English, 936
Standardized tests
    analogies in, 854–855
    English skills items in, 853–855
    objective, 848–849
    practice handbook, 857
    preparing for, 847, 851–853
    purpose of, 851

reading comprehension in, 851–852
sentence completion in, 853
synonyms in, 853
tips for taking, 850, 855
types of items in, 851–855
States, abbreviations of, 767
Stationary, stationery, 834
Story writing. *See* Narrative writing
Student models, 14, 18, 20, 22, 26, 46–48, 51, 69, 72, 92, 130, 134, 172, 178, 181, 190, 194, 199, 250, 302, 349–355
Study skills
  evaluating what you read, 839–840
  mnemonic devices, 839
  note taking in class, 836
  outlining, 836
  reading graphs and diagrams, 842–845
  reading and remembering, 836–839
  SQ3R method, 836–839
  time management, 837
Style, 360–363, 936
Subject
  complete, 498
  compound, 394, 500–502
  diagraming, 575
  indefinite pronoun, as, 395
  noun clause as, 553–555
  position in sentence, 392–393, 503–505
  problems of agreement of, with verbs, 392–395
  simple, 497
  who as, 642–643
Subject complements, 509
  diagraming, 576
Subjective pronoun, as subject, 637, 642
Subject-verb agreement
  checking for, 613
  with collective nouns, 393, 618
  with compound subjects, 394–395, 660
  correcting problems with, 392–395
  and indefinite pronouns, 395, 623–625
  with intervening expressions, 621–622
  and intervening prepositional phrases, 392, 614

and intervening words, 392, 395
  in inverted sentences, 392–393, 616–617
  with linking verbs, 615
  with nouns of amount, 393, 619
  with number and person, 613
  with predicate nominatives, 392
  with special nouns, 618
  with special subjects, 618–619
  with titles of works, 619
Subordinate clauses, 469–470, 544, 929, 936
  adjective, 549
  adverb, 551
  noun, 553
  and sentence combining, 376
  who versus *whom* in, 642–643
Subordinating conjunctions, 478, 544, 930
  to introduce adjective clauses, 549
  to introduce adverb clauses, 551
Suffixes, 825–826, 828–830
Summarizing, 195
  in note taking, 326
Summary, 936
Superlative form, of modifiers, 460–461, 663–665, 928
Supplemental material, parentheses to set off, 753
Supporting details, 127, 128, 226
  See also Details
Suspense, 936
Symbols
  in beginnings of language, 787
  definition of, 936
  forming plural of, 762
  as persuasive technique, 794
Synonyms, 137
  on standardized tests, 853
  See also Thesaurus

Tables, reading, 842
Tag lines, in dialogue, 186
Tag questions, and commas, 750
Take, bring, 694
Teach, learn, 698
Technical writing, 428–430
Tenses of verbs, 581–598
Tests
  essay, 252–257
  fill-in, 849
  matching, 849
  multiple-choice, 848

short answer, 849
  standardized, 851–856
  time management in, 850
  true-false, 849
  See also Study skills
Than, personal pronouns following, 641
Than, then, 699, 834
Theater arts, writing topics in, 85
Theme, 936
Then, than, 699, 834
Thesaurus, 137, 817
  on computer, 139, 261, 816
  dictionary form of, 816–817
  original form of, 816
These kinds, this kind, 697
Thesis statement
  in conflict analysis, 199
  definition of, 936
  developing, 330, 331
  modifying, 330
  varieties of, 330
  See also Topic sentence
They, indefinite use of, 399, 645
Third-person limited point of view, 90–91, 93
Third-person omniscient point of view, 91, 93
Third-person pronouns, 445, 645
This here, that there, 700
This kind, these kinds, 697
Time
  numerals to express, 770
  transition showing, 74
Time expressions, colon in, 739
TIME Facing the Blank Page, 109–119
Time line, reading, 845, 936
Time management
  in essay question answers, 253
  in studying, 837
  in tests, 850
Time order, 936
Title, of persons, 715
  abbreviations of, 768
  commas with, 749
Titles of works
  capitalizing, 720
  italics for, 308, 758
  and subject-verb agreement, 619
Tone, 936
Topic, 50–55, 60–63
Topic selection, for research paper, 323
Topic sentence
  definition of, 936

focusing, 129
importance of, 69
writing, 71
See also Thesis statement
Trade names, 717
Tradition, oral, 944
Trains, capitalizing names of, 719
Transitions
 in cause-and-effect writing, 74, 334
 to show comparison, 74
 to show contrast, 74
 definition of, 74, 936
 in descriptive writing, 130
 evaluating and revising, 81
 for importance, 74
 list of, 74
 to show location, 74
 to show time, 74
 using, 75
Transitive verbs, 454–455
Tree diagrams, reading, 844
Troubleshooter, 386–411
True-false tests, 849

U

Underlining, title of work, 308, 758
Understood subject, 556
Unity, 76–80, 81, 936
URL, 810, 913, 937
Usage
 subject-verb agreement, 613–625
 Troubleshooter, 387–410
 using modifiers correctly, 663–675
 using pronouns correctly, 637–651
 verb tenses and voice, 585–601
Usage glossary, 691–703
Usage guidelines, in dictionary, 814–815
Usage information, in dictionary entries, 815
Using Computers
 for checking spelling, 247
 for formatting poetry, 147
 for keeping learning log, 15
 for organizing notes, 293
 for outlining, 235
 for research, 27
 for revising anecdotes, 191
 for revising transition words, 81
 for search and replace

commands, 251
 for sharpening keyboard skills, 85
 for thesaurus, 139, 261
 for writing scripts, 67

V

Vantage point, 140–143
Variety in sentences, 936
Venn diagram, 937
Verbals and verbal phrases, 527–530, 937
 gerunds, 529
 infinitives, 529, 932
 participles, 529
Verb phrases, 458–459, 934
Verbs
 action, 454–455
 active voice, 600–601
 agreement with subject, 392–393, 613–624
 auxiliary, 457
 choosing exact, 137
 compatibility of tenses of, 598–599
 conjugation of, 589
 definition of, 453, 937
 effective use of, 459
 emphatic forms of, 596
 future perfect tense of, 595, 937
 future tense of, 591, 937
 incorrect tense or form of, 402–403
 intransitive, 454, 455, 937
 irregular, 586–587, 937
 linking, 455–456
 in passive voice, 600–601, 934
 participle form, 934
 as part of predicate, 935
 past perfect tense of, 594, 937
 past tense of, 590, 937
 present perfect tense of, 593, 937
 present tense of, 589, 937
 principal parts of, 585
 problems of agreement of, with subject, 392–395
 progressive forms of, 596, 937
 regular, 586, 937
 shift in tense, 401
 tense of, 453, 937
 transitive, 454, 455
 voice of, 600–601
Video making, 905–906
Viewing and representing

analyzing media messages, 903–904
creating a Web site, 906–907
creating media messages, 904–907
examining media messages, 902–904
film techniques, 899–901
identifying media genres, 902–903
interpreting visual design, 895–898
making a video, 905–906
understanding visual messages, 895–901
Viewpoint. *See* Point of view
Visual analysis, 921–923
Visual communication, 917–920
Visual design, interpreting, 895–898
Visual learning. *Writer's Choice contains numerous instructional visuals.* 48, 54, 56, 88, 142, 181, 233, 283, 673, 790, 799–780, 802–804
Visual messages, understanding, 895–901
Vocabulary
 acronyms, 785
 analyzing the general context, 821
 analyzing specific context clues, 820
 antonyms, 813
 borrowed words, 795–796
 and dictionary, 819
 homographs, 813
 idioms, 791
 jargon, 797
 malapropisms, 788
 prefixes, 825
 remembering new words, 821
 suffixes 825
 synonyms 813
 word roots, 822
Voice
 of verbs, 600–601, 928, 934
 as tone, 937

W

Weasel words, 794
Webbing. *See* Clustering
Web site, 937
 creating, 906–907
 home page on, 932

Well, good, 671
"What if" questions, 315
Where at, 700
Who, use of, as subject, 451, 642–643
Who, whom, 642–643
Wholly, holy, holey, 834
Whom, use of, as object, 642–643
Word division, hyphens in, 765
Word parts
  base word, 822
  prefixes, 824–825, 866
  roots, 822–824, 935
  suffixes, 825, 826
Word processing, 937
  for design, 917–918
  producing multimedia presentations, 924–927
  the writing process, 909–912
Words as words
  forming plural of, 762
  italics with, 759
Wordworks, 785, 791, 794, 797
Works-cited list, 337–340, 346, 355–356
World Wide Web, 810, 913, 937
Would of, might of, must of, should of, could of, 695
Writing
  anecdotes, 191
  annotations, 19
  coherence in, 929
  cohesive, 929
  collaborative, 434, 929
  complaint letters, 305
  descriptive, 930
  dialogue, 184–187
  effective use of adjectives in, 460–461
  effective use of adverbs in, 467
  effective use of conjunctions, 480–481
  effective use of phrases in, 532–538
  effective use of sentences in, 548
  explanatory, 931
  expository, 931
  expressive, 931
  to learn, 13
  lyrics, 7
  personal, 934
  persuasive, 934
  pronoun reference in, 633
  rubrics. *See* Writing rubrics
  for self-discovery, 11

  sentence variety in, 501
  specific nouns in, 444
  technical, 428–430
Writing about literature
  analyzing conflict, 196–198, 933
  analyzing point of view, 90–92
  analyzing setting in a short story, 148–150
  comparing and contrasting works of literature, 258–260
  plot summary, 194–196
  responding to imagery in poetry, 144–146
  responding to a short story, 24–26
  reviewing a nonfiction book, 306–308
  using a reader-response journal, 20–22
  writing, 933
Writing across the curriculum. *See* Cross-Curricular writing
Writing, application, 421–422, 495, 521, 541, 573, 611, 635, 661, 689, 711, 731, 779
Writing in the Real World, 4–7, 42–45, 122–125, 166–169, 216–219, 278–281
Writing process, 40–108, 937
  drafting, 49, 95–96, 109, 110, 114–115, 154, 201–202, 263–264, 311–312
  editing, 31, 97, 109, 111, 118, 155, 203, 265, 313
  electronic resources and, 909–912
  presenting, 31, 97, 109, 111, 119, 155, 203, 265, 313, 935
  prewriting, 29, 95, 109, 110, 112–113, 153, 201, 263, 311, 935
  revising, 30, 96, 109, 111, 116–117, 154, 202, 264, 312
Writing prompts, 11, 15, 19, 23, 27, 49, 55, 59, 63, 67, 71, 75, 81, 85, 89, 93, 131, 135, 139, 143, 147, 151, 173, 179, 183, 187, 191, 195, 199, 223, 227, 231, 235, 239, 243, 247, 251, 257, 261, 285, 289, 293, 297, 301, 305, 309, 327, 331, 335, 341, 345, 356
Writing rubrics, 11, 15, 19, 23, 27, 49, 55, 59, 63, 67, 71, 75, 81, 85, 89, 93, 125, 131, 135, 139, 143, 147, 151, 173, 179, 183,

187, 191, 195, 199, 219, 223, 227, 231, 235, 239, 243, 247, 251, 257, 261, 281, 285, 289, 293, 297, 301, 305, 309, 417, 419, 421, 423, 426, 430, 432, 433, 435
Writing skills and strategies, 109–119
Writing systems 787
Writing, technical, 441–443
Writing techniques
  brainstorming, 94, 263, 311, 929
  clustering, 53, 55, 255, 287, 929
  freewriting, 11, 17, 46, 48, 49, 50, 51, 932
  journals, 29, 200
  listing, 29, 153, 263
Writing tool, computer as, 53, 54, 55, 59, 75, 89, 93, 151, 123, 183, 423–427

You
  avoiding indefinite use of, 399
  indefinite use of, 399
  and pronoun-antecedent agreement, 396–397
  understood, as subject, 556

ACKNOWLEDGMENTS

Text

UNIT ONE From *Blue Highways: A Journey Into America* by William Least Heat-Moon. Copyright 1982 by William Least Heat-Moon. By permission of Little, Brown and Company.

UNIT TWO From "Bombing Down the Interstates Nuclear Loads Carry Safety Questions" by Mark Trahant. *Arizona Republic*, January 21, 1990. Reprinted by permission of Pheonix Newspapers, Inc.

"My Furthest-Back Person-The African" by Alex Haley. Copyright 1972 by Alex Haley. Reprinted by permission of John Hawkins & Associates, Inc.

UNIT THREE From *Equator* by Thurston Clarke. Copyright © 1988 by Thurston Clarke. Reprinted by permission HarperCollins Publishers, Inc.

The lines from "Corsons Inlet" are reprinted from *Collected Poems, 1951-1971*, by A. R. Ammons, by permission of W. W. Norton & Company, Inc. Copyright 1972 by A. R. Ammons.

"The Solace of Open Spaces," from *The Solace of Open Spaces* by Gretel Ehrlich. Copyright 1985 by Gretel Ehrlich. Used by permission of Viking Penguin, a division of Penguin Putnam Inc.

UNIT FOUR From "Perseus and the Gorgon" by Bobby Norfolk. Reprinted by permission of Bobby Norfolk and Folktale Productions.

"User Friendly" by T. Ernesto Bethancourt, copyright 1989 by T. Ernesto Bethancourt. From *Connections: Short Stories by Outstanding Writers for Young Adults* by Donald R. Gallo, Editor. Used by permission of Dell Publishing, a division of Random House, Inc.

From *Tortuga* by Rudolfo A. Anaya. Published by University of New Mexico Press, 1720 Lomas Blvd. NE, Albuquerque, New Mexico 87131. Copyright 1979 by Rudolfo A. Anaya.

UNIT FIVE From "Drowsy America" by Anastasia Toufexis. Copyright © 1990 Time Inc. Reprinted by permission.

From *A Book of Bees . . . and How to Keep Them* by Sue Hubbell. Copyright 1988 by Sue Hubbell. Reprinted by permission of Darhansoff & Verrill Agency.

UNIT SIX "A Plague on Tennis" by Mark Mathabane. Reprinted by permission of the author.

UNIT SEVEN From *The Concord Review*, Fall 1990, Volume Three, Number One. Copyright 1991 by The Concord Review, P.O. Box 661, Concord, Massachusetts 01742. Reprinted by permission.

Photo

Cover KS Studios; **vi** (l)Ralph J. Brunke, (r)Stephen Kennedy; **vii** (t)Eric Futran, (b)Wadsworth Atheneum, Hartford/ Ella Gallup Sumner and Mary Catlin Sumner Collection; **viii** Stephen Kennedy; **ix** (t)Giraudon/Art Resource, NY, (b)*THE CIVIL WAR: Confederate Ordeal*, photograph by Larry Sherer © Time-Life Books, Inc; **x** (t)Stephen Kennedy, (c)Michael Holford, (b)Art Resource, NY; **xi** (t)The Howard University Gallery of Art, Washington, DC. Permanent Collection, (c)Billy E. Barnes/Tony Stone Images, (b)Ralph J. Brunke; **xii** James Porto; **xiii** Eric Futran; **xiv** (t, c) Stephen Kennedy, (b)SCALA/Art Resource, NY; **xv** PhotoDisc, Inc; **xvi** (t)Andy Keech/Photo Trends, (bl)Zao-Grimberg/The Image Bank, (br)courtesy The Collection of Mildred Hart Bailey; **xvii** Roger Tully/Tony Stone Images; **xviii** (t)HMS Images 1990, (b)P. Markow/FPG International; **xix** Milwaukee Art Museum, Gift of Mrs. Edward R. Wehr; **xx** The Metropolitan Museum of Art, Gift of Robert W. de Forest, 1925; **xxi** PhotoDisc, Inc; **xxii** (l)Artville, (r)PhotoDisc, Inc; **xxiii** Artville; **xxiv** PhotoDisc, Inc; **xxv** Carmen Lomas Garza; **xxxi-1** The Corcoran Gallery of Art/CORBIS; **2-3** Michael Boys/CORBIS; **4 5** Chel Beeson; **6** (t, bl)Chel Beeson, (br)Ralph J. Brunke; **7** Ralph J. Brunke; **8** SCALA/Art Resource, NY; **11** Carmen Lomas Garza; **12 16** Stephen Kennedy; **17** Ralph J. Brunke; **20** John G. Herron/Stock Boston; **21** Eric Futran; **24** Courtesy Mrs. Mary Weatherall; **27** Henri Rousseau, *The Sleeping Gypsy*, 1897. Oil on canvas, 51"x 6'7" Collection, Museum of Modern Art, NY. Gift of Mrs. Simon Guggenheim; **33** The Oakland Museum, Bequest of Abilio Reis; **35** Courtesy Bernice Steinbaum Gallery, NY; **37** Field Museum of Natural History, Chicago; **39** Michael Boys/CORBIS; **40-41** Nathan Benn/CORBIS; **42** Monty Roessel; **43** Eric Futran; **44 45** Ralph J. Brunke; **55** Edna Davis Jackson; **56** Eric Futran; **60** Greg Mancuso/Stock Boston; **63** Art Resource, NY; **64** Reprinted by permission: Tribune Media Services; **68** Sisse Brimberg; **72** Paul Explaining Pictures to Mie Kakigahara, Tokyo, February 1983. Photographic Collage 30 3/4 x 42 1/2". © David Hockney; **77** Eric Futran; **82** The Far Side cartoon by Gary Larson is reprinted by permission of Chronicle Features; **86** Eric Futran; **87** Stephen Kennedy; **90** The Far Side cartoon by Gary Larson is reprinted by permission of Chronicle Features; **93** Courtesy Muzeum Narodwe w Poznaniu, Poznan, Poland; **101** Wadsworth Atheneum, Hartford, Ella Gallup Sumner and Mary Catlin Sumner Collection; **119** Nathan Benn/CORBIS; **120-121** Douglas Peebles/CORBIS; **122** Jerry Bauer, Courtesy Julian Bach Agency; **124** Eric Futran; **125** M. Scheler/The Image Bank; **125** (l) Suzanne L. Murphy/FPG International, (r)Graphic House/FPG International; **126** J. W. Meyers/Stock Boston; **128** Courtesy Bernice Steinbaum Gallery, New York; **131** Blackbear Bosin, Courtesy The Philbrook Museum of Art, Tulsa, Oklahoma; **134** Stephen Kennedy; **135** The Cleveland Museum of Art, Anonymous Gift; **136** Reprinted from Green Lantern #15 Copyright 1991 DC Comics, Inc. All rights reserved. Reprinted by permission. Art by M.D. Bright, Romeo Tanghal, Anthony Tollin; **140** Robert Bishop; **145** Milwaukee Art Museum, Gift of Mrs. Edward R. Wehr; **146** Giraudon/Art Resource, NY; **157** Frederic Remington, *The Fall of the Cowboy*, 1895. Oil on canvas (1961.230) Amon Carter Museum, Fort Worth, Texas; **159** Ann Taylor; **165** Douglas Peebles/CORBIS; **166** Stephen Kennedy; **166-167** Richard Reynolds/TxDOT; **167** (t)Michael Holford (b)Eric Futran; **168** (t, c) Stephen Kennedy, (b) Chattanooga Free Press. Photo by Laura Walker; **169** Stephen Kennedy; **170** Ralph J. Brunke; **174** from *THE CIVIL WAR: Confederate Ordeal*. Photograph by Larry Sherer © Time-Life Books, Inc; **176** (t) Robert Tringali Jr./Sportschrome, Inc., (b) Sportschrome; **179** Courtesy Donald Morris Gallery, Inc; **180** File Photo; **183** Des Moines Art Center, Purchased with funds provided by the AVA Program, 1982.7; **187** Gilberto Ruiz/Courtesy of the Barbara Gillman Gallery; **188 192** File Photo; **196** Nasjoonalgalleriet, Oslo, Norway; **199** Private Collection, Courtesy of the Texas Gallery, Houston. Photo by Bill Kennedy; **203** Fundación Rufino Tamayo/Art Resource, NY; **213** Richard Reynolds/TxDOT; **214-215** Simon Fraser/SPL/Photo Researchers; **216** Ellen Denuto; **219** Peter Southwick/Stock Boston; **220** Eric Haase; **223** Russian Museum, St.

Petersburg, Russia; **224** Wyoming Division of Tourism; **227** The Howard University Gallery of Art, Washington, DC. Permanent Collection; **228** Ralph J. Brunke; **231** M.C. Escher/Cordon Art-Baarn-Holland/Art Resource, NY; **232** Bettman/CORBIS; **239** Alma Thomas (American, 1891-1978). *Iris, Tulips, Jonquils and Crocuses,* 1969. Acrylic on canvas, 60 x 50 in. The National Museum of Women in the Arts. Gift of Wallace and Wilhelmina Holladay; **240** Billy E. Barnes/Tony Stone Images; **243** Collection of the Chase Manhattan Bank, N.A; **244** Kent Knudsen/Stock Boston; **248** Dave Clendenen; **252** Reprinted by permission: Tribune Media Services; **258** Erich Hartmann; **262** Scala/Art Resources, NY; **268** Giraudon/Art Resource, NY; **271** Art Resource, NY; **272** Ernest Lawson 1873-1939, *Garden Landscape,* 50.8 x 61.0. The Brooklyn Museum. Bequest of Laura L. Barnes; **275** Simon Fraser/SPL/Photo Researchers; **276-277** Joseph Sohm/ ChromoSohm/CORBIS; **278** Ralph J. Brunke; **279** (l)Eric Futran, (r)Steven Wohlwender; **280** Eric Futran; **282** James Porto; **284** Rainforest Action Network; **285** Jonathan Franklin/Courtesy of the Collection of Wendy Spatz; **286** Ralph J. Brunke; **289** Courtesy of Roslyn Oxley Gallery, Paddington, Australia; **292** Courtesy of the National Wildlife Federation, photo by Ralph J. Brunke; **294** Larry Pierce/The Image Bank; **296** Consumers Union of United States, Inc., Yonkers, NY 10703; **300** Courtesy of Elgin Syferd/Drake and the Idaho Travel Council; **301** SCALA/Art Resource, NY; **302** Herman © 1976 Jim Unger. Reprinted with permission of Universal Press Syndicate; **306** Ralph J. Brunke; **315** The Bridgeman Art Library Ltd; **319** Joseph Sohm/ChromoSohm/CORBIS; **320-321** John McAnulty/CORBIS; **328** Eric Futran; **336** The Granger Collection; **346** Courtesy of

Historical Pictures Service; **358-385** CORBIS; **386-387, 388** Al Young/CORBIS; **436** SuperStock; **493** Ando Hiroshige, Japanese, 1797-1858, Imagiri Promentory for Maizaka from the Hocido Tokaido, 1833 color wood-block print 266 x 351 mm Elvehjem Museum of Art, Univeristy of Wisconsin-Madison; **503** Andy Keech/Photo Trends; **519** SCALA/Art Resource, NY; **529** Zao-Grimberg/The Image Bank; **539** Magnum Photos; **545** Roger Tully/Tony Stone Images; **571** The Carnegie Museum of Art, Pittsburgh, Museum Purchase; gift in memory of Elizabeth Mellon Sellers from her friends. 74.17; **609** Courtesy Ashmolean Museum, Oxford; **621** P. Markow/FPG International; **633** Stanley I. Batkin; **642** HMS Images; **659** Courtesy of the Collection of Mildred Hart Bailey; **687** The Metropolitan Museum of Art, Gift of Mrs. Earl W. Koeniger, 1966 (66.114); **709** The Metropolitan Museum of Art, Gift of Robert W. de Forest, 1925 (25.173); **729** Bettman/CORBIS; **755** AP/Wide World; **777** The Mary and Sylvan Lang Collection, Marion Koogler McNay Art Museum, San Antonio, Texas; **782** Archivo Iconografico, S.A./CORBIS; **783** Susan Anderson; **785** John Elk III/Stock Boston; **785-797** (gears)VCG/FPG International; **787** SCALA/Art Resource, NY; **788** The Far Side © 1987 Universal Press Syndicate. Reprinted with permission; **792** (l)SCALA/Art Resource, NY, (r)Courtesy Ashmolean Museum, Oxford; **793** Bettman/CORBIS; **796** (l)The Bridgeman Art Library Ltd./Art Resource, NY, ©Martha Swope, (r)NASA; **797** By permission of Johnny Hart and Creators Syndicate, Inc; **813** File Photo; **891** (l)The Kobal Collection, (r)Reuters/Gregg Newton/Archive Photo; **918** (t)Aaron Haupt, (b)Bob Daemmrich/Stock Boston.